'No living person is a greater authority on the life [of]
Dickens than Michael Slate[r]'
—Claire Tomalin

'A superb piece of literary detective work. ... If this loyal and generous book
resembles any previous biography, it is Forster's. Like Forster, Slater has
written a book that distils a lifetime of affectionate study, and as Dickens once
said of his friend, the great novelist is fortunate to have "so sympathetic, acute
and devoted a champion".'
—Robert Douglas-Fairhurst, *The Daily Telegraph*

'[A] captivating biography. [Slater] seems to have consulted every scrap ...
that Dickens scribbled on in his 58 years, to produce exactly what the book's
subtitle promises: "a life defined by writing".'
—David Propson, *The Wall Street Journal*

'Slater leaves no stone unturned, and we must be immensely grateful to him
for introducing us to so many unfamiliar pieces on Dickens's writing ... This
book gives us the best account yet of how the "clutching eye" served to enlarge
everyone's vision.'
—Claire Harman, *The Sunday Telegraph*

'There have been many lives of Dickens, so what makes Slater's stand out?
First, he has a matchless knowledge of all things Dickensian, and second ...
he is ideally equipped to enrich his biography by dipping into the ocean of
Dickens's writings aside from the novels. ... [A] fine biography [which] aligns
life and works.'
—John Carey, *The Sunday Times*

'Michael Slater's research has been compendious and his judgements are
clear-eyed ... This is a microscopically attentive account of what Dickens was
writing when, and how he went about it ... a nuanced and interesting account
of Dickens as a literary craftsman and publishing professional.'
—Sam Leith, *The Spectator*

'[A] fine, meaty and careful book, a notable addition to the literature on our
most formidable novelist.'
—Paul Johnson, *Literary Review*

'An authoritative and engaging biography.'
—*The Economist*

'Brilliant in its insight ... Slater untangles the DNA of the writer's life and by knitting its sequences into the spiral of immense energy, observation and commitment provides an unmatched ladder of evidence to the plots and characters of the novels.'
—Mary Leland, *Irish Examiner*

'This book is like a cake, rich with fruit, appropriately for Dickens a Christmas cake, which will keep and be sliced into for years; or maybe, as he saw it, "the layers of red and white in a side of streaky, well-cured bacon" – white for comedy – red for mortality.'
—P.J. Kavanagh, *The Tablet*

'Well written, clear headed, even keeled. Slater's biography will stand now as Edgar Johnson's once did – as the definitive narrative account of Dickens's crowded career.'
—Brian Murray, *First Things*

'Michael Slater's subtle and searching account of Dickens's life is a very welcome addition to Dickens studies.'
—Catherine Peters, *Dickens Quarterly*

'Slater, who has edited Dickens's journalism, emphasizes the variety of his subject's activities—the tireless writing, performing, and hosting ... [and] assiduously annotates the emotional background that gave rise to each text.'
—*The New Yorker*

'The full measure of Dickens the writer, in all the forms of writing, is taken here with a finesse and attention to detail unlikely to be surpassed.'
—*The Dickensian*

'Slater's mastery of Dickens's works, combined with his use of new material, gives us a Dickens far more complex and nuanced than was hitherto assumed.'
—*Contemporary Review*

'An engrossing story of a writer at work. New even to devotees of Dickens biography are wonderful vignettes of Dickens the journalist, honing his knowledge of London by reporting on actual events and personalities that became wonderfully transmogrified into his baroque fiction.'
—*The Star Tribune*

CHARLES DICKENS

MICHAEL SLATER is Emeritus Professor of Victorian Literature at Birkbeck College, University of London, and a Past President of both the International Dickens Fellowship and the Dickens Society of America. He was for many years the editor of the Dickens Fellowship's journal *The Dickensian*. His publications include *Dickens and Women* (1983) and *An Intelligent Person's Guide to Dickens* (1999). During 1994–2000 he edited *The Dent Uniform Edition of Dickens's Journalism* (4 vols; vol. 4 co-edited with John Drew). He has lectured on Dickens and other Victorian writers to a wide variety of audiences in North America, Europe and Japan, where he was Visiting Professor at the University of Kyoto in 2005. He lives in London.

CHARLES DICKENS

MICHAEL SLATER

YALE UNIVERSITY PRESS
NEW HAVEN AND LONDON

For information about this and other Yale University Press publications please contact:
U.S. Office: sales.press@yale.edu   www.yalebooks.com
Europe Office: sales@yaleup.co.uk   www.yalebooks.co.uk

Set in Minion by IDSUK (DataConnection) Ltd.
Printed in United States of America

Library of Congress Cataloging-in-Publication Data

Slater, Michael.
    Charles Dickens : a life defined by writing / Michael Slater.
        p. cm.
    Includes bibliographical references and index.
    ISBN 978–0–300–11207-8
    1.   Dickens, Charles, 1812–1870. 2.   Authors, English—19th
century—Biography.   I. Title.
    PR4581.S6155 2009
    823'.8—dc22
    [B]
                                                                                2009026834

A catalogue record for this book is available from the British Library

ISBN 978–0–300–17093–1 (pbk)

10 9 8 7 6 5 4 3 2 1

This book is dedicated to the memory of
Kathleen Tillotson
1906–2001
mentor and friend

Contents

Illustrations in the text

Nos 2, 14, 36 and 50 are taken from Robert Langton, *The Childhood and Youth of Dickens* (1891), nos 9 and 20 from Frederic G. Kitton, *Charles Dickens by Pen and Pencil* (1889–90), nos 12, 15, 24, 46, 51, 53–56, 58 and 59 from B. W. Matz, ed., Dickens in Cartoon and Caricature (Boston Bibliophile Society, 1924); no. 40 is reproduced by courtesy of the Museums and Archives Service, Great Ormond Street Hospital for Children, NHS Trust, and no. 52 by courtesy of the Morgan Museum and Library, New York; the Claudet daguerreotype of Dickens is reproduced by courtesy of the Library Company of Philadelphia; all other images are reproduced by courtesy of the Charles Dickens Museum, London.

Plates

Preface

CHARLES DICKENS was indeed, as he said himself, 'an amazing man'. And for the last century and a half memoirists and biographers have written extensively about his extraordinary dynamism, his organisational genius and notable capacity for business, his lifelong concern for the poor, especially children, his multifarious and energetic charitable activities, his deep interest in crime and punishment, prisons and the detective police, his intense love/hate relationship with, and need for, London and its teeming streets, his passion for the theatre and his own histrionic brilliance, his love of Christmas, his obsession with order and fascination with disorder, his worship of the domestic hearth and his strong attraction towards what he called 'vagabondage', his complex family relationships and his secret connection for the last twelve years of his life with a woman twenty-seven years his junior.

Discussion of all these things will be found in this book too. But, mindful of Dickens's words in his will about resting his claims to the remembrance of his country upon his published work, I have focused primarily upon his career as a writer and professional author, and have been particularly concerned to place his novels in the context of the truly prodigious amount of *other* writing that he was constantly producing alongside the serial writing of those books, and to explore the web of connections between them and it, as well as connections with his superlative letters and his personal life. These other writings of Dickens – short stories, sketches, topical journalism, essays, travel writings and writings for children, polemical pieces in verse as well as prose – contain much fine work highly characteristic of him but are mostly known only to specialists and so will be given more attention here than they generally receive.

It is a propitious time for a new life of Dickens along the lines indicated. A four-volume edition of his journalism, the Dent Uniform Edition, was completed in 2000. The magnificent twelve-volume *British Academy Pilgrim Edition of Dickens's Letters* was finished two years later. The latter work particularly, together with those scholarly editions of his novels so far published in the Oxford Clarendon Dickens and the Norton Critical Editions series, provides new insights into, and much new and detailed information about, Dickens's life and work on which I have been able to draw in this book, which appears as we prepare to celebrate the bicentenary of his birth in 2012.

Acknowledgements

I WISH TO THANK the following friends who read all or part of this book in manuscript (some of them in more than one version) and suggested innumerable improvements: Michael Allen, the late Richard D. Altick, the late Philip Collins, Edward Costigan, Ashby Bland Crowder, Jean Elliott, Beryl Gray, John Grigg, and Toru Sasaki. This book has benefited enormously from their close involvement with it and I am profoundly grateful to them all. I am likewise indebted to the reader appointed by Yale University Press for submitting so detailed and constructive a report on my final draft.

I have also received valuable help and advice in connection with this book from other friends and colleagues during the past six or seven years; and in several cases, as will be evident from my end-notes, I have greatly benefited from their published work. In this respect I would like specifically to thank the following: Malcolm Andrews, Rosemary Ashton, Robert Bledsoe, Laurel Brake, Margaret Brown, Duane DeVries, John M. L. Drew, Angus Easson, the late Kenneth J. Fielding, Barbara Hardy, the late Peer Hultberg, Leon Litvak, David Paroissien, Robert L. Patten, Andrew Sanders, Paul Schlicke, Fred Schwarzbach, Grahame Smith and Tony Williams. I am very grateful also to Michael Baron and Robina Barson, Joss Burton, Jan and Pia Lokin, Q Love, Chris Lungley and Ann Watkins for their continued interest in this book, and all their invaluable encouragement during the writing of it.

The idea of attempting a biography of Dickens was first mooted to me by Robert Baldock and Malcolm Gerratt of Yale University Press and it is a pleasure to record my appreciation of their help and support during my subsequent labours. I would also like to thank Michael Rogers for his meticulous proof-reading, and David Atkinson for once again providing a work of mine with an excellent index.

At the Charles Dickens Museum Florian Schweizer and Andrew Xavier have been unfailingly helpful and resourceful in supplying me with important material from the rich resources of the Museum's collections, and their unflagging enthusiasm for the project, like that of the late Cedric Dickens, was a constant stimulus. I am also indebted to Dr Schweizer for his note on the history of the Guild of Literature and Art following chapter 14. Martin Nason has generously shared with me the riches of his fine Dickens Collection, and I have over the years received tremendous help from past and present members of staff of the Senate House Library, University of London (formerly the University of London Library), where most of the work for this book was carried out. I am especially grateful to Kate Gazzard of the Charles Dickens Museum and to Dave Jackson of the Senate House Library for their help in assembling the illustrations, and to Steve Kent of Yale University Press for his great care in the presentation of them.

I am indebted to Mark Dickens for his permission to quote from unpublished material written by Dickens or by members of his family, and to Oxford University Press and the Pilgrim Trust for permission to quote from *The British Academy Pilgrim Edition of the Letters of Charles Dickens*. I greatly appreciate the Pilgrim Trust's generosity in waiving all permission fees. Quotations from the texts of Dickens's speeches in K. J. Fielding's edition of *The Speeches of Charles Dickens* (OUP, 1960) are made by permission of the K. J. Fielding Estate, and quotations from Dickens's *Book of Memoranda*, edited by Fred Kaplan (New York Public Library, 1981), and from the holograph of Dickens's pocket diary for 1867, are made by permission of The Henry W. and Albert A. Berg Collection of English and American Literature, The New York Public Library, Astor, Lenox and Tilden Foundations.

Preface to the paperback edition

I have taken the opportunity to correct a number of errors in the first edition of this book and would like to record my thanks to the following friends, reviewers and correspondents for having drawn my attention to a number of them: Professors Joel J. Brattin, Donald Hawes, Catherine Peters, Dr Beryl Gray and Mr Roy Sloan.

Since the letter purportedly written by Dostoevsky in 1862 describing an interview with Dickens which appeared on p.502 of the first edition cannot be satisfactorily authenticated I have removed it from this edition.

Michael Slater, 2011

Note on monetary values

Making monetary comparisons over time is always a difficult and approximate exercise and, since Dickens's day, not only has the value of money changed dramatically but the introduction of decimal currency in 1971 has added further complexity. The traditional 'pounds, shillings and pence' were then replaced by a system (partly adopted to ensure the parity of old and new pounds) in which the pound was divided into one hundred (new) pennies. Before 1971 there were twelve pennies in a shilling, and twenty shillings, or 240 (old) pennies, in the pound. One new penny thus became equivalent to 2.4 old ones. Right up to decimalisation some older denominations had continued to be widely used, notably the half-crown and the guinea. The former was equivalent to two shillings and sixpence, and the 'gentlemanly' guinea, used primarily for professional charges and salaries (also, in Dickens's time, for paying contributors to periodicals and for pricing books), was worth one pound and one shilling.

The mid-nineteenth century did not experience the sustained inflation which has been a feature of the period since World War II. Within Dickens's lifetime there were price fluctuations, sometimes quite considerable from year to year, reflecting such things as the quality of the harvest or the demands of a war budget, but the value of the pound in 1870 was not greatly different from its value in the 1820s. Writing in *All the Year Round* in 1864 (XI, 464) Andrew Halliday noted, 'Three hundred [pounds] a year is a salary upon which a family may live comfortably; but not luxuriously'. If the vastly different composition of the average family budget in Victorian times (Halliday allowed for one live-in servant) is born in mind, a multiplier of about 75 will give some general notion of Victorian prices in modern terms. See further Philip Collins's entry, 'money values', in *The Oxford Reader's Companion to Dickens*, ed. Paul Schlicke, 1999, the House of Commons Research Paper 99/20 (available on line from www.parliament.uk), and www.measuringworth.com.

CHAPTER 1

Early years

FROM PORTSMOUTH TO CHATHAM,
1812–1822

Do you care to know that I was a great writer at 8 years old or so – was an actor and a speaker from a baby – worked many childish experiences and many young struggles into Copperfield?

Dickens to Mary Howitt, 7 September 1859

THE EARLIEST specimens of any writing by Charles Dickens of which we have a record consist of a formal note of invitation and a facetious schoolboy letter. The first was written when he was 'between eight and nine years of age' (that is, 1820 or 1821) and his family was living in Chatham where his father, John, was an Assistant Clerk in the Navy Pay Office. The letter was written some five years later, when Dickens was 'between thirteen and fourteen', thus three or four years after the family had moved to London and just after John had retired from the Pay Office on health grounds and was embarking on a new career in journalism to supplement his pension. From the time between the dates of these two items no scrap of Dickens's writing seems to have survived, though three notable samples of it that did once exist are mentioned by his great friend John Forster in his *Life of Charles Dickens*. While the Dickens family was still in Chatham, Forster tells us, the young boy wrote a tragedy called *Misnar, the Sultan of India* based on a favourite story of his. Then later, after the family had moved to London, he wrote a couple of character-sketches, one of an eccentric old barber obsessed with Napoleon, and the other of a deaf old woman who cooked for the family in Bayham Street. According to Dickens himself, writing in 1850 in the preface to a new edition of his first book, *Sketches by Boz, Misnar* had had its predecessors and/or successors in the form of 'certain tragedies achieved at the mature age of eight or ten, and represented with great applause to overflowing nurseries'. As to the schoolboy letter, by the time Dickens wrote this he had perhaps already taken to the writing of 'small tales' for the amusement of his schoolfellows, one of whom later recalled that they had had 'a sort of club for lending and circulating them'. It seems likely, then, that there was a fair amount of Dickens juvenilia which has not come down to us.[1]

The note of invitation reads as follows: 'Master and Miss Dickens will be pleased to have the company of Master and Miss Tribe to spend the evening on . . . [date, etc.]'. It is redolent of genteel middle-class life as it was lived in the early nineteenth-century with its little social ceremonies and mutual courtesies – just such a composition, in fact, as one would expect the children of Mr John Dickens of the Navy Pay Office and his lady to send to the children of Mr Tribe, owner and landlord of the handsome old Mitre Tavern in Chatham High Street, and a good friend of the highly convivial John. It was at the Mitre that the Dickens children, Charles and his beloved little sister Fanny, one year older than he, used sometimes to sing, 'mounted on a dining table for a stage', while their impresario-father looked proudly on.[2]

Five years later, in London, Dickens sent the following letter to a schoolfellow called Owen Peregrine Thomas:

Tom

I am quite ashamed I have not returned your Leg but you shall have it by Harry to morrow. If you would like to purchase my Clavis you shall have it at a very *reduced price*. Cheaper in comparison than a Leg.

Yours &c
C. Dickens

PS. I suppose all this time you have had a *wooden* leg. I have weighed yours every Saturday night.

1 Dickens's schoolboy letter as reproduced by Forster

When he wrote this Dickens was a pupil at Wellington House, William Jones's 'Classical and Commercial Academy' in the Hampstead Road, and the 'Leg' and 'Clavis' to which he refers would have been standard Latin school-books. The letter is very much the work of the lively, fun-loving schoolboy so vividly recalled by Thomas and others who gave Forster their reminiscences of Wellington House Academy for his biography. Forster comments that there is 'some underlying whim or fun in the "Leg" allusions'. He does not, however, point out that this is, in the language of nineteenth-century playbills, 'positively the first appearance' in all Dickens's writings of a wooden leg, the subject of numerous comic allusions throughout his work, culminating in Silas Wegg's versatile appendage in *Our Mutual Friend*. It goes to the heart, in fact, of that fascination with the borderline between the animate and inanimate that is central to so much Dickensian comic writing. Forster, who reproduces the letter in facsimile, as I do here, does, however, note that 'in the signature the reader will be amused to see the first faint beginning of a flourish afterwards famous'.[3]

These earliest specimens of Dickens's writing belong to two very important phases of his early life. The first is a product of what he came to think of as the golden period of his Chatham childhood, when he was aged between five and ten years. The second comes from what we might call his rally, that took place between the ages of thirteen and fifteen, when his interrupted schooling was at last resumed, and he could once more publicly enjoy the status of a middle-class young gentleman after the humiliation of drudging in a blacking factory. Considered together, therefore, the two items derive considerable poignancy from our knowledge of the decidedly grim – albeit highly stimulating imaginatively – time that intervened between the writing of the childhood note and of the schoolboy letter. Some twenty-five years later this period was to inspire in Dickens some very passionate writing indeed, the so-called 'autobiographical fragment', which, as will become apparent in the next chapter, is our primary source of knowledge about what happened to him during that dark time. Now, however, we must go back to his very earliest years and the date when, long before he himself could write a word, he was a cause of writing for his father.

On Monday 10 February 1812 readers of *The Hampshire Telegraph* and *The Hampshire Courier* found this advertisement in their respective journals: 'BIRTHS – on Friday, at Mile-end Terrace, the Lady of John Dickens, Esq., a son'. It is a self-consciously genteel announcement placed by a man who, in 1785, had been born as the second son of upper servants in the household of John Crewe of Crewe Hall in Cheshire. He had apparently received a good education, probably thanks to Crewe, and since 1805 had been pursuing a successful career, with a steadily rising income, in the Navy Pay Office, his initial appointment there being also most likely owing to Crewe's patronage. He worked first at Somerset House in London and while there wooed and won the petite and pretty nineteen-year-old Elizabeth Barrow, daughter of Charles Barrow and sister of his friend and fellow-clerk Thomas Barrow, who held the important post of Chief Conductor of Money in Towns. John had been posted to Portsmouth, thereby qualifying for an 'outport allowance' of five shillings a day in addition to his regular salary. His total income for 1808 had been nearly £200, quite enough on which to marry respectably. On 13 June 1809 he made a flying visit to London to marry Elizabeth, returning with her to the brand-new Portsea house he had taken at annual rental of £35. On 28 October 1810 their first child, Frances, always known as Fanny, was born there, her birth being announced in the local press in similar fashion to Charles's.[4]

Born on 7 February, Charles was baptised Charles John Huffham Dickens in the local parish church on 4 March. He was named after his maternal grandfather even though, two years before, that distinguished relative had been obliged to flee the country in disgrace, having been detected in systematically defrauding the Pay Office of the huge sum of £5,689, over several years. Happily, his exposure seems to have had no adverse effect whatever on the careers of either his son or his son-in-law. Charles's third given name, Huffham (a baptismal-register misspelling for Huffam), complimented his godfather, a prosperous rigger to the Royal Navy who lived in Limehouse. His business must often have required Huffam to visit Portsmouth Dockyard where he would have met John, who was doubtless happy to cultivate the friendship of so flourishing and well-connected a man.

During the first six years of Dickens's life his parents moved house no less than five times and it seems likely that this restlessness affected Dickens in his later life when he seemed to have some sort of need for constant changes of environment. Within four months of his birth John and Elizabeth moved to a lodging-house in Hawke Street, Portsea, 'a most respectable locality'. From there they soon after moved to more spacious premises in Wish Street, Southsea, where Elizabeth's recently-widowed sister, the twenty-six-year-old Mary Allen, came to join them, her annual £50 pension as the widow of a naval officer being doubtless a welcome addition to the household income. Dickens's earliest memory as told to Forster probably belongs to Wish Street though Dickens himself specified Portsea.

> He has often told me that he remembered the small front garden to the house at Portsea, from where he was taken away when he was two years old, and where, watched by a nurse through a low kitchen-window almost level with the gravel walk, he trotted about with something to eat, and his little elder sister with him.

It was an idyllic memory that, over forty years later, and two years after Fanny's sadly early death from consumption, was to inspire Dickens to write a brother/sister fantasy-piece called 'A Child's Dream of a Star' for his journal *Household Words* (6 April 1850). His earliest experience of a sibling death took place, in fact, in Wish Street when his little brother, Alfred Allen Dickens, born in March 1814, died (of 'water on the brain' according to a notice in the local press) at the age of six months.[5]

Other memories of Dickens's earliest years in Portsea and Southsea may be found in his journalism though we must always keep in mind that his essays are brilliantly *composed* pieces, the work of a master of language seeking to achieve particular effects – comic, humorous, pathetic, indignation-rousing, and so on. It is always risky, therefore, for biographers to take them as straight-forwardly autobiographical, even though Dickens himself may have been happy for his readers so to interpret them. The purported memories of his earliest Christmases, which would have been in Portsea and Southsea, do seem very authentic, however, especially the description of his reaction to certain disturbing toys detailed in 'A Christmas Tree' (*HW*, 21 Dec.1850) – like the startling jack-in-the-box, 'a demoniacal Counsellor in a black gown, with an obnoxious head of hair and a red cloth mouth, wide open, who was not to be endured on any terms'. So also does the incident described in his essay 'New Year's Day' (*HW*, 1 May 1859) describing how he was carried downstairs in a woman's arms on New Year's Eve to be shown 'a very long row of ladies and gentlemen sitting against a wall, all drinking at once out of little glass cups with handles, like custard cups' and looking like his first idea of 'the good people in Heaven, as I derived it from a wretched picture in a Prayer-book'.[6]

In January 1815 John Dickens was recalled to London and Dickens always remembered the family coming away from Portsmouth in the snow. The loss of the outport allowance meant a drop in John's income but this was partly offset by a rise in his basic salary in respect of his ten years' service. The family went into lodgings in Norfolk Street (now Cleveland Street), Marylebone, where a fourth child, Letitia Mary, was born in April 1816, John describing himself on the baptismal register not as a Government clerk but as 'Gentleman'. Thus it was in his fifth and sixth years that Dickens had his first experience of the city that was to become the main setting for – and in a sense the main character in – most of his writings. His only published remembrance of this period, however, if it is indeed a genuine memory and not an invented comic set-piece, occurs in the already-cited essay 'New Year's Day'. There he describes how 'a grim and unsympathetic old personage of the female gender' frog-marched him to a huge toy bazaar in Soho Square and ordered him to choose a present costing not more than half-a-crown.[7]

At the end of 1816 John was posted to Chatham Dockyard and, after a brief stay in Sheerness, the family, which still included Mary Allen, moved into No. 2 Ordnance Terrace, a newly-built house advertised for sale as 'commanding beautiful views' and 'fit for the residence of a genteel family'. Here they were to

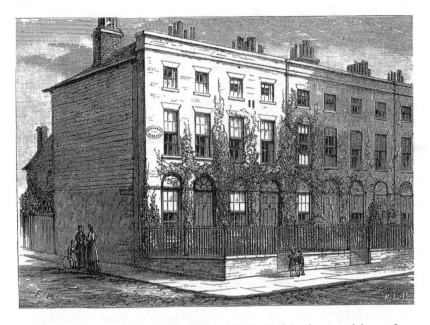

2 Ordnance Terrace, Chatham. The Dickens family lived in the second house from the left

live for four years, waited on by two live-in servants, a young nursemaid called Mary Weller and an older woman called Jane Bonny. These four years, plus a further one in a smaller house in St Mary's Place, Chatham, seem to have been extremely happy ones for the young Dickens, and richly nourishing to the life of his imagination. Vividly detailed memories of places, people and incidents belonging to this time were to feed into his writings from his 'Our Parish' sketches in *Sketches by Boz* in the 1830s right up to the 'Uncommercial Traveller' essays he wrote for his second weekly journal, *All The Year Round*, in the last decade of his life. Particularly notable in this respect are 'Dullborough Town' (*AYR*, 30 June 1860) and 'Nurse's Stories' (*AYR*, 8 Sept. 1860). These were the titles Dickens gave the essays when he collected them in volume form but in the magazine itself they are indexed under the joint title 'Childhood Associations'. In 'Dullborough Town' he feigns to be returning for the first time since childhood to the town in which he had passed his 'earliest days'. He depicts Dullborough as an amalgam of the three Medway towns of Chatham, Strood and Rochester, and serio-comically evokes the glamour and excitement they had held for him as a child when they were, in Forster's phrase, 'the birthplace of his fancy'. In 'Nurse's Stories' he remembers another, and more sensational, source of imaginative stimulation in his childhood. From an amused but still responsive adult perspective he retells some of the comic/horrific bed-time stories purportedly told to him by his nurse, the ironically named Mercy (who may or may not have been based on Mary Weller), which he finds still lurking in the 'dark corners' of his mind.[8]

Chatham itself with its busy dockyard and bustling streets crowded with soldiers and sailors, 'the gay bright regiments always coming and going', and the quiet old adjoining city of Rochester with its ruined castle, ancient cathedral and picturesque old High Street, 'full of gables, with old beams and timbers carved into strange faces', were places that might have fired any child's imagination, let alone a child so richly endowed in this respect as the young Dickens. Then, because of his father's job, he had privileged access to the Dockyard where he 'never tired of watching the rope-makers, the anchor-smiths (nine of them at once, like "the muses in a ring"), and the block-makers at their work'. He would have seen, too, the convict labourers in the Yard, lined up each evening under guard for return to the sinister-looking 'hulks' or prison-ships moored off the coast. He would have had a ringside seat on St Clement's Day, 23 November, to see the blacksmiths processing in honour of their patron saint and singing their chorus 'Beat it out, beat it out – old Clem!' that, long afterwards, he was to describe the child Pip and Miss Havisham singing together in *Great Expectations*. Other special treats were trips on the River Medway aboard the Navy Pay Office yacht with his father and Fanny when John had business to transact in Sheerness, or being taken to see the spectacular military exercises and reviews, sham sieges and sham defences held on the 'Chatham lines' near Fort Pitt, a setting he was to use later for one of Mr Pickwick's earliest misadventures. It is in *Pickwick Papers*, too, that he evokes, in comic mode, the picturesque appeal of old Rochester and its ruined castle. Mr Jingle the strolling player celebrates it in his own staccato style in *Pickwick*, chapter 2:

> glorious pile – frowning walls – tottering arches – dark nooks – crumbling staircases – Old cathedral too – earthy smell – pilgrims' feet worn away the old steps – little Saxon doors – confessionals like money-takers' boxes at theatres – queer customers those monks . . . old legends too – strange stories: capital.[9]

John Dickens's subscription to the publication by a local bookseller of *The History and Antiquities of Rochester and its Environs* in 1817 might suggest that he too responded to the old city's picturesque appeal. But his subscription probably primarily reflected his desire to present himself as a cultivated member of society, a leading citizen and a patron of the arts. He owned a small collection of cheap reprints of eighteenth-century literary classics and other books, a cut-price version of a gentleman's library, which, as we shall see, was hugely important to little Charles. John was also praised as 'an active and conspicuous member' of a local relief committee formed after a major fire in

Chatham High Street had gutted thirty-eight houses. He subscribed two guineas to the fund set up to relieve the victims. And, together with his admiring family, he had the pleasure of seeing published, albeit anonymously, in *The Times* on 4 March 1820 his lengthy account of what he called 'this melancholy accident' with its elegant references to 'the devouring element' and 'the active exertions of the military'. John favoured a richly orotund style in speech and writing on which Dickens later modelled Mr Micawber's idiolect, and Forster states that no one could know John 'without secretly liking him the better for these flourishes of speech, which adapted themselves so readily to his gloom as well as to his cheerfulness'. He was a father to be proud of and his encouragement and approbation must have meant a great deal to Charles, whom he coached to perform comic poems and songs before admiring audiences at the above-mentioned Mitre Tavern and also at his school's 'show day' (Mary Gibson, née Weller, told Langton how vividly she remembered Charles's rendering of Isaac Watts's poem 'The Voice of the Sluggard', given with '*such action* and *such attitudes*'). John also made a companion of his little son, taking him for walks, telling him stories about the neighbourhood, and encouraging him to aim high in life. He noticed that the boy particularly admired a handsome country house situated at the top of Gad's Hill just outside Rochester and, according to Dickens's later testimony, would often tell him, 'If you were to be very persevering and were to work hard, you might some day come to live in it'. It was presumably John, also, who organised family trips to London in 1819 and 1820 to see the greatest of all clowns Joey Grimaldi performing in pantomime at Sadler's Wells. Little Charles, who was later to edit Grimaldi's *Memoirs*, clapped his hands with what he later called 'great precocity'.[10]

During all this time at Chatham John was earning a good salary, rising to £441 in 1822, but was evidently living beyond his means so that in 1819 he needed to borrow what was then the very considerable sum of £200. He borrowed this from a certain James Milbourne of Kennington Green, Surrey, guaranteeing him an annuity of £26 as long as he, John, then only in his early thirties, should live. Within two years he found himself unable to keep up the payments whereupon his brother-in-law, Thomas Barrow, who had imprudently underwritten the arrangement, had to refund Milbourne's capital as well as a half-year owing on the annuity. He never recovered this money from John and barred him from his house, a ban still in force when Dickens married in 1836. John also borrowed money from his Ordnance Terrace neighbour, Richard Newnham, and at some point also from his widowed mother. The move to a smaller house in St Mary's Place, Chatham, in 1821 may have been an economy measure, though the leading authority on Dickens's childhood has described it as a 'not inferior' locality to Ordnance Terrace and comments that the saving on rent would have been very slight. Mary Gibson is reported by Langton, however, as 'sorrowfully remembering the altered circumstances under which [the family] now lived'.[11]

It may be that in St Mary's Place Dickens was no longer able to enjoy games of make-believe with the children who had been his neighbours at Ordnance Terrace, notably George Stroughill from next door, 'a frank, open, and some-what daring boy'. There had been outside games like the one described in 'Dullborough Town', played in a hayfield with Dickens pretending to be a British captive in the dungeons of the Indian city of Seringapatam, conquered by the British in 1799, and being rescued by his victorious countrymen in the persons of George plus two cousins and his 'affianced one', probably George's fair-haired little sister Lucy. Lucy may have been the 'red-cheeked baby' mentioned by Forster with whom Dickens had been 'wildly in love' at Chatham and who seems to have had a lasting effect upon his imagination. And then there had been the indoor games as described to Langton by Mary Gibson. Dickens would come downstairs to her and say, 'Now Mary, clear the kitchen, we are going to have such a game,' after which George Stroughill would bring in his magic lantern and 'they would sing, recite, and perform parts of plays'. Speaking of the house in St Mary's Place, Gibson told Langton, 'There were no such juvenile entertainments at this house as I had seen at the Terrace'.[12]

The first record we have of little Charles going to school belongs to the time in St Mary's Place, unless we are to take the Dame's School mentioned in 'Our School' (*HW*, 11 Oct. 1851), with its fearsome pug-dog guardian, as factual – which it may well be (Forster locates it in Rome Lane, Chatham). According to Dickens, it was from his mother that he received his earliest education. It was from her that he acquired 'his first desire for knowledge, and his earliest passion for reading', no doubt using those thin books 'with deliciously smooth covers of bright red and green' that he was lovingly to recall in his already-mentioned *Household Words* essay 'A Christmas Tree'. He remembered, he told Forster, that his mother 'taught him regularly every day for a long time, and taught him, he was convinced, thoroughly well'. She even guided him as far as the rudiments of Latin. We should bear this in mind when we read Dickens's contemptuously amused description in his autobiographical fragment of his mother's unavailing efforts, a year or two later, to help the family's dire finan-cial situation by starting a school. Elizabeth is a more difficult figure than her ebullient husband, her beloved 'D' as she called him, to bring into focus but she evidently had a lively curiosity about people, liked dancing and amateur dramatics, and enjoyed clothes (poignantly, almost the last glimpse we have of her in Dickens's surviving letters records a senile desire 'to be got up in sables like a female Hamlet'). The wife of the surgeon under whose care her dying husband was later placed described her as being 'as thoroughly good-natured, easy-going, companionable a body as one would wish to meet with'. As for her teaching of Fanny and Charles, it seems likely that the arrival of Harriet Ellen born in 1819 (and destined for an early death two years later) and Frederick William born in 1820 (always known as Fred) would have made it difficult for Elizabeth to continue her daily instruction of her two older children. They were therefore sent to a school a short walk away belonging to William Giles, a young Baptist minister, who had attended St Aldate's School in Oxford.[13]

Giles was, according to Langton, who was relying on the evidence of a very elderly surviving sister of the schoolmaster, 'an accomplished scholar, and a very conscientious, painstaking man'. He was much struck by the young Dickens's 'bright appearance and unusual intelligence' and gave him 'every encouragement in his power, even to making a companion of him of an evening'. He was evidently a man who inspired his pupils with lasting gratitude and a quarter century or so later a number of them gathered to honour his fiftieth birthday. Dickens could not attend but sent a warmly-worded letter recalling that he 'was very young indeed' when he lost the advantage of Giles's tuition. Already in 1838 he had told Giles that he retained a 'vivid remembrance of your old kindness and excellence', and he happily adopted the nickname of 'The Inimitable' after Giles had sent him, half-way through the publication of *Pickwick Papers*, a silver snuff-box inscribed to 'the inimitable Boz'. The boys attending Giles's school wore distinctive white beaver hats and Dickens hung on to his when he and his family moved to London and his schooling was broken off. His 'poor white hat', as he calls it in the autobiographical fragment, must have then been a poignant reminder for him of his lost middle-class status and we may note that he makes 'a much-worn little white hat' a feature of the young David Copperfield's apparel when he is sent off by the Murdstones to the bottling warehouse.[14]

Two of Giles's younger brothers, John and Samuel, who were also pupils at his school, became great friends with Dickens who, speaking in Manchester in 1843 when John Giles was present, vividly recalled how he and John had 'rambled together through the same Kentish fields and mingled in the same sports'. Among the places they rambled to was a stretch of waste ground just outside Chatham known as 'Tom-all-alone's', a haunting name that Dickens stored away in his memory and made powerful use of many years later when writing *Bleak House*. Giles's aged sister remembered Dickens as 'a very handsome boy with long curly hair of a light colour' who enjoyed parties and especially 'Fifth of November festivities round the bonfire'. It was here in Chatham, according to Langton, that Dickens invented the schoolboy lingo that his later schoolfellows in London believed he did not devise until he was one of them.[15]

So far Dickens may sound like any normal lively schoolboy but he was exceptional in his passion for reading stories, essays and travel literature ('a terrible boy to read', Mary Gibson famously called him) and fortunate in that he had the run of his father's little library. Here he could steep himself in the writings of Defoe, Fielding, Goldsmith, Smollett, Addison and Steele as well as *The Arabian Nights* and *Tales of the Genii* (an eighteenth-century imitation of *The Arabian Nights* purporting to be of ancient origin), *Don Quixote*, Le Sage's *Gil Blas* and Elizabeth Inchbald's collection of farces (1806–09). Defoe's *Robinson Crusoe*, Goldsmith's *The Vicar of Wakefield* and *The Arabian Nights* and *The Tales of the Genii* seem especially to have seized his imagination judging by the way that specific allusions and generalised references to them, along with Shakespearean ones, pervade all his writings, both public and private. In addition, *The Arabian Nights* with its overarching framework story and stories within stories was to have as profound an effect upon his later structuring of his own work as Addison and Steele's *Tatler* and *Spectator* were to have upon his journalism. During his thirties and forties, from the time of writing *A Christmas Carol* onwards, Dickens celebrated the wonder and delight of all this childhood reading many times, always with an apparently effortless total recall of details of plots, settings and characters. A much-quoted passage in *David Copperfield* is the most famous example but we might also remember the description of the window display in a children's bookshop in Salisbury that entrances Tom Pinch in *Martin Chuzzlewit*, chapter 5, and two of Dickens's finest *Household Words* essays, the already-cited 'A Christmas Tree' and 'Where We Stopped Growing' (1 Jan. 1853).[16]

The *Copperfield* passage occurs in chapter 4 of the novel. David remembers how, as a child, he was consoled under the Murdstone tyranny by reading the books his dead father had left in a small room upstairs and how such characters as Roderick Random, Tom Jones, Don Quixote and Robinson Crusoe had emerged from that room 'a glorious host to keep me company' and how they 'kept alive my fancy, and my hope of something beyond that time and place'. Forster tells us this is one of the many passages in the novel that are 'literally true' and that, as far as Dickens's biography is concerned, 'its proper place is here', that is, in his first chapter describing Dickens's early years in Chatham. At that time, however, as we have seen, the boy's imagination was already being richly nourished by the place itself, his father's stories and his books, his role-playing games, his visits to the theatre and so on. Years later, for good fictional purposes, he conflates in *Copperfield* memories of his 'glorious' Chatham reading with others belonging to the desolating months in Camden Town that followed the family move to London, when in time he found himself sent on errands to sell piecemeal the little volumes that had meant so much to him. Forster, by inserting the *Copperfield* passage where he does (not even troubling to alter the local references to the novel's Blunderstone) and presenting it as 'literally' autobiographical, distorts the biographical record, wittingly or unwittingly.[17]

As far as we know, there was only one thing that cast a shadow over Dickens's bright Chatham years and that was his propensity to what Forster calls 'attacks of violent spasm' in his side, from which he continued to suffer to a greater or lesser degree for the rest of his life and which he attributed to inflammation of his left kidney. These agonising attacks left him for a time weak and unable to join in games or rambles with other boys and it would have been then that the pleasures of the imagination derived from all his omnivorous reading would have been an especial resource for him. He was thinking of such times, no doubt, when he pictured himself in his 1848 preface to *Nickleby* as having been a 'not very robust child, sitting in bye-places near Rochester Castle, with a head full of Partridge, Strap, Tom Pipes, and Sancho Panza [characters from Fielding, Smollett and Cervantes]'.[18]

A few months after the Dickens family moved to St Mary's Place, on 11 December 1821, Mary Allen married again and left to join her new husband Dr Matthew Lamert, a surgeon attached to the Ordnance Hospital in Chatham. He was a middle-aged widower with three sons and, according to Forster, Dickens later based the character of the peremptory Dr Slammer in *Pickwick* upon him. His oldest son James, born in 1802, came to lodge with the Dickenses after his father's remarriage and was kind to little Charles. James Lamert was a keen theatre-goer and encouraged the boy's strong attraction to the delights of live theatre, first stimulated, presumably, by those trips to London to see the great Grimaldi. Lamert took him to shows in Rochester's Theatre Royal and in 'Dullborough Town' Dickens, richly blending the comic and the nostalgic, as he does throughout this fine essay, celebrates his rapt childhood absorption in a milieu where the world of imaginative delight is so often intertwined with the humours of the all-too-mundane in the shape of makeshift props and scenery, inadequate actors, and jocose interventions by the audience.[19]

James Lamert was, it seems, no passive theatre-goer but would sometimes organise private theatricals in the Ordnance Hospital, at that time 'almost uninhabited', and it was most likely he who encouraged his young protégé to write a play himself. One of *The Tales of the Genii*, 'The Enchanters, or, Misnar the Sultan of India', seems to have made a particularly strong impression on Dickens – a lasting one, too, since there is a strikingly elaborate allusion to it at a climactic point in *Great Expectations* (end of ch. 38) – and, as noted at the outset of this chapter, he precociously composed an entire tragedy based on this long, wandering but also highly sensational story.[20]

By the time young Lamert took him up Dickens's happy time at Chatham was drawing to a close. Within the year John Dickens was posted back to London. With six children now to feed – a fourth son, Alfred Lamert Dickens, having been born on 11 March 1822 – and debts still owing, he and Elizabeth had also to cope with the drop in income this move inevitably entailed because of losing the outport allowance. John's salary, £441 in 1822, fell to £350 in 1823. We do not know what their mood was on leaving Chatham but, given their natural buoyancy, it is hard to think that they were much engloomed. Whether

Dickens left with them and the rest of the family, including an orphan from Chatham Workhouse who replaced Mary Weller – Jane Bonny had gone with Dr and Mrs Lamert – is not clear. His later reference to William Giles's appearing among the packing-cases 'on the night before we came away' to give him a precious parting present, a copy of Goldsmith's short-lived weekly *The Bee*, collected in volume form, suggests that he did. However, Giles's elderly sister told Langton that Dickens was, 'almost at the last minute', left with her brother and stayed with him 'some little time longer' before leaving to join his family in London (possibly to finish the school term). In that case, the Uncommercial Traveller's moving rite-of-passage description of his forlorn and solitary departure from Dullborough Town might be, as Forster asserts, truly autobiographical:

As I left Dullborough in the days when there were no railroads in the land, I left it in a stage-coach. Through all the years that have since passed, have I ever lost the smell of the damp straw in which I was packed – like game – and forwarded, carriage paid, to the Cross Keys, Wood-street, Cheapside, London? There was no other inside passenger, and I consumed my sandwiches in solitude and dreariness, and it rained hard all the way, and I thought life sloppier than I had expected to find it.[21]

CHAPTER 2

Early years

LONDON, 1822–1827

When I tread the old ground, I do not wonder that I seem to see and pity, going on before me, an innocent romantic boy, making his imaginative world out of such strange experiences and sordid things!

David Copperfield, ch.11

THE DICKENSES' new home, 16 Bayham Street in Camden Town, was appreciably smaller than their last house in Chatham, though the rateable value (£22 p.a.) was higher than that of the Ordnance Terrace house (£5. 10s.). John Dickens needed to retrench but the evidence indicates that he was soon running up bills with his baker and other tradesmen. For her part, Elizabeth Dickens continued to be landlady as well as wife and mother and so arranged the new home that, even within the confined space of its four rooms on two floors, young Lamert could continue lodging with the family, at least for the time being. He probably had the front room on the first floor, as Tommy Traddles does in *Copperfield* (ch. 27) when he lodges with the Micawbers in Camden Town, in a house Dickens seems to have based on his memories of Bayham Street. The family, now six in all, would have been squeezed into the remaining accommodation and the little orphan maid-of-all-work whose 'sharp little worldly and also kindly ways' Dickens was later to recall when depicting the Marchioness in *The Old Curiosity Shop* would have bedded down in the basement kitchen. Dickens himself slept in a kind of rear garret which had its own little staircase but was no more than 'a sort of cupboard some four and a half feet high, hanging over the [main] stairway'.[1]

Forster, doubtless echoing what he had often heard from Dickens himself, described the area as being then 'about the poorest part of the London suburbs' and the house itself as 'a mean small tenement, with a wretched little back-garden abutting on a squalid court'. This description of Bayham Street and its environs was objected to by some *Daily Telegraph* readers when Forster published it in vol.1 of his *Life of Dickens*. One reader signing himself or herself 'F. M.' called it 'a perfect caricature of a quiet street in what was then but a village' while another opined that such a grim description 'must have been prompted by [Dickens's] personal privations'.[2]

3 16 Bayham Street, Camden Town

Forster's treatment of Bayham Street exemplifies, in fact, the problematic nature of attempting any sort of objective account of Dickens's life during 1822–24. Over twenty years later Dickens himself wrote very powerfully and eloquently about this period in the so-called 'autobiographical fragment' which he used in *Copperfield* and then gave to Forster (though in quite what form is a puzzle). Forster quotes extensively from it in the second chapter of his *Life of Dickens* and, since neither anyone involved with the Dickens family at this time nor even anyone who simply came across them has left any record, we have nothing against which to check this strongly emotional account by Dickens himself of his experiences and way of life during these two years. We should also remember that by the time he wrote it he had long been vividly aware of himself as 'the Inimitable', a phenomenally gifted and hugely popular creative artist – of being, in fact, what Carlyle was to call 'a *unique* of talents'. Moreover, after the profound effect that his 1842 American journey had had upon his sense of self, he had begun, from the time of writing *A Christmas Carol* onwards, to draw on his own early life for fictional purposes at a much deeper level than before. It is from the standpoint of an established and much-acclaimed literary prodigy, a man in his own words 'famous and caressed and happy', that he looks back in anger, grief and pity, as well as something close to incredulity, at what was done to him in his eleventh and twelfth years.[3]

There must certainly have been much that was bewildering and disturbing about the new family situation for a sensitive and imaginative ten-year-old like Dickens. The abrupt termination of his schooling with, apparently, no plan for its resumption and an only partial comprehension of his father's increasing financial difficulties – a partial comprehension later turned to richly comic account when he was writing the Micawber chapters of *Copperfield* – must have been uppermost among his concerns, as well as his sudden isolation from friends of his own age. It may have been about this time, too, that his infant sister Harriet died which, along with the news of Mary Lamert's death in Ireland in September 1822, would have added further gloom to the already beleaguered household. Then in April 1823 Fanny, his dear companion and confidante, left home, having been admitted as a boarder and piano pupil at the newly-founded Royal Academy of Music. It was not only the loss of her company that would have distressed Dickens but also what must have seemed to him the sheer unfairness of this. Somehow thirty-eight guineas a year could be found to pay Fanny's board and tuition fees at the Academy but apparently nothing could be spared for the continuance of *his* education. There would have been a bitter personal resonance for him many years later in what he wrote in chapter 8 of *Great Expectations*, 'In the little world in which children have their existence . . . there is nothing so finely perceived and so finely felt as injustice.'

Today we may well understand how Fanny's harassed parents must have welcomed Thomas Tomkison's willingness to recommend her to the Royal Academy of Music. Tomkison was a piano-maker in Dean Street, Soho, and perhaps came to know the Dickenses through Thomas Barrow, who lodged close by in Gerrard Street. The young Dickens could hardly have been expected to reflect that this privileging of Fanny's education was, from his parents' point of view, entirely reasonable. Yet, as a close student of Dickens's early life has observed (surely correctly), 'Although Charles had given promise of a precocious literary bent . . . Fanny's talent as a pianist and her possession of a good soprano voice were deemed to be a surer guarantee of potential earning power.' In fact, John and Elizabeth had precious little evidence for detecting a 'precocious literary bent' in their eldest son. True, he had written *Misnar* and maybe some other 'juvenile tragedies' but this had more to do with his passionate response to theatre than with literature. They would not have seen his two sketches of curious London characters mentioned in the previous chapter (above, p. 1) as he had not dared to show them to anyone. What *was* remarkable was his talent for comic recitals and comic songs, something that proved to be also very useful at this time for entertaining his godfather Christopher Huffam and his cronies, one of whom pronounced the boy a 'progidy'. But a career for his eldest son as a 'professional gentleman' entertaining the boozy patrons of 'harmonic evenings', like Mr Smuggins in *Sketches by Boz* or Little Swills in *Bleak House*, would hardly have been something that even the convivial and generally easy-going John would have contemplated with equanimity.[4]

So the puzzled boy was left alone to fall into a mooching way of life, in which he would often, as he later told Forster, spend time gazing dreamily at the distant city of London from a spot near some almshouses at the top of Bayham Street, 'a treat that served him for hours of vague reflection afterwards'. He made himself useful about the house, cleaned his father's shoes, and ran domestic errands, all the time doubtless feeling both bewilderment and hurt that no-one seemed to have any plans for him. He knew he had a 'kind-hearted and generous' father who had watched by him when he was ill 'unweariedly and patiently, many days and nights', and who had encouraged him to dream of one day coming to live in a fine house like Gad's Hill if he worked hard enough. Yet this same father seemed, he later wrote, 'in the ease of his temper and the straitness of his means . . . to have utterly lost at this time the idea of educating me at all, and to have utterly put from him the notion that I had any claim upon him, in that regard, whatever'. Whether this was John Dickens's actual state of mind with respect to his eldest son or whether, as is most likely, he was simply unable to pay a second set of tuition fees we cannot now know. Nor can we know what answer he gave when Dickens asked him, as surely he must have done, when he was going back to school. All we know for sure is that, whatever the situation was at the time, the way Dickens recalled it twenty years or so later was that John's attitude towards his education seemed, incomprehensibly, to have been one of total obliviousness.[5]

Dickens's life, if devoid of schooling, was not without its treats and pleasures at this time, however. Lamert made a toy theatre for him to play with, and perhaps even took him again to some actual theatres. He found a new source for books, among them Jane Porter's *Scottish Chiefs* and Holbein's *Dance of Death*, borrowing them from Uncle Thomas Barrow's landlady in Gerrard Street, who was a bookseller's widow (he went there often to visit and help Barrow, laid up with a broken leg). Many of these pleasures can be related directly to his later emergence as the supreme novelist of London, the writer who, both as novelist and journalist, was to describe the city 'like a special correspondent for posterity'. Among the books he borrowed was the same collection of comic verse, Colman's *Broad Grins*, in which his father had found the recitation piece with which he had scored such a triumph at the 'annual display' at Giles's school in Chatham. Whether or not this now gave him a pang, he was entranced by the description of Covent Garden he found in another of Colman's doggerel poems and one time 'stole down to the market by himself to compare it with the book'. Telling Forster this, he remembered how he went 'snuffing up the flavour of the faded cabbage-leaves as if it were the very breath of comic fiction'. This seems to have been a solo expedition, as perhaps were his visits to Gerrard Street, but more usually he was accompanied by an adult – sometimes James Lamert perhaps – on visits to the city, responding with fascination and delight to all the sights and sounds of the place. In particular, he was strongly attracted (the 'attraction of repulsion' as Forster calls it) to the so-called 'rookery' or labyrinthine slum sheltering many criminals of St Giles, located at the southern end of the Tottenham Court Road, the kind of locality he was later to describe in his 1841 preface to *Oliver Twist* as full of 'foul and frowsy dens, where vice is closely packed and lacks the room to turn'. Forster records him as saying that 'if he could only induce whomsoever took him out to take him through Seven-dials [an area forming part of the "rookery" or crime-infested slum of St Giles and later the subject of one of his Boz sketches], he was supremely happy: "Good Heaven!" he would exclaim, "what wild visions of prodigies of wickedness, want, and beggary, arose in my mind out of that place!" He loved also the visits to Godfather Huffam in Limehouse which gave him glimpses of the riverside and boatyard life there while "the London night-sights as he returned were a perpetual joy and marvel". These visits must have seemed a bit like the old days at the Mitre in Chatham come back again as Huffam's friends applauded the boy's comic singing, and his kindly godfather gave him also more tangible proof of his appreciation in the form of a very handsome half-crown tip. Huffam was, as Dickens was to put it later, the kind of godfather "who knew his duty and did it".[6]

The essay in which this phrase appears is 'Gone Astray', which Dickens published in his magazine *Household Words* on 13 August 1853. Written in the first person, it purports to describe, 'literally and exactly', how the writer was taken as a child for a sight-seeing walk in London, got accidentally separated from his escort, and spent a whole day wandering about the city with his head full of stories about Dick Whittington and Sinbad the Sailor and wondering at all the mysteries and marvels of the place like the huge images of the giants Gog and Magog in the Guildhall. Whether this essay was based on an actual experience of being lost we do not know but one distinguished Dickens scholar has noted that the vividness of his description of little Florence Dombey's feelings when she finds herself lost in a similar situation (*Dombey and Son*, ch. 6) suggests that he is indeed remembering an actual occurrence. However this may be, what is certainly true is that one of the main effects Dickens seeks to create in 'Gone Astray' is to make the reader experience a romantic child's thrilled and attentive response to the city with all its multi-tudinous wonders and dangers and this is something that we may certainly take as reflecting autobiographical truth.[7]

For it was at this time that Dickens's lifelong fascination with the sights and sounds of London, and with the myriad strange human life-forms bred or shaped by the city, really took hold of him, and even found its first expression in writing. As already noted in the previous chapter, he tried his hand at sketching a couple of ripe London characters. He came across the eccentric old barber (who may have been none other than the father of Turner) through Thomas Barrow, who was shaved by him. The deaf old woman who helped his mother in Bayham Street had a skill in making 'delicate hashes with walnut-ketchup' that put Dickens in mind of a character in one of his favourite stories Le Sage's *Gil Blas*, the pampered canon's housekeeper who could soften dishes down 'to the most delicate or voluptuous palate'. It seems very likely that the old barber, 'who was never tired of reviewing the events of the last war', also reminded Dickens of Sterne's Uncle Toby in another of his favourite books *Tristram Shandy* (Toby is obsessed by memories of certain events of the Seven Years' War). We seem to have here, in fact, traces of the earliest example of something that was to become a leading characteristic of Dickens's later writings both fictional and non-fictional, that is, his use, for a variety of purposes, of literary allusion, especially to Shakespeare and to many of the best-loved books of his childhood such as those just mentioned and *The Arabian Nights*.[8]

John Dickens's affairs, meanwhile, went from bad to worse. He fell behind with payment of the rates and got deeper into debt. He could hardly expect further help from Thomas Barrow nor from his widowed mother, former housekeeper at Crewe Hall, who was now living in retirement in Oxford Street. From her he had, as she recorded in her will in January 1824, already had 'several Sums of Money some years ago' and she therefore left him £50 less than she left to his childless elder brother William. To young Charles she gave her husband's silver watch but no more money to John. In the autumn of 1823 Dickens's mother, feeling that she must 'do something', decided to open a school. Dickens presents this in the autobiographical fragment and in *Copperfield* as a comically hopeless undertaking and was still mocking it years later, after his mother's death (in *Our Mutual Friend*, Bk I, ch.4), even though it really was not such a hare-brained idea. By Dickens's own account, Elizabeth Dickens was a good teacher and it was reasonable to hope that Christopher Huffam might, through his contacts with parents going out to India, be able to get her some pupils. Bigger and better-situated premises were certainly needed for the purpose, however, and shortly before Christmas, the family moved into 4 Gower Street North, Bloomsbury, which had a rental value of £50 per annum. A large brass plate on the front door read 'Mrs Dickens's Establishment', circulars were printed and Charles helped to distribute them but not a single pupil appeared. For Huffam the timing was unpropitious as he was verging on bankruptcy. Charles's errands now mainly consisted of taking household items (as well as precious books from his father's library) to the pawnbroker's while his parents made a last desperate struggle to stay afloat. Eleven years later, after Dickens had begun publishing sketches of London under the pen-name of 'Boz', his enthusiastic readers would have no suspicion of the wretched personal experience on which he was drawing for the harsh comedy and pathos of his *Evening Chronicle* sketch (30 June 1835) of a pawn-broker's shop, with its 'little dens, or closets' for the concealment of the more timid or respectable customers.[9]

By early February 1824 it was clear that the school idea was a non-starter. Then came an opportunity for Charles, now just twelve years old, to become largely self-supporting. A cousin of James Lamert's had bought a business and installed him as its manager. The business in question was a small riverside manufactory of blacking for use on boots and stoves, located at Old Hungerford Stairs, just off the Strand. A certain Jonathan Warren had started it, having quarrelled with his brother Robert, owner of a well-established blacking factory at 30 Strand. Lamert offered to employ Charles to make neat wrappers for the pots of blacking, and to paste labels onto these. For six or seven shillings a week the boy would work a ten-hour day six days a week, with an hour allowed for a mid-day meal and a half-hour for tea. Dickens's parents accepted this offer, perhaps believing in their optimistic way that this humble 'factory-floor' job might prove to be the first step on the ladder of a business career. Six or seven shillings a week was, moreover, by no means a bad wage for a twelve-year-old in 1824. Three years later, for example, Charles's starting-wage as an attorney's office-boy was only ten shillings and sixpence per week. Lamert undertook to give him some schooling in the dinner-hour and initially kept him segregated from two other boys similarly employed. Both these arrangements soon proved impracticable, however. The lessons lapsed and Charles moved downstairs to work alongside the other two whose names were Bob Fagin and Poll Green.

Dickens's laconic later comment about Bob Fagin in the autobiographical fragment, 'I took the liberty of using his name, long afterwards, in *Oliver Twist*', has – not surprisingly – been much discussed. Clearly, something much deeper and more complex was going on in Dickens's psyche when he named his diabolic arch-villain Fagin than when he borrowed Poll Green's first name, as he also confessed to having done, for the minor character Poll Sweedlepipe in *Martin Chuzzlewit*. It is something best discussed later, however, in the context of the writing of *Oliver Twist*.[10]

The exact date when Dickens began work at Warren's is unknown but seems likely to have been 9 February 1824, two days after his twelfth birthday. Hardly had he had a chance to deal with this apparent extinction for ever of all hopes of the kind of professional or genteel middle-class career he had been brought up to expect than there came another terrible blow. His wonderful gentlemanly father was arrested for debt. After a brief interval in a sponging-house, during which Charles (presumably granted leave from the blacking factory) ran frantic errands trying to borrow some ready money from one source or another, John

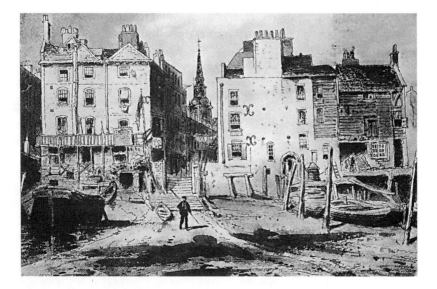

4 Old Hungerford Stairs

Dickens entered the Marshalsea Prison, Southwark, on 20 February. 'The sun', he declared with characteristic grandiosity, 'had set on him for ever'. This humiliation of his father must have been an appalling thing for Charles, made worse by his lurid memories of Smollett's description of Marshalsea prisoners in *Roderick Random*. 'I really believed at the time', Dickens told Forster later, 'that they [his parents] had broken my heart.' John had been arrested at the suit of a baker to whom he owed £10 but it has been pointed out that this debt (which, with costs, amounted to £40) was only a holding one and others would doubtless have been put in after his detention. Remarkably, he was still getting his Navy Pay Office salary but next quarter-day was a whole month off and meanwhile there were the outgoings on the house in Gower Street to meet as well as the family's general living expenses. 'Quarter-days', 'Boz' was later to write, no doubt remembering John's difficulties, 'are as eccentric as comets: moving wonderfully quick when you have a good deal to pay, and marvellously slow when you have a little to receive.' On 2 March John addressed a petition from 4 Gower Street North to the Navy Treasurer William Huskisson asking for superannuation on account of ill health ('chronic affection of the Urinary Organs'). He was entitled to a pension of five-twelfths of his salary because of his length of service and retirement would leave him free to seek other employment with which to supplement this.[11]

Meanwhile he and Elizabeth had to address the present crisis. A debtor's family could join him or her in the Marshalsea if, like John, he or she could pay for a private room. The Gower Street house, now presumably mostly denuded of furniture, was given up, probably early in April, and Elizabeth and the three younger children, Letitia, Fred and Alfred, moved into the prison while a lodging for the orphan servant-girl was found nearby. Dickens himself was sent to lodge in Little College Street, Camden Town (just around the corner from Bayham Street), with an old family friend, Mrs Roylance, on whose character and personality he later drew when creating the rebarbative Mrs Pipchin in *Dombey and Son*. From Little College Street to Warren's Blacking was nearly three miles. On Sundays he would call for Fanny at the Music Academy and they would go together to the Marshalsea which would mean a twelve-mile walk for him in total. All this must have intensified his sense of banishment from the family bosom, as well as adding such long treks to either end of his working day. His later account of this period in the 'autobiographical fragment' is full of bitterness towards his parents and pity for his younger self (as well as not a little pride in his capacity for survival) but there can surely be no doubt that at the time he would have been deeply unhappy and miserably bewildered both by what was befalling him and by his parents' apparent insouciance. The result was that the figures of inadequate, or downright culpable, parents and hapless, innocent child-victims were deeply imprinted upon his imagination at this time and later became central to his fictional world.[12]

Dickens later told Forster that 'in every respect ... but elbow-room' his parents and siblings 'lived more comfortably in prison than they had done for a long time out of it' and experienced 'no want of bodily comforts' there. In fact, they were crammed into a low-ceilinged room ten and a half feet square in a stale-smelling, crowded tenement. Although recently rebuilt, the Marshalsea was still a very confined place, unlike the more spacious and comfortable King's Bench Prison to which Dickens later sent Mr Micawber. John may indeed have been able to afford some 'bodily comforts' and he certainly made himself a person of consequence inside the prison by becoming chairman of the inmates' committee that effectively ran the place. Nevertheless, life within the Marshalsea walls would still have been pretty oppressive – though much less so, of course, than for the destitute debtors living 'on the poor side'.[13]

Meanwhile, Dickens was unwittingly continuing that education in the teeming street-life and strange old corners of London that was to be so fundamental to his later artistic triumphs, and to which he was to pay wry tribute in chapter 20 of *Pickwick* when Tony Weller answers Mr Pickwick's enquiry about his son Sam's education by saying he had 'let him run in the streets when he was wery young, and shift for his-self', this being 'the only way to make a boy sharp'. The young Dickens now had ample opportunity, for example, to explore the 'fine, dissipated, insoluble mystery' of Covent Garden, or the differently mysterious 'dark arches' beneath the Adelphi Terrace, to come upon unexpected sights like coal-heavers dancing outside a riverside public-house, or to observe and hear stories about such weird London characters as the half-crazed 'White Woman of Berners Street' who was always dressed as a bride and who was, years later, to contribute to the creation of Miss Havisham in *Great Expectations*. He could make a close study, too, of his father's fellow-prisoners in the Marshalsea, remembering them all, as he later wrote, 'when I looked with my mind's eye, into the Fleet prison during Mr Pickwick's incarceration', and recalling them again later both in *Copperfield* and in *Little Dorrit*. In the evenings he would listen avidly to his mother as she relayed to him all the stories she had heard about, or from, various of the debtors.[14]

These evening talks took place after more congenial lodgings had been found for him closer to the prison, in Lant Street (later to be humorously sketched in chapter 32 of *Pickwick*) so that he could breakfast and sup with his family. His new landlord was 'a fat, good-natured, kind old gentleman' who was lame and had 'a quiet old wife' and 'a very innocent grown-up son, who was lame too'. He was to remember them all when he came to depict the Garland family in *The Old Curiosity Shop*. Sometimes, when waiting for the prison-gates to open in the morning, he would meet his parents' little maid on London Bridge and tell her 'quite astonishing fictions about the wharves and the tower'. Perhaps some of them derived from a twopenny magazine he bought every Saturday called *The Portfolio of Entertaining and Instructive Varieties in History, Science, Literature, the Fine Arts, etc.* This paper, although it included much crude sensationalism ('All of us are in Danger of being Buried Alive' runs one typical headline), was also full of 'smart schoolboy humour' and had definite pretensions to literary merit and middle-class cultural values, as its title indicates. These pretensions, together with the magazine's fondness for reprinting tales from his beloved *Arabian Nights*, must have represented for Dickens a precious link back to his Chatham schooldays and altogether happier times.[15]

John Dickens meanwhile was beginning the process of regaining his freedom through getting himself declared insolvent. His mother died while his application to the Insolvent Debtors' Court was still in process but he could not touch his £450 bequest since it had to be applied to the settlement of his debts. He was, in fact, discharged from the Marshalsea, 'per Insolvency Act', on 28 May, a whole week before his mother's will had been proved by his brother, the sole executor.[16]

The family at first went back to stay with Mrs Roylance in Little College Street and then, according to Forster, moved to somewhere in Hampstead. This meant that Charles's walks to and from the Strand once again became even longer treks, though he perhaps now had his father for company since John had resumed his duties at Somerset House whilst awaiting the result of his superannuation request. On 29 June 1824 Charles witnessed the ceremony at which Fanny received the Royal Academy of Music's silver medal and the second prize for the piano and wept to think that he himself had no opportunity to compete for such honours. All he could do was to rival Bob Fagin's dexterity in dealing with the blacking-pots. Unfortunately, the boys' remarkable speed and skill made passers-by stop to stare admiringly in at the window by which they worked in the Chandos Street premises, just a bit south-west of Covent Garden, to which Jonathan Warren had moved his establishment. This exposure of his status as 'a common labouring boy' to the public gaze must have been a searing experience for the young Dickens and it has been persuasively argued that it left an indelible mark upon his art. It may also have been the means of securing his release from Warren's. This public exhibition of his son and heir working at a menial job might, Dickens later believed, have offended his father and have caused the sharp quarrel between him and Lamert that resulted in John's taking his son away. To the boy's incredulous horror, his mother (presumably only too aware of the continuing precariousness of the family finances) exerted herself to patch up the quarrel and came back from Chandos Street with a request for the boy to return the next day. John would not allow this, however, and declared that he should return to school. And so the notorious blacking factory episode, which, according to the latest research, may have lasted much longer than was once assumed – thirteen or fourteen months, an eternity for a twelve-year-old – came at last to a close.[17]

At the close of 1824, a couple of months before John Dickens began drawing his pension, the Dickens family moved to Johnson Street, Somers Town, described by the Dickens scholar Frederic Kitton in 1905 as having been 'a poverty-stricken neighbourhood even in those days'. It was a colourful district, however. Successive waves of French and Spanish political refugees had come to live there, as well as a large artistic colony, noted in Hone's *Year Book* for 1826. Many years later, when he was writing *Bleak House* and located the dilettante Harold Skimpole in this neighbourhood, Dickens remembered, and included in his topographical description, the 'poor Spanish refugees walking about in cloaks, smoking little paper cigars' whom he had noticed in his boyhood.[18]

The first evidence we have of John's having a new job occurs in September 1826 when we find him writing articles on marine insurance for *The British Press* but it seems likely that he had been working for this paper as a parliamentary reporter for some time previously. The presumption is that some time during 1824/25 he had decided to try journalism, taught himself Gurney's fiendishly complicated system of shorthand, and had begun picking up what reporting and other journalistic work he could. He most likely had help from another brother-in-law, John Henry Barrow, who had contributed to *The British Press* in the past. His financial difficulties continued, as shown by his letter to the Royal Academy of Music of 6 October 1825, asking for an 'order', or I.O.U., to be accepted in lieu of present payment for Fanny's next quarter's fees. 'A circumstance of great moment to me,' he wrote, 'will be decided in the ensuing term [i.e., legal term of Michaelmas] which I confidently hope will place me in comparative affluence, and by which I shall be enabled to redeem the order before the period of Christmas Day.' Whether this 'circumstance' related to the first pay-out to his creditors, which happened in Rochester on 2 November, we do not know but that would most likely have had to do with his mother's legacy. Here he may have been referring to the possibility of becoming a staffer on *The British Press*, though that would hardly make him 'affluent' – unless, of course, the 'comparative' relates to near-indigence.[19]

Continuing difficulties notwithstanding, John was evidently now able to dispense with Charles's six or seven shillings a week and to send him back to school. Charles emerged from Warren's 'with a relief so strange that it was like oppression' and went, as a day boy of course, to the grandly-named Wellington House Academy in the Hampstead Road, which had a reputation, evidently thoroughly undeserved, as 'a very superior sort of school, one of the best indeed in that part of London'. The school was owned and run by one William Jones, whom Dickens later described in a speech in 1857 as 'by far the most ignorant man I have ever had the pleasure to know, who was one of the worst-tempered men perhaps that ever lived, whose business it was to make as much out of us and to put as little into us as possible, and who sold us at a figure which I remember we used to delight to estimate, as amounting to exactly £2.4s.6d a head.' Jones's fondness for thrashing his pupils, especially plump, tightly-clad boys, is well attested in the memories of Dickens's schoolfellows as communicated to Forster and Robert Langton. Dickens afterwards made it a notable attribute of David's brutal schoolmaster, Mr Creakle for whom it was 'like the satisfaction of a craving appetite'.[20]

Such reminiscences as are on record all agree in describing Dickens as a very lively schoolboy with 'a more than usual flow of spirits', something that the letter quoted at the beginning of the last chapter seems to bear out. An anonymous contributor to *The Dickensian* in 1911 remembered attending a 'juvenile party' in Johnson Street at which young Charles sang a popular comic song, 'The Cat's Meat Man', with 'great energy and action, his tone and manner displaying the full zest with which he appreciated and entered into the vulgarity of the composition'. Evidently, his time in the blacking-factory had left no outward mark upon him unless it were to make him more self-consciously gentlemanly in his bearing and appearance. He held his head 'more erect than lads ordinarily do' and was 'very particular with his clothes . . . a blue sailor costume and a blue cloth cap', appearing always 'like a gentleman's son, rather aristocratic than otherwise'. He seems to have imported into Wellington House from his Chatham schooldays the 'lingo' joke (pretending to be speaking in a foreign language). A favourite occupation among Jones's pupils was, according to two of them who wrote to Forster, the getting up of amateur theatricals, either in the school – though this is categorically denied by the anonymous writer in *The Dickensian* – or in each other's homes. One of Forster's correspondents remembered Dickens getting up a play in the back-kitchen of a friend's house with an improvised plot and speeches: 'when we had finished, we were quite sure that if there had only been an audience they would all have cried, so deep we made the tragedy'. As already noted, Dickens also belonged to a little club that wrote and circulated small tales, and with a fellow-pupil called John Bowden, he produced something they called *Our Newspaper*, written on scraps of copy-book paper and loaned out on payment of marbles or pieces of slate pencil. As to academic studies, although the personal oddities of some of the ushers (assistant masters) are recalled in these various reminiscences, hardly anything is said about their actual teaching. Dickens may or may not have been taught some Latin at the school (the evidence is conflicting) but as to English, 'his wonderful knowledge and command of English must have been acquired by long and patient study after leaving his last school.' In fact, the foundations of this 'wonderful knowledge and command' had been laid three or four years earlier during his voracious private reading of literary classics in his Chatham days.[21]

From the point of view of Dickens's development as a writer, therefore, the only effect of his two years' schooling at Wellington House would seem to have been to provide him with some good copy for future use. Besides supplying Jones as a model for Creakle Wellington House also provided rich material for Dickens's fanciful reminiscent essay 'Our School' in *Household Words* (11 Oct. 1851). As to what mainly fed his imagination during these two years we must look for this not to the school curriculum but to the various cheap weekly magazines to which he and his schoolfellows were addicted. One that he specially mentioned to Forster was called *The Terrific Register*. With this he could, at the cost of a penny, frighten the very wits out of his head, which, as he told Forster, 'considering there was an illustration to every number, in which there was always a pool of blood, and at least one body, was cheap'. It has been noted that the stories featured in it 'range into torture, incest, the devouring of human bodies, physical details of various horrible methods of execution, and a variety of other such pleasant and profitable subjects'. Clearly, it was stronger meat than *The Portfolio* and had none of that magazine's pretensions to middle-class culture and 'improvement', but Dickens, now restored to his rightful place in society, had no longer any need to be anxious about this and so could dispense with *The Portfolio*. A normal schoolboy now, he could feel free to indulge in 'a taste for crude sensationalism'.[22]

We know little about John Dickens's financial situation during 1826/27 except that there was a second pay-out to his creditors on 13 November 1826, and that he experienced repeated difficulties in paying Fanny's fees at the Academy. A severe blow to him must have been the closure of *The British Press* at the end of October 1826 and on 6 February he petitioned Lloyds Insurance Company, which he had always boosted in the paper, for some compensation since this closure had 'caused him serious pecuniary inconvenience' (he was awarded ten guineas). The failure of the paper may have deprived Charles of some little income too in that, as 'a smart, intelligent, active lad', he had, according to Samuel Carter Hall, who also worked on *The British Press*, taken to bringing to the paper voluntary reports of accidents or fires not covered by the paper's regular reporters and to being paid for them as a 'penny-a-liner'. There was evidently some sort of crisis in the Dickens family finances in March 1827 when they were evicted from their Johnson Street house for non-payment of rates and moved into temporary lodgings in the Polygon, a circle of houses facing outwards in nearby Clarendon Square. Fanny had to leave the Academy in June but returned two months later as a part-time 'sub-professor' paid seven shillings for six hours work a week. Meanwhile, Charles left Wellington House for good. He quitted it, one presumes, with little regret, eager to 'begin the world' again, as the phrase then went, but this time to do so in a respectable situation.[23]

Elizabeth Dickens had a married aunt, Elizabeth Charlton, who kept a boarding-house in Berners Street (the notorious White Woman's beat). She often visited this aunt and sometimes took Charles or Fanny with her. Lodging with Mrs Charlton was a young solicitor called Edward Blackmore whom Elizabeth begged to find employment for Charles. Since, as Blackmore later recalled, the boy was 'exceedingly good-looking and clever' and had very prepossessing manners, he was happy to take him on as a junior clerk, and in May 1827 Dickens began working for the firm of Ellis and Blackmore in Gray's Inn, where he was to remain until November 1828. Both Blackmore himself and the firm's articled clerk George Lear contributed their memories of Dickens to Frederic Kitton's 1890 compilation *Charles Dickens by Pen and Pencil*. Both men recall something that happened on Dickens's first day at the office. He had turned up wearing 'a military-looking cap which had a strap under the chin' and carried it 'rather jauntily on one side of his head'. He was sent out on an errand and returned with a black eye. Asked by Lear how he had come by it, he explained:

a big blackguard fellow knocked my cap off as I was crossing over Chancery Lane from the Lincoln's Inn gateway. He said 'Halloa, sojer!' which I could not stand, so I at once struck him and he then hit me in the eye. A gentleman who was crossing at the same time said to the fellow, 'You blackguard! how could you dare to hit a little fellow in that way?' His answer was ready, – 'Vy, he hit me fust!'

This reads like a miniature 'Sketch by Boz' and prompts us to recognise the extent to which Blackmore's reminiscences, and still more Lear's, show how the writer of the 1834 *Morning Chronicle* 'Street Sketches' was already stirring

in the fifteen-year-old junior clerk they are recalling. They certainly recognised
this themselves. Blackmore wrote, 'His knowledge of London was wonderful,
for he could describe the position of every shop in any of the West End streets'
and Lear remembered that 'having been in London two years, I thought I knew
something of town, but after a little talk with Dickens I found that I knew
nothing. He knew it all from Bow to Brentford.' Lear also remembered how his
new colleague 'could imitate, in a manner that I have never heard equalled, the
low population of the streets of London in all their varieties, whether mere
loafers or sellers of fruit, vegetables, or anything else'.[24]

It was very soon after Dickens had started work for Ellis and Blackmore, in
fact, that the original Boz was born, in the shape of his last sibling, Augustus
Newnham Dickens (the second name honouring a former neighbour in
Ordnance Terrace who had just died and left a little money to Letitia). The new
baby was given the family nickname of Moses after Dr Primrose's gullible son
in *The Vicar of Wakefield*, a name that he pronounced as 'Boses' when he began
to talk. The family adopted this and shortened it to Boz (ardent Dickensians
still dispute as to whether it should be pronounced with a short or long o), the
pen-name Dickens adopted when he first wrote for money.

Both Blackmore and Lear also comment on Dickens's passion for the
theatre, something he shared with a salaried clerk in the office called Potter,
who carried his enthusiasm so far as to pay to act in a cheap theatre in
Catherine Street, off the Strand. Dickens and Lear sometimes went to watch
him and Dickens drew richly on his memories of such visits, at the same time
distancing himself from this somewhat tawdry former activity, several years
later in his sketch 'Private Theatres' published in the *Evening Chronicle* on
11 August 1835. There he describes such establishments as being patronised
mainly by 'dirty boys, low copying-clerks in attorneys' offices . . . and a choice
miscellany of idle vagabonds.' He also introduces Potter by name into another,
more raffish, sketch involving a theatre, 'Making a Night of It' (*Bell's Life in
London*, 18 Oct. 1835), where Potter features as a city rather than an attorney's
clerk, and is distinguished by an 'off hand, dashing, amateur pickpocket sort of
manner'. Nor, if we are to believe Blackmore and Lear, was Potter the only
figure Dickens encountered during his two years in the offices of Ellis and
Blackmore who would later serve him as a model for an eccentric character.
They also mention a broken-down farmer called Newman Knott who called
regularly at the office to collect an allowance made to him by friends from his
more prosperous days and link him with Newman Noggs in *Nickleby*. Lear also
mentions an original for Miss Flite in *Bleak House* who was known as 'the
Little Old Lady of the Court of Chancery'. She was 'the victim of some
prolonged Chancery suit which had turned her head'.

Far and away the greatest contribution these two years made to Dickens's
later literary achievements, however, was the experience it gave him of some of

the arcane mysteries of legal London, and the opportunity to observe the habits and hear the talk of the men, mainly of low or middling professional status, who made their living from the law. Lear admired the pinpoint accuracy of Dickens's portrayal of the various gradations of lawyers' clerks in chapter 31 of *Pickwick*, and the law and its practitioners feature prominently in his writings from the clerks, attorneys and barristers of *Pickwick* right through to Grewgious and Bazzard in *Edwin Drood*, most notably, of course, in his great masterpiece *Bleak House*. Lear also mentions that his firm did much work as agents for country solicitors and remembers that Dickens 'soon became very handy in doing the work at the public offices, and the old clerks who presided over the business in them, both Chancery and Common Law, came in for his imitations and descriptions'. Among the public offices young Dickens would have had to attend for business were 'the Alienation Office, the Affidavit Office, the Clerk of the Escheats, the Dispensation Office, the Filazer's, Exigenter's and Clerk of the Outlawry's Office, the Hanaper Office, the Enrolment Office, the Pell Office, the Prothonotaries' Office, the Six-Clerks Office and the Sixpenny Receivers Office'. The sheer oddity of many aspects of the world in which he was now moving must, one feels, have been some compensation to Dickens for the 'drudgery' of much of his office work. It was this drudgery that Blackmore believed was the reason for Dickens's leaving the firm in the winter of 1828. The literary barrister, and later judge, James Fitzjames Stephen, who delighted to lambaste Dickens in *The Saturday Review* from the mid 1850s on, crushingly (and snobbishly) observed in 1857 that Dickens's 'notions of law, which occupy so large a space in his books, are precisely those of an attorney's clerk'. But it was having occupied that very position that gave Dickens the opportunity to observe, at ground level, so to speak, ways in which the law could affect individuals – sometimes in the most mystifying and alarming way – and also how it specialised in making business for itself, how legal processes could become ends in themselves with very comfortable results for many of the law's practitioners. Both these perceptions were to be fundamental to the later presentation, both comic and sinister, of law and lawyers in his fiction and also in some trenchant journalistic pieces.[25]

When he left Ellis and Blackmore Dickens transferred for a few months to the office of another solicitor, Charles Molloy of New Square, Lincoln's Inn, but was beginning to chafe at the routine and restrictions and life as an attorney's clerk ('a lawyer's office', he wrote a few years later in a letter outlining the very brief and sanitised version of his biography that he was prepared to make public, 'is a very little world, and a very dull one'). For all his continuing enjoyment of larks, he was now past the stage of being one of those 'office lads' he later described in *Pickwick* chapter 31 who 'in their first surtouts . . . feel a befitting contempt for boys at day-schools: club as they go home at nights for saveloys and porter: and think there's nothing like "life" '. He was, after all, no longer an undersized boy but, in the latter months of his time at Ellis and Blackmore's, had, as it seemed to George Lear, 'grown into a young man at once' who one day, Lear remembered, presented himself in 'a new suit of clothes, brown all alike, coat cut like a dress coat, and with a high hat'.[26]

Dickens seems to have decided, after a few months working for Molloy, that the time had come for him to strike out in a different line, in a wider world. The one lasting benefit he derived from his time there was the close friendship he formed with Molloy's articled clerk Thomas Mitton whose family lived near to the Dickenses in Somers Town (they had resumed occupation of the house in Johnson Street but it is not clear on what basis). Mitton seems to have been a rather eccentric, and somewhat prickly, character but he and Dickens stayed close friends for decades, with Dickens relying on his advice in many matters. Mitton acted, in fact, as Dickens's solicitor until the 1850s, and continued to deal with certain business matters for him after that. He was especially helpful to Dickens in the 1830s and 1840s, responding to requests for small loans early on and generally helping to deal with the recurrent difficulties caused by John Dickens's fecklessness in financial matters.[27]

As far as change of career was concerned, the most obvious thing for Dickens to do was to follow his father's example and try for success as a journalist. The fact that he had a close family relative active in that world, his uncle John Henry Barrow, who might be able to give him a helping hand, must have been an added incentive. Another, but riskier, possibility was the stage. Dickens had apparently boasted to Lear of his father's intimacy with some of the leading actors of the day but we have no evidence for this, and, if he tried for an acting career, he would have to rely on his own talents. These were indeed considerable (Lear marvelled at his ability to imitate to perfection the speech and manners of so many of the contemporary stars of the stage) but, even so, the lack of contacts would have been a drawback. As will appear later, he by no means abandoned the idea of a stage career but evidently decided to try journalism first. Accordingly, he set vigorously to work to tame what David Copperfield was later to call 'that savage stenographic mystery', just as his father had done before him.[28]

CHAPTER 3

'The Copperfield days'

1828–1835[1]

I have taken with fear and trembling to authorship.

David Copperfield, ch. 43

WHEN ON 22 November 1831 John Dickens's name appeared in the *London Gazette* as someone whose finances were yet again to be examined by the Insolvent Debtors Court, he was listed as

> Dickens, John (sued as John Dickenson) first of No.13, Johnson-Street, Somer's-Town, then of No.10, Norfolk-Street, Middlesex Hospital, then of No.21, George-Street, Adelphi, and of North-End, Hampstead, and last of No.3, Belle Vue, Hampstead, all in Middlesex. . . .

This dry official notice brings home to us just how nomadic an existence the Dickens family led after leaving Johnson Street (and the variant surname prompts the idea that it may have resulted from some effort on John Dickens's part to evade his creditors). It certainly points to a restless domestic background for young Charles as he struggled, having left Molloy's law office, to establish himself in a new and more congenial career.

He considered the stage, inspired by the great comic actor Charles Mathews, an immense favourite with London audiences since 1803. Mathews was famous for his 'At Homes', solo performances including what he called a 'monopolylogue' in which he brilliantly impersonated various comic and eccentric characters of both sexes and different nationalities, the impersonations being strung together on a thread of fast-moving narrative, usually describing a journey. Comic songs, often sung in character, and short farces with Mathews playing every part generally also formed part of his programme. During 1828–32 Dickens, aware of what he called his own 'strong perception of character and oddity' and 'natural power' of reproducing in his own person what he observed in others, was a keen student of Mathews's art. He learned many of the 'At Homes' by heart, and composed at least one original one for himself. He later told Forster that after he became a jobbing shorthand writer he had spent most of his evenings in the theatre, 'really studying the bills first, and going to where there was the best acting: and always to see Mathews whenever he played'. He spent many hours every day practising 'even such things as walking in and out, and sitting down in a chair'. In early 1832 he obtained an audition at Covent Garden but a bad cold intervened and he wrote postponing his application until the following season. By then, however, a career as a parliamentary reporter was opening up before him and he did not re-apply. Mathews's histrionic versatility remained vivid in his memory, however, and as has been long recognised, contributed not a little to his development both as a writer and, later, as a public reader.[2]

The foundations of the career on which Dickens did embark, that of journalist, were laid by one of his maternal uncles, John Henry Barrow. Barrow, born in 1796, had reported the proceedings of Doctors' Commons for *The Times*, and in 1820 had achieved a great reputation with his coverage, also for *The Times*, of the trial for adultery of George IV's rejected queen, Caroline of Brunswick. He had also published a novel called *Emir Malek, Prince of the Assassins* (1827). In January 1828 he launched a major new publishing enterprise, *The Mirror of Parliament*, a weekly record of parliamentary debates with its own reporters in the press gallery, unlike *Hansard* which simply copied from the daily papers. John Dickens became one of Barrow's reporting team but it was apparently not he but John Barrow who taught Charles shorthand on the Gurney system. It was probably Barrow, too, who advised Charles to become a freelance shorthand reporter in Doctors' Commons when the young man had the opportunity, some time in 1829, of sharing a freelance reporter's box there with one Thomas Charlton, possibly a relative by marriage, as well as an office, again with Charlton (and one other), at 5 Bell Yard, near St Paul's. Charles was also following in his uncle's footsteps when he acquired, the day after his eighteenth birthday, a ticket for the British Museum reading room. There he embarked on a course of miscellaneous literary and historical reading, including Goldsmith's *History of England*, the works of Shakespeare and Addison and, rather startlingly, in September 1830, an old book about female sexuality called *Thoughts on the Times, but Chiefly on the Profligacy of Our Women* (1779).[3]

Doctors' Commons was a good place for Dickens, with his eye for the grotesque and his ear for pomposity and jargon, to start his reporting life. An antiquated institution, it was both picturesque and preposterous. It consisted of three different courts dealing respectively with 'wills, wives and wrecks' as well as with people accused of misbehaving in church or at vestry (parochial) meetings. Offenders of the last kind were punished with fines which they much resented and periods of excommunication about which they cared nothing at all. The Doctors themselves, who were holders of the degree of Doctor of Civil Law from Oxford or Cambridge, swapped around among themselves the roles of judge and advocate, depending on which court was in session. They, and the self-important proctors (attorneys) who employed them, inspired in Dickens a mixture of scornful contempt for such arcane legal procedures and amusement at the contrast between the pomposity of the proceedings and the frequently trivial or sordid realities with which they were concerned. He turned this scornful amusement to excellent literary account six years later in one of the last of his London sketches to be published in *The Morning Chronicle* (4 Oct.1836). The funniest section of this, describing Michael Bumple 'promoting', as the Doctors' Commons phrase went, a case against Thomas Sludberry for 'brawling' in a vestry meeting and using such injurious expressions as 'You be blowed' was long ago shown to have been closely based on an actual case, Jarman *v.* Wise, that Dickens reported on 18 November 1830. He was to mine his memories of this 'lazy old nook near Saint Paul's Churchyard' still more richly in *David Copperfield* thirteen years later, when he has innocent young David opt for a genteel career in Doctors' Commons, undeterred by Steerforth's ridiculing of the institution as 'a very pleasant profitable little affair of private theatricals, presented to an uncommonly select audience'.[4]

Six months before he reported Jarman *v.* Wise Dickens fell violently in love with Maria Beadnell, a pretty banker's daughter, petite and vivacious. For the next three or four years, he wrote long afterwards in one of his 'Uncommercial Traveller' essays, Maria 'pervaded every chink and crevice' of his mind. His passion also involved him in much literary composition, intended to impress both her and her parents. No doubt there is some comic exaggeration in the later essay about all the unposted letters, 'more in number than Horace Walpole's', that he indited to Maria's mother, who could never even get his name right, but we may, I think, safely believe in the actual composition of *some* such epistles at any rate, and believe also that they varied greatly in style and tone depending on the mood of hope or despair he was caught up in and acting out at the time:

> Sometimes I had begun, 'Honoured Madam. I think that a lady gifted with those powers of observation which I know you to possess, and endowed with those womanly sympathies with the young and ardent which it were more than heresy to doubt, can scarcely have failed to discover that I love your adorable daughter deeply, devotedly.' In less buoyant states of mind I had begun, 'Bear with me, Dear Madam, bear with a daring wretch who is about to make a surprising confession to you, wholly unanticipated by yourself, and which he beseeches you to commit to the flames as soon as you have become aware to what a towering height his mad ambition soars.'

His letters to Maria herself contain much heightened language not far short of this. One would, of course, expect this in love-letters written by a lover so

passionately enamoured as was Dickens, but even so the rhetorical and
theatrical element is very marked, as, for example, the use of the register of
melodrama in the following: 'I have . . . too often thought of our earlier correspondence, and too often looked back to happy hopes the loss of which have
made me the miserable restless wretch that I am . . .'.[5]

His passion for Maria stimulated another sort of writing, too, drawing on
his talent for brilliant literary mimicry. He can be seen flexing his parodic
muscles, so to speak, in various writings evidently composed to flatter, amuse
and impress the Beadnells and their circle. He wrote, probably in the autumn
of 1831, 'The Bill of Fare', a clever imitation of Goldsmith's poem 'Retaliation',
in which the poet describes all his friends as though they were dishes at a
banquet and writes mock epitaphs for them. During the course of 360 lines
Dickens compliments both Mr and Mrs Beadnell (Mr Beadnell is 'good fine
sirloin of beef' and his wife 'an excellent *Rib* of the same') and many of their
friends. Himself he describes as follows: 'A young Summer Cabbage without
any heart; – / Not that he's *heartless* but because, as folks say, / He lost his
a twelve month ago, from last May.' Maria naturally receives some pretty
compliments and even her lapdog, later immortalised as Dora's Jip, gets a
mention. Dickens contributed another clever and fluent pastiche, several
verses long, to the album that Maria kept, like most contemporary young
ladies. He parodies Southey's 'The Devil's Walk' in which the Devil finds
himself at one point near Maria's home in Lombard Street where he catches
sight of

> a face so fair
> That it made him start and weep
> For a passing thought rushed over his brain
> Of days now beyond recall.
> He thought of the bright angelic train
> And of his own wretched fall.

Dickens also contributed to Maria's album an acrostic on her name together
with other verse offerings, all jostling for attention with similar ones from her
numerous other admirers.[6]

Judging by the dates appended to Dickens's pieces, November 1831 would
seem to have been the high point of his courtship of Maria. It was about this
time, too, that he first set up his own establishment. He shared rooms in
Buckingham Street just off the Strand with another young man called James
Roney, a law student, and it was here that, in chapter 23 of *David Copperfield*,
he was to locate the young David – but in solitary splendour. Roney migrated
seven years later to Demerara in British Guiana, now Guyana, where he eventually became Chief Justice. His interest in this remote colony had perhaps

5 Maria Beadnell as milkmaid, drawn by Henry Austin for Maria's album

originated in 1831 when a Mrs Hadfield, related to the Barrows by marriage, met Dickens before returning to Demerara after a lengthy visit in England. Roney may have been present when she met Dickens who was, she recalled in later life, 'brooding over the choice of a career' and 'questioned her very closely as to the prospects for pushing his fortune in the West Indies, wanting but a little encouragement to try his luck there'. Whether he thought such a move might help him with Maria, or would serve as an escape from the torment she was causing him, we do not know, but the idea of the young Dickens 'beginning the world' among the swamps and tropical forests of Guyana is certainly a fascinating one. The place evidently stayed in his mind as it is where he has Mr Pickwick send Jingle to start a new life and also where Little Nell's grandfather vainly sends her scapegrace brother Fred for a similar purpose.[7]

His unrequited love for Maria notwithstanding, a great deal of jollity alternating with ferociously hard work seems to have been very much the mode of Dickens's existence during this period – as indeed it was for the rest of his life. There were numerous 'flares' or parties. Sometimes these were just the assembling of a few choice spirits to 'knock up a chaunt or two'. Sometimes they were more elaborate, like the group river excursion to Greenwich in spring 1833 which he invites one of his fellow-contributors to Maria's album, a trainee architect and civil engineer called Henry Austin, to join – 'We take our grub (which I provide) on board' – and which later supplied good material for one of Dickens's earliest published stories, 'The Steam Excursion' (*Monthly Magazine*, Oct. 1834). Austin, who later married Dickens's sister Letitia, became a good friend. Another friendship dating from this time was the one with the journalist Thomas Beard, five years Dickens's senior, whose family became acquainted with the Dickenses when John Dickens joined the parliamentary reporting staff of the *Morning Herald* some time after the closure of *The British Press*. Both Austin and Beard were to remain important figures in Dickens's life, unlike other close friends of this time such as the bank clerk Henry Kolle, who in 1833 married Maria's sister Anne with Dickens acting as best man.[8]

John Dickens's appearance in the Insolvent Debtors Court on 15 December 1831 did not prevent him and his wife holding a birthday party for Charles at their new home in Margaret Street, Marylebone, on 8 February 1832. By this date Dickens's fortunes were definitely improving. He had graduated from Doctors' Commons work to reporting parliamentary debates for his uncle's *Mirror* and was considered by John Barrow 'the best reporter in the gallery'. He was now also recruited by a new Radical evening paper, *The True Sun*, which began publication on 5 March. It was for the *True Sun* that he reported on the dramatic last few months of the great battle for the implementation of the Reform Bill which was passed by Parliament in March. And he was seemingly happy to supplement his salary by – astonishingly – exercising his gift for verse parody and pastiche on behalf of Warren's Blacking, of all places. A series of rhyming puffs for 'Warren's Jet Blacking – the pride of mankind' appeared in *The True Sun* between 13 March and 14 May and it does seem most probable that they were of Dickens's writing. If we believe this was the case then we surely have to reconsider his later assertion, in the autobiographical fragment, about the abiding intense horror of the blacking factory and everything connected with it that he was left with after his servitude there came to an end.[9]

The big problem for both Dickens and his father at this time as far as a regular salary was concerned was that when Parliament was not in session their occupation was gone. Such was the case from 16 August 1832 to 29 January 1833, after the dissolution of Parliament following the enactment of the Reform Bill. Both father and son, therefore, would have been glad of the remunerative work obtained for them by John Henry Barrow in late November or early December 1832. In Charles's case this work concerned the recruiting and organising of poll clerks in Lambeth for Barrow's friend the strongly pro-Reform Whig M.P. Charles Tennyson, uncle of the poet.[10]

Things must have gone reasonably well for the family on the financial front because, within a week of the re-opening of Parliament, the Dickenses were established at 18 Bentinck Street, Marylebone, in rather grander lodgings than any they had had before. Soon Elizabeth was sending out printed invitations to a party to celebrate Charles's coming of age on 7 February ('Quadrilles. 8 o'clock'). Among the guests would surely have been Maria Beadnell. She may or may not have called Dickens a mere 'boy' on that occasion, as later described in his Uncommercial Traveller essay 'Birthday Celebrations', but her behaviour seemed to him at the time yet one more example of the 'displays of heartless indifference' to which she had been subjecting him. A few weeks later, on 18 March, he reproached her with this in a long and anguished, but also self-consciously noble, letter breaking off the affair: '. . . nothing will ever afford me more real delight than to hear that you the object of my first, and my last, love, are happy'. Private misery coincided with a signal recognition of his professional competence. Lord Stanley, the Secretary for Ireland, admired the accuracy with which he had been reported by one of the Mirror of Parliament staff and asked for that person to be sent to him to take down a fair copy of the whole speech. When Dickens presented himself Stanley was astonished by his youthful appearance.[11]

Unhappiness over Maria evidently did not affect Dickens's work nor did it prevent him from throwing himself into planning and organising an ambitious programme of amateur dramatics performed in Bentinck Street on 27 April. This began with an 'Introductory Prologue', undoubtedly written by Dickens himself, followed by three dramatic pieces. The first was Henry Bishop's 1823 opera Clari the Maid of Milan which calls for elegant and complicated sets as well as a cast of sixteen and a band ('numerous and complete', according to the printed playbill drawn up by Dickens). The great song of the opera is 'Home, sweet home', sung by the heroine who was, of course, played by Fanny, and it must have had not a little resonance for the Dickens family after their very peripatetic existence in recent years. Dickens himself played Clari's old father, who wrongly believes his daughter has been ruined by the nobleman who enticed her to leave her simple country home. His role was confined to the last scene but gave him the chance to launch such lines as 'I am the scathed tree of the heath that cannot drop' directly at the head of Maria, who was sitting in the audience. Quintessentially Dickensian was his ability in the next piece, the interlude of The Married Bachelor, to parody his own passion for Maria in the role of an uncontrollably flirtatious husband. Finally, he acted the part of a strolling player (with

Mrs Joseph Porter

6 'Mrs Joseph Porter': private theatricals depicted by Cruikshank in *Sketches by Boz*

a song about being the victim of Cupid's tyranny) in R. B. Peake's farce *Amateurs and Actors*. This piece concerns the preparations for an amateur production for which the performers have hired a professional manager and includes many lines which no doubt greatly tickled the Bentinck Street audience, such as the manager's 'As Garrick observed, one easily sees when the amateurs are acting that there is not an *actor* among them.'[12]

The evening was no doubt a great triumph for Dickens but seems to have done nothing to soften Maria towards him. He made one last appeal to her in 'a very conciliatory note sans pride, sans reserve sans anything but an evident wish to be reconciled', declaring, 'I never have loved and I never can love any human creature breathing but yourself', but all to no avail. She answered him, as he was to remind her when she suddenly re-entered his life over twenty years later, 'very coldly and reproachfully' and he 'went his way', though with a heart sadder, he said, than anyone could possibly have known. A quarter of a century was to pass before he would experience again such abiding intensity of love for a woman.[13]

His wretched situation regarding Maria probably made him all the keener on masterfulness in other aspects of his life. When in October he was again organising some amateur theatricals, for example, he circulated a memo-randum to his fellow-players calling their attention to various 'Regulations' he had drawn up. This production may have been O'Thello, Dickens's burlesque operatic version of Shakespeare's tragedy, acted in Bentinck Street some time in the autumn of 1833. We know it only from the pages preserved by John Dickens containing his own part, that of 'the Great Unpaid', that were later sold or given away by him. From these surviving fragments it would seem to have been a very spirited business making adroit use of the tunes of many contem-porary popular songs of which Dickens evidently had a vast repertoire (later bestowed upon the incomparable Dick Swiveller in The Old Curiosity Shop). Here, for example, is one of Desdemona's solos, to be sung to the tune of 'There's nae luck about the house': 'Oh! let us pass a merry night,/ Our house is rather small,/But being recovered I invite/All present to a ball./There is some cold duck in the house,/ There's wine enough for all;/ Likewise some spirits and some grouse/ So we'll enjoy the ball.'[14]

Dickens seems to have given up working for the True Sun after just a few months. On 6 June he wrote a very polite letter to Lord Stanley's secretary asking Stanley to recommend him as a shorthand writer if ever the opportu-nity should arise. John Barrow also approached John Payne Collier of the Morning Chronicle for help in getting Dickens a place on that paper's parlia-mentary reporting staff. His nephew, said Barrow, was not only an excellent reporter but also 'a good singer of a comic song'. Collier met the uncle and nephew, with some others, for dinner and found Dickens very reluctant to perform to order. He did eventually get a couple of songs out of him, including one of Dickens's own compositions, 'Sweet Betsey Ogle' (about a flirtatious milkmaid), but only 'after a good deal of pressing'. If there was any entertain-ment going on, Dickens now wanted to be the organiser and not the one who was organised – as he had been in his childhood days when his father showed off his talents at the Mitre in Chatham.[15]

No position on the Chronicle was forthcoming and so this ambitious young-man-in-a-hurry decided to make his bid for success in another line. This line was authorship for which, it seems, he had been grooming himself for some while though not with the intensity with which he had earlier tried to prepare himself for a stage career. Years later he was famously to describe, in a preface to *Pickwick Papers*, how he dropped his 'first effusion' as he called it 'stealthily one evening at twilight, with fear and trembling, into a dark letter-box, in a dark office, up a dark court in Fleet Street'. When he afterwards bought a copy of the magazine and found his story printed therein he had to go and walk in Westminster Hall for half an hour because his eyes 'were so dimmed with joy and pride, that they could not bear the street'. It is hard for us to imagine such a furtive and timorous Dickens as here presented, even when he contrives to make submitting the story sound an almost perilous, Gothicky sort of enterprise ('one evening at twilight' was originally 'one summer's night'). But, after rejection by Maria, and apparent rejection by the *Chronicle*, he was doubtless highly anxious about this new experiment. Another rejection would have been hard to bear and there is no reason to disbelieve his description of his reaction when he found his offering had been accepted.[16]

The title of Dickens's 'first effusion' was 'A Sunday Out of Town', re-titled when published as 'A Dinner at Poplar Walk'. It is a facetious account of the sufferings of a wealthy, fastidious old bachelor forced to spend a day with scheming and obstreperous relatives during which he has to make a speech, enabling Dickens to draw directly on his own recent experiences for comic purposes: 'as the newspapers sometimes say in their reports of the debates, "we are quite unable to give even the substance of the honourable gentleman's observations" '. The letter-box into which he dropped his manuscript belonged to the long-established *Monthly Magazine*, recently purchased by a certain Captain Holland. It was not exactly flourishing for it had a circulation of only around six hundred. Unsurprisingly, Dickens found Holland ' "rather backward in coming forward" with the needful'. In fact, he was never paid for the stories that he continued to publish in the journal for over a year, even after he had begun to be paid for his sketches by the *Morning Chronicle*. No doubt this continuance had something to do with the fact that contributions to monthlies and quarterlies got reviews whereas newspaper-pieces never did.[17]

Announcing, in early December, his first appearance in print, Dickens told Kolle that he had for some time been planning a series of magazine papers with the collective title *The Parish*. The word 'parish' was a very resonant one at this period. The new Parliament had turned its attention to the nation's Poor Laws, basically unchanged since Elizabethan days, and the highly controversial New Poor Law that came into operation in August 1834 retained the parish, usually a union of several old ecclesiastical parishes, as the basic administrative unit. We do not know when Dickens wrote the opening sentences of the first of his 'Parish' sketches, eventually published as 'Sketches of London No. 4' in *The Evening Chronicle* for 28 February 1835, but they make clear the contemporary force of the word: 'How much is conveyed in those two short words – "The Parish"! And with how many tales of distress and misery, of broken fortune and ruined hope, too often of unrelieved wretchedness and successful knavery, are they associated!' In his letter to Kolle Dickens tells him that if his 'Parish' papers are successful, he will 'cut [his] proposed Novel up into little Magazine Sketches' since 'publishing is hazardous'. We do not know what this 'proposed Novel' was but the juxtaposition of its mention with that of the 'Parish' papers suggests that the germ of the story that eventually became *Oliver Twist, or the Parish Boy's Progress* may already have been in Dickens's mind.[18]

For the moment he concentrated on writing more comic tales of follies, rivalries and social embarrassments in middle- and lower-middle-class life. All but one appeared in the *Monthly*, the exception being 'Sentiment', published in *Bell's Weekly Magazine* on 7 June under the heading 'Original Papers'. Perhaps Dickens switched to *Bell's* because he got paid, but if he was hoping to find a profitable outlet for his writings he was disappointed. *Bell's Weekly* folded (after only twenty-eight issues) and he returned to the *Monthly*. The form the tales take and the characters they present owe much to the contemporary theatre, especially to the kind of farces and interludes played by Mathews and his co-manager of the Adelphi Theatre Frederick Yates. As he wrote successive tales Dickens rapidly refined and improved his art, and working on them must have taken up a good deal of his time during the first half of 1834. Meanwhile he evidently continued to work for, or with, his uncle on *The Mirror of Parliament*, staying with him out at Barrow's home in Norwood in December, for example, to help deal with 'business in the shape of masses of papers, plans and prospectuses'. He may also have already been doing some work for the 'French employer' he mentions in a letter towards the end of 1834 but nothing definite is known about this.[19]

A noticeable feature of these *Monthly* tales is the number of theatrical and literary jokes and allusions, also of references to the anxieties, frustrations and self-deception of would-be authors. Theodosius Butler in 'Sentiment', for example, writes incessantly but 'in consequence of some gross combination on the part of publishers, none of his productions appear in print.' What do find a market, however, are the novels about high society written by Mr Simpson in 'The Boarding House', novels based on his experiences as a fashionable hairdresser. They prompt the acid authorial comment that 'so long as good taste, unsullied by exaggeration, cant and maudlin quackery continues to exist [these books] cannot fail to instruct and amuse the thinking portion of the community'. But what comes across most strongly of all in these stories, and still more so in the newspaper sketches that succeed them, is the writer's astonishing knowledge of London. He can describe equally well the contents of the window of a fashionable barber's shop in Regent's Street and the contents of the window of a distinctly *un*fashionable linen-draper's shop in Tottenham Court Road. He knows the *sounds* of the city, too, and can tell just how many minutes elapse between the striking of the hour by the clock on New St Pancras Church and the striking of the same hour by the clock on the nearby Foundling Hospital.

In the summer of 1834 the old-established but latterly struggling newspaper *The Morning Chronicle* was acquired by a trio of bankers and stockbrokers headed by a Liberal M.P., a successful businessman called John Easthope. The intention was to make the paper into a strongly pro-Government organ supporting Lord Melbourne and the Whigs in all the post Reform Bill measures they were seeking to enact, especially the New Poor Law, the centrepiece of their legislative programme. Easthope retained as editor of the *Chronicle* the characterful old Scots bookman John Black but needed some good new reporters. Thomas Beard was recruited from the *Herald* and Black also received an application from Dickens, which John Dickens supported both by going in person to see the influential Radical politician Joseph Parkes and by writing him a follow-up letter extolling Charles's 'competence in every respect for the duties he will be required to perform'. And in August 1834 Dickens was duly appointed a regular member of the *Chronicle*'s parliamentary reporting team at a salary of five guineas a week and celebrated in characteristic fashion by buying some fine new clothes, being, Charles Mackay recalled, 'rather inclined to what was once called "dandyism" in his attire, and to a rather exuberant display of jewellery on his vest and on his fingers'.[20]

Dickens had hinted at the end of his fifth *Monthly* story 'The Boarding House' (May 1834) that he might provide a sequel and now in August he did so, leaving the way open for further instalments in the future if called for. The comic climax of this second instalment of 'The Boarding House' deprives Mrs Tibbs of all her lodgers in one fell swoop and, despairingly, she decides to call it a day. 'We fear', Dickens writes at the end, that 'Mrs Tibbs's determination is irrevocable. Should she, however, be induced to rescind it, we may become once again her faithful biographer.' And for the first time he signs his work, an indication that he was now beginning to wish to be identified as the author of a particular body of work. He uses the pseudonym 'BOZ', derived, as we have seen, from a Dickens family joke.

The parliamentary session ended on 15 August immediately after the passing of the New Poor Law and a month later Dickens was being sent off with Beard on his first major *Chronicle* assignment. They travelled by sea to Leith and thence to Edinburgh to cover a festival held in honour of the just-retired Prime Minister, Earl Grey, who had been chiefly responsible for the passing of the Reform Bill, and Dickens was delighted to notice a commercial traveller on board laughing out loud, no doubt at a humorous stroke by Boz, while reading a copy of the *Monthly Magazine*. The picturesque townscape of Edinburgh evidently made a great impression on him, judging by the vividness with which, three years later, he recalled its 'tall gaunt straggling houses, with time-stained fronts. . . . Six, seven, eight stories high, as children build with cards' when writing 'The Story of the Bagman's Uncle' (*Pickwick Papers*, ch. 49). His and Beard's first report from the city – headed 'From Our Own Correspondent' – appeared in the *Chronicle* on 13 September, an account of some preliminary civic celebrations. Even without Beard's authority for attributing the following section to Dickens, readers familiar with the latter's early fiction would surely recognise his style and technique in this description of inept official arrangements, crowd behaviour, and the pathetic spectacle of the blind children attending the ceremony:

> A marquee was erected in the centre of a parched bit of ground, without a tree or shrub to intercept the rays of a burning sun. Under it was a military band, and around it were the company. The band played, and the company walked about; and when the band was tired, a piper played by way of variation, and then the company walked about again; and when the piper was tired, such of the visitors as could find seats sat down, and those who could not looked as if they wished they had not come; and the poor blind-school pupils, who occupied the warmest seats in the inclosure were very hot and uncomfortable, and appeared very glad to be filed off from a scene in which they could take little interest, and with which their pensive careworn faces painfully contrasted.

On 18 September the *Chronicle* team's full report of the banquet appeared in the paper. This included the celebrated description, also by Dickens, of the man who could wait no longer to begin eating his dinner until the guest of honour should have arrived:

> ... having sat with exemplary patience for some time in the immediate vicinity of cold fowls, roast beef, lobsters and other tempting delicacies ... [he] appeared to think that the best thing he could possibly do, would be to eat his dinner, while there was anything to eat. He accordingly laid about him with a right good-will; the example was contagious, and the clatter of knives and forks became general. Hereupon, several gentlemen, who were not hungry, cried out 'Shame!' and looked very indignant; and several gentlemen who were hungry, cried out 'Shame!' too, eating nevertheless, all the while, as fast as they possibly could. . . .[21]

This incident so described would not have been out of place in one of Boz's *Monthly* tales and indeed Dickens links it directly with the next of these to appear, 'The Steam Excursion' in the October *Monthly*, where the gourmandising life and soul of the party, Mr Hardy, is dismissed at the end in the following paragraph (omitted when this sketch was republished in volume form):

> Having been for some months past subject to indigestion, and loss of appetite, he was recently persuaded to try a keener air and a more northern climate for the removal of the one, and the improvement of the other. We are

credibly informed that he was present at the Edinburgh dinner, and, moreover, that he is the individual to whose eager appetite on that occasion we
find allusion made in *The Morning Chronicle* of a few days since.

It was on 26 September, just a few days after the dinner report that Dickens
made his Bozzian début in the *Chronicle* with a 'Street Sketch' called 'Omnibuses'
over the signature 'BOZ' with four more such sketches following before the end
of the year. We do not know whether this series was commissioned by Black or
first proposed by Dickens himself but Boz was certainly establishing himself as
a *Chronicle* presence. On 18 December the paper featured a vehemently anti-
Tory squib under the title 'The Story Without a Beginning (Translated from the
German by Boz)'. This, a pastiche of a well-known German fairy-tale, was
Dickens's fierce response to William IV's sudden dismissal of the reforming
Whigs and request to the Duke of Wellington to form a Tory government. The
dominant emotions of the piece are contempt for the King ('it was not his first
but his second childhood') and a visceral loathing for the Tories ('insects and
reptiles that bask in the sunshine, and retreat to small dark corners when the
air is cold').[22]

'Boz' was rapidly becoming Dickens's established alter ego, his writing self,
even in private life. He signed himself Boz, for example, when on 20 September
he contributed a versified offering with the title 'A Fable (Not a *gay* one)' to the
album of Thomas Beard's sister Ellen, an offering in which he seems still to be
brooding on the failure of his love for Maria Beadnell. Boz's public persona,
on the other hand, as seen in Dickens's five 'Street Sketches' published in the
Chronicle during the last four months of 1834, is very different. Here he is
the same amused observer of human follies and foibles as the narrator of the
earlier *Monthly Magazine* tales but extends his social range downwards
through the world of the 'shabby genteel' to that of streetwise omnibus cads
[conductors] and petty criminals. The people he presents are, like the impa-
tient diner at the Grey banquet, no longer borrowed from contemporary farces
but men and women that Dickens himself has actually seen, and heard, as
he travels to and from work on his Oxford Street omnibus, or observes the
pathetic attempts to keep himself respectable of a down-at-heel reader in the
British Museum, or is entertained by the antics of a prototype Artful Dodger
at the Old Bailey, or simply roams about the streets of London which provide
for him such 'inexhaustible food for speculation'. The sprightly cad described
in 'Omnibuses' who boasts 'that he can chuck an old gen'lm'n into the buss,
shut him in, and rattle off, before he knows where it's a -going to' has some
claim to be considered the first original 'Dickens character'.[23]

Another development noticeable both in the October *Monthly* story, 'The
Steam Excursion', and in the second *Chronicle* sketch 'Shops and Their Tenants'
(10 Oct.) is the emergence of the closely-linked compassionate and socially

indignant sides of Dickens. Boz now introduces a note of pathos, as Dickens had done in his reporting of the blind children at the Grey Festival. It sounds in the description of the 'thinly clad' prostitutes with their 'wan looks' and 'forced merriment' who appear in an early morning street scene in 'The Steam Excursion' (itself quite unlike anything in the preceding *Monthly* tales) and of the motherless young girl in 'Shops' struggling to care for her younger siblings and help her father eke out a bare existence as a 'fancy stationer'. This girl may well be driven into prostitution ('a last dreadful resource') as a result of 'thoughtless females' of the middle classes who, motivated by 'an immodest love of self-display', hold fancy fairs and interfere with her 'miserable market'. Dickens, it seems, has already begun that study of prostitutes to which he looked back several years later when defending the truthfulness of his portrayal of Nancy in the 1841 Preface to *Oliver Twist*:

> Suggested to my mind long ago – long before I dealt in fiction – by what I often saw and read of, in actual life around me, I have, for years, tracked it [the nature and behaviour of prostitutes] through many profligate and noisome ways, and found it still the same.

The subject of the last sketch in the series, 'Brokers' and Marine Store Shops' (*Morning Chronicle*, 15 Dec. 1834) may well have been suggested to Dickens by what was happening in his own life and that of his family during November. It is all about the variety of second-hand furniture shops to be found in London, some stocked with 'groves of deceitful, showy-looking furniture', others, in poorer neighbourhoods, offering 'the most extraordinary confused jumble of old, worn-out, wretched articles, that can well be imagined'. Most wretched of all are those in the neighbourhood of a debtors' prison like the Rules of the King's Bench (a few streets adjacent to the prison where prisoners who could afford to pay for the privilege were allowed to reside). Dickens writes with telling detail about the 'contamination' of such a prison, and in his grim account of how the prisoners first dispose of whatever luxury items they may have and gradually sink to having to sell even articles of their children's clothing the image of the hapless Mr Dorrit seems to be already hovering on the point of his pen.

In fact, John Dickens had come very close to seeing the inside of a debtors' prison again that autumn. He was arrested in late November at the suit of some wine merchants (he was also overdue with the Bentinck Street rent) and taken to a 'lock-up house' in Cursitor Street, that is, a secure house for the accommodation of debtors while they tried to raise some funds to keep them out of the prison. In between his *Chronicle* duties Dickens had to rush about getting together, with the help of his solicitor friend from Molloy's office, Thomas Mitton, enough money to settle the debt, release his father and reorganise the family's living arrangements. He had already been planning to set up a home of his own in rented chambers and this crisis no doubt accelerated the move. He rented a three-roomed apartment in a block of chambers called Furnival's Inn, Holborn, at an annual rental of £35 and took his fourteen-year-old brother Fred with him, 'to instruct and provide for as I best can', while settling his mother and the younger children 'in comfortable quarters, where they are not Strangers'. John himself retreated to stay with a laundress friend of the family's in Hampstead. Dickens had given him some money, borrowed from Beard on the strength of £5 due to him from someone he calls his 'French employer', but within a fortnight John was asking Beard for a couple of sovereigns for shoe repairs, a preposterously large sum for such a purpose.[24]

There must have been some hasty second-hand furniture buying for the Furnival's Inn chambers and Dickens quickly turned the experience to serio-comic account in a sketch of brokers' shops for the *Chronicle*, just as he intro-duced a vivid description of the lock-up house in Cursitor Street in the second part of his next *Monthly* tale, 'A Passage in the Life of Mr Watkins Tottle' (Feb. 1835). But the sudden resurgence of the shadow of the debtors' prison and desperate poverty (was he merely joking when he wrote to Mitton, 'I have not yet been taken, but no doubt that will be the next act in this "domestic tragedy" '?) had surely given him quite a shock and led to the writing of the powerful paragraph about the shops near the King's Bench. He had, in fact, intended to write even more fully about this subject, he says in conclusion, but does not want to exceed the normal space allocated for his sketches (one column) or 'to trespass at greater length on the patience of our readers'. He does, however, have more of 'these imperfect sketches' to offer and hopes to have many opportunities of doing so 'when the partial absence of matter of pressing and absorbing interest again enables us to occupy a column occasion-ally'. He was also, in less apologetic fashion, keeping his *Monthly* option open and the second and last instalment of 'Watkins Tottle' ends with the informa-tion that the unfortunate protagonist 'left a variety of papers in the hands of his landlady – the materials collected in his wanderings among different classes of society – which that lady has determined to publish, to defray the expenses of his board and lodging. They will be carefully arranged, and presented to the public from time to time, with all due humility, by BOZ.'[25]

Dickens seems here to be preparing for a continuation of his *Monthly* contri-butions in the form of sketches like the ones he had begun writing for *The Morning Chronicle*. A longer-term plan was that he should at some later stage enrol himself as a law student in case his literary career should not prosper and he had written to the Steward of New Inn on 13 November, when enquiring about hiring a set of chambers there, 'I intend entering at the bar, as soon as circumstances will enable me to do so'. At this point, however, a promising opportunity opened up in journalism. The *Chronicle*'s owners determined to establish a sister paper, *The Evening Chronicle*, to be published three times a week and aimed, as all evening papers were at this time, rather at country readers than at metropolitan ones. The appointed editor was George Hogarth, a distinguished Scottish music critic and former editor of *The Halifax Guardian*. He asked Dickens to contribute an original sketch to the first number of the new paper (31 Jan. 1835). Dickens made a counter-proposal, reflecting his rapidly growing confidence in Boz's marketability. He suggested that he might write 'a series of articles under some attractive title' for the new paper for '*some* additional remuneration'. Hogarth agreed and Dickens's salary went from five to seven guineas a week, a substantial rise. The first of the new series, 'Sketches of London. No.1. Hackney-coach Stands', duly appeared in the first issue of *The Evening Chronicle*. It was to be followed over the next seven months by fourteen more such sketches intermingled with half a dozen of those 'Parish' papers that he had for some time had in mind. All were reprinted in the morning paper but at irregular intervals and often after a gap of several weeks.[26]

Dickens once referred to 'dear old [John] Black' as 'my first hearty out-and-out appreciator' but, so far as his literary rather than his reportorial work was concerned, George Hogarth might seem to have had a better claim. It was he who first suggested that Dickens might write a sketch for the new paper and then welcomed the proposal for a series, and it was he who wrote what Dickens called a 'beautiful notice' of the first collected edition of *Sketches by Boz* in 1836. Hogarth's praise would have meant a great deal to Dickens coming as it did from a man who had been the good friend (and trusted legal adviser) of Sir Walter Scott himself. Moreover, Hogarth was a kindly, genial man who made Dickens welcome at his family home in Brompton. There Dickens promptly fell in love with Hogarth's eldest daughter, Catherine, a pretty little blue-eyed young woman of eighteen with a retroussé nose and rosebud lips. She was gentle and amiable, quite unlike the coquettish Maria, proficient in all the 'accomplishments' required of an early nineteenth-century young lady, with a particular gift for needlework. She was evidently quite free from those female follies criticised by Boz in the *Evening Chronicle* for 17 March ('Sketches of London no. 6. London Recreations'). These stem, he believes, from 'the course female education has taken of late days', that is, 'the pursuit of giddy frivolities and empty nothings, [that] has tended to unfit women for that quiet domestic life, in which they show far more beautifully than in the most crowded assembly'. By the spring Dickens had become engaged to Catherine and was beginning eagerly to look forward to the time when, as he wrote to her, he would have the delight of being 'able to turn round to you at our own fireside when my work is done, and seek in your kind looks and gentle manner the recreation and happiness which the moping solitude of chambers can never afford'.[27]

Meanwhile, he had much work to do, being liable to be sent off at a moment's notice to review a new play or to travel long distances by stage coach to report on elections in different parts of the country (1835 was a year of two General Elections), as well as having his series of London sketches to keep going. He moved to temporary lodgings in Selwood Terrace, Chelsea, in order to be near to Catherine but still found himself often having to write her a note explaining that his work commitments prevented him from coming to see her and sometimes having to deprecate her resulting discontent. His courtship letters to her are very different in tone from those he had written to Maria and would seem to show that he was never really in love with Catherine for her own sake but more concerned with her potential for being a loving and supportive wife, a creator of that haven of domestic tranquillity that he so passionately longed for, or believed that he did. Thus, he liked her to come and preside at his breakfast-table, chaperoned by her younger sister Mary, and he longed for the time when she would do it every day as of right. A strong hortatory element runs throughout the letters amidst all the affectionate playfulness. He is certainly not prepared to tolerate anything savouring of the tormenting behaviour in which Maria had allowed herself to indulge: 'if you really love me I would have you do justice to yourself, and shew me that your love for me, like mine for you, is above the ordinary trickery, and frivolous absurdity which debases the name and renders it ludicrous'.[28]

He no longer had the leisure to organise amateur theatricals but he did apparently treat Catherine and her family to at least one brief but dazzling one-man show. His eldest daughter, Mary, records her mother's story of how one summer evening when the Hogarths were sitting in their drawing-room which had French windows opening on to a lawn,

> suddenly a young sailor jumped through one of the open windows into the apartment, whistled and danced a hornpipe, and before they could recover from their amazement jumped out again. A few minutes later my father walked in at the door as sedately as though quite innocent of the prank, and shook hands with everyone; but the sight of their amazed faces proving too much for his attempted sobriety, his hearty laugh was the signal for the rest of the party to join in his merriment.

Outside of his letters to her, this is the only glimpse we have of Dickens when he was courting Catherine. It adds a dimension of playfulness and sheer fun that comes across in the letters only in the comic pet-names he invents for her, such as 'dearest Mouse' and 'Pig', and in a lively description (written in response to a complaint of Catherine's that his previous letter had been too 'stiff and formal') of his adventures and misadventures on the road while reporting a by-election in Northamptonshire in December 1835.[29]

The *Evening Chronicle* sketches show Dickens experimenting with a variety of new effects, including some polemical ones, as at the end of 'Gin Shops'

(7 Feb. 1835) when he turns on his comfortable middle-class readers in a way that he will later learn how to use with what he would call 'sledge-hammer' effect (most famously in the 'Dead, Your Majesty!' passage at the end of chapter 47 of *Bleak House*): 'Gin-drinking is a great vice in England, but poverty is a greater; and until you can cure it, or persuade a half-famished wretch not to seek relief in the temporary oblivion of his own misery, with the pittance which, divided among his family, would just furnish a morsel of bread for each, gin-shops will increase in number and splendour.'[30]

In these sketches Dickens continues to draw upon the comic potential of experiences undergone in the line of duty. In 'Early Coaches', for example, he makes comic capital out of the discomforts of having to rise at five o'clock on a miserable wet morning while in 'Public Dinners', reporting the rituals associated with fund-raising dinners on behalf of one charity or another, he notes with delight how uninitiated diners applaud the sung grace *Non nobis* 'as vehemently as if it were a capital comic song'. This sketch and the half-dozen similar ones describing London recreations are, in fact, more elaborate and worked-up versions of the kind of special reports on the same theme he was contemporaneously writing for the *The Morning Chronicle* – like his report of a grand opening fête at the Colosseum pleasure-dome by Regent's Park on 9 July. His description of arriving guests having to run the gauntlet of the onlookers is wholly 'Bozzian' in both style and substance: '... a numerous concourse of people were assembled in the road, who beguiled the time and enlivened the occasion, as the different carriages set down, by urgently entreating the visitors to "flare-up"; imploring smartly-dressed gentlemen "not to cut it too fat, but just to throw in a bit of lean to make weight", and similar *facetiae*.'[31]

Many of the *Evening Chronicle* sketches develop the theme of 'amateur vagrancy', that habit of roaming the streets of London at all hours and looking in at all sorts of strange places that we have already touched on and that, from the beginning of his career through to its end, was absolutely essential to Dickens the writer. Eleven years later, living in Lausanne and trying to get started on *Dombey and Son*, he lamented to Forster that the absence of that great 'magic lantern' the streets of London was causing him 'immense' difficulty (his characters, he said, seemed 'disposed to stagnate without crowds about them'). In 'Thoughts About People' (*Evening Chronicle*, 23 April) Boz focuses on a solitary poor clerk wandering aimlessly in St James's Park and extrapolates from his appearance and demeanour a whole existence of monotony, loneliness and privation – creates a character, in fact. It is a small-scale *tour de force* of the imagination. In 'The Pawnbroker's Shop' (*Evening Chronicle*, 30 June) Boz moves still further towards being a novelist as he imagines the story that two middle-class female customers seem doomed to enact as he observes them in their private box juxtaposed with two other women, a gaudily-dressed young prostitute in an adjacent box and a slovenly drunkard in the 'common shop'.[32]

Other sketches deal with various kinds of popular entertainment – exhilarating shows like Richardson's at Greenwich Fair and the circus acts at Astley's Amphitheatre, a venue that five years later will feature memorably in *The Old Curiosity Shop*. In these particular sketches Dickens first practises what will become, from *Nickleby* through to *Great Expectations*, one of the surest and funniest of his comic routines, the description of preposterous melodramas, inadequate acting, bathetic productions of Shakespeare, absurd stage conventions of his day, and so on. Stage fathers, for instance, often

> have to discover, all of a sudden, that somebody, whom they have been in constant communication with during three long acts, without the slightest suspicion, is their own child, in which case they exclaim, 'Ah! what do I see! This bracelet! That smile! These documents! Those eyes! Can I believe my senses? – It must be! – Yes – it is – it is – my child!' – 'My father!' exclaims the child, and then they fall into each other's arms, and look over each other's shoulders; and the audience give three distinct rounds of applause.[33]

Much less good-humoured is his portrayal of the 'dirty boys' and 'low copying-clerks in attorneys' offices' who patronise the private theatres ('Private Theatres', *Evening Chronicle*, 11 Aug.). We get the distinct impression that Dickens is here distancing himself from his time as a theatre-loving clerk at Ellis and Blackmore's just as, somewhat more genially, he is concerned in other sketches to distinguish himself and his stylish dandyism from proletarian youths who swagger about in would-be fashionable attire – pink shirts, blue waistcoats, and so on. 'Some of the finery of these people provokes a smile', he loftily writes in 'London Recreations' (*Evening Chronicle*, 7 March) and in 'Thoughts About People' (*Evening Chronicle*, 23 April) he remarks of some apprentices in their Sunday best: 'Were there ever such beautiful efforts at the grand and magnificent as the young fellows display in their own proper persons!'

Most of these *Evening Chronicle* sketches are distinctly metropolitan, though the paper was, as already noted, aimed primarily at a provincial readership, which was, in the case of the two dealing with the Houses of Parliament, particularly unlikely to be familiar with what is being described. At the end of the second one, 'Bellamy's' (*Evening Chronicle*, 11 April), Boz apologises to his readers 'for selecting for the second time, a subject involving allusions which they may not understand'. His intermingling of half-a-dozen 'Our Parish' sketches, presumably derived from the papers he mentioned in his letter to Kolle of the previous winter, was perhaps an attempt to achieve a more nation-wide appeal. The series-heading 'Sketches of London' is still used and references to the Lord Mayor in the first of these sketches make it clear that Boz's parish is a metropolitan one but the various officials he describes were, of course, to be found in all parishes, nor are the individual parishioners he sketches presented as specifically London types. In at least one case, in fact, the 'Old Lady' in 'Sketches of London No.12', it has been shown that Dickens was drawing on childhood memories of Mrs Mary Newnham, a neighbour of the Dickenses in Ordnance Terrace, 'a neat row of houses in the most airy and pleasant part of [the parish]'.[34]

The first 'Parish' sketch appeared on 28 February 1835 with a promise at the end of others in the same vein should Boz 'be induced to imagine' that his readers liked them. No further such sketches appeared, however, until 19 May after which they alternated with non-parish ones until the unheralded termination of the whole series on 20 August. This suggests that the real reason for their introduction was that Dickens was under such pressure of other commitments during the summer that he had to draw on notes for the projected 'Parish' series to maintain a steady flow of sketches for Hogarth. On 1 May Black sent him to report Lord John Russell's nomination speech in Exeter, where Russell was standing as Liberal candidate for South Devon (thirty years later Dickens remembered taking down the speech 'in the midst of a lively fight maintained by all the vagabonds in the neighbourhood, and under such a pelting rain, that I remember two good-natured colleagues ... held a pocket-handkerchief over my notebook, after the manner of a state canopy in an ecclesiastical procession'). His letters to Catherine over the next three months make it clear that his routine parliamentary reporting duties were very heavy. He is often 'completely worn out' and is struggling to get a sketch finished – one night, having not finished work at the office until eleven, he still had to go back into the gallery for half an hour at 1 a.m. He also had special assignments to deal with, like reporting on the attractions offered by the Colosseum (*Morning Chronicle*, 13 Oct.) as well as a certain amount of theatre reviewing. On top of all this, he naturally wanted to spend as much time as possible with Catherine and presumably needed also to devote some time to the education of his young boarder-brother Fred, whom he sent about on errands rather as his father had once sent him. It would not be surprising, if under the circumstances he sometimes worked up for *The Evening Chronicle* sketches material he already had by him, and there are certainly a couple of the 'Parish' ones ('The Four Sisters' and 'The Ladies' Societies', 18 June and 20 August) that seem to belong more with the farcical *Monthly* tales than with the wonderfully sharp and vivid metropolitan sketches Dickens was now writing.[35]

The 'Parish' sketches also gave Dickens an opportunity to tease the rigorously Benthamite John Black about the Poor Laws ('How often used Black and I', he wrote later, 'to quarrel about the effect of the poor-law bill!'). Knowing that his *Evening Chronicle* sketches would all be reprinted in Black's *Morning Chronicle* Dickens must have taken great delight in writing the following signing-off paragraph at the end of the second 'Parish' sketch (19 May), just before he begins alternating them with his regular London sketches (it also reads like a covert apology for the kind of recycling I have suggested):

We are not sufficiently acquainted with the details of the recent alteration in the Poor-laws, to know whether we have a legal settlement anywhere or not; but we hope our readers will not object, when subjects are scarce, and we distressed, to our deriving assistance from the parochial funds. We are perfectly willing to work for their amusement: but we openly avow our determination, on some future occasions, to throw ourselves again upon – 'Our Parish'.[36]

One of the 'Parish' sketches, the last but one to be published ('The Broker's Man', *Evening Chronicle*, 28 July) features Dickens's first attempt at a characterised narrator within the narration. Mr Bung, who works for a broker, that is, someone whose job it is to value goods seized for unpaid rent or other debts, tells Boz various anecdotes, comic and pathetic, of his professional life. There is some evidence to suggest that Dickens's friends and admirers considered this sketch a particularly fine one. George Hogarth evidently treasured a proof of it which Dickens asked him to loan to Thomas Beard who wanted to show it to a friend.[37]

The last of Boz's 'Sketches of London' to appear in *The Evening Chronicle* ('Our Parish', 20 Aug.; subsequently renamed 'The Ladies' Societies') ends with the words 'to be continued'. Earlier on, in the Greenwich Fair sketch (16 April), Boz had exuberantly announced his intention to continue his series 'until it reaches something under its two hundredth number'. Yet he suddenly vanished from *The Evening Chronicle* after 20 August though his already-published sketches continued to be reprinted in *The Morning Chronicle* until the end of the year. On 27 September he began a new series of twelve sketches, entitled 'Scenes and Characters', in the highly popular weekly *Bell's Life in London and Sporting Chronicle*. Its circulation (24,000) exceeded that of any other daily or weekly paper. In terms of circulation, and no doubt also of payment, it was a better vehicle for Dickens's sketches, which always featured on the front page instead of being tucked away inside as had been the case with all but one of his sketches for the *Morning* and *Evening Chronicles*. And whereas *The Evening Chronicle* was, as already mentioned, directed at a provincial and rural audience, *Bell's Life* was very much targeted at a metropolitan one (true, the sketches written for Hogarth were all reprinted in *The Morning Chronicle* but only at irregular intervals and sometimes after long gaps). Influenced by some or all of these considerations, Dickens must have been easily seduced by *Bell's* Vincent Dowling on whose behalf it was later claimed that he had been 'the first to discover the genius for sketching characters of Dickens'. Dickens's engagement to Hogarth's daughter and Black's keen appreciation of his journalistic work no doubt helped to smooth over Boz's desertion and he may not even have had to forfeit his two extra guineas per week from the *Chronicle*.[38]

As part of the adjustment he may have been asked, or persuaded, by Hogarth, not to use the name 'Boz' in *Bell's* since it was now so closely associated in the public mind with *The Morning Chronicle* and its sister-paper. For his *Bell's* nom de plume Dickens humorously adopts the name of a character from one of his *Monthly* tales, clearly expecting his readers to enjoy the joke – another sign that he is beginning to see himself as the author of a distinct body of work. Tibbs, ironically named after Beau Tibbs in Goldsmith's *Citizen of the World*, is the put-upon husband of a boarding-house landlady. He is always trying to tell a story but getting cut short by his wife and is thus 'a melancholy specimen of the story-teller'. The twelve sketches and stories Dickens publishes in *Bell's* between 27 September and 17 January are anything but 'melancholy specimens' of course. They include several comic tales of misplaced self-confidence and punctured pretentiousness, rather like the *Monthly* ones. However, they are mostly set rather lower down the social scale than those and in inner-city local-ities like 'the most secluded portion of Camden Town', or 'the populous and improving neighbourhood of Gray's-inn-lane', rather than in the suburbs. Also, they teem with sharply individualised vignettes of a great variety of lower and lower-middle class Londoners (brilliant thumbnail sketches abound) as opposed to the stock farce types that tend to predominate in the earlier tales.[39]

In one sketch, 'The Prisoners' Van' (*Bell's Life*, 29 Nov.), Dickens for the first time talks to his readers (in a relaxed and confident tone) about how he works and where he finds his material of choice, a passage omitted when the sketch was reprinted in the first volume edition of *Sketches*:

> We have a most extraordinary partiality for lounging about the streets. Whenever we have an hour to spare, there is nothing that we enjoy more than a little amateur vagrancy – walking up one street and down another, and staring into shop windows, and gazing about us as if, instead of being on inti-mate terms with every shop and house in Holborn, the Strand, Fleet-street and Cheapside, the whole were an unknown region to our wondering mind. We revel in a crowd of any kind – a street 'row' is our delight. . . .

There follows a wonderfully vivid mini-sketch of a fatuous street row, of a somewhat milder kind than the all-female brawl featured in his first Tibbs sketch, 'Seven Dials' (*Bell's Life*, 27 Sept.). Then, having softened up his readers with this comic reportage, Dickens goes on to depict a disturbing scene of two girls, a brazen sixteen-year-old prostitute and her as yet unhardened younger sister, being carted off to Coldbath Fields (the Middlesex House of Correction). He challenges his readers, some of whom, certainly, would have occasionally been clients of such girls, to deny that this is a common scene: 'These things pass before our eyes day after day, and hour after hour – they have become such matters of course, that they are utterly disregarded'.[40]

At some point during 1835 Dickens became acquainted with the dazzling new literary star, William Harrison Ainsworth, the Manchester solicitor's son,

seven years his senior, who in the previous year had had an enormous success
with *Rookwood*, a historical romance featuring Dick Turpin. Handsome and
dressed in the height of fashion, Ainsworth ranked with fellow-novelist and
dandy Edward Bulwer, later Bulwer Lytton, as one of the greatest of London's
literary lions. Like Bulwer Lytton, he was an habitué of Lady Blessington's celebrated salon at Gore House, Kensington, where reigned the greatest dandy of
all, Count D'Orsay, Lady Blessington's son-in-law, rumoured by some to be also
her lover. We do not know exactly how Ainsworth and Dickens met but it seems
likely, as Ainsworth's biographer suggests, that the older writer sought Dickens
out because of his admiration for Boz's sketches, and we can be sure that
Dickens as an aspirant to literary fame and fortune, and to dandyism also,
would have responded warmly to any such approach. Ainsworth advised
Dickens to publish his sketches in volume form and 'introduced him to his
own publisher [an enterprising young man called John Macrone], and also to
George Cruikshank'. In fact, Dickens did not meet the forty-three-year-old
Cruikshank, by this time the most famous of all contemporary illustrators,
until some while after he had accepted Macrone's offer of £100 for a collection
of his sketches, which Cruikshank had agreed to illustrate.[41]

Dickens set about the work of selecting sketches for publication and extensively revising them in such interstices of time as he could find between his
fulfilling his regular *Chronicle* duties, keeping up his quota of new sketches
for *Bell's*, seeing Catherine (who fell ill from scarlet fever in October), being ill
himself, and working on the libretto for an operetta which – as if he did not
already have enough on hand – he had undertaken at the suggestion of John
Hullah, a fellow-student of Fanny's at the Royal Academy of Music. As regards his
Chronicle work, he had, of course, his regular late-night stints in the reporters'
gallery but he was also sent off on various special assignments. Among these
was reporting on a 'calamitous' fire at Hatfield House in which the Dowager
Marchioness of Salisbury was burned to death. Dickens's detailed account of this
appeared in the paper on 2 December and culminated in a description of two
things that were always to fascinate him, a miscellaneous jumble of articles (here
the heaped-up furniture rescued from the flames) and striking visual contrasts:

> rich couches and sofas, handsome mirrors, high-backed damask-covered old
> chairs, and fantastic cabinets of ancient date, with Turkey carpets, chrystal
> ornaments, pictures, and suits of armour, and a thousand other heterogeneous
> articles – contrast singularly enough with the old heavy chimney-pieces, and
> oaken pannels which have worn the same appearance for centuries and seem
> to defy the ravages of time . . .

His accounts, both to Catherine in his private letters and in his *Chronicle* reports,
of another assignment, covering a rowdy by-election in Northamptonshire,

7 William Harrison Ainsworth, drawn by Maclise for *Fraser's Magazine*'s 'Gallery of Illustrious Characters', 1834

are filled with energetic contempt for the blatant corruption and intimidation indulged in by the Tories. Their candidate was returned, he reports on 19 December, by 'ignorant, drunken, and brutal electors' who have been 'treated and fed, and driven up to the polls the whole day, like herds of swine'. Within a year, as a rapidly rising literary star, he was turning this Northamptonshire experience most richly to account in his description of Mr Pickwick involved in the rumbustious electoral proceedings at Eatanswill.[42]

Dickens's first surviving letter to Macrone (?27 October 1835) shows that the two had been discussing a title for the two projected volumes into which it had been decided to collect the sketches. Dickens now proposes *Sketches by Boz and Cuts by Cruikshank* in preference to a more cumbersome joke-title they had been toying with that rather pointlessly parodied a contemporary travel-book. Cruikshank, as a long-established and highly popular cartoonist and illustrator, would naturally have equal billing with Boz and indeed it was quite a coup for Macrone to have secured his collaboration. The artist was cele-brated for his political cartoons but it was his illustrations to Pierce Egan's best-selling *Life in London* (1820–21) that perhaps suggested him to Macrone as a natural illustrator for Boz's sketches. Dickens's appreciative and flattering reference to the artist in the modest preface he wrote for the two volumes (see next chapter) shows he was fully alive to the importance of Cruikshank's contribution. In his private communications with Macrone, however, the eager and increasingly self-confident young author was rather less respectful, telling Macrone on 21 December that he thought Cruikshank 'requires the spur' (it had been originally hoped – somewhat unrealistically, given Dickens's many other commitments – that the two volumes would be out in time for Christmas).[43]

In late October, before printing began, Dickens assured Macrone that he could easily supply 'two or three new Sketches', if necessary, to fill up the volumes, having memoranda by him for another nine or ten pieces. In the event, he had more than enough material and it was decided to omit eight of the tales and sketches published before 1 November to make room for three new pieces, a hitherto unpublished comic tale called 'The Great Winglebury Duel', written for the *Monthly*, and two pieces written specially for Macrone. The latter are of great interest as being the first things Dickens wrote for initial publication in permanent volume form, rather than in a magazine or newspaper. Both are certainly 'dark'. The first, 'A Visit to Newgate', was written after Dickens and Macrone had been on a conducted tour of the prison (5 Nov.), undertaken by Dickens specifically to collect material. He took great pains with the writing and was highly gratified by the praise bestowed on it by Hogarth, Black and others, including Macrone himself. Newgate had haunted his imagination since child-hood, especially as the last home of those condemned at the Old Bailey to die upon the gallows. In his paper he evokes a Piranesi-like atmosphere ('tortuous and intricate windings, guarded in their turn by huge gates and gratings . . .') which envelops the miserable men, women and children that he finds huddled together or moping solitarily in the labyrinthine building's various wards and yards. These descriptions have all the sharpness of Boz's observation of London's street people but with no touch of the comic. Dickens is clearly aiming at high seriousness. Although he promises Catherine that he has some 'rather amusing' anecdotes to tell her about his visit, there is no hint of any such matter in the sketch as published. At one point a horror-stricken description of '*the condemned pew*' (Dickens's italics) in the prison chapel erupts into the sober, socially-concerned journalist's prose. The last five paragraphs take us inside the head of an increasingly panic-stricken man in the condemned cell as he lives through the last night of his life – a sort of dress rehearsal for the tremendously powerful description of Fagin's last night alive in *Oliver Twist*, written just two years later.[44]

Dickens had visited Coldbath Fields as well as Newgate with a view to writing another paper for the two volumes but abandoned the idea since this prison for minor offences could not provide the material for the kind of heightened prose he was wanting to write at this point: 'You cannot throw the interest over a year's imprisonment, however severe, that you can cast around the punishment of death. The Tread-Mill will not take the hold on men's feelings that the Gallows does'. And it was the gallows that inspired 'The Black Veil', the other piece written specially for the two volumes. This is a story, 'his first proper story', observes Peter Ackroyd, 'no longer a sketch or a scene or a farcical interlude but a finished narrative'. It was based, Dickens told Catherine, on 'an extraordinary idea' that suddenly came to him (and that surely related to his experiences in Newgate) about a woman crazed with grief for her son who has been hanged. Madly hoping she can still save his life, she causes his body to be immediately brought away from the gallows and tricks a young doctor into attending it in the belief that it is a desperately ill patient. Telling the story from the doctor's point of view, Dickens skilfully builds up the suspense and memorably describes the desolate and threatening outer-London neighbourhood in which the doctor finds himself as he searches for the address the black-veiled woman has given him.[45]

Newgate, the gallows, murder, madness, dysfunctional families, the bad old days when inadequately-policed London was a more dangerous place ('The Black Veil' is set a quarter-century in the past): all these themes figure prominently in the two pieces written specially for Dickens's first volume publication and they were all central to the conception of Dickens's first planned novel, *Gabriel Vardon, the Locksmith of London* which he was to agree to write for Macrone in May 1836. At just that moment, however, his developing authorial career would take a sudden major and very unexpected turn, pushing the projected *Gabriel Vardon* on to a back burner until 1841 when it was finally brought back to the boil as *Barnaby Rudge*. This is matter for later but it is worth noting here that 'The Black Veil' and whatever can be surmised about Dickens's ideas for *Gabriel Vardon* do suggest that, not surprisingly, during 1835/36 he was thinking along Ainsworthian lines with regard to what he was writing, or planning to write, for volume publication. Historical settings and melodramatic passions characterise Ainsworth's fiction and, though Dickens may not have been a whole-hearted admirer of *Rookwood*, he would certainly have noted its enormous and lucrative success. He was, he told Macrone in early January, 'highly gratified with Ainsworth's opinion of the Visit to Newgate' and asked, 'Has he seen the Black Veil?'[46]

By the turn of the year Dickens had finished his careful revision of the proofs for the two volumes of *Sketches* and also published his first piece on a theme his treatment of which would in due course become a corner-stone of his great popularity ('Christmas Festivities', *Bell's Life*, 27 Dec. 1835). He was still waiting to see Cruikshank's proposed illustrations for his first book but had every reason to feel a growing confidence that his 'pilot balloon' would '*go off well*', as he wrote in his preface to the two volumes and that he might soon thereafter make his début as a novelist, stepping forward to take his place beside his dazzling new friend Ainsworth. He could also reasonably look forward to continued success as a journalist, to increased earnings from his sketch-writing, and, above all, to marriage with his 'dearest girl' and his own domestic hearth. No wonder that both 'Christmas Festivities' and his next *Bell's* piece, 'The New Year' (*Bell's Life*, 3 Jan.) are both very upbeat in tone, determinedly putting aside all thoughts of what in the first piece Dickens calls 'past misfortunes': 'here goes our glass to our lips, and a hearty welcome to the year one thousand eight hundred and thirty-six say we.'[47]

Just how much of an *annus mirabilis* the year he was thus welcoming in would prove to be for him Dickens could not possibly, for all his ambition and self-confidence, have imagined.

CHAPTER 4

Break-through year

1836

. . . he is such a nice creature and so clever he is courted and made up to by all the literary Gentlemen, and has more to do in that way than he can well manage.
Mary Hogarth writing about Dickens to her cousin
Mary Scott Hogarth, 15 May 1836

DURING THE month before Parliament reconvened on 2 February 1836 *The Morning Chronicle* kept its star gallery reporter busy on other assignments. On 22 January he covered the ceremonial laying of the foundation-stone for a charity school by Lord Melbourne, the Prime Minister, for example, and had often, sometimes at short notice, to review some new theatrical piece. In his personal life he naturally tried to spend as much time as possible with Catherine but had frequently to deprecate her disappointment at not seeing him. He had also to look after Fred, now sixteen, and to supervise a regular programme of studies for him, as well, presumably, as keeping an eye on his parents and younger siblings, now lodged in Edwards Street, Marylebone. There was also the libretto for Hullah's operetta to be written and the final preparations for the volume publication of his sketches to be dealt with. He resisted the idea, apparently mooted by Macrone, of changing the title from *Sketches by Boz* since this was 'both unaffected and unassuming – two requisites which it is very desirable for a young author [not] to lose sight of'. He did, however, add an important defining sub-title: 'Illustrative of Every-day Life and Every-day People'.[1]

Dickens kept in close touch with Cruikshank over the illustrations and wrote a deferential preface thanking the celebrated artist for agreeing to be his fellow-passenger in this 'pilot balloon'. His own aim, he wrote, had been 'to present little sketches of life and manners as they really are' and, if the book were well received, he hoped to 'repeat his experiment with increased confidence, and on a more extensive scale'. He wrote a paragraph advertising (or 'puffing', as it was called) the book for insertion in the *Chronicle* on 2 February and apologised to Macrone for its being so low-key: 'it is not affectation; I really *cannot* do the tremendous in puffing myself' (he did, nevertheless, bring

8 'Public dinners'. In this illustration to *Sketches by Boz* Cruikshank has depicted Dickens (second from left) and himself (furthest right) among the ushers

himself to call attention to the presence in the book of 'a very powerful article, entitled "A Visit to Newgate" '). He also wrote covering letters to accompany review copies and urged Macrone to be prompt in distributing the latter. As many copies as possible should be sent to his friends in London and to Hogarth family connections in Edinburgh, all of whom, he wrote, 'not only *can* but *will* do the work a great deal of good'.[2]

It must have been a tense time for him and the tension, aggravated by constant overwork, perhaps caused the sudden recurrence of his old malady. Once, after working hard till 3 a.m., he had to spend what was left of the night, he told Catherine, 'in a state of exquisite torture from the spasm in my side ... I have not had so severe an attack since I was a child'. She is not to worry, however, since he has everything under control: 'I am so used to suffer from this cause that it never alarms me.'[3]

Meanwhile, the twelfth and last of his *Bell's Life* sketches, 'The Streets at Night', appeared in that paper on 17 January. It is a winter piece to match his summery 'The Streets – Morning' (*Evening Chronicle*, 21 July 1835) and shows how far he had, in five months, advanced in working out his concept of narrative/descriptive art. Aiming at truth to life ('life and manners as they really are'), he has recognised this necessarily involves depicting grimness as well as gaiety and often juxtaposing tragic, horrific and pathetic aspects of life with comic, pleasant and heart-warming ones. And, indeed, he who as a boy revelled in the 'Awful Instances of Despair, Grief and Madness' promised in each issue of *The Terrific Register*, and whose imagination was so stirred by glimpses of the squalor and brutality of St Giles's, was naturally drawn strongly towards such material by that very 'attraction of repulsion' already mentioned (above, p. 18). In 'The Streets at Night', he shows how effortlessly he can, within the one sketch, modulate from humorous description (preparations for the evening meal in the humbler suburbs) to strong pathos (a beggar carrying her child and feebly singing for alms in the freezing street) and then back again to lively comedy in the presentation of a rowdy and bibulous late-night 'harmonic meeting'.

He was also working on a purely comic tale at this point for a new monthly publication called *The Library of Fiction*. Here he reverted to his old farcical *Monthly* vein but again the new story showed a distinct advance on his earlier work. 'The Tuggses at Ramsgate' describes a London grocer and his family aiming at gentility who patronise the fashionable resort of Ramsgate. There they fall easily into the hands of 'three designing impostors', immediate precursors of Jingle in *Pickwick*, and end up both fleeced and ludicrously humiliated. Embellished with two illustrations by the popular comic artist Robert Seymour, the tale exactly suited the new journal which was subtitled *Family Story-Teller; consisting of Original Tales, Essays, and Sketches of Character*. This periodical was a venture by a newly-formed publishing firm of booksellers, Edward Chapman and William Hall, and Dickens had probably been recommended to them by their *Library of Fiction* editor, Charles Whitehead, who was an old *Monthly* hand. They quickly recognised that Dickens's skill in devising farcical anecdotes made him an ideal collaborator for Seymour in a major publishing venture that the artist was urging on them. They approached Dickens about the matter on 10 February and found that he was already concerned in various other projects. He had, as he told Catherine, 'more irons in the fire', and, like Kelmar's men in that favourite melodrama of his childhood, Isaac Pocock's *The Miller and His Men* (1813), was busy carrying 'more grist to the Mill'.[4]

The project most concerning him during January and February, apart, of course, from the publishing of *Sketches by Boz*, was the operetta. He had got Hullah to change the setting from Venice to an English village in 1729 and the format to that of a traditional English ballad-opera like Gay's *Beggars' Opera*. He devised a plot that owed not a little to *The Vicar of Wakefield* (intended seduction of innocent but over-impressionable village maidens by the local squire and his flash London friend). The title became *The Village Coquettes* and Dickens's by now well-practised talent for light verse stood him in good stead as he set to work on the words for the various songs, starting with a rousing opening chorus beginning, 'Hail to the merry Autumn days, when yellow cornfields shine,/Far brighter than the costly cup, that holds the monarch's wine!'[5]

Hogarth recommended the operetta to the celebrated tenor and impresario John Braham, letting him know the libretto was by the same *Morning Chronicle* reviewer who had so praised Braham's singing at his own theatre, the fashionable St James's, on 15 January. Librettist and composer then worked hard to prepare as full a script and score as possible ready for the manager's consideration. Dickens was keen to involve Catherine and planned to take her to the St James's, 'as I should very much like you to see a place and a set of people in which we are likely to be so much interested'. He also tells her he is using a suggestion of hers for opening the second act. By the beginning of February he could tell Cruikshank that Braham had accepted the piece 'with the most flattering encomiums; and an assurance that it *must* succeed'. Many months were to pass, however, before it was finally produced.[6]

Meanwhile, Dickens was also busy dramatising his tale 'The Great Winglebury Duel' as a vehicle for the popular comedian James Pritt Harley with whom he was on friendly terms, and who belonged to Braham's company at the St James's. Written originally for the *Monthly*, this story was not printed until it was included in the two-volume *Sketches By Boz* that Macrone published in February. Dickens beefed up its farcical elements by bringing on stage characters who are referred to but do not actually appear in the narrative, devising a set with lots of doors, and developing the low-comedy role of the inn servant, Tom Sparks the Boots, a sort of prototype Sam Weller without the 'Wellerisms'. He offered the play, titled *The Strange Gentleman*, for publication to Chapman and Hall on 18 February but it seems then to have remained on a back burner until the summer when Braham began to get interested in the idea of producing it.[7]

On 8 February, one day after Dickens's twenty-fourth birthday, *Sketches by Boz* finally appeared, in two volumes and priced at one guinea. Dickens's appreciation of Hogarth's 'beautiful notice' in the *Chronicle* (11 Feb.) has already been mentioned; the praise Hogarth bestowed upon the 'terrible power' of the last section of 'A Visit to Newgate' (which he found 'even more pathetic and impressive' than Victor Hugo's *Dernier jour d'un condamné*) must have greatly pleased Dickens. Many other reviews – overwhelmingly favourable – followed in the weeklies and some dailies. ' "Boz" ', declared the *Court Journal* on 20 February, 'is a kind of Boswell to society – and of the middle ranks especially'. The March issue of the *Metropolitan* recommended the book to the Americans as 'a perfect picture of the morals, manners and habits of a great portion of English Society'. (The Americans were not slow in producing their own edition of *Sketches* as, of course, they were free to do in the absence of any international copyright agreement: the Philadelphia firm of Carey, Lea and Blanchard published *Watkins Tottle, and other sketches, illustrative of every-day life and every-day people* in 1836, and followed up with further collections of Dickens's sketches in 1837.) Reviewers sometimes expressed reservations about Boz's tendency to caricature and also his choice of subject-matter, but always in the context of a high overall estimate of the author's qualities. Dickens's future close friend and biographer John Forster wrote in *The Examiner* (28 Feb.) for example:

> The fault of the book is the caricature of Cockneyism, of which there is too much. This common-place sort of thing is unworthy of the author, whose best powers are exercised obviously with great facility on the less hackneyed subjects. He shows his strength in bringing out the meaning and interests of objects which would altogether escape the observation of ordinary mortals.[8]

Macrone's energetic advertising of the book helped to get it wide coverage. Meanwhile, Dickens himself made sure that a copy got into the hands of the only peer he had ever met, Lord Stanley, reminding him in his covering letter of 8 February about his attendance on him as a *Mirror of Parliament* reporter and defending himself against the charge of presumption as follows:

> The wish of Authors to place their works in the hands of those, the eminence of whose public stations, is only to be exceeded by the lustre of their individual talents, is, and always has been, so generally felt, even by the greatest Men who have ever adorned the Literature of this Country, that I hope it may be pardoned when it displays itself in so young, and so humble a candidate for public favor, as / My Lord /Your Lordship's most obedient, Humble servant./ Charles Dickens.

There is, I think, a remarkable mixture here of that elaborate kow-towing to aristocracy that crops up so disconcertingly from time to time in Dickens's correspondence (at all periods of his life), a young writer's pride in his first book, his assertion of himself as someone now properly to be ranked among 'Authors', and a parade of modest self-deprecation ('so young, and so humble'). Dickens is, of course, hoping for Stanley's patronage to promote his book; but he also, I think, wants to ensure that this great lord, who may recall him only as a very competent newspaper reporter, should be made aware of the literary feat that he, the 'humble' reporter, has now achieved.

By 31 March Dickens could write proudly to his uncle Thomas Barrow, in a letter announcing his imminent marriage, about 'the great success of my book, and the name it has established for me among the Publishers'. It augured well for the production of a second series of sketches, as hinted at in his preface to the collection already published, and on 18 March Boz fans must have been pleased to find half-way down one of the columns of *The Morning Chronicle* the heading 'Sketches by Boz – New Series No.1'. This sketch, entitled 'Our Next Door Neighbours', is an oddly discontinuous one, however. Starting out as a whimsical piece about resemblances between street door-knockers and their owners, it ends up with a sympathetic Boz attending the deathbed of an impoverished youth of gentle birth who came from the country in a doomed attempt to make a living for himself and his widowed mother in London. The sketch is much less assured in touch than 'The Streets at Night' and was perhaps a false start, experimenting with the use of the Boz persona in rather a different way by having Boz become personally involved in the scenes he is describing. However that may have been, Dickens published no further sketches in the *Chronicle* until 24 September when a 'New Series' was again announced with the superbly-achieved 'Meditations in Monmouth Street' appearing as 'No.1'. 'Our Next Door Neighbours' was not discarded, however, but collected later in the year in *Sketches by Boz. Second Series*. Dickens would, I believe, have taken some pride in this his first attempt at a deathbed scene.[9]

The non-appearance of further 'New Series' sketches in the *Chronicle* in the spring and summer of 1836 may have resulted from the additional pressure Dickens was now under because of a long-term enterprise he had taken on. A couple of days after the publication of *Sketches by Boz* William Hall of Chapman and Hall approached him about writing the letterpress for a new work that the firm was, at the popular artist Robert Seymour's suggestion, proposing to publish in twenty shilling monthly numbers. Seymour would supply four plates for each number depicting the laughable misadventures of a club of newly-affluent Cockney sportsmen seeking to imitate the hunting, shooting and fishing activities of genuine country folk (among those already mining this popular vein of contemporary humour was Cruikshank in his *Comic Almanack* series and the author Robert Surtees with his hunting grocer Mr Jorrocks in the *New Sporting Magazine*). Dickens could hardly have regarded this as a very prestigious proposal. Flushed with the success of *Sketches*, he was now looking towards the writing of his first novel *Gabriel Vardon* (he later changed the surname to Varden), intended to be the foundation-stone of his literary career. This novel, a historical one, naturally, was to appear in all the dignity of the guinea-and-a-half, three-volume format hallowed by Scott and required by the all-powerful circulating libraries. Of shilling monthly numbers, he had, he wrote later, only 'a dim recollection of certain interminable novels in that form, which used, some five-and-twenty years ago, to be carried about the country by pedlars, and over some of which I remember to have shed innumerable tears before I served my apprenticeship to Life'.[10]

Such memories notwithstanding, here was an offer of £14.3.6 per month for writing twenty instalments of 12,000 words (with the possibility of more money if the work should prove successful). This, coming on top of his *Chronicle* salary, would enable him to move to a better apartment in Furnival's Inn and to get married sooner rather than later. The work, he wrote to Catherine on 10 February, 'will be no joke, but the emolument is too tempting to resist'. He disregarded those friends (presumably Ainsworth and Macrone) who warned him against involvement with 'a low, cheap form of publication by which [he would] ruin all his rising hopes' for he evidently felt himself to be in a strong enough position to make conditions. Seymour should illustrate his text instead of him writing the letterpress for Seymour's plates, the Cockney sporting club idea should be dropped, and Dickens should 'take [his] own way, with a freer range of English scenes and people'. Chapman and Hall readily agreed to all this on 12 February (how far Seymour was consulted about these major changes to his project we do not know) when acknowledging with praise copy for 'The Tuggses at Ramsgate'. They requested a prospectus for the new work 'as soon as possible', copy for the first number by 1 March (publication to be at the end of the month, the same date as for the first volume of *The Library of Fiction*) and copy for the second by mid-March. The actual content of the work was defined only as being 'illustrative of manners and life in the Country', a rural counterpart, therefore, to *Sketches by Boz*.[11]

'My views being deferred to,' wrote Dickens in a famously tantalising sentence a decade later, 'I thought of Mr Pickwick, and wrote the first number.' *How* did he 'think of Mr Pickwick'? The proprietor of a line of stage-coaches plying between London and Bath was called Moses Pickwick and the comic-sounding surname probably stuck in Dickens's mind because of its being incongruously joined with Moses, a family nickname and, indeed, the very origin of 'Boz' (above, p. 28). He substituted for Moses another and, among gentiles, much commoner Old Testament name, Samuel (and saved up a joke about the real-life Moses Pickwick for later use, in ch. 35 of the novel). Mr Pickwick himself Dickens seems to have conceived of as being rather like one of those prosperous, self-satisfied old bachelors, often with a hobby-horse, who figure in some of the *Monthly* tales. Pickwick's hobby-horse was to be amateur scientific investigation, Dickens having noticed the comic potential existing in the reports of the speeches and activities of the more vainglorious members of the recently-formed British Association for the Advancement of Science, a target that was to be in his sights again eighteen months later in *Bentley's Miscellany*. He kept Seymour's club notion and Pickwick has three companions, all stock farce types.[12]

One, Mr Winkle, a false pretender to sporting prowess, was included, Dickens later wrote, especially for Seymour's sake. Seymour's original idea of Pickwick as a tall thin man was replaced at Chapman's suggestion by a rotund elderly man dressed in old-fashioned tights and gaiters, a type that Seymour already had in his repertoire. Dickens seems to have taken kindly to the idea of a plump Pickwick, perhaps because it helped him to emphasise the amiability of this figure with his 'beaming' and 'twinkling' eyes. Pickwick was to be a figure of fun, certainly, but more sympathetic than any of the comic old bachelors in *Sketches*.

Dickens quickly dashed off an ebullient mock-heroic prospectus. Pickwick is praised as a great and intrepid traveller while the text makes clear that his travels do not take him more than thirty miles from London. Dickens left himself and Seymour scope for any number of rural scenes ('races, fairs, regattas, elections, meetings, market days . . .') and emphasised the miscellaneous nature of the work ('The Pickwick Travels, the Pickwick Diary, the Pickwick Correspondence . . .'). By 18 February he could report to Chapman and Hall, 'Pickwick is at length begun in all his might and glory'.[13]

For his first chapter Dickens falls back on his experience of Parliament to present a report of a meeting of the Pickwick Club parodying parliamentary language and debating conventions. The rest of the number deals with Pickwick and his friends setting out from a London coaching-inn on their rural travels (naturally, they head first for Rochester, where Dickens could draw most easily on personal knowledge of the terrain). Pickwick's farcical gullibility is established through his contretemps with the pugnacious cab driver and this is used to introduce a trickster figure to get the action going. This trickster is a strolling player called Jingle who, Dickens tells Catherine, 'is a very different character from any I have yet described' and will, he hopes, 'make a decided hit'. Jingle's most distinctive trait is, as his name suggests, his staccato speech, 'delivered with extraordinary volubility'. It was a trick Dickens had often seen Mathews using in his 'At Homes' and that he himself had already used briefly in one of his sketches (see the Irish orator in 'The Ladies' Societies', first published in *The Evening Chronicle*, 20 August 1835).[14]

Most of the rest of the number, which took him longer to write than he had anticipated ('the sheets are a weary length', he lamented to Catherine; 'I had no idea there was so much in them'), is essentially a *Monthly Magazine* type tale, based like 'The Great Winglebury Duel', on the standard comic theme of the reluctant duellist. But Dickens the author of 'A Visit to Newgate' would have wanted to introduce some contrasting 'dark' material into *Pickwick* as quickly as possible. He invented another strolling player (this time a 'dismal' one, to contrast with Jingle) who tells about a drunkard's death. Dickens must have written this immediately after, or maybe contemporaneously with, 'Our Next Door Neighbours'. Like that sketch, it features a death-bed scene but now involving horror as well as pathos. 'Many literary friends,' he told Seymour, 'on whose judgment I place great reliance, think it will create considerable sensation.' He could not include the tale in the first number, however, since he found he had overwritten his allowance of twenty-four printed pages. The first number therefore ended at the point where 'The Stroller's Tale' was about to begin. It appeared on 31 March, the last weekday of the month, known as

'Magazine Day', when the new numbers of all monthly journals were published. The green covers that were to become Dickens's trade-mark bore the title *The Posthumous Papers of the Pickwick Club containing a faithful record of the Perambulations, Perils, Travels, Adventures and Sporting Transactions of the Corresponding Members. Edited by "Boz".*[15]

With his marriage-day (2 April) fast approaching, Dickens had to work extra hard during March to finish *Pickwick* II, scheduled for publication 30 April, in order to gain time for his honeymoon. As he also often had to do 'heavy turns' in the reporters' gallery it is hardly surprising that there are so many apologies for absence in his letters to Catherine. One Sunday-evening note tells her he will have to work into the small hours because, not having got to bed until three that morning, he had not been able to start writing until nearly one. Astonishingly, his writing and his inventiveness in these early numbers of *Pickwick* show no sign of strain or fatigue. The second chapter opens with a good joke comparing the rising sun to a maid-of-all-work which is followed by the image of Mr Pickwick 'bursting like another sun from his slumbers' to embark with boyish enthusiasm upon his adventures. 'The Stroller's Tale', opening the second number, has tremendous drive and linguistic energy, as do the succeeding descriptions of the Pickwickians' misadventures at some military manoeuvres, their joyous picnic with the Wardles (introducing, among more stock types from contemporary farce, a striking new minor character, Joe the narcoleptic Fat Boy), and their troublesome journey to Dingley Dell, with horses as refractory as one that Dickens himself had had to contend with the year before, on the Chelmsford–Braintree road.[16]

Catherine being still a minor, Dickens had to return to his old haunts in Doctors' Commons to obtain a special marriage licence confirming she had her father's consent, a piece of legal/ecclesiastical business he turned to comic account in *Pickwick* IV when Jingle, bent on eloping with Rachael Wardle, obtains from Doctors' Commons 'a highly flattering address on parchment, from the Archbishop of Canterbury to his "trusty and well-beloved Alfred Jingle and Rachael Wardle" '. The wedding itself took place at the Hogarths' parish church, St Luke's in Chelsea. Over a half-century later Tom Beard, the best man, could recall only that it was 'altogether a very quiet piece of business', something that was to be true of all happy weddings in Dickens's subsequent fiction. Henry Burnett, a singing-partner of Fanny's at the Royal Academy of Music and perhaps already her fiancé (they married in September 1837), also remembered the wedding breakfast as having been 'the quietest possible'. Macrone was invited, indeed was going to be best man until Dickens reported that 'the ladies' all told him that, as he put it, 'I *must* be attended to the place of execution, by a single man'. Burnett recalled:

A few common pleasant things were said, healths drunk with a very few words said by either party – yet all things passed off very pleasantly, and all seemed happy, not the least so Dickens and his young girlish wife. She was a bright, pleasant bride, dressed in the simplest and neatest manner, and looked better perhaps than if she had been enabled to aim at something more.

Since 'neat' was always to be one of Dickens's highest terms of praise for a woman's appearance, he was no doubt more than happy with Catherine as, with joyful pride, he helped her out of the carriage and took her up the steps into her father's house after returning from the church. He was proud also of Catherine's notable cultural connections, describing her in his letter of 31 March to his uncle Thomas Barrow as 'the daughter of a gentleman who has recently distinguished himself by a celebrated work on Music, who was the most intimate friend and companion of Sir Walter Scott, and one of the most eminent among the Literati of Edinburgh'.[17]

For their brief honeymoon the young couple went to the village of Chalk, near Rochester, with its blacksmith's house and adjoining forge later to feature so memorably in *Great Expectations*. Their first child Charles, always known as Charley, was to be born exactly nine months later. By 14 April they were back in Furnival's Inn enjoying their new domesticity. Catherine's next oldest sister, the sixteen-year-old Mary, who as Catherine's faithful chaperone had endeared herself to Dickens during his courtship, came for a month's visit. To judge by two surviving letters from her to her cousin, Mary Scott Hogarth, and by the few comments about her recorded by people she met, Mary was a very charming young woman and her being there must have helped Catherine to begin adjusting to the long periods during the day, and often the evening too, when Dickens would either be working for the *Chronicle* or shut away, writing *Pickwick* against the calendar. The first of Mary's letters (15 May) gives us a vivid picture of life in Furnival's Inn:

> I have just returned from spending a most delightfully happy month with dearest Catherine in her own house! I only wish you could see her in it . . . she makes a most capital housekeeper and is as happy as the day is long – I think they are more devoted than ever since their Marriage if that be possible – I am sure you would be delighted with him if you knew him he is such a nice crea-ture and so clever he is courted and made up to by all the literary Gentlemen, and has more to do in that way than he can well manage. . . .

What Mary does not mention in this letter – the painful nature of the details involved no doubt restrained her from doing so – was a sudden dramatic turn of events in Dickens's budding authorial career that occurred during her visit and had momentous consequences for the development of *Pickwick Papers*.[18]

On the evening of 17 April Dickens and Seymour met for the first and last time. Dickens was not quite happy with Seymour's illustration for 'The Stroller's

9 Mary Hogarth: engraving of a lost portrait by Hablot Knight Browne ('Phiz')

Tale' and asked for some alterations to be made. Somewhat patronisingly – perhaps one might even say 'impudently', given the relative status of the two men at this time – Dickens invited Seymour to join him and the publishers for 'a glass of grog' on the Sunday evening ('the only night I am disengaged'), when he would explain his objections more fully. Three days after this meeting, Seymour, having worked till late in the night on the troublesome plate, went in the morning into his Islington garden studio and shot himself through the heart. He had had money worries, and perhaps suffered from other anxieties to do with his illegitimacy and defective education. He had also a history of some mental instability. And now it was becoming brutally clear that the project he had proposed to Chapman and Hall, and by which he had set such store, was passing out of his control. Also, with Dickens's introduction of the grim 'Stroller's Tale' the project was beginning to include subjects unsuitable for his particular talents, which lay very much in the field of comic caricature. Dickens's request for him to rework his plate of 'The Dying Clown' could well have been the final vexation that tipped him towards suicide.[19]

His death could well have put a stop to *Pickwick*. Sales of the first number had been disappointing and the print run for the second had been halved (from one thousand to five hundred). Now the more famous of the two names connected with the enterprise would no longer be on the cover. But Chapman and Hall were sufficiently impressed by Dickens's work for them so far, and by the success of his *Sketches*, to take a gamble on him. They proposed increasing his letterpress allowance from twelve to sixteen thousand words per month (thirty-two pages in place of twenty-six), the equivalent, as has been noted, of seven or eight sketches, 'an impressive leap for a young author to make'. At the same time the number of plates per part would be reduced from four to two. Dickens accepted the proposal provided that his monthly payment was raised initially to twenty guineas, with more to come if the work 'should be very successful'. Along with his acceptance he sent Chapman and Hall copy for nearly half of *Pickwick* IV, the number in which Sam Weller makes his first appearance.[20]

May 1836 was an extraordinarily productive month for Dickens, even by the standards he was now setting himself. He wrote the third number of the newly-enlarged *Pickwick*, which carries on the Jingle seduction plot but features also a highly melodramatic tale of near-parricide called 'The Convict's Return', plus a very effective 'graveyard' poem, 'The Ivy Green', recycled from an offering in a young lady's album. Most notably, it is in this number that we find the first example of Dickens's extraordinary power to create a tableau which, often as a result of a particular line of dialogue, quickly achieved mythic status in British culture, Oliver Twist asking for more being probably the best-known example. In this case it is Joe the fat boy petrifying Old Mrs Wardle with his sublime threat, 'I wants to make your flesh creep'.[21]

In this same month Dickens also wrote his second piece for *The Library of Fiction*, 'A Little Talk About Spring and the Sweeps', purportedly – and perhaps actually – inspired by seeing a traditional May Day parade of sweeps in fancy dress soliciting money from passers-by. On 9 May he agreed to deliver to Macrone by the end of November, 'or as soon after as I can possibly complete it' (that Macrone allowed this glaring loop-hole clause shows his eagerness to sign Dickens up), the manuscript of his projected three-volume novel *Gabriel Vardon, the Locksmith of London* in return for a payment of £200, a sum that, as Ainsworth was later to tell Macrone, was 'preposterously small' for a writer of Dickens's already demonstrated worth. The month ended with more reporting work outside London when Black sent him down to Ipswich to cover meetings held there by 'the Liberator', Daniel O'Connell, M.P., who was campaigning for 'Justice for Ireland'. The turbulence of the crowd (the Tories' behaviour, Dickens wrote to Catherine, was 'most outrageous and disgraceful') provided him with good copy for the Eatanswill election episode he was already planning for the next number of *Pickwick*. During this month also he dashed off his first piece of crusading journalism. He was infuriated by what he perceived as the class bias and fanaticism of speeches made by the Scottish baronet Sir Andrew Agnew and supporters during Agnew's third attempt to get his Sunday Observance Bill through the Commons on 18 May, when it was defeated by only thirty-two votes. Dickens's 12,000-word pamphlet pointedly imitates the format of a sermon divided into heads of an argument, its full title being *Sunday Under Three Heads. As It Is. As Sabbath Bills Would Make It. As It Might Be Made.*[22]

Dickens snipes at the Sabbatarians in each of the three things he writes this month and in *Sunday Under Three Heads* he pours a whole broadside in on them. We may assume, I think, that this pamphlet was the result of an initiative by Dickens himself and was the first major manifestation of that '*generously angry*' Dickens whose face was so memorably evoked by George Orwell at the end of his landmark essay on Dickens in 1939. Sabbatarianism with, as Dickens saw it, its perversion of Christian teaching, was, like teetotalism, to be one of his lifelong bugbears. Agnew is lampooned in *Nicholas Nickleby*, ch. 16 (Aug.1838) as the Sabbatarian M.P. Mr Gallanbile and, nearly twenty years later, we have the famous denunciation of gloomy London Sundays in *Little Dorrit*, Book I, chapter 3. Here, in this early pamphlet, Dickens shows how Agnew's bill is blatantly 'directed exclusively, and without the exception of a solitary instance, against the amusements and recreations of the poor' while leaving the rich unaffected. His vivid descriptions (more 'sketches' by Boz, in fact) of ordinary people harmlessly enjoying various forms of Sunday recreation that would be banned under Agnew's bill, such as cricket, greatly strengthen his argument. He must have found time also for a return visit to the British Museum Reading Room since he makes effective satirical use of a seventeenth-century pamphlet containing 'sundry memorable examples of God's Judgements upon Sabbath Breakers, and other like Libertines in their unlawful Sports'.[23]

Dickens's own pamphlet with its scathing foreword addressed to Charles Blomfield, Bishop of London and a prominent supporter of Sabbatarian legislation, was published under the *nom de guerre* of 'Timothy Sparks'. Presumably Dickens did not want Boz to be seen as too openly polemical at this time when he was still gathering his audience and carefully cultivating 'an excellent character as a quiet, modest fellow' (reviewers praising the 'good sense' of this little work clearly had no idea that it was the work of Boz). However, he did not hesitate in this month's number of *Pickwick* to ridicule the inhabitants of Muggleton who have presented to Parliament eighty-six petitions 'for abolishing Sunday trading in the street' (this mocks the many tradesmen's petitions presented by Agnew), or to bait the Sabbatarians again in 'A Little Talk about Spring and the Sweeps' when lamenting the demise of 'merry [springtime] dances round rustic pillars'.[24]

When *Pickwick* III appeared on 31 May it carried a publisher's announcement, written by Dickens, deploring Seymour's 'melancholy' death and apologising for the fact that there were only three plates in the issue (a ransacking of the artist's studio had unearthed no sign of a fourth one in preparation). Arrangements were being made, the announcement continued, glossing over the disappointing sales figures, to present ensuing numbers 'on an improved plan, which we trust will give entire satisfaction to our numerous readers'. Meanwhile, another illustrator was appointed, Robert William Buss, who had already provided an illustration for Dickens's 'Little Talk about Spring and the Sweeps'.

His work proved unsatisfactory, however, owing to his lack of experience in etching on steel, and he lasted for only one number before being replaced by a self-effacing younger man called Hablot Knight Browne, nineteen years old, who had trained as an engraver and had already supplied admirable illustrations for 'The Tuggses at Ramsgate' and *Sunday Under Three Heads*. Browne (chosen in preference to Thackeray, then a struggling young artist) entered the *Pickwick* enterprise very much as a junior partner. Unlike Cruikshank or Seymour, he carried no baggage of established reputation and *amour-propre* and proved an ideal collaborator for Dickens. His work in its vitality, tumultuous yet precise detail, and elements of grotesquerie was strongly responsive to Dickens's, he was compliant and amenable to requests for alterations, and, like Dickens, he could work with amazing rapidity. As 'Phiz', a name abbreviated from 'physiognomy' and chosen to chime with 'Boz', he was to remain Dickens's chief illustrator for the next twenty-four years.[25]

Later commentators have rightly seen *Pickwick* IV, the number being written in early June, as the great turning-point in Dickens's career. In it he introduces Sam Weller, the character he had commended to Macrone as his 'specimen of London life'. But there is no sign in Dickens's surviving correspondence that he felt at this stage that Sam was the harbinger of any momentous development in his literary career. The sparkling brilliance with which this character is presented no doubt partly results from Dickens's relief at having got Pickwick back to London, the teeming streets of which provide, as he was well aware by now, the richest food for his imagination. But we should note that in the same breath as he commends Sam to Macrone he commends with equal emphasis something else in the number, the highly sensational 'Madman's Manuscript'. The remainder of *Pickwick* IV is somewhat desultory, the Jingle seduction plot having been worked out in the first two chapters, but Dickens would have been encouraged by the increasing public notice taken of the work, and gratified to see the *Sunday Times* comparing him on 12 June with two of his literary heroes, Fielding and Smollett. He would have appreciated also the tangible evidence of the growing commercial success of the work provided by the four pages of advertisements appearing in this number, the first 'Pickwick Advertiser' (by *Pickwick* X this extended to sixteen pages). But his main literary concerns and expectations during this month of May seem to have been centred on *The Village Coquettes*. Braham had been 'speaking highly', Dickens told Hullah, 'of my Works and "fame" (!)', and saying he wanted to be the first to introduce Boz to the public as a dramatist. Braham wanted a low-comedy, non-singing part inserted for the benefit of his star comedian John Pritt Harley and Dickens happily obliged, dashing in the character of Martin Stokes, a bumbling farmer, complete with the obligatory tag-lines. He seized every opportunity to work with Hullah on the operetta over the next few weeks and it was finally ready for a private reading before a group of literary and musical friends on 23 July. This was Catherine's first essay in formal entertaining

10 Hablot Knight Browne ('Phiz'): self-portrait

and things seem to have gone very well; writing to her grandfather George Thomson on 30 July, Dickens described her as still retaining some of the 'high and mighty satisfaction she derived from a supper of her own invention and arrangement which we gave to our first little party a week ago'.[26]

Among Dickens's major *Chronicle* assignments in the summer of 1836 was helping to cover the sensational Melbourne trial on 22 June in which the Prime Minister was sued by the Hon. George Norton for 'crim con.' (that is, adultery) with Norton's beautiful wife, the writer Caroline Norton. It was a blatant put-up job. The prosecution offered farcically inadequate evidence and the jury eventually acquitted Melbourne, at eleven thirty that evening, without even leaving their box. The *Chronicle* report next morning occupied twenty-six and a half columns and, even though Dickens would have had colleagues relieve him from time to time, it is hardly surprising to find him writing to Macrone on 23 June that he had been in bed all day, the trial having 'played the devil with me'. The trial report is deadpan in tone and it is not possible to distinguish the parts written by Dickens though there are some sharply-worded comments at the beginning which sound very much like him. These concern the inconvenient structure of the court building and the offensive behaviour of 'a large concourse' of fledgeling barristers. From these 'youths', writes Dickens (if it is indeed he), very much on his social and professional dignity, reporters 'experienced nothing but a series of gratuitous annoyances and ungentlemanly interruptions' from the beginning to the end of the trial.

Dickens's experience of seeing at such close quarters how an older man's totally innocent behaviour towards a woman could be deliberately misrepresented by unscrupulous lawyers seems likely to have suggested to him an idea for developing a main plot for *Pickwick Papers*. The farcical business of Jingle and Rachael Wardle was concluded and Dickens now needed to lay the foundations of a more sustainable plot centred on Pickwick, the book's protagonist. Memories of Uncle Toby lodging with Widow Wadman in Sterne's *Tristram Shandy* and of her mistaking his innocuous remarks for an amorous approach may also have helped inspire the introduction of Pickwick's landlady, the widowed Mrs Bardell. The re-appearance of Sam Weller in this connection was an added bonus since Dickens knew this character had made a hit (William Jerdan, editor of the influential *Literary Gazette*, had urged him to develop this 'novel character' as much as possible) and he knew he could make much of him. Moreover, if Pickwick were going to metamorphose from farcical pedant into a Dickens version of Don Quixote he would need a Sancho Panza to ground him in reality, and Sam would fit the bill perfectly. Dickens entitles the first chapter of *Pickwick* V (ch.12), which he was writing in July, 'Descriptive of a Very Important Proceeding on the Part of Mr Pickwick; No Less an Epoch in His Life, than in This History'. He was thereby signalling a turning-point in this series of monthly 'papers' even as he continued with his original sketches-and-tales formula: the number includes the wildly satirical Eatanswill election sketch and a comic-fantastic tale told by a 'bagman' (commercial traveller), as well as the scene between Mr Pickwick and Mrs Bardell. There is, however, a distinct thematic connection between the three different elements in this number, whether consciously intended or not. The innocent Pickwick is mocked by the Eatanswill mob for supposedly flirting with Mrs Pott ('I see him a vinkin' at her, vith his vicked old eye', shouts one man in the crowd) and the bagman's tale is all about wooing and winning 'a buxom widow'. Gradually, *Pickwick* was turning into a coherent novel and ceasing to be merely a series of miscellaneous 'papers', even though reviewers continued to notice it under 'periodicals' rather than under 'new novels'. It would be a little while yet before they, or indeed Dickens himself (still dreaming of dignified 'three-deckers', that is, novels published in three volumes, as representing true 'literature'), recognised that he had decisively changed received ideas about the format of the novel.[27]

Writing to George Thomson, Catherine's grandfather, on 30 July to excuse himself and Catherine from accepting Thomson's invitation to visit Edinburgh, Dickens includes a succinct summary of his authorial and job commitments at this point:

I am at present engaged in revising the proof sheets of the second Edition of the Sketches which will shortly appear; I am preparing another series which must be published before Christmas, I have just finished an opera which will be produced at Braham's Theatre in October, I have to get Mr Pickwick's lucubrations ready, every month; and have, in addition, to perform the duties (neither slight nor few) which my engagement with The Morning Chronicle imposes upon me.

All his life Dickens took pride (with good reason) in his efficient time-management and ability to keep many balls in the air at once. Here he is evidently concerned to impress Thomson with these qualities, to present himself as an author who, while energetically pursuing his career in a well-organised way, still has to cope with a day job, though in his case 'night job' might be a more appropriate phrase. What he does not say is that, despite his already crowded schedule, he is taking on more and more work with the object of getting himself into a position in which he will be able to turn full-time author. He devoutly hoped, he wrote to Macrone in late July, that before the next session of Parliament he might be able to 'make some arrangements which will render its sittings a matter of indifference to me – as the story books say "for ever after" '.[28]

By now Macrone realised he had a potential gold mine in 'Boz the magnificent', as the ebullient William Maginn hailed Dickens in the August number of *Fraser's Magazine*. He did everything to bind Dickens closer to him. He had already made an agreement to publish his first novel, though without any firm delivery date. He now found a stool for young Fred Dickens in his counting-house, and he and his wife maintained a close 'young marrieds' friendship with Dickens and Catherine. Macrone was in considerable financial difficulties so he was eagerly looking forward to the publication, in time for the Christmas market, of a second series of Boz's sketches, as well as the promised novel *Gabriel Vardon*. The Boz series was to appear in two volumes like the first series. It would gather up nearly all those pieces published earlier than December 1836 and not yet collected, and add new ones. Meanwhile, Macrone duly produced on 10 August a second edition of the first series. His advertisement for it in *The Athenaeum* for 30 July was apparently the first public identification of Boz as 'Mr Charles Dickens'.[29]

Dickens's preface to this second edition may be seen as the first letter relating to what has been called Dickens's 'lifelong love-affair with his reading public . . . by far the most interesting love-affair of his life'. He expresses his 'warmest thanks' and 'deepest gratitude' to the public for 'the kindness and indulgence' shown towards his work, and for all the 'patronage' and encouragement given to 'a young and unknown writer'. In affectionately teasing vein, he neatly paves the way for the second series of *Sketches* and even for the novel he has agreed to write for Macrone. His sketches have been so well received, he writes, that

if the pen that designed these little outlines, should present its labours frequently to the Public hereafter; if it should produce fresh sketches, and even connected works of fiction of a higher grade, they have only themselves to blame.

Notably disingenuous here is the phrase 'little outlines' as we can be sure that Dickens would certainly not have really felt this an appropriate description for either 'A Visit to Newgate' or for 'The Black Veil'.[30]

Macrone must have been startled by Dickens's sudden announcement on 3 August that he had contracted to write a fortnightly series of 'short sketches', half the length of those written for the *Chronicle* or *Bell's*, for a new periodical called *The Carlton Chronicle and National Conservative Journal*, the first number of which would appear in three days' time. The *Carlton's* editor, Percival Banks, would pay well, Dickens told Macrone, and as his circulation was small these sketches would not injure sales of Boz's second series – in fact, since the magazine circulated 'all among the nobs' they would probably enhance the book's sales. The *Carlton* series was to be called 'Leaves from an Unpublished Volume by Boz (which will be torn out, once a fortnight)'. Robert Patten's comment is apposite: 'One wonders just how happy Macrone was to find out that Dickens was selling his copyright a second time over.'[31]

In the event Dickens contributed just two sketches to the *Carlton*, 'The Hospital Patient' (6 Aug.) and 'Hackney Cabs and Their Drivers' (17 Sept.). The long gap between the appearance of the first and the second sketch probably resulted from the sheer pressure of Dickens's other commitments at this time. Not only was he busy negotiating with two other publishers, as we shall see, but he also had *The Strange Gentleman* and, above all, the operetta to finish. Meanwhile, there was always *Pickwick* to attend to. *Pickwick* VI, written early August, reintroduces Jingle in the course of another comic sketch, Mrs Leo Hunter's 'fancy dress *déjeuner*'. This subject came naturally to hand for it was about now that 'Mr Dickens', the man behind 'Boz', became, wrote the critic Abraham Hayward later, 'the grand object of interest to the whole tribe of "Leo Hunters", male and female, of the metropolis'. But Dickens may have also felt he was not getting sufficient contrast into the work since the only touch of darkness amidst all the fun of *Pickwick* V and VI is Sam's teaching Pickwick (ch.16) about those lost in destitution's abyss, 'the worn-out, starving, houseless creeturs as rolls themselves up in the dark corners 'o them lonesome places'. Sam's description of the dry arches under Waterloo Bridge is, in fact, a Boz sketch in miniature, and he can be seen as, among other things, a racier, fully characterised, successor to Boz in Dickens's oeuvre.[32]

Chiming with this passage in *Pickwick* is the starkness of Dickens's first *Carlton* piece 'The Hospital Patient', written more or less contemporaneously. His discrete sketches give him another outlet for the non-comic writing that has to be confined to the inserted tales in *Pickwick*, and he may well have preferred making his début in this journal of the 'nobs' with something more in the vein of his much-admired 'Visit to Newgate' than with the kind of humorous/satirical street sketch for which Boz was most celebrated, and of which his second *Carlton* piece, about metropolitan cab-drivers, was to be a fine example. In 'The Hospital

Patient' he comments on the 'miserable creatures' who can be seen lingering about the streets late at night and the sketch culminates in his third deathbed scene, one that is rather more complex in its effect than its predecessors. A woman lies dying in a hospital having been savagely beaten by her partner, but the scene is neither simply pathetic as at the end of 'Our Next Door Neighbour' nor simply horrific as in 'The Stroller's Tale'. The description of the woman's continued love for the man and her frantic attempts to save him from the gallows touches on the tragic, for all the melodramatic expression involved. Its power derives from Dickens's horrified fascination with the subject of brutal treatment of loving and submissive women by their partners – he had already dramatised this once in 'The Pawnbroker's Shop' (*Evening Chronicle*, 30 June 1835) and was to revisit the subject in spectacular fashion in *Oliver Twist* two years later.[33]

Despite all he now had on hand Dickens, astonishingly, signed yet another contract on 11 August. He agreed to write for the bookseller Thomas Tegg a children's book aimed at the Christmas market and provisionally entitled *Solomon Bell the Raree Showman*. Tegg, a sharp businessman who dealt mainly in cheap reprints, remainders and abridgments, beat Dickens's price down from £120 to £100 and did not want Boz's name attached to the work, probably because this persona might seem inappropriate – too streetwise, as it were – for a children's book. Dickens's ready agreement suggests that he may already have been getting anxious about over-exploiting his 'Boz' persona, especially in such a piece of blatant hackwork as this. Then, on 22 August, he signed an altogether more formidable contract with yet another publisher, Richard Bentley, with whom he had been negotiating about a novel for more than a week. He agreed to write not one but *two* three-volume novels for £500 each, and promised to engage in no other 'literary production' until the first of these was completed. Quite how he justified all this to himself, given his existing commitments to Macrone (who did not even learn of this new agreement for three months) we do not know.[34]

No reference is made in the Bentley agreement to *Pickwick Papers* so it was presumably classed by both Dickens and Bentley as a 'periodical' rather than as a 'literary production'. It was with the first of the two novels he was to write for Bentley that Dickens expected, as he said, to create 'a work on which I might build my fame'. About this time also, realising more material will be needed for *Sketches by Boz. Second Series*, he re-inaugurated the aborted 'New Series' in the *Morning Chronicle*. On 25 August he accepted £30 from Braham for the copyright of *The Strange Gentleman*. Meanwhile, he and Hullah sold their joint copyright in *The Village Coquettes* music to Cramer's the music publishers 'for a good round sum', and they resolved to publish a book of the songs, for sale in the theatre, on their own account. Dickens suggested to Bentley that he might make an offer to publish the text of the opera. If it should prove 'a very great hit' (and he ticks off its selling points for the publisher's benefit: ' "Boz's" first play – an old English story, and an attempt to revive the rustic opera') the book would have 'a considerable sale'. He seemed bent, in fact, on raising money, and the promise of money, by all possible means, presumably so that he could now turn full-time writer.[35]

Around 20 August, after Parliament had risen, he and Catherine began their summer holiday in the pretty little village of Petersham in Surrey, where they stayed until 24 September. Dickens described it in Jingle-ese when inviting Hullah to visit: 'Beautiful place – meadow for exercise – horse for your riding – boat for your rowing – room for your studying – anything you like' (neither then nor later were Dickens's house-guests encouraged just to relax). Another local attraction for him would have been the Theatre Royal, Richmond, then managed by the 'grandiloquent' actor-manager Thomas Davenport, supposedly Dickens's model for Crummles in *Nicholas Nickleby*. Davenport's nine-year-old daughter, an 'Infant Phenomenon', made her Richmond début as a diminutive Venus in a burlesque called *Cupid* on 29 August, and it is pleasant to imagine that Dickens and Catherine, and perhaps Mary too, might have been there, though this may well have been one of the days when Dickens had to go to London. He was constantly travelling up to town for the day, either by stage-coach or on horseback, to see Hullah, or a publisher, or John Pritt Harley or Braham at the St James's where both actor and impresario were full of enthu-siasm about the prospects for *The Strange Gentleman* and also *The Village Coquettes*. Sometimes what his great friend the actor William Macready would later call Dickens's 'clutching eye' would en route catch a scrap of copy for the new series of sketches. In the first one, 'Meditations in Monmouth Street' (*Morning Chronicle*, 24 Sept.), for example, Dickens conjures up the figures of the jolly market-gardener, whom he has seen 'coming up to Covent Garden in his green chaise-cart, with the fat tubby little horse, half a thousand times', and a 'coquettish' maidservant 'in whom we at once recognised the very girl who accepted his offer of a ride, just on this side the Hammersmith suspension-bridge, the very last Tuesday morning we rode into town from Richmond'.[36]

With all these trips to town the writing of *Pickwick* VII (chs 18–20) proceeded slowly. Not until 21 September did Chapman and Hall get all the copy, just nine days before 'Magazine Day' (the first fragment of the manuscript to survive belongs to this number and shows evidence of 'fast, energetic compo-sition'). It was copy worth waiting for since it contained the richly comic episode of Mr Pickwick's ignominious confinement in a village pound after he has been found in postprandial torpor on private land. Also, it introduced some major new characters, the rascally lawyers Dodson and Fogg, and Sam's magnif-icently ripe 'old stager' of a father, Tony Weller with his mortal dread of 'widders'. With each monthly part the unity and thematic coherence of this rambling story of Pickwick and his friends was clearly growing and the book itself was, as Forster finely puts it, 'teaching him what his power was'. Dickens was also now well embarked on the process of bringing the time of year in which the action is set in each monthly part into synchronicity with the actual month in which that part appears, something that must have seemed to his readers to impart to the serial the very rhythm of life itself.[37]

The last week or so before 29 September when *The Strange Gentleman* opened at the St James's was especially hectic with Dickens spending hours at the theatre 'superintending [the play's] preparation, morning, noon, and night'. A copy of the manuscript (mainly in John Dickens's hand, interesting evidence that he was making himself useful to his increasingly celebrated and hectically busy son) was submitted, as required by law, to the Lord Chamberlain's office for approval. This copy shows that Dickens's text underwent much revision during rehearsals, and at the same time the various songs were also added that were needed to turn it into a so-called 'burletta' (the St James's, like most other London theatres, was not permitted to do straight plays or 'legitimate' drama). The result was a triumph. The little play was, according to *The Times*, 'very well received throughout, and announced for repetition with great applause'. It was, the reviewer noted, 'from the pen of a gentleman who has very much amused the town by the broad humour and downright fun of sketches published by him under the *sobriquet* "Boz"', and it abounded 'in those strokes of quaintness and happy perception and rich description of the ludicrous for which his writings are remarkable'. It enjoyed a remarkably good run of fifty nights (an excellent return for Braham on his £30) and was proudly viewed more than once by its young author sitting in a private box, accompanied by various family members and friends. Further theatrical triumphs might be anticipated when the much-postponed production of *The Village Coquettes* would eventually take place.[38]

Meanwhile, he had his new *Morning Chronicle* series (every sketch being almost immediately reprinted in *The Evening Chronicle*) to keep up: 'Scotland Yard' appeared on 4 October, later than intended, and 'Doctors' Commons' on 11 October, again later than intended. Like 'Meditations in Monmouth Street', and 'Vauxhall Gardens By Day', which followed them on 26 October, these are superbly crafted essays, descriptive of quaint or curious London localities, in which Boz no longer sounds the least hesitant or apologetic in his approach to his readers. They are now assumed to be pretty familiar with him as a columnist/reporter whose foibles and interests they are likely to share – see, for example, the opening of 'Scotland Yard':

> If our recollection serves us, we have more than once hinted, confidentially, to our readers that we entertain a strong partiality for the queer little old streets which yet remain in some parts of London, and that we infinitely prefer them to the modern innovations, the wide streets with broad pavements, which are every day springing up around us.

These sketches, like all the others as yet uncollected (except for 'The Tuggses at Ramsgate' which Dickens, seeing the success of *The Strange Gentleman*, may have been thinking of dramatising) were to be collected in the two-volume *Sketches by Boz, Second Series,* he had planned with Macrone. During October Dickens must have continued the work of polishing and revising this material that he had begun back in the summer. His revision was detailed and extensive. It mainly consisted of removing ephemeral references and political allusions and eliminating slang expressions, but his first publication, 'A Dinner at Poplar Walk', was substantially revised and retitled 'Mr Minns and His Cousin' while in two instances two original sketches were amalgamated into one. By this time Cruikshank was fast losing patience as he had still been sent only two sketches to illustrate. Dickens, being 'so over head and heels in work' on his return to town, could not meet Cruikshank until about 5 October when they settled the illustrations for the first volume (it had not yet become clear to all concerned, as it did shortly afterwards, that there would be only enough material to fill one volume). When Dickens heard from Macrone that the artist had regretted not having seen all the manuscript earlier since this would have allowed him to suggest 'little alterations to suit the Pencil' as he had done for other authors, he exploded, calling Cruikshank 'mad'. Had any such emendations come to hand Dickens would, he wrote scornfully, have preserved them as 'curiosities of Literature'. This storm quickly blew over, however, and had no lasting effect.[39]

Pickwick VIII (chs 21–23), written during the earlier part of October, must have made curious reading for Dickens's parents. A strange old man called Jack Bamber tells Mr Pickwick, who is gradually being drawn more and more into the meshes of the law, a grim story about a 'queer client' and the fearful things that can be done by unscrupulous lawyers. It opens with a description of no less a place than the Marshalsea Prison in all its wretchedness and insalubriousness ('The condemned felon has as good a yard for air and exercise in Newgate, as the insolvent debtor in the Marshalsea Prison'). This may be an early instance of Dickens's extraordinary power of responding to some contemporary burning issue in a way that contributes strongly to the plot or theme or ambiance of whatever fictional work he happens to have on hand, since imprisonment for debt was very much in the news at this time owing to a parliamentary rejection in July of a proposal to abolish this penalty. The intense personal resonance of this subject for Dickens can be felt in his description of the wretched debtor's wife and little son lingering so early every morning on 'the old bridge' (the one that, many years later, he will make Little Dorrit's favourite retreat). There they wait for the prison gates to open as they watch 'all the bustling preparations for business and pleasure that the river presents at that early hour', just as Dickens himself and his parents' little servant-girl from the Chatham workhouse had done only twelve years earlier.[40]

The number opens with a long disquisition by the weird old man who will tell the story of the Queer Client on those 'strange old places' the Inns of Court and the peculiar and often desperate lives that have been lived in them 'when young men shut themselves up in those lonely rooms, and read and read, hour after hour, and night after night'. It is like a macabre variation on 'Scotland Yard' and the other *Chronicle* sketches Dickens was writing this month. His Petersham 'ruralising' had perhaps renewed and sharpened his intense fascination with the great labyrinth of London and its wealth of strange, often tucked-away, localities. The Marshalsea Prison with so much 'want and misfortune' pent up in its narrow bounds, Scotland Yard where a lonely little boy, wandering the London streets after his day's drudgery, once sat down on a bench to watch the coal-heavers dancing, Doctors' Commons with all its flummery, bachelor chambers like those in the Inns of Court with their gloom and solitude and frowsy 'laundresses' (cleaning women) – all these places had strong personal associations for Dickens, some involving not a little pain and anxiety. Yet this October, needing copy, he presses them all into service and writes them up in assured 'Bozzian' mode. He finds himself able to do this, even with the Marshalsea, by means of an invented narrator given to melodramatic and sensational effects, whom he can use to mediate its miseries to the reader.

Pickwick VIII was hailed in *The Examiner* as 'the best *Pickwick* we have had' by Forster who was not yet personally acquainted with Dickens. In this number Dickens continues to develop innocent Mr Pickwick's tendency to get into difficulties with the opposite sex in his adventure with the middle-aged lady in yellow curl-papers. It also carries on the secondary plot of the pursuit of the trickster Jingle. Feeling his power as a writer more and more, Dickens was now looking out for commissions that would enable him to leave his job on the *Chronicle*. Some negotiations with the *Sunday Times*, perhaps for more sketches, fell through: 'I could not get enough and saw no reason for doing it *cheap*', he wrote to Beard, adding that he thought that as a result he would continue to 'exhibit in the Gallery' at least until the following Easter. But then two things occurred that changed the situation very considerably and left him, he felt, free to write that resignation letter.[41]

First, he received, at the end of October, a 'very kind' letter from Chapman and Hall. By this time the phenomenal success of *The Pickwick Papers* was becoming more apparent by the day. It was showing itself in ways very familiar to us in these days of 'product endorsement' but still quite novel then (and, of course, of no direct profit to the author). Abraham Hayward, writing in the *Quarterly Review* a year later, remembered that 'in less than six months from the appearance of the first number'

Pickwick chintzes figured in linen-drapers' windows, and Weller corduroys in breeches-makers' advertisements; 'Boz' cabs might be seen rattling through the streets, and the portrait of the author of 'Pelham' [Bulwer] or 'Crichton' [Ainsworth] was scraped down or pasted over to make room for that of the new popular favourite in the omnibuses.

Dickens's remuneration for *Pickwick* was already set to rise from £14.3.6 to £25 per month in November, as specified in the agreement made in August, and now Chapman and Hall evidently proposed that Dickens should write, whether on these or on still better terms, another story in twenty monthly parts after the conclusion of *Pickwick* in eleven months' time. The publishers must have ventured on some remonstrance about Dickens's lateness in supplying copy as he rather uncomfortably jokes that he is 'well aware of the lingering disease under which Mr Pickwick has recently laboured' and promises that it 'will now take a favourable turn'. He asks them only to remember that he has 'many other occupations' and that spirits 'are not to be forced up to Pickwick point, every day'.[42]

For all the greater unity that he is now consciously imparting to *Pickwick*, its format still prevented Dickens, and others, from thinking of it as a novel. His first story to be properly so designated was to be *Gabriel Vardon, the Locksmith of London*, for which he was now contracted twice over, first to Macrone and then to Bentley, with, in the latter case, the proviso that he would engage in no other 'literary production' until it was finished. This did not, apparently, preclude him from writing further serial works – considered *sub*-literary, presumably – for Chapman and Hall, whom he appoints as his sole 'periodical publishers'. He would never, he wrote them, take such pride in any future novel as he did in the (as yet unfinished) *Pickwick* which 'has made its own way'. Meanwhile, Chapman and Hall will continue to be his periodical publishers 'until I am advertised in the daily papers, as having been compressed in my last edition – one volume, boards, with brass plates'.[43]

The second thing that happened was that Richard Bentley ('almost frantic', according to his chief clerk, with delight at the notion of producing a monthly journal which might outsell his former business-partner and now hated rival Henry Colburn's *New Monthly Magazine*) asked Dickens to become the editor, and Cruikshank to become the illustrator, of the projected new periodical to be called *The Wits' Miscellany*. Both men accepted immediately. Under an agreement signed on 4 November Dickens was to get £20 per month for editing the *Miscellany* but Bentley was to retain the power to veto the appearance of any article. This arrangement was to be guaranteed for a year, even if the journal should fold within that time, as was the further twenty guineas per month in respect of Dickens's contributing sixteen pages (equivalent to one printer's sheet) of original writing to each number. The copyright in such contributions by Dickens was to be Bentley's, however. Dickens bound himself not to conduct or write for any other periodical – apart from *Pickwick* and the subsequent 'similar work' he had by now agreed to write for Chapman and Hall. Ominously, no reference was made to his earlier agreement to write a three-volume novel for Bentley with the publisher having an option on a second novel. Evidently, this was presumed to remain in force.[44]

Dickens had now secured a guaranteed regular income, for the next year at least, of a basic £65.20 per month (£25 from Chapman and Hall, £40.20 from Bentley). With such ample evidence of his rapidly rising market value, to which he does not fail to direct Bentley's attention, he now felt himself able, even though he would soon have three mouths to feed, to resign from *The Morning Chronicle*. Accordingly, on 5 November he gave a formal month's notice to the proprietors, enclosing with it a personal letter to Easthope, thanking him for his 'courtesies and kindnesses' (perhaps somewhat sarcastically, given Easthope's reputation for roughness – his nick-name among his staff was 'Blast-Hope'), and saying, with elegant and pointed emphasis, how sorry he was to be leaving 'an Establishment where I have uniformly discharged my duties with so much pleasure to myself, and I hope I may add, with so much satisfaction to my Employers'. Finding Easthope's response to be insufficiently appreciative, Dickens replied on 18 November with a prime example of what have been called his 'Great Protester' letters, fairly seething with a sense of injured merit:

> wherever there was difficult and harassing work to be performed . . . leaving hot and crowded rooms to write, the night through, in a close damp chaise – tearing along, and writing the most important speeches, under every possible circum-stance of disadvantage and difficulty – for that duty have I been selected.[45]

Over thirty years later, speaking at a dinner of the Newspaper Press Fund, Dickens vividly evoked these same experiences in a very different tone. He recalled transcribing important speeches from his shorthand notes 'writing on the palm of my hand, by the light of a dark lantern, in a post chaise and four, galloping through a wild country, all through the dead of night, at the then surprising rate of fifteen miles an hour'. It was a job that brought the strong 'machismo' element in his character into pleasurable play, much stimulated by the fierce competition offered by his colleagues on *The Times* ('they had the start two or three minutes', he wrote to Beard on 2 May 1835 from Wincanton, on his way back from reporting Lord John Russell's speech in Exeter; 'I bribed the post boys tremendously & we came in literally neck and neck – the most beautiful sight I ever saw . . .'). Well may we believe that the silver-gilt inscribed goblet presented to him by his grateful and admiring *Morning Chronicle* colleagues shortly after his resignation, and which he kept all his life, greatly pleased him and that that special warmth and affection evident in all his letters to Tom Beard had its roots deep in their shared experience of the heady days of his reporting triumphs.[46]

CHAPTER 5

Editing *Bentley's Miscellany*

1836–1837

The popularity of this writer is one of the most remarkable literary phenomena of recent times, for it has been fairly earned without resorting to any of the means by which most other writers have succeeded in attracting the attention of their contemporaries.

Quarterly Review, 59 (October 1837)

IN NOVEMBER and December 1836 Dickens was a leading partner in a highly flourishing project undertaken by one publishing firm, Chapman and Hall. He was also in the process of severing his connection with another firm, that of the unfortunate Macrone, whose terms were no longer acceptable. And he was entering into a (for him) quite new kind of relationship with yet another publisher, Richard Bentley, to whom he was already heavily committed on a different basis. Lastly but still pressingly there was the little matter of the plot, dialogue and lyrics of *The Village Coquettes*, all still to be completed by himself and Hullah.

Troubled as he was by violent headaches and attacks of 'rheumatism in the face' (influenza was rampant during the exceptionally severe winter of 1836/37), Dickens found it tough going. Telling Cruikshank on 28 November that he would be late with copy needed for illustrating *Sketches by Boz, Second Series*, he lamented, 'For the last fortnight I have been very unwell – unable for many days to put pen to paper, and the unlooked-for extent of the preparations for the opera occupies my whole day. I cannot do more than one pair of hands and a solitary head can execute, and really am so hard pressed just now that I must have breathing time.' Because most of his letters at this period are dated just by the day of the week we cannot chart the dates of his bouts of illness with any accuracy nor determine the precise order in which he wrote things. The Pilgrim Editors show good reason, however, for dating his draft prospectus for Bentley's new journal to early November. In it Dickens promises 'a feast of the richest comic humour' to be provided by 'the ablest and merriest caterers of the age', leaving a blank for the names of the said caterers to be filled in later. His self-introduction as editor strikes the same note of decent modesty (more assumed than actual, we may

believe) as that sounded in the Prefaces to the first and second editions of the first
series of *Sketches by Boz*, but it is now tempered by growing confidence in the
warm relationship that Boz has established with the public:

> The management of the Wits' Miscellany has been entrusted to 'Boz' – a
> gentleman with whom the public are on pretty familiar terms, and who – his
> time not being wholly engrossed by the weighty affairs of his far-famed
> 'Club' – has consented to undertake the task. As he feels considerable diffidence
> in occupying so high a station among so many more distinguished individuals,
> however, and begs not to have his bashfulness increased by any further mention
> of him here, it will be best to let him speak for himself in the first number.

That this self-deprecating demeanour was not something Dickens adopted
only in print appears from his letter to Bentley of 5 December, following a star-
studded dinner-party at the publisher's, in which he wrote: 'I kept very quiet,
purposely. Since I have been a successful author, I have seen how much ill-will
and jealousy there is afloat, and have acquired an excellent character as a quiet,
modest fellow. I like to assume a virtue, though I have it not; it has served me
with a subject more than once.'[1]

There could hardly have been a bigger contrast than between this attitude
and the demeanour of the editor of *Fraser's Magazine*, the highly successful
monthly on which Bentley was clearly modelling his journal. *Fraser's*, a Tory
monthly founded by the publisher James Fraser in 1830, was edited by William
Maginn (1793–1842), one of the most colourful characters in the colourful
world of early nineteenth-century journalism. Described by Carlyle as 'a
rattling Irishman, full of quizzicality and drollery', his convivial personality was
a major factor in moulding his contributors into a company, the so-called
'Fraserians'. His journalistic pre-eminence in the late 1830s is shown by
Bentley's inviting him to contribute a 'Prologue' to the first number of the new
journal (now renamed *Bentley's Miscellany*, much to Dickens's relief). Maginn
complied in characteristically ebullient vein. But the surmise is surely correct
that it was Dickens who wrote the latter part of this Prologue, following the
words, 'Here, then, ladies and gentlemen . . .'. In it the writer disclaims any
attempt to 'jostle with' already existing journals, lavishly compliments a wide
range of well-known periodical writers, insists the new magazine will be
entirely non-political, and begs 'with all due humility' that readers unimpressed
by the first number will suspend judgment until they have seen the next one.[2]

During November Dickens busied himself with recruiting contributors and
did not decide how to fill the sixteen pages of original writing he was contracted
to supply for this and each succeeding issue until towards the end of the month
when, ahead of the actual writing, he had to settle with Cruikshank about the
illustration for it. They agreed on what Dickens described to Bentley as 'a

capital subject'. The tale he had thought up may have come into his head as a result of depicting in the December instalment of *Pickwick* (*Pickwick* IX), the fatuously pompous Mr Nupkins, J.P., Mayor of Ipswich. In his *Bentley's* contribution Dickens describes the workaday riverside town of Mudfog and its Mayor Nicholas Tulrumble who succumbs to *folie de grandeur*. November is the month in which the Lord Mayor of London's Show takes place and this may well have been what sparked off in Dickens's mind, already running on provincial mayors for his *Pickwick* number, the idea of a vainglorious specimen of the breed intent on mounting his own 'Show'. Tulrumble recruits a local 'vagabond' Ned Twigger, alias 'Bottle-nosed Ned', to appear in full armour as the equivalent of the Lord Mayor's Champion and Cruikshank's 'capital subject' was Ned's imprudent carouse thus accoutred in the kitchen of Mudfog Hall.[3]

11 'Ned Twigger in the kitchen of Mudfog house', depicted by Cruikshank for *Bentley's Miscellany*, January 1837

In early November Dickens evidently informed Macrone that he deemed the agreement he had made with him in May to write a three-volume novel for £200 to be null and void because the money was now too little for a writer of his current market value. He also revealed that he had signed up with Bentley to write two novels for £500 each. Understandably upset, Macrone vainly tried to embarrass Dickens into fulfilling his contract by advertising *Gabriel Vardon* as forthcoming. Dickens persisted in regarding his one-sided breaking of his contract with Macrone as merely a 'misunderstanding' and the two men ceased to be on speaking terms. Dickens dealt directly with Macrone's printer Thomas Hansard over the printing of *Sketches by Boz, Second Series*, which Macrone had by now been compelled to accept would consist of one volume only. As mentioned in the previous chapter, Dickens had, since the summer, somehow been finding time extensively to revise those sketches that were as yet uncollected, polishing them up for the more mixed audience of book buyers or borrowers that would now replace their predominantly masculine and metropolitan original readers. In order, as he put it, 'to finish the Volume with *eclat* [*sic*]', Dickens wrote, as he had done for each volume of the 'First Series', a sombre tale, 'The Drunkard's Death', which, like 'The Black Veil', explored an extreme, pathological state of mind. He bestowed 'great pains' upon it but was distracted by the long-anticipated first night of *The Village Coquettes* (6 Dec.) so that it did not reach the printer's hands until 9 December, just six days before *Sketches by Boz, Second Series* was published.[4]

The first night of *The Village Coquettes* was very much 'Boz Night' at the St James's since the 'New Operatic Burletta', as it was described in the playbill, was followed by the fiftieth performance of *The Strange Gentleman*. Both pieces were enthusiastically received and at the end the audience 'screamed' for Boz. There was at this time, however, no tradition of playwrights appearing to take a bow and Dickens's coming forward to do so was much ridiculed. *The Weekly News* commented, 'When Sir Walter Scott cast aside the veil which had previously concealed the author of the Waverley Novels, a great "sensation" was produced, but, unfortunately, Mr Charles Dickens is not *yet* Sir Walter Scott, and the effect was rather ludicrous.' John Forster in *The Examiner* (in which Dickens had been particularly anxious to have the work reviewed), after roundly condemning both the music and the libretto, also had some fun with the curtain calls at the end. If Braham could 'parade the real living Boz every night', he wrote, this feeble show might enjoy a long run. After expressing 'great respect and liking for Boz' Forster described how Dickens 'appeared, and bowed, and smiled, and disappeared, and left the audience in perfect consternation that he neither resembles the portraits of Pickwick, Snodgrass, Winkle or Tupman. Some critics in the gallery were said to have expected Sam Weller.'[5]

Dickens's reaction to all this seems to have been one of rueful amusement. *The Examiner*'s critique was so well done that he could not help laughing, he told Hullah, and he mentioned three other papers 'which blow their little trumpets against unhappy me, most lustily'. He mildly protested against the criticism of his libretto in a preface written for *Coquettes* when Bentley published it, at Dickens's pressing solicitation, towards the end of the month: any libretto must be 'to a certain extent, a mere vehicle for the music: and . . . it is scarcely fair or reasonable to judge it by those strict rules of criticism which would be justly applicable to a five-act tragedy, or a finished comedy'. Dedicating his 'dramatic bantling' to John Pritt Harley, he goes out of his way to compliment the comic actor on 'the honour and integrity' of his private life, which suggests some private anxiety on his part about the possible reaction of middle-class readers, now his target audience, to his association with what was widely seen as the 'immoral' world of the theatre.[6]

With the operetta's first night behind him, Dickens at once turned to finishing his story for *Sketches by Boz, Second Series*. 'The Drunkard's Death' with its alcoholic father, abused wife and blighted children reprises two of the 'terrific' stories that had already appeared in *Pickwick*, 'The Stroller's Tale' and 'The Convict's Return', but it is more skilfully constructed. The sinisterly jovial police agents who entrap the drunkard into betraying his fugitive son, and the culminating horror of the man's death by drowning, are powerfully evoked, the latter anticipating by four years the haunting description of Quilp's death in *The Old Curiosity Shop*.

The subject of drink was, not surprisingly given the time of year, at the forefront of Dickens's mind. *Pickwick* X to which he had to turn immediately after writing 'The Drunkard's Death' introduces a comic drunkard, the red-nosed preacher Stiggins, but also dwells happily on all the jolly Christmas imbibing at Dingley Dell. It features, moreover, the tale of Gabriel Grub, misanthropic sexton and solitary toper, who is converted to a more wholesome frame of mind towards his fellow-men (but whether also to total abstinence we are not told) by a goblin vision he experiences in the graveyard one Christmas Eve. Nor was drink purely a matter of authorial imaginings with Dickens during this festive month if we are to believe his merry report to Beard: 'I arrived home at one oClock this morning dead drunk, & was put to bed by my loving missis'.[7]

Pickwick X (published 31 Dec.) marks the beginning of that popular identification of Dickens with Christmas that was to be consolidated for all time, by his *Christmas Carol* a few years later. The revels of Mr Pickwick and his friends at Wardle's Manor Farm in Dingley Dell were not the product of Dickens's own unaided imagination, however. He was plugging into a great revival of interest in traditional English Christmas customs and festivities that had been in progress since the early years of the century. This had been given considerable impetus by certain writings of the Anglophile American writer

Washington Irving who glowingly describes an old-fashioned English country Christmas at 'Bracebridge Hall' in his *Sketch Book of Geoffrey Crayon, Gent* (1820). Dickens had soaked himself in this book as a child, as he told Irving in 1841, and it was a labour of love for him to adapt the Bracebridge Christmas for his own purposes. He diversified Irving's basic scenario with some quintessentially 'Bozzian' episodes such as Pickwick and Winkle on the ice as well as the rather startling Dickens-idiosyncratic one of the Pickwickians, two of them middle-aged and decidedly corpulent, going for a twenty-five mile walk after a lavish and highly bibulous Christmas wedding-breakfast! [8]

It is at this half-way point in *Pickwick*, in the monthly number that people are reading just after the appearance of *Sketches by Boz, Second Series*, that Dickens as Boz steps forward to say a few personal words. Up to now in *Pickwick* the voice of Boz has always been, with one exception, ironic, that of the ostensibly admiring editor of *The Posthumous Papers of the Pickwick Club* (Dickens was most probably influenced here by Carlyle's use of the device of a seemingly over-awed editor in his *Sartor Resartus*, serialised in *Fraser's* 1833–4). The one exception comes at the beginning of chapter 16 (*Pickwick* VI, the September number) in the two paragraphs extolling the beauties of autumn. The first two paragraphs of chapter 28 are a paean of praise for Christmas with an emphasis on the 'pure and unalloyed delight' of family reunions which it is hard not to relate to how the young Dickens, saviour son and brother and happy father-to-be, must have been feeling in the autumn/winter of 1836. But then comes this:

> We write these words now, many miles distant from the spot at which, year after year, we met on that day [Christmas], a merry and joyous circle. Many of the hearts that throbbed so joyfully then, have ceased to glow; the hands we grasped grown cold; the eyes we sought have hid their lustre in the grave; and yet the old house, the room, the merry voices and smiling faces, the jest, the laugh, the most minute and trivial circumstances connected with those happy meetings, crowd upon our mind at each recurrence of the season, as if the last assemblage had been but yesterday! Happy, happy Christmas, that can win us back to the delusions of our childish days. . . .

This seems quite unrelated to the Pickwickians, whom the narrative keeps 'waiting in the cold on the outside of the Muggleton coach' while Boz soliloquises. Apart from Mr Pickwick's later mention of sliding on the ice when he was a boy, the Pickwickians have no history, no memories. But Dickens, now that the mask of Boz has become transparent and he finds himself fast emerging into the spotlight as a celebrated author, seems to be keen on building up an idea of himself as a writer not only in the modes of both Fielding and Smollett, as remarked by several reviewers, but also in that of Henry Mackenzie's still popular novel of sensibility *The Man of Feeling* (1771).[9]

In *Pickwick* X Dickens/Boz directly addresses his readers outside the text as well as within it. In an appended 'Address', in which, interestingly, he presents himself as 'Mr Pickwick's Stage-Manager', he confirms that he will complete the work in twenty numbers as originally announced even though he has every temptation to prolong it ('brilliant success, an enormous and increasing sale, the kindest notice, and the most extensive popularity'). This number appeared on 31 December, the same day as the first number of *Bentley's Miscellany* and just two weeks after Macrone's publication of *Sketches by Boz, Second Series*. This had received less notice than the earlier *Sketches*, perhaps because it was overshadowed by *Pickwick*, or because this time Dickens was not spurring Macrone on to promote it. He did, however, write a jokey little preface for it, mostly in comic dialogue form, representing himself and Macrone knocking like charity boys on the public's door to offer their 'Christmas piece' (in real life, of course, as we have seen, they were no longer speaking).

Bentley's with its hundred and four pages of mingled comic tales and verses and biographical anecdotes began prosperously. *The Athenaeum* warmly welcomed it but opined that Boz should 'have opened the work after his own humour' rather than have let writers from *Fraser's* do so. 'The Public Life of Mr Tulrumble' is praised ('it is Boz every line of it') and was a great hit with other reviewers as well, like the one in *The Monthly Review* who congratulated Boz on becoming 'one of our most indefatigable labourers in periodical literature . . . treading the paths of humorous life with a sure and constant step'. As regards 'Tulrumble', the *Monthly* reviewer went so far as to say, somewhat surprisingly, 'nothing, perhaps, that has yet appeared in the Pickwick Club can excel [it] for genuine humour and knowledge of character'.[10]

Before this first number appeared Dickens discovered how much time was required by his editorial work. One morning, for example, he laboured in vain for three hours trying to get one article into printable shape. Such work, coming on top of his other commitments, left him 'really half dead with fatigue'. He also became aware of Bentley's evident intention to be a sort of co-editor and by mid-January was having to write, 'I must beg you once again, not to allow anybody but myself to interfere with the Miscellany'. He was nevertheless full of confidence, telling Bentley that he thought the next number would be 'an exceedingly good one' and that he had 'hit upon a capital notion for myself, and one which will bring Cruikshank out'. He made time to compose a facetious three-page advertising circular for insertion in the February issues of various periodicals. Once more, he drew on his parliamentary experiences for comic effect. The circular parodied the Royal Speech at the beginning of a parliamentary session. It was titled *Extraordinary Gazette* | *Speech of his Mightiness* | *on opening the second number of* BENTLEY'S MISCELLANY | *Edited by 'Boz'*. with a Phiz cartoon showing Dickens leading a fat porter

12 Heading of *The Extraordinary Gazette*, an advertisement leaflet inserted into the third
number of *Bentley's Miscellany* with this illustration by Hablot Knight Browne ('Phiz')
showing Dickens leading a *Bentley's* porter

carrying a vast number of copies of *Bentley's*. For all its jokey style this *Gazette*
served as a meaningful editorial manifesto:

> It has been the constant aim of my policy to preserve peace in your minds, and
> to provoke merriment in your hearts; to set before you the scenes and charac-
> ters of real life in all their endless diversity; occasionally (I hope) to instruct,
> always to amuse, and never to offend. I trust I may refer you to my Pickwickian
> measures, already taken and still in progress, in confirmation of this assurance.[11]

The 'capital notion', discussed with, and indeed perhaps partly originated by, Cruikshank, was the idea for the story that became *Oliver Twist*. Why it so pleased Dickens is not hard to imagine. He was determined to be seen as something more than a mere chronicler of 'humorous life' as is evident from the importance he clearly attached to the various pathetic, horrific and would-be tragic tales and sketches interspersed amid the comic reportage of Boz and the comic adventures of the Pickwickians. He wanted to make the world a better place, to champion the poor and oppressed, to 'instruct' readers in social justice matters and, as he later put it when writing *The Chimes*, his most fiercely polemical story, 'to shame the cruel and canting'. One of his dearest women friends, who first met him nine years after this time, remembered how 'his face used to *blaze* with indignation at any injustice or cruelty'. This was Dickens in his 'Timothy Sparks' mode, as already seen in *Sunday Under Three Heads* and in certain passages in the original periodical versions of the Boz sketches, though this aspect of them was generally toned down for volume publication (it was not altogether expunged, however – his challenging conclusion to 'The Prisoners' Van', for example, was left untouched). Now he was once again writing for a journal, this time one edited by himself, and, even though it presented itself as comic in nature, he evidently felt (whether or not he was following up hints from Cruikshank) that, within the Mudfog frame-work, he could move from the essentially traditional social satire of the Tulrumble story to something more sharply topical. He had prepared the way for further Mudfog stories at the end of 'Tulrumble' ('Perhaps, at some future period, we may venture to open the chronicles of Mudfog'). Among Mudfog's public buildings would be one which, as Dickens writes in the first sentence of *Oliver Twist*, 'is common to most towns great or small, to wit, a workhouse', that most prominent and most dreaded manifestation of one of Dickens's greatest *bêtes noires*, the New Poor Law. His 'Mudfog chronicles' scheme thus gave him a perfect opportunity to attack this (as he saw it) iniquitous measure. Nor, since the Tories hated the New Poor Law as much as the Radicals, would Bentley, 'loyal to the backbone' though he was, be much disturbed by such polemics in his comic journal. Accordingly, Dickens's chief contribution to the second (February) issue of *Bentley's*, the lead article, carries the title 'Oliver Twist, or, The Parish Boy's Progress. By Boz. Illustrated by George Cruikshank. Chapter the First.' The allusion to Hogarth's famous 'Progresses' would not have been lost upon his readers but they would not have thought of this as the start of a serialised novel any more than did Dickens himself. Rather, they would have thought of it as resembling earlier Boz sketches that had been published in chapters.[12]

By now Dickens had written several death scenes but not yet a birth one. It was no coincidence that he should write one now, within a week or two of the birth of his first child. Charles Culliford Boz Dickens ('Charley') was born on

6 January after 'a day and night of watching and anxiety'. Dickens may well, as he joyfully watched his first-born gasping, sneezing and finally beginning to exercise his lungs, have been struck by the thought that Charley would have looked and reacted much the same even had he been born not into the loving warmth of a prospering family but into the bleak world of a parish workhouse. It could well have been the sight of his little firstborn, just come 'naked into the world', that inspired Dickens's comment, towards the end of the first chapter of his new story, that it is not until Oliver is clothed in 'the old calico robes' of the workhouse that any stranger, seeing him, could have assigned him to his correct station in society. Now the danger is past he can joke, too, in his description of Oliver's birth, about all the fuss and anxiety surrounding that of his son, at which both grandmothers had been present: 'Now, if during this brief period [before he began to breathe] Oliver had been surrounded by careful grandmothers, anxious aunts, experienced nurses, and doctors of profound wisdom, he would most inevitably and indubitably have been killed in no time.'[13]

Dickens completed what he called his 'glance at the new poor Law Bill' with an account of Oliver's sufferings at a 'baby-farm'. This was highly topical in early 1837 following a great scandal about child deaths at such an establishment in St James's, Westminster, to which Cruikshank claimed to have drawn Dickens's attention. Dickens introduced the character of Bumble the parish beadle, who gloriously transcends the beadle figure as already established in popular folklore (and used by Dickens in *Sketches*) and offers a devastating caricature both of the Utilitarian philosophy underlying the New Poor Law and of its often grotesque results in practice. The whole instalment is superbly clinched by the now legendary scene of Oliver asking for more. As a counterweight, perhaps, to such a startlingly grim follow-up to 'Tulrumble' and perhaps also because the *Oliver* chapters are well short of the sixteen pages he was contracted to contribute, Dickens dashed off a knowing one-page 'Theatrical Advertisement, Extraordinary', full of in-jokes about the contemporary London theatre world that many of *Bentley's* men-about-town readers would doubtless have taken great delight in decoding. But the parish-boy story was his trump card. 'I have thrown my whole heart and soul into Oliver Twist,' he wrote to Bentley on 24 January, 'and most confidently believe he will make a feature in the work, and be very popular'.[14]

Before writing these opening chapters of *Oliver* Dickens had had to finish *Pickwick* XI (chs 30–32). He had been helped by being able to draw freely on memories of his time as a lawyer's clerk and of convivial occasions in bachelor lodgings in his 'Copperfield days'. On the other hand, he had been constantly distracted not only by Catherine's being 'in a very low and alarming state' after finding she could not feed her baby (he alone could persuade her to take even 'ordinary nourishment') but also by his own violent headaches and general physical wretchedness resulting from taking 'about as much medicine as would be given to an ordinary-sized horse'.[15]

Writing to her cousin Mary on 26 January, Mary Hogarth reported Catherine's distress with great sympathy, adding that Dickens was 'kindness itself to her'. His literary career meanwhile, she wrote, 'gets more and more prosperous every day and he is courted and flattered on every side by all the great folks of this great City – his time is so completely taken up that it is quite a favour for the Literary Gentlemen to get him to write for them. He is going to begin a Novel very soon.' Telling his family that he is 'very soon' going to begin that much-deferred first novel (that is, *Gabriel Vardon* – he was not yet thinking of *Oliver* as a novel) even as he struggles to fulfil his quota of pages for the next *Miscellany*, and to keep control also of the increasingly subtle and complex development of *Pickwick*, strikingly illustrates the young Dickens's boundless confidence in his own powers as a writer. He did, however, decline to write a new farce for Harley, offering instead a 'little piece in one act' written 'long before I was Boz'. Harley, of course, accepted it and Dickens revised it in such interstices of time as he could find. The title was altered from *Cross Purposes* to *Is She His Wife? or, Something Singular!* and the piece was successfully produced at the St James's on 3 March. Harley took his benefit performance ten days later and Dickens somehow found time to write a special monologue (now sadly lost) for the actor to deliver in the character of Mr Pickwick describing his experiences at a whitebait dinner at Blackwall.[16]

By the end of March Dickens had completed both *Pickwick* XIII and the third instalment of *Oliver* ready for the April number of *Bentley's*. During the previous weeks he had had to turn quickly from grim sketches of a brutal chimney-sweep and a mercenary undertaker (March instalment of *Oliver*), to the humours of Sam Weller's Valentine and the grand comic climax of the Bardell *v.* Pickwick trial (*Pickwick* XII), then back again to writing in early March the horrific description of a pauper's funeral and depicting Oliver's desperate attack on Noah Claypole (April instalment of *Oliver*) and finally back again to composing for *Pickwick* XIII the quintessentially 'Bozzian' sketches of fashionable society disporting itself at Bath and of the footmen aping their betters at a 'swarry' (that is, soirée) attended by Sam Weller.[17]

Dickens was certainly under enormous pressure. There was the ceaseless grind of *Miscellany* editorial work ('I really have done, with anxiety and sickness about me, more than nine people out of ten could have performed,' he told Bentley on 24 January), the need to take Catherine into the country for her health, and the whole distracting business of house-hunting – they were rapidly outgrowing their chambers in Furnival's Inn. Unsurprisingly, both the March instalment of *Oliver* and *Pickwick* XIII needed supplementing. The shortfall in the *Miscellany*, in which *Oliver* occupied just over twelve pages (so far it had in fact never extended to the sixteen pages called for by Dickens's agreement with Bentley) was offset by a fluently-written piece of seven pages

called 'The Pantomime of Life'. This appeared under the series-heading 'Stray
Chapters. By "Boz" ', a useful catch-all title for such future make-weight pieces
as might be needed. Boz argues that the pantomime, an art-form in which he
'revels', is truly a 'mirror of life' ('Is there any man who cannot count a dozen
pantaloons in his own social circle? . . ?') and rounds off the piece with a hit at
Parliament where 'we are particularly strong in clowns'. It has been persuasively argued that this essay, hastily improvised though it was, may be seen as
a sort of artistic manifesto by Dickens, justifying the essential theatricality of
his art. Its equivalent make-weight piece in *Pickwick* XIII is an interpolated
tale, 'The True Legend of Prince Bladud [the supposed founder of Bath]'.
This differs greatly from the gloomy melodrama of the earlier inset stories,
as well as from the Christmas story of Gabriel Grub, being in the same vein
of social/political satire as 'The Story Without a Beginning' (above, p. 44) but
less heavy-handed and more generalised. It looks forward to a certain very
effective genre of Dickens's later satirical journalism involving the use of
legends, fairy-tales and fantasy.[18]

By March the success of *Bentley's* was assured. In the new agreement, drawn
up between himself and Bentley on the 17th, Dickens settled for a system of
bonus payments instead of phased increases in his editorial salary. Whenever
Bentley's sales figures reached 6,000 copies a month Dickens would get an extra
£10 on top of his regular £20 and a further £5 for each succeeding increase of
500 copies. The agreement did not, however, settle the vexed matter of
Bentley's continued interference in editorial matters, such as the selection and
rejection of articles, which remained a sore point for Dickens. It was also
explicitly stated that he would continue to contribute 'an original Article of his
own writing of about 16 pages' to each issue.[19]

Meanwhile, *Pickwick's* sales continued to be phenomenal. On 8 April
Chapman and Hall, who were rather better at handling their sensitive superstar
than was the too legalistically-minded Bentley, gave a dinner to celebrate this
ongoing success, having previously presented Dickens with a bonus cheque for
£500. Reviewers vied with each other in eulogising *Pickwick's* astonishing
'verisimilitude' and 'inexhaustible fun'. They continued to treat it, however, as a
periodical, 'a series of monthly pamphlets', rather than as a connected story, just
as *Oliver* in *Bentley's* was considered 'a clever series of articles'. Inevitably, the
parasitic swarm of popular dramatists and plagiarists, unrestrained by any
effective copyright laws, got busy with it. Edward Stirling's *The Pickwick Club,
or The Age We Live In* (City of London Theatre, 27 March) was the first of many
such hastily-improvised dramatisations, many appearing before the serialisation of the story was complete so the dramatists had to invent material to
bulk out their offerings. A month later appeared *The Penny Pickwick: the
Post-Humorous Notes of the Pickwickian Club. Edited by Bos* [i.e., Thomas
Peckett Prest] *with engravings by Phis*, issued in weekly parts by a downmarket

publisher called Edward Lloyd. Chapman and Hall failed to obtain an injunction against Lloyd in the Court of Chancery and there seemed to be nothing that either they or Dickens himself could do to abate this brazen exploitation which increased alongside his popularity.[20]

During the first weekend of April, having at last found a suitable house, Dickens moved himself, wife, baby and brother Fred into 48 Doughty Street. An advance of £100 from Bentley on *Gabriel Vardon*, the first of his two promised novels, helped to cover expenses. This move coincided with the first anniversary of his marriage and was tangible proof of the amazing upturn in his fortunes that had taken place during the year. 48 Doughty Street, today the Charles Dickens Museum, is an elegant late eighteenth-century terrace house, with six rooms on three floors, together with a basement comprising a kitchen and other offices and three attic rooms. It stands in a handsome street which at this period had gates and a porter at either end. Just east of it runs the then insalubrious Gray's Inn Road, along which cattle were driven towards Smithfield on market days, while to the north and west lay the fashionable squares and terraces of the estates of the Foundling Hospital and the Duke of Bedford. Dickens agreed to rent the house for three years in the first instance for £80 a year, an increase of £30 on his Furnival's Inn rent (which he had to go on paying for another eighteen months, having been unable to sublet the chambers for the unexpired term of his lease).

He and Catherine now had a much better home in which to indulge his love of entertaining. The house had an attractively shaped dining-room, also a spare bedroom, of which Mary as visitor was the first occupant, and a pleasant little study, adjacent to the drawing-room on the first floor and overlooking the small back garden. This last room he proceeded to furnish with a complete set (fifty-eight volumes) of 'Bentley's Standard Novels', a highly successful series of cheap reprints. From the cash-book recording domestic expenditure (kept by Dickens himself, we note, rather than by Catherine) we find that the household establishment included a cook, a housemaid and a nurse, while Dickens also had, or soon acquired, a manservant or groom.[21]

April 1837 was a good month for the rising young author even though he seemed to have to read 'as many papers for the Miscellany, as all the Editors and Sub Editors of all the other Magazines put together'. His swiftly increasing fame and prosperity and his great domestic happiness, to which the presence on a visit of his delightful young sister-in-law evidently contributed, made a stunning contrast with his situation a mere dozen years earlier with his parents in prison and himself under Bob Fagin's tutelage and protection at Warren's Blacking and left to wander the exciting but dangerous streets of London in his free time. It was perhaps Dickens's consciousness of this great contrast that lay behind the dramatic developments in *Pickwick* and in Oliver's story in *Bentley's* this month in which both protagonists are respectively introduced to a sensational new scene. Mr Pickwick enters the Fleet Prison and Oliver runs away to London where he is promptly decoyed into the clutches of an old villain who runs a gang of street-boy pickpockets (and whose squalid Saffron Hill lair Dickens locates only a short walk east from where he now lives in his 'first-class family mansion' in Doughty Street). Pickwick goes to the Fleet rather than the Marshalsea since Dickens had already featured the latter in *Pickwick* and he would hardly have wanted readers to begin wondering about his apparent preoccupation with one particular prison. Never having visited the Fleet himself, he used a recently-published compilation, *Scenes and Stories by a Clergyman in Debt. Written during his Confinement in the Debtors' Prisons*, to supply several details in the description of the prison in this and the next number, though the overall atmosphere of misery and despair that he builds up, and the sketches of the prisoners themselves, derive primarily from his childhood memories. 'When I looked, with my mind's eye,' he later told Forster, 'into the Fleet Prison during Mr Pickwick's incarceration, I wonder whether half a dozen men were wanting from the Marshalsea crowd that came filing in again . . .'[22]

With *Pickwick* Dickens knew by now just where he was going. He kept Mr Winkle's love-story on the boil in this May number (*Pickwick* XIV) as the minor comic plot and filled it out with yet another variation on the reluctant-duellists joke, while his imagination warmed to the work of continuing the development of Pickwick himself into a specimen of that most difficult to portray of all fictional characters, the convincingly good human being. He had a congenial model to hand in Goldsmith's Vicar of Wakefield, Dr Primrose, another good man who has to suffer unjust imprisonment. In the case of *Oliver*, however, the evidence seems to show that, despite the dramatic incident of Oliver's flight to London, he was still undecided about how the story should ultimately develop.

In making Oliver flee to London Dickens may have been in the first instance motivated by a desire to shift his story's setting from the one-dimensional satirical creation of the town of Mudfog to the real city in which his childhood had undergone such a sensational change and which had so thoroughly captivated his imagination. But it was surely his image of his childish self, apprenticed to a degrading trade and roaming the London streets at risk of becoming 'a little robber or a little vagabond', that was the main motivating factor. This seems clear from his deadpan comment about Bob Fagin in the autobiographical fragment, 'I took the liberty of using his name, long afterwards, in *Oliver Twist*.' The use he made of it was to name the powerfully-evoked, hideous and yet also alluring, 'merry old gentleman' (a common nickname for the devil) who gives the fugitive boy food, warmth, companionship and even a job. In real life Bob Fagin's kindness and protectiveness towards, and general mentoring of, himself as a young boy in Warren's must, at some level, have featured in Dickens's mind, both at the time and in retrospect, as the most insidious and dangerous threat of all to whatever hope he might have had of restoration to that genteel world from which he seemed to have been expelled for ever, and it was surely felt by him as an added twist of the knife when Bob 'settled' another boy, Poll Green, who objected to the blacking factory custom of calling Charles 'the young gentleman'.[23]

The ending of chapter 7 of *Oliver* in *Bentley's* tells us that Oliver remembered little Dick's blessing 'through all the troubles and changes of many weary years', suggesting that a long period of suffering and hardship lay ahead of him. This proves in the event not to be the case, however, Dickens clearly having changed his mind over the summer about how to develop the story, and he subsequently deleted the phrase 'of many weary years' when *Oliver* was published in volume form. Now, in the May number of *Bentley's*, the introduction of two such striking criminal characters as the Artful Dodger (already adumbrated in one of Boz's sketches, 'Criminal Courts') and Fagin greatly helped to move the serial away from being essentially an episodic series of scenes or 'sketches', like the depiction of the pauper funeral in chapter 5, and towards the form of a thrilling narrative with promise of a strong 'Newgate' interest.[24]

Even with so much happening in this instalment, *Oliver* still did not stretch to the sixteen pages of Dickens's writing required for the May number so he dashed off another 'Stray Chapter by Boz'. This one, 'Some Particulars Concerning a Lion', would surely have been seen as an amusing in-joke by many *Bentley's* readers since Boz himself was now an even greater lion than when he had described Mrs Leo Hunter's *fête champêtre* in *Pickwick* VI (Sept.1836). In this *Bentley's* paper he writes as an awed spectator of a great literary lion on show among the guests at an evening party. According to Henry Burnett, Dickens 'resented and hated' all attempts to lionise him but loved to be the life and soul at private gatherings. Such was the family dinner-party at Doughty Street on 29 April where Bentley, the only outsider, recorded that after dinner 'Dickens sang two or three songs, one the patter song, "The Dog's Meat Man", & gave several successful imitations of the most distinguished actors of the day'.[25]

Dickens did perform, albeit somewhat differently, in public a few days later, however, at the anniversary dinner of the Literary Fund on 3 May, where the chairman, the Duke of Somerset, proposed 'the health of Mr Dickens and the rising Authors of the Age'. Dickens returned thanks in a gracefully modest speech ('. . . overpowered by receiving such an honour from such a company . . . [looking around] he saw many more distinguished for ability than he could ever hope to be . . .'). He may seem to us to have been over-doing the flattery and the self-deprecation but this first public manifestation of the esteem in which he was held by his literary brethren would have been a very important occasion for him. Throughout his whole career he was always to set great store by showing his solidarity with fellow-writers and being, as he liked to put it, 'true to his order' in his constant quest to uphold and enhance the 'dignity of literature'.[26]

Three days later he took Catherine and Mary, along with his parents, to see a performance of *Is She His Wife?* Mary returned to Doughty Street with him and Catherine and, Dickens wrote later to *Bentley's* contributor Richard Johns with whom he was on friendly terms, 'went up stairs to bed at about one o'Clock in perfect health and her usual delightful spirits; was taken ill before she had undressed; and died in my arms next afternoon at 3 o'Clock. Everything that could possibly be done *was* done but nothing could save her. The medical men imagine it was a disease of the heart.' Although they had, according to Catherine, often said they 'had too much happiness to last', this totally unexpected sudden death came as a devastating shock to the whole family. The intensity and duration of Dickens's grief was something extraordinary, however. He wore the ring he took from Mary's finger for the rest of his life. He kept her clothes, looking at them from time to time and thinking how they would 'moulder away in their secret places', like her body in the ground. He wanted, when his time came to die, to be buried next to her and was much distressed four years later when her grandmother and one of her brothers were buried there instead ('I cannot bear the thought of being excluded from her dust . . . It seems like losing her a second time'). Memories of the dead girl had, as has long been recognised, a profound effect on the portrayal of many of the heroines of his subsequent fiction, beginning with Rose Maylie in *Oliver*. The immediate effect, however, was to stop him writing fiction altogether for a week or two. There would be no June instalment of either *Pickwick* or *Oliver*. Dickens wrote many grief-stricken letters memorialising and idealising the dead girl ('the grace and ornament of our home', 'so perfect a creature never breathed', 'the dearest friend I ever had') and composed an epitaph for her tombstone in Kensal Green Cemetery: 'Young, beautiful, and good./ God in His mercy/ numbered her with His angels /at the early age of /seventeen.'[27]

Dickens wrote to a friend that Catherine, for whom the shock of Mary's death had brought on a miscarriage, had 'borne up through her severe trial like what she is – a fine-hearted noble-minded girl' but now needed rest and quiet. He rented a cottage at North End, Hampstead, where they stayed for a few weeks during which Dickens made regular trips into town to deal with *Miscellany* business, which included the composing of an editorial address marking the completion of the magazine's first volume with the June number. For this address he adroitly used the same stage-manager/showman persona as for the address in *Pickwick* X. His bland editorial assertion, 'we have eschewed everything political', would surely have surprised admirers of *Oliver* and its fierce satirising of the New Poor Law. Moreover, Fagin's eulogy of capital punishment in chapter 9 in the very next (July) instalment was highly political, having direct reference to certain legislation about the criminal law that was just at this time passing through Parliament.[28]

At North End Dickens was visited by John Forster, now literary editor of *The Examiner*. This was the beginning of a deep and lasting friendship which quickly became of central importance to Dickens both in his personal and in his writing life. He and Forster had first met through Ainsworth the previous winter and had liked each other but had not yet had much opportunity to develop the acquaintance. Now when he was 'more than ordinarily susceptible . . . to all kindliest impressions', Dickens's heart 'opened itself' to Forster who left him, as he recorded many years later, 'as much his friend, and as entirely in his confidence, as if I had known him for years'. Forster had been born in the same year as Dickens, the son of a Newcastle butcher, had attended a grammar school, and had early become devoted to literature and the theatre. Arriving in London as a law student in 1828, he had shown great promise but soon began to make his mark also as a historian through a series of studies of anti-monarchical seventeenth-century statesmen for *The Englishman's Magazine* in 1831. This accomplishment led to his being commissioned to write a multi-volume *Lives of Statesmen of the Commonwealth* (1836–9). In 1832 he became drama critic on *The True Sun* on which Dickens also briefly worked. Forster was struck by his 'keen animation of look' but did not actually meet him. At this time Forster was already a close friend and much-needed business adviser of the poet and essayist Leigh Hunt, twenty-eight years his senior, and was the well-loved friend, too, of another great survivor from the golden age of English Romantic literature, Charles Lamb. As his literary career developed (by the end of 1831 he was drama editor of *The Examiner*) Forster's acquaintanceship widened. Through writing for the *New Monthly* he became the friend and adviser of its distinguished editor, Edward Bulwer. In 1833 he favourably impressed his hero Macready, whom Dickens and so many others worshipped, above all for his powerful interpretations of Shakespeare's tragic heroes. Forster quickly became an intimate and valued friend and counsellor of the 'eminent tragedian'. He was unmarried (a love-affair with 'L.E.L.', the poet Letitia Landon, ended abruptly and unhappily in 1833) and his biographer plausibly suggests that his penchant for disciple-like friendships with distinguished figures older than himself may have reflected not only his passion for the arts but also a certain loneliness or sense of emptiness in his own personal life.[29]

In Dickens Forster found, the equality of their ages notwithstanding, a sort of ideal younger brother and protégé. Here was a brilliantly original fellow-writer whose career was developing with such spectacular swiftness that all agreements with publishers quickly became obsolete. What he desperately needed was the help of a clear-headed friend with knowledge and experience both of the law and of the London publishing and literary scene – just such a person as Forster was, in fact. On his side, the young Dickens was a dazzlingly attractive figure, whose charm at this time Forster sought to convey over thirty years later in a famous passage of his *Life of Dickens*:

He had a capital forehead, a firm nose with full wide nostril, eyes wonderfully beaming with intellect and running over with humour and cheerfulness, and a rather prominent mouth strongly marked with sensibility. The head was altogether well-formed and symmetrical, and the air and carriage of it were extremely spirited. The hair so scant and grizzled in later days was then of a rich brown and most luxurious abundance, and the bearded face of his last two decades had hardly a vestige of hair or whisker; but there was that in the face as I first recollect it which no time could change, and which remained implanted on it unalterably to the last. This was the quickness, keenness, and practical power, the eager, restless, energetic outlook on each several feature, that seemed to tell so little of the student or writer of books, and so much of a man of action and business in the world. Light and motion flashed from every part of it. . . .

Moreover, through Dickens, as through Macready, the domestically solitary Forster obtained an entrée into a loving family circle. 'You are a part, and an essential part, of our home, dear friend,' Dickens was to tell him in 1842. A great affection developed between him and Catherine and twenty years later, when he himself was at last about to marry, he wrote to her, 'I have never felt so strongly as within the last few months how much of the happiness of past years I owe to you.'[30]

Dickens fully shared Forster's ardent concern with such matters as the social status and rewards of authors and with the heroic (if misguided) efforts of Macready and others to restore to the English drama the literary greatness of its Elizabethan and Jacobean days. It was through Forster that he met Macready whom he had long idolised and who became one of his most cherished and most intensely revered friends. Two other important friendships Dickens also owed to Forster were those with the antiquarian painter George Cattermole and with the lawyer and dramatist Thomas Noon Talfourd, M.P. for Reading, who was working hard to get a new copyright bill through Parliament. Very quickly Forster became Dickens's trusted guide and adviser with regard to all aspects of his career. From the summer of this year onwards, Forster records, 'there was nothing written by him which I did not see before the world did, either in manuscript or proofs'. Dickens relied on him implicitly as a proof-corrector, for example, and was even happy for him to make minor textual alterations, 'knocking a word's brains out here and there' or counteracting Dickens's tendency to slip into blank verse at moments of great intensity. Above all, Dickens was grateful for Forster's championship in his continued troubles with publishers. The grandly overbearing manner that many people – even, on some later occasions, Dickens himself – found objectionable, allied to Forster's legal expertise, made him a formidable advocate. 'He had a knack', wrote Ainsworth, 'of making people do what he liked, whether they liked it or not.'[31]

In fact, Forster did *not* succeed in the first campaign he undertook for Dickens, at the latter's urgent request, which was to stop Macrone from cashing in on the success of *The Pickwick Papers* by republishing both series of *Sketches by Boz*, the copyright of which belonged to him, in the same green-covered monthly-number format as Chapman and Hall were using for *Pickwick*. Dickens was much distressed by this prospect, which would result in Macrone making yet more money out of his writings without Dickens himself becoming one penny the richer. Forster refused to countenance demands by Macrone that he considered exorbitant and, after a little muddying of the waters by Bentley, the matter was finally resolved by Chapman and Hall and Dickens, using money advanced to him by the publishers, jointly paying Macrone his price (£2,250) for the copyrights.[32]

'The next Pickwick', Dickens promised Forster in late June, 'will bang all the others.' He was writing *Pickwick* XV (chs 41–43) which appeared at the beginning of July and included Dickens's address to readers contradicting the wild rumours about himself that had been generated by the non-appearance of a June number ('By one set of intimate acquaintances . . . he has been killed outright; by another, driven mad . . .' when he had, in fact, 'been seeking in a few weeks' retirement the restoration of that cheerfulness and peace of which a sad bereavement had temporarily deprived him'). This fifteenth number describes Mr Pickwick's eye-opening and heart-rending experiences amid the 'noise and riot' of the Fleet with streetwise Sam acting as his guide and interpreter. It is not Sam, however, but the unsavoury trio on whom Pickwick is first billeted who provide the crucial information that 'money was in the Fleet, just what money was out of it' and would procure him almost anything he wanted, including a private room. Meanwhile, Pickwick's previously somewhat unfocused benevolence is particularised in the description of his generosity towards Jingle, now his fellow-prisoner. His ordeal continues in *Pickwick* XVI. He witnesses the death of the poor Chancery prisoner (a foretaste here of *Bleak House*) and a mass of other wretchedness, which gives him such heart-ache that he declares, 'Henceforth I will be a prisoner in my own room.'

During June Dickens was also writing chapters 9–11 of *Oliver*. Oliver experiences a rude awakening on his first outing with the Dodger when the true nature of the work done by Fagin's boys 'rushes upon his mind'. Worse still, he is himself condemned as a thief and narrowly escapes imprisonment at the hands of Mr Fang (whom Dickens intended to be recognised as a lampoon of a notoriously bullying Hatton Garden magistrate called Laing). Chapter 11 closes with his rescue by the benevolent Mr Brownlow, for whose name Dickens was probably indebted to a well-known Secretary of the Foundling Hospital.[33]

A notable sign of Dickens's phenomenal success was the appearance of a lengthy article, written by a friend and disciple of Carlyle's called Charles Buller, on Dickens and his cultural significance in the July number of the highly intellectual *London and Westminster Review*. In this month also Dickens made his first trip to the Continent, a short visit to France and Belgium, accompanied by Catherine and his *Pickwick* illustrator H. K. Browne. Browne's inclusion in the party suggests that the expedition may have had a prospecting-for-copy aspect to it. Dickens was perhaps thinking of a paper for *Bentley's*, with an illustration by Browne, about visiting the site of the battle of Waterloo, a very popular tourist destination for the English in the 1830s. If so, the paper was never written but memories of his experience on this trip may well have contributed years later to Dickens's powerful description, at the beginning of his fourth Christmas Book, *The Battle of Life* (1846), of the site of a long-ago bloody battle, now a smiling agricultural landscape but with grim relics of bygone slaughter constantly coming to light.[34]

Dickens returned from Belgium to his own battles with Bentley. And it may well be that the preoccupation with the theme of beleaguered innocence that we have noticed as prominent in both *Pickwick* and *Oliver* this summer stemmed not only from dark memories of his boyhood but also from his feelings about his treatment by some publishers. Macrone had made ten times more money than he from *Sketches* and now he was, as he saw it, being ruthlessly exploited by Bentley. Indeed, by early August he was actually identifying Bentley with Fagin, quoting, in a note to Forster, Sikes's description of Fagin in chapter 13 as an 'infernal, rich, plundering, thundering old Jew'. He was still contracted to write two novels for the man, in addition to his regular monthly stint for *Bentley's*. On 14 July he wrote to Bentley designating *Oliver* as the first of the novels. The second one would then be *Gabriel Vardon*, now renamed *Barnaby Rudge* – this renaming providing evidence that he was managing to give some thought to this as yet very embryonic work despite all his other commitments. Bentley, unsurprisingly but unwisely, objected to making *Oliver* do double duty as both Dickens's main magazine contribution each month *and* as one of the contracted novels. After much acrimonious dispute, during which Dickens threatened to stop writing *Oliver* altogether (in fact, did stop it for one month), and also announced that he was resigning from the editorship, Bentley had, of course, to back down. A new agreement between him and Dickens, signed on 28 September, increased Dickens's editorial salary by £10 a month and accepted *Oliver* as the first of the two novels he had promised to write. On its completion Dickens was to receive £500, additional to the twenty guineas he had been getting for each monthly instalment and Bentley was to have the copyright for only three years, after which he was to share it with

Dickens. The work was to be completed by midsummer 1838 while *Barnaby Rudge*, for which Dickens was to have £700, was to be finished before the end of October of the same year and published at once in three-volume format with the same copyright arrangements as for *Oliver*.[35]

In the August instalment of *Oliver* (chs 12–13), in keeping with his resolve to make Bentley accept the work as the first of the two novels he had contracted to write for him, Dickens began introducing details hinting at future plot-complications, such as Oliver's intense reaction to the female portrait he sees at Brownlow's. In the next instalment he smuggled in a joke at Bentley's expense about how much better it was to be a bookseller than a book-writer, and wrote, provocatively, in a long passage about hypocritical philanthropists that harks back to the satirical tone of the opening chapters and was subsequently deleted before volume publication, about 'my long-considered intentions and plans regarding this prose epic (for such I mean it to be)'. Bentley having still not come to terms, Dickens then suspended *Oliver*, substituting instead in the October number a paper titled 'Full Report of the First Meeting of the Mudfog Association for the Advancement of Everything' and disingenuously claiming on the wrapper of the October number that the length of this 'report' prevented the insertion of an *Oliver* instalment. This 'First Report' mocks the proneness to self-congratulation of the British Association for the Advancement of Science (founded 1831) and the pompous vacuity of press reports of its proceedings. The paper was a kind of outgrowth of *Pickwick* which had started out as a lampoon on the Association with Mr Pickwick's paper, 'Speculations on the source of the Hampstead Ponds, with Some Observations on the Theory of Tittlebats'. Satirical references to the Association had recurred in later numbers, most recently in the May one (the excitable 'scientific gentleman' in *Pickwick*, chapter 39) but only very incidentally. Now, doubtless prompted by elaborate newspaper reports of the Association's annual meeting, begun on 9 September in Liverpool, Dickens returned to the charge (his paper, he tells Cruikshank, is 'the best I can make it of it's [*sic*] kind'). It harks back to his original conception of Mudfog as a suitable location for utilitarian 'philosophers' obsessed by statistics, such as Mayor Tulrumble, who 'contracted a relish for statistics and got philosophical', and the 'very sage, deep, philosophical men' who oversee the workhouse in which Oliver is born.[36]

The story of *Oliver* as it had been taking shape since its protagonist's flight to London was no longer a suitable vehicle for the kind of satirical-polemical writing that had created Mr Bumble and the Board of Guardians of Mudfog Workhouse. But this October 'paper by Boz' allowed Dickens to return to that mode, and he used it to express for the first time something that was to become a major theme in all his writing, most prominently in *Hard Times*. This was the vital importance of preserving the life of the imagination or

'fancy' in an age increasingly dominated by facts and figures. Most especially is
it important to cultivate the life of the imagination in children if they are not
to grow up into emotionally and morally stunted adults. We can already see
Mr Gradgrind in perspective in Mr Slug who, addressing the Statistics Section
of the Mudfog Association's conference deplores the 'state of infant education
among the middle classes of London'. 'The ignorance that prevailed was
lamentable', he declares, since the children had not 'the slightest conception of
the commonest principles of mathematics, and considered Sindbad the Sailor
the most enterprising voyager that the world had ever produced'.[37]

After finishing this paper Dickens took his family down to the Kentish fishing-
village of Broadstairs for a late summer holiday. He found this quiet place so
congenial that he and the family returned there every summer but two for the
next fourteen years. He celebrated its quaint charms in many letters to friends
and also in a lovingly-detailed essay, 'Our Watering Place' (*HW*, 2 Aug.1851).
Briefly fashionable when patronised by the Duchess of Kent, its day had passed
and the little place now provided Dickens, increasingly encumbered by his
celebrity, with an ideal retreat from the heat, noise and crowds of London in the
summer. Here in early September he continued, after a brief illness, with his
winding up of *Pickwick*, a process that he had begun in the just-published
Pickwick XVII.

With Pickwick's self-release from the Fleet Prison, capitulating to Dodson
and Fogg from the most humane motives, Dickens had really come to the end
of his main plot for the serial and the only narrative suspense left, such as it was,
related to the humours of Mr Winkle's love-story, the sorting out of which at
least gives Mr Pickwick something to do for the last three and a half numbers.
To fill out those numbers Dickens reverts, as Peter Ackroyd has noted, to
theatrical convention by re-introducing many of the leading secondary characters for a final 'turn' and/or exit speech. Among these re-introduced characters
is the Bagman (commercial traveller) who had contributed a fantastic yarn
about a talking chair to *Pickwick* V. Dickens fills almost half of *Pickwick* XVII
with another such story, this time set in Edinburgh which enables him to draw
very effectively on his memories of his brief visit three years earlier – a good
early example of the fruits of his amazing skill in 'fanciful photography' he was
later to call it. The tale itself reprises the Bacchanalian element of *Pickwick* as a
lead into a lively parody of Ainsworth-style historical melodrama.[38]

By this time Dickens had improved his acquaintance with Talfourd, to whom
he wrote a very flattering letter on 30 August, telling him that nothing in his
'brief career' had pleased him so much as Talfourd's kind words about his work –
'my sketches I should rather say'. Now he composed a long, and equally fulsome,
dedicatory epistle to Talfourd, to be printed in the final double number of
Pickwick, thanking him on behalf of all authors for the efforts he had been
making in Parliament to strengthen the laws regarding copyright. During early

October Dickens worked hard on this final *Pickwick* before turning, in the latter part of the month, to the development of *Oliver* as a novel by seeking, as Jane Austen would have put it, to 'promote the general distress of the work' (chapters 16 and 17 describe Oliver back in Fagin's clutches and Bumble traducing him to Brownlow). As if this were not already a sufficient work-load, Dickens had also been for some weeks carefully revising and re-arranging the contents of both series of *Sketches by Boz* (the three volumes published by Macrone) for Chapman and Hall's planned publication of the sketches in monthly parts. Dickens grouped the sketches in the order in which they have ever since been printed ('Our Parish', 'Scenes', 'Characters' and 'Tales') and which disguises the chronology of their composition. He finally included 'The Tuggses at Ramsgate', and made a great number of stylistic changes suited to his increasing respectability as a writer. The monthly parts, with a specially-designed cover by Cruikshank, were published in pink wrappers to distinguish them from the green covers reserved for *Pickwick* and the, as yet untitled and unwritten, second monthly-part work Dickens was contracted to write for Chapman and Hall. The first number of *Sketches* was published simultaneously with the last number of *Pickwick* at the end of October.[39]

Dickens used the *Pickwick* preface to respond, implicitly rather than explicitly, to the long critique of his work in the October number of the leading Tory journal *The Quarterly Review*, from which I have already quoted twice (see above, pp. 81 and 85). Dickens knew the author was a well-known barrister and essayist called Abraham Hayward and thought some personal resentment was probably involved since he had not responded to some friendly overtures from Hayward. In his notice Hayward dissented from the comparisons of Boz to Fielding and Smollett that were becoming more frequent in reviews. Dickens, he claimed, rather too sweepingly, had no trace of Fielding's 'skill in the construction of the prose epic' nor (and this was still more unjust) of Smollett's 'dash, vivacity, wild spirit of adventure and rich poetic imagination'. The Pickwickians' adventures were 'too disconnected . . . to admit of that concentration of interest which forms the grand merit of a narrative'. Hayward did concede, however, that there was 'a sustained power, a range of observation, and a continuity of interest' in what he called the 'series' of 'the memoirs of "Oliver Twist" ' that was superior to anything Dickens had yet achieved. But, he concluded, Dickens 'writes too often and too fast' as a result of having accepted 'all engagements that were offered to him'. If he continues in this way, wrote Hayward, 'it requires no gift of prophecy to fore-tell his fate – he has risen like a rocket, and he will come down like the stick', words that, as we shall see, rankled with Dickens though he did admit that Hayward's critique as a whole 'contains a great deal that I know to be true'.[40]

Dickens, having won his battle with Bentley to have *Oliver* accepted as a novel, began this October to stake his claim to be treated not as a writer of sketches and periodicals but, in the teeth of Hayward's demurrer, as a novelist in the great tradition of Fielding and Smollett. He did this both in the *Pickwick* preface and in the November instalment of *Oliver*. In the preface he presents the idea for *Pickwick* as having been entirely his own, his intention having been to depict a 'succession of characters and incidents' as vividly as he could, but making them 'at the same time, life-like and amusing'. Despite the 'detached and desultory form of publication' (and he offers no clue as to why he might have chosen to write in this apparently unsatisfactory form), he has tried to ensure that the twenty monthly parts should, when collected together, 'form one tolerably harmonious whole'. He goes on to observe that, clearly, no complexity of plot could be attempted under such circumstances and

> if it be objected to the Pickwick Papers, that they are a mere series of adventures, in which the scenes are ever changing, and the characters come and go like the men and women we encounter in the real world, [the author] can only content himself with the reflection, that they claim to be nothing else, and that the same objection has been made to the works of some of the greatest novelists in the English language.

Foremost among these 'greatest novelists' were, of course, Fielding and Smollett. The reader of this preface is encouraged to feel that its writer is a true novelist who has triumphantly overcome the problems inherent in the limiting form in which he has, for some reason, chosen to write. There is no hint that Dickens has signed up with Chapman and Hall to write another book in precisely this same apparently limiting monthly-number format – and, subsequently, Chapman and Hall did not seem to be supporting *Pickwick*'s pretensions to novel status when they published the completed work not in the standard three-volume format used for novels (the format Bentley was to use for *Oliver*) but bound in one fat volume, like an annual or semi-annual volume of a periodical.[41]

In the November instalment of *Oliver*, Dickens began for the first time to talk to the reader about his narrative method in the manner of Fielding. Chapter 16 ends just after the intensely dramatic episode of Oliver's recapture by the thieves and Nancy's fierce intervention to save him from Fagin's violence. Chapter 17 then returns us to Mudfog and the satirical comedy of Bumble but, before we meet the beadle again, Dickens justifies his switch from terror to comedy by invoking the custom, found in 'all good murderous melodramas', of alternating tragic and comic scenes 'as the layers of red and white in a side of streaky, well-cured bacon'. This, he argues, simply reflects real life in which transitions from 'well-spread boards to death-beds, and from mourning weeds to holiday garments, are not a whit less startling'. His own experience to date certainly bore witness to the truth of this, both in the vicissitudes of his childhood and, more recently, in the sudden catastrophe of Mary's death immediately following the happy family outing to the theatre. He then shifts his ground, assumes a more teasing tone and pleads 'long usage' as justification for sudden changes of scene in novels, such changes even being considered by many as 'the great art of authorship'. But he at once repudiates any idea that this convention might be what is motivating him here. He has, he disingenuously observes, simply too much material to get through in narrating 'this history' (no longer, we note, merely a 'progress', presented in a series of scenes, but a proper joined-up 'history', like Fielding's *History of Tom Jones*) to allow him to indulge in literary tricks, or digression for digression's sake. *Pickwick* may be open to Hayward's charge of disconnectedness and digressiveness as a result of the form in which it was published but in *Oliver Twist* Dickens's 'sole desire', he straight-facedly asserts, is 'to proceed straight through this history with all convenient despatch', keeping faith and 'a good understanding' with his readers.[42]

Finding he had no copy of the February issue of *Bentley's* to hand, he had to get one from the printers so that he could check up on his description of the circumstances of Oliver's birth in order to build on it, if possible, for the novelistic plot he was now hastily constructing. He intended, he told Forster, that Nancy should figure prominently in this: 'If I can only work out the idea I have of her, and of the female who is to contrast with her [the pure young Rose Maylie], I think I may defy Mr Hayward and all his works'. In the event, Nancy was to replace Oliver as hero in the latter part of the story.[43]

On 31 October Dickens took Catherine off to Brighton for a week's break. *Pickwick* was concluded, *Oliver* was decisively upgraded from a series of sketches to novel status, and a regular three-volume novel, now called *Barnaby Rudge*, was firmly promised to Bentley for delivery the following October. Boz the periodical journalist and editor of a comic monthly was fast becoming Mr Charles Dickens the rising, indeed already risen, young novelist. He had risen on both sides of the Atlantic, moreover. The Philadelphia firm of Carey, Lea and Blanchard that had produced partial editions of *Sketches by Boz* without reference to the author now wrote to 'Mr Saml. Dickens' offering him, as a goodwill gesture, £25 for the twelve parts of *Pickwick* they had so far also published. On 26 October Dickens courteously declined their offer saying he would not feel 'quite at ease' in accepting it but also saying how pleased he was about *Pickwick*'s American popularity, and offering to enter into a business arrangement with Carey, Lea and Blanchard to facilitate their publication of *Oliver Twist*, due to be completed in Britain the following June.

CHAPTER 6

Periodicals into novels

1837–1839

I suppose like most authors I look over what I write with exceeding pleasure and think (to use the words of the elder Mr Weller) 'in my innocence that it's all wery capital'.

Dickens to G. H. Lewes, [?9 June 1838]

THE EVENING of 18 November 1837 would have been a proud one for Dickens as he hosted a dinner at the Prince of Wales Hotel, Leicester Place, to celebrate the completion of *Pickwick*. Macready, Talfourd and Ainsworth joined Forster, John Dickens, George Hogarth, Browne, Chapman and Hall and others in hearty applause when Degex the landlord brought in 'a glittering temple of confectionery . . . beneath the canopy of which stood a little figure of the illustrious Mr Pickwick'. Dickens replied to Talfourd's toast to him 'under strong emotion – most admirably', and a highly festive atmosphere prevailed. The young author, whom the dinner had cost £41.7s, must certainly have felt that he had had his money's worth.[1]

He had every reason for contentment with Chapman and Hall whose behaviour contrasted so markedly with that of the 'Burlington Street Brigand', as Dickens called Bentley when writing to Beard on 17 December. Having, at considerable expense, retrieved his first two books from Macrone, Chapman and Hall had worked with him to produce a more polished and coherently-organised, and more fully-illustrated, edition of *Sketches*. Now they entered into two new contracts with him, the first giving him a third share in the copyright of *Pickwick* after five years so that he could share in profits from that work's continuing success, and the second, signed the very day of the dinner, commissioning him to write a new periodical work, the title still to be decided on, 'of the same extent and contents in point of quantity' as *Pickwick*. Like *Pickwick,* it was to be published in twenty monthly numbers for each of which he was to receive £150. The manuscript of the first instalment was to be with the publishers by mid-March. Chapman and Hall had also presented him with a cheque bringing his total remuneration for *Pickwick* up to £2,000. Two days later he opened an account at Coutts' Bank with a deposit of £500.[2]

In *Oliver* he was now focusing intensely on Fagin, Sikes and Nancy (chs 18–19, written during November). Inspired, perhaps, by his recent holiday reading of Defoe's *Political History of the Devil*, Dickens develops Fagin into a grotesque devil-figure and during December (chs 20 and 21) builds up interest in Nancy as a woman torn by inner conflict. His first major attempt at a non-comic female character, she evidently owes something to his memory of the battered woman trying to protect her brutal partner described in 'The Hospital Patient' in *Sketches*. Wilkie Collins was later to assert that Dickens never surpassed his achievement in Nancy as far as his female characters were concerned. The narrative of the abortive burglary at Chertsey is powerfully written throughout and provides a suspenseful end to chapter 21. This is also the close of what Dickens now boldly announces as 'the end of the first book' of the novel into which his initial satirical sketches of a 'parish boy's progress' have metamorphosed. The chapter ends with Oliver, bleeding from a gunshot wound and fainting as he is dragged along by Sikes: 'a cold deadly feeling crept over the boy's heart, and he saw or heard no more.' *Bentley's* readers had to wait a full three months before finding out what became of him while Dickens, in the February and March instalments (Bk II, chs 1–5), attends to some urgent, and distinctly makeshift, retrospective plot-construction, necessitating a return to Oliver's birthplace, the Mudfog Workhouse. During January Dickens wrote the first three chapters of Book II. The comic scene of Bumble's wooing of the workhouse matron Mrs Corney (Dickens finds he needs them to be married) is followed by the grim scene of the death of old Sally, the nonce-character 'Mrs Thingummy' retrieved from the very first instalment of *Oliver*. She dies with Oliver's name on her lips after confessing to stealing a gold locket from his mother's corpse. The dying woman had shown it to her and told her that the baby might one day 'not feel disgraced to hear its poor mother named'. Dickens has to rely on his readers not remembering the first instalment of *Oliver* well enough to recall that there had been no opportunity for such a confession as he now works to reassure them that Oliver comes from a good family and hints at a happy and prosperous ending to the story to come. Fagin's frenzied reaction, in the last chapter of this February instalment, to the news that Oliver has been lost creates further mystery and provides an effective cliff-hanger ending.[3]

Developing *Oliver* into a three-volume novel, planning the new periodical for Chapman and Hall, and the regular grind of editing *Bentley's* should have been enough to keep even such a dynamo as Dickens fully occupied during the winter of 1837/38. He had, however, yet another task on hand. Surprisingly, he had agreed to edit for the vexatious Bentley a long rambling manuscript containing the memoirs of the recently-deceased prince of clowns Joey Grimaldi, as revised by a journalist called Wilks. Of course, Dickens, with his passion for pantomime and glowing childhood memories of seeing Grimaldi, would have been strongly attracted to the subject and it may also be that, as he later claimed, he took the job on partly as a favour to Cruikshank whom Bentley had commissioned to illustrate the work. He made sure, however, that a rather bristling contract with Bentley was drawn up (29 Nov. 1837) whereby he was to receive £300 down and a half share of the profits. He then set to work, severely curtailing Wilks's 'dreary twaddle' and using as his amanuensis John Dickens, who evidently revelled in being of use to his famous son and mingling in his ever-expanding social life. Dickens wrote an introductory chapter extolling the delights of pantomime, also a concluding one, and set much store by both of them. Throughout the work there are unmistakeable Dickens touches, like the description of Grimaldi 'coughing very fiercely' in an attempt to frighten off some suspected burglars, and ironic asides like the one about two night watchmen having been 'chosen, as the majority of that fine body of men were, with a specific view to their old age and infirmities'. Moreover, in certain places Dickens has completely changed the original Grimaldi/Wilks text, 'telling some of the stories in my own way'. He sometimes ends up with something that could well be an episode from *Pickwick*, like the anecdote in chapter 10 about the fraudster who invites Grimaldi and a friend of his down to his non-existent country estate for a day's shooting and lands them in a ludicrous scrape. Dickens also speaks of giving the book a 'colouring' throughout to bring out the kind-heartedness of Grimaldi. We can already see in his recension of this manuscript the brilliant future editor of *Household Words* and *All The Year Round* 'diffusing himself', as he was later to express it, throughout every issue, improving, sharpening and 'brightening' his contributors' offerings.[4]

Dickens prided himself on his power to transmute 'twaddle' into good writing: 'The Grimaldi', he told Bentley, 'grows under the alterations much better than I had supposed possible' and was pleased when the book sold very well, though no doubt irritated by Bentley's advertising in it, among 'New Novels in the Press', three volumes of 'A New Work of Fiction' by 'Charles Dickens, Esq. ("Boz")'. Dickens perhaps perceived some striking affinities between himself and Grimaldi as he presented him. The great clown had been the darling of a vast public, as Dickens himself had now become, but his 'attention to his duties, and invariable punctuality was always remarkable', and he always claimed that he had reached the height of his profession through 'strict attention, perseverance, and exertion'. These were qualities that Dickens felt he, too, possessed, in ample measure, and believed to have been fundamental to his success.[5]

No sooner had Dickens finished with Grimaldi in early January than he took up another new commission, this time from Chapman and Hall. They signed him up to write a little three-shilling comic book entitled *Sketches of Young Gentlemen*, illustrated by Browne, to be published as a follow-up to *Sketches of Young Ladies*, also illustrated by Browne and written by 'Quiz' (the

Rev. Edward Caswall). The *Young Gentlemen* book was published anonymously, probably because Dickens was breaking his contract with Bentley which prohibited him from writing for anyone else apart from the new periodical work promised to Chapman and Hall. His fee was £125 which, he noted in the short-lived diary he began keeping on New Year's Day, 'for such a little book without my name to it, is pretty well'. It was the kind of thing that by now he could almost write in his sleep but, as always, it is the contemporary theatre and its conventions that inspire some of his best comic touches. He creates a joyous caricature, for example, of the kind of stage-struck young man with whom he must often have rubbed shoulders in the days when he was going almost nightly to the theatres. This young man is 'a great advocate for violence of emotion and redundancy of action'. If a father has to curse a child 'it is essential that the child should follow the father on her knees, and be knocked violently over on her face by the old gentleman as he goes into a small cottage, and shuts the door behind him'. A couple of weeks earlier, in another anonymous 'moonlighting' assignment, this time for Forster's *Examiner*, Dickens had enjoyed himself lambasting just such acting as this in *Pierre Bertrand*, a preposterous melodrama at the Haymarket.[6]

Meanwhile, he seems to have planned that his promised new periodical for Chapman and Hall would, like *Oliver*, focus upon the theme of abused children. Cheap boarding schools in Yorkshire had achieved notoriety as places to which unwanted children were sent by those responsible for them, and where they suffered much cruelty and neglect. The announcement 'No Vacations' was used as a further inducement, besides distance and cheapness, to those parents or guardians who, for whatever reason, wanted children for whom they were responsible kept permanently out of the way. Dickens remembered to have seen in his own childhood a boy who had been sent home with a 'suppurated abscess . . . in consequence of his Yorkshire guide, philosopher and friend, having ripped it open with an inky pen-knife'. He never forgot the impression this made on him and later 'fell . . . into the way of hearing more about' these schools. He would, like everyone else, have seen many grandiloquent advertisements for them in the newspapers and 'at last', as he later recorded, 'having an audience, resolved to write about them'. Chapman and Hall may have been hoping for another *Pickwick* but the evidence shows that Dickens himself was thinking more along the lines of *Oliver*.[7]

This is not surprising for, proud as he was of *Pickwick*'s success, Dickens did not want to be thought of as *primarily* a comic writer, a sort of superior Surtees or Pierce Egan, but rather as an effective satirist and a master of pathos, crusading on behalf of the poor and the powerless. In the January issue of *Bentley's* there appeared a 'Poetical Epistle', seven verses long, addressed to himself by one of his chief contributors, 'Father Prout' (the ex-Jesuit Francis Mahony). The publication of this effusion is so contrary to Dickens's carefully

cultivated public modesty that some explanation seems called for, and it may
be that he felt the 'Epistle' might serve him as a sort of writer's manifesto. Here
is the third verse:

> But neither when you sport your pen, oh, potent mirth-compeller!
> Winning our hearts 'in monthly parts' can Pickwick or Sam Weller
> Cause us to weep with pathos deep, or shake with laughter spasmodical,
> As when you drain your copious vein for Bentley's periodical.

The sixth verse compares Dickens, to his advantage, both to the greatest of all
British satirists and to the nation's most celebrated narrative humorist:

> Write on, young sage! still o'er the page pour forth the flood of fancy;
> Wax still more droll, wave o'er the soul, Wit's wand of necromancy.
> Behold! e'en now around your brow th'immortal laurel thickens;
> Yes, SWIFT or STERNE might gladly learn a thing or two from DICKENS.[8]

As far as his personal life was concerned, what was preoccupying Dickens at
the turn of year, according to his diary, was his grief over the loss of Mary who,
he recorded, had sympathised with all his 'thoughts and feelings more than any
one I knew ever did or will'. She was always in his thoughts and in November,
when he was working on the end of chapter 20 of Book One of *Oliver*, a
memory of how she had looked just after dying in his arms had obtruded itself
into his writing as he described how Oliver sleeping the sleep of exhaustion
looked like death but not 'as it shows in shrouds and coffins, but in the guise it
wears . . . when a young and gentle spirit has but an instant fled to heaven . . .'.
Dickens copied out passages of desolate widower's grief from Scott's diary and
noted, 'I know but too well, how true all this is'. No doubt he talked much to
Catherine about those domestic evenings of 'merry banterings round the fire'
in Furnival's Inn when the 'sweet words' Mary bestowed upon what he had just
been writing were 'more precious' to him than 'the applause of a whole world'.
All this may have been in part conscious preparation for the attempt he was to
make a month or two later to create a stained-glass version of Mary in Rose
Maylie, the pure young girl who is to contrast with Nancy and who will make
her first appearance in the April number of *Bentley's* (Bk II, ch.7). It is rather
like the way in which, later on, he will hold Mary very much in his mind as he
approaches that part of *The Old Curiosity Shop* in which he will recount the
death of Little Nell. Every night he dreamed of his beatified young sister-in-law
until he mentioned the fact to Catherine whereupon, interestingly, the dreams
abruptly ceased.[9]

On 15 January he temporarily discontinued his journal: 'Here ends this brief
attempt at a Diary. I grow sad over this checking off of days, and can't do it. C.D.'

He did, in fact, resume it a few weeks later but thereafter kept it only intermittently and mainly as a memorandum of engagements, travel expenses and so forth. Meanwhile his family, social and cultural life continued apace. He went for exhilarating rides, sometimes as far as Richmond and Twickenham, with Forster, Ainsworth or Talfourd, entertained frequently at home, both family and friends, one notable occasion being the christening of that 'infant phaenomonon [sic]', his son and heir, on 9 December. He was now very much at the heart of the London literary and theatrical establishment, gossiping with Forster, for example, about Macready's unexpected reservations about putting on a new tragedy by Talfourd ('looks to me like the last stage of imbecility'). But he did not leave old friends behind as he made newer, grander ones, and Mitton and Beard were frequent guests. He had as lively a curiosity as ever about the sights and characters of the metropolis, such as the morning-after scene following some great urban fire, or the town's latest sensation, Dr John Elliotson demonstrating the power of mesmerism at University College Hospital. Elliotson's crowded public demonstrations, which were highly controversial because of his use of young female patients as subjects, interested Dickens deeply. He made repeated visits to the hospital, alone or with Ainsworth, and became a great friend and champion of the beleaguered Elliotson, who was eventually dismissed from his post. Later Dickens was to discover that he himself had definite mesmeric powers (below, p. 186).[10]

All this activity jostled for time with his various commissioned writings and produced recurrent work crises which he lamented with gusto: 'I am as badly off as you are', he writes to Forster on 16 January, 'I have not done the young gentlemen, nor written the preface to Grimaldi, nor thought of Oliver Twist, or even suggested [to Cruikshank] a subject for the plate'. When he went on 9 January to insure his life, for Catherine's sake, with the Sun Insurance Office, the Board, Dickens noted, 'seem disposed to think I work too much', adding wryly that, after 'an interesting interview' with them, he 'came away – to work again'. The Board declined his proposal. Only six weeks later he added yet another publishing commitment, albeit a rather more distant one, to the growing list when he agreed to write, for £300 down and a half-share of the profits, a Christmas volume for Chapman and Hall to be called Boz's Annual Register and Obituary of Blue Devils ('blue devils' was contemporary slang for melancholia or depression). This project remained on the stocks for a year before vanishing in the excitement of preparations for the new weekly journal, Master Humphrey's Clock.[11]

Dickens also wrote occasional book and theatre reviews for Forster's Examiner, among them an enthusiastic report of Macready's new production of Lear, which restored the Fool to the cast from which the adaptor Nahum Tate had banished him in 1681. After Macrone's sudden death in September, leaving his wife and children destitute, Dickens generously rallied to Ainsworth's side in an effort to help the widow by collecting contributions from distinguished writers to be published in a volume for her benefit. He was also keen to write a farce or a comedy to help Macready's efforts to 'revive the drama' during the actor's management of Covent Garden Theatre but made little progress with it – it was December before he managed to complete it. Another project he toyed with was a collaboration with Ainsworth 'to illustrate ancient and modern London in a Pickwick form' (that is, in monthly parts) with illustrations by Cruikshank. Ainsworth wrote of this project as a settled thing in a letter to a friend on 8 February but the scheme fell through after Dickens had to begin work on his new periodical for Chapman and Hall, a major addition to his existing commitment to Bentley.[12]

On 30 January, in hard winter weather, Dickens and Browne travelled by stage-coach up to Yorkshire to see at first hand the ill-famed schools. Dickens carried a letter of introduction from Mitton's partner to a local attorney saying that he was looking for a school to which a poor London widow he knew might send her son. Dickens stored up the comicality of some of his fellow-passengers for use in the new periodical. They included a tippling mistress of a Yorkshire school who, Dickens wrote to Catherine, showed him a long letter from one of her charge's parents 'containing a severe lecture (enforced and aided by many texts from Scripture) *on his refusing to eat boiled meat*'. On 2 February Dickens and Browne saw the one-eyed William Shaw, proprietor of Bowes Academy, one of the biggest schools in the area, and Dickens made a note to himself to research newspaper reports of prosecutions brought against this man fifteen years earlier after two boys had gone blind at his school. Later, he wrote about this 'scoundrel' to the literary philanthropist Anna Maria Hall and about his stumbling on a gravestone in the local churchyard erected in memory 'of a boy, eighteen long years old, who had died – suddenly, the inscription said; I suppose his heart broke . . . at that wretched place [Shaw's school]'. He added, 'I think his ghost put Smike into my head, upon the spot.' The local attorney he met confidentially urged Dickens, as revealed in the preface to the Cheap Edition of *Nickleby* ten years later, to keep the little boy from scoundrels like Shaw as long as there was 'a harse to hoold in a' Lunnun, or a goother to lie asleep in!' Author and illustrator returned to London with plenty of 'copy' for the new periodical. But, with his already well-developed instinct for just how much squalor and misery his readers could bear, Dickens realised that he would have to throw over what he had seen 'as much comicality . . . as [he] could, rather than disgust and weary the reader with its fouler aspects'. Before he could begin this work, however, he had the March instalment of *Oliver* to write and some further easing of his commitment to Bentley to negotiate – in effect, to demand.[13]

He proposed that *Barnaby Rudge*, the first novel of their agreement of 22 August 1836, should now follow *Oliver* as a serial in *Bentley's* rather than be published in three volumes in October. He would, Dickens argued, have to begin another serial if *Bentley's* was 'to keep its ground' after the end of *Oliver* and doing this simultaneously with the new periodical for Chapman and Hall *and* writing *Barnaby* for volume publication 'would have been beyond Scott himself'. Bentley agreed immediately but was not destined to see Dickens fulfil this agreement any more than any of the previous ones they had made, the *Grimaldi* alone excepted.[14]

Over the next five months (Feb.–June 1838) Dickens was simultaneously writing the second section (Bk II) of *Oliver* and the first four monthly numbers of *The Life and Adventures of Nicholas Nickleby*, as the new 'periodical' for Chapman and Hall was finally titled. The full title, used for the monthly wrappers and modelled on *Pickwick*, was designed to allow Dickens maximum scope as regards story-line: *The Life and Adventures of Nicholas Nickleby; containing a faithful account of the Fortunes, Misfortunes, Uprisings, Downfallings, and Complete Career of the Nickleby Family, Edited by* 'BOZ'. Dickens seems to have been undaunted by this workload. The Pilgrim Editors interestingly note a 'major change' in his handwriting, 'reflecting, perhaps, a mood of confident optimism', that clearly began in the second half of February. The pothooks used for forming capital M or N that he would have learned at school now yielded to a more dashing way of writing them, for example. As to content, these first four *Nickleby* numbers constitute the first movement, as it were, of the new work. They noticeably replicate the pattern of its predecessor in that they end with Nicholas's thrashing Squeers and absconding from Dotheboys Hall just as Oliver absconded from Mudfog after thrashing Noah Claypole. Dickens, having once again reached a climactic point in his satirical narrative, found that he now needed to shift into another fictional mode. He naturally turned to modes of proven success, either contemporary or from an earlier period. For *Oliver* this had been the 'Newgate' model; for *Nickleby* it was the picaresque model, so brilliantly used by Smollett.[15]

By February 1838 Dickens had reached a point in *Oliver* where a second mode-shift was needed. He had to connect his Bumble-dominated Mudfog Workhouse story with the Fagin-dominated London-criminal-underworld one. Accordingly, he switched into the Gothic mode with the sudden introduction (Bk II, ch. 4) of Monks, whose name, language, gestures and general appearance all proclaim his ultimate derivation from the Gothic romances of the previous century that Ainsworth (from whom Dickens probably got the idea of 'going Gothic') was avowedly copying in *Rookwood*. Monks is Oliver's villainous but legitimate half-brother competing with the unwitting Oliver for the family inheritance, a reversal of the pattern of the bastard Luke Bradley and his half-brother Sir Ranulph Rookwood in Ainsworth's best-seller. Monks cuts but a feeble figure alongside Fagin but, pasteboard as he is, he works well enough to connect the two disparate novels Dickens has found himself successively writing in *Oliver*. He makes the link at the end of Book II, in the July

Bentley's, when Monks, in quest of the locket stolen from the corpse of Oliver's mother, tracks down Mr Bumble.[16]

From March to early June, Dickens wrote the chapters of *Oliver* (Bk II, chs 6–13) set in the Maylie household. At the centre of the picture is Rose Maylie:

> in the lovely bloom and spring-time of womanhood; at that age, when, if ever angels be for God's good purposes enthroned in mortal forms, they may be, without impiety, supposed to abide in such as hers. Oh! where are the hearts which following some halting description of youth and beauty, do not recal a loved original that Time has sadly changed, or Death resolved to dust.

Dickens deleted the last sentence of this passage in manuscript, no doubt recognising that he was slipping from fiction into personal lamentation, but otherwise found the established formula for depicting the angelic young heroines of Gothic romance was ideally suited to the literary evocation of Mary. Remembering those evenings of 'merry banterings' by the fireside, however, he does not want Rose to be too ethereal so writes of her 'cheerful, happy smile . . . made for Home; for fireside peace and happiness'.[17]

The chief excitement in these chapters, apart from a few Gothic moments like the terrifying apparition of Fagin and Monks at the jessamine-and-honeysuckle-framed window of Oliver's study in chapter 34, is Rose's sudden illness, the hectic fever that brings her close to death. Dickens makes this episode help the plot in that it brings upon the scene Rose's suitor, Harry Maylie, and enables Dickens to work up some mystery about a blot on Rose's name that makes her so determined not to marry him though she loves him. But there is a compelling biographical explanation for the writing of this episode too, as has long been recognised. Dickens was working on it in May, the first anniversary of Mary's fatal seizure, and he evidently had a need to re-live in imagination that terrible night and day of 6/7 May 1837. He needed to dwell upon 'the suspense, the fearful acute suspense, of standing idly by while the life of one we dearly love is trembling in the balance . . . the desperate anxiety *to be doing something* to relieve the pain, or lessen the danger which we have no power to alleviate . . .'. In reality he had not been able to save Mary but now in his imagined world he can bring about a happier outcome.

He had, however, killed off another Mary-figure just a week or two previously in the first of the two interpolated tales that helped to bulk out *Nickleby* II. But this was a comfortably-distanced story of medieval times, 'The Five Sisters of York', inspired by his viewing of the Five Sisters Window in York Minster. The youngest sister, Alice, is a 'fair girl' whose heart 'bounded with joy and gladness' and who was the 'very light and life' of their home (just as Mary, Dickens told Ainsworth, had been 'the grace and life of our home'). This story, together with its mock-Gothic companion-piece about the Baron of Grogzwig and his defeat of 'the Genius of Despair and Suicide', may or may not have been dashed off to fill out the May number but is clearly another offering to the memory of Mary. This preoccupation with her results in his first exploration of a question that was to emerge as a leading theme in his writings ten years later, culminating in the writing of *Copperfield*. This question was how to live with memories of pain and sorrow without becoming embittered or ceasing to believe that 'the good in this state of existence preponderates over the bad' and that 'memory, however sad, is the best and purest link between this world and a better'.[18]

The Dickenses' second child, a daughter, was born on 6 March. Inevitably, the baby was named after Mary and was, significantly, the only child of theirs to have only one Christian name. From the next arrival onwards Dickens took the opportunity offered by the necessity of naming the new baby to compliment a friend, or pay homage to a literary hero, or even to signal something about his writing plans, as with his eighth child Henry Fielding Dickens, but Mary's name was too sacred to be yoked with any others – apart from his own, of course. Shortly after this new Mary's birth Catherine became 'alarmingly' ill, perhaps suffering from anaemia as a result of two births and a miscarriage within the space of fifteen months, as well as from postnatal depression (once again, she was unable to breastfeed her baby). Dickens's already desperately tight writing schedule – at this period, Forster recorded, he 'never wrote without the printer at his heels' – was complicated by the need to care for Catherine, and at the end of the month he took her to the Star and Garter at Richmond for a few days' convalescence, on the eve of the triumphant publication of the first number of *Nickleby*. Nearly fifty thousand copies were sold on the first day, a truly staggering number. Forster joined the couple on 2 April to celebrate their wedding anniversary together with his own birthday, an annual festival the three of them continued to keep up for many years, with interruptions only when Dickens and Catherine happened to be abroad.[19]

Though by 21 February he had written only the first chapter, Dickens succeeded in completing *Nickleby* I in time for publication on 'Magazine Day', 31 March, and thereafter kept both it and *Oliver* going together like some brilliant literary juggler, working first on *Oliver* each month and then *Nickleby*. It perhaps helped him to do so in that he was at this point writing the two stories in such very different veins. In contrast to the predominantly sentimental-idyllic narrative of *Oliver* during these months, *Nickleby*, after the first chapter, was very much a return to Dickens's *Sketches by Boz* vein. He gave readers a succession of striking sketches of metropolitan and provincial (Yorkshire) 'scenes' and 'characters' including Golden Square in Soho, the usurer Ralph Nickleby and his eccentric clerk, Miss La Creevy the miniature-painter, Squeers the rascally schoolmaster, Dotheboys Hall, and the Kenwigs family. His continuing problems with Bentley are reflected in a pointed joke in *Nickleby* IV (ch.14) about the meekness of the Kenwigses' revered uncle, Mr Lillyvick the water rates collector : 'if he had been an author who knew his place, he couldn't have been more humble'.

Despite the basic 'sketch' format and the interpolated tales in these initial numbers of *Nickleby* Dickens was clearly paying attention to characterisation, plot and structure. Ralph Nickleby represents his first attempt, however crude and perfunctory, to 'psychologise' a character, accounting for villainous behaviour in terms of response to early experience and upbringing. He looks forward to more complex characters like Jonas Chuzzlewit, Uriah Heep, Steerforth, Tom Gradgrind and Henry Gowan. As regards plot, Dickens lays the ground for a two-strand narrative by providing not only a young hero who has to leave his family to seek his fortune but also a heroine (sister to the hero) whose trials and tribulations will be set in London, and he loses no time in setting his wicked-uncle villain to work. Despite all this, reviewers tended to see *Nickleby* as simply another *Pickwick*, promising to be 'as humorous and amusing as its great predecessor'. It is, unsurprisingly, to Forster's notices in *The Examiner* that we must turn to find a critic alert to new developments in Dickens's writing. Forster would, of course, have been well aware of Dickens's ambitions and intentions as a writer so we may feel some confidence in interpreting these *Examiner* notices as reflecting Dickens's own view of his developing work or, at the very least, not conflicting with it. The review of the first number of *Nickleby* (1 April 1838) noted that it showed the same qualities that had made *Pickwick* so popular but 'with the addition of even better promise on the score of a well-laid design, and of greater truth and precision of character'. Smike's portrait in the second number is found 'more terrible and affecting than anything in *Oliver Twist*' (6 May), the description of Dotheboys Hall in *Nickleby* III is compared to Hogarth whilst Mrs Nickleby is pronounced to be 'hit off to the life' (3 June), and the 'utter absence of the forced or melodramatic' is praised in *Nickleby* IV which shows a 'most affecting mixture of the ludicrous and terrible'.[20]

These *Examiner* notices apart, there was little critical discussion of the new work by reviewers, though much enthusiastic excerpting from it as there had been from *Sketches* and *Pickwick*. Inevitably, it fell prey to the hack dramatists and the plagiarists, wholly unabashed by Dickens's 'Proclamation' against them beginning 'Whereas we are the only true and lawful "Boz" . . .' written at the beginning of March and published both in the periodical press and as a handbill. *Nickelas Nickelbery* by 'Bos' (eight pages for a penny) appeared simultaneously with *Nickleby* I. Seeking to steal a march on his theatrical plunderers, Dickens offered to dramatise *Oliver* himself for the actor-manager Frederick Yates. He describes the plot as being 'involved and complicated' and says he himself does not yet know how it will end so no hack dramatist will be able to anticipate him. Nothing came of this proposal but between March and December 1838 no less than five unauthorised adaptations of *Oliver* appeared in the London theatres. Forster tells us how Dickens attended one and was so mortified that 'in the middle of the first scene' he lay down upon the floor of his box and stayed there until the final curtain. A year later he included a swingeing attack on these piratical dramatists in *Nickleby* XV but to no avail whatever and he continued to suffer their depredations for many more years.[21]

At the beginning of June Dickens took his family for a two-month sojourn in a villa at Twickenham. He and Catherine entertained a stream of family visitors and other guests, even the irritating Bentley. Beard and Forster, of course, were frequently there and Dickens established a 'balloon club' with them. Ostensibly intended for his children's amusement, it gave Dickens another outlet for the Mudfoggian style of comic writing in which he so clearly delighted, like his spoof letter to *The Times* describing a balloon ascent from 'Gammon Lodge' by 'that intrepid aeronaut Mr Forster'. He had some more private epistolary fun with an impassioned love-letter to Forster written as from the pen of a young lady admirer who had just learned he was to marry another whilst, about the same time, he was composing for *Nickleby* V what is surely the greatest comic letter in English literature, Fanny Squeers's hilarious report to Ralph Nickleby of Nicholas's assault upon her father leaving two benches 'steeped in his Goar'.[22]

On 7 July Dickens finished the first instalment (two chapters) of what had now become *Oliver Twist* Book III. Three days later he told Bentley he had planned *Oliver* to the close, 'and if I have any fortune in preparing the next No. of Nickleby expeditiously, hope to make a great start [on the rest of *Oliver*'s final volume] this month'. *Nickleby* V, to which he turned that same day, is essentially four Bozzian sketches, including two of a fatuously pompous and shameless M.P. They are written with tremendous verve and we certainly have no sense of reading stuff which has been dashed off to clear the decks for another task. But nor do we feel any sense of a plot gathering momentum, even though experienced novel-readers would certainly have expected to see more of the beautiful young lady, 'scarcely eighteen' and possessed of 'an exquisite shape', whose brief appearance in the employment agency in chapter 16 makes such an impression on Nicholas. At this point all Dickens's plotting skills have to be focused on *Oliver*.[23]

Bentley had been hoping for this first Dickens novel, as Oliver had now become, to be finished ready for three-volume publication in September (under the Agreement of 28 Sept. 1837 the deadline had, in fact, been midsummer 1838). It would then still have had several months to run in *Bentley's*. It was becoming evident, however, that completion could not now be expected until October. Dickens had, after all, now to work out not one plot but two. The first

is the powerful 'Newgate' one involving Fagin, Sikes and Nancy which ends with
Fagin in the condemned cell. The second is the 'Gothic' one involving Oliver,
now a passive 'heroine' figure, Monks, Brownlow and the Maylies. The elaborate dénouement of this latter plot bogs down the novel in Book III, chapter 11,
when even Monks complains about the long-windedness of Brownlow's explanations, and again in Book III, chapter 13, when the explanations are resumed.
Dickens contrived to yoke the two plots together through the iconic virgin-and-
whore scene between Rose and Nancy in Book III, chapter 3 [ch. 40]) but then
needed someone to 'dodge' Nancy, clearly not a suitable job for a likeable character like Charley Bates or the Dodger. The sneaking Noah Claypole was ideal
for the work and Dickens happily retrieved him from the early 'Mudfog' chapters. He also brilliantly solved the problem of how to dispose of the Dodger, the
novel's greatest comic character, for whom neither penitence nor punishment
fitted the bill (a reformed Charley Bates is all very well but a repentant Dodger
is as unimaginable as a sober Mrs Gamp). Remembering his model for this
character, the irrepressibly impudent boy-thief in 'Criminal Courts' in *Sketches*,
he contrived a splendidly unrepentant comic-triumphant exit for the Dodger
in Book III, chapter 2 [ch. 43].[24]

During late July and all of August Dickens was clearing the decks for a
concentrated final assault on *Oliver*. Having made Bentley agree to the suspen-
sion of this work for the September number so he could concentrate on
writing the dénouement of the story 'straight through', as it were, he supplied
his statutory sixteen pages (with two pages extra) by means of another facetious piece on the British Association, then holding its annual conference in
Newcastle. Internal evidence shows that he was still working on his 'Full
Report of the Second Meeting of the Mudfog Association for the Advancement
of Everything' as late as 22 August. He somehow also found time to write a two
thousand word polemical review for *The Examiner*, published 2 September, of
a pamphlet issued on behalf of the Ballantynes, Scott's printers and business
partners. This pamphlet strongly defended the Ballantynes against the accusation that they had been partly responsible for Scott's financial collapse, an
accusation made in John Gibson Lockhart's massive biography of Scott, his
father-in-law, which Dickens had been poring over during the past year.
Dickens vehemently defended Lockhart (his piece, he told Forster, was 'very
moderate in tone, if not in length'). No doubt the tensions between himself
and Bentley, the increasing tendency of reviewers to hail him as Scott's
successor, and his own linking of himself with Scott as a phenomenally
successful and prolific writer who was hugely enriching his publishers but not
himself would have given a distinct edge to his championship of Lockhart.[25]

With all this on hand Dickens sometimes found himself writing till half-
past midnight and having 'the steam to get up afresh' the next morning. On
3 September he retreated with Catherine to the Isle of Wight for nine days 'for

Oliver purposes' and there, intent as he must have been on working on the last stages of the novel, he still found enough writing energy to compose forty-four lines of doggerel verse instructions to the landlord of their hotel in Alum Bay. Back in London on 12 September, he set about negotiating, with the help of Forster and Mitton, yet another agreement with Bentley. This one, signed on 22 September, dealt with the editorship of the *Miscellany*, the publication of *Oliver Twist* (always referred to in the Agreement as a 'series of original papers') and the writing of 'an original novel' entitled *Barnaby Rudge: a Tale of the Great Riots*, which it was now agreed would be serialised in *Bentley's* for eighteen months following the conclusion in the journal of *Oliver*. Everything was settled to Dickens's satisfaction. Meanwhile, in the September *Nickleby* he had placed Kate Nickleby in the household of the posturing Wititterleys, and Nicholas and Smike in the company of Mr Crummles and his troupe of strolling players. He knew, therefore, that he had two (for him) highly congenial comic veins to work as regards this story during the next month or so when *Oliver* would be making such heavy demands on him. From his hilarious description of the 'Affairs, Domestic and Theatrical' of Mr Crummles Dickens switched immediately back to the dark and desperate world of Fagin's London and the gruesomely bloody murder of Nancy. Following this (the murder was written by 2 Oct.) Dickens was for the next fortnight 'incessantly occupied night and day' on the book, much heartened by Thomas Lister's highly laudatory survey of his work in the October *Edinburgh Review*. Lister compared him to Hogarth but without Hogarth's touches of misanthropy and 'coarseness' and singled out *Oliver* as 'calculated to give a more favourable impression of Mr Dickens's powers as a writer than anything else which he has yet produced . . . more interest in the story, a plot better arranged, characters more skilfully drawn . . .'.[26]

Dickens told Bentley on 3 October that he was writing this final volume of *Oliver* 'with greater care, and I think with greater power than I have been able to bring to bear on anything yet'. It must have been around this time that, besides pressing ahead with the writing, he was also going back over the first eighteen instalments as printed in *Bentley's* and making over two hundred deletions and emendations. Many are simply stylistic but over a dozen relate to the way in which Dickens transformed, during the work of composition, his 'glance at the New Poor Law' of spring 1837 into a novel, beginning with the deletion of the reference to Mudfog in the first sentence of the first instalment. As to the 'greater power' in the writing to which Dickens refers, the flight of Sikes and his death, the empathetic description of Fagin's sensations during his trial, and his frenzied behaviour in the condemned cell certainly comprise the most psychologically intense scenes that Dickens has written to date. He seems to have astonished even himself with Fagin who, he told Forster, 'is such an out and outer I don't know what to make of him'. His readers would have been

surprised by his flouting of convention at the end of the novel. It has been
pointed out that in Bulwer Lytton's *Paul Clifford* and other popular novels
featuring a hero of doubtful or mysterious origins this hero is invariably
revealed in the end to be legitimate. This does not happen with Oliver,
however, where Dickens prefers to follow the example of Fielding's *Tom Jones*
but, unlike Fielding, he seems more concerned with Oliver's 'weak and erring'
mother, the dead Agnes, than with Oliver himself. The challenging last few
words of the story are devoted to her, and Dickens insisted on Cruikshank's
changing his final plate, which at first made no reference to Agnes but instead
portrayed Oliver in a happy fireside group with the Maylies. Even though it
was too late for the substitution of a different plate in the first impression of
the first volume edition, published 9 November, Cruikshank was obliged
thereafter to replace his fireside scene with one showing Oliver and Rose
standing alone together in a church. They are looking at the memorial tablet
to Agnes described by Dickens in the text – fully aware, of course, that the idea
of a memorial to a 'fallen woman' in a church would cause raised eyebrows –
and this final image and the last words of the novel serve to underline the fact
that Oliver is illegitimate.[27]

Another remarkable feature of the last chapter, and one that connects with
the contretemps over Cruikshank's last plate, is the long, yearning paragraph
in which Dickens says how much he wishes he could continue the story to
show Rose Maylie 'in all the bloom and grace of early womanhood . . . the life
and joy of the fireside circle and the lively summer group', to 'recall the tones
of that clear laugh, and conjure up the sympathising tear that glistened in that
soft blue eye', and so forth. It is, in fact, a kind of elegy for Mary Hogarth,
Rose's original, and perhaps the real offence of Cruikshank's plate was that,
while it illustrated one of the very scenes of Rose's future that Dickens longed
to describe, for him it fell painfully short of his intensely personal concern
with the subject. A few years later Phiz's illustration of another fireside scene,
little Paul Dombey with Mrs Pipchin, was to cause him similar distress, in this
case definitely intensified by strong personal memories.[28]

With *Oliver* done, Dickens could turn his full attention to *Nickleby*. Once
again, he went on a journey, partly to be out of London when *Oliver* was
published, a practice he followed with all his subsequent novels, and partly to
reconnoitre possible new scenes for the developing action of *Nickleby* – that
this was part of his motivation is suggested by the fact that Browne accompanied him. Forster was left to deal with proofing the last chapters of *Oliver*
(Bentley was making 'prodigious exertion' to get the book out on the advertised date of 7 November) and Dickens and Browne set out from London on
29 October. They went first to Leamington and visited Warwick Castle, later
recalled in *Dombey and Son*, Kenilworth with its strong Scott associations
(Dickens found the place 'beautiful beyond expression', an ideal spot for a lazy

13 The cancelled 'fireside plate' from *Oliver Twist*

summer holiday), and Stratford. At this last place Dickens stored up material ('the birth-place, visitors, scribblers') which he later used to delicious comic effect in the December number of *Nickleby* (ch. 28) in which Mrs Wititterly languidly discourses about the effect on writing one's name in the visitors' book: 'it kindles up quite a fire within one'. Dickens and Browne then travelled to Shrewsbury via Birmingham and Wolverhampton, through landscape that proved a real eye-opener for Dickens, as he wrote to Catherine on 1 November: 'miles of cinder-paths and blazing furnaces and roaring steam engines, and such a mass of dirt gloom and misery as I never before witnessed'. This grim

scenery found no place in *Nickleby* but a year or more later Dickens made
effective use of it in *The Old Curiosity Shop* when describing Little Nell's flight
with her grandfather through the Black Country. From Shrewsbury he and
Browne took the scenic route to Llangollen, where their hotel bill included
payments for a harpist, something Dickens remembered years later, in 'The
Holly-Tree Inn' (1855), when he described Welsh inns 'with the women in
their round hats, and the harpers with their white beards (venerable but
humbugs, I am afraid)'. From there they went to Liverpool where Forster
joined them and then, armed with letters of introduction from Ainsworth, all
three travelled to Manchester, Ainsworth's native city, on 6 November.[29]

Ainsworth had written to his friend Crossley, 'I rather suspect he [Dickens]
is reconnoitring for character', and to another friend, a solicitor called Gilbert
Winter, he 'gave . . . a hint that Dickens wishes to see the Grants'. These were
two brothers of humble origin who had become immensely prosperous
merchants, widely celebrated for their seemingly boundless benevolence.
Dickens would have been naturally curious to meet them but may also have
been thinking they might serve him as models for a character or characters
who might befriend and help his beleaguered young hero. Winter gave a
dinner party with the Grants among the guests so Dickens could meet them.
He also gave a breakfast-party in honour of the London visitors, and a cousin
of Ainsworth's who was present recorded that 'Mr Dickens was then writing
Nicholas Nickleby, and I well remember his reading the proofs of his novel, and
smiling at his own writings.' The famous writer, he added, was then 'a smart-
looking young man of rather effeminate appearance, wearing long hair, very
much like the pictures of the hero of his story. . . . I still call to mind his
polished boots and drawing-room like attire'. No reference to the Grants
appears in Dickens's surviving correspondence from this period but there is an
allusion to another possible Nicklebeian outcome of this trip in a letter of
29 December to the Irish journalist Edward Fitzgerald in which Dickens writes
that he has been shown the worst cotton-mill and the best and found 'no great
difference between them'. The experience, he writes, has 'disgusted and astonished' him 'beyond all measure' and he intends 'to strike the heaviest blow in
my power for these unfortunate creatures, but whether I shall do so in the
"Nickleby", or wait some other opportunity, I have not yet determined'.[30]

He made a sudden decision to return to London with Forster 'in order to
ensure there shall be no mistakes in Oliver' on 8 November but it was already too
late to change Cruikshank's last plate, as we have seen he wanted to. He also
wanted to change the way he was named on the title-page. He wanted his first
proper novel to appear under the name of 'Charles Dickens' rather than that of
'Boz', a clear signal that he now considered himself to have arrived as a
fully-fledged author, no longer just a writer, no matter how successful, of sketches
or *Pickwick*-style periodicals. Both the changes he wanted had to wait until

the first impression of this first edition of *Oliver* in volume form had been exhausted. *Nickleby* meanwhile was approaching the half-way mark and Dickens had to apply himself to it at once in order to ensure that the December number would appear on time. He found himself unable to write with his normal speed because, he believed, of the intensity of his *Oliver* work the previous month, and it was 24 November before he had finished the number. Despite the pressure under which it was composed, it proved to be a sparkling one with some splendid comic 'business' both for Mrs Nickleby and for the Crummles troupe.

Dickens then turned to *The Lamplighter*, a farce he was writing for Macready. This was very much in his facetious 'Mudfog Association' vein, featuring a foolish astrologer and an absurdly flimsy plot. The only good thing in it is the lamplighter himself, a role written for Harley. Always alert to the comic potential of people defining themselves by their trade or profession, Dickens gave the lamplighter what he quite rightly thought was a funny speech about a lamplighter unable to survive the advent of gas: 'At last he went and hanged himself on a lamp-iron in St Martin's Lane, that he'd always been very fond of; and as he was a remarkably good husband, and never had any secrets from his wife, he put a note in the two-penny post as he went along, to tell the widder where the body was'. On 5 December he read the piece to Macready who thought the dialogue good but the plot 'meagre'. He was much impressed by Dickens's reading, however: 'He reads as well as an experienced actor would – he is a surprising man.' But the farce did not survive a second reading and Dickens later recycled it as a short story for the volume being got up for the benefit of Macrone's widow.[31]

Dickens's diary entries for December record much conviviality, including two meetings of the Trio or Cerberus Club which consisted of three members only, Forster, Ainsworth and himself. It succeeded an earlier 'club' consisting of Dickens and Forster alone, for which Dickens, with characteristic exuberance, had drawn up a set of mock rules and regulations. He dined out with Cruikshank on 11 December and on the 12th supped out (after chairing a dinner of the Literary Fund) with the distinguished antiquarian artist George Cattermole, a man twelve years his senior, with whom he was developing a close friendship. After that he buckled down to writing *Nickleby* X (chs 30–33) and to getting the stage ready for the entry in the next number of the Grants in the guise of the Cheeryble Brothers. Once *Nickleby* X was finished there was more jollity: a Christmas Eve visit to Covent Garden with Forster and Forster's young poet-friend Robert Browning to watch Macready rehearse the pantomime, dinner with Elliotson on 28 December, with Ainsworth on the 29th, with Talfourd on the 30th and on the 31st a final dinner of the year at home in Doughty Street with Forster, Ainsworth and Cattermole among the guests.[32]

For two years now Dickens had had the labour of editing *Bentley's Miscellany* in addition to his own writing commitments. That this editing involved a huge

amount of toil and dispensation of practical advice on his part can be deduced
from his surviving letters to contributors and would-be contributors, doubtless
a tiny percentage of the totality of such correspondence. As is clear from his
later editorial work for his own journals, this was a kind of labour he delighted
in, except, perhaps, when dealing with such an independent-minded contributor as Elizabeth Gaskell. He enjoyed literary collaboration at all levels provided
always that he was *primus inter pares* and had a major financial stake in the
resulting publication. This was not his situation with regard to Bentley, who
presumed to behave virtually like a co-editor and whom he perceived to be
making enormous profits from the success of *Oliver*. Nor was this the only
difficulty with Bentley. He now expected Dickens to begin work on *Barnaby
Rudge* so that its serialisation could begin, as called for in the Agreement of
22 September, in the month following the one in which the last instalment of
Oliver should appear – this was expected to be March but in the event was April.

Dickens did, in fact, start work on *Barnaby* on 3 January, writing 'four slips'
that evening. 'The beginning is made,' he told Forster the next day, 'and –
which is more – I can go on, so I hope the book is in training at last'. He soon
found, however, that he could *not* go on, because of his distracting consciousness that his books were 'enriching everybody connected with them but
myself, and that I, with such a popularity as I have acquired, am struggling in
old toils, and wasting my energies in the very height and freshness of my fame,
and the best part of my life, to fill the pockets of others'. He demanded a respite
of six months before working any more on *Barnaby*. Bentley agreed but in
such a legalistic way that Dickens became infuriated and decided to withdraw
from the editorship forthwith, rejecting Bentley's rather desperate offer of £40
a month just to keep his name on the masthead. The January 1839 *Miscellany*
was thus the last issue of the magazine to appear under his editorship. The last
instalments of *Oliver* being now relegated to the back pages, the *Miscellany*'s
lead piece was the first instalment of Ainsworth's 'Newgate' tale *Jack Sheppard*,
about the notorious young thief and escape-artist, hanged at Tyburn in 1724.
It was Ainsworth who, urged on by Dickens, successfully proposed himself to
Bentley as Dickens's successor. To smooth the transition Dickens promised to
write gratuitously a paper for the next number 'announcing, in the pleasantest
manner in which he can possibly state it, the termination of his present
connexion with [the magazine]' as well as two further papers to be supplied
within the following six months, also gratuitously. These two papers were
never forthcoming but the 'pleasant' announcement duly appeared in *Bentley's*
February number under the title 'Familiar Epistle from a Parent to a Child
Aged Two Years and Two Months'. Dickens presents himself as a concerned
father handing over his infant journal to 'one of my most intimate and valued
friends, Mr Ainsworth' and, pursuing the theme that it is a world of change,
derives considerable comic mileage from something he had observed on the

Manchester–London train. This was the 'disconsolate demeanour of the Post Office Guard' when the train stopped to take in water and 'he dismounted slowly from the little box in which he sits in ghastly mockery of his old condition with pistol and blunderbuss beside him, ready to shoot the first highwayman (or railwayman) who shall attempt to stop the horses' and looked mournfully about him 'as if in dismal recollection of the old roadside publichouse'. Dickens must have spotted this melancholy official when returning from his December excursion (as far as we know, his first rail journey) or on the journey back from a second visit to Manchester (12–17 Jan.) when he, Ainsworth and Forster had attended a public dinner on the 14th in honour of himself and Ainsworth. 'Pleasant' as was the 'Familiar Epistle' Dickens wrote on his return to London, it had a sting in it nevertheless. Dickens says to his 'child', 'I reap no gain or profit by parting from you, nor will any conveyance of your property be required for, in this respect, you have always been literally "Bentley's Miscellany", and never mine.' His long-standing exasperation with Bentley's continual interference with the conduct of the magazine is only just below the surface.[33]

This exasperation may have been the determining factor in Dickens's demand for a six-month postponement of *Barnaby* and subsequent abrupt decision to withdraw from *Bentley's*. He probably also wished to create a kind of *cordon sanitaire* between Ainsworth's new 'Newgate' serial and his own *Barnaby Rudge*, a work that had for so long now carried such a weight of significance for him. *Barnaby* had first been envisaged as a novel appearing in all the dignity of three volumes and challenging comparison with Scott. More precisely, it would challenge comparison with *The Heart of Midlothian* in that the most dramatic scene of that novel is the storming of the Edinburgh Tolbooth during the Porteous Riots of 1736 and, given Dickens's strong fascination with Newgate, it was more than likely that the most dramatic scene in his 'Tale of the Riots of 'Eighty' would be the burning down of the prison by the Gordon rioters. Since Dickens had already introduced a powerful Newgate scene into the end of *Oliver* he must have had mixed feelings about *Jack Sheppard*'s being the very next story to be serialised in *Bentley's* as it was bound to feature Newgate scenes also. Ainsworth's tale was on such a different, more straightforwardly sensationalist, level, however, compared with *Oliver* that only 'jolter-headed critics', as Dickens wrote in his 1841 preface to *Oliver*, could see his and Ainsworth's work as comparable.

Nevertheless, the unfortunate juxtaposition of their two stories was there in the magazine though the last thing Dickens would have wanted was that his long-deferred début as a novelist in the Scott tradition should first appear as what might simply seem from its context to be yet one more Newgate-related serial. When telling Talfourd on 31 January that he had broken with Bentley he said he was sure that Talfourd would be glad to hear 'that Barnaby Rudge will

be published next year as a Novel and not in portions', adding that he had
'two thousand pounds certain, on the delivery of the Manuscript, and two
thousand more conditional upon the Sale!'. This was the agreement sealed on
27 February, hammered out between Bentley's lawyers and Mitton acting for
Dickens. Dickens was to deliver *Barnaby* to Bentley ready for volume publication on 1 January 1840, the basic payment he was to receive for this still
unwritten novel having increased more than fourfold in two and a half years.[34]

For the first nine months of 1839 Dickens's main writing concern was
Nickleby, the enormous popularity of which continued undimmed. One
journal, describing 'magazine day' at the end of January, reported that both
sides of the Strand 'looked almost verdant with the numerous green covers' of
the February *Nickleby* 'waving to and fro in the hands of the passengers along
that busy thoroughfare'. Dickens provided readers with a succession of great
comic episodes like that of 'the gentleman in small clothes' (old-fashioned
knee-breeches) who woos Mrs Nickleby with showers of vegetables in the
April number, a scene that, Dickens told Forster, he thought would 'come out
rather unique'. But he worked away at the plot too, retrieving Squeers and
other of the Yorkshire characters from the early numbers to involve them,
either as (somewhat improbable) helpers or as hinderers of Ralph's dastardly
plotting against Nicholas and Kate.[35]

He celebrated his 27th birthday with a party in Doughty Street on
7 February. Among the family and friends who were present was the sculptor
Angus Fletcher, already perhaps working on the bust of Dickens he made some
time this year. Dickens's image was now in request. He was a major celebrity in
a lionising age, whom even the grandest of London's *grandes dames*, Lady
Holland, the great Whig hostess, having assured herself that he was 'presentable', invited to her salon, and whose acquaintance was cultivated by such
eminent literary figures as Leigh Hunt and Bulwer Lytton. From *Pickwick* to
Oliver to *Nickleby* the reading public followed him with ever-increasing
acclaim and delight while thousands more enjoyed his work at second-hand,
much to his chagrin, through all the unauthorised dramatisations. The more
he demanded of himself as a writer the more he found he could supply, no
matter how tight the deadline, even if he did occasionally fear he might
' "bust" the boiler'. He had got the better of two publishers and knew that
Chapman and Hall, his 'trusty friends' as he now called them, were only too
aware that their rapidly-escalating prosperity depended on him. He was the
happily-married father of two thriving children and the centre of an ever-
expanding circle of admiring friends and a loved companion of the great
Macready. He lived at a highly respectable address and kept his own carriage
with a groom to attend on him. He summed it all up in his birthday entry in
his diary: 'The end of a most prosperous and happy year, for which and all
blessings I thank GOD with all my heart and soul.'[36]

One distressing drain on his prosperity, however, was the continued financial fecklessness of his father and other family members. He complained to Forster, 'Directly I build up a hundred pounds one of my dear relations comes and knocks it down again.' His father sponged off Chapman and Hall: 'The want of £15', he wrote to them at one point, 'places me in a situation of the most peculiar difficulty – as regards home affairs ... the subject is one of settlement by two o'clock, and unless I so arrange it, I am lost.' Having failed to repay them as promised, he still asks for further loans though writing 'under feelings of the most pregnant and heartrending distress at my own want of common honesty'. Dickens had to do something. Having decided, after consultation with Forster, that his parents needed to be removed a long way from metropolitan temptations, he acted with an energy and rapidity worthy of his current hero. In *Nickleby* the antithesis of the rich and bustling metropolis with all its dangers is that 'sequestered part of the county of Devonshire' where Nicholas's father has his farm, as his father had before him, and from which his newly-impoverished widow and children come, innocently hopeful, to the 'wilderness' of London. This rural retreat was the idyllic setting of Nicholas's and Kate's childhood described in chapter 58; it is where poor Smike will be taken in the vain hope that its beneficent influence will restore him to health; and it is the place to which all the good characters will retire at the end of the story to live happily ever after (reprising the finale of *Oliver Twist* with the blameless Smike's tomb taking the place of the erring Agnes's memorial tablet). It was the very place, obviously, for Dickens to send his irresponsible parents to. There they could, in the scenario that he quickly devises for them, settle down to tranquil rural domesticity, devoting themselves to the upbringing of their youngest child, the twelve-year-old Augustus, and basking (at a safe distance) in the reflected glory of their famous son.[37]

In a whirlwind trip to Exeter and back (4–11 March) Dickens found, and rented for only £20 a year, what seemed to him an ideal cottage at Alphington, one mile from Exeter, a 'jewel of a place' with a 'splendid garden' in 'the most beautiful, cheerful, delicious rural neighbourhood I was ever in', with the landlady, 'the finest old countrywoman conceivable', living next door and certain to be a great comfort to his mother (in his letter to Forster he develops her and her family into richly comic characters). The paint and paper were new 'and the place clean as the utmost excess of snowy cleanliness could be'. He set to and furnished it throughout – carpets, curtains, tables, beds, chairs, everything down to all 'the kitchen necessaries', garden tools 'and such like little things'. His parents, he believed, would hardly miss the bustle of London as the cottage was on the high road to Plymouth and 'there is as much long-stage and posting life, as you would find in Piccadilly'. All in all, he felt sure 'they may be happy there, if they will', adding, with what we must think truly staggering self-deception, 'If I were older and my course of activity were run, I am sure *I* could, with God's blessing, for many and many a year'.[38]

14 Mile End Cottage, Alphington

Dickens had, in fact, written the (idyllic) end of their story for his parents, complete with a cast of comic extras (the name of their maidservant, a certain Betty Peek, sounds promising) and it only remained for them to conform to it. Having also dealt with his brother Fred, now nineteen, by getting him a junior Treasury clerkship, he then turned back to the fictitious story of Nicholas and Kate, which the real-life script he had suddenly had to write for his parents had interrupted. *Nickleby* now being more than half way through its run, it was more than high time for Nicholas's unknown beloved, briefly featured in *Nickleby* V, to reappear and she duly does so but in a manner that only heightens the mystery surrounding her both for Nicholas and the reader. In *Nickleby* XIV, written during April and comprising chapters 43–5, Dickens is clearly starting on the home run. Clumsily, or brazenly, repeating a melodramatic situation already used in *Nickleby* X (ch. 32), he introduces a secondary hero, Frank Cheeryble, for Kate to marry eventually, which also helps to intensify one aspect of the Smike plot, the boy's hopeless love for Kate. Dickens also introduces the mysterious figure of Brooker, who is signalled as Ralph's shabby-sinister nemesis. Meanwhile, Dickens makes time to write another anonymous piece for *The Examiner* (published 31 March 1839) further excoriating Scott's printers and publishing partners for claiming they had been ruined by him. He is now far more vehement in his condemnation of them: the wrong was all on the side of these 'pigmies', not on that of 'the giant who upheld them . . . under the shadow of whose protection they gradually came to lose sight of their own stature, and to imagine themselves as great as he'.

At the end of April, in order to work on *Nickleby* with fewer routine distractions and interruptions, he hired Elm Lodge, a villa in Petersham, Hampshire and moved his household there for four months. Here he wrote *Nickleby* XV–XVIII in between entertaining a stream of his closest friends (the extensive gardens, Forster notes, encouraged 'much athletic competition' in which Dickens 'distanced every competitor'), visits to the Hampton Races (turned to good account in *Nickleby* XVI where they are the setting for the fatal quarrel between the secondary villain Sir Mulberry Hawk and his young dupe Lord Frederick Verisopht), and trips back to London to dine with such notable new acquaintances as the banking heiress Angela Burdett Coutts, Sir David Wilkie and the Rev. Sydney Smith. He returned to town also on 20 July to speak at a public dinner for Macready, who was retiring after three years as manager of Covent Garden. The writer Mary Cowden Clarke, watching from the ladies' gallery, saw how observant Dickens was of everyone round him: 'No spoonful of soup seemed to reach his lips unaccompanied by a gathered oddity or whimsicality, nor morsel to be raised upon his fork unseasoned by a droll gesture or trick he had remarked in someone near'. His speech, she added, was 'like himself, genial, full of good spirits, of kindly feeling and cheerful vivacity'.[39]

Among the friends visiting Dickens in Petersham was a comparatively new one who quickly became very dear to him, replacing Ainsworth as a member of the 'Cerberus' trio. This was the brilliant and handsome young Irish artist Daniel Maclise, celebrated for his gallery of portraits of literary celebrities in *Fraser's*. Chapman and Hall had commissioned him to paint a cabinet portrait of Dickens, which they then had engraved for the frontispiece to the bound volume of *Nickleby*. It thus became the first widely-disseminated image of Dickens, conveying to the general public a strong sense of his dynamic and charismatic presence. Thackeray was among those contemporaries who thought the likeness 'perfectly amazing': 'Here we have the real identical man Dickens: the artist must have understood the inward Boz as well as the outward before he made this admirable representation of him.'[40]

Maclise must indeed have understood something of 'the inward Boz' for such a close and strongly affectionate friendship to develop between the two men. Dickens greatly admired Maclise's art but it was above all to the man himself that he responded, as his younger daughter, herself an artist, recalled in her essay on her father as a lover of art and artists: 'Maclise . . . was very handsome in person, and had a singular fascination and charm of manner, little personal attractions for which my father had invariably an almost boyish enthusiasm, and the charming warmth and geniality of his nature completely won my father's heart.' Male friendships were a hugely important element in Dickens's life and 'friend' was not a term he used loosely, as he told an

American correspondent who wrote to ask if he 'might command [Dickens] as a friend' in pursuing a literary career: 'My inability to answer that question, is in exact proportion to the great weight I attach to the name, and the care with which I bestow it upon but a few out of troops of acquaintances.'[41]

With the April and May numbers (XIII and XIV) of *Nickleby*, the reintroduction of the mysterious young lady with whom Nicholas is smitten and the appearance of Brooker, Dickens was getting all his characters into place for the story's dénouement. He had yet to introduce another auxiliary villain, the stage-miser figure of old Arthur Gride, so that Nicholas will have someone from whom to save his beloved (at last given a name, Madeline) besides her parasitic father. With Madeline rescued, the way would be clear for Dickens to move towards the ending involving the pathetic death of Smike, the revelation that he was Ralph's long-lost son, and Ralph's subsequent horrific suicide. Just at this point there opened, on 20 May at the Strand Theatre, a theatrical piece called *Nicholas Nickleby and Poor Smike or, The Victim of the Yorkshire School* by William Moncrieff, one of the most brazen of Dickens's dramatic plagiarists. Moncrieff anticipated Dickens's revelation that Ralph is Smike's father but made his mother a relation of Sir Mulberry's, cast off by her rich uncle General Hawk. Infuriated by this crude travesty of his story, Dickens seized the opportunity provided by his reintroduction of the Crummles troupe to make their final bow in *Nickleby* XV, the June number, fiercely to lampoon Moncrieff, though not by name, as a 'literary gentleman ... who had dramatized ... two hundred and forty-seven novels, as fast as they had come out – some of them faster than they had come out – and who *was* a literary gentleman in consequence'. Nicholas, somewhat improbably, berates this brazen character for 'cutting, hacking and carving' authors' books and 'hastily and crudely vamp[ing] up ideas not yet fully worked out by their original projector, but which have doubtless cost him many thoughtful days and sleepless nights'.[42]

We have no record of Dickens enduring 'sleepless nights' at Petersham but what he described to Laman Blanchard on 11 July as the 'very difficult' task he had 'to wind up so many people *in parts*, and make each part tell by itself' doubtless cost him many 'thoughtful days' amid all the entertaining of friends and attendance at London dinner-parties. It would not have been such a problem for him in *Pickwick*, even though he then had to worry about writing *Oliver* as well, because in *Pickwick* the interest depends primarily on the sayings and doings of Pickwick and Sam and Sam's father, so once the Bardell/Pickwick plot is over Dickens can use Pickwick and the Wellers to distribute rewards and punishments in an episodic fashion – though the law in the form of Dodson and Fogg is beyond even Pickwick's power to reform or punish. At Petersham Dickens managed the *Nickleby* winding-up process very deftly. In successive numbers (*Nickleby* XV–XVIII) he carefully balanced needful plot-development against comic, sensational or pathetic 'last appearance' scenes by important secondary characters. We learn from Forster that, for all his fecundity and his growing skill in managing a continuous story in monthly parts, Dickens was anxious about the 'strain on his fancy' of keeping such a long story going – and, of course, there was the Bentleian *Barnaby* commitment awaiting him as soon as he should have finished *Nickleby*. This anxiety, as well as a fear that the public might tire of the monthly-part format, strongly influenced the nature of the proposition for a new literary project that he made through Forster to Chapman and Hall in mid-July. They were to be urged, he told Forster, to 'do something handsome, even handsomer perhaps than they dreamt of doing', if they wished to keep him, and 'to step gallantly forward' in response to his proposal. This was that they should launch a new periodical, one that, unlike *Pickwick* and *Nickleby*, would not be one continuous story but a mixture of shorter fiction and articles of various kinds. Dickens would, of course, be sole editor and a major contributor but there should be work by other hands too. The details of this proposal, which Chapman and Hall were only too happy to agree to (what choice had they, after all?), will be more appropriately discussed at the beginning of the next chapter.[43]

On 3 September, in another household move of the kind that became a standard annual pattern for them, Dickens and his family removed to Broadstairs for a month where he could work uninterruptedly on the final double number of *Nickleby*. From 5 to 19 September the daily entry in his diary consists of one word 'Work', apart from a note on 13 September that Fred had arrived for a short holiday, and another on Sunday 15th specifying that he wrote the preface to *Nickleby* that day and that the famous elderly banker-poet Samuel Rogers had called. Chapman and Hall visited him on 9 September to show him Browne's sketches for the last illustrations and nine days later he wrote to Forster:

I have had pretty stiff work as you may suppose, and I have taken great pains. The discovery is made, Ralph is dead, the loves have come all right, and I have now only to break up Dotheboys and book together. I am very anxious that you should see this conclusion before it leaves my hands. . . . .

He had just completed chapters 62 and 63. In the former he describes Ralph's final defeat, appalled recognition of what he has done, and his cursing of the whole world as he dies, like some great villain in Jacobean tragedy. Chapter 63 is a grand-finale scene copied from the theatre with all the principal characters assembled in the Cheerybles' drawing-room to be paired off. That might seem to be the natural end of the story, with the irrepressible (and unpaired-off) Mrs Nickleby rightly having the last word, but Dickens still needs, as he notes, to have a Dotheboys dénouement (nor has he yet managed to give the glorious Mr Mantalini a curtain call) so he tacks on a second ending (ch. 64), hovering awkwardly between farce and pathos, and then a third and final one (ch. 65), modelled, as noted above, on the conclusion of *Oliver*.[44]

All was finally done by 2 p.m. on 20 September and he went over to Ramsgate with Catherine and Fred to send the last copy to the printers. His final diary entry was 'Thank God that I have lived to get through it happily.' It only remained to ask Macready's permission to dedicate the book to him, which Dickens did the next day. 'Surely this is something to gratify me,' Macready recorded in his diary. Then, before leaving Broadstairs, Dickens hastily wrote for *The Examiner* yet another piece (published 29 Sept.) lambasting Scott's publishers, who were still sniping away at Lockhart over the great man's financial catastrophe. The Dickenses finally returned to Doughty Street at the beginning of October, Catherine being in the last weeks of her third pregnancy. On 5 October Chapman and Hall hosted what Macready thought was a '*too splendid dinner*' at the Albion in Aldersgate Street to celebrate the completion of *Nickleby*. Among those present were three distinguished artists, Cattermole, Sir David Wilkie and Maclise, whose portrait of Dickens hung in the room. Macready proposed a toast to Dickens, referring to him as 'one who had made the amelioration of his fellow-men the object of all his labours'. He went on to compare him, Wilkie reported to a correspondent, to Wordsworth in his genius for combining 'the bold adventure and the startling incident' with 'all the little details and minute feelings, of the every-day intercourse of life'. This led Dickens to speak to Wilkie about his love for Wordsworth and his particular admiration for the poem 'We Are Seven' which divested death of its horror 'by treating it as a separation and not an extinction' (it had perhaps helped him in coming to terms with Mary's death). In his reply to Macready he said that *Nickleby* 'had been to him a diary of the last two years: the various papers preserving to him the recollection of the events and feelings connected with their production'.[45]

The way in which Dickens speaks of *Nickleby* here, not as a novel but as a series of 'various papers', echoes what he had written in the preface to the volume edition (one volume like *Pickwick*, not three like *Oliver*) published on 23 October. After defending himself against charges of exaggeration, either of the foulness of the Yorkshire schools on the one hand, or of the benevolence of the Cheerybles on the other (he does not name the Grants but states that the fictional brothers truly portray living originals), Dickens quotes approvingly from the last number of Henry Mackenzie's periodical *The Lounger* (1785–7) in which Mackenzie argues that 'the author of a periodical performance has indeed a claim to the attention and regard of his readers more interesting than that of any other writer' because 'he commits to his readers the feelings of the day, in the language which those feelings have prompted'. This should conduce towards feelings of intimacy and tender friendship between the writer and his readers. Dickens, referring to himself neither as novelist nor as story-teller but as 'periodical essayist', confesses that he shares these feelings and these hopes. There is no word here about plots or the novelistic difficulties of 'winding up so many people in parts'. Rather, Dickens's preface, together with his portrait featuring as the frontispiece to the volume, is concerned to build up an image of himself as the intimate friend and well-loved literary companion of every individual among his phenomenal readership, preparing them for the new periodical to be launched the following spring.[46]

Had Dickens been concerned at this time to present himself as a novelist, he might, after all his struggles with plot in *Nickleby*, have been somewhat depressed by certain passages in Leigh Hunt's long (of course, anonymous) *Examiner* review of the completed book on 27 October. After extolling Dickens's 'strong power of reality' in the book, Hunt asks if he is yet a 'perfect novelist' and convincingly answers in the negative because 'he has yet to acquire the faculty of constructing a compact and effective story, without which that rank can never be obtained'. Hunt holds up *Tom Jones* as the supreme example of successful novel-construction and comments that *Nickleby*'s plot 'seems to have grown as the book appeared by numbers, instead of having been mapped out beforehand'. If only Dickens will work on this and curb 'his common-place exuberance', he may hope, concludes Hunt, to become 'the not unworthy successor of our GOLDSMITHS and FIELDINGS'. Dickens was certainly eager to follow in the footsteps of these great predecessors but in the autumn of 1839, thinking of his new periodical, it was the Goldsmith of *The Bee* and the Fielding of *The Covent Garden Journal* that he had in mind rather than the authors of *The Vicar of Wakefield* and *Tom Jones*.[47]

Nickleby is full of jokes about literature, high and low, authorship, scholarship and criticism and to this aspect of the work we may perhaps relate an amusing *jeu d'esprit* in which Dickens collaborated with Cruikshank in the summer of 1839 (their last but one joint production). Dickens was charmed by a Cockney ballad called 'The Loving Ballad of Lord Bateman' which Cruikshank delighted in singing as he had heard it sung in a London pub, and which his publisher Charles Tilt was proposing to publish with Cruikshank's illustrations. Cruikshank happily accepted Dickens's offer to supply some spoof editorial apparatus in the shape of a preface and notes, and the little book duly appeared at the beginning of July. Dickens's notes form a critical commentary on the text worthy of *Nickleby*'s Mr Curdle himself. Thus the line, 'This Turk he had one ounly darter' ('This Turk he had only one daughter') is annotated as follows:

> The poet has here, by that bold license which only genius can venture upon, surmounted the extreme difficulty of introducing any particular Turk, by assuming a fore-gone conclusion in the reader's mind, and adverting in a casual, careless way to a Turk unknown, as to an old acquaintance. '*This* Turk he had –' We have heard of no Turk before, and yet this familiar introduction satisfies at

once that we know him well. . . . 'This Turk he had –' is a master-stroke – a truly Shakspearian touch. There are few things like it in the language.[48]

Dickens himself ceased to have 'one ounly darter' on 29 October when Katherine Macready Dickens was born. It was now becoming imperative for the family to move to a larger house. So began a distracting period of house-hunting with Elizabeth Dickens, temporarily released from exile in Devonshire, assisting by going to 'scrutinise' various properties. Catherine herself was not yet able to undertake this though she does not seem to have been so ill after this birth as after the previous ones – her request for reading matter forwarded to Forster by Dickens on 7 November suggests that she was certainly convalescent by then (Dickens's adding, 'If you have any literary rubbish on hand, please to shoot it here' indicates his opinion of the kind of reading desired). In the same letter he announces that a suitable house 'of great promise (and great premium) "undeniable" situation, and excessive splendour' has been found. This was 1 Devonshire Terrace, opposite to the York Gate entrance to Regent's Park, a handsome house of thirteen rooms with a large garden for which Dickens paid £800 for an eleven-year lease, plus an annual rental of £160. He had also to make arrangements with his Doughty Street landlord about the remainder of his lease there, fixtures and fittings, etc. He was soon in 'the agonies of house-letting, house-taking, title proving and disproving, and other ills too numerous to mention' and the move to Devonshire Terrace finally took place in early December.[49]

During all this upheaval, Dickens, who had also to contend with a series of bad colds, had been trying to work at *Barnaby*. On his return from Broadstairs he had written to Cruikshank, currently illustrating Ainsworth's *Jack Sheppard* in *Bentley's*, that he was 'going forthwith tooth and nail at Barnaby' and promised to have copy to show the artist by mid-October. By the beginning of November, however, he had written only ten pages, progress having been much hampered by all the house-hunting. It seems likely, too, that, quite apart from his preoccupation with his new Chapman and Hall project, he would have had in any case little appetite to return to work for Bentley. The latter's pertinacity in advertising *Barnaby* as 'preparing for publication' and his linking of *Jack Sheppard* with *Oliver Twist* in another advertisement infuriated Dickens and he seized on these things, vehemently exaggerating their injuriousness to himself, as a pretext for a final break with the obnoxious publisher: 'War to the knife and with no quarter on either side, has commenced with the Burlington Street Brigand,' he announced in a letter to Beard on 17 December. He stopped work on *Barnaby* and defiantly instructed his solicitors to inform Bentley that he would not be delivering the manuscript on 1 January as called for by the Agreement he had signed on the previous 27 February. A prolonged period of legal wrangling then ensued and matters were not resolved until the following summer, when Dickens and Bentley signed a final agreement on 2 July. Under this Dickens bought all rights in *Oliver* and his other writings from Bentley for £1,500 and paid a further £750 for the Cruikshank plates and unsold stock of the novel. Chapman and Hall advanced him the money against the £3,000 they agreed to pay him for *Barnaby* (to be published first in monthly numbers and then in volume form).[50]

Dickens was now committed only to Chapman and Hall, to whom he had recently given a copy of *Pickwick* inscribed with a quotation from *Oliver* (Brownlow's conversation with Oliver in ch.14 about book-writers and book-sellers) followed by the words, 'the old gentleman does *not* say, though I *do* that Chapman and Hall are the best of booksellers past, present, or to come; and my trusty friends'. With the triumphs of *Oliver* and *Nickleby* behind him, he was now eagerly looking forward to the start of the new periodical which he hoped would prove equally, if not more successful, while being a much less onerous and stressful undertaking as far as he himself was concerned. It may seem surprising that he should also at this time register himself as a law student as he did at the Middle Temple on 6 December. But, aware as he was of the vagaries of literary fame, and haunted as he was by the spectre of Scott writing himself out in order to pay off his debts, Dickens was determined to contrive a safety net for himself, and what safer one could there be than that invincible, all-powerful legal system that had defeated even Mr Pickwick?[51]

CHAPTER 7

The *Master Humphrey* experiment

1840–1841

My great ambition is to live in the hearts and homes of home-loving people, and
to be connected with the truth of truthful English life.

Dickens to Mary Novello, 27 December 1841

DICKENS ENVISAGED the new periodical that he asked Forster to propose on
his behalf to Chapman and Hall in the summer of 1839 as a threepenny
weekly consisting of twelve quarto pages, to begin publication on 31 March
1840. He was to have complete editorial control and to be guaranteed a certain
sum for the portion of the work that he would bind himself to write every
week. He would also be a proprietor 'and a sharer in the profits' which he anticipated would be substantial. The weekly numbers would also be collected as
monthly ones and, 'at regular intervals', published in volume form. Dickens's
concept harked back to those magazines of the previous century he had read
so avidly in his childhood. It would be based on the 'pleasant fiction' that it
originated with 'a little club or knot of characters', like Isaac Bickerstaff and his
friends in Steele's *Tatler* (1709–11) or Sir Roger de Coverley and his friends in
Addison and Steele's *Spectator* (1711–12), but it would be 'far more popular'
both in subject-matter and mode of treatment than those journals.[1]

These imagined characters would, as in the *Spectator*, play a continuing role in
the publication and others would be added, including Mr Pickwick and Sam
Weller. Among ideas for ongoing features of the work Dickens himself would
write was one for 'a series of satirical papers purporting to be translated from
some Savage Chronicles' which should 'keep a special look-out upon the magistrates in town and country'. Another was for a series of stories about London
past, present and future, told to each other nightly by the statues of the giants
Gog and Magog in Guildhall, who would break off their narratives at dawn, like
that great mistress of serial fiction Scheherezade. This device, says Dickens,
would open up 'an almost inexhaustible field of fun, raillery and interest'. Now
this field, at least as far as the first two elements are concerned, does not sound
much like *The Arabian Nights*, so it was probable that Dickens envisaged his Gog
and Magog tales as being like Scheherezade's in their form only. Another

suggested London-based series was the 'Chapters on Chambers' of which, he reminds Forster, 'I have long thought and spoken', and of which he had already given readers a taste in Jack Bamber's 'Queer Client' tale in *Pickwick*. All these series he would write himself but there would be contributions from others, too, so that he would not have to carry the whole project single-handed. Dickens's final suggestion is that he might give 'fresh novelty and interest' to the magazine once it has been got going by travelling either to Ireland or to America and sending back sketches of what he saw there featuring in their local tales and traditions as Washington Irving had done in his *Legends of the Alhambra* (1832).[2]

Chapman and Hall agreed to all Dickens's suggestions and further gratified him by giving him a bonus of £1,500 for *Nickleby*. 'Proposals for Agreement' were signed by both parties on 15 October 1839 followed by the lengthy formal Agreement for the periodical, now named *Master Humphrey's Clock*, on 31 March 1840. Dickens was to have £50 for each weekly number and, over and above this, was to receive 50 per cent of the net profits, to be paid to him at half-yearly intervals. Chapman and Hall were to be entirely responsible for all production costs, including the wood-engravings which were intended to be an important feature of the new work. When the first number, published on 4 April, sold 70,000 copies Dickens exultantly told Macready that if sales kept up at this level he would be earning £10,000 a year ('at which', noted Macready, 'I heartily rejoice').[3]

After he propounded his initial scheme for this new, but at the same time old-fashioned, periodical Dickens had had to devote himself to finishing *Nickleby* and after that, as mentioned in the last chapter, he turned back to the long-deferred *Barnaby Rudge* and wrote the first two chapters (chs 1–3 in the published text).

Having seized on a pretext to stop writing *Barnaby Rudge* for which he had been contracted to Bentley, Dickens was free to concentrate wholly upon his new project, though not without some apprehension that Bentley might resort to litigation. He also agreed to write for Chapman and Hall another little comic book like *Sketches of Young Gentlemen*, to be illustrated by Browne as that had been. *Sketches of Young Couples* was intended to cash in on the Queen's marriage to Prince Albert, irreverently referred to by Dickens in a private letter as a 'German Sassage [sausage]' from 'Saxe Humbug and Go-to-her' (Albert's title was Prince of Saxe-Coburg-Gotha), and Dickens got for it nearly double what he was paid for the *Young Gentlemen* book two years earlier. It appeared on the day of the royal wedding, 10 February. It was published anonymously for the same reason that *Young Gentlemen* was, namely that Dickens was breaking his contract with Bentley to write nothing other than certain specified items for any other publisher before delivering *Barnaby*. 'Dickens was a very clever man but he was not an honest man' was, many years later, the understandable verdict of Bentley's son George, on Dickens's dealings with his father.[4]

Young Couples begins with an 'Urgent Remonstrance to the Gentlemen of England (being Bachelors or Widowers)'. Single men are warned that the perils of Leap Year are greater than normal in 1840. Women may conspire to follow the example set by Victoria who had announced her intention to 'ally herself in marriage' with Prince Albert: '. . . a very distressing case has occurred at Tottenham, in which a young lady not only stated her intention of allying herself in marriage with her cousin John, but, taking violent possession of her said cousin, actually married him.' With his mind running on the Gordon Riots as a result of revisiting *Barnaby*, Dickens introduces some spoof anti-Catholicism: 'such plot, conspiracy or design, strongly savours of Popery as tending to the discomfiture of the Clergy of the Established Church, by entailing upon them great mental and physical exhaustion'. The book has been alleged to contain an affectionate portrait of William Hall and his wife and Edward Chapman in 'The Nice Little Couple' Mr and Mrs Chirrup and their bachelor friend (the Halls were both small in stature and Chapman was a bachelor). Mrs Chirrup is described as having 'the neatest little foot, and the softest little voice, and the pleasantest little smile, and the tidiest little curls, and the brightest little eyes, and the quietest little manner' and the couple's bachelor friend is always to be found at their agreeable little dinner-parties. Dining with the Dickenses in Devonshire Terrace was an altogether grander affair, it seems. Lord Jeffrey, the editor of *The Edinburgh Review*, having been a guest there, described the event to his friend the Scottish judge Lord Cockburn as having been 'rather too sumptuous a dinner for a man with a family, and only beginning to be rich, though selling 44,000 copies of his weekly issues'.[5]

Lord Jeffrey, important as he was to become to Dickens in his self-appointed role as the young writer's admiring 'Critic Laureate', was only one among the increasing number of distinguished new friends Dickens was making during 1840–41. He already had his entrée at Holland House and some time during the winter of 1839/40 Forster introduced him into London's other great literary salon, that of Lady Blessington at Gore House, Kensington. The beautiful, charming and highly literary Countess of Blessington had a complicated marital history and her closeness to her beautiful son-in-law, Count D'Orsay, who was estranged from his wife, was the subject of scandal. D'Orsay was an amateur artist and successor to Beau Brummel as London's acknowledged 'dandy *par excellence*, the very Prince and Pope of tailors'. Respectable ladies could not associate with Lady Blessington but men eminent in the worlds of literature, art and politics flocked to her salon. Prominent among them were Daniel Maclise, Edward Bulwer and Benjamin Disraeli, the latter two being dandies only slightly less lustrous than D'Orsay himself. It was at Gore House in January that Dickens first met the volcanic sexagenarian man of letters Walter Savage Landor, famed for his entertainingly erudite *Imaginary*

Conversations (1824–9). Dickens became greatly attached to him – more, one suspects, for Landor's colourful personality than for his writings, which Dickens probably found 'desperately learned' like his table-talk. He named his second son Walter Landor, and, thirteen years later, painted an affectionate portrait of the writer and his eccentricities in Boythorn in *Bleak House*.[6]

It was at another aristocratic mansion, that of the prominent Whig politician Edward Stanley, that Dickens first met, in March 1840, a still more formidable senior in the world of letters, 45-year-old Thomas Carlyle. Carlyle's *History of the French Revolution* had brought him widespread fame in 1837 and his admirer John Stuart Mill, seeing Dickens for the first time at Macready's home in that same year, was reminded of Carlyle's description of Camille Desmoulins in the *French Revolution* with his 'face of dingy blackguardism irradiated with genius'. He commented with mingled condescension and fascination, 'such a phenomenon does not often appear in a lady's drawing-room'. In the distracted England of 1840, alarmed by Chartist riots and Anti-Corn Law agitation, wars in China and Afghanistan, and widespread social distress at home, Carlyle was fast becoming a revered, prophet-like figure. The publication in late 1839 of *Chartism*, his wake-up call to England, further enhanced his status in this respect. Dickens soon became one of his most ardent disciples and later told Forster, 'I would go at all times farther to see Carlyle than any man alive.' As for Carlyle's view of Dickens, he has left us an affably patronising description of Dickens as he first saw him in the Stanleys' drawing-room. There, it seemed to Carlyle, the assembled Lords and Ladies 'did not seem to mind him overmuch', which suggests a certain upper-class resistance to the lionisation of the young writer at this time (Carlyle is writing to his brother John on 17 March 1840):

> He is a fine little fellow, Boz, as I think; clear blue intelligent eyes, eyebrows that he arches amazingly, large protrusive rather loose mouth, – a face of most extreme *mobility*, which he shuttles about, eyebrows, eyes, mouth and all, in a very singular manner while speaking; surmount this with a loose coil of common-coloured hair, and set it on a small compact figure, very small, and dressed rather à la D'Orsay than well: this is Pickwick; for the rest a quiet shrewd-looking little fellow, who seems to guess pretty well what he is, and what others are.[7]

Other notable persons with whom Dickens was becoming better acquainted during 1839/40 and who, like Carlyle, were to play important roles in his life, were the heiress Angela Burdett Coutts and the celebrated forty-six-year-old marine and landscape painter Clarkson Stanfield, who was also famous for painting scenery for Covent Garden and other theatres. Within a few years Dickens was acting as a tireless unofficial almoner to Burdett Coutts as well as volunteer administrator of her 'Home for Homeless Women', while Stanfield

was to become one of his most dearly-loved friends and an enthusiastic collaborator in his amateur theatricals. Meanwhile, Dickens's fervent commitment to
help and cherish Macready in every possible way remained undimmed. In late
May 1840, just when he would have been most preoccupied with radically
changing the nature of his new periodical, Dickens nevertheless exerted himself
to help promote arrangements for Macready's production of Talfourd's new
tragedy *Glencoe*. In his 'Advertisement to the Second Edition' of his play (1840)
Talfourd acknowledges Dickens's 'generous devotion to my interests among his
own triumphant labours'.

Daniel Maclise, meanwhile, had become Dickens's favourite companion for
outings of one kind or another. These might take the form of what Dickens
called a 'great, London, back-slums kind of walk', seeking nocturnal adventures
'in knight-errant style', a teasing reference to the handsome Irishman's notorious propensity for romantic entanglements. Alternatively, they might involve
a hearty 'rustic walk' to Eel Pie Island, ending in the eating of lamb chops
'and drinking beer, and laughing like a coal-heaver'. When Maclise was unwell
in the summer of 1841 Dickens eagerly pressed him to join the family encamp-
ment at Broadstairs for a six-week holiday: 'No one loves you better than I,' he
wrote and he hinted – just how seriously we cannot be sure – at the possibility
of some sexual escapades: 'There are conveniences of all kinds at Margate (do
you take me?) and I know where they live.' Maclise seems to have been, like
Wilkie Collins later, a correspondent with whom Dickens felt he could indulge
himself in the mildly naughty badinage that was one of the epistolary games he
sometimes enjoyed playing. At the height of their pretence (in which Forster
also joined) of being madly in love with the young Queen, Dickens wrote
pathetically to Maclise about the distress caused to him and Forster by seeing
pubs called The Queen's Head and the Queen's Arms: 'Oh our dear friend, what
dreadful thoughts does not that . . . sign awaken, what visions of Albert in the
Queen's Arms calling for what he likes and having it. The thought is madness.'[8]

Forster, who must have cut a rather ponderous figure in this particular lark,
was by now firmly established as Dickens's chief literary and business adviser
though there were times when Dickens, like everyone else, found Forster's
overbearing behaviour intolerable. We know from Macready of at least one
violent dinner-table quarrel between the two over some matter in the summer
of 1840 that resulted in Dickens ordering Forster out of the house and drove
Catherine from the room in tears. Such upsets notwithstanding, he remained
always Dickens's indispensable chief literary confidant and counsellor and so
was the first to learn, ten days or so into the new year, of his friend's latest ideas
about the new periodical, ideas in which certain elements reappear from the
opening chapters of the suspended *Barnaby Rudge*, notably an emphasis on
quaint antiquity not present in the scheme for the journal as originally
proposed to Chapman and Hall via Forster the previous summer.[9]

Dickens now elaborated to Forster on his conception of 'this old file in the queer house', who is soon to be antiquely styled 'Master' Humphrey, the surname being taken from that of a clockmaker Dickens had met in Barnard Castle on his Yorkshire schools expedition. Dickens's Humphrey is deeply attached to his 'old quaint queer-cased clock' and hoards manuscripts in 'the old, deep, dark, silent closet where the weights are'. The description of the old file's favourite custom of physically retrieving these writings from this very Dickensian emblem of times past indicates just how much Dickens's conception of the new project has changed in the six months since he first broached it. The busy, bustling daylight world of the eighteenth-century periodical essayist has given place to the mysterious and shadowy world of romance and poetic allegory. Outwardly, Dickens's life was becoming ever busier, ever more involved in society at all levels, and ever more crowded with events (including a harrowing one on 14 January when he had to serve on a jury at an inquest on a new-born baby found dead in a family house where the maidservant mother was suspected of infanticide). It was crowded, too, with commitments like the one to Macready already mentioned, and the remarkable amount of time and attention he was giving to the encouragement of a poor cabinet-maker with literary ambitions called John Overs. His own literary energies overflowed into the high-spirited letters about his mock passion for the Queen mentioned above. Yet, in contrast to all this, his main literary project at this time seems to be suffused with what has been well defined as a 'tendency to retreat', to turn away from the busy, practical, workaday world towards the secluded, the fanciful, the dreamlike, and to be much concerned with the past, either with the personal past of individual characters or with earlier periods of London's turbulent history.[10]

This regression to the past showed itself also in Dickens's ideas for the new periodical's illustrations. Browne would continue as his illustrator-in-chief but Dickens also approached his friends George Cattermole and Daniel Maclise, both chiefly celebrated as history painters, to work alongside Browne. Cattermole, who had illustrated both Scott and Bulwer Lytton, was 'England's foremost painter of scenes commemorating bygone times'. He had married a distant relation of Dickens's and lived in an intensely antiquarian ambience at Clapham Rise where Dickens and Forster often visited him. Leonardo Cattermole recalled that his father's studio, where Dickens would brew punch expertly despite 'refractory lemons' squirting onto 'his floreate waistcoat', was full of old carved furniture, including an escritoire 'with hideous, gaping, "Old Curiosity Shop" faces on it', armour, tapestry and 'romantic appurtenances of ancient warfare'.[11]

Cattermole was, therefore, a highly desirable illustrator for the *Clock* as Dickens now conceived of it. Just how keenly Dickens wanted him is evident from the tone and phrasing of the nervously jocular, but also highly deferential,

letter he wrote to Cattermole on 13 January soliciting his help. He explained
that he had decided to go for 'wood-cuts dropped into the text' rather than
separate steel engravings such as had accompanied all his publications to date.
Not only would this be cheaper but it would also enable him to impart another
dimension to the text by having the cuts dropped into the text at places where
they would best complement the letterpress, something that would be facilitated by the large page size to be used. He asked Cattermole to name his own
terms and mentioned that he was also inviting Maclise to participate but, curiously, made no reference to Browne, the hard-working 'mere' illustrator, who,
in the event, was to supply nearly three-quarters of all the *Clock* illustrations
while Maclise would supply only one. Cattermole accepted Dickens's flattering
invitation and his first illustration, Master Humphrey's 'old quaint room with
antique Elizabethian [*sic*] furniture, and in the chimney-corner an extraordinary old clock', Dickens pronounced '*most famous*', even though Cattermole
had not placed the clock where the text specifies. He continued to profess
himself thoroughly delighted with, and grateful for, Cattermole's contributions
throughout the run of the *Clock*. He himself responded eagerly to the challenge
of this new way of illustrating his work, giving Cattermole and Samuel Williams
(and, presumably, Browne, though we have no documentary evidence in this
case since he destroyed his letters from Dickens) 'full, detailed and enthusiastic
instructions for the cuts', and taking great pains over the precise placing of them
in his text.[12]

By 28 February, with just over a month to go before publication day,
Dickens had written the first three weekly numbers of *Master Humphrey's
Clock*. The advertisement for the new periodical in *Sketches of Young Couples*
expresses very clearly his hopes regarding the relationship that might develop
between himself and the *Clock*'s readers, hopes already adumbrated, as we have
seen, in his Preface to *Nickleby*:

> *Master Humphrey* hopes (and is almost tempted to believe) that all degrees of
> readers . . . may find something agreeable in the face of the old clock. That
> when they have made its acquaintance its voice may sound cheerfully in their
> ears, and be suggestive of none but pleasant thoughts. That they may come
> to have favourite and familiar associations connected with its name, and to
> look for it as a welcome friend.
>
> From week to week, then, Master Humphrey will set his clock, trusting
> that while it counts the hours, it will sometimes cheat them of all their
> heaviness, and that while it marks the tread of Time, it will scatter a few slight
> flowers on the Old Mower's Path. . . .

Boz, smart and satirical, frequently boisterous and sometimes sensational, is, it
seems, to metamorphose into a quite different, much gentler, authorial persona

(a modern reader might be tempted to add 'more soft-headed'). The point is that Dickens does not just want to be popular, he wants to be the beloved friend, pleasant and comforting, of every individual among his hordes of readers, his weekly visit being eagerly anticipated by (to quote the advertisement again) 'all degrees of readers, young or old, rich or poor, sad or merry, easy of amusement or difficult to entertain'. As to what the *Clock*'s contents will actually consist of no clue is offered, apart from the swarm of bizarre, or picturesquely historical, little figures that Dickens is shown releasing from the innards of the clock in Browne's illustration for the prospectus. The only recognisable figure is the incongruous one of Mr Pickwick, whose reintroduction, as we have seen, had been part of Dickens's plan from the beginning.

15 Illustration for prospectus advertising *Master Humphrey's Clock* by H. K. Browne ('Phiz')

In writing his first three weekly issues Dickens concentrated on building up the character and filling in the history of Master Humphrey, who is to conduct the journal – 'It is my intention constantly to address my readers from the chimney-corner,' he announces at the beginning of the second weekly issue, *Clock* 2. Humphrey himself is, he tells us, 'a mis-shapen, deformed, old man', reclusive but lovingly disposed towards his fellow human beings, especially children. His relationship with his creator is quite a complex one. Like Humphrey, Dickens is strong on benevolence but, unlike Humphrey, he is young and positively pulsating with social and philanthropic as well as creative energy – anything but a recluse, in fact. Like Humphrey again, he has his little club of intimates but its leading members are Forster and Maclise, two lively young high-achievers like himself, whereas the members of Humphrey's are quiet-going, older men who, like Humphrey himself, have been somehow defeated or incurably wounded by life, and have subsequently retreated from the real world into one of imagination and midnight story-telling. As a child Humphrey used often to dream of the terrible moment when he discovered that his deformity set him apart from other children, adding 'and now my heart aches for that child as if I had never been he, when I think how often he awoke from some fairy change to his old form, and sobbed himself to sleep again' (*Clock* 1). He also remembers how keenly his mother had felt 'for her poor crippled boy' – very unlike the attitude of Elizabeth Dickens, as recalled by Dickens, after her bright schoolboy son had been transformed into a little labourer in a blacking factory.

Dickens's feelings about having had his education broken off when he was sent to work in Warren's may also be reflected in the history of one of Humphrey's companions, Jack Redburn, who was betrayed as a child, having been 'reared in the expectation of a fortune he has never inherited' (*Clock* 3). Unlike Dickens, however, Redburn has conspicuously failed to make his way in the world. He is 'something of a musician, something of an author, something of an actor . . .' but has been unable to concentrate his energies in one direction as his creator so formidably did. It is as though Dickens is imagining the sort of man he might have become had he not been possessed of that strongly-focused 'earnestness' by which he set such store. Redburn is, however, endowed with one very well-known idiosyncrasy of his author's (well known in Dickens's domestic circle, at least): a compulsion to re-arrange the furniture in any room of his inhabiting. Just a week or so after he had introduced Redburn into the *Clock*, for example, we find Dickens joking about his obsessive behaviour in a letter to Catherine from Bath on 1 March: 'Of course I *arranged* both the room and my luggage before going to bed, and had everything very tidy.'

At the end of February Dickens went with Forster on a four-day visit to Landor in Bath and it was in that city, always seen by him as being populated with ancient grotesques, that he first conceived a poetic idea for a story to be told by Master Humphrey about an innocent, beautiful little girl who asks him to help her find her way home on one of his nocturnal wanderings in the streets of London (like Dickens again, Humphrey is much addicted to night walks). Once again, the image, hugely powerful and resonant for him, of a beautiful, vulnerable child wandering in the dark city seized his imagination as it had done in the case of *Oliver*. This image can only have been intensified by what he had continued to witness since the days when he himself was such a child, those terrible sights involving children about which he wrote to his fellow-novelist Catherine Gore on 31 January 1841: 'I . . . see in London whenever I walk alone into its byeways at night, as I often do, such miseries and horrors among these little creatures – such an impossibility of their growing up to be good or happy – that these aristocratic dolls [referring to pictures of children of the nobility] do turn me sick.' Nell, the child Humphrey encounters, does have a home to go to but with its 'old dark murky rooms' full of 'lumber and decay and ugly age' it proves to be nearly as grim and threatening as the London streets themselves. It was surely thoughts of Cattermole's gloomily picturesque studio, as well as the similar interior of Landor's house, that helped to inspire in Dickens the idea of Nell's home being an old curiosity shop, thus hitting upon what became a master-image or *leitmotif* for the full-length novel that was soon to take over the whole Master Humphrey project and prove to be crucial in the development of Dickens's art.[13]

Back in London, Dickens's first concern was to rearrange the contents of *Clock* I–3 to achieve more effective contrasts between Humphrey's musings and the sensational tales he retrieves from the bowels of his ancient clock. One of these tales, 'A Confession Found in a Prison in the Time of Charles the Second', revisits that most compelling theme for Dickens, a criminal's last night in the condemned cell (thirty years later, the climax of his last, unfinished, novel, *Edwin Drood* was intended to be just such a scene). This tale, like most of the others, was set back in Tudor or Stuart times. But the story he had conceived in Bath, about Humphrey's mysterious night-time encounter with Nell in the city, would have a greater immediacy for readers because of its contemporary setting and would greatly help in establishing Humphrey as a character. Dickens planned to feature it in *Clock* 4, which would be an important number in that it would complete the magazine's first monthly number and would be just the place to introduce a new interest. The tale's general heading, 'Personal Adventures of Master Humphrey', implied a series of which this story with its individual title, 'The Old Curiosity Shop', strikingly printed in Gothic type, was to be the first. The only other item in *Clock* 4 was also a direct result of Dickens's Bath visit and was doubtless intended to contrast with Humphrey's tale of dark London mysteries. It is a superb comic letter, almost as good as Fanny Squeers's, sent to Humphrey from Bath by a lady signing herself 'Belinda'. She has recognised, in Browne's sketch for *Clock* 2 of the 'devilish gentlemanly fellow' who proposes himself as a member of Humphrey's little club, a faithless former beau ('that cane dangling as I have seen it dangle from his hands I know not how oft – those legs that have glided through my nightly dreams and never stopped to speak . . .') and implores Humphrey to divulge his address.

We do not know exactly when Dickens wrote *Clock* 4 but we do know that he and his publishers had concluded weeks before the first number appeared (and so maybe before he had even conceived of Master Humphrey's 'Personal Adventure') that he was going to have to write the whole of the *Clock* himself, as he told Beard on 22 March. It is, of course, sufficiently ironic that as a result of his seeking to ease the strain of having to produce 18,816–19,584 words per calendar month, as for *Pickwick* or *Nickleby*, Dickens should now end up having, for the next nineteen months, to produce between 26,800 and 33,376 in the same time! But the whole concept and atmosphere of the *Clock*, even before the introduction of Little Nell, is so idiosyncratic, so highly personal to Dickens himself, that he must have realised quite soon that it would be very difficult, if not impossible, to accommodate literary collaborators, as opposed to illustrators, on such a project.[14]

The first weekly number appeared on 4 April and sold, as we have seen, a phenomenal seventy thousand copies. Forster carried the joyful news to Dickens and Catherine in Birmingham where they had gone, consistent with the superstitious custom that Dickens had established for himself that he should always be out of London on the day any new periodical work of his began publication. Alfred Dickens, studying engineering in Tamworth, joined the party and, elated by the tremendous success of the *Clock* ('What will the wiseacres say to the success of weekly issues *now*?', crowed Dickens to Hall of Chapman and Hall) they prolonged their jaunt so long they ran out of money. Alfred had to be sent to pawn Dickens's and Forster's gold watches to pay their expenses.[15]

Dickens's elation was very short-lived, however, since sales quickly dropped when purchasers found the *Clock* was not a new full-length story by Dickens but a strange miscellany of tales within tales with a reclusive old cripple for its central figure. Some reviewers were harsh. Noticing the first two weekly issues, the *Monthly Review* critic wrote in May, 'How Dickens, with his talents and experience, could have suffered such a *thing* to go forth under the sanction of his name, is to us a matter of unfeigned marvel.' And five numbers had appeared, including Humphrey's 'Old Curiosity Shop' adventure and the reintroduction of Mr Pickwick in *Clock* 5, when Thackeray reported to his mother, 'Dickens is sadly flat, with his Old Clock: but still sells 50000.'[16]

Dickens deftly rewrote the publication history of *The Old Curiosity Shop* in his preface to the Cheap Edition of the novel (1848). 'The first chapter of this tale', he wrote, had appeared in *Clock* 4 'when I had already been made uneasy by the desultory character of that work [i.e., the *Clock*] and when, I believe, my readers had thoroughly participated in the feeling.' Master Humphrey's adventure was not, in fact, announced as the 'first chapter' of anything, and even the phrase 'and

16 Publication day, *Master Humphrey's Clock*: one of the sketches done by the fifteen-year-old Richard Doyle to illustrate his journal for 1840: 'It was just six and all the men and boys from the booksellers were just rushing out with their bundles'

to which I shall recur at intervals', following 'An adventure which I am about to relate', was added as an afterthought. In the 1848 preface Dickens wrote, 'The commencement of a story [meaning a long story] was a great satisfaction to me.' This is, I think, both true and misleading. It is misleading in that he clearly had no intention of beginning a long story when relating Humphrey's encounter with Nell. However, once the central idea for the story, the contrast between the beautiful child and her grotesque surroundings, had gripped his imagination, and the need had simultaneously arisen of somehow reversing the decline in *Clock* sales, we may well believe that he did indeed find artistic satisfaction in developing this idea. Thus, as Forster writes,

> [there] was taking gradual form, with less consciousness of design on his own part than I can remember in any other instance throughout his career, a story which was to add largely to his popularity, more than any of his other works to make the bond between himself and his readers one of personal attachment, and very widely to increase the sense entertained of his powers as a pathetic as well as a humorous writer.

Dickens himself was well aware of the last-named fact and referred to it in the 1848 preface when he wrote of the story, 'The many friends it has won me and the many hearts it has turned to me when they have been full of private sorrow, invest it with an interest, in my mind, which is not a public one, and the rightful place of which appears to be "a more removed ground".[17]

Forster tells us that it was after Dickens had written half a dozen chapters of *The Old Curiosity Shop,* thus after the publication of *Clock* 10 or 11 (30 May or 6 June), that he decided to run the story on for four whole weekly issues 'to give it a fair chance'. In fact, the story ran on for the next thirty-five weekly issues. Dickens had to disembarrass himself of Humphrey's first-person narration, which he did, awkwardly enough, at the end of the third chapter in *Clock* 8 (23 May 1840). Then, having brought the endlessly fascinating and entertaining characters of Quilp and Dick Swiveller fairly into play, he started Nell and Grandfather on their wanderings, and established the dynamic rhythm of alternating between a sequence of Quilp or Swiveller-centred chapters set in London and a sequence of Nell-centred ones set outside London. Sales of the *Clock* soared until by the end of *The Old Curiosity Shop*'s serialisation, its circulation touched the staggering figure of 100,000.[18]

This being the first of Dickens's novels for which the complete manuscript survives (together with corrected galley-proofs for just under half of the chapters) we can now get closer than ever before to observing him actually at work – we can, as it were, peer over his very shoulder. As we might expect in this case, when he is for the first time writing in short weekly instalments, Dickens complains of not having 'room to turn' and of having to 'cramp most dreadfully'. We see that he frequently misjudged length, quite often over-writing and having to cancel substantial passages in proof. Less often, he actually under-wrote and had to supply more text at proof stage. His most substantial cuts are, with one exception, not plot-related but are passages either of free-wheeling comedy or of social criticism. The one exception is the passage towards the end of the story in which Sally Brass disconcertingly reveals that she is the mother of the Marchioness and Quilp the father.[19]

Something else shown by the corrected proofs is the extent of Forster's involvement in the work. He was often authorised to make cuts or alterations at his own discretion and Dickens constantly discussed his characters and the story's development with him. He was delighted, for example, that Forster at once recognised the great potential of Dick Swiveller's character, and confided, 'I *mean* to make much of him'. And it was Forster whose '*valued suggestion*', as Dickens called it, first made him recognise – probably in early July when he was writing *Clock* 20 (*Shop,* chs 25 and 26) – that the whole sense of the story as it was developing pointed inexorably towards its ending with Nell's death.[20]

Once Dickens had finally decided the *Shop* was to occupy most, if not all, of the weekly issues (that he took a little while to come to this decision is suggested by the introduction of Tony Weller in *Clock* 11 [13 June]), he decided to move his household to Broadstairs for a month so that he could concentrate uninterruptedly on the work. 'With that tremendous energy which characterises the proceedings of this establishment,' he told Beard on 1 June, 'we thought of coming here one day last week, and accordingly came this very morning.' He proceeded to issue pressing invitations, as was his wont, to Beard and other close friends to come and visit but was nevertheless characteristically self-disciplined about getting his writing done on time. Allowing himself Mondays off, 'in common with other vagabonds', as he told Edward Chapman's brother George, he followed a routine of rising at 7, getting to his desk by 8.30 and working there till 2 p.m. or later. 'It is now four o'clock and I have been at work since half-past eight', he told Forster on 17 June, adding, 'I have really dried myself up into a condition, which would almost justify me in pitching off the cliff, head first – but I must get richer before I indulge in a crowning luxury.' He had, he said, pleased himself greatly in the writing of chapter 15 of the *Shop*, as well he might have done since it is a superlative description, packed with effective visual detail, of Nell and Grandfather slowly making their way out of London: 'If I had read it as anybody else's writing,' Dickens confided to Forster, 'I think I should have been very much struck.'[21]

Before returning to London Dickens found time to exercise his talent for a form of writing different from fiction or straight journalism, a form that he was quite often to use for his public-discourse interventions, the 'Letter to the Editor'. Under a pseudonym he wrote two letters to *The Morning Chronicle*, published 23 and 29 June, deploring barristers' abuse of the rules when cross-examining witnesses – the very thing he had satirised in *Pickwick*. The trial that provoked these letters was that of a Swiss valet François Courvoisier who had cut the throat of his master, Lord William Russell, Lord John Russell's uncle, as the elderly peer lay in his bed. This case naturally created a huge sensation and we may be sure that Dickens, given his deep fascination with the subjects of murder and capital punishment, would have eagerly followed the newspaper reports. He may also have been startled by the way in which life seemed to be imitating his own (as yet unpublished) art. Both the nature and the circumstances of the murder seemed uncannily to echo those of Reuben Haredale's murder recounted in the first chapter of *Barnaby Rudge*, which Dickens had written the previous year. Courvoisier was sentenced to be hanged on 6 July. On the eve of the execution Dickens impulsively decided to go to Newgate to witness the preparations for the hanging. He took Burnett and Maclise with him and ended by hiring a room opposite the gallows to view the actual hanging. He was both appalled and fascinated by the gross licentiousness and the brutal indifference to the suffering of the condemned man exhibited by the enormous and unruly crowd that had assembled (Dickens was astonished suddenly to spot Thackeray crushed in among the mob of ruffians, prostitutes and pickpockets), and he vividly recalled the scene in another of his Letters to *The Morning Chronicle* six years later. Undoubtedly he was also remembering this experience, which Burnett compared to 'a ghastly night in Hades with demons', when he came to depict the scenes of rioting mobs and Hugh's execution in *Barnaby Rudge* the following year.[22]

On 2 July Dickens signed, as we have seen, the deed that finally released him from the last of his 'Bentleian bonds'. Another agreement was then drawn up with Chapman and Hall under which he was within the next five years to write *Barnaby Rudge* for them in ten parts, each part being equivalent to a monthly number of *Pickwick* or *Nickleby*. The publishers would hold the exclusive copyright of the work for six months after the completion of its publication, and they would be free to issue it in fifteen, rather than ten, monthly numbers. Under this arrangement Dickens would receive £3,000, the £2,250 advanced to him to pay off Bentley being included in this sum. Throughout all these negotiations Dickens relied on Forster's good counsel and practical help and gave him, as a token of his great gratitude, an elegant claret jug accompanied by a letter expressive of the warmest friendship. Further adjustments were made in November when it was mutually agreed that *Barnaby Rudge* was immediately to follow *The Old Curiosity Shop* in *Master Humphrey's Clock*. And thus this long-planned historical novel, having been originally projected as Dickens's first dignified 'three-decker', finally saw the light of day in the humble form of serialisation in a magazine initially designed as a cheap weekly miscellany.[23]

Meanwhile, the *Clock* was not turning out to be quite the gold-mine Dickens had anticipated. The number of illustrations had been severely cut back after the first few issues, steadying at two per issue, but this still meant eight cuts had to be produced every month (as against only two, admittedly more expensive *pro rata*, steel engravings for *Pickwick* or *Nickleby*), and this contributed largely to the production costs that ate so deeply into the profits. And he needed money. He was overdrawn at Coutts by £27 2s at midsummer 1840 and over the next year or so had to borrow from his publishers sums amounting to £769.9.5. These were, of course, additional to the money they had advanced him to pay off Bentley so that he was, by 31 July 1841, owing them a mortifying total of £3,019.9.5. This caused some difficulty when the firm's solicitor, Chapman's brother William, began tactlessly to agitate about proper legal security. Dickens, 'disgusted . . . and thoroughly sick at heart', signed a bond drawn up by William. It was, he bitterly commented, 'the least offensive way of putting me in double irons'.[24]

The life-style that by 1840 Dickens had established for himself and his family in Devonshire Terrace certainly required the support of a rising income. The house had been lavishly refurbished when the Dickenses moved in and the census return for 1841 shows that there were no fewer than five live-in servants as well as Dickens's groom Topping, who lived out. There was much entertaining, occasionally on quite a grand scale, as later censoriously noted by Jane Carlyle: 'Such getting up of the steam is unbecoming to a literary man who *ought* to have his basis elsewhere than on what the old Annandale woman called "Ornament and Grander" '. The Dickenses also dined out a good deal and generally 'moved in society', as the phrase went. Sometimes, indeed, they moved in very high society. Dickens had already had to don court dress on at least one occasion before July 1840. Then for several weeks a year the family moved into lodgings suitable to their status at Broadstairs. Dickens's parents and his youngest brother Augustus were also a continual drain on his purse (no doubt he also helped to subsidise both Alfred and Fred from time to time), especially as John Dickens continued shamelessly to borrow money on the strength of Charles's name and fame. At the end of July Dickens and Catherine paid a flying visit to the 'perfect little doll's house' in Alphington, after receipt of an apparently reproachful letter from John. 'They *seem* perfectly contented and happy,' he reported to Forster, somewhat wistfully.[25]

All the time Dickens had to keep 'winding his Clock': 'Mr Shandy's Clock was nothing to mine,' he wrote to Landor on 26 July, adding, 'I am more bound down by this Humphrey than I have ever been yet – Nickleby was nothing to it, nor Pickwick, nor Oliver – it demands my constant attention.' It is all the more astonishing, therefore, to find him writing in this same month to the Home Secretary, Lord Normanby, offering to write 'a strong and vivid description of the terrors of [the penal settlement of] Norfolk Island and such-like places, told in a homely Narrative with a great appearance of truth and reality'. Such a narrative would, he believed, if placed '*on the pillow of every prisoner in England*', have a strongly deterrent effect in making criminals think twice before committing such serious crimes as might render them liable to transportation. At present this prospect was no deterrent, thanks to newspaper tales of men transported many years ago who had since realised great fortunes in Australia – Dickens himself would remember such reports a quarter-century later when he came to write *Great Expectations*. He did not, he told Lord Normanby, expect any payment for the pamphlet but offered it as 'a humble tribute of my respect for the liberal and wise Government under which the people live at present'. His offer was not taken up. We are left uncertain which aspect of this episode to wonder at most, Dickens's readiness to add such a *pro bono* item to his already tremendous work-load, his apparently seeing no contradiction between the idea of 'a liberal and wise Government' and the toleration of such a hell-hole as Norfolk Island, or his supreme confidence in the power of his writing to sway hearts and minds – a confidence buoyed up, no doubt, by the fervour of the ongoing public response to his current serial.[26]

By late August Dickens had been working only on the *Shop* for nearly three months. Four successive weekly issues having been devoted to Nell (chs 25–32), it was time to turn back to the London of Quilp and Swiveller and this is achieved by a notably clumsy transition at the start of ch. 33. One of Dickens's last activities before leaving London, with his family, for Broadstairs again on 30 August, was to go searching in a Whitechapel street, Bevis Marks, for a suitable-seeming house for Sampson Brass, to form the setting for *Clock* 24.

Then, during the Dickens family's five-week residence in Broadstairs, he began drawing various narrative threads together as he looked towards the end of the story – also, more immediately, towards the publication of the *Clock*'s first half-yearly volume, announced for publication 'early in October' in *Clock* 24 and 25.

At Broadstairs there was the customary stream of visitors, both family and friends. Dickens was now beginning to suffer from some of the inconveniences of celebrity, such as gawping fellow holiday-makers, begging-letter writers, and gossip about his private life. A persistent rumour that he had gone mad so vexed him that he seized the chance to ridicule it in his preface to the *Clock*'s first half-yearly volume: 'It may be some consolation to the well-disposed ladies or gentlemen who, in the interval between the conclusion of his last work and the commencement of this, originated a report that he had gone raving mad, to know that it spread as rapidly as could be desired. . . .' He stuck rigidly to his writing routine but, away from his desk, delighted in behaving like a sort of super-dynamic Master of the Revels, ably supported by Fred. He took the lead in organising games, charades, singing comic songs, expeditions to Pegwell Bay to feast on prawns and bottled stout, and suchlike diversions. He also flirted preposterously with a dazzled twenty-year-old called Eleanor Emma Picken and her somewhat older friend Milly. Eleanor was holidaying at Broadstairs with the family of Charles Smithson, Mitton's partner. She later recalled Dickens calling Milly his 'charmer' and 'the beloved of his soul' and herself his 'fair enslaver', inviting her to 'tread a saraband' with him, and so on, and how 'Mrs Charles Dickens entered into the fun with great gusto and good humour' (Catherine was again pregnant so perhaps not over-keen on treading sarabands herself). Eleanor, who was not well off, also remembered Dickens on one occasion, when she was wearing her only silk dress, rushing her down to a pole at the end of the jetty and holding her fast there as the tide was coming in. As she struggled to free herself he told her to think of the next day's report in the *Times* 'wherein will be vividly described the pathetic fate of the lovely E[mma] P[icken], drowned by Dickens in a fit of dementia!' adding, 'Don't struggle, poor little bird! You are powerless in the claws of such a kite as this child.' Dickens seems, in fact, to have delighted in acting out versions of Dick Swiveller and Quilp in his own person, as well as writing about them, during this month when his story was so much concentrated on these partic-ular characters. But there were other times when his demeanour and his wonderful eyes flashing like 'danger-lamps' made it clear to Emma and Milly that he was intensely preoccupied with (they presumed) 'the throes and agonies of bringing forth his conceptions' and definitely not to be accosted. Another much impressed young lady visitor, a friend of Catherine's, called Eliza Franklin seems, however, when visiting Devonshire Terrace, to have been allowed to watch Dickens while he was writing and observe the 'extraordinary' varied expressions passing over his countenance.[27]

The first half-yearly volume of the *Clock* appeared in October with a dedication to old Samuel Rogers, widely regarded as a leading poetical exponent of sensibility since the publication of his *Pleasures of Memory* in 1792. He was, therefore, a writer whom Dickens would have been keen to associate publicly with the *Shop*, quite apart from any desire he may have had to flatter a distinguished senior literary figure with whom he was on friendly terms. His description of Rogers's writings as 'replete with generous and earnest feeling', and of his personal life as 'one of active sympathy with the poorest and humblest of his kind' expresses Dickens's own ideals, and his readers would at this time have been further encouraged to see him in this light by his paean of praise for the 'household affections and loves' of the poor in the opening chapter of the new volume (*Clock* 27, ch. 38 of the *Shop*). His appeal to the nation's rulers to 'turn aside from the wide thoroughfares ... and strive to improve the wretched dwellings in bye-ways where only Poverty may walk' struck a chord that had been heard before in his writing. From now on it will become a dominant one in both his fiction and his journalism, contributing strongly towards giving him that unique public status as deeply compassionate champion of the poor, accorded to him alone among all the writers of the age.[28]

Dickens's urgent concern about what Carlyle famously called 'the Condition of England Question' manifested itself in chapters of the *Shop* written after he had returned to Devonshire Terrace in October. The newspapers were full of accounts of distress in the manufacturing districts and Dickens, remembering his journey along the Birmingham–Wolverhampton road of two years before, paints in chapter 45 of the *Shop* a Tartarean landscape populated by a desperate semi-savage population, bands of unemployed labourers, 'clustered by torchlight round their leaders, who told them in stern language of their wrongs' or rushing forth 'on errands of terror and destruction, to work no ruin so surely as their own'. The fascinated horror, as well as the fear, of self-defeating mob violence which will fuel Dickens's narrative of the Gordon Riots in *Barnaby Rudge* is already strongly present in this passage which refers to the so-called 'physical force' Chartists, whose violent exploits in Birmingham and Newport the previous year would have been fresh in everyone's mind. Nell overhears a woman upbraiding a magistrate for sentencing her son to transportation for theft though he has never been taught to know right from wrong, or indeed taught anything at all, because all schemes for national education remain stalled by sectarian disputes ('you gentlemen quarrelling among yourselves'). For Dickens, with his passionate belief in education and better social conditions as the sovereign remedies for crime among the lower orders, this was a shameful situation against which he never ceased to campaign.

The publication of the first volume of the *Clock* was celebrated with the now customary lavish dinner (held in Devonshire Terrace) on 21 October. By now Dickens's imagination was thoroughly seized with this extraordinary narrative, half dream-like and half in the Pickwickian/Nicklebeian mode, and during the winter of 1840/41 he wrote on with seeming ease. More and more, he must, consciously or unconsciously, have come to realise that the grand unifying theme of the story was the creative imagination itself, the telling of stories. The man in chapter 44 who tends the furnace reads stories in his fire (this was a scene, wrote Dickens to Forster, that 'would have been a good thing to have opened a new story with'), the Bachelor in chapter 54 loves to indulge in 'teeming fancies' with regard to the antiquities in his village church, and Dick Swiveller's improvisation of fantastic legends and magical transformations of reality is central to the tender comedy of his relationship with the little Marchioness. The original intention for *Master Humphrey's Clock* survives, in fact, but in an altered form. Dickens was much gratified by a lengthy *Athenaeum* review (7 Nov.) of the first volume of the *Clock* in which the writer, whom he soon learned to be the poet Thomas Hood, especially praised the depiction of Nell both in words by Dickens and in a woodcut by Samuel Williams (Dickens had asked Williams to alter his original 'very pretty drawing' for this scene to make more of a contrast between the child and her grim surroundings). Williams's illustration of Nell asleep in the Shop is, wrote Hood, 'like an Allegory of the peace and Innocence of Childhood in the midst of Violence, Superstition, and all the hateful or hurtful Passions of the world'. On Dickens himself Hood commented:

> . . . no writer's personal character seems more identified with his writings than that of Boz. We invariably rise from the perusal of his volumes in better humour with the world; for he gives us a cheerful view of human nature, and paints good people with a relish that proves he has himself a belief in, and sympathy with, their goodness.

Dickens wrote to thank Hood, with whom he was at this time only slightly acquainted, for his review, and must have been still more gratified when Hood in his reply likened him to his beloved Goldsmith: '. . . books which put us in a better humour with the world in general must naturally incline us towards the Author in particular. (So we love Goldsmith for his Vicar of Wakefield).'[29]

Clock 34 and *Clock* 35 (chs 52–55 of the *Shop*) appeared on 28 November and were full of intimations of Nell's mortality, reinforced by Maclise's dramatically-composed illustration on the last page of *Clock* 35, his single contribution to the periodical. Dickens's readers were not slow to take the hint and already by 24 November he found himself, as he reported to Chapman and Hall, 'inundated with imploring letters recommending poor little Nell to mercy. – Six yesterday, and four today (it's not 12 o'Clock yet) already!' He made them wait seven long weeks before discovering whether their pleas had been of any avail while he, knowing that Nell had indeed to die, prepared himself for what he foresaw would be the most harrowing scene he had yet attempted to write, more harrowing even than the murder of Nancy. In staging Nell's death, moreover, he would be challenging comparison with one of the most sublime scenes of Shakespearean tragedy, the death of Cordelia. To prepare for it, the novel's decks had to be cleared of all other interest and from *Clock* 36 to *Clock* 42 (chs 56–68 of the *Shop*) Dickens, briefly distracted by efforts to ensure that a dramatic version of the *Shop* about to be staged by Yates at the Adelphi should not be too much of a travesty, concentrated on the dénouements of the plot centred on Quilp and the Brasses and the related one centred on Dick Swiveller and the Marchioness. To help him plan the story to the end, he sketched out in mid-December number-plans for *Clock* 42–43 and half of *Clock* 44 (chs 66–71), the first time, as far as we know, that he had done such a thing. No such number-plans, if they ever existed, have survived for the next novel *Barnaby Rudge* but Dickens used them for almost all his novels thereafter. He also drew up, either then or a week or two later, a memorandum to himself about the Single Gentleman's identity and personal history as well as a check-list of all the main characters to be used for reference when composing the last chapter with its conventional round-up of characters giving their after-histories.[30]

The autumn and winter of 1840/41 must have been an exhilarating time for Dickens. The popular success of the *Shop* was far outstripping that of all his previous work. Tens of thousands of eager purchasers could hardly wait to get hold of the next instalment of his story, and he took the opportunity, speaking at the Southwark Literary and Scientific Institution on 2 December, publicly to celebrate the fact that writers no longer needed to truckle to those whose 'only title to eminence' derived from their ancestors' achievements. Now they could look instead to the patronage of the kind of educated and enlightened public that such places as the Southwark Institution were helping to foster: 'That huckstering, peddling, pandering to patronage for the sale of a book, the offspring of intellect and genius, would not now remain a stain upon their most brilliant productions.' Significantly, when speaking of poets who might have been better appreciated earlier if literature had not been so much in thrall to aristocracy, he invoked the name of Wordsworth, whose spirit can be felt hovering throughout *The Old Curiosity Shop*.[31]

It was to be a basic principle of Dickens's professional life that, in contrast to the patronage system that obtained in the literary world of the previous century, in the nineteenth-century struggling writers, especially struggling young writers, should be helped and encouraged by their successful colleagues. He devoted a remarkable amount of time to answering letters soliciting help that he constantly received from would-be writers. Included in Pilgrim II (covering 1840–41), for example, are six letters written to Robert Horrell, a young solicitor's clerk in Exeter with poetic aspirations. Undoubtedly, there were sheaves of similar letters that have not come down to us, and it is just amazing that Dickens, given the enormous pressures of his own writing schedule, should have made time to send such detailed replies to such correspondents, including much sensitive criticism of their work and some excellent practical advice as, for example, about the best way to submit their work to magazine editors. On 25 November he sent Horrell a long constructive critique of his poems, the sort of thing that students in creative writing courses today would give their eye teeth for. Another aspect of Dickens's 'standing by his order', as he would have put it, was his willingness to relieve less successful fellow-writers whenever he could. 'I do verily think', wrote Eliza Franklin in her letter already cited, '[Dickens] the most noble minded dear man. His constant Charity is Giving away things to distressed authors.' Obviously, there was a limit to what he could do as an individual, as he explained to one George Fletcher on 2 November 1841: 'if I were the richest man in England, I should have to disappoint, almost as often as I helped.' Later on, as we shall see, he was constantly projecting, or involving himself in, elaborate fund-raising schemes designed to benefit impoverished writers, whether individually or collectively.

John Overs the literary cabinet-maker was a special case. Thirty-two years old in 1840, he was married with five children and suffering from tuberculosis. He would soon be no longer able to ply his trade, which involved his standing for up to twelve hours a day. He sought to make some small financial provision for his family through writing, in his scanty leisure time, poems, sketches and historical tales for the magazines and had submitted some poems to *Bentley's* just as Dickens was relinquishing the editorship. They caught Dickens's interest and, finding that Overs was 'none of your maudlin gentry who think themselves neglected geniuses, but a straightforward hardworking, earnest man – above his station in nothing but having read and remembered a great many books', he determined to help him, not only by reading and criticising his writings, often in personal interviews, but also by giving him money occasionally, arranging for Elliotson to examine him, and finding him work (but only as an odd-job man, somewhat to Overs's chagrin) under Macready at Drury Lane. He also loaned him books, among them a copy of *Chartism* which Overs returned with a long and detailed critique of Carlyle's polemical pamphlet from the point of view of a thoughtful and articulate working man. Dickens seems to have paid only perfunctory attention to this response. As long as Overs knew his place and did not presume to anything approaching equality with gentlemen (he received a stinging reproof from Dickens on 23 November when he dared to complain about Macready), Dickens was even by his own standards quite exceptionally kind, encouraging and practically helpful to him. He was particularly appreciative of this (clearly far from revolutionary) working-man's plan to make a carving for him of what John Dickens claimed to be the Dickens family crest (why on earth, one wonders, did Dickens tell Overs about this family pretension to gentility?).[32]

As he looked forward to Christmas and New Year 'charades and other frolics' Dickens was simultaneously, as he told Cattermole when sending him instructions for the last *Shop* illustrations, breaking his heart over the story and could hardly bear to finish it. He had to work himself into a certain state of mind for writing the end of the story by deliberately reviving painful memories of Mary Hogarth's death. 'Old wounds bleed afresh when I only think of the way of doing it,' he told Forster. 'Dear Mary died yesterday, when I think of this sad story.' Then follows the remarkable comment that he would go nowhere till the writing was finished: 'I am afraid of disturbing the state I have been trying to get into, and having to fetch it all back again.' He finally finished the book at 4 a.m. on Sunday 17 January and was afterwards 'very melancholy to think that all these people are lost to me for ever'. Master Humphrey echoes this sentiment in *Clock* 45 (6 Feb. 1841), at the beginning of the bridging-passage needed to introduce *Barnaby Rudge* and also to provide matter for the 'four mortal pages' of the number that remained to be filled after the concluding chapter of the *Shop*. Master Humphrey's speculations about Sir Christopher Wren's feelings when viewing his completed master-piece, St Paul's Cathedral, seem to echo Dickens's own at this point of completing the *Shop*: 'I imagined him far more melancholy than proud, and looking with regret upon his labour done.'[33]

A reference to the great bell of St Paul's striking the midnight hour gives a thrilling hint about the nature of the new story that Humphrey and his circle are about to read. Opened to such music as this, says Humphrey, it ought to be a tale 'where London's face by night is darkly seen . . .'. This leads Dickens on to what one critic has called 'a panoramic vision of the sleeping city, in an essay poised inchoately between investigative journalism, imaginative sketch and allegory'. Besides introducing the new story Dickens is also concerned in this Master Humphrey section to establish some continuity between the beginning of the *Shop* narrative with its original title 'Personal Adventures of Master Humphrey' and its ending. Hence Humphrey's wildly unconvincing claim that he himself was the Single Gentleman in the *Shop*, and his strong hint that another member of the club has a personal involvement in the new story to begin in the next issue.[34]

For Dickens the next eight months were dominated by the weekly serialisation of *Barnaby Rudge* in the *Clock*. This 'Tale of the Riots of 'Eighty' had now been in his mind for five years, and the surmise that it was the historical fact of the rioters' tearing down of Newgate that had first gripped his imagination is surely right. This fact retained so strong a hold upon it that he never gave up the idea of writing this story despite all the difficulties with publishers it had caused him. Fictionalising this event would also allow him to challenge explicit comparison with Scott, as readers would inevitably be put in mind of the famous description of the Porteous riot in *The Heart of Midlothian*. His first plan, to take for his hero Gabriel Varden, a London locksmith, was changed within two years, and a mentally afflicted youth named Barnaby Rudge became the central figure. Here again, readers would be likely to be reminded of Davie Gellatley in Scott's *Waverley* as well as of Madge Wildfire in *Heart of Midlothian*. Echoes of 'The Idiot Boy' and other poems by Wordsworth, whose presence had already been felt in the *Shop*, would further emphasise the distinguished literary antecedents of his new work.[35]

As we have noted, Dickens had made an abortive start on writing *Barnaby* two years earlier when it was scheduled to begin appearing in monthly instalments in *Bentley's*. Presumably, the main outlines of the plot in this his first non-improvised full-length narrative, and the way in which he would involve his fictional characters in the historical events to be depicted in the work's grand climactic set piece, were already in his mind, and he had perhaps even begun the detailed research into contemporary accounts that lies behind his description of the Gordon Riots. Now, however, he had to readjust his plans so as to fit the story's serialisation into the same brief instalments as those used for the *Shop*, and this was on top of the basic difficulty of beginning a new story with 'all [his] thoughts and interest hanging about the old one'. To complicate matters further, Catherine's pregnancy was making her 'exceedingly unwell', and Dickens had not, he wrote to Ainsworth on 25 January, 'been to bed for eight and forty hours'. What he rather strangely refers to as 'this business of Kate's' was still not over when he wrote to Cruikshank ten days later; his mind, he unfeelingly joked, was beginning to 'run very much on Joanna Southcote'. Once the baby had finally been born, on 8 February, Dickens reverted to a more sympathetic tone when writing about Catherine. She had had, he wrote to Mitton the same day, 'a very hard trial indeed, but thank God is thriving now, amazingly'. She seems, as usual, to have had no say in naming the child, however. Dickens was going to call him Edgar ('a good honest Saxon name, I think') but then decided to name him Walter Landor in honour of his friend. This dedication of his sons to famous writers, as though they were books, was a practice he followed with regard to all three of Walter's successors.[36]

Meanwhile, he had *Barnaby* to attend to. On 29 January he reported to Forster:

> I didn't stir out yesterday, but sat and *thought* all day; not writing a line; not so much as the cross of a t or dot of an i. I imaged forth a good deal of *Barnaby* by keeping my mind steadily upon him; and am happy to say I have gone to work this morning in good twig, strong hope and cheerful spirits. Last night I was unutterably and impossible-to-form-an-idea-of-ably miserable. . . .

He was not always so buoyant about the writing as this, and would often lament the constraints of the weekly instalments ('I want elbow-room terribly'). Nevertheless, he does not generally seem to have found the actual writing difficult, and produced what George Gissing considered to be 'taking it all in all, . . . perhaps the best written of his novels . . . in the sense of presenting the smoothest and closest strain of narrative'. Surviving letters reveal none of the agonising involved in writing the later chapters of the *Shop*. He had a number of characters like old John Willet, Mrs Varden and the gloriously spiteful Miss Miggs for whom he could easily write as much comic dialogue as might be needed, allowing himself to mark time with the plot whenever he needed a breather, so to speak. Above all, there was his second great animal character (Sikes's dog Bullseye in *Oliver* being the first), Grip the raven, whom Ruskin thought perfect, 'like all Dickens's animals'. Grip was closely based on two remarkable pet ravens that Dickens owned in succession during the writing of *Barnaby*, the first of which gave him a comic/pathetic idea of the sort that appealed strongly to his imagination: 'Barnaby being an idiot my notion is to have him always in company with a pet raven who is immeasurably more knowing than himself.' As with Mrs Varden or Miggs, he could, to use his own phrase, 'put in more relief' from Grip at any point in the writing – as he does, for example, in chapter 17 when he fills eight paragraphs with a description of the bird's response to the news that it was Barnaby's birthday.[37]

The writing of *Barnaby* went steadily on throughout the summer, which included the visit to Scotland (19 June to 18 July) shortly to be described. By the time he got to the Gordon Riots, he was comfortably ahead of the printers and enjoying himself immensely: 'I have just burnt into Newgate, and am going in the next number to tear the prisoners out by the hair of their heads', he wrote to Forster on 11 September and, a week later, 'I have let all the prisoners out of Newgate, burnt down Lord Mansfield's, and played the very devil. . . . I feel quite smoky when I am at work.' Hardly any corrected proofs survive but the evidence of the manuscript shows that there was a great deal of alteration at proof stage, much of it entrusted to Forster on whom Dickens particularly relied to cut out anything that was 'too strong'. Dickens confessed that it was difficult for him, in the actual writing, 'to judge what tells too much and what does not'.[38]

Barnaby carries on from *Oliver* the idea of the State as the criminally neglectful or brutally repressive parent of its poorest children, which was to become so prominent in all Dickens's social writings. It pervades his presentation of late eighteenth-century London in *Barnaby* and is embodied in the relationship between Mr Chester and his natural son Hugh (Chester is Dickens's version of Lord Chesterfield, whose *Letters . . . to his Son* (1774) he regarded as the epitome of eighteenth-century cynicism). It flares up in Hugh's scaffold speech in chapter 77 when he points to his innocent fellow-sufferer Barnaby's courage and love for him and cries out:

What else should teach me – born as I was born, and reared as I have been – to hope for mercy in this hardened, cruel, unrelenting place! Upon these

human shambles, I, who never raised this hand in prayer till now, call down
the wrath of God! On that black tree of which I am the ripened fruit, I do
invoke the curse of all its victims, past, and present, and to come. . . .

Hugh goes on to curse 'that man who, in his conscience, owns me for his son'
and it is a notable feature of *Barnaby* that Dickens seems to have deliberately
constructed it around a series of actual father/son relationships in which the
father is either tyrannically stupid like John Willett or downright evil like
Rudge or Chester. There is one good father in the novel, Gabriel Varden, but
he is shown as powerless to save his surrogate son, the vain and vicious
apprentice Sim Tappertit, from catastrophe.[39]
During the earlier part of 1841, when he was getting *Barnaby* under way,
Dickens's relations with his own father were under particular stress. On
18 February he was caused 'great grief and distress' by a letter from his acquaintance Thomas Latimer, editor of the Exeter-based *Western Times*, about money
John had borrowed from him: 'his making your note of hand payable at my
publishers', wrote Dickens to Latimer, 'was a moral outrage which words can
scarcely censure enough.' By 6 March he had become so exasperated that he
instructed Mitton to put an advertisement in all the daily newspapers to say he
would not be responsible for any debts other than those incurred by himself and
Catherine. He also instructed Mitton to tell John that, if he did not wish Dickens
to cast him off altogether, he must go and live abroad, taking Augustus with him,
also Elizabeth if she were willing to go (if not, John would have to allow her £40
a year out of his pension of £145.16.8). Dickens would pay for Augustus's
schooling and allow his father £20 a year. However, the irrepressible John, who
had described himself to Eleanor Picken in Broadstairs the previous year as
being 'like a cork – if he was pushed under water in one place, he always bobbed
"up to time" cheerfully in another, and felt none the worse for the dip', seems to
have weathered this particular storm without having to go into even more
remote exile. Meanwhile, Dickens perhaps found some relief for his feelings by
having the appalling Chester smoothly expatiate in chapter 12 of *Barnaby*
(published as *Clock* 52 on 27 March) on 'those amazingly fine feelings and those
natural obligations which must subsist between father and son' and how the
relationship between father and son 'is positively quite a holy kind of bond'.[40]
Dickens was by now more and more concerned to present himself as a
novelist rather than as 'the periodical essayist' of the *Nickleby* Preface. It is
Fielding's introduction to *Tom Jones*, not Mackenzie's observations in *The
Lounger*, that he invokes in the preface to the second half-yearly volume of
Master Humphrey, published in April, and he continually revises the history of
the genesis of *The Old Curiosity Shop* so as to disguise the improvisatory nature
of the early stages of the work. To Thomas Latimer, John Dickens's Exeter cred-
itor, he wrote on 13 March: 'It is curious that I have always fancied the Old

Curiosity Shop to be my XXX [i.e., his best work, a brewing metaphor], and that I never had the design and purpose of a story so distinctly marked in my mind, from its commencement. All its quietness arose out of a deliberate purpose; the notion being to stamp upon it from the first, the shadow of that early death . . .'. When the story was first issued on its own in one volume (15 Dec. 1841), it was reprinted from the *Master Humphrey* plates with all the *Humphrey* matter excised. This resulted in some blank pages which gave Dickens the opportunity to insert four new paragraphs in chapter 1 before the final paragraph. In them he echoes Hood's *Athenaeum* review when he describes Nell as seeming 'to exist in a kind of allegory', and generally to foreshadow the development of the story as it eventually got itself written. The effect of these deftly-inserted paragraphs is to present the *Shop* as a far more consciously and deliberately crafted work than the actual history of its writing shows it to have been.[41]

Earlier in 1841 Dickens had promulgated what was in effect a critical manifesto in his lengthy preface to the so-called 'Third edition' of *Oliver Twist*, published by Chapman and Hall on 15 May and printed from the unbound sheets of the novel they had enabled Dickens to buy from Bentley. As he was to do with the *Shop*, Dickens presents his second book as having been carefully planned from the beginning (and making it sound very like the *Shop* in its basic conception):

> . . . when I wished to show in little Oliver, the principle of Good surviving through every adverse circumstance, and triumphing at last; and when I considered among what companions I could try him best, having regard to that kind of men into whose hands he would most naturally fall; I bethought myself of those who figure in these volumes.

He is concerned now to distance *Oliver* both from Bentleian 'Mudfog' chronicles and from Ainsworthian 'Newgate novels', and to assert his own status as claimant to a place 'in the noblest range of English literature' (here he lists the great novelists of the previous century). He defends himself vigorously as a writer of realistic fiction, aiming to show life in the criminal underworld as it really is in all its 'squalid poverty' and perpetually overshadowed by 'the great, black, ghastly gallows'. Such remorseless realism, he maintains, serves a great moral purpose in the deterrent effect it must have on 'the young and ill-disposed' who may be seduced into a life of crime by romantic tales of high-waymen in 'crimson coats and ruffles' cantering on moonlit heaths or roistering in snug taverns. He makes clear, however, that his realism will stop short of reproducing the real-life language used by the characters he is depicting. Quite apart from its distastefulness to him personally and its unsuitability to 'the manners of the age', such reproduction is simply not needed to achieve the end he is seeking which is to show the life of a professional criminal as being 'of the most debased and vicious kind'. In a kind of coda to the preface the last two paragraphs are a vigorous rebuttal (or rather, a shouting down in capital letters) of Thackeray's critique of Nancy, but avoiding the use of Thackeray's name: 'It is useless to discuss whether the conduct and character of the girl seems natural or unnatural, probable or improbable, right or wrong. IT IS TRUE.'

While Dickens was working on the *Oliver* preface in early March he was also writing *Clock* 50 (*Barnaby* chs 8–9) and, once again, a connection shows itself between two disparate pieces of writing going on at the same time. In chapter 8 of *Barnaby* we follow the decidedly 'ill-disposed' Sim Tappertit (who wishes he had been born a corsair, a pirate or a 'gen-teel highwayman') into a squalid recess of the London underworld, 'reeking with stagnant odours', where he and his similarly ill-conditioned fellow-prentices seek to glamorise their nefarious activities with a tawdry masquerade in a tavern that is anything but 'snug' ('the floors were of sodden earth, the walls and roof of damp bare brick tapestried with the tracks of snails and slugs; the air was sickening, tainted, and offensive . . .'). Proclaiming in his *Oliver* preface that he will not, for the sake of refined and delicate readers, 'abate one hole in the Dodger's coat, or one scrap of curlpaper in the girl's dishevelled hair', Dickens is meanwhile taking care not to spare his readers a single disgusting detail in his elaborate description of Stagg's foul cellar.

In the early summer Dickens and Catherine travelled to Edinburgh for a public banquet in his honour on 25 June and for him to receive the Freedom of the City. The banquet at the Waterloo Hotel was a dazzling affair. Over two hundred and fifty people paid a guinea per ticket, Whigs and Tories mingling happily together on this occasion despite Edinburgh's reputation for fierce political divisions, and the ladies who, following custom, came in with Catherine after the banquet to listen to the speeches also numbered two hundred and fifty plus. Lord Jeffrey not being well enough to take the chair, the task fell to Professor John Wilson, famous for his gruff animadversions on literature and politics as 'Christopher North' in the strongly Tory *Blackwood's Magazine*. Wilson acclaimed Dickens's 'almost divine insight into the workings of human nature', compared him with Defoe, Fielding, Richardson and Scott, and praised 'the benign spirit' found in all his work. The applause and shouting that greeted the 'little, slender, pale-faced, boyish-looking' Dickens when he rose to speak, was tremendous but, he told Forster, he managed to stay 'as cool as a cucumber'. Privately, he relished the sight of so many distinguished grey heads gathered around his 'brown flowing locks' to do him honour but modestly presented himself as a writer activated only by 'an earnest and humble desire . . . to increase the stock of harmless cheerfulness'. He did, however, refer to having had a more exalted purpose in *The Old Curiosity Shop*. He hoped, he said, that, through his treatment of Nell's death, he might have softened thoughts of death in young minds, and helped to assuage the grief of those who mourned by substituting 'a garland of fresh flowers for the sculptured horrors which disgrace the tomb'. He made two other speeches during the evening, delivering them with the same remarkable fluency and eloquence as the first one. 'He is as happy in public speaking as in writing,' declared one of his hearers, '– nothing studied, nothing artistical; his were no written speeches, conned, and got by heart, but every sentence seemed to be suggested on the impulse of the moment.' From now on for the rest of his life, public speaking was to be another medium by which Dickens most effectively communicated with his adoring public.[42]

Elated by his rapturous reception in Edinburgh (the banquet was followed by a week of intense lionisation), Dickens, accompanied by Catherine and with the young sculptor Angus Fletcher acting as their exuberant native guide, set off for a tour in the 'tremendous wilds' of the Highlands. Dickens's fine descriptions of the journey, the awe-inspiring scenery he saw, and a terrifying experience the party had in crossing a foaming river are quoted at length by Forster, providing us with the earliest specimens we have of Dickens the brilliant travel-writer. After writing about Fletcher's eccentricities in one letter, he jokingly promises to 'soar to the sublime' in his next and does so in his subsequent enthralled descriptions of Glencoe with the high glens surrounding it forming 'such haunts as you might imagine yourself wandering in, in the very height and madness of fever'. The travellers have to retrace their steps through Glencoe in a violent thunderstorm which, satisfyingly, renders the place 'perfectly horrific'. And Dickens found it easier to get on with writing *Barnaby* amid all this sublimity than among the social distractions of Edinburgh. By 9 July he had finished chapters 45–8 ready for *Clock* 69 and 70, duly published on 24 and 31 July. The story, he wrote to Forster on 30 June, is 'progressing . . . to good strong interest' and has been brought to 'an exciting point, with a good dawning of the riots'.[43]

During Dickens's Scottish tour a General Election was in progress which, it soon became clear, would mean the return to power under Sir Robert Peel of the Tories, 'people', Dickens wrote a few weeks later, 'whom, politically, I despise and abhor'. In May he had been half-tempted to stand for the Liberals in Reading, where he would have joined Talfourd in representing the borough, but financial considerations deterred him (M.P.s received no salary at this time). Dickens's dismay at the way things were going politically gave an edge to his fiercely satirical portrait in chapter 47 of *Barnaby* of the so-called 'fine old country gentleman' and Justice of the Peace, the sort of man exalted by the Tories who is, in fact, a brutal sot. A month later he elaborated on this figure with some spirited verses entitled 'The Fine Old English Gentleman. New Version. (*To be said or sung at all Conservative Dinners*)' which Forster anonymously published in *The Examiner.*

> The good old laws were garnished well with gibbets, whips and chains,
> With fine old English penalties, and fine old English pains,
> With rebel heads, and seas of blood once hot in rebel veins;

For all these things were requisite to guard the rich old gains
    Of the fine old English Tory times;
    Soon may they come again!

This squib, eight verses long, appeared in *The Examiner* signed 'W' on 7 August, and was followed by two others, of similar length, in the same month, respectively attacking Peel's 'Tamworth Manifesto' (which repackaged the Tories as 'Conservatives') as the prescription of a quack doctor, and lampooning the ultra-right-wing Colonel Sibthorp, whose election by the voters of Lincoln while they rejected the reformist Bulwer particularly outraged Dickens. 'By Jove, how radical I am getting!' he wrote to Forster on 13 August, 'I wax stronger in the true principles every day.' He may well have written more squibs than the three just mentioned since Forster comments, 'I doubt if he ever enjoyed anything more than the power of thus taking part occasionally, unknown to outsiders, in the sharp conflict the press was waging at this time.' In Edinburgh he had accepted an invitation to make a weightier intervention in the public debate when he promised Macvey Napier, editor of the great Whig quarterly *The Edinburgh Review*, to write an article (it would appear anonymously like all other articles in the *Review* but his authorship would quickly have become known) on the appalling revelations that were expected to appear in the report of the Parliamentary Committee on the 'Employment and Condition of Children in Mines and Manufactories'. Though occasionally reminded of his promise by Napier and utterly horrified by the report when it finally appeared in May 1842, Dickens never did, in fact, write this article, nor any of the others he later mooted for the *Edinburgh*, from time to time. Rather than writing weighty pieces for the quarterlies, it better suited his talent for being a 'skirmisher and sharpshooter' (to borrow Macaulay's phrase) to write a letter to *The Morning Chronicle* or to contribute anonymous polemical pieces to *The Examiner*. And in the autumn of 1843 he was to discover in *A Christmas Carol* a form of fictional writing, unique to himself, that was infinitely more effective for social-propagandist purposes, more of a 'hammer-blow', to use a favourite metaphor of his, than any journalistic article or pamphlet could conceivably have been.[44]

By mid-August Dickens and his family had been established in Broadstairs for nearly two weeks. During his time in London between Scotland and the Kentish coast he had finally brought about the completion and publication of *The Pic Nic Papers*, the three-volume illustrated anthology he had edited for Mrs Macrone's benefit (she eventually received £450 from this publication). For this Dickens had rewritten his *Lamplighter* farce as a short story, and the illustration Cruikshank supplied for this proved to be the artist's last collaboration with him. For the next three months or so Dickens was free of other commitments (it took him no time at all to reject Henry Colburn's offer of the editorship of *The New Monthly Magazine*) and could concentrate on the completion of *Barnaby*. 'I am hideously lazy,' he wrote to Hall on 14 September, 'always bathing, lying in the sun, or walking about. I write a No. when the time comes, and dream about it beforehand on cliffs and sands – but as to getting in advance –! where's the use, too, as we so soon leave off!' For he and Chapman and Hall all agreed the time had come to end the *Clock*, though the publishers could legally have insisted on his continuing it for another three years. With the Dickens/Bentley imbroglio so recent a memory, however, they were hardly likely to start invoking the letter of law.

Dickens was obviously eager to be released from the intense pressure of writing in weekly instalments. But there was also the fact that *Barnaby* had not taken hold of the public as *The Old Curiosity Shop* had done (Chittick notes that it was 'barely reviewed at all'). Not being a beautiful and threatened child, Barnaby could not be the kind of focus for fear and pity that Oliver and Nell had been. Lord Jeffrey certainly spoke for many readers when he besought Dickens, 'pray give us something to love and weep over – better than Dolly – and more touching than even Mrs Rudge'. Dickens could not have been other than deeply concerned about the *Clock's* falling circulation figures, now hovering round the 30,000 mark. He and Catherine had visited Scott's Abbotsford before returning to England and there he had seen a 'tumbled and bent' old white hat of Scott's that powerfully focused his Scott-centred anxieties. Just as he had, with astonishing speed, become Scott's acknowledged successor as the greatest, and infinitely most popular, British novelist of the day, so he might now, if he did not take care, suffer a similar fate to Scott's and end up writing himself to death in a desperate effort to keep up the sales of his books. Ten years later he could still vividly recall this hat at Abbotsford, in its 'vile glass case', exhibiting the last clothes Scott had worn. The hat seemed to have been 'tumbled and bent and broken by the uneasy, purposeless wandering hither and thither of his heavy head' and made Dickens think of Scott's biographer Lockhart's 'pathetic description' of the great writer in his last illness still struggling to write but letting the pen fall from his hand while silent tears coursed down his cheeks.[45]

Scott was certainly very much in Dickens's mind as he pondered the draft of an address to the readers of the *Clock* informing them that the periodical would cease publication with the conclusion of *Barnaby* in November, and that he would begin a new book in monthly parts 'under the old green covers' the following March, the first number to appear at the end of that month. Walking about Lincoln's Inn just before a meeting to discuss the new work with Chapman and Hall in Forster's chambers on 21 August, he began thinking that 'Scott failed in the sale of his very best works . . . *because he never left off*' and reflected that his own great success 'was, in a manner, spoiling itself, by being run to death and deluging the town with every description of trash and rot [i.e., the numerous plagiarisms and piracies of his work]'. He briefed Forster to propose to Chapman and Hall that he should have a year's sabbatical after *Barnaby* and then come out with a new three-volume novel 'and put the town in a blaze again'. The publishers were staggered but agreed (what choice had they, after all, when the proposal came from their most golden of geese?), and agreed again when Dickens reverted to the idea of the new work's being in monthly parts, 'which', as he wrote to Mitton on 30 August, 'gives me a much longer rest'. Accordingly, an agreement was signed on 7 September whereby Dickens would get an advance of £150 per month at 5 per cent interest from Chapman and Hall during the period between the end of *Barnaby* and the beginning of the new work. For the latter he would receive a monthly 'salary' of £200, and both this new loan (£1,800 in total) and the still outstanding one of £3,019.9.5 were to be repaid from Dickens's three-quarters share in the profits of the new work. As has been pointed out, this Agreement, however satisfactory it may have seemed to Dickens at the time, hardly boded well for his financial future.[46]

Meanwhile, he was becoming more and more excited about a dramatic new project. He was not the sort of person to take a year out from the punishing writing schedule he had been following for the past five years without feeling the need for some major new scheme to mop up some of his extraordinary energies. Forster well understood the danger: 'some fear as to the use he was likely to make of the leisure afforded him [by the proposed sabbatical] seemed to me its only drawback'. The new scheme soon emerged. It will be remembered that one of Dickens's original ideas for the *Clock* was that he might at some point travel to Ireland or America and write about his experiences for the journal. The idea now returned with much greater force. America had long been a place in his mind as it was for so many of his fellow-countrymen, a Utopia for the Radicals and a Dystopia for the Tories. He was always especially thrilled by fan mail from the American interior: 'simple and honest hearts' writing to him from those 'vast solitudes'. His transatlantic literary hero Washington Irving had assured him that a visit by him 'would be such a triumph from one end of the States to the other, as was never known in any Nation'. He would again experience public adulation as in Edinburgh, and sublime scenery as in the Highlands but this time both experiences would be on a stupendous scale. No wonder he soon found himself 'haunted by visions of America, night and day' and became adamant that the trip '*must* be managed somehow!' By 19 September he had made up his mind to go, accompanied by Catherine and leaving as soon after Christmas as it would be safe to do so. Macready, who had toured in America in 1826, discouraged Dickens from taking the children. Catherine at first 'cried dismally' at the thought of being separated from them for so long but was reluctantly reconciled to it after Macready had promised that he and his wife would keep a close eye on them. Charley, Mamie, Kate and baby Walter, who was not yet weaned, were to be left in lodgings in Osnaburgh Street, close to the Macreadys' home, under the care of a nurse, other servants and their uncle Fred – presumably Dickens felt that, financially, he just could not trust his parents to run the household in his absence – while Devonshire Terrace was to be let. Catherine was further comforted by her maid Anne Brown's willingness to accompany her, and by Maclise's prompt response to her request that he make a group portrait of the children for her to take with her to America.[47]

Details of Dickens's arrangements with his publishers about the American trip belong to the next chapter. Of equal importance to him were his arrangements with his readers. They had to be kept in the picture. He returned to the draft announcement he had prepared about stopping the *Clock* and, with Forster's help, produced a final version which duly appeared in *Clock* 80 (9 Oct.). During the course of the *Clock*, and particularly as a result of the intensity of readers' reactions to the life and death of Little Nell, Dickens's sense of his relationship with his public, and the peculiar power over it that he exercised, had deepened. The relationship had become more intimate, 'personally affectionate, and like no other man's', as he later expressed it. He more and more took on the role of the reader's 'guide, philosopher and friend' (to use one of his favourite quotations from Pope), something reflected in *Barnaby* in the numerous passages of authorial exhortation or consolation, praised by Forster as 'manly, upright thinking' and noted by Gissing, who termed it 'old-fashioned moralizing, generally on the compensations of life'. Dickens now addresses his *Clock* readers as his 'Dear Friends'. He says that to commune with them 'in any form' is for him 'a labour of love' but confesses that, in using the weekly-instalment format, he has 'often felt cramped and confined in a very irksome and harassing degree', and that he was finally no longer able to bear 'these jerking confidences which are no sooner begun than ended'. The *Clock*, he announces, will therefore cease publication when *Barnaby* ends and for his new story he will revert to what he calls 'our old and well-tried plan [as though it had been devised jointly by himself and his readers], which has only twelve gaps in the year, instead of fifty-two'. Finally, he reveals that he is to visit America, his pleasure in the prospect being subdued only 'by the reflection that it must separate us for a longer time than other circumstances would have rendered necessary'.[48]

The day before this address appeared, in *Clock* 80, Dickens, back now in London, had to undergo an exceedingly painful operation for a fistula, caused, he believed, by too close an application to his writing over the last year or so. The operation was performed, of course, without anaesthetic. Shortly afterwards he suffered severe emotional distress through having to sanction the opening of Mary Hogarth's grave to receive the body of one of her and Catherine's brothers who had died suddenly. 'It seems like losing her a second time,' he agonised to Forster. Despite all these miseries, and the fact that he could only write standing up or lying on a sofa, the sheer intensity of his engagement with the writing of *Barnaby* at this stage carried him along, as well as the extraordinary nature of his writing experience as described to Forster;

... may I not be forgiven for thinking it is a wonderful testimony for my being made for my art, that when, in the midst of this trouble and pain, I sit down to my book, some beneficent power shows it all to me, and tempts me to be interested, and I don't invent it – really do not – *but see it*, and write it down.... It is only when it all fades away and is gone, that I begin to suspect that its momentary relief has cost me something.

Forster quotes this letter when attacking George Henry Lewes in his *Life of Dickens* for invoking 'the phenomena of hallucination' to explain Dickens's extraordinary artistry and one can see how the apparent glibness of Lewes's attempt to account for the extraordinary intensity of the working of Dickens's creative imagination would have angered him. Dickens's own preferred term, presumably, would have been 'inspiration'.[49]

He finally finished *Barnaby* just after he and Catherine arrived in Windsor for a fortnight's rest and recreation, on doctor's orders. Before leaving London, on 6 November, he sent a very interesting reply to a correspondent enquiring why he had not introduced into his novel the historical figure of the former Lord Mayor and maverick politician John Wilkes (who played a prominent part in putting down the Riots). Dickens's reply shows his own awareness of that extraordinary quality much found in his writing that we have come to perceive as proto-cinematic:

In this kind of work the object is, – not to tell everything, but to select the striking points and beat them into the page with a sledge-hammer. ... No man in the crowd who was pressed and trodden here and there, saw Wilkes. No looker-on from a window ... beheld an Individual, or anything but a great mass of magistrates, rioters, and soldiery, all mixed up together. Being always in one or the other of these positions, my object has been to convey an idea of multitudes, violence and fury: and even to lose my own dramatic personae in the throng, or only see them dimly, through the fire and smoke.[50]

The last two chapters of *Barnaby* appeared in *Clock* 87 (pub. 27 Nov.) together with a further address to readers, as promised by Dickens. In this he thanked all those 'friends' who had written to him in response to his first address and declared his happiness in the idea that his writings might associate themselves in readers' minds with their 'firesides, homes and blameless pleasures'. Lest they should fear he might be about to stray into pastures new and strange, or embark upon another historical novel, he is explicit about the nature of the story he will write after his American trip. It will, he promises, be 'another tale of English life and manners', in other words, a successor to *Pickwick* and *Nickleby*. A week later came the final number of the magazine itself. This features a last reverie by Master Humphrey on the pleasures of memory and imagination in which Dickens borrows from Charles Lamb's 'Dream Children' (*Essays of Elia*, 1823) to describe the solitary and childless old man imagining himself as a happy grandfather in the midst of a loving family circle. A peculiar, and characteristically Dickensian, twist is given to his fantasy-imaginings in that the one child among his imagined grandchildren whom he especially cherishes is, in fact, a cripple, a version of his younger self. Then follows another highly Dickensian vision of London, 'this struggling town', wherein 'what cheerful sacrifices are made; what toil endured with readiness; what patience shown and fortitude displayed; for the mere sake of home and its affections!' Entranced by this glowing vision, Master Humphrey passes tranquilly from this world. One of his companions, known only as the Deaf Gentleman, supplies a coda detailing the subsequent history of all the *Clock* characters and suggesting a (not very plausible) connection between Jack Redburn's personal history and the story of Edward Chester in *Barnaby* – the last glimmer of Dickens's original wish to make the stories in the *Clock* personal to their tellers. Also in this last *Clock* was Dickens's preface to *Barnaby* and the frontispiece for the third and last half-yearly volume which Dickens had hoped Cattermole would design but which was done by Browne as Cattermole was ill (Cattermole did, however, manage to do the tailpiece illustration showing Master Humphrey's empty chair). In his preface Dickens, responding no doubt to certain contemporary events such as the newly-formed Protestant Associations set up to petition against favours allegedly shown to Catholics in various spheres, notably that of education, points the moral of his tale. He deplores the pernicious ease with which 'what we falsely call a religious cry', begotten of 'intolerance and persecution', is raised 'by men who have no religion'. He also disclaims any special sympathy with the Catholic Church and defends the historical accuracy of his description of the Riots. Vol. 3 of the *Clock* was published on 15 December, together with the first separate editions of *The Old Curiosity Shop* (with the inserted paragraphs in ch.1 mentioned above, p. 165) and *Barnaby Rudge*.[51]

Ever resilient, Dickens quickly recovered his health and returned to London on 20 November, brimming with excitement over the coming American trip whilst at the same time sad at the idea of leaving home – 'for my household Gods . . . take a terrible deep root' – and wishing himself already back home again. An American journalist found him in a study 'piled high with . . . Travels in and Descriptions of America', and ablaze 'with highly-coloured maps of the United States, whose staring blues, reds, and yellows, so much in contrast with the colourless maps of Europe, greatly amused him'. He lived 'in a perpetual state of weighing anchor' but found time in the mornings to sit for his portrait to Count D'Orsay, and for his bust to Samuel Joseph. D'Orsay had told him, 'I have set my heart on giving the representation of the outside of a head, the inside of which, has furnished delight to countless thousands.' Evenings were taken up with theatre visits, including going to see Macready play Shylock on

17 Dickens drawn by Count D'Orsay in 1841. D'Orsay portrayed Dickens twice; under this version he has written 'the best of the two'

the first night of his new managerial reign at Drury Lane (27 Dec.), and dinner parties both at home and at friends' houses ('Every day this week I am engaged', he had to apologise to Burdett Coutts on 14 December). There was also the christening of little Walter to arrange as well as the usual Christmas and New Year festivities, which culminated in a last dinner with Catherine and Forster at Devonshire Terrace on New Year's Day before the sealing of the wine cellar and the handing over of the keys of the house to General Wilson, the incoming tenant. On 2 January Dickens and Catherine, accompanied by Forster as far as Liverpool, left London on the first lap of their journey to that beckoning land, the soil of which, he wrote to the editor of the New York *Knickerbocker Magazine*, Lewis Gaylord Clark, on 28 September, he had so many times trodden in his day-dreams.[52]

CHAPTER 8

America brought to book

1842

This is not the Republic I came to see. This is not the Republic of my imagination.
Dickens to Macready, 22 March 1842

'IT WOULD be a good thing, wouldn't it,' Dickens had written to William Hall on 14 September 1841, 'if I ran over to America about the end of February, and came back, after four or five months, with a One Volume book – such as a ten and sixpenny touch?' In a follow-up letter he apparently mentioned that he intended keeping a 'notebook' which would be his quarry for the proposed travel book, along with the descriptive letters he would send from America to Forster and others. Chapman and Hall responded enthusiastically and the thing was settled. No formal agreement was made but on New Year's Day 1842, Dickens sent his publishers an acknowledgment of the receipt of £885 on account of the profits to be realised from the book's sale (of which he was to have a three-quarter share). He acknowledged also receipt of a further £800 from the £1,800 advance agreed in respect of the new periodical work he was scheduled to begin for Chapman and Hall in the autumn. This sum was placed to his credit at a New York bank in correspondence with Coutts's. Chapman and Hall were authorised to settle all housekeeping bills passed to them by Fred during Dickens's and Catherine's absence and to receive, also from Fred, as a set-off against these the quarterly rent (150 guineas) for 1 Devonshire Terrace. Dickens ends this business letter by once more testifying to his strong sense of his publishers' 'honorable, manly, and generous' behaviour towards him.

Good sales for anything Dickens might choose to write about his American travels could be expected not only because he was the author but also because books on this topic were in great demand in post-Reform Bill Britain. John Gibson Lockhart began his review of a couple of them in the *Quarterly Review* for September 1841 by noting there had lately been 'no scarcity' of such books, written by 'soldiers, sailors, divines, dandies' and many others. Public curiosity about the great new democratic Republic across the ocean was intense. As already noted, it had a strong political element. Many writers saw American society as a dire warning of what could befall Britain if ideas of political reform were carried much further. In her *Domestic Manners of the Americans* (1832), written after a three-year struggle to get a living for herself and her family in America, Frances Trollope, mother of Anthony, wrote, 'The social system of Mr Jefferson, if carried into effect, would make of mankind an unamalgamated mass of grating atoms.' She asserts that the merely theoretical assumption of equality where no such thing exists has poisoned the American political system: men 'attain to power and fame, by eternally uttering what they know to be untrue'. Dickens himself had comically registered the English appetite for such denunciations of America in *Pickwick* (ch. 45), where Tony Weller recommends that Mr Pickwick, having been smuggled out of the Fleet Prison, should abscond across the Atlantic. Eventually he could return and 'write a book about the 'Merrikins as'll pay all his expenses and more, if he blows 'em up enough'. The Americans for their part showed themselves highly sensitive to criticism by European visitors, the most striking example of this being their near-hysterical vilification of Trollope, whose volumes were among the American travel-books by which John Sherwood had found Dickens surrounded on his visit to him in Devonshire Terrace. Sherwood also spotted among Dickens's books two other Tory-biased accounts, Captain Basil Hall's *Travels in North America* (2 vols, 1829) and Captain Marryat's *Diary in America* (6 vols, 1839). On 12 October 1841 Dickens wrote to Andrew Bell, yet another reactionary commentator (not a naval captain, for once), that dedicating his *Men and Things in America* (1838) to the Tory leader Sir Robert Peel seemed 'to denote a foregone conclusion'. 'My notion', wrote Dickens, 'is that in going to a New World one must for the time utterly forget, and put out of sight the Old one and bring none of its customs or observances into the comparison.' This was admirable advice but he did not always follow it himself once he was in the States and writing up his experiences on the spot. Another error he found in foreigners' descriptions of America, and which in the event he himself did not always avoid, was a readiness 'to draw wide national conclusions from isolated exceptional facts – to charge the nation with the peculiarities of a few individuals met by chance on steamboats and railroad cars'.[1]

A writer of the opposite political persuasion to the Tories was the redoubtable and progressive-minded Harriet Martineau. After an investigative tour lasting two years she published her three-volume *Society in America* in 1837, followed by a further three volumes, *A Retrospect of Western Travel* in 1838. Even she, though an ardent admirer of the new Republic, was far from uncritical of it, especially in respect of its treatment of women, its meretricious and slanderous newspaper press, and its toleration of slavery (not, of course, that even the most Tory of other British commentators actually condoned this last atrocity). Sherwood does not mention Martineau's books but Dickens certainly knew them (both works feature in an 1844 inventory of his library), and of all his predecessors in the field of the American travel book it is Martineau with whom he seems to be most in dialogue in *American Notes*. As to what is now generally regarded as the most significant of all early nineteenth-century European reports on America, Alexis de Tocqueville's *Democracy in America* (vol.1, 1835; vol. 2, 1840), there appears to be no hard evidence that Dickens ever read it.[2]

Whether or not he knew De Tocqueville, Dickens clearly did read widely in preparation for his American tour. He borrowed a copy of George Catlin's *Letters and Notes on the Manners, Customs, and Conditions of the North American Indians* (2 vols, 1841) and described himself as 'shaking hands' with its author in every page. He was evidently hoping to meet some Native Americans and was eagerly anticipative of this when he travelled to St Louis 'on the confines of the Indian territory', as he repeatedly described it in his letters. In the event, however, he met, and that by chance, only one representative of the race albeit an impressive one. This was the Choctaw chieftain Pitchlynn, not mentioned in Dickens's surviving letters but described at some length in *American Notes*. Otherwise, he had romantically to imagine the Native Americans as they once picturesquely roamed in their 'solitudes', and noted sadly of those he came across still living in white-controlled areas (reaching, we note, for an Old World comparison): 'They are a fine people, but degraded and broken down. If you could see any of their men and women on a race-course in England, you would not know them from gipsies.' As for America's other subjected race, he did manage, at least to a certain limited extent, to carry out his intention expressed to Lady Holland when taking leave of her 'to go into the slave districts', being 'determined to ascertain by personal inspection the condition of the poor slaves'. As we shall see, however, he spent very little time in the slave states, so deeply repugnant did he find the experience, and when he came to treat the subject in *American Notes*, as of course he could not avoid doing, he mainly relied on simply transposing into his text large sections of material from a pamphlet published by the Anti-Slavery Society in 1839.[3]

He took a passage for himself, Catherine and Anne Brown from Liverpool to Boston on board the S. S. *Britannia*, a wooden paddle-steamer, part of what was to become the Cunard Line. She had made her maiden voyage across the Atlantic in 1840, cutting the crossing-time to just fourteen days. Undeterred by the fate of the *Britannia*'s sister-ship the *President*, lost at sea in the spring of 1841, Dickens had characteristically opted for this, the fastest and most up-to-date form of transatlantic transport. He and Catherine were accompanied to Liverpool by Forster. Alfred Dickens came over from Birmingham, and the Burnetts from Manchester, to join the party at the Adelphi Hotel where Angus Fletcher and other friends also appeared. Dickens perhaps paid a reluctant visit to his maternal grandmother, who lived in Liverpool ('as you very well know,' he had written to Fanny on 22 December, '[she] never cared twopence about us until I grew famous and then sent me an affectionate request for Five Pounds or so') but carefully avoided all public appearances. Dickens and Catherine were initially disconcerted by the smallness of their cabin ('like one of those cabs you get in at the back', he wrote to Maclise on 3 January). But Catherine's 'cheerfulness about the whole thing', even though she was suffering from toothache, quickly helped to reconcile her husband to the situation. In a postscript to Dickens's letter to Maclise Forster wrote of her, 'She deserves to be what you know she is so emphatically called – the Beloved'. It was a good augury for the vital support and loving companionship she was to give her superstar husband in the testing time that lay ahead. There is no record of what Anne's accommodation was like or what she thought of it.[4]

The *Britannia* sailed on 4 January and reached Boston on 22 January, after a very rough crossing indeed and the experience of further terrors for her passengers when, as a result of pilot's error, the ship had gone aground off the Canadian port of Halifax, Nova Scotia, on the night of the 19th. She was got off through the skill of the ship's captain, John Hewitt, whose calmness and competence throughout the difficult voyage was much admired by Dickens. The following morning Dickens was among the many passengers who went ashore and he had a gratifying foretaste of the kind of welcome awaiting him in America. Crowds cheered him in the streets and a place of honour was reserved for him at the state opening of the provincial parliament which happened to take place that day. Forty-eight hours later the *Britannia* finally docked in Boston.

On the ship Dickens had held himself aloof from most of his fellow-passengers, consorting mainly with two or three congenial companions including Lord Mulgrave, a young Guards officer on his way to rejoin his regiment in Montreal. According to another fellow-passenger, a young clerk and amateur artist called Pierre Morand, Dickens left Catherine to represent him at social gatherings 'while he sought fresh air in another direction'. Once arrived in Boston, however, and settled, through the good offices of Dr Palmer, editor of the *Boston Transcript*, at America's 'pioneer first-class hotel', the Tremont House, he found himself absolutely engulfed by a tidal wave of lionisation that was at first exhilarating but before long started to become both exhausting and frustrating. That first Saturday evening, however, he bounded into the Tremont's foyer shouting out 'Here we are!', Grimaldi's famous catchphrase and as such entirely appropriate for a great and cherished entertainer making his entrance upon a new stage. He half-felt he was actually doing this next morning when the brightly-painted, unsubstantial buildings made him think, as he wrote later in *American Notes*, that 'every thoroughfare in the city looked exactly like a scene in a pantomime'. After a private dinner with Lord Mulgrave, interrupted by numerous messages inviting the Dickenses to attend divine service the next day at this or that place of worship (all declined), and a

18 The S.S. *Britannia*

deputation of 'Young Men of Boston' inviting him to a public banquet (accepted), he and Mulgrave rushed out for a midnight ramble through the streets. A group of young men including James Fields, later to become Dickens's American publisher and close friend, trailed the visitors' footsteps and could hear the 'one continual shout of uproarious laughter as [Dickens] went rapidly forward, reading the signs on the shops and observing the architecture of the new country into which he had dropped as from the clouds'.[5]

The next day Dickens began sitting for his portrait to an enterprising painter called Francis Alexander, who had arranged with him for the sittings before he had left England, and also to a hardly less quick-off-the mark sculptor, Henry Dexter. He was swiftly inundated with letters, invitations, requests for autographs, appointments, and so on: 'I have', he lamented, 'the correspondence of a secretary of state, and the engagements of a fashionable physician.' At his urgent request, Alexander found him a secretary, George Washington Putnam, the same age as Dickens, a very active Abolitionist, and a pupil of Alexander's. Putnam, fondly nicknamed 'Hamlet' by Dickens on account of the cloak he liked to wear, subsequently accompanied Dickens and Catherine on their tour as a general factotum with a salary of $10 a month, rising eventually to $20. Shortly after Dickens's death he published a reverential account of the experience in *The Atlantic Monthly*.[6]

Crowds followed Dickens everywhere, including to the Tremont Theatre on the 24th, where the enterprising manager, having secured Dickens's promise of attendance, proclaimed the fact on his playbill for the evening advertising, *inter alia*, a piece called *Boz! A Masque Phrenologic* (with the manager as Boz) as well as an act from a dramatisation of *Nicholas Nickleby*. Young ladies wrote to Dickens soliciting a lock of his flowing hair, everyone who was anyone in Boston society paid him a visit, and the local papers loudly celebrated the arrival of this writer, who was 'the solace of the lonely, the companion of the gay, the beloved and admired of all ages and classes'. Only the more Puritanical papers (mindful, no doubt, of Stiggins and the Brick Lane Branch of the Ebenezer Temperance Association) declined to join in such 'servile adoration of a mere pleasant story teller or novelist'. For a 'mere pleasant story-teller' Dickens's heavy programme of visits of inspection to prisons, hospitals and asylums might seem somewhat remarkable, likewise his breakfasting with the famous Unitarian divine, Dr William Ellery Channing, and his devotion of one whole day to visiting the celebrated model factories at Lowell. On 1 February he spoke at the Young Men of Boston's banquet in his honour. He referred to his own writings in much the same terms as he had done in Edinburgh six months earlier but greatly expanded his reference to Little Nell, with romantic mention of all the touching letters about her he had received in England from 'dwellers in log-houses among the morasses, and swamps, and densest forests, and deepest solitudes of the Far West'. It must have surprised his audience when Dickens in his peroration passed from such rhetoric as this to some very plain speaking on the potentially explosive topic of international copyright. America's failure to ratify any agreement on this subject of course cost him dear but he seems, as modern scholars have pointed out, to have been unaware that America was passing through a period of deep economic depression. His pleas for international copyright were singularly ill-timed, therefore.[7]

Dickens left Boston on 5 February, well pleased with the city ('Boston is what I would have the whole United States to be,' he later wrote) and having formed warm friendships with a number of prominent Bostonians. Among them were the city's Mayor, Jonathan Chapman, and several Harvard professors, notably the poet Henry Wadsworth Longfellow, who found Dickens 'a glorious fellow . . . a gay free-and-easy character', with 'a slight dash of the Dick Swiveller about him', and a portly, oyster-loving Professor of Greek, Cornelius Conway Felton, who became one of Dickens's most cherished friends. As for the travel book promised to Chapman and Hall (a project which he was carefully concealing from his hosts), Dickens exulted to Forster: 'The American poor, the American factories, the institutions of all kinds – I have a book, already.' To Mitton he wrote on 31 January: 'There is a great deal afloat here, in the way of subjects for description. I keep my eyes open, pretty wide; and hope to have done so to some purpose, by the time I come home.'[8]

From Boston the Dickens party went by rail to Worcester, Massachusetts, for a weekend before travelling on to Hartford, Connecticut. In Worcester a reporter from *The Worcester Aegis* saw Dickens at a gubernatorial reception and published a profile of the celebrity guest that was apparently 'more widely reprinted in other papers ... than any other single article written during Dickens's tour'. It was a highly personal description of a kind that Dickens was to find more and more offensive as his tour continued:

> We found a middle sized person, in a brown frock coat, a red figured vest, somewhat of the flash order, and a fancy scarf cravat, that concealed the dickey, and was fastened to the bosom in rather voluminous folds by a double pin and chain. His proportions were well rounded .... His hair, which was long and dark, grew low upon the brow, had a wavy kink where it started from the head, and was naturally or artificially corkscrewed as it fell on either side of his face. ... The whole region about the eyes was prominent, with a noticeable development of nerves and vessels, indicating, say the phrenologists, great vigor in the intellectual organs with which they are connected. The eyeballs completely filled their sockets. ... The nose was slightly acquiline – the mouth of moderate dimensions. ... His features, taken together, were well proportioned, of glowing and cordial aspect, with more animation than grace and more intelligence than beauty.

Having noted that Dickens sports a gold watch chain and 'a shaggy coat of bear or buffalo skin that would excite the admiration of a Kentucky huntsman', the reporter sums up by comparing him to all those 'similar looking young men' who frequent the theatres and other public places. Dickens does not, he continues, look at all like a literary man – appropriately enough since

> it is well understood that he draws his characters and incidents less from imagination than from memory, depending for his resources less upon reflection and study, than upon observation. His writings bear slight evidence of reading, and he seldom, if ever, quotes from books. His wonderful perceptions, his acute sensibility, and his graphic fancy, furnish the means by which his fame has been created.[9]

At Hartford Dickens's strenuous programme continued. He visited the law courts and some of the public institutions, such as the Insane Asylum, and was obliged to hold a regular 'levee' for two hours every morning. On his birthday, he spoke at another public banquet in his honour and reverted to the question of international copyright, speaking of it still more pointedly than at Boston. Invoking the shade of Scott, he said that his great predecessor 'might not have sunk beneath the mighty pressure on his brain' but have lived to give more wonderful books to the world had he only been able to enjoy the income that should by rights have accrued to him from his massive American sales. 'My blood so boiled', he wrote to Forster, 'that I felt as if I were twelve feet high when I thrust it [his comment on Scott] down their throats.' The *Hartford Times* was quick to respond: 'It happens that we want no advice on this matter, and it will be better for Mr Dickens, if he refrains from introducing the matter hereafter'. *The Boston Morning Post* was blunter: 'You must drop that, Charlie, or you will be dished; it smells of the shop – rank.' Two days later the New York *Courier* declared that Dickens was wrong to 'intrude his *business* upon those who assemble to do homage to his genius'.[10]

From Hartford the Dickens party proceeded by train and steamboat to New York via New Haven, where Dickens and Catherine had to hold two two-hour 'levees' during their short stay, each time having to shake hands with between two and three hundred people. Finally, on 12 February, they reached New York where they stayed in some splendour until 5 March at the Carlton House Hotel, where Washington Irving was among their first visitors, coming in alone 'with open arms'. Dickens now found himself under even greater celebrity pressure than he had been at Boston. On 14 February the 'Great Boz Ball' was held at the Park Theatre, organised by a group of New York citizens eager, as they told Dickens, to honour him for 'the value of your labours in the cause of humanity, and the eminently successful exercise of your literary talents'. The theatre was transformed into a 'magnificent saloon' lavishly decorated with 'flowers, garlands, draperies, and trophies emblematical of the different States of the Union' and designs representing scenes from Dickens's novels, as well as a bust of Dickens himself 'surmounted by an eagle holding a laurel wreath'. Over three thousand people attended the event and the dances, executed with much difficulty owing to the tremendous crush, alternated with *tableaux vivants* presenting scenes and characters from the novels. Dickens described the ball to Maclise in a letter of 27 February as 'the most splendid, gorgeous, brilliant affair you . . . can possibly conceive'. So many were disappointed in getting tickets that a second Ball was planned for two nights later but by then Dickens had, not surprisingly, fallen ill with a sore throat. For three days he was confined to his hotel room where he had the opportunity to acquaint himself with some of the newspapers' commentary on himself and his visit. This probably did not much help to bring down his temperature. *The New York Aurora*, for example, reported that he was going to a private dinner party at the Coldens' (the lawyer David Colden, a friend of Macready's, was his chief host in New York and he and his wife became good friends of the Dickenses),

19 The 'Great Boz Ball' in New York, from an American newspaper

and commented that in England Dickens had probably never been admitted 'into such really good society, as since he landed in this country'. The knowledge that Dickens had risen from fairly humble origins to such glittering success in an England seen as wholly dominated by its monarchy and aristocracy made him a true hero for the Americans, even if there was sometimes a certain vagueness about the precise nature of the humble origins. In its 'Welcome to Thee, Charles Dickens!' the *Aurora* rather charmingly describes him as the brilliantly successful son of 'an honest haberdasher'.[11]

By 18 February Dickens had recovered enough to speak at a splendid banquet in his honour, held at the City Hotel and chaired by Washington Irving. He here announced his resolve to decline all further public banquets for the rest of his time in America. From now on he would 'pass through the country more quietly' (as if this option was really open to him!), the better to observe and understand what he was seeing in 'this land of mighty interest'. Then, after boldly referring once more to International Copyright, the rest of the speech consisted of an eloquent personal tribute to Washington Irving with a copious flow of well-remembered details from Irving's sketches and stories. It is worth noting the terms in which he praised Irving as a creator of unforgettable characters whose imaginative writings permanently informed and enriched his readers' response to the real-life places in which he set his stories. Dickens undoubtedly relished this public opportunity to praise a fellow-writer whose work had been so nourishing for him, but he was by now feeling both highly stressed ('I have no rest or peace, and am in a perpetual worry') as well as infuriated by the newspaper attacks on him over the question of international copyright. He told Forster he could do nothing he wanted to do, go nowhere that he wanted to go and see nothing that he wanted to see. It seems clear, however, both from his letters and from *American Notes*, that he did nevertheless manage to do a fair amount of his preferred kind of sightseeing while in New York. He visited asylums, workhouses and prisons, including the notorious 'Tombs' (New York House of Detention), described in *American Notes* as a 'dismal-fronted pile of bastard Egyptian, like an enchanter's palace in a melo-drama'. Once he was 'out half the night' in the slums with a police escort, replicating similar forays in London. Starting at midnight, he and the two constables allocated to him visited 'every brothel, thieves' house, murdering hovel, sailors' dancing place, and abode of villainny [*sic*], both black and white, in the town'. Apart from the strong interest these places would have had for him, such expeditions would have enabled him to escape for a few hours from the ubiquitous gawpers who, he complained, would stare down his throat whenever he opened his mouth to drink a glass of water. Despite this, however, he still managed to escape from the limelight some nights to enjoy incognito champagne-and-oyster-fuelled rambles with the highly congenial Felton, 'heartiest of Greek professors' as he called him in *American Notes*, who had travelled down from Harvard to see him again.[12]

On 5 March the Dickens party arrived in Philadelphia by rail from New York. They were in the city for only four days, one of which Dickens devoted to a detailed, and, as it proved, somewhat harrowing, tour of the celebrated Eastern Penitentiary, opened twelve years before and operating on the much-vaunted 'Solitary System' (prisoners being thought to corrupt each other, every inmate was held in strict solitary confinement for the whole of his or her sentence, no matter how long, a system that Dickens found appallingly cruel). He had, of course, a stream of visitors calling at his hotel, among them Edgar Allan Poe, whose high praise of *The Old Curiosity Shop* in *Graham's Magazine* in May 1841 must have greatly gratified him if he saw it. Poe and Dickens had two long interviews during which Dickens promised to try to find Poe an English publisher, which he did after returning home but without success. Visitors like Poe were one thing but quite another was the general 'levee' which Dickens was tricked into holding at his hotel. Putnam recalled that 'for two mortal hours or more the crowd poured in and [Dickens] shook hands and exchanged words with all, while the dapper little author of the scene [a certain local politician called Colonel Florence, who had set Dickens up for this] stood smiling by, giving hundreds and thousands of introductions, and making, no doubt, much social and political capital out of his supposed intimacy with the great English author.' As on all such occasions, Catherine was Dickens's 'perfectly game' faithful fellow-sufferer, invariably impressing the Americans with her good humour and truly ladylike demeanour.[13]

From Philadelphia the party proceeded by steamboat and rail to Washington, where Dickens visited both Houses of Congress, delivered two petitions signed by American writers in favour of international copyright, was received by President Tyler, and attended a presidential reception. Whenever Dickens moved in the crowded assembly, it was, according to the correspondent of the New York *Express*, 'like throwing corn among hungry chickens' as the people came flocking round him. On a quieter occasion, a private dinner in his honour, he offered in his speech the following grandly democratic version of his career as a writer: '. . . every effort of my pen has been intended to elevate the masses of society; to give them the station they deserve among mankind. With that intention I commenced writing . . .'. The next evening the Dickens party boarded a night steamer and at Potomac Creek next morning transferred to a stage-coach which bumped and jolted them as far as Fredericksburg over one of the notorious 'Virginny' roads and from there they completed the final leg of their journey to Richmond by train.[14]

Now brought face to face with slavery in all its brutal reality, Dickens found the experience so hateful that he changed his plan to go as far south as Charleston and instead travelled some two thousand miles westward, to St Louis. The idea of having devoted readers in the remotest, and most scenically sublime, parts of America strongly appealed to him, as we have seen, and his imagination had clearly been fired by an invitation to be guest of honour at a public dinner in St Louis. By the time he reached that city, however, this event had metamorphosed into a soirée with no speechifying so it was at a Richmond 'social supper' that he made what was to be his last speech in America for twenty-five years. He could hardly have failed to be struck by the incongruity of being toasted in a slave-owning community as a writer whose work makes us 'feel for the humblest' and 'creates in all of us a sympathy for each other – a participation in the interests of our common humanity, which constitutes the great bond of equality'. Prudently, however, he refrained from all reference to slavery in his response, even though he found himself absolutely forced to speak his mind on the subject in more private circumstances. He and Catherine (they were like 'a kind of Queen and Albert', he wrote to Maclise) were obliged to hold the usual daily two-hour 'levees' with 'people coming in by hundreds – all fresh and piping hot, and full of questions'. He visited a tobacco manufactory employing slave labour as well as a slave-owner's plantation before returning to Washington en route for Baltimore. Here, despite the usual routine of 'levees' and prison-inspecting, Dickens found time to write, on 22 March, a series of

sparkling letters to Maclise, Macready, Mitton, Lady Holland, Angela Burdett
Coutts, and others. He tells Burdett Coutts that he is by now beginning to feel
that he was accumulating almost too much material for his travel book: 'I don't
see how I shall ever get rid of my gatherings', he writes to her, little foreseeing
what devastating satirical use he would be provoked into making of some of
said 'gatherings' in his next novel. To Mitton he wrote that he had already had
'a great store of oddity and whimsicality' and hinted that he would shortly be
enriching it still further as he was about to travel 'into the oddest and most
characteristic part of this most queer country'.[15]

The Dickens party left Baltimore on 24 March for St Louis via Pittsburgh
and Cincinnati, arriving at St Louis on 10 April. One segment of the journey
was achieved by means of a canal boat, a real endurance test involving
cramped living-quarters and annoying, or downright antisocial, behaviour by
some fellow-passengers, notably the incessant expectoration of the ubiquitous
tobacco-chewers. During a four-day stopover in Pittsburgh Dickens startled
himself by the dramatic way in which he proved, in front of Putnam and
another witness, his conviction that he had mesmeric powers: 'Kate sat down,
laughing, for me to try my hand upon her. . . . In six minutes, I magnetized her
into hysterics, and then into the magnetic sleep.' They resumed their journey,
now travelling on the Ohio by a steamboat far more spacious and salubrious
than the canal boat had been. Dickens liked Cincinnati and gave it his highest
accolade of imaginative approval when he described it as seeming to have
'risen out of the forest like an Arabian-night city'. Indeed, he found it almost
as attractive as Boston with comparably excellent public institutions, such as
its renowned free schools. The last leg of the journey, also by steamboat, was
on the Mississippi, a river to which Dickens reacted even more negatively than
Fanny Trollope had done. Nor did he care for the famous Looking Glass
Prairie, on his overnight expedition there from St Louis: it was, he thought,
decidedly inferior to Salisbury Plain. The St Louis soirée proved to be yet
another trial-by-levee and Dickens was glad enough to leave the place and its
'intolerably conceited' society on 14 April in order to return to Cincinnati,
even though this meant another dose of what modern tourist brochures would
no doubt call 'the Mississippi Experience'.[16]

It was not until Dickens and Catherine reached Niagara Falls on 26 April that
Dickens at last found that sublimity of nature he had been so ardently hoping
to experience in America. He recaptured the exalted mood that had possessed
him in Boston when he first felt upon his pulses, as it were, the really stupendous nature of the New World's welcome to him. It was in Boston that he had
first invoked the Guardian Angel figure of Mary Hogarth ('that spirit which
directs my life') in order to express his sense that more was involved here than
just mass enthusiasm for a very popular writer – that there was, in fact, an
actual spiritual dimension to what he was experiencing. Now, at Niagara, he

again invokes Mary – this time, it seems, as some kind of spiritual tourist: 'she has been here many times, I doubt not, since her sweet face faded from my earthly sight'.[17]

Dickens and Catherine rested for nine days at the dramatically-sited Clifton House Hotel, where their bedroom and sitting-room windows looked straight down upon the Falls. Here, in the intervals of his entranced exploration of his spectacular surroundings Dickens caught up with letter-writing. He confided to Forster his growing sense of what he described as 'a perplexingly divided and subdivided duty' regarding the travel-book promised to Chapman and Hall. Readers would be eager to learn his considered opinions about the country, its institutions and so forth, but so many aspects of his experience of 'this most queer country' seemed to demand a comic or satirical approach, as he had already indicated to Mitton. Now he exclaims, 'Oh! the sublimated essence of comicality that I *could* distil, from the materials I have!' One thing certainly was no laughing matter, however. This was the International Copyright question and it was at Niagara that he at last received the memorial from his fellow-writers on the subject that he had asked Forster to organise back in February. Addressed to the American people, and urging the need for an international copyright agreement for the sake of American writers as much as foreign ones, this memorial carried the signatures of twelve British authors, including Bulwer Lytton, Tennyson, Talfourd, Leigh Hunt, Sydney Smith, Samuel Rogers and, of course, Forster himself. It was accompanied by an open letter addressed to Dickens, signed by the same twelve writers, as well as a separate one on the same subject from Carlyle. Dickens promptly forwarded copies of all three documents (without, however, mentioning that he was their instigator) to certain newspapers in Boston, New York and Washington, as well as to Representative J. P. Kennedy from Baltimore, a strong proponent of an international copyright bill, with whom he had been in touch earlier on.[18]

During his brief 'vacation' at Niagara Dickens also busied himself with preparations for some private theatricals in which he had engaged to participate with Lord Mulgrave and other officers of the British garrison at Montreal, all members of a well-established troupe called the Garrison Amateurs. With his zeal for perfection of theatrical effect Dickens was especially anxious to procure the right kind of comic wig for one of his parts and succeeded in getting one from William Mitchell, a New York actor-manager originally from England whom Dickens had known in London before Mitchell moved to the States. On 4 May the Dickens party made a steamboat crossing over Lake Ontario to Toronto. There they stayed long enough for Dickens to be shocked by what he calls in *American Notes* the city's 'wild and rabid Toryism' before proceeding to Kingston, at that time capital of the United Province of Canada. They reached Montreal on 11 May and stayed there until the 30th, with a side-trip (escorted by Lord Mulgrave) to picturesque Quebec on 26/27 May. This side-trip took place between the two performances by the Garrison Amateurs, the private one before an invited audience on 25 May and the public one on the 29th.

Dickens was 'Stage Manager and Universal Director', as well as leading actor, of the Montreal theatricals, just as he had been nine years earlier when organising and starring in the *Clari* production in the family drawing-room in Bentinck Street. There was nothing he liked better than being the orchestrator of a group of people who had come together for some purpose, whether it was just for fun, to have a party or make an excursion (he was a born master of ceremonies), or, more creatively, to produce a play, or a magazine. In the case of amateur dramatics, he intensely enjoyed being the prime mover in the contrivance of brilliantly realistic 'stage-pictures'. Also the bringing a character to vivid stage life through voice, movement, gesture, facial expression, make-up and costume gave him a satisfaction similar to that of bringing a character to life through words on the printed page. In some ways, indeed, it was the more exciting process of the two because of the immediate audience response involved and, eventually, he would in his public readings find a sensational way to combine both satisfactions. Meanwhile, Montreal's Garrison Amateurs provided him with the first opportunity for the exercise of his creative powers (apart from various comic or pathetic scenes elaborated in many of his letters) since he crossed the Atlantic and he seized it with both hands.

The plays chosen for performance were four farces, three of them being performed on each of the two evenings (one for a private and one for a public audience), and it was in the one for which he had needed the special comic wig that Dickens scored the greatest triumph of both evenings. This farce, or 'comic scene', was a double act called *Past Two o'Clock in the Morning* in which Dickens played Snobbington, a fussy, quiet little man, intruded upon in the middle of the night by a noisy and excitable stranger. One Montreal reviewer wrote:

> The helpless, hypochondriacal Cockney, fond of his little creature comforts, methodical as a Quaker . . . who is disturbed in his night's rest, and put to all kinds of shifts and inconveniences by the boisterous inroad of the Tom-and-Jerry sort of stranger, who instals himself, bongré, malgré, in his quarters, is performed to the life by Mr Dickens. His style is a sort of mixture of the late Charles Mathews and Mr Buckstone's, and would do no discredit to either of those eminent performers.

'I really do believe', Dickens wrote to Forster, 'that I was very funny . . . and made the part a character, such as you and I know very well.' He had created the character very much as he created a fictional character, by mixing together elements from various real people. Catherine acted in another farce, playing only on the private evening. Dickens exulted to Forster, 'Only think of Kate playing! and playing devilish well, I assure you!' He underlined his delighted astonishment by adding no less than eight exclamation marks against her name in the playbill for the evening that he sent to Forster with all the performers' names written in.[19]

At the end of May Dickens and Catherine, by now 'FEVERED with anxiety for home', headed back to New York by steamboat, rail and stage-coach, for their last week on American soil. They made a last excursion, with the Coldens, to visit the Shaker Village, to which Dickens, with his dislike of closed communities, had a predictably negative response, and the West Point Military Academy, to which, with his love of order and discipline, he had a predictably positive one. Back in New York, there was a final dinner-party on 6 June and on the following day, Dickens, Catherine and the faithful Anne Brown, who had amused Dickens by remaining steadfastly unimpressed by everything she saw (Niagara was, she opined, 'nothing but water' and 'too much of that'), joyfully embarked for home on board the sailing packet the *George Washington*. With them was Timber Doodle, a little shaggy white terrier given to Dickens by Mitchell the theatre manager, the first of Dickens's many memorable and much-loved dogs. The *Washington* had a fair and prosperous voyage home, with Dickens at his most exuberant, very different from his reserve on the *Britannia*. He played the accordion and, with a few other choice spirits, formed a club called the 'United Vagabonds' which delighted to commit 'all kinds of absurdities'.[20]

In more reflective moods, he would study what he calls in *American Notes* the 'little world of poverty' that was travelling steerage on the *George Washington*. This consisted of failed emigrants (many of them victims of what we would now call 'people-traffickers') returning to the Old Country disappointed and disillusioned. Dickens was fascinated to learn from the ship's carpenter some of these people's individual histories just as – not so very many years before but in how different a life! – he had loved to hear from his mother the life-stories of some of his father's fellow-prisoners in the Marshalsea.

The *George Washington* docked at Liverpool early on 29 June. With as little loss of time as possible Dickens and Catherine took the train for London, looking out eagerly from their carriage-windows on to the so-much-pined-for beauties of the English countryside, 'the pretty cottages, the beds of flowers, the old churchyards, the antique houses, and every well-known object'. It was dark by the time they arrived at Osnaburgh Terrace for an ecstatic reunion with their children, the joy of which threw Charley into alarming convulsions from which, however, he happily soon recovered. Next day the family re-occupied No.1 Devonshire Terrace and Dickens, of whom Forster later wrote, 'no man was so inclined naturally to derive his happiness from home concerns', was, after six tumultuous months, once more back where he most desired, and most needed, to be.[21]

Throughout those six months Dickens sent Forster a regular series of long, journal-type letters. Often written under difficult circumstances, they nevertheless show, as Forster claims, 'unrivalled quickness of observation . . . the irresistible play of humour . . . unwearied unforced vivacity' and, he adds, 'there is not an erasure in them'. Forster shared these journal-letters with others, as was Dickens's intention, both with intimate friends like Maclise and Mitton (who also received occasional letters of their own, in the same vein as Forster's but shorter and, in Mitton's case, partly business-related) and with a wider circle of Dickens's friends and acquaintances. On 20 June he read from them to Crabb Robinson who wrote in his diary, '. . . better letters I never heard read. The descriptions most animated, satire and sublime painting admirably intermixed.'[22]

The letters to Forster, and one or two others, like the one written specially for the leading political journalist Albany Fonblanque about Washington and 'the political oddities of this land' of 12 March, were intended to serve a twofold purpose. First they, together with the eagerly-awaited replies to them, had to substitute for that daily or near-daily, personal contact with family and friends – chief among them Forster himself, of course – that was always of such huge importance to Dickens's diurnal well-being in every respect. They would have helped to assuage the travellers' pangs of home-sickness whilst at the same time enabling Dickens to keep up his 'Sparkler of Albion' role as the brilliant life and soul of his familiar circle ('my pen has so long supplied the place of a voice', he wrote to Lady Holland on 22 March). Secondly, the letters were intended to serve as quarry for the American travel book, a method of travel-book writing that had been strongly recommended to Dickens by Captain Basil Hall. Mingled, therefore, with all the personal and particular news about his and Catherine's travelling experiences in various conveyances and in various hotels, the staggering nature of his reception, the formation of new friendships, and the hornets' nest stirred up by his international copyright campaign, is much bravura reportage, as well as set-piece descriptions and vivid sketches. These last might be comic, like the wonderful description of the roaming, foraging pigs on New York's Broadway; they might aim at the sublime, like the description of Niagara, or at evoking horror, like the depiction of prisoners held in solitary confinement in Philadelphia; or they might be exercises in sentiment, like an elaborate account of a bright little woman with her very young baby on the Mississippi steam-boat travelling to join her husband who has not yet seen the child. These were all among the passages that, during the four months following his return to England, Dickens extracted, and edited for public consumption, before incorporating them into the book that became *American Notes*.[23]

When Forster, writing the first volume of his *Life of Dickens*, came to the chapters dealing with the 1842 journey, he naturally turned back to the letters Dickens had written him during that time. Knowing that Dickens had himself mined them for *American Notes*, he was not expecting to find much left worth quoting and was quite astonished by the riches he discovered. The travel book may give us Dickens's considered report on what he saw and heard in the States but, Forster insists, 'the *personal narrative* of this famous visit . . . is in the letters alone'. Only in the letters, too, do we find such gems as the perfectly-paced comic scene that Dickens constructs for Fonblanque's delectation, following his formal visit to the beleaguered President Tyler, whom he finds sitting alone by a hot stove on a hot day with 'a great spit box' beside him:

The President got up, and said, "Is *this* Mr. Dickens?" – "Sir", returned Mr. Dickens – "it is." "I am astonished to see so young a man Sir", said the President. Mr. Dickens smiled, and thought of returning the compliment – but he didn't for the President looked too worn and tired, to justify it. 'I am happy to join with my fellow citizens in welcoming you, warmly, to this country', said the President. Mr. Dickens thanked him, and shook hands. Then the other Mr. Dickens, the secretary, asked the President to come to his house that night, which the President said he should be glad to do, but for the pressure of business, and measles. Then the President And [*sic*] the two Mr. Dickenses sat and looked at each other, until Mr. Dickens of London observed that no doubt the President's time was fully occupied, and he and the other Mr. Dickens had better go. Upon that they all rose up; and the President invited Mr. Dickens (of London) to come again, which he said he would. And that was the end of the conference.

These letters, too, are full of such quintessentially Dickensian descriptions as the following of the behaviour of some of those who crowded into the dreaded 'levees':

We had very queer customers at our receptions, I do assure you. Not least among them, a gentleman with his inexpressibles imperfectly buttoned and his waistband resting on his thighs, who stood behind the half-opened door, and could by no temptation or inducement be prevailed upon to come out. There was also another gentleman, with one eye and one fixed gooseberry, who stood in a corner, motionless like an eight-day clock, and glared upon me, as I courteously received the Pittsburgians.[24]

Recognisable in such passages is the raw material for various aspects of the satirical vision of America that Dickens was to develop in *Martin Chuzzlewit* months later, during the spring and summer of 1843. Indeed, it seems probable that he still had his letters to Forster, borrowed back for *American Notes*, by him at that time, so clear are some of the echoes. Among the crowd, for example, at the levee young Martin is (very improbably) compelled to hold in chapter 22 is a 'silent gentleman with glazed and fishy eyes, and only one button on his waistcoat (which was a very large metal one, and shone prodigiously), [who] got behind the door, and stood there, like a Clock, long after everybody else was gone'.

Macready was, naturally, among the friends with whom Forster shared Dickens's letters but the great actor also wrote directly to Dickens during the American trip, and received at least three letters back from him. These, especially the last two (22 March and 1 April), are very different from Dickens's journal-letters to Forster or Fonblanque. Macready had successfully toured America in 1826/27, he liked the country and the people, and seriously considered going to live there. Republican America was more congenial to him than monarchical England. Aware of this, Dickens is anxious that Macready should not think he has been over-hasty in arriving at a critical stance towards America but, on the contrary, had come to a well-considered verdict. The passage quoted as epigraph to this chapter continues:

> I infinitely prefer a liberal Monarchy – even with its sickening accompani-ments of Court Circulars . . . to such a Government as this. In every respect but that of National Education, the Country disappoints me. The more I think of its youth and strength, the poorer and more trifling in a thousand respects, it appears in my eyes.

Knowing how sensitive to press criticism Macready was, he scouts the idea of his ever living comfortably in a country with 'a press more mean and paltry and silly and disgraceful than any country ever knew'. Dickens then seeks (protesting too much, we may feel) to conciliate his friend by lavishing praise on the 'generous, open-hearted' nature of the American people themselves before he returns to the charge. He asserts his own Liberal credentials and lack of (class) pride, illustrating the latter by mentioning the great pleasure he had had in receiving a deputation of Hartford carmen who had read his books 'and perfectly understood them'. Both Macready and Dickens would have been oblivious of the condescension that we can now detect in his comments here which point us, I think, towards one of the root causes to be found in Dickens himself for much of his discomfort in America, that is, his very English class-consciousness.

Ironically, he had to spend the first part of his next letter to Macready (1 April) urging him to shrug off attacks in 'certain rotten sins called Sunday newspapers' (the English equivalent of the scurrilous American press of the time). The letter ends, no doubt in response to some deprecation by Macready of his criticisms of America, with perhaps the fiercest, most concentrated and most comprehensive denunciation of the new nation that Dickens ever wrote. He introduces it by quoting something he had written to Forster just over a month before: 'I believe the heaviest blow ever dealt at Liberty's Head, will be dealt by this nation in the ultimate failure of its example to the Earth.' And we notice that it is now only a minority of Americans who for him are worthy citizens: ' "*the Mass*" (to use our monarchical term) are miserably dependent in great things, and miserably independent in small ones'.

Amid all this Dickens does not fail to express his gratitude for the watchful eye the Macreadys are keeping on his children (rather to the children's discomfort, it would seem). As far as actual family letters were concerned, Dickens wrote some chatty ones to Fred, occasionally containing instructions, and one to Henry Austin containing a glowing paragraph about Niagara later recycled for *American Notes*. If Dickens wrote to either his father or his mother, no letter has survived and it seems unlikely that he did so. He does send love to his mother via Austin but John Dickens was still in disgrace in his son's eyes, and made matters worse while Dickens was away by trying, unsuccessfully, to borrow money from 'Miss Coutts & Co'. This must have been what Mitton reported to Dickens, eliciting in reply the wearily wry comment, 'How long he is, growing up to be a man!' It was just as well, perhaps, that Dickens did not know that John had had more success with Macready, borrowing £20 from him on 21 February.[25]

The last group of letters written by Dickens in America consists of those to certain friends he made there, pre-eminently to Jonathan Chapman, to Colden (to whose wife he also sent, on 29 April, one of his elaborately facetious comic love-letters, accompanied by doggerel verses) and to Felton. It is noticeable that with these friends Dickens felt comfortable enough to write to them about their country critically, and even satirically. Chapman was literary and liked expressing his affection for Dickens (who had proposed an 'alliance' with him) in somewhat high-flown terms ('I feel as if Providence had marked us as friends. I seemed to read it in your face the first moment I looked upon it.'). Dickens responded in the same key with a passionate tirade about the agony caused him as a result of press attacks on his stance on international copyright:

> I have never in my life been so shocked and disgusted, or made so sick and sore at heart, as I have been by the treatment I have received here . . . in reference to the International Copyright question. . . . there fall upon me scores of your newspapers; imputing motives to me, the very suggestion of which turns my blood to gall; and attacking me in such terms of vagabond scurrility as they would denounce no murderer with. I vow to Heaven that the scorn and indignation I have felt under this unmanly and ungenerous treatment has been to me an amount of agony such as I have never experienced since my birth.

He has not, he adds, shared these feelings with anyone, not even Catherine – which, if true and not merely a rhetorical flourish, certainly seems pretty strange, suggesting an oddly limited intimacy in this particular marital relationship. We do not have Chapman's reply to this outpouring ('I open my whole heart to you, you see!' Dickens tells him) but we do have his later impassioned farewell letter to Dickens (1 July) in which, like a forerunner of Silas Wegg in *Our Mutual Friend,* he is moved to 'drop into poetry'.[26]

Dickens's friendships with the Coldens and with Felton, though also very warm, seem to have been less high-pitched and produced some wonderful epistolary comedy. In one letter, for example, he extemporises a fine outburst from Miss Miggs in *Barnaby* after Colden had mistakenly referred to her as 'Moggs':

> . . . Her name is but a short one, but she considers that it come direct from Evins, and was there invented for her ancestors' use and distinction. She thanks her blessed Stars that she has no shame in connections with her name, and has no call to disguise it; and she is of opinion that it hill becomes a 'Publican and Sinner (she is supposed to mean *Re*publican) to miscall his feller creeturs as isn't clothed in purple through no faults of their own, but may fly equally up'ards ven the time comes, in calico, notwithstanding.

As for Felton, it is with him above all among his American correspondents that Dickens seems to be at his most unbuttoned. Their shared running joke about Felton's passion for oysters gives rise to one of those splendid passages of comic fantasy scattered so profusely throughout his letters, passages that are as good as anything of the kind in his published journalism. What, Dickens asks, happens to oyster-openers when oysters are not in season? 'Do they commit suicide in despair, or wrench open tight drawers and cupboards and hermetically-sealed bottles – for practice? Perhaps they are dentists out of the oyster season. Who knows?'[27]

As his biographers have long recognised, Dickens's 1842 American experiences profoundly affected his sense of his own identity both as man and as artist. He had had the exhilarating experience of being fêted by cheering crowds as no 'King or Emperor upon the Earth' had ever been before, and of realising that at the 'core', as he put it, of all this was love and admiration for him personally and sheer delight in his invented stories and characters. 'It is no nonsense, and no common feeling', Channing wrote to him, 'It is all heart'. The feeling of enormous, benign power this reception gave him must surely have made him believe that he was in a unique position to help bring about the passing of an international copyright agreement, something he may or may not have had it in mind to do before coming to America (the evidence is ambiguous but he always strenuously denied having gone there as any kind of 'ambassador' for the cause). Of course, he could hardly pretend to be unaware that he himself was, as he wrote to Jonathan Chapman, 'the greatest Loser by the existing law, alive' but he could not very well take this line publicly, though the fact was obvious enough. Instead, he made Scott, whose literary heir he was now recognised to be, his surrogate as chief victim of the unjust current situation, as in his Hartford speech (above, p. 182). The American press was not deceived, however, and Dickens was soon shocked and furious to find his ruse ignored and himself directly attacked by sections of the press for bad taste, intruding as he did '*pecuniary* considerations' (that favourite adjective of his reprobate father's!) into occasions meant to honour him. 'It is well known', asserted 'A Friend' in *The New York Courier* on 14 February, 'that the object of Mr Dickens's visit to this country is for the purpose of making further engagements for the publication of his work.' As has been shown, he became in his own person the subject of controversy:

> By one side he was pictured as the self-made man whose rapid rise in the world had not given him the time to learn all the fine points of good manners; by the other he was described as the struggling bread-winner, a man with 'a wife and four children, whom his death may very possibly leave destitute'.[28]

In addition to the copyright imbroglio Dickens's physical appearance, dress and behaviour were, as already shown, freely commented upon, often unflatteringly. The situation was that he had come there to get materials for writing about America but here was America first writing about him! He was even pressed into the service of those wishing to advertise their wares. His 'rather yellow teeth' showed, said the Philadelphia *Spirit of the Times* on 9 March, that he did not avail himself of 'Teaberry Tooth Wash' or 'Hufeland's Dentifrice', the virtues of which commodities were described elsewhere in the paper, while an enterprising grocer in the New York Bowery advertised 'Boz Pork and Beans'.[29]

Thus Dickens's initial sense of power and glory must soon have yielded to a sharp awareness of just how much he was being used and exploited for the benefit of others, whether it was those exhibiting him and Catherine at 'levees', newspaper editors seeking to gratify their readers' vulgar curiosity, or tradesmen jumping on the Boz bandwagon. This is likely to have been deeply disturbing to Dickens's sense of self and of his relationship to the world, especially coming after the seven years of ever-increasing public adulation he had experienced in Britain. This adulation, moreover, had, apart from the Edinburgh banquet, been mainly expressed in print and so had not involved intrusive multitudes wanting to stare into his face and shake his hand. Now he found himself on show to anyone who wanted to stand and gawp at him, very much as he had been long before, when working in the window of Warren's blacking factory, but this time the gawping was positively voracious: 'People *eat* him here!' wrote the Boston sculptor William Wetmore Story on 3 February.

Dickens remained outwardly always self-possessed and affable, even when he was hardly able to stand from fatigue, but inwardly he was increasingly distressed and exasperated by all this frenzied and intrusive lionisation.[30]

Above all, he was shaken by what he saw as the scurrilous response to his (as he saw it) utterly reasonable and appropriate call for an International Copyright agreement. With regard to this, however, and also with regard to the general lionisation, Dickens's response must have been complicated by a recognition in himself, at some level, of a hitherto unsuspected capacity for deviousness. It was one thing to keep secret from his readers, as he was to do all his life, boyhood experiences involving circumstances now recalled as shameful and degrading; but it was quite another to conceal from his American readers that he was indeed intending, as many of them more than suspected, to put them in a book – to make money from them, in fact. He even inserts a teasing reference to this in *American Notes* (Bk2, ch. 6) when describing a fellow-passenger on the Lake Erie steamboat whom he overhears supposing 'that Boz will be writing a book bye and bye, and putting all our names in it'. Again, it was one thing to campaign openly for international copyright, whether or not the campaign had been premeditated, but quite another secretly to get Forster to organise public support of his stance by fellow English writers that was then presented to the American public as the result of spontaneous action on their part. Just how conscious Dickens himself was of his own deviousness in these matters is, as has been observed by one of the most perspicacious of modern Dickens critics, impossible to determine – any more than one can confidently point as this critic does, to Dickens's increased self-awareness, however muffled, as clearly leading on to his conception of the arch-hypocrite Pecksniff as the chief villain of his first post-American novel.[31]

One alteration in himself as a result of his American experiences of which Dickens was very clearly aware, however, was the shift in his political attitudes from the boisterous Radicalism of his 1841 *Examiner* squibs. This shift involved a modification of his critical stance both towards monarchy and aristocracy as governing institutions, and towards pro-democratic sentiments. America had helped him to realise just how English he was, and this included an enhanced appreciation of traditions and old-established customs, written, as it were, on the very landscape with its 'old churchyards' and 'antique houses' that he and Catherine had so rejoiced to behold again on their train journey back from Liverpool to London. 'The man who comes to this Country a Radical', he wrote to Macready from Baltimore on 22 March, glancing perhaps at Harriet Martineau, 'and goes home again with his old opinions unchanged, must be a Radical on reason, sympathy, and reflection, and one who has so well considered the subject, that he has no chance of wavering.' For himself, he returned from the great new democracy across the Atlantic not only with an altered sense of self but also with, as he put it in the suppressed first chapter to

American Notes, 'a corrected and sobered judgment' in regard to matters of political and social organisation.

Whatever profound changes were taking place within himself, however, Dickens's outward life during the months following his return home continued very much as it had been before he went abroad. He socialised with his friends (a high point being a great welcome-home dinner for him in Greenwich on 9 July at which Cruikshank became gloriously drunk), gave lavish dinner parties in Devonshire Terrace and revelled in jolly family life – inventing, for example, comic nick-names for the children, each one being pronounced, as he told Austin on 25 September, 'with a peculiar howl'. The family made their customary summer move to Broadstairs where he and Catherine entertained the customary stream of visitors, invited by Dickens, throughout August and September. Nor did such hospitality end when the Dickenses were back in London in early October. Longfellow was a house-guest for a fortnight during which Dickens took him into literary society, on an excursion to Rochester and, with Maclise, on one of his police-escorted night-tours round some of London's shadiest districts.

The most significant event in the Dickens household this year was the arrival in it as a permanent resident of fifteen-year-old Georgina, the third of the four Hogarth sisters. We do not know what brought this arrangement about but Catherine, with four young children to care for, the whole household to organise around the needs and complex requirements of her exceptionally dynamic and ultra-meticulous husband, and, on top of all this, a great deal of formal entertaining to attend to, clearly stood in need of more domestic assistance than could be provided by the usual complement of servants. Georgina could make herself useful in the nursery and elsewhere, and her move meant one less mouth for her father to feed. She was a pretty, blue-eyed girl (Maclise used her as a model for his 1843 painting 'Girl at a Waterfall', anonymously purchased by Dickens) of a helpful and obliging disposition, but for Dickens she also seemed at times to be almost like Mary returned to life: 'The perfect like of what she [Mary] was, will never be again,' he wrote to Mrs Hogarth on the anniversary of Mary's death in 1843, 'but so much of her spirit shines out in this sister [as it did not in Catherine, apparently] that the old time comes back again at some seasons, and I can hardly separate it from the present.' From now on Georgina's home was with her sister, her dazzling brother-in-law, and their ever-growing family. She and Catherine became his 'pair of petticoats', as he once called them, indulging a little harem fantasy that may have dated from his childhood reading of *The Arabian Nights*.[32]

As for his writing, before he had had much chance to begin work on his travel-book, Dickens was fired by the idea of becoming the leading contributor ('literary articles as well as political') to a new Liberal daily there suddenly seemed to be a good chance of establishing. A Conservative evening paper, *The*

20 Dickens, Catherine and Georgina Hogarth; engraving of a drawing by Maclise

Courier, had just ceased publication and its 'premises and types and so forth' were available for purchase and use in launching a brand new paper, 'nailing the true colours to the mast'. With his 'corrected and sobered judgment', his fervent Radical-Liberalism now tempered and refined by America, Dickens was eager to become a force in the political arena by placing his pen at the service of the Liberal cause. His 'old training' as a journalist, his literary powers and his phenomenal popularity (which would 'command immediate attention' for whatever he wrote) should all, he felt, make him a potential godsend to any newspaper. Only capital was needed and on 8 July he besought Lady Holland to ascertain from Lord Melbourne and others whether this might not be forthcoming from 'Members of the late Government or from the Reform Club'. Fortunately, it was not and Dickens was saved, for the time being anyway, from massively over-committing himself by taking on the job of star writer on a new national daily. Three and a half years later, he would not again be saved from himself in this way and the result would be the only public failure of his whole career, apart from the concept of *Master Humphrey's Clock*.[33]

Meanwhile, 'sketches' of America had been 'shaping themselves' in his head and by 13 July he had already begun 'working like a dray-horse' on the book. Within twenty-four hours he had completed a combatively-worded first chapter headed 'Introductory, And Necessary To Be Read' in which he listed all the things the book would *not* be. It would not be statistical or gossipy or political, nor would it be concerned with his own reception in America. He anticipates that it will be objectionable to all those many Americans apt to be 'dissatisfied with all accounts of the Republic . . . which are not couched in terms of exalted and extravagant praise'. And he adds that as he has not been accustomed to be lenient with what he deemed to be follies and abuses at home, he has 'no intention of softening down, or glozing over' those he saw abroad. All this, he wrote to a correspondent, might 'seem to prepare the reader for a much greater amount of slaughter than he will meet with; but it is *honest* and *true*'.[34]

He certainly lost no time in returning to attacks on injustice and abuses at home. On 25 July there appeared in the *Morning Chronicle* a lengthy letter from him signed 'B' (for 'Boz', presumably). As in the introductory chapter to the American book, he goes on the offensive by anticipating, and scathingly denouncing, the strong opposition to Lord Ashley's Mines and Collieries Bill sure to be deployed in the House of Lords that evening by Lord Londonderry and other colliery-owning peers. This Bill, inspired by the appalling revelations contained in the First Report of the Children's Employment Commission, was aimed at stopping the employment underground of women and children below the age of ten. Dickens savages the argument that this would constitute 'an interference with the rights of labour', as well as the fatuous assertion that miners were wholly contented with their lot. It is just as well, he writes, that miners do work underground otherwise 'society would be deafened by their shouts of merriment'. With his memories of the American South still fresh, Dickens recalls how the institution of slavery (as well as 'every other grade of poverty, neglect, oppression, and distress') is similarly defended: 'happiness capers and sings on a slave plantation, making it an Eden of ebony'. He includes a powerful passage about the brutal exploitation of children in factories and mines, the very topic on which he had promised to write an article for the *Edinburgh Review* a year before. But this kind of *Morning Chronicle* to-the-minute polemical writing suited his journalistic talents far better than composing long 'think-pieces' for heavyweight journals like the *Edinburgh*. It is very much the same sort of thing as he might have written for the new Liberal paper had it been set up. He is, however, careful not to mention his *Chronicle* letter when – perhaps seeking to square his conscience? – he writes the very next day to the *Edinburgh's* editor, Macvey Napier, saying that he was still 'really desirous' to contribute to that journal. And by not appending his name to the *Chronicle* letter he was probably hoping to hide from Napier the fact that he had written for a daily paper what is, in effect, a moderately long leading article on the very subject he had long promised to treat in the *Edinburgh*.[35]

During the summer and into October work on *American Notes* continued. By the end of July he had decided, after looking over his journal, that the work, as yet untitled, would stretch to two volumes and calculated that he had compiled about half of the first one. I use the word 'compiled' because he had pasted into the manuscript of the chapter on Boston eight and a half printed pages from a pamphlet written by Dr Samuel Gridley Howe, Director of the Massachusetts Asylum for the Blind, detailing his caring (and astonishingly effective) treatment of Laura Bridgman, a young woman born blind, deaf and dumb, and also of a blind and dumb boy. This was not book-making but a tribute Dickens wanted to pay to a man he saw as a great and inspiring healer, and to an aspect of American society that he found, with some exceptions, to be wholly admirable, and wholly shaming to England, namely the establishment and conduct of American public institutions. No doubt Dickens thought wistfully of Dr Howe and his Asylum when the best he could do for 'a wretched deaf and dumb boy' whom he found 'half-dead' upon the Broadstairs sands was to get him into a workhouse infirmary.[36]

As for the travel book, he was evidently finding some difficulty in getting the tone right (another way of putting this would be to say that there seems to have been some confusion in his mind about his target audience). How was he to reconcile the concept of 'sketches' of scenes and characters with more traditional travelogue, with a fair amount of investigative journalism (especially in relation to prisons and asylums), and with numerous polemical passages denouncing this or that aspect of American life and manners? As he worked on the early chapters, he lamented to Forster that his subjects were not the kind that he could '*dash* at' – as a sketch-writer might – but he believed things would go easier in this respect once he reached Washington. In fact, he has already managed to achieve a predominantly 'sketch' mode by the time he reaches New York. The first time we feel his imagination is really deeply engaged (stirred as it undoubtedly had been by the Laura Bridgman case) is when he comes to describe the effect, as he sees it, on its victims of the system of solitary confinement in Philadelphia's Eastern Penitentiary, a chapter he himself thought 'very good'. His intensely empathetic account of the experience of a generic prisoner under this system looks back to the powerful ending of 'A Visit to Newgate' in *Sketches by Boz* and forward, through many years, to the moving depiction of Dr Manette in *A Tale Of Two Cities*.[37]

Though Dickens told Chapman that he had written the book 'kindly and good-humouredly', few readers would agree with him. A definite animus against America and the Americans runs through it, intensifying in the later chapters, and is hardly counterbalanced by the rhapsody on Niagara. Dickens's choice of title, made in late August, was certainly aggressive: *American Notes for General Circulation*. This may have been meant to glance at the many bank failures that had afflicted America in 1837, leaving banks with worthless paper currency on their hands (Dickens alludes to the stoppage of the United States Bank and its 'ruinous consequences' in his chapter on Philadelphia). Meanwhile the 'motto' or epigraph that he proposes for the title-page slyly prophesies what will be the nature of the American publication of the book: 'In reply to a question from the Bench, the Solicitor for the Bank observed, that this kind of notes circulated the most extensively, in those parts of the world where they were stolen or forged. *Old Bailey Report*'. Forster persuaded Dickens to forego such blatant provocation as this but the title remained intact. As it was generally abbreviated to *American Notes*, however, the jibe contained in it rather lost its force.[38]

The rejected epigraph was clearly intended as another shot in his ongoing copyright campaign. On 7 July he sent a printed circular to many of his fellow British authors, and to the *Morning Chronicle* and other papers, announcing that, pending the agreement of a treaty, he would no longer have dealings with any American publishers (his self-denying ordinance, which he kept for ten years, extended even to Carey, Lea and Blanchard from whom, as we have seen, he had received money, most recently payment for early proof-sheets of *Master Humphrey's Clock*). He ends the circular by denouncing those American editors and proprietors of cheap newspapers 'who battened off English writers' and conspired to mislead the American public on the question of copyright. 'We can at least', he wrote on 26 July to fellow-novelist G. P. R. James, a mass-manufacturer of historical romances, 'shew [the Americans] that we, the robbed, entertain for them, the robbers, a very disdainful and contemptuous disgust'. This might, he hopefully added, eventually shame them into doing what no 'considerations of abstract justice' would ever move them to.[39]

The American press was not slow in striking back. A forged letter, purportedly written by Dickens to *The Morning Chronicle* on 15 July, began appearing, in whole or in part, in various American papers. The letter is a crudely-worded attack on American meanness, rudeness and so on in which the writer complains of the attentions forced upon him in America, 'many times to the serious inconvenience of myself and my party', and of 'the awkwardness, the uncouth manners, and the unmitigated selfishness which meet you everywhere in America'. The attribution to Dickens was eventually corrected but the damage was done; many Americans were left believing that Dickens had shown himself guilty of what *The Boston Courier* called 'absolute *baseness of heart* . . . spleen, ingratitude and depravity'. Dickens himself did not deign to take any public notice of this cheap trick but kept his powder dry for the crushing denunciation of most of the American press as a mere 'monster of depravity' delivered in the 'Concluding Remarks' to *American Notes*.[40]

At the beginning of September he finished the first volume and was pleased to find that both publishers and printers thought he was doing too much for the money so he could end the first volume earlier and carry over the Washington to Baltimore chapter to the second one. With Forster's help he refined the dedication of the book to his American friends, a group which, as one modern scholar has observed, 'almost with each new line [of the dedication] becomes a more limited subset of itself', amply demonstrating the problems he was experiencing in defining for himself the book's target audience: 'I DEDICATE THIS BOOK TO / THOSE FRIENDS OF MINE/ IN AMERICA / who, giving me a welcome I must ever / gratefully and proudly remember, / left my judgment / FREE; / and who, loving their country, can bear / the truth, when it is told good / humouredly, and in a / kind spirit.'[41]

He had determined to write nothing about his own reception in the States and the book is rather hamstrung as a result with the great celebrity-narrator presenting his travel report as though he had been just another European tourist but with a special interest in prisons, hospitals and other such institutions. His pride in the fact that the tremendous welcome he received resulted solely from his achievements as a writer has to be projected on to the figure of Washington Irving ('my dear friend') at the presidential reception described at the end of the first volume:

> . . . I have seldom respected a public assembly more, than I did this eager throng, when I saw them turning with one mind from noisy orators and officers of state, and flocking with a generous and honest impulse round the man of quiet pursuits: proud in his promotion [to American ambassador to Spain] as reflecting back upon their country: and grateful to him with their whole hearts for the store of graceful fancies he had poured out among them.

When it came to dealing with the unavoidable topic of slavery, which the manuscript of *American Notes* shows he had originally fiercely broached in the first chapter set on American soil, the one dealing with Boston, he was disadvantaged by having spent such a short time in the South. In lieu, therefore, of incorporating into the narrative of his journey any first-hand 'sketch' of a scene in the slave states, or any account of the actual institution of slavery, Dickens deals with the subject in a chapter appended, as it were, to the narrative. This chapter is more of an anthology than anything else, consisting as it mainly does of advertisements for runaway slaves copied out by Dickens from an anti-slavery pamphlet by an abolitionist called Theodore Weld. These advertisements document the extreme brutality of the treatment experienced by such slaves, followed by a dozen extracts from Southern

1 John Dickens
Painted by John W. Gilbert

2 Elizabeth Dickens
Painted by John W. Gilbert

3 Fred Dickens
Miniature painted by his
aunt Janet Barrow, n.d.

5 Fanny Dickens
Drawn by Samuel Laurence
in chalk and crayon,
about 1837

4 Charles Dickens aged eighteen
Miniature painted by his aunt Janet Barrow, 1830

6 Scene from 'Misnar, the Sultan of India', *Tales of the Genii* (1805)

7 Grimaldi as Clown

8 'Seven Dials' (*Sketches by Boz*)

𝕻𝖗𝖎𝖛𝖆𝖙𝖊 𝕿𝖍𝖊𝖆𝖙𝖗𝖎𝖈𝖆𝖑𝖘.

STAGE MANAGER, MR. CHARLES DICKENS.

ON SATURDAY EVENING, APRIL 27, 1833,

At Seven o'clock precisely. The performances will commence with

AN INTRODUCTORY PROLOGUE;

THE PRINCIPAL CHARACTERS BY

MR. EDWARD BARROW; MR. MILTON; MR. CHARLES DICKENS; MISS AUSTIN;
AND MISS DICKENS.

IMMEDIATELY AFTER WHICH WILL BE PRESENTED THE OPERA OF

CLARI.

The Duke Vivaldi	MR. BRAMWELL,
Rolamo, a Farmer, (Father to Clari)	MR. C. DICKENS,
Jocoso, (Valet to the Duke) .	MR. H. AUSTIN,
Nicolo	MR. MILTON,
Geronio	MR. E. BARROW,
Nimpedo	MR. R. AUSTIN,
Pages to the Duke . . .	MASTERS F. DICKENS & A. DICKENS.
Clari	MISS DICKENS,
Fidalma (her Mother) . .	MISS L. DICKENS,
Vespina	MISS AUSTIN,
Ninette	MISS OPPENHEIM.

CHARACTERS IN THE EPISODE.

The Nobleman	MR. HENRY KOLLE,
Pelgrino, a Farmer . . .	MR. JOHN DICKENS,
Wife of Pelgrino . . .	MISS URQUHART,
Leoda	MISS OPPENHEIM.

AFTER WHICH THE FAVOURITE INTERLUDE OF

The Married Bachelor.

Sir Charles Courtall . . .	MR. C. DICKENS,
Sharp	MR. JOHN URQUHART,
Lady Courtall	MISS L. DICKENS,
Grace	MISS DICKENS.

TO CONCLUDE WITH THE FARCE OF

Amateurs & Actors.

David Dulcet, Esq. (a Musical Dramatic Amateur, who employs Mr. O. P. Bustle, and attached to Theatricals and Miss Mary Hardacre)	MR. H. AUSTIN,
Mr. O. P. Bustle, (a Provincial Manager, but engaged to superintend some Private Theatricals)	MR. BRAMWELL,
Wing, (a poor Country Actor) .	MR. C. DICKENS,
Berry, (an Actor for the heavy Business) . . .	MR. BOSTON.
Elderberry, (a retired Manufacturer, simple in wit and manners, and utterly unacquainted with Theatricals)	MR. J. DICKENS,
Timkins, (Elderberry's Factotum)	MR. R. AUSTIN,
Geoffry Muffincap, (an elderly Charity Boy, let out as a Servant at Bustle's Lodging) .	MR. E. BARROW,
Miss Mary Hardacre, (a fugitive Ward of Elderberry's) . .	MISS DICKENS,
Mrs. Mary Goneril, (a Strolling Tragedy Actress, and a serious evil to her Husband) .	MISS OPPENHEIM

The Scenery by Messrs. H. Austin, Milton, H. Kolle, and Assistants.——The Band which will be numerous and complete, under the direction of Mr. E. Barrow.

J. & G. Nichols, Printers, Earl's Court, Cranbourn Street, Soho.

9 Playbill for the Dickens family private theatricals, 27 April 1833

10 George Hogarth
Dickens's father-in-law, from a miniature

11 John Black
'my first hearty out-and-out appreciator'

12 Robert Seymour
Published by his widow, 6 May 1841

13 George Cruikshank
Drawn by Maclise for *Fraser's* 'Gallery of Literary
Characters' (1833); see Robert L. Patten, *George
Cruikshank's Life, Times and Art*, I (1992), 386

MR BOZ   MR TINTO   MR MAC   MR PROUT

*Drawn by W. M. Thackeray
at St James's grove 1838.*

14 Dickens, Thackeray, Maclise and Francis Mahony ('Father Prout')
Sketched by Thackeray in 1836

15 Letter from Dickens to Chapman and Hall (?6 August 1836)

16 John Forster
Portrait by Daniel Maclise (1830)

17 Daniel Maclise
From his self-portrait, *Fraser's* 'Gallery of Literary
Characters' (1838)

18 48 Doughty Street, now the Charles Dickens
Museum

19 Thomas Talfourd
From a painting by Sir Thomas Lawrence

S U N D A Y

UNDER THREE HEADS.

AS IT IS;

AS SABBATH BILLS WOULD MAKE IT;

AS IT MIGHT BE MADE.

BY TIMOTHY SPARKS.

LONDON:

CHAPMAN AND HALL, 186, STRAND.

1836.

21 Charles Dickens
By Samuel Laurence, chalk and crayon (1837)

22 Catherine Dickens
By Samuel Laurence, chalk and crayon (1837)

Dickens standing triumphant on the head of Mr Pickwick; etched by Thomas Sibson for his *Sibson's Racy Sketches of Expeditions, from the Pickwick Club* (1838)

27 Page of the manuscript of *Nicholas Nickleby*

28 Browne's original pencil and wash drawing for 'A sudden recognition, unexpected on both sides' (see *Nicholas Nickleby*, ch. 38); on it Dickens has written in pencil (words partly obscured by mount), 'I don't think Smike is frightened enough or that Squeers is earnest enough – for my purposes'

29 'The Nickleby portrait', engraved from the oil painting by Maclise (1839) for use as frontispiece to first volume edition of *Nicholas Nickleby*

30 1 Devonshire Terrace
From a sketch by Maclise

31 The Countess of Blessington and Count D'Orsay

32 Sir Edward Bulwer Lytton

33 Broadstairs
Engraved from a drawing by George Shepherd (working between 1830 and 1858)

"How should you like to grow up a clever man, and write books?" said the old gentleman.

"I think I would rather read them Sir" replied Oliver.

"What! Wouldn't you like to be a book-writer?" said the old gentleman.

Oliver considered a little while, and at last said he should think it would be a much better thing to be a bookseller; upon which the old gentleman laughed heartily, and declared he had said a very good thing, which Oliver felt glad to have done, though he by no means knew what it was.

<u>Vide Oliver Twist</u> in which the old gentleman does not say, though I do that Chapman and Hall are the best of booksellers past present or to come; and my trusty friends. Which I give under my hand for the benefit of Edward Chapman, his book, this fourteenth day of November 1839.

Witness Boz.   [signature: Charles Dickens]

34 Inscription in a copy of *Pickwick Papers*, written by Dickens for Edward Chapman, 14 November 1839

35 Dickens in Lord Byron's chair in Cattermole's studio, sketched by Leonardo Cattermole

" A black and dreadful place !" exclaimed the child.
" Look in," said the old man, pointing downward with his finger.
The child complied, and gazed down into the pit.

" It looks like a grave, itself," said the old man.
" It does," replied the child.
" I have often had the fancy," said the sexton, " that it might have been
dug at first to make the old place more gloomy, and the old monks more
religious. It's to be closed up, and built over."
The child still stood, looking thoughtfully into the vault.
" We shall see," said the sexton, " on what gay heads other earth will
have closed, when the light is shut out from here. God knows ! They'll
close it up, next spring."

" The birds sing again in spring," thought the child, as she leant at her
casement window, and gazed at the declining sun. " Spring ! a beautiful
and happy time !"

36 Page from *Master Humphrey's Clock* showing woodcut by Maclise (his only contribution to the
periodical) dropped into the text of *The Old Curiosity Shop*

37 'Boz's Introduction to Christopher North and the Caledonian Youth' (1841). Caricature engraving by A.Lesage showing Dickens being presented by Lord Jeffrey to Professor John Wilson and Peter Robinson ('Christopher North' and 'The Caledonian Youth' of *Blackwood's Magazine*) while Scott and Shakespeare look down approvingly on the event

38 The Dickens children, Charley, Mamie, Katey and Walter, portrayed, with Grip the raven, by Maclise for Catherine Dickens to take with her to America (1841)

39 Washington Irving

newspapers, supplied to Dickens by his publishers, reporting violent crimes committed against each other by Southern whites. These latter extracts were intended to show the brutalising effects on the community as a whole of the existence of slavery. Dickens pasted the extracts into his manuscript, adding italicisation marks here and there, and by 5 October, re-installed in Devonshire Terrace, he could tell Forster that he had finished the slavery chapter (which Longfellow thought 'grand') after working all day until midnight on the previous day.[42]

The last chapter, 'Concluding Remarks', features Dickens's denunciation of the 'mortal poison' diffused by the vast mass of American newspapers with its 'evil eye in every house, and its black hand in every appointment in the state, from a president to a postman'. A footnote refers the reader for corroboration of his charges to 'an able and perfectly truthful article' in the October issue of the *Foreign Quarterly Review* (published by Chapman and Hall) to which, says Dickens, 'my attention has been attracted, since these sheets [i.e., of *American Notes*] have been passing through the press'. In fact, Dickens is once more being more than a little disingenuous here since he had certainly been deeply involved in the production of this article. Its anonymous author was Forster, who in fact edited the *Foreign Quarterly* but seems to have kept very quiet about the fact, and it is a swingeing attack on the 'loathsome slander', 'positive obscenity' and 'blackguardism' characteristic of such mass-circulation papers as *The New York Herald* and *The Morning Courier and New York Enquirer*, containing certain details that Forster could have derived only from Dickens. American newspapers that supported the campaign for international copyright were singled out for praise. Copies of the October *Foreign Quarterly* reached New York on 18 October and Dickens was at once widely credited with being the author. Indeed, the *Herald* reprinted the article with the heading 'Boz's First Words on America'.[43]

Within a few more days Dickens had finished his book completely, inserting at the last minute, at his brother-in-law Henry Austin's instigation, a recommendation to the Americans to study Edwin Chadwick's *Report on the Sanitary Condition of the Labouring Population of Great Britain* (1842), and having been persuaded by Forster to drop the introductory chapter (subsequently printed in Forster's *Life of Dickens*). He did, however, rescue from it one aggressive phrase for use as the last words of the book, thus giving the phrase much greater prominence. In the cancelled chapter he had written of the crowds who welcomed him to America that he saw them as carrying in their hospitable hands 'a home-made wreath of laurel; and not an iron muzzle disguised beneath a flower or two' (in other words, he was not made to feel threatened if he did not write what the Americans wished to read). The book as published ends with a paragraph in which Dickens says that he has made no reference in it to his reception, nor has he allowed that to influence him in what he has written:

'in either case I should have offered but a sorry acknowledgment, compared with that I bear within my breast, towards those partial readers of my books across the Water, who met me with an open hand, and not with one that closed upon an iron muzzle.'

It was an unfortunate decision to drop the introductory chapter because it makes clear what kind of a book it is, explains less aggressively why Dickens makes no reference to the welcome given to him by the 'most generous and affectionate-hearted' American people ('it would ill become me to flourish matter necessarily involving so much of my own praises, in the eyes of my unhappy readers'), and mounts a strong defence against charges of national prejudice. Such preliminary clarification would have been all the more useful because of the enormous anticipation of the book that existed. *American Notes* was, as has been well said, 'news rather than literature' in that it brought Dickens out 'in a new field'. British readers and reviewers 'waited to see whether he would show himself a universal genius or be exposed to his critics'. As to the Americans, they were waiting, after the excitement of the forged letter, to see whether the man they had so lavishly honoured would prove a mere 'Trollopizing' ingrate, or would produce a fair-minded book reporting on their 'go-ahead' young country. In Britain orders for the book from the trade were, he told his sister Fanny, 'much larger than have ever been known since Scott's time – taking off 3000 copies in two days, a week before its publication'. The book appeared on 19 October and three days later John Dickens, who ('fearing' that he might be 'overlooked at such a distance') had previously solicited a publication-day copy from Chapman and Hall, wrote to the publishers from Alphington, 'Your account of the subscriptions I presume to be most satisfactory, in as much as the *whole* of your contemplated first issue was not sufficiently extensive to reach it.' He added, 'To describe the pleasure and gratification I have had in reading the volumes, is out of the question. That they will add greatly to Charles's character [that is, reputation] I have no doubt, and I trust very considerably to your mutual pecuniary profit and advantage also.'[44]

The latter portion of John's comments was justified in that, as Dickens could tell Felton on 31 December, 'Four large Editions' had been sold by that date, yielding him a profit of £1,000 which more than covered his advance of £885. The critical reception was decidedly mixed, however. Forster highly praised the book in an anonymous *Examiner* review but it was severely criticised by Tory novelist Samuel Warren in *Blackwood's*, by an anonymous reviewer in *Fraser's* (Dickens knew his identity and it was, he told a correspondent on 8 November, someone 'to whom, I need scarcely add, I have ever been kind and considerate'), by John Croker in the *Quarterly* and – embarrassingly for Macvey Napier – by Tennyson's friend James Spedding in the *Edinburgh*. There was in these reviews, as has been shown, a distinct element of putting down this Radical-leaning young writer, with what Spedding called his 'desultory education,' who had sprung from no one knew where. As to the book's fate in America, it was promptly pirated and sold in prodigious quantities. *The New York Herald* printed and sold 50,000 copies in two days. Reviewers were generally and predictably hostile, a reviewer in *The Southern Literary Messenger*, for example, calling it 'one of the most suicidal productions, ever deliberately published by an author, who had the least reputation to lose'. In the January 1843 issue of the influential *North American Review*, however, Felton stoutly defended his friend's work – to Dickens's great delight, of course. It was, he argued, very much the kind of book that readers had a right to expect from the author of *Pickwick*, neither didactic nor philosophical but 'full of graphic touches, good feeling, and pleasant observation' and abounding in 'touches of the poetical and imaginative'.[45]

With *American Notes* behind him Dickens could begin to think more fully about the new 'tale of English life and manners', to be issued in the old monthly-part format, promised to his readers nearly a year before, in the closing numbers of the *Clock*. He seems now, after his immersion in America and things American, to have wanted the new story to be not just English but really unmistakeably English both in the 'life and manners' to be depicted and in its physical setting. With regard to the latter, he happily fell in with Forster's suggestion that, once he had finished *American Notes*, he and Dickens should, as it were, 'challenge' Dickens's memories of American scenery by taking a trip into some picturesque and preferably unfamiliar English county. Maclise and Stanfield would also be of the party. By early August Cornwall had been fixed upon and Dickens's imagination was busy conjuring up powerful visions of bleak and desolate landscapes, of deep mines extending beneath the sea (Cornish tin and copper mines were still in full production at this time), of St Michael's Mount and dramatic seascapes, of Land's End and the Eddystone Lighthouse. Meditating a more striking opening for the new tale than any he had written for its predecessors, he told Forster, 'I have some notion of opening the new book in the lantern of a lighthouse!' Six weeks or so later, as he beavered away on *American Notes*, his imagination continued to dwell on the idea of sea-girt Cornwall, and on the descriptions of God-forsaken mining areas he had read about in the Children's Employment Commission Report. The new book might open in 'some terribly dreary iron-bound spot' and, two days after *American Notes* is published, Dickens writes to Southwood Smith asking for his help in locating 'the very dreariest and most desolate portion of the sea-coast of Cornwall', as well as 'the next best bleak and barren part'. Tintagel was Smith's nomination for the most cheerless spot: 'here shall you see nothing but bleak-looking rocks and an everlastingly boisterous sea'.[46]

It is as though Dickens, having been disappointed in his expectation of finding inspirational wildernesses in America, landscapes that might parallel the sublimity of Glencoe even though lacking a comparable grim history, is now bent upon realising such a setting in England. As to 'life and manners', he finds himself dealing zestfully with a quintessentially English thing in this area too, immediately after writing the last pages of *American Notes*. Lord Ashley's bill, which Dickens had, as we have seen, made time to write a long impassioned defence of in a letter to *The Morning Chronicle* on 25 July, finally passed the Lords on 1 August but with many watering-down amendments. The Tory peer and colliery-owner Lord Londonderry thereupon published his would-be magnificently crushing *Letter to Lord Ashley on the Mines and Collieries Bill*. Dickens had asked to have the reviewing of this document for the *Chronicle* and his notice, to which he must have turned immediately upon finishing *American Notes*, and over which, as the much-corrected manuscript shows, he took considerable care, appeared on 20 October. It brilliantly mocks the noble Lord's self-satisfied pomposity and the absurdity of some of his assertions, e.g., that a certain ornately-phrased letter of support quoted by him was written by a little trapper-boy. It makes allusion to a 'piscina' and this, writes Dickens, 'is particularly natural, for it is well known that trapper boys are always thinking of piscinae, and from their earliest infancy constantly ruminate, at the bottom of mines, in the Latin tongue'. It seems likely that Londonderry's grandiose style and sublime self-conceit may well have contributed towards the creation of 'the moral Pecksniff'.[47]

But Pecksniff was probably not yet even a twinkle in Dickens's eye when he and his friends set off for Cornwall on 27 October. Not even the title of the new story scheduled to begin publication in just over two months' time had been settled. In *The Athenaeum* of 29 October it was advertised as, simply: 'A New Tale of English Life and Manners. By "Boz". To be Completed in Twenty Monthly Numbers, and illustrated with Two etchings on steel.' Even the question of who would provide the illustrations, whether Browne alone or Browne sharing the work with another artist as on *Master Humphrey's Clock*, was apparently still undecided. The first and most urgent task that awaited Dickens on his return from the Cornish tour would be to choose his title, always for him a vital first step in beginning a new work. For the moment, however, he launched himself into what proved to be a thoroughly joyous, though short, expedition. This, and the publication of his travel book, he might reasonably have felt, would provide closure for his (in many respects decidedly *un*joyous) engagement with America, even though such closure might mean that that 'sublimated essence of comicality' he had apprehended during his transatlantic adventures would have to remain for ever undistilled.

CHAPTER 9

'The turning-point of his career'

ENGLAND, ITALY, ENGLAND, 1842–1845

'Ah!' he [Dickens] said to me, 'when I saw those [Venetian] places, how I thought that to leave one's hand upon the time, lastingly upon the time, with one tender touch for the mass of toiling people that nothing could obliterate, would be to lift oneself above the dust of all the Doges in their graves, and stand upon a giant's staircase that Samson couldn't overthrow!'

Forster, *Life of Dickens*, 348

FROM 27 OCTOBER to 4 November 1842 Dickens and his friends toured Cornwall in an open carriage amid much jollity and boisterous fun. Dickens later described to Felton their exploration of 'earthy old Churches' and 'strange caverns on the gloomy seashore' as well as their going 'down into the depths of Mines, and up to the tops of giddy heights where the unspeakably green water was roaring I dont know how many hundred feet below!' Unlike America, Cornwall lived up to all his expectations yet the first scene of his 'New Tale of English Life and Manners' was not laid there after all but in Wiltshire. It was some time, however, before he altogether abandoned the notion of setting part of the 'new tale' in Cornwall and his imagination continued to be haunted by its rugged landscape, mines and dramatic coastline. They appear in the *Carol*, for example, when Scrooge finds himself transported to 'a bleak and desert moor, where monstrous masses of rude stone were cast about as though it were the burial-place of giants', and then whirled out to sea where his ears are 'deafened by the thundering of water, as it rolled, and roared, and raged among the dreadful caverns it had worn, and fiercely tried to undermine the earth'.[1]

Home again in Devonshire Terrace, Dickens plunged into what he described to Burdett Coutts on 12 November as 'the agonies of plotting and contriving a new book'. In fact, this was the first time he had ever been in quite this situation, though he makes it sound a familiar one when he writes: 'In starting a work which is to last for twenty months, there are so many little things to attend to, which require my personal superintendence that I am obliged to be constantly on the watch.' Neither *Pickwick* nor *Nickleby* had been begun in that way, nor, for that matter, had *Oliver* or *The Old Curiosity Shop*. The long-gestated *Barnaby*

had been plotted out as a novel as none of its predecessors had been but this is
the first time that Dickens begins a story having in mind an overall *design*, a
unifying theme, intended to pervade and shape the whole work. 'I set out on this
journey', he was to tell his readers in the preface written for *Chuzzlewit*'s publication in volume form, 'with the design of exhibiting, in various aspects, the
commonest of all the vices'. Forster tells us that Dickens's plan was to show,
'more or less by every person introduced, the number and variety of humours
and vices that have their root in selfishness'. Self-interest was, as Dickens saw it,
the age's besetting sin. Unconcern for others manifested itself in individuals, in
social grouping and in religious denominations. He sought to startle his readers
at the outset by means of an 'overture' chapter reminiscent of the second one in
Fielding's satirical novel *Jonathan Wild* (1743) and quite unlike the opening of
any of his previous books. All notions of pride of birth and breeding are reduced
to absurdity. The seedy Chuzzlewit family, 'descended in a direct line from Adam
and Eve', represent all humanity and the Chuzzlewits in his tale, writes Dickens,
will be found to have 'many counterparts and prototypes in the Great World
about us'. The family name is derived from the verb 'to chizzle' (variant of
'chisel'), meaning 'to cheat or defraud', which, according to the *Oxford English
Dictionary*, was 'quite a current word in England in 1835'.[2]

According to Forster, 'the notion of taking Pecksniff for a type of character
was really the origin of the book'. This might seem to recall Dickens's famous
'I thought of Mr Pickwick and began' but denotes a very different process.
Pickwick as first conceived by Dickens is simply a stock farcical type, the vainglorious pedant. He has a comic appearance and a comic-sounding name
(borrowed from a real-life one that had caught Dickens's eye), and is a
perfectly adequate protagonist for the sequence of ludicrous misadventures
intended to constitute *The Pickwick Papers*. But Mr Pecksniff, a prominent
member of the Chuzzlewit clan, is a great 'humour' character in the tradition
of Ben Jonson (whose play *Every Man in His Humour* Dickens was later to
produce and perform in). Pecksniff expresses his 'humour', or dominating
characteristic, an endlessly resourceful moral hypocrisy, in everything he says
and does – even in everything he wears. His name expresses him perfectly,
suggestive as it is both of carping criticism and of supercilious disapproval.
Dickens is generally agreed to have modelled the character to quite an extent
on a certain public figure called Samuel Carter Hall. Hall edited *The Art Union
Monthly Journal of the Fine Arts*, was a zealous teetotaller and a loquacious
supporter of many worthy causes, a man whose 'smooth self-righteousness'
and 'conspicuous puritanism' irritated many besides Dickens. His nickname
was 'Shirt Collar Hall', and Dickens lays emphasis on the 'jutting heights of
collar' that set off Pecksniff's 'moral' throat. Hall seems to have been quite
unabashed by the Pecksniff portrayal. After reading a report of one of Hall's
speeches years later Dickens raged to Wilkie Collins about 'the snivelling

insolence of it, the concentrated essence of Snobbery in it, the dirty Pecksniffianity that pervaded it'.[3]

Dickens seems to have hit at once upon the name for Pecksniff but he evidently had more trouble with the surname of the new story's eponymous hero, experimenting with 'Sweezleden', 'Sweezleback' and 'Sweezlewag', then (abandoning the hint of 'swindling' for that of 'chiselling') 'Chuzzletoe', 'Chuzzleboy', 'Chubblewig' and 'Chuzzlewig' before finally settling on 'Chuzzlewit'. 'Martin', however, was fixed upon from the start. Dickens still clung to the formula of a long, facetious title that would not tie him down too much even though he meant this story to mark a distinct artistic advance on its monthly-part predecessors. He also reverted (for the last time in his career) to the pseudonym of 'Boz' as belonging to this mode of publication. Some time around 12 November he sent a first draft of the title to Forster which went through several minor changes before it appeared in the following form in an *Athenaeum* advertisement on the 26th: *The/ Life and Adventures/ of/ Martin Chuzzlewit /His relatives, friends and enemies. /Comprising all/ His Wills and His Ways, /With an Historical record of what he did /and what he didn't;/ shewing moreover/ who inherited the Family Plate; / Who came in for the Silver spoons, /and who for the Wooden Ladles./ The whole forming a complete key / To The House of Chuzzlewit. / Edited by Boz / With illustrations by Phiz'.*[4]

He had thought of recruiting a young artist called John Leech to work with Browne on the new story. Leech, he thought, might perhaps share the illustrating of *Chuzzlewit* with Browne rather as Cattermole had shared the illustrating of *Master Humphrey's Clock*. Browne seems to have resisted the arrangement, however, and Dickens gave up the notion, though he cultivated Leech's friendship. In the event Browne rose splendidly to the challenge of the new work, developing his own art in parallel with Dickens's.[5]

'Unless', Dickens told Burdett Coutts in the letter already cited, 'I were to shut myself up, obstinately and sullenly in my own room for a great many days without writing a word, I don't think I should ever make a beginning.' Yet, on the same day that he wrote this he dashed off another letter to Macready, offering to write a Prologue for a new five-act blank-verse tragedy Macready was shortly to produce and star in at Drury Lane. *The Patrician's Daughter* was the first dramatic effort of a young man called John Westland Marston, and is quite unreadable today. But it was seized upon by Macready, and fervent supporters of his like Forster and Dickens, as the sort of play that would help to 'revive the drama', as the phrase went – that is, to restore to the English stage the glories of Shakespeare's day (when, of course, all tragedies were five acts long and written in blank verse).

Dickens's eagerness to promote the play probably stemmed not just from his constant desire to be serviceable to Macready but also from the fact that it chimed with many of his current preoccupations. It had a contemporary setting and revolved, as the title suggests, around issues of class. The low-born hero is a man who has risen to eminence through his own strenuous efforts but whose mind and heart have been scarred in the process and we can understand how this theme would have resonated with Dickens. Macready was, naturally, happy to accept Dickens's offer and, after passing through three drafts, the Prologue finally got itself written. Composed of forty-eight lines of heroic couplets, its key phrase is 'Awake the Present!' Just as Dickens himself is now turning from the Scott-style historical fiction of *Barnaby* to a story of contemporary 'English life and manners', so he admonishes fellow-writers to turn their attention to the present day and instructs the audience to learn from Marston's play 'How social usage has the pow'r to change/ Good thoughts to evil; in its highest range/To cramp the noble soul, and turn to ruth/ The kindling impulse of our glorious youth,/ Crushing the spirit in its house of clay.' His final line turns the spotlight on the audience: 'Yourselves the actors, and your homes the scene.' Dickens briefly thought of using a version of this line as an epigraph for *Chuzzlewit* – '*Your* homes the scene. *Yourselves* the Actors, here' – but Forster wisely dissuaded him from so confrontational an approach to his readers.[6]

In fact, the English world of *Chuzzlewit* is somewhat distanced in time from that of its first readers (the American scenes by contrast are markedly contemporary). Although Dickens *is* concerned with current social ills as well as moral failings, and once or twice breaks into a fierce polemic on the subject, he does not yet seem ready to give his main story a fully modern setting. Indeed, the English part of *Chuzzlewit* sometimes seems to be pervaded by a 'nooks and corners' antiquarianism somewhat reminiscent of Master Humphrey. It is not until he comes to write his next novel, *Dombey and Son*, that Dickens gives his whole story a firmly present-day setting and, in place of the nostalgic celebration of stage-coach travel in chapter 36 of *Chuzzlewit* we find in chapter 20 of *Dombey* a powerful description of Mr Dombey's train ride to Leamington.

The prologue for Marston's play was not the only distraction for Dickens as he began *Chuzzlewit*. He busied himself to get a grant from the Literary Fund for the widow of the old Radical satirist William Hone, who had asked for a visit from him on his deathbed and whom Dickens described to the Fund, in a tactfully anodyne way, as a writer who had contributed 'to the stock of cheerful blameless literature'. He wrote a short anonymous piece for *The Morning Chronicle* (published 29 Nov. 1842) in support of the sanitary reformer Dr Southwood Smith's projected Sanatorium, a subscription-run London nursing-home for impoverished members of the middle classes – clerks, young students, governesses – alone in the city who fell ill, either physically or mentally. Also, some mysterious family business, 'not the most pleasant in its nature', required his attention. He also found himself bowled over by another new blank-verse five-act drama Macready was considering. This was Browning's *A*

Blot in the 'Scutcheon, which, like Marston's play, dramatised the tragic consequences of aristocratic pride but was set back in the eighteenth-century. Dickens
responded with extraordinary intensity to the pathos of the heroine's repeated
line about the terrible carnal error into which she and her equally innocent
young lover had fallen: 'I was so young – I had no mother.' He knew, he told
Forster, 'nothing that is so affecting' in any book he had ever read. The extremity
of this reaction, together with his responsiveness to Marston's play and its
portrayal of the hardening of a man's nature as a result of his having been
socially shamed in his early years, suggests that Dickens was now beginning to
allow into the forefront of his mind, as it were, disturbing memories of his own
blacking-factory days, and of what he now remembered as his mother's abandonment of him. This led to thoughts about 'how all these things have worked
together to make me what I am', a development that was to become centrally
important to his writing of the mid to late 1840s.[7]

Distractions notwithstanding, he managed to finish *Chuzzlewit* I (chs 1–3)
soon after 8 December. He rushed round to Forster to try the effect upon him
of Pecksniff and of Pecksniff's idolater, victim, and moral opposite, Tom
Pinch, the most elaborate example to date in Dickens's fiction of that favourite
and most indulged character of his, the guileless grown-up child. Forster tells
us that 'perhaps no story was ever begun by [Dickens] with stronger heart and
confidence' and this confidence manifests itself even in the very texture of the
prose – in the self-delighting, virtuoso quality, for example, of the satirical
writing in the first chapter. This quality is found also in the second with its
richly evocative description of an autumn evening in the countryside. In this
chapter, too, and in the next, exuberant changes are rung upon Pecksniff's
wonderfully unctuous idiolect. Finally, at the end of the number, our attention
is firmly directed to the story's overall theme, 'Universal Self!'. Dickens 'strikes
the key-note before pursuing [his] tune' as he later describes himself doing in
a very different novel, *Hard Times*.[8]

Dickens's sense of mastery in this new story is shown not only in the
virtuosity of his prose, and the unprecedented sense of overall purpose and
direction that we apprehend from the outset, but also in his introduction of a
new style of punctuation. This involves the lavish use of colons and semi-
colons to mark pauses in long sentences (sometimes in short ones too) that
will be a prominent feature in his first Christmas Books. This punctuation is
rhetorical rather than grammatical in nature, as though Dickens were *telling*
rather than writing his story, and contributes towards a further strengthening
of that peculiarly personal intimacy with his readers already established as the
hallmark of the writer Charles Dickens.

With *Chuzzlewit* I completed, Dickens turned to writing a satirical piece,
'Snoring for the Million', for anonymous publication in Fonblanque's
Examiner. The Government was encouraging the establishment of singing

classes for the masses ('Singing for the Million' was the catchphrase) and Dickens seizes the opportunity to express his growing anxiety about the state of the nation. How much better it would be, suggests Dickens with heavy irony, if, instead of singing, people could be taught to pass most of their time sleeping:

> Oppressive and unequal laws will be no more remembered; the justice dealt out by Magistrates to Poverty, instead of . . . goading the irritated on to fury, and arming the wicked and designing with their sharpest weapons, will be forgotten save in dreams; . . . there will be no fast-widening gulf between the two great divisions of society: all will be peace and comfort. . . .

This little piece appeared on Christmas Eve and is worth noting as a slight foretaste of the 'sledgehammer' social messages that Dickens was to deliver to the British public under his own name for Christmas 1843 and Christmas 1844. He was also, as always, busy at this time on the domestic front, especially in making elaborate preparations for a great Twelfth Night party in honour of Charley's birthday. This would feature not only a magic lantern but also a dazzling display of conjuring by himself for which he had bought from the great toy-shop Hamley's a complete conjurer's outfit. This must have been one of the earliest of those memorable Dickens children's parties so fondly recalled by Thackeray's elder daughter as 'shining facts in our early London days'. 'There were', she wrote, 'other parties, and they were very nice, but nothing to compare to these: not nearly so light, not nearly so shining, not nearly so going round and round.'[9]

During the first six months of 1843 the writing of *Chuzzlewit* proceeded steadily. Dickens tried to adhere to a routine of keeping himself 'strictly at home, with the exception of a long country walk or ride every day, during one half of the month', a régime which, he told Lady Holland on 28 February, he found 'a capital one, both for health and pleasant authorship'. Towards the end of March, however, he found it necessary, in order to concentrate on the writing and planning of the novel, to retreat to 'a sequestered Farm House at Finchley', Finchley being still very much a rural area at this time. He remained based at Cobley's Farm, as the place was called, for upwards of two months and it was here, Forster remembered, Dickens first told him, 'walking and talking in the green lanes as the midsummer months were coming on', about the eccentric monthly nurse he intended introducing into the story (Mrs Gamp first appears in *Chuzzlewit* VIII, the July number). In Finchley his immediate concern was *Chuzzlewit* V, which contains a number of important plot-developments and ends with Martin's sudden announcement of his decision to go to America. A surviving note made for the preceding number shows that one major strand of the plot was already clear in his mind ('Old Martin's Plot to degrade and punish Pecksniff in the end') and progress reports in his letters indicate ease of composition. He was struck, he told Forster, by the way in which two of the story's main characters 'opened out' to him as he wrote ('one of the most surprising processes of the mind in this sort of invention'), and to Felton he had written on 2 March that he was 'powdering away' at the story with 'all manner of facetiousness' rising up before him as he went on. But he was also able to curb his own exuberance, as shown by his jettisoning of the first seven slips of chapter 6, which contain amusing but essentially repetitive material.[10]

During these weeks Dickens also found time to do Macready another good turn. He published in *The Examiner* (4 March) an appreciation of Macready's Benedick in the actor-manager's own production of Shakespeare's *Much Ado About Nothing*. His defence of Macready's acting against the criticism that it is 'broad, or farcical, or overstrained' at the climactic point of Benedick's confusion (Act II, sc. 3) is also a defence of his own comic art. Macready's performance, he asserts, is entirely natural, a true enactment of how any 'master of fiction' would have described Benedick's behaviour at this juncture, and he proceeds to invoke his novelistic pantheon of Goldsmith, Swift, Fielding, Smollett, Sterne, and Scott – that great tradition of novelists to which he might now feel confident that he himself belonged, whatever Abraham Hayward might say. That he was seen by his fellow-writers as a leading figure in the field is shown by the efforts made to involve him this month in the ill-fated Society, or Association, of British Authors. He chaired one meeting (8 April) but afterwards withdrew from the Society, believing it to be a hopeless project. Two months later, however, he did chair another meeting, this time of authors, publishers and printers in the publisher Longman's office to establish an Association for the Protection of Literature, to ensure compliance with copyright laws. This proved to be a quite ineffectual organisation that struggled on for a few years before collapsing in 1849.[11]

Meanwhile, his deep concern over 'the Condition of England' was losing nothing of its urgency. He was 'perfectly stricken down' by the harrowing evidence contained in Southwood Smith's Second Report of the Parliamentary Commission on Children's Employment ('Trades and Manufactures'). He is thinking, he writes to Smith on 6 March, of publishing, as soon as he has finished his monthly *Chuzzlewit* stint, 'a very cheap pamphlet, called "An appeal to the People of England, on behalf of the Poor Man's Child" – with my name attached, of course'. Four days later, however, he defers this purpose until the end of the year when he believes he will be able to write something that will have 'twenty thousand times the force' that could be exerted by his first idea. It seems that he is already thinking of the power of the Christmas factor as regards appeals on behalf of the poor. Meanwhile, his anger about contemporary social issues burns away beneath the Pickwickian/Nicklebeian surface of *Chuzzlewit*, sometimes bursting through, as in chapter 13. This chapter was written during the first half of May, just after he had been especially disgusted by the speeches made by certain City merchants at a charity dinner, 'sleek, slobbering, bow-paunched, overfed, apoplectic, snorting cattle – and the auditory leaping up in their delight!' In the *Chuzzlewit* passage written immediately afterwards he bids the complacently prosperous to go 'into the mine, the mill, the forge, the squalid depths of deepest ignorance, and uttermost abyss of man's neglect, and say can any hopeful plant spring up in air so foul that it extinguishes the soul's bright torch as fast as it is kindled!'[12]

Dickens was especially angered by the failure of the various religious denominations to do anything to save children and give them a chance of a better life through education, a failure stemming from sectarian rivalry or even rifts within denominations themselves. Even the Americans put England to shame in the matter of national education, Mr Bevan, *Martin Chuzzlewit*'s 'good American', was to declare in the novel's June number (ch.17). Dickens finds himself growing 'horribly bitter', for example, about the Church of England's preoccupation with its own internal divisions about 'Puseyism' (the Oxford, or High Church, Movement). In 'Snoring for the Million' he had attacked the 'intolerant and bigoted insanity' of this Church that 'loves, in its greatest danger, ever to exhibit itself with its hand at its own throat'. Now, in late May after finishing *Chuzzlewit* VI, he fired off another scathing anonymous piece for *The Examiner*, cleverly aping the format of Southwood Smith's Report. Dickens's 'Report of the Commissioners Appointed to Inquire into the Condition of the Persons Variously Engaged in the University of Oxford' (published 3 June 1843) likens the bigotry of the University's bickering clergy to the benighted ignorance of factory children. His utter disgust with the Church of England moved him to join the Unitarians (we recall how impressed he had been by Channing in Boston). The Unitarians, he wrote to Felton on 2 March, '*would* do something for human improvement if they could', and they 'practise Charity and Toleration'. His rage against sectarianism expressed itself again four months later when he redeemed a four-year-old promise to Lady Blessington to write something for her annual *The Keepsake*. His verses, entitled 'A Word in Season', describe England as a country 'Where darkness sat upon the living waters/ And brutal ignorance, and toil, and dearth / Were the hard portion of its sons and daughters', whilst those churchmen who should have worked to remedy this situation 'Squabbled for words upon the altar-floor, / And rent The Book, in struggles for the binding'.[13]

At the end of *Chuzzlewit* V, the May number, young Martin Chuzzlewit, following his show-down with Pecksniff, suddenly announces he will go to America. Nothing has prepared the reader for this, nor is there any evidence that Dickens, for all his determination, retrospectively announced in his Preface, to 'keep a steadier eye upon the general purpose and design' of this work than he had done with its predecessors, had envisaged such a picaresque-style development from the beginning. No doubt a desire to increase the disappointing sales of the monthly parts had much to do with the decision. Sales had been sticking at around 20,000 per month, barely half of the circulation of *Pickwick* and *Nickleby*, while *Master Humphrey*, in the cheaper weekly parts, had at its peak sold around 70,000 copies. This situation was frustrating for Dickens, believing, as he told Forster on 2 November, that *Chuzzlewit* was 'in a hundred points immeasurably the best of my stories'. It was also a matter of great concern to Dickens as a man with a large household and a highly sociable lifestyle to maintain. He had had only £20 in his bank account at Coutts's at the end of 1842, and he still owed Chapman and Hall the £1,800 advanced to him before he went to America. We have already noted Jane Carlyle's comment on his lavish entertaining, and another of his dinner-guests at Devonshire Terrace, Dr Gridley Howe, Director of the Perkins Institution for the Blind that Dickens had visited in Boston, thought his host was 'by the style of his living, endangering his *biler*, as the Kentucks say'. Dickens had constantly to cope, moreover, with the ever-recurrent drain on his finances caused by the shame-less sponging of his father and other family, his 'blood-petitioners', as he once bitterly called them.[14]

While Dickens's decision to start drawing on his recent American experi-ences may have been primarily motivated by the hope of increasing sales (which it did only very moderately, however), it was also, Forster tells us, because of his continuing anger with American journalists, whom he later called 'a herd of rascals, who are the human lice of God's creation'. He was aware, though he claimed not to read them, of the strident attacks on him and his integrity being made in the American press, and he had been much annoyed by a pro-American, and somewhat supercilious, review of *American Notes* that had appeared in the January *Edinburgh*. Here now was a golden opportunity both to 'make good' his *Notes* and to produce that 'distilled essence of comi-cality' that he had eschewed in his travel book. He could at the same time give a dramatic new turn to his current serial and also deliver a 'sledgehammer' counter-blow to his American attackers. The blow certainly hit its target: 'Martin has made them all stark staring raving mad across the water,' he exulted to Forster a few months later.[15]

Chuzzlewit VII, the first American number, describes Martin's and Mark Tapley's New York baptism of fire (no European-friendly Boston for them), Martin's introduction to the nefarious procedures of the *New York Rowdy Journal*, his grim experience of an American boarding-house, and his disastrous visit to the snobbish Norrises. Dickens starts to pay off old scores when he has Martin discover that the *Rowdy Journal* is happy to publish forged letters. He found, he told Mitton on 7 June, that it took him 'at least twice as long' as normal to write these two chapters – not surprisingly, perhaps, since he is cramming into them most of the basic ingredients of the anti-American satire he will develop later.

Having finished these demanding initial American scenes, Dickens was now intent upon introducing the figure of Mrs Gamp, originally inspired by

Burdett Coutts's anecdotes about an eccentric monthly nurse she had recently hired to nurse her companion Hannah Brown. 'I mean to make a mark with her,' he told Forster, and indeed it was soon apparent that Mrs Gamp was one of the supreme achievements of his comic art to date. It was at this point that poor William Hall made a disastrous faux pas. Fearing that the *Chuzzlewit* profits might not be enough to allow Dickens to pay off his debt, he made some tactless allusion to a clause in the Agreement of 7 September 1841 which, under certain circumstances, allowed Chapman and Hall to deduct £50 from Dickens's agreed monthly stipend for *Chuzzlewit* of £200 and apply it towards the repayment of the £1,800 he had received from them during the period between the end of the *Clock* and the beginning of *Chuzzlewit*. Dickens was enraged. Here, as he saw it, was the wretched history of his relations with previous publishers repeating itself yet again. Chapman and Hall, having profited hugely from his labours, were now showing themselves to be just as hard and grasping as their predecessors. 'A wrong kind of fire' was burning in his head and he was finding it hard to write at all. He determined to separate himself from his one-time 'trusty friends' as quickly as possible: 'I am bent upon paying Chapman and Hall *down*', he told Forster, 'And when I have done that, Mr Hall shall have a piece of my mind.' Meanwhile he insisted that £50 should be immediately deducted from his monthly stipend for *Chuzzlewit* and requested Forster to open negotiations on his behalf with Chapman and Hall's printers, Bradbury and Evans, with a view to their becoming his publishers.[16]

Dickens took Catherine, now expecting her fifth child, and Georgina, on a visit to his friend the solicitor Charles Smithson, Mitton's partner, at his beautiful home, Easthope Park, near Malton in Yorkshire for the first two and a half weeks of July. He enjoyed rides and walks in the beautiful surrounding countryside, as well as 'forfeits, pic-nics, rustic games, inspections of ancient monasteries at midnight when the moon was shining', but had also to work on the proofs of *Chuzzlewit* VIII, dealing with hundreds of misprints resulting from the printers' difficulties with Mrs Gamp's highly idiosyncratic vocabulary. This excursion must have been a welcome break after a very busy London spring and early summer. Not only had he had this major new serial to get under way but he had also begun what was to become virtually a second dazzling career, that of speaking at grand public dinners in aid of this or that charity. These events, which as Boz he had mocked in one of his London sketches, were immensely popular in nineteenth-century England and Dickens had performed at no fewer than four such between early April and late June.[17]

No sooner was he back in London than he added to John Overs and others who already figured in his charitable casebook the family of an actor called Edward Elton, drowned as he was returning home from an Edinburgh engagement. A widower, he left his seven children utterly destitute. On 26 July Dickens chaired a fund-raising committee and within months the impressive sum of over £2,300 had been raised. As one of the fund's trustees Dickens's involvement in the upbringing of the orphans continued for many years. Esther, the eldest, who trained as a teacher, was to please him very much with her 'quiet, unpretending, domestic heroism', and thoughts of her may well have later contributed something to his conception of her namesake, the heroine of *Bleak House*. Meanwhile, his own finances were still problematic and on 22 July he had to arrange for Mitton to supply him with £70 to tide him over until September.[18]

At the beginning of August the Dickens family began a two-month sojourn in Broadstairs. Apart from various dashes up to London as, for example, to chair the farewell dinner given to Macready on 26 August before he left for an American tour, Dickens kept to his established routine of writing for four hours every morning: 'a gentleman with long hair and no neck-cloth who writes and grins as if he thought he were very funny indeed. His name is Boz.' Then, after 'a strong lunch', would come a walk of 'a dozen miles or so'. The only variants on his London régime were his pre-lunch dip in the sea and the times when he lay on his back on the sand reading. He wrote *Chuzzlewit* IX–XI in Broadstairs, working with unflagging invention and great confidence in the story. 'I have nearly killed myself with laughing at what I have done of the American No.', he wrote to Mitton on 13 August, adding, 'I seem to hear the people talking again.' *Chuzzlewit* X, which Dickens believed would 'bang all the others', wonderfully 'opens out' Mrs Gamp as the reader is initiated into the 'fearful mystery' surrounding her invisible adulatory friend Mrs Harris and is given, as promised in one of the chapter-titles, 'valuable hints in relation to the management of a sick chamber'.[19]

Just as he was completing *Chuzzlewit* X Dickens ran up to London to investigate, for Burdett Coutts, a Ragged School that had been set up in Field Lane off Saffron Hill in Clerkenwell – Fagin's territory. Ragged Schools were charitable institutions established in slum areas, mainly by Evangelical clergymen, to provide some basic instruction in literacy and knowledge of the Scriptures to the very poorest children, including those who lived on the streets. Dickens visited the Field Lane School, which he found housed in premises resembling 'an ugly dream', and on 16 September sent Burdett Coutts a powerful account of it and of its desperate need of help. He had, he told her, 'very seldom seen . . . anything so shocking as the dire neglect of soul and body exhibited in these children'. Not only was the thing shocking in itself but it was also ominous: 'in the prodigious misery and ignorance of the swarming masses of mankind in England, the seeds of its certain ruin are sown'. Within a month or so of writing this Dickens would be creating those two child-monsters, 'horrible and dread', Ignorance and Want, whose apparition, 'yellow, meagre, ragged, scowling, wolfish', so appals Scrooge.[20]

Shortly after Dickens and his family returned from Broadstairs he travelled to Manchester to speak at the 'First Annual *Soirée*' of the Athenaeum on

5 October. The Manchester Athenaeum, founded in 1835 to provide educational and recreational facilities, including a library, for the working classes,
was in financial difficulties as a result of the trade depression of the early 1840s
and Fanny Burnett had persuaded her famous brother to come and support
the institution by speaking at the Soirée. He shared the platform with two
notable M.P.s, Benjamin Disraeli and the doughty anti-Corn Law campaigner
Richard Cobden. In his well-crafted address Dickens spoke of how his
heart 'died within him' when he saw in jails and night-refuges 'thousands of
immortal creatures condemned . . . to tread, not what our great poet calls, "the
primrose path to the everlasting bonfire" but one of jagged flints and stones,
laid down by brutal ignorance', and he warmly praised the Manchester
Athenaeum for its strong commitment to popular education.[21]

Back in London, he got to work on *Chuzzlewit* XI, depicting the fraudulent
Anglo-Bengalee Disinterested Loan and Life Assurance Company, based upon
the notorious case of the West Middlesex General Annuity Company of 1840
when the directors, a cobbler and a tallow-chandler, absconded with a fortune.
The Anglo-Bengalee was to play an important role in first the thickening and
then the dénouement of that part of the plot (by far the most compelling part)
centred on the murder committed by Jonas Chuzzlewit. This character, whose
degeneration clearly counterpoints in Dickens's design his cousin Martin's
regeneration, is a spectacular example of just how terrible may be the results
of an upbringing by a bad father. The intensity of Dickens's depiction of
this malign father/son relationship does seem to me to point, like his
sudden enthusiasm for writing a Prologue for *The Patrician's Daughter*, to an
increasing imaginative engagement with the subject of the moulding of
character by early experiences and influences. It seems likely that this would
have led to his reflecting more deeply on his own case.

The idea of the State as a bad or neglectful parent to the children of the poor
was central to his social thinking at this time and, shortly after his return from
Manchester, the two concerns about childhood and children, the personal and
the social, seem to have come together in his mind to create *A Christmas Carol*.
The basic notion for this 'Ghost Story of Christmas', as he sub-titled it, derived,
as has long been recognised, from a Christmas tale he wrote for *Pickwick* seven
years earlier, describing the misanthropic sexton Gabriel Grub's overnight
conversion to benevolence as a result of goblin intervention. Once Dickens had
conceived of the more elaborate supernatural machinery of Marley's Ghost and
the Christmas Spirits, and also of the definitive mean old skinflint, Ebenezer
Scrooge, he had his story, to be presented as 'A Christmas Carol in Prose',
divided into five staves like a real carol. The result was the first and greatest of
his five 'Christmas Books', written in a white heat of excitement during the
month or so following the completion of *Chuzzlewit* XII. Dickens told Felton
he had 'wept, and laughed, and wept again, and excited himself in a most

extraordinary manner, in the composition', walking about 'the black streets of London, fifteen and twenty miles, many a night when all the sober folks had gone to bed'. The result more than justified his having deferred until the end of the year his projected 'Appeal to the People of England on behalf of the Poor Man's Child'. No pamphlet, no matter how fiercely written, could have had half the impact of the pathetic figure of Tiny Tim, or of those wolf-children with whom the Ghost of Christmas Present confronts Scrooge. As to its relationship with the full-length novel Dickens was in the midst of writing, the *Carol* becomes, as Peter Ackroyd has pointed out, 'almost a dream reworking of *Martin Chuzzlewit* in which the themes of "Selfishness", money, greed and the commercialised society which results from them, are conveyed in condensed and fantastic form'. He might have added, too, the theme of moral conversion, or change of heart, and, indeed, it is in *Chuzzlewit* XIII (chs 33–35), written immediately after the *Carol*, that Dickens describes Young Martin's sudden conversion, in the dismal swamp of Eden, from the careless selfishness that has hitherto been his dominant characteristic.[22]

The *Carol* also shows a notable development in the consciously autobiographical element in Dickens's writing. The story actually *turns* on memory, specifically on the deleterious consequences of blanking out one's past, as he himself had perhaps often fantasised about doing. Scrooge, made literally to revisit his past, weeps to see his 'poor forgotten self as he had used to be'. In a passage that looks forward to *Copperfield*, the abandoned child Scrooge in his bleak schoolroom derives comfort and companionship from the marvellous figures his fancy conjures up from his reading of *The Arabian Nights* and *Robinson Crusoe*. As a writer Dickens cannot yet, it seems, directly confront the blacking factory itself but he nevertheless comes closer here to the factual truth of his boyhood sufferings than ever before. The schoolroom setting adds, moreover, a layer of irony, conscious or unconscious, because it was to a school that the boy in the blacking-factory had so yearned to be sent. To complicate matters still further, the young Scrooge's desolate and decaying schoolhouse, 'a mansion of dull red brick, with a little weather-cock-surmounted cupola, on the roof', recalls Gad's Hill Place as seen from outside. The forsaken-child image of the young Dickens sits, deprived of hope but comforted by imaginative literature, in the ruins of his own dream home.[23]

The Dickens of 1843, meanwhile, was dreaming of large profits from the *Carol* to help him realise his scheme of letting Devonshire Terrace and moving his whole household to the Continent for a year, a scheme first expounded to the startled Forster on 1 November. It was partly motivated by the need to economise, since it would certainly be much cheaper to live abroad, but also by his desire to develop as a writer, to 'enlarge [his] stock of description and observation' through experience of different countries. Moreover, the disappointing *Chuzzlewit* sales figures had re-awakened fears that his popularity might drop as suddenly as it had risen, and over-exposure might contribute to this. He shrank from the prospect of 'putting myself before the town as writing tooth and nail for bread'. This made him wary of Bradbury and Evans's suggestions that, if they became his publishers, he might at once start a new magazine or embark upon a collected cheap edition of his works. He wanted to give the public time to miss him, and he needed also the stimulation of fresh experiences before beginning the new story that he was already thinking of, one that he had an idea might best be first published in Paris, or at any rate in volume form, 'all at once – no parts – sledge hammer blow'. He could also, he suggested to Forster, write him the same kind of journal-letters from France or Italy as he had done from America to be worked up into a travel-book as his American letters had been. He was already taking Italian lessons from the exiled Italian patriot Antonio Gallenga, who recorded in an autobiography written in 1884 going almost daily to Dickens's house, 'where, like a Napoleon, he kept his tame eagle – a bright-eyed, ready-witted, somewhat gushing, happy man, cheered by the world's applause, equally idolised by his wife, by his children, by every member of his family, while as yet not even the shadow of a cloud had risen to darken the light of his household.'[24]

The realisation of Dickens's scheme depended on his getting some money together, which he hoped to do mainly as a result of the *Carol*. He was determined that the lion's share of the anticipated profits should find its way into his own pockets rather than into those of any publisher. Therefore Chapman and Hall, who were still desperately hoping to remain his publishers, would publish the book on commission, all production expenses being met by Dickens. He was not sparing of these: wanting to make the book as physically attractive as possible, a Christmas present in itself, he had it bound in salmon-brown and gilt, commissioned Leech to supply eight illustrations, half to be printed as hand-coloured plates, while the title-page would be printed in two colours, first green and red and then blue and red. At the same time he insisted that the selling price of the book should not exceed five shillings. This price, however, given the high production costs, proved in the event to leave a very narrow profit margin while it put the book beyond the reach of most of the nation's Cratchits, whose cause it championed.[25]

The *Carol* was published on 19 December 1843 and was greeted with almost universal delight. It sold six thousand copies in five days and was soon reprinting. Reviewers vied with each other in praise, especially of the book's humanity and its sympathy for the 'real grinding sorrows of life'. Lord Jeffrey wrote to Dickens that it had done more good than 'all the pulpits and confessionals in Christendom' since Christmas 1842, and later Thackeray publicly hailed it as 'a national benefit and to every man and woman who reads it a personal kindness'. It was, Dickens exulted, 'a most prodigious success – the greatest, I think, I have ever achieved'. No wonder he was in such tremendous form at Mrs Macready's children's party on 27 December, capering away in country dances like his own Fezziwig. 'You would have thought', he wrote to Felton on 2 January, 'I was a country Gentleman of independent property, residing on a tip-top farm, with the wind blowing straight in my face every day.' A certain wistfulness surely underlies this fantasy of settled prosperity, given Dickens's current financial anxieties, anxieties that may help to account for his unfeeling irritation with Catherine who was about to add another burden to the family exchequer – she is 'nervous and dull,' he tells Felton, 'but her health is perfectly good, and I am sure she might rally, if she would'. Thirteen days later, another young Dickens was born and named Francis Jeffrey in honour of Lord Jeffrey, Dickens's adulatory self-styled 'Critic Laureate'.[26]

The New Year opened with Dickens determined to stop the blatant piracy of his books by Grub Street. As already noted, he could do nothing about the hack dramatists – he even went to see one of the numerous unauthorised stage adaptations of the *Carol* which, he told Forster, was 'better than usual . . . but *heart-breaking* to me'. But when, on 6 January, there appeared in *Parley's Penny Library* something called 'A Christmas Ghost Story Reoriginated from the original by Charles Dickens', he instructed Mitton to instigate Chancery proceedings against the publishers and the 'reoriginator'. He thereby plunged himself into a world of injunctions, motions for dissolution, affidavits, vice-chancellors, and other such intricate and costly legalities from which he eventually emerged having won his case but facing a substantial bill for costs (the 'vagabond' pirates escaped scot-free by declaring themselves bankrupt). Eight years later, with bitter remembrance of his own experience, Dickens would write in the opening chapter of *Bleak House* that all Chancery lawyers who were also men of honour advised potential clients to 'suffer any wrong that can be done you, rather than come here!'[27]

Vexatious pirates notwithstanding, Dickens began the new year in buoyant mood, delighted by the large sales of the *Carol*. On his birthday he wrote to Stanfield, 'two and thirty years ago, the planet Dick appeared on the horizon. To the great admiration, wonder and delight of all who live, and the unspeakable happiness of mankind.' Five days later, on 11 February, came an unpleasant shock. Chapman and Hall sent him the first statement of accounts for the first 6,000 copies of the *Carol* and his profit, after all expenses and the publishers' commission had been paid, turned out to be substantially less than he had anticipated. He was convinced that Chapman and Hall had failed to advertise the book properly, and had also 'run the expences [*sic*] up, anyhow, purposely to bring me back [and deter him from any further publishing on his own account], and disgust me with charges'. He now resolved, therefore, to break with them completely. Aided as always by Forster, he set about negotiating new publishing arrangements with Bradbury and Evans which would allow him the sabbatical year abroad upon which he was now set.[28]

On 26 February he spoke at the annual Soirée of the Liverpool Mechanics'
Institution and on the 28th at a Conversazione of the Birmingham Polytechnic
Institution. Catherine was not well enough to accompany him but the Burnetts
joined him in Liverpool as well as an old friend, Thomas James Thompson. In
both places, Dickens, resplendent in his 'magpie waistcoat', was received with
overwhelming enthusiasm. In Liverpool he entered the hall to the strains from
the organ of 'See the Conquering Hero Comes' while in Birmingham he found
himself facing the words 'Welcome Boz!' in six-foot-high letters, made of arti-
ficial flowers, adorning the front of the gallery. In Liverpool he was eloquent
upon the theme of the Mechanics' Institution as a force for 'human improvement and rational education' (referring to the wives of its members as angels on
the hearth), and also for promoting 'mutual forbearance among various classes'.
In Birmingham he deftly invoked *The Arabian Nights* to echo the Ghost of
Christmas Present's warning to Scrooge, speaking of the terrible threat to
society represented by 'the Spirit of Ignorance, long shut up in a vessel of
Obstinate Neglect . . . and sealed with the seal of many, many Solomons'. In
both places he experienced the special thrill that such occasions had for a writer
like himself, always seeking to achieve a *personal* intimacy with his thousands of
readers. 'It is a brave thing, by Heaven it is,' he rejoiced to his fellow-writer
Thomas Powell, 'to walk out of the room where one is shut up for so many
hours of such a short life, into a sea of agitated faces, and think that they are
always looking on –.'[29]

One Liverpool face in particular, whether agitated or not, had an extraordinary effect upon him. It belonged to Christiana Weller, eighteen years old, who
gave a piano recital at the Soirée. Dickens made a humorous public reference
to the significance for him of her surname but wrote very differently about her
in private. 'Good God what a madman I should seem, if the incredible feeling
I have conceived for that girl could be made plain to anyone!' he wrote a couple
of days later to Thompson, who was also smitten by Christiana but in a rather
more straightforward way. A widower, he was able to woo, and eventually
marry her, a proceeding not open to Dickens. If Christiana did resemble Mary
Hogarth, as Mrs Hogarth apparently believed, this no doubt had something to
do with the electric effect she produced on Dickens, and with his strange idea
that she was 'destined to an early death' (she lived, in fact, to 'disappoint him
very much' as a married woman and died at the ripe old age of 85).[30]

Mary may have been especially in Dickens's thoughts just before he went to
Liverpool. He was working on *Chuzzlewit* XV in which there was much focus
upon the brother–sister relationship of Tom and Ruth Pinch, who had set up
home together in the previous number. They were, as he later confessed to
Lady Holland (10 June), 'two of the greatest favorites I have ever had'. He could
hardly have written as he did about 'pleasant little Ruth' – so pretty, so young
and innocent, so domestic, so admiringly devoted to her brother – without

some conscious thought of Mary. Dickens's sudden obsession with Christiana, and subsequent excited concern with the chequered progress of Thompson's courtship (the couple did not marry until October 1845), is surely a case of the world of his imagination and personal fantasies impinging upon the real world rather than the other way around. As far as his 'real' life is concerned, this strong response to Christiana may, like his impatience with Catherine during the final weeks of her latest pregnancy, relate to some settled marital discontent, but this can only be a matter of speculation.[31]

During these first six months of 1844 Dickens, having got Young Martin and his cheery 'squire' Mark Tapley safely back in England, completed the serial writing of *Martin Chuzzlewit*. Back in November he had told Forster that he was feeling his power more than ever before and the latter part of *Chuzzlewit* amply demonstrates this. All the great scenes show Dickens writing at the top of his bent, and with no sign of strain or fatigue but rather fully displaying for the first time, as one critic later expressed it, 'at once the versatility and the strength of his genius'. And yet *Chuzzlewit*'s monthly sales figures never rose above twenty-three thousand. This made Dickens all the more determined to 'leave the scene' for a time. It was not only a question of reducing his living expenses, or of stopping the public from taking him for granted. His creative faculties, he was convinced, needed a long rest. 'It is impossible', he had written to Forster the previous November, after noting that he had been writing continuously for eight years, 'to go on working the brain to that extent for ever. The very spirit of the thing, in doing it, leaves a horrible despondency behind, when it is done; which must be prejudicial to the mind, so soon renewed and so seldom let alone.' In the light of his subsequent work, from *Dombey and Son* onwards, Forster's judgement that Dickens's final decision in early 1844 to go abroad for a sabbatical year was 'the turning-point of his career' can be seen as entirely justified.[32]

The financing of this sabbatical remained problematic, however. Might he perhaps start writing regularly for his old paper *The Morning Chronicle*? His anti-Tory sentiments, so strong at this time (see, for example, his caricature of a Tory M.P. as the 'member for the Gentlemanly Interest' in *Chuzzlewit*, ch. 35) had already moved him to fire off some anonymous, anti-Corn Law leaders for the *Chronicle*, only one of which, the heavily ironic 'The Agricultural Interest' (9 March 1844), has been positively identified. Now he was asked if he might consider contributing regularly, either supplying further articles or, if he were to follow his plan of going abroad, a weekly letter 'with such scraps of descriptions and impressions as suggested themselves to my mind'. These negotiations came to nothing, however. Such other writing as Dickens did manage while completing *Chuzzlewit* was motivated by compassionate or charitable feelings, not by money. He had no time to produce 'scattered scraps of writing here and there', he told Anna Maria Hall (who presumably resolutely ignored the popular identification of her husband with Pecksniff) when she solicited an article as a matter of business. He did respond to a request from Hood, however, on account of their friendship and his high regard for Hood's work. Struggling with ill-health and poverty, Hood was seeking to revive his fortunes with a new magazine and Dickens helped him with quite a substantial article (roughly two and a half thousand words), which he wrote in time for publication in the May issue of *Hood's Magazine* even though this was just when he was striving hard to get ahead of his usual *Chuzzlewit* schedule and busy revising certain key passages in the manuscript. In his 'Threatening Letter to Thomas Hood from an Ancient Gentleman' Dickens satirises diehard Toryism through reference to the contemporary mania for such live exhibitions as that of the Ojibwa Indians or of the American midget, 'General Tom Thumb', both at the Egyptian Hall in Piccadilly. His 'ancient gentleman' also applauds a certain judge (the 'only one who knows how to do his duty, now') who had sentenced to death a desperate pauper woman convicted of infanticide, a case to which Dickens would return six months later when planning the *Carol's* 1844 successor, *The Chimes*.[33]

During these last months of writing *Chuzzlewit* Dickens made time for other charitable work, too, in the form of more after-dinner speeches, this time for the benefit of those enduring the hardships peculiar to genteel poverty. Prominent among such folk were governesses whose cause Dickens had already championed in *Chuzzlewit* IV and XIV (chs 9, 36) when describing Ruth Pinch's miserable situation in a *nouveau riche* family. On 20 April he supported them again by speaking at their Benevolent Institution. On 11 May he spoke at the Artists' Benevolent Society, and on 4 June on behalf of the Sanatorium once again (with further reference to the plight of governesses). On the last occasion the shade of Mrs Gamp would have been felt by many in his audience to have been hovering about the hall when Dickens inveighed against that 'odious anomaly called a sick nurse . . .'.[34]

Meanwhile, he had had to decide where in Italy he and his family would live. He had been fantasising to Thompson for months about the colourful and leisured life which he, together with Thompson and Christiana, would lead in the warm South (his own domestic establishment seems not to have featured in such imaginings): 'I see myself', he wrote on 13 March, 'in a striped shirt, moustache, blouse, red sash, straw hat, and white trousers, sitting astride a mule, and not caring for the clock, the day of the month, or the day of the week.' Lady Blessington and Count D'Orsay had advised Pisa but by mid-May he had settled on Genoa, then part of the Kingdom of Sardinia. He seems to have been persuaded to settle there by his eccentric sculptor friend Angus Fletcher, who was living not far from Genoa. Dickens commissioned him to hire, for three months in the first instance, a villa suitable for the accommodation of Dickens himself, Catherine, Georgina, the five children and three women servants under the command of Anne Brown. By this time Catherine had joined him for Signor Gallenga's weekly Italian lessons, he had purchased from the Pantechnicon, the great London furniture warehouse, an enormous second-hand coach (as large, he said, as Forster's library) to transport himself, his family and his servants to their new home and had hired a courier, Louis Roche, native of Avignon, to escort them.

He arranged to let 1 Devonshire Terrace to 'a most desirable Widow (as a tenant, I mean)' from 28 May. His eagle and his raven were sent to Landseer to look after, and he and Catherine made a detailed inventory of the contents of the house, including the library. The family moved to temporary accommodation in nearby Osnaburgh Square where Dickens, money worries notwithstanding, promptly held a very grand dinner-party. Earlier, he had written out a full account of his literary property for Bradbury and Evans. This showed that the only copyrights belonging wholly to him were *Oliver Twist, American Notes* and *A Christmas Carol* (he was wrong about *American Notes*, in fact, having given Chapman and Hall a quarter-share in this book). Subsequent negotiations resulted in an Agreement (no longer surviving) dated 1 June whereby Bradbury and Evans advanced him £2,800, interest-free, for which they were to have a quarter-share in any future books Dickens might write. He was not, in fact, committed to writing anything, not even a travel book, but there was an understanding that he should write a successor to the *Carol* for Christmas 1844 and that, possibly, a magazine edited, or partly edited, by himself might be started after his return to England. He received £2,000 on 1 June and the balance of £800 in two instalments in January and March 1845. As security Dickens gave the printers his Britannia Life Assurance policy for £2,000. It was by far the most favourable arrangement he had yet made with a publishing firm. Further immediate cash in hand was provided by Bradbury and Evans's purchase for £200 of a quarter-share in the copyright of the *Carol*, and for £1,000 a half-share in that of *Oliver*.[35]

June 1844 was an exceptionally busy month, even by Dickens's standards. The first half was dominated by finishing *Chuzzlewit*. Browne received detailed instructions for the design of the frontispiece and title-page vignette to appear, along with his preface, in the last double number, and for the two plates to be published with the number. Dickens wanted the frontispiece centred on Tom Pinch (made 'as interesting and amiable as possible'), seated at his organ with 'any little indications' that Browne might like of Tom's history seeming to rise out of the organ and float about it, and must have been delighted by Browne's splendid execution of this idea. On 4 June he spoke at the Sanatorium Dinner and also busied himself in promoting the London concert performances Christiana Weller was giving at this time. With *Chuzzlewit* at last finished in mid-June, he paid a flying visit to Landor in Bath and was back in London in time to be fêted at a grand farewell dinner-party in his honour at Greenwich.

Shortly afterwards he took a two-day break to go yachting with Albany Fonblanque, the first and only time he is recorded as indulging in this form of recreation.[36]

Amidst all this he still found time to compose a long inscription to be engraved on a silver salver to be presented to his Unitarian pastor Edward Tagart. He praises Tagart for his 'labours in the cause of that religion which has sympathy for men of every creed and ventures to pass judgment on none'. He also wrote a preface to *Evenings of a Working Man*, a collection of Overs's verse and prose. Overs was now too ill to work any longer (by the end of September, indeed, he would be dead) and the publication of this Dickens-sponsored little book was intended to raise money to support his wife and children. The title emphasises that the contents are the product of Overs's scanty leisure time. He does not presume to present himself as an aspiring professional writer, something that Dickens had strongly warned him against doing. Dickens's preface is written in the *de haut en bas* tone characteristic of all his letters to his protégé. He commends Overs for seeking not to climb the social ladder but to exercise whatever small literary talent he might have only to help secure a modest competence for his family. Also commendable are 'the instinctive propriety of his manner, and the perfect neatness of his appearance'.[37]

'On the first of July', wrote Dickens to Thompson on 24 March, 'Dick turns his head towards the orange groves.' And it was on that date that Dickens's 'good old shabby devil of a coach' carrying himself, his family, his servants and his 'brave courier' (as Louis Roche soon came to be called) duly set out for Dover on the first leg of its two-week journey to Genoa. For Dickens this journey through the country that he was later to call (in an 1860 essay vividly recalling this experience) 'the dear old France of my affections' was a revelation, almost like acquiring a whole new view of the world. 'Surrounded by strange and perfectly novel circumstances,' he wrote to Forster from Marseilles, 'I feel as if I had a new head on side by side with my old one.' If the French countryside, with its vines, avenues, swarming beggars, highly *un*pastoral shepherdesses, and 'steady old Curés' jolting along in ramshackle coaches, was a revelation for Dickens, Paris, where the travellers stayed two nights in the Hotel Meurice, favourite port of call for English travellers, was a sensation. To register the effect on him of his first experience of this city that was to become so important to him both as man and as writer we have to go to his letter of 7 August to Count D'Orsay: 'My eyes ached and my head grew giddy, as novelty, novelty, novelty; nothing but strange and striking things; came swarming before me. . . . almost every house, and every person I passed, seemed to be another leaf in the enormous book that stands wide open there. I was perpetually turning over, and never coming any nearer the end.' A day or so later he wrote in a letter to Mitton, 'There is no such place for material in my way, as Paris.'[38]

From Chalons the party travelled down the Rhone to Lyons which Dickens later described as a nightmarish place with 'all the undrained, unscavengered qualities of a foreign town' grafted upon 'the native miseries of a manufacturing one'. Another great urban centre that gripped his imagination, and which he revisited from Genoa, was Marseilles, and already present in his description of this city in *Pictures from Italy* are details that will reappear thirteen years later in the opening chapter of *Little Dorrit* – the 'staring white' houses, the foul water of the harbour contrasting with the beautiful blue of the open sea, and a place of incarceration in the midst of all the city's sunlit bustle. From here the Dickens party sailed to Genoa and finally found themselves entering the Albaro villa chosen for their residence by Fletcher – 'the most perfectly lonely, rusty, stagnant old staggerer of a domain that you can possibly imagine', Dickens reported to Forster, adding that it reminded him of nothing so much as a 'pink gaol'. It had superb views but would have been uninhabitable in winter. Dickens looked for more suitable accommodation to which to move after his three months' tenancy was up and found a splendid Renaissance palazzo within the walls of Genoa but built on an eminence overlooking the city. Known as the Palazzo Peschiere, it was built around 1560 and the interior walls and ceilings

21 The Palazzo Peschiere, Genoa

were painted with a series of striking frescoes which may still be seen today. It was surrounded, Dickens told Mitton on 12 August, by 'the most delicious gardens (filled with fountains, orange trees, and all sorts of lovely things)', including the fishponds that gave the Peschiere its name.[39]

At Albaro the Dickens party acclimatised themselves to their new surroundings – to the terrific heat, the ubiquitous fleas (poor little Timber the dog had to be shaved in an effort to moderate his torments), stunning views of the Mediterranean with its glorious blueness that never ceased to enrapture Dickens, delicious new fruits like green figs, the drunken local postman and his maudlin penitence after losing the letters he was carrying, and other such phenomena. Dickens also happily plunged into exploring Genoa's maze of streets and narrow 'vicos', with their frescoed houses, great decaying palaces, veil-wearing women, picturesque taverns, theatres (including the famous puppet theatre), swarming monks and priests, 'gorgeous' church processions, and fiercely gesticulating mora players (mora was a gambling game played using the fingers only). He returned to Marseilles to collect Fred, on holiday from the Treasury, and went back to Genoa by the Cornice road from Nice, 'not being satisfied to have seen [from the sea on his initial journey to Genoa] only the outsides of the beautiful towns that rise in picturesque white clusters . . . upon the margin of the sea', towns from which he found most of the romance evaporated when seen at close quarters, many of them being 'very miserable'.[40]

He swam every day, skimming about 'like a fish in high spirits', cultivated a moustache, and wandered about, he told D'Orsay on 7 August, in a comfortable 'dreamy sort of way', reading Tennyson and Manzoni's *I Promessi Sposi*. This letter is one of a series of characteristically vivid and entertaining ones to D'Orsay, Forster, Maclise, and others. He had not yet settled on any definite plan about using them as the basis for a travel book but the idea had certainly been floated. In early August, having at last received from London his writing-paper, inkstand and customary desk ornaments and arrayed them on his desk in the way he liked ('my paper is arranged and my pens spread out in the usual form', he told Forster), he began shutting himself up in the morning to think about his projected Christmas Book. He was distracted by domestic concerns, however, and a sudden short-lived return of his old malady with its accompanying excruciating pain in his side, so was no further forward with the work when the time came to move to the Peschiere, probably on 23 September.

One of his first experiences in his spectacular new home was that of having an intensely vivid dream involving Mary Hogarth, the first such dream for six years. He dreamed that what he knew to be Mary's spirit appeared to him in Madonna-like blue robes, and he begged it to tell him which was 'the True religion'. The answer, delivered with 'heavenly tenderness', was that for *him* the best religion was Roman Catholicism (since arriving in Genoa he had been exposed as never before to the way in which this religion can affect the daily lives of ordinary people). He woke Catherine to tell her about the dream and later reported it in some detail, but with surprising objectivity to Forster. To him Dickens presented it mainly as a remarkable mental phenomenon and mused about its ingredients, adding, 'I wonder whether I should regard it as a dream, or an actual Vision!' Whatever he decided about this had no effect whatever in modifying the sharp hostility towards Roman Catholicism that was to pervade the pages of *Pictures from Italy*, though it stayed in his mind and he was to refer back to it at least twice in later writings. Meanwhile, he really had to begin writing a successor to the *Carol* but was hampered for want of a title. Suddenly, the tolling of the church and convent bells of Genoa, which he thought might have been partly responsible for his dream, inspired him with his title, which he announced to Forster, probably on 8 October, by means of a Shakespeare quotation on an otherwise blank piece of paper: 'We have heard THE CHIMES at midnight, Master Shallow!' Simultaneously he hit upon an idea for the 'machinery' that was to work the story. It was to be an intense dream or vision experienced by the tale's humble protagonist, the little old street-messenger Trotty Veck, who has made an imaginary friend of some London church bells. His guide in the world of the vision is the spirit of a young girl whose pathetic death he is forced to witness in the dream itself.[41]

'Never did I so stagger upon a threshold before,' Dickens told Forster as he tried to begin the new story: 'I want a crowded street to plunge into at night.' Soon, however, he was in a 'regular, ferocious excitement' with the story and 'blazed away' at it every day until mid-afternoon. He sent it to Forster in instalments (keeping a shorthand copy 'in case of accidents'), the first one being accompanied by a sketch of his 'general idea' for the tale, interestingly different in several details from the published work (Forster comments that when Dickens got fairly into the writing of any story 'his fancies controlled him'; characters who were so real to him 'as to be treated as existences' would make him modify his planned story-line). He had, he told Forster, found it very harrowing to narrate the death of the beautiful young girl Lilian, who had been forced into prostitution by penury, but intended to begin the last section the next day 'with a broad grin' and end it 'with the very soul of jollity and happiness'. He finished the story at precisely 2.30 p.m. on 3 November, having had 'what women call "a real good cry" '.[42]

We notice in the progress reports Dickens sent Forster, along with instalments of the story, such terms as 'ferocious' and 'wrathful'. All the pity and anger that had been building up in him over the past two years or so in relation to the increasingly desperate plight of the English poor, emotions fuelled by Carlyle's fierce polemics, now burst forth to create the most overtly Radical fiction he ever wrote. *The Chimes*, a New Year's story rather than a Christmas one (its full title was *The Chimes: A Goblin Story of Some Bells that Rung an Old Year out and a New Year in*), was scorchingly topical, a sensational exposé of the desperate lengths to which the poorer classes were being driven, and for which they were then savagely punished – all as reported in the daily newspapers. Dickens's story touched on prostitution, arson, and infanticide. His satire was directed against the complacent and unfeeling magistrates like Sir Peter Laurie, a former Lord Mayor of London, who had expressed his determination to 'put down' suicide, as well as the pseudo-philanthropy of certain politicians, the fanaticism of bigoted political economists (like the reviewer of the *Carol* in the *Westminster Review* who had objected to Scrooge giving the Cratchits a turkey when there weren't enough turkeys to go round everyone), and the cant about the so-called 'good old times' so dear to diehard Tories. At one stage in his vision Trotty even seems to be prophesying some kind of social revolution, using the very metaphor for it that Dickens will re-use many years later in *A Tale of Two Cities*: 'I know that our [i.e., the poor's] Inheritance is held in store for us by Time. I know there is a Sea of Time to rise one day, before which all who wrong us or oppress us will be swept away like leaves. I see it, on the flow!' To get Dickens's Radicalism into perspective, however, we should place against this another passage from Trotty's vision in which he sees the labourer Will Fern pleading to the gentry for 'better homes' and 'kinder laws' and saying, 'There an't a condescension you can show the Labourer then, that he won't take, as ready and as grateful as a man can be; for he has a patient, peaceful, willing heart.'[43]

Throughout *The Chimes* Dickens used the same rhetorical punctuation that he had introduced in *Chuzzlewit*, as though he were speaking rather than writing (at the end, indeed the reader is directly addressed as 'Listener'), and he was now possessed by a strong desire actually to read his 'tremendous book' to a live audience. He asked Forster to assemble some of their mutual friends together on a certain date and then set out, with only Roche for company, on a fortnight's whirlwind tour (6–21 Nov.) of northern Italian cities before heading for London. His itinerary included Piacenza, Parma, Modena, Bologna, Ferrara, Padua, Venice, Verona, Mantua and Milan (where he enjoyed a brief reunion with his 'pair of petticoats'). This rapid travelling produced what he later described in *Pictures from Italy* as 'an incoherent but delightful jumble in my brain'. He wrote some letters on the road, including a long one to Catherine (with a postscript much quoted by his biographers: 'Keep things in their places. I can't bear to picture them otherwise') and others to Forster, in which he strives to convey his overpowering sense of the 'magnificent and stupendous reality' of Venice, with its fabulous architecture (beyond 'the wildest visions of *The Arabian Nights*'), its streets made of water, and its stupendous Titians and Tintorettos. He confesses that he will have to wait until he is back in the Peschiere before he will be able to compose anything like an adequate record of his adventures and impressions. From Milan he travelled to England via the Simplon Pass, Switzerland, Strasbourg and Paris, reaching

London on 30 November. After a joyous reunion with Forster, he busied himself with the proofs and illustrations for *The Chimes*, which was to be published in the same format as the *Carol*, only with a bright red rather than a salmon-brown cover, and minus the costly coloured plates. For this book Leech was part of a team of illustrators, the other members being Maclise, who did the elaborate frontispiece and title-page, Stanfield, and the young *Punch* artist Richard Doyle. The ten illustrations in the text, half of them by Leech, were more closely integrated with the letterpress than had been the case with the *Carol* and Dickens, after getting Leech and Doyle to make some minor alterations, was very happy with the result. 'The book is quite splendid,' he reported to Catherine on 2 December, adding, with a rueful memory of those *Carol* accounts, 'the expences [*sic*] will be very great, I have no doubt.'[44]

The day after his arrival in London he read *The Chimes* to Macready and wrote to Catherine on 2 December, 'If you had seen Macready last night – undisguisedly sobbing and crying on the sofa, as I read – you would have felt (as I did) what a thing it is to have Power.' Macready's response to his work must have been doubly gratifying to the young writer in that he himself had so often been deeply moved by his revered friend's own formidable brand of 'Power'. Two days later Forster assembled a hand-picked group of friends, including Carlyle, Jerrold and Maclise, in his apartment in Lincoln's Inn Fields to hear Dickens read the new Christmas Book. On this occasion, too, Dickens must have felt 'what it was to have Power'. In the sketch of the occasion he sent to Catherine, Maclise gave visual representation to this power by drawing radiant beams of light emanating from the reader's head. There were, he wrote, 'shrieks of laughter' and 'floods of tears as a relief to them', and added, 'I do not think that there was ever such a triumphant hour for Charles.' A second reading in Forster's chambers on 5 December had Fonblanque and Richard Barham, author of *The Ingoldsby Legends*, among the audience and was equally successful. Dickens had now tasted blood, as it were, as far as reading his own work aloud was concerned and this led in time, as Forster somewhat drily notes, to 'rather memorable issues'.[45]

By 9 December Dickens was again in Paris, where he made a short stay, and finally arrived back at the Peschiere on the 20th. Meanwhile, *The Chimes* had been published on 16 December and had amply justified Dickens's prediction that it would 'make a great uproar'. *The Globe* said (31 Dec.) that it was 'attacked and defended with an ardour which scarcely any other subject is capable of inspiring'. At one extreme the Tory weekly *John Bull* accused Dickens (28 Dec.) of pandering to 'the low Radical doctrines of the day' while at the other the Chartist daily *The Northern Star* was rejoiced (also 28 Dec.) that, 'expressing views of man and society far more comprehensive than he has before put forth, Mr DICKENS enters the public arena, as *the champion of the poor!*' Sales were brisk and the following April Dickens was able to report to Mitton that

22 Dickens reading *The Chimes* to a group of friends in Forster's chambers, drawn by Maclise and showing (left to right): Forster, Jerrold, Laman Blanchard, Carlyle, CD, Fred Dickens, Maclise, W. J. Fox, Stanfield, Alexander Dyce, Rev. William Harness

Bradbury and Evans's gross profits on the first twenty thousand copies (up to 31 Dec.) had been between £1,400 and £1,500. After payment of all expenses and deduction of the publishers' quarter-share, Dickens's net profit amounted to £1,065.8s.2d. Contrasting these figures with Chapman and Hall's for the *Carol*, he crowed, 'Bradbury and Evans are the Men for me to work with'.[46]

The Christmas, New Year and Twelfth Night jollifications at the Peschiere (the last-named of these festivals being enhanced by a magnificent Twelfth-cake sent from England by Angela Burdett Coutts in honour of Charley's birthday) were intermingled with Dickens's intense involvement in his mesmeric (hypnotic) treatment of the petite English wife of a Swiss banker resident in Genoa called Emile de la Rue. Mme de la Rue suffered from an acute neurasthenic disorder which caused spectral illusions, convulsions, even catalepsy at times. Dickens found he could use those mesmeric powers he had discovered himself to possess in America to relieve her. From 23 December onwards he threw himself (with M. de la Rue's full support and co-operation) into an intensive course of treatment that was increasingly presented, in his detailed correspondence with de la Rue, as a struggle between himself, acting as a sort of combined therapist and exorcist, and a malign 'Phantom' which manifested itself in Madame de la Rue's hallucinations. Dickens clearly found this campaign to save a young woman from her demons immensely stimu-lating, and could funnel most of his formidable energy towards it since the only literary work in which he was currently engaged was writing up his travels of the previous November. He continued treating Mme de la Rue for several months and succeeded in considerably alleviating her symptoms. During February, as he and Catherine were travelling to Naples via Rome, he regularly mesmerised his 'patient', as he called Mme de la Rue, long-distance, and when the Dickenses returned to Rome he persuaded the de la Rues to join them. Here he resumed face-to-face treatment – though this hardly seems the right phrase when we think of the occasion when he was summoned to the de la Rues' bedroom one night to find Madame 'rolled into an apparently impossible ball, by tic in the brain' and was only able to find where her head was 'by following her long hair to its source'.[47]

The situation made Catherine, who was once more in the early stages of pregnancy, understandably very uneasy. Greatly to Dickens's annoyance, and, no doubt to his embarrassment also, he had to communicate this to the de la Rues. We may imagine how hotly he would have denied, to himself as to others, any erotic, or even romantic, element in what he would have seen as a purely therapeutic relationship with Mme de la Rue. It is, however, worth noting that in the only direct literary outcome of this whole episode, a tale of the uncanny set in Italy and called 'To Be Read At Dusk' that he wrote seven years later, Dickens makes the relationship between powerful male mesmerist and female subject explicitly sexual in nature.[48]

On 19 January Dickens and Catherine set out for Rome via Pisa and Siena. They reached Rome on the 30th and stayed there one week, which happened to be Carnival Week ('a great scene for a description', he told Mitton). Dickens was especially enthralled by the Coliseum, 'most stupendous and awful' by day or by night: 'The ancient part of Rome, and a portion of the Campagna, are *what I meant* when I came here,' he wrote to Burdett Coutts on 18 March; 'the rest a little below my imaginary mark, and very unlike it'. From Rome the travellers went south to Naples where Georgina joined them. They visited Pompeii and Herculaneum and made a highly dramatic ascent of Vesuvius with Dickens insisting on climbing up to the very edge of the crater to look down 'into the flaming bowels of the mountain'. They returned to Rome on 2 March, where the de la Rues joined them and Dickens continued his treatment, and a few days later he witnessed the public beheading of a murderer, going close up to the scaffold immediately afterwards to view the corpse and severed head, and noting how strangely the neck seemed to have been 'annihilated'. The ceremonies of Holy Week – 'unmitigated humbug' in Dickens's view – offered further spectacle, much enlivened by the comical behaviour of some of the English tourists. From Rome the travellers proceeded to Florence, finally returning, on 9 April, to Genoa, a city to which Dickens had now become deeply attached. There they found 'all well and flourishing' and the children 'looking beautiful'.[49]

Dickens now had nearly two clear months before it would be time to return to England. He wrote a series of letters to Forster and others going over all his Italian travels, especially Venice, Rome and Naples, and providing what Forster calls 'such rich filling-in to the first outlines sent, as fairly justified the title of *Pictures* finally chosen for them'. To Mitton Dickens wrote on 20 May that he had by that date 'elaborately *painted*' at least three quarters of his travels to Rome and Naples. At this stage, however, he was still undecided as to the form in which he might publish some version of these 'shadows in the water', as he called them in a phrase he retrieved for use in his 'Reader's Passport' preface to *Pictures from Italy* a year later. He postponed a decision until his return when Forster and he could discuss the matter with Bradbury and Evans. Meanwhile, no more is heard of his eagerness, mentioned the previous autumn when he was trying to get going with *The Chimes*, to write 'a story about the length of that most delightful of all stories, the *Vicar of Wakefield*'. Instead, we find him telling Amédée Pichot on 10 April that he intends at some point to write his autobiography, a plan, he says, that he has formed 'il y a longtemps'. During this 'sabbatical' pause in his career he was evidently beginning to think more about his early life – witness the detailed account in his New Year letter to Forster of his abortive attempt to become a professional actor – and perhaps beginning to think also about how he might draw on such material for fictional as well as autobiographical purposes, having already tapped it in the *Carol*.[50]

It seems likely that it was during this relatively tranquil period also that Dickens systematically revised the text of *Oliver Twist* in order to introduce into it the rhetorical punctuation he had pioneered in parts of *Chuzzlewit* and used throughout *The Chimes*. The copyright of *Oliver* now belonged to him and Bradbury and Evans and at some point during 1844 the decision must have been made to re-issue the novel in monthly parts beginning in January 1845. It may not have been until later in the year that Dickens carried out this revision but it is difficult to see when he would have had the sustained leisure for it after his return to London. Meanwhile, just before leaving Genoa, he put his histrionic abilities to the test again when he gave a private reading of the *Carol* at the house of the British Consul (whose son remembered him as having been 'extremely nervous' on the occasion).[51]

On 9 June the Dickens ménage left the Peschiere and set out for home via the St Gothard Pass. Like many another Victorian tourist, Dickens was enraptured by Switzerland's scenic beauties, little thinking that within the year he would be resident among them. The travellers proceeded via Zurich and Cologne to Brussels where Forster, Maclise and Douglas Jerrold had come to meet them. They eventually reached Devonshire Terrace on 3 July, and Dickens had hardly been re-installed there a week before he was writing to Forster about a major new literary project.

This project was one that had been mooted some while before and is alluded to in the Agreement with Bradbury and Evans of 1 June 1844. It was for a new weekly periodical to be edited by Dickens, like *Master Humphrey's Clock* but unlike the *Clock* would not result in his having to write the whole thing himself. Jerrold had just successfully launched his own periodical, a monthly called *Douglas Jerrold's Shilling Magazine* and published by Bradbury and Evans. Dickens preferred more frequent contact with his readers via a weekly journal but was happy to write a piece for Jerrold's August number extolling the work of Maclise, whom a Royal Commission had chosen, along with five other artists, to submit designs for frescoes to decorate the new Houses of Parliament. Dickens's confident references to 'the glories of the Vatican' and 'the galleries of Florence', likewise his equally confident comments on the art of fresco and on the Raphael tapestries in Rome in relation to the famous Cartoons at Hampton Court (now in the Victoria and Albert Museum), clearly reflect his recent Italian experiences.[52]

As to Dickens's ideas for *his* new periodical, as outlined to Forster, they make an interesting contrast with his plans for *Master Humphrey's Clock* back in 1840. It was to be called *The Cricket* and was basically an extension of the *Christmas Carol* formula to cover the whole year, and an exploitation of the now well-established Dickens public persona: '*Carol* philosophy, cheerful views, sharp anatomization of humbug, jolly good temper; papers always in season, pat to the time of year . . .'. 'It is a name and aim', he tells Forster, 'which people would readily and pleasantly connect with *me*.' The concept of the *Clock* had interposed a 'little club or knot of characters' between Dickens the journalist and his readers. Now, as 'The Cricket' ('a cheerful creature that chirrups on the hearth') he could locate himself in their homes with a genial intimacy, 'dashing' at their fenders and arm-chairs and at once sitting down 'upon their very hobs'. The *Clock* had had a marked antiquarian bias whereas *The Cricket* would be highly topical, 'pat to the time of the year'. It would review new books and plays and supply 'notices of all good things, notices of all bad ones' as well as reprinting items from its contemporaries. The *Clock* had been primarily literary in content whereas *The Cricket* was evidently thought of as definitely journal-istic. In many ways it looked forward, as the Pilgrim Editors note, to *Household Words*, the title of which more directly proclaims its targeting of readers in their own domestic context. However, the projected *Cricket*'s 'vein of glowing, hearty, generous, mirthful, beaming reference in everything to Home, and Fireside' links it more closely with the 1840s Christmas Books than with Dickens's strongly socially-investigative magazine of the next decade.[53]

All thoughts of *The Cricket* were suddenly swept aside on 25 July when Bradbury and Evans 'perfectly amazed' Dickens with their proposal that he should become the first editor of a new national daily paper they were plan-ning to found in partnership with Joseph Paxton, the Duke of Devonshire's remarkable head gardener and chief man of business. In this year of 'Railway Mania' he had invested some £35,000 in railway schemes and the projected new paper, to be called *The Daily News*, was intended to promote railway interests, as well as those of capital and labour generally. It would thus be Liberal and progressive in politics, and was especially intended to spearhead the campaign for the repeal of the Corn Laws, a proposal fiercely opposed by the Tories on behalf of the so-called 'agricultural interest' (farmers and landowners). Dickens's phenomenal popularity, and his strong public image as a great champion of reform, would be tremendous assets for the projected new paper.[54]

The wonder is not that the projectors of the new paper should want Dickens but that he should – even on the very handsome terms he eventually negotiated for himself – contemplate for one moment taking on, even for a limited period, such an onerous and responsible full-time job, one hardly reconcilable with any continuation of his career as a novelist in the immediate future. He was probably influenced by two main considerations. The first was financial security. The moderate (by his standards) sales of *Chuzzlewit* had been something of a shock, as had the similarly moderate profits on the *Carol*, and the number and demands of his dependents seemed to be ever-increasing. He confided to Forster, who expressed misgivings about acceptance of the proffered editorship, 'I have sometimes that possibility of failing health or fading popularity before me, which beckons me to such a venture when it comes my way.' The second reason was surely his strong ambition to 'leave his hand upon the time', to address by every means possible that formidable 'Condition of England Question' and to help ameliorate the lot of the poor in any way he could. He was evidently in campaigning mood this summer and on 28 July renewed his offer to Napier of an article for the *Edinburgh Review*. This time he proposed to write against capital punishment, arguing *inter alia* that its fearfulness tended to engender a 'diseased sympathy' for murderers 'among the well-conducted and the gentle' (he had probably been irritated by R. H. Horne's recent charge that he had in *Oliver Twist*, 'made the criminal an object of sympathy', albeit inadvertently). However, like all his previous proposals for an *Edinburgh* article this one also came to nothing, though he did a year later write not one but a whole series of articles on this topic. These were published in *The Daily News*, a daily or weekly paper being a vehicle better suited than a heavyweight monthly to his particular brand of crusading journalism.[55]

Meanwhile, the concept of *The Cricket* was not wholly abandoned. It metamorphosed into what Dickens described as 'a delicate and beautiful fancy for a Christmas book, making the Cricket a little household god – silent in the wrong and sorrow of the tale, and loud again when all went well and happy'. Work on this little book was not to begin until October, however. From mid-July onwards Dickens was gleefully busy organising some amateur theatricals on a decidedly more elaborate scale than those performed in Montreal three years before. Following his sabbatical, he needed as many outlets as possible for his creative energy. He told Cattermole on 3 September, 'I have been bottled up so long that I bless this play for serving as a corkscrew.' The play was Ben Jonson's *Every Man in His Humour* (1598), probably because it offers a whole range of character-parts giving nearly every cast member a chance to shine. Dickens was, naturally, producer, director and stage-manager and had the juiciest role, that of swaggering Captain Bobadil, the boastful soldier. The programme was rounded off by the farce in which he had had such delirious success in Montreal, *Past Two o'Clock in the Morning*. Originally, he was to be partnered in this by Stanfield but, the latter having enough to do with painting the scenery, the burly artist was replaced by the still more rotund Mark Lemon, editor of *Punch*, who became known to Dickens's children as 'Uncle Porpoise'.

23 'Mr Charles Dickens as "Captain Bobadil"' by Kenny Meadows. *Illustrated London News*, 22 November 1845

Lemon and Dickens played together brilliantly in this and many later farces staged by the Amateurs.[56]

Between mid-July and the night of the performance at a private theatre in Soho on 20 September, Dickens recruited and drilled his cast, the female parts being played by professional actresses. Characteristically, Dickens attended to every last detail of the production, and the parallels with his later 'conducting' of *Household Words* and its contributors are evident, as has been pointed out. As, however, his histrionic achievements, remarkable though they were, do not – at least at this point – bear very directly on his life as a writer, I refrain from much detailed discussion of them here. Suffice to say that the performance, which took place before a fashionable and appreciative audience, was an enormous success. By popular demand a public performance followed, with Prince Albert and his suite in attendance, at the St James's Theatre on 15 November (a charity event to raise money for the Sanatorium).[57]

Intermingled with all this histrionic activity in Dickens's schedule during the autumn and winter of 1845–46 were the mighty preparations going forward for the launching of *The Daily News*, preparations which at one point in early November Dickens believed would have to be abandoned because of sudden financial reverses affecting Paxton and another backer. This proved a temporary set-back, however, and he was soon again involved in much correspondence, a journey to Chatsworth to confer with Paxton, and another to Liverpool 'to blow vague Trumpets' for the new paper. His formal acceptance of the editorship, at a salary of £2,000 (he demanded and got double what he was first offered), took place on 3 November and by 17 November he was working on the prospectus for *The Daily News* (his draft does not seem to have survived) which appeared in the press on 1 December, and was much involved in the recruitment of staff.[58]

All this considerably hindered the writing of his third Christmas Book, now named *The Cricket on the Hearth: A Fairy Tale of Home*. Such a seasonal offering from him was now, commented *The Mirror of Literature* (27 Dec.) 'as regularly expected as a pantomime, and his appearance on the publishing stage is hailed with as much delight as that of Grimaldi used to be on the boards of the theatre'. Once again, Maclise, Doyle, Stanfield and Leech supplied illustrations and, to Dickens's delight, the great animal painter Landseer agreed to provide a vignette of the splendid dog Boxer, who is by far the best character in this Dickensian pastoral, which is a rather thin little tale of threatened conjugal happiness in humble rural life, with a curiously personal and wistful postscript.[59]

Dickens had had a struggle to get the little book under way but was able to report to Burdett Coutts on 1 December that it was finished. 'It is', he told her, 'very quiet and domestic' and he hoped that it was 'interesting and pretty'. It was the first of his Christmas Books to have a dedicatee and the fact that this was Lord Jeffrey, the worshipper of Little Nell, sufficiently indicates what particular aspect of his literary genius Dickens believed it represents. It certainly marks a distinct departure from the pattern established by the *Carol* and *The Chimes* in that there is no particularly seasonal element in the story and not the least vestige of social criticism. Partly, perhaps, because of this latter absence, the *Cricket* proved, at least initially, far more popular than either of its predecessors. Reviews were generally very favourable (*The Times*'s savage attack on it was attributed to hostility towards the nascent *Daily News*) and no fewer than seventeen different stage versions appeared in London within a month of the book's publication. Acting on the principle of 'if you can't beat them, join them', and in order that he might be, as he put it, 'slaughtered as gently as possible', Dickens agreed, allegedly for 'golden reasons', to supply leading comic actors Robert and Mary Ann Keeley (a husband-and-wife team, who managed the Lyceum) with early proofs of the story from which their house-dramatist, the showman Albert Smith, might work up an adaptation and get the story on the boards ahead of all competition.[60]

On the domestic front, the latter part of 1845 was marked by the birth on 28 October of the Dickenses's sixth child and fourth son. The baby was not christened until the following April when he was named Alfred D'Orsay Tennyson Dickens after his two bizarrely contrasting godfathers ('Ah, Charlie', wrote Browning to Elizabeth Barrett, 'if this don't prove to posterity that you might have been a Tennyson and were a D'Orsay – why excellent labour will have been lost!'). Some three months before Alfred's birth his eighteen-year-old uncle, Augustus Dickens, seemed to Thomas Powell, who had helped to find him employment, to be forming an unsuitable attachment. Dickens declined to intervene, justifying his not doing so by reference to his own early life (he himself had been just eighteen when he fell so passionately in love with Maria Beadnell). He wrote to Powell on 2 August:

> I broke my heart into the smallest pieces, many times between thirteen and three and twenty. Twice, I was very horribly in earnest; and once I really set upon the cast for six or seven long years, all the energy and determination of which I am owner. But it went the way of nearly all such things at last, though I think it kept me steadier than the working of my nature was, to many good things for the time. If anyone had interfered with my very small Cupid, I don't know what absurdity I might not have committed in assertion of his proper liberty; but having plenty of rope he hanged himself, beyond all chance of restoration.[61]

This first extant retelling by Dickens of the Maria Beadnell affair is fascinating from many points of view – the (doubtless unconscious) exaggeration of the duration of his suffering (1820–21) becomes 'six or seven long years' in his memory, which contrasts with the apparent light-heartedness of the writing ('my very small Cupid', etc.), and the belief that the emotional distress was character-building in a good way. It is one of the most striking examples of the way in which Dickens's mind during these immediately post-America years was continually turning back to revisit and re-imagine painful passages in his early life. The most painful passage of all he could not, of course, allude to, even in general terms, but the fact that Charley was now in his ninth year and Dickens was corresponding about his education with Burdett Coutts, who had offered her help in placing him in a good school, must also have turned his thoughts back to his forlorn ten-year-old self with his schooling broken off and his happy life in Chatham exchanged for a dismal one in Camden Town. Generally, one can say of the period between the summer of 1842 and the winter of 1845 that, whilst most of what Dickens actually wrote related in one way or another to the Condition of England Question, he had mentally and emotionally begun to travel the road that would lead through *Dombey and Son* to *David Copperfield*. 1846, however, was to open with a spectacular detour which was to prove the one unmitigated failure of his dazzling career.

CHAPTER 10

An interlude

'DAILY NOOSES' AND THE NOOSE ITSELF, 1846

We'll have, please God, the old kind of evenings and the old life again, as it used to be before those daily nooses caught us by the legs and sometimes tripped us up.
Dickens to Forster, 26–29 October 1846

THE DEED of partnership establishing *The Daily News* (21 Jan.1846) lists those who had invested capital in the project, principally Paxton and Bradbury and Evans, and the number of shares accruing to each but also names others who held 'literary shares', allocated to those who supplied labour (in the form of editorial or printing work) rather than capital. These shareholders were not required to invest any money but could participate in Proprietors' meetings, though without voting rights. Dickens received ten such shares, equivalent, it has been calculated, to an investment of £4,000. He therefore stood to gain more from the enterprise than just a handsome salary (£2,000 p.a.), and this additional income would continue after he had ceased to be an employee. Bradbury and Evans became the paper's 'managers' with the right to appoint or remove anyone on the staff from the editor downwards. Dickens was, in fact, once more putting himself in a position he had found irksome whilst editing *Bentley's* though he seems to have been unconcerned about this in the general euphoria of launching the new paper.[1]

He apparently had a free hand in the recruitment and remuneration of staff, and in organising the initial reporting arrangements. With Beard, now working for the *Herald*, he arranged an unprecedented news-gathering pact on behalf of their two papers and the *Daily News* historians McCarthy and Robinson note that he 'appears to have made the most liberal arrangements for the compensation of all those who worked with him and under him':

His one idea was to make *The Daily News* the first really Liberal daily paper of England, as complete and well appointed in every qualification of English journalism as the very best of those which were got up for the use of the classes rather than of the masses. . . . Men were not to be invited to take the paper simply because it advocated their own political opinions. They were invited to take it because, while it did advocate their political opinions, it was also to be regarded as the best newspaper, simply regarded as newspaper, that they could get anywhere. This was Mr Dickens' idea, and that idea he enforced in action.[2]

To help him carry out his idea, Dickens recruited leader-writers from among his most prominent friends and acquaintances in the world of journalism, including Forster, Fonblanque and Jerrold. A strong team of parliamentary reporters was assembled and placed under the management of John Dickens, who had been released from his West Country exile and whom his long-suffering son had allowed to return from his Devonshire banishment. John seems to have risen to the challenge and was remembered as being exceedingly efficient in the 'regular marking and orderly despatch to the printers of the numerous manuscripts thrown off at lightning speed' by his team, and as showing a 'most enviable stamina'. Dickens fired up at once when he thought Bradbury was slighting John, roundly declaring that there was not 'a more zealous, disinterested or useful gentleman attached to the paper' than his father. That John merited such praise is suggested by the fact that he kept his post until his death in 1851. Writing in the previous year, Dickens may have had his father's zealous work for *The Daily News* in mind when writing Traddles's praise of Micawber in chapter 54 of *David Copperfield*: 'I must do Mr Micawber the justice to say . . . that although he would appear not to have worked to any good account for himself, he is a most untiring man when he works for other people.'[3]

Dickens did not stop at his father as far as relatives were concerned when recruiting staff for the new paper. George Hogarth became theatrical and musical editor, and John Henry Barrow was sent off as a foreign correspondent to India, where the Sikh Wars were beginning ('Great attention will be paid to foreign matters,' Dickens wrote to an old India hand called Stocqueler in early December, 'and we are particularly anxious to shine in reference to India'). Friends and former colleagues were also enlisted: Lady Blessington, for example, undertook to provide society news, known in the trade as 'fashionable intelligence' (a journalistic genre Dickens later parodied brilliantly in *Bleak House*, chapter 2). His right-hand man in everything connected with the paper, as in all other aspects of his professional life, was Forster but he was also greatly helped by 'a very good fellow', the quietly tactful and efficient William Henry Wills, formerly assistant editor of *Chambers' Edinburgh Journal*, who was appointed as his secretary.[4]

The paper's premises were some old houses owned by Bradbury and Evans in Bouverie Street, Whitefriars. Gutting them and converting them into offices in the time available required huge efforts by the workmen involved. They were supervised by Bradbury and Evans's master printer, a Mr Jones, and when a 'dummy number' of the paper dated 'Monday, 19 January' was put together on the 17th, Dickens, 'torn to pieces' as he was with 'overwhelming pressure of business', nevertheless found time to dash off for it an amusing spoof leader reporting Jones's trial for the 'wilful and malicious' murder of 'five bricklayers, seven carpenters, two furniture-warehouse porters, three painters, and a plasterer'. Also included in this dummy (otherwise largely composed of material extracted from other newspapers) was a version of the first of a series entitled 'Travelling Letters Written on the Road', the title under which Dickens had decided to publish in serial form an account of his Italian experiences before bringing it out as a book.[5]

The first issue of *The Daily News* nearly failed to appear owing to an incompetent printer (an exhausted Mr Jones perhaps?). 'All our efforts was [*sic*] nearly being floored at four O clock this morning,' Paxton wrote to his wife, 'and it was only by exertion almost superhuman that it was got out at all.' Although the Charles Dickens Museum has a copy of the issue carefully inscribed by Catherine, 'brought home by Charles at two o'clock in the morning, January 21st', Dickens was not, in fact, able to leave the office until 6 a.m. when, perhaps with happy memories of earlier races against *The Times* in his *Chronicle* days, he dashed off a note to Forster to say they had 'been at press three quarters of an hour and were out before the *Times*'. However annoyed the *Times* people may have been about this, they were, according to their crack reporter William Howard Russell (later celebrated for his damning reports from the Crimean war front) relieved to find the first number of the *News* 'ill-printed on bad paper, and "badly made up" '. Though he admired Dickens's 'brilliant picture from Italy' (the first 'Travelling Letter' which, in fact, is entirely devoted to travelling through France) Russell thought the issue as a whole was 'a fiasco'. This was too harsh but there were certainly enough typographical errors for Dickens to insert a jokey letter of protest about this in the next issue, ending, 'I have an interest in the subject, as I intend to be, / If you will allow me, /YOUR CONSTANT READER', together with an apologetic reply to himself laying the blame on 'disadvantageous circumstances'. Of this second issue he wrote to Beard on 22 January, 'we have a Capital paper today', adding, 'I sat at the Stone [the slab used by printers on which pages of type were set up], and made it up myself.'[6]

The first issue features Dickens's opening editorial address in which he announces that

The Principles advocated by The Daily News will be Principles of Progress and Improvement; of Education, Civil and Religious Liberty, and Equal Legislation; Principles, such as its conductors believe the advancing spirit of the time requires: the condition of the country demands: and Justice, Reason and Experience legitimately sanction. Very much is to be done, and must be done, towards the bodily comfort, mental elevation, and general contentment of the English People.

24 'Titania Dickens to Bottom – The Daily News': Cartoon published in *Mephystopheles*, 14 February 1846

This might seem to be going well beyond the aims of the middle-class Anti Corn Law League but Dickens goes on to say that the people's 'true interests' cannot be considered as 'a class-question', being, as they are, inseparable from 'the interests of the merchant and the manufacturer'. The mission of *The Daily News*, therefore, would be to heal, rather than widen, any breach 'that may unhappily subsist, or may arise, between Employer and Employed'. The paper would also seek 'to elevate the character of the Public Press in England' by avoiding the kind of 'sordid' attacks on rival publications prevalent in England and America.[7]

A total of sixty-four leading articles written by Forster, Jerrold and the rest of the team appeared during Dickens's three-week editorship. They show the paper sticking closely to Liberal/Utilitarian doctrine with over a third directly attacking the Corn Laws. But the paper also opposed Lord Ashley's bill seeking to limit factory workers' hours to ten a day, which it saw as class legislation undermining the workers by reducing their wages. This may seem odd given Dickens's reputation as a great humanitarian, as may the absence of leaders calling for the redress of social injustices. We should recall, however, that Will Fern in *The Chimes* pleads with the gentry not for Parliament to remedy social evils but for a more sympathetic *understanding* of the plight of the poor, the provision of better housing by landlords, and so on – more *noblesse oblige*, in other words, on the part of the upper and middle classes. Nine years later this will also be the stance of that model working-man Stephen Blackpool in *Hard Times*. In Dickens's view there were bad laws that needed to be abolished, such as the harsh penal ones favoured by the Tories and, above all, the hateful Corn

Laws that hampered free trade and kept the price of bread high in order to
benefit 'the agricultural interest'. As regards new legislation, however, the less
there was of this the better for the country. What was needed was that existing
laws, like those relating to Chancery, that had become overly complex in their
operation should be drastically simplified, and access to legal help should not
depend on wealth (as poor Stephen finds to be the case with regard to the
divorce courts). In all this Dickens was typical of all Liberals who had leanings
towards certain aspects of Radicalism.[8]

One area in which Dickens did very much want Government action,
however, was that of national education, and he recalled his experience of
visiting the Field Lane Ragged School in September 1843 in a piece he
wrote for *The Daily News* in the form of a letter published in the issue for
4 February under the heading 'Crime and Education'. He describes the horror
of seeing London's 'careless maintenance from year to year . . . of a vast hopeless nursery of ignorance, misery and vice; a breeding place for the hulks and
jails' in the hordes of feral street-children, abandoned to their fate in this
'capital city of the world'. In the absence of any system of national education,
the Ragged School movement was at least a tiny, faltering step in the right
direction. He vividly evokes the Field Lane School and the terrible sight
of some of the children there – 'low-browed, vicious, cunning, wicked;
abandoned of all help but this; speeding downward to destruction; and
UNUTTERABLY IGNORANT'.[9]

Dickens appeals to his readers' Christian charity to help these schools but at
the same time deplores their volunteer teachers' over-emphasis on religion and
'religious mysteries'. This kind of overloading of children with scriptural
quotations and allusions was a continuing preoccupation of his. Twenty years
later, he would present a devastatingly satirical picture of the teacher at
Charley Hexam's Ragged School 'drawling on to My Dearerr Childerrenerr . . .
about the beautiful coming to the Sepulchre; and repeating the word
Sepulchre (commonly used among infants) five hundred times, and never
once hinting what it meant.' In the version of the New Testament that he began
writing in this year of 1846 for reading to his own children, whose ages now
ranged from nine down to just a few months, he was careful to gloss scriptural
terms wherever he needed to use them. Having mentioned miracles, for
example, he writes, 'I wish you would remember that word, because I shall use
it again, and I should like you to know that it means something very wonderful
and which could not be done without God's leave and assistance.'[10]

Scriptural references were very marked in his second verse contribution to
the *News*, published on 9 February, after he had ceased to be editor. This was
'The Hymn of the Wiltshire Labourers' which appeared with his signature.
Dickens wrote it in response to a report of a meeting of agricultural workers
at Bramhill in Wiltshire at which a woman was reported to have cried out,

'Don't you all think that we have a great need to Cry to our God to put it in the hearts of our greassous Queen and her Members of Parlerment to grant us free bread!' The second of Dickens's five verses runs as follows:

The God, who took a little child,
And set him in the midst,
And promised him His mercy mild,
As, by Thy Son, Thou didst:
Look down upon our children dear,
So gaunt, so cold, so spare,
And let their images appear
Where Lords and Gentry are!

The last two lines recall the scene in *The Chimes* in which the starving Will Fern suddenly appears at the Bowley Hall banquet. The day after they were published Dickens himself was at a grand dinner (but in his case, one presumes, by invitation), where the host was Lord John Russell, and he was gratified to find that his hymn had 'made some impression'.[11]

Dickens seems to have written anonymously various short pieces for the paper during his brief editorship, such as the enthusiastic review of Hood's *Poems* that appeared on 29 January, but his main contribution was a series of articles that continued for several weeks after he ceased being editor before it suddenly terminated without warning or explanation. Called 'Travelling Letters Written on the Road' and published under his name, they appeared irregularly between 21 January and 11 March. They describe his family's journey through France and residence in Genoa, and his visits to various north Italian cities, stopping with Bologna. He seems to have followed the same practice as he did for *American Notes* in borrowing back from Forster and others letters written to them on the spot in order to use them as a basis for his published version. In this case, however, there were two stages of publication. These letters served, in an amplified and revised form, for the basis of the first part of his travel book, *Pictures from Italy*, published two months later. Dedicated as *The Daily News* was to 'the advancing spirit of the time', *Pictures* made a good vehicle for conveying Dickens's artfully-constructed vision of Italy as being, for all its dreamy picturesqueness, a stagnant, priest-ridden country, full of places like Piacenza 'gone to sleep and basking in the sun'. And, before he even reaches Italy, Letter No. 2 provides the *News*'s enlightened readers with a thrill of horror about the badness of the bad old days, and a reminder that some of that badness still lingers on. It features a striking Dickens character called 'Goblin', an ancient spitfire who guides visitors round the Palace of the Popes in Avignon. She descants on the terrors of the Inquisition – a vivid reminder to his readers of what a very different Dickens goblin, the Goblin of the Great Bell in

The Chimes, calls those 'ages of darkness, wickedness and violence' that had now so mercifully passed away. Dickens's *Fidelio*-like moment of exultation at the sight of sunlight streaming through the broken wall of the Inquisition's dungeons typifies for him 'the light that has streamed in, on all persecution in God's name, but which [referring to such bigoted régimes as the one governing the Papal States] is not yet at its noon!'[12]

The Goblin describes with equal relish a ghastly massacre carried out at Avignon in the name of Liberty during the French Revolution, and we see that Dickens has already fully developed that Carlyle-inspired interpretation of the Revolution that will, almost two decades later, underpin *A Tale of Two Cities*. When 'monstrous institutions' work 'for scores of years . . . to change men's nature' they end by tempting them 'with the ready means of gratifying their furious and beastly rage'. The Liberty proclaimed and worshipped by the Revolutionaries is 'an earth-born creature, nursed in the black mud of the Bastille moats and dungeons, and necessarily betraying many evidences of its unwholesome bringing-up'.

On the day that the fourth of his 'Travelling Letters' appeared, 9 February, Dickens abruptly resigned from the editorship of the *News* and was replaced by Forster (he continued to be paid his editorial salary until the end of April, however). He had never intended to stay long in the post but had simply wanted, as he wrote to his old Edinburgh friend Lord Robertson on 17 January, to do all he could 'to establish the Paper well' since his share of it, meaning his ten literary shares, 'would then be a fine property'. His resigning the post sooner rather than later was not owing to incompetence. There is little evidence to support W. J. Fox's assertion that Dickens 'broke down in the mechanical business' of editing. His reasons for giving up the editorship included the enormous daily pressure of the job ('very laborious work indeed', he told de la Rue), objections to the 'one-sided' railway-boosting policy imposed by Paxton and his fellow-proprietors, resentment of Bradbury's managerial interference in the day-to-day running of the paper, and – most importantly from our point of view – his increasing preoccupation with ideas for a new story that would be published in the tried-and-tested shilling-numbers format. Before considering this, however, we should note the remarkable series of five letters arguing for the abolition of capital punishment that he wrote for the *Daily News* between 23 February and 16 March under the heading 'Letters on Social Questions'.[13]

Once again, as with 'Crime and Education', we find an idea Dickens first mooted for the *Edinburgh* eventually emerging in *The Daily News* but this time on a much more expansive scale. As we have seen, he had offered the previous summer to write an article in favour of the abolition of capital punishment in the *Edinburgh* and had, in fact, outlined his argument in some detail to Macvey Napier. The movement to end hanging was at its strongest during the early 1840s and Dickens had his own individual take on it, which related to the

baleful fascination exercised upon the public mind by what he had called in
the 1841 preface to *Oliver Twist* 'the great, black, ghastly gallows'. Now the
Daily News gave him the opportunity of treating the subject in his favourite
serial form, and in a format which would allow of more imaginative treatment
than a fact-grinding piece for a highbrow quarterly. The manner and matter of
this letter-series would also make it quite distinct from his other series, the
'Travelling Letters'. True, the powerful description in these, mentioned in the
previous chapter, of the public beheading he witnessed in Rome clearly relates
to his current preoccupation with capital punishment, but the 'Travelling
Letters' series did not get as far as Rome and Dickens did not write up his
account of this 'ugly, filthy, careless, sickening spectacle' until some weeks later,
as part of *Pictures from Italy*.

In the *Daily News* letters he deploys with effect all the usual arguments
against capital punishment (possibility of error, etc.), using statistical evidence
and relevant quotations from an 1841 report recommending abolition to
the New York legislature. More telling, however, are the passages in which
he recalls the hideous scenes he witnessed at Courvoisier's execution
(above, p. 153), or those where his writer's empathetic imagination takes over
as he explores from the inside the mental processes of different kinds of
murderers, as he had explored those of the prisoner on the eve of execution in
'A Visit to Newgate', Fagin in the dock in *Oliver Twist*, Sikes on the run, and
Jonas Chuzzlewit both before and after he kills Tigg. His object is to show how
in some cases the gallows is no deterrent at all while in others it is a positive
incitement to murder. An example of the latter category is the man who nurses
'a slow, corroding, growing hate' for his partner and begins to tell himself 'that
he wouldn't mind killing her, though he should be hanged for it':

> With the entrance of the Punishment into his thoughts, the shadow of the
> fatal beam begins to attend – not on himself, but on the object of his hate. At
> every new temptation, it is there, stronger and blacker yet, trying to terrify
> him. When she defies or threatens him, the scaffold seems to be her strength
> and 'vantage ground'. Let her not be too sure of that; 'though he should be
> hanged for it'.
>
> Thus, he begins to raise up, in the contemplation of this death by hanging,
> a new and violent enemy to brave. The prospect of a slow and solitary expi-
> ation would have no congeniality with his wicked thoughts, but this throt-
> tling and strangling has. There is always before him, an ugly, bloody,
> scarecrow phantom, that champions her, as it were, and yet shows him, in a
> ghastly way, the example of murder. (*DN*, 9 March 1846)

Later Dickens retreated from the total-abolition position adopted in these
letters and concentrated instead on campaigning for an end to the depraved

spectacle of public executions. He seems to have come – or perhaps we should rather say (remembering such creations as Fagin and Quilp) he returned – to a belief in the existence in some individuals of innate, irredeemable evil, not resulting from influences or circumstances, a matter of nature and not nurture. It is the belief expressed by the landlady of The Break of Day in *Little Dorrit* when she declares 'that there are people who have no good in them – none', 'who must be dealt with as enemies of the human race' and be 'crushed like savage beasts and cleared out of the way'. For his final position on capital punishment we may turn to an 1864 letter asking a correspondent to distinguish when quoting him between public executions and capital punishment. He comments, 'I should be glad to abolish both, if I knew what to do with the Savages of civilization. As I do not, I would rid Society of them, when they shed blood, in a very solemn manner but would bar out the present audience.'[14]

Dickens had intended to write a sixth and final letter for the *Daily News*, dealing with secondary punishments, but ran out of time as he had to concentrate on preparing his Italian travel book, which needed to be published not later than May so as to leave a sufficient gap between its appearance and that of the first monthly part of his new story. This preparation involved some revision of the 'Travelling Letters', which he had pasted into a little memorandum book for editing purposes, and also the writing up of the rest of his Italian itinerary: 'The greater part of the descriptions', he wrote to Mme de la Rue on 17 April, 'were written in letters to Forster, but the putting of them together, and making additions to them, and touching them up, is rather a long job.' He continued the narrative mode already established in the 'Letters', one of reminiscence, fantasy and dreamy reflectiveness, sometimes verging on nightmare, as at the end of the wonderfully evocative section on Venice. It is variegated with some splendid comic episodes, like the hilarious description of a performance of the Milanese Theatre of Puppets in Genoa, and frequent caustic comments both on Italian Catholicism (the Jesuit priests in Genoa, for example, 'muster strong in the streets, and go slinking noiselessly about, in pairs, like black cats') and on the foreign tourists who cannot look at paintings and antiquities for themselves but have to be told what to think by their cicerones or guide-books. The title Dickens chose for his second travel book, *Pictures from Italy*, fits it as perfectly as *American Notes* had fitted its predecessor, containing, as that title had done, a joking reference to one of the things most frequently associated with the country concerned.[15]

It had been intended that Stanfield should illustrate *Pictures*. But he was soon to be received into the Catholic Church and by mid-March had seen enough of what Dickens had written to make him so uneasy about the way in which Roman Catholicism was being mentioned that he felt obliged to withdraw. Dickens's affection for his 'Dear Stanny' was undimmed but he was uncompromising over the point at issue. A new illustrator had urgently to be found and, through the good offices of Colnaghi, the West End print-dealer, Dickens discovered Samuel Palmer, the idealist landscape painter and disciple of Blake. Palmer was supporting himself and his family mainly by teaching and welcomed the proposed work for Dickens (though he was uncertain how much to charge for it). He had spent some years in Italy and had exhibited Italian landscapes at both the Royal Society and the Royal Society for Painters in Water Colours. He was unaccustomed to wood-engraving, however, and this, given the time pressures involved, probably accounts for the little book's containing only four vignettes instead of the twelve illustrations originally envisaged. It was finally published, to decidedly mixed reviews, on 18 May.[16]

As he finished *Pictures* Dickens's mind and imagination were beginning to be busy with the as yet untitled new story now scheduled to begin publication at the end of September. The only thing clear at this stage was that it should be set in England and it was accordingly advertised by the publishers on 18 April as 'A NEW ENGLISH STORY, by Mr Dickens, /To be published in Twenty Monthly parts'. His own first distinct reference to the work ('a new book in shilling numbers') dates from 30 January. Thereafter as we study the surviving records of his life during the time of the new story's gestation we can, I believe, distinguish two interconnected strands of thought and feeling relating to it. The first is primarily moral and social in nature and the second highly personal and autobiographical.

At some point during this period he told Forster the new story 'was to do with Pride what its predecessor had done with Selfishness'. He had lately been closely involved with a world where a species of pride was to be found that differed from pride of birth or breeding. This was pride of wealth which flour-ished in this world of 'deposit men, and provisional directors and committee men', as Dickens called it, into which *The Daily News* had plunged him, not altogether happily. Drawing on his experience of it he had perhaps already begun to develop the figure of Mr Dombey, head of the great mercantile firm of Dombey and Son. Mr Dombey was, Barnaby Rudge excepted, the first Dickens protagonist since that very different City personage Mr Pickwick to be neither a child nor a Fieldingesque or Smollettian young man with his way to make in the world.[17]

The Daily News and its proprietors were much concerned with railways so it is not perhaps surprising that, after Dickens's brief but intense involvement with the paper, the railway, which he had hitherto drawn on only for a comic diatribe by Tony Weller in the *Clock*, or for descriptive purposes in *American Notes* and the American scenes in *Chuzzlewit*, should figure prominently in certain crucial chapters of the first novel he wrote after quitting the editorship, the first English novel in which the villain meets his death under the wheels of a train. Mr Dombey is no railway magnate, however, and Dickens will keep clear of the contemporary 'Railway Mania' (frantic trading in railway stocks and shares) in the new story, apart from making a comic allusion to it in the naming of Staggs's Gardens, 'stag' being Stock Exchange slang for a speculator who buys heavily on a new share issue in anticipation of a rise in its price and hence the chance of a quick profit.[18]

Dickens appropriately locates Staggs's Gardens, the area that is to be totally transformed by the coming of the railway, in Camden Town. This was a part of London that would, of course, have had a distinct personal resonance for him as it had done in the *Carol*, and this points us to the second strand of thought and feeling in the novel mentioned above. Dickens seems to have continued during 1845/46 that recuperation of his earlier years for fictional purposes that we first noticed emerging in the *Carol*. Indeed, he may well have started work on an actual formal autobiography as early as the spring of 1845. Now, in February 1846, at the very moment when he made the decision to extricate himself from 'daily nooses' and to begin looking purposefully towards his new story, he took Catherine, Forster and Douglas Jerrold on a jaunt to Rochester to revisit the scenes of his boyhood. He was, moreover, just at this time discussing with Burdett Coutts the kind of school that might be best for nine-year-old Charley, the cost of whose education she wished to defray as a mark of her high esteem for Dickens's philanthropic zeal. It would have been strange if this had not sharpened Dickens's memories of his own abruptly halted schooling at the age of ten and of what he now recalled as a period of desolating parental neglect. Memories of his precious early brother/sister relationship with Fanny were also integral to Dickens's own version of the story of his life and these, too, surely fed into the early chapters of *Dombey*.[19]

While Dickens was 'contemplating' his new story 'with great ardour', as he wrote to Lord Robertson on 28 February, his deep concern with Ragged Schools continued unabated. He even proposed to the prominent educationalist Dr James Kay-Shuttleworth on 28 March that they should jointly try the experiment of raising subscriptions to set up a 'Normal Ragged School', outside the Ragged School Union, in which children could be taught without being 'wearied to death' by 'long Pulpit discourses'. And, only five days before leaving London for his second year abroad, he wrote at great length, and in remarkable detail, to Burdett Coutts about a project to be realised (if she agreed) on his return to London for her financing the setting up of an 'asylum' for homeless women, including those just released from prison but with nowhere to go to. Operating on a marks system pioneered by Captain Maconchie when Governor of Norfolk Island and much admired by Dickens, it would function as a rehabilitation centre, training such women in 'order, punctuality, cleanliness, the whole routine of household duties – as washing, mending, cooking' before sending them to British colonies overseas as potential wives and mothers. The 'Normal Ragged

School' did not become a reality but the Asylum certainly did and was to become a major commitment for Dickens for over a decade.[20]

Dickens's decision to move his household abroad again for a year was made at the end of January though he did not settle definitely for Switzerland until April (Catherine, he disloyally told Mme de la Rue, had positively refused to contemplate a return to Genoa). He wanted partly to mark publicly his disengagement from the *Daily News* and, as he later put it to Forster, to fill up 'the Pit in my literary life, made by that unhappy paper', and partly to give himself some respite from the pressures he was always under in London in order to concentrate on the new book. These pressures included the endless flood of begging letters, for example, or requests to speak at charity dinners, as he had done, very effectively, on 6 April for the newly-formed General Theatrical Fund. Financial considerations were also important. It would be cheaper for the family to live abroad and, as *Chuzzlewit* had not been the money-spinner he had hoped for, Dickens's finances were still rather shaky. The re-issue of *Oliver Twist* in ten monthly parts (Jan.–Oct.) with a new cover-design by Cruikshank made no profit for him. Bradbury and Evans's delay in paying his *Daily News* salary into his account meant that he found himself, to his great distress, to be overdrawn on 5 March. His concern about keeping his name as a law student on the books at the Middle Temple (see above, p. 139) so that he might one day be called to the Bar where 'there are many little pickings to be got' is another indication of ongoing financial anxiety, like his enquiring about the possibility of his being appointed 'to the paid magistracy of London' – not that, to outward appearance, he seemed to be in the least weighed down by his financial worries. Lord Jeffrey described him at this time as looking 'radiant with happiness and health & looking like an airy Cornet just vaulted out of a Cavalry Saddle'.[21]

Dickens decided on moving his household to Switzerland because the country had impressed him so favourably when he was travelling through it the previous year, and by 19 May, the day after *Pictures* was published, he had arranged to let Devonshire Terrace to an M.P. for £300 per half-year. He mentions his intention of 'getting up some Mountain knowledge' for fictional purposes but it was to be more than four years before he set a scene in Switzerland (chapter 58 of *Copperfield*) and, even then, the description is somewhat perfunctory. Meanwhile, he was keen to bring his wider circle of friends up to date with his plans. By that I mean, of course, his devoted readers, many of whom he must have somewhat disconcerted by becoming editor of a daily paper. His preface to *Pictures* provided an ideal opportunity to reassure them. Headed 'The Reader's Passport', it serves several purposes, in fact. Readers are warned not to expect a lot of conventional, guide-book information about Italy's antiquities and art treasures, or disquisitions on the country's political situation. Also, Dickens deftly invokes *Barnaby Rudge* to defend himself against potential accusations of anti-Catholicism. His readers, he writes, should regard

Pictures as 'a series of faint reflections – mere shadows in the water – of places to which the imaginations of most people are attracted in a greater or less degree, on which mine had dwelt for years'. *The Athenaeum* wittily commented, welcoming the book in its columns on 23 May, 'The substance of the small volume is not so much Italy visited by Mr Dickens as Mr Dickens visited by Italy.'

This preface to *Pictures*, like all Dickens's prefaces, is essentially an open letter to his readers, so 'dear to him in all his visions', but it is unique in that it contains something approaching an apology. He refers to the *Daily News* interlude as 'a brief mistake I made, not long ago, in disturbing the old relations between myself and my readers, and departing for a moment from my old pursuits'. But, the apology made, he can now reassure them that he is about to resume those pursuits, 'joyfully, in Switzerland; where I can at once work out the themes I have now in my mind, without interruption: and while I keep my English audience within speaking distance, extend my knowledge of a noble country, inexpressibly attractive to me'.[22]

CHAPTER 11

Dombey and other dealings

1846–1848

Dealings with the Firm of Dombey and Son Wholesale, Retail, and for Exportation
                          Full title of the monthly part-issue of *Dombey and Son*

Although Literature as a profession has no distinct status in England, I am bound to say that what I experience of its recognition, all through Society, in my own person is honorable, ample, and independent.
                                    Dickens to D. M. Moir, 17 June 1848

THE DICKENS household, with Roche the 'Brave Courier' again in attendance, left London on 31 May 1846 and reached Lausanne nine days later. It was here in this attractive, steep-hilled little town that Dickens decided to settle, notwithstanding his fear that, once he was at work again, he might sorely miss the populous streets of London for his customary night walks. He rented a villa called Rosemont, 'a kind of beautiful bandbox', with pleasant grounds sloping down to the lake and a fine view of mountains on the opposite shore. He re-arranged the furniture throughout the whole house before preparing his first-floor study, which was 'something larger than a Plate Warmer', for the work he was now so eager to begin. He was enraptured by the scenery and charmed by the Swiss. They were 'a good wholesome people to live near Jesuit-ridden kings on the brighter side of the mountains' and he rejoiced in the overthrow, with minimal force, on 7 October of Geneva's reactionary government by a group of radicals. Writing to Macready on the 24th he described the revolutionaries as 'free spirits, nobly generous and moderate, even in the first transports of victory – elevated by a splendid popular Education – and bent on Freedom from all tyrants, whether their crowns be golden or shaven'.[1]

He found himself and his family welcomed into a congenial little society of Anglo-Swiss led by William Haldimand, a retired banker and former M.P. A philanthropist after Dickens's heart, Haldimand was co-founder of a local asylum for the blind and Dickens would always remember him fondly as 'one of

25 Rosemont Villa, Lausanne

the noblest-hearted gentlemen in the world'. Two other wealthy philanthropists
were also of the circle, William and Maria de Cerjat, and another former M.P.,
the Hon. Richard Watson of Rockingham Castle in Northamptonshire, and
his wife Lavinia. Until de Cerjat died in 1869 Dickens wrote to him annually,
long and interesting letters sending personal news but commenting also, often
in some detail, on national and world affairs. These letters were, doubtless, a
continuation of the kind of conversations he, the de Cerjats and the Watsons had
enjoyed during this time in Lausanne with the always stimulatingly argumenta-
tive Haldimand. As to the Watsons, they quickly became two of Dickens's very
dearest friends, especially Lavinia, who was a woman of great charm, intelligence
and strong artistic interests.[2]
    Watson's diary records an agreeable round of dinners, whist, outdoor games,
and exploring expeditions, including one to the spectacular Great St Bernard
Pass, memorably described by Dickens in a letter to Forster. This place 'always
had a weird fascination for him', his eldest son recalled. It features vividly in an
article 'Lying Awake' written five years later and again in the opening of Book II
of *Little Dorrit* in 1856. For Watson Dickens was 'the most natural unaffected
distinguished man I ever met' and he comments more than once on what fun
he was to be with and on the 'wonderful charm and spirit' of his readings aloud
of his own work. Dickens gave three such private readings in Lausanne, one of

each of the first two numbers of his new story, *Dombey and Son*, and one of his new Christmas Book, *The Battle of Life*. His friends' responsive enthusiasm led Dickens to write, semi-seriously, to Forster about how 'in these days of lecturings and readings, a great deal of money might possibly be made (if it were not infra dig) by one's having Readings of one's own books'. Forster made light of this but secretly feared (with good reason, as things turned out) that this would not be the last he would hear of it.[3]

These readings from his current work show that, as we might expect, Dickens was not spending all his time socialising and sight-seeing. His first task at Rosemont had been to clear the decks for work on his new novel. This involved writing a long letter to Lord John Russell about the Ragged Schools and another to Burdett Coutts about her projected home for homeless women. He had also to finish his 'children's New Testament', a redaction of the gospels written in appropriately plain and simple language with, of course, none of the bravura touches to be found in his later *Child's History of England*. Dickens's depiction of Jesus as primarily a great teacher and healer is in continuity with his social journalism and with religious references in his fiction. Thus he exhorts his children never to be 'proud or unkind' to any of the poor: 'If they are bad, think that they would have been better, if they had had kind friends, and good homes, and been better taught.' Nearly two years later, in the final number of *Dombey*, he would sum up for adult readers his interpretation of the New Testament in his description of it as 'the blessed history, in which the blind, lame, palsied beggar, the criminal, the woman stained with shame, the shunned of all our dainty clay, has each a portion, that no human pride, indifference, or sophistry . . . can take away'.[4]

He had been at Rosemont a few days before his 'big box' arrived. This contained his preferred writing materials and what Forster calls 'certain quaint little bronze figures' that he always liked to have on his writing-desk, including a pair of duelling frogs and a dog thief/salesman with 'lots of little dogs in his pockets and under his arms'. By 28 June everything was in order and he could send Forster the awaited message 'BEGAN DOMBEY!' after making what he called 'a plunge over head and ears' into this story, the writing of which was to dominate the next twenty months of his life, first in Switzerland, then in Paris, and lastly in London and Broadstairs. He seems to have arrived at the title without any of the hesitation seen in the case of *Chuzzlewit*, or of *Dombey*'s immediate successors, and was anxious that it should be kept profoundly secret until publication day, no doubt because of its surprise departure from his traditional 'life and adventures' formula and its revelation that he was venturing into a new sphere of human activity. Its original version, used as an epigraph to this chapter, puts the emphasis on the family firm, which perhaps Dickens might first have thought would figure more prominently in the story than it ultimately does. When the novel appeared in volume form, however, the title became simply *Dombey and Son*, thus putting the emphasis squarely on the family. Both versions of the title conceal an irony not revealed to readers until five months into the story when they would discover that 'Dombey and Son' was to be 'a Daughter after all!'[5]

The plot of *Dombey* was planned out in much greater detail previous to the actual writing than had been the case with any of its predecessors, with the possible exception of *Barnaby Rudge*. On 25 or 26 July Dickens sent Forster the first four chapters of the new novel together with a general outline of the plot which Forster reproduces, with some omissions, in his *Life*. The outline describes Dombey's pride in his son and his indifference towards his daughter which will turn to 'positive hatred' after the boy's early death. But 'this rejected daughter . . . will come out better than any son at last' when the firm crashes and Dombey becomes a broken man. Eventually, he will come remorsefully to understand that his daughter has been his 'unknown Good Genius always' and so end 'the struggle with himself'. Hardly any other characters are mentioned, apart from two or three who appear in chapters 1–4. There is no hint of Dombey's disastrous second marriage, which, together with Carker's villainy, also unmentioned in the synopsis as we have it, precipitates the novel's catastrophe. But, as Dickens tells Forster, he is here giving him only 'what cooks call "the stock of the soup" ' and 'all kinds of things will be added to it'. It already represents, however, a remarkable advance in depth of conception and detailed planning when compared with the over-arching melodramatic device mentioned in Dickens's notes for *Chuzzlewit* IV, 'Old Martin's Plot to degrade and punish Pecksniff in the end'.

The novel was to be illustrated by Browne, as all the previous monthly-number novels had been, and Dickens must have sent him an outline similar to that sent to Forster in order to facilitate the designing of a cover for the monthly parts 'shadowing out' the story's 'drift and bearing'. Dickens was very anxious Browne should avoid caricature in depicting the protagonist of the new, more character-driven, kind of story he was attempting and wanted the artist to view a certain City magnate whose appearance he had had in mind when describing Mr Dombey. Browne was unable to do this but sent Dickens a sheet of twenty-nine sketches of potential Dombeys for him to choose from. Stimulated perhaps by the new developments in Dickens's art, Browne showed considerable enterprise in his own contribution to *Dombey* and Dickens was pleased with his work, with one notable exception to be mentioned below, his depiction of Mrs Pipchin. Their collaboration was of course greatly facilitated once Dickens was back in London and communication by word of mouth or brief, rapid notes could be resumed. This applied also to Forster's contribution – proof-correcting, suggesting cuts and changes, and acting as a general sounding-board for Dickens's ideas. Writing from Lausanne, Dickens asked for his response to the notion that young Walter Gay might be made a more pathetic version of Hogarth's Idle Apprentice, 'gradually and naturally trailing away, from that love of adventure and boyish light heartedness, into negligence, idleness, dissipation,

26 Some of Browne's trial sketches for Mr Dombey submitted to Dickens and reproduced by Forster in his *Life of Dickens*

dishonesty and ruin'. 'Do you think it may be done', he asked, 'without making people angry?' Forster evidently thought not and Dickens 'ultimately acquiesced' despite all the literary advantages he perceived in it.[6]

Dombey is the first Dickens novel for which there exists a complete set of preparatory notes for each monthly number (an isolated set, quoted above, exists for *Chuzzlewit* IV), a working practice Dickens followed for all his subsequent novels in this format, as well as for *Hard Times* which was published as a weekly serial but planned in five monthly numbers. For each number he prepared a sheet of paper approximately 7×9 inches by turning it sideways, with the long side horizontal, dividing it in two, and then using the left-hand side for what he called 'Mems'. These were memoranda to himself about events and scenes that might feature in the number, directions as to the pace of the narrative, particular phrases he wanted to work in, questions to himself about whether such-and-such a character should appear in this number or be kept waiting in the wings (usually with some such answer as 'Yes', 'No', or 'Not yet' added later) – in short, what has been succinctly described as 'brief aids in decision making, planning and remembering'. Among the 'General Mems for No 3', for example, we find that wonderful image for little Paul's desolation at Mrs Pipchin's, '– as if he had taken life: [*sic*] unfurnished, and the upholsterer were never coming' while 'The Major', Carker, and 'the offices in the City' are all marked 'to stand over'. In the notes for later numbers we find such 'mems' as 'Uncle Sol to die?' answered by 'No – Run away to look after Walter' (*DS* VII); 'Carry on the Servants as a sort of odd chorus to the story' (*DS* X); and 'Be patient with Carker – Get him on very slowly, without incident' (*DS* XII). In *DS* VII Mrs Skewton and Edith make their début and are the subject of an elaborate 'mem':

> The mother and daughter. The mother, and her cant about 'heart', and nature – Daughter who has been put through her paces, before countless marrying men, like a horse for sale – Proud and [disgust] weary of her degradation, but going on, for it's too late now, to try to turn back – <u>These to be encountered at Leamington</u>.[7]

On the right hand side of the sheet Dickens would generally write the numbers and titles of the three chapters that make up each monthly part and jot down, either before or after writing them, the names of the main characters and events featuring in each chapter, with occasionally a crucial fragment of the dialogue like little Paul's 'Papa what's money?' in chapter 8, or a note of significant events like 'Death's warning to Mrs Skewton' in chapter 36. In the notes for the climactic chapter 47 ('The Thunderbolt'), which contains the highly sensational scene of the discovery of the scandalous flight of the second Mrs Dombey, we find the following: 'Opening [reflectio] matter – sanatory'. In the chapter as written the narrator pauses near the beginning to reflect upon nature and nurture and upon 'the millions of immortal creatures' whose moral nature is warped by having to live in foul conditions. This chapter was, Dickens notes, originally intended to close the number but was then transposed with chapter 48 in which Florence finds refuge with Captain Cuttle in the Little Wooden Midshipman, so as 'to leave a pleasanter impression on the reader'. Particularly interesting as showing Dickens's continual experimentation as a writer is a note for chapter 14 ('Paul Grows More and More Old-fashioned and Goes Home for the Holidays'). It reads: 'His illness only expressed in the child's own feelings – Not otherwise described.' Dickens told

Forster he found the episode difficult to write in this way but it was 'a new way of doing it . . . and likely to be pretty'. Certainly this technique greatly enhances the effectiveness of *Dombey* V (March 1847), the number that ends with Paul's death, and famously caused Thackeray, whose *Vanity Fair* had just begun appearing in monthly numbers, to bang this number of *Dombey* down on the table in Bradbury and Evans's printing-office and exclaim, 'There's no writing against such power as this – one has no chance! Read that chapter describing young Paul's death: it is unsurpassed – it is stupendous!'[8]

Alongside his new system of making detailed notes and memoranda for each number two important developments in Dickens's novelistic art manifest themselves in *Dombey*, one concerning technique and the other content. The first involves a more detailed and patterned use of emblems than heretofore. Some part of the natural world, or some human institution important for the plot is depicted as imaging or emblematising some spiritual, moral or political reality. Thus the sea in *Dombey* is both that mighty mass of water across which the firm of Dombey and Son sends its trading vessels, including the ill-named, ill-fated *Son and Heir*, emblem of little Paul, to gather riches for itself; but it is also an image of that 'dark and unknown sea that rolls round all the world' out upon which the Dombey children's dying mother drifts at the beginning of the book. The reader is carefully reminded of this aspect of the sea at various crucial points in the narrative and Dickens's final note for his final chapter reads: 'End with the sea – carrying through, what the waves were always saying, and the invisible country far away.' Looking ahead to such later triumphs of this emblematising art as the depiction of the London fog and the Court of Chancery in *Bleak House*, the prison and the Circumlocution Office in *Little Dorrit*, and the river and the dust-heaps of *Our Mutual Friend*, we recognise in them successors to this presentation of the sea in *Dombey*.[9]

The second development in Dickens's art marked by *Dombey* is that this novel featuring a rejected daughter and a bartered bride inaugurates a ten-year period in his writing career during which all his novels, with the exception of *Copperfield*, have female rather than male protagonists. They also explore (and here we may certainly include *Copperfield*) a number of more complex female characters, new in Dickens's fiction, like Rosa Dartle in *Copperfield*, Louisa Gradgrind in *Hard Times*, and Miss Wade in *Little Dorrit*. At the same time many of the central concerns of these books relate closely to the difficulties, social restrictions, humiliations and consequent resentment experienced by women from widely different backgrounds in the male-oriented world of Victorian England.[10]

For the first eight months of the writing of *Dombey* Dickens continued living abroad, first in Lausanne and then in Paris, returning to London just before the publication of *Dombey* VI. He wrote frequently to Forster and, since Forster draws lavishly on these letters in his *Life*, we know a great deal about the stresses and strains of composing this particular novel. 'You can hardly imagine', Dickens wrote on 30 August, 'what infinite pains I take, or what extraordinary difficulty I find in getting on FAST.' This was partly, he continued, because he was now putting a deliberate curb on himself: 'I seem to have such a preposterous sense of the ridiculous, after this long rest . . . as to be constantly requiring to restrain myself from launching into extravagances in the height of my enjoyment.' He suffered, too, from the absence of crowded streets: 'For a week or a fortnight I can write prodigiously in a retired place (as at Broadstairs), and a day in London sets me up again and starts me. But the toil and labour of writing, day after day, without that magic lantern is IMMENSE! . . . *My* figures seem disposed to stagnate without crowds about them.' Twice during his sojourn in Lausanne he had to gather up Catherine and Georgina and dash over to Geneva for a week or so for the sake of the streets, afterwards finding himself 'greatly better' both in himself and as a writer. Another problem was that he took a little while to get his hand in again as regards writing the right amount to fit the thirty-two printed pages of each number. The first four numbers were all over-written and needed cutting in proof.[11]

Superimposed upon these difficulties was another, hitherto unprecedented, one that proved formidable indeed. He had agreed with Bradbury and Evans to write a Christmas Book for 1846 (such keenly-anticipated annual productions from his pen were guaranteed money-spinners) and now found himself having to begin this book when he had just got started on *Dombey*. It was, he told Mitton on 25 September, 'desperate work'. He had in earlier days managed to write two stories simultaneously but the first one had always been well under way before he had begun the second. Now, not only did he have to begin both books at the same time but the situation was aggravated in that his idea for this particular Christmas offering, to be called *The Battle of Life: A Love Story*, was more like the leading idea for another novel than for any Christmas ghost-story or fairy-tale and it is, indeed, the only one of the Christmas Books to be devoid of any supernatural element, Dickens wanting, as he told Forster, to make it 'a simple domestic tale'. The setting is the site of a long-ago great battle in which 'thousands upon thousands had been killed' and he wanted to contrast such carnage with the nobler moral and emotional battles fought out every day in the hearts and minds of ordinary men and women. His somewhat bizarre illustration of this deals with two devoted sisters. The younger one, Marion, sacrifices her own love for her reciprocally loving suitor because she realises that her sister Grace selflessly loves him too and believes (rightly as it turns out) that he will transfer his affections to Grace if she removes herself for some years. This story must have had an intense personal resonance for Dickens, relating in some convoluted way to his memories of Mary Hogarth and his current relationships with Catherine and Georgina. No doubt this contributed to his intense frustration over the narrow limits within which he had to work – 'What an affecting story I could have made of it in one octavo volume,' he lamented to Forster. He would, we may be sure, have been especially gratified by the *Daily News*'s reviewer's comparison of the *Battle* to *The Vicar of Wakefield* on 26 December since this favourite novel (its length would have been ideal for the *Battle*, he thought) was running in his head as he toiled at his atypical Christmas Book. It was at his suggestion that the characters were depicted in 'the coats and gowns of dear old Goldsmith's day'.[12]

As Dickens agonised over writing this little book, 'constantly haunted by the idea that I am wasting the marrow of the larger book and ought to be at rest', his spirits sank so low that, he told Forster later, he felt himself to be 'in serious danger', and he came close to abandoning the *Battle* altogether. With characteristic bravado, he added that, despite everything, he nevertheless 'walked my fifteen miles a day constantly, at a great pace'. Meanwhile, the first number of *Dombey* appeared (30 Sept.). It had been eagerly awaited and well advertised so that it sold like the hottest of cakes. To Dickens's great joy, it outstripped the sale of the first number of *Chuzzlewit* by more than twelve thousand. Succeeding numbers more than maintained what he described to Beard as this 'prodigious success', with the reading public in general endorsing the judgment of the reviewer in *Chambers's Edinburgh Journal* who declared on 24 October that 'the good ship Boz' was now 'righted and once more fairly afloat'.[13]

Buoyed up by this triumph, Dickens managed, after further struggles, to finish the *Battle* and sent the last section to Forster on 18 October. Maclise, Leech, Stanfield and the young *Punch* artist Richard Doyle were supplying the all-important illustrations and Forster was double-checking the proofs with special instructions to be on the watch for lapses into blank verse. 'I *cannot* help it, when I am very much in earnest,' Dickens told him, and asked him to 'knock out a word's brains here and there' if necessary. Dickens revisited Geneva from 19 to 28 October in order to concentrate on the writing of *Dombey* III. In this number Paul, accompanied by Florence, is sent to board with Mrs Pipchin, Dickens's number-plan showing clearly that he was modelling this character on Mrs Roylance with whom he had lodged while his parents were in the Marshalsea, though memories of a seaside lodging-house keeper from an earlier period in the family's history seem also to have contributed to his depiction of his Brighton 'ogress and child-queller'. Sending the number to Forster he wrote, 'I hope you will like Mrs Pipchin's establishment. It is from the life and I was there – I don't suppose I was eight years old.' He was, in fact, all of twelve but had evidently already begun remembering himself as several years younger than he actually was at the time of the Warren's blacking episode, with a resulting intensification of the pathos of his forsaken condition as he recalled it to his mind.[14]

Clearly, the process of consciously revisiting his past for literary purposes that had begun in the *Carol* was continuing in *Dombey*. Dickens may even have begun working on an actual autobiography or memoir before he thought of using Mrs Roylance in the novel since he goes on to ask Forster: 'Shall I leave you my life in MS. when I die? There are some things in it that would touch you very much, and that might go on the same shelf with the first volume of Holcroft's.' This does not, of course, mean that he *had* actually begun writing such a work, only that he had at least thought about doing so. His allusion to the first volume of the *Memoirs* of the dramatist Thomas Holcroft (1745–1809) strongly hints at his having suffered boyhood hardships comparable to Holcroft's when Holcroft's family's fortunes had suddenly changed for the worse. Rather oddly, Forster does not seem to have risen to the bait. Nor was his curiosity aroused, as it might have been, by the intensity of Dickens's disappointment with Browne's portrayal of Mrs Pipchin which doubtless stemmed from his comparing it with his vivid memories of Mrs Roylance, Pipchin's real-life original.[15]

On 9 November Dickens finished writing *Dombey* III ('marvellously rapid work', Forster notes) and he and his family left Lausanne for Paris a week later, arriving in the French capital on the 20th. They settled in at 48 Rue de Courcelles in the fashionable Faubourg St Honoré, in a house the eccentric construction of which caused Dickens much delighted amusement. Here he quickly set to work on *Dombey* IV, having decided to 'slaughter' Paul at the end of No.V. Perhaps because of the upset over his depiction of Mrs Pipchin, Browne was sent very detailed instructions for the two plates for *Dombey* IV, later pronounced by Dickens to be 'much better than usual'. No sooner had he finished his monthly stint than a variety of business required his presence in London. Arriving there on 15 December he plunged into the Keeleys' rehearsals of Albert Smith's dramatisation of *The Battle of Life* at the Lyceum (once again, they had paid him for the head start this gave them on their competitors) and on 19 December the little book, 'Cordially inscribed to my English Friends in Switzerland', appeared in the by now traditional dress for a Dickens Christmas Book of crimson and gold. Despite a predominantly hostile reception by the reviewers, it had an immediate sale of twenty-three thousand copies (by contrast, Thackeray's first venture into the increasingly crowded Christmas Book field, *Mrs Perkins's Ball*, sold a mere one and a half thousand). According to Wilkie Collins, Dickens told a friend that he had made '*four thousand guineas*' by the *Battle*, a book which, Wilkie noted, 'everybody abused and nevertheless, everybody read'.[16]

By 24 December Dickens was back in Paris, where he finished *Dombey* V on 16 January and was so shattered by the writing of Paul's deathbed scene that, as he wrote to Burdett Coutts two days later, sleep deserted him and he 'walked about Paris until breakfast-time the next morning' (he later shared this confidence with his readers in the preface to the Cheap Edition of *Dombey*, rather oddly referring to Paul as 'my little friend', just as Dr Blimber does in the novel). Paul's death caused a great sensation, later described as having plunged the British reading public into a veritable 'national mourning', and the publishers happily increased the serial's press run to thirty-three thousand.[17]

Dickens now allowed himself to enjoy Paris, pursuing a love affair that he had already begun and that was to last the rest of his life. His way of enjoying the city was characteristic. It consisted of 'wandering into Hospitals, Prisons, Dead-houses [the Paris Morgue never ceased to fascinate him], Operas, Theatres, Concert Rooms, Burial-grounds, Palaces, and Wine shops', all this producing on him the effect of 'a rapid Panorama'. Returning to his desk in early February, Dickens found great difficulty in obeying the overall injunction in his memoranda for *Dombey* VI: 'Great point of the No to throw the interest of Paul, at once on Florence'. He managed to do so, albeit somewhat heavy-handedly (having to dash over to London to write some extra copy when the proofs showed the number underwritten by two pages) and then began looking towards the introduction of Edith and her appalling mother. With the business of Dombey's second marriage under way, he could now continue writing the novel without more than the usual monthly 'agonies', so carefully had he laid its foundations. Moreover, he could do this in spite of all the pressures, self-generated and otherwise, of life outside his study walls during 1847. Charley, now studying at King's College School, succumbed to scarlet fever which brought Dickens and Catherine, now five months pregnant, back to London permanently. Georgina followed with the other children and, Devonshire Terrace being let until the end of June, the family moved into temporary quarters in Chester Terrace. There the Dickenses' seventh child, Sydney Smith Haldimand, was born on 18 April. 'My dear Kate suffered terribly,' Dickens told Macready the following day and he himself was so shaken that he had been temporarily unable to write. But, he continued, he was working 'with such an infinite relish for the story I am mining at, that I don't care twopence for being behindhand'. His choice of metaphor indicates that as he followed out his plan for *Dombey* he was joyfully finding more and more in the way of novelist's gold. Moreover, as a result of the book's great success (each number was earning him £460) his actual bank balance was growing ever stronger. Whereas in the summer of 1846 he had still been actively seeking some form of public employment to boost his income, by 4 July 1847 he could tell Mitton that he was looking around for good investments. 'His accounts for the first half-year of *Dombey*', Forster tells us, 'were so much in excess of what had been expected ... that from this date all embarrassments connected with money were brought to a close.'[18]

Dickens's main business during his December visit to London had been connected with preparations for the launching of the highly innovative 'Cheap Edition' of his works, advertised somewhat misleadingly as 'carefully revised and corrected throughout, by the Author', and featuring a specially-written preface for each volume. This edition was scheduled to begin publication on 27 March with

Pickwick as the first title. It owed its name to its being issued in weekly double-columned fascicules of sixteen pages each at 1½ d. and sewn-up monthly parts at 7d. When the serialisation of a title had been completed it was published in volume form, in wrappers at 4s.6d. and in cloth at 5s. The edition thus combined the dignity of a Collected Works (looking back to Constable's so-called '*Magnum Opus*' edition of Scott's Waverley novels, 1829–33, which, however, appeared only in volume form at 5s. per volume) with the targeting of a much wider readership among the less prosperous. It was, too, a remarkable tribute to Dickens's status as a writer that his works were being collected, not towards the end of his career as in Scott's case but when he had only just turned thirty-four. Moreover, with his advertised revision of his texts (though actually this was pretty minimal with the interesting exception of *Sketches by Boz*), and his specially-written prefaces for each book setting out his version of its genesis and writing, Dickens was evidently seeking to achieve for himself with the Cheap what a modern critic has noted the 1829–33 edition of the Waverley Novels achieved for Scott, namely the clarification of 'the retrospective shape of a career – a life in writing'.[19]

He hoped 'to get a great deal of money out of the idea' of the Cheap Edition, and so he did in the long run though the immediate financial returns proved rather disappointing. The considerations he had in mind in this resourceful 'working' of his copyrights (to use his own word for the activity of republishing in new forms books of which he either wholly or partly owned the copyright) were by no means solely financial, however. He makes this clear in his 'Address' published in *Dombey* VI and elsewhere. After asserting the projected new edition to be 'unprecedented … in the history of Cheap Literature' he makes a brief reference ('manly', he would have called it) to his hopes of 'increased personal emolument', and then takes care to reassure potential or actual purchasers of already existing editions of his books that the Cheap would not replace these. It would not, for example, include the original illustrations though each volume would have a specially-drawn frontispiece by a leading artist (the artists involved included Cruikshank, Browne, Cattermole and Stone). Dickens ends with what is, in effect, an impassioned love-letter to his public in which he draws attention to the unprecedented, and warmly intimate, nature of the relationship this new venture might create between his writing self and his readers:

> To become, in his new guise, a permanent inmate of many English homes, where in his old shape, he was only known as a guest, or hardly known at all; to be well thumbed and soiled in a plain suit that will bear a great deal, by children and grown people, at the fireside and on the journey: to be hoarded on the humble shelf where there are few books, and to lie about in libraries like any familiar piece of household stuff that is easy of replacement: and so see and feel this – not to die first, or grow old and passionless: must obviously be among the hopes of a living author, venturing on such an enterprise. . . .[20]

During the period 1846–49 Dickens's correspondence contains many refer-ences to his lofty sense of the writer's profession. Writing on 8 November 1847 to George Henry Lewes about the latter's novel *Ranthorpe*, for example, he comments, 'When Literary men shall begin to feel the honor and worth of their pursuit, as you would teach them to, Literature will be a happier calling.' And on 9 January 1848, answering a letter from Thackeray praising *Dombey*, he writes:

> I *do* sometimes please myself with thinking that my success has opened the way for good writers. And of this, I am quite sure now, and hope I shall be when I die – that in all my social doings I am mindful of this honour and dignity and always try to do something towards the quiet assertion of their right place. I am always possessed with the hope of leaving the position of literary men in England, something better and more independent than I found it.

Famously, he goes on to deplore Thackeray's hilarious series of parodies of contemporary fellow-novelists in *Punch* (from which he tactfully excluded Dickens): 'I think it is a great pity to take advantage of the means our calling gives us . . . of at all depreciating or vulgarizing each other'. On 22 April 1848 he acclaimed Forster's new biography of Goldsmith as 'a noble achievement', praising especially his friend's insistence on the high status that should prop-erly be accorded to writers: 'I don't believe that any book was ever written . . . half so conducive to the dignity and honor of literature'. Seeming to assume that he will predecease Forster though they are the same age, he declares, 'I desire no better for my fame when my personal dustyness shall be past the controul [*sic*] of my love of order, than such a biographer and such a Critic.'

Dickens's passion for amateur theatricals and the way in which, two years earlier, he had channelled this enthusiasm towards raising money for Southwood Smith's Sanatorium doubtless prompted him to conceive of what he called a great 'demonstration by Literature on behalf of Literature' when the Government was slow to grant a pension to the ever-impecunious literary veteran and Radical icon Leigh Hunt. In June 1847, just before the annual family move to Broadstairs, Dickens reconvened his troupe and again began intensive rehearsals at a little West End theatre belonging to the veteran actress Frances Kelly. The Amateurs acquired some new recruits, including George Henry Lewes and Cruikshank, and, as before, professional actresses were engaged for the female parts. The object was to raise a fund for Hunt by reviving *Every Man in His Humour* and adding Shakespeare's *Merry Wives of Windsor* to the repertoire with Dickens as Shallow, plus a repertoire of short farces to round off the evening. After two performances at Covent Garden the Amateurs were to appear also in Manchester and Liverpool, one night in each place. His *Dombey* commitment notwith-standing, Dickens threw himself with all his usual fervour into all aspects of the business and into the voluminous correspondence it involved. Although he enjoyed complaining, in comic-desperate vein, of being 'lost in abysses of work', he evidently thrived on the situation. The number-plans for *Dombey* IX–XV (chs 26–48), written between May and November 1847, show him, according to the editor of the Clarendon Edition of the novel, 'clearly moving forward with very few queries and second thoughts'. The July Number (X), which includes two great scenes, Edith's passionate denunciation of her mother's scheming on the eve of her marriage to Dombey and the resplendent, barren marriage-ceremony itself, was not even begun by 13 June and was finished in eleven days, with barely a week to go before publication day.[21]

On 2 July Hunt finally got his government pension (£200 p.a.) but the Amateurs decided to go ahead anyway with the Manchester and Liverpool performances of *Every Man* to supplement the pension, and to raise money for another impoverished writer, the elderly dramatist John Poole. As part of this great 'demonstration' of Literature for Literature, Dickens asked Talfourd to write a prologue for him to speak at the Manchester performance, and Forster got Bulwer Lytton to write another for the Liverpool one. On both occasions (26 and 28 July), Dickens wrote to Mitton on 8 August, a large theatre was 'crammed to the roof with people in full dress, who "took" everything in a manner I never saw equalled'. In the two-hander farce *Two o'Clock in the Morning* he and Lemon made the audiences laugh so much that they were drooping over the fronts of the boxes 'like fruit'.[22]

Dickens decided to contribute to this 'demonstration' as a writer as well as actor-manager. Perhaps he thought it might also help him to 'blow off' a little of that 'superfluous steam' that, he told Lewes on 11 August, he found himself troubled with now the play was over, adding 'but that is always my misfortune'. He planned to publish a little pamphlet, giving Mrs Gamp's account of the Amateurs' Northern tour. This might, he reckoned, add as much as another £100 to the profits on the play. The basic joke would be that Mrs Gamp had joined the excursion on the off-chance that her services might be needed by some of the married ladies (both John Leech's wife and – one is tempted to add 'inevitably' – Catherine were, in fact, pregnant, with the former only narrowly escaping actually having to give birth in a railway carriage). Dickens did not carry the pamphlet idea through but the few pages of vintage 'Gampese' that he did write, first printed by Forster, show how seemingly effortlessly he could revert to an extraordinary idiolect invented for a character in *Chuzzlewit* even when he was simultaneously so deeply involved in writing the very differently-textured *Dombey*. Nor does he miss the chance to work in a timely jibe at the nation's indifference to the plight of impoverished writers. When Gamp tells her alter ego Mrs Harris that the Amateurs are 'agoin play-acting, for the benefit of two litter'ry men', she is sharply reproved: ' "Sairey", says Mrs Harris, "you're an Inglish woman, and that's no business of you'rn." '[23]

The success of the Amateurs' efforts caused Dickens to begin planning repeat performances which would broaden their repertoire and increase their commitment very considerably. He wanted, as he told Mitton on 8 August, 'to shame the English Government, by giving as much every year to the reduced professors of Art, Literature, and Science, as the whole Civil List gives, on account of Great Britain'. During the winter of 1847/48 he and Lemon worked on a scheme for a 'Provident Union of Literature, Science and Art' whereby the Amateurs would give four performances annually, both in London and the provinces. Each year they would revive 'some sterling English play' and produce it 'with the utmost care'. The proceeds would be devoted to the establishment of a contributory insurance scheme for writers and artists. Had it come to fruition, the scheme would have involved monthly committee meetings as well as the actual productions. Coming on top of all the work he was about to undertake for Burdett Coutts's home for homeless women, this would have been a staggering commitment, even for a man of Dickens's prodigious energy and outstanding administrative genius – while all the time, of course, his primary concern had to remain his own writing career. In the event, however, the scheme was set aside, to be revived in a different form by Dickens and Bulwer Lytton two years later.[24]

Contrasting with his organisation of such spectacular public activities on literature's behalf as the Amateurs' productions but similarly related to Dickens's keen sense of the responsibilities attaching to his position as a sort of *de facto* president of what was often referred to as 'the Republic of Letters' are the private replies, often very detailed, that he was always making time to send to many of the aspirant writers who besieged him with manuscripts and requests for help or advice. His surviving letters of this kind must be the merest tip of a colossal iceberg. Inevitably, he most often found himself having to send discouraging replies, as to a certain Mrs Price whose specimen poems, though 'very agreeable and womanly', were, he rather crushingly wrote, devoid of 'any novelty, either of thought or expression'. When, however, he was able to discern any potential worth in what was submitted to him, as he had earlier done in Overs's case, he would often send his correspondent a detailed and constructive critique, witness his reply to a woman who had sent him a five-act tragedy, a response all the more remarkable in that he wrote it during the frenetic few days immediately before the launching of the *Daily News*. After 1850, of course, this kind of letter would have been largely merged in the unending torrent of correspondence involving would-be or actual contributors to his magazines.[25]

In the summer of 1847 Dickens was half-way through the writing of *Dombey* and it was at this point that he began to devote a truly prodigious amount of his time and energy first to the establishment and then to the week-by-week running of Burdett Coutts's home, a commitment he was to continue honouring for the next ten years. Dickens located suitable premises at Shepherd's Bush, west London, in what is now Lime Grove, arranged the lease, supervised the necessary alterations and the purchase of furniture, interviewed potential inmates (initially restricted to young women about to be released from prison), appointed staff, and laid down what the daily routine of the place should be. The house was called Urania Cottage and Dickens and Burdett Coutts decided to keep the name, probably because of the association with Aphrodite Urania the goddess of heavenly love, as opposed to Aphrodite the goddess of physical love. Also, the word 'Cottage' evoked a non-institutional domestic atmosphere which contrasted reassuringly with what has been well described as the 'forbiddingly explicit' names of already existing institutions like The British Penitent Female Refuge. In the course of his voluminous correspondence with Burdett Coutts Dickens had gently to coach her into understanding that the Cottage's inmates needed not so much lessons in penitence as to be '*tempted* to virtue'. This depended on kind treatment and, above all, on giving the women hopes of eventually becoming happy wives and mothers in a distant but still British land – Australia or South Africa – where wives were needed, and to which they would be assisted to emigrate when they were deemed to be sufficiently educated in 'the whole routine of household duties'. This phrase appears in Dickens's long and detailed account of the project, published anonymously five years later under the title 'Home For Homeless Women' in *Household Words*. This article shows that admission to the Home ceased at some point, perhaps even before it opened, to be restricted to prostitutes, maybe because, as Dickens's prison-governor friend, Captain George Chesterton reported, this class of women proved very reluctant to apply. Dickens records that the sixty-six women who had been admitted since the Home was opened had included, in addition to 'young women from the streets', 'starving needlewomen of good character, poor needlewomen who have robbed their furnished lodgings, violent girls committed to prison for disturbances in ill-conducted workhouses, poor girls from Ragged Schools, destitute girls who have applied at police offices for relief . . . domestic servants who have been seduced, and two young women held to bail for attempted suicide'. Of the eight case-histories he cites in the article only two in which the subject had actually 'gone wrong', in both cases involving a fall from respectability. One wonders just how many women there were, in fact, among the sixty-six past and present inmates of Urania Cottage in 1853 who were truly representative of those hundreds of thousands of contemporary prostitutes whose plight Dickens had already presented in his fiction – Nancy in *Oliver*, sexually exploited from childhood, or Lilian in *The Chimes*, driven by sheer grinding poverty to yield to what she calls 'the dreadful thoughts that tempt me in my youth'.[26]

While the actual histories and situations of Nancy and of Lilian in Trotty's vision are grimly realistic, the young women's high-flown expressions of despair or penitence are anything but, likewise the rhetorical pleas to Nancy to

save herself made by Brownlow and Rose Maylie. Similar melodramatic rhetoric appears again in the 'Appeal' (signed 'YOUR FRIEND') written by Dickens
in October 1847 for distribution to the prison-cells of potential recruits to
Urania Cottage, at this point assumed all to be unhappy prostitutes. His
description of what he assumes will be their own view of their situation might,
apart from the reference to his quasi-brotherly rather than quasi-fatherly
concern, have been written by Brownlow himself: 'You know what the streets
are; you know how cruel the companions that you find there are; you know
the vices practised there, and to what wretched consequences they bring you,
even while you are young . . .'. Burdett Coutts herself in her Stratton Street,
Piccadilly, mansion is shadowed forth as a sort of grander, more aware, and
more potent Rose Maylie: 'There is a lady in this town who from the windows
of her house has seen such as you going past at night, and has felt her heart
bleed at the sight. She is what is called a great lady, but she has looked after you
with compassion as being of her own sex and nature, and the thought of such
fallen women has troubled her in her bed.' The last paragraph of the Appeal
with its refrain 'think of it then . . . think of it then . . . oh think of it then'
seems like a straight-faced version of Mr Pecksniff's hilarious valedictory
address to Old Martin in *Chuzzlewit* chapter 20, and affords a notable example
of Dickens's remarkable ability to make serious use at times of the hortatory
element in what we might call the 'pulpit-discourse' of his day whilst gloriously parodying it at others.[27]

The so-called 'Case Book' in which Dickens, like a modern therapist, wrote
down with 'perfectly imperturbable face' and avoidance of all leading questions
and expressions of his own opinion, each woman's account of her own history,
is apparently lost. For the most direct literary result of his long and close
involvement with Urania Cottage we must look to the vivid glimpses we get of
various of the inmates scattered throughout his letters to Burdett Coutts, as well
as in the few surviving ones to successive resident superintendents of the
Cottage – particularly his reports of some of the women's occasional relapses
and misdemeanours, leading in some cases to expulsion. Such a failed inmate
was Jemima Hiscock who 'forced open the door of the little beer cellar with
knives and drank until she was dead drunk; when she used the most horrible
language and made a very repulsive exhibition of herself'. But no drunken
Jemima appears in Dickens's subsequent fictional writings. Those 'fallen
women' characters who do appear all conform to the melodramatic mode. The
first is Alice Marwood who first appears in *Dombey* XI, the number for August
1847 published three months before the opening of Urania Cottage. Dickens
presents her as a lower-class parallel to Edith, she having been marketed by her
mother just as cruelly as Edith has been in her very different sphere. Later on,
we have the anonymous prostitute whom Redlaw encounters in *The Haunted
Man* (and who virtually reprises the battered girl in 'The Hospital Patient' in

Sketches by Boz), Martha Endell and Little Em'ly in *Copperfield*, and in *Little Dorrit* (Bk I, ch. 14) another unnamed prostitute who mistakes Little Dorrit for a child. The roles of all of these young women, except for the gloomily-named Martha Endell, are wholly determined by thematic and/or plot considerations pertaining to the story in which they appear. As for Martha, Dickens does find her something of her own to do in the plot of *Copperfield* (she rescues Em'ly from falling still further) but, essentially, she is a journalistic rather than a fictional creation, written into *Copperfield* as an advertisement for the Urania Cottage project. Even here, however, Dickens's conventional, fallen-woman characterisation of her ('making the same low, dreary, wretched moaning in her shawl', and so on), together with the complete absence of any explanation of just *how* she fell from grace, shows little sign of being informed or influenced by that 'most extraordinary and mysterious study . . . interesting and touching in the extreme' of which he wrote to Burdett Coutts, when commenting on his interviewing of prospective recruits for the Home.[28]

Neither does Dickens's subsequent portrayal of philanthropic characters or organisations seem to be at all modified by his deep and prolonged involvement in such a commendably successful experiment in organised philanthropy (in his *Household Words* article Dickens states that of the fifty-six women who had passed through the Home since its opening no fewer than thirty, 'of whom seven are now married', had fulfilled its founders' hopes and done well in their new lives overseas). The good-hearted old boys of the early novels, the Pickwicks, Brownlows and Cheerybles, have a successor, albeit a rather toned-down one, in Mr Jarndyce of Bleak House. Like them, he is no organiser of philanthropic projects but a prosperous elderly bachelor who goes in for acts of individual benevolence. Organised philanthropy does indeed appear in Dickens's fiction from now on but it is invariably presented as self-interested, ridiculous or downright odious, like Mrs Jellyby's African mission or Mr Honeythunder's Haven of Philanthropy in *Drood*, or else as hopelessly muddled and ineffectual like the Ragged School that Charley Hexam attends in *Our Mutual Friend*. As the Uncommercial Traveller, however, Dickens did write very effectively about one small-scale charitable project. This was the East London Hospital for Children, set up and run by a young doctor and his wife, and described by Dickens in 'A Small Star in the East'.[29]

In September 1847, as he was working on *Dombey* XIII (chapters 39–41) and busy with preparations for the opening of Urania Cottage, Dickens needed to write a preface for the Cheap Edition of *Pickwick*, now about to appear in volume form. This gave him a fine opportunity not only to provide his own 'authoritative' version of the origins of the book and of his writing career in general but also to impress upon his readers, now avidly following the intricate plot of *Dombey*, just how effectively he as a novelist has reconciled literary artistry and serial publication. In *Pickwick*, he writes, 'no ingenuity of plot was attempted, or even at that time considered very feasible by the author in connexion with the desultory mode of publication adopted'. Nor can he resist a little general crowing: 'My friends told me it [publishing in monthly parts] was a low, cheap form of publication, by which I should ruin all my rising hopes; and how right my friends turned out to be, everybody now knows'.

By November Urania Cottage was ready to open its doors and a major new commitment had to be factored into Dickens's already crowded schedule, with six more numbers of *Dombey* still to write. He had already decided, mindful, no doubt, of his agonies over *The Battle of Life*, that the Christmas Book promised to Bradbury and Evans for 1847, for which he had conceived 'a very ghostly and wild idea' as far back as the summer of 1846, would have to be postponed. He was 'loath to lose the money', he told Forster on 19 September, but was even more concerned (and we may certainly believe him) about not fulfilling what he now evidently thought of, with good reason, as a duty he owed to his public. He was, he declared, still more loath 'to leave any gap at Christmas firesides which I ought to fill'. Presumably Forster advised strongly against attempting to go on with the little book and it was deferred.[30]

Before he could get started on the climactic *Dombey* XV (chs 46–48) Dickens had to write, on 3 November, an immensely long letter to Burdett Coutts dealing with every aspect of getting the Home ready for its first residents, and assuring her that there was 'nothing whatever, in the business arrangements, which is not in working order'. About ten days later the first inmates were admitted and by the 27th Dickens had finished the number. He and Catherine went on a visit to the Watsons at Rockingham and from there Dickens went over to Leeds to boost the cause of popular education at a 1 December soirée of the Leeds Mechanics' Institute where he was rapturously received ('a most brilliant demonstration', he reported to Forster) with one enthusiastic gentleman on the platform calling for 'one cheer more for the author of Little Nell'. He was touched and delighted to learn later that the man, having recently lost a little daughter, 'had held to [*The Old Curiosity Shop*] as a sort of comfort ever since'.[31]

While he worked with Burdett Coutts for the rehabilitation of 'fallen' women in real life he had in *Dombey* two female characters, one fallen and the other apparently about to fall, for whom he wished to keep his readers' sympathy. He decided to do this in the traditional way, by having them die a penitential death. He might feel confident of gaining the reader's sympathy for poor ruined Alice, Carker's discarded lower-class mistress, as she lay dying, comforted by readings from the New Testament such as he had arranged for the women in Urania Cottage. But the creating of similar deathbed sympathy for Edith, an upper-class woman who had revenged herself on her tyrannical husband by committing adultery, was more problematic. This probably accounted for his ready responsiveness to a letter from Jeffrey that arrived in late December positively refusing to believe that Edith had become Carker's mistress. If she did not, in fact, become an adulteress then Dickens would not have to kill her. So, for the second time in this very carefully planned novel, he made a major change in his intention regarding a character by creating 'a kind of inverted Maid's Tragedy'. This opened up the opportunity for 'a tremendous scene' (rather too 'tremendous' for most modern readers) which duly appeared in the February number with Edith disabusing Carker in the highest melodramatic style of the notion that she had ever had any intention of becoming his mistress and flying with him to Sicily ('You have fallen on Sicilian days and sensual rest, too soon,' she taunts him). The reader is then free to feel sympathy for her when she later expresses to Florence a sort of conditional contrition for her conduct before departing for a life of exile under the bumblingly benign protection of Cousin Feenix: 'When you leave me in this dark room, think that you have left me in the grave.' It was by such adroit avoidance of dangerous territory that Dickens could continue to be hailed, as he had just been in Glasgow, as 'one of the few novelists' who 'might be read . . . without a blush'.[32]

In Glasgow he had been presiding at a soirée of the Glasgow Athenaeum on 28 December, when, as he had done at Leeds, he had championed popular education as a supreme means of alleviating 'social miseries'. Urania Cottage cannot have been far from his mind when he spoke of the 'due cultivation of domestic virtues' as being as important an aspect of education for the adult as for the child. Catherine, who had again accompanied him, was unable to witness yet another of his public-speaking triumphs, having suffered a miscarriage during the railway journey (a rueful reminder for Dickens, perhaps, of his Gampian *jeu d'esprit* of the previous year?). The following day was devoted to Dickens's special brand of socially-investigative sight-seeing (visiting the city's prison and lunatic asylum) and then, with Catherine apparently recovered, they went on to Edinburgh where they had to prolong their visit after she had been suddenly taken ill again. Whilst in the city Dickens, conscious as he always was of his special relationship to Scott, would have looked with particular interest at the newly-erected Scott Memorial. He did not approve. The Memorial was, he thought, 'a failure', being 'like the spire of a Gothic church taken off and stuck in the ground'.[33]

Dombey's sales remained extremely buoyant. The story was so popular that Bradbury and Evans thought it worthwhile to issue two sets of large extra illustrations of the leading characters, drawn by Browne and approved by Dickens. By 17 February he was 'deep in No.18', working towards the great showdown scene between Carker and Edith, after finishing which he must have turned immediately to the writing of a long review-essay for Forster's *Examiner*, published on 26 February. He was reviewing *The Night Side of Nature or, Ghosts and Ghost-seers* by the novelist Catherine Crowe. Paranormal phenomena was a subject of intense, lifelong interest to him and he thought Crowe's book 'one of the most extraordinary collections of "Ghost Stories" that has ever been published'. In his review-essay he includes a veiled reference to his mesmeric treatment of Mme de la Rue and notes that this article will be the first of two. In this one, he announces, he will deal with arguments against the existence of ghosts and in a follow-up piece the next week will consider 'what may be said in their favour'. Unfortunately, this second piece remained unwritten, probably owing to the pressure on space in *The Examiner* as a result of the revolution in France.[34]

At the end of February he took Catherine for a week to Brighton to concentrate on writing the final double number of *Dombey*. The place had figured significantly in the story and he would be within sight and hearing of the sea that supplied one of the book's master-emblems. On 21 March he was still 'lingering over' the work, wanting, as he told Burdett Coutts, to 'carry his care' of Dombey and his family to the last. His 'General Mems' for Nos XIX–XX include a sort of roll-call of the characters as a check-list to make sure that none is left unaccounted for, and the chapter-notes are unusually full, including the final direction to himself about ending with the sea, though he had in the event to cut this last passage in proof since he had somewhat over-written the number. On 24 March he finished and wrote a brief preface and a dedication. Using the former as a 'greeting-place', he addresses his readers in comradely fashion, thanking them for 'the unbounded warmth and earnest-ness of their sympathy in every stage of the journey we have now concluded', and stressing the bond of fellowship he feels with them by saying how fully he himself had shared in whatever sorrow they might have felt over the death of little Paul. The novel was dedicated to the Marchioness of Normanby with whose husband he had been on friendly terms for some years, and who had been British Ambassador in Paris during Dickens's residence. He and his wife were therefore probably closely associated in his mind with Paul's death. On 11 April Dickens held the by now customary dinner to celebrate the conclu-sion of the story's serialisation and the following day it appeared in volume form. He had, he wrote to George Hogarth when inviting him to the dinner, 'great faith in Dombey, and a strong belief that it will be remembered and read years hence'. 'Its success in these days', he added, 'is quite prodigious'.[35]

CHAPTER 12

From *Dombey* to *Copperfield*

1848–1849

'*Thus,' said the Phantom, 'I bear within me a Sorrow and a Wrong. Thus I prey upon myself. Thus, memory is my curse; and, if I could forget my sorrow and my wrong, I would!'*

The Haunted Man and the Ghost's Bargain, ch.1

'IN THE strangeness of my separation from all those people', Dickens wrote to Lady Blessington on 4 April 1848, referring to the characters in *Dombey and Son*, 'I am quite forlorn.' He needed distraction and soon found it in a highly congenial direction, namely in a chance for the Amateurs to make another 'great demonstration' on behalf of literature. A body called the London Shakespeare Committee had recently bought the Stratford Birthplace and Dickens now reactivated the Amateurs to fund-raise for the endowment of a Birthplace curatorship, the intended appointee being a distinguished elderly playwright, now in poor circumstances, called Sheridan Knowles. His tragedy *Virginius* (1820) had provided Macready with one of his most acclaimed roles and many regarded him as the modern Shakespeare. Dickens's troupe added *The Merry Wives of Windsor* to their repertoire and admitted the first and only female Amateur to their ranks, Mary Cowden Clarke, the author of *The Complete Concordance to Shakespeare's Plays* (1844–5). Dickens himself played Justice Shallow, which earned him as many plaudits as his Bobadil. Triumphant performances to capacity audiences were given at London's Haymarket Theatre in May, followed by similar ones in Manchester, Liverpool and Birmingham in June, and in Edinburgh and Glasgow in July. As always, Dickens was the life and soul of the whole enterprise, attending to every last detail of the arrangements both theatrical and logistical, and ensuring the maintenance of what he called 'that unanimity, punctuality, and attention, without which we should be all astray'. Forster wistfully recalls 'his animal spirits, unresting and supreme' which were 'the attraction of rehearsal at morning, and of the stage at night'. 'There seemed', he writes, 'to be no need for rest to that wonderful vitality.'[1]

As far as authorship was concerned, Dickens's published writings for the next twelve months were, with the exception of his 1848 Christmas Book

The Haunted Man, wholly journalistic in nature. They comprised reviews and short topical pieces, presumably either requested for *The Examiner* by Forster, who had just become the magazine's editor, or suggested to him by Dickens. Dickens's contributions during spring and summer 1848 were written between his bouts of theatrical activity or after those particular revels had ended. Other contributions followed in December after he had finished *The Haunted Man*. Like everything else in *The Examiner*, his articles were published anonymously. However, given the general style, matter and outlook of Dickens's articles and his well-known close friendship with Forster, their authorship was probably an open secret, at least in metropolitan literary circles.

During the spring and summer Dickens's contributions were mainly polemical or satirical and dealt with social rather than political matters. In his private letters he exulted at the downfall of Louis Philippe, King of the French, and laughed at the 'epidemic' of 'special constable-ing' caused by fears of a Chartist uprising but he was too preoccupied with finishing *Dombey* to respond in *The Examiner* even to such headline events as these. When he was at last free to contribute he seized such opportunities as presented themselves either to strike a blow for one of his favourite causes or to attack one of his favourite *bêtes noires*. Thus the Metropolitan Police Report for 1847 provided an opportunity to raise the subject of national education, which he did in two articles, 'Ignorance and Crime' and 'Ignorance and Its Victims' (22 and 29 April 1848). He would doubtless have had Urania Cottage in mind when drawing attention in the first article to the lack of knowledge of 'the commonest household duties, or the plainest use of needle and thread' among the women 'constantly passing and repassing' through 'our great prisons'. A review of *The Drunkard's Children*, Cruikshank's follow-up to his celebrated temperance-propaganda sequence called *The Bottle*, gave him an opportunity to revert to his polemic in *Dombey* XV and highlight the pressing need for sanitary reform (8 July). A description of his visit to the *Keying*, a working Chinese junk on show in the East India Docks, offered a fine chance to deride both stick-in-the-mud British politicians and squabbling Anglican clergymen (24 June). His most substantial contribution, written in Broadstairs in August, was a long and trenchant review (19 Aug.) of *A Narrative of the Expedition sent by her Majesty's Government to the river Niger in 1841*. He mercilessly dissects the *Narrative* as the record of an egregious example of that misdirected and self-vaunting philanthropy which was later to provide him with rich materials for the creation of Mrs Jellyby and her ludicrous Borrioboola-Gha scheme in *Bleak House*.[2]

During the autumn there seems to have been a three-month gap in Dickens's *Examiner* contributions and then in December he wrote three more reviews and a piece called 'Judicial Special Pleading', sharply pointing out how Tory distortions of history play directly into the hands of Radical extremists like the 'physical-force' Chartists. The first of the three reviews is of particular interest as being the only known example of Dickens writing directly about science (if we discount his unfortunate excursion into combustion theory in the preface to *Bleak House*). He was reviewing *The Poetry of Science, or Studies of the Physical Phenomena of Nature*, published anonymously by Robert Hunt, a lecturer at the Royal School of Mines. This review, like the references in his notice of Crowe's *Night Side of Nature* and his omnivorous appetite for African and other travel-books, is a salutary reminder of the breadth of Dickens's reading. He shows a keen enthusiasm for contemporary scientific advances and his admiring allusions to Robert Chambers's (also anonymously-published) *Vestiges of the Natural History of Creation* (1844) suggest that he may have espoused Chambers's 'Theory of Development', a notable forerunner of Darwin's *Origin of Species*, but, as the book's title indicates, a good deal less alarming to Christian susceptibilities. Throughout the review Dickens makes effective use of poetic imagery to demonstrate how the scientific truths that are fast replacing old myths and superstitions are proving to be 'at least as full of poetry' as the latter while 'always [bearing] testimony to the stupendous workings of Almighty Wisdom'.[3]

Dickens's ready access to the *Examiner*'s columns gave him the opportunity to develop his journalistic skills as he looked forward to one day having a periodical of his own. In that connection we can detect a note of regret in the reply he sent to a German author who had written to him about international copyright: 'not being the conductor of any newspaper or literary journal, I have but scant means of directing general attention to such a wrong as you have suffered.' His use here of the term 'conductor' rather than 'editor' looks forward to the founding, a year or so later, of *Household Words* with its masthead announcement 'Conducted by Charles Dickens'. It conveys his desire to mould his staff and contributors into an ensemble, as he did his Amateurs, rather than simply recruiting, overseeing and controlling them. In November 1846, Forster tells us, Dickens wrote to him from Paris about 'another floating fancy for the weekly periodical which was still and always present in his mind'. He strongly inclined, Dickens wrote, 'to the notion of a kind of *Spectator* (Addison's) – very cheap and pretty frequent. . . . If the mark between a sort of *Spectator*, and a different sort of *Athenaeum*, could be well hit, my belief is that a deal might be done.' He was evidently still hankering for elements of the kind of eighteenth-century periodical that had so influenced the concept and content of *Master Humphrey's Clock* but now recognised that it must be a nineteenth-century journal too.[4]

The Athenaeum was at this time enjoying considerable success and esteem as a literary weekly under the ownership and editorship of the critic and antiquary Charles Wentworth Dilke (1789–1864) who had been close to Keats and who was also a friend of John Dickens, having been a colleague of his in the Navy Pay Office and being now his line-manager on *The Daily News*. It was he who in the spring of 1847 had mentioned to Forster (in what conversational context Forster does not reveal) that he had once, when in company with John Dickens, seen young Charles working in a warehouse near the Strand. He had tipped the boy half-a-crown and received in return 'a very low bow'. Dickens remained silent 'for several minutes' when Forster asked him about this and made it clear the subject was painful to him. Forster does not tell us what Dickens said after this silence, only that it was 'very shortly afterwards' that he learned the details of what he called, in the title of the second chapter of his *Life of Dickens*, Dickens's 'hard experiences in boyhood'. His reporting of Dilke's remark seems to have initiated a two-year process in Dickens's mind and imagination that led eventually to the writing of *David Copperfield*, the novel in which, as Forster put it (rather overstating his case), he took 'all the world into his confidence'.[5]

As already noted, Dickens had in November 1846 offered to bequeath to Forster his life in manuscript. If such a manuscript was in existence surely Dickens would now have given it to Forster to read? It seems more likely that he had been jotting down various scattered passages of autobiography during the previous three years or so and was continuing to do so. This would accord with Forster's statement that it was during 1847/48 that he gradually came to learn 'in all their detail the incidents that had been so painful' to his friend. Some of these he learned about from written communications and some from conversations, like, for example, those which, he tells us, he 'perfectly recollects', about young Charles's Saturday night treats during his months in the blacking factory. Among the autobiographical passages apparently committed to paper by Dickens either during this period or perhaps earlier, and printed by Forster in his *Life*, are the sketch of his father quoted in Forster's first chapter, and the description of the Marshalsea prisoners signing a petition to the King drawn up by his father praying for a bounty to drink the King's health on his birthday. This latter description was written down, according to Forster, a full 'three or four years' before Dickens incorporated it into chapter 11 of *Copperfield*. Another passage that Forster quotes, this time directly from *Copperfield*, as 'literally true' and as having been 'every word' written down as fact 'some years before' it was used in the novel in 1849, is the famous account, mentioned in chapter 1 above, of David's avid childhood reading of Fielding, Smollett, *The Arabian Nights* and other classics from his father's little library.[6]

Forster's account of just how he learned about Dickens's boyhood sufferings, and especially what he says about the relationship between the fragment of autobiography that he quotes and the text of *Copperfield* is hard to unravel. But that he was already in possession of the main facts by 7 May 1847 seems clear from Dickens's writing to him on that date (a significant one for Dickens, being, as he observes, the eleventh anniversary of Mary Hogarth's death), 'I am more at rest for having opened all my heart and mind to you.' During the next twelve months part of his mind continued to run on his early years and he refers to them in May 1848 in the preface he writes for the Cheap Edition of *Nickleby* where he shares with his readers a remembrance of himself as 'a not very robust child, sitting in bye-places, near Rochester Castle, with a head full of Partridge, Strap, Tom Pipes [characters in Fielding and Smollett], and Sancho Panza'. Meanwhile, his elder sister Fanny's health was fast deteriorating and she died of consumption on 2 September, a distressful situation that also took him back into his past. The dying woman spoke to him, as he recalled in an essay written many years later, about the scent of fallen leaves in the woods in which they had walked as children, telling him that she felt so aware of this scent at night that she 'moved her weak head to look for strewn leaves on the floor at her bedside'. Fanny's cruelly early death 'vividly reawakened all the childish associations which made her memory dear to him' and on the day of her funeral he spoke to Forster about 'his tender and grateful memory' of her in their 'childish days'.[7]

Fanny's presence may be strongly felt in *The Haunted Man* with which Dickens reported himself to Forster to be 'a mentally matooring' in late September. Before setting to work on this, however, he had a preface to write for the third of his novels to appear in the Cheap Edition. This was *The Old Curiosity Shop*, the Cheap Edition serialisation of which, in both weekly and monthly parts, had just concluded. A preface was needed for the volume publication with its Cattermole frontispiece. Dickens's aim in the preface is to make the novel's genesis appear to have been a more deliberate and dignified business than it actually had been. Little Nell's story, he writes, 'was constructed from the beginning . . . with a view to separate publication when completed' and he indulges in some rueful regret for Master Humphrey, now condemned to 'the trunk and butter business', that is, becoming scrap paper used to line trunks or wrap butter. This preface also echoes the one written for *Dombey* a few months earlier in the way it invokes the special bond that Dickens felt to exist between himself and readers grieving over the deaths of children. Nor, I believe, is it fanciful to see a parallel between the image of himself that he was now evoking in his fragmentary autobiographical writings and Little Nell as described in his revisionist account of her creation. In the autobiographical writings he pictures himself as a pure and innocent child cast amidst uncouth companions in the antiquated premises of Warren's Blacking, while of Little Nell he writes: 'I had it always in my fancy to surround the lonely figure of the child with grotesque and wild, but not impossible companions.'[8]

The earlier, happier, period of his childhood was also sometimes in his thoughts during this period, for example at the end of September when Forster accompanied him on a visit to Chatham and Rochester. In Rochester he called upon a local vicar, the Reverend W. H. Drage, who as a curate in Chatham in the 1820s had been the Dickens family's next-door neighbour in Ordnance

Terrace (Dickens 'perfectly well' remembered him, correct initials and all). Past and present must have strangely merged for Dickens as he talked with Drage about a candidate of the vicar's for admission to Urania Cottage. Soon afterwards Dickens heard from another, more significant, figure of his Chatham childhood. This was his old schoolmaster William Giles, to whom he wrote in reply on 31 October: 'When I read your handwriting, I half believe I am a very small boy again. . . . I call to mind how you gave me Goldsmith's Bee when I first left Chatham (that was my first knowledge of it) . . .'. He ends, 'I am half inclined to say, now, "if you please Sir, may I leave off?" – and if I could make a bow in writing, I should certainly do it.'[9]

With all these memories, both bitter and sweet, now swirling around in his head, it is hardly surprising that his new Christmas Book (at which, he reported to Burdett Coutts on 6 November, he was 'grinding away') should return to the theme of memory which had been central to the *Carol*. But whereas Scrooge had suppressed all memory of his past, Redlaw goes to the opposite extreme and, incited by an evil doppelgänger, broods much over his past wrongs and sorrows. These centre on his parents', and especially his mother's, neglect of him as a child ('I was easily an alien from my mother's heart') and a devastating disappointment in love suffered in early manhood. Redlaw bitterly remembers how, inspired by this love, he 'strove to climb' and 'toiled up' only (and here fiction takes over from autobiography) for his beloved to run off with his treacherous best friend, a shadowy forerunner of *Copperfield*'s Steerforth. The story's blend of autobiography and fantasy is further thickened by Redlaw's having a devoted sister ('How young she was, how fair, how loving!') who deeply loved the treacherous friend, believing her love was returned. After his betrayal she lived on in her brother's home, 'doubly devoted', to see him become a famous man and then died, 'gentle as ever; happy; and with no concern but for her brother'.[10]

Redlaw succumbs to the temptation to have all memory of his past wrongs and sorrows blotted out but finds he has thereby been drained of all human kindness and can no longer feel love or compassion towards others. Worse still, he is doomed to pass on this curse to everyone he meets. Two people only are immune, a savage London street-urchin, successor to Ignorance in the *Carol*, and Milly, a version of Dickens's feminine ideal – 'the very spirit of morning, gladness, innocence, hope, love, domesticity, &c &c &c &c', according to his, somewhat breezy, description of the character to his old artist friend Frank Stone, who was to illustrate her (other illustrations were provided by Leech, Stanfield, and a newcomer on the art scene, John Tenniel). Redlaw is redeemed through Milly, his memory fully restored and with it his power to feel compassion for others. 'Of course,' Dickens wrote to Forster, 'my point is that bad and good are inextricably linked in remembrance, and that you could not choose the enjoyment of recollecting only the good. To have all the best of it you must remember the worst also.' The self-therapy he is seeking to practise here, whilst still providing his readers with a 'pretty' story having what he calls 'a good Christmas tendency', seems clear enough.[11]

On 22 November he went down to Brighton to finish writing the little book. 'When one laughs, and cries, and suffers the agitation that some men experience over their books', he told Stone, 'it's a bright change to look out of window and see the gilt little toys on horseback [that is, the fashionably-dressed equestrians] going up and down before the mighty sea and thinking nothing of it' (one notices the echo of one of *Dombey*'s leading motifs, the sea as emblem of eternity). He finished the story on 30 November and next day wrote to Bradbury that he had been 'crying [his] eyes out over it – not painfully but pleasantly as I hope the readers will'. But that he was expecting more than just a sentimental reaction in some quarters is shown by his letter to George Hogarth on 15 December in which he says, 'I have no doubt of its doing me good with all thoughtful readers.' On 5 December he gave a wedding breakfast for his youngest brother, Augustus, the original 'Boz', who was marrying the orphan daughter of a former official of the East India Company. He did not, however, even attend Fred's marriage to Anna Weller at the end of this month, it being a match of which, as we have seen, he strongly disapproved. On 11 December he gave a private reading of *The Haunted Man* to the Watsons and some other friends. He also helped Lemon to arrange a dramatised version of this very undramatic little book, for which he was paid £100. It was little enough compensation for the misery involved: 'every word the actors say is a rack to me,' he told Burdett Coutts. The book itself appeared on 19 December and, although on 6 January he described it as an 'immense success', it had, for a Dickens Christmas Book, very moderate sales – six thousand less, in fact, than *The Battle of Life* – resulting in a net profit of just over £793. There was general enthusiasm for the Tetterby family, worthy successors of the *Carol*'s Cratchits, but many readers found the story of Redlaw's emotional and spiritual journey both confused and confusing.[12]

Dickens's last publication in 1848 was a warmly appreciative discussion of the art of his good friend John Leech as shown in *The Rising Generation*, a portfolio of Leech's cartoons from *Punch* poking gentle fun at middle-class children, mostly very charmingly depicted, behaving precociously. Written at Forster's request, Dickens's review appeared in *The Examiner* on 30 December. He lavishly praises Leech's constant endeavour 'to refine and elevate' the increasingly popular art of caricature by introducing 'beautiful faces or agreeable forms' into his drawings. He could well have added that it was this very quality that made Leech such an appropriate illustrator-in-chief for his own Christmas Books, related as they were to another part of popular culture. He had, Forster tells us, 'a secret delight' in believing that in them he was giving a 'higher form' to 'old nursery tales' of which he was so 'intensely fond'.[13]

27 Example of 'The rising generation' series by John Leech in *Punch,* 1848. *Juvenile*: 'I tell you what it is, governor, the sooner we come to some understanding, the better. You can't expect a young feller to be always at home, and if you don't like the way I go on – why I must have chambers, and so much a week'

Ideas for a new monthly-part serial, as well as for the new periodical about which he had been thinking, on and off, for over two years, were now beginning to ferment in Dickens's mind. With regard to the former, he eagerly caught at Forster's suggestion that the new serial might be written in the first person. His responsiveness may well have been influenced by remembering the great success in 1847 of a remarkable first-person novel, Charlotte Brontë's *Jane Eyre* (Dickens was later reported as saying he had never read this book but that is hard to believe), or it may have been due to a dawning realisation that the autobiographical narrative on which he was, probably intermittently, working might provide a basis for such a work. He perhaps also reflected that a first-person narrative starting in childhood would afford a grand opportunity for developing further the technique so successfully pioneered in *Dombey* with little Paul's illness 'expressed in the child's own feelings – not otherwise described'. Also, he seemed inclined to look back with a certain wistfulness to his one attempt so far at a long first-person narrative, the use of Master Humphrey as narrator in the *Clock*, an attempt which had had to be abandoned with such clumsy abruptness. This could well have been another reason for his ready response to Forster's suggestion.[14]

Before beginning work in earnest on the new story Dickens organised another of those jolly bachelor jaunts in which he so evidently delighted. He, Leech and Lemon made a two-day trip to Norwich during 7–9 January. This expedition was, in fact, more macabre than jolly in that their destination resulted from curiosity to view the scene of a sensational double murder that had taken place near the city the previous November when the Recorder of Norwich and his son had been killed by a grudge-bearing farmer named Rush, now awaiting trial. Dickens and his friends visited the victims' home, which, he was pleased to think, had 'a murderous look that seemed to invite such a crime', also Rush's farm, where they scornfully observed the police's incompetent search for the murder weapon. The big surprise of the trip, however, was Yarmouth, briefly visited on impulse after Norwich had, apart from the site of its gallows ('fit for a gigantic scoundrel's exit'), proved disappointing. The wide flatness of the Yarmouth sea-shore and the 'hill-less marshes' inland from the town made it 'the strangest place in the wide world', Dickens wrote to Forster, adding, 'I shall certainly try my hand at it.' It may be, as has been suggested by some commentators, that the place made such an impression on him partly because of its resemblance to the Medway estuary and the marsh country of his childhood. His brilliant evocation of Yarmouth three months later through the astonished eyes of young David Copperfield is certainly striking testimony to his powers of observation since he was only in the town for a day and a night, and much of the day was taken up with walking to Lowestoft and back. On the walk Dickens noticed the name Blundeston painted on a signpost. This was later transmuted into the 'Blunderstone' of *Copperfield*, a nicely suggestive name for the native village of the kind of Fieldingesque hero Dickens was now thinking about – a hero, that is, destined to make mistakes and encounter many obstacles in his progress towards maturity. That Fielding was much in Dickens's mind at this time was shown when he named his eighth child and sixth son, born 15 January, Henry Fielding Dickens 'in a kind of homage to the style of work he was now so bent on beginning'. Happily, Catherine was spared much of her usual suffering at this birth as a result of Dickens's insistence, against medical advice, that she should be allowed chloroform. It may be that it was his greater-than-usual involvement in this particular birth that influenced his decision to begin his new story with a chapter entitled 'I Am Born', in which the protagonist relates what he has been told about his own birth-history.[15]

It was on 20 January, Forster tells us, that he first saw what Dickens had so far written of his autobiography 'in its connected shape'. It has been plausibly suggested that Dickens showed this manuscript to Forster at this point because he was thinking about incorporating much of it into the new story and wanted his friend's opinion about this. Forster came at last to read as a continuous narrative Dickens's impassioned account of how he, 'a child of singular abilities, quick, eager, delicate, and soon hurt, bodily or mentally', had been consigned by his parents to what he saw as degrading menial work in a 'crazy, tumble-down old house . . . literally overrun with rats', working with 'secret agony of soul' alongside Bob Fagin and Poll Green, how his whole nature had been 'penetrated' with grief and humiliation, and how he had felt 'utterly neglected and hopeless'. This account forms the substance of most of Forster's second chapter, though he seems not to be quoting from the actual manuscript he was shown in January 1849 but from a later, more fragmentary, copy since he says at one point, 'I lose here for a little while the fragment of direct narrative' and at another, 'There is here another blank'. In what Forster gives us Dickens relates how he, 'so young and childish', had all week to fend entirely for himself with 'no advice, no counsel, no encouragement, no consolation, no support, from any one that I call to mind, so help me God'. He describes his various survival-strategies, such as ensuring that he could do his work quite as well as the other boys and preserving always a sense of his own gentility. This involved shunning over-familiarity even with kindly Bob Fagin, who cared tenderly for him when he had 'a bad attack of [his] old disorder' and towards whom he would seem to have had a very complex emotional response. He describes occasional acts of bravado, too, as when he walked into a pub one day and boldly ordered a glass of the establishment's 'VERY *best*' ale 'with a good head to it'. He gives evidence of his remarkable powers of observation through a vividly detailed description of the ceremonious occasion in his father's Marshalsea existence already mentioned in this chapter. He piercingly recalls the heartbreak he felt when he saw Fanny being presented with two prizes at the Royal Academy of Music whilst he himself seemed to be 'beyond the reach of all such honourable emulation and success'. And in the very next paragraph he describes the (to him) deeply humiliating success that did fall to his lot when he and Bob Fagin were watched admiringly, often by 'quite a little crowd', as they sat by a window dexterously tying up the blacking pots. The 'fragment' ends with the narrow avoidance of a final horror. His father, having quarrelled with the manager, decided his son should work there no longer and the boy 'with a relief so strange that it was like oppression' left the place for good, only to find when he got home that his mother, of all people, 'was warm for [his] being sent back'. She was, however, overruled by his father who decreed that he should resume his interrupted schooling.[16]

The outstanding literary craftsmanship of this autobiographical fragment has been much commented upon. Forster thought indeed that it gave us 'a picture of tragical suffering, and of tender as well as humorous fancy, unsurpassed in even the wonders of his published writings'. In it Dickens depicts his twelve-year-old self primarily as a figure of intense pathos, like the significantly-named Little Dick in *Oliver Twist* or Oliver himself. At other points in the fragment its protagonist is seen in a more heroic light, proudly hiding his anguish and preserving his 'gentlemanly' self even in the abyss. At still other points lively comic anecdotes show him as a resourceful and streetwise, even cheeky, survivor, like a young Sam Weller or an Artful Dodger. Elements of all three of these versions of his younger self will reappear in the fictional child David Copperfield. As to the fragment itself, it seems from some diary notes Forster made at the time it was shown to him and quoted by him in the *Life*, that Dickens declared himself to be in two minds about whether or not it should ever be published. Despite all its vivid circumstantial detail and the impassioned language used in certain passages, he doubted that what he had written would convey to the reader the full horror of what had happened to him: 'The description may make none of the impression on others that the reality made on him.' In the course of the fragment itself, indeed, he insists that no words could ever convey the extent to which he suffered. The 'deep remembrance' he has of the misery and shame experienced by his younger self simply 'cannot be written'. Nevertheless, he was, he told Forster, content to leave open the possibility of posthumous publication, the decision to be taken by Forster himself or by 'others'. Himself, he had 'no wish' in the matter. Of the now vanished manuscript itself Forster notes, 'No blotting, as when writing fiction; but straight on, as when writing ordinary letter.' This might suggest that what he saw was a fair copy made by Dickens, drawn from scattered passages written earlier, but we have no way of verifying such speculation.[17]

What *is* certain is that Dickens, whether or not he was influenced by Catherine, as Charley later claimed, was to go on to reproduce in some early chapters of his new story, as yet untitled, many details from this finished picture (as it were) of his time in the blacking factory. According to Forster, the basic idea for the story was 'itself suggested by what he had so written of his early troubles'. As it happened, the subject of the sufferings of neglected children, of a far worse kind than anything that the young Dickens had had to endure, was also very much in the news just at this time and he quickly responded to this. At a huge baby-farm in Tooting, just south of London, large numbers of pauper children were dying of cholera in appalling circumstances. The newly-constituted Board of Health, of which Henry Austin was General Secretary, had issued a general warning of the likelihood of an outbreak of cholera but Drouet, the owner of the Tooting farm to which many metropolitan parishes sent their pauper babies, had ignored it. He had escaped detection because of the incompetence or connivance of parish inspectors (the Board itself had no jurisdiction within a twelve-mile radius of London). As a result by mid-January the children in his care were dying in their hundreds. On 20 January *The Examiner* printed a ferocious article written by Dickens, called 'The Paradise at Tooting', which

28 Drouet's baby-farming establishment at Tooting

concluded that the establishment had been devastated by the cholera because it was 'brutally conducted, vilely kept, preposterously inspected, dishonestly defended, a disgrace to a Christian community, and a stain upon a civilised land'. Dickens contributed three further trenchant articles on this topic during the three months immediately preceding the appearance of *Copperfield* I at the end of April. Drouet's cruelty and negligence was a scandal that would have aroused his fury at any time (his fictitious baby-farmer Mrs Mann in *Oliver* seems insignificant indeed by comparison with this man) but, coming just when he, having resurrected in detail his own sufferings in the blacking factory, was more than usually sensitive on the subject of children abandoned to their fate, we may well believe he felt compelled to write so much about it, even in the throes of conceiving *Copperfield*.[18]

By 2 February Dickens was, he told Macready, 'revolving new books in his mind and walking perpetually'. (He was also, we should bear in mind, regularly attending to Urania Cottage business and dealing with problems like the 'atrocious temper' of one staff member whom he found on one visit behaving like 'a Stage Maniac in a domestic drama'.) Having conceived of the theme of innocence as a central concern of the new novel, he imparts to Forster his idea for the character who will become Mr Wickfield, a sort of 'more innocent

Pecksniff', always asking about anyone's action, 'now, *What's his motive?*' In preparation for introducing Yarmouth characters he makes a careful study of Edward Moor's *Suffolk Words and Phrases* (1823) to ensure the authenticity of the characters' speech. And his 'clutching eye' was always capturing odd or bizarre details and storing them away for future use. A lady whom he notices as having taken to dining out 'in immense black velvet hats', for example, will feature a year later in *Copperfield* IX as the similarly-attired Mrs Henry Spiker, who strikes David as 'looking like a near relation of Hamlet's – say his aunt'.[19]

He still had not got his title, however, and for him this was always a crucial first step. He made another trip to Brighton (14–21 Feb.), accompanied by Catherine and the Leeches, to grapple with the problem (he can hardly have been helped by their landlord and his daughter both going mad, obliging the Dickens party to decamp to the Bedford Hotel). Bound up with the manuscript of *Copperfield* are no fewer than sixteen different attempts at a title for the new story, each on a fresh sheet. His first notion was to call it *Mag's Diversions. Being the personal history of Mr Thomas Mag the Younger of Blunderstone House*, the title being explained by a quotation showing that the phrase 'Mag's diversions' meant something like 'mischief' or 'the deuce and all'. His protagonist's name soon became changed to David Copperfield: one sheet, probably the earliest in the sequence, shows Dickens experimenting with combining certain words – 'flower', 'brook', 'field', 'boy', etc. – with others to produce a surname that satisfied him – 'Flowerbury', 'Copperboy', etc., and, finally, 'Copperfield', written twice. On another sheet David Copperfield shares equal billing with 'his Great-Aunt Margaret', the first hint of Betsey Trotwood ('Trotfield' and 'Trotbury' are among the experimental names on the putative earliest sheet). Dickens was 'much startled' when Forster pointed out that David Copperfield's initials were his own reversed and declared it to be 'just in keeping with the fates and chances which were always befalling him'. On 26 February he sent Forster a list of six possible titles to choose from, all containing the name David Copperfield and ringing the changes on the formula to be used in describing this first-person narrative – 'Disclosures', 'Records', 'Last Living Speech and Confession', 'Survey of the World as it Rolled', 'Last Will and Testament' and 'Copperfield Complete' as well as on the name of David's home – 'Blunderstone House/Lodge/ Rookery' and 'Copperfield Cottage'. The one phrase constant in these six, and all the earlier versions, is 'personal history'. Forster chose no.4, *The Copperfield Survey of the World as it Rolled. Being the personal history, experience, and observation of David Copperfield the Younger, of Blunderstone Rookery*, as had Catherine and Georgina, whereupon Dickens declared it had been his favourite from the first. Once he began writing, however, he found that he needed to drop the 'survey' idea in order to keep focused on David's 'personal history'. 'Being' was also necessarily dropped and the word 'adventures' was added after 'personal history'. And to this final version was added a phrase that had already appeared in one of the variants: '(Which He never meant to be Published on any Account)'. At this stage, it seems, Dickens was still planning that David's auto-biography should be presented as being posthumously published, just as would be the case with his own, if he should ever, in fact, complete it and his executors should decide to publish it.[20]

Since the first number of the new story was scheduled to appear on 1 May Bradbury and Evans needed to open their advertising campaign for it before Dickens had settled on the title. Accordingly, the first advertisement to appear, in *The Athenaeum* on 3 March, was simply headed 'New Work by Mr Charles Dickens'. It announced that the first number would appear in May and that the illustrations for this 'New Story' would be by Browne. By the end of the month, however, the publishers could announce Dickens's finally-chosen title, which duly appeared in all subsequent publicity – coloured bills, posters and show-cards, as well as press advertisements. Oddly, the discarded *Copperfield Survey of the World as it Rolled* turned up in one or two of the latter but quickly disap-peared again, surviving only as an image of a baby contemplating the globe in the cover-design for the monthly parts. For this design Browne, lacking advance plot-information such as he had had for *Dombey*, took his cue from the title and designed a monthly-part cover showing, in a generalised way, on the left-hand side the progress of a man from infancy up to maturity and on the right-hand side his descent into old age and finally death with the goddess Fortune presiding at the top centre of the design.

With the title settled Dickens could finally get to work on the first number of the new story. He had, he wrote to Burdett Coutts on 24 March, made a 'virtuous resolution to be beforehand' and was able to report himself as being near to finishing the number with over a month to spare before publication date. He had, he told Austin four days later, been 'wallowing' in the new story 'very comfortably, and (I hope) successfully'. It was an auspicious beginning for the writing of this new story that was to become, among all his works, his 'favourite child'.

CHAPTER 13

Interweaving and conducting

WRITING *DAVID COPPERFIELD* AND BEGINNING *HOUSEHOLD WORDS*, 1849–1850

I really think I have done it ingeniously, and with a very complicated inter-weaving of truth and fiction.

Dickens writing to Forster about the fourth monthly number
of *David Copperfield*, 10 July 1849

R EPLYING ON 29 January 1855 to Arthur Ryland of the Birmingham and Midland Institute who had asked for a Reading from *David Copperfield*, Dickens lamented the 'huge difficulty' of creating one. He had 'so woven and blended [the book] together' that he could not find a way to extract from it for the Reading the two episodes he wanted, a comic one (David's and Dora's chaotic housekeeping) and a pathetic one (Mr Peggotty's quest for his lost niece). Unlike some of the remarks in his Cheap Edition prefaces to *Copperfield*'s predecessors, this one about his careful structuring of the novel did not derive from hindsight. Dickens's notes for the first monthly number (even in the incomplete form in which we have them) and the text itself show that certain major plot-lines, to be gradually 'woven and blended' together, were already clear in his mind from the start. One involved David's great-aunt Betsey Trotwood who disappears at the end of chapter 1 but is clearly going to reappear later on. The other evidently concerned the fate of Little Em'ly. In a long passage inserted into chapter 3, after the first draft was completed, Em'ly speaks of her longing to be a lady and David the narrator hints very broadly at some future shameful catastrophe awaiting her. The novel's dominant elegiac tone is also established in these early chapters. Chapter 2 includes the first of those beautiful retrospective passages, written in the present tense and delicately mingling pathos and humour, that mark significant stages in David's life as he progresses from blissful infancy to eventual union with 'the real heroine', as Agnes is called in Dickens's notes for *Copperfield* V in which she first appears.[1]

One real child's voice pierced Dickens's heart as he worked on *Copperfield* II, a number strong in pathos as young David's fortunes take a desolating turn following his mother's marriage to Mr Murdstone. On 16 April the Drouet trial ended with the defendant's acquittal on a technicality and, despite his pressing *Copperfield* deadline, Dickens promptly dashed off yet another scathing article for *The Examiner*, published on 21 April. In it he quoted from the evidence given by one of the workhouse nurses who received the sick and dying children from Drouet's establishment into the Royal Free Hospital. She testified to giving milk and bread to one of them and, when asked if the child had eaten the bread, replied, 'No; he held up his hand, and said, "Oh nurse, what a big bit of bread this is!" ' This was, wrote Dickens, a 'little touch . . . of a peculiarly affecting kind, such as the masters of pathos have rarely excelled in fiction'. The child's head 'was lifted up for a second but it sank again. He could not but be full of wonder and pleasure that the big bit of bread had come, though he could not eat it.'[2]

So fired up was Dickens by the whole Drouet business that at a big dinner party he gave at Devonshire Terrace on 18 April he could not stop fulminating about it. Next day he found writing difficult. 'Though I know what I want to do, I am lumbering on like a stage-waggon,' he wrote to Forster, 'I am quite aground . . . and the long Copperfieldian perspective looks snowy and thick, this fine morning.' He was perhaps paying the penalty for the intensity of his response to the Drouet case. A year later he explained to Austin why for the sake of *Copperfield* he had to miss a meeting of the Metropolitan Sanitary Association, at which the shocking state of over-full metropolitan graveyards was on the agenda: 'If I get fierce and antagonistic about burials, I can't get back to Copperfield for hours and hours. This is really the sort of condition on which I hold my inventive powers: and I can't get rid of it.'[3]

He managed to finish *Copperfield* II a week before he was due to host another, still grander, dinner-party on 12 May. Among the guests were the Carlyles and Carlyle delighted Dickens by calling himself 'a lone, lorn creetur' like Mrs Gummidge. Another guest was Elizabeth Gaskell, making her second visit to Devonshire Terrace and taking note of the arrangement of Dickens's study ('books all round, up to the ceiling and down to the ground; a standing-desk at which he writes; and all manner of comfortable easy chairs'). Gaskell's first novel, *Mary Barton* (1848), had brought her fame and she was soon to figure largely in Dickens's professional life, the sometimes vexatious 'Scheherazade' of his *Household Words*. Also present was Thackeray, the great success of whose *Vanity Fair* (published in monthly numbers Jan. 1847–July 1848) had shot him to the top of the literary tree where, he jokingly told his mother, he was having 'a great fight' with Dickens. To a certain extent, he had anticipated *Copperfield* with his *History of Pendennis*, the first number of which had appeared in November 1848. This also was a story about a young man growing up from childhood to maturity into which its author had 'interwoven' many of his own experiences. It is not, however, a first-person narrative, nor does it begin with the hero's infancy. Thackeray, always generous in his appreciation of Dickens,

was enraptured by the first number of *Copperfield*. 'O it is charming,' he wrote
to his friend Jane Brookfield, 'Bravo Dickens. It has some of his very prettiest
touches – those inimitable Dickens touches wh. make such a great man of him.'
But he could not forebear adding that he believed *Copperfield* showed that,
although Dickens had ceased to make any public mention of his, Thackeray's,
work, he had nevertheless been influenced by it into 'greatly simplifying his style
and foregoing the use of fine words'. 'By this', he added, 'the public will be the
gainer.' That Dickens himself was aware of having in *Copperfield* toned down
some of his customary stylistic effects is suggested in his jocose reference, in a
letter to Lemon of 25 June, to his just-written description of David's mother's
death: 'Get a clean pocket-handkerchief ready for the close of "Copperfield"
No. 3; "simple and quiet, but very natural and touching." – *Evening Bore*.'[4]

Unlike David, destined by his creator to become a writer, Dickens himself
was always keenly aware of that other career he once came so near to embarking
on. As an actor he would also have had to make his own way but neither he
himself nor anyone who had seen him act could have had any doubt that he
would have risen to the very top of the profession. Most actors had no such
success, however, and many turned for help at times to the General Theatrical
Fund. On 21 May Dickens spoke at the Fund's annual festival and defended
actors against 'the sweeping charge of improvidence' so often brought against
them. It was no doubt with his proud and ever-present sense of his own
phenomenal achievement against tremendous odds, which he was currently
fictionalising in *Copperfield*, that he remarked in his speech:

> if you are born to the possession of a silver spoon, it may not be very difficult
> to apply yourself to the task of keeping it well polished on the side-board,
> but ... if you are born to the possession of a wooden ladle instead, the
> process of transmuting it into that article of plate is often a very difficult and
> discouraging process.[5]

The problems Dickens had complained of in progressing *Copperfield* II soon
vanished. As he got into the number, he found himself able seamlessly to weave
into his fictional narrative of the child David's experiences his already-written
description of his own passionate childhood absorption in the books from
his father's little library, as well as memories of Wellington House Academy
and its sadistic proprietor, wonderfully transmogrified into the malevolently
whispering Mr Creakle. This must have strengthened him, if indeed he needed
any strengthening, in his intention to draw directly in the new story on what
had by now become his most acutely distressing memories, centred on his
blacking factory experience. For a man so secretive about his personal history
as Dickens this might seem like playing with fire. *Copperfield*, after all, was a
first-person narrative tracing the story of a young man from a very modest

background who would, just like Dickens himself, become through his own determined and unaided efforts first a successful parliamentary reporter, and then a hugely popular novelist. Inevitably, it would be – and was – widely read as being, at least to some extent, autobiographical. 'It is supposed', the Queen was briefed many years later, before receiving Dickens in audience, 'that [*Copperfield*] gives or at least gives a hint of the author's early life.' Dickens could hardly have been unaware of such belief, and indeed he would sometimes encourage friends to look for autobiographical elements in the novel. But he could feel confident that no one outside his immediate family (excepting perhaps a few long-standing close family friends like Dilke) would even remotely suspect that all the part about young David's degradation into a 'little labouring hind', the desperate visits to the pawnbroker's, and the Micawbers' time in a debtors' prison was based on autobiographical fact – any more, apparently, than they believed the all-consuming intensity of David's passion for Dora reflected his creator's actual experience. 'People used to say to me', he wrote later to Dora's original, Maria Winter née Beadnell, when heaping coals of fire upon her hapless middle-aged head, 'how pretty all that was, and how fanciful it was, and how elevated it was above the little foolish loves of very young men and women. But they little thought what reason I had to know it was true and nothing more nor less.'[6]

The sales figures for *Copperfield* in its monthly parts were disappointing. The first number sold far fewer copies than the first number of *Dombey* (twenty-six as opposed to nearly thirty-two thousand), and this remained the pattern throughout the run, with the monthly sales struggling to reach twenty thousand, and fewer advertisers taking space in the numbers than had been the case with *Dombey*. Yet when in September Dickens saw the sales figures for *Copperfield* I–III he was not disheartened. 'Passing influences' were responsible, he told Forster: 'as *Chuzzlewit* with its small sale [in monthly parts] sent me up, *Dombey*'s large sale has tumbled me down.' This was a view that might seem vindicated by the initial monthly-part sales of his next book, *Bleak House*, which considerably exceeded those of *Copperfield*. Moreover, Dickens knew that David's story was winning golden opinions everywhere, and knew also, from Bradbury and Evans, that the back numbers were selling briskly. He was further heartened to receive at this time a letter from a Russian translator, I. I. Vvedensky, telling him that his books were being 'read with avidity . . . from the banks of the Neva to the remotest parts of Siberia'. Subsequently, it became a standing joke between him and Forster when anything had vexed him that he 'had ordered his portmanteau to be packed for the more sympathising and congenial climate of "the remotest parts of Siberia" '.[7]

By 6 June he was half-way through *Copperfield* III (chs 7–9) and, as he told Forster, 'quite confident in the story'. He had introduced and effectively established his Byronic-hero figure, James Steerforth, a new type for him, and attentive readers might already be anticipating that this golden boy would be the cause of Emily's ruin, though it would be another four numbers before Dickens was to bring them together. His letter to Forster about his development of the story continues, 'I have a move in it ready for this month [referring to the death of David's mother]; another for next; and another for the next'. The 'move' for *Copperfield* IV (chs 10–12) was, of course, David's being sent to do menial work washing bottles and pasting labels in Murdstone and Grinby's wines and spirits warehouse. On 21 June Dickens found he needed an exceptionally long country walk of fourteen miles to begin thinking through what he later called, with reference to the whole novel, that 'very complicated interweaving of truth and fiction' that was to constitute this number. And even so, Forster tells us, still another week or so had to pass before he could 'see his way'. If he were to be 'dragged forth to a dungeon for contempt of court' for ignoring a jury summons, as he had just done, it might, Dickens told him, help 'with a new notion or two in my difficulties'. No doubt Forster appreciated the point of this joke, knowing as he did that John Dickens's Marshalsea experience was somehow going to have to figure in the number. To complicate matters, Dickens had a bad fall on 1 July, which resulted in some debilitating cupping and blistering during the next few days. Nevertheless, he managed to send at least part of the first chapter to the printers on the 4th. Five days later, he was responding to the Lord Mayor's toast to the 'Honour and Prosperity of those engaged in the Pursuits of Literature' at a Mansion House banquet, which proved to be a rather prickly occasion since Dickens, always highly susceptible to the least hint of patronage, thought he detected such a hint in the Lord Mayor's speech. Afterwards, he fled to Broadstairs for a week to recover his health and there he finally managed to finish this emotionally-charged number, his sole 'mem' for which consisted of one poignant line: 'What I know so well'.[8]

Either at Broadstairs, or just before going there, he must have conceived of the Micawbers and soon afterwards reported that he was getting on 'like a house afire'. The introduction of the Micawbers enabled him to get his parents into the book while distancing them from what he saw as the terrible thing they had done to him when he was, like David Copperfield, 'a child of excellent abilities, *and with strong powers of observation*, quick, eager, delicate, and soon hurt bodily or mentally' (a description that was imported verbatim into the novel from the autobiographical fragment, with the addition of the words I have italicised). Not being David's parents, the Micawbers are freed from all responsibility for his degradation. Indeed, they do much to alleviate his loneliness and are a source of comfort, and even enjoyment, in his forlorn existence. John Dickens's financial fecklessness, his affected gentility and delight in grandiloquent phrases, Elizabeth's ill-fated school scheme, their resilience and 'gypsy-like' way of life in the prison, the ceremonial display of John's grand petition to the king – Dickens is now free to transfer all these things, more or less intact, from the autobiographical fragment into the novel.[9]

John Dickens does not seem to have been embarrassed by being so identifiably depicted with such a financially irresponsible character as Micawber, sometime inmate of a debtors' prison. The former London journalist Shelton Mackenzie wrote in his *Life of Charles Dickens* (1870), 'It was a constant joke among newspaper-men, that Charles Dickens had drawn upon his father's actual character, when he was writing *David Copperfield*, and put him into that story as Micawber.' John, apparently, 'considered himself rather complimented in thus being converted into literary "capital" by his son'. Mackenzie implies that the resemblance related to personal mannerisms rather than to financial history but comments sympathetically on how hard it must have been for John to raise a family of eight on 'four or five guineas a week'. He might well, Mackenzie speculates, have needed to resort to 'little bills' (raising money on credit), or even, on occasion, to pawnbrokers. But Mackenzie, who was writing within weeks of Dickens's death (thus long before Forster's publication of the revelatory fragment), makes no allusion to John's having seen the inside of the Marshalsea as Micawber sees the inside of the King's Bench. This dramatic fact seems to have been something of which he, like John's other journalistic colleagues, was wholly ignorant – thanks in part, it would seem, to Dilke's discretion.[10]

With *Copperfield* IV successfully completed, Dickens was ready to organise the usual household migration to the seaside for the summer. This year, instead of returning to Broadstairs, he joined forces with Leech to look for another congenial resort for them and their families somewhere on the south coast. They soon fixed upon the Isle of Wight. Leech rented a villa at Ventnor while Dickens rented another at Bonchurch, one of the chief charms of which for him seems to have been the fact that he was able to rig up an open-air shower-bath under a waterfall in the grounds. The owner was an old friend of Dickens called James White, a clergyman-author whom Forster describes as a great lover of 'jest and merriment' with a charming wife. The Dickens family's move to Bonchurch took place on 23 July and on Ryde pier they ran into Thackeray who reported to Mrs Brookfield his encounter with 'the great Dickens with his wife his children his Miss Hogarth all looking abominably coarse vulgar and happy . . .'.[11]

At Bonchurch Dickens established the rigid rule that he should be invisible between breakfast and 2 p.m. During those sacrosanct hours he was for the first fortnight or so of each month in his study planning and writing his next number. Even in the later, 'leisure part' of the month he still needed some private time: 'If it be only half an hour's sitting alone in a morning', he wrote to Watson on 21 July, 'and half an hour's look at pen, ink and paper, it seems to keep me in the train.' He was very conscious, he said, of how much lay before him (that 'long Copperfieldian perspective' he had mentioned earlier) and also of the 'necessity' of sustaining his reputation 'at its highest point', a necessity given an extra edge, no doubt, by the thought of the new journal trading on his name that he and his publishers planned to launch in the near future. Outside his study, however, he was in full holiday mode, his 'hard Copperfieldian mornings' being followed by picnics, outdoor games of rounders or leap-frog, indoor games of forfeits, and some spectacular displays of conjuring with Dickens billing himself as 'the Unparalleled Necromancer Rhia Rhama Roos'. There was also the usual stream of visitors, among them Talfourd, newly made a judge, who recorded 'a glorious walk with Dickens . . . all the way talking as authors talk'. Eventually, however, Dickens found the climate enervating and in late August treated Forster to an epistolary extravaganza on the subject, reporting on himself as though he were a very sick patient: '. . . a ball of boiling fat appears to be always behind the top of the bridge of his nose, simmering between his haggard eyes. . . .'. And so, at the end of September, the family sought the familiar benefits of Broadstairs, remaining there for something over two weeks before returning to London on 18 October.[12]

Whilst at Bonchurch Dickens kept in touch with events at Urania Cottage, though he did not attend committee meetings so regularly. Also, his passionate commitment to the cause of sanitary reform ensured that he kept track of Austin's battles with the Metropolitan Commission of Sewers and he may even have helped his brother-in-law to write two articles on the subject, published in *The Examiner* on 14 July and 4 August. He also found time, between finishing one number of *Copperfield* and starting the next, to write an impassioned appeal, published in *The Examiner* and elsewhere, on behalf of the Italian patriot Mazzini and his fellow Republican refugees, expelled from Rome by French troops. He refers to the Republicans as having 'built upon the ruins of a monstrous system [the Papal government] which had fallen of its own rottenness and corruption, one of moderation and truth', and to the French intervention as an act of 'such stupendous baseness that it will remain an ineffaceable stain upon the honour and the name of France, through all the coming ages of the world'. Two numbers of *Copperfield* were completed at Bonchurch before the retreat to Broadstairs. No. V introduces Agnes, and No. VI concludes what might be called, in musical terms, the first movement of this novel. It marks the end of David's childhood. Prominent among Dickens's 'mems' for this number are the words, 'The Progress from childhood to youth' and the last chapter (ch. 18) is the second of those 'Retrospects' already mentioned that, briefly and poignantly, arrest the temporal flow of the novel.[13]

I quoted Dickens's telling Mary Howitt that he had been 'a great writer' as a child at the head of my first chapter. His David Copperfield shows no such precocious literary talent, however. From beginning to end of this first-person narrative whose composer becomes a famous and successful novelist we hear very little indeed about his work. In these early numbers such acts of writing as we do find are invariably comic, perpetrated by child-like adults – Mr Micawber's petition, Mr Dick's 'Memorial', Dr Strong's dictionary. In his notes for *Copperfield* V Dickens reminds himself to link Mr Dick with the Doctor and, characteristically, he makes self-referential jokes in connection with both Mr Dick and Dr Strong. 'Dick' was one of his own nick-names (his first thought had been to call this character Robert) and in the book's final 'Retrospect' we hear of Dr Strong still labouring on his dictionary 'somewhere about the letter D'. Mr Dick's obsession with King Charles's head was highly topical in 1849, the bicentenary of the King's execution, and was inspired by a suggestion of Forster's (Dickens's original, much weaker, notion was that Mr Dick should be obsessed with the proverbial bull in the china shop). The depiction of Mr Dick is, in fact, a fine example of Dickens the novelist blending with Dickens the engaged social journalist. It builds up the wise benevolence of Betsey Trotwood whilst at the same time enabling Dickens to pay a second public tribute to the work of a man he admired, Dr John Conolly, whose activities at the Hanwell Asylum, pioneering the more humane treatment of the mentally ill (substituting kindly care for forcible restraint and providing the sufferers with something to do) he had already found occasion to praise directly seven years before, in *American Notes.*

From Bonchurch Dickens had corresponded with Burdett Coutts, Charley's patroness, not only about Urania Cottage but also about sending Charley to Eton. Concurrently, he was describing in *Copperfield* Aunt Betsey's decision to send David to Dr Strong's school at Canterbury, and the boy's experiences when he gets there. Dr Strong's school is only vaguely sketched, a sort of bourgeois dream of what a good public school might be like. Insofar as Dickens does supply much detail he does so mainly by contrasting it with Salem House but one thing that *is* very sharply realised is David's fear that his fellow-scholars might find out his shameful secret, his warehouse-boy past. This sharpness surely derives from Dickens's mingling of memories of himself at Wellington House with imagining his twelve-year-old son at Eton, blissfully unaware of the sensational contrast between his situation and the one in which his own father had found himself at his age.

Happily ensconced in Broadstairs in early October, Dickens wrote the splendid November number, *Copperfield* VII. In his notes he directs himself to 'pave the way' with various characters who have been already introduced, that is, to prepare the ground for the roles they are to play in the developing story, and he introduces some new ones. Among the latter is Rosa Dartle, unmentioned in the 'mems', who evidently 'grew under his hand', as the editor of the Clarendon *Copperfield* puts it, her individuality having been originally confined only to certain turns of speech copied from Hannah Brown. Dickens was now able to think purposefully about 'the old notion of the Periodical' which, he wrote to Forster on 24 September, was 'at last gradually growing into form'. On 7 October, even before he had finished his monthly *Copperfield* stint, he sent Forster a long letter elaborating his ideas for a weekly journal. It was to be cheaply priced at 1½ or 2d., and would mingle original matter and informative articles reprinted from other journals with 'a little good [original] poetry'. All contributions written especially for the journal were to be 'as amusing as possible' but also 'distinctly and boldly going to what in one's own view ought to be the spirit of the people and the time'. In other words, although the papers in the magazine were to be miscellaneous and multi-authored, they should all aim at both entertainment and social comment, and this comment should be conformable to Dickens's by now pretty widely known views on the state of the nation. To bind it all together, and to give the journal a personality of its own, Dickens elaborated the peculiar notion of a 'semi-omniscient, omnipresent, intangible creature' called 'the Shadow', a figure that in its conception harks back to the Boz of the *Sketches* and hovers strangely between Master Humphrey and the Uncommercial Traveller in the history of Dickens's long, and ultimately successful, quest for a journalistic persona. Forster failed to 'make anything out of it that had a quite feasible look' but Dickens clung to the idea, still referring to the magazine as 'The Shadow' in a letter to Bradbury of 29 October.[14]

Home again in Devonshire Terrace, Dickens happened upon an obnoxious pamphlet describing drunkenness as the chief cause of 'juvenile depravity', written by one Thomas Beggs, a former secretary of the National Temperance Association. Dickens promptly dashed off for *The Examiner* a long article entitled 'Demoralisation and Total Abstinence', published 27 October, in the same issue as his eulogistic review of Macready's new production of *King Lear*. He was always incensed by the failure of people like Beggs to make any connection between the prevalence of drunkenness among the lower classes and what he describes in this article as 'the social filth, indecency, and degradation in which scores upon scores of thousands are forced to wear out life'. At this particular moment, however, he may have been more than usually inflammable as regards crude equations of drunkenness with moral depravity. For it was just at this time that, in *Copperfield* VI–VII, he was, among other things, seeking delicately to prepare the reader for Mr Wickfield's gradual enslavement to the bottle (and thereby to Uriah Heep also) as a result not of any depravity but of over-anxious paternal love.[15]

Like the Drouet articles, 'Demoralisation and Total Abstinence' is a forerunner of the veritable stream of essays on various social questions that Dickens would soon be writing, either alone or in collaboration, for his own journal. This *Examiner* piece has some biographical interest also in that we catch in it a glimpse of the shrewd interviewer of Urania Cottage's inmates, both potential and actual, a person not to be imposed upon by woeful tales evidently shaped by what the interviewee thinks will go down well with her interlocutor. Beggs reported that criminals in prison frequently blamed their crimes on drink. This, Dickens writes, is simply because they know this is what their interrogators want to hear: 'If a notion arose that the wearing of brass buttons led to crime, and they were questioned to elucidate that point, we should have such answers as, "I was happy till I wore brass buttons," "Brass buttons did it," "Buttons is the cause of my being here," all down long columns of a grave return.' He was to revisit this topic of the fatuousness of encouraging prisoners to profess penitence and reformation in an article called 'Pet Prisoners' in the 27 April issue of *Household Words* and again in the final double number of *Copperfield* itself (ch. 61) when it provides a splendid opportunity for two of the villains of the story to take their curtain call, along with the odious Creakle, somewhat improbably transformed into a soft-headed magistrate. Meanwhile, in his own charitable work, Dickens was characteristically brisk and incisive in dealing with a small group of Urania Cottage women and their tales of unjust treatment by the staff. Isabella Gordon, the ringleader, quickly found herself summarily expelled, as did one of her followers, a 'most deceitful little Minx' called Sesina who, Dickens wrote, 'would corrupt a Nunnery in a fortnight'.[16]

Having eventually decided that David should begin his career as a trainee proctor (solicitor) working for the doctors of civil law in the antiquated courts of Doctors' Commons, Dickens could draw freely on his memories of 1829/30 in writing *Copperfield* VIII. 'I am wonderfully in harness', he told Forster on 17 November, 'and nothing galls or frets.' Aspects of both his past and present lives feed into the number. He introduces his 'fallen woman' character, Martha, 'the girl already lost', who is to become a sort of advertisement for the Urania Cottage project, and he locates young David in his own old Buckingham Street lodgings and revels in describing, as 'a piece of grotesque truth', his first dissipation. Again, drunkenness is featured but this time purely as comedy: 'His first time of getting tipsy. Description of it exactly', reads one of Dickens's notes for this number.[17]

Evidently, he felt safely enough 'in harness' to risk being distracted before he had finished his *Copperfield* stint by the strong feelings that, remembering Courvoisier's execution, would, he knew, be stirred up in him if he witnessed another public hanging. At midnight on 12 November he, Leech, Forster, and two other friends took possession of a hired rooftop overlooking the gallows that had been erected outside Horsemonger Lane Gaol. Leech wanted to get copy for his cartoon published in *Punch* on 24 November and scathingly entitled 'The Great Moral Lesson at Horsemonger Lane', and Dickens joined him after initially demurring. At 8 the next morning Frederick Manning and his elegant, fiery-tempered Swiss wife Maria were hanged for the brutal murder of Maria's lover, killed purely from mercenary motives. The behaviour of the huge crowd of onlookers was such that Dickens was impelled to write to *The Times* forcefully describing the immorality and degradation of the scene, and demanding an end to public executions. He followed this up with an even longer letter in the same vein (*Times*, 17 Nov.) and the result was that, even before he had finished his *Copperfield* number, he found himself wallowing in 'a roaring sea of correspondence'. He had not yet abandoned his view, so fully argued in the 1846 *Daily News* letters, that capital punishment should be abolished but was very urgent that the horrific and socially harmful spectacle of public executions should be stopped forthwith.[18]

'Two days' very hard work indeed' had enabled him to complete *Copperfield* VIII, he reported to Forster on 20 November, adding that he thought it 'a smashing number'. It is certainly a rich one, including not only the scenes already mentioned but also two great new comic characters, Miss Mowcher and Mrs Crupp. He was ready for a holiday and, after speaking at the first anniversary dinner of the Newsvendors Benevolent Institute, went with Catherine on a long-promised visit to the Watsons at Rockingham. He described his four-day stay there to Forster in one of his brilliant epistolary parodies, aping the sycophantic style of an impressionable American tourist whose account of visits to various English country-houses he had earlier mocked in *The Examiner*. America and the Americans would have been on his mind at this point just after he had written a preface for the Cheap Edition of *Martin Chuzzlewit* in which he had defended himself vigorously against accusations both of a general animosity towards America, and of much 'violent exaggeration' in his depiction of scenes like the meeting of the Watertoast Association (*MC*, ch. 21). In this preface he appears more concerned to argue for the novel's truthfulness to life rather than for literary merit, discussing it almost as if it were more a series of journalistic pieces than a work of fiction. Thus, he omits the original preface's comment about keeping 'a steadier eye upon the general purpose and design' but defends at some length the psychological truth of his portrait of Jonas Chuzzlewit, linking this defence with some fierce social polemic. He defends also the accuracy of his depiction of both Mrs Gamp and Betsey Prig as specimens respectively of hired sick-room attendant and hospital nurse.[19]

At Rockingham he enjoyed himself hugely, performing conjuring tricks, organising country dances, talking politics with his host, and play-acting with the Hon. Mary Boyle. Boyle was a relative of Mrs Watson's, diminutive, vivacious, and just two years Dickens's senior. He later called her 'the very best actress I ever saw, off the stage – and immeasurably better than a great many I have seen on it'. To the great delight of the assembled Watson household, she and Dickens performed a scene between Sir Peter and Lady Teazle from Sheridan's *School for Scandal* and another based on the wooing of Mrs Nickleby by her lunatic neighbour in ch. 41 of *Nickleby*. Dickens prolonged the latter joke into his subsequent friendship with his 'dearest Meery', as he sometimes called her, by making her the object of one of the longest lasting of his comic epistolary mock-flirtations.[20]

Meanwhile he was about to make David fall in love in earnest, for which purpose he began mining memories of his own desperately ardent wooing of Maria Beadnell between the ages of eighteen and twenty-one. This retrieval of past love-torments does not seem to have been a particularly painful process for him whatever he said about it later when, five years after *Copperfield* was published, he was to react with an intensity extraordinary, even by his standards, after suddenly receiving a letter from Maria following many years of no direct contact between them. In the course of the ensuing brief sequence of impassioned correspondence between them he told Maria about having destroyed his unfinished autobiography, 'just before Copperfield', because his unrequited love for her had proved just too agonising for him to recall and record. He does not, however, explain how it was that he could nevertheless bear to depict in David's love for Dora what he calls 'a faithful reflection of the passion I had for you'. True, he did say later to Forster that this fictionalising of the affair had caused him great distress: 'No one can imagine in the most distant degree what pain [it] gave me'. But this comment also belongs to early 1855, by which time Dickens's state of mind with regard both to his emotional life and his emotional history was very different from what it had been in 1849/50. His letter to Maria's father of 19 October 1849 commiserating with him on the death of his wife (she for whom he had always been 'Mr Dickin') is purely conventional in tone. There seems to be no trace in it, any more than there is in the notes for – or the actual writing of – the Dora part of *Copperfield*, of the acute distress of which he speaks in 1855, nothing equivalent to that poignant 'mem' for *Copperfield* IV, 'What I know so well'. 'Some beautiful comic love' is the phrase Dickens uses in February 1850, about the chapter describing David's engagement and the phrase well expresses the nature of all those passages in the Dora chapters that most obviously derive from Dickens's own early love for Maria. Chapter 33 (entitled 'Blissful') ends with David recalling his days of loving Dora as 'an unsubstantial, happy, foolish time' and saying, 'Of all the times of mine that Time has in his grip, there is none that in one retrospection I can smile at half so much, and think of half so tenderly', a passage Dickens highlights by copying it out (or maybe first jotting it down) in his notes for this number. Five years later, it seems, in a highly characteristic revision of his own authorial history, he comes to believe, quite genuinely, that he had written those scenes not tenderly smiling but in searing pain.[21]

Back in 1849, as the year drew to a close Dickens found himself caught up in two cases of the kind of embarrassment and/or annoyance to which writers are subject when they copy, or are believed to have copied, directly from life.

A former friend of his, Thomas Powell, had absconded to America after being detected in embezzling large sums of money from his City employers, John Chapman & Co. In New York Powell published *The Living Authors of England*, which included a patently malicious sketch of Dickens and his writings. In the course of this he asserted that Dickens had based Mr Dombey upon Thomas Chapman, senior partner in the firm. Since Dickens was on friendly terms with this Chapman, and indebted to him, moreover, for finding employment for Augustus, this assertion was a major embarrassment. Apprehensive that Powell's book might gain wide currency and perhaps even be published in London, he moved swiftly to discredit its author in the American press, helped by Lewis Gaylord Clark, editor of *The Knickerbocker*. He drew up and caused to be circulated a privately-printed dossier documenting Powell's rascality. The other difficulty over 'originals' might surely have been anticipated by a writer less strange than Dickens. Miss Mowcher, the exuberantly vulgar and 'volatile' dwarf hairdresser and manicurist who appears in *Copperfield* VIII was closely modelled on a dwarf chiropodist, Mrs Seymour Hill, who lived near Devonshire Terrace and may have attended Catherine. Mowcher is clearly intended to play a villainous role, helping Steerforth to seduce Em'ly, and Mrs Hill sent Dickens a piteously reproachful letter ('Should your book be dramatised and I not protected madness will be the result . . .') and followed it up with another from her solicitor. Dickens, somewhat disingenuously, offered the standard novelist's defence ('I never represent an individual but always a combination of individuals in one') but, professing himself distressed by her distress, promised 'to alter the whole design of the character' and to make Mowcher an exemplary character. This he managed to accomplish, though with some awkwardness – how could it have been otherwise, now that his novels were so carefully planned and structured? 'I am at present repairing Miss Mowcher's injury', he wrote to Burdett Coutts on 12 February 1850 when working on chapter 32, 'with a very bad grace, and in a very ill humour.' To Forster he described Mrs Hill's distress as 'serio-comic' but added, 'there is no doubt one is wrong in being tempted to such a use of power'. It was a temptation to which he was to yield again, however, and a good deal more spectacularly, in his next novel.[22]

On 27 December Bradbury and Evans began the distribution of handbills advertising 'A New Weekly Miscellany of General Literature' to be published in March, price twopence, 'conducted by Mr Charles Dickens' and 'designed for the Entertainment and Instruction of all classes of readers, and to help in the discussion of the most important social questions of the time.' During the next three months Dickens, while continuing to be for roughly half of each month 'the slave of the lamp called Copperfield', in the other half joyfully plunged into all the multifarious business connected with the new journal. He contacted prospective contributors, notably Gaskell, whom he wooed assiduously, and shared with them his ideas about what sort of magazine it should be, for example (to James White), 'We hope to do some solid good and we mean to be as cheery and pleasant as we can', or (to Mary Howitt), 'All social evils and all home affections and associations, I am particularly anxious to deal with, well.' He made it clear that his concept of the journal as being closely identified with him required that all contributions should be anonymous (though authors would be free to reprint under their own names). He tried out on Forster and the publishers many different titles for the new periodical, including *Charles Dickens. A weekly journal . . . Conducted by Himself*, before eventually settling for *Household Words*, 'a very pretty name', drawn from the famous Agincourt speech in Shakespeare's *Henry V*. The whole line, '*Familiar in their Mouths as HOUSEHOLD WORDS*', was to be printed above the title of every issue. Office premises were leased at 16 Wellington Street, just off the Strand, with additional rooms converted into a flat for Dickens's use, his 'Town Tent' as he came to call it. He recruited his former *Daily News* secretary, William Henry Wills, as his sub-editor, which proved an ideal appointment. Wills might not have 'the ghost of an idea in the imaginative way', as wrote Dickens to Austin on 21 March, but he was utterly reliable, a shrewd and hard-working manager whose punctuality, diligence and efficiency were up even to Dickens's ferociously high standards. For the next nineteen years he was to be 'the Inimitable's Indispensable', so to speak, in everything connected with the 'conducting' of both *Household Words* and its successor *All The Year Round*, as well as an admirably discreet confidential man of business in matters relating to Dickens's complicated private life in his later years.[23]

Copperfield X, the February number, climaxes with Em'ly's flight. In the next one Mr Peggotty sets out on his long search for her, and Dickens gives his readers another cliff-hanger ending with Betsey's abrupt announcement to David of her financial ruin. The next four numbers (April–July) focus primarily on David and Dora, with more skilful interweaving of fiction with autobiographical fact, notably David's heroic conquest of 'that savage stenographic mystery' and his becoming a crack parliamentary reporter and (rather more hazily dealt with) the beginnings of his career as a professional writer. Dickens's notes show clearly that he knows where he is going and just what effects he wants to achieve: '<u>Express that very delicately</u>' he warns himself regarding his depiction of Dora's inability to take on wifely responsibilities. He keeps an eye on continuity, reminds himself of the need to 'carry the thread of Agnes through it all', or 'To carry on the thread of Uriah, carefully, and not obtrusively'. David's growing uneasiness about his marriage is steadily directed towards the grand *éclaircissement* scene to take place at Dr Strong's in chapter 45 (No. XV, the July number) when David will be so heart-struck by Annie Strong's words, 'There can be no disparity in marriage like unsuitability of mind and purpose'. Dickens's only uncertainty seems to have been about whether or not Dora should meet with an early death, thus clearing the way for David's eventual union with Agnes. He was 'still undecided' about this on 7 May, he told Forster, adding 'but MUST decide today'. It is remarkable that he was, even at this comparatively late stage of writing such a book, still considering an ending so different from the happy one, tinged with pathos, that his public had long since come to expect of him. Had Dora not died, David, sadly aware of his terrible mistake, would have ended still married to her, perhaps fathering many children by her, while Agnes, still guarding the secret of the true nature of her love for him, would, presumably, have ended up as some sort of devoted sister/housekeeper to the couple. It has been suggested that Dickens might have rejected such an ending as being embarrassingly close, at least in outward appearance, to his own domestic situation in 1850 but I doubt if such a thought consciously occurred to him. He would, I feel sure, have been both astonished and indignant had Forster argued for killing off Dora on these grounds. There were areas of his personal life that this intensely autobiographical genius seems to have been able to fence off, temporarily or permanently, from the world of his imagination.[24]

Public life was another matter, however. In his Cheap Edition preface to *Chuzzlewit* Dickens somewhat sweepingly claimed, 'In all my writings I hope

29 Jacob's Island, Bermondsey

I have taken every possible opportunity of showing the want of sanitary improvements in the neglected dwellings of the poor.' He had not, in fact, touched on this topic in *Copperfield* but on 6 February, speaking at a meeting of the Metropolitan Sanitary Association (which campaigned against the preposterous exclusion of London from the remit of the new General Board of Health), he made a reference to one of his most celebrated descriptions of an insanitary district, the Jacob's Island chapter of *Oliver Twist*. He was about to write a preface for the Cheap Edition of this novel and must have been delighted when his old butt, Sir Peter Laurie, responding to newspaper reports of his speech, provided him with some choice copy. Speaking at a meeting of the Marylebone Vestry, Laurie triumphantly announced that there was, in fact, no such place as Jacob's Island. 'It only existed', he said, 'in a work of fiction, written by Mr Charles Dickens ten years ago [*roars of laughter*]'. The new *Oliver* preface gave Dickens a golden opportunity to have the last laugh. He copied into it the report of Laurie's speech, and ironically agreed that anything described in fiction of course promptly ceased to exist in the real world ('when Smollett took Roderick Random to Bath, that city instantly sank into the earth . . .'). This led to the neat conclusion that Laurie himself must be a fiction, 'having been himself described in a book (as I understand he was, one Christmas time, for his conduct on the seat of justice)'. To give the widest possible publicity to this devastating counter-attack, as well as to advertise the Cheap Edition, Dickens caused a two-page insert carrying the new *Oliver* preface to be included in all copies of *Copperfield* XII, immediately after the text of the instalment and preceding the end adverts.[25]

Simultaneously with this number of *Copperfield* there appeared, on 30 March, the first number of *Household Words*. Dickens's new journal entered a market dominated at the respectable end by *Chambers's Edinburgh Journal*, founded in 1832, and at the disreputable end by *Reynolds' Miscellany*, founded in 1846. *Chambers's*, selling at one penny and a half, was primarily factual and instructive, though it did occasionally offer suitably bland or improving fiction reprinted from other sources. It seems to have had a steady circulation of between 60,000 and 70,000. *Reynolds's*, selling at one penny, specialised in a heady mixture of serialised melodramatic fiction, sometimes verging on the pornographic, like its opening serial *Wagner the Werewolf*, and the republican, pro-Chartist politics of its editor, G.W.M. Reynolds. Reliable circulation figures for *Reynolds's* are hard to come by but in his *The English Common Reader* Richard D. Altick quotes one for 1855 of two hundred thousand. Both *Chambers's* and *Reynolds's* were squarely aimed at a working-class or lower-middle-class readership. With *Household Words* Dickens, relying on the prestige of his name as guaranteeing high literary quality, impeccable respectability, and strong commitment to the values of hearth and home, was able to extend the weekly-magazine-buying audience upwards into the middle and even upper-middle classes. An important factor here was his decision to feature new, high-quality fiction both in serialised form and as separate short stories. His inaugural offering was Gaskell's *Lizzie Leigh* which ran through the first four issues of the new journal. As it happened, Gaskell's theme, the loving redemption of a fallen woman by a near relation, in this case her mother, chimed well with the story of Em'ly as he was developing it in the pages of *Copperfield*.[26]

Household Words was 25 per cent dearer than *Chambers's*. For their two pennies Dickens's readers got twenty-four, unillustrated, double-columned pages (so as to cover all marketing bases, it was also available monthly in paper-bound fascicules as well as bound in half-yearly volumes, suitable for shelving in gentlemen's libraries, just like the regular monthlies). Dickens's contract, signed on 28 March, guaranteed him complete editorial freedom together with a half-share of all profits, the other half being divided between the publishers on the one hand, and Forster and Wills on the other. Over and above this, Dickens was to receive £500 a year for his editorial work with additional payments for all articles contributed by him, whether these were solely or jointly authored. Over the next nine years the magazine, with only one worrying dip in sales (quickly counteracted by Dickens's serialisation of *Hard Times* in its pages), amply fulfilled his hopes of success. It seems to have had a fairly steady circulation of around forty thousand copies, and, together with his annual profits from the sales of the Cheap Edition, greatly helped to cushion his finances against the fluctuations in income that inevitably resulted from his novel-writing.[27]

For the first number he wrote a very upbeat 'Preliminary Word', in which we, reading with the 20/20 vision of hindsight, can clearly discern foreshadow-ings of the next two novels he was to write after *Copperfield*. *Household Words*, Dickens proclaims, will seek to nourish its readers' imaginations by showing them 'that in all familiar things . . . there is Romance enough, if we will find it out', a sentiment to be echoed in the famous last sentence of his preface to *Bleak House*: 'In Bleak House, I have purposely dwelt upon the romantic side of familiar things.' He states that a leading aspect of the new journal's mission will be the tender cherishing of 'that light of Fancy which is inherent in the human breast', a light which if neglected may 'sink into a sullen glare' but which cannot be extinguished – 'or woe betide that day!' Four years later, under the necessity of having quickly to invent a story for serialisation in the journal, he embarked upon *Hard Times* which powerfully dramatises this very concept. And, just as he will do in that novel, so here in this 'Preliminary Word', he makes lavish use of fairy-tale and *Arabian Nights* imagery as an integral part of his campaign against the 'iron binding of the mind to grim realities'.

Towards the end of his 'Preliminary Word' Dickens shares with his readers his vision of himself as a widely and uniquely loved writer, one 'admitted into many homes with affection and confidence . . . regarded as a friend by children and old people . . . thought of in affliction and in happiness . . . [peopling] the sick room with airy shapes "that give delight and hurt not" . . . associated with the harmless laughter and the gentle tears of many hearths.' Such a position carries 'great responsibility' as well as bringing a 'vast reward'. Dickens defines this reward in terms of power and we might recall here his confessing to a misuse of power in the Miss Mowcher business. Here now, in his brief prologue, Dickens describes the writer in his 'hours of solitary labour' imagining those who will read the result of this labour as 'a multitude moved by one sympathy'. This, one might say, represents Dickens's concept of his ultimate 'conductorial', or even mesmeric, achievement. And he gently reminds his readers, as if they needed reminding, that 'the hand that writes these faltering lines ["faltering", presumably, because the writer is so possessed by the grandeur of his vision]', has been 'happily associated with *some* Household Words before to-day'. Thus, he is already well aware of the great privileges and responsibilities, and of the tremendous rewards, accruing to a writer so uniquely integrated as he is into his readers' intimate domestic life. Potential purchasers of the magazine may have complete faith, therefore, that he will 'enter in an earnest spirit upon this new task'.[28]

Thus does Dickens, half-way through the writing of *Copperfield*, embark 'cheerily' (this adverb is the last of his 'Preliminary Words') upon another major literary enterprise, this time an open-ended one. For the rest of his life he was to spend a high proportion of his working hours 'conducting' and writing for *Household Words* and its successor *All The Year Round*. His biographers have marvelled ever since at the strength and extent of this commitment to his journals, the first of which he described to Leigh Hunt on 31 January 1855 as 'that great humming-top . . . which is always going round with the weeks and murmuring "Attend to me!" '. He was sole or joint author of over one hundred and fifty articles published in *Household Words* between 30 March 1850 and 1 January 1859, including some of the finest essays he ever wrote. He also serialised in its pages his *Child's History of England* and *Hard Times* as well as, jointly with Wilkie Collins, *The Lazy Tour of Two Idle Apprentices*. From 1851 onwards also he originated and 'conducted' a special extra Christmas Number in which he collaborated with a number of other established writers invited to join him in this enterprise. He read shoals of manuscripts and corresponded, often in considerable detail, with actual or would-be contributors about their offerings – also, of course, with Wills constantly, and with Bradbury and Evans. Once a number had been set up in type he would work meticulously over the proofs, often spending hours on the job and making so many alterations in some articles that the resulting proof-sheets would often look, as he once said, like 'an inky fishing net'. From the very beginning, too, he kept a close eye on the composition and balance of each number to ensure that it did not become too heavy. A good example of all this unremitting, week-in-week-out attention to detail is a letter to Wills of 5 August 1853, commenting on the proofs of the issue due to appear a fortnight later. The whole number, Dickens declares, is as heavy as 'stewed lead' and needs 'lightening'. He alters the title of one article, and supplies it with a lively introductory paragraph while in another he singles out 'a forlorn attempt at humour' that 'cannot be too ferociously decapitated', as well as a clumsy sentence needing to be struck out 'with a pen of iron'. In yet another piece, contributed by Leigh Hunt, a particular paragraph must be deleted, in still another Wills must pay attention to 'the slang talk' ('don't let "Ya" stand for "You" '), and so on. A famous postscript instructs Wills with regard to the whole number: 'Brighten it, brighten it, brighten it!'[29]

Dickens was proud of his first number which contained, besides the first instalment of Gaskell's *Lizzie Leigh*, poems by Leigh Hunt and the Irish poet William Allingham, the first of two brilliant articles by Dickens himself on popular theatre, showing the 'light of Fancy' being 'cherished' in a very down-market setting. It also featured another lively piece by him and Wills on the workings of the Post Office (the first of a series of so-called 'process' articles, describing the working of some organisation or the manufacture of some article) which became a regular feature of the journal, a historical anecdote by George Hogarth, and an article about the advantages for poor families of emigration to Australia under Caroline Chisholm's Family Colonisation Loan Society. This last article was written by Dickens as a frame for presenting 'a bundle of emigrants' letters'. From Brighton, where he had retreated for a fortnight 'to pursue Copperfield in peace', Dickens wrote to Bradbury on 14 March, 'I really think it is an extraordinary production; and if the Public be not satisfied, I don't know what they would have. *I* never read such a Number of anything else'. And then he adds one of those exulting appreciations of his own 'inimitability' that he delighted in:

> And here's a man for you! – They sent me today the proposed No. 2, in a list of articles. The amazing undersigned feels a little uncomfortable at a want of Household tenderness in it. So he puts away Copperfield, at which he has been working like a Steam Engine – writes (he thinks) exactly the kind of thing to supply the deficiency – and sends it, by this post, to Forster!
> What an amazing man!

This piece, so quickly written and here referred to in such jauntily self-congratulatory terms, was a little spiritual fantasy, very much in Dickens's death-of-little-Paul-Dombey vein, about childhood love between a brother and a sister, the sister's early death and her brother's eventual joyful reunion with her among the angels after death. Called 'A Child's Dream of a Star', it was given pride of place in the second number. Dickens had been primed to write it by gazing at the stars during a nocturnal rail journey down to Brighton

(a railway carriage was, he told Forster, 'always a wonderfully suggestive place'
to him when alone), which had reminded him of himself and Fanny gazing up
at the stars as children. The piece is worth noting as the first example in
Dickens's authorial history of a kind of essay-writing in which he was to
achieve some of his finest non-fictional work through drawing directly on the
events and experiences of his early life, the way for this having been paved by
his turn to autobiography in the writing of *Dombey* and *Copperfield*.[30]

'A Child's Dream' certainly fulfils its purpose of providing a counterbalance
of domestic sentiment to Gaskell's harrowing tale of 'fallen' Lizzie Leigh and all
the informative articles on coal mining and Australian ploughmen that,
together with a polemical one contrasting heathen and Christian burial
customs, and 'Perfect Felicity', another piece by Dickens himself, make up the
rest of the number. 'Perfect Felicity' is an exercise in what we might call
'scatter-gun' satire. It is supposedly uttered by a raven in one of the so-called
'Happy Families', little menageries of small animals and birds exhibited in the
streets of London, showing natural enemies like a cat and a mouse peaceably
co-existing in the same cage. It was no doubt memories of the keen delight
he had taken in the personalities of his own pet ravens that caused Dickens
to present his topical satirical observations in this novel and comic fashion,
which he found so congenial that three more 'Raven' pieces followed in
subsequent issues. He had not had scope to practise this kind of writing, so
satisfying to him in its combination of fancy and social purpose, since the
days of *Bentley's* and the writing of such satirical *jeux d'esprit* as 'The
Pantomime of Life'. In 'Perfect Felicity' and its successors he directs his
fire against some familiar Dickensian targets such as opponents of sanitary
reform (the raven gets in a good peck at the hapless Laurie), the workhouses,
lack of education for poor children, the Court Circular, funeral ceremonies,
and so on. The coming into existence of *Household Words* while *Copperfield*
was still appearing in monthly numbers also gave him the means of having
two shots at the same target. Thus, in chapter 33 of *Copperfield* XI, the March
number, he has David expose the Prerogative Office, where all wills made
in the diocese of Canterbury had to be deposited, as a thoroughly corrupt
institution and 'a pernicious absurdity'. The Office is again in his line of fire in
the 28 September issue of *Household Words*, in an article written jointly with
Wills, the first of a series of four called 'The Doom of English Wills'. He
reminds his readers about the passage in *Copperfield*: 'The public have lately
heard some trifling facts relative to Doctors' Commons, through the medium
of a young gentleman who was articled, by his aunt, to a proctor there . . .'.
Another *Household Words* article, 'Pet Prisoners' (27 April), fiercely attacks the
new system of solitary confinement being pioneered in the purpose-built
Pentonville Prison, and Dickens returns to the charge in the final double
number of *Copperfield* in which David is shown, in chapter 61, 'two interesting

penitents', Uriah Heep and Littimer, who are clearly happily exploiting the misconceived system for their own ends.[31]

During the next three months, April, May and June, as work on *Copperfield* proceeded smoothly, Dickens had the capacity (so to speak) to write, or collaborate in the writing of, no fewer than thirteen articles for *Household Words*, several of them quite substantial. In one, the amusing but undoubtedly also deeply-felt essay, 'The Begging-Letter Writer' (18 May), Dickens treats his readers to a behind-the-scenes glimpse of a punitive aspect of his life as a writer famous for his compassion towards the poor, and for his loyalty towards his 'order', that is, his fellow-writers: 'For fourteen years, my house has been made as regular a Receiving House for such communications [begging letters] as any one of the great branch Post-Offices is for general correspondence' (this is a topic he will revert to in both *Bleak House* and *Our Mutual Friend*). In another he, the great scourge of the workhouse system, reports on a visit to one such institution ('A Walk in a Workhouse', 25 May 1850). It is a moving account of monotony and deprivation that culminates in the image, perhaps deliberately intended to recall the most famous scene in *Oliver*, of the 'morsel of burnt child' with something in his face that seems to plead 'in behalf of the helpless and the aged poor, for a little more liberty – and a little more bread'. Both the begging-letter writers and the depressing 'groves' of old men he saw in the workhouse were to reappear later in his fiction. Very different in tone from these articles is 'Old Lamps for New Ones' (15 June 1850), a furious onslaught on the Pre-Raphaelite Brotherhood, sparked off partly by Dickens's intense revulsion at what he seems to have regarded as the virtually blasphemous ultra-realism of Millais's 'Christ in the House of His Parents', on exhibition in the Royal Academy's Summer Show.[32]

Already by 12 April Dickens felt able to tell Burdett Coutts that he was confident that *Household Words* would become 'a *good property*'. He admitted, however, that 'the labor in conjunction with Copperfield, is something rather ponderous'. He and Wills had begun to assemble a group of regular contributors such as Richard Hengist Horne, whom we have already met, and a young graduate of King's College, London, called Henry Morley, whom Forster had employed as a leader-writer on *The Examiner*. Morley soon proved his ability to supply good articles in the style Dickens required and covering a very wide range of topics. Sometimes he wrote in collaboration with Dickens himself. After a year he was taken on as a staffer with a salary of five guineas a week and remained one of the journal's most prolific contributors until its demise. A more imposing recruit was Harriet Martineau, distinguished author of *Illustrations of Political Economy, Society in America* and many other works, whose services Dickens had been eager to acquire. Martineau, who held strong opinions and was later described to Wills by Dickens (14 Oct. 1854) as 'grimly bent upon the enlightenment of mankind', proved in the event to be a troublesome colleague. In 1854 she withdrew from the journal altogether following a disagreement with Dickens over factory legislation but for the present he was glad to have her on board. He was delighted also to secure the co-operation of the great scientist Michael Faraday in publishing two articles in the journal, 'The Chemistry of a Candle' and 'The Mysteries of a Tea-kettle' (3 Aug. and 16 Nov.), based upon Faraday's hugely popular 'Friday Evening Discourses' to lay audiences at the Royal Institution.

At the end of April Dickens and Bradbury and Evans launched a monthly supplement to *Household Words* called *The Household Narrative of Current Events*, initially under Forster's direction with George Hogarth acting as compiler-in-chief. It continued for five years and was then stopped for some unknown reason, presumably because it proved uneconomic. It was the same length and price as a weekly issue of the journal and had to be bought separately. According to Dickens's brief announcement in *Household Words* (13 April) it aimed to be 'a comprehensive Abstract or History of all the occurrences of that month, native and foreign' forming 'a complete Chronicle of all that year's events . . . systematically arranged for easy reference' and would be cumulated in annual volumes. It would share the journal's great objective – here expressed (somewhat cloudily) as the enablement of 'those who accept us for their friend, to bear the world's rough-cast events to the anvil of coura- geous duty and there beat them into shape'. For modern readers who dip into the *Narrative's* columns the interest is rather to see how he bore some of the 'rough-cast events' he found in this supplement to the anvil of his novelist's imagination and there, months or even years later, 'beat them into shape'. For example, in the January 'Narrative of Law and Crime' (published after 1 May as the beginning of a catch-up exercise so that subscribers could have a complete volume for 1850) we find George Ruby, the real-life original of Jo the crossing- sweeper, who first appears in *Bleak House* IV (June 1852), as well as Martha Joachim, the wealthy recluse always dressed in white, whom Dickens remem- bered a decade later, along with the White Woman of Berners Street (see above, p. 23), when he came to create Miss Havisham in *Great Expectations*.[33]

By 22 June, with *Copperfield* XV (chapters 44–46) completed, *Household Words* well launched, and a defiantly unapologetic preface written for the Cheap Edition *American Notes*, Dickens, feeling he had 'again broken his head with hard labour', ran off for nine days to a blazingly hot Paris, accompanied by Maclise. He 'looked in at the Morgue' where, he reported to Catherine, he saw 'a body horribly mutilated with a musket ball in the head, and afterwards drowned' (it made Maclise so sick he had to sit outside on a doorstep for ten minutes to recover). In less macabre fashion, he enjoyed socialising with his actor-friend François Régnier. His new publishing enterprise was of course always very much in his mind. Perhaps as a result of some art-gallery visit, or perhaps because he was still brooding about Millais, he was moved to compose

Mr. Peggotty's dream comes true.

30 'Mr Peggotty's dream comes true' (*David Copperfield* No. XV1) by H. K. Browne ('Phiz')

a piece called 'The Ghost of Art' (published 20 July), a splendidly comic recapit-ulation of a complaint he had made earlier, in *Pictures from Italy*, about the use of stereotypical models by modern artists. Composing it, he wrote to Catherine on 28 June, had been 'all things considered . . . pretty sharp work'.[34]

Back in London by 1 July, he had the last four numbers of *Copperfield* ahead of him. He was full of confidence in '*your* book', he told Mrs Watson on 3 July (*Copperfield* was to be dedicated to her and her husband). Everyone was 'cheering David on' and he himself liked the book very much, 'thoroughly believed it all', and went to work on it every month with 'an energy of the fieriest description'. To Bulwer Lytton he wrote on 26 July that he was 'keeping his mind very steadily upon it' and expressed the hope that there would be found in it 'some heretofore deficient qualities' in his writing. Presumably, it was structural qualities that he was primarily referring to – a few days earlier he had told James White that he had 'carefully planned out the story, for some time past, to the end', and was 'making out his purposes with great care'. *Copperfield* XV1, the August number (chs 47–50), begins preparing the reader for Dora's death, paves the way for Micawber's exposure of Heep, and climaxes with the great 'sensation' scene of Mr Peggotty's reunion with Em'ly. Dickens's 'careful planning' is evidenced by his having written down his basic 'mems' for Nos XVI–XX all at the same time, presumably early in July, with subsequent additions and changes being made later as he wrote each monthly part in the usual way.[35]

The grand climactic chapter of the whole novel (ch. 55, 'Tempest') was to be set in Yarmouth, and Dickens was eagerly looking forward to finishing the book to the sound of the 'hoarse music' of the sea, 'that old image of Eternity that I love so much'. At Broadstairs he had secured, he told Horne on 6 July, 'a good bold house on the top of a cliff, with the sea Winds blowing through it, and the gulls occasionally falling down the chimneys by mistake', and he planned to go there as soon in August as Catherine should have given birth to her ninth child, for, as Dickens wrote merrily on 14 August to Timothy Yeats Brown, a friend from Genoese days, his household was 'in an Anti-Malthusian state'. Meanwhile, domestic concerns and Urania Cottage notwithstanding, he made good progress with *Copperfield* XVII in which there was a great deal to be done. The way had to be paved for Mr Peggotty and Em'ly to emigrate to Australia (which would also provide a neat comic exit for Mrs Gummidge), he had to 'Smash Uriah Heep by means of Mr Micawber' (as he puts it in his notes), to settle the fate of the irrepressible Micawbers by having them join the emigration party, and, finally, to describe the death of Dora. This last he does in another movingly elegiac 'Retrospect' chapter. 'I hope I shall have a splendid number', he wrote to Forster, 'I feel the story to its minutest point'. As was usual with him, the actual business of writing involved a continuous process of selection and rejection: 'Am eschewing all sorts of things that present themselves to my fancy – coming in such crowds!'[36]

On 16 August Catherine bore a third daughter, who was named Dora Annie. Why did Dickens choose to call the new baby after a much-cherished fictional character he was about to kill? Surely the answer lay, as Forster seems to imply, in his desire to give, through the life of his own child, some sort of posthumous existence to David's Dora who, born of such tender memories of his own youth, had become a favourite of his. The fictional Dora survived the arrival of the real-life one by only a week or so. On 21 August Dickens wrote from Broadstairs to Catherine, still in London and not yet sufficiently recovered to join the rest of the family, 'Even now, I am uncertain of my movements, for, after another splitting day, I still have Dora to kill – I mean the Copperfield Dora – and cannot make certain how long it will take to do' (he had been uncertain as to whether Dora should die in this number or in the final double one but had decided that it had to be in this). His letters to Catherine during this period, it is worth noting, are not only comradely (he knows that she will understand his jokes) but also very affectionate, giving her much news of the children and telling her, 'Without you we shall be quite incomplete and a great blank everywhere.' 'I think of you all day', he tells her, 'God bless you, my darling.'[37]

During these last months of *Copperfield*, July–October 1850, Dickens was also revisiting his earliest published volumes. *Sketches by Boz* was contemporaneously appearing as the last title in the Cheap Edition in weekly fascicules and monthly parts, and he was extensively revising the text. His primary concern, apparently, was to soften down what might now seem crude and unworthy of the author of *Copperfield* in the language of his first book, and to update some of the social comment. Outside his study, he continued to work hard for Urania Cottage. While 'clear[ing] the way for Emigration' in *Copperfield* XVII, as he instructs himself to do in his working notes, he energetically prosecuted his search for real-life Em'lys and Marthas who might be suitable cases for Urania Cottage treatment. He investigated the Ragged Schools as a potential source of supply and reported fully to Burdett Coutts on his (not very optimistic) findings. On top of all this, he had, now and always, to ensure the continued spinning of that 'great humming-top' *Household Words*. This included sifting through the heaps of manuscripts continually submitted for publication. As he sifted he marvelled at the number of people who, though devoid of literary talent, were nevertheless eager to break into print: 'People don't plunge into churches and play the organs without knowing the notes or having a ghost of an ear. Yet fifty people a day will rush into manuscript for these leaves only, who have no earthly qualification but the actual physical art of writing.' 'Our Voluntary Correspondent', as he generically termed such would-be contributors, were clearly far removed from the model contemporary author as depicted by Dickens in David Copperfield with his emphasis on 'patient and continuous energy' and 'thorough-going . . . earnestness' as the very bases of his achievement as a writer.[38]

As for his own journalistic writings during these last *Copperfield* months, Dickens had by him a good stock of vivid real-life stories of crime and detection garnered at his two brandy-and-cigar soirées held at the *Household Words* office, either just before or soon after his Paris trip, for the benefit of a group of officers from the recently-established Detective Branch of the Metropolitan Police. He drew on their yarns for a series of three substantial articles published between 27 July and 14 September (following up an initial one by Wills on the detective police). These articles show Dickens experimenting with a comparatively new genre of journalism, the interview, which he 'would work up . . . with lively and comic touches all his own'. The admiring, almost hero-worshipping tone he adopts towards the police in these pieces, as also in his later fiction, has been much commented on. So has his particular admiration for Inspector Charles Field of the Detective Branch, who was to escort Dickens and his friends on a number of nocturnal tours of the so-called 'rookeries' (slum areas and criminal neighbourhoods) of London, and on whom he was in certain respects to model Inspector Bucket with his 'confidential forefinger' in *Bleak House*.[39]

Besides these police articles, Dickens was sole author of four more *Household Words* pieces published between the end of August and the end of October and he collaborated in the writing of three others. His increasing exasperation with the reactionary forces, antiquated institutions and vested interests still so strong in English public life not only found a vent in the last two 'Doom of English Wills' articles (28 Sept. and 5 Oct.), written jointly with Wills, but also in 'A Poor Man's Tale of a Patent' (19 Oct.) which looks forward to the Circumlocution Office tribulations of the working-class inventor Daniel Doyce in *Little Dorrit*, and 'Lively Turtle' (26 Oct.), a splendidly grotesque satire on the City Corporation, provoked by its entrenched opposition to the removal of Smithfield Market from its original site in the City. Dickens first began thinking about this last article back in July and evidently some of it was written by 17 September when he told Wills he would have to defer finishing it because of the pressures of writing *Copperfield* XVIII. The progressive, reforming, anti-Establishment spirit that breathes through all these articles also appears, in a milder and more humorous form, in the last double number of *Copperfield*. In chapter 59 David, returning to London from his Swiss tour, is snubbed by the ancient chief waiter of the Gray's Inn Coffee House and finds himself oppressed by the place's 'prescriptive, stiff-necked, long-established, solemn, elderly air'.

Copperfield XVIII (chs 54–57) contains the great 'Tempest' chapter which, David tells us, describes an event 'so bound by an infinite variety of ties to all that has preceded it' that he has seen it 'growing larger and larger' as he advanced in his narrative, 'like a great tower in a plain, and throwing its forecast shadow even on the incidents of my childish days'. By means of this extraordinary image Dickens seems to be deliberately calling his readers' attention to the way in which he has 'woven and blended' his novel together so carefully that every part contributes to the whole. No longer is his work open to criticism on grounds of formlessness and lack of structure. As to the chapter itself, he reports himself to Forster on 15 September as having worked on it 'eight hours at a stretch yesterday, and six hours and a half today', adding that it 'has completely knocked me over – utterly defeated me!' Two days later he described himself to Wills as being 'in that tremendous paroxysm of Copperfield – having my most powerful effect in all the Story, on the Anvil', his smithy image well conveying the sheer physical strenuousness of the work. When the number was finished, he wrote to Lavinia Watson on 24 September, 'There are some things in the next Copperfield that I think better than any that have gone before.' He was, of course, alluding to his magnificent description of the great storm in which both Ham and Steerforth perish but also to the unforgettably bleak scene of David's last visit to Steerforth's stricken home and to the beautifully quiet and poignant ending of the number with David gazing his last upon the emigrant ship as it sails away in 'the calm, radiant sunset'.

After finishing this number Dickens travelled up to London for a meeting at the *Household Words* office on 20 September to finalise the arrangement of contents of the 5 October issue. As he had not been able to complete the 'Lively Turtle' piece in time, it was decided to make the second piece on 'the Doom of English Wills' the lead article, and Dickens 'then and there', as he had said he would, wrote a very spirited first half for the piece, amounting to just over four columns of the printed issue. During the next two and a half weeks he finished the 'Turtle' article, wrote 'The Poor Man's Tale of a Patent', read the proofs of *Copperfield* XVIII and revised the latest section of the Cheap *Sketches*. And all the while he was conducting an extensive correspondence with Mary Boyle and others about the elaborate private theatricals he was organising to take place at Rockingham and Knebworth after he had finished *Copperfield* (he knew from past experience that he would absolutely need the bustle and strong excitement of this activity to counteract the feelings that would beset him when the book was finished). 'This is quite a Managerial letter', he apologised in a postscript to Boyle on 20 September, 'but I write with all manner of appointments and business-discussions going on about me – having my pen on the paper, and my eye on "Household Words" – my head on Copperfield – and my ear nowhere particularly.'

On 7 October he told Burdett Coutts that he was 'looking very hard at a blank quire of paper' and trying to persuade himself that he was going to begin the final double number of *Copperfield* 'in earnest'. Two weeks later he was, he told Forster, 'within three pages of the shore' and 'strangely divided, as usual in such cases, between sorrow and joy'. What was *not* usual was what resulted from his subtle and complex intertwining of David's story with the only partially written story of his own life with its secret griefs and loves. From this stemmed a haunting sense that in finishing his novel he was sending some part of himself 'into the Shadowy World'. Even Forster, with all his knowledge of his friend's childhood shames and sorrows, would be astonished, says Dickens, if he were to tell him only 'half of what *Copperfield* makes me feel tonight'.[40]

His working notes for this final double number begin with the words, 'After Lapse – dreamily described – in Italy &c / David to come back from abroad / All his love for Agnes and all her love for him to be worked out'. But before Dickens could begin to 'work out' David's 'mature' and responsible (but inevitably less romantic) love for his 'good angel' time had to elapse for him to recover from the deaths of those beautiful, fallible people whom he had so loved, Steerforth and Dora. The recovery could not be complete because part of him would always love the memory of them (as well as that of the pretty, loving, weak young mother so early lost to him) in a way that he could not love Agnes. It has been suggested, in one of the best essays ever written about this novel, that a good epigraph for it might be some lines from Wordsworth's 'Immortality Ode', 'Though nothing can bring back the hour / Of splendour in the grass, of glory in the flower; / We will grieve not, rather find / Strength in what remains behind . . .'. The description in this last number of David's experience of spiritual healing among the mountains of Switzerland has a definite Wordsworthian flavour to it, and it is noteworthy that Dickens had bought a copy of *The Prelude*, recently published for the first time, shortly before he wrote this last *Copperfield*.[41]

By 23 October, on the eve of the family's return to Devonshire Terrace, Dickens was able to send the concluding chapter, 'A Last Retrospect' ('Close with Agnes' reads the last of his chapter-notes) to the printers, together with the preface. All the queries and uncertainties in his working notes had been answered and resolved (not forgetting a last mention of Miss Mowcher as having been the agent of Littimer's capture, thereby showing that she is most definitely on the side of the angels). The *Copperfield* preface is not much longer than the *Dombey* one but is still more intimate in tone, and more tantalising. He hints strongly at the novel's autobiographical strain in writing of his concern not to '[weary] the reader whom I love, with personal confidences, and private emotions'. And he repeats the image he used in his letter to Forster, taking care to generalise it, when he comments on 'how an Author feels as if he were dismissing some portion of himself into the shadowy world, when a crowd of the creatures of his brain are going from him for ever'. Then, as if feeling a need to counteract the sense of somewhat wistful melancholy he has evoked, he ends the preface with 'a hopeful glance' towards his next novel.

It was a difficult preface to write because of the unusual intensity of his emotions on finishing this particular book. He later told the Duke of Devonshire that finishing it had made him 'really unhappy'. Significantly, he wrote to Burdett Coutts on 23 October that he had 'an idea of wandering somewhere for a day or two – to Rochester, I think, where I was a small boy – to get all this fortnight's work out of my head'. It is almost as though, having so wonderfully recreated the idyll of his early childhood as the point of departure for this novel, now that he has finished it, he needs to revisit the real-life setting of that time to get all the intervening years 'out of his head'.[42]

A week or so later he had another preface to write, this time for the Cheap Edition of *Sketches by Boz*, the final weekly fascicule of which was published on 16 November, completing the whole Edition. Dickens had requested that *Sketches* should come last in the series as he feared it might make 'a dangerous break in the continuity of the Sale, and perhaps damage what followed'. Aware that in *Dombey*, and now still more in *Copperfield*, he had scaled new heights in his art and had at last moved on definitively from the work of Boz, Dickens writes of *Sketches* as though his first book was now a source of some embarrassment to him. He had, moreover, just finished depicting in David Copperfield a very un-Bozzian figure, the very model of the kind of novelist held highest in contemporary esteem. He was, Dickens pleads (but it is something of a boast also, of course) 'a very young man' when he first wrote the Boz sketches. They were his 'first attempts at authorship', apart from 'certain tragedies achieved at the mature age of eight or ten', and he now perceives that they are often 'extremely crude and ill-considered' and bear 'obvious marks of haste and inexperience', especially in the 'Tales' (the earliest written items). He concludes:

> But as this collection is not originated now, and was very leniently and favourably received when it was first made, I have not felt it right either to remodel or expunge, beyond a few words and phrases here and there.

Dickens here contrives to remind the reader of his remarkably successful début as a writer, pre-dating *Pickwick*, whilst at the same time deliberately misrepresenting the extent to which he had been so meticulously revising and polishing *Sketches by Boz* over the years, not least during the previous five or six months. What is being here presented to the reader as very much apprentice work has, in fact, been subject to at least as careful a revision as any of the articles accepted for *Household Words*. This preface remained Dickens's last word on his earliest publications (he reprinted it unaltered in 1868 as the preface to the last lifetime edition of *Sketches*), leading Forster to protest that Dickens 'decidedly underrated' these specimens of 'the first sprightly runnings of his genius'.[43]

14 November saw Dickens established with his Amateurs at Knebworth, Bulwer Lytton's Gothic mansion, preparing to stage a revival of their production of *Every Man in His Humour* for the delectation of its owner (now 'My dear Bulwer Lytton' to Dickens, having previously been 'My dear Sir Edward') and his county neighbours. Plans to perform first at Rockingham and then at Knebworth had had to be reversed owing to some private trouble that apparently befell the Watsons. Far from wandering off to Rochester as he had thought of doing, Dickens had spent a characteristically bustling three weeks at Devonshire Terrace. He organised and superintended rehearsals (at one of which Catherine, who was to have acted for the first time since performing 'devilish well' in Montreal, unfortunately sprained her ankle and had to withdraw from the cast), attended to the costumes, worried about lighting arrangements, investigated a huge semi-mechanical keyboard instrument called a 'Choremusicon' for possible use in the production, dealt with an outbreak of petty theft at Urania Cottage, resolved some drainage problem that was troubling that establishment, and of course attended constantly, and with all his accustomed assiduousness, to *Household Words*. The next piece solely from his pen to appear in the journal was the leading article for the 23 November issue, 'A Crisis in the Affairs of Mr John Bull, as Related by

Mrs Bull to the Children', which was Dickens's ferociously partisan anti-Papal contribution to the public hysteria stirred up by the so-called 'Papal Aggression', that is, the Pope's restoration of the Catholic hierarchy in England.[44]

As he set out for Knebworth that November morning Dickens was no doubt anticipating that the theatricals to be staged there would induce in him the same exhilaration and delight that such activity had always done since the far-off days of *Clari* and *O'Thello*. Indeed, this delight had already, as his letters clearly show, been diffusing itself through all the multifarious preparations into which he had plunged himself, providing him with the perfect antidote to the 'postnatal depression', so to speak, that followed his conclusion of *Copperfield*. In the event, however, the Amateur Company's three triumphal performances of Jonson's comedy in the hall of Bulwer Lytton's 'Gothick' mansion were to give Dickens something beyond the customary thrills of greasepaint, gas lamps, assumed identities and enraptured audiences. They would point him towards attempting the fulfilment of one of his greatest ambitions as a professional author, the striking of a 'sledgehammer blow' (to borrow a favourite phrase of his) on behalf of 'the Dignity of Literature'.

CHAPTER 14

The year of the Guild

1850–1851

I do devoutly believe that this plan, carried, will entirely change the status of the Literary Man in England, and make a revolution in his position which no Government, no Power on earth but his own, could ever effect. . . . I have a strong conviction that we hold in our hands the peace and honor of men of letters for centuries to come, and that you are destined to be their best and most enduring benefactor.

Dickens to Bulwer Lytton, 5 January 1851

THE KNEBWORTH performances of *Every Man in His Humour* went off, Dickens reported to Lavinia Watson on 23 November, in 'a whirl of triumph' which 'fired the whole length and breadth of the County of Hertfordshire'. The regular Amateurs were augmented by members of the local gentry, while female roles were played by Lemon's wife Nelly (substituting for Catherine), Georgina, and a professional actress, Anne Romer. The Knebworth Banqueting Hall accommodates one hundred and seventy spectators and on the first night was filled mainly with Bulwer Lytton's tenants and other locals. The two following nights were for the benefit of the county families and their guests. Dickens, having drilled his cast to his required standards both in London and at Knebworth, and having devoted as always the minutest attention to every single aspect of the play's *mise en scène*, revelled once more in swaggering as Jonson's Bobadil and afterwards, perfectly partnered (again, as always) by Lemon, reduced successive audiences to helpless mirth in a well-honed performance of *Animal Magnetism.*

Bulwer Lytton was deeply impressed by this close-up view of the Amateurs in action and saw clearly how Dickens himself was the essential driving force of the whole enterprise. Like Dickens, he was a highly successful novelist who had shown generous concern for the plight of less successful fellow-writers and was aware of the Amateurs' earlier performances to raise money for them. He now said to Dickens, as the latter subsequently related to Burdett Coutts (23 March), 'this is a great power that has grown up about you, out of a winter night's amusement, and do let us try to use it for the lasting service of our

order', meaning writers. Dickens caught eagerly at the idea. Through the
Amateurs he might revive, in a somewhat different form, the Provident Union
scheme, already canvassed by him and Lemon, and he was delighted when
Bulwer Lytton, as popular a playwright as he was a novelist, proposed writing
a full-length five-act comedy for the Amateurs to perform. All proceeds were
to go towards the setting up of a new institution intended to help not only
writers but also artists in need. Part of the money was to go towards the cost
of erecting, on land at Knebworth donated by Bulwer Lytton, some houses,
later called 'lodges', for the temporary or long-term accommodation of writers
or artists whom misfortune, illness or old age had reduced to penury. It was
proposed to elect a Warden, Members and Associates of the Guild, all salaried
at between £200 and £100 p.a. and assigned certain duties, like lecturing at
Mechanics' Institutes. As in the case of the earlier scheme, self-help was to be
of the essence. Writers and artists who applied to join the Guild would be
expected to make regular contributions to the Guild's chosen Life Insurance
Company while they could do so. In other words, it was not to function like
a charity but more like a hardship or pension fund. Furthermore, genuine
literary or artistic achievement was to be a criterion for the reception of benefits by members so that it should 'bear the character of a tribute to merit, not
of an alms to destitution'. This was the approach Dickens had taken when he
successfully solicited the Prime Minister, Lord John Russell, for a government
pension for aged dramatist John Poole. He was able to send Poole a congratu-
latory Christmas Eve letter telling him he now had a pension of £100 p.a.[1]

The grand new scheme became Dickens's chief non-writing preoccupation
throughout 1851, apart from what he called in a letter of 5 September to Frank
Stone, 'Shepherd's Bush, and my Virgin charges there'. Immediately after his
return to London from Knebworth, however, he had, as always now, to attend
to *Household Words*. In particular, the issue to appear on 21 December had
to be planned as a special Christmas number. The public would be expecting
some sort of seasonal celebration from the writer of the *Carol* and its
successors, and an ideal vehicle was to hand in the form of his new journal,
deliberately targeted as it was at its readers' hearths and homes. Accordingly,
he devoted the whole of 30 November to planning what he now called 'the
Christmas No.' He himself would write the initial section which was to be
followed by seven essays ('Christmas in Lodgings, Christmas in the Navy',
and so on) and some seasonal verses by Horne. Dickens's contribution, 'A
Christmas Tree', is a richly evocative memory-piece, a seemingly effortless total
recall of the terrors and delights of the toys and books and theatre-visits associated with each stage of his infancy and childhood. It modulates from this
into a sequence of Christmas-fireside ghost stories, thus providing Dickens's
readers with some continuity with the Christmas Books in all but one of which
the supernatural element had been essential. The earlier part of the essay, with

Dickens looking into the 'dreamy brightness' of his 'youngest Christmas recollections', could hardly have been written before the composition of the autobiographical fragment and *Copperfield* had enabled him to deal in writing with his oppressive blacking factory memories, thus making his earlier, happier, ones available to him for direct autobiographical use.[2]

It is not until 21 February that we find in his surviving letters the first clear reference to thoughts about a new novel: 'the first shadows of a new story', he tells Mary Boyle, are 'hovering in a ghostly way about me'. Two *Household Words* essays he wrote this winter, 'A December Vision' (14 Dec.) and 'Last Words of the Old Year' (4 Jan.), show that his mind and imagination were already much engaged with certain topics, not new with him, that later emerged as central themes in *Bleak House*. Prominent among these were the ruinous delays and labyrinthine complexity of the Court of Chancery, the State's abandonment of the children of the poor to ignorance, starvation and crime, already powerfully depicted in the *Carol* and *The Haunted Man*, and the dire necessity of sanitary reform. Indeed, in 'A December Vision' we find Dickens already using that 'miasma' image that will be so central to his description of Tom-all-Alone's with its stark warning to the middle and upper classes that 'There is not a drop of Tom's corrupted blood but propagates infection and contagion somewhere'. Here is the passage from 'A December Vision':

> I saw innumerable hosts fore-doomed to darkness, dirt, pestilence, obscenity, misery, and early death. . . . I saw, from those reeking and pernicious stews, the avenging consequences of such Sin issuing forth, and penetrating to the highest places. . . . I saw that not one miserable wretch breathed out his poisoned life in the deepest cellar of the most neglected town, but, from the surrounding atmosphere, some particles of his infection were borne away, charged with heavy retribution on the general guilt.

Even Sir Leicester Dedlock's 'family gout' is foreshadowed in this article when a 'minister of state' boasts of his ancestors' longevity: 'We have the gout, but bear it (like our honours) many years.'[3]

Throughout 1851 we find in Dickens's letters and journalism many examples of his responding to people, places, publications, events and beliefs in a way that will bear fruit in the presentation of characters, settings and ideas in *Bleak House*. He notes the dirty faces of the philanthropic Caroline Chisholm's children, and he reads the Board of Health's shocking 1850 report on London's overflowing graveyards and the newspaper accounts of a coroner's rejection of a young crossings-sweeper's evidence because of the boy's ignorance. London itself is still for him a fascinating conglomeration of very different neighbourhoods, as depicted in all his writings from *Sketches* onwards, but he also seems now to have a sense of it as a dark and gloomy totality, a sense that pervades *Bleak House* from the first chapter onwards. Here he is writing to Bulwer Lytton on 10 February: 'London is a vile place, I sincerely believe. I have never taken kindly to it since I lived abroad. Whenever I come back from the Country, now, and see that great heavy canopy lowering over the housetops, I wonder what on earth I do there, except on obligation.' And it is in this lowering city that he sees, in his 'December Vision', 'Thirty Thousand children, hunted, flogged, imprisoned, but not taught – who might have been nurtured by the wolf or bear, so little of humanity had they, within them or without.'[4]

By New Year's Day Dickens had already received a draft of Bulwer Lytton's comedy which, he told Lavinia Watson, 'raised a sea of business' for him in connection with 'the great scheme' that they had in hand. He did not, however, at all relax in his attention to preparations for the postponed theatricals at Rockingham about which he had been so busily corresponding for months with both Lavinia Watson and Mary Boyle. The performance took place on 15 January in the 'very elegant little theatre' Dickens had had constructed in the Castle's long drawing room (one of the estate workers remembered him as a 'wonderful clever man with his hands, a reg'lar carpenter'). The programme consisted of three farces, one being the Irish playwright Dion Boucicault's *Used Up!* In this Dickens played a blasé young nobleman pretending to be a ploughboy who falls in love with a farmer's daughter, played by Boyle. This gave him scope for developing in their subsequent correspondence the mock-flirtatious relationship he had already established with her. How far Catherine knew about this and what she thought of it we do not know. She herself also acted in the Boucicault play, taking the minor role of Lady Maria Clutterbuck, little suspecting that, before the year was out, this would become her *nom de plume.* After the performance Dickens ebulliently organised some country dances that lasted well into the small hours before returning to London the next day, a railway journey of a hundred and twenty miles, in time to dine with the Prime Minister.[5]

'Green-hearted Rockingham', as he called it in a verse tribute to the Watsons he composed as a tag to the theatricals, had always a special place in Dickens's own heart and he later drew on some aspects of the Castle's architecture and surroundings when, at some point during this year, he found that he would be needing a fine old aristocratic country seat as one of the settings in his new novel. For his fictional purposes, however, he wished to evoke an atmosphere of magnificent stagnation, tinged with an ominous sense of approaching catastrophe. Unsurprisingly, therefore, he took pains to throw readers off the scent by locating Chesney Wold in Lincolnshire and seemed anxious to minimise the extent to which he had modelled the place upon Rockingham when, towards the end of the serialisation of *Bleak House*, he wrote to Lavinia Watson: 'In some of the descriptions of Chesney Wold, I have taken many bits, chiefly about trees and shadows, from observations made at Rockingham. I wonder whether you have ever thought so!' Perhaps his dream, after writing one of the Chesney Wold episodes, of Watson pursuing him 'with a Revolver' resulted from uneasiness about how the Watsons might feel about the use of their home in *Bleak House*.[6]

About the time of his visit to Rockingham Dickens began his first serial work for *Household Words*. This was his *Child's History of England*, successive chapters of which appeared at irregular intervals in the magazine between 25 January 1851 and 10 December 1853. At this point his nine children ranged in age from five-month-old Dora to fourteen-year-old Charley and when the *Child's History* was published in three volumes (1852–54) Dickens dedicated it 'To my own dear children, whom I hope it may help, bye-and-bye, to read with interest larger and better books on the same subject'. He used as a crib a *History of England* compiled 1837–39 by a hack writer called Thomas Keightley and was reviving an intention first expressed (and perhaps briefly acted on) in May 1843 when he told Douglas Jerrold that he was writing 'a little history of England' for five-year-old Charley intended to counteract any 'conservative or High church notions' to which the child might be exposed when a little older: 'the best way of guarding against any such horrible result, is, I take it, to wring the parrots' necks in his very cradle'. By 'parrots' Dickens meant all those who extolled 'the good old days', those Tory times before the Reform Bill of 1832 which stretched back into those 'ages of darkness, wickedness and violence' denounced by the Goblin of the Great Bell in *The Chimes*. In his 'Preliminary Word' in the first number of *Household Words* Dickens had expressed the hope that everything in the magazine would have the effect of making its readers 'thankful for the privilege of living in this summer-dawn of time', this great new age of human progress and enlightenment that he, like so many of his contemporaries, believed was opening up. His *Child's History* would play its part in this by showing, with plenty of gory detail, how the English people had been for so long afflicted, down to the Glorious Revolution of 1688, by a succession of weak or vicious rulers and meddling, over-mighty priests (beginning with the Druids), with Henry VIII, 'a blot of blood and grease upon the History of England', featured as villain-in-chief. Only two rulers meet with Dickens's unqualified approval, namely Alfred the Great (very sound on the administration of justice and on national education) and Carlyle's great hero Cromwell, whose brisk way with parliaments Dickens wishes would serve as a warning to all such assemblies 'to avoid long speeches, and do more work'.

During the first two months of 1851 Dickens and Bulwer Lytton worked on the prospectus for their proposed new institution, which Bulwer Lytton wanted to call, rather grandly, 'Our Order'. The name eventually chosen was 'The Guild of Literature and Art', inspired by 'the name given by old Saxon custom to societies in which the members of a class contributed to the benefit of each other'. Dickens declared himself delighted with Bulwer Lytton's as yet unnamed comedy, which he himself eventually titled *Not So Bad As We Seem; or, Many Sides to a Character*. He lamented that he could not play the character part of the heroine's father because, as he wrote to Bulwer Lytton on 5 January, 'Assumption has charms for me – I hardly know for how many wild reasons – so delightful, that I feel a loss of O I can't say what exquisite foolery, when I lose a chance of being some one, in voice &c not at all like myself.' He felt, however, that he had to play the hero because he alone could 'hold the play together' in this role. The character, Lord Wilmot, 'a young man at the Head of the Mode more than a Century ago', in fact offered Dickens plenty of histrionic scope, to say nothing of rich costumes, elaborate wigs and other accoutrements dear to the heart of amateur actors. Wilmot is a witty fop with a heart of gold who role-plays within the play, pretending to be the scandal-mongering bookseller Edmund Curll in a scene with the impoverished author David Fallen. Fallen's hapless dependence on haughty aristocrats or unscrupulous publishers is depicted as representative of the writer's plight in the previous century and the scene ends with Wilmot promising to become Fallen's patron, which sits rather oddly with the Guild's anti-patronage stance.[7]

Dickens seized the chance to begin advertising the Guild on 1 March at a public banquet honouring Macready's retirement from the stage. Bulwer Lytton was in the chair and Dickens, dressed for the occasion with spectacular elegance, proposed his health. After praising Macready for being 'ever anxious to assert the order of which he is so great an ornament', Dickens humorously alluded to what he called the 'popular prejudice' that authors were 'not a particularly united body' but claimed that 'among the followers of literature' there could hardly have been one further above 'those little grudging jealousies, which do sometimes disparage its brightness' than Bulwer Lytton. He then spoke briefly about their collegial scheme 'to smooth the ragged way of young labourers, both in literature and the fine arts, and to soften, but by no eleemosynary means, the declining years of meritorious age'.[8]

Three days later Dickens approached the Duke of Devonshire to ask if the première of the new comedy might take place in the grand setting of Devonshire House, Piccadilly, before (if they would come) Victoria and Albert. As has been pointed out, however, this invocation of aristocratic, and even royal, patronage at the outset underlines a certain confusion at the heart of the Guild scheme which we have already noted as present in Bulwer Lytton's play. The Duke of Devonshire was well known for his graciousness and for being a generous patron of writers – he had, for example, come very handsomely to the rescue of the ever-impecunious Leigh Hunt. Dickens possibly met him in 1845 when he had had to dash up to Chatsworth, the Duke's country seat, to see Paxton in connection with *Daily News* arrangements. The Duke now responded very positively to Dickens's letter, revealing himself to be a great fan of its writer ('I never missed reading a number of his beginning with Pickwick, and told him I could pass examination on all his histories') and placing his London mansion at Dickens's command. In due course he also obtained the promise of royal attendance. Immediately following this Dickens plunged with 'utmost rapture and vehemence' into detailed preparations for the production of the comedy, which it was intended afterwards to perform publicly at the Hanover Square Rooms.[9]

The Guild project and the production of Bulwer Lytton's comedy were major preoccupations for Dickens for the first four months of 1851. During that time he nevertheless managed to write, besides the first three chapters of his *Child's History*, no fewer than six articles for *Household Words* as well as collaborating in six more. Some of these articles are campaigning ones like 'Birth, Mrs Meek, of a Son' (22 Feb.) and 'A Monument of French Folly' (8 March), respectively protesting against the antiquated practice of swaddling new-born babies and the continuance of Smithfield Market in the heart of London. Others were 'process' or exploratory ones like 'Plate Glass' (1 Feb.) and 'Spitalfields' (5 April). In the case of the three last-named articles research trips had been required prior to the writing. Finest of all is 'Bill-Sticking' (22 March) to which Dickens subsequently chose to give pride of place in *Reprinted Pieces*, the collection of his own *Household Words* articles made for the 1858 Library Edition of his works. This article, which occupies just over a quarter of the issue in which it appears, concerns the large advertising vans, plastered all over with sometimes garish advertisements and driven at a walking pace, that were a notable, and frequently inconvenient, feature of London's streets at the time. Dickens imagines himself riding inside one of them with a quintessentially Dickensian character, full of comic professional pride, whom he calls the King of the Bill-Stickers and from whom he learns much about the tricks of the trade.[10]

From the beginning of 1851 he was beset by even more domestic concerns than usual. He had to embark on a search for a new house as his lease of Devonshire Terrace was coming to an end and apparently could not be renewed. He also had trouble with Fred who was now in financial difficulties and trading on Dickens's name to obtain credit: he 'is rasping my very heart just now', Dickens told Burdett Coutts on 18 January. Then, in early March Catherine became seriously ill with some kind of nervous trouble that caused violent headaches as well as giddiness and dimness of sight. Dickens believed she had been for some years intermittently suffering, albeit in a milder form, from this disorder, which he called 'an alarming disposition of blood to the head'. The so-called 'cold water cure' at Malvern in Worcestershire for nervous and other diseases was at the height of its vogue at this time and Dickens arranged for Catherine to go there at once, attended by Anne Brown. He placed her under the care of Dr James Wilson, founder of the Malvern hydropathic establishment, who had earlier treated Bulwer Lytton. Dickens himself immediately followed her down to Malvern as did Georgina a bit later (though she seems to have returned to London subsequently) and he planned for some of the children to move there as well.[11]

Dickens took lodgings for himself, Catherine and Anne Brown in Knutsford Lodge, Malvern, and began a commuting existence. He travelled up to London at least once or twice a week in order to continue house-hunting, attend to *Household Words* and Urania Cottage business, and, on top of all this, to begin twice-weekly, five-hour rehearsals of Bulwer Lytton's comedy (this 'trifling addition to my usual occupations' he calls it in a letter to Burdett Coutts of 20 March). In Malvern he continued the *Child's History* (he has great fun in chapter 3, published on 29 March, excoriating St Dunstan as an overweening priest and Queen Elfrida as a melodramatic villainess) and worked on a new farce, to be played as an afterpiece to *Not So Bad As We Seem*. But he did not feel, he told Bulwer Lytton on 23 March, that farce-writing 'quite suited' him, nor was it what his public now expected from him: 'I have an uneasy sense of the impossibility of expressing anything, through such a medium, that people would expect from me'. He wrote also to Forster, 'I am constantly striving, *for my reputation's sake*, to get into it a meaning that is impossible in a farce' (my italics). This seems to connect with the apologetic tone of his preface to the Cheap Edition of *Sketches*. 'Boz' with his farcical tales and dramatic pieces about the follies and misadventures of a bunch of comic stereotypes belonged to earlier days. From 'Charles Dickens' in 1851 the reading public expected much more in the way of 'meaning'.[12]

Suddenly, alarming news about his father cut across everything else. John and Elizabeth Dickens were lodging with Robert Davey, an eminent surgeon, in Keppel Street, Bloomsbury. Dickens had asked Davey to accommodate his parents so that a close eye could be kept on John's state of health, which had evidently been causing some concern. On the morning of 25 March John suddenly became very ill and had to undergo, without anaesthetic, an extremely painful bladder operation – he had been suffering pain a long time but had concealed the extent of the problem. Dickens, who was in London, visited his father immediately after the operation (when his room was 'a slaughter house of blood') and found him, he reported to Catherine, 'wonderfully cheerful and strong-hearted'. But his condition slowly deteriorated and on Saturday 31 March he died, 'O so quietly', at about five in the morning. Dickens had, as it happened, come up from Malvern the previous day and had been at the dying man's bedside for many hours. During this vigil he was doubtless remembering, amidst much else, the father of those earlier days about whom he had written to Forster: 'By me, as a sick child, he has watched night and day, unweariedly and patiently, many nights and days.' His own old trouble came back to him as it always did in times of great emotional stress:

'All this goes to my side directly,' he told Catherine on 25 March, 'and I feel as if I had been struck there by a leaden bludgeon.' Mrs Davey recalled that Dickens's conduct towards his mother after his father died was 'noble': 'He took her in his arms, and they both wept bitterly together.' Telling her that she must rely on him for the future, he relieved her mind by promptly discharging all John's debts. But all memories of the troubles and annoyances that the financial irresponsibility of the man he now called 'my poor father' had caused him in earlier days seem to have been much softened by now, and it was John's 'zealous, useful, cheerful spirit' that he commemorated on his father's Highgate Cemetery tombstone.[13]

Dickens did not allow his grief and sadness to distract him from his work for the Guild nor, of course, from work for *Household Words*. He decided to turn the sleeplessness from which he was suffering to account by arranging with Wills to spend the night of 3 April in Bow Street police station, something that would be sure to yield material for 'a splendid paper'. Ten days later, he sent back from Malvern the proofs of a very substantial article (in the writing of which Wills had collaborated), having worked on them '9 hours without stirring'. Entitled 'The Metropolitan Protectives', it eulogises the police, graphically describing 'the patience, promptitude, order, vigilance, zeal and judgment, which watch over the peace of the huge Babylon when she sleeps' and appeared as the lead article on 26 April. Other commitments had also to be honoured besides *Household Words*. On 14 April Dickens once more chaired the annual General Theatrical Fund dinner, and must surely have delivered with more than usual feeling a certain passage in his speech. This was the one in which he spoke of the actor having sometimes to come 'from scenes of affliction and misfortune – even from death itself – to play his part before us' just as 'all men must do that violence to their feelings, in passing on to the fulfilment of their duties in the great strife and fight of life'. This most deeply-held belief of his was put to a severe test when he left the hall to find Forster and Lemon waiting to tell him of the cruelly sudden death of his infant daughter Dora with whom he had been happily playing just before leaving home.[14]

His immediate task was to tell Catherine. That he did not go to Malvern to break the news to her himself, give her what comfort he could in their joint loss, and bring her back to London, suggests the psychological and emotional distance that existed between husband and wife. It was Forster who went to Malvern, bearing with him a letter from Dickens to Catherine, tenderly expressed but written as though to a child who might not fully grasp the terrible thing that has happened. The second and third paragraphs read as follows:

> Little Dora, without being in the least pain, is suddenly stricken ill. She awoke out of a sleep, and was seen in one moment to be very ill. Mind! I will not deceive you. I think her *very* ill.

There is nothing in her appearance but perfect rest. You would suppose her quietly asleep. But I am sure she is very ill, and I cannot encourage myself with much hope of her recovery. I do not – why should I say I do, to you, my dear! – I do not think her recovery at all likely.

Catherine seems to have responded well to such treatment. The day after little Dora's funeral (18 April) Dickens told Bulwer Lytton she was as well as he could hope, resigned to the baby's death and able to 'speak of it tranquilly'. He added, 'She is so good and amiable that I hope it may not hurt her.' She was, inevitably, 'very low' and he tried to distract her by taking her out a good deal in connection with their impending move. He looked forward, too, to getting her away to Broadstairs – this time for five months from the end of May, in order to avoid the crowds who were now pouring into London for the Great Exhibition, due to open on 1 May. He himself had been so shaken by the deaths of his father and his 'poor little pet' that he had to ask for a postponement of the Royal Gala Performance at Devonshire House, the event being rescheduled for 16 May.

By 25 April Dickens was, he reported to de la Rue, very much back in harness, 'amidst a mob of carpenters, gasmen, decorators, scene-painters, upholsterers, theatrical supernumeraries, tailors, wig-makers, and Heaven knows what else'. Rehearsals were resumed with great intensity: 'My legs swell so, with standing on the stage for hours together, that my stockings won't come off,' Dickens wrote to Beard on 13 May. In such interstices of time as he could find he worked with Lemon at a new farce, set in Great Malvern and called *Mr Nightingale's Diary*. This was originally drafted by Lemon but Dickens, having overcome his earlier misgivings, contributed so much in the way of gags and comic dialogue (reviving the idiolects of Sam Weller and Mrs Gamp for the purpose) that it soon became very much a joint work. Dickens thought it would be a 'Screamer' and so indeed it proved to be when it was first played as an afterpiece to *Not So Bad As We Seem* at the second Devonshire House performance on 27 May before a very exclusive audience of 'fashionables'. It subsequently became one of the most sure-fire items in the Amateurs' repertoire. Although there were other roles in it (including one played by the young Wilkie Collins, whom Dickens had invited to join the Amateurs), everything depended on the extraordinary stage rapport between Dickens and Lemon. Their brilliantly-improvised comic dialogue and stage routines varied wildly from night to night as Dickens, emulating Charles Mathews, played Gabblewig, a comic young lover who in turn plays in swift succession an astonishing variety of different characters, including a Gamp-like old woman and an ancient, stone-deaf sexton.[15]

Dickens wrote an account of the Guild for *Household Words* (10 May) but did not allow this new cause to distract him from prosecuting his old campaigns. 'Cain in the Fields' (10 May), written jointly with R. H. Horne, dealt with rural murders and with what Dickens saw as very much a related matter, the lack of educational provision for the rural poor, and with the deleterious effects of public executions. Connected with this last concern was his sole-authored, highly topical, article, 'The Finishing Schoolmaster' (17 May), which shows by printing application letters written by would-be deputy hangmen the baleful attractiveness of this office. 'I bestow more time than you suppose on Household Words', wrote Dickens on 25 April to fellow-author David Moir who had evidently been asking about his next novel, 'and do not contemplate any immediate resumption of my green leaves [that is, publishing a new monthly-part novel].' He hopes, however, '(reversing the order of vegetable things) to come out again, about the dead of winter'. It was, in the event, to be a bit longer than this before he began *Bleak House* but this is further evidence that the outlines of a new novel were slowly forming in his mind and mingling with his increasingly urgent concerns about the state of the nation. His disdain for parliamentary politics was not lessened by the 'ministerial crisis' of February, when Russell and his Whig colleagues resigned after losing a vote in the Commons but the Tories' leader Lord Stanley would not 'come in' with the result that, after more politicking, Russell's government returned to office. Nor did the electoral bribery and corruption scandal that erupted at St Alban's in April do anything to increase Dickens's respect for parliamentary democracy. In due course both things were to be satirically reflected in the new novel he was now (to borrow a fine phrase from George Eliot) 'simmering towards'.

One major contemporary event about which Dickens wrote very little is the Great Exhibition. Of course he applauds it as stupendous evidence of the social, technological and scientific progress of mankind in this 'summer-dawn of time' and he fully shares in the national pride that it was conceived and realised in Britain. However, as a spectacle and an experience it failed to stir his imagination but was, on the contrary, 'a very Fortunatus's purse of boredom'. 'I have a natural horror of sights', he told Lavinia Watson on 11 July, 'and the fusion of so many sights in one has not decreased it'. He then proceeds to regale her with a very funny, fantastical account about something that *does* stimulate his comic imagination, namely visitor reactions to the Exhibition – in this case those of a party of very young schoolchildren. Ultimately, however, Dickens believed the whole thing was a massive distraction from what should have been major and pressing concerns for England's ruling classes. This was something he had already expressed in his 'Last Words of the Old Year' (4 Jan.): 'Which of my children shall behold the Princes, Prelates, Nobles, Merchants, of England, equally united, for another Exhibition – for a great display of England's sins and negligences, to be, by steady contemplation of all eyes, and steady union of all hearts and hands, set right?'[16]

Dickens's last public duty before the Royal Gala Performance at Devonshire House was to toast the Board of Health at the first anniversary banquet of the Metropolitan Sanitary Association on 10 May. In his speech he reverted to the infection image in 'A December Vision' noted above that was to become a leading motif in *Bleak House*. The winds, he warns, will carry pestilence-laden air from the seething slums to the fashionable quarters of town and 'if you once have a vigorous pestilence raging furiously in Saint Giles's, no mortal list of Lady Patronesses can keep it out of Almack's.'[17]

By 16 May all was finally ready at Devonshire House and the Queen and Prince Albert and their suite arrived to attend the première of Bulwer Lytton's comedy. Everything went well and the Queen was sufficiently impressed to contribute £150 to the Guild's funds as well as paying £50 for her ticket. Altogether this performance and the second one on 27 May raised £2,500. The second performance saw the joyous première of *Mr Nightingale* and the evening was rounded off with an elegant supper and a ball, all munificently funded by the Duke. The following day Dickens finally managed to get away to Broadstairs where Catherine, Georgina and the family were already installed. On 1 June he wrote to the Duke from Fort House that 'the freshness of the sea, and the associations of the place (I finished Copperfield in this airy nest)' had set him to work 'with great vigor' so that he could hardly believe he sometimes transformed himself into a theatre manager and went about 'with a painted face, in gaslight'. The family stayed in Broadstairs for the next five months with

31 Royal performance of *Not So Bad As We Seem* at Devonshire House, 16 May 1851, *Illustrated London News*, 24 May 1851

Dickens making frequent trips up to London, staying in his 'gypsy tent' at the *Household Words* office, Devonshire Terrace being let to a tenant. In addition to routine *Household Words* and Urania Cottage business there was house-hunting to be done and all the preparations for the first three public performances of *Not So Bad As We Seem*. These took place on 18 June, 2 July, and 4 August and realised profits of £60 per night. Besides his frequent London journeys, Dickens made many others – with Catherine to visit Macready in his Dorset retirement, with Beard to Eton to take Charley and some of his schoolfriends on a jolly boating excursion, to Chatsworth for a flying visit to the Duke of Devonshire in early October. Among the most well-thumbed items in Dickens's library at this time must have been the successive issues of *Bradshaw's Monthly Railway Guide*, a compilation of train timetables first published in 1839, that seems to have caused him not a little vexation (a letter to Austin on 22 August begins, 'I write this note, with a brain addled by severe study of Bradshaw') but which also provided him with material for an entertainingly exasperated *Household Words* essay, 'A Narrative of Extraordinary Suffering' (12 July).

His hunt for a new home ended on 25 July when he paid £1,542 for a 45-year lease of Tavistock House, a grand, stone-porticoed, eighteen-roomed house in Bloomsbury, not far from his first house in Doughty Street. Frank Stone was relinquishing the lease and moving next door but one. He and his family had lived there for some years so Dickens, and presumably Catherine also, would have already been somewhat familiar with its interior. Standing in Gordon Street, across the northern end of Tavistock Square, it was the westernmost of a terrace of three houses, an original 1796 mansion which had later been extended by the addition of two large wings, closed off from the public road by iron gates and with a handsome carriage sweep before it. It had spacious bay windows at the back on the ground and first floors, over-looking a garden that boasted a fine mulberry tree. Dickens had relied greatly on the advice of his civil-engineer brother-in-law throughout all his house-hunting and in early September took Austin's advice to call in Cubitt the builders to carry out the extensive programme of alterations, refurbishment and redecoration he was planning (we do not know just how much involvement Catherine had in all this but she clearly had some as shown by an 11 September letter to her from Dickens about bedroom-allocation and other matters). Dickens naturally concerned himself with every detail including plumbing and bathroom arrange-ments. 'A Cold Shower of the best quality, always charged to an unlimited extent', he told Austin, 'has become a positive necessary of life to me.' And he yields to what he calls the 'whim' of having some panels of comically-titled dummy book-backs, like *Hansard's Guide to Refreshing Sleep* ('As many volumes as possible'), specially made for his study. Some titles, like this one ridiculing parliamentary speechifying, are satirical, others merely facetious, but several relate to what he was writing or was now looking forward to writing. One sees, for example, why the author of *A Child's History* might amuse himself with devising titles like *A History of the Middling Ages*, or *King Henry the Eighth's Evidences of Christianity*, and why an author moving towards the writing of *Bleak House* might enjoy the idea of multi-volumed *Short History of a Chancery Suit*.[18]

During this summer and early autumn Dickens either wholly wrote or collaborated on a dozen or so articles for *Household Words*. By 9 June he had completed the brilliant 'On Duty With Inspector Field' (14 July), recounting a recent nocturnal tour with Field of St Giles and other notorious London slum districts. He greatly elaborates Field's portrait as already drawn in 'A Detective Police Party', highlighting the irresistible authority, geniality and apparent omniscience which will form the leading characteristics of *Bleak House*'s Inspector Bucket. 'On Duty With Inspector Field' anticipates that novel in other ways too. It shows that Dickens has made himself a master of many of the rhetorical forms such as free indirect speech and apostrophe, whether to his readers or to one of his own characters, that he will deploy to such effect in *Bleak House* – in the inquest scene in chapter 11, for example, or in the famous ending to chapter 47 ('Dead, your Majesty. Dead, my lords and gentlemen....'). The first-person narration of *Copperfield* had precluded the use of these forms and, though Dickens had used them in earlier books, not always happily (we remember with a shudder his 'Blessings on thy simple heart, Tom Pinch!' in *Chuzzlewit*), it was not with the subtlety and complexity that he shows here. Dazzling stylistic virtuosity is also very much present in another article, 'A Flight' (30 Aug.), his 'fanciful paper', as he calls it, in which he re-lives his experience of travelling twice (once the previous year, and more recently, in February 1851), on the South Eastern Railway Company's 'Double Special Express' eleven-hour service from London to Paris.[19]

'A Flight' is written throughout in the present tense ('Everything is flying. The hop-gardens turn gracefully towards me, presenting regular avenues of hops in rapid flight, then whirl away.' ...). On 27 July, a few weeks before he wrote it Dickens had counselled Charles Knight to use the present rather than the past tense in one of his 'Shadow' articles for *Household Words* (essays on famous people of the past):

> I understand each phase of the thing to be *always a thing present, before the mind's eye* – a shadow passing before it. Whatever is done, must be *doing*.
> ... If I did the Shadow of Robinson Crusoe, I should not say he *was* a boy at Hull, when his father lectured him against going to sea and so forth – but he *is* a boy at Hull – there he is, in that particular Shadow, eternally a boy at Hull. ...

It was, of course, the technique he himself had used in the 'Retrospect' passages in *Copperfield* and no less than half of his next novel was to be written in the present tense alternating with another first-person narrative.

Other of Dickens's *Household Words* articles written this summer look back-wards in his art (and his life) as well as forwards. One is a reprise of one of the quasi-autobiographical episodes in *Copperfield*. 'Our School' (11 Oct.) revisits Jones's Wellington House Academy, fiercely caricatured as Creakle's Salem House in *Copperfield*. The article was said by some of Dickens's former schoolfellows, in touch with Forster when he was beginning his biography, to have reproduced 'the general features of the place . . . with wonderful accu-racy'. Another article, 'One Man in a Dockyard' (6 Sept.), looks both backward and forward in his life and work. Looking back to what he describes to Wills (30 July) as 'an old idea I once had (when I was making my name) of a fanciful and picturesque Beauties of England and Wales', he decides to experiment by taking Horne down to Chatham with him to 'take certain bits of the Dockyard and fortifications'. The resultant collaborative article includes a picturesque description, undoubtedly written by Dickens, of those favourite haunts of his boyhood, Rochester Castle and Rochester High Street.[20]

Despite all the family anxieties and bereavements he had suffered in the spring, and all the distractions of the Guild performances and of moving house, Dickens seems to have been in excellent writing form in Broadstairs this summer as is shown by the richness and variety of his work for *Household Words*. There is no suggestion in his letters to Wills that he is at any loss for subjects or having to work against the grain. Even the *Child's History*, which might have become something of a chore, continued to be written with evident gusto and on 27 July he called Wills's attention to 'a very pretty bit' in his chapter on Henry I (9 Aug.) – a pathetic account of the sinking of the White Ship carrying the King's son and his companions with the loss of everyone on her apart from one sole survivor, 'a poor butcher of Rouen'. We know, too, that he pleased himself 'exceedingly' with his humorously affectionate pen-portrait of Broadstairs, 'Our Watering Place' (2 Aug.1851).[21]

All this time ideas about the new novel were growing in his mind and causing him, he told Burdett Coutts on 17 August, 'violent restlessness'. He fantasised about running away to Switzerland but contented himself instead with a brief trip to the Stroud Valley in Gloucestershire, a location that offered, he said, 'a natural picture I wish to look into' (he was perhaps already envis-aging Jarndyce's delightful home in the English countryside and looking for an appropriate setting). He agonised to Austin on 7 September about the seemingly interminable delay in the builder Cubitt's men beginning work at Tavistock House while all the time his new book was 'waiting to be born'. Once the men *had* begun he lamented the slowness of their progress. 'I am wild to begin a new book', he told Beard on 6 October, '– and can't, until I am settled'. The following day he wrote to Austin, 'O! If this were to last long – the distraction of the new book – the whirling of the story through one's mind, escorted by workmen – the Pantechnicon's [i.e., the furniture depository's] imbecility, the wild necessity of beginning to write, the not being able to do so – the – O! – I should go – O! –'.

Meanwhile, there was something that simply *had* to be written, whatever the circumstances. This was a promised contribution to one of the fashionable annuals, *The Keepsake*, edited by Lady Blessington's niece, Margaret Power. Sometime during the early autumn Dickens sent her two stories of the uncanny collectively entitled 'To Be Read At Dusk'. They were, in one reviewer's judgment, 'in the very best style of phantasmagory . . . hit off in that free and easy manner, without effort . . . brimful of the spontaneous charm belonging to all [Dickens] writes'. One can only hope Dickens did not see this review because it was just the kind of thing that enraged him – the belief that any of his writings could be dashed off in a 'free and easy manner' rather than as a result of the exercise of that 'patient and continuous energy' he had desiderated in *Copperfield* as essential for any writer worth his salt. Unfortunately, however, there was one 'free and easy' aspect to the first of these two stories. Wittingly or unwittingly, Dickens seems to have appropriated for its basis an anecdote of Mrs Gaskell's. This told of a young married woman haunted by the face of a man she has never met nor seen in any picture. During a visit to Rome she suddenly vanishes and is later glimpsed in a carriage, sobbing and weeping, with, seated next to her, the owner of the mysterious face she had so often described. Gaskell, accustomed to dining out on this tale, was annoyed with Dickens for his appropriation of it. Rather than its having been an act of conscious plagiarism on his part, however, it may well be the case that the story stirred up in him such vivid memories of Augusta de la Rue in Genoa and her fearful hallucinations that these came to overlay his memory of the original story and its source. Once alerted to what he had done, he at once wrote his 'Dear Scheherazade' an elaborate comic apology (25 Nov.) that may or may not have mollified her.[22]

Catherine ventured into authorship this year using the pen-name of 'Lady Maria Clutterbuck', the character she was to have played in *Used Up*. In October Bradbury and Evans published what was labelled as the 'second edition' of a small volume entitled *What Shall We Have For Dinner? Satisfactorily Answered by Numerous Bills of Fare for from Two to Eighteen Persons*, written by 'Lady Maria Clutterbuck'. 'Second edition' indicates that there must have been a first edition earlier in the year, compiled by Catherine between Rockingham and Malvern perhaps, but no copy of this seems to have survived. Dickens gave his backing to the enterprise, perhaps first undertaken at his initiative to help Catherine recover from her troubles, by contributing a brief comic preface, written in the character of Lady Clutterbuck. The book must have met with some success since a 'new edition' followed in 1852 and this was reissued in 1856 and 1860.[23]

Dickens's urgency to get settled into his study at Tavistock House so that he could start on his new book was no doubt intensified by the fact that, even though the back numbers of *Copperfield* were selling well, he did not have a lot coming in just at this time when he was spending so much on the grand new house ('so remarkable for nothing as for its Drainage', he joked to Frederick Evans on 2 September). Moreover, ideas for the new novel continued to ferment in his mind, stimulated even more than usual by the contemporary events and social and political developments reported in the press. *The Times* continued its vigorous campaign against the monstrous delays and labyrinthine complexities of the Court of Chancery, High Church 'Puseyism' continued to cause havoc in the Church of England, and there was an American-inspired attempt to introduce a more practical style of dress for women (derisively called 'Bloomerism' after Amelia Jenks Bloomer, its first proponent). This provoked an outbreak of press hysteria and culminated in a near-riot at the so-called 'Bloomer Ball' at the Hanover Square Rooms. Dickens was, alas, more than happy to contribute to the sexist merriment. In *Household Words* for 8 November he published 'Sucking Pigs', the title harking back to his earlier article, 'Whole Hogs' (23 Aug.), in which he had lampooned all-or-nothing campaigners for such causes as pacifism and vegetarianism. He imagines being married to Mrs Bellows, an indefatigably campaigning wife and mother: 'She must agitate, agitate, agitate. . . . She must go in to be a public character. She must work away at a Mission. . . '. In the course of all this she neglects her family, 'say, for the sake of argument, nine little Bellowses to mend, or mar, at home'. It will be another three months before Mrs Jellyby and Mrs Pardiggle will appear in the first monthly number of *Bleak House* but one feels they are here very much waiting in the wings.[24]

The new novel's title, always so crucial for Dickens, was not yet fixed, though he must certainly have been experimenting with it by 26 September when he joked about 'raising the (East) wind' in a letter to Evans. 'The East Wind' is one of the phrases he plays with on the ten undated 'slips', or half-sheets of paper, containing trial titles bound up, in an apparently random order, with the manuscript of *Bleak House* in the Forster Collection at the Victoria and Albert Museum. On all but one of these slips the title that stands first is 'Tom-All-Alone's', that desolate-sounding place-name remembered from his Chatham childhood. It does not seem, however, that Dickens was at this stage imagining it as the name of a ruinous London slum but rather as that of a sort of forerunner of Satis House. Just beneath 'Tom-All-Alone's', again on all but one of the slips, appear the words 'The Ruined House' or 'The Solitary House', always followed by some phrase indicating desolation or stasis (on half the slips the phrase is, 'That got into Chancery and never got out'). Briefly considered as alternatives to 'House' are 'Building', 'Factory' and 'Mill', the last two terms raising the interesting possibility that Dickens might have had thoughts of setting this story, or at least part of it, in the industrial north – where, in fact, he does set its immediate successor, *Hard Times*.

Although we cannot date these slips, nor do more than put them into some sort of conjectural order, it seems likely that the last one included in the binding is actually the latest in terms of composition. It reads 'Bleak House/ and the East Wind/ How they both got into Chancery/ and never got out', followed by a line drawn across the slip and under it the final title: 'Bleak House'. Perhaps Dickens suddenly realised that if he used 'bleak' instead of 'ruined' or 'solitary' he could dispense with any adjectival phrase. His planning notes for the first two numbers of the new story show, however, that his working title was initially *Bleak House and the East Wind* (the last four words were subsequently scored through in the notes for the first number). By this time, evidently, he must have decided that Bleak House, despite its name, should be a benign place, home of benevolent Mr Jarndyce – a place by no means sealed off, however, from the manifold vexations and miseries of the outside world. Jarndyce's fanciful way of responding to the situation at times when the influence of these things is particularly obtrusive is to remark that the wind is in the east.[25]

Tantalisingly, we have no clue as to just when it was during the 1851 gestation of *Bleak House* that Dickens decided upon the sensationally new narrative technique he used for the book, dividing the narration between a third-person (but by no means 'omniscient') narrator and commentator, writing in the historic present tense, and a first-person narrative in the past tense, supposedly written by a young woman who has been asked (by whom we never know) to recount the story of her life. At the beginning of her narrative she refers to 'my portion of these pages' but thereafter makes no further reference to the other 'portion'. Nor does she ever appear (though she is once alluded to) in the third-person narrative. As just stated, we have no hint from Dickens as to why he chose this double narrative form for *Bleak House* but it is possible that in writing *Copperfield* he had found that combining satire with first-person narration where the narrator is supposed to be as ingenuous as the young David Copperfield posed a serious difficulty. In the case of a young woman narrator like Esther Summerson this difficulty would have been much increased, hence, perhaps, Dickens's decision to split the narration in this novel. Apart from anything else, Esther's 'portion' of the narrative was to be his first attempt at first-person female narration, and autobiographical narration at that, something that, he confessed the following year to a young American woman admirer, 'had cost him no little labor and anxiety': 'Is it quite natural,' he asked her, 'quite girlish?'[26]

The title was, presumably, still undecided by 12 October when he drafted a preliminary advertisement for the new story and sent it to Evans. This proposed announcement simply mentions a 'New Serial Work . . . In Twenty Monthly Numbers' and 'A New Story by Charles Dickens with Illustrations by H. K. Browne' with no date given for the beginning of publication. In the event, no advertisement for the new serial appeared until 14 February 1852, just two weeks before the first number was published, and then, of course, the title was given. This delay in announcing it may have been prudence on the publishers' part since Dickens had not even begun writing the book on 12 October. After his return to London from Broadstairs on the 20th his first priority was to plan the first special extra Christmas number of *Household Words* and on the 27th he met at the office with Wills, Horne and Morley to set about this. Invited contributors, including Harriet Martineau and the young George Augustus Sala (a new recruit whom Dickens considered very promising), were asked to write about what Christmas meant to different people at different times or in different situations. He had also to deal with arrangements for the various projected provincial tours of the Guild players. The first of these took them to Bath and Bristol for four days on 10 November. In Bath Dickens saw again his dear old friend Landor, whom he was intending to put into the new novel as the warm-hearted eccentric Lawrence Boythorn. Meanwhile, he was obliged to leave Catherine, now seven months pregnant with what was to be her last child, in day-to-day charge of all the business of moving into Tavistock House. She seems to have risen to the occasion. Writing to her on 13 November from Clifton, he expressed himself 'quite delighted' to see from her latest letter 'that all is going on so vigorously, and that you are in such a methodical, business-like and energetic state'. He ends the letter by saying, 'I am continually thinking of the House in the midst of all the bustle, but I trust it with such confidence to you that I am quite at my ease about it'. The letter is signed 'With best love to Georgy and the girls, ever my Dearest Kate, Most affectionately Yours . . .'.

A day or so after returning from the Guild tour Dickens was at last able to establish himself in his study. 'I am beginning to find my papers, and to know where the pen and ink are,' he happily reported to Burdett Coutts on 17 November. 'Order is re-established.' It may have been about this time that he went on a field-trip with Wills to observe the functioning of a pawnbroker's shop in preparation for their collaborative article 'My Uncle' (6 Dec.), which contains a brilliantly impressionistic scene in the shop from Dickens's pen. Contemporaneously, he must have been writing those celebrated opening paragraphs of *Bleak House* about the London mud and fog and the waddling Megalosaurus, a creature who would have been fresh in Dickens's memory from Morley's mention of it ('a sort of crocodile, thirty feet long, with a big body, mounted on high thick legs') in his 'Antediluvian Cruise' article (*HW*, 16 Aug.) At the beginning of December he again annoyed Gaskell when he altered her reference to himself (as Boz) and to *Pickwick* in her first Cranford story, 'Our Society at Cranford' (*HW*, 13 Dec.). Without consulting her, Dickens substituted Thomas Hood and his comic journal *Hood's Own* for himself and *Pickwick*, feeling that it would be inappropriate to have his own works boosted in his journal. Gaskell protested but too late. The number had already gone to press, and she had to content herself with restoring her original text when *Cranford* was separately published.

On 7 December Dickens reported to Evans that he had finished the first number of *Bleak House* apart from 'the last short chapter' (this chapter, 'In Fashion', was repositioned before publication as chapter 2). He had also the reign of King John to 'knock off' to complete the first volume of the *Child's History* which he wanted to be published to catch the Christmas market ('We *cannot be out too soon*,' he admonished Evans). But both novel and history had to be put on hold while he wrote his own contribution for the *Household Words* Christmas Number. The other contributions were all to hand and Dickens, on reading through them, decided the number needed 'something with no detail in it, but a tender fancy that shall hit a great many people'. He promptly wrote a short piece entitled 'What Christmas Is, as we Grow Older'. Towards the end he exhorts his readers not to let fear of pain cause them to shut out from their Christmas memories their dead loved ones: 'Of all days in the year, we will turn our faces to that City [the City of the Dead] upon Christmas Day, and from its silent hosts bring those we loved, among us.' Without naming names, Dickens personalises this piece by drawing on his own poignant memories, recent and not so recent, of little Dora, of Fanny and her 'poor mis-shapen boy' who died soon after her, and of Mary Hogarth ('a dear girl – almost a woman – never to be one'), dead now these fourteen years but as present as ever in his heart and mind. He had, he told Evans, 'taken great pains with the Xmas No.' and thought it 'a very good one'. He was proportionately furious, therefore, when a bad misprint in his own contribution jumped out at him from the published version: 'we commit his body to the Deep' was printed as 'we commit his body in the Dark'. Dickens raged, 'I don't believe there is a beastly unstamped newspaper in London in which such a flagrant and unpardonable mistake would be made.' He added, 'I am so disgusted by it that I throw down my pen in absolute despair, and could as soon paint an historical picture as go on writing.'[27]

As 1851 drew to its close Dickens continued to focus much of his energy on the Guild but now also on the actual writing of his carefully-planned and very ambitious new novel. The last Guild performance of the year took place in Reading on 23 December and Dickens looked forward to the organisation of further ones in the North in February and in the Midlands in the spring. That he could contemplate with equanimity the addition, in the near future, of these considerable histrionic and 'Managerial' exertions to all his other commitments, including the major new literary work upon which he had just embarked, suggests that he felt very confident indeed about the latter. It was a confidence which the acclaim of many generations of readers of *Bleak House*, right down to our own day, has shown to have been entirely justified.

CHAPTER-NOTE ON THE GUILD OF LITERATURE AND ART, 1852–1897, BY
FLORIAN SCHWEIZER

Dickens remained involved with the Guild's activities until his death, missing only five out of forty-six committee meetings between 1852 and 1870. Despite its initial success as a publicity and fund-raising stunt (£3,615 was raised in the first year), the Guild was beset with problems. Fellow-authors – including Macaulay and Thackeray – criticised the scheme severely, and there was virtually no interest in it within the literary community. Furthermore, the bill of incorporation restricted the activities of the Guild, ruling, to Dickens's fury, that no pensions could be awarded until seven years had elapsed. According to committee member John R. Robinson, the Guild was 'all ready' by 1854, but 'it was standing still'. There were no applications for the life assurance scheme, and even after the Guild was finally allowed to grant pensions the only people who approached it were relatives of deceased authors. Apart from the regular committee meetings, at which grants were occasionally awarded, Dickens spent little time on Guild affairs. But the office of *Household Words* served as the Guild's headquarters and Wills took on the role of secretary. Dickens's campaign, together with Forster and Dilke, to reform the more successful Royal Literary Fund probably resulted from his frustration with the Guild but this only led to increased scrutiny of the failed Guild scheme. Some Guild houses were eventually built in Stevenage in 1865 and Dickens spoke optimistically at the opening ceremony (see below, p. 538) but no writer or artist ever moved into this accommodation.

The Guild never recovered from the blows it had received in its early years. New problems arose in the 1860s when, after no suitable recipient of an annuity could be found, the compulsory life assurance for membership and compulsory subscription to a sickness fund were given up. By 1868 various ideas for the future of the Guild were mooted, including the establishment of literary scholarships and the sale of the Guild houses. The houses were soon sold but the Guild continued to exist in a dormant state until it was finally dissolved by an Act of Parliament in 1897, its fund being distributed between the Royal Literary Fund and the Artists' General Benevolent Fund.

CHAPTER 15

Writing *Bleak House*

1852–1853

. . . never in any former work has Mr Dickens made use of a plot so evidently planned before-hand with minute consideration, or throughout so elaborately studied.

The Examiner, 8 October 1853

DICKENS HAD, as we have seen, been working towards *Bleak House* for nearly a year. At some point during this period he decided to have two very different but related settings at the heart of the novel's plot and its social message. These are a festering London slum and the High Court of Chancery, the latter being the subject of much adverse publicity at this time. He had also decided on a particular theme, adumbrated in his 1851 speech to the Metropolitan Sanitary Association, that would, in a way unprecedented in his earlier books, pervade and give a remarkable unity to this long story with its ramifying plot and large cast of characters. This was a much more closely planned procedure than the one outlined in his *Dombey* 'prospectus' where his project was simply to 'carry the story on, through all the branches and off-shoots and meanderings that come up'. *Bleak House*'s unifying theme is that of infection, both physical and moral. The putrescence of Tom-all-Alone's infects other, very different, places, reaching even as far as Mr Jarndyce's pleasant rural home, while the malign rigmarole of Chancery infects its suitors with mania and madness. At plot level the London slum and the High Court are linked because Tom-All-Alone's is itself 'in Chancery'. Finally, there is the already-mentioned highly innovative form of narration that Dickens devised for telling this story. In all important respects, then, he knew just where he was going with this new novel, just what he wanted to achieve, and just how he would seek to achieve it. One indication of this was his evident ability to provide Browne with a good deal more information than usual at this stage about plot, themes and characters. Browne's wrapper-design for the monthly parts is consequently much more specific in its details than the more gener-alised one he had created for the *Copperfield* monthly wrapper. Dickens's relations with Browne seem to have been generally good during their work together on *Bleak House* (as indeed they had been during *Copperfield*) and Dickens was keen to have his 'cher Brune' join him in Boulogne to celebrate the conclusion of the novel in July 1853. *Bleak House* is generally regarded as the last of Dickens's novels in which artist and writer seem to be working well together, with Browne evidently responding to new developments in Dickens's art. The most striking example of this is provided by the famous 'dark plates' which Browne began providing in No. XII, primarily to illustrate the darkening story of Lady Dedlock, though there is also a powerful plate of Tom-All-Alone's in *Bleak House* XIV. The Lady Dedlock sequence culminates, very dramatically, in the plate entitled 'Morning' (*Bleak House* XVIII), depicting Lady Dedlock's corpse lying in the gateway of the pestiferous London churchyard where her lover is buried.[1]

Dickens's previous working-out of the new novel's overall design, and his meticulously-structured working week (at his desk in his study from 10 to 2 every day, Tuesdays for Urania Cottage committee meetings, Wednesday evenings and Thursdays for *Household Words* business, and so on), enabled him to make steady progress month by month with the writing of *Bleak House* whilst continuing to fulfil his numerous outside commitments. Among the latter was the tremendous task of organising no fewer than three more provincial tours by the Amateurs for the Guild during 1852. He continued, too, to be inundated with requests to speak at public dinners on behalf of this or that charitable institution and dealt with this by making it a rule to accept only two such invitations ('very rarely more') at the beginning of the public-dinner season and to stick to those. The begging-letter writers he had always with him, of course, and here the remarkable thing is the number of individual cases he actually made time to follow up, with help from Wills who seems to have replaced Fred in this role. Sometimes he also took the trouble to refer apparently deserving cases to Burdett Coutts for possible relief. Almost as troublesome as this class of correspondents were the visitors to London bearing letters of introduction to him. They forced him to retreat to Folkestone in early July, ahead of the usual date for his household's annual move to the seaside. At another point (March 1853) incessant 'invitations to feasts and festivals', added to his heavy work-load, made him feel, he wrote, that his head would split 'like a fired shell' if he stayed in London. He bolted to Brighton for ten days to concentrate on his writing.[2]

While in London he sought relief from his punishing schedule by impromptu 'outs', as he called them, when he would suddenly summon a friend or two, Frank Stone or Lemon or (increasingly) Wilkie Collins, to accompany him on a London ramble, a theatre visit or a day at the seaside. These occasions were, of course, different in kind from the frequent research trips he would make, often with Wills or Morley, for *Household Words* purposes, like his Boxing Day visit to St Luke's Hospital for the insane on 26 December 1851, subsequently written up jointly with Wills in the 17 January issue of the journal as 'A Curious Dance

32 Admission ticket to an Amateurs' performance in aid of the Guild of Literature and Art

Round a Curious Tree'. Such visits could feed into his current fictional work in addition to supplying material for his journal. It seems very likely, for example, that the memory of a patient he saw at St Luke's, 'the old-young woman with the weird gentility', contributed to the creation of the comic-pathetic little madwoman Miss Flite, introduced at the end of *Bleak House*, chapter 3. And we can, I think, be certain that the utterly forlorn dying orphan boy, observed by Dickens on a late February visit to a Ragged School dormitory for homeless men and boys, and described with such unforgettable poignancy in his subsequent article 'A Sleep to Startle Us', contributed much, along with the crossings-sweeper George Ruby, to his depiction of Jo, who makes his first appearance in *Bleak House* IV, written just a couple of months later.[3]

Some of Dickens's previous journalistic concerns also feed into the early numbers of *Bleak House*, written during the first three months of 1852. The ill-fated Niger expedition of 1841, ridiculed by him in *The Examiner* in 1848, lies behind Mrs Jellyby's plan for sending colonists to cultivate the coffee bean and educate the natives of Borrioboola-Gha. His 1843 spoof Commissioners' Report on the Oxford Movement in the Anglican Church is recalled in the Puseyite figure of Mrs Pardiggle with her fondness for attending matins 'very prettily done' and in the ladies who demand money from Mr Jarndyce to help found a 'Sisterhood of Medieval Marys'. His *Examiner* denunciations of Drouet are echoed in his account of Guster, Mrs Snagsby's epileptic maid-of-all-work, who was 'contracted for, during her growing time, by an amiable benefactor of his species resident at Tooting'. Of a rather different order of borrowing from life is his modelling of the parasitic dilettante Harold Skimpole on Leigh Hunt, now approaching seventy and (thanks largely to Dickens) in receipt of a government pension but, despite this, still as improvident as ever. Dickens defended this recognisable depiction of his friend and fellow-writer both to Hunt himself and, after his death, publicly in *All The Year Round*, by claiming he had only copied a few of Hunt's surface mannerisms. To Lavinia Watson, however, he confided, on 21 September 1853, that Skimpole was 'the most exact portrait that ever was painted in words!', adding, 'There is not an atom of exaggeration or suppression' though he had kept the 'outward figure away from the real man'. Responding at the time of writing to Forster's uneasiness about the matter, he changed the character's first name from Leonard to Harold and made other manuscript alterations designed to diminish Skimpole's resemblance to Hunt. He also noted, when returning the proofs of *Bleak House* II, that Browne's depiction of Skimpole had 'helped to make him singularly unlike the great original'. Nevertheless, in Forster's opinion 'the radical wrong remained'. The fact is that, whatever personal affection or gratitude for his literary work Dickens may have felt for Hunt, he could not have failed to recognise in him a prime example of the irresponsible artist, heavily dependent on patronage, pensions and the generosity of friends, whose presumed typicality made people sceptical about the success of the projected Guild of Literature and Art. Skimpole is just the kind of ostentatiously amateur artist whom Sir Leicester Dedlock is delighted to patronise, and the way he is presented in *Bleak House* undoubtedly reflects Dickens's preoccupation with the Guild project at this time (the novel is indeed dedicated 'to my Companions in the Guild of Literature and Art').[4]

The Skimpole question is complicated, however, by the fact that Dickens evidently became fascinated by his own depiction of Hunt, finding, as he put it, 'a delightful manner reproducing itself under my hand', so that the fictional character soars almost as free of his 'great original' as Pecksniff had done of Samuel Carter Hall or Micawber of John Dickens. Micawber remains a very engaging character, however, whereas Dickens makes Skimpole a hypocritical villain similar to Pecksniff but less comic, so that it is hardly surprising Hunt was deeply hurt. No such complexities occur in the case of Boythorn, brought in as a foil both to Skimpole and Sir Leicester. This character is, Dickens boasted to Lavinia Watson (who seems to have anticipated later Dickens enthusiasts in her curiosity about his 'originals') 'a most exact portrait' of his cherished friend and old admirer Landor. He faithfully copies the old poet's loudness of speech, vehemence of expression and uproarious laughter but in this case his imagination does not ignite and he fails to make the character anything more than a Dickensian 'turn', complete with a pet canary put in to suggest the gentle nature that lies beneath all the boisterousness.[5]

The first number of *Bleak House* appeared on 28 February. The initial printing of 25,000 copies (based on the sales of *Copperfield* in parts) sold out within three days and Bradbury and Evans had to reprint again and again. *The Athenaeum* hailed the number on 3 March as 'rich in promise of powerful interest and abundant amusement' and quoted at length from the descriptions of the Court of Chancery and of Chesney Wold. By the end of June a total of 38,500 of the first number had been printed and the initial print run for No. V was set at 35,000. 'It is a most enormous success,' Dickens wrote to de Cerjat on 8 May, 'all the prestige of Copperfield (which was very great) telling upon it, and raising its circulation above all my other books.' It was also the occasion of Dickens's breaking his 1842 pledge to have no more dealings with American publishers. He entered into an agreement with Harper & Brothers to supply them with advance sheets of *Bleak House* for £360 and was later to make similar arrangements with them for *Little Dorrit*, *A Tale of Two Cities*, *Great Expectations* and *Our Mutual Friend*, amounting to a total profit for him of £2,860.[6]

Altogether, it was a triumphant time for him. He had been, he reported to Catherine on 13 February, most rapturously received at Liverpool during the Guild tour of 11–14 February. With what I am sure he would have thought of as 'manly' sobriety, he added, 'the earnest admiration and love of the people towards one, is something quite bewildering – or would be, if one were not steady in such matters'. He is forced to close his letter 'abruptly', he tells her, but we may nevertheless feel some surprise at the absence of any special enquiry about her health, she being at this point eight months pregnant (one might almost think he was trying to ignore the fact). On 13 March their tenth and last child (inevitably

33 Section of Browne's monthly-part cover for *Bleak House*

named, in the midst of all the Guild excitement, Edward Bulwer Lytton Dickens)
arrived and Dickens wrote to Burdett Coutts as follows: 'I am happy to say that
Mrs Dickens and the seventh son – whom I cannot afford to receive with perfect
cordiality, as on the whole I could have dispensed with him – are as well as
possible.' Not the least strange thing about this very strange genius was his jocose
assumption in such letters that these regular childbirths were events for which he
had no responsibility. Once a baby had actually arrived, however, he seems always
to have responded warmly to it. Edward, always called 'Plorn' (an abbreviation of
the fantastic nickname 'The Plornishghenter' Dickens bestowed on him) became,
in fact, a particular favourite, as little Dora had been before him. As to Dora,
continuing grief for his lost child can be sensed behind a passage Dickens wrote
at this very time, in an article publicising the newly-opened Children's Hospital
in Great Ormond Street. The article, 'Drooping Buds', was written jointly with
Morley but the passage beginning, 'Baby's dead, and will be never, never, never
seen among us any more!' is certainly from Dickens's pen. In it he alludes not
only to Dora but, as he had done in 'What Christmas Is, as we Grow Older', also
to his late nephew Harry Burnett. The passage connects also with the great infection theme of *Bleak House*. Dickens imagines hearing the voices of children
(compositely called 'Baby') who may have died in years gone by in the old
mansion occupied by the new Hospital. Among them is one belonging to a child
'who lived to walk and talk . . . and to influence the whole of this great house and
make it very pleasant, until the infection that could not be stopped was brought
here from those poorer houses not far off, and struck us one day while we were
at play, . . . and killed us in our promise!'[7]

Dickens's 'mems' for the early numbers of *Bleak House* show him looking
far ahead to later plot-developments. In his notes for No. 2, for example, he
instructs himself to 'Introduce the old Marine Store Dealer who has the papers',
and to include the 'Foreshadowing legend of the country house'. Similarly, one
of his notes for No.V, in which Lady Dedlock seeks out her lover's grave, is
'shadowing forth of Lady Dedlock at the churchyard', looking forward to the
very end of the book (after the last number had been published on 1 September
1853 Dickens wrote to Cerjat, 'It was necessary to kill Lady Dedlock, and to kill
her so. I had intended it from the first, and everything worked to that end.').
No.V also includes a description of Mr Tulkinghorn at home in Lincoln's Inn
Fields, and Dickens reminds himself to refer to the painted ceiling of the old
lawyer's room with the words 'Pointing hand of Allegory', looking forward
ten numbers to the description of Tulkinghorn's murder. But, as always, he
readily makes use of any suitable new material that happens to come to hand
while he is in process of composition. William Challinor, a solicitor, after
reading the first number, sent Dickens, at work on No. III, a copy of his 1849
revised pamphlet *The Court of Chancery: its inherent Defects, by a Solicitor*
and Dickens, as he later made clear in his preface to *Bleak House*, proceeded to

base the history of the maddened Chancery suitor Gridley, which he brings in two numbers later, on one of the cases of grievous injustice recorded by Challinor. Another, more minor, example is the detail in chapter 13 about Richard Carstone's having spent eight years at a public school merely learning how to make Latin verses. This doubtless owes something to Dickens's suspicion, expressed in a letter to Burdett Coutts a few weeks before, that Charley's Eton schoolmaster 'would like nothing better than to keep him making Latin verses for the next five years' which would be 'not quite rational in such a case'.[8]

Dickens had hoped to finish no. IV (chs 11–13), which, with good reason, he thought 'rather a stunner', on 1 May. This number introduces the reader to Jo in the virtuoso inquest scene, as well as to Hortense, Lady Dedlock's tigerish maid whose creation was inspired by memories of Maria Manning, and develops two important relationships, that between Ada and Richard and that between Jarndyce and Esther. It continues the anti-Puseyite satire in describing the 'Dandies in Religion' at Chesney Wold and opens the satire on party politics with rival party leaders speechifying at Sir Leicester's dinner-table. And all the time Dickens is continuing carefully to lay the ground for future plot-developments – as, for example, in this note about creating a suspenseful ending to the number: 'Mr Tulkinghorn and Lady Dedlock. Each watching the other. Open that interest and leave them so.' Dickens did not, in fact, manage to finish the number until 8 May, having on the 3rd to speak at a Royal Academy Banquet, and on the 4th to chair a meeting of authors calling for the removal of 'Trade Restrictions on the Commerce of Literature' (among those present was young Mary Anne Evans, the future George Eliot, who admiringly noted Dickens's ability to preserve a 'courteous neutrality of eyebrow' and to speak 'with clearness and decision'). At last, however, the number was done and Dickens could report to Cerjat that he could now begin to look forward to 'good things' to come in his novel, 'whereof the foundations are built'. In June he made a brief trip to St Alban's to look about him 'for Bleak House purposes', and visited the gaol which suggests that he may have been thinking ahead to when Jo comes to St Alban's as a vagrant in *Bleak House* X, the December number. It was in May, we might note, that, in order to ease the writing pressure on himself, he seems to have begun experimenting with dictating, perhaps to a clerk, the successive instalments of the *Child's History* (by now he had reached Edward III). Later on, apparently, he would dictate the *History* regularly to Georgina 'while walking about the room, as a relief from his long, sedentary imprisonment' working on *Bleak House*.[9]

During the next thirteen months Dickens worked steadily on *Bleak House*, encouraged by the high sales of the monthly parts. He worked to his customary pattern of three, or occasionally four, chapters to a number. Generally, two of these are written in the past tense by Esther and one is in third-person and present tense. Five numbers, however, those dealing primarily with the Tulkinghorn /Lady Dedlock plot, in which Dickens's political satire is interwoven with the presentation of Chesney Wold, are entirely third person. And in the final, double, number only two chapters are third-person while six are narrated by Esther, the whole novel ending on her significantly unfinished sentence, 'even supposing –'. It does not seem, from the evidence of the *Bleak House* manuscript, that Dickens had greater problems when writing as Esther than he did when writing the third-person chapters. Nevertheless, he would have been conscious of setting himself a peculiarly difficult task in ventriloquising Esther and was much gratified when a young American journalist called Grace Greenwood congratulated him on such a 'wonderful instance of mental transmigration':

> Mr Dickens . . . confessed that the character of this young lady, as autobiographically evolved, had cost him no little labor and anxiety. 'Is it quite natural,' he asked 'quite girlish?' I replied that if an American could speak for English young-womanhood, it certainly was; and when he said he was about to get Esther in love, and hardly knew how he should be able to manage the delicate difficulties of the case, I told him that I was sure he would carry her triumphantly through – and he did.[10]

This conversation must have happened during July 1852 when Dickens was working on *Bleak House* VI (in which Esther receives a nosegay, tantamount to a declaration of love, from Alan Woodcourt, whom she has mentioned only very coyly and obliquely up to this point). It seems pretty clear from what Dickens wrote to various female friends a few months later that he felt confident he was managing 'the delicate difficulties of the case' very well, 'triumphantly', indeed. By this time he was at work on *Bleak House* X–XI (chs 30–35) in the course of which Esther first strongly hints at, and finally confesses, her love for Alan Woodcourt. He told Lavinia Watson on 22 November he had just come to 'the point I have been patiently working up to in the writing, and I hope it will suggest to you a pretty and affecting thing'. He is most probably here referring to Esther's disfigurement as a result of an infection (presumably smallpox) caught while she was nursing her little maid who had been infected by Jo. The 'pretty and affecting thing' he hopes it may suggest to Mrs Watson is Esther's heartbreaking resolve to abandon, for Alan Woodcourt's sake, all dreams that he might one day return the love she has for him. Dickens's working notes for No. X include this: 'Esther's love must be kept in view, to make the coming trial the greater and the victory the more meritorious'. Her disfigurement must also be the 'great turning idea of Bleak House' that he mentions to Burdett Coutts on 19 November, telling her that leading up to it had kept him 'in a perpetual scald and boil'. On Christmas Day, shortly before the publication of no. XI, he sent Mary Boyle one of his mock-flirtatious effusions in the character of Joe as assumed by Sir Charles in *Used Up*: 'O Mary wen you come to read the last chapter of the next number of Bleak House [i.e., ch. 35] I think my ever dear as you will say as him what we knows on as done a pretty womanly thing as the sex will like and will make a sweet pint for to turn the story on.' The 'pretty womanly thing' to which Dickens draws attention is Esther's renunciation and her agonised thankfulness that Woodcourt was not her accepted lover: 'What should I have suffered, if I had had to write to him, and tell him the poor face he had known as mine was quite gone from me, and that I freely released him from his bondage to one whom he had never seen!' Esther's 'womanly' sacrifice 'turns' the story in that it leads on to her emotionally confused acceptance of Jarndyce's proposal of marriage and to her later discovery, with a kind of awed joy, that Jarndyce's still greater selflessness has ensured that she is finally united with her one true love.[11]

Esther was widely, but not universally, admired by the first readers of *Bleak House*. *Bentley's Monthly Review* found her 'perfectly *lovable* in every way', for example, but Charlotte Brontë thought her style 'too often weak and twaddling', and George Brimley in *The Spectator* wished she 'would either do something very "spicy", or confine herself to superintending the jam-pots at Bleak House'. Dickens himself, however, evidently felt sufficiently comfortable about his writing as Esther to use female autobiographical narrators again, albeit very different ones, in *Little Dorrit* (Miss Wade and Little Dorrit herself in her long letters to Clennam from Italy, which are very much in Esther's self-abnegating mode) and in his 1863 and 1864 Christmas stories (Emma Lirriper).[12]

The dominant tone adopted by Dickens in the third-person chapters of *Bleak House* is very different from Esther's. It is mainly ironic and satirical, often caustic, frequently polemical and sometimes downright accusatory, as, most famously, in the 'Dead, Your Majesty!' passage that ends chapter 47 describing Jo's death. Not surprisingly, readers were sometimes provoked into responding, like the clergyman who wrote to Dickens to protest against what he saw as an attack on Christian overseas missions in chapter 16 (Jo marvelling at the imposing premises of the Society for the Propagation of the Gospel in Foreign Parts, having 'no idea, poor wretch, of . . . what it costs to look up the precious souls among the cocoa-nuts and bread-fruit'). That great *Pickwick* fan Lord Denman publicly criticised the Borrioboola-Gha satire, linking it with what he saw as pro-slavery bias in *Household Words*, and also accused Dickens of opportunistically jumping on the bandwagon of the press campaign against Chancery abuses. Dickens vigorously defended himself on both occasions.[13]

He had more of a problem with a different kind of objection that was raised, also publicly, by George Henry Lewes, with whom he was on friendly terms and who was a member of the Amateurs. *Bleak House* X (chs 30–32), the December 1852 number and the mid-point of the book's serialisation, ends with Krook's sensational death by spontaneous combustion. Dickens means the reader to be startled into a fearful realisation that a corrupt and unjust institution like Chancery (emblematic of contemporary British society as a whole) will, if not radically reformed, suffer the fate that Carlyle in his great history *The French Revolution*, read over and over again by Dickens, shows befalling the *ancien régime*. It will collapse or disintegrate as a result of its own inner rottenness. This invocation of the notion of spontaneous combustion was too much for Lewes. Writing on 11 December in *The Leader*, a new radical weekly he had co-founded with Leigh Hunt's son, Thornton (who, presumably, was also upset with Dickens on account of the Skimpole caricature), he reproached Dickens for promoting bad science. He was doing so by subscribing to the 'vulgar error' that people, especially drunkards, might perish by 'spontaneous combustion', an idea Dickens had perhaps picked up 'among the curiosities of his reading'. Dickens was evidently stung by this attack. It was not only Lewes's patronising attitude towards his reading but the fact that the literal truth underlying his emblematic art (as distinct from his use of 'fancy') was always of immense importance to him. The fog at the beginning of *Bleak House* had to be a real London fog as well as a perfect symbol for the Court of Chancery. Spontaneous combustion had to be a real, if rare, occurrence in nature for it to function as a perfect symbol for future institutional collapse. He promptly went on the offensive with a response to Lewes in the January number of *Bleak House*. Rather heavy-handedly, he inserts into his description in chapter 33 of the local aftermath of Krook's death (otherwise a brilliant reprise of the description of the same thing after Nemo's death in ch.11) a raft of decidedly arcane authorities for the existence of spontaneous combustion as a natural phenomenon, and lists citations of various actual occurrences – all dating from the previous century, however. Lewes responded in successive issues (5 and 12 Feb.) of *The Leader*, confuting Dickens's claims by reference to more recent authorities. Dickens, fortified by advice from Elliotson, next wrote privately, and somewhat irritably, to Lewes, still asserting his belief in this bizarre medical myth but kept most of his powder dry for a final broadside in the preface he would write for the publication of the novel in volume form.[14]

During the period he was composing *Bleak House* Dickens wrote, or collaborated in the writing of, no fewer than twenty-five articles for his journal. He also, of course, continued with his irregular serialisation in its pages of the lively *Child's History*: he laments Joan of Arc's refusal to become 'a good man's wife', relishes the chance to lambast his 'favourite ruffian' Henry VIII, and really goes to town on James I, or 'His Sowship' as he called him ('He used to loll on the necks of his favourite courtiers, and slobber their faces . . .'). As to the articles, the majority of them dealt with political and social matters and included a fair amount of the kind of writing that he characterised as 'savage and zoological roaring'. Many relate closely, as we might expect, to the satire and social criticism in the novel. He pillories the Prime Minister Lord Derby as 'the Honourable Member for Verbosity' in 'Our Honourable

Friend' (31 July) and in such articles as 'Boys to Mend' (11 Sept.) and 'In and Out of Jail' (14 May 1853), both written jointly with Morley, he continues that fierce exposure of the national disgrace of governmental neglect of all the teeming children of the slums represented in *Bleak House* by Jo. The scathing condemnation in 'Trading in Death' (27 Nov.) of the 'barbarous show and expense' of pompous funerals, provoked by the widespread commercial exploitation of the Duke of Wellington's state funeral on 18 November, looks forward to the satirical description six months later of Tulkinghorn's grand funeral (ch. 53) with its procession of 'inconsolable carriages' and 'bereaved worms, six feet high' (that is, footmen dressed in mourning). In 'Proposals for Amusing Posterity' (12 Feb.1853) he echoes Esther's (somewhat uncharacteristic) satirical observations on the British Honours system which had just appeared, topically enough because of the publication of the New Year's Honours List, in chapter 35 in *Bleak House* XI, the January number. Dickens's anger at society's abandonment of Jo because he is 'not one of Mrs Pardiggle's Tockahoopo Indians ... not a genuine foreign-grown savage' but only 'the ordinary home-made article' (ch. 47, written April 1853), also fuels his ferocious contempt for the public's adulation of the 'Zulu Kaffirs' currently on exhibition in London. Published under the title 'The Noble Savage' in *Household Words* on 18 June, this diatribe makes for uncomfortable reading today, sharply reminding us, like his later response to the Indian Mutiny, of the limitations of Dickens's sympathies in certain respects.[15]

One of the most remarkable of his *Household Words* essays written during this period seems to belong more to the world of *Our Mutual Friend* than that of *Bleak House*, however. This is 'Down With the Tide' (5 Feb. 1853), describing a nocturnal excursion with the Thames police (the article may have been based on his interview with a police inspector at the *Household Words* office rather than on actual experience), which he had first thought of asking Sala to write before taking the subject himself. With its powerful evocation of the dark river itself, discussion of suicides, and detailed description of the variety of nefarious trades that are plied along the river's banks, it shows that the setting for the story of Gaffer Hexam, his daughter and his sometime partner Rogue Riderhood was already present in Dickens's imagination long before he began the novel to which they belong. It is, so to speak, eleven years ahead of its time in his writing life.

Likewise anticipative of later developments in his art are certain other remarkable essays of this *Bleak House* period such as 'Lying Awake' and 'Where We Stopped Growing' (as well as a long nostalgic passage about childhood pleasures in another article called 'First Fruits', which was mostly the work of Sala). Like two earlier pieces, 'A Christmas Tree' and 'Our School', these writings are in the personal/reminiscent mode, a genre of essay-writing that Dickens was to bring to perfection in his 'Uncommercial Traveller' series seven years later. The second of them, 'Where We Stopped Growing', was written for the 1853 New Year's Day issue of *Household Words*. In it Dickens focuses on his childhood memories of stories, people and places, and on the importance for our happiness and moral health in later life of preserving the child in us by never outgrowing such memories. A few months earlier, he had introduced the Smallweed family into *Bleak House* as horrible specimens of the dehumanising result of depriving children of 'all amusements . . . all story-books, fairy tales, fictions, and fables', something he will make a leading theme in his next novel *Hard Times*.[16]

As we have seen, Dickens's work for his magazine was by no means confined to writing the articles credited to him, wholly or in part, in the Contributors' Book. 'I diffuse myself with infinite pains through Household Words and leave very few pages indeed, untouched,' he told de la Rue on 4 December 1853. In addition to all the endless revision and rewriting this involved he was in constant correspondence with staffers and other contributors, often entering into considerable detail. One would-be contributor, for example, who had used the 'gentle reader' formula, was adjured (28 Feb. 1853), in imagery reminiscent of the opening of *Bleak House*, 'to dismiss the Gentle Reader as a monster of the Great Mud Period, who has no kind of business on the face of the literary Earth'. On another occasion, Morley received a virtual tutorial by post, reflecting light on Dickens's own journalistic practice as well as on the missionary zeal that lay behind his writings. The sort of papers needed for *Household Words*, Dickens told him on 31 October 1852

> are not to be done without trouble; and the main trouble necessary to them, is the devising of some pleasant means of telling what is to be told. The indis-pensable necessity of varying the manner of narration as much as possible, and investing it with some little grace or other, would be very evident to you if you knew as well as I do how severe the struggle is, to get the publication down into the masses of readers, and to displace the prodigious heaps of nonsense and worse than nonsense, which suffocate their better sense.

Nothing annoyed Dickens more than the idea that any kind of worthwhile writing could be done easily. In late March and early April 1853 he was hard at work on a particularly demanding number of Bleak House, No. XV, in which several climactic events occur: the death of Jo (among Dickens's 'mems' for this number is the famously laconic 'Jo? Yes. <u>Kill him</u>'), the murder of Tulkinghorn, and the arrest of George Rouncewell. He happened also at this point to be collaborating with Morley on 'H.W.' dealing with the production of the magazine itself. He seized the opportunity to try to disabuse readers of any illu-sions they might be under with regard to the life of a writer – the kind of illu-sion, for example, apparently harboured by the typical perpetrator of the kind of hopelessly badly written offering that was constantly pouring into the maga-zine's office. Dickens comments:

He has a general idea that literature is the easiest amusement in the world. He figures a successful author as a radiant personage whose whole time is devoted to idleness and pastime – who keeps a prolific mind in a sort of corn-sieve, and lightly shakes a bushel out of it sometimes, in an odd half hour after breakfast. It would amaze his incredulity beyond all measure, to be told that such elements as patience, study, punctuality, determination, self-denial, training of mind and body, hours of application and seclusion to produce what he reads in seconds, enter into such a career. He has no more conception of the necessity of entire devotion to it, than he has of an eternity from the beginning. Correction and re-correction in the blotted manuscript, consideration, new observation, the patient massing of many reflections, experiences and imaginings for one minute purpose, and the patient separation from the heap of all the fragments that will unite to serve it – these would be Unicorns or Griffins to him – fables altogether.

Dickens wrote *Bleak House* VI–VIII (chs 17–25), the August, September and October numbers, together with half-a-dozen sole or joint-authored articles for *Household Words* during his family's summer seaside residence (in Dover this year) which ended on 3 October. The children were then sent back to Tavistock House while Dickens and Catherine, accompanied by Georgina, went across to stay in a hotel in Boulogne for a couple of weeks. This was partly, no doubt, to avoid the bustle of the re-occupation of the London home so Dickens could concentrate on *Bleak House* IX (chs 26–29). But he probably also wanted to reconnoitre Boulogne as a possible summer destination for the family next year, Broadstairs being now so notorious as the place where Dickens spent his summers that it could no longer serve him as a bolt-hole, and Dover had evidently not proved to be a wholly satisfactory substitute. He found Boulogne 'as quaint, picturesque, good a place as I know' and determined to bring the family there the following summer, when he would be finishing the novel. Returning to London, he had to turn his mind to the *Household Words* Christmas number for which he was evidently hankering to find some framework that should make it more than just a random collection of stories. Asking James White for a contribution on 19 October, Dickens told him the number was to 'consist entirely of short stories supposed to be told by a family sitting round the fire' at Christmas time, with titles like 'The Grandfather's Story', 'The Father's Story', and so on. He had another tussle of wills with Gaskell (who had been keeping him waiting more than six months for the last instalment of *Cranford*) over her ghost tale 'The Old Nurse's Story', which he greatly admired but the ending of which he vainly tried to persuade her to alter. He himself contributed two items. The first, 'The Poor Relation's Story', is an exercise in the mode of Charles Lamb's 'Dream Children' on the theme, very resonant for Dickens, of how imagination may compensate for unsatisfactory reality. The second, 'The Child's Story', was written in the same allegorical register as 'A Child's Dream of A Star' and shows how neither our former selves nor our dead loved ones are really lost to us but live on with us in our memory. This last story doubtless reflects Dickens's sorrow over the many bereavements he had suffered during the previous year or so – his father, his infant daughter and, more recently, three dear friends, Richard Watson, Count D'Orsay, and Macready's wife Catherine. 'This tremendous sickle certainly does cut deep into the surrounding corn, when one's own small blade has ripened,' he wrote to Forster, adding, 'But *this* is all a Dream, may be, and death will wake us.'[17]

Dickens continued to fulfil what he saw as the responsibilities flowing from his position as a leader of the literary profession ('our order', as he liked to call it). With these responsibilities came certain rewards. On 6 January he was fêted as a 'national writer' in Birmingham by a civic association formed to award prizes in the Fine Arts and was presented with a silver-gilt salver and a diamond ring. Returning thanks, he spoke of his high estimation of 'the working people' in remarks that connect with his admiring presentation of Mr Rouncewell the ironmaster, who had made his first appearance in *Bleak House* two months earlier. Rouncewell represents Dickens's idea of a Carlylean 'Captain of Industry' but his characterisation may well owe something to his creator's admiration for Paxton also. At a banquet following the presentation, Dickens replied to a toast to 'The Literature of England', coupled with his name. Mindful of the Guild, he rejoiced in the passing of Grub Street with its miserable dependence on aristocratic favour. 'From all such evils', he declared, 'the people have set Literature free.' Any 'true man' with something to say could now be sure of an audience, 'always supposing', he added, bringing in one of his own guiding principles, 'that he be not afflicted with the coxcombical idea of writing down to the popular intelligence ...'. His hosts joyfully accepted his spontaneous offer to give a public reading of *A Christmas Carol* in Birmingham the following Christmas in aid of a projected new Industrial and Literary Institute (Dickens specified that he would want large numbers of workfolk to be given free admission to the reading).[18]

While he was working on *Bleak House* Dickens extended his Burdett Coutts portfolio, so to speak, by involving himself in various of Burdett Coutts's schemes for improving the dwellings of the poor, either by new building (he favoured apartment blocks rather than small houses) or by trying to bribe or pressure slum landlords into improving their properties. His tone in his voluminous correspondence with her about this, as about other matters, is generally pretty brisk. On one notable occasion, however, the day after his Birmingham apotheosis in fact, when he was reconnoitring a Southwark slum called Hickman's Folly as a potential site for rehabilitation, he was inspired to send her a pen-portrait of the scene as powerful and unforgettable as any passage in *Bleak House*. Southwark, location of the Marshalsea, had been the setting for some of his sharpest boyhood sufferings, and distressful memories must have stirred in him that dreary winter afternoon as he stood contemplating the 'wooden houses like horrible old packing-cases full of fever' and noticed 'a wan child' standing on a broken-down gallery at the back of one of them, looking over at 'a starved white horse who was making a meal of oystershells'. The setting sun meanwhile was 'flaring out' at the child 'like an angry fire'. Dickens, the forlorn child and the horse staring at one another seemed to him, he wrote, like 'so many figures in a dismal allegory'. The entrance to the house on the gallery of which the child was standing proved, upon investigation, to be all boarded up and Dickens closes his haunting description with the words:

> God knows when anybody will go in to the child, but I suppose it's looking over still – with a little wiry head of hair, as pale as the horse, all sticking up on its head – and an old weazen face – and two bony hands holding on to the rail of the gallery, with little fingers like convulsed skewers.

He did not forget the horse but introduced him a few weeks later, endowed with Apocalyptic resonance, into the wonderfully sinister and foreboding ending of *Bleak House* chapter 37, in which Esther vividly recalls the 'gaunt pale horse with his ears pricked up' harnessed to the gig that drove Mr Vholes and Richard away from St Alban's, 'at speed to Jarndyce and Jarndyce'.[19]

From January to August 1853 Dickens worked away steadily at the last eight numbers of *Bleak House* (the last 'double' number counting as one as usual). The continued interweaving of the stories of Esther, of Lady Dedlock, of Richard and Ada, and of Jo, whilst at the same time steadily working out the novel's overall 'purpose', surely demanded more of him than any of his previous literary endeavours had done. He was delighted by what he called the 'noble and glorious balance' of £3,264.8.0 in his favour shown in Bradbury and Evans's statement of his earnings up to the end of December 1852, which reached him on 11 March. No less than £3,106.13.6 of this balance derived from the sales of *Bleak House* I–VI. He reminds his publishers that their current agreement with him (that of 1 June 1844) will run out at the conclusion of *Bleak House* and invites them to think about future arrangements. He has, he tells them, somewhat grandly, been entirely satisfied with them and he hopes that he and they may continue business partners 'until the printer in stone who will have to be employed at last, shall set up F.I.N.I.S over our last binding in boards'.[20]

A month later, declining an invitation from Rev. Gaskell to speak at a meeting promoting the new Manchester and Salford Sanitary Association, Dickens wrote, 'since I got rid of the heavy demands upon my leisure, made by the Guild, I have accepted *no public engagement whatever*, being entirely and completely occupied with Household Words and Bleak House'. He does not mention his ongoing heavy commitment to Urania Cottage, perhaps because the Gaskells already knew about it (he was, as it happens, about to publish a long-planned account of the place in *Household Words*, in which, of course, Burdett Coutts's involvement and his own was kept wholly out of sight). He is, he tells Gaskell, very anxious to devote himself entirely to the writing of *Bleak House* 'without interruption' and will leave London 'for some months expressly for that purpose' as soon as the weather becomes more settled.[21]

One 'public engagement' he could not avoid was the Mansion House banquet in honour of the judges on 2 May at which Talfourd was to propose a toast to 'Mr Charles Dickens and the Literature of the Anglo-Saxons'. The phrasing of the toast complimented Harriet Beecher Stowe who was seated across the table from Dickens. Her *Uncle Tom's Cabin*, first published serially in America 1851–52, had sold a million and a half copies during the first year of its publication in Britain and she was now on a triumphal European tour. Dickens had distinct reservations about her art but in a *Household Words* article on 'North American Slavery' (18 Sept. 1852; written jointly with Morley) he had extolled the novel as 'a noble work; full of high power, lofty humanity'. He now again described it as 'noble' but resisted the opportunity this occasion gave him to respond publicly to Lord Denman's attacks on him the previous autumn for ridiculing anti-slavery campaigners, including Beecher Stowe, in his portrayal of Mrs Jellyby. With regard to another matter, however, Dickens could hardly fail to rise to the bait that had been dangled in front of him in an earlier speech. Sir William Page Wood, a Chancery judge, defending his Court, blamed 'the parsimony of the public' for the notorious slowness of its procedures, the number of Chancery judges having been until recently limited to two. Now they had been increased to seven all cases would be decided 'within a few months'. Professing himself delighted with this news, and picking up on the clear allusion Wood had made to Jarndyce and Jarndyce, Dickens got a laugh by saying that he 'had reason to hope that a suit which had been going on for some years past, and in which he was interested, might, by the learned judge's intervention, be brought to a satisfactory termination'.[22]

At the beginning of June Dickens, who had been complaining to Forster of overwork, was so unwell with his old kidney trouble as to be confined to bed for several days, followed by a recuperative stay in Folkestone. He could not, therefore, begin writing *Bleak House XVII*, which was to include Lady Dedlock's flight, until after he had got himself to Boulogne with Catherine and Georgina (the children were to follow when the family's accommodation had been settled) and had rented a place, discovered by Georgina, just outside the town which he described to Wills as 'the best doll's house of many rooms in the prettiest French grounds and the most charming situation I have ever seen'. He must surely have felt that he had come to live in a French version of

Jarndyce's Bleak House. Certainly, his description to Forster of the delightful irregularities of the architecture of the Château des Moulineaux, as the house was called, with doors opening on to gardens at different levels, and so on, seems almost consciously to echo Esther's description of Jarndyce's house at the beginning of the novel. By the time that he and his family had moved into Les Moulineaux Dickens had fully recovered and was cultivating a moustache. He reported himself to his writer friend Peter Cunningham as 'Vigorous, brown, energetic, muscular. The pride of Albion and the admiration of Gaul'. He was, Georgina reported to Felton on 10 August, 'at once restored to health by the change of the sea air & got to work the very day after & wrote the number which he had almost feared he would have to postpone in an incredibly short time'.[23]

Dickens was also delightedly discovering the numerous endearing eccentricities of his landlord, Ferdinand Beaucourt-Mutuel. Devoted to the memory of the great Napoleon, Beaucourt was infinitely proud of the two Boulogne properties he owned, and for which he was constantly designing some ingenious new improvement or other (rather as Dickens himself would do later when he, too, had become the proud proprietor of a little country estate). Dickens depicted Beaucourt as the gentle, endlessly courteous, 'M. Loyal Devasseur' in the article celebrating Boulogne as 'our French Watering-place' that was already forming in his mind – he was, he told Wills on 10 July, 'gathering capital materials together' for it but he must have put it aside for a while as it did not appear in *Household Words* until 4 November 1854, after the family had passed a second summer in Boulogne.

No sooner had he finished *Bleak House* XVII on 23 June than Dickens began issuing the usual stream of pressing invitations to various friends to come and visit. Wilkie Collins was asked to come for a long stay and promised a garden-room in which to write (guests were expected to employ themselves usefully for that portion of each day when Dickens was incommunicado). By about mid-July Dickens had finished no. XVIII which, Collins believed, contained in the description of Sir Leicester's reaction to the exposure of his wife's shame and her flight, 'some of the finest passages [Dickens] has ever written'. On 25 July Dickens told Wills he hoped to begin the final number in a week's time and meanwhile would *try* to write something for *Household Words* but is 'so full of the close of Bleak House' that he cannot get at a good subject. Within forty-eight hours, however, he was sending Wills the first instalment of an article with the rest promised for the next day. The article thus rapidly produced was 'Gone Astray', one of the finest of all his personal essays, which, as noted above (p. 18), may have been literally autobiographical. Even if this is not the case, this evocative memory-piece about being lost in the city as a child does read like a benignly comic, almost fairy-tale, variation on Dickens's poignant account in the autobiographical fragment of his miserable, yet also imaginatively stimulating, wanderings in the London streets as another kind of lost or abandoned child during the blacking-factory time. Just as he had then made up 'quite astonishing fictions about the wharves and the tower' for the wonderment of the little servant-girl from the workhouse, so now the child he portrays wanders about the City 'inspired by a mighty faith in the marvellousness of everything'. This emphasis on a child's stimulated imagination seems to connect the piece with another essay that Dickens tells Wills he wants to write as soon as he shall have completed *Bleak House*, to be called 'Frauds upon the Fairies'. He had been provoked by something just read in *The Examiner*, namely Forster's review of Cruikshank's new *Fairy Library* which was enthusiastic but did note (though not critically) that the artist, now a strong temperance campaigner, was altering traditional fairy-tales for propagandist purposes. His version of *Hop-o'-my-thumb*, for example, ends in a welter of propaganda for a variety of causes such as free trade, anti-gambling, total abstinence and compulsory national education (the last-named of which might have appealed to Dickens, one would have thought). Even before he had seen Cruikshank's book Dickens determined to attack it, so outraged was he by this (as he saw it) fanatical tampering with these time-honoured tales that, if left alone to work upon children's imaginations, would encourage 'gentleness and mercy' and many other virtues. [24]

Returning to 'Gone Astray', we may wonder what can have prompted Dickens, urgently needing an article for *Household Words*, to return so effectively to the lost/abandoned-child-in-the-city theme just as he was about to write the final pages of *Bleak House*? May it not have been in his mind because in this great London novel he had depicted in Jo, the benighted crossings-sweeper who 'don't know nothink', his starkest example yet of such a child? Jo is killed by the city whereas the young Dickens had not only survived but was inspired by it to write. Jo, abandoned utterly from his very birth, has never had access to such things as fairy tales and romances such as 'kept alive' the young Dickens's 'fancy' even in his darkest days, just as they do young David Copperfield's, and that help the lost child in 'Gone Astray' to turn potential terror into adventure. The young Dickens in the autobiographical fragment has enough money to buy himself a pastry or a slice of pudding, the child in 'Gone Astray' can treat himself to a German sausage, but Jo's treat consists of the bits of broken meat furtively pressed on him by the benevolent Snagsby. As he sits gnawing them and staring at the shining cross on top of the dome of St Paul's, that object is for Jo simply 'the crowning confusion of the great, confused city', whereas for the child in 'Gone Astray' St Paul's is an enchanting wonder to feast upon ('how was I to get beyond its dome, or to take my eyes from its cross of gold?'). Jo has no way of responding even to street music beyond listening to it as a dog might. In the autobiographical fragment, however, the young Dickens's story-book-fed passion for the marvellous often leads him on Saturday nights to a street show-van which he enters 'with a very motley assemblage, to see the Fat-pig, the Wild-indian, and the Little-lady'. The child in 'Gone Astray' goes one better by finding his way into an actual theatre, albeit a cheap one (Dickens here conflating happier childhood memories of Rochester Theatre with his blacking factory ones) where, once his anxieties about winning the draw for a donkey are allayed, he finds plenty on which to feast the well-nourished capacity for imaginative pleasure that he has brought with him. Jo cannot even roam freely like the young Dickens or the young David Copperfield when off duty, or like the child in 'Gone Astray'. He is always in fear of the ubiquitous Mr Bucket and his myrmidons who keep ordering him to 'move on' (among Dickens's 'mems' for Bleak House VI we find the following note: 'The great remedy for Jo and all such as he. Move on!'

By 1 August, after a brief excursion to look at Amiens, Dickens reports himself to be going 'tooth and nail' at Bleak House. Studying his plan for the final double number, we note that the left-hand half of the folded sheet, headed 'Richard's death', is a kind of check-list or roll-call of all of the novel's main surviving characters. Ticks added later against their names indicate that they duly appear, or at least get a mention, in the number. Perhaps appropriately, the only rejected character is unassuming little Mr Snagsby against whose name a later 'No' is firmly written. In any earlier book Dickens would have found some way of inserting the Snagsbys along with Guster and the wonderfully oleaginous Chadband, into the book's closing chapters (we remember the final bows taken by Mr Creakle, Uriah Heep and Littimer in *Copperfield* XIX–XX) but *Bleak House* is a very different sort of book.

Despite the intense demands on his concentration and literary skills made by bringing this long and complex novel to a conclusion, Dickens does not let up on his 'Conductorial' labours for *Household Words*. Besides the occasional article, he continues to supply regular instalments of the *Child's History*, having by this time reached the reign of Charles I, a man with 'monstrously exaggerated notions of the rights of a king'. Wills receives back from Dickens in Boulogne page after page of detailed comment on the proofs of the successive numbers of the magazine. The imperious Conductor may re-order the contents of an issue or change them altogether, he may re-title articles, delete passages (one such casualty was a passage Dickens saw as pure Skimpole in an article by Leigh Hunt), get rid of 'forlorn attempts at humour', rewrite introductory sentences, and so on. Above all, he constantly seeks to 'lighten' and 'brighten' every number. Wills receives other instructions too. He is asked to get together some informa-tion about a notorious ongoing Chancery case (one that, piquantly enough, involves the estate of a wealthy blacking manufacturer) since Dickens plans to use the preface to *Bleak House*, as he has used other prefaces before, as a platform to defend the truth to life of his art as a novelist. Meanwhile, he is also planning to publish in *Household Words*, as soon as he shall have finished the novel, an attack on another legal scandal. Over many years Burdett Coutts had been harassed and victimised by a blackmailing con man who claimed (on the basis of some grotesquely unconvincing forged 'evidence') that she had promised to marry him. Despite the absurdity of his case, he was repeatedly allowed by the Courts to exploit every possible legal loophole in order to carry on his persecution of her, even forcing her to appear in court. For Dickens it was, as he had pointed out to Burdett Coutts back in February, simply another example of that great principle of the English law that he had just identified in ch. 39 of *Bleak House*, namely the principle of making business for itself.[25]

By the time he made a flying visit to London (18–20 August) Dickens had written all but the last short chapter of *Bleak House* and this he finished, as he told Burdett Coutts 'very prettily indeed', on 27 August at the *Household Words* office. He used the same words about it in a letter of the same date to Lavinia Watson, 'I like the conclusion very much, and think it *very pretty indeed*'. The 'prettiness' presumably consisted for Dickens and, he doubtless hoped for his readers also, in the modest, affectionate, thoroughly 'womanly', way in which he has Esther tell us about the after-lives of the chief characters in her story, those in the Lady Dedlock story having been accounted for by the third-person narrator in the preceding chapter. Esther tells us how happy and busy and useful and mutually loving she and her family and her dearest friends all are. Even the initially shocking detail about Caddy's baby being born deaf and dumb tends to serve the 'prettiness' of the chapter because Esther can tell us what a tender, caring mother Caddy is to the poor child. The final 'pretty' touch is Esther's modest bashfulness about her own prettiness which prevents her from finishing her last sentence. Even allowing for the incorrigibility of those bad parents, Mrs Jellyby (now going in for 'the rights of women to sit in Parliament') and Mr Turveydrop (still exhibiting his Deportment about town), the close of Esther's narrative still seems an oddly sweet ending to such a dark, and in many ways tragic, book. It may remind us, in fact, of nothing so much as the ending of *Oliver Twist* in which all the good characters withdraw from the dark city (the portrayal of which in the earlier novel is, in fact, almost wholly confined to the criminal underworld) to form 'a little society, whose condition approached as nearly to one of perfect happiness as can ever be known in this changing world', with benevolent old bachelor John Jarndyce in place of benevolent old bachelor Mr Brownlow. Dickens, it might seem, is still struggling, in this great new phase of his art, to keep to his old 'happy ending' formula and only just managing to achieve this through the somewhat fairy-tale ending of Esther's story. He will do something similar, this time with much clearer fairy-tale overtones, with the end of Bella Wilfer's story in *Our Mutual Friend*.

Dickens, accompanied by Wills, was by 23 August back in Boulogne whither Forster, Lemon, Bradbury and Evans, and Wills had travelled to join him and the still-resident Wilkie Collins. They all dined together to celebrate the completion of *Bleak House*. Two days later Dickens read the final number to everyone who was still there. 'It made a great impression, I assure you,' he told Lavinia Watson on 27 August, adding that the story had kept its 'immense circulation from the first'. This was not quite accurate but the circulation never fell below 31,500, still stupendous in comparison with other respectable writers of the day. Also, it was substantially more than the monthly-part sales of *Copperfield*, but Dickens's assertion in the Preface, which he must have written on or about this date, that he had never had so many readers still seems a little odd when we recall that *The Old Curiosity Shop* achieved a sale of 70,000 copies a week. As regards prefaces in general, we know that he did not believe that authors should use them to explain their intentions. He thought, for example, that Collins's long 'Prefatory Letter' to *Basil* explaining his moral purpose in the book 'would have been better away', believing that 'a book (of all things) should speak for, and explain, itself'. He might seem to have somewhat broken his own rule in the brief preface he had recently written for the Cheap Edition of *The Christmas Books* (Sept. 1852) in which he asks the reader to see each of them as a 'whimsical kind of masque', intended to 'awaken some loving and forbearing thoughts, never out of season in a Christian land', but the peculiarly intimate tone adopted in these stories makes this preliminary communication to the reader seem almost integral to the stories themselves. Now, however, in his preface to the first volume edition of *Bleak House* he somewhat abruptly announces, immediately following his apologia for spontaneous combustion, 'In Bleak House, I have purposely dwelt upon the romantic side of familiar things,' – a sentence which, as has been often noted, echoes his 'Preliminary Word' to *Household Words*. His final words to his readers in this preface, or 'greeting-place' (to use the term he had used in the brief preface to *Dombey*), enhance that sense of personal contact with his ever-growing number of readers so dear to him and to them: 'May we meet again!'[26]

During the next six weeks or so, before Dickens went off, accompanied by two of his fellow-Amateurs, Collins and the artist Augustus Egg, who was four years his junior, on a long-anticipated holiday jaunt to Italy, he made a couple more trips to London, dealing with *Household Words* and Urania Cottage business. He wrote entertainingly to Catherine and to Lavinia Watson about the West End being like a veritable desert at this time of year (memories of which he would draw on seven years later for an 'Uncommercial Traveller' article for *All The Year Round*, 'Arcadian London'). He finished off the *Child's History*, covering in the last instalment (published 10 Dec.) the whole period from 1688 to the present day in a few paragraphs, asserting that the events of this period 'would neither be easily related nor easily understood in a book such as this'. Most likely, he had simply become tired of the thing, especially as the little annual volumes into which the *History* had been regularly collected for the Christmas market had not sold particularly well. Somewhat disappointing too were Bradbury and Evans's accounts for the first half of 1853 which showed that his profits were £200 less than his publishers'. He would receive only £2,300, he told Catherine, and, because of this and the expenses of his forthcoming trip, had decided against having any party this coming Christmas, apart from one for the children. Meanwhile, he wrote 'Frauds on the Fairies' and 'Things That Cannot Be Done'. When sending 'Frauds on the Fairies' to Wills on 14 September Dickens told him that, 'between ourselves', he thought it 'ADMIRABLE. Both merry and wise'. His re-telling the story of Cinderella as a temperance tract is indeed very funny, though it is a pity that in the conclusion he carries over from the end of *Bleak House* his mockery of the campaign for women's rights. He was also beginning to think about the special Christmas Number for 1853, adopting the same format as for 1852, and writes to Gaskell (as always, in the most flattering terms) and others, soliciting contributions. During the first week of October he made another trip to London to be fêted at a dinner at the London Tavern, given by all those who had acted with him in the Amateurs' fund-raising performances for the Guild. It was, he reported to Catherine, 'a most amazingly gorgeous and brilliant affair'.[27]

No comment by Dickens on the reception of *Bleak House* seems to have survived. He had long since claimed not to read any reviews of his work and perhaps his being mainly in Boulogne during September made it easier for him to avoid them this time. In London 'What do you think of *Bleak House?*' was a question that, according to *The Illustrated London News* (24 Sept.), 'everybody has heard propounded within the last few weeks', and this was certainly reflected in the number of column-inches devoted to the book by the reviewers, mixing praise and blame in pretty much equal measure. On the whole, it was the pathos of Jo and the comedy of 'the immortal Bucket', as Forster calls him (he was felt to be a worthy successor to such great Dickensian characters as Gamp and Micawber), that drew the most praise from reviewers. Amid the grumbles about 'disagreeable exaggeration', and also (incredibly) about the novel's complete lack of plot and structure, there seems to have been an almost total lack of recognition of a fundamental change or advance in Dickens's novelistic art – the double narrative, for example, is barely mentioned, though there is some enthusiasm for Esther herself. The one big exception, already cited in the epigraph to this chapter, is the long and thoughtful review in *The Examiner*, probably written by Forster and most probably read by Dickens. This does praise highly the novel's 'singularly skilful' conduct of its story and the care bestowed upon its construction. In his comments on the novel in his biography, however, Forster sees Dickens as perhaps too comprehensively and unrelentingly enforcing the book's fierce social message. We are not allowed to escape 'into the old freedom and freshness of the author's imaginative worlds', and this seems to have been a general feeling among Dickens's vast readership, a feeling that would intensify over the next five years as *Bleak House* was succeeded by two more dark, 'condition-of-England', novels.[28]

On 10 October Dickens, Collins and Egg together with their courier, Edward Kaub (Roche was dead by this time) set out for Paris en route for Lausanne, Milan and Genoa. Lausanne and Genoa were places that held many good memories for Dickens both as a man and as a writer and must have seemed to him ideal battery-recharging destinations after the long strain and pressure of writing *Bleak House*. He was eager to re-explore Italy generally, perhaps even to get as far as Sicily this time, and had been brushing up his Italian. His companions were both younger than he, Wilkie Collins twelve years younger. The group dynamics in this case therefore worked very differently from the way they did during Dickens's Cornish jaunt with Forster, Stanfield and Maclise back in 1842. This time Dickens was very much the leader, in charge of every detail. The trip was to be one of his 'outs' writ large, commensurate in scale with the twenty months of sustained intensive work that had preceded it. Moreover, Dickens, who had, he confided to Burdett Coutts on 18 September, 'vague Swiss notions' in his mind, also wanted, as he put it, to 'look about me' (his usual phrase for checking out local colour). Evidently, he was thinking of setting part, at least, of his next novel in Switzerland. Having dwelt so long and so intensely on the 'romantic side of familiar things' he was now perhaps thinking of using a contrasting, more traditional, romantic setting, rather as he had contemplated using wild and desolate Cornish scenery eleven years before. Financial considerations, however, were to cut across any such intentions if he had them. Not only would the setting of his next story be very different from Switzerland (though to many of his readers it perhaps seemed almost as exotic) but also the very format of the story, and hence its mode of reception by readers, would be quite different from the one he had been working with so successfully for the past ten years.

CHAPTER 16

Writing 'For These Times'

1853–1854

To interest and affect the general mind in behalf of anything that is clearly wrong –
to stimulate and rouse the public soul to a compassionate or indignant feeling that
it must not be – without obtruding any pet theory of cause or cure, and so throwing
off allies as they spring up – I believe to be one of Fiction's highest uses. And this is
the use to which I try to turn it.

Dickens to Henry Carey, 24 August 1854

FROM PARIS where Dickens, Collins and Egg dined with Burdett Coutts, Dickens sent the first of the series of long, gossipy, and affectionate letters he wrote to Catherine during his Swiss/Italian excursion, interspersed with similar ones to Georgina. He found Paris as exhilarating as ever and 'wonderfully improving' in appearance with its newly macadamised quaysides and the grand new extension of the Rue de Rivoli. By 16 October the travellers had reached Lausanne where Dickens had a joyous reunion with the Cerjats and Haldimand. He also renewed his acquaintance with the Mer de Glace in an adventurous expedition during which, he gleefully reported to Catherine, he was hailed by the guides as an 'Intrepid'. From Lausanne the party journeyed on to Milan and Genoa, where Dickens enjoyed more reunions with, amongst others, the Thompsons and the de la Rues. Catherine was treated to an entertaining description of the Thompsons' dishevelled domesticity but for the time being the de la Rues remained significantly unmentioned. From Genoa the travellers embarked for Naples where they stayed a few days and then, abandoning the idea of crossing to Sicily, proceeded to Rome, reaching there on 12 November.[1]

During this trip Dickens could not, of course, be as closely involved as usual with the day-to-day editing of his journal but he sought to keep Wills up to the mark with his 'solemn and continual Conductorial Injunction', promulgated on 17 November, 'KEEP "HOUSEHOLD WORDS" IMAGINATIVE!' He was mindful, too, of the need to organise the Christmas Number, a second 'round of stories by the Christmas fire'. From Rome he sent Wills the first of his own offerings, 'The Schoolboy's Story', which, he commented, 'is in a character that nobody else is likely to hit, and which is pretty sure to be considered pleasant'. It is indeed a heart-warming tale of evil repaid with good, saved from sentimentality by being mediated to us through its convincingly ventriloquised, schoolboy narrator. After a few days in Rome, where Dickens rejoiced especially to observe the electric telegraph wires piercing 'like a sunbeam through the cruel old heart of the Coliseum', he and his party moved on to first Florence and then Venice. In Venice he wrote 'Nobody's Story', his second Christmas piece – which was very far from being 'pleasant'. Nobody, the leading character, embodies the vast anonymous mass of the poor but honest, overburdened and endlessly toiling English people, and he echoes Jo's confusion when preached at by the missionaries who visit him in his slum dwelling where, he says, 'every minute of my numbered days is new mire added to the heap under which I lie oppressed'. He cannot get his children educated, nor the fetid lairs in which they have to live cleansed, neither will the powerful Bigwigs who rule him permit him and his family any 'mental refreshment and recreation' or 'humanising enjoyments' as a relief from the unremitting squalor and harshness of their existence. This last detail looks forward to a central concern of Dickens's next novel *Hard Times*, but in the main 'Nobody's Story' reads like a scathing postscript to *Bleak House*. The pestilence engendered in Nobody's slum becomes a deadly miasma threatening the grand homes of the Bigwigs, briefly terrifying them into trying to improve his lot but 'as their fear wore off . . . they resumed their falling out among themselves, and did nothing'. This was certainly a pretty ferocious Christmas offering from Dickens to the English public – the fiercest, in fact, since *The Chimes*, the only previous such offering to have been written in Italy.[2]

Dickens felt his touring holiday was doing him good after the long haul of writing *Bleak House*. 'I feel that I could not have done a better thing to clear my mind and freshen it up again, than make this expedition,' he wrote to Catherine on 14 November. He knew, however, that he had to keep on the move. 'I am so restless to be doing', he wrote to Burdett Coutts from Milan on 25 October, '– and always shall be, I think, so long as I have any portion in Time – that if I were to stay more than a week in any one City here, I believe I should be half desperate to begin some new story!!!' For the moment, however, his main literary output was epistolary. In his letters to Catherine, for example, he builds up his travelling-companions as a pair of comic characters. They amuse him especially when they discourse on 'Art, Color, Tone, and so forth'. As *Pictures from Italy* demonstrates, Dickens was a man who knew what he liked when it came to paintings and sculpture. He wanted no guidance from self-appointed experts. To Forster he wrote scornfully, 'the intolerable nonsense against which genteel taste and subserviency are afraid to rise, in connection with art, is astounding'. As to literature, Collins diverted him by expounding 'a code of morals taken from modern French novels' which, Dickens reports to Catherine, 'I instantly and with becoming gravity Smash'. Meanwhile he was sending to Forster a number of vivid little travel-sketches, among them a hilarious account of some very Chuzzlewittian-sounding Americans making fools of themselves at the Rome opera, and a powerfully sinister description of the fever-haunted desolation of the Roman Campagna.[3]

From Rome the Dickens party returned to Paris arriving there on 10 December. Charley, who had been studying German with Dickens's European publisher, Baron Tauchnitz, in Leipzig with a view to a career in commerce, joined them and they all crossed to England the following day. Dickens wrote his last letter to Catherine from Turin on 5 December. It differed from its predecessors in that it was primarily a marital lecture about her attitude towards his involvement with the de la Rues nine years earlier, and was prompted, presumably by his having seen them again in Genoa. He strongly recommends (it is, he insists, a recommendation *not* an order, and he will never enquire into whether or not she has acted on it) that Catherine should send Augusta de la Rue a friendly and sympathetic letter. As to his mesmeric treatment of Augusta, Catherine, of all people, should by now have come to understand that

> the intense pursuit of any idea that takes complete possession of me, is one of the qualities that makes me different – sometimes for good; sometimes I dare say for evil – from other men. Whatever made you unhappy in the Genoa time had no other root, beginning, middle, or end, than whatever has made you proud and honoured in your married life, and given you station better than rank, and surrounded you with many enviable things. This is the plain truth . . . .

In the absence of much knowledge of how the relationship between husband and wife actually worked, or failed to work, it is hard to know how Catherine would have felt about receiving such a letter as this which shows Dickens still resentful of the embarrassment he felt she had caused him (she would surely have been greatly hurt had she seen the letter he wrote to Burdett Coutts only a few weeks later, blaming her for Charley's 'indescribable lassitude of character', claiming this had been inherited from her along with 'tenderer and better qualities'). Whatever she may have thought, she did dutifully write to Mme de la Rue.[4]

On his return to Tavistock House *Household Words* and its plummeting circulation figures demanded his attention. Profits had dropped from between £900 and £1300 per half-year to £527.15.10 for the same period by the end of September. Dickens at once fell 'tooth and nail' upon the task of editing the extra Christmas number. Also, drawing on his great stock of knowledge of travel literature (a genre for which he had always, Forster tells us, 'an insatiable relish') he quickly produced another 'fireside' piece, 'The Long Voyage' (somewhat of a scissors-and-paste job), for the lead article in the New Year's Eve issue. Bradbury and Evans and Wills clearly felt, however, that to restore the fortunes of the magazine something more was needed from the pen of its 'Conductor'. By late December they, together with Forster, had persuaded him to begin a serialised story in the journal as soon as possible, even though, as he later told Lavinia Watson, he 'had intended to do nothing in that way for a year'. Not for the first time, nor for the last, Dickens, confronted with a decline in the sales of a periodical for which he was responsible, turned to and began a serial story to save the day. But there was a difference between the situation with *Household Words* in late 1853 and either that with *Master Humphrey's Clock* in 1840, or that with *All The Year Round* in 1860. In the two latter cases Dickens had already actually created, or at least conceived of, two central characters in a particular relationship (Nell and her Grandfather, and what Forster calls 'the germ of Pip and Magwitch') on whom he could build. But here the story had to be invented *ab initio*. The agreement drawn up by his *Household Words* partners on 28 December simply requires Dickens to write, as soon as possible, 'a story for Household Words equal in length to five single monthly numbers of Bleak House', to be published in continuous weekly instalments. For this he was to receive £1,000, which sum was to be kept quite apart from the magazine's regular accounts. The copyright was to remain solely and entirely his.[5]

On the day his partners drew up this agreement Dickens, accompanied by Catherine and Georgina, was in Birmingham for the public readings from his Christmas Books (the *Carol* and the *Cricket*) that he had promised to give for the benefit of the new Birmingham and Midland Institute. This was the first occasion of his giving such readings and the first night had gone brilliantly. On the 28th he was taking a day off before further readings on the two following days. He made a solo rail excursion from Birmingham to Wolverhampton, observing from the train ('always a wonderfully suggestive place' to him when travelling alone – see above, p. 308) the industrial landscape covered by a heavy fall of snow. He used this as the basis for 'Fire and Snow', published in the 21 January issue of *Household Words*, into which he introduced some fairy-tale imagery ('clanking serpents ... writhing above coal-pits') which he was to revisit in the story he was now committed to writing. The third night's reading was targeted at a working-class audience with tickets priced accordingly. Over two thousand people attended. Before he read the *Carol* Dickens made a short speech in which he was interrupted at the first word by 'a perfect hurricane of applause' so that he had to stop and begin again. He called for greater mutual understanding and co-operation between employers and employed and voiced the hope that these things would be promoted by improved educational opportunities for the workers, 'educational of the feelings as well as of the reason', and a greater trustfulness towards the workers on the part of the employers. He then read virtually the entire text of the *Carol*. This lasted three hours but his enraptured hearers, he told Lavinia Watson on 13 January, 'lost nothing, misinterpreted nothing, followed everything closely, laughed and cried with most delightful earnestness, and animated me to that extent that I felt as if we were all bodily going up into the clouds together'.[6]

His impassioned plea for greater understanding between workers and employers had a particular resonance in the winter of 1853 because of the bitter industrial dispute raging in the Lancashire industrial town of Preston since the previous summer. The workers in the cotton-mills had demanded the restoration of the 10 per cent of their wages cut as (they claimed) a temporary measure when trade was bad in 1847. The masters having rejected this, most of the workers had struck whereupon most masters had responded by closing their mills, thus locking out the entire workforce. Nothing stood between the workers and their families and outright starvation except the voluntary contributions sent in by their fellow-workers in Blackburn and other industrial towns and distributed by a committee of the Preston hands. The dispute had attained national importance, and attracted international interest also (Dickens had read reports in the Italian newspapers). *Household Words* carried an article entitled 'Locked Out' in the issue for 10 December in which the writer argued, as Dickens himself had done in 'Railway Strikes' (*HW*, 11 Jan.1851), that strikes generally resulted from disastrous ignorance on the part of the workers and meddling by professional political agitators and 'mob-orators'.

At some point in early January, while he was enjoying the afterglow of his Birmingham triumph and busily organising some private theatricals to be performed by his children on Twelfth Night, Dickens got the idea for his new story. Later, he was to tell Lavinia Watson (1 Nov. 1854) that the idea had 'laid hold of me by the throat in a very violent manner', implying that it was this sudden seizure rather than any commercial considerations that had led to the writing of this particular story. It seems more probable, as I have suggested, that the idea occurred to him shortly after he had agreed to write the story, as a result of two things merging in his mind. The first was the urgent need, as most recently expressed in his Birmingham speech, for more inter-class co-operation ('fusion ... without confusion') and the equally urgent need for setting in place a system of national education addressing the feelings as well as the reason, that should help to promote this. The second was his growing concern over the continuing grim news of the bitter worker/employer conflict taking place in Preston.[7]

The strict limits within which the new story was to be confined (one quarter the length of one of his monthly-part novels) favoured the creation of a fable-like tale and Dickens evidently decided to use this fictional mode to demonstrate what he was sure would be the disastrous consequences, both for individuals and for society, of what he later called, when writing to Carlyle to ask permission to dedicate the book to him, 'a terrible mistake of these days'. His reference here seems to be to the contemporary national obsession with the so-called 'science' ('the Dismal Science', Carlyle called it) of Political Economy, fuelled as it was by a widespread faith in facts and figures, statistics and averages. As he saw it, this was leading to the neglect of other, vitally important, forms of education, especially those aimed at developing a child's emotional and imaginative life. Political economy pervaded the theories and practice of many leading educationalists, notably the pedagogic procedures inculcated at the new Teacher Training Colleges which had been established in 1846 under the aegis of Sir James Kay-Shuttleworth, a founding member of the Statistical Society in 1834, and the first secretary of the Committee of Council on Education (1839–49). On 25 January Dickens asked Wills to get him, 'for the story I am trying to hammer out', the Education Board's questions for the examination of schoolteachers. His decision to set the story in a northern industrial town was undoubtedly in response to what was happening in Preston, but may have been influenced also by the great success of Gaskell's *Mary Barton* in 1848 (he was also planning to serialise in *Household Words* a second novel on which she was working, and for which he was eventually to supply the title, *North and South*). Perhaps he believed also that using this more circumscribed and – to most of his readers – quite unfamiliar industrial setting would help to focus attention on his message. The tighter format of this serial, with its stripped-down narrative, sparseness of detail, and strong, rapidly-sketched contrasts of scene and character, would also help to convey his meaning to the reader with great immediacy.[8]

On 20 January, a Friday (always regarded by him as an auspicious day on which to begin any new enterprise), Dickens began planning the new story. He had already got the name 'Gradgrind', brilliantly combining the notion of grading or measuring with that of harsh mechanical process. He now jots down 'Mr Gradgrind', followed by 'Mrs Gradgrind', and then proceeds to list no fewer than thirty-six different possible titles for the story. As in the case of *Bleak House* and, later, *Great Expectations*, he wants a title relating to the central theme and meaning of the book rather than to its protagonist. He makes a short list of thirteen titles, adds a new one ('The Gradgrind Philosophy') and sends it to Forster, asking him to choose three. 'Hard Times', one of the few suggestions that did not somehow refer to facts and figures, was one of the three Forster picked out. Dickens himself had also chosen three and since 'Hard Times' was the only title common to his list and to Forster's, it became his final choice. The neatness of its dual reference to the hard-headedness (and, by extension, the hard-heartedness) of Gradgrindian political scientists, and to the hardship of the workers' lives in Coketown makes it difficult to imagine a better choice.[9]

Dickens also planned out the new story in five monthly numbers each of which he then sub-divided into four weekly instalments consisting of one or two chapters. Each weekly instalment would occupy five of the magazine's double-column pages, give or take a paragraph or two. Seven and a half pages of his writing would, he calculated on 20 January, be required to yield this amount of copy. As far as the mechanics of the thing went this was fine but his calculations concealed the real problem, namely that he had to present the story's successive episodes (characters, setting, action) within five and a bit octavo pages rather than in the ampler space of the thirty-two page monthly number, or even the twelve quarto pages of the weekly numbers of *Master Humphrey's Clock*. Not surprisingly, we find him, shortly after he had begun writing, complaining to Forster that he found the difficulty of space 'CRUSHING'. 'Nobody', he lamented, 'can have any idea of it who has not had an experience of patient fiction-writing with some elbow room always, and open places in perspective.' In the event, he rose magnificently to the new challenge and subsequently found that, when necessity demanded it, he could with comparative ease return to the weekly-serialisation mode in *A Tale of Two Cities* and, later, *Great Expectations*.[10]

Dickens's careful planning of *Hard Times* was not confined to the problem of weekly serialisation. As he later told Carlyle, he also 'constructed it patiently, with a view to its publication altogether in a compact cheap form', that is, as a single unillustrated volume to be priced at five shillings. Thus we find among his working notes for the second monthly number the following: 'Republish in 3 books? / 1. Sowing / 2. Reaping / 3. Garnering'. For the first time since *Oliver* Dickens follows Fielding in *Tom Jones* and Sterne in *Tristram Shandy*, in dividing his novel into 'books', a practice he was to continue in all his subsequent completed novels. Unlike his eighteenth-century predecessors, however, Dickens now gives his 'books' titles, (except in the case of *Great Expectations* where the divisions are called 'stages'), and numbers his chapters consecutively throughout. In the case of *Hard Times*, the biblical echo in the books' titles points to the story's message that basing a whole educational system on a wholly secular and dehumanising social theory must inevitably lead to dire results. The third title, 'Garnering', does suggest, however, that there will be some positive element in the story's ending. Something will be saved from the bad harvest, some good will result, even for Mr Gradgrind. He is no villain, after all, but simply a bigoted believer in a tragically mistaken theory.[11]

On 23 January Dickens told Burdett Coutts he had written the first page of the new story. Five days later he made a weekend visit to Preston with Wills, partly to get some general background, and partly to report for his *Household Words* readers on the situation there. His resultant article, 'On Strike' (*Household Words*, 11 Feb.), begins with Dickens encountering on the Preston train a forerunner of Mr Bounderby, an overbearing opponent of the workers, whom Dickens mentally names 'Mr Snapper'. This allows him to make clear that he himself supports neither the masters nor the workers but is a concerned observer who wishes to be a friend to both. In Preston, where his presence and his luxuriant new moustaches were much commented upon by the local press, he walked about the streets, inspected the various placards, and briefly attended a meeting in which delegates from neighbouring towns handed over the money raised by their fellow-townsmen to support the striking Preston workers. 'I am

34 'Payment of the operatives, in the Temperance Hall, Preston', *Illustrated London News*, 12 November 1853

afraid I shall not be able to get much here,' he wrote to Forster just before going to this meeting: 'It is a nasty place (I thought it was a model town).' The next day he attended another meeting at which the money was distributed. In 'On Strike' he emphasised the quiet good order of the proceedings at both meetings, which was only briefly broken in the first one by the fiery oratory of one speaker, Mortimer Grimshaw (here called 'Gruffshaw'), who later modelled for Dickens's revolutionary agitator Slackbridge. Finally, he describes a visit to one mill that had stayed open where those workers who had reported for duty resembled 'a few remaining leaves in a wintry forest'. As this image suggests, 'On Strike' is essentially an impressionistic piece of reportage, concerned to reassure his middle-class readers that the Preston strikers were nothing like the revolutionary, industrial-town mobs he had once described in *The Old Curiosity Shop*. Dickens does not examine the arguments for and against the strike. For him it is simply 'a deplorable calamity' for all those directly concerned, and for the nation at large, and the only way for it to be satisfactorily settled was by means of some 'authorised mediation and explanation'.[12]

The figure most fully described – and most extensively reported – in 'On Strike' is the chairman of the first meeting, George Cowell. Dickens depicts him as an impressive-looking, calm, quietly-spoken man with 'a placid attentive face' and 'a persuasive action of his right arm'. His Lancashire dialect is sensitively reproduced and Dickens recalls it later when writing dialogue for the Coketown worker Stephen Blackpool. Hapless, confused Stephen, destined to martyrdom as his name suggests, is not, however, modelled on George Cowell in the way that Slackbridge clearly is on Mortimer Grimshaw. The latter was a local man, mentioned only briefly in the article. In *Hard Times*, however, he appears as a rabble-rousing outsider, an emissary of the United Aggregate Tribunal, whose rant fills several columns of *Household Words* in the eleventh weekly instalment of the serial (Bk II, ch. 4 in the volume edition). The absence from the novel of a Cowell figure shows Dickens's fictional purposes were somewhat different from his journalistic ones. Unlike the Preston workers, the Coketown ones are unionised and they do not go on strike – Dickens had to reassure Gaskell, who was planning to include a strike in her new story for his journal, that she need not worry about his pre-empting her in this respect. *Hard Times* is primarily concerned with educational matters and the need for inter-class understanding and co-operation and Dickens did not want it to be too narrowly related to the Preston strike in readers' minds but rather to be understood as having a much wider application to the contemporary condition of England.[13]

Hence his annoyance with *Household Words* contributor Peter Cunningham when, in *The Illustrated London News* for 4 March (the same day that *Hard Times* was first advertised in Dickens's journal) Cunningham chattily informed his readers that Dickens's 'recent enquiry into the Preston strike is said to have origi- nated the title [of the new tale], and, in some respects, suggested the turn of the story'. Writing privately to Cunningham on 11 March, Dickens told him he was 'altogether wrong' and that 'the title was many weeks old, and chapters of the story were written, before I went to Preston or thought about the present Strike'. This was certainly stretching the truth but does not affect the main ground of Dickens's complaint which he expressed as follows:

> The mischief of such a statement is twofold. First, it encourages the public to believe in the impossibility that books are produced in that very sudden and Cavalier manner . . .; and Secondly in this instance it has this pernicious bearing: It localizes (so far as your readers are concerned) a story which has a direct purpose in reference to the working people all over England, and it will cause, as I know by former experience, characters to be fitted on to individuals whom I never saw or heard of in my life.

Many years later, advising the actor-manager Charles Fechter on producing a dramatic adaptation of Gaskell's *Mary Barton*, Dickens recommended using a fictitious name for the setting instead of the real one, Manchester. 'When I did "Hard Times" ', he wrote (4 Sept. 1866), 'I called the scene Coketown. Everybody knew what was meant, but every cotton-spinning town said it was the other cotton-spinning town.'

During February and early March Dickens was, as he expressed it to Burdett Coutts, 'cracking my head' over the new story. By 7 March he had managed to complete the first five chapters, enough copy for the first two weekly instalments. They bring the story to the point at which Mr Sleary and his circus troupe are about to enter (Dickens had asked Lemon to send him 'any slang terms among tumblers and Circus-people' that he could think of, to supplement those he himself had already noted down). The reader has already met Gradgrind and his family, McChoakumchild the fact-grinding schoolmaster (wittily presented as a character out of *The Arabian Nights*), and the self-vaunted self-made man Josiah Bounderby.[14]

During March Dickens wrote only one piece for *Household Words*, a warm tribute to his old friend Talfourd which appeared in the 25 March issue. Talfourd had died very suddenly at the Stafford Assizes on 13 March whilst in the midst of his charge to the jury. With his last breath he 'feelingly deplored the want of sympathy which existed between the higher and lower classes'. This chimed perfectly with Dickens's most urgent concerns in *Hard Times*. 'Who,' he wrote, 'knowing England at this time, would wish to utter with his last breath a more righteous warning than that its curse is ignorance, or a miscalled education which is as bad or worse, and a want of the exchange of innumerable graces and sympathies among the various orders of society, each hardened unto each and holding itself aloof?'[15]

Dickens greatly feared, and with good reason, that both politicians and people would be distracted from problems at home by the Crimean War which began in March, though he believed the Emperor of Russia was a dangerous tyrant who had to be stopped. Some months into the war, on 1 November, he wrote to Lavinia Watson that he 'felt something like despair to see how the old cannon smoke and blood-mist obscure the wrongs and sufferings of the people at home'. It was all the more imperative, therefore, that he should get the message of *Hard Times* across to as wide a readership as possible. The first instalment of the story, comprising the first three chapters, appeared in the issue dated 1 April 1854. Dickens's name was given as author and there were no chapter-titles nor, of course, any illustrations. It was the lead item in this issue and in all subsequent ones until the end of its run so that, as has been noted, each instalment seemed to resemble a leading article (Dickens's editorial commentary on the times) as well as being an instalment of a story by him. Gaskell's *North and South*, which followed *Hard Times* in *Household Words*, was not granted such pride of place, nor did it carry her name (it was billed as 'by the Author of *Mary Barton*'). This duality of *Hard Times* appears at its most striking, perhaps, in two places. The first is the opening paragraph of chapter 10, half-way through the fifth weekly instalment, which reads: 'I entertain a weak idea that the English people are as hard-worked as any people upon whom the sun shines. I acknowledge to this ridiculous idiosyncrasy, as a reason why I would give them a little more play.' The second is the direct hortatory address to the 'Dear reader' at the end of the very last instalment of the story, which is reminiscent of the ending of *The Chimes*,

" Familiar in their Mouths as HOUSEHOLD WORDS."—SHAKESPEARE.

HOUSEHOLD WORDS.

A WEEKLY JOURNAL.

CONDUCTED BY CHARLES DICKENS.

Nᵒ. 210.]   SATURDAY, APRIL 1, 1854.   [PRICE 2d.

HARD TIMES.

BY CHARLES DICKENS.

CHAPTER I.

"Now, what I want is, Facts. Teach these boys and girls nothing but Facts. Facts alone are wanted in life. Plant nothing else, and root out everything else. You can only form the minds of reasoning animals upon Facts : nothing else will ever be of any service to them. This is the principle on which I bring up my own children, and this is the principle on which I bring up these children. Stick to Facts, sir !"

The scene was a plain, bare, monotonous vault of a school-room, and the speaker's square forefinger emphasised his observations by underscoring every sentence with a line on the schoolmaster's sleeve. The emphasis was helped by the speaker's square wall of a forehead, which had his eyebrows for its base, while his eyes found commodious cellarage in two dark caves, overshadowed by the wall. The emphasis was helped by the speaker's mouth, which was wide, thin, and hard set. The emphasis was helped by the speaker's voice, which was inflexible, dry, and dictatorial. The emphasis was helped by the speaker's hair, which bristled on the skirts of his bald head, a plantation of firs to keep the wind from its shining surface, all covered with knobs, like the crust of a plum pie, as if the head had scarcely warehouse-room for the hard facts stored inside. The speaker's obstinate carriage, square coat, square legs, square shoulders,—nay, his very neckcloth, trained to take him by the throat with an unaccommodating grasp, like a stubborn fact, as it was,—all helped the emphasis.

"In this life, we want nothing but Facts, sir ; nothing but Facts !"

The speaker, and the schoolmaster, and the third grown person present, all backed a little, and swept with their eyes the inclined plane of little vessels then and there arranged in order, ready to have imperial gallons of facts poured into them until they were full to the brim.

CHAPTER II.

THOMAS GRADGRIND, sir. A man of realities. A man of facts and calculations. A

man who proceeds upon the principle that two and two are four, and nothing over, and who is not to be talked into allowing for anything over. Thomas Gradgrind, sir—peremptorily Thomas—Thomas Gradgrind. With a rule and a pair of scales, and the multiplication table always in his pocket, sir, ready to weigh and measure any parcel of human nature, and tell you exactly what it comes to. It is a mere question of figures, a case of simple arithmetic. You might hope to get some other nonsensical belief into the head of George Gradgrind, or Augustus Gradgrind, or John Gradgrind, or Joseph Gradgrind (all suppositious, non-existent persons), but into the head of Thomas Gradgrind—no, sir !

In such terms Mr. Gradgrind always mentally introduced himself, whether to his private circle of acquaintance, or to the public in general. In such terms, no doubt, substituting the words " boys and girls," for " sir," Thomas Gradgrind now presented Thomas Gradgrind to the little pitchers before him, who were to be filled so full of facts.

Indeed, as he eagerly sparkled at them from the cellarage before mentioned, he seemed a kind of cannon loaded to the muzzle with facts, and prepared to blow them clean out of the regions of childhood at one discharge. He seemed a galvanising apparatus, too, charged with a grim mechanical substitute for the tender young imaginations that were to be stormed away.

"Girl number twenty," said Mr. Gradgrind, squarely pointing with his square forefinger, "I don't know that girl. Who is that girl ?"

"Sissy Jupe, sir," explained number twenty, blushing, standing up, and curtseying.

"Sissy is not a name," said Mr. Gradgrind. "Don't call yourself Sissy. Call yourself Cecilia."

"It's father as calls me Sissy, sir," returned the young girl in a trembling voice, and with another curtsey.

"Then he has no business to do it," said Mr. Gradgrind. "Tell him he mustn't. Cecilia Jupe. Let me see. What is your father ?"

"He belongs to the horse-riding, if you please, sir."

Mr. Gradgrind frowned, and waved off the objectionable calling with his hand.

"We don't want to know anything about

VOL. IX.   210.

35 Front page of *Household Words*, 1 April 1854, with first instalment of *Hard Times*

the closest thing to *Hard Times* in Dickens's oeuvre to date – Mr Filer, for example, can be seen as a first sketch for Mr Gradgrind and Will Fern as a rural forerunner of Stephen Blackpool.[16]

During the serialisation of *Hard Times* Dickens took some trouble to publish in *Household Words* articles bearing on events in his story. He had a very specific connection in mind when on 24 March he asked Wills to ask

Morley to write, for 'immediate publication', an article on preventable factory accidents. Morley's 'Ground in the Mill', full of horrific examples gleaned from official reports of deaths and maimings caused by factory machines, duly appeared one month later. In his note to Wills Dickens was doubtless thinking ahead in his story to chapter 13, to be published in the issue for 13 May. In that chapter as first written Stephen speaks of the death of a little sister of Rachael's following such an accident and complains bitterly about the callous irresponsibility of the mill-owners. Rachael begs him to leave such matters as 'they only lead to hurt' and he solemnly promises her to do so. This is important for the plot since it is the 'promess' which Stephen later mentions, in his second interview with Bounderby. It prevents him joining the Union with the result that he is sent to Coventry by his fellow-workers in addition to being sacked by Bounderby. When first proofing the passage, Dickens even added a footnote referring his readers to Morley's article but must have had second thoughts and deleted both the passage and the footnote in a later proof. Most likely, he cancelled them because the passage would have detracted too much from Stephen's saintliness. The result is that this character's later refusal to join the Union (Bk II, ch. 4 of the text as printed) simply mystifies the reader.[17]

From early March until mid July 1854 Dickens was preoccupied with *Hard Times*. He seems to have completed each instalment about four weeks ahead of the publication date. Ever conscious of the remorseless need for compression, he reported on 18 April to Wills, temporarily hors de combat because of ill health, that he was 'in a dreary state, planning and planning the story of Hard Times (out of materials for I don't know how long a story), and consequently writing little'. His working notes show him sometimes deciding against the introduction of characters or the development of situations for which twenty monthly numbers would have allowed him ample space. Thus, Gradgrind's three younger children, Adam Smith, Malthus and Jane, will have 'no parts to play' (though Jane does, eventually, make a brief but telling appearance); the query 'Bitzer's father and mother?' gets the answer 'No' while another one, 'Lover for Sissy?', is answered by, 'No. Decide on no love at all'. Under the circumstances it is astonishing how much vintage Dickensian comedy he manages to distil, in such limited space, out of the mutually exploitative relationship between the vulgar Bounderby and his steely housekeeper Mrs Sparsit with her 'Coriolanian nose'. Remarkable, too, is the way he manages to end each weekly instalment on a greater or lesser degree of suspense, with strong climaxes coming at the ends of chapters 16 and 28 (Louisa's marriage to Bounderby, and her later collapse at the feet of her devastated father) which, in the volume edition, conclude Books One and Two respectively. One thematically and structurally important character appears in the earliest working notes but is kept waiting for sixteen chapters (which make up Book One) before making his appearance. This is the would-be seducer

James Harthouse, described, though not yet named, in Dickens's notes as 'the man who by being utterly sensual and careless, comes to very much the same thing in the end as the Gradgrind school'. He cannot, of course, begin to play his crucial role in the plot until after Louisa has become Bounderby's wife.

The words 'Open Law of Divorce' in Dickens's notes for chapter 10 mark his decision to introduce another highly topical subject into this story of the effects of Utilitarianism and Political Science on national education and industrial relations. A Royal Commission on the divorce laws had submitted its report in 1853, and a Divorce and Matrimonial Causes Bill was to be introduced, unsuccessfully, into the House of Lords in June 1854. The existing laws, unchanged since the Reformation, made the cost of full divorce proceedings prohibitive except for the very wealthy – ultimately, they involved the procurement of a special Act of Parliament for each individual case. This enormous expense kept chained together many couples in all classes of society who might otherwise have been able to free themselves. The laws were also heavily weighted against women, as the redoubtable journalist Eliza Lynn Linton had demonstrated, with reference to the notorious Caroline Norton case, in her *Household Words* article 'One Of Our Legal Fictions', published the week before the instalment of *Hard Times* in which Stephen asks Bounderby if there is any way he can legally extricate himself from his nightmare marriage.[18]

The contemporary debate about the divorce laws may well have sharpened certain feelings Dickens had begun to have, or perhaps had had for some time, about his own marriage, which, like Stephen Blackpool's, was now nearly twenty years old. It was in this year, 1854, Forster tells us, that Dickens first began writing to him about 'the drawbacks of his present life'. He alluded to feelings that Forster describes as comparable to those he had already attributed to his hero in *David Copperfield* (that 'old unhappy loss or want of something' which haunts David in his early adulthood) – though Dickens did not yet, it seems, make an explicit comparison between himself and his fictional creation. His emotional distress, Dickens tells Forster, is inevitably intensified because he is an artist, a writer, and thus fated to lead that 'so happy and yet so unhappy existence which seeks its realities in unrealities, and finds its dangerous comfort in a perpetual escape from the disappointment of heart around it'.[19]

During the months *Hard Times* was being serialised in *Household Words* even Dickens, with all his phenomenal energy, had no time to write anything else – leaving aside, of course, his prolific correspondence. This included several long, vividly-detailed letters to Burdett Coutts about Urania Cottage, numerous editorial missives to Wills, and business letters to Gaskell about the projected serialisation of her new novel in *Household Words*. He undertook no public engagements, though he did chair a Garrick Club dinner to celebrate Shakespeare's birthday on 22 April and, on 12 June, the first meeting of the Council of the newly-incorporated Guild of Literature and Art. Six days later, the whole Dickens family moved to Boulogne for their customary summer and early autumn retreat from London. The amiable M. Beaucourt was once again their landlord but this time it was his second property they rented, the 'airy and fresh' hilltop Villa du Camp de droite. Roomier than Les Moulineaux, it had a private road and a beautiful garden and altogether, Dickens told Wills, 'beat the former residence all to nothing'. It had also the great advantage of being more sequestered, further away from the town and therefore from unwanted visitors. 'It is like being up in a balloon,' Dickens wrote to Wilkie Collins on 12 July: 'Lionizing Englishmen and Germans start to call, and are found lying imbecile in the road half way up. Ha-ha-ha!'[20]

In these congenial surroundings he finished the writing of his novel. 'I am three parts mad and the fourth delirious, with perpetual rushing at *Hard Times*,' he told Forster on 14 July, adding, 'I have done what I hope is a good thing with Stephen, taking his story as a whole.' He had, he said, 'been looking forward through so many weeks and sides of paper to this Stephen business, that now – as usual – it being over, I feel as if nothing in the world, in the way of intense and violent rushing hither and thither, could quite restore my balance.' 'This Stephen business' is what Dickens calls in his chapter-notes for the 19th weekly number (chs 33 and 34) '<u>The great effect</u>', namely the belated discovery of Stephen lying badly injured at the bottom of 'Old Hell Shaft', the disused mining shaft into which he had fallen in the dark, his being brought to the surface, and his dying prayer (echoing Talfourd's words and pointing the moral of Dickens's fable) 'that aw th' world may on'y coom toogether more, an' get a better unnerstan'in o' one another, than when I were in 't my own weak seln'. The last three chapters ending the story were finished by 17 July and Dickens returned to London for a few days to supervise the final stages of publication. On the 22nd he was able to send Catherine a complete set of the uncorrected proofs.

He found he needed more elbow-room in the last instalments. 'Weekly Nos to be enlarged to 10 of my sides each – about' reads one of his notes for the third notional monthly number. Despite this, he found himself planning for an extra, twenty-first, weekly number. That would, rather awkwardly, have carried the story over into a new volume of *Household Words* and Wills persuaded him to get the whole conclusion into one number (equivalent to the final double number in the regular monthly format). Accordingly, in the issue for 12 August the last two chapters of *Hard Times* occupied over eighteen columns of the journal, more than twice the normal amount. Five days earlier, the novel had appeared in volume form with an extended title underlining its urgent topicality: *Hard Times. For These Times.* It carried the dedication to Carlyle but no preface (nor did Dickens ever write one for this particular book, any more than he did for a later weekly serial *Great Expectations*). He made some revisions in the re-set text, though hardly enough to justify the phrase 'carefully revised' used in the advertisements. He also supplied chapter-titles, and introduced the book-divisions. The novel was published at five shillings – for only sixpence more, in fact, readers could buy the ninth volume of the magazine, containing the whole story and much else besides. Reviewers, other than Forster in *The Examiner*, were mainly unenthusiastic; nevertheless the volume had sold over 5,000 copies by the end of the year. This, together with the £1,000 Dickens received for the story from his *Household Words* partners, enriched him by nearly £1,500. Finally, and most importantly, the serial had succeeded, we learn from Forster, in more than doubling the journal's circulation.[21]

With *Hard Times* finished Dickens plunged into strenuous leisure in his Boulogne retreat, organising ball games and other such diversions for the family and visiting friends; also, as he wrote to Gaskell on 31 July, spending much time lying on the grass, 'reading books and going to sleep'. He continued to be scornful of what he and others, notably *Punch*, saw as the doddering ineptitude of the Prime Minister, Lord Aberdeen, and his colleagues and thought of writing for *Household Words* a series of papers satirising Parliament under the title of 'The Member for Nowhere'. For some reason he gave up this idea – reluctantly, as he told Forster, 'and with it my hope to have made every man in England feel something of the contempt for the House of Commons that I have'. He did not, in fact, altogether abandon this hope since he wrote for *Household Words*, over the next six months, no fewer than seven articles lambasting governmental negligence and folly. He excoriates the shameful frivolity of M.P.s when debating sanitary reform, the indecision of Lord Aberdeen (whom he depicts in one article as 'Abby Dean', John Bull's somnambulist housekeeper), the 'corruption, confusion and waste' of enquiries conducted by Commons Committees ('the very worst tribunals conceivable by the mind of man'), the 'classes and families and interests' that had brought the administration of public affairs to such a low ebb, and the catastrophic effects of red tape in all departments of government. Two more articles he wrote at this time expose miscarriages of justice in the County Courts and ridicule the pomp attaching to London's Lord Mayor. Also, like other readers of William Howard Russell's *Times* reports from the Crimea, Dickens was appalled and angered by Russell's revelation of what he (Dickens) calls 'the confused heap of imbecility, mismanagement and disorder, under which the nation's bravery lies crushed and withered'. 'I have made up my mind', he wrote to Burdett Coutts on 25 January 1855, 'that what one can do in print to wake the sleepers [i.e., Aberdeen and his colleagues], one is bound to do at such a serious juncture.' And, referring to one of his satirical articles called 'That Other Public', he adds that he has 'fired off a small volley of red hot shot, in Household Words next week'. Nor, in his view, can Mr Gradgrind and his statistical sect escape all responsibility for the Crimean débacle. When the popular educator Charles Knight, having read *Hard Times*, wrote to say that he feared being classed as 'a cold-hearted political economist', Dickens answered, 'My satire is against those who see figures and averages, and nothing else – the representatives of the wickedest and most enormous vice of this time . . . the addled heads who would take the average of cold in the Crimea during twelve months, as a reason for clothing a soldier in nankeen on a night when he would be frozen to death in fur. . . . Bah! What have you to do with these?'[22]

One article, 'To Working Men', stands out from this group with regard to its form. During August and September there had been a new, and truly devastating, outbreak of Asiatic cholera in London, killing some 10,000 people and leading to the cordoning off of certain poor areas south of the river. From Boulogne Dickens wrote to Wills on 25 September 1854 saying he was 'quite shocked and ashamed' to see no mention of this terrible visitation in the issue of *Household Words* which was about to go to press, and he sent copy for an article, 'To Working Men', with instructions to unmake the number and put this address first. His zealous concern in the piece is unmistakeable, and he does not fail to point to his track record as a veteran campaigner for sanitary reform: 'Long before this Journal came into existence, we systematically tried to turn Fiction to the good account of showing the preventible [*sic*] wretchedness and misery in which the mass of the people dwell . . .'. Despite the article's title, Dickens does not address himself directly to 'working men'. His target audience seems to be very much the normal *Household Words* one, namely, middle middle-class and lower middle-class readers who would not have thought of themselves as 'working men'. The piece is therefore indirectly addressed to the latter saying what they should be doing rather than directly exhorting them. If, collectively, they would agitate, vigorously but peacefully, for the installation of a new and better Government at Westminster then, according to Dickens, 'the powerful middle class of this country, newly smitten with a sense of self-reproach,' would unite with them to ensure that the change should take place 'by Christmas'. No wonder the deeply Tory Burdett Coutts was worried. Dickens had to write to reassure her that he was trying to *avert* a revolution rather than to foment one.[23]

The cholera eventually passed but the war went on. Horrified as he was by the catastrophic misconduct of the Crimean campaign, Dickens, like Tennyson, whose 'Charge of the Light Brigade' appeared in *The Examiner* on 9 December 1854, continued to believe whole-heartedly in the rightness of the War, and to extol the heroism of the British troops. He involved himself, with all his customary promptness and practicality, in the realisation of Burdett Coutts's scheme to provide an industrial-sized drying machine to facilitate the laundering of the soldiers' clothes in the Crimea. He arranged for copies of his books to be sent in response to appeals for reading-matter for the troops, and sought to promote solidarity with our French allies. He did this partly (somewhat paradoxically perhaps) through his allusions to the military glories of the first Napoleon's Grande Armée but also more generally by presenting the French in a favourable light. To this end, he at last wrote his long-meditated, wholly charming, essay on Boulogne, 'Our French Watering-place', published in *Household Words* on 4 November. In this 'M. Loyal Devasseur', a lovingly detailed portrayal of his landlord, the ex-soldier Ferdinand Beaucourt-Mutuel, represents all that is best in the French character whilst Boulogne itself is praised because 'a long and constant fusion of the two great nations there, has taught each to like the other, and to learn from the other, and to rise superior to the absurd prejudices that have lingered among the weak and ignorant in both countries equally.' Moreover, his Christmas tale for 1854 was, on one level at least, a celebration of both British and French military prowess and heroism.

He and Wills had planned the 1854 Christmas number at Boulogne during August. It represented a significant advance on its predecessors and established a model for its successors. Reverting yet once more to the format of his beloved *Arabian Nights*, Dickens produced a framing narrative to accommodate the stories to be contributed by his invited collaborators. He himself supplied the first tale in the series, subsequent linking passages where needed, and a fine concluding description of a Christmas Day country walk. He may have conceived the idea for his framing narrative as far back as 11 May when he and Lemon had made an excursion to Rochester and there visited Watts's Charity which stood, as it still does (now a museum), in the High Street. Founded in 1579 under the will of Richard Watts, a leading citizen of Rochester, the Charity's purpose was to provide for six 'poor travellers' one night's free lodging and 'Four-pence each'. Dickens now imagines himself in Rochester on Christmas Eve arranging for a festive dinner and 'a temperate glass of hot Wassail' to be served up in the Charity for the six poor travellers who would randomly come to lodge there that night. His inn would supply the turkey, beef and 'sundries' while he himself would mix the wassail or punch (Dickens notoriously prided himself on this art). 'Being withal as poor as I hope to be', he imagines himself as being a seventh poor traveller and describes his telling of the first of a sequence of tales related in turn by the travellers as they sit round a blazing fire after their unexpected banquet. Each tale is written to suit the character of the traveller as described by Dickens or by one of his contributors. These latter included Wilkie Collins, here making his début in a department of the magazine in which he was, in due course, to become Dickens's chief, and sometimes sole, collaborator.[24]

Dickens's own tale is set in the time of the Napoleonic Wars and its protagonist, feigned to be a relative of his, is Richard, 'better known as Dick', who, having brought shame on his own name, invents for himself the surname of Doubledick. He has 'gone wrong and run wild' after a traumatic disappointment in love, and has become so careless of himself that he enlists as a soldier at Chatham Barracks with a suicidal 'determination to be shot'. The somewhat convoluted story of Doubledick's moral and spiritual redemption involves an English officer and a French officer, both equally brave and honourable.

36 Watts Charity, Rochester High Street

Dickens adds a highly topical Crimean-war postscript to the story, telling us that the 'time has since come' when the sons of Doubledick and of the French officer 'fought side by side in one cause: with their respective nations, like long-divided brothers whom the better times have brought together, fast united'.

The public aspect of this little story, clearly very much written 'for these times', is obvious enough and it is hardly surprising that it proved such a great popular success – by 3 January the special Christmas Number in which it appears had sold 80,000 copies. But the Rochester/Chatham setting and Dickens's play upon his own name in 'Doubledick' should alert us to its other aspect, a very private and personal one. Addressing his companions after a toast to Christmas Eve, Dickens-in-the-story describes human life as 'a story more or less intelligible' and confesses to being 'so divided this night between fact and fiction, that I scarcely know which is which'. We hardly need such a hint as this to perceive in this stilted and sentimental fiction a strange mirror-image of Dickens's evidently still troubling memories of the Maria Beadnell affair and its bitter dénouement. In one of those confidences of his that conceal much more than they reveal Dickens tells Arthur Ryland on 22 December that the writing of this Christmas tale had deeply affected him. When the idea for it came into his head, he tells Ryland, it 'obtained such strong possession' of him that 'it cost me more time and tears than most people would consider likely'. Then, passing quickly on to its public aspect, he adds, 'The response it meets with is payment for anything.'

Another striking confluence of public concerns and strong personal feelings also belongs to this increasingly unsettled time in Dickens's life. On 22 October 1854 the Arctic explorer Dr John Rae returned to England with some sensational news, reported at length in *The Times*, about the possible fate of the Franklin Expedition. In May 1845 two ships under the command of the veteran explorer Sir John Franklin had sailed for the Arctic in search of the supposed North West Passage. Since the July of that year nothing had been heard or seen of Franklin and his men and from 1847 onwards many expeditions had gone in search of them without success. Dickens, with his passionate interest in stories of exploration, took a keen interest in the subject and a number of articles about Arctic exploration had appeared in *Household Words*. Now Rae reported having met with some Innuit who claimed to have seen the emaciated and mutilated corpses of the last survivors of Franklin's expedition. The Innuit told Rae that the state of the bodies and the contents of some kettles found with them made it clear that the men had been driven to cannibalism in their efforts to stay alive. This was a horrific idea for the British public with its much-vaunted faith in the valour and high honour of its soldiers and sailors. Dickens, fully sharing in this faith, would have been deeply disturbed, like everyone else, by Rae's report but his strong 'attraction of repulsion' towards the topic of cannibalism would have given an extra intensity to his response. On 20 November he wrote to Wills asking for a cutting of the report and adding, 'It has occurred to me that I am rather strong on Voyages and Cannibalism and might do an interesting little paper for next No. on that part of Dr Rae's report, taking the arguments against its probabilities.' This sounds like a good journalist seizing on a topical issue but Dickens's intervention was surely a prime example of something about his writing that he had earlier indicated to the composer Jules Benedict when declining (on 20 July) to write songs for Benedict to set to music: 'what I do, I do in the main because I can't keep it – it *will* come out of me, somehow'. This seems borne out by the fact that he wrote on this particular personally resonant subject at such length that his 'little paper' had to be serialised in two numbers (2 and 9 Dec.). His impassioned rejection of Rae's report as far as the cannibalism allegations were concerned depends first upon attacking the Innuit as being, at best, unreliable witnesses and, at worst, killers and robbers of the last Franklin survivors. They are, after all, 'savages', and every such being is, Dickens asserts, 'in his heart covetous, treacherous and cruel'. His second line of attack is to draw attention, by citing case after case, to the extreme rarity of recorded examples of cannibalism among survivors of maritime disasters. At the end of his second piece Dickens reverts to what had been his grand target in *Hard Times*: 'Utilitarianism will protest "they are dead; why care about this?" ' In response he again invokes human and non-Utilitarian concepts and values – in this case gratitude for endeavours made on behalf of all humanity by a few courageous individuals, reverence for their memory, and pity for their terrible fate.[25]

Dickens's fiercely polemical journalism of the autumn and winter of 1854/55 provided a safety valve for his ever-growing restlessness and a distraction from what he had called the disappointments of his heart, but it was not enough. His sense of dissatisfaction went deep, and it is from this period that Forster dates the doom of his marriage: 'An unsettled feeling greatly in excess of what was usual with Dickens, more or less observable since his first residence at Boulogne, became at this time almost habitual, and the satisfactions which home should have supplied, and which indeed were essential requirements of his nature, he had failed to find in his home'. He began to be possessed by 'dreadful thoughts' of fleeing from his home and isolating himself in some inaccessible world of snow and ice where he would write his next novel – going on his own authorial Franklin Expedition, so to speak. His imagination was especially haunted by memories of the Great St Bernard monastery, above the snow-line in the Alps. He did not, in fact, return there but it would figure prominently in the new novel he was beginning to incubate. Predicting that Forster would ascribe his feelings simply to '*Restlessness*', he wrote, 'Whatever it is, it is always driving me, and I cannot help it. I have rested nine or ten weeks, and sometimes feel as if it had been a year – though I had the strangest nervous miseries before I stopped. If I couldn't walk fast and far, I should just explode and perish.'[26]

Dickens's journalistic sallies certainly provided him with opportunities for blowing off what he elsewhere calls his 'superfluous steam'. But, as always, it was performing in public that was his supreme salve for discontent. Between 19 and 28 December he gave public readings of the *Carol* to enraptured audiences in Reading (at the Mechanics' Institute where he had succeeded Talfourd as president), in Sherborne (for the sake of Macready, now living in retirement there), and in Bradford, for the town's Educational Temperance Institute. In this last place he urged the members of his audience of three thousand seven hundred to think of themselves as 'a small social party assembled to hear a tale told round the Christmas fire'. They rewarded him with 'loud and repeated applause' and he began, unsurprisingly, to think seriously about developing this activity on a paid basis. Bradford had already offered to pay him a £50 fee, and he might have begun his career as a professional reader now instead of three years later had he not yielded to Forster's argument that 'to become publicly a reader [would] alter without improving his position publicly as a writer', an alteration only to be justified 'when the higher calling should have failed of the old success'.[27]

At home, too, performing helped to alleviate his restlessness and the children's theatricals were more strenuously organised this year than last. He arranged for the temporary conversion of the Tavistock House schoolroom into a little theatre and set about master-minding an elaborate production of J. R. Planché's 'Fairy Extravaganza', *Fortunio and His Seven Gifted Servants*. He adapted the piece for performance by himself and his children with the participation also of Lemon and *his* children, Wilkie Collins, and one or two other friends. Happily resuming his 'managerial' hat, Dickens proceeded to drill his domestic troupe as thoroughly as he had always drilled the Amateurs. Costumes and wigs were supplied by the same costumiers and wig-maker and as a finishing touch he composed and had printed a special playbill headed 'Theatre Royal Tavistock Square'. He himself featured among the dramatis personae both as 'Mr Passé' (playing Baron Dunover) and as 'Mr Measley Servile' (playing a character of his own invention, 'The Expectant Cousin of the Nobility in General'). Tavistock House was soon full, as he gleefully reported to de Cerjat on 3 January, 'of spangles, gas, Jew theatrical tailors, and Pantomime Carpenters'. Five days later, *Fortunio* was triumphantly performed before an invited audience (including Planché himself) and Charley long remembered his father as Measley Servile, acting with 'a fixed and propitiatory smile . . . the very type of the smile of the sycophant and toady' and constantly pervading the stage 'whence he was better able, than from the wing, to direct the performance'.[28]

His growing friendship with Wilkie Collins, twelve years his junior but already very much a professional writer and one whose work he admired, seems to have provided another source of relief and relaxation for Dickens. Although on the Italian tour he had felt called upon to 'smash' Collins's defence of the morality found in French novels, he seems nevertheless to have found the younger man's Bohemian attitude to life attractive, perhaps partly because it was such a change from Forster's increasing staidness and intense respectability, qualities Dickens was later to mock in the figure of Mr Podsnap in *Our Mutual Friend*. Over his outings with Collins Dickens enjoyed casting an air of loucheness (perhaps 'Bohemianism' would be a more appropriate term) rather as he had done in early years with Maclise, who had since become very reclusive. Writing from Boulogne on 12 July 1854, for example, Dickens tells Collins that he is coming to London briefly and urges him to join him in his intended 'career of amiable dissipation and unbounded license in the

metropolis' before returning with him to France: 'If you will come and breakfast with me about midnight – anywhere – any day – and go to bed no more
until we fly to these pastoral retreats – I shall be delighted to have so vicious
an associate.' Collins is again his chosen companion when, at the beginning
of February, he decides on a trip to Paris, having, as he tells Burdett Coutts,
'motes of new stories floating before my eyes' (he adds that he might possibly
go on to Bordeaux since the motes 'seem to drive somewhere in that direction'). Dickens writes to Régnier at the beginning of February asking him to
find an apartment for himself and Collins, saying that he wanted to throw
himself 'en garçon on the festive diableries of Paris', a project for which Collins
would be an ideal companion.

At the same time as all this, however, he is writing in a very different
vein to Forster, though using the same image for the intimations of his new book
that he had used to Burdett Coutts. He expresses his political despair ('I am
hourly strengthened in my old belief, that our political aristocracy and our tuft-
hunting are the death of England. In all this business [of the Crimean War] I
don't see a gleam of hope') and also his personal wretchedness. Having re-read
Copperfield with a view to deriving a public reading from it, he has been struck
by how he has prefigured in it his own current emotional state:

Am altogether in a dishevelled state of mind – motes of new books in the
dirty air, miseries of older growth threatening to close in upon me. Why is it,
that as with poor David, a sense comes always crushing on me now, when I
fall into low spirits, as of one happiness I have missed in life, and one friend
and companion I have never made?[29]

That image of 'motes' of the new book floating in the air is noteworthy.
Dickens did not yet have any clear overall vision of the new book he was
intending to write in the standard twenty-monthly-number format. Forster
suggests that he may even have been experiencing, for the first time in his
life, some anxiety that his powers of invention, hitherto always so abundant,
might some day fail him and this is why in January he began jotting down in a
notebook (since published as *Charles Dickens' Book of Memoranda* with the
memoranda numbered in sequence) ideas for the opening of a story, such as
no.7: 'beginning with a house; abandoned by a family fallen into reduced
circumstances. Their old furniture there, and tokens of their old comforts.
Inscriptions under the bells downstairs. "Mr John's Room" – "Miss Caroline's
room . . .". He also noted down ideas for particular characters and incidents,
scraps of dialogue, and long lists of possible names for characters, some of
which were used in later books: 'Tippins, Minnit, Radlowe, Pratchet, Mawdett,
Wozenham, Snosswell, Lottrum . . .'. A second list includes Bangham, Chivery,
Merdle, Dorret-Dorrit, Carton, Plornish, and Magwitch. The very first entry in

the book, 'The unwieldy ship taken in tow by the snorting little steam Tug', later provided the defining image for Casby and Pancks in *Little Dorrit*, and a number of other early entries relate to characters in that novel, for example, a sketch for someone in Mrs Clennam's situation (no.13): 'Bedridden [or room-ridden] twenty – five and twenty years – any length of time. . . . Brought out of doors by an unexpected exercise of my latent strength of character, and then how strange!' Several also relate to characters and incidents in later novels and stories. Internal evidence shows that Dickens added new entries only rather irregularly after May 1855 (over half the entries in the book were made during the first five months of this year) but evidently he continued to consult the book thereafter, and marked entries he had used. The one about the bedridden person, for example, is annotated, in a different ink, '*Done in Mrs Clennam*'.[30]

One 'mote' identifiable to us among those that floated before Dickens's eyes seems to have been the idea of setting some or all of the new story abroad, in places he had visited, France or Switzerland or Italy. Another must surely have been related to prisons and imprisonment because, although we have no clear evidence that Dickens was at this point thinking about such matters in connection with his new story, the emergence of imprisonment as a theme as soon as he began to jot down his 'mems' and number-plans for the first two numbers suggests that it was in his mind from a very early stage.

Whether or not it related to his present, the idea – and indeed the reality – of prisons and imprisonment related, obviously enough, to his past, and his writings during the autumn and winter of 1854/55 show that his imagination was much engaged with his earlier life. We have already noted the autobiographical element in his Christmas tale of Richard Doubledick. There is also a masterly *Household Words* essay, 'An Unsettled Neighbourhood', published in the issue for 11 November 1854, in which Dickens recalls, with a wealth of vivid detail, the Camden Town of his childhood, a 'neighbourhood as quiet and dismal as any about London', and describes how it has now been changed for ever by the coming of the London to Birmingham railway. On his birthday he was drawn back to the scene of a happier phase of his childhood and told Burdett Coutts that he had 'walked from Gravesend to Rochester between walls of snow varying from three to six feet high'. On the walk he made an exciting discovery. Gad's Hill Place in Higham, the very house, he told Wills, that was 'literally "a dream of my childhood" ', was up for sale. He wanted to view it before leaving with Collins for Paris but this proved to be impractical. And then, just two days later, on the very eve of his departure, there came out of the blue a startling reminder of another, and altogether more poignant, dream of his early years, his reaction to which was extraordinary, even by his own standards of intensity.[31]

CHAPTER 17

Writing *Little Dorrit* – among other things

1855–1857

How strange it is to be never at rest, and never satisfied, and ever trying after something that is never reached, and to be always laden with plot and plan and care and worry, how clear it is that it must be, and that one is driven by an irresistible might until the journey is worked out! It is much better to go on and fret, than to stop and fret. As to repose – for some men there's no such thing in this life. . . . The old days – the old days! Shall I ever, I wonder, get the frame of mind back as it used to be then?

Dickens to Forster, 13 April 1856

A writer with a great audience, who deeply feels certain salient public vices of his time, must not let them altogether go by him. He has his duty to do, and he must do it – yoking it to his pleasanter fancy as well as he can.

Dickens to the Reverend Archer Gurney, 25 April 1857

DICKENS, AS we have seen, thought of Friday as a special day of the week for him, one often associated with momentous happenings in his life, and Friday 9 February 1855 proved to be no exception. That evening he found himself unable, after glancing at the envelopes of some newly-delivered letters, to concentrate again on the book he was reading. His thoughts kept wandering back to much earlier days. Looking again at the envelopes, he was startled to recognise on one of them the well-remembered handwriting of Maria Beadnell. It was now ten years since she had become Mrs Henry Winter, wife of the manager of a Finsbury saw-mill, and Dickens had not seen her for a long time, perhaps not even since the end of his courtship of her – though he and her father had kept in touch. Now he was suddenly flooded with nostalgia for his old 'Copperfield days'. 'Three or four and twenty years vanished like a dream,' he told Maria in his reply to her letter, which he had opened, he said, 'with the touch of my young friend David Copperfield when he was in love'. An increasingly impassioned exchange of correspondence followed over the next two weeks, during his absence in Paris. Only his side survives in the form of three long letters in which he blends intense and vividly-detailed memories of his courting days with not-so-veiled reproaches of her for her failure to return his love, and with a deep and admiring pity for his younger self: 'I shall never be half so good a fellow any more.' Maria is left in no doubt that his passion for her was inextricably intertwined with the roots of his great success: 'Whatever of fancy, romance, energy, passion, aspiration and determination belong to me, I never have separated and never shall separate from the hard-hearted little woman – you – whom it is nothing to say I would have died for, with the greatest alacrity!' Maria seems to have been swept along – as well she might have been – by the torrent of emotion that her 'busy and pleasant' letter (as Dickens called what was probably just a chatty, re-establishing of contact sort of missive) had released in this man, now loved and idolised by thousands. She even went so far, it appears from what he writes in one letter, as to tell him that she really had loved him but had been overborne by others. Dickens was evidently bent on resuscitating their relationship as some kind of *amitié amoureuse*. 'Remember,' he told her in grandly vague fashion, 'I accept all with my whole soul, and reciprocate all'. Perhaps he had some idea of achieving, through such an *amitié*, that 'one happiness' he felt he had missed in life and about which he had just written so yearningly to Forster. Might he not have found at last in the person of his old flame 'that one friend and companion' he had 'never made'? Poor unsuspecting Maria could hardly have chosen for her re-entry into his life a moment when his feelings were in a more combustible state.[1]

Dickens's fire was soon quenched, however. Some time between his return to Tavistock House on Tuesday 20 February and the following Saturday he contrived a tête-à-tête meeting with Maria and found himself confronted with a stout woman of forty-four. She had warned him that she was 'toothless, fat, old, and ugly' but he had simply brushed this aside. Now, after meeting her again in the flesh he wrote to her in a very different tone – treated her to one of his standard jocular, 'Sparkler-of-Albion' letters, in fact – reverting in the salutation from 'My dear Maria' to 'My dear Mrs Winter'. The serio-comic nature of his disconcerting reunion with her was to provide him with some rich fictional material ten or eleven months later, when writing *Little Dorrit* and describing Arthur Clennam's reunion with his old sweetheart Flora after a separation of more than twenty years. For the moment, however, he probably had no notion of pressing Maria into service for the new story which, as yet, existed only in the form of those 'motes' floating in the air of his imagination.[2]

The thrilling anticipation of seeing Maria again when he got back to London, together with the fact that Collins was unwell, probably militated against much exploration of the 'festive diableries' of Paris, though the two friends do certainly seem to have gone in for a veritable orgy of theatre-going and Dickens's evocative description in a letter to Forster of one performance they saw, Frédéric Lemaître, in *Trente Ans; ou, la vie d'un joueur*, shows us what a finely observant drama critic he was. As to his published journalism, he must have already written, before leaving London, three lead articles that appeared in successive issues of *Household Words* on 3, 10, and 17 February. One, 'Gaslight Fairies', is a seasonal piece describing with sympathy and humour the children and young girls who play fairies and such-like roles in the Christmas pantomimes. Back in his blacking-factory days, when his fellow-worker, Poll Green spoke of his little sister who 'did imps in the pantomimes', the young Dickens had been deeply ashamed of his contact, even at second hand, with such a shabby class of thespians. Now, however, he defends them against those who are 'so often pleased to think ill of those who minister to our amusements' and ends by sketching a generic 'Miss Fairy'. She is three and twenty years old and her whole family depends upon her meagre earnings. Her exploitative father is a superannuated and drunken old actor whom Miss Fairy still loves, admires and fervently believes in, and she has an equally exploitative ne'er-do-well brother, John Kemble Fairy (Kemble was the name of a great acting dynasty in the early nineteenth-century). This image of a devoted young woman toiling to support her parasitic family stayed with him and became central to his conception of the heroine of his new novel, while the contrast between the shabby and down-at-heel lives of corps de ballet dancers and the glamour that surrounds them on stage is also revisited in the book in the heroine's sister Fanny, who is a dancer at a cheap theatre.[3]

The other *Household Words* articles Dickens wrote before he went to Paris were both topical and fiercely polemical, as also were eleven further ones that he wrote between the end of February and the end of August. He was becoming ever more disgusted by the contemporary political situation. The disastrously incompetent conduct of the Crimean War led to the independent M.P. John Roebuck's motion calling for a Committee of Enquiry into the matter and, when on 29 January this motion was passed by a large majority, the Government resigned. One member of it, Lord John Russell, the only leading politician in whom Dickens had any faith, had already resigned, believing that Roebuck's motion could not honourably be opposed. After much manoeuvring for places, a new ministry, which included many of the old faces, was formed on 5 February under one of Dickens's chief *bêtes noires*, the veteran Tory politician Lord Palmerston. 'Pam' was now in his seventies but still as smart a political operator, and as aristocratically insouciant, as ever and – mainly because of his bellicose patriotism – still hugely popular with the electorate. The Radical M.P. and distinguished archaeologist Henry Layard ('Layard of Nineveh'), who had been to the Crimea and seen for himself what was happening, denounced the calamitous ineptitude of the aristocratic high command and demanded its replacement. In response, Palmerston simply invoked 'that glorious charge of the cavalry at Balaklava . . . where the noblest and wealthiest of the land rode foremost, followed by heroic men from the lowest classes of the community', and then proceeded to put every possible obstacle in Layard's way so that the M.P. was driven to carry on his campaign outside Parliament.[4]

Layard helped to form the Administrative Reform Association, inaugurated on 5 May, with a second public meeting, held at Drury Lane Theatre, following on 13 June. Dickens felt strongly enough about governmental maladministration to join the Association, the only time in his life that he joined a political movement, but he could not attend on the 13th. On 2 June, however, he assured Layard, 'I am constantly putting the subject in as sharp lights as I can kindle, in Household Words.' He plumed himself especially, and with justice, on one 'fine little bit of satire' which took the form of 'an account of an Arabic MS. lately discovered very like the *Arabian Nights* – called the Thousand and One Humbugs'. Three articles with this title, published on 21 and 28 April and 5 May, derided Parliament, personified as 'Howsa Kummauns (or Peerless Chatterer)', the nepotistic and routine-bound Civil Service ('Scarli Tapa and the Forty Thieves'), and 'the Grand Vizier Parmarstoon (or Twirling Weathercock)'. Palmerston is lampooned also as the 'Talkative Barber' – 'an accomplished diplomat, a first-rate statesman, a frisky speaker, an easy shaver, a touch-and-go joker, a giver of the go-by to all complainers, and above all a member of the aristocracy of barbers'. Two other articles clearly anticipate themes that Dickens soon afterwards wove into his new novel. 'The Toady Tree' (*HW*, 26 May 1855) anticipates Mr Meagles's lamentable worship ('toadying') of the aristocratic Barnacles and the Stiltstalkings in *Little Dorrit*. The second, 'Cheap Patriotism' (*HW*, 9 June 1855), purports to be written by a clerk in a public office who blandly records the nepotistic appointments to well-salaried positions, idleness, insolence towards the public, and other abuses rife in the Civil Service. This highly topical piece – contemporary readers would have been aware of the Northcote–Trevelyan Report of 1854 with its as yet unacted-on proposals for radical reform of the Service – clearly anticipates the great Circumlocution Office satire in the third number of *Little Dorrit*, that 'scarifier' with which, three months later, Dickens was to 'relieve his indignant soul'.[5]

Besides firing off such 'volleys of red hot shot' in his magazine Dickens joined forces with Forster and Charles Dilke in attacking a bastion of aristocratic patronage that loomed large in the field of his own profession as a writer. This was the Royal Literary Fund, established in 1790 to relieve authors of 'approved literary merit ... being in want or distress' which had been granted a royal charter in 1818. Dickens had belonged to the Fund for many years but had become more and more dissatisfied with the way the institution's business was organised by its long-serving secretary, Octavian Blewitt. The Fund had plenty of money but the grants it made tended to be very small, its running expenses seemed exorbitant, and it operated under heavy aristocratic patronage whereas, Dickens argued, it 'should be entirely in the hands of literary and scientific men, and that no other human being had any business there whatever'. At the Annual General Meeting on 14 March Dickens denounced the Fund's Charter as 'utterly defective and rotten' and successfully moved that a committee should be appointed to prepare an application for a new one, the details to be debated at a Special General Meeting. Dickens wrote to Collins on 19 March, 'Virtually, I consider the thing done' but he and his fellow-reformers had seriously underestimated their conservative opponents. At the special meeting on 16 June their proposals for entirely reforming the Fund so as to make it in some respects more like the Guild of Literature and Art were decisively rejected. The result of this was to increase Dickens's antagonism; his, Forster's and Dilke's tenacious battle with 'the obstructives' as he called Blewitt and the conservatives on the Fund's Committee was to continue unabated for the next four years.[6]

Meanwhile, he had been made 'sick and sour' by a Royal Proclamation that 21 March should be a day of 'Solemn Fast, Humiliation and Prayer'. 'The gentlemen who have been so kind as to ruin us are going to give us a day of humiliation and fasting', he wrote to his American friend, Captain Ely Morgan, and he made bitter references to the event in two *Household Words* articles. In the same letter he reports himself as being 'in the first stage of a new book, which consists in going round and round the idea, as you see a bird in its cage go about and about his sugar before he touches it'. He gives Morgan no indication of what this idea was. By the beginning of May he could tell Forster that 'the story was breaking out all around' him, and he was 'going off down the railroad to humour it'. As this last sentence indicates, and as he vividly describes in letters to a number of correspondents, he was in a state of extreme restlessness, one which seems to have been even more intense than was usual with him at the start of a new novel. He either rushed about or sat making 'all kinds of notes' but was as yet unable to settle down steadily to the actual writing.[7]

As usual, settling on the title was an essential first step. By 8 May he had got hold of a 'capital' one. This was *Nobody's Fault* which, as his working notes show, remained the title for the next five months during which he wrote the first three numbers (Bk I, chs 1–11). The title was no doubt meant as an ironic comment on how Britain's ruling class managed to deny or evade responsibility for national disgraces and disasters. Forster would seem to have confused matters by linking this working title to an idea he remembered Dickens having 'of a leading man for a story who should bring about all the mischief in it, lay it all on Providence, and say at every fresh calamity, "Well, it's a mercy, however, nobody was to blame you know!" '. Such a character (unnamed) is mentioned in Dickens's notes for the second number but with 'Not yet' written against him. By the end of the fourth number he has still not appeared. Clearly, therefore, he was not going to be the story's 'leading man', merely a minor character who was to personify the comfortable irresponsibility which is to be a target for satire in the novel. But, as seems clear from the way he begins the story, Dickens had a deeper purpose than simply the satirising of politicians and civil servants. Drawing on his memories of Marseilles nine years before, first written up in *Pictures from Italy* (see above, p. 227), he creates a dramatic opening scene with strong contrasts between purity and foulness, and between blazing light and gloomy darkness, as well as between two prisoners, the swaggering, sinister Rigaud and the childlike Cavaletto. Succeeding chapters develop the theme of confinement or imprisonment both literal and metaphorical and – inevitably, one feels – lead Dickens back to the Marshalsea of his childhood and to the creation of his heroine, Little Dorrit, the selfless, toiling, loving Child of the Marshalsea. The stage was set for his most profound fictional exploration to date of his traumatic childhood experience.[8]

It was not until September, when Dickens wrote the second chapter of *Little Dorrit* III, depicting the Circumlocution Office, that his 'capital' title seemed, for this chapter anyway, to fit his story. By that time, however, he had not only created his heroine (not yet called 'Little Dorrit' but simply 'Dorrit'), her parasitic family and her whole Marshalsea environment, but had brought her into contact with his strangely subdued forty-year-old hero, Arthur Clennam, a man undergoing, like Dickens himself, what we should today term a mid-life crisis. He had evidently begun to register what was to be the essential dynamic of the story, the earnest love, self-sacrifice and active New Testament goodness of a gentle young woman pitted against a 'prison' world of fraud, confusion, corrosive pretence, sycophancy, Old Testament vengefulness and criminal irresponsibility, as well as the sheer, diabolic evil represented by her polar opposite in the novel, the 'gentlemanly' villain Rigaud/Blandois. By the time he was writing the fourth number in November, just a few weeks ahead of the date set for publication of no.I, the absolute centrality to the novel of the character Little Dorrit, as she was now first called, was evident and Dickens dropped *Nobody's Fault* in favour of *Little Dorrit*.

Back in May, however, he was still very much casting about. His working notes for the first number of *Little Dorrit* when compared with those for earlier novels reflect much uncertainty (there are, in fact, no general 'mems' at all for the first number of *Bleak House*, just some brief chapter-notes). The *Dorrit* 'mems' begin with a series of questions: 'Waiting Room? No / Office? No / French Town? Yes / Man from China? Yes / Prison? Yes / Quarantine? Yes / Family and two daughters? No / Working jeweller and his daughters? No'. Then comes this idea:

> People to meet and part as travellers do, and the future connexion between them in the story, not to be now shewn to the reader but to be worked out as in real life. Try this uncertainty and this not-putting of them together, as a new means of interest. Indicate and carry through this intention.

He decided against this notion but when working on the second number in August told Forster that he had more than half a mind to return to it and to begin the book again 'and work in what I have done, afterwards'. He did not do this but, as the first chapter of Book II of the novel, the Great St Bernard one, shows, kept the idea in mind and adapted it, very effectively, for use at this mid-point of his story. It is not until the end of the chapter that the names of the various characters meeting at the convent 'as travellers do' are confirmed for the reader by their signatures in the travellers' book with the last one, that of Blandois, Rigaud's assumed name, ending in sinister fashion 'with a long lean flourish, not unlike a lasso, thrown at all the rest of the names'. This powerful image hints that any future connections between these characters, 'to be worked out in real life', are not going to be happy ones.[9]

As Dickens worked at laying the foundations of his new book his extreme restlessness urgently required some immediate outlet. The campaign to reform the Royal Literary Fund provided some relief, as did reading the *Carol* to an audience of railway workers at Ashford on 27 March, and baiting the Government in a speech to the General Theatrical Fund on 2 April but something more strenuously distracting was needed. To Collins he wrote on 11 May:

> The restless condition in which I wander up and down my room with the first page of my new book before me, defies all description. I feel as if nothing would do me the least good, but setting up a Balloon. It might be inflated in the Garden in front [of Tavistock House] – but I am afraid of its scarcely clearing those little houses.

Fortunately, his correspondent was in a condition to provide at that moment the means for precisely the kind of distraction Dickens found most congenial and invigorating, namely organising and starring in some theatrical production. 'Distraction' is not, in fact, quite the right word since this activity was essentially a continuation of his novel-writing by other means, the pleasure he derived from 'feigning to be somebody else' being, as he wrote to the *Quarterly Review* editor Whitwell Elwin on 7 June, 'akin to the pleasure of inventing'. Collins was experimenting with drama and asked if Dickens would read a play called *The Lighthouse* that he had derived from his own story, 'Gabriel's Marriage', published two years earlier in *Household Words*. This play was, Dickens was delighted to find, 'a regular old-style Melo Drama' with a wonderfully meaty role for the central character, Aaron Gurnock. Gurnock is an old lighthouse-keeper haunted by guilty memories of having been an accessory years before to the murder of a woman. In the climactic scene of the action, which all takes place in the lighthouse, he is struck with terror by being suddenly confronted with a figure that he at first believes to be the murdered woman's ghost but that, as he gradually comes to realise, is flesh and blood, the intended victim having survived the attempt to kill her. Gurnock's better feelings then take over and he ends by begging for, and obtaining, the woman's forgiveness.

Fired by this script, Dickens promptly threw himself into highly elaborate preparations to stage the play in the converted schoolroom at Tavistock House that had been used for the children's theatricals. He recruited Lemon, Collins and Egg as fellow-actors, likewise Georgina, Mamie and Katey. He revived *Mr Nightingale's Diary* for performance as a sprightly afterpiece, persuaded Stanfield to paint the scenery, drilled Charley and Frank Stone's son Marcus in how to produce the storm-at-sea sound-effects for the first act of the drama ('half a dozen cannon-balls to roll about on the floor to simulate the shaking of the Lighthouse as it was struck by the waves', etc.). He commissioned a young musician friend of Charley's, Francesco Berger, to compose an overture and incidental music, and himself wrote both a prologue and an eight-verse 'Song of the Wreck' for Mamie to sing during the performance. This song was printed on the elegant playbill Dickens also composed, which was headed 'The Smallest Theatre in the World! /TAVISTOCK HOUSE / Lessee and Manager Mr Crummles'. At all three performances (16, 18, 19 June) the invited audiences responded with enthusiasm. One of them included Carlyle, who was much impressed by Dickens's 'wild picturesqueness' as Gurnock, and also a famous retired actress Elizabeth Yates, who noted that he was modelling his acting style in Gurnock on that of Lemaître. According to Dickens's letter to Burdett Coutts of 19 June, Yates exclaimed at the end, '(with a large red circle round each eye), "O Mr Dickens what a pity it is you can do anything else!" ' Charley comments that it was in acting Gurnock that CD first showed 'that extraordinary dramatic intensity and force, with which his readings were afterwards to make the public so familiar'. The whole affair ended in characteristic Dickensian fashion. Following the last performance there was a jovial supper after which the company turned to Scottish reels and, Dickens wrote to Stanfield on 20 June, 'danced in the maddest way until 5 this morning', adding, 'It is as much as I can do, to guide the pen.'[10]

A week later matters theatrical were still in his mind when he made a long and brilliant speech at the third meeting of the Administrative Reform Association. Palmerston had scornfully referred to the Association's previous meeting, held at the Drury Lane Theatre, as 'the Drury Lane private theatricals'. Dickens, claiming 'some slight acquaintance with theatricals, private and public', neatly turned the joke against the Prime Minister: 'if I wanted to form a company of Her Majesty's servants, I think I should know where to put my hand on "the comic old gentleman"'. Referring to the activities of Parliament in general, he said, 'We have seen the *Comedy of Errors* played so dismally like a tragedy that we cannot bear it.' He then prefaced his main remarks by reassuring his audience that, despite his presence before them, he was not about to exchange his writer's life for one in politics. Referring to his warm 'attachment' to his multitudes of readers stemming from 'the confidence and

44 John Dickens in later life

45 William Charles Macready
By H. P. Briggs

46 Dickens acting in *Used Up* by Dion Boucicault
By Augustus Egg (1849)

47 W. H. Wills

48 Wilkie Collins
From the portrait by Sir John Millais

49 Clarkson Stanfield
From a drawing by Daniel Maclise

50 John Leech
From the portrait by Sir John Millais

51 Dickens in his study in Tavistock House
By Edward Matthew Ward (painting completed 1854)

52 China monkey
One of the objects that Dickens liked to have
always on his writing desk

53 Tavistock House

54 Leigh Hunt
'Skimpole' in *Bleak House*. Lithograph by
G. H. Ford (1850)

55 Walter Savage Landor
'Boythorn' in *Bleak House*

56 Thomas Carlyle

57 Angela Burdett Coutts
Mezzotint after a painting by J. R. Swinton (1865)

58 'Tom-All-Alone's'
One of H. K. Browne's 'dark plates' for *Bleak House*

The office boy for ever looking out of window, who never has anything to do. Done in Our Mutual

The lady, un peu passée, who is determined to be interesting. No matter how much I love that person — nay, the more so for that very reason — I must flatter and bother, and be weak and apprehensive and nervous and what not. If I were well and strong, agreeable and self-denying, my friend might mistrust.

How as to a story in two periods — with a lapse of time between, like a French Drama ?

Titles for such a notion. Time!

The Leaves of the Forest	Five and Twenty Years
Scattered Leaves	Years and Years.
The Great Wheel.	
Round and Round.	Rolling Years.
Old Leaves.	Day after Day.
Old and New Leaves.	Memory Carton
Leaves of Years	Rolling Stones.
Leaves	Dead Leaves.
Long ago	Fallen Leaves.
Far apart	Two Generations.
	Many Years Leaves.

Felled Trees.

59 Page from Dickens's *Book of Memoranda*

60 Maria Winter, *née* Beadnell

61 Georgina Hogarth *c.* 1850
By Augustus Egg

62 Catherine Dickens
Daguerreotype by John Jabez Edwin Mayall, between 1852 and 1855

63 Nelly Ternan (1857)

64 Charles Dickens
Copy made by Frith in 1870 of his 1859 painting of
Dickens in his study

65 Henry Morley

66 James Emerson Tennent

67 Hans Christian Anders

68 Charles Dickens photographed in reading pose (1859)

69 John Forster
Carte de visite by H. Watkins (?), formerly owned by Percy Fitzgerald

Five ~~chapters~~ *chapters.*

THE STORY

OF

LITTLE DOMBEY.

I.

his Wife's

Rich Mr DOMBEY sat in the corner of ~~the~~ darkened ~~room~~ *bedchamber* in the great arm-chair by the bedside, and ~~Son lay~~ *rich Mr Dombey's* tucked up warm in a little basket ~~bedstead~~, carefully ~~disposed~~ *placed* on a low settee ~~immediately~~ in front of the fire and close to it, as if his constitution were analogous to that of a muffin, and it was essential to toast him brown while he was very new.

Rich ~~Mr~~ Dombey was about eight-and-forty years of age. ~~Son~~ about eight-and-forty minutes. ~~Mr~~ Dombey was rather bald, rather red, and ~~though a hand~~ *rather* ~~some well made man, too~~ stern and pompous in

B

Rich Mr Dombey's son

70 Page from the specially printed reading text of *The Story of Little Dombey* showing Dickens's emendations

71 Arthur Smith

Well, Mr. Dickens, on the eve of our departure, I present you with $300,000, the result of ...tures in America."
" What! only $300,000 ? Is that all I have made out of these penurious Yankees, after ...ues of them? Pshaw! Let us go, Dolby!"

72/73 American newspaper cartoons of Dickens and Dolby on Dickens's American Reading Tour
The right-hand cartoon, entitled 'The British Lion in America', is based on a widely-distributed studio portrait-photograph taken by Jeremiah Gurney, New York, in Dec. 1867 (see Noel C. Peyrouton, 'The Gurney Photographs', *D* 54 (1958), 145–55)

74/75 James T. Fields and his wife Annie Fields

76 Dickens sketched by Leslie Ward (1870)

77 Gad's Hill Place
The Illustrated London News, 18 June 1870

78 From the last words of fiction written by Dickens (*Mystery of Edwin Drood*, ch. 23)

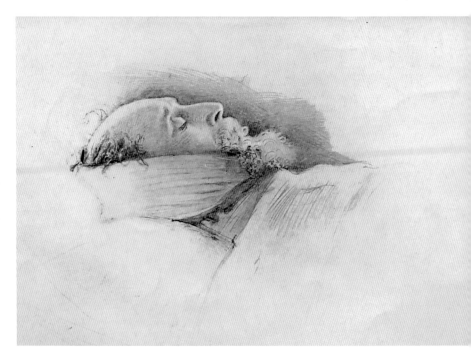

79 Dickens on his deathbed
By Sir John Millais

80 'The empty chair. Gad's Hill – Ninth of June 1870'
By Luke Fildes

friendship that they have long reposed in me', he described himself as 'one who lives by Literature, who is content to do his public service through Literature, and who is conscious that he cannot serve two masters'. It was always, he said, within his chosen sphere of action that he had 'for some years, tried to understand the heavier social grievances and to help to set them right'. He then proceeded to lambaste the delays, obfuscations, inefficiency and obsolete procedures of Parliament and its servants in a speech that may be seen as a stirring overture to the Circumlocution Office satire in *Little Dorrit*. In particular, Dickens's allusion to 'that class of gentlemen of good family, who are not particularly fit for anything but spending money which they have not got', and who think it extraordinary 'that these Administrative Reform fellows can't mind their own business', looks forward to Clennam's encounter at the Circumlocution Office with Barnacle Junior (he of the recalcitrant monocle) and the latter's wonderfully anguished protest, 'Look here. Upon my soul, you mustn't come into the place saying you want to know, you know.'[11]

Dickens had this year decided upon Folkestone for the family's annual summer retreat and reported this to Burdett Coutts on 8 May, saying that it would be convenient for the family's proceeding to Paris for six months in October 'to complete the polishing of Mary and Katey' – had he, one wonders, already begun to think about employing a professional 'varnisher' for his daughters as, a year and a half later, he was to describe Mr Dorrit as doing for his? Before the move to Folkestone another private performance of *The Lighthouse* was staged on 10 July at Campden House, the Kensington mansion of a certain Colonel Waugh, to raise funds for a charitable cause. Keen to enhance the likelihood of Collins's play being taken up for professional production by one of the London theatres, Dickens actively promoted extensive press coverage of this performance and many appreciative reviews duly appeared, especially of his Gurnock. Meanwhile, the Government's attempt to introduce a bill aimed at stopping Sunday trading had led to serious rioting in Hyde Park. Dickens, the one-time author of *Sunday Under Three Heads*, recognised an old enemy in this blatantly class-biased legislation (which had ultimately to be withdrawn) and strongly denounced the bill, even at Lord John Russell's dinner-table. The introduction of this bill most likely helped to inspire the opening of Chapter 3 of his new story with its desolating picture of what his chapter-note designates as a 'Dismal London Sunday', as well as yet another anti-Parliamentary piece for the 4 August issue of *Household Words* called 'The Great Baby', in which he seizes the opportunity again to attack Cruikshank, here lampooned as 'Mr Monomaniacal Patriarch', for his extreme Temperance views.[12]

In Folkestone, once the usual routine of a Dickens family summer with its customary stream of visitors (which this time included Wilkie Collins for a six-week stay) had been established, Dickens gradually settled down to the writing of the new monthly-part serial that he was still calling *Nobody's Fault*.

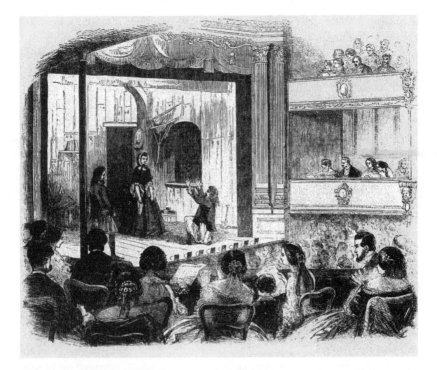

37 Performance of *The Lighthouse* at Campden House, 10 July 1855 (Dickens is the kneeling figure on the right)

He felt able to tell Baron Tauchnitz on 5 September that the first number would be published at the end of November, and by mid-month he had finished the second one (chs 5–8) which introduces the Dorrit family and tells their history. Dickens's notes for the number show that he was consciously developing the prison theme. The situations of Mrs Clennam and Mr Dorrit, for example, are noted as '<u>Parallel Imprisonments</u>'. When writing a bit later on to Browne, 'at full explanatory length', about the cover-design, he must have specified the central position of the image of Little Dorrit leaving the prison in rays of sunlight but the fetters linking together the letters of her surname in the bottom half of the vignette's border were presumably Browne's inspired embellishment. On 16 September Dickens told Forster he had made 'an enormous outlay' in chapter 5 (this subsequently became chapter 6). This 'outlay' included a description of how Mr Dorrit became 'The Father of the Marshalsea' and how his younger daughter Amy's being born there made her 'The Child of the Marshalsea'. He also told Forster that he now had a 'great idea of overwhelming [the Dorrits] with wealth', adding, 'their condition would be very curious'. Curious for *us* here, as scholars have noted, is to see just how

38 Section of Browne's monthly-part cover for *Little Dorrit*

far Dickens had progressed in the writing of his new story before hitting upon this basic structural idea, one that we might reasonably assume to have been central to its very conception. He had also begun to see the fictional potential of Amy Dorrit, whom he was still referring to in his notes as 'Dorrit'; he believed, he told Forster, that he could make her 'very strong' in the story. On 16 September he told Wills he was now 'steeped in my story' and alternating between enthusiasm and depression. To Lavinia Watson he expressed himself more lyrically, telling her he could feel the story all around him, 'heaving in the sea, flying with the clouds, blowing in the wind'. He evidently now felt sufficiently possessed of it to be able to put its actual composition briefly on hold while he wrote for *Household* Words a splendidly evocative tribute to Folkestone. He called the place 'Pavilionstone' after its chief hotel, the Pavilion, which he praised highly, remembering the manager's great kindness to him when he was convalescing there two years before (above, p. 355). This piece appeared in the issue for 29 September under the title 'Out of Town' and was a kind of holiday postcard from Dickens to his readers: 'Sitting, on a bright September morning, among my books and papers at my open window on the cliff overhanging the sea-beach, I have the sky and ocean framed before me like a beautiful picture.' His morning's work done, he took to 'the neighbouring downs and grassy hill-sides' and reported, 'I find I can still in reason walk any distance, jump over anything, and climb up anywhere'.[13]

By the end of September Dickens had, by 'sticking at it day after day', nearly finished *Dorrit* III and had at last, with the bravura account of the great Circumlocution Office, introduced into the story the overt political satire fore-shadowed by Browne's brilliant cartoon at the top of the monthly cover-design. This showed a procession with Britannia dozing in a wheel-chair preceded by blind old cripples, fools and a cane-sucking dandy. She is propelled from behind by more dandies wearing fool's-caps and being fawned on by syco-phants. Significantly, however, the appearance of 'the man who comfortably charges everything on Providence' – crucial to the 'Nobody's Fault' idea but clearly becoming more and more peripheral to the plot as it was evolving – was again deferred with the query about introducing him once more firmly answered by 'not yet'. And now it was already time to be thinking of the next *Household Words* Christmas number. Having, during a flying visit to London, discussed with Collins his idea for another framework narrative, Dickens soon afterwards circulated an outline of this to prospective contributors. He was 'beset' at this time, as he later told Forster, by recurrent notions 'of a book whereof the whole story shall be on the top of the Great St Bernard' (a region that had always a 'weird fascination' for him). He now imagined a homely English variant, that would also chime with the images of confinement, actual or virtual prisons, that had more generally 'beset' him since the inception of *Little Dorrit*. A solitary stage-coach passenger, snowed up one Christmas at a lonely inn on the Yorkshire moors, is driven to beguile the time by getting the people of the inn to tell him about 'some curious experience each has had' or else has heard about. These stories were to be supplied by Collins and other invited contributors writing as 'The Landlord', 'The Barmaid', and so on.[14]

Other business, too, required Dickens's attention before the family's move to Paris for a six-month stay. Thackeray was shortly to embark for America where he was to make a lecture-tour and there was a farewell dinner to him to be presided over; there was a promised charity reading of the *Carol* to be given at Folkestone; and there was Charley to be settled as a clerk in Baring's Bank. By 19 October, however, Dickens had managed to get himself to Paris and, 'after going through unheard-of bedevilments', had succeeded, with Georgina's help while Catherine waited with the children at a Boulogne hotel, to find a small house with 'rooms rather larger than meat-safes' but plenty in number, in a splendid situation on the Champs Elysées. He inaugurated his writing residence there by dashing off, in response to an urgent request for more copy from Wills, another satirical piece for *Household Words*. Entitled 'A Slight Depreciation of the Currency', it addressed the contemporary prevalence of money-worship in Britain, a theme that was to become very prominent in the new novel following the introduction in the May number (VI) of 'the great and wonderful Merdle'. Dickens began this article by citing Sydney Smith's observation that Englishmen often seemed to 'have a remarkable satisfaction in even speaking of large sums of money', an observation that would certainly have been again in his mind when he came to invent the small-talk of Merdle's high-society guests:

'I am told', said Bishop magnate to Horse Guards [a general or senior civil servant from the War Office], 'that Mr Merdle has made another enormous hit. They say a hundred thousand pounds.'

Horse Guards had heard two.

Treasury had heard three.[15]

Having evidently now firmly decided on 'overwhelming' the Dorrits with wealth at some later point in the story, Dickens told his publishers on 29 October that he intended to divide the novel into two books, respectively entitled 'Poverty' and 'Wealth'. He had already written to Browne some weeks earlier, as noted above, giving him detailed guidance for designing the monthly-part cover and, presumably, subjects for the two plates for the first number. Browne's failure to respond, about which Dickens complained to Wills on 19 October, did not augur well for the writer/ artist collaboration on this book, which was to be the last but one of Dickens's to be illustrated by Browne. And, indeed, the sparse evidence that survives does suggest that Dickens was quite often asking Browne to make changes. Browne's *Dorrit* illustrations have often been said to show a marked decline in quality from those for *Copperfield* and *Bleak House*, which is, I think, too sweeping a judgment. One of the plates for *Dorrit* X, for example, 'The Marshalsea becomes an Orphan', brilliantly complements Dickens's text, Mr Dorrit's anatomically questionable left arm notwithstanding. As to Browne's cover for the monthly parts, it is excellent. In its overall design and witty deployment of detail it highlights the novel's main themes and, though a clear narrative line like the one found on the *Dombey* cover is lacking, the story's inner meaning is 'clearly "shadowed forth" '.[16]

Once installed in Paris, Dickens greatly took to life there. He was much gratified to find that he was now truly famous and very widely read in France, though he cannot have been altogether happy about an unauthorised translation of *Chuzzlewit* that was at this time appearing in *Le Moniteur*. People greeted him warmly in shops and, he reported to Forster, he found 'much of the personal friendliness in my readers, here, that is so delightful at home'. He was lionised and lavishly entertained, insofar as he allowed himself to be, by the leading lights of the Paris arts world: the prolific dramatist Eugène Scribe, the writer and politician Emile de Girardin with his 'three gorgeous drawing-rooms with ten thousand wax candles in golden sconces', and the celebrated actress Pauline Viardot. It was at Viardot's house that Dickens and Catherine were introduced to George Sand – not a writer with whose passionately romantic novels Dickens would have felt much sympathy, if indeed he knew them. Sand herself he was amused, and perhaps pleased, to find 'just the kind of woman in appearance whom you might suppose to be the queen's monthly nurse.' These grand invitations would have been awkward to refuse but he tried generally to keep himself free of dining-out commitments. To one would-be hostess, evidently one with some claims of acquaintance, he carefully explained that after a day's writing, 'I cannot relieve my mind or prepare myself for the morrow, unless I am perfectly free from promises and engagements, and can wander about in my own queer way.' 'At such times,' he told her, 'hot rooms and society, worry me more than you can easily imagine – nothing but the open air will set me right.' He did agree to sit for his portrait to the well-known painter Ary Scheffer, 'a most noble fellow', at whose house he made 'all sorts of acquaintances', but in the event was much unsettled by having to 'sit, sit, sit' to the artist (and, as it turned out, simultaneously to Scheffer's brother Henri) with *Little Dorrit* weighing on his mind. A rather more tiresome, but inevitable, concomitant of his celebrity was the crowd of obscure local authors seeking to present themselves to him; and, of course, Parisian begging-letter writers proved to be just as numerous and assiduous as their London *confrères*.[17]

For Dickens the writer the supremely important thing was that he had a whole fascinating city to wander in whenever he wanted or needed to do so, a city teeming with life and much prettier than London, as was borne in upon him during his frequent business trips back to England. He happened to be in London on his birthday and wrote to Catherine that the streets were 'hideous to behold' and the ugliness of the city 'quite astonishing'. In Paris whenever his head was '[stinging] with visions of the book' he could, as he reported to Forster, 'disembarrass it by plunging out into some of the strange places I glide into of nights in these latitudes'. Wilkie Collins was an ideal companion for such 'glidings' and likewise, when he was away, the ideal recipient for news about such solo expeditions on Dickens's part. 'On Saturday night,' Dickens wrote to him on 22 April, 'I paid three francs at the door of that place where we saw the wrestling, and went in, at 11 o-Clock, to a Ball'. Having compared the place to London's National Argyll Rooms ('virtually a high-class brothel', according to the Pilgrim editors), Dickens described the women there, making particular mention of one who sat alone in a corner wearing a rich shawl, 'handsome, regardless, brooding, and yet with some nobler qualities in her forehead'. He would have liked to know more about her and told Collins, 'I mean to walk about tonight, and look for her'. Then there was the Parisian theatre scene which was quite as lively as London's, indeed more so in some respects, and, as usual, some of Dickens's most entertaining letters are about various plays he has seen. Another Parisian spectacle of a very different kind into which, as he later wrote in *The Uncommercial Traveller*, he seemed 'dragged by invisible force' whenever he was in the city (see also above, p. 310)– an extreme instance of 'the attraction of repulsion' – was the one to be found in the Paris Morgue where corpses pulled out of the Seine, or else found somewhere, were exhibited for identification purposes. This grim place is mentioned many times in Dickens's journalism and features prominently in 'Railway Dreaming', the great celebration of Paris that he wrote on the spur of the moment for *Household Words* (published 10 May 1856) at the end of his time in the city, to strengthen a number of the journal that he considered weak. It would surely have been again in his mind a year later when he came to describe, in *Dorrit* XVII, the finding of Merdle's dripping corpse in the warm baths.

Stimulated as he was by Paris, Dickens yet found himself hampered during the autumn of 1855 in his work on the fourth number of his new story – now definitively titled *Little Dorrit* – by several things, among them the need to help Burdett Coutts with arrangements following the sudden death of Dr Brown, her dear companion's husband, and also much 'botheration' over the Christmas number, now titled *The Holly-Tree Inn.* With the honourable exception of Collins's, most of the contributions offered for the number were disappointing (one, indeed, Dickens rejected as 'unmitigated, bawdy Rot'). As far as his own scene-setting contribution went, however, that seems to have flowed easily enough and by 18 November he had finished all eight-and-a-half-thousand words of it. The snowbound traveller-narrator is a comically bashful young man who has been disappointed in love. Yielding to histrionic despair, he is running away to America, 'on my way', as he puts it, 'to the Devil'. His description of the tedium of his temporary 'imprisonment' at the inn soon merges into a stream of reminiscences about inns, the details of which hardly seem to fit what little we have been told about his character and history. The narrator is, in fact, Dickens himself, writing under the thinnest of fictional disguises, and mingling autobiography and fancy in a way that very much looks forward to his later 'Uncommercial Traveller' essays. For example, the description of his ghoulish nurse terrifying him as a child with horrific tales about murderous landlords clearly anticipates the much-quoted 'Nurse's Stories' of his later journalism. He goes on to recall the Mitre Inn of his Chatham childhood as well as the many different inns encountered during his travels in Britain, Europe and America. Memories of 'a lonely Inn in a wild moorland place' (i.e., the inn at Greta Bridge where he and Browne stayed in February 1838 and which may have been the 'original' of the Holly-Tree itself) lead on to memories of Mary Hogarth, here called 'a dear lost one', and the remarkable history of his dreams of her after her death. He perhaps needed once more to commemorate this idealised young woman from his early years now that the image of another one had been so shattered by the reality of Mrs Winter – a shattering he was about to fictionalise in *Dorrit* IV.[18]

Besides 'The Guest' Dickens also wrote 'The Bill', a brief conclusion to the Christmas number in which the dejected lover, whose name – unsurprisingly – turns out to be Charles, does get the girl after all. Then, feeling that – apart from his own contribution and Collins's – the number as a whole was still rather weak, Dickens quickly dashed off a fourth contribution to it. This was 'The Boots', a story supposedly related by the inn-servant named in the title about two eight-year-olds who, having fallen romantically in love, turn up at the Holly-Tree en route for Gretna Green. Its twinkling sentimentality is off-putting for today's readers but Dickens told Collins he thought it 'an odd idea' that succeeded in getting 'something of the effect of a Fairy Story out of the most unlikely materials'. Everyone at the Holly-Tree, including the Boots, is enchanted by the runaway children (rather as the kindly publican and his wife had been by the very young Dickens boldly asking them to draw him a pint of their 'very

best – the VERY best – ale') and delights in humouring them while their families are being secretly sent for. This story was at once eagerly seized upon by the
dramatisers and later became one of the most popular of all Dickens's public
readings. It ends with Boots expressing a sentiment which, for all its jocoseness,
might – if the author in question were anyone else but Dickens – be seen by
modern readers as consciously striking an ominous note with regard to developments in his personal life at this time: 'it would be a jolly good thing for a great
many couples on their way to be married, if they could only be stopped in time,
and brought back separately'.[19]

On 30 November the first number of *Little Dorrit* went on sale and it became
an immediate best-seller. Reviews were well-nigh universally favourable and
mostly very enthusiastic – *The Athenaeum*, for example, praised 'this evidence
of an ever-ripening genius and an ever-progressing art'. Within a month
38,000 copies had been sold and Dickens exulted to Forster that the new story
had 'beaten even *Bleak House* out of the field'. Equally gratifying were the
'enormous' sales achieved by *The Holly-tree Inn* when that hit the bookstalls on
15 December. That same day Dickens began a nine-day trip to England (his
third since settling in Paris) to visit Rockingham, and to give charity readings
of the *Carol* in Peterborough and Sheffield. In both cities he was received
with rapturous enthusiasm. In Sheffield, he told Lavinia Watson, they greeted
the line 'and to Tiny Tim who did <u>not</u> die' with 'a most prodigious shout and
roll of thunder'. After the reading the Mayor presented him with a service of
cutlery and Dickens responded with a proclamation of his writer's credo. This
credo makes clear his perception of his dual role as a personal friend to every
one of his individual readers and at the same time a champion of their collective rights in the body politic: 'Believe me, ladies and gentlemen, that to the
earnestness of my aim and desire to do right by my readers, and to leave our
imaginative and popular literature more closely associated than I found it at
once with the private homes and public rights of the English people, I shall ever
be faithful, – to my death – in the principles which have won your approval.
[*Loud applause.*]. . .'.[20]

When *Dorrit* II appeared on 31 December Dickens was only two numbers
ahead of the printers, having begun three ahead. With the *Household Words*
Christmas number now behind him, however, he was able to make better
progress with the fourth number, though still 'beset' by his earlier idea for a
story entirely set 'on the top of the Great St Bernard'. In due course he would
find a way to work this setting into *Little Dorrit*; more immediately, he could
compensate himself for his disillusionment following his meeting with Maria
Winter by building on his perception of her as she was now to create Flora
Finching, arguably his greatest comic achievement since Micawber, and one
which made him laugh very much as he was writing it. Such qualms as he
might have had after the Skimpole/ Leigh Hunt business about the misuse of

authorial power in basing characters on living people in such a way that the originals could be recognised did not apparently trouble him in this case. This may have been because poor Maria, unlike Leigh Hunt, or before him even little Mrs Seymour Hill, was in no sense a public figure, and Flora, moreover, for all her foolishness is presented as essentially kind-hearted. Meanwhile, a still more recent experience, of a very different kind, contributed towards the powerful ending of the fourth number describing Little Dorrit and her pathetic 'child' Maggy forced to spend a cold, wet night in the streets; like the prostitute who mistakes Little Dorrit for a child, they become part of 'the shame, desertion, wretchedness, and exposure, of the great capital'. Dickens had been horrified, on one of his nocturnal London walks the previous November, to come across what appeared to be five rain-sodden 'bundles of rags' crouching against the wall of Whitechapel workhouse. These 'bundles' were, in fact, young females, barred out because the place was already over-crowded. He described the incident in a *Household Words* piece sent to Wills on 9 January ('A Nightly Scene in London', *HW*, 26 Jan. 1856) but was clearly also drawing on it here in *Dorrit* IV.[21]

His sojourn in France helped Dickens to perceive the many ways in which, as it seemed to him, they ordered things better there, however much such English patriots as his Mr Meagles might disparage the French people's proneness to 'allonging and marshonging'. It served to confirm his gloomy view of the state of his own nation. He found in France, he told Bradbury and Evans in mid-November 1855, a general impression 'that England has become a mere second-rate power and is perfectly unable to do anything for herself – [the] result of toadyism and mismanagement'. In another letter, this time to Forster, he compared the English paintings with the French ones on view at the Exposition Universelle and was depressed to see 'mere form and conventionalities' usurping 'in English art, as in English government and social relations, the place of living force and truth'. He urged Wills, in a long business letter of 10 January, including suggestions for a whole raft of possible articles for *Household Words*, to try to find someone 'to write popularly about the monstrous absurdity of our laws, and to compare them with the Code Napoleon'. He took up some of these themes himself in a *Household Words* article, 'Insularities', published on 19 January. Despite the fact that he was portraying the most villainous character in his current novel as a thoroughly English caricature of a perfidious and melodramatic Frenchman, Dickens was clearly going through one of the more intense phases of his lifelong Francophilia.[22]

It was an auspicious moment, therefore, for the French publishing firm of Hachette, wishing to take advantage of a recent reciprocal copyright agreement between France and Great Britain, to approach him about publishing new and faithful translations of all his novels. Having consulted Tauchnitz

about the terms offered, Dickens was happy to make an agreement with
Hachette whereby he would receive 11,000 francs (approximately £440) in
eleven monthly instalments. He wrote to Forster on 30 January, 'Considering
that I get so much for what is otherwise worth nothing, and get my books
before so clever and important a people, I think this is not a bad move?' One
of his books he did discourage Hachette from translating, however. This was
Sketches by Boz, the contents of which he referred to dismissively as being
among his 'juvenile productions'. Meanwhile he toyed with the idea of collaborating with Wilkie Collins on a series of articles about Paris. This scheme did
not materialise but there was one *Household Words* article by another writer –
very much on an English theme, however – in the composition of which
he did become deeply involved at this time. This was Morley's 'Our Wicked
Mis-statements' (*HW*, 19 Jan. 1856), responding to a pamphlet published by
Harriet Martineau (her 'vomit of conceit', Dickens called it) strongly critical of
the series of articles about factory accidents published in *Household Words* as
part of a campaign for the introduction of legislation compelling factory-
owners to fence in their dangerous machinery. A staunch Liberal, Martineau
was strongly opposed to all forms of government interference with trade.[23]

On 31 January *Little Dorrit* III was published and Dickens took 'a grim
pleasure' in thinking that his Circumlocution Office satire would now see the
light and in 'wondering what effect it will make'. Carlyle was predictably
delighted. 'Recommend me to Dickens;' he wrote to Forster, 'and thank him
a hundred times for "The Circumlocution Office", which is priceless after its
sort! We have laughed loud and long over it here; and <u>laughter</u> is by no means
the supreme result in it. – Oh Heaven.' In other quarters it gave, equally
predictably, great offence. That hard-working civil servant and writer Anthony
Trollope, who had recently lampooned Dickens the social crusader as
'Mr Popular Sentiment' in his novel *The Warden* (1855), now, apparently,
composed a riposte to the Circumlocution Office satire in the form of an article
sent to *The Athenaeum* but its editor, Hepworth Dixon, would certainly have
been highly nervous about Dickens's reaction to such a notice so it was not
printed. Overall, the new Dickens serial, so eagerly anticipated, continued to be
very favourably received (*The Atlas*, a London weekly, opined on 9 February, for
example, that Dickens had never 'wielded pen to better purpose') but without
any picking out of the Circumlocution Office for special mention.[24]

The Dickens household remained in Paris until the end of April with
Dickens making frequent trips to London not only on *Household Words* or
Urania Cottage business but also in connection with his buying of Gad's Hill
Place, which he had now decided upon (the purchase price, paid on Friday
14 March, was £1,790). Another concern was renewing the assault upon the
Royal Literary Fund, which he represented both in a *Household Words* article
(8 March; written by Morley and revised by himself) and in an aggressive

speech at the Fund's Annual General Meeting on 12 March, as very much a microcosm of the Britain he was currently depicting in *Little Dorrit*. It was in his view disgracefully mismanaged by a set of Barnacles and thoroughly infected by 'the vulgar and common social vice of hanging on to great connexions at any price' while perverting 'the project of a working literary man'. During February he finished the writing of *Dorrit* V (chs 15–18) in which he introduced the character of the well-connected, cynically exploitative artist Henry Gowan, precisely the kind of meretricious dilettante who, like comparable litterateurs too prevalent in the Royal Literary Fund, brought discredit on his profession.

Dickens now embarked, much afflicted by the extreme restlessness usual for him at such a time, upon *Dorrit* VI in which he introduced 'Society', the Merdles and the mystery of 'Mr Merdle's Complaint' which, his chapter-notes reveal, will be shown to be 'Fraud and Forgery bye and bye'. Just a few days before Dickens made this note a swindling financier called John Sadleir, who had got himself elected to Parliament and risen to be for a time a junior lord of the Treasury, poisoned himself on Hampstead Heath after the collapse of his Tipperary Bank had ruined thousands of investors. Dickens had seized on what he called this 'precious rascality' as quarry for the figure of Merdle but told Forster that he had had 'the general idea of the Society business' before Sadleir's suicide, adding, 'Society, the Circumlocution Office, and Mr Gowan, are, of course, three parts of one idea and design.' He saw them as three interconnected, hollow shams flourishing mightily in contemporary Britain and to be exposed in his novel. By now he clearly had firmly in his mind a definite overall 'idea and design' for *Little Dorrit*, which was less concentrated and more complicated in its ramifications (and in its plot) than had been the case with *Bleak House*.[25]

During April he worked on *Little Dorrit* VII (chs 23–25), relishing the rich seam of 'drollness' he had opened up with the creation of Flora and Mr F's Aunt, and looking forward as 'a fine point in the story', to the showering of wealth upon the Dorrits in No. X. In his non-writing life, however, things were not going well. He was experiencing ever-increasing tension together with a keen sense of emotional loss linked to a certain nostalgia for 'the old days', and a kind of growing fatalism about life, which he envisaged as an arduous journey that the heavily-burdened traveller must 'work out' to its appointed end. All this found expression in the letter to Forster of 13 April part of which I quoted as an epigraph to this chapter. Later in the letter comes a sentence that points towards what may have been the heart of the matter: 'I find that the skeleton in my domestic closet is becoming a pretty big one.' This suggests long concealment of some ugly truth, a concealment that was becoming ever harder to maintain and presumably refers to Dickens's growing awareness that he had not only long ceased to love his wife (many commentators since, including his

younger daughter, have doubted if he ever really did love her) but was now
beginning to find her very presence and ordinary behaviour irritating or
displeasing. We get a glimpse of this irritation a few days later, I think, when
he tells Collins on 22 April about having treated Catherine, Georgina and the
girls to a dinner at his favourite restaurant, the Trois Frères; Georgina, Mamie
and Katey hardly did justice to the meal, he thought, but 'Mrs Dickens nearly
killed herself'.

Once more it was Wilkie Collins who helped to provide Dickens with a
desperately-needed new outlet or distraction. 'Collins and I', Dickens wrote to
Wills, on 6 April, 'have a mighty original notion (mine in the beginning) for
another Play at Tavistock House', to be performed the following January. From
his asking in this same letter if Wills's wife Janet would be willing to play a
Scotch housekeeper, 'in a supposed country house' with Georgina, Mamie
and Katey, it is evident that the planning of the play was already fairly well
advanced. It was another six months before Dickens revealed its title, *The
Frozen Deep*, in a letter to Burdett Coutts, but he and Collins must already have
devised the basic plot and decided to set the main action in the Arctic, scene
of the ill-fated Franklin Expedition (thoughts of which would have been
revived in Dickens's mind at this time, Lady Franklin having been recently in
touch with him). Both the concept of courageous men destined to go on a long
and hazardous journey, like the Arctic explorers, and the concept of a flawed
hero who has to fight against dark passions in himself (very unlike the kind
of heroes Dickens had so far created), were, as has been so well demonstrated
by the leading authority on *The Frozen Deep*, personally very important and
significant for Dickens at this time. Almost certainly, 'the mighty original
notion' for the new play, which he claimed was his in the beginning, involved
both these things.[26]

In his 22 April letter to Collins already cited Dickens wrote, 'The first blank
page of Little Dorrit No. 8 now eyes me on this desk with a pressing curiosity'
but it would get nothing out of him that day, he felt sure. As the time
approached for his family to leave No. 49 Champs Elysées and return home
Dickens found he could not work on *Dorrit* in the midst of such 'unsettled
domesticity'. This instability did not affect his journalistic writing, however.
Before leaving Paris he wrote what he described to Wills on 20 April as
'a capital paper, with an odd and novel idea in it' and, immediately following,
the splendid 'Railway Dreaming' already referred to. The 'capital paper' was
'Proposals for a National Jest-Book' (*HW*, 3 May 1856) in which he made
clever use of the jest-book format to carry on his campaign against Palmerston
and the whole aristocratic ruling class (Palmerston figures here both as 'First
Lord of the Jokery' and as a merry footpad, 'an old hand', who mocks John Bull
even as he fleeces him). It was nearly three weeks, however, before he could get
back to writing *Little Dorrit*. He did not return directly to his London home

because of Catherine's parents, who had apparently been staying there while the Dickenses were in Paris, and who now seem to have become intolerable to him – he could not, he told Wills on 27 April, 'bear the contemplation of their imbecility any more'. On 29 April, therefore, he took up residence in the Ship Hotel at Dover where he stayed until 2 May – not, it seems, writing anything but enjoying some beneficial 'twenty-mile walks in the fresh air' and storing up some good material for another article, 'Out of the Season' (*HW*, 28 June 1856). This piece has in it a good running joke about his finding any number of excuses not to begin the 'chapter of unheard-of excellence' that he has gone there specifically to write.[27]

Once back in Tavistock House, Dickens found that he and his manservant John had to turn to and give the place a thorough spring clean, the 'imbecile' Hogarths having apparently left it in a very dishevelled state, and it was not until 9 May, just five days before Catherine, Georgina and the children returned, that he got back to *Little Dorrit*. He was much encouraged, of course, by the knowledge that, as he was able to report in a letter of 2 May, 'Little Dorrit, has beaten all her predecessors, in circulation'. The story was, in fact, as the Pilgrim editors note, selling around 35,000 copies per number, 1,000 more than *Bleak House* and no fewer than 13,000 more than *Copperfield* at the same point in their respective serialisations. Still just about managing to keep two numbers ahead of publication, Dickens worked away at the last ten chapters of Book I during the next three months, first in London and then in Boulogne, where on 7 June the family were welcomed back to the Villa des Moulineaux by the solicitous Beaucourt-Mutuel. A few days after this Dickens, on the point of beginning No. IX, told Forster, 'The story lies before me, I hope, strong and clear. Not to be easily told; but nothing of that sort <u>is</u> to be easily done that I know of'. With Gowan's marriage to Pet Meagles Dickens bound the Barnacles and Stiltstalkings more tightly into the plot. At the same time he showed Clennam's deepening sadness, but also the nobility of his nature. He must now abandon all hope of winning Pet's love but remains unconscious of Little Dorrit's love for him, 'putting before her', as Dickens's note for chapter 32 has it, 'his condition as that "much older man who has done with that part of life"', and unconsciously stabbing her to the heart'. His unusually full notes for this important chapter also include the following: '<u>Prepare for the time to come</u> – in that room, long afterwards', looking forward to the final chapter of the whole novel, still eleven months away; and '<u>Pancks immensely excited</u> – <u>strong preparation for the end of the book</u>'. Also carefully woven into the narrative are the sinister activities of both Miss Wade and Rigaud, alias Blandois, who is always accompanied, in true melodramatic fashion, by his own 'music', the 'mysterious noises' heard in Mrs Clennam's house first mentioned in Dickens's notes for chapter 15 and now again mentioned in those for chapter 29. The great tragicomic chapter 31 (in *Dorrit* IX) showing

Mr Dorrit's grotesquely condescending reception in his narrow Marshalsea room of Nandy, his 'old pensioner' from the workhouse, skilfully foreshadows, as Dickens noted in his 'mems' for this number, 'what they [the Dorrit family] are likely to be in a higher station'. His chapter-note about Nandy with its reference to 'Groves of old men in Marylebone Workhouse' shows him remembering his investigative visit to that institution six years before, written up in 'A Walk in a Workhouse' (*HW*, 25 May 1850), and provides a rare instance of his recycling his journalistic treatment of a subject for later fictional purposes (see above, p. 309).

During these summer months of intense work on *Dorrit* and preoccupation with developing *The Frozen Deep* Dickens wrote very little for *Household Words*, though he continued to lavish his conductorial energies upon it. On 22 June, for example, he told Forster that he had just spent four hours 'of close attention' hacking and hewing a contributor's story into acceptable shape for publication, making a 'dreadful spectacle' of the proofs 'which look like an inky fishing-net'. He was provoked by newspaper reports of the trial of the Rugeley poisoner William Palmer, convicted at the Old Bailey on 27 May, into dashing off 'The Demeanour of Murderers' (*HW*, 14 June), a vehement protest against admiring accounts of Palmer's unfailing composure and self-confidence throughout the trial and after his conviction, and about the difficulty of reconciling such behaviour with belief in his guilt. This behaviour indicated nothing but 'cruelty and insensibility', argued Dickens, who had not the least doubt that Palmer had committed the crimes of which he was accused, and he might have pointed to his current villain Rigaud/Blandois as strikingly illustrating his conviction that 'Nature never writes a bad hand'. Indeed, it was in the very number of *Dorrit* on which he was working at this point, IX, that he made the same remark with regard to this character: 'On this man ... Nature, always true, and never working in vain, had set the mark, Beware!' The attentive observer of humanity will never be deceived by surface behaviour into mistaking a murderer (always for Dickens the worst of all criminals) for an innocent man. The Palmer article was followed in *Household Words* by 'Out of the Season' on 28 June and there was then a two-month gap before the writing of another of his satirical/polemical pieces, 'Nobody, Somebody and Everybody', which in its title and conception reverts to the idea of 'Nobody's Fault'. This renewed attack on Palmerston and Britain's aristocratic ruling class was Dickens's infuriated response to the Report, presented to Parliament on 21 July, of the Board of Enquiry into the conduct of the Crimean War, held at the Chelsea Hospital. In their Report the members of the Board, all senior military personnel, absolved Lords Lucan, Cardigan and their colleagues, from all blame for what Dickens calls the 'intolerable misery and loss' of the war. He was certainly not alone in seeing what he described to Forster as 'the no-result of our precious Chelsea enquiry' as an utter whitewash. He also notes that 'Nobody' seems to have been responsible for the late Sadleir's appointment as a Junior Lord of the Treasury under the Aberdeen government. His article is continuous with the first two chapters of *Dorrit* X (chs 33 and 34), written a few weeks earlier. Chapter 33 elaborates his fictional version of Sadleir, and chapter 34 describes Gowan's marriage to Pet Meagles which 'a shoal of Barnacles' condescend to honour with their presence, pre-eminent among them being their great chief Lord Decimus Tite Barnacle, whom Dickens clearly intends as a hit at Palmerston.[28]

With the opening of Book II of *Little Dorrit* the newly-enriched Dorrits travel to Italy via Martigny and the Great St Bernard, and Dickens began to be able to draw freely upon his memories of Switzerland and Italy from the 1840s and 1853. These were all evidently still so vivid to him that he hardly ever in his 'mems' and chapter-notes for No. XI and the subsequent numbers set in Italy needed to prompt himself by specifying a particular place seen on his own travels. 'All those remembrances were fresh in my mind – as they often are –', he wrote to Lavinia Watson on 7 October about the Great St Bernard chapter, referring to the expedition he, Catherine, Georgina and the Watsons had made to the place in 1846, 'and gave me an extraordinary interest in recalling the past'. A small exception appears in his notes for Book II, chapter 6 in no. XII, describing the Gowans' Venetian apartment, where he reminds himself to 'Remember the Bank at Venice'. This jotting was enough to bring forth three richly-detailed paragraphs evoking the Gowans' highly picturesque location, not forgetting 'the prevailing Venetian odor of bilge water and an ebb-tide on a weedy shore'.

Dickens was working on *Dorrit* XI when Wilkie Collins arrived in Boulogne on 16 August to continue collaboration on *The Frozen Deep*. His high opinion of Collins's work grew in proportion with his personal liking for him. He was actually moved to tears in a railway carriage whilst reading Collins's 'The Diary of Anne Rodway' (*HW*, 19, 26 July) and wrote to him on 13 July, that it was 'done with an amount of honest pains and devotion to the work, which few men have better reason to appreciate than I, and which no man can have a more profound respect for'. Collins, was, in other words, the kind of thoroughly professional fellow-writer who met with Dickens's entire approval. On 10 July he instructed Wills to pay Collins £20 for 'The Diary of Anne Rodway', and to tell him that he, Dickens, 'wished to remove it from ordinary calculations' on account of its great merit. He confided to Wills his thoughts that, once he had completed *Little Dorrit*, he and Collins 'might do something in Household Words together'. 'He and I', wrote Dickens, 'have talked so much within the last 3 or 4 years about Fiction-Writing, and I see him so ready to catch at what I have tried to prove right, and to avoid what I thought wrong, and altogether go at it in the spirit I have fired him with, that the notion takes some shape with me.' In the event, he and Collins would be collaborating closely on a 'something' for *Household Words* well before the conclusion of *Little Dorrit*.

We do not know how far advanced they were at this stage with the planning of *The Frozen Deep* (still, as far as we know, untitled) but the basic concept of the role to be played by Dickens, that of the rugged and tormented hero Richard Wardour, must have been already worked out. Since boyhood Wardour has loved with a deep passion Clara Burnham, his junior by some years. He steadily refuses to accept that she can love him only as a brother. She falls in love with, and becomes engaged to, Frank Aldersley, a man of her own age, whom Wardour has never seen but whom, in despairing rage, he threatens to harm if ever their paths should cross. By chance both men find themselves on the same expedition to the Arctic and the audience is led first to fear what Wardour may do to his unwitting rival when he discovers his identity, and then to suspect that he has actually killed him. In a sensational dénouement it transpires that Wardour has, in fact, triumphed over his own murderous passions and saved Aldersley even at the cost of his own life. Interestingly, it is just at this time that Dickens makes, in a letter to Forster of 15 August, his famous attack on the hypocrisy of English readers like those he meets in France 'who pass their lives with Balzac and with Sand' and who protest that the heroes of English novels are 'always uninteresting – too good – too natural, &c.' He rounds bitterly upon such 'shining impostors' who affect not to recognise that it is, in fact, their own morality that compels English novelists to deny to their heroes 'I will not say any of the indecencies you like, but not even any of the experiences, trials, perplexities and confusions inseparable from the making or unmaking of all men!' He was evidently beginning – perhaps partly as a result of increasing stresses and tangled feelings in his own personal life and partly owing to his continuing development as an experimental artist – to want to create a more complex and challenging kind of hero, one who might even alienate the reader's sympathies at some points in the narrative. Participating in the writing and then enacting on stage the role of Collins's Richard Wardour was to be Dickens's first, highly sensational, experiment along these lines.

Collins's stay at Les Moulineaux was brief. An outbreak of diphtheria in Boulogne determined Dickens to cut short his family's residence there. Catherine took the children back to Tavistock House before the end of August, followed a few days later by first Dickens and then Georgina. 'After a plunge of four and twenty hours duration among the wrecks of my dismantled study', he informed Burdett Coutts on 8 September, 'I have happily fished up all the fragments of that noble ship and pieced them together. The neat result is afloat again, and looks none the worse.' He moved swiftly to re-establish the normal routines of his London life, including the regular weekly committee meetings at Urania Cottage. He even managed to write another angry article, 'The Murdered Person', published in the 11 October issue of *Household Words*, in which he again castigated the philanthropical approach to criminals already denounced by the landlady of the Break of Day in *Dorrit* III and reverted to in *Dorrit* XII, the one he had in hand, where he describes Rigaud/Blandois's appearance in Venice as such that 'any real philanthropist could have desired no better employment than to lash a great stone to his neck, and drop him into the water flowing beyond the dark arched gateway in which he stood'. In 'The Murdered Person' he recurred also both to the blatant whitewashing of Lucan and Cardigan by the Chelsea Board of Enquiry the previous July and (perhaps significantly) to the iniquity of the current Divorce Laws. But the disruption of his plans for the autumn, worries about Katey's health (she had returned from France with a bad cough), and coping with what he described to Burdett Coutts on 26 September as the 'immense arrear of demands on my attention' meant that he fell behind schedule with the writing of *Little Dorrit* so that his 'in hand' material threatened to shrink to only one number. In the same letter he reported that he had been hard at work all week on *Dorrit* XII, due for publication at the end of October. That there was much needing considera-tion both as regards the planning and the actual writing of this number is shown by the numerous detailed 'mems' and chapter-notes Dickens made for it. The query 'Pave the way – with the first stone – to Mr Merdle's ruining everybody?' is answered with a five-times-underlined 'Yes', while in another 'mem' he instructs himself as follows: 'And work through Fanny, suspicion of Mrs General's having a design on Mr Dorrit. <u>Also the Sparkler affair</u> [his infatuation with Fanny]. Lead, very carefully, on.'[29]

Despite the concentration demanded by *Little Dorrit* Dickens continued exchanging ideas for *The Frozen Deep* with Collins, whom he had now recruited to the staff of *Household Words* at a salary of five guineas a week ('He is very suggestive, and exceedingly quick to take my notions,' he wrote to Wills on 16 September, when proposing the arrangement). About *The Frozen Deep* he was exultant: 'Turn it how you will, the strength of the situation is <u>prodigious</u>,' he wrote to Collins on 12 September 1856. The actor in him clearly scented a part in which he would bring the house down. But the next *Household Words* Christmas number was now looming and immediately after finishing *Dorrit* XII Dickens had to attend to it. By 30 September he was able to circulate to potential contributors his scheme for the framework narrative. This scheme showed that the idea for this number was, like *The Frozen Deep*, inspired by Dickens's continuing fascination with the Franklin Expedition, and the notion of the courageous, disciplined British sailors surviving in a ferociously hostile environment; any suggestion that they might ever resort to cannibalism was to be specifically rebutted. Evidently, he no longer considered it necessary to tie the now well-established special Christmas number to the Christmas season. For this one he envisages an English trading vessel carrying some passengers and bound for Australia (later the ship's destination is altered

to California) being wrecked by an iceberg south of the southernmost tip of
South America. The Captain, 'a cool man with his Wits about him' named
Ravender, organises the evacuation of nearly everyone aboard into an open
boat. With barely enough provisions to sustain life they have then to endure
many days and nights in the boat and the captain calls on all those who can do
so to tell stories in order to keep up the company's spirits (Dickens, devoted
student as he was of the history of voyages and travels, is here copying from
what he mistakenly remembered as a real-life initiative of Captain Bligh's).
Dickens invited potential contributors to write their stories either as one of the
crew or as one of the passengers and suggested a whole string of possible identities in both categories ('. . . the Bride Passenger, the Bridegroom Passenger,
the sister passenger, the brother passenger . . . the child passenger, the Runaway
passenger, the old Seaman, the toughest of the Crew, &c &c').

    Shortly after sending out his circular Dickens must have invited Collins to
co-author the number with him, writing as the First Mate John Steadiman,
the Captain's devoted and thoroughly capable second-in-command, who is
in charge of a second boatload of survivors, now added in the framework
narrative. Collins was apparently at first nervous of such collaboration and
needed to be taken for a reassuring walk in the woods near Gad's Hill. In the
event, he came fully up to the mark and Dickens wrote to Burdett Coutts on
9 December, shortly after the number had been published, 'the way in which
[he] has got over the great difficulty of falling into my idea, naturally, is very
meritorious indeed'. Collins took over the writing of the main narrative of *The
Wreck of the Golden Mary*, as the number came to be titled, after Dickens had
written the long first part, with its detailed presentation of Captain Ravender,
his crew of 'good men and true', and the various passengers, and also its
powerful description of the actual shipwreck. Dickens wrote this first part
immediately after finishing the highly plot-thickening *Dorrit* XIII (Bk II, chs
8–11) and said of the former to Wills in a letter of 13 November, 'I never wrote
anything more easily, or I think with greater interest and belief.' It was perhaps
a relief for him to be able to give full throttle to a Franklin-style man-of-action
hero like Captain Ravender at a time when the male protagonist of the big
novel he was writing was so understated a figure as Arthur Clennam. The
tender care of Ravender for his two female passengers and for Lucy, the angelic
little golden-haired child of one of them, and the description of Lucy's gentle
death, also gave him what was perhaps a welcome chance for what he would
have called 'pretty' touches in the writing. The big sombre novel on which he
was so deeply engaged was not affording him much opportunity for these. To
Burdett Coutts he wrote in the letter already cited that he thought *The Wreck*
'the prettiest Christmas No. we have had' (he was no doubt referring also to
some of the contributions such as Harriet Parr's 'Poor Dick's Story' as well as
to his own contribution). It certainly sold very well when it was published on

6 December, early because Dickens wanted it 'to get all over England Ireland and Scotland, a good fortnight before Christmas Day'. The following February Dickens told James White, one of the contributors to *The Wreck*, that this Christmas number had done *Household Words* 'great service' and had 'decidedly told upon its circulation'. This must have been a great relief to him as the half-year's balance on the magazine up to the end of September 1856 had been, he had written to Catherine on 8 November, 'very indifferent indeed'.[30]

Contemporaneously with their collaboration on the Christmas number Dickens and Collins were also hard at work on *The Frozen Deep* and on the preparations for its production. On 2 October Collins arrived at Tavistock House, 'in a breathless state', with the first two acts of the play, Dickens reported to Burdett Coutts the following day, adding that the play (in which he was very keen to get her interested, being well aware that she was generally less than enthusiastic about his theatrical ventures) was 'extremely clever and interesting – very serious and very curious'. He heavily revised Collins's script, being careful to mention his readiness to defer to 'Authorial sanction' but we may well feel a little sceptical about this. Dickens's extensive cuts and other changes are all concerned with keeping the dramatic interest tightly focused on Wardour and on making him less savage, and with building up the suspense both on stage and in the audience as to whether he might in the end prove to be a murderer. By late October the play had been cast, with Dickens as Wardour and Collins as Frank Aldersley, and a characteristically strenuous and precise schedule of rehearsals drawn up by Dickens, who told Collins he had learned his part during a twenty-mile walk, 'to the great terrors of Finchley, Neasden, Willesden, and the adjacent country'.[31]

Dickens was hardly exaggerating when he told Alfred that his arrangements for producing *The Frozen Deep* were 'of stupefying grandeur'. Not only was Stanfield once again recruited to paint the scenery for the maritime scenes but another artist, William Telbin, celebrated especially for his Panorama paintings, agreed to paint the domestic interior for Act I. 'The mazy Berger', as Dickens called him, once more wrote the music; machinery and properties were borrowed from the Adelphi Theatre; costumes were supplied by Nathan's; and, most spectacular of all, the schoolroom at Tavistock House was completely remodelled into a private theatre. The large bay window overlooking the garden, which had provided a perfectly good acting area for *The Lighthouse*, was taken out and the floor joined with a large wooden structure that Dickens himself had designed and caused to be erected in the garden. The result was a stage thirty feet deep. This left a much bigger area of the room available for the auditorium which could then hold about ninety people. Dickens also had new gas lines installed in order to produce elaborate lighting effects. Of the production as a whole Dickens wrote to Frank Stone on 20 November, 'I want to make it something that shall never be seen again.' As to the actors, Charley Dickens, who played one of the young naval officers, remembered how they 'pegged away at the "Frozen Deep" for quite three months, three and sometimes four times a week' but added 'the enjoyment of the rehearsal-night suppers would have made amends for even harder work than we had'. Berger recalled that the refreshments on these occasions included 'a huge joint of cold roast beef, a tongue, a ham, several cold roast fowl, a few raised pies, tarts and jellies, dozens of bottled Guinness and Bass, and ended with punch brewed by the "manager's" own hand'. Given all this ample provision we can hardly be surprised by Charley's anecdote: 'the butcher called in person on my mother one day, to point out that he was supplying such an abnormal quantity of joints that he thought it his duty to mention it to her, in order to be sure that there was no mistake'. This is one of the very few mentions of Catherine in connection with all this major and prolonged domestic upheaval at Tavistock House during the autumn and early winter of 1856. Another is Dickens's telling Wills on 4 January that he was going to take Catherine to Newgate Market the next day 'to shew her where to buy fowls' (the butcher was not to be the household's sole resource for meat during its theatrical season, apparently). The whole business must have put the mistress of the house under enormous pressure, quite apart from the responsibility of having to send out to so many friends and acquaintances, no doubt under Dickens's close supervision, all the invitations to the actual performances. One can only hope that the early November visit Catherine made to the Macreadys fortified her enough to cope well with the subsequent demands on her as the hostess and catering manager of Tavistock House.[32]

It is astonishing enough to think of Dickens master-minding all this activity and working towards what he was confident would be the most stupendous effect he had yet produced as an actor whilst at the same time continuing to write such a profound and complex work as *Little Dorrit*. But it becomes still more so when we remember that he was also as assiduous as ever in his 'conductorial' attention to *Household Words*, and in his work for Urania Cottage – busy, for example, in persuading Burdett Coutts, in a letter of 15 November, to reject the drab material called Derry she had chosen for making the women's everyday clothing: 'Color these people always want, and color (as allied to fancy, I would always give them) ... who is Derry that he is to make quakers of us all, whether we will or no!' But the keen delight that he always took in his own 'inimitable' virtuosity, powers of concentration, and seemingly inexhaustible energy seems to have more than sustained him. Writing on 13 December to Macready, with whom he had always a running joke about their both being very ancient, he vividly described the chaos into which Tavistock House had descended and continued: 'Calm amidst the wrack, your aged friend glides away on the Dorrit stream, forgetting the uproar for a stretch of hours – refreshes himself with a ten or twelve mile walk – pitches himself head-foremost into foaming rehearsals – placidly emerges for Editorial purposes – smokes over buckets of distemper with Mr Stanfield aforesaid – again calmly floats upon the Dorrit waters'.

During these months of November and December the 'Dorrit waters' were flowing strongly. Writing numbers XIII and XIV Dickens developed mysterious, evidently sinister, connections between Miss Wade, Tattycoram and Rigaud/Blandois, ventriloquised another delicate letter from Little Dorrit to Clennam, and superbly described the grand dinner at Mr Merdle's 'for the great patriotic purpose of making Young Sparkler a Lord of the Treasury' (a variant on the scandal of Sadleir's appointment). He described also the beginning of the Merdle 'epidemic', drawing on his observation of the gambling mania in Paris which he had so vividly described in *Household Words* a few months earlier, and took pains sensitively to trace out the process of Fanny's engagement to Sparkler, 'shewing how it came about, and how such a mind in such a person naturally worked that way'.[33]

Meanwhile Twelfth Night, the date scheduled for the first performance of *The Frozen Deep*, was drawing ever nearer. Everyone involved from Dickens himself and his fellow-actors to his eagerly-expectant invited guests was looking forward to something remarkable, though just *how* remarkable no one except Dickens himself probably anticipated. But what even he could hardly have imagined was how 'this winter evening', given, in the words of the prologue he wrote for Forster to speak, 'to the union of three sister arts', would lead on, aided by the fortuitous death of an old friend, to such momentous changes in his own life, both as man and as artist, and in the lives of so many of those closest to him, as well as in the life of a certain young actress of whose existence he may at this point have been only dimly aware.

CHAPTER 18

Drama and dénouement

PERFORMING *THE FROZEN DEEP* AND FINISHING *LITTLE DORRIT*, 1857

... the interest of such a character [as Richard Wardour] to me is that it enables me, as it were, <u>to write a book in company</u> instead of in my own solitary room, and to feel its effect coming freshly back upon me from the reader. ... I could blow off my superfluous fierceness, in nothing so curious to me.

Dickens to Maclise, 8 July 1857

DURING THE summer of 1856 Dickens had, in the course of what he described in a letter to Forster as 'my numerous refreshings at those English wells', re-read yet again that childhood favourite *Robinson Crusoe*. He had been confirmed in his belief that it was 'the only instance of an universally popular book that could make no one laugh and could make no one cry', achieving its effect by 'mere homely force and intensity of truth'. It was to *Crusoe* that he turned for an arresting opening when writing a Prologue for *The Frozen Deep* (spoken by Forster to 'soft music' after the curtain had risen upon 'Mists and darkness'):

> One savage footprint on the lonely shore,
> Where one man listened to the surge's roar;
> Not all the winds that stir the mighty sea
> Can ever ruffle in the memory.
> If such its interest and its thrall, O then
> Pause on the footprints of heroic men,
> Making a garden of the desert wide
> Where PARRY conquer'd and FRANKLIN died.

Dickens first invokes the supreme classic of all imaginative literature dealing with civilised man's struggle to survive in the wild and, immediately following, the memory of two real-life 'heroic men' of recent fame. Both Admiral Sir William Parry and Sir John Franklin and their respective teams had, in their arctic expeditions, pitted themselves against an environment infinitely more hostile than Crusoe's island yet had conducted themselves throughout in as civilised a fashion as if they had been strolling in a garden. Dickens was wanting to prepare *The Frozen Deep*'s audience for a drama that sought to penetrate deeper into human nature than Defoe's story. Richard Wardour's struggle will not only be against the forces of external nature but also against those dark forces within himself that have frozen his humanity. The audience was about to witness not simply a 'faint reflection' of real-life heroes in the arctic waste but a dramatist's attempt to explore the secrets of that 'vast Profound' existing within every one of us,

Testing the region of the ice-bound soul,
Seeking the passage at its northern pole,
Soft'ning the horrors of its wintry sleep,
Melting the surface of that 'Frozen Deep'.[1]

Dickens, now three-quarters of the way through the composition of *Little Dorrit*, was eager to embark upon the simultaneous creation, in his actor-manager mode, of another work, one that should be a comparable artistic triumph. Because of the circumstances of its creation, however, a private production in his own house, it could not be experienced by any part of that mass audience currently devouring *Dorrit* in serial form, that audience with which he had long since established such a strong personal relationship. The only way this new work, or at least a version of it, could be delivered to this audience was through hearsay or published reviews. This may have been part of the reason for Dickens's taking the highly unusual step of inviting several professional drama critics, including *The Times*'s John Oxenford, to attend the first night at Tavistock House, making it clear that he would be happy for them to review the production. Ostensibly, his reason for so doing was that it would otherwise be, as he wrote on 30 December to the drama critic of *The Morning Herald* (very much a family newspaper), 'hardly fair' to 'the other public men' who had 'taken pains with it'. He was here primarily referring, I presume, to Collins as the play's author and to Stanfield and William Telbin, whose splendid scene-painting contributed so greatly to the production's overall impact.

The first performance, on Monday 5 January 1857, was, in fact, a dress rehearsal. It took place before an audience of servants and tradesmen together with their families and friends and had its own specially-printed playbill. From this and the bills for the subsequent nights we see that Dickens allowed half-an-hour for recovery and refreshments at the end of the play before the evening ended with a performance of the farce *Animal Magnetism*. The programme ended at 11.30, having begun at 7.45 p.m. Four performances before audiences of invited guests took place on 6, 8, 12 and 14 January with a different farce, J. B. Buckstone's *Uncle John* (1833), being, for some reason, substituted for

39 Dickens performing in *The Frozen Deep* at Tavistock House, January 1857

Animal Magnetism from the 8th onwards. Each audience numbered about ninety, the new fashion for crinoline making it especially difficult to squeeze everyone in. Among those who accepted invitations were Macready, Burdett Coutts, Thackeray, the Dean of St Paul's, the President of the Royal Academy, and, on the last evening, an impressive showing from the judiciary – 'judges enow to hang us all', as Douglas Jerrold was heard to remark. Dickens's Wardour electrified everyone. 'I certainly have never seen people so strongly affected by theatrical means,' he wrote to Hannah Brown on 14 January and in another letter of the same date, to the Countess Gigliucci, he reported, 'Our Audiences have been excellent, with a wonderful power of crying.' Thackeray was heard to exclaim, 'If that man would now go upon the stage he would make his £20,000 a year.' Macready thought it 'remarkably, extraordinarily clever, in all respects . . . [it] excited me very much'. Oxenford eulogised Dickens's acting in *The Times* (7 Jan.) but some very interesting comments also appeared in a later review (*The Times*, 13 July 1857) of one of the subsequent, genuinely public, performances that took place in the summer:

The performance of Mr Dickens as the vindictive and (afterwards) penitent Richard Wardour is, in the truest sense of the word, a creation. Nay, we may go further and say that it is the creation of a literary man – that it is doubtful whether any mere actor, unless under the influence of extraordinary sympathy with the part assumed, would attempt to fill up an outline with that elaborate detail that is introduced by Mr Dickens into Mr Collins's sketch. We feel that if Mr Dickens had had to describe in narrative form the situations of the *Frozen Deep*, instead of acting them, he would have covered whole pages in recording those manifestations of emotion, which, not having his pen in hand, he now makes by the minutest variations of voice and gesture. . . .

Oxenford could well see that Dickens was indeed doing what he told some of his friends he was doing, something akin to 'writing a book in company'. This, as he wrote to his diplomat friend Sir James Emerson Tennent on 9 January, afforded him 'a satisfaction of a most singular kind', one which he said 'had no exact parallel in my life'. Inevitably, he suffered keenly from withdrawal symptoms. A letter to Collins on 19 January ended with the words 'O reaction, reaction!', and he was kept on tenterhooks by rumours that the Queen wished to see a performance of the play at Windsor: 'I . . . slink about holding my breath', he wrote to Burdett Coutts on 3 February, but no request came from the Palace.[2]

Immediately following the last night of *The Frozen Deep*, with the sounds of the demolition of his private theatre dinning into his ears, Dickens turned to catching up on his correspondence. He also had to deal with the routine heavy work-loads relating to *Household Words* and Urania Cottage (including, in the latter case, the unwelcome addition of some newly-developed drainage problems), and to the final preparations for sending his second son out to India. Walter was now sixteen and for the past three years his education had been directed towards his entering the service of the East India Company, having been nominated for an infantry cadetship in the Company by Burdett Coutts, a major shareholder. Dickens had also to write an 'Address' to the French public to be printed in French and English in the first volume (*Nicholas Nickleby*) of the Hachette edition of his works in translation, which was about to be launched upon the French public. In this address he praised the care taken by Hachette's translating team working under the direction of the publisher's friend Paul Lorain, Rector of the Academy of Lyons, and expressed his pleasure in being so well presented to 'the great French people . . . to be known and approved by whom *must be* an aspiration of every labourer in the Arts, for which France has done so much, and in which she has made herself renowned throughout the world'.[3]

Above and beyond all this he urgently needed to get on with the writing of *Little Dorrit* XVI, over which, he told Macready on 28 January, his 'knitted brows' were 'turning into cordage'. He knitted them to some effect, however. The number includes the great scene of Mr Dorrit's mortifying relapse into his old Marshalsea self at Mrs Merdle's grand Roman dinner-party. Browne rose to the occasion with another of his animated crowd scenes, to which Dickens gave the title 'An Unexpected After-Dinner Speech', but apparently made

Dorrit look too comic for Dickens's purposes. On 10 February Dickens asked him to change Dorrit's expression to one 'much more in accordance with that serious end which is so close before him' and Browne skilfully complied, altering the character's expression to one of confusion and pathos. As for his own work on the number, the biggest challenge Dickens had set himself was how to integrate into it Miss Wade's narrative of her own life – 'unconsciously laying bare all her character', as one of his notes for chapter 20 puts it. Evidently, Forster had reservations about Dickens's first version which had Miss Wade telling her story direct to Clennam, and Dickens wrote to him, 'I had an idea, which I thought a new one, of making the introduced story so fit into surroundings impossible of separation from the main story, as to make the blood of the book circulate through both. But I can only suppose, from what you say, that I have not exactly succeeded in this.' He then split the chapter into two, the second one, titled 'The History of a Self-Tormentor', being presented as written by Miss Wade. He evidently saw the writer as a woman imprisoned by her own psychology – her 'paranoia', as we would say today – and his phrase 'the blood of the book' is perhaps an allusion to the novel's grand, all-pervading prison metaphor. He chose not to spell this out, preferring, as always, to focus on his art's truthfulness to actual life. A few weeks later, he told a correspondent that, having observed Miss Wade in real life (he does not identify this original), he knew the character he had created to be 'true in every respect': 'It quite fascinated me in its singular anatomy and I devoted great pains to it in the little narration.'[4]

By 14 February Dickens had started work on *Dorrit* XVII in which he had, as he prompted himself in his chapter-notes, first to 'pave the way' towards the 'catastrophe' that will ultimately befall Mrs Clennam's gloomy mansion and then to deal with another kind of collapse, Merdle's 'suicide and demolition'. He found the writing hard going as evidenced by the fact that he seems to have looked back for help with the plotting to an unauthorised dramatisation of the first part of the novel by Frederick Fox Cooper that had run briefly at the Strand Theatre in November 1856. Cooper had had to invent a dénouement for his drama, certain details of which now appear in Dickens's own. Dickens was yearning for the kind of carefree break he could experience with Collins and on 14 February asked the younger writer, who was at this time toiling away at his *Household Words* serial *The Dead Secret*, to come and canvass 'Brighton and other trip-possibilities' with him. Meanwhile, he distracted himself with furniture-buying for Gad's Hill, now legally his property, and with consulting Austin about the extensive alterations he wanted made to the house. On 28 February he described himself in a letter to Macready, in which he reverted to the blood-imagery he had used once before with regard to the novel's structure, as 'transcendently busy, drawing up the arteries of Little Dorrit', adding that it was 'Very hard work, but deeply interesting to me'. This suggests that he went straight on from finishing *Dorrit* XVII not only to compile the 'mems' for *Dorrit* XVIII (Bk 2, chs 27–29) but also to compile two sheets (four pages) of further 'Mems' for 'working the story round' in the final double number. The left-hand pages of these 'Mems' were headed 'Retrospective' and the right-hand ones 'Prospective'. In them he elaborately worked out *Little Dorrit*'s extraordinarily convoluted back-story ('drew up its arteries') which would eventually be force-fed to the reader through a series of lengthy speeches by Mrs Clennam and others in the novel's final chapters.[5]

Before turning to these 'Mems' Dickens must have written a long satirical essay for *Household Words*, 'Stores for the First of April'. Printed as the lead article, this occupies just over five pages (approximately 4,800 words), in the issue for 7 March. Dickens had been outraged by a recent exposé of the gross pro-Government bias of the Board of Enquiry into the conduct of the Crimean War, a bias amply documented in Col. Alexander Tulloch's *Review* of the Board's proceedings (published in January). In 'Stores for the First of April' Dickens revisited the topic of the 'murderous muddle and mismanagement, by English administrators of one kind or another in the Crimea, on every imaginable head on which it was possible to do wrong'. He also made scathing reference to an airy defence of both Government and Civil Service by his old detractor Abraham Hayward in the August 1856 number of the *North British Review*. According to Hayward, all the sufferings of the English army might 'be accounted for without imputing any blame to any minister, civil or military officer, or chief of department, whether in London or whether in the Crimea'. 'Nobody's fault' indeed! Dickens's ire may be responsible for the unlikely reappearance in *Dorrit* XVIII of Ferdinand, the 'sprightly young Barnacle', the very personification of insouciant irresponsibility. Ferdinand visits the Marshalsea to express his hope that the Circumlocution Office had had no part in Clennam's imprisonment. 'I was rather afraid', he tells Clennam, '. . . that we might have helped to floor you, because there is no doubt that it is our misfortune to do that kind of thing now and then. We don't want to do it; but if men will be gravelled, why – we can't help it.' His parting words to Clennam reflect directly on the Court of Enquiry's whitewashing report: 'We must have humbug, we all like humbug, we couldn't get on without humbug.'[6]

Dickens's disillusionment and disgust at this time with the workings of parliamentary democracy knew no bounds. To Paxton, who was Liberal M.P. for Coventry, he wrote on 1 March, 'direfully against my will, I have come to the conclusion that representative Government is a miserable failure among us.' Parliament seemed preoccupied with party squabbles and the mass of the people appeared either indifferent to how they were ruled, or else were easily duped and betrayed by such cynical grandees as Palmerston. He continued, of course, flatly to reject the frequent invitations he received to stand for Parliament himself, telling one such enquirer, 'I believe no consideration would induce me to become a Member of that amazing Assembly.' To the Earl of Carlisle he wrote on 15 April that, although he had 'no sympathy with Demagogues', he was 'a grievous Radical'. Carlisle, in his previous incarnation as Viscount Morpeth, had been an active member of Russell's socially reforming government of 1846–50 and had carried the Public Health Bill of 1848, so had certainly shown himself to be, even though an aristocrat, one of that rare breed, M.P.s who met with Dickens's approval.[7]

Dickens could attack the iniquities of Parliament only through his articles in *Household Words* but in the case of what he saw as another pernicious 'Humbug', located in Bloomsbury rather than Westminster, the Royal Literary Fund, he still felt he could do a great deal more. He returned from his refreshing three-day break with Collins in Brighton on 9 March not only to resume work on *Dorrit* XVIII but also to deliver yet another scathing speech at the Fund's Annual General Meeting in support of a resolution proposed by Dilke, similar to resolutions he had proposed, with Dickens's support, at previous meetings. This year Dilke's resolution asked the Fund's General Committee to 'reconsider the whole of the management and expenses'. The would-be reformers were out-manoeuvred but Dickens refused to admit defeat since in his lexicon 'defeat' was a word that could apply only to his opponents. Writing to Macready about the Fund on 14 May in his most '*sic volo sic jubeo*' mood, he announced, 'I am resolved to reform it or ruin it – one or the other'. Ultimately, he found he could do neither and he, Dilke and Forster had to abandon their hard-fought campaign. Meanwhile, however, he was at least able, in a speech at the annual dinner on 6 April of the very differently-run Royal General Theatrical Fund, publicly to praise the achievement of a rather more successful reformer in the field of the arts. This was the actor-manager Samuel Phelps, who had transformed Sadler's Wells Theatre from a veritable bear-garden into a worthy home for Shakespearean and other classic drama, attracting and retaining 'one of the most intelligent and attentive audiences ever seen'.[8]

On 3 April Dickens responded to a letter from Hans Christian Andersen with a very warm invitation to his admired fellow-writer to come on a summer visit to what Dickens described as his newly-acquired 'little country house . . . in a very beautiful part of Kent'. He hoped to finish *Little Dorrit* by the end of the month, he told Andersen, and in the summer would be a free man 'playing at cricket and all manner of English open-air games'. On 7 April he took Catherine, Georgina and the two youngest boys to stay in a hotel in Gravesend from where he could more easily keep an eye on the building works at Gad's Hill whilst he concentrated on the writing of the final double number of the novel in which he was, as he put it in a letter of 11 April, declining an invitation to go to the Derby, busy with a race of his own 'bringing a pretty large field of characters up to the winning-post, and spurring away with might and main'. He compiled four pages (two sheets) of notes, the left-hand pages headed 'Mems: for <u>working the story round</u> – Retrospective' and the right hand ones 'Mems: for working the <u>story round</u> – Prospective. (<u>To work out in Nos. XIX and XX</u>)'. The 'retrospective' notes are reminders to himself of events and conversations earlier in the story that are crucial to the plot, like Clennam's speech to his supposed mother about his father's deathbed anxiety in Bk I ch. 5. The 'prospective notes' explicate the very convoluted back-story, tracing it all the way back to Clennam's father's uncle's will. His page of notes headed 'Mems: to be done' for *Dorrit* XIX / XX contains the customary roll-call of all the major characters, plus one or two of the minor ones, with 'Yes' or 'No' against their names to indicate whether or not they are to make a last appearance. In a few cases the word 'Generally' appears instead, indicating that they will not actually appear in these last pages of the narrative but the reader will hear what became of them. Against Mrs General's name he notes a comic idea for the last mention of her: 'Enthusiastic recommendations on the part of her connexion – (Yes) Nobody recommending, wants her though!' On the right-hand page are his chapter-notes as usual. These show that in Book II, chapter 30 he wanted the plot-unravelling to be done '<u>as much as possible through Mrs Clennam herself</u>, so as to present her character very strongly'. He had, as we have seen, already sketched the idea of a paralysed character galvanised into movement some months before, in one of the earliest notes made in the *Book of Memoranda*.[9]

His notes show his plan to 'set the darkness and vengeance' of Mrs Clennam's Old Testament beliefs 'against the New Testament' of Little Dorrit's (ch. 31) and how, after the comic dénouement of the Pancks/Casby sub-plot (ch. 32), he planned to build towards the mutual-declaration-of-love scene between Little Dorrit and Arthur. His last chapter-note reads, 'They [i.e., Little Dorrit and Clennam] will go out of the Marshalsea to be married – straight to be married – Very quiet conclusion'. The conclusion is indeed 'quiet' but there is no retreat to pastoral bliss for the heroine and her partner as there was at the end of *Bleak House*. Dickens's mood was darker than it had been in 1853. Little Dorrit and Clennam will have to live and effect what limited good they can in the busy world of 'roaring streets' where, as the novel's famous last sentence puts it, 'the noisy and the eager, and the arrogant and the froward and the vain, fretted, and chafed, and made their usual uproar'.

For the first week or so of May Dickens concentrated intensely on completing *Little Dorrit* and declined all engagements. 'I am forced,' Dickens wrote to Paxton on 3 May, 'really forced by the peculiar nature of my own work which cannot be left and resumed at pleasure – to stick to my writing.' He was, he said, 'in the full flight and mid career of the close of my book, and must finish it at a heat, and until it is finished am fit for nothing else'. In this same heat he wrote the preface, to be published as usual in the final double number along with the title and contents pages, the dedication to Clarkson Stanfield (no doubt to commemorate their close association at this time over *The Frozen Deep*), and two last illustrations (in addition to the normal two plates for the number), the title-page vignette and the frontispiece. These two last illustrations face each other and their subjects were chosen, presumably by Dickens, to point up the parallel shown in the story between the literal prison of the Marshalsea and the figurative prison of Society. In the vignette Little Dorrit emerges from the Marshalsea, seeming to bring with her into the outside world a shaft of sunlight, and in the frontispiece, dwarfed by majestic footmen, she timorously follows Fanny into the grand Merdle mansion.[10]

As we have seen, Dickens customarily used his prefaces, those 'meeting-and-greeting places' for him and his readers, to defend the truthfulness to life of anything in his story that might be considered too far-fetched or fanciful. Here he defends the truth of his portrayal of the Barnacles, the Circumlocution Office and Merdle by reference to recent actual events. But how was he to assert the truthfulness of his depiction of life in the Marshalsea as it had been thirty years ago? He could hardly say to his public as he had said to Forster about Mrs Pipchin's establishment, 'It is from the life and I was there'. Something about the prison had to be said, however, since it would have been odd indeed if the Preface made no reference to the place that casts its shadow over the whole novel. Moreover, Dickens has here an opportunity to do something he seems always to have taken a special delight in, namely to share his most intimate secrets with his readers but in some coded fashion, to be understood only by himself (Forster and perhaps Catherine, having read the autobiographical fragment, would have been privileged readers in this respect). In his *Dorrit* preface he related, as he also told Forster in a letter, that he went to Southwark on 6 May to see if anything of the Marshalsea still survived, the prison having now been closed for fifteen years. Much of it was still there, including the block containing the rooms in which debtors had been housed.

At the site Dickens met a strange apparition, whom he describes in the preface as 'the smallest boy I ever conversed with, carrying the largest baby I ever saw', which is interestingly reminiscent of Little Moloch in his deeply personal Christmas Book, *The Haunted Man*. This small boy who was much too young to have known the place when it was still a prison, nevertheless gave Dickens, according to the preface, 'a supernaturally intelligent explanation of the locality in its old uses, and was very nearly correct'. The last five words were surely somewhat risky – how, a thoughtful reader might have asked, could Dickens have been so certain about the near-correctness of the boy's description? It is a curious passage and, were it not that Dickens also described this knowing boy in his letter to Forster, we might be tempted to see him as a fictional version of the child Dickens – rather like the 'very queer small boy' who tells the Uncommercial Traveller all about Gad's Hill in 'Travelling Abroad'. However that may be, it is hard to resist the idea that Dickens was projecting his younger self of the Marshalsea days on to this small boy (who also, incidentally, seems able to summon up Dickensian-sounding characters like 'Joe Pythick' and his uncle Tom). The coincidence that Dickens was revisiting a place so strongly associated in his mind with the darkest days of his early years just when he was preparing to move, as owner, into the fine old house that had so stirred his childish admiration before those dark days began, would surely not have been lost upon him.[11]

The actual writing of *Little Dorrit* was completed on 8 May, and the final double number and the bound volume appeared together on the last day of the month. The sales of the monthly parts had remained buoyant throughout the serialisation, yielding Dickens a handsome profit of between £542 and £600 for each number. Recalling that in his Preface to *Bleak House* he had written that he 'had never had so many readers', he now wrote in the *Little Dorrit* Preface that he had 'still to repeat the same words'. He was perhaps deliberately thumbing his nose at the widespread hostile criticism that had been directed at the later instalments of the story, and gratefully resting on that special 'affection and confidence' that had – he claimed and not without justice – grown up between himself and his readers.[12]

Normally he felt a strong need for some immediate and violent distraction after finishing a long book. Such feelings would have been mitigated at the end of *Dorrit* by the purchase of Gad's Hill. His new house was providing him with plenty of occupation, there being, as he told James White on 22 May, a 'tremendous number of ingenuities to be wrought out' as part of the preparations for the family's taking up residence there for the summer. At this stage Dickens still seemed not to have had any idea of making Gad's Hill his permanent home, though he evidently took great delight in his new role as an 'Inimitable Kentish Freeholder' as well as in the Shakespearian associations of Gad's Hill as the scene of Falstaff's robbery of the Canterbury pilgrims in *Henry IV Part One*. He formally inaugurated his 'Freeholdership' on 19 May, Catherine's birthday, when a group of his closest friends – among them Beard, Collins, and Wills – joined him and Catherine to enjoy a cold collation at the new house. On 1 June the family moved in and a few days later received Andersen as their first house-guest. Dickens's first piece of writing done at Gad's Hill may have been the satirical piece called 'The Best Authority' which appeared as the lead article in the 20 June issue of *Household Words*. This mocked the public's readiness to credit whatever 'the Best Authority' is reported as saying, much as credulous investors had believed in the idea of Merdle's infallibility.[13]

His new house alone, however, would not have been enough to distract Dickens at this time. Suddenly, however, there came a golden opportunity for him to plunge into a mass of business that was of a kind especially congenial to him, involving as it did the co-ordination of the activities of many people in an act of professional solidarity and targeted benevolence, with theatrical doings very much to the fore. His old and valued friend Douglas Jerrold, having, at the age of fifty-four, finally achieved some measure of financial stability as editor of *Lloyd's Weekly Newspaper*, died unexpectedly on 8 June, after a very short illness. Jerrold left behind him a widow, three sons struggling to make their way in the world (the eldest, Blanchard, was a journalist contributing regularly to *Household Words*) and an unmarried daughter. Within hours of hearing of the death, which he did by chance as he was travelling up to London by train, Dickens was busy organising an extensive programme of literary, musical and theatrical events to raise money for the benefit of the widow and her daughter, to be called the Jerrold Fund. He quickly recruited a distinguished committee to oversee the proceedings including Forster, Bulwer Lytton, Macready and Stanfield, arranged to give a public reading of the *Carol* and organised both Thackeray and William Howard Russell to give a lecture each. He also planned a concert at St Martin's Hall, two gala evenings at the Haymarket and the Adelphi theatres of professional performances of some of Jerrold's best plays (including, of course, *Black Eyed Susan*, with T. P. Cooke coming out of retirement to play the role of the sailor-hero that he had created nearly thirty years before), and – most exciting prospect of all for Dickens no doubt – a subscription performance of *The Frozen Deep* at the Gallery of Illustration in Lower Regent Street. Protests from the Jerrold family that they were by no means destitute and did not want this public fund-raising were swept aside as Dickens plunged eagerly into detailed negotiations with fellow-writers, theatre managers, actors, singers and musicians. 'I have got hold of Arthur Smith as the best man of business I know', he had told Forster on 10 June, 'and go to work with him tomorrow morning. . . . My confident hope is that we shall get close upon two thousand pounds.' Smith, the brother and business-manager of Dickens's friend the author and showman Albert Smith, was later to become Dickens's indispensable manager for his professional readings, that new career towards which events, and Dickens's own needs, now seemed to be driving him.[14]

On 30 June Dickens read the *Carol* to an audience of over two thousand people in St Martin's Hall. The event lasted two hours and the reception was ecstatic. A reviewer in *The Leader* wrote on 4 July:

> Mr Dickens's voice, naturally powerful and expressive . . . is completely under his control, and he modulates it with the practised ease of one accustomed to address the public from the platform rather than through the pen. . . . At the close there was an outburst, not so much of applause as of downright hurrahing, from every part – the stalls even being startled from their propriety into the waving of hats and handkerchieves, and joining heartily in the contagious cheer.

To Macready Dickens wrote on 13 July, 'The two thousand and odd people were like one, and their enthusiasm was something awful.' As in his writing, this fusing of a huge audience into one was above all the effect that he aimed at, and the advantage of the readings was that he could actually *feel* this happening as he read ('the effect coming freshly back upon me'). In response to popular demand he gave another reading of the *Carol* for the Jerrold Fund on 24 July and a third one in Manchester on 31 July.[15]

There was likewise such a demand for tickets for the planned performance of *The Frozen Deep* that extra ones had to be scheduled. As noted above, the Queen had been rumoured earlier as wanting to see the production and now Dickens was directly approached about this. She could not support fund-raising efforts for the benefit of individuals so proposed to Dickens through an equerry that he and his troupe should give a private performance of the play at Buckingham Palace. He answered that he would not 'feel easy as to the social position of my daughters at the Court under such circumstances' and, emboldened by the fact that the Queen had, he wrote to Burdett Coutts on 20 June, 'always been most kind and considerate to me on other occasions', counter-proposed that she and the Prince should come to see the play privately at the Gallery of Illustration, bringing her own guests. The Queen readily agreed and a special performance for the royal party was accordingly given at the Gallery on 4 July. This was the famous occasion when Dickens twice respectfully declined the Queen's summons to him after the play to attend her to be personally congratulated on the play generally and his performance in particular (his acting she considered 'beyond all praise and not to be surpassed'). He declined to come because he was already dressed in the ludicrous costume needed for the farce *Uncle John* that concluded the evening's entertainment ('I was mighty glad when I woke this morning', he told Forster on 5 July, 'that I had carried the point'). For the general public there was the already advertised performance on 11 July but also two further ones on the 18th and the 25th, all of them taking place before enraptured audiences.[16]

Absorbed as he was in his Jerrold Fund activities, and much as he might eschew reading any reviews of his own work, Dickens cannot have been unaware that *Little Dorrit*, had, as mentioned above, latterly not been getting a good press. A detailed study of the novel's reception has shown that twenty-five out of thirty-six traced reviews or notices of the complete, or nearly complete, novel were hostile, using such opprobrious terms as 'unartistic', 'unnatural' and 'uninteresting'. Dickens had certainly been upset by one such notice (in *Blackwood's Magazine*) that he had stumbled upon earlier in the year. The reviewer, whose article was entitled 'Remonstrance with Dickens', lamented a perceived decline in Dickens's art: 'in that wilderness [of *Little Dorrit*] we sit down and weep when we remember thee, O *Pickwick!*'. *Blackwood's*, we should remember, was a Tory periodical and there can be no doubt that much of the critical hostility to *Dorrit* was politically motivated, as John Hollingshead pointed out in *The Train* for August 1857. Tories were offended by the attacks on the aristocracy, and Liberals by the attacks on Parliament and the Civil Service. Writing anonymously in the new intellectual weekly *The Saturday Review* on 3 January 1857, James Fitzjames Stephen, whose father, the distinguished civil servant Sir James Stephen was believed by some to have been the model for Mr Tite Barnacle in *Dorrit*, described Dickens as a writer hardly able to 'attract the attention of the more intelligent classes of the community' but who exercised 'a very wide and very pernicious political and social influence' among the vast, unreflective and imperfectly educated, majority of the population. When Stephen returned to the charge in a long article headed 'The License of Modern Novelists' in the July number of the *Edinburgh Review* (a journal once edited by Dickens's very own 'critic laureate', Lord Jeffrey) he got somewhat carried away and made a couple of slips that gave Dickens a chance to produce a crushing retort in *Household Words* on 1 August, in a lead article called 'Curious Misprint in the *Edinburgh Review*'.[17]

Accusing Dickens of cultivating an opportunistic topicality in his fiction, Stephen asserted that the fall of Mrs Clennam's house at the end of *Little Dorrit* was inspired by a recent (9 May 1857) collapse of some houses in the Tottenham Court Road. Dickens leapt eagerly to the defence of the integrity of his art. Invoking two of his favourite images for the work involved in the writing of serial fiction, paving and weaving, he observed that the way to the collapse of the house, and the crushing of the villainous Rigaud with it, 'is paved all through the book with a painful minuteness and reiterated care of preparation, the necessity of which (in order that the thread may be kept in the reader's mind through nearly two years), is one of the adverse incidents of that serial form of publication'. Stephen had also sought to ridicule Dickens's concept of the Circumlocution Office by citing the case of Rowland Hill, the founder of the penny post. Hill, Stephen claimed, was an outstanding but not untypical example of someone with a brilliant scheme for 'what amounted to a revolution in a most important department of the Government' who, far from being fobbed off and frustrated at every turn by the Circumlocution Office, had found his scheme promptly adopted and himself given a leading role in implementing it. Gleefully, Dickens set about demonstrating how singularly unfortunate Stephen had been in his choice of example. Hill, he had no difficulty in showing, was a particularly notorious example of someone who had suffered a severe ordeal by Circumlocution and the appearance of his name in the *Edinburgh* article, Dickens ironically concluded, must surely have been owing to a misprint.[18]

To Macready Dickens later wrote (3 August) one of his bravura, 'here's an amazing man!', letters about the circumstances of the writing of this article:

I saw the chance to answer it [the *Edinburgh* article] last Friday week, as I was going down to read the Carol in St Martin's Hall. Instantly turned to, then and there, and wrote half the article. Flew out of bed early next morning and finished by Noon. Went down to Gallery of Illustration (we acted there that night), did the day's business, corrected the proof in Polar costume in dressing room, broke up two numbers of Household Words to get it out directly, played in Frozen Deep and Uncle John, presided at Supper of company, made no end of speeches, went home and gave in completely for four hours, then got sound asleep, and next day was as fresh as – you used to be in the far off days of your lusty Youth.

Much as his admirers have always marvelled at Dickens's fantastic energy and quite extraordinary capacity for dealing with many things at the same time, he himself delighted to marvel at it quite as much. During all this summer when he was, as he later wrote to Lavinia Watson, 'rending the very heart out of my body by doing that Richard Wardour part' and master-minding all the Jerrold Fund activities he was also attending as closely as ever to both Urania Cottage and *Household Words* business.

On the strained domestic front, he had to cope with all the problems of settling into Gad's Hill, especially problems of drainage and water supply. These last are chronicled in his comically distraught letters appealing for Austin's help and advice, like the one written on 28 August about 'the aggrava-tion of knowing that the water is at the bottom of the well – and of paying for that accursed water-cart that comes jogging backwards and forwards – and of looking at the dry bath, morning after morning – is gradually changing the undersigned honey-pot into a Mad Bull'. He had also the stress of dealing with Hans Christian Andersen, whose projected two-week visit extended to five weeks. Andersen's eccentricities did not endear him to Georgina and the children (Katey later remembered him as a 'boney bore who stayed on and on') but Catherine was always kind to him and Andersen persuaded himself that Dickens must have modelled Agnes in *Copperfield* on her. Dickens also was unfailingly kind, comforting Andersen when he was distressed by a bad review, but confessed to Burdett Coutts on 10 July, 'We are suffering very much from Andersen' before going on to give her a hilarious account of Andersen's misadventures in a London cab.[19]

Towards the end of his response to the attack in the *Edinburgh Review* Dickens introduced a personal note. The *Review* might not be able to apolo-gise to him in its next issue, he wrote, because 'it will, too possibly, have much to do by that time in championing its Circumlocution Office in new triumphs on the voyage out to India (God knows the Novelist has his private as well as his public reasons for writing the foreboding with no triumphant heart!)'. He was here referring to Walter, whom he had, just four days earlier, seen off at

Southampton on his way to India. On 19 July, the day after the second of the public performances of *The Frozen Deep*, Dickens took Charley with him down to Southampton to see Walter off, the first of four sons whom he was to send overseas to make their careers. He found this farewell brought into focus, sharply and disconcertingly, what seemed to him a strange duality in the mode of his existence. As a writer he drew, constantly and deeply, on the matter of his early life, on those scenes, relationships and experiences of his childhood, youth and young manhood that were always present to his imagination and integral to his emotional life, and that had, most recently, powered so much of the writing of *Little Dorrit*. In his daily, domestic, professional and public life, however, he was Charles Dickens, the responsible father of a large family and a highly respected, indeed greatly loved, public figure, almost an institution of British life. This parting with his sixteen-year-old son strangely fused the past and the present so that, as he wrote on 19 July to Edmund Yates (who had three infant sons), 'I dont at all know this day how he [Walter] comes to be mine, or I, his': '. . . seeing Charley and he going aboard the Ship before me just now, I suddenly came into possession of a photograph of my own back at 16 and 20, and also into a suspicion that I had doubled the last age'. His public allusion to Walter's departure in the *Household Words* article relates, of course, to the other strand in *Little Dorrit*, the one attacked by Stephen. News was just beginning to reach England of the outbreak of the Indian Mutiny in early May although the scale and ferocity of the event was not yet fully known. Whatever it was that was happening there, Dickens feared that the Circumlocution Office would make as big a hash of dealing with it as it had done in the case of the Crimean War.[20]

Meanwhile in his zeal to drive the Jerrold Fund to its £2,000 target Dickens had been exploring the possibility of taking *The Frozen Deep* to Birmingham for a couple of nights if a venue could be found that would not be 'too large for the ladies', who would not be able to project their voices in the way that would be necessary in a large auditorium. This project came to nothing but when on 31 July he went to give a *Carol* reading at the four-thousand-seater Free Trade Hall in Manchester (an extra event, not scheduled in the original Jerrold Fund programme) he was pressed by some leading Mancunians to bring the play there also. The Hall was crowded in every part for his reading and the whole of this huge audience was, the *Manchester Guardian* reported on 1 August, 'completely under the sway of the story and its reader'. After such an exhilarating experience it is hardly surprising that Dickens promptly accepted the invitation to bring *The Frozen Deep* to the Free Trade Hall. No doubt he was motivated, as he told Collins, by his desire to reach the Fund's target sum but at work in him also must have been a keen desire (one might even speak of a real emotional and psychological need, at this critical time in his life) to continue 'writing' and 'rewriting' the tragic-heroic story of Richard Wardour 'in company'. The challenge and the potential rewards of doing this attended by such an immense company as that which would be assembled in the Free Trade Hall, a company he already had proved to himself he could control and unify as a reader, was surely irresistible. He at once began the search for some professional actresses, 'the best who *have been* on the stage', to take over the roles hitherto performed by his daughters, sisters-in-law and family friends. His choice of players was to have consequences for both his life and his art that were truly momentous.[21]

CHAPTER 19

Writing off a Marriage

1857–1858

Do not think me unimpressed by certain words in your letter concerning forgiveness and tenderness when I say that I do not claim to have anything to forgive ... but that a page in my life which once had writing on it, has become absolutely blank, and that it is not in my power to pretend that it has a solitary word upon it.

Dickens to Angela Burdett Coutts, 12 February 1864

DICKENS FOUND the professional actresses he needed through the help of an old friend, the actor-manager Alfred Wigan. Wigan drew his attention to the fact that the highly respected Frances Ternan, who had been a star performer in her younger days, and two of her three actress daughters, Maria and Ellen, were without an engagement for the summer (the oldest girl, twenty-two-year-old Fanny, was playing Oberon in Charles Kean's *Midsummer Night's Dream* at the Princess's). Frances Ternan, née Jarman, had made her London début in 1827 and had played opposite both Edmund Kean and Charles Kemble. She had acted also with Macready, who had been kind to her when her Irish actor-husband Thomas Ternan died in poverty in 1846. Now she was semi-retired, devoting herself mainly to the fostering of her daughters' careers. Her vivacious second child, Maria, born in 1835, had been on the stage since infancy and was now gaining a reputation as a comédienne and singer. Eighteen-year-old Ellen, always known as Nelly, had also played juvenile roles in her earlier years and had now just finished playing her first adult role which had required her to show her legs in the breeches part of Hippomenes in Frank Talfourd's burlesque *Atalanta* at the Haymarket Theatre (April–July 1857).[1]

In *The Frozen Deep* Frances Ternan took over the role of Nurse Esther, Maria the role of the heroine Clara Burnham, and Nelly the minor role of Lucy Crayford. The Ternans also took over Georgina's, Mamie's and Katey's parts in *Uncle John*. Together with two other actresses recruited for the other minor parts, they were subjected to 'three days drill' at Tavistock House by their dynamic new manager and leading man before the whole company set off, in festive mood, for Manchester on 20 August. Determined to 'make a family party of it', Dickens had arranged for everyone to travel on the same train and stay at the same hotel, 'just as though we were staying in a country house'. Catherine, who, according to Dickens, had been 'extremely unwell' recovered in time to travel with the rest.[2]

By this time Dickens had written nothing for *Household Words* for a couple of months, apart from his riposte to the *Edinburgh*, and he promised Wills on 13 August that he would 'try to knock out a subject or two' but even he found this to be impossible under such bustling circumstances. The success of *The Frozen Deep* before packed and palpitating audiences in the enormous Manchester Free Trade Hall on 21, 22 and 24 August was, because of the much vaster audience, even more spectacular than at the Gallery of Illustration. The second of these performances Collins considered to have been 'the finest of all the representations of "The Frozen Deep" '. 'Dickens surpassed himself,' he wrote, adding, 'The trite phrase is the true phrase to describe that magnificent piece of acting. He literally electrified the audience.' Dickens certainly startled his own troupe with the power and pathos of his big death scene. In it, he glee-fully reported in later accounts written separately to two of his dearest female friends, Maria Ternan almost drowned him with her tears as she knelt over him as he lay dying and he had to whisper to her to compose herself. This simply made her weep still more as she sobbed out, 'Oh it is so sad, it is so dreadfully sad. Oh don't die! Give me a little time! Don't take leave of me in this terrible way – pray, pray, pray!!' When one checks the actual text of the last page of *The Frozen Deep*, one wonders whether Maria spoke all this aloud as improvised dialogue (in which case it would have been rather in competition with Wardour's nobly pathetic dying speech), or whether she, too, was whis-pering (in which case the audience would have been treated to rather a long pause before the resumption of the play's dialogue). Could it possibly be that Dickens was writing most of this speech for her retrospectively?[3]

Despite having to soothe Maria, and his own excitement over 'the crying of two thousand people over the grave of Richard Wardour', or perhaps stimulated by all these emotional displays, Dickens was struck by 'new ideas' for his next book. These, he told Burdett Coutts, came into his head as he lay upon the floor 'with surprising force and brilliancy' and some weeks later he noted them down in what he called 'a little book I keep', perhaps the *Book of Memoranda*. When he came to write a preface for *A Tale of Two Cities* just over two years later he mentioned that he had first conceived that story's 'main idea' whilst acting in *The Frozen Deep*. He refers to 'acting with my children and friends', thus making the occasion specific to the London rather than to the Manchester perform-ances, perhaps as a result of his wish, in view of all the gossip there had been since the spring of 1858, to keep the Ternans out of the picture.[4]

Back at Gad's Hill after his Manchester triumphs and with the £2,000 target for the Jerrold Fund comfortably achieved (as he informed the world through the columns of *The Times*), Dickens was tormented by the usual restlessness following great artistic effort but this time it took a particularly acute form. This restlessness was, he told Hannah Brown on 28 August, 'the penalty of an imaginative life and constitution' and so beset him now 'that I feel as if the scaling of all the Mountains in Switzerland . . . would be but a slight relief'. He told her also how much he suffered from 'the vague unhappiness which tracks a life of constant aim and ever impels to some new aim in which it may be lost'. To Collins he wrote the following day still more dramatically, mentioning his 'grim despair' and urging his younger friend, on the pretext of seeking copy for *Household Words*, to come away with him to 'any place in the world' because 'when I *do* start up and stare myself seedily in the face, as happens to be my case at present, my blankness is inconceivable – indescribable – my misery, amazing'. It has been generally and surely correctly assumed that the peculiar intensity of Dickens's desperation at this time must be connected with his response to one or both of the two younger Ternan sisters. Indeed, when we find him writing a few days later to the Angel Hotel at Doncaster, booking rooms for Races Week (13–20 Sept.) we can be certain of it since that was the date, and Doncaster Theatre Royal the place, of the young actresses' next engagement. Dickens and Collins agreed that they would start off by exploring Cumberland and, in default of Swiss Alps, climb the 'gloomy old mountain' of Carrick Fell, just to the north of Skiddaw, which had caught Dickens's fancy in looking over a volume called *The Beauties of England and Wales*. They would call their expedition 'The Lazy Tour of Two Idle Apprentices' in honour of Hogarth, and jointly compose a series of papers under this title for October publication in *Household Words*. They would present themselves as holidaying apprentices of the 'highly meritorious lady' Literature, adopting the names of the protagonists of Hogarth's 1747 series of engravings called *Industry and Idleness*. Dickens became Francis Goodchild and Collins Thomas Idle, and the running joke of the successive chapters was to be the contrast (based, at least as far as Dickens was concerned, upon their real-life characters) between the desperate intensity of Goodchild's nature and the extreme strenuousness of his so-called 'idleness' and Thomas Idle's comfortably relaxed disposition and contented indolence.

Dickens was also concerned about a somewhat grander literary enterprise. At Forster's urging, he suggested to Bradbury and Evans that they should embark, with Chapman and Hall's necessary co-operation as far as the books they controlled were concerned, on the re-issue of all his books in a handsome edition directed at what he called in a letter to Evans of 6 September, 'the better class of readers who would buy them for well-furnished bookshelves', hence its being in due course designated the 'Library Edition'. Not only would this, it was hoped, make money – Dickens was naturally always keen on what he called 'working the copyrights' – but it would enhance the status and dignity of his oeuvre. This was something the Cheap Edition (of which a second series, consisting of the novels written after *Chuzzlewit*, was now in course of publication) could not, and clearly was not intended, to achieve.

Meanwhile, the Ternans loomed large in his emotional and imaginative life. It is not altogether clear whether it was Maria or Nelly who was having such an effect on him at this point – given his lifelong fascination with sisters and sisterly feelings, it could well have been both. In any case, the result seems to have been an intensification of his negative feelings towards his marriage. Inevitably, he began in his letters to Forster, and to certain other intimate friends, to construct an autobiographical narrative to explain and justify these feelings. Forster, it seems clear, evidently felt great affection for Catherine. Only a year before, he had written to her when he himself was about to marry, 'I have never felt so strongly as within the last few months how much of the happiness of past years I owe to you'. Now he sought to modify Dickens's attitude towards her. When, however, he came to write the biography that his friend had virtually commissioned him to write, he felt himself constrained to present Dickens's narrative about ending his marriage without any 'balancing' comment from himself. He does, however, touch on what he calls 'defects of temperament' in Dickens resulting from his early experiences and relates these to the collapse of the marriage and 'sorrowful misunderstandings' between husband and wife. He quotes without comment a letter of early September 1857 in which Dickens, appealing to him as a witness, wrote,

> Poor Catherine and I are not made for each other. . . . Her temperament will not go with mine. . . . What is now befalling me I have seen steadily coming on, ever since the days you remember when Mary was born; and I know too well that you cannot, and no one can, help me.

In other words, Dickens is saying that his marriage conformed to the dismal pattern he had feelingly described just a few months earlier in *Dorrit* XV, when writing about the Roman wedding of Fanny Dorrit and Edmund Sparkler: 'after rolling smoothly over a fair pavement' the bridal carriage 'had begun to jolt through a Slough of Despond, and through a long, long avenue of wrack and ruin'. To this striking image Dickens had added the glum comment, 'Other nuptial carriages are said to have gone the same road, before and since.'[5]

'No one can help me.' No individual person could help him, perhaps, but there was always his adoring public, the great and abiding love of his life, and the idea that had been growing ever stronger in his mind, nourished by the huge success of all his *Carol* readings for charity, that he should give public readings of his work for his own benefit, now came very much to the fore. He asked Forster, who had consistently opposed this idea, to think again about it but that great champion of the Dignity of Literature still maintained the same objections, as he later recalled in his *Dickens*:

It was a substitution of lower for higher aims; a change to commonplace
from more elevated pursuits; and it had so much the character of a public
exhibition for money as to raise, in the question of respect for his calling as
a writer, a question also of respect for himself as a gentleman.

In Forster's opinion, Dickens himself perhaps did not realise 'how much his
eager present wish to become a public reader was but the outcome of the restless domestic discontents of the last four years'. Once he had embarked on such
an unsettled mode of life as that of a touring professional performer, however,
all hope of 'resettling his disordered home' would inevitably be lost.[6]
　　Whether Forster recognised it or not, all hope of Dickens's 'resettling his
disordered home' was past well before he and Collins took the express from
Euston Station to Carlisle on 7 September to begin their 'Lazy Tour'. At this
stage, Dickens could see no escape from the situation. 'For her [Catherine's]
sake as well as mine, the wish will force itself upon me that something might
be done,' he wrote, but wrote also that he knew this to be impossible. Already,
however, he was beginning the process of gradually writing Catherine out of
his life that was to reach its culmination the following April. During the two
weeks that he and Collins were away his only letters home were to Georgina
(we can infer this from the fact that Catherine seems to have kept every letter
he ever wrote to her and when dying asked her younger daughter to deposit
them in the British Museum 'that the world may know he loved me once').
In his letters to Georgina Dickens sent his love to the children, especially to
'the darling Plorn', but never to Catherine. It was to Georgina or to Forster that
he sent 'inimitable' accounts of the chief event of his and Collins's week in the
Lakes. This was their ascent and dramatic descent of Carrick Fell in heavy rain
and black mists, with an incompetent local guide. Coming down, Collins
sprained his ankle so badly that Dickens had to carry him the rest of the way
('Wardour to the life!', wrote Dickens to Forster). They returned to Carlisle on
11 September, going on the next day to Lancaster and from there to Doncaster
for Races Week. Here Dickens saw the Ternans again, as he had all along
intended.[7]
　　Writing to Wills about copy for the 'Lazy Tour' chapters, Dickens teased
his unromantic sub-editor with hints about what was happening: 'Lord bless
you, the strongest parts of your present correspondent's heart are made up of
weaknesses. And he just come to be here at all (if you knew it) along of his
Richard Wardour! Guess *that* riddle, Mr Wills!' He and Collins, who must surely
have had a pretty shrewd idea of what was happening even if Dickens did not
directly confide in him, found themselves plunged into the frenetic atmosphere
of Races Week full of what Dickens later described as 'Lunatics, horse-mad,
betting-mad, drunken-mad, vice-mad, and the designing Keepers [that is,
bookies] always after them'. These ruthlessly exploitative 'Keepers' struck

Dickens as all bearing an uncanny resemblance to the famous murderers Thurtell and Palmer, both of whom had been murkily involved in the world of the turf. On 15 September he and Collins went to the theatre to see Maria and Nelly perform (Nelly in two very minor parts). Dickens was so outraged by the coarse behaviour of the rowdy audience, especially by the lewd interjections of one hopelessly drunk young 'gent', that he momentarily doubted the whole-someness of an art 'which sets women apart on a high floor before such a thing as this' (meaning the young drunk). The next day, St Leger Day, he and Collins took both girls and their mother in an open carriage to the racecourse where he distinguished himself by picking out the winners of the three chief races despite knowing nothing whatever about any of the runners. Four days later he was again teasing Wills: 'I am going to take the little – riddle – into the country this morning' (they made an excursion to see the ruins of Roche Abbey). He pro-mised that he would still be on time with his copy for chapter 3 of the 'Tour', however: 'So let the riddle and the riddler go their own wild way, and no harm come of it!'[8]

Clearly, he was in a very excitable state – he had described 'Mr Goodchild' in the first chapter of 'The Lazy Tour' as being 'always in love with somebody' – and perhaps he was not behaving quite as discreetly as befitted such a celebrated champion of domesticity. The *Doncaster Gazette* was busy tracking his movements (he would not have appreciated the paper's reference to him on 18 September as 'the distinguished author of *The Pickwick Papers* – his greatest work') and it may have been an anxious word from Mrs Ternan, or, just possibly, some sort of rebuff from either Maria or Nelly, that decided him to leave Doncaster earlier than he had intended. None of the Ternans could control what he wrote for *Household Words*, however, and we may wonder what they would have made of Francis Goodchild's rhapsodic memories of the St Leger which featured in the fifth and last chapter of the 'Lazy Tour' (*HW*, 31 Oct. 1857):

O little lilac gloves! And O winning little bonnet, making in conjunction with her golden hair quite a Glory in the sunlight round the pretty head, why anything in the world but you and me! Why may not this day's running – of horses, to all the rest: of the precious sands of life to me – be prolonged through an everlasting autumn-sunshine, without a sunset! . . . Arab drums, powerful of old to summon Genii in the desert, sound of yourselves and raise a troop for me in the desert of my heart, which shall so enchant this dusty barouche . . . that I, within it, loving the little lilac gloves, the winning little bonnet, and the dear unknown wearer with the golden hair, may wait by her side for ever, to see a Great St Leger that shall never be run!

It is no wonder that Forster was careful in his *Dickens* to ascribe the whole of this last chapter to Collins, thereby seeking to avoid unwelcome identifications.

One of Nelly's most striking features was her 'golden hair' and we may therefore guess that by the time Dickens wrote this it was she and not Maria who was the object of his romantic adoration. The *Arabian Nights* imagery of the passage just quoted anticipates the fairy-tale motifs Dickens later invoked in another veiled reference to Nelly in his letter to Lavinia Watson of 7 December:

> I wish I had been born in the days of Ogres and Dragon-guarded Castles. I wish an Ogre with seven heads . . . had taken the Princess whom I adore – you have no idea how intensely I love her! – to his stronghold on the top of a high series of Mountains, and there tied her up by the hair. Nothing would suit me half so well this day, as climbing after her, sword in hand, and either winning her or being killed. – *There's* a state of mind for you, in 1857.

The first three chapters of the 'Lazy Tour' were the ones actually written during the tour and to them Dickens contributed the framework narrative as well as various set-piece descriptions of places they visited. These descriptions were written in what he was to characterise the following year as his 'fanciful photographer' mode, a genre of journalism that, following his own instruction to keep the magazine imaginative, he thought particularly suited to *Household Words*. He was, he told Forster, very much 'tickled' by these passages and their 'fantastic fidelity' and he took especial pride, as well he might have done, in the bravura depiction in chapter 3 of the great railway-junction at Carlisle, described in its alternating states of 'Lethargy and Madness'. By the time he finished correcting proof of this chapter (26 Sept.) he had been for some days back home (which now seems mainly to have meant Gad's Hill), and was once more brought face to face with the misery of being, as he saw it, hopelessly trapped in a failed marriage. It may well have been as a result of this that so much of both the style and substance of the last two chapters of the 'Tour' are, as we shall see, rather different from the style and substance of the first three.[9]

It seems from the surviving letters written by Dickens during these weeks that Catherine remained alone in Tavistock House. Anne Brown, who had left Dickens's and Catherine's service in 1855 to marry a French polisher called Edward Cornelius, returned temporarily to act as housekeeper there, whilst Georgina and the children, including the paternal favourite, five-year-old Plorn, were all at Gad's Hill with Dickens. When he needed to come up to London he often stayed in his bachelor flat at the *Household Words* office. One night in early October he did stay at Tavistock House, however, and something occurred, perhaps an argument with Catherine connected with the Ternans or with Georgina, which so angered him that he turned out of bed at 2 a.m. and walked thirty miles through 'the dead night' down to Gad's Hill. 'I had been very much put-out,' he told Lavinia Watson when writing to her on 7 December about this pedestrian feat, memories of which would later contribute to the writing of a stunning *Uncommercial Traveller* essay 'Night Walks' (*ATYR*, 21 July 1860). It may have been immediately after this contretemps that Dickens sent his notorious letter of 11 October to Anne Cornelius, instructing her to have his dressing-room at Tavistock House converted into a single bedroom and for the door between it and Catherine's room to be sealed up with some plain deal bookshelves built into the recess. He had already, he told Anne, arranged for his new bed and bedding to be delivered to Tavistock House. Catherine, it seems, would have had the humiliation of learning first from her former maid of this definitive withdrawal of her husband's from the marital bedroom. Just one week later she received the last cheque for household expenses she was ever to get from him. Almost simultaneously he was sending another cheque (£50) to J. B. Buckstone, manager of the Haymarket and Adelphi Theatres, apparently in connection with Buckstone's giving Nelly a Haymarket engagement. 'I need hardly tell you', Dickens wrote to him on 13 October, 'that my interest in the young lady does not cease with the effecting of this arrangement . . .'.[10]

On 23 October Dickens wrote to de la Rue, the only other friend apart from Forster to whom, because of past history, he felt he could write openly about his domestic 'skeleton'. His would-be comic use of melodramatic conspiratorial imagery in the letter perhaps implies some uneasy consciousness on his part that he might be thought to be acting dishonourably towards Catherine in writing like this about her to the de la Rues, his relations with whom had once caused her so much marital unhappiness.

> Between ourselves (I beckon Madame de la Rue nearer with my fore-finger and whisper this with a serio-comic smile), I don't get on better in these later times with a certain poor lady you know of, than I did in the earlier Peschiere days. Much worse. Much worse! Neither do the children, elder or younger. Neither can she get on with herself, or be anything but unhappy. (She has been excruciatingly jealous of, and has obtained positive proofs of my being on the most confidential terms with at least Fifteen Thousand Women of various conditions in life, every condition in life, since we left Genoa. Please to respect me for this vast experience.)

He makes Catherine into a 'humour' character out of Ben Jonson, dominated by the emotion of jealousy. He also describes her as a failed mother, an accusation to which he will return, more insistently, later on. The heroine of all this domestic drama is, of course, Georgina: 'She is the active spirit of the house, and the children dote upon her.'

It was during these turbulent autumn weeks that Dickens wrote his part of chapter 4 of the 'Tour' – all of it, that is, apart from the second interpolated story which is by Collins – and all of chapter 5. As already noted, these last

two chapters read rather differently from the first three. There is a peculiar
intensity in Dickens's description of an inmate of Lancaster Lunatic Asylum
absorbed in studying a little piece of matting as he tries to trace a pattern in its
fibres. This sight makes Dickens think 'how all of us, GOD help us! in our
different ways are poring over our bits of matting, blindly enough, and what
confusions and mysteries we make in the pattern'. He proceeded to 'pore over'
his own little piece of matting in writing the eerie tale about a wife-murder
(told by the murderer's ghost) which immediately follows, and which he
described to Wills on 2 October as 'a very odd story, with a wild, picturesque
fancy in it' (he seems to have developed rather a fondness for the adjective
'wild' about this time). The story, generally called 'The Bride's Chamber', was
probably first suggested to his imagination by a very recent, and notably cruel,
case of wife-murder he would have heard about in Lancaster – the fact that the
victim's name was Ellen would have been enough to arrest his attention, one
imagines. In his story he gave this name to the wife, whom he creates as a
strange conflation of Catherine and Nelly. She is described to Francis
Goodchild by the ghost of her murderer-husband, who had been old enough to
have been her father, and who had, in fact, been her guardian from the age of
ten and had 'formed [her] in the fear of him' as her destined husband. He had
reduced her to being 'a weak, credulous, incapable, helpless nothing' whom he
literally *willed* to death: 'she had long been in the way, and he had long been
weary'. But immediately after her death he was confronted by, and forced to kill,
'a slender youth' with, like the young Dickens, 'long light brown hair', who had
loved Ellen and had vainly tried to rescue her from her cruel imprisonment.
The murder eventually came to light, with Dickens reworking a sensational
device from a story in *Master Humphrey's Clock* to bring about the exposure,
and the murderer was hanged. His ghost is condemned to tell his story every
year, on the anniversary of his execution, to whoever occupies the bride's
chamber, which is now one of the sitting-rooms in the inn into which the old
house has been converted and where Goodchild and Idle are now staying.[11]

The last chapter of 'The Lazy Tour', nearly all written by Dickens, features a
lurid description of Doncaster in Races Week as a place pervaded by sinister or
nightmarish figures, and contains the already-quoted ecstatic description of
the little golden-haired beauty sitting in an open carriage at the Races, as well
as the appalled description of the 'Satyr-like' behaviour of the drunken audience at the theatre. As with the 'Bride's Chamber' story, a certain feverishness
or extremity of emotion pervades all of this writing which we do not find in
the first three chapters of the 'Tour', and which would seem most likely to have
stemmed from the increased turbulence in Dickens's emotional life following
his time in Doncaster.

It was about this time, too, that Dickens began to write more feverishly than
hitherto about the Indian Mutiny. This event had been featuring in British

newspapers since late June/early July but Dickens's reference, in a letter to his Liverpool acquaintance Dr Sheridan Muspratt on 4 September, to 'these distracted Indian times' and to Walter's likely involvement in them, seems quite moderate. A month later, however, perhaps in delayed reaction to the massacre of British women and children at Cawnpore which had occurred on 15 July, he wrote in a very different tone to Burdett Coutts, declaring that if he were Commander-in-Chief in India he would do his utmost 'to exterminate the Race upon whom the stain of the late cruelties rested . . . to blot it out of mankind and raze it off the face of the earth', and he wrote in similar terms in the letter to de la Rue quoted above. Sensational press reports of the horrible fate suffered by the victims of Cawnpore and elsewhere were perhaps beginning to resonate in Dickens's mind with his image of Nelly and his fantasies about rescuing her from ogres. Meanwhile, it had become high time to begin planning the next Christmas number of *Household Words* for 1857.

Here was an opportunity for devising a story in which Dickens might elaborate a realistic version of his fantasy about defending or rescuing Nelly whilst at the same time 'shadowing out', as he expressed it in a letter to Morley of 18 October, 'the bravery of our ladies in India'. The result was 'The Perils of Certain English Prisoners, and Their Treasure in Women, Children, Silver, and Jewels', written jointly with Wilkie Collins during November (the first and last of the three chapters are by Dickens, the middle one by Collins) and published on 7 December. Dickens wanted, he told Morley, to avoid direct reference to India but write a story 'in which a few English people – gentlemen, ladies and children – and a few English soldiers, would find themselves alone in a strange wild place and liable to hostile attack'. He settled for an imaginary island off the coast of South America where a small colony of English are working a silver mine, and set the story back in the previous century. The narrator is an illiterate common soldier called Gill Davis, a foundling child formerly employed to scare birds 'at Snorridge Bottom, betwixt Chatham and Maidstone'. From afar, across the barrier of class, he worships his Captain's sister, a gentle and beautiful young lady called Marion Maryon. The English are betrayed into the hands of an international band of ruthless pirates by the – apparently motiveless – treachery of Christian King George, one of the native half-castes or 'Sambos', whereupon Davis devotes himself especially to Marion's protection. She and some others of the English women behave with great courage and resourcefulness in support of him and his fellow-soldiers, both in hand-to-hand fighting with the pirates and afterwards when the surviving English have all been taken prisoner. Some time after these dramatic events (which fall a long way short of the horrific ones at Cawnpore) Marion marries Captain Carton. Carton, whose name Dickens plucked from one of the lists in his *Book of Memoranda*, commands the forces that eventually defeat the pirates and later becomes an admiral and is knighted.

Davis ends as Lady Carton's faithful old retainer and the story we read is what he dictates to her, as he still cannot read or write. In this way he at last makes his 'singular confession' to her that, despite 'the immense and hopeless distance' between them he had loved her as a woman. Knowing very well how 'presumptuous and impossible to be realised' were his 'unhappy thoughts', he had still loved her and had suffered just as much 'agony' from the impossibility of his love's being returned as if he had been a gentleman. So strongly affected was Dickens by his own writing in this concluding section that, he told Lady Duff Gordon on 23 January 1858, he was 'for days and days, really unable to approach the Proofs':

> As often as I tried to correct them, I turned them over, looked at the last page, and was so completely overcome that I couldn't bear to dwell upon it. It was only when the Steam Engine roared for the sheets, that I could find it in my heart to look at them with a pen in my hand dipped in any thing but tears!

Apparently, Dickens was not the only one to be moved by this story of ardent but hopeless love. Years later, after Dickens's death, and after she had become the wife of a Margate headmaster, Nelly took to giving Dickens readings for charity and one of her favourite recital-items was 'The Perils of Certain English Prisoners'.[12]

'Perils' tells, like *The Frozen Deep*, the story of a man passionately in love with a woman he cannot have, a situation that was to be at the heart of all Dickens's major fiction from now on. Hitherto his hopeless-lover figures, from Smike to John Chivery, had always been secondary ones, pathetic or comic, but for the last eleven years of his life they were to be very much centre-stage, and seriously presented. Captain Carton's namesake in *A Tale of Two Cities* will, in fact, owe more to Richard Wardour than to Gill Davis in that he will not have to contend with any class barrier but with the still more insuperable difficulty that the object of his adoration, Lucie Manette, has given her love to another. Closer to Davis's situation will be that of Pip in *Great Expectations*, another poor boy from Davis's, and Dickens's, part of the world, who will suffer greatly through his hopeless love for a beautiful, socially-superior girl (in his case, one quite unlike the gentle Marion, however). But there is another aspect to the characterisation of Davis that looks back towards *Little Dorrit* rather than forward to succeeding novels. The young soldier's initial hostility towards his upper-class officers reflects Dickens's anger at the way in which the Army was almost entirely officered by scions of the aristocracy who had bought their commissions, a system that, as he wrote to Burdett Coutts on 4 October, 'has blighted generous ambition, and put reward out of the common man's reach'. Davis's mocking portrayal of Mr Commissioner Pordage, the British Government's representative on the island, continues the Circumlocution Office satire in

Little Dorrit and the severe criticism of the maladministration of India that had appeared in *Household Words* before the Mutiny. In Pordage Dickens lampoons Lord Canning, the Governor-General of India, whose order seeking to restrain indiscriminate bloody reprisals against the Indians on the part of British troops infuriated some sections of the London press. *Punch*, for example, ridiculed him as 'Clemency Canning' in its 'big cut' (main cartoon) for its 24 October issue. Dickens, who called Canning's order 'a maudlin proclamation', has Pordage warn Carton when the latter is setting out in pursuit of the pirates, 'Government requires you to treat the enemy with great delicacy, considera-tion, clemency, and forbearance.' Carton's reply closely echoes the speech Dickens told de la Rue he himself would make if he were made Commander-in-Chief in India: 'Believing that I hold my commission by the allowance of God, and not that I have received it direct from the Devil, I shall certainly use it with all avoidance of unnecessary suffering, and with all merciful swiftness of execution, to exterminate these people from the face of the earth.'[13]

On 25 November Dickens invited Burdett Coutts and Hannah Brown to a private reading of 'Perils' at Tavistock House. He had, he told Burdett Coutts, planned the story with great care 'in the hope of commemorating, without any vulgar catchpenny connexion or application, some of the best qualities of the English character that have been shewn in India'. He added, 'I hope it is very good, and I think it will make a great noise.' The previous day he had offered to send Benjamin Webster, manager of the Adelphi and Haymarket Theatres, an advance copy of the text so that he could steal a march on all the other managers who would be bound to seize upon it. 'It lights up all the fire that is in the public mind at this time,' Dickens told Webster, 'and you might make your Theatre blaze with it.' Webster declined the offer but the story *was* drama-tised at four other London theatres – not, however, with any remarkable success. Nor did the story itself make any 'great noise' despite praise from both *The Times* and, surprisingly, *The Saturday Review* (though the latter did predictably deplore the 'exaggerated' figure of Pordage).[14]

The period December 1857 to March 1858 was, on the whole, very much one of 'business as usual' for Dickens the professional and public man. He wrote only two articles for *Household Words*, both of them fairly routine tilting at such familiar targets as spiritualist séances and wretched railway refresh-ment rooms, but continued to keep a close editorial eye on every issue and to give detailed advice to would-be contributors about how to present their work to best advantage. He continued also to be generously encouraging towards new talent coming into the field, and gratified George Eliot by sending her a fan letter (18 Jan.) about her first book, *Scenes of Clerical Life*. He had already praised the stories it contained to Forster the previous spring when they were appearing in *Blackwood's Magazine* and, writing now directly to their author, he took leave to doubt the masculine authorial name: 'if they [the sketches] originated with no woman, I believe that no man ever before had the art of making himself, mentally, so like a woman, since the world began'. He gave several *Carol* readings for charity – in Coventry, where he was presented with a handsome watch, in Chatham and Bristol, and in Edinburgh, where he was presented with a massive silver wassail cup. The Edinburgh reading (26 March) was 'a wonderful go', he wrote to Beard on 5 April: 'Certainly the most intelligent audience (2000 strong) I have ever had to do with; and showing a capacity of being affected by the pathetic parts, such as I never saw before.' He was as indefatigable as ever in his efforts to help fellow-writers – taking the lead, for example, in raising a £200 fund for Lady Blessington's niece, Marguerite Power, who was struggling to make a living as a novelist, or sitting for three stricken hours one Saturday evening to hear Westland Marston 'read a very bad play' in order to advise him how to exploit it commercially. Meanwhile, he continued as implacable as ever in his campaign against the managers of the Royal Literary Fund. He was the main, if not the sole, author of a pamphlet entitled *The Case of the Reformers in the Literary Fund stated by Charles W. Dilke, Charles Dickens and John Forster*, published just before the Fund's Annual General Meeting on 10 March. In it he again accused the Fund's committee of 'dealing with the followers of Literature as beggars only' and of gross extravagance with regard to its administrative costs. He spoke at the meeting but he and his fellow-reformers were once more heavily defeated and shortly afterwards a Committee member published a detailed refutation of the *Case*. Dickens quickly responded with yet another pamphlet which he described, in a letter to Wilkie Collins of 29 April, as 'a facetious facer' given 'con amore' to 'those solemn impostors'.[15]

Rather more constructive than his prolonged bickering with the Royal Literary Fund was Dickens's superb speech, arguably the finest of his whole life, delivered on 9 February when presiding at a fund-raising banquet for the struggling Hospital for Sick Children in Great Ormond Street. This was an institution for which he felt a particular warmth, having, shortly after its foundation, celebrated it in *Household Words*, in a jointly-written article by himself and Morley called 'Drooping Buds' (*HW*, 3 April 1852). At the heart of the speech is a moving passage, comparable in power to the description of Jo's death in *Bleak House*, in which he recalled a 'little feeble, wasted, wan, sick child' with 'bright attentive eyes' whom he had once seen lying in an egg-box in one of the worst slums in darkest Edinburgh. This child lay 'quite quiet, quite patient, saying never a word' but, as his mother said, 'seeming to wonder what it was a' aboot':

> There he lay, looking at us, saying in his silence, more pathetically than I have ever heard anything said by any orator in my life, 'Will you please to tell us what this means, strange man? And if you can give me any good reason why I should be so soon, so far advanced on my way to Him who said that children

were to come into His presence, and were not to be forbidden, but who scarcely meant, that they should come by this hard road by which I am travelling – pray give that reason to me, for I seek it very earnestly and wonder about it very much.

Even though the Freemasons' Hall, where the dinner was held, was not as crowded as one might have expected it to have been, over £3,000 was raised in subscriptions and Dickens pledged himself to give also a Reading of the *Carol* on behalf of the Hospital. This he did on 15 April and it led to momentous consequences for Dickens himself, as well as to more funds to the Hospital. The huge success of the Reading and the overwhelming public demand for far more places than could possibly be provided finally bore down, as Forster ruefully recorded, Dickens's last lingering doubts as to whether or not he should begin to give Readings for his own profit.[16]

Six weeks or so after his speech for the Hospital for Sick Children Dickens proposed Thackeray's health at the Theatrical Fund dinner, describing him as 'a gentleman who is an honour to literature, and in whom literature is honoured', which was perhaps a clever way of enlisting Thackeray in the ranks of the upholders of 'the Dignity of Literature' when he was, as Dickens well knew, in fact, opposed to them. Adapting Thackeray's own description of himself as the 'showman' of *Vanity Fair*, Dickens linked it to his proclaimed belief in the essentially dramatic nature of the novelist's art: 'every writer of

40 The Girls' Ward at the Hospital for Sick Children in April 1858

fiction, though he may not adopt the dramatic form, writes in effect for the stage'. As far as the personal relationship between Thackeray and Dickens was concerned, this dinner may be said to have marked its high point. By the end of the year they would have ceased to be on speaking terms.[17]

Beneath all this public activity of Dickens's during the winter and early spring of 1857/58 there ran an ever-increasing strain of domestic tension and unhappiness. One outward sign of this was the lack of any of the usual Christmas or New Year festivities at Tavistock House. As to Gad's Hill, Dickens told Forster that though he was constantly improving the place, he had no interest in it, apparently still regarding it primarily as an investment. At this time he must have been more than usually emotionally reliant on Forster, his main, if not his sole, confidant with regard to his marital problems, and this may be reflected in the warmth of the dedication he composed in December for the Library Edition, by then in active preparation: 'This best edition of my books is, as of right, inscribed to my dear friend John Forster, Biographer of Oliver Goldsmith. In grateful remembrance of the many patient hours he has devoted to the corrections of proof-sheets of the original editions: and in affectionate acknowledgment of his counsel, sympathy and faithful friendship, during my whole literary life.'

As to what was currently happening in that life, Dickens told Lady Gordon in his New Year letter already cited, 'Wild and misty ideas of a story are floating about somewhere' before going on to imagine a very wild story indeed: 'Nothing would satisfy me at this present writing, but the having to go up a tremendous mountain, magic spell in one hand and sword in the other, to find the girl of my heart (whom I never did find), surrounded by fifty Dragons – kill them all – and bear her off triumphant.' Lady Gordon might have been startled by this frank avowal that he had never loved his wife (something he had certainly taught himself to believe by this time) but she could not, of course, have suspected that the image of a real-life young actress lay behind this fantasy, as it had done behind the 'princess and ogres' fantasy in Dickens's earlier letter to Lavinia Watson. As to ideas for a new novel, Dickens's thinking had, in fact, got rather beyond the 'wild and misty' stage by this time, as his contemporary correspondence with Forster shows. 'Nothing whatever', he told Forster, would do him 'the least "good" ' in the way of abating 'the one strong passion of change impending over us that every day makes stronger', that is, his desire to make some radical alteration in his domestic circumstances. But it might help him to endure the situation if he could 'discipline his thoughts' towards steady work on a new book so that the 'anxious toil' always involved in such labour 'would have its neck well broken before beginning to publish, next October or November'. His first suggested title was *One Of These Days*, which is not very revealing, but a few weeks later, in mid-March, he was proposing others – *Buried Alive, The Thread of Gold, The Doctor of*

Beauvais – which indicate that the plot, the setting and at least two of the leading characters of the story that was to become *A Tale Of Two Cities*, Dr Manette and his golden-haired daughter, were beginning to form themselves in his mind.[18]

But it was the notion of embarking on a new, and potentially highly lucrative, career as a professional reader of his own work that held out a stronger and more immediate promise of distraction from domestic miseries than work on a new novel. Apart from the money, there were two very powerful considerations in its favour. It would take him away from Tavistock House for long periods of time and it would constantly bring him face to face with sections of his adoring public, affording him, night after night, that supreme pleasure he had experienced in his amateur theatricals of 'seeing the house rise at you, one sea of delightful faces, one hurrah of applause!' But he needed to reassure himself that his special relationship with his readers, upon which his regular income depended, would not be adversely affected by this new departure. A letter to Evans of 16 March shows that he had already thought far ahead, envisaging a programme of London readings during the May/June lecture season to be followed by performances in the provinces and in Scotland during August, September and October, returning to give more readings in London over Christmas with 'a new Christmas Story written for the purpose'. This plan would still leave untouched Ireland and America, 'if I could resolve to go there', with the likelihood of clearing no less than £10,000 on a tour of the latter country. The big question, however, was 'would such an use of the personal (I may almost say affectionate) relations which subsist between me and the public, and make my standing with them very peculiar, at all affect my position with them as a writer? Would it be likely to have any influence on my next book?' (meaning its sales, of course). Evans probably sent him a reassuring answer and, once Dickens had learned that even Miss Coutts and Hannah Brown saw no objection to the scheme, he felt able to put aside Forster's opposition to it as what he called in a letter to Collins 'extraordinarily irrational'. The ecstatic reception of his charity reading in Edinburgh on 26 March further convinced him that this new career was what he needed at this time. 'My determination is all but taken,' he wrote to Forster on his return from Scotland: 'I must do *something*, or I shall wear my heart away. I can see no better thing to do that is half so hopeful in itself, or half so well suited to my restless state.'[19]

We do not know whether it was some particular quarrel that precipitated the end of the Dickens marriage in March or April, though most biographers favour a gossipy tale about an item of jewellery purchased by Dickens for Nelly and delivered by mistake to Catherine. It seems clear enough that his growing involvement with Nelly and her family was the thing that finally made the situation no longer bearable for him, if not also for Catherine whom he apparently ordered to pay a social call on Mrs Ternan. Just what the extent of that involvement was at this particular time, and what the attitudes of Nelly and her mother and her sisters were towards Dickens we simply do not know. We *do* know, from the evidence of playbills, that Nelly was still pursuing her stage career during 1858 but as a person she is, unlike her livelier sisters, a complete blank to us. And she remains so until after Dickens's death and her re-emergence as the wife of George Wharton Robinson. Plenty is known about her in this highly respectable phase of her existence, though nothing that really helps us to understand the enormous impact she had upon Dickens in her late teens. Dickens told Collins on 21 March that 'the Doncaster unhappiness' remained still so strong upon him that he could find no rest and that he had 'never known a moment's peace or content since the last night of the Frozen Deep'. This confidence perhaps refers to his having recognised in Doncaster that Nelly was the love of his life but a love that could never lead to marriage and the wording suggests that Collins was in the know but this can only be guesswork.[20]

Similarly, we can only assume that he might be making a coy reference to Nelly in the only piece that he wrote for *Household Words* this spring. 'Please To Leave Your Umbrella' (*HW*, 1 May 1858) describes a visit to Hampton Court one rainy spring day. Dickens writes that he has his 'little reason for being in the best of humours' with the place though 'that little reason is neither here (ah! I wish it were here!) nor there'. Later he indulges a fantasy about how 'I and my little reason . . . would keep house here, in perfect contentment', and the article ends with him and his 'little reason' leaving the palace, 'dreaming away' together under his umbrella, 'through the fast-falling spring rain, which had a sound in it that day like the rustle of the coming summer'. This certainly strikes a very different note from that reference to 'Doncaster unhappiness' but, again, we can only try to guess as to what has caused the change. One thing is clear, however. There could be no role for Nelly in Dickens's official narrative about the failure of his marriage, the one that Forster was faithfully to transmit to posterity as Dickens had trusted him to. At the actual period of the break-up Forster, who, as we have seen, had a genuine affection for Catherine and a deep concern for his friend's mental and emotional state at this time, seems to have struggled to keep the marriage going, as Georgina claimed she also did in a letter, very disloyal to her sister, that she sent Maria Winter on 31 May. In it she claimed that 'by some constitutional misfortune & incapacity, my sister *always* from their infancy, threw her children upon other people'. Fairly obviously, this letter was written at Dickens's instigation and one wonders if he could possibly have feared that Maria might flightily think herself and their former love somehow involved in his marital difficulties, especially given those remarkable letters he had written her in February 1855. It would, of course, have been very much in Georgina's own interests for the marriage to continue, at least as far as appearances were concerned. All mediation was unavailing, however, and on 30 March Dickens wrote to Forster, 'It is all despairingly over. . . . A dismal failure has to be borne, and there an end.'[21]

The only other narrative about the end of the marriage that we have, apart from Dickens's as transmitted to us by Forster, is contained in a long letter written at the end of August to a family friend of the Hogarths by Catherine's maternal aunt, Helen Thomson. There are also Katey's later comments on the subject, somewhat randomly set down by a friend of her extreme old age, Gladys Storey. Some of these are very striking but they hardly amount to a narrative. Thomson's letter tells us that 'all this distress [Dickens's determination to end the marriage, in fact if not appearance] came upon us like a thunder clap, just after his reading in Edinburgh last April when we had been so gratified by hearing him'. The Edinburgh reading, the one that had been such 'a wonderful go', in fact took place, as already noted, on 26 March so this would fit in with the date of Dickens's announcement to Forster about everything being 'despairingly over'. Weeks of painful negotiations followed during April and May. Initially Dickens made, according to Thomson, various 'absurd' and 'insulting' proposals to Catherine as, for example, that she should keep to her own apartments in his house in daily life, appearing as his hostess on social occasions, or else that she should live with a servant at Gad's Hill while he and the family were in Tavistock House and vice versa. These being all rejected, it became a question of a formal separation (divorce, even under the new Matrimonial Causes Act, was not an option). In dealing with the lawyers acting for Dickens and Catherine respectively Forster represented Dickens and Mark Lemon, so long the Dickens children's beloved 'Uncle Porpoise', represented Catherine. A provisional settlement seems to have been agreed by 7 May and two days later Dickens wrote to inform Burdett Coutts about the situation.[22]

In his letter to Burdett Coutts he continued to portray himself and Catherine as both victims of a tragic mistake: 'I believe that no two people were ever created, with such an impossibility of interest, sympathy, confidence, sentiment, tender union of any kind between them, as there is between my wife and me.' The marriage has been 'an immense misfortune' to both of them. He ends the letter by depicting Catherine as a truly pitiful creature, married to a man she is incapable of understanding: 'I think she has always felt herself at the disadvantage of groping blindly about me, and so has fallen into the most miserable weaknesses and jealousies' (this is a pre-emptive strike, perhaps, in case any rumours about Nelly should have reached Burdett Coutts's ears). For good measure he adds, 'Her mind has, at times, been certainly confused besides.' In between these two pathetic presentations of Catherine, however, he evidently feels a need to return to the 'bad mother' line he used in the letter to de la Rue and to elaborate on it. He begins with a proposition that hardly makes sense:

> If the children loved her, or ever had loved her, this severance would have been a far easier thing than it is. But she has never attached one of them to herself, never played with them in their infancy, never attracted their confidence as they have grown older, never presented herself before them in the aspect of a mother. I have seen them fall off from her in a natural – not *un*natural – progress of estrangement and at this moment I believe that Mary and Katey (whose dispositions are of the gentlest and most affectionate conceivable) harden into stone figures of girls when they can be got to go near her, and have their hearts shut up in her presence as if they closed by some horrid spring.

One does not need to know very much about the history of Catherine and her children to realise that the Bad Mother figure presented here must be seen as largely a creature of Dickens's imagination (complete with his hallmark fairy-tale element, introduced at the end). But clearly it was important for him to get himself to believe it – perhaps, as I have suggested before, as a way of enabling him to pity himself through pitying his children. Three months later, after his attitude to Catherine has evidently become much harsher, Dickens will, for some as yet undiscovered reason, carry the charge still further, telling Burdett Coutts (23 Aug.) that she must disbelieve the evidence of her own eyes when she sees Catherine together with any of her children: 'The little play that is acted in your Drawing-room is not the truth, and the less the children play it, the better for themselves, because they know it is not the truth.'[23]

Meanwhile, he had finally taken 'the Plunge' as he called it and embarked on his career as a paid public reader with a reading of *The Cricket on the Hearth* at St Martin's Hall in Long Acre on the evening of Thursday 29 April. Given all the gossip that was beginning to circulate about his domestic affairs, he might reasonably have been somewhat apprehensive about his reception but, if so, he was quickly reassured. The capacity audience of three thousand received him, recalled Edmund Yates, 'with a roar of cheering which might have been heard at Charing Cross, and which was again and again renewed'. He made a brief introductory speech stressing his conviction that becoming a paid performer of his own works involved 'no possible compromise of the credit and independence of literature', also that 'in these times whatever brings a public man and his public face to face, on terms of mutual confidence and respect' was 'a good thing'. In his case, it could only strengthen that special relationship amounting almost to 'personal friendship' which it was his privilege, pride and responsibility to have with his multitudinous readers. 'And thus it is', he concluded, 'that I proceed to read this little book, quite as composedly as I

41 St Martin's Hall, Long Acre

might proceed to write it, or to publish it in any other way.' This event was not, Yates wrote in a *Daily News* review the following day, like a public entertainment but rather 'a very large family party, gathered round the kindest, the dearest, the best of their friends', which was very much the atmosphere that Dickens always sought to evoke on these occasions.[24]

For the next three months, greatly dependent always upon the support and skill of his excellent manager Arthur Smith for whom he had considerable personal fondness, Dickens read at St Martin's Hall every Thursday and most Wednesdays. His choice and treatment of texts for this programme will be discussed in the next chapter. Then on 2 August he embarked upon a very demanding tour of England, Ireland and Scotland which lasted until 13 November and comprised 85 performances in all. This was an average of five or six a week so that it is not surprising that he should sometimes have felt himself to be 'a perfect galley-slave' whilst at the same time being exhilarated by both the tremendous financial and emotional rewards of this experience. To Wilkie Collins he confessed on 11 August that he would be 'heartily glad' when the tour was over because he missed his 'quiet room and desk' – but immediately added, 'perhaps it is best for me not to have it just now, and to wear and tear my Storm away – or as much of it as will ever calm down while the water rolls – in this restless manner'.[25]

During the weeks following Dickens's inauguration of his career as a professional reader London's 'chattering classes' (as we would now call them) were busy with speculations about the collapse of his marriage and about who else, besides himself and Catherine, might be involved. Georgina had made herself an obvious target for gossip by choosing to remain with her brother-in-law, asserting, according to Helen Thomson's letter, that 'a man of genius ought not to be judged with the common herd of men'. Gossip about her in relation to Dickens was potentially very damaging indeed for him since at this time sexual relations between a brother and sister-in-law would have been regarded as incestuous. Others had somehow got wind of Dickens's involvement with the Ternans, with Mrs Hogarth and her youngest daughter Helen apparently being one source of such stories. To help Smith counteract these last rumours in case they should lead to problems in making arrangements for the forthcoming Readings tour, Dickens gave him a written statement on 25 May with a covering letter authorising him to show the document to whomever he thought fit. This document became known as 'the Violated Letter' after it had, three months later, been published, apparently without Smith's connivance, in the American press and copied thence into certain English newspapers. In this statement Dickens took the same line about both Catherine and Georgina that he had taken in his earlier letter to Burdett Coutts. But Catherine is also now represented (notwithstanding Dickens's grand words about 'that manly consideration toward Mrs Dickens which I owe to my wife') as believing that the stresses of their marriage aggravated 'a mental disorder under which she sometimes labours'. She had, Dickens claims, long been asking him for a separation because 'she felt herself unfit for the life she had to lead as my wife' but he had always replied that they had to stay together, at least in appearance, for the children's sake. But, he continues, Forster has now persuaded him it would be better, even for the children, if he and Catherine were to separate. Referring to what he calls, using a favourite adjective of his father's, the 'pecuniary part' of the separation agreement, he writes, with a distressing vulgarity that will surface again in connection with the same topic in his will, that it is 'as generous as if Mrs Dickens were a lady of distinction, and I a man of fortune'. He imprudently ends the letter with a mysterious and tantalising reference to 'two wicked persons' who were spreading rumours about the involvement in the matter of 'a young lady for whom I have a great attachment and regard' and whom he passionately declares to be most 'virtuous and spotless ... innocent and pure ... as good as my own dear daughters'.[26]

The result of this statement, which Smith seems to have begun showing to people almost immediately, was naturally to fuel the gossip with speculation about the identities of the 'two wicked persons' and the spotless young lady. Thackeray knew of the statement's existence but had not yet seen it when he heard at the Garrick that Dickens had banished his wife on account of an intrigue he was having with Georgina. Writing to his mother, he described his response: 'No says I no such thing – its with an actress – and the other story [about Georgina] has not got to Dickens's ears but this has – and he fancies that I am going about abusing him.' He goes on to say that he got his story from a man at Epsom: 'There is some row about an actress in the case, & he [Dickens] denies with the utmost infuriation any charge against her or himself – but says that it has been known to any one intimate with his family that his and his wife's tempers were horribly incompatible & now the children are grown up [Edward was only six in fact] – it is agreed they are to part . . . '. He has not seen Dickens's letter but would give £100 for the story not to be true: 'To think of the poor matron after 22 years of marriage going away out of her house! Oh dear me its a fatal story for our trade.' One cannot help thinking how enraged Dickens would have been with the suggestion that his behaviour was damaging to what he liked to call his 'order', and Thackeray's use of the word 'trade' speaks volumes about the opposed attitudes of himself and Dickens in the great 'Dignity of Literature' debate.[27]

The final terms for the Deed of Settlement seem to have been agreed by 26 May but then Dickens heard that his mother-in-law and her youngest daughter were still going about repeating 'those amazing slanders', presumably about his involvement with Nelly. He refused to proceed any further until they had been forced to sign a sworn statement (subsequently attached to the 'Violated Letter') that they did not believe such rumours and knew that Catherine did not believe them either. Dickens was at this stage still seeing Catherine as someone more to be pitied than blamed and he asked his lawyer to convey to her, through her lawyer, his assurance that he did not at all accuse her of involvement in this scandal-mongering: 'She has a great tenderness for me, and I sincerely believe would be glad to shew it. . . . It would be a pleasure to her (I think) that I had begun to trust her so far; and I believe that it would do her lasting good if you could convey that assurance to her.' It must have been a delicate business for Catherine's lawyer to convey this message to her, perhaps in front of her mother, after tracking her down to Brighton where Mrs Hogarth had taken her for a fortnight's rest, hoping to alleviate her 'distress and agitation'. Here she finally signed the deed of separation on 4 June.[28]

At this point, with everything legally settled, Dickens seems to have decided that it was not enough to have his vindication of his actions circulating only in manuscript form, in the statement given to Smith. Reassured as he may have been by audiences' reception of him at St Martin's Hall, he still wanted to ensure that his wider public should know the truth (the truth as he saw it, that is). He had been for the past month labouring under a tremendous 'sense of Wrong', he wrote to Yates on 8 June, so that his heart was 'jagged and rent and out of shape'. Despite strong objections by Forster and other friends, he determined, after conferring with John Delane the formidable editor of *The*

Times, to seek relief by issuing what we should now call a press statement. This first appeared in *The Times* on 7 June, from which it was copied into other daily papers, and then in the issue of *Household Words* for 12 June, under the heading 'Personal'. After a brief preamble about the history of his special relationship with the public and an appeal to all his 'brethren', knowing as they do how true he has always been to 'our common calling', to help in the dissemination of his words, Dickens wrote:

> Some domestic trouble of mine, of long-standing, on which I will make no further remark than that it claims to be respected, as being of a sacredly private nature, has lately been brought to an arrangement, which involves no anger or ill-will of any kind, and the whole origin, progress, and surrounding circumstances of which have been, throughout, within the knowledge of my children. It is amicably composed, and its details have now but to be forgotten by those concerned in it.
>
> By some means, arising out of wickedness, or out of folly, or out of inconceivable wild chance, or out of all three, this trouble has been made the occasion of misrepresentations, most grossly false, most monstrous, and most cruel – involving, not only me, but innocent persons dear to my heart, and innocent persons of whom I have no knowledge, if, indeed, they have any existence – and so widely spread, that I doubt if one reader in a thousand will peruse these lines, by whom some touch of the breath of these slanders will not have passed, like an unwholesome air.

He concludes with a declaration, both in his own name and in Catherine's, that all the 'whispered rumours' are 'abominably false' and anyone now repeating them 'will lie as wilfully and as foully as it is possible for any false witness to lie, before Heaven and earth'. Before sending this statement for publication he sent a copy to Catherine asking if she had any objection to the allusion to herself. In a covering note he wrote, 'Whoever there may be among the living, whom I will never forgive, alive or dead, I earnestly hope all unkindness is over between you and me'. She made no difficulty, it seems, and Dickens may still have had some idea of maintaining a friendship with Catherine, or so she was told. 'Surely he cannot mean it', she wrote to her aunt, 'as I feel that if I were ever to see him by chance it would almost kill me'.[29]

In this statement Dickens is writing directly to his public. Contrastingly, there is a kind of private – one could almost say coded – writing that he seems to have enjoyed practising at this time. This was the copying out, presumably for autograph-hunters, of substantial extracts from *David Copperfield*. No fewer than three examples dated by Dickens on dates between 28 April and 26 June 1858 have come to light in the sale-rooms in recent years. They are drawn from chapters 37 and 44, which deal with David's mistaken marriage to Dora (who saves the day by obligingly dying of weakness soon after the loss of her baby). That Dickens should, at this crisis in his personal life, be so much revisiting this particular episode of this particular novel is certainly remarkable.[30]

The result of the publication of Dickens's 'Personal' statement was, naturally, to publicise his domestic difficulties far beyond the world of the metropolitan literati but this does not seem to have done him much damage, certainly not to have had any effect on the numbers and enthusiastic responsiveness of his audiences either in London or in the provinces, Scotland or Ireland. The most dramatic consequence of his insistence on publishing this statement was his quarrel with Bradbury and Evans and, more sadly, with his old friend and fellow-actor Mark Lemon over their failure as, respectively, proprietors and editor of *Punch* to publish his 'Personal' statement in that magazine. That he should have wished, or should have thought it appropriate, for such an item to appear in the pages of a comic miscellany marks, as the Pilgrim editors aptly comment, 'the extremity of his irrational behaviour' at this time. He would have viewed that matter very differently of course. He had called upon his 'brethren', that is, all his fellow writers, members of a profession he had done so much to champion and to raise in public esteem, to help in disseminating his words and here were his own publishers and one of his closest and oldest literary friends refusing to do so. On 17 June, according to a statement published the following year by Bradbury and Evans, they learned 'from a common friend [presumably Forster], that Mr Dickens had resolved to break off his connection with them'. He wrote very harshly to Evans on 22 July that he could no longer deal with anyone who had been false to him 'in the only great need and under the only great wrong' he had ever known and from that time on the fate of *Household Words* was sealed. Preoccupied with his reading tour, Dickens decided to wait until the next half-yearly audit day, 9 November, before initiating steps to dissolve his partnership with Bradbury and Evans. His intention, which in due course he relentlessly carried out, was to shut down *Household Words* at the end of the nineteenth volume (28 May 1859). He would 'conduct' one last Christmas number for the journal, therefore and inaugurate a completely new weekly journal which he would own and publish himself.[31]

Bradbury and Evans could not be excluded from the new venture of the Library Edition, however. Chapman and Hall had launched this in the spring with some of the novels they controlled, *Pickwick, Nickleby, Chuzzlewit*, and the first volume of *The Old Curiosity Shop* (the edition was being simultaneously published in America by Ticknor and Fields who bought 3,500 copies of each volume from Chapman and Hall). The *Shop* was not long enough to fill out a second volume so Dickens supplied the shortfall by collecting, under the somewhat uninspired title of *Reprinted Pieces*, as many *Household Words* essays written solely by himself as were needed to fill the volume. This brought in Bradbury and Evans and on 3 July Dickens sent Bradbury's son Henry a list of the thirty-one items he had selected (out of a potential eighty or so) saying he wanted them published in the order in which he had listed them and not in chronological order of first publication. *Reprinted Pieces* opens with the dramatic/pathetic narrative of 'The Long Voyage' and ends with the richly retrospective 'A Christmas Tree', counted nowadays as the first 'Christmas Story'. In between, and grouped together wherever such grouping was appropriate, came the earliest Christmas stories, all his seaside sketches (Broadstairs, Boulogne, Folkestone, Dover) and all his police-related articles, together with a few satirical pieces and a number of his finest familiar essays, not including, however, some others equally fine such as 'Where We Stopped Growing' and 'Gone Astray'.[32]

Dickens's life at this time offers two contrasting pictures. On the one hand, there is the resplendent Public Reader with his fully-documented itinerary and his dazzling, fully-reported performances before packed and rapturous audiences in cities throughout England, Scotland and Ireland. On the other, there is Dickens the private man whose personal life was undergoing a tremendous sea-change about which his adoring public knew virtually nothing. True, plenty of scurrilous rumours were afloat both about his relations with Georgina and about his relations with the Ternan family. At one stage Dickens even had to threaten an action for slander against a certain Glaswegian journalist who, after returning from a visit to the capital, was reported to have gone about saying Dickens was 'the outcry of London' and that Georgina had already borne him three children. Other scandalmongers seized on the Ternans but on the wrong sister. Gossip about Dickens's connection with Fanny reached the ears of her American cousin Richard Spofford and Dickens was quick to send him a letter glowing with conscious virtue and disinterested benevolence. The publication of the so-called 'Violated Letter' in the American and English press during August inevitably spread the gossip more widely. But no one beyond Dickens's immediate family and two or three intimate friends like Wills, Forster and Collins (as well, of course, as the Ternans themselves) knew anything about what was really going on. The Hogarth family's perception of the situation we can gather from Helen Thomson's letter, which also gives us a glimpse of a remarkable document now lost, namely a letter written by Dickens to his older children that was clearly one of the more striking examples of the way in which he wrote Catherine out of the family. Thomson writes:

> As to the platonic attachment he [Dickens] has had the bad taste and boldness to profess to a young actress, and which he wrote to his elder children their mother had not character to appreciate, and which he intruded on the notice of the public in his foolish and egotistical statement, I can only compare it to 'the wicked fleeing where no man pursueth'. What has the public to do with what ought to be his private affairs? . . .[33]

Today, for all the intensive researches that, for well over a century, have been made into every aspect of Dickens's existence, we know little more about his personal life during the latter half of 1858 than did his contemporaries. From such scraps of evidence as have chanced to survive, it is, however, clear enough that he was involving himself more and more in the affairs of Nelly and her family. He no doubt master-minded Fanny's late-September move to Florence in order to pursue her musical education there. The intention was that she should remain a year abroad, and Mrs Ternan went with her to get her settled. Dickens wrote letters of introduction for her and most likely made some contribution towards the costs of the arrangement (indeed, he may well have paid most of the expenses but his bank records are unrevealing on this point). Having persuaded Mrs Ternan that the little Canonbury house in which she and her daughters were living was 'unwholesome', he probably helped to settle Maria and Nelly in the lodgings they took in Berners Street, off Oxford Street, a convenient location for returning home late at night from the respective theatres (the Haymarket and the Strand) at which the two girls had engagements. That he was much concerned for their well-being is evidenced by his asking the discreet Wills on 25 October to enquire at Scotland Yard about some 'dangerous and unwarrantable conduct' towards them on the part of a certain policeman. Dickens suspected this officer might have been suborned by some 'Swell' with designs upon one or other of the sisters or, indeed, both. Meanwhile, his attitude towards Catherine seems for some reason to have taken a turn for the worse and in the letter to Burdett Coutts of 23 August already cited he not only reiterated his 'bad mother' charges against her but wrote of her as a treacherous enemy: 'the weak hand that never could help or serve my name in the least, has struck at it – in conjunction with the wickedest people, whom I have loaded with benefits [i.e., her mother and sister Helen]'. Writing to Georgina on 12 September, he cannot even bear to name her but refers to her as 'your sister'.[34]

In the midst of all his public triumphs he seems to have been smarting from a sense of injured merit, something that only the nightly-renewed love and adulation of his great audiences, the 'personal affection' that they 'poured out' upon him, could assuage. When he performed at Manchester on 18 September the audience's welcome of him was, he told Forster, 'astounding in its affectionate regard of the late trouble' and quite 'unmanned' him. Ten days or so later in Edinburgh (where his daughters had joined him) he seems to have reached some sort of crisis-point. It was at that time, he later told Mary Boyle (9 Dec.), that 'my sense of cruel wrong was strongest within me'. He responded by resolving 'to put the subject away from me, and to know no more of it'. But his imagination, stimulated by the need to begin thinking about a last Christmas Number for *Household Words*, was playing with the idea of a very different sort of reaction on the part of someone with a grievance against the world. On 6 September he outlined to Collins a possible scheme for a story: 'some disappointed person, man or woman, prematurely disgusted with the world for some reason or no reason (the person should be young I think) retires to an old lonely house, or an old lonely mill, or anything you like, with one attendant, resolved to shut out the world and have no communion with it' (making the protagonist a young person would, of course, help to distance the story from his own situation, as well as accentuating the folly of the character's behaviour). Through the agency of the attendant this folly would be gradually exposed and the recluse made to learn that 'you can't shut out the world – that you are in it to be of it – that you get into a false position the moment you try to sever yourself from it – and that you must mingle with it, and make the best of it, and make the best of yourself into the bargain'.

Dickens continued to make the best of his world in all respects. Whatever modus vivendi he had established with Nelly in particular, and with the Ternan family in general, by the time he finished his gruelling Readings tour in mid-November, it seems to have been one that worked for him, as did his domestic life at Gad's Hill, meticulously organised for him by Georgina. Certain family problems he had always with him. The incorrigible Fred's marital problems, if linked with Augustus's earlier and widely publicised desertion of *his* wife and subsequent flight to America with another woman, could have become a major public embarrassment for him. This did not happen since Victorian journalists did not hound the families of the famous in the way they do today. Another source of tension was the so-called 'Garrick Club Affair' involving Thackeray and Edmund Yates, who had published a somewhat derogatory account of Thackeray, including his demeanour at the Garrick, in a new gossip magazine called *Town Talk*. This brouhaha had been running on since the summer and now ended with Yates's expulsion from the Club, Dickens's resignation from it, and his ceasing to be on speaking terms with Thackeray – as a consequence, Thackeray believed, of 'pent up animosities and long cherished hatred'. On the whole, however, Dickens seems now to have been in a more emotionally stable state than he had been for some time. He had been reassured and re-energised by the heady triumphs of his Readings tour and had established some sort of a settled – necessarily very private – relationship with Nelly. He could return to his pen with renewed zest and begin to look forward to launching his new journal and the new serial that he was planning for it.[35]

Meanwhile there was the last *Household Words* Christmas number to be organised. Dickens's original notion of a self-deluding recluse was abandoned (or perhaps 'shelved' would be a better word since it resurfaced three years later, prompted by Dickens's encounter with a real-life hermit) though the 'lonely house' element was retained. The number was called 'A House To Let', the house in question being a desolate-looking one across the road from another house taken by an old lady, the narrator of the number, who becomes curious about it and gets her manservant Trottle and her elderly beau Jarber to investigate its history. This framework story allows for narratives by other hands to be brought in, but Dickens and Collins ultimately wrote the whole number between them apart from two contributions, Gaskell's 'The Manchester Marriage' and a poem by Adelaide Anne Procter. Dickens and Collins worked on the number together at Gad's Hill at Dickens's suggestion and later, on 29 November, put in a whole day at the *Household Words* office, to finish it. They collaborated on the framework narrative and wrote one story each. Dickens's story, 'Going into Society', is narrated by a showman called Magsman (an echo of 'Thomas Mag', the first name Dickens thought of for the hero of *David Copperfield*). Magsman tells the story of Mr Chops, a remarkable dwarf who was once part of his freak show. Chops suddenly came into a fortune as a result of winning in the lottery and 'went into society' with unhappy consequences. The themes of showmanship and of society's attitude towards those who exhibit themselves for money would, for obvious reasons, have been more present than usual in Dickens's mind at this time. Another theme, that of unrequited love, is here treated in serio-comic form, with Mr Chops nourishing a hopeless passion for a Fat Lady whose love is already bestowed elsewhere. It is tempting to think that this might be an indication that Dickens's feelings towards Nelly were no longer so turbulent as they had been a year earlier when he was at work on 'The Perils of Certain English Prisoners'.

After finishing 'Going into Society' Dickens found himself so taken with the story and its 'odd idea' which was 'so humorous, and so available at greater length' that he thought of withdrawing it and making it 'the Pivot round which my next book shall revolve'. He could hardly have been referring here to *A Tale of Two Cities*, the general scheme for which was already in his head by this time, but his comment does seem to fit the next novel after that, *Great Expectations*, which does indeed 'pivot' around another ill-fated foray into society. In the event, Dickens did not hold back the story and it duly appeared in what was to be the last Christmas number of *Household Words*, published on 7 December. He added a pleasant touch to the end of the story by having the old lady buy the house to let and turn it into a Hospital for Sick Children, thereby avoiding the 'unseasonable grimness' which the working out of the framework-story plot as proposed by Collins would have involved.[36]

The last thing Dickens wrote in this momentous year, which had seen such enormous changes in all aspects of his life, was a remarkable retrospect of that life entitled 'New Year's Day'. It was to be the last thing he would ever write for *Household Words* and appeared as the lead article in the issue for 1 January 1859. This beautifully-crafted essay, written in reminiscent – ostensibly autobiographical – vein, vividly evokes scenes, real or imaginary,

from the writer's past with mingled humour and nostalgia and looks forward
to some of the finest of the Uncommercial Traveller's 'samples' that were to
feature in *All The Year Round* during the next decade. Dickens conjures up
scenes from his infancy, childhood, young manhood and more recent years,
interweaving fact and fiction in such a way as to baffle the unravelling powers
of the biographer's art. The use of Mrs Pipchin's name for 'the grim and
unsympathetic old personage of the female gender . . . dressed in black crape'
who drags him as a child along Oxford Street should alert us to the kind of
interweaving process that is evidently going on here (see above, p. 5). The
adventure Dickens describes that he shared with his little sister involving a
man with a wooden leg may be a much embroidered memory or it may be
pure comic invention (Dickens can never keep wooden legs out of his writings
for very long); but the description of the same beloved sister on her deathbed
believing she could smell the fallen leaves in the woods in which they had
walked as very young children is a moment of piercing factual truth. Memories
of Mr Beadnell, advanced to country-house status, and of Maria must lurk
somewhere behind those memorable figures of the writer's young manhood,
prosperous and hospitable old Mr Boles and Miss Boles, 'a blessed creature: a
Divinity' who is now a matron, 'and I have outlived my passion for her, and
I perceive her appetite to be healthy and her nose to be red'. The splendours
of the Peschiere in Genoa are recalled as though the place belonged in *The
Arabian Nights* but Dickens also includes the historical detail of the great
Twelfth Cake that was sent all the way from London to Genoa in January 1845.
From Genoa the memory-trail leads on to Paris and the essay ends with an
elaborately-detailed evocation of Dickens's Parisian New Year of 1856, and all
his enchanted delighted theatre-going in that 'brilliantly lighted' city which
'shines out like the gardens of the Wonderful Lamp'.

What is completely absent from the essay is any allusion, however remote,
to the fact that the writer had ever been a married man. The Twelfth Cake was,
as we know, sent to Genoa by Burdett Coutts for Charley's birthday but this
detail is not mentioned because to introduce any of the children would have
been to introduce, at least by implication, their mother. The 'we' who are
described as celebrating this Genoese New Year may be the writer's family but
they melt into the 'handful of English dwelling in that city' and attention is
quickly diverted to the 'rare old Italian Cavaliere' who is also of the party and
who is developed into a richly comic figure. In this wonderful essay for the
New Year Dickens finally completes the process of writing off his marriage and
altogether banishing Catherine from his life. 'That figure', he was to write
grimly to Burdett Coutts sixteen months later, 'is out of my life for evermore
(except to darken it) and my desire is, Never to see it again'.[37]

CHAPTER 20

Stories into scripts

THE PUBLIC READINGS, 1858

When I first entered on this interpretation of myself . . . I was sustained by the hope that I could drop into some hearts, some new expression of the meaning of my books, that would touch them in a new way. To this hour that purpose is so strong in me . . . that, after hundreds of nights, I come with a feeling of perfect freshness to that little red table, and laugh and cry with my hearers, as if I had never stood there before.

Dickens to Robert Lytton, 17 April 1867

DICKENS'S FIRST reading as a professional, *The Cricket on the Hearth* at St Martin's Hall on 29 April 1858, was, as we have seen, rapturously received. He had read the *Cricket* publicly just once before, for charity, and performed it only once more during his London readings, and also once in Edinburgh in September, but never again thereafter. He perhaps felt that in order to work well this little 'fairy tale of home' needed a more intimate venue, such as Ary Scheffer's Parisian atelier, where he gave a private reading of it in December 1855. His chief prompt-book for the *Cricket* shows, however, that he worked just as hard on it as he did on the other readings. He worked over it more than once, in fact, as is shown by the different-coloured inks used, trying to shorten it enough to make it fit into the two hours that was the standard length, punctuated with a ten-minute interval, for a reading.[1]

Dickens's prompt-books are specially-prepared copies that he had printed of the texts he chose for his readings. In the case of the Christmas Books he had the pages of a copy of the published text inlaid in larger-sized paper, and then had the volume bound in red half-morocco gilt so as to look good on the platform. The larger 'frame' page gave plenty of space for deletion marks, the insertion of new copy and stage-directions ('Tone to Mystery', 'Cheerful', 'Tone to Pathos', and so on). When long passages of the original printed text, usually descriptive or narrative, were cut Dickens stuck the unwanted pages together with postage-stamps or sealing wax. He had reading copies of two more of the Christmas Books, *The Chimes* and *The Haunted Man*, similarly bound up and then marked them up with additions and deletions as he had done the *Carol* prompt-book. In the case of *The Haunted Man*, however, he gave up working on the text two-thirds of the way through the book, probably after deciding that this brooding tale could not be made dramatic enough in form to be developed into a reading – especially since, in keeping the focus on its gloomy hero Redlaw, he had to cut so much from the book's liveliest passages, those dealing with the family life of the Tetterbys and their Moloch of a baby.[2]

The Christmas Books were an obvious quarry for Dickens's readings repertoire not only because their novella-type length meant that any one of them could, with careful cutting, be adapted as a whole for a two-hour reading but also because in their original format they already exemplified a more intimately personal mode of communication between Dickens and his readers than did his full-length novels. This is pre-eminently the case in the *Carol* in which the narrator says at one point, 'I am standing in the spirit at your elbow' – a sentence superfluous in the reading text and therefore cut – but *The Chimes* and the *Cricket* do both also convey the strong sense of a narrating voice and both end with personal little codas, which Dickens naturally retained in the reading versions. But the *Carol* as a potential reading text definitely scores over *The Chimes* and the *Cricket* in another respect, and that is in terms of dramatic form. The *Carol*'s plot is clear, simple and highly effective and calls for some twenty distinct voices (the boy Scrooge sends to buy the turkey was one of the highlights of this reading) whereas both *The Chimes* and the *Cricket* have more elaborate plots, like miniature novels, but yet involve fewer voices in each case.

While he was still reading only for charity Dickens stuck to the *Carol*, apart from that one performance of the *Cricket*. But he yearned, he told Arthur Ryland in 1855, for 'a swim in the broader waters of one of my long books'. He had been trying, he told Ryland, to evolve a reading from *Copperfield* which, with its first-person narration, might seem favourable material for such an enterprise but which proved recalcitrant. With *Dombey and Son*, however, he managed better. Memories of the enthusiastic reception of his readings of the first two numbers of this novel to private audiences in Lausanne in 1846, which had first made him think of the idea of reading for his own profit, probably prompted him to turn his attention to this particular book. He saw that a coherent, and dramatically effective, reading focused on little Paul Dombey could be developed from the first five numbers (chs 1–16). The story of Paul's brief, beleaguered life has a clear beginning, middle and end, and could therefore very well stand alone as a complete story when extracted from the novel. Moreover, Paul's death, like Little Nell's and the pathos of Tiny Tim, had occasioned periods of particularly strong empathy between Dickens and his readers, an empathy that surely might not only be revived but also enhanced by his actually telling the story in person to a live audience, 'touching them in a new way'. The reading that he did evolve, *The Story of Little Dombey*, was first performed at St Martin's Hall on 10 June and next day Dickens reported to

Maclise, 'We had an amazing scene of weeping and cheering . . . certainly I never saw a crowd so resolved into one creature before, or so stirred by any thing.' *Little Dombey* became one of the most popular of all his readings after the *Carol*, though he gave it only rarely after 1861 – partly, perhaps, because the intense description of Paul's deathbed scene, and the very last words of the reading about 'the swift river' that is bearing us 'to the ocean', became steadily more uncomfortable for the increasingly mortality-haunted Dickens to read.[3]

The prompt-copy for *Little Dombey* could not be created in the same way as those for the readings from the Christmas Books since the pages of the novel were too densely printed to serve as the basis of a script to be read on stage. Dickens therefore had the pages he wanted extracted from a copy of the novel and collated. After he had made various manuscript additions and deletions, these pages were reprinted in larger type with wide margins. He then worked again, in great detail, over the newly-printed text, once in black ink and once in blue, painting out major deletions with a red wash, making numerous manuscript alterations, and underlining many words for emphasis. The reading as first devised occupied a whole two-hour programme and covered Paul's birth, christening, successive sojourns at Pipchin's and Blimber's, return home, illness and death. It was later cut to accommodate a half-hour afterpiece and still further reduced later on. The christening chapter disappeared completely, together with many secondary characters like Miss Tox. The effect of these successive prunings was to focus ever more strongly upon Paul and Florence. Mr Toots, whose well-meaning inanities were much relished by audiences, provided comedy that does not detract from but rather enhances the pathos attached to Paul whose littleness never ceases to astonish Toots. The one part of *Little Dombey* that was not cut over the years was Paul's deathbed scene which is almost word for word as in the novel (ch.16), with only the passage about Walter Gay excised.

A similar process to that used for making the prompt-book for *Little Dombey* was followed in the case of the three short readings Dickens introduced, as a group, into his repertoire in the ninth week of his tour: *The Poor Traveller, Boots at the Holly-Tree Inn* and *Mrs Gamp*. What reasons, apart from their convenient length, could he have had for choosing the first two of these items? In the case of *The Poor Traveller* (the tale of Richard Doubledick and the French officer from the 1854 Christmas number of *Household Words*) Dickens was perhaps influenced by the fact that the Crimean War was recent enough for the story still to have a certain topical resonance for audiences (he rarely performed it after 1859). In *Boots at the Holly-Tree Inn* and *Mrs Gamp* he was evidently going for strong ventriloquial effects, using two of his most popular characters to date. His impersonation of the Cockney Boots from the 1855 Christmas number of *Household Words* was much admired, and Boots's sentimental anecdote about the runaway infant lovers, the text of which Dickens found he needed to change hardly at all for the reading, evoked an expression of 'playful pity' on the faces of audiences that he thought 'tender and pleasant'. When he read Boots at Plymouth, he reported to Wills, 'the people gave themselves up altogether (Generals, Mayors, and Shillings equally) to a perfect transport of enjoyment of him and the two children'. In *Mrs Gamp* he stitched together passages from different parts of *Chuzzlewit* involving a good deal of Gamp dialogue and went to much trouble over the years to achieve a satisfactory balance between Mrs Gamp's speeches and the rest of the reading, speeches by others and passages of narrative. But he could not ultimately satisfy himself with a reading like this that consisted only of parts of a whole: 'You cannot feel the fragmentary nature of a broken reading without a continuous story, more than I do,' he wrote to the Rev. William Brookfield on 20 June 1859. 'I detest it. But the Public always like it, occasionally, and therefore I give it them.'[4]

With the addition of these three shorter pieces, at first always performed together to make up a full evening's programme, Dickens's repertoire for his first readings tour was almost complete. As already noted, he virtually dropped the *Cricket*, and there was one other reading he performed only very occasionally even though audiences apparently always found it powerfully effective. This was *The Chimes*, and one reason for his performing it less frequently may have been that he could not so easily tone down the social-protest, 'Hungry Forties', element in it as he could in the *Carol*. In the reading version of the latter Scrooge's confrontation with Ignorance and Want disappears and, in successive prunings of the readings text, the emphasis falls more and more upon the Cratchits' joyous Christmas dinner, the only part of the original *Carol* text to survive almost untouched. *The Chimes* may have come to seem somewhat dated in the more prosperous days of the late 1850s and Dickens, on the rare occasions when he did present it, felt it necessary to make a little prefatory speech in which he recalled the circumstances of its composition in 1844 and expressed his belief that, although there might now be less need for his message of social protest, 'a few hints for compassionate and merciful remembrance are never out of date in the Christian calendar'.[5]

Copies of Dickens's readings text were published by Bradbury and Evans with green paper covers for sale to his audiences. In the case of the readings derived from the Christmas Books they were simply the texts of the *Carol*, *Chimes* and *Cricket* as first published and with none of the changes made in the prompt-copies. The reading edition copies of *Little Dombey* and of *The Poor Traveller, Boots at the Holly-Tree Inn* and *Mrs Gamp* printed together, are simply the texts of the prompt-copies as Dickens had them privately printed before he began to edit them. In his letters Dickens mentions these reading books as selling well but their publication was not, apparently a profitable venture.[6]

42 Dickens giving a public reading, woodcut by C. A. Barry in *Harper's Weekly*, 7 December 1867

Dickens's hugely successful series of London readings ended on 22 July and only two weeks later he embarked on his gruelling three-month tour of the English provinces, Ireland and Scotland. With him went the team that had supported him in his London performances, headed by the amiable and admirably efficient Arthur Smith, whom Dickens described as 'something between a Home Secretary and a furniture-dealer in Rathbone Place. He is always either corresponding in the genteelest manner, or dragging rout seats [hired chairs] about without his coat.' Dickens was also accompanied by John Thompson, his manservant of many years' standing, Boycett, his gasman who rigged up the special lighting he required, and Berry, a general assistant. He had designed his own reading-desk which came up only to his waist so that the audience could see as much of his figure as possible. It was covered with green baize, changed at some later date to crimson, and had on it, on the left-hand side, a box, similarly covered, which could act as a book-rest or a prop. Behind him he had a large screen which helped to project his voice into the audience and before him stood his lighting-apparatus, two gas-pipes about twelve feet high which held in place a batten of gas-jets that concentrated a powerful light on his face so that it was clearly visible from every part of the hall. All this equipment travelled with him and was erected in each new venue. He always wore immaculate evening dress as part of his seeking to create, just as his great model Charles Mathews had done before him in his 'At Homes', that desired drawing-room ambiance so important for reassuring those many members of the middle classes who would have been horrified by the thought of witnessing a regular theatrical representation.[7]

Once the tour was under way Dickens introduced only one new reading into his repertoire. This was *Bardell and Pickwick*, or *The Trial from Pickwick* as it was more often called, a short virtuoso piece for eight voices, just under thirty minutes long and adapted from chapter 34 of what was, apart from the *Carol*, his best-known and best-loved book and had now become, like the *Carol*, part of the very fabric of English life. In a letter to Beard of 20 October he says he just 'took it into his head' to read the *Trial* (the main reading of the evening was *Little Dombey*) but this is misleading. The *Trial* would certainly have been as thoroughly prepared and intensively rehearsed as any of the other readings. He would subsequently often read it as an afterpiece to *Little Dombey* or to a similarly shortened *Carol*, so that his regular evening's programme began to resemble the standard nineteenth-century theatrical format of a full-length play followed by a farce to round off the evening and send the audience home in high good humour. The *Trial* became, in fact, after the *Carol* the most popular of all his readings, with Dickens's physical transformation of himself into the person of the fat little judge, Mr Justice Stareleigh being particularly admired. Another of its high points was the inclusion in it of Sam Weller, one of the most popular of all his characters. In the letter to Beard about the first performance of the *Trial* quoted above he reported that when Sergeant Buzfuz said, 'Call Samuel Weller!' the audience 'gave a great thunder of applause, as if he were really coming in'. It became customary, in fact, for audiences to cheer and applaud at that point, a phenomenon that one American commentator rightly saw as 'such an unaffected tribute of admiration as few authors have ever obtained'.[8]

Dickens's letters during the autumn and winter of 1858–59 are full of delight and gratification over the success of the readings, the responsiveness of his audiences, and the substantial financial rewards the venture was bringing him. 'My clear profit', he tells Burdett Coutts on 27 October, '– my own, after all deductions and expenses – has been more than a Thousand Guineas a month'. He quickly goes on to say, however, what was undoubtedly true, that the greatest thing for him has been the way in which audiences everywhere have 'delighted to express that they have a personal affection for me and the interest of tender friends in me'. This, he tells her, 'is (especially at this time) high and far above all other considerations'. There is a certain note of emphasis, perhaps, in Dickens's 'at this time', resulting from his awareness that Burdett Coutts was unhappy about the recent upheaval in the Dickens household and was particularly concerned by the treatment of Catherine, whom she had apparently invited to make her home with her.[9]

The money and the great personal affection demonstrated by his audiences were both highly important to Dickens the man but perhaps the most important

thing of all for Dickens the writer was that each performance allowed him literally to 'write a book in company' in a more literal and even more exhilarating way
than did performing Richard Wardour with the necessary aid of his fellow-actors.
He performed alone just as he wrote alone in his study. Here, however, he was
working not with his mind's eye upon a host of imaginary readers but with his
physical eyes upon real readers present before him in flesh and blood, and
responding, as he sometimes expressly encouraged them to, with audible sobs
and laughter to his narrative as it came from his lips. Enchanter-like, he could
'resolve' his thousands of eager auditors into 'one creature' but at the same time
was vividly conscious of them as distinct individuals, like the two audience
members at a Harrogate matinée performance of *Little Dombey* on 11 September:

> There was one gentleman ... who exhibited – or rather concealed – the
> profoundest grief. After crying a good deal without hiding it, he covered his face
> with both his hands, and laid it down on the back of the seat before him, and
> really shook with emotion. He was not in mourning but I supposed him to have
> lost some child in old time. There was a remarkably good fellow of 30 or so,
> too, who found something so very ludicrous in Toots that he *could not* compose
> himself at all, but laughed until he sat wiping his eyes with his handkerchief.
> And whenever he felt Toots coming again he gave a kind of cry, as if it were
> too much for him. It was uncommonly droll, and made me laugh heartily.[10]

For this audience the thrilling feeling of hearing a book being written for
them there and then would have been intensified by Dickens's habit of impro-
vising new text as he was actually reading – sometimes passages that would
then become part of the regular performed text. A famous example occurs in
the *Trial* when Sam Weller responds to Buzfuz's saying about Sam's service
with Mr Pickwick, 'Little to do and plenty to get, I suppose?', 'Oh, quite enough
to get, sir, as the soldier said ven they ordered him three hundred and fifty
lashes.' In the prompt-copy Dickens expanded the judge's rebuke, 'You must
not tell us what the soldier said,' with 'unless the soldier is in court, and is
examined in the usual way.' Then in performance he would elaborate on this
in a variety of fantastic ways, to the delight of the audience for whom he
was creating this unique new, one-night-only, text.[11]

Ultimately, the readings were a way for Dickens the writer to bring his characters out of the study and on to the platform. Some of them at least he would,
it seems, have already actually performed in the study, as evidenced by a
famous anecdote told by Mamie about watching her father in the very act of
creating a character on the page. He was busy writing, she recalls,

> when he suddenly jumped from his chair and rushed to a mirror which hung
> near, and in which I could see the reflection of some extraordinary facial

43 Audience member at one of Dickens's readings ('whenever he felt Toots coming again he gave a kind of cry, as if it were too much for him'); drawn by Fred Barnard for the Household Edition of Forster's *Life of Dickens* (1892)

contortions which he was making. He returned rapidly to his desk, wrote furiously for a few moments, and then went again to the mirror. The facial pantomime was resumed, and then turning toward, but evidently not seeing me, he began talking rapidly in a low voice. Ceasing this soon, however, he returned once more to his desk where he remained silently writing until luncheon time. . . .[12]

The continuity between Dickens the writer and Dickens the public reader could hardly be better illustrated.

CHAPTER 21

Serials, series and stories

WRITING FOR *ALL THE YEAR ROUND*, 1859–1861

*As to my art, I have as great a delight in it as the most enthusiastic of my readers;
and the sense of my trust and responsibility in that wise, is always upon me
when I take pen in hand. If I were soured, I should still try to sweeten the lives
and fancies of others; but I am not – not at all.*

Dickens to Angela Burdett Coutts, 8 April 1860

'SOURED' DICKENS may not have been but the events of 1858 had certainly left
their scars. He felt very bitter towards various individuals, notably the
hapless Bradbury and Evans whom he saw as having betrayed him in his hour
of need. Now he wanted them out of his life. No sooner had his triumphal
readings tour ended on 13 November than he began taking steps towards
the closing down of *Household Words*. He could not even bear to be in the
same room as the 'Whitefriars Gang', as he now called Bradbury and Evans,
and gave Forster power of attorney to act for him in this matter, ignoring all
Evans's attempts to deal directly with himself. Forster tried unsuccessfully to
pressure the publishers into selling Dickens their quarter-share in *Household
Words* (or perhaps, with Dickens's connivance, he was deliberately provoking
them into refusing) but this had not the slightest effect on Dickens's determination to cease 'conducting' *Household Words* on 28 May 1859 at the end of its
nineteenth volume. That would be just one month after the appearance of his
projected new journal which was intended, of course, completely to sabotage
the old one.[1]

Having decided that the first number of the new journal would feature
the first instalment of a new serial of his own writing, Dickens, still busy with
his Christmas readings at St Martin's Hall which continued until 10 February,
found himself in urgent need of two new titles – one for the journal and one
for the serial. Incredibly, he chose *Household Harmony* as an ideal title for
the former and responded huffily to Forster's objection that this might not be
altogether appropriate given his own recent domestic history: 'I am afraid we
must not be too particular about the possibility of personal references and
applications', he wrote, 'otherwise it is manifest that I can never write another

book.' He did withdraw the suggestion, in fact, but continued to hanker after a title that, like *Household Words* or *Household Harmony*, would have a Shakespearian echo. At last he hit upon one that he thought 'really ... admirable' and sent it to Forster on 28 January. It was *All the Year Round*, derived from a line in *Othello* which, slightly altered, would serve as the journal's tag-line: 'The story of our lives, from year to year'.[2]

The right name for the new serial took a bit longer to find and in its absence he had problems with beginning the story. Eventually, he achieved what were to become the best-known opening words of all his books: 'It was the best of times, it was the worst of times . . . .' And by 11 March he had got 'exactly the name' he needed, 'exactly what will fit the opening to a T.'. This was *A Tale of Two Cities*. It was to be his second and last attempt at a historical novel and, like the previous one, was to appear in weekly instalments. Like *Barnaby Rudge*, too, it was to be set in the latter half of the eighteenth-century, to have a five-year time-gap in the narrative, and to feature a sensational episode of a frenzied mob tearing down a great grim prison. Unlike *Barnaby*, however, it would not be written in the shadow of Sir Walter Scott, it would be mainly set in two great cities rather than in one, and – a major new departure for Dickens the novelist – it would be plot- rather than character-centred. In August 1859, when he was nearing the end of its composition, Dickens explained to Forster just what kind of novel he had been attempting:

I set myself the little task of making *a picturesque story*, rising [that is, increasing in interest and excitement] in every chapter, with characters true to nature, but whom the story itself should express more than they should express themselves by dialogue. I mean in other words, that I fancied a story of incident might be written (in place of the bestiality that *is* written under that pretence [a reference to the sensational serials of such writers as the prolific G. W. M. Reynolds]), pounding the characters in its own mortar, and beating their interest out of them. If you could have read the story all at once, I hope you wouldn't have stopped halfway.

Dickens's decision to use a French Revolution setting may have related to what had become for him the prison of his marriage and also, as has been persuasively argued, to the political tensions between Britain and France in 1858–59. The inspiration for Dr Manette, 'buried alive' in the Bastille, goes back to the horror Dickens had experienced in meeting those condemned to long-term solitary confinement in Philadelphia's Eastern State Penitentiary and, beyond that, to the old man he had read about as a child who was at last freed from long imprisonment in the Bastille and 'brought his white face, and his white hair, and his phantom figure, back again to tell them what they had made him . . . and prayed to be shut up in his old dungeon till he died'. The idea of Carton's self-sacrifice for love by becoming a substitute guillotine-victim was of more recent origin in Dickens's imaginative life and blended together two things. One was his memory of a play called *The Dead Heart* which Benjamin Webster had read to him and other friends early in 1857 and the other was the train of ideas for a story that came into his mind with such 'surprising force and brilliancy' just a few months later when he was enacting the death of Wardour in *The Frozen Deep*. Nelly had played a minor character called Lucy in this drama so it is not surprising to find that his new heroine is named Lucie nor that she physically resembles Nelly, even down to a characteristic expression of countenance: she has 'a short, slight, pretty figure, a quantity of golden hair, a pair of blue eyes . . . and a forehead with a singular capacity (remembering how young and smooth it was), of lifting and knitting itself into an expression that was not quite one of perplexity, or wonder, or alarm, or merely of bright fixed attention, though it included all the four expressions' (*Tale of Two Cities*, Bk I, ch. 4). Apart from her physical appearance, however, Lucie Manette has proved a sad disappointment to Dickens biographers. Heroine of a novel that is plot- rather than character-centred, and being unable as a model Victorian daughter/wife/mother to originate any action that might 'pound out' her character 'in its own mortar', she remains a blank for all those wanting to find in her traces of Nelly, or at least some clue as to Dickens's feelings towards his 'little riddle' at this time. Biographers soon abandon her for the more suggestive and rewarding figures of her successor-heroines Estella, Bella Wilfer and Helena Landless.[3]

By now Dickens was leading three distinct lives – in addition, of course, to his writing one in which he was engaged with 'the children of his brain' who, Charley recalled, 'were much more real to him at times than we were'. There was the public figure, the celebrated author and reader, shown seated by his desk in casual but vibrant pose in the portrait, commissioned by Forster from William Powell Frith, for which Dickens began sitting in January 1859. A striking 1858 photograph by Herbert Watkins shows him in the actual act of writing while another, also by Watkins, shows him, a commanding and mesmerising presence, standing at his reading desk. Then there was the genially hospitable paterfamilias of an oddly organised but thoroughly respectable household, who commuted between Tavistock House and his 'little Kentish freehold', as Dickens delighted to call Gad's Hill Place. This Dickens had, of course, to concern himself with the education of, and the finding of careers for, those of his sons still under his roof, Francis, Alfred, Sydney – who entered the Navy in 1859 – Henry and 'the noble Plorn', as Dickens called his youngest and favourite son, now seven. Lastly, there was Dickens the discreet friend and, to borrow an apt phrase from a recent writer on Dickens, 'fairy godfather' of the Ternan family. It seems – hard though it is to credit – that at the beginning of 1859 Dickens actually had some idea of leasing Tavistock House to the Ternans, presumably at a nominal rent, but Forster and Wills managed to dissuade him from so massive an indiscretion. Instead, he – almost certainly – supplied the money for Fanny and Maria Ternan to purchase a long lease of a hardly less grand four-storied terrace house on the Bedford Estate, 2 Houghton Place, near Mornington Crescent, a lease which they transferred to Nelly on her twenty-first birthday in March 1860. Here Francesco Berger, who knew the Ternans well, would often find himself during the 1860s playing cards with 'the mother, daughter, and Dickens, on Sunday evenings . . . generally followed after supper by Ellen and Dickens singing duets to his [i.e., Berger's] pianoforte accompaniment'. 'The charmer', as Dickens called Nelly in letters to intimate friends, evidently figured in his London social life outside Houghton Place as well, as, for example, when, with Georgina acting as a sort of chaperone, she accompanied him to the French actress-manager Madame Celeste's opening of the Lyceum Theatre (across the road from the *All the Year Round* office) on 30 September 1859. That Nelly was also, to some extent, involved in his writing life seems evident from his reporting to Bulwer Lytton on 15 May 1861 that he had read the proofs of the first instalment of the story Lytton was writing for *All the Year Round* to 'a woman whom I could implicitly trust, and in whom I have frequently observed (in the case of my own proofs) an intuitive sense and discretion that I have set great store by'.[4]

Given all the different lives that Dickens himself was simultaneously living by this time, it is hardly surprising that characters leading double lives, and even actual doubles should now become more prominent in his writings. The upright hero of *A Tale* Charles Darnay, the significance of whose first name and initials has not escaped commentators (though none, I believe, has remarked on the fact that he is a much younger man than his creator whereas Lucie is Nelly's age) has his double and dark shadow in the dissipated Sydney Carton. For Carton's secret relationship with his arrogant and unscrupulous former schoolfellow Stryver, which also has a doubling element, Dickens retrieved a notion from his *Book of Memoranda* jotted down in 1855: 'The drunken? – dissipated? – what? – LION and his JACKALL and Primer – stealing down to him at unwonted hours'. The authorial meditation on the 'wonderful fact' that 'every human creature is constituted to be that profound secret and mystery to every other' which opens the third chapter of the *Tale* in the first number of *All the Year Round* also seems likely to have stemmed from Dickens's new situation with its carefully compartmentalised relationships. His keenness that Nelly, at least, should be helped to read the secrets of his heart is shown by his concern in June that she should be sent clean proofs, or 'fair revises', of Book II, chapters 10 to 13, in which, in their very different ways, both Darnay and Carton declare their love for Lucie.[5]

Dickens's primary source for historical material in the *Tale* is, very obviously, that 'wonderful book', as he calls it in his preface to the novel, Carlyle's *The*

French Revolution (1837), which he told Forster in July 1851 he was reading 'for the 500th time'. For his scene-setting opening chapter he also made good use of the volumes of *The Annual Register* for 1774–76 that he had in his library, and he read extensively in contemporary accounts of the condition of France under the *ancien régime*. Some of these accounts, like that of Louis-Sébastien Mercier in his *Le Tableau de Paris* (1782–8), would have been among the famous 'two cart-loads of books' that Carlyle arranged to be sent to Dickens from the London Library. Nor was Dickens's extensive background reading for the *Tale* confined only to the obvious historical sources. He later reminded Forster that while he was working on the story he had read 'no books but such as had the air of the time in them'.[6]

With the *Tale* Dickens was not only returning after a long gap to historical fiction and experimenting with what was for him a new method of plot-centred novel-writing. He was experimenting also with a new kind of publishing schedule whereby his story was to be serialised in *All the Year Round* between 30 April and 26 November 1859 in thirty-one weekly instalments markedly shorter than the weekly instalments of *Hard Times* had been. These instalments were to be divided into three books instead of waiting until volume publication for such division, as had happened with *Hard Times*. The story would be simultaneously published by Chapman and Hall from 1 July to 1 December in shilling monthly numbers, numbers seven and eight being published together as the final double number. These monthly numbers would have the familiar green covers, for which Browne provided an excellent cover-design, as well as the usual two plates for each number. This 'rather original and bold idea' of simultaneous weekly and monthly publication, Dickens wrote to Forster, 'will give *All the Year Round* always the interest and precedence of a fresh weekly portion during the month; and will give me my old standing with my old public, and the advantage (very necessary in this story) of having numbers of people who read it in no portions smaller than a monthly part'.[7]

In the event, Dickens was to be disappointed by the monthly-number sales and recognised that the 'very great sale' of the weekly instalments 'forestalled the market to a considerable extent'. As regards overseas sales, he showed himself to have become by now quite a sharp operator. For a fee of £1,000 he arranged with an enterprising New York journalist called Thomas Coke Evans, to send stereotype plates of each number of *All the Year Round* to America two weeks ahead of the London publication date so that the number could appear almost simultaneously, in New York just one day after in London. (Later in the year Evans found he could not keep up the payments and sold the contract on to the New York publishing firm of Emerson & Co.) Then, for another fee of £1,000, he arranged with the mighty New York firm of Harper's, which had pirated him so ruthlessly in the past, for advance sheets to be sent to them of every number containing an instalment of the *Tale* so that it could appear in

Harper's Weekly one week later than it had appeared in London. These were indeed profitable arrangements but they had a major side-effect in helping to make the new journal a much less topical publication than *Household Words* had been.[8]

By far the most sensational (in more senses than one) literary arrangement that Dickens entered into at this time with an American publisher was that with Robert Bonner, owner of *The New York Ledger*. About Bonner's stunning offer of £1,000 for a short story Dickens might have used the same words he had used twenty-three years earlier when Chapman and Hall offered him £14 a month to write the letterpress to accompany Seymour's Cockney-sportsmen plates: it was 'an emolument too tempting to resist'. He accepted the commission on 29 March and, writing the story alongside the early chapters of *A Tale*, managed to finish it by 3 May. It was titled 'Hunted Down' and was divided into two 'portions'. Dickens partly developed the story from some notes in his *Book of Memoranda*. One of these related to the celebrated art critic, forger and poisoner for gain of his own relatives Thomas Griffiths Wainewright (1794–1852), whom Dickens had seen in Newgate back in 1837. He had had Wainewright in mind back in the summer of 1843 when he was describing Jonas Chuzzlewit's attempted poisoning of his own father but why should he return to him now as a model for the villain of 'Hunted Down', Julius Slinkton, who poisons one of his nieces and intends poisoning the other for the sake of the insurance money? Surely it was because among the books having 'the air of the time' that Dickens read for the *Tale* he would, given his vast admiration for its author, have returned to Bulwer Lytton's *Lucretia, or the Children of Night* (1846). This novel, which begins during the French Revolution, was avowedly based upon the life and career of Wainewright. Besides giving Dickens a notion for 'Hunted Down', *Lucretia* may also have suggested to him an idea for the great climactic scene of the *Tale* since it opens with a description of a blood-thirsty crowd surging around the tumbril that is carrying to the guillotine a calmly self-possessed and handsome young aristocrat together with a terrified young working-girl.[9]

All this while Dickens was forging ahead with plans for the new journal. He hired a new office in Wellington Street a few doors away from the *Household Words* office and later in the year turned the third floor of the building into a comfortable apartment for himself, his 'Town Tent', as he often called it. To 'strengthen' the first number of *All the Year Round*, published on 30 April, he dashed off an article, 'The Poor Man and His Beer', describing a notable example of 'temperate temperance', a club that Austin had just taken him to see, which a Hertfordshire landowner had encouraged his labourers to set up and run for themselves so they could have their beer independent of the public-house. Dickens also contributed a few satirical squibs under the heading 'Occasional Register', including the following echo of 'Nobody's Fault':

'MISSING./ ON ALL OCCASIONS, the man who is responsible for anything done ill in the public service. He will particularly oblige by coming forward.' He and Wills also orchestrated a massive publicity campaign with a quarter of a million handbills being distributed through the newsvendor W. H. Smith, who by this time had a stall on almost every railway station. The bills announced that Dickens would be transferring himself and his 'strongest energies' from *Household Words* to *All the Year Round* and taking his staff of writers with him. They concluded with the words, 'On Saturday, 28th May Mr Charles Dickens will CEASE TO CONDUCT HOUSEHOLD WORDS; that Periodical will be DISCONTINUED, and its Partnership of Proprietors dissolved.' Bradbury and Evans's legal attempt to stop the distribution of these bills failed, leaving them with no option but to agree to an auction of *Household Words* at which they might perhaps acquire full rights over the title and then re-launch it as a competitor to *All the Year Round*. The auction took place on 16 May and Bradbury and Evans were outmanoeuvred as a result of some crafty sale-room tactics by Frederic Chapman and Arthur Smith, the latter acquiring the journal and its stock for Dickens for £3,550. Since the stock, valued at £1,600, was to be bought from him by Chapman and Hall, and since he and Wills already owned three-quarters of *Household Words*, the net cost to Dickens was, in fact, only £500, as he gloated in a letter to Georgina immediately following the auction.[10]

The last issue of *Household Words* duly appeared on 28 May with the prospectus for *All the Year Round* on its front page and a triumphal third-person 'Last Household Word' from Dickens on its back page ('He knew perfectly well, knowing his own rights, and his means of attaining them, that *it could not be* but that this Work must stop if he chose to stop it'). The same day was published the fifth weekly number of *All the Year Round* with the beginning (chs 1 and 2) of Book II of *A Tale* and with the following words added to the masthead, 'With Which is Incorporated Household Words'. The new journal quickly proved 'a phenomenal financial success', selling on average more than three times the number of copies sold by *Household Words*. Dickens being resolved 'to work what I do, with my own capital, and to have no publisher at all' for the journal 'except as a paid Agent and Instrument', *All the Year Round* was wholly owned by himself and Wills. Dickens had a three-quarters share and Wills one quarter and the profits, averaging £3,292 per year between 1859 and 1867, were divided proportionately. Dickens also drew an annual salary of £504 as editor while Wills as sub-editor and general manager drew one of £420. The actual title of the journal was, as Dickens made crystal-clear to his partner, entirely owned by himself and he had complete power to close the magazine down whenever he wished.[11]

Dickens was, at any rate during the magazine's early years, just as much a hands-on editor of *All the Year Round* as he had been of *Household Words* but after the first number did not write any more articles for it, with one brief exception ('Five New Points of Criminal Law', 24 Sept. 1859) until after the last instalment of *A Tale of Two Cities* had appeared on 26 November. His major overall concern was to ensure a succession of good serials to follow the *Tale* as the lead feature in each issue. In the summer Wilkie Collins began work on a new serial story *The Woman in White* ('I have not the slightest doubt', Dickens wrote to him on 16 August after Collins's struggles to arrive at a title had ended with this one, 'that The Woman in White is the name of names, and very title of very titles') and the first instalment was published in the same issue as the one in which *A Tale of Two Cities* concluded. Between the ending of his story and the beginning of Collins's Dickens inserted the following notice:

> We purpose always reserving the first place in these pages for a continuous original work of fiction, occupying about the same amount of time in its serial publication, as that which is just completed. . . . And it is our hope and aim, while we work hard at every other department of our journal, to produce, in this one, some sustained works of imagination that may become a part of English Literature.

He tried hard to get George Eliot, whose new book *Adam Bede* he fervently admired (it had, he wrote to her, 'taken its place among the actual experiences and endurances of my life'), to agree to supply a serial to follow Collins's. He told her partner George Henry Lewes on 14 November that he was ready to 'close the matter on any terms satisfactory to Mrs Lewes and yourself' but she declined. 'Adam (or Eve) Bede', he wrote on 21 February 1860 to the Irish novelist Charles Lever, whose offer of a serial he had gladly accepted, 'is terrified by the novel difficulties of serial writing; can not turn in the space; evidently will not be up to the scratch when Collins's sponge is thrown in.' It was Lever, therefore, who succeeded Collins in August 1860 – ultimately with a rather dramatic result.[12]

The writing of the *Tale* proceeded with great intensity between April and October 1859. He told Yates on 19 May that he was completely enslaved to the story 'and must do it in its own time and way'. He seems to have been able to dispense altogether with any kind of 'mems' or number-plans since he had such a clear idea of where he was going with the story. On 8 July, when he would have been working on Book II chapters 15–21, the mid-point of the text, he told Wills that he could see the story as 'in a wonderful glass'. But the summer heat and some apparently venereal health problem (he described it to his doctor Frank Beard, brother of Thomas, as a 'small malady' caused by his 'bachelor state') rather slowed him down so that he could get no further ahead with the actual writing than his 'old month's advance'. Nevertheless, he was, as he told Forster on 9 July, 'getting the *Tale of Two Cities* into that state that IF I should decide to go to read in America late in September I could turn to at any time, and write on with great vigour', despite being driven 'frantic', just as he had been when writing *Hard Times*, by the problems of dividing the story into brief weekly instalments or 'Teaspoons' as Carlyle called them. The American project had been under consideration since January when Thomas Coke Evans had first proposed it to him. Dickens did not rule it out, even though he had, as he told Arthur Smith on 26 January, referring to his relationship with Nelly, 'a private reason' which would make 'a long Voyage and absence particularly painful' to him at this time. To be weighed against this consideration was the potentially enormous sum that might be gained (Evans was offering him a down payment of £10,000 upon signature of the agreement). It was not until the late summer that he finally abandoned the idea, having – apart from other considerations – begun to doubt Evans's ability to come up with the money.[13]

He was much heartened by the way in which the *Tale* had evidently taken 'strong hold' of its readers, reflected in the soaring sales of *All the Year Round*. That this resulted from the *Tale*'s being serialised in weekly instalments was clear to *The Illustrated London News*'s critic who wrote on 13 November: 'in the form in which it [the *Tale*] has been produced, whether artfully or not we cannot say, it has the effect of keeping up the desire to ascertain what it is all about through every successive number'. Wilkie Collins, when he came to write a preface for *The Woman in White*, hailed the *Tale* as 'the most perfect piece of constructive art that has ever proceeded from his [Dickens's] pen'. Privately, however, he told Dickens that he would have constructed it somewhat differently. He himself would have given the reader some inkling of the fearful connection between Dr Manette's terrible Bastille experience and Darnay's family history well before that connection is sensationally revealed at Darnay's trial by the Revolutionary Tribunal (Bk III, ch.10). Dickens's response to Collins's criticism is worth quoting at length since it is one of the most interesting and important surviving statements of his artistic credo (it also points us towards the great gulf existing between his genius and Collins's):

> I do not positively say that the point you put, might not have been done in your manner; but I have a very strong conviction that it would have been overdone in that manner – too elaborately trapped, baited and prepared – in the main, anticipated and its interest wasted. This is quite apart from the peculiarity of the Doctor's character, as affected by his imprisonment; which of itself would – to my way of thinking – render it quite out of the question to put the reader inside of him before the proper time, in respect of matters that were dim to himself through being, in a diseased way, morbidly shunned by him. I think the business of Art is to lay all that ground carefully, but with the care that conceals itself – to shew by a backward light, what everything has been working to – but only to SUGGEST, until the fulfilment comes. These are the ways of Providence – of which ways, all Art is but a little imitation.[14]

Dickens finished writing the *Tale* just before embarking on his second provincial readings tour in Ipswich on 10 October. Back at Gad's Hill for the weekend, shortly before he let the place for six months, he wrote to Edward Chapman on the 16th about arrangements for the novel's publication in volume form a few days before the appearance of the final instalment in *All the Year Round* on 26 November. He dedicated this tale set in a time of social catastrophe brought on by a rotten political system to Lord John Russell, the great proponent of the Reform Bill of 1832 and in Dickens's view the polar opposite of those Tory aristocrats whose arrogant incompetence was threatening to produce a disaster comparable to the French Revolution nearer home. Among those to whom he sent a complete set of proofs was François Régnier, whom he had previously asked to advise Fanny Ternan about studying singing in Paris. Thanking Régnier for his help, Dickens asked if he thought the *Tale* ('the best story I have ever written') might with advantage be adapted for the French stage. Given his long-standing hatred of having his books mangled by hack dramatists, it might seem odd that he is here positively encouraging such action. In the case of the *Tale*, however, I believe he might well have seen dramatisation as the natural continuation of his experiment in writing a more plot-based kind of novel, his 'best *story*' to date (my italics). Such a work might even gain in power from being staged. Best of all for Dickens, of course, would have been to play the lead himself. To Mary Boyle he wrote on 8 December: 'Yes, Mary dear: I must say that I like my Carton. And I have a faint idea sometimes, that if I acted him, I could have done something with his life and death' (a tour de force, Dickens is hinting, that would have put even his Wardour in the shade). In the event, Régnier having confirmed that a stage version of the *Tale* would run into political problems in Paris, Dickens was happy to turn to Madame Celeste to direct the stage version of the novel written by the accomplished adaptor Tom Taylor, with herself as Madame Defarge, which opened to good notices at the Lyceum on 30 January.

Back in late October, the first literary work that claimed Dickens's attention once he had finished his highly successful readings tour (which included both Cambridge and Oxford, where the Prince of Wales was in the audience) was the assembling of the first Christmas number of *All the Year Round* which was to be twelve pages longer than the *Household Words* Christmas numbers and so, at forty-eight pages, double the size of an ordinary number of the magazine and costing twice as much. His idea for the number originated in an increasingly tetchy semi-public correspondence into which he had been ensnared by William Howitt, a former *Household Words* contributor. Howitt was now a spiritualist fanatic whom Dickens, alluding to the contemporary craze for communicating with spirits by table-rapping, called 'a kind of arch-rapper among the rappers'. He was a great enthusiast for haunted houses and now Dickens, drawing on an idea noted in his *Book of Memoranda*, devised a framework narrative in which a group of friends agree to spend the Christmas season in a reputedly haunted house, each one being allocated to a particular room. Before the party broke up each would tell the rest about any ghostly visitations he or she might have experienced in this room. The various stories were to be supplied by Dickens himself, Collins, Gaskell and others who had regularly contributed to the *Household Words* Christmas numbers.[15]

As usual, his contributors appeared unable to grasp Dickens's concept although it was, he told Forster, 'the simplest in the world' and he had described it to them 'in writing, in the most elaborate manner'. It was that the sojourners in the house should be haunted only by memories of their own past lives. On 20 November he told Lewes he was 'in a state of temporary insanity (Annual) with the Xmas No.', a state which he expected to last 'for ten days or a fortnight to come'. He nevertheless managed to get it published on schedule, on 13 December. His own story, 'The Ghost in Master B's Room', is a remarkable mixture of the uncanny, of imagined (or maybe recollected?) childhood fantasy-games inspired by *The Arabian Nights*, and of fictionalised autobiography. With regard to the last-named element, it is anybody's guess whether he intended his readers to connect Master B with 'Boz' but, when he describes Master B's parents suffering a financial collapse as his own had done (no debtors'-prison experience, though – Master B's father just dies suddenly) and having to sell up, it certainly does look like the kind of private joke with himself (here of a rather grim kind) that he always delighted to smuggle into his writing.[16]

Writing the framework narrative and 'The Ghost in Master B's Room' for this 1859 Christmas number surely showed Dickens how, now that the serialisation of *A Tale of Two Cities* was finished (the novel appeared in volume form on 21 November) he might continue contributing regularly to his new journal in a less pressurised, non-fictional mode that would be responsive to his current emotional and psychological state. He was still more than capable of firing off the kind of fiercely topical satirical paper he had so often written for *Household Words* but this was not a genre that really suited *All the Year Round*. It was not an up-to-the-minute crusading magazine like *Household Words* (its continued campaign on behalf of Italian unity was necessarily a more long-term business). Apart from anything else, it had, as we have seen, to go to press two weeks ahead of its English publication date because of its American publication arrangements. Nor was Dickens himself any longer so generally embattled with regard to public affairs as he had been during the 1850s. Another genre of essay that he had also written for *Household Words*, descriptive and reflective like so many of those that he had chosen to include in *Reprinted Pieces*, was wholly appropriate to *All the Year Round*. In *Household Words* these pieces had been anonymously published with no authorial persona or other device to link them together beyond the fact that they were generally recognised to have been written by Dickens himself. But now that his

THE HAUNTED HOUSE.

THE EXTRA CHRISTMAS NUMBER OF **ALL THE YEAR ROUND.**

CONDUCTED BY CHARLES DICKENS.

CONTAINING THE AMOUNT OF TWO ORDINARY NUMBERS.

CHRISTMAS, 1859.

Price 4d.

INDEX.

THE MORTALS IN THE HOUSE.

UNDER none of the accredited ghostly circumstances, and environed by none of the conventional ghostly surroundings, did I first make acquaintance with the house which is the subject of this Christmas piece. I saw it in the daylight, with the sun upon it. There was no wind, no rain, no lightning, no thunder, no awful or unwonted circumstance, of any kind, to heighten its effect. More than that: I had come to it direct from a railway station; it was not more than a mile distant from the railway station; and, as I stood outside the house, looking back upon the way I had come, I could see the goods train running smoothly along the embankment in the valley. I will not say that everything was utterly common-place, because I doubt if anything can be that, except to utterly common-place people—and there my vanity steps in; but, I will take it on myself to say that anybody might see the house as I saw it, any fine autumn morning.

The manner of my lighting on it was this.

I was travelling towards London out of the North, intending to stop by the way, to look at the house. My health required a temporary residence in the country; and a friend of mine who knew that, and who had happened to drive past the house, had written to me to suggest it as a likely place. I had got into the train at midnight, and had fallen asleep, and had woke up and had sat looking out of window at the brilliant Northern Lights in the sky, and had fallen asleep again, and had woke up again to find the night gone, with the usual discontented conviction on me that I hadn't been to sleep at all;—upon which question, in the first imbecility of that condition, I am ashamed to believe that I would have done wager by battle with the man who sat opposite me. That opposite man had had, through the night—as that opposite man always has—several legs too many, and all of them too long. In addition to this unreasonable conduct (which was only to be expected of him), he had had a pencil and a pocket-book, and had been perpetually listening and taking notes. It had appeared to me that these aggravating notes related to the jolts and bumps of the carriage, and I should have resigned myself to his taking them, under a general supposition that he was in the civil-engineering way of life, if he had not sat staring straight over my head whenever he listened. He was a goggle-eyed gentleman of a perplexed aspect, and his demeanour became unbearable.

It was a cold, dead morning (the sun not being up yet), and when I had out-watched the paling light of the fires of the iron country, and the curtain of heavy smoke that hung at once between me and the stars and between me and the day, I turned to my fellow-traveller and said :

"I beg your pardon, sir, but do you observe anything particular in me?" For, really, he appeared to be taking down, either my travelling-cap or my hair, with a minuteness that was a liberty.

The goggle-eyed gentleman withdrew his eyes from behind me, as if the back of the carriage were a hundred miles off, and said, with a lofty look of compassion for my insignificance:

"In you, sir?—B."

"B, sir?" said I, growing warm.

"I have nothing to do with you, sir," returned the gentleman; "pray let me listen—O."

He enunciated this vowel after a pause, and noted it down.

At first I was alarmed, for an Express lunatic and no communication with the guard, is a serious position. The thought came to my relief that the gentleman might be what is popularly called a Rapper: one of a sect for (some of) whom I have the highest respect, but whom I don't believe in. I was going to ask him the question, when he took the bread out of my mouth.

long-established, 'personally affectionate', relationship with the readers of his fiction had been intensified by his experience of audiences' responses at the readings, he would have been keen to create a similar feeling of intimacy with the readers of his journalism. Moreover, the dramatic break with the past and subsequent reorganisation of his life that had dominated 1858, together with other changes that life was bringing such as the growth towards adulthood of his children and whatever relationship he was developing with Nelly, meant that his feelings about his earlier life had become rather more complex than those that had powered the writing of the autobiographical fragment, *The Haunted Man* and *David Copperfield*.[17]

Dickens managed both to achieve the desired greater intimacy with his readers and to find an ideal vehicle for the exploration and expression of his changed attitude towards his past in the series of essays that he began publishing under the collective heading of *The Uncommercial Traveller* in the issue for 28 January 1860. His framing narrative and 'Master B's Room' story for *The Haunted House* anticipate these 'Uncommercial' essays both in style and tone, while the genre of the essays themselves clearly harks back to the work of Charles Lamb and the other Romantic essayists so eagerly devoured by him in those childhood days when he was reading 'as if for life'. His referring to these essays, in a letter to Collins of 7 January, as 'my series of gossiping papers' indicates the kind of intimate, chatty relationship he was seeking to establish with his readers. And it would certainly not have escaped his notice that Thackeray as editor of a hugely successful new monthly magazine, *The Cornhill*, the first number of which had just appeared, was setting up just such a relationship with *his* readers by means of the first of his 'Roundabout Papers'. The idea of the Uncommercial Traveller was certainly a great improvement on Dickens's earlier notion of adopting a very peculiar sort of journalistic persona called 'the Shadow', 'a kind of semi-omniscient, omnipresent, intangible creature'. The brilliant name he now hits upon most probably derived from his recent contact with the Commercial Travellers' Schools Society. He had chaired this Society's second anniversary festival on 22 December and been hailed there by an enthusiastic clergyman as one whose writings had done 'immense good' and as having been 'specially appointed to break down with a sledge-hammer the anointed iniquity of high places'. Dickens would surely have relished this application to himself of one of his favourite images for forceful writing. In his speech he had reminded his hearers 'that we are all Travellers, and every round we take converges nearer and nearer to our home', but he also affirmed his belief that 'the good we do, and the virtues that we show . . . survive us through the long and unknown perspective of time'. Just one week later, he was on his way to remote Anglesey to meet someone who had recently done great good and shown conspicuous virtue. The Rev. Stephen Roose Hughes, a Church in Wales vicar, had risen magnificently to a most

terrible occasion when the steam clipper *The Royal Charter*, homeward bound
from Melbourne to Liverpool, was wrecked in a most terrible storm on 26
October off the coast near Hughes's village, Llanallgo, with the loss of over four
hundred and fifty lives. Hughes and his family had shown tremendous energy,
resourcefulness and compassion in managing the burial of all those bodies
that could be recovered and in dealing with great numbers of bereaved relatives both in person and by correspondence. Among those drowned were four
members of the Hogarth family, cousins of Catherine and Georgina, and this
may have been the reason for Dickens's visit; or it may have been that, moved
by all the newspaper accounts of what Hughes had done, he decided to use the
first of his planned 'gossiping papers' to celebrate such an outstanding example
of human goodness and practical Christianity.[18]

A long account of his visit duly appeared as the first 'Uncommercial
Traveller' paper in the 28 January issue of *All The Year Round*, immediately
following the Traveller's brief introduction of himself into which Dickens
wove that all-important word for him both as writer and as editor, 'fancy':

> Figuratively speaking, I travel for the great house of Human Interest Brothers,
> and have rather a large connexion in the fancy goods way. Literally speaking,
> I am always wandering here and there from my rooms in Covent-garden,
> London – now about the City streets: now about the country bye-roads –
> seeing many little things, and some great things, which, because they interest
> me, I think may interest others.

The description of his visit to Llanallgo, devoid as it is of 'fancy' and quoting
freely from the heartfelt letters of gratitude sent to Hughes by bereaved relatives, made rather a solemn beginning for 'a series of gossiping papers' but the
succeeding fifteen 'Uncommercials', published at the rate of one or two a
month over the next eight months, were mostly very different. Only one, called
'The Great Tasmania's Cargo' when collected in volume form, harks back to
Household Words style. It is a ferocious attack on the India Office, 'the Pagoda
Department of that great Circumlocution Office', inveighing against the
appalling conditions under which some British soldiers had been repatriated
from India. And in the last paper in the series, 'The Italian Prisoner'(13 Oct.),
Dickens seems to have abandoned his 'Uncommercial' persona to tell what he
calls 'strictly a true story' from the time of his sojourn in Italy in 1844–45.
Apart from these two, however, the essays are all thoroughly imbued with fancy
and with a strong sense of the Traveller's distinctly Dickensian personality and
they contain in many cases much detailed reference to the Traveller's personal
history. Advertised in *All the Year Round* itself as a 'series of Occasional
Journeys by Charles Dickens', these essays were the first journalism he had ever
published for the first time under his own name. This, of course, strongly

encouraged readers to identify the Traveller as a transparent mask for Dickens himself, and to regard whatever he, the Traveller, told them about his personal history (which was quite a lot) as factual autobiography on Dickens's part, a response later encouraged by Forster in his *Life of Dickens* when he noted how many of these essays had supplied 'traits, chiefly of his younger days, to portions of this memoir'.[19]

Like the readings, then, the Uncommercial Traveller papers served to strengthen that (to Dickens) vital sense of personal intimacy between himself and his readers. They provided him, too, with an ideal medium for his favourite game of telling and not telling his readers about his past, a past now viewed by him in a rather different light. Just before returning to live in Gad's Hill Place at Easter, for example, he introduced the house and what it meant to him into his sixth Uncommercial Traveller paper (7 April; called 'Travelling Abroad' when collected in volume form), which also reminisced about his travels in France and Switzerland. He shared with his readers his cherished story about his father's having often told him as a child that if he 'were to be very persevering and to work hard' he 'might some day come to live' in Gad's Hill. Now he had decided that it should become his only home and in August began negotiations for the sale of Tavistock House, drawing yet another line under his pre-Nelly existence, as he did also with the famous bonfire he made of his correspondence at Gad's Hill the following month. Another 'Uncommercial Traveller' paper (30 June) was devoted to the subject of returning to 'the birthplace of his fancy', the Medway towns of Rochester and Chatham, with Dickens writing as though he had never been back to these places since his childhood exile from them thirty-eight years before. Blending the two towns together as 'Dullborough Town', Dickens deals, in masterly and moving fashion, with nostalgia, disillusionment and the renewing of the life of the imagination. In the event, Rochester, Chatham and the contiguous marsh country stirred Dickens's adult imagination even more deeply than they had done his childish one and became primary settings for two of the three novels he was yet to write. Some of the other papers among these 'Uncommercial' ones, such as those subsequently called 'Night Walks' (21 July) and 'Chambers' (18 August) also clearly prefigure the dark and gloomy, frequently sinister, London of *Great Expectations* and *Our Mutual Friend*.[20]

Meanwhile, on 17 July Gad's Hill, the house of his childhood dreams which had also been the setting for the painful beginning of the end of his marriage, became the house in which the first of his own children's marriages, that of his beloved Katey was celebrated. 'Lord, how the time and life steal on!', he wrote in his 12 June letter of invitation to his friend of nearly forty years, Thomas Beard. 'It was but yesterday that Kate always had a scratched knee – and it was but the day before yesterday when there was no such creature.' The creature's mother was, of course, excluded from the occasion – not that Catherine could have borne to be there, in any case, feeling as she did that the mere sight of Dickens would almost kill her. Katey's husband was Charles Allston Collins, Wilkie's gentle and sweet-natured younger brother, a Pre-Raphaelite artist and the author of a series entitled 'The Eye-Witness' in *All the Year Round*. He was eleven years Katey's senior and in poor health. Katey apparently told Gladys Storey, the great confidante of her declining years, that her father had not desired the marriage. If so, this may have been owing to Collins's state of health, or because Dickens knew it was not a love match, or because his attitude towards matrimony was decidedly negative at this time ('N.B. No connexion, I hope,' he wrote in his letter to Beard, who had been his best man, 'with a similar ceremony performed in a metropolitan edifice some four and twenty years ago'). As for Katey herself, Storey reports her as saying that she saw in the marriage an escape from 'an unhappy home' and that her father knew this. She said Mamie had told her that on the evening of the wedding-day she had found Dickens on his knees in Katey's bedroom sobbing into her wedding-gown. When at last he rose and saw Mamie, 'he said in a broken voice, "But for me, Katey would not have left home", and walked out of the room.' Ten days later came more cause for distress. Dickens's thirty-eight-year-old brother Alfred, the steady one who had never caused him trouble, died suddenly, leaving a wife and five children, the oldest a boy of thirteen, for whom Dickens had to provide. This he at once set about doing with his customary promptness and generosity: 'Day after day', he wrote to a close friend, Frances Dickinson, on 19 August, 'I have been scheming and contriving for them, and I am still doing so, and I have schemed myself into broken rest and low spirits.' Nor were Alfred's widow and orphans his only family worries at this time. His third son, Frank, now sixteen, was proving difficult to settle into any groove. Also, he had had to concern himself, back in March, with making suitable arrangements for the care of his mother, now lapsing into senile dementia. He tells Dickinson:

> My mother, who was also left to me when my father died (I never had anything left to me but relations), is in the strangest state of mind from senile decay; and the impossibility of getting her to understand what is the matter, combined with her desire to be got up in sables like a female Hamlet, illumines the dreary scene with a ghastly absurdity that is the chief relief I can find in it.

More complex his attitude towards his own past life may have become but one thing seems unchanged, his old feeling of bitterness towards his mother which here allows him to write jokingly about the pitiable state to which she has been reduced.[21]

The last thrilling instalment of *The Woman in White*, which had been greatly helping to keep up the sales of *All the Year Round*, appeared in the issue for 18 August and was followed by the first instalment of Charles Lever's *A Day's*

Ride: a Life's Romance. Back in June, Dickens had hailed the first portion of this story with great enthusiasm, calling it 'full of life, vivacity, originality and humour' though making ominous mention of the need to get more quickly to 'the action of the story'. A few weeks later he was telling Lever he had made what he euphemistically called 'a few short cuts' in the proofs. Such brisk editorial intervention makes a marked contrast with Dickens's hugely deferential approach to Bulwer Lytton on 3 August, delicately enquiring if there might be 'any possibility' of Lytton's contributing a serial for *All the Year Round*, for whatever sum he cared to name. His journal, urged Dickens, 'has the largest Audience to be got that comprehends intelligence and cultivation', quickly adding, 'but that audience is already your own, and *that* is no temptation.' No definite answer was immediately forthcoming from Bulwer Lytton and meanwhile Lever's story took its dilatory course.

Dickens himself was now gravitating towards the writing of a new book to be published by Chapman and Hall in the traditional twenty-monthly-number format. On 8 August he told Lord Carlisle, referring perhaps to his 'Uncommercial' wanderings, that he was 'prowling about, meditating a new book' and on 24 August informed Chapman and Hall that they would probably soon hear from him about 'a new Serial Story'. The first clues we have as to the setting, content or plot of this story are supplied by Forster. He tells us how he

45 Stone lozenges in Cooling churchyard

stood with Dickens in the churchyard of the 'desolate Church' of Cooling, 'lying out among the marshes seven miles from Gadshill!', while Dickens told him that he intended setting the opening scene of his new novel there, in the country of his childhood. Dickens would certainly have shown Forster those thirteen little stone lozenges, commemorating thirteen siblings who died in infancy, which were to feature (reduced to five in order to avoid charges of exaggeration!) in the opening chapter of *Great Expectations*. Forster also quotes a letter, dated to mid-September by the Pilgrim editors, in which Dickens reports that in the course of writing 'a little piece', presumably for his 'Uncommercial Traveller' series, 'such a very fine, new, and grotesque idea has opened upon me, that I begin to doubt whether I had not better cancel the little paper, and reserve the notion for a new book'. Forster is told he must judge about this when he has seen a proof of the piece. The idea 'so opens out before *me*', Dickens tells him, 'that I can see the whole of a serial revolving on it, in a most singular and comic manner'. This idea, Forster tells us, 'was the germ of Pip and Magwitch which at first he intended to make the ground work of a tale in the old twenty-number format'. What Forster tells us nothing about is where the concept of Miss Havisham came from, and it was left to an outstandingly industrious Dickens scholar of the late twentieth-century to trace the origins of the various disparate elements that came together in Dickens's imagination at this time to create his own 'woman in white' and her decaying house. Some of these elements reached back into his childhood, like memories of 'the White Woman of Berners Street', about whom he had already written in his 1853 *Household Words* essay 'Where We Stopped Growing', and some were of more recent date like certain disparate news items in the January 1850 issue of *The Household Narrative* that linked themselves together in his memory.[22]

It was, presumably, in order to clear the decks for this big new book that Dickens began unusually early in the year on the planning of the next Christmas number. This was to be mainly written by himself and Wilkie Collins and they met to confer about it on 11 September. By this time, however, sales of *All the Year Round* were tumbling as Lever's meandering tale failed to hold the public's interest (seven instalments had appeared by this time). A 'council of war', as Dickens described it to Forster on 4 October, was promptly held in Wellington Street as a result of which it was decided that, in order to save the journal, he himself had to 'strike in'. He had, in fact, already begun writing his new novel for monthly-part publication but was confident, he told Forster, that he could make what he was doing 'run into another groove', meaning that of weekly serialisation. It was settled that the first instalment would appear in *All the Year Round* on 1 December and that the story itself would be compressed into the same length as *A Tale of Two Cities* (in the event, it was longer by five weekly instalments, the equivalent of one monthly part). By the time he wrote to Forster he had already divided the beginning of the story into the first two or three weekly parts and promised Forster sight of them the following day. 'The name', Dickens added, 'is GREAT EXPECTA-TIONS. I think a good name?' In all his previous novels in which an innocent provincial boy or youth comes to London to seek his fortune the book is named after that boy or youth but the title of *Great Expectations* 'reaches for more', as has been well said, 'suggesting the fantasies not just of an individual but of a whole society, or at least of a generation'. Two days after hitting so felicitously on his title Dickens had the delicate task, which he discharged with the utmost consideration for the sensitivities of an older fellow-writer no longer as popular as he had once been, of telling Lever that *Great Expectations* would be replacing *A Day's Ride* as the magazine's lead serial. On the same day he wrote to Forster, who had evidently regretted the squeezing of the projected full-length novel into a series of weekly instalments, 'The sacrifice of *Great Expectations* is really and truly made for myself,' adding that, 'The property of *All the Year Round* is far too valuable, in every way, to be much endangered.' If Dickens were now to commit himself to a twenty-monthly-number serial for Chapman and Hall, he would, as he said, have put it beyond his power to do 'anything serial' for the journal 'for two good years' and that would be 'a most perilous thing' for it. Given the number of households he had by now to maintain, any decline in the profitability of his journal would have been dangerous indeed and for the same reason he was no doubt glad to get the £1,250 that Harper's agreed to pay him for the American weekly serialisation rights of *Great Expectations* (£250 more than he had received for *A Tale of Two Cities*).[23]

The manuscript of *Great Expectations*, now in the Wisbech and Fenland Museum, shows that Dickens still planned the novel in terms of monthly parts, though only nine parts instead of the usual twenty. Each part consisted of four weekly instalments and was separately paginated by Dickens. These parts were not separately published, however, no doubt because of the disappointing sales of the monthly parts of the *Tale* as published during that story's weekly serialisation. Three parts of *Great Expectations* made one 'stage' of Pip's Expectations, there being three stages in all, looking ahead towards final publication in three volumes. For the first time since *Oliver Twist*, a new Dickens novel was to appear in this traditional form following its serialisation. In the manuscript and weekly instalments Dickens indicates the future volume-divisions in a way that is integral to the text. At the end of chapter 19 appears the line, 'THIS IS THE END OF THE FIRST STAGE OF PIP'S EXPECTA-TIONS'; at the end of chapter 39 there is a similar line, 'THIS IS THE END OF THE SECOND STAGE OF PIP'S EXPECTATIONS'; and at the end of the final chapter we find the significantly different formula, 'THIS IS THE END OF GREAT EXPECTATIONS'. The first stage ends with Pip's departure from the forge to become 'a London-made gentleman' and the second one with the devastating return of the convict Magwitch who reveals himself as Pip's true benefactor and 'second father'. The third and final line follows the account of Pip's meeting again with Estella many years after the action of the story has ended. Dickens's original manuscript makes it clear that this was to be their last meeting but, famously, Bulwer Lytton persuaded him to alter what he had written in order to give the work a happier ending.[24]

As had happened in the case of *A Tale of Two Cities*, Dickens was so thoroughly possessed by his plan for *Great Expectations* and by his general conception of the story that he seems to have had no need of 'mems', number-plans, or notes of any kind. Only when he was about to begin writing the last 'stage' of Pip's expectations, including Pip's enthralled unravelling of the mystery of Estella's birth, did he find a need to jot down a few calculations about the characters' relative ages and the story's elaborately-signalled internal chronology (he also made some notes for the sequence of action in the climactic scene of Magwitch's recapture). He was now living for much of the time among the scenes of his early childhood which were to provide one of the two main settings for the novel, the other being the dark London of *The Uncommercial Traveller*. He was also drawing on his whole emotional and imaginative history – on childhood dreams, anxieties and terrors, on the raptures and miseries of passionate youthful love, and on deep-seated, lifelong concerns around money and social status. He did not need to resort to his *Book of Memoranda* for notions for characters, incidents or situations as he had done whilst writing his two previous novels, though he evidently plundered his long lists of possible character-names. These supplied him with Compey (later elaborated into Compeyson), Pumblechook, Gargery, Wopsle, Skiffins, and one or two other names. The only notion that he took from it, however (apart from a couple that may have gone towards the creation of Bentley Drummle), was one about a 'House-full of Toadies and Humbugs' who all feign to be ignorant of each other's true characters. He adapts this for use in chapter 11 when describing Miss Havisham's vulture-relatives, though the *Book of Memoranda* entry contains no hint of the wild Dickensian comedy of this episode in which Camilla's admiring husband tells her, ' "Camilla, my dear, it is well known that your family feelings are gradually undermining you to the extent of making one of your legs shorter than the other." '[25]

By 24 October four weekly instalments (the first notional monthly part, covering chs 1–7) had been 'ground off the wheel', Dickens told Wilkie Collins, but he added that the next instalment needed to be likewise ground off before he and Collins could set out on a brief expedition they had planned. The image used here for writing makes an interesting contrast with that of 'the story-weaver at his loom' that Dickens uses for the process of writing his next monthly-part novel. The expedition was to be to Devon and Cornwall in quest of local colour for the next Christmas number which was to be set in those parts (Dickens, we recall, had had a hankering to use this part of the country for fictional purposes as far back as 1842). We can see why he had to get the fifth weekly instalment of *Great Expectations* done before interrupting his work on the novel to travel to the South-west since this instalment consists of the crucially important eighth chapter, describing Pip's fateful first visit to Satis House. By the end of the chapter most of the novel's major characters have made their appearance and the 'pivot' on which the story will turn has been put in place. Forster was given a short preview of the book, one notably omitting any reference to Miss Havisham and Estella – perhaps because Dickens was clearly keen to emphasise to his friend that the new tale would contain plenty of humour:

> The work will be written in the first person throughout, and . . . you will find the hero to be a boy-child, like David. Then he will be an apprentice. You will not have to complain of the want of humour as in *The Tale of Two Cities*. I have made the opening, I hope, in general effect exceedingly droll. I have put a child and a good-natured foolish man in relations that seem to me very funny. Of course I have got in the pivot on which the story will turn too – and which indeed, as you will remember, was the grotesque tragic-comic conception that first encouraged me [he must here be referring to what Forster earlier called the 'germ' of Pip and Magwitch]. To be quite sure I had fallen into no unconscious repetitions, I read *David Copperfield* again the other day, and was affected by it to a degree you would hardly believe.

Knowing what he now did about Dickens's childhood, it would surely not have been too difficult for Forster to imagine the effect that a re-reading of *Copperfield* might have upon its author. Nor is it hard for us to think how strongly Dickens must have been affected not only, of course, by re-reading the episode of the young David in Murdstone and Grinby's warehouse but also by the contrast between his elaborate description of David's domestic bliss at the end of the novel and the subsequent shipwreck of his own real-life marriage. As to 'unconscious repetitions', Dickens had no need to worry about these given the great difference in character, personal history and situation in life between David and Pip, his first-ever working-class hero in a full-length novel, impishly described by Shaw as CD's 'apology to Mealy Potatoes'. Moreover, though both novels are written in the first person, the narrators' voices could hardly be more different.[26]

With the first five instalments of the new story in hand, Pip introduced to Satis House (based on Restoration House in Rochester, with the name borrowed from another house in the city) and its remarkable inhabitants, and a whole month still to go before the advertised starting-date for the beginning of serialisation in *All the Year Round*, Dickens could now safely interrupt his work on the story in order to concentrate on the Christmas number, which, like its predecessors, was certain to be a money-spinner. Its title was to be *A Message from the Sea* and he and Collins were to collaborate in writing the framework story. This was the most elaborate of such stories to date and, like *Great Expectations*, it involved mystery but in form is much closer to a detective story, in this case one full of preposterous coincidences. Its main character, the amiable Captain Silas Jonas Jorgan who turns amateur sleuth, was based upon a dear American friend of Dickens's, Captain Elisha Ely Morgan of the American merchant service (Jorgan was 'a portrait . . . exactly like the man', Dickens told Hannah Brown). In thus presenting an American hero, and a highly sympathetic one at that, for the first and last time in his oeuvre Dickens may have had his eye upon that much-canvassed possible readings tour in America but he still could not resist putting some choice 'Chuzzlewitticisms', as we may call them, about America into Jorgan's mouth. He sent out the usual circular asking for contributions to compose the interpolated stories in the number, specifying stories of adventure or 'peril of any kind', before he and Collins went off to spend five days in Devon and Cornwall, 1–5 November. The excursion inspired some very fine descriptive writing by Dickens, no whit inferior to comparable passages in *Great Expectations*, for example, his description of 'the true Cornish moor':

> None but gaunt spectres of miners passed them here, with metallic faces, ghastly with dust of copper and tin; anon, solitary works on remote hill-tops, and bare machinery of torturing wheels and cogs and chains, writhing up hill-sides, were the few scattered hints of human presence in the landscape; during long intervals, the bitter wind, howling and tearing at them like a fierce wild monster, had them all to itself. (Ch. 2, 'The Club-Night')

The two writers spent the rest of November pulling together the Christmas number, with a certain amount of 'high-shouldered desperation' on Collins's part. The result was a work of genuine collaboration and, in the absence of manuscript and proofs, it is impossible to distinguish exactly between the work of Dickens and Collins. We can, however, be sure that everything Collins wrote would have been subject to much revision and editing by Dickens – we know, for example, that Dickens made him rewrite the opening of chapter 4 because he thought Collins had written it too much in the style of *The Woman in White*. The contributions from other writers accepted by Dickens, including one from his new son-in-law, were accommodated in the number through the invention of a story-telling Club. The members are absurdly pompous and self-satisfied and I think it more than likely that Dickens, who forgot nothing and forgave very little, was here seizing an opportunity to settle scores, in his own mind at least, with the Garrick Club Committee for its ludicrous self-importance, as he saw it, in dealing with Thackeray's complaint against Edmund Yates.[27]

By the end of the month the Christmas number was done leaving Dickens feeling overworked, indeed positively unwell and in need of rest. It was published on 13 December and sold very well. The same day Tauchnitz published the collected 'Uncommercial Traveller' essays in volume form and Chapman and Hall followed suit two days later. Dickens was 'greatly pleased' by the appearance of this volume, for which he had written a short preface stating that 'the Series is, for the time, complete' but adding that 'it is the Uncommercial Traveller's intention to take to the road again before another winter sets in'. It was, in fact, to be two and a half years before he could resume his 'uncommercial' wanderings mainly owing to the great pressure of his other commitments, though he did, as we shall see, use the name 'Mr Traveller' for the protagonist of the next Christmas number, thereby associating it with his 'Uncommercial Traveller' essays and keeping his readers mindful of them.

In the meantime *Great Expectations* was wonderfully reviving the fortunes of *All the Year Round*. Urging Mary Boyle to read it, Dickens told her on 28 December that it was 'a very great success, and seems universally liked – I suppose because it opens funnily [!] and with an interest too'. He considered it, he told her, 'very droll'. Work on it was resumed under the difficulties of continued illness (he asked Francis Beard to 'inspect' him on 29 January) as well as other distractions. Prominent among these was the taking of legal steps, together with Wilkie Collins, to stop an unauthorised dramatisation of *A Message from the Sea* at the Britannia Theatre (he and Collins had earlier published a few copies of a semi-dramatic synopsis of the story in an attempt to establish their copyright). He was also chairman of a fund to raise money for his old friend John Hullah whose St Martin's Hall, the venue for Dickens's London readings, had burned down in August. He was engaged, too, in the business of negotiating a four-months' rental, from the end of January, of a grand London house, No. 3 Hanover Terrace, primarily so that Mamie could have her London season. One very welcome development on the *All the Year Round* front was Bulwer Lytton's agreeing to write the next serial for the journal, following on immediately after the end of *Great Expectations*. This was not only a source of tremendous pride and pleasure to Dickens, who was happy to pay Lytton an exceptionally high fee (£1,500), but, with Collins agreeing to follow on from Lytton with a new serial, it must also have greatly reassured him about the magazine's future.[28]

For the first five months and a half of 1861 Dickens worked steadily at the writing of *Great Expectations*, buoyed up by its continued popularity. The result was a much deeper and more complex work than its immediate predecessor. It is all the more astonishing, then, that Dickens seems to have been able to dispense with the usual 'mems'. The manuscript and proofs reveal only one major change of mind during the course of composition – apart, of course, from the famous change at the very end. This earlier substantial change occurs

in chapter 23 when Mrs Pocket was changed in proof from being simply a farcically incompetent, if sweetly amiable, wife and mother to being also 'the only
daughter of a certain quite accidental deceased Knight', which causes her to be
obsessed with class and titles. Bentley Drummle, also, becomes in proof 'next
heir but one to a baronetcy', which further contributes to the class theme. The
'toady neighbour' Mrs Coiler, who plays up to Mrs Pocket, was originally envisaged by Dickens as being simply that lady's gushingly devoted mama. The
change enhances the novel's unity in that some run-of-the-mill Dickensian
farce is replaced by a satirical episode that wittily contributes to the novel's
overall critique of gentility and class snobbery.[29]

Biographers and biographical critics have detected various connections
between Dickens's personal life and characters in *Great Expectations* – that he
may have drawn on Charley for certain aspects of Herbert Pocket, for example.
Above all, there has been a general assumption since the revelations about his
relationship with Nelly Ternan that Pip's anguished love for 'heartless' Estella
reflects Dickens's passion for a cold and unresponsive Nelly. But, as will have
become abundantly clear, we have very little evidence as to what Dickens and
Nelly's relations actually were at this time, apart from Berger's story about
Dickens's going to Houghton Place to play cards with Nelly under her mother's
eye (they did not, one assumes, play 'beggar my neighbour' as did Pip and
Estella under Miss Havisham's) and to sing duets with her at the piano, none
of which sounds particularly lacerating. To me, it has always seemed more
likely, in fact, that in this novel of sadly chastened retrospection, Dickens's
depiction of the young adult Pip's sufferings at the hands of Estella owes more
to memories of those now distant years of tormenting enslavement to Maria
Beadnell that he had earlier turned to such favour and such prettiness when
writing *David Copperfield*.[30]

The most interesting thing about *Great Expectations* from a biographical
point of view is what we know of Dickens's general state of mind when he was
at work on the story. He found, he confided to Forster in the following year,
that 'a certain shrinking sensitiveness' bred in him in the old blacking factory
days had returned in 'the never-to-be-forgotten misery of this later time' (that
is, I take it, since 1857/58) and this 'shrinking sensitiveness' is very much one
of Pip's characteristics. Dickens was not only psychologically distressed but
also physically unwell. He was afflicted in particular with what he called
'neuralgic pains in the face', pains that vanished the moment he had written
the last word of the story. He was, moreover, feeling oppressed by all the heavy
demands on his purse, what he calls in a letter to Wills of 11 March those
'enormous drags upon me which are already added to the charges of my
own large family' – and also, presumably, to the cost of supporting Nelly and
her family: 'I declare to you', he told Wills in this same letter (remembering,
perhaps, that terrifying Atlantic crossing of January 1842) 'that what with my

mother – and Alfred's family – and my Angel Wife – and a Saunders [seemingly an applicant for financial help] or so – I seem to stop sometimes like a steamer in a storm, and deliberate whether I shall go on whirling, or go down'. Against all these troubles and vexations he found public solace in his contact with his fervently responsive audiences, who flocked to his new series of London public readings, and, no doubt, private solace in the company of Nelly and her family. He began the readings, which would greatly help to shore up his finances, of course, on 14 March, continuing on a weekly basis until 18 April. Above all, he would have taken intense pleasure and satisfaction in the writing of this journal-rescuing, highly personal, totally achieved novel. It was being received with greater enthusiasm by his public than anything he had written (Christmas stories apart) since *David Copperfield*, and, little though his beloved readers realised it, he was by its means communing with them in a far more intimate and honestly self-revelatory way than had been the case with the earlier, ostensibly part-autobiographical, novel. It is, I think, significant that he never at any time wrote a preface for *Great Expectations*. What, after all, was there for him to say about it?[31]

Despite all the stresses and strains Dickens was suffering at this time, the writing of *Great Expectations*, strenuous though it was, seems to have proceeded with the greatest smoothness. Writing to Forster, probably in mid-April when he was embarking on the writing of the third 'stage' (vol. 3 of the separately-published text), following Magwitch's return, he regretted that this final part could not be read 'all at once'

> because its purpose would be much more apparent; and the pity is the greater, because the general turn and tone of the working out and winding up will be away from all such things as they conventionally go [no conventional happy ending therefore]. But what must be, must be. As to the planning out from week to week, nobody can imagine what the difficulty is, without trying. But, as in all such cases, when it is overcome the pleasure is proportionate. Two months more will see me through it, I trust.

He ends with an image of making well suited to this particular story: 'All the iron is in the fire, and I have "only" to beat it out.' The following month he organised a research trip preparatory to writing the climactic chapter 54 in which Magwitch is captured just as Pip and Herbert are trying to smuggle him aboard a steamer bound for Hamburg and Compeyson perishes in an underwater struggle with him. Dickens hired a steamer for the day to go down the Thames from Blackwall to Southend 'to make himself sure', Forster tells us, 'of the actual course of a boat in such circumstances, and what possible incidents the adventure might have'. Accompanied by friends and family members, he 'seemed to have no care, the whole of that summer day (22nd of May, 1861), except to enjoy their enjoyment and entertain them with his own in shape of a thousand whims and fancies; but his sleepless observation was at work all the time, and nothing had escaped his keen vision on either side of the river.' Forster rightly hailed the resultant gripping, and highly atmospheric, chapter as 'a masterpiece'.[32]

Immediately after this steamer trip Dickens retreated for three days to the Lord Warden Hotel in Dover for some healthy seaside walking and to give himself space to concentrate on writing ('I work here, like a Steam Engine, and walk like Captain Barclay,' he reported to Wills). He calculated on finishing the book by 12 June and, in fact, finished a day ahead of schedule. 'The work', he confessed to Macready, 'has been pretty close,' adding that he hoped the book was a good one and that he was sure he would very soon throw off 'the little damage it has done me'. He chose to dedicate this most personal to him of all his books to his much-loved old friend, and fervent fellow-believer in mesmerism, Chauncy Hare Townshend, of whom he was to write to Georgina after hearing of Townshend's death in 1868: 'I never, never, never was better loved by man than I was by him, I am sure. Poor dear fellow . . .'. Not only did Dickens dedicate the book to Townshend, he also presented him with the manuscript, a puzzling departure (repeated in the case of his next novel) from his practice, ever since the writing of *The Old Curiosity Shop*, of giving the manuscripts of his novels to Forster, his closest literary friend and chosen biographer.[33]

Four days after finishing *Great Expectations* Dickens took Georgina and Mamie for a short stay with Bulwer Lytton at Knebworth. During the visit he went to see James Lucas the 'Hertfordshire Hermit'. This unfortunate had succumbed to severe paranoia and barricaded himself in his house. He had ceased to wash himself or to cut his hair and nails and, dressed only in a blanket, he held court for the many visitors attracted by his condition, talking with them through a barred window. One might have expected the creator of Miss Havisham to have had some sympathy for this mind diseased, but Dickens either could not or would not recognise that Lucas was mentally ill, attributing his behaviour to a morbid kind of vanity. His disgust had a positive outcome in that it inspired him with an idea for the frame story of his next Christmas number. Meanwhile, and more momentously for literature, Bulwer Lytton had – astonishingly – persuaded him to change the ending of his novel.

Even given Dickens's extraordinary reverence for Bulwer Lytton, this seems, on the face of it, a strange development. Only a year before he had strongly, and entirely persuasively, defended his depiction of Madame Defarge's death in *A Tale of Two Cities* against Bulwer Lytton's criticism that it was too 'accidental'. But now, in what has rather cruelly been called his only lasting contribution to English literature, Bulwer Lytton (who had, Dickens reported, been 'extraordinarily taken by the book') was able to persuade Dickens to scrap the brilliantly economical downbeat ending he had written, an ending that resonated perfectly with this novel of ruined lives and lost illusions, and substitute for it an ending in which, apparently, boy finally gets girl and they live happily ever after. It would be interesting indeed to know just what were those 'good reasons', as Dickens called them, that persuaded him to make this regrettable change. Were they primarily sentimental or economic (the public would not stand for such a sad ending)? Dickens's telling Forster that he had substituted for the original ending 'as pretty a little piece of writing as I could' and that he had no doubt that the story would be 'more acceptable through the alteration' does seem to suggest that it was done for the latter reason but those who detect a telling ambiguity about the second ending are surely in the right. Dickens, while providing a romantic happy ending for those who want or need it (though nothing like so crudely as Charlotte Brontë does at the end of *Villette*), has also written the new ending in such a way that attentive readers can understand very well that, while Estella now has a heart to pity Pip, irretrievable damage has been done to them both and she and he will, as she says, 'continue friends apart'.[34]

This last instalment with the altered ending appeared in *All the Year Round* for 3 August 1861. It had indeed continued to be the 'immense success' Dickens had claimed back in January (he used the same phrase when writing to Macready on 31 July). It met with a fair amount of disdainful, and to us today astoundingly obtuse, criticism, as did all his post-*Copperfield* work, but *The Saturday Review* praised the book as 'new, original, powerful, and very entertaining' while the *Times* critic, Eneas Sweetland Dallas rejoiced that 'Mr Dickens has in the present work given us more of his earlier fancies than we have had for years'. Judging by its popularity as a serial and its prodigious sales in volume form, both to circulating libraries (the greatest of these, Mudie's, took fourteen hundred copies) and to individuals, it was received by the reading public with the greatest enthusiasm. On 31 August Dickens told Wills jubilantly, 'There are only 90 copies left of the Third Edition, and we are now going to press with the Fourth.' The novel was greeted in the shops with a widespread display of a caricature of Dickens with a big head and little legs 'tapping his forehead to knock an idea out'. Captioned 'From Whom We Have Great Expectations', it occasioned its subject great delight, making him when he first saw it, as he reported to Lavinia Watson, shake with laughter 'in open sun-lighted Piccadilly'.[35]

The three-volume, unillustrated, edition of *Great Expectations* was not the only literary production of financial interest to Dickens that was selling well in the summer of 1861. The sales of *All the Year Round* were being kept up 'bravely' by Bulwer Lytton's *A Strange Story*, which had increased the journal's circulation by about one and a half thousand. Dickens felt free to return to his

46 Cartoon of Dickens by Charles Lyall used as advertisement for *Great Expectations*

second, and even more lucrative, career and began intensive work on new items for possible addition to his readings repertoire in preparation for the new tour which he planned to begin in October. Remembering the physical distress he had suffered while writing *Great Expectations*, he resolved, he told Forster, 'to do nothing in that way for some time if I could help it'. In the event, three whole years were to pass before he again embarked upon a full-length novel, the longest gap in his writing career so far.

CHAPTER 22

Christmas numbers, public readings, and 'uncommercial' travels

1861–1863

The last report of the Writer's Progress was made to me from the office on Christmas Eve. He had then sold the rather extraordinary number of one hundred and ninety-one thousand, odd hundred copies!

Dickens to Macready, 27 December 1862, reporting sales
of the Christmas number of *All the Year Round*

'I CANNOT REGARD myself as having a home anywhere,' Dickens wrote to Wilkie Collins on 22 April 1863 – adding, however, that he was becoming very fond of Gad's Hill because 'the place gets so pretty . . . and I am always touching it up with something new'. He was indeed spending 'a good deal of money' on enlarging and improving his Kentish property, a favourite activity that continued until his death and became a standing family joke, but he had not yet settled into his 'Squire of Gad's Hill' mode. The period between finishing *Great Expectations* in the early summer of 1861 and beginning to write his long-gestated next novel *Our Mutual Friend* towards the end of 1863 was a remarkably peripatetic one, even by Dickens's standards. In late October 1861 he embarked upon another strenuous readings tour of England and Scotland that lasted four months. The following February, in order for Mamie to have her London season, he arranged a four-month exchange of Gad's Hill with the owner of a house in Hyde Park Gate South, which he was soon denouncing as 'an odious little London box' in which it was impossible for him to write. In the summer of 1862 he embarked upon a year and a half's frequent coming and going between his apartment over the *All the Year Round* office in Wellington Street and Gad's Hill Place or between Paris and rural northern France. During this period references in his letters to his actual or proposed movements are often very vague (at one point, for example, he writes that he is going to 'vanish into space' for a few days) and even sometimes contradictory. Dickens scholars have persuasively linked all this 'oscillation', as he called it at one point, to the idea that he may have been regularly visiting Nelly and her mother, who perhaps were living in France during this time, for some part of it (perhaps again) in a cottage at Condette. Condette is a hamlet to the south of Boulogne where we know that Dickens stayed at various times during the early 1860s. The cottage, which still exists and is now called the Chalet Dickens, belonged to Dickens's amiable former Boulogne landlord, Ferdinand Beaucourt Mutuel, whom he introduces by name into his Christmas Story for 1862, *Somebody's Luggage*, where he describes him as a markedly older man than the M. Loyal Devasseur of the 1854 *Household Words* essay 'Our French Watering Place'.[1]

The notion of travelling a good deal further afield than France also haunted these years as Dickens considered and reconsidered the offer of £10,000 from the Melbourne catering firm of Spiers and Pond (who brought the first English cricket-team to the Antipodes in December 1861) for a six-month readings tour in Australia. At one point he asked Tom Beard to accompany him if he did decide to go. Such an expedition, he wrote to Beard, might, besides being highly lucrative, also be valuable to him as a writer: 'I could perhaps see that country in its present early state of transition, from some point of view (for after-use in fiction) that has not yet struck any man's fancy.' He had consulted Bulwer Lytton whose 'unlimited confidence in this possibility was almost absurd'. He even went so far, Forster tells us, 'as to plan an Uncommercial Traveller Upside Down'. He finally declined the offer, however. No doubt the very long separation from Nelly such a tour would have involved would have influenced him ('I know perfectly well before-hand how unspeakably wretched I should be,' he told Forster) as well as the fact that on 1 October 1861 the early death of Arthur Smith had robbed him of the wonderfully efficient services of his much-loved manager.[2]

Smith's death was only the first of several that affected Dickens during these early years of the new decade. It was followed only a week later by that of his ever-helpful brother-in-law Henry Austin, as a result of which he had to devote time over the next two years to obtain a government pension for his widowed sister Letitia and to help her make a new start in life. Later came the deaths of a number of friends who had been especially dear to him – Cornelius Felton, Angus Fletcher, James White and Augustus Egg. Well might he exclaim, 'What a great Cemetery one walks through, after forty!' He found comfort and support in his Christian beliefs, writing to Letitia, 'in this world there is no stay but the hope of a better, and no reliance but on the mercy and goodness of God'. Deaths stirred up memories too, of course. Eighty-nine- year-old George Beadnell died in November 1862 and Dickens wrote to Maria: 'all the old Past comes out of its grave when I think of him, and the ghosts of a good many years stand about his memory.' An unforgiven figure from the rather more recent past who also died about this time was Mrs Hogarth and we can only speculate about the welter of strong emotions, positive and fiercely negative, that must have been swirling away beneath Dickens's coldly business-like note to Catherine of 5 August 1863. It concerned the authority for opening Mary

Hogarth's grave so that her mother might be laid to rest beside her and her other child George. Dickens's note was more than cold; it was, in fact, downright cruel in the way it transformed his and Catherine's joint past into his alone, by beginning, 'When I went to America (or to Italy: I cannot positively say which, but I think on the former occasion) . . .'. A month later came the death of Dickens's own mother and his terse comment on her demise (in a postscript to a letter to Wills of 14 September) forms a notable contrast with his elaborate response to his father's death in 1851: 'My poor mother died quite suddenly at last. Her condition was frightful.' Christmas Eve brought another, far more unexpected, sudden death – that of Thackeray. This occurred only a few days after Dickens's chance encounter with him in the entrance hall of the Athenaeum when the two men shook hands and broke the hostile silence maintained between them since the foolish Garrick Club quarrel. And then, on the very last day of the year, far away in India, died Walter, Dickens's second son, though he did not, of course, learn about this loss until early in the New Year.[3]

When writing of friends' deaths Dickens was fond of invoking a military metaphor about the necessity for the survivors to 'close up the ranks'. He made telling use of it in a fund-raising speech for the Royal Free Hospital on 6 May 1863 when (perhaps with an eye to the Queen whose prolonged seclusion after the Prince Consort's death in December 1861 he considered 'very unsatisfactory') he deftly connected the subject of coping with grief following bereavement with the plight of the sick poor, condemned to die in their thousands for want of adequate medical care:

> . . . the most prosperous and best cared for among men and women know full well that whosoever is hit in this great and continuing battle of life, howsoever vast the gap may be that is made, however dear the companion may be that is down, we must close up the ranks and march on, and fight out the fight. But it happens that the rank and file are many in number, and the chances against them are many and hard, and they necessarily die by thousands, when the captains and standard-bearers only die by ones and twos.

This powerful speech was one of only four Dickens made for charity dinners during 1861–63, noticeably fewer than in previous years.[4]

During these years Dickens had numerous family matters, beyond those already mentioned, to worry and concern him. His incorrigible brother Fred, wrangling with his wife over a legal separation and continuing his career of financial fecklessness, remained a source of trouble and embarrassment. Dickens still had to find suitable careers or 'grooves', to use his word, for Frank and Alfred, likewise a congenial school for his shy and sensitive youngest child,

Edward ('Plorn'). There was the ongoing need to look after the welfare of his two sisters-in-law, the blind Harriette, deserted by Augustus in 1857, and Helen, Alfred's widow, with her five children. During the summer and autumn of 1862 he was also extremely concerned about Georgina, who was suffering from some kind of heart trouble. 'I (who know her best, I think)', he wrote to Macready on 2 July, 'see much in her that fills me with uneasiness. . . . All that alacrity and "cheer of spirit" that used to distinguish her are gone'.

Something was clearly troubling him at an even deeper level than all this, and it seems most probable that it related to Nelly. He had already told Forster in June 1862 how 'the never to be forgotten misery' of the blacking-factory time had bred in him a 'shrinking sensitiveness' which had returned in 'the never to be forgotten misery of this later time'. He referred specifically to 'the last five years', the period since Nelly's appearance in his life and his breaking up of his marriage with all the attendant painful publicity that he had, to a large extent, brought upon himself. To Wilkie Collins he wrote on 20 September 1862 about 'some rather miserable anxieties' about which he would tell him some day. He will, says Dickens, 'fight out of them . . . being not easily beaten' but 'they have gathered and gathered'. In a letter to Forster the following month he alluded to 'all this unsettled fluctuating distress in my mind' and, writing to Lever from Paris on 4 November, he referred to 'sundry ties and troubles' that 'confine my present oscillations to between this place and England'. Again, it is reasonable to suppose that these allusions to anxieties, or stresses, or difficulties must be connected, at least to some extent, with his relationship with Nelly. Certainly, his strongly emotional reaction at a performance of Gounod's *Faust*, described to Georgina on 1 February 1863, would seem to relate pretty clearly to the situation of himself and Nelly: 'I could hardly bear the thing, it affected me so, and sounded in my ears so like a mournful echo of things that lie in my own heart.' A subsequent letter to Macready (19 Feb.) shows that the scene that had specially moved him so was the one in which the innocent young Marguerite takes up the jewels that Mephistopheles has left in her path to help Faust seduce her. 'I couldn't bear it,' Dickens told his old friend, 'and gave in completely.' Nelly and he may or may nor have become lovers by this time (and we do not know for *sure* that they did so at any time), but, in any case, he had totally compromised her by becoming the chief source of financial support for her and her family. He could hardly have failed to realise that, if this were to become known, everyone would naturally believe he had seduced her.[5]

A domestic event that greatly displeased him during these years was Charley's marriage, in the autumn of 1861, to Bessie, daughter of Frederick Evans, now implacably seen by Dickens as an enemy. The young couple had been childhood sweethearts but Dickens chose to see their marriage (he did not attend the wedding) as something his unfortunate first-born could not help and largely the fault of Catherine. 'The dear fellow does what is unavoidable – his foolish mother would have effectually committed him if nothing else had,' he wrote to Hannah Brown, knowing, of course, his comment would be relayed to Burdett Coutts. His letter makes painful reading, as do Dickens's savage jibes at his old friend Mark Lemon ('as poor and mean a Hound as lives'), but such vindictive comments help us to take some measure of the sheer bitterness of that substratum of pain and anger left by the events of 1857–59 in Dickens's psyche, lying beneath the mysterious newer distresses of 1862–63. As far as Charley's marriage is concerned, it seems clear from Dickens's fierce and unrelenting hostility towards Evans, and also towards Lemon, that he continued to see their failure in June 1859 to publish his 'Personal' statement in *Punch* as both personally and professionally treacherous in the highest degree. He and Lemon were at least formally reconciled in 1867, after Clarkson Stanfield on his deathbed had appealed to Dickens to make it up with his erstwhile 'dear old Boy'. But Dickens never forgave Evans, even though he did come to accept Charley's marriage to Bessie Evans and showed great affection for the grandchildren it brought him. Evans himself seems to have retaliated by spreading scandal about Dickens in the literary world. Harriet Martineau, for example, reported to her friend Fanny Wedgwood (20 Oct., 1860) that Evans had told her, with what sounds like malicious exaggeration or even downright malicious invention, that Dickens's 'cruelty' to Catherine ('Swearing at her, in the presence of guests, children and servants') had caused him, and even the devoted Wills, to decline invitations to Gad's Hill for some while before the end of the marriage. If reports of any gossip of this kind reached Dickens's ears it would of course have greatly strengthened his enmity towards his former publisher.[6]

The one source of almost unalloyed happiness for Dickens during this fraught time lay in his public readings, those 'great experiences of the public heart', as he called them, and the 'blazes of triumph' that they ignited. The only problem was Smith's successor as Dickens's manager, the hapless Thomas Headland, 'the worthy man with the genius for mistakes', who became 'Blockheadland', or simply 'Block', in Dickens's private correspondence. That problem was still ahead, however, when Dickens settled down at Gad's Hill, in the summer of 1861, to prepare several new readings for his second provincial tour planned for the autumn. He went back to trying to get a reading out of *Copperfield* and this time managed to construct a reading that he described to Forster as being 'a continuous narrative', though the only continuity, in fact, is that provided by the presence of David himself in every episode. Unlike the three earlier readings derived from novels rather than from the shorter Christmas writings, the *Copperfield* reading does not focus on a limited section of its parent novel, like *The Story of Little Dombey*, or on one episode or one character, like *Bardell and Pickwick* or *Mrs Gamp*. In four chapters (originally six before Dickens pruned it down to a more manageable length from the two-hour version he first produced) it tells the tragic story of Steerforth and little Em'ly, interleaved, as it were, with the comedy of David's dinner for the Micawbers at Mrs Crupp's, his courtship of Dora, and her chaotic house-keeping after their marriage. Dickens thus managed to get into the one reading his benign version of his father as Micawber, his own younger and (as he saw it) better self of the Maria Beadnell days, and the most compelling seducer of innocent maidenhood he had ever created. The reading culminates in the great tempest scene from chapter 55 and ends, as does that chapter, with David viewing, with anguished memories of love and betrayal, the corpse of his boyhood's hero. Aware as he was of how closely his readers associated him personally with this novel, Dickens would surely have looked forward with a particular zest to sharing this reading with his public. It is no surprise to find him confiding to a friend a year later that *Copperfield* is 'far more interesting' to him 'than any of the other readings', and that he is 'half ashamed to confess' the tenderness he has for it.[7]

Dickens also prepared at least three other readings drawn from his full-length novels this summer but in these he followed the *Little Dombey* formula, focusing on one particular episode or sequence of events in the book concerned. The readings were *Nicholas Nickleby at the Yorkshire School* and *Mr Bob Sawyer's Party* from *Pickwick*, both of which became enormously popular, and *The Bastille Prisoner* (from Book One of *A Tale of Two Cities*) which, for some reason, was never performed, although Dickens worked on the prompt-book as thoroughly as on the others, altering the text and inserting stage-directions. *The Bastille Prisoner* focuses strongly upon Lucie Manette's reunion with her broken father and Dickens perhaps felt that the almost complete absence of any comic element (no Miss Pross) made it unsuitable for reading purposes. It is probable that Dickens also devised his reading version of *Great Expectations* this summer although he does not mention it in the late-August letter to Forster cited above (but then neither does he mention *Mr Bob Sawyer's Party*). He had a prompt-book prepared as for the other readings but seems never to have worked on it. The adaptation is drawn from the novel as a whole and like it is divided into three 'stages' (not corresponding to those in the novel, however) but it omits everything relating to Pip's love life, focusing instead on the story of Pip, Joe and Magwitch, the original 'germ' of the story. Dickens turns his novel, in fact, into a novella, and does so very effectively. He would still have had to cut it considerably for a reading, however, so that may be why he did not proceed with it. He got even less far with ideas for readings from *Bleak House*, no further than a couple of jotted notes: 'Mrs Jellyby and Mr Turveydrop / or Mrs Pardiggle./ Chesney Wold'. Another reading, also prepared this summer, that he does mention in the letter to Forster is *Mr Chops, the Dwarf*, taken from his contribution to 'A House to Let', the *Household Words* Christmas number for 1858. This item remained unperformed, however, until Dickens's Farewell Tour in 1868, when Magsman's description of Chops's ending each of his entertainments by walking 'three times round the Cairawan' with his 'Chaney sarser' [china saucer] to collect tips from the spectators before retiring behind the curtain would have had a certain comically poignant appropriateness.[8]

Dickens began his second provincial readings tour in East Anglia on 28 October 1861 and was soon reporting to Wilkie Collins that 'for a certain fantastic and hearty enjoyment' *Nickleby* 'tops all the Readings' while to Hannah Brown he wrote (in the same letter that contained the sour remarks about Charley's marriage) that the *Copperfield* reading 'seems to have ... an expression of a young spirit in it, that addresses people of sensitive perception curiously'. Meanwhile, the annual chore of compiling the lucrative Christmas number was looming. This year's offering, Dickens decided, should be based on his visit to Lucas's 'hermitage' the previous summer and he got Wills to send out the usual circular to prospective contributors. This called for stories that would show the 'absurdity' of the hermit's situation and attitudes and exemplify 'the wholesome influences of the gregarious habits of humanity'. Dickens began drafting the framework story of 'Mr Traveller's' visit to 'Mr Mopes' and tried it out on Collins. He agreed with Collins's response that it was too 'hurried and huddled up' and needed some elaboration. 'Much more can be made of it,' he replied to Collins, 'Much more, therefore (please God), *shall* be made of it, when we get to work.' In the event Collins was so busy with his (as yet unnamed) new novel, slated to follow Lytton's *A Strange Story* in *All the Year Round*, that he could not collaborate in the writing of this Christmas number in the way he had done for four of its five immediate predecessors. He did, however, contribute a comic anecdote about two babies being irretrievably mixed up at birth which Dickens thought 'exceedingly droll' though he must also, as has been suggested by a modern Dickens scholar, have recognised how out of keeping it was with the serious message the number as a whole was intended to convey. Collins also gave Dickens the idea for one of the hermit's visitors, Miss Kimmeens, a little girl who is left all alone at her school for an entire day and whose flight from the self-pitying solitude that was threatening to make her 'go wrong' emotionally is used by Mr Traveller as his trump card against Mr Mopes. 'The child notion enchants me,' Dickens wrote to Collins on 31 October, adding, 'With my love for the blessed children, I could sit down and do it out of hand, if I could do anything with the gas-lights of the night looming in the eight o'clock future.' As soon as he can get a respite from the readings, he tells Collins, he will turn over the idea so that he can work on it 'briskly and quickly' when he returns to London. This he did and only a fortnight later he had, in fact, finished work on the whole Christmas number. Called *Tom Tiddler's Ground* after a children's game, it sold very well indeed when published on 12 December. 'The news of the Xmas No. is indeed Glorious,' Dickens wrote to Wills the next day and sales eventually topped a

47 'The Committee of Concoction': Cartoon in *The Queen*, 21 December 1861 showing (left to right) George Augustus Sala, Wilkie Collins, Dickens, W. H. Wills (?), John Hollingshead

quarter of a million, making Mr Mopes's original, 'Mad Lucas', into such a national celebrity that the following spring special excursion trains had to be laid on for the hordes of Dickens's readers who wanted to come and stare at him. He himself was, not surprisingly, much distressed by the fiercely hostile nature of Dickens's depiction of him and made a rather confused counter-attack in the local press.[9]

After putting the Christmas number to bed, Dickens headed north to continue his readings tour which ended in Chester on 30 January 1862. The previous autumn he had written to a correspondent that he had 'the most pressing reasons against committing myself to any new engagement whatever, in February and March' but nothing in his February/March letters gives us much clue as to what those 'pressing reasons' might have been. They may have related to Nelly or it may simply have been the case that he was wanting to keep himself free to begin work on the new book he was now meditating. He and Mamie moved into Hyde Park Gate on 25 February and he had no public engagements before or after that until he began a series of weekly readings at St James's Hall on 13 March. He wrote one short article for *All the Year Round* to allow himself a bit of crowing over the catastrophe that was befalling America with the beginnings of the Civil War. In this piece, 'The Young Man from The Country' (*AYR*, 1 March 1862), he quotes lavishly from those parts of *American Notes* in which he had most fiercely criticised American political

life and the American press, and concludes: 'The foregoing was written in the
year eighteen hundred and forty-two. It rests with the reader to decide whether
it has received any confirmation, or assumed any colour of truth, in or about
the year eighteen hundred and sixty-two'. His private view of the Civil War was
expressed in a letter to Cerjat of 16 March in which he claimed that there was
not 'a pin to choose between the two parties': 'They will both rant and lie and
fight until they come to a compromise; and the slave may be thrown into that
compromise or thrown out of it, just as it happens.'[10]

On 28 March he spoke on behalf of the Artists' Benevolent Fund and seized
the chance to pursue his vendetta against the Royal Literary Fund and its high
administrative costs. It was, he declared, in all benevolent institutions necessary to ensure that money donated was spent on the purpose for which it was
given; otherwise, 'though flowing knee-deep in all the cardinal virtues, and
chin-deep in all the gentilities and respectabilities . . ., it would be but like the
unhappy man on whom a verdict was delivered, "found drowned" '. This
phrase 'found drowned' he had previously jotted down in his *Memoranda*,
followed by the words, 'The descriptive bill upon the wall, by the waterside'
(entry 36), and it was probably again in his mind at this time in connection
with the projected new novel, as was the related entry (no. 40) which reads,
'A "long shore" man – woman – child – or family. qy. Connect the Found
Drowned Bill with this?' Here we find the first traces of the Hexam family in
Our Mutual Friend and indeed Dickens has annotated the first of these two
entries '*Done in Our Mutual*'. The dating of all entries in *Memoranda* can only
be tentative but some, like these and others that clearly relate to *Our Mutual
Friend* (even if they were not subsequently so annotated by Dickens) can from
internal evidence be fairly confidently dated to early 1855. Presumably,
Dickens picked them out during 1862–63 when he was trawling through
Memoranda as part of the process of revolving in his mind ideas, scenes and
characters for the new novel. Among other entries relative to *Our Mutual
Friend* to be found in this 1855 section of *Memoranda* are the following:
'And by denying a thing, supposes that he altogether puts it out of existence'
(no.16), which Dickens later annotated '*Done in Podsnap*', and 'the office-boy
for ever looking out of window, who never has anything to do' (no.19), later
annotated '*Done in Our Mutual*'. Also in this section there are lists of possible
character-names (nos 12 and 14) many of which were eventually used in
Our Mutual Friend, as well as a list of possible book-titles (no. 22) among
which appear, along with the final choice, 'Our Mutual Friend', the following:
'Rokesmith's Forge', 'The Cinder Heap', and 'Dust'.[11]

The dating of other entries in *Memoranda* that clearly relate to *Our Mutual
Friend* is puzzling and Forster has confused the issue by quoting some of them
as having been included in letters written to him between 1860 and 1864. What
seems clear is that, throughout the spring and summer of 1862, Dickens was

trying to begin the writing of this new long novel and finding himself unable to do so, presumably as a result of his unsettled state and the mysterious anxieties and distresses mentioned earlier. 'I am trying to plan out a new book, but have not got beyond trying,' he told Cerjat on 16 March 1862. 'Alas! I have hit upon nothing for a story', he wrote to Forster the next month; 'Again and again I have tried but this odious little house [16 Hyde Park Gate South] seems to have stifled and darkened my invention.' Three months later things were no better – worse, in fact, because of his worries about Georgina. He wrote to Collins on 20 July, 'Sometimes, in a desperate state, I seize a pen, and resolve to precipitate myself upon a story. Then I get up again with a forehead as gnarled as the oak tree outside the window, and find all the lines in my face that ought to be on the blank paper.' This situation was to continue on into 1863, through more readings, in Paris as well as in London, and sundry 'vanishings into space' in France, and it would not be until early October of that year that he would be able to tell Forster he was at last ready and indeed 'exceedingly anxious' to begin writing his new novel.[12]

On 25 August 1862, following a couple of trips to France after his London readings had ended, he wrote to Forster that he was trying to 'coerce' his thoughts into 'hammering out the Christmas number' and also that he had an idea for beginning a longer story 'by bringing together two strongly contrasted places and two strongly contrasted sets of people, with which and with whom the story is to rest, through the agency of an electric message . . .'. Forster quotes this letter in a footnote but also quotes in his main text on the same page (p.751) an entry from *Memoranda* (no. 89) which is so close in wording to the letter that we may presume it must also belong to this date (that is, if Forster did not actually fabricate the passage in the letter from it, as he may well have done). The electric message notion was dropped before Dickens began writing *Our Mutual Friend* but the idea of beginning with two strongly contrasting places and sets of people stayed with him and was the basis of the opening of the novel that, he told Forster thirteen months later (12 Oct.1863), he could see 'perfectly'. This particular entry in *Memoranda* is followed by some fifteen or so others many of which relate directly to *Our Mutual Friend*. Among them we find the germs of ideas for various major and minor situations and characters in the novel such as Rokesmith's pretending to have died so that he can assume another identity (he '*is* dead to all intents and purposes external to himself'), the mutual deception of the Lammles, the Veneerings ('the perfectly New people'), one character reading Gibbon's *Decline and Fall* aloud to another one, and certain aspects of Eugene Wrayburn. If Forster's dating of the electric message idea entry is correct, these entries following it must all belong to late summer/early autumn 1862. If this is the case, it does seem somewhat surprising that Dickens had already imagined so many characters and situations of the novel, major as well as minor (no Bella Wilfer as yet, though, no 'Boffin's Bower', and no Bradley Headstone), and yet he was still not ready to settle down to the actual writing of it for another year. It reinforces the idea conveyed by the mysterious allusions in his letters quoted above that during 1862–63 he was subject to an unusual amount of mental and emotional distraction.

No amount of mental and emotional distraction, however, could be allowed to interfere with his constant close attention to *All the Year Round*. He corresponded regularly with Wills about contributions either accepted or to be rejected and about the make-up of particular numbers. He was also closely in touch with Bulwer Lytton about his *A Strange Story* which ran in the journal from 10 August 1861 to 8 March 1862. Dickens was predictably deferential in his dealings with Bulwer Lytton and constant in praising his story, but persuaded him to eschew footnotes. 'The difficulty', he wrote, 'of getting people to read notes (which they invariably regard as interruptions of the text – not as strengtheners or elucidators of it), is wonderful.' He also strongly counselled Bulwer Lytton against explanatory prefaces and appendices. Such things were always anathema to Dickens the novelist. 'Let the book explain itself,' he advised Bulwer Lytton, adding, with that unswerving admiration for his friend's grandiose writing that puzzles us today, 'It speaks *for* itself with a noble eloquence.' Bulwer Lytton's successor in the serial slot was Wilkie Collins. Dickens had earlier regarded him as a literary protégé in whom he took especial pride, but now addressed him much more as an equal while Collins, for his part, evidently felt no difficulty in rejecting en masse the twenty-six different titles Dickens offered him for his new story, settling eventually on one of his own inventing, *No Name*. He was now very much established as a successful author on the strength of *The Woman in White* and resigned – with Dickens's full agreement and approval – from the staff of *All the Year Round* in January 1862, as he could well afford to do with an offer of £5,000 for a new novel from the firm of Smith and Elder in his pocket. His resignation did not affect his continuing importance to Dickens, either as close friend or as fellow-artist. 'To hold consultation', Dickens wrote to him on 31 October 1861, 'on the quiet pursuits in which we have had so much common interest for a long time now – is a delightful and wholesome thing in the midst of this kind of life [his provincial readings tour] – in the midst of any kind of life.' *No Name* ran, with great success, in *All The Year Round* from 15 March 1862 to 17 January 1863 and Dickens extolled it as '*wonderfully fine*' with touches in the comic-scoundrel figure of Captain Wragge 'which no one but a born (and cultivated) Writer could get near'. His general praise in the same letter of Collins's development as a professional writer shows how much Dickens saw him as a younger version of himself, '[combining] invention and power, both humorous and pathetic, with that invincible determination to work, and that profound conviction that nothing of worth is to be done without work, of which triflers and feigners have no conception.'[13]

As Dickens was seeking to 'hammer out' an idea for the Christmas number in August 1862 and trawling through *Memoranda* his eye must have been caught by one of the items in the 1855 list of possible titles (no. 22). This was 'Somebody's Luggage', and just beneath it appears 'To Be Left 'Till Called For'. These two phrases evidently sparked off something in his imagination that led to the creation of his most brilliant and original Christmas number to date. He had always had a good eye for waiters and in recent years, since beginning on his readings tours and his general wanderings, 'uncommercial' and otherwise, he would have been having quite a varied experience of them. Stimulated by the title he had rediscovered, he made the narrator of this Christmas number a quintessential London waiter named Christopher. Born and bred to the business, he is now in his sixties, a highly dignified and self-satisfied head waiter in a good old-fashioned establishment ('We are a bed business, and a coffee-room business. We are not a general dining business, nor do we wish it. . . .'). His opening professional disquisition 'includes (I hope)', Dickens wrote to Forster, 'everything you know about waiters, presented humorously'. By mid-September he had written this monologue, which ends with Christopher's description of how he was manoeuvred into buying a lot of luggage that had long been left 'till called for' at his hotel. Every item of it is stuffed with untitled manuscripts completely unrelated to each other, all written by the 'Somebody' who owns the luggage. Christopher assigns titles to these manuscripts according to which article of luggage they were found in – 'His Boots', 'His Umbrella', and so on. In this way Dickens wittily solved his perennial problem of trying to invent a framework tale into which his contributors' stories could fit, and avoided the resulting frustration when, as usually happened, they failed to understand his idea. He now produced what he described to Collins as 'a comic defiance of the difficulties of an Xmas No.' and in his usual circular to potential contributors could announce that the number's 'slight leading notion' had been 'devised with a view to placing as little restriction as possible on the fancies of my fellow-writers'. By mid-September he had not only completed the waiter's opening monologue but also written a 'ridiculously comical and unexpected end' for the number. Entitled 'His Wonderful End', this takes the form of an elaborate in-joke about *All the Year Round* and its Christmas numbers, would-be authors, the correcting of proofs and Dickens himself as editor.[14]

When telling Wills on 14 September that he had written the beginning and end of *Somebody's Luggage*, Dickens mentioned that he planned soon 'to be at work on a pretty story for it' and by 8 October had finished writing 'His Boots'. The description of the little French garrison town in which the story is set was a distillation of his observations during his summer wanderings in northern France when he visited a number of such towns which still retained their fortifications created by Louis XIV's great engineer Vauban. 'I wonder', he mused in a letter to Beard after the number had been published and had sold prodigiously, 'how many people among those purchasers have an idea of the number of hours of steamboat, railway train, dusty French walk, and looking out of window, boiled down in His Boots?' He prided himself on the accuracy of his description, telling Hannah Brown that he had sought 'to make a complete Camera Obscura picture of a dull fortified French town ... trying how much I could possibly suggest – of the truth – to the fancy or the recollection, in the compass of five or six pages'. The 'prettiness' Dickens claimed for the little story set in this town derives from the tender care taken by a French corporal of a neglected little child, Bebelle, who, it is implied, is illegitimate. After the corporal's heroic death fighting a fire Bebelle is rescued by a middle-aged Englishman, known as 'Mr the Englishman', staying in the town. He affects moroseness, having left home after harshly repudiating his daughter (the implication is that it was over an illegitimate baby). As a result of his observation of, and later contacts with, the corporal and little Bebelle he undergoes a change of heart. He adopts the child and takes her back to England with him, to his forgiven daughter. His actions are observed throughout with benevolent approval by two of the townsfolk, one of them being old M. Mutuel. The idea for this story came to him, Dickens told Hannah Brown in the letter cited above, 'by seeing a French soldier acting as nurse to his master's – a captain's – little baby girl, and washing her and putting her to bed, and getting her up again in the morning, with the greatest gravity and gentleness'. It has been suggested that this tale of the adoption of an illegitimate child might have been inspired by Nelly's bearing Dickens a child somewhere in France at this time. There is a certain amount of circumstantial evidence which might seem to indicate such an event as having occurred, and a couple of later 'Bebelle' references in Dickens's letters and journalism may seem to support this idea, but in the absence of any hard evidence it has to remain only speculation.[15]

In his letters Dickens seems more concerned with the topographical accuracy of the setting of 'His Boots' than with the actual story, which he called 'very slight in itself' in a letter to Collins of 8 October. Collins had written to say that he would not be able to contribute a story to *Somebody's Luggage* because of the pressure he was under to complete *No Name* while suffering greatly from complicated health problems. Dickens replied, 'I think I shall now go at some short odd comic notion, to supply your place.' The result was 'His Brown-Paper Parcel', another lively first-person piece, the speaker being a brilliant but lazy young pavement-artist disgusted by seeing his own work passed off as that of others. In it Dickens seems to be having some kind of private, 'lazy apprentice', type of joke with himself about his hordes of imitators, especially, perhaps, those who copied his Christmas numbers and who were a contributing factor when, five years later, he resolved to terminate the series despite the huge sales successive numbers commanded. Ironically, just as he was writing this piece Dickens himself, anxious about Collins's state of health – and also, no doubt, anxious editorially with regard to the continuity of the serialisation of *No Name* – was offering to write imitation-Collins if his friend became too ill to carry on: 'Absurdly unnecessary to say that it would be but a make-shift! But I could do it, at a pinch, so like you as that no one should find out the difference'. In the event, Collins with the constant medical attention of Frank Beard (whose bedside ministrations sometimes extended to taking dictation) did not require Dickens's proffered help though he greatly appreciated the offer.[16]

Having finished all his part of *Somebody's Luggage*, Dickens crossed to France on 16 October and seems to have spent a few days wandering in the French–Flemish country near the Belgian border before going to meet Georgina and Mamie at Boulogne on the 19th. He was to take them on to Paris where they were all three going to remain until just before Christmas in the hope that the change would be beneficial to Georgina, who seemed to be recovering from her summer illness. He wrote to Wills from Hazebroucke on the 17th, sending corrected proofs of articles to appear in *All the Year Round* and announcing that, as he had 'leisure for adventure', he was 'going to have a look at Dunquerque – in the Uncommercial interest'. This is the first hint we have that he may have been thinking about embarking on the promised new 'Uncommercial Traveller' series, even though he was constantly struggling to get started on the new book. In fact, it was to be another seven months before the Uncommercial would reappear in the pages of *All the Year Round*, and Dunkirk had evidently not proved very inspiring since Dickens wrote about no visit to it. He tells Wills also that he has been in 'two old Vauban defended towns' and was gratified to find that the description in 'His Boots', which he had been checking against the reality, was 'amazingly accurate'. He was similarly gratified to notice 'only . . . one thing missed in the Copperfield storm' (he does not say what) when he stood for five tempestuous hours at the end of Boulogne pier waiting for Georgina and Mamie while their packet-boat made repeated vain attempts to reach harbour, having in the end to put in at Calais.[17]

Dickens's letters to Wills about his relaxed sightseeing tour in northern France seem difficult to reconcile with the notion that there might have been some kind of crisis going on involving Nelly and an illegitimate child. True, he had written to Lever in November 1862 about 'sundry ties and troubles' that kept him 'oscillating' between Paris and England but it seems to me more probable that he is there referring to ongoing concerns about his sons, sister, sister-in-law, mother, and so on, rather than to Nelly. However, if she and her mother were at this time indeed domiciled somewhere in northern France – possibly, as her biographer speculates, in the Paris region – this may have been part of the reason for Dickens's decision to make a three-month sojourn in

Paris at a time when so much was demanding his attention at home. No doubt
the desire to give the convalescent Georgina a change also played a part in this
decision, and this may well have been the time, if Dickens and Nelly were in
regular contact, when Georgina and Nelly began to form that close and affectionate friendship which was to continue after Dickens's death and Nelly's
marriage.[18]

Dickens found Paris, which Haussmann was transforming into a city of
grand boulevards and sumptuous new buildings, 'more amazing than ever'
with 'the Genius of the Lamp always building palaces in the night'. The beauty
and civilised charm of the city became a recurrent theme in his writing of the
1860s, as, for example, in 'The Boiled Beef of New England' (first published as
'The Uncommercial Traveller' in *AYR*, 15 Aug. 1863):

48 Charles Fechter as Hamlet

The meanness of Regent-street, set against the great line of Boulevards in Paris, is as striking as the abortive ugliness of Trafalgar-square, set against the gallant beauty of the Place de la Concorde. London is shabby by daylight, and shabbier by gaslight. No Englishman knows what gaslight is, until he sees the Rue de Rivoli and the Palais Royal after dark.

His interest in French theatre, always strong, was now perhaps even stronger as a result of the close friendship he had formed with the thirty-eight-year-old romantic actor Charles Fechter, born of a German father but brought up in Paris, whose work he had long admired; he had written him a fervent fan letter when Fechter first appeared on the London stage and was now advising him about his forthcoming period of management at the Lyceum Theatre. Wills came over to Paris in mid-November to settle the contents of *Somebody's Luggage* and Dickens himself made a few lightning trips to London, one of them motivated by concern for his old mesmeric friend Dr John Elliotson's financial situation, a false alarm as it turned out. There is no mention in any of Dickens's surviving letters from these months in Paris of any attempts at writing and his plans for the immediate future as outlined in a letter to Letitia of 20 December do not suggest that he was contemplating much activity in that line for some time. He had already told her that, after a family Christmas at Gad's Hill, he would return to Paris in January to give a reading at the British Embassy for an English charity. Now he wrote that there was no likelihood of his returning until 'at the earliest, the middle of February'. He might go on to see friends in Genoa and in any case wanted to look about him 'in many odd places'. On the other hand, we find him telling Chapman and Hall on 2 January that he hoped 'shortly' to decide 'on the subject of a new book'. He does not, we notice, yet use the title *Our Mutual Friend* so perhaps he had not yet finally settled on it and, as we know, he always needed to have his title settled before he could begin writing. He assured Chapman and Hall that 'the matter [of the new novel] is continually in my mind and occupying my thoughts' (witness those notes in *Memoranda*, no doubt) but that he could not foresee finding time for it before February. Then, only a week later, he told another correspondent that he had promised to visit Lausanne, and perhaps also Genoa, after the Paris Reading. *Somebody's Luggage*, meanwhile, was doing amazing business as he happily reported to Macready in the letter quoted above as epigraph to this chapter.

Writing from Gad's Hill on 6 January 1863, Dickens told his friend Sir Joseph Olliffe, physician to the British Embassy, that he would reach Paris on the 15th, just two days before the date set for the reading, after visiting 'a sick friend [presumably Nelly] concerning whom I am anxious'. In Paris such was the demand for tickets for his Embassy reading that he had to agree to give two more, on the 29th and 30th. Between them he 'vanish[ed] into space for a day or two', returning (again presumably) to Nelly. These Paris readings were a great success, with the audiences' enthusiasm inspiring Dickens to surpass himself. 'I got things out of the old *Carol*', he told Wills on 4 February, '– effects I mean – so entirely new and so very strong, that I quite amazed myself.' As to the *Copperfield* reading, 'When David proposed to Dora, gorgeous beauties all radiant with diamonds, clasped their fans between their two hands, and rolled about in ecstasy.' Now, in search of a reading calculated to produce an even greater sensation than any he had so far included in his repertoire, he turned to *Oliver Twist* and the murder of Nancy but in the event decided that it was just too terrible: 'I have got something so horrible out of it', he wrote to William Brookfield, on 24 May, 'that I am afraid to try it in public'. Six years were to pass before he was able to overcome this apprehension.

He left Paris on 5 February to spend ten days or so touring in the French–Flemish country. On his birthday he found himself in Arras, Robespierre's birthplace which he had been curious to see. During this little excursion he gathered some good material for possible use in future 'Uncommercial Traveller' papers, like the comically homely 'Théâtre Religieux' he happened upon at a fair in Arras and which he for some reason relocated to Hazebroucke in the first of the new 'Uncommercial Traveller' series (*AYR*, 2 May 1863; indexed as 'From Dover to Calais' in the *AYR* volume and subsequently reprinted with the title 'The Calais Night Mail'). By 17 February he was back in England, summoning Georgina to meet him in London, where a predictable heap of business awaited him. He was soon in full swing again with various activities but these did not include beginning to write the new novel. On 6 March he began a new series of London readings at irregularly-spaced intervals, which continued until 27 June. Howitt's publication of his strongly-opinionated *History of the Supernatural* and the appearance of an autobiography written by the celebrated American medium Daniel Dunglass Home provoked him into writing two devastatingly funny reviews for *All the Year Round*, 'Rather a Strong Dose' (21 March) and 'The Martyr Medium' (4 April). 'The stupendous absurdity of Howitt's book is inconceivable,' he wrote to Collins on 22 April, whereas 'Home's is clearly (to me) the book of a scoundrel without shame.'

On 4 April he spoke, as eloquently as ever, on behalf of the Royal General Theatrical Fund, implicitly pleading the cause for respect for all entertainers of the public including writers, and he spoke also, as already mentioned, for the Royal Free Hospital (6 May). As to writing, he may or may not have been intending to embark at this time on the now long-promised new series of 'Uncommercial Traveller' papers but his hand was forced in any case. Sales of *All the Year Round* were beginning to slip. Dickens believed this was because the new serial he had commissioned, Charles Reade's *Very Hard Cash*, was not holding the readers' interest as Collins and Lytton had done in their very different ways, even though it came from the pen of a well-established novelist whose hugely popular *The Cloister and the Hearth* had only recently appeared. It was necessary, Dickens decided, that he himself once again should 'strike in', and a new series of the Uncommercial, for which he had recently been researching copy in France, was the obvious choice. The drop in sales was, fortunately, nothing like so serious as the one that had forced him to push Lever aside and re-conceive *Great Expectations* as a weekly serial – fortunately, because his slowly-forming ideas for the big book that became *Our Mutual Friend* could hardly have been so deftly adapted to serialisation in weekly 'teaspoonfuls' as the Pip and Magwitch idea had been. Accordingly, the issue of *All The Year Round* for 25 April announced 'THE UNCOMMERCIAL TRAVELLER, / A New Series of Occasional Papers / By CHARLES DICKENS, / WILL BE RESUMED NEXT WEEK'.[19]

Between April and October he wrote twelve new 'Uncommercial Traveller' pieces for *All the Year Round*. Some reported on visits to particular places like the admirable Stepney pauper schools that he had visited with the great sanitary reformer Edwin Chadwick on 27 May (*AYR*, 20 June; reprinted as 'The Short-Timers' in the *UT* volume of the Cheap Edition in 1866) or a Mormon emigrant ship on the eve of sailing for America (*AYR*, 4 July; reprinted as 'Bound For the Great Salt Lake'). Others were familiar essays, on such themes as birthday festivities, old City churchyards, funeral ceremonies, and London alms-houses. Some contained the same kind of apparently autobiographical material as had featured in various similar essays from the previous series. Dickens scholars can sometimes verify this material from external sources but mostly not. Contemporary readers, however, would naturally have tended to identify the Traveller with Dickens himself. They would have been led to believe, for example, that Dickens had been educated at a regular middle-class boarding-school where a hamper of treats from his loving parents would regularly arrive on his birthday (*AYR*, 6 June; reprinted as 'Birthday Celebrations'). 'The Calais Night Mail' clearly reflected his recent Channel-hopping and travels in northern France and provided the opportunity for a comic excursus on sea-sickness (a malady that much afflicted Dickens) and gave him also a chance to remind his readers of his last Christmas story which had so delighted them. The little caged bird which the Traveller imagines twitteringly addressing him all the way from Calais to Hazebroucke tells him, 'Scattered through this country are mighty works of VAUBAN, whom you know about, and regiments of such corporals as you heard of once upon a time, and many a blue-eyed Bebelle.' The second essay (*AYR*, 16 May; reprinted as 'Some Recollections of Mortality') contains a wonderful set-piece on a visit to the Paris Morgue. Memories of this macabre theatre of death, always so fascinating to Dickens on the 'attraction of repulsion' principle, surely fed into those descriptions of corpses fished out of the Thames that supply Gaffer Hexam with his grisly wallpaper in the third chapter of *Our Mutual Friend*. A third 'Uncommercial' paper had been published and at least two, probably three, more had been finished by the time Dickens wrote to Georgina from London on 18 June, 'My head is addled with Uncommercial Travelling – done for the time, I am happy to say.' A period of relaxation at Gad's Hill followed, somewhat marred by a temporary swelling on the back of his neck and the fact that, with five of his sons at home, Gad's Hill was, as he put it, 'pervaded by boys to a fearful extent': 'They boil over (if an affectionate parent may mention it), all over the house.'[20]

He was surprised one day to receive a letter from Eliza Davis, wife of the Jewish solicitor who had bought Tavistock House, and whom he had privately referred to at the time as a 'Jew Money Lender'. Inviting Dickens to contribute to a Jewish charity, Davis expressed her regret that 'Charles Dickens the large-hearted, whose works plead so eloquently and so nobly for the oppressed of his country' should, through his creation of Fagin, have been responsible for encouraging 'a vile prejudice' against people of her race. Just as he had done when attacked by Lewes over spontaneous combustion in *Bleak House*, Dickens defended himself on historical grounds, pointing out that at the time in which the story was set most London receivers of stolen property were, in fact, Jewish. His constant reference to Fagin as 'the Jew', he told Davis, simply 'conveys that kind of idea of him which I should give my readers of a Chinaman, by calling him a Chinese'; it implied no hostility towards Jews as such – still less, as Davis had charged, towards the Hebrew religion. Unsurprisingly, Davis was not wholly appeased by this answer, which rather side-stepped (how consciously on Dickens's part who can say?) the main point, namely that Fagin is an unforgettable figure of pure evil – diabolic indeed, yet also fascinating and seductive – and that in depicting him Dickens had very obviously drawn on anti-Jewish folklore and stereotypes, as well as, consciously or unconsciously, on that devastating period of his own personal history from which the character's name was taken. The resultant fictional figure had, we may remember, bemused him ('the Jew . . . is such an out and outer I don't know what to make of him') so how was he now to explain Fagin away on rational historical grounds? The fact that he had recently been toying with the idea of performing Fagin in his most diabolic aspect as part of a sensational new addition to his readings repertoire, may well have added to his evident discomfort regarding this matter.[21]

He could not alter or soften Fagin's role and character in the way he had done Miss Mowcher's in *Copperfield*. Later, when the sheets of the Charles Dickens Edition *Oliver Twist* were passing through the press in 1867, he probably had Davis's remonstrance in mind when he suddenly began, from chapter 39 onwards, altering references to Fagin as 'the Jew', substituting instead 'he' or 'Fagin'. More immediately, Davis's remonstrance had suggested to him a way in which he might make some immediate amends. Replying to his letter, Davis wrote, 'I hazard the opinion that it would well repay an author of reputation to examine more closely into the manners and character of the

British Jews and to represent them as they really are, to "Nothing extenuate nor aught set down in Malice". Dickens did not answer this letter but he must have decided, either at this time or soon afterwards, to add to the ingredients of the new novel he was brewing an elaborately described and documented, thoroughly good, Jewish character. The result was the appearance in *Our Mutual Friend* the following year of the (unfortunately thoroughly tiresome) character of Jenny Wren's 'fairy godfather', saintly old Riah.

'I am always thinking of writing a long book, and never beginning to do it,' Dickens told Wilkie Collins on 9 August. Instead, he wrote two more 'Uncommercial' pieces, one about cheap dining-halls for working men (*AYR*, 15 Aug.; reprinted as 'The Boiled Beef of New England') and the other about a visit to Chatham (*AYR*, 29 Aug.; reprinted as 'Chatham Dockyard'). In this last piece a mysterious 'wise boy' emerges from an old fort in the marsh country near Chatham to instruct the Uncommercial Traveller in local lore. 'He has also greatly enlightened me', writes the Traveller, 'touching the mushrooms of the marshes, and has gently reproved my ignorance in having supposed them to be impregnated with salt.' He has also proved to be a mine of information about all the different vessels to be seen on the Medway. Like the 'very queer small boy' of 'Travelling Abroad' and the 'supernaturally intelligent' small boy of the *Little Dorrit* Preface, he seems to be – at least in part – another avatar of Dickens himself as a child, and in the essay the Traveller does indeed refer to his childhood familiarity with the Dockyard. This boy may equally well be, as has been suggested, a playful portrait of Dickens's sailor son, Sydney the 'little Admiral', who was among the boys at home this summer, his ship being in dry dock at Chatham, and who might well have accompanied his father on the visit to the Dockyard described in the essay. Dickens does not refer to his Uncommercial writings in the 9 August letter to Collins but mentions that he was 'thinking of evaporating for a fortnight on the 18th'. His variant here on his earlier phrase about 'disappearing into space' strongly suggests to us today that his journey probably involved spending some time with Nelly who was, presumably, still resident in France.[22]

Dickens went to France on 18 August and on the 31st reported himself to his solicitor Frederic Ouvry as being just back 'from a fortnight's Uncommercial Travelling abroad'. He had been once more in northern France and distilled his experience of the country into a vivid paper for *All the Year Round* (12 Sept.; reprinted as 'In the French–Flemish Country'), doubtless drawing also upon his earlier visits to this part of the world. During this August excursion he had had time and space to concentrate on the projected, and as yet still untitled, new novel and told Forster on 30 August that he 'was full of notions for the new twenty numbers'. First, however, there was 'the Christmas stone' to be 'clear[ed] out of the road' – in other words, the 1863 Christmas number of *All the Year Round*. Once he had finished that, he wrote, 'I think I can dash into it [i.e., the road] on the grander journey'. It would seem, though we have no hard evidence on which to base such a surmise, that at least some of the mental or emotional distress (probably connected with Nelly in some way) that had been troubling him had now somehow been assuaged. He was at last really ready to start work on the big new book about which he had been thinking, on and off, for so long and jotting down ideas for in his *Book of Memoranda*. As to 'the Christmas stone', that was soon shifted. Stimulated perhaps by his discussions with Letitia, middle-aged and childless, about her idea of supplementing the government pension he had obtained for her by letting lodgings, Dickens, as he had once 'thought of' Mr Pickwick, now thought of Mrs Lirriper, a kindly, garrulous, middle-aged, and childless widow who lets lodgings at 81 Norfolk Street, Strand (at that time Norfolk Street led down from the Strand to the Thames). She became the narrator of the Christmas number and proved herself a fully worthy successor in this role to Christopher the waiter. Indeed, she may be said to represent a higher reach of Dickens's art in that Christopher, wholly defined as he is in both speech and behaviour by his profession, is very much a characteristic figure of Dickensian comedy. Mrs Lirriper, on the other hand, is a genuinely humorous creation. She is certainly comic but also moving, one of Dickens's most successful depictions of a good woman, hidden away now in a little-read minor work.[23]

Mrs Lirriper's Lodgings also represents a notable artistic development in Dickens's Christmas numbers series. Hitherto the story element in the framework devised for each Christmas number from *The Seven Poor Travellers* onwards had been distinctly vestigial, apart from the collaborations with Wilkie Collins between 1856 and 1860. These had, not surprisingly, all revolved around a plot including sensational events and/or mystery and detection. Now in the story of Mrs Lirriper and her touching mutually-dependent relationship with her lodger 'Major' Jemmy Jackman and their joint adoption of the little orphan child, whom they name Jemmy Lirriper, Dickens seems to be giving his readers a Dickens novel in miniature. Indeed, he told Percy Fitzgerald that he 'really put as much into Mrs Lirriper as would almost make a novel' and to many readers this story must have seemed like a welcome reprise of the Betsey Trotwood/ Mr Dick/ young David story in *Copperfield*. This framework story meant that the dovetailing into it of stories written for the number by others was far less problematic than usual. Dickens's circular letter to potential contributors, sent out by Wills on 10 September, is brief and virtually all-permissive. The stories, supposedly told to Major Jackman over the years by various of Mrs Lirriper's lodgers and now committed to paper by him, may be written in the third person or the first and may relate to any season or period; they may be told to an audience, or to the reader, or written without the writer knowing how they will come to light, if they ever do, and so on. Dickens was confident that, given this frame story, he would be able to accommodate them all.[24]

He was about to begin writing when he was delayed by the sudden death of his mother on 12 September and the need to make the funeral arrangements. Coping with this latter necessity would have stirred up his abiding scorn for the fatuous and costly pomposity of Victorian funerals, to which he had last given vent in chapter 35 of *Great Expectations* (first published 20 April 1861). He quickly 'jobbed up', as he wittily put it (meaning, put together in a meretricious manner), a scathing 'Uncommercial' article on the subject (*AYR*, 26 Sept. 1863; reprinted as 'Medicine Men of Civilisation'). That done, he returned to Mrs Lirriper. He told Wills on 14 September that he was about to tackle her and hoped 'to make something of her'. He had his title, *Mrs Lirriper's Lodgings*, and thought it 'a good one'. He had presumably finished the story by 7 October, when he told Georgina that he had a 'still-unbegun Uncommercial' to write before he could come down to Gad's Hill. This piece, which completed the series of twelve he had decided upon, depicted a typical London almshouse and its inhabitants (could it, one wonders, have been partly a long-delayed riposte to Anthony Trollope's 1855 lampoon of Dickens in *The Warden* as 'Mr Popular Sentiment' writing a highly-coloured account of Hiram's Hospital in his novel *The Almshouse*?). It appeared in *All The Year Round* on 24 October and was reprinted in *The Uncommercial Traveller* as 'Titbull's Alms-Houses'. He had been distracted from writing it by, among other things, an earthquake that occurred in London in the early hours of the morning of 6 October. He felt impelled to send an account of his experience to *The Times*. He was awoken, he wrote, by a violent swinging and heaving motion 'as if some great beast had been crouching asleep under the bedstead and were now shaking itself and trying to rise'. At their weekly gathering that evening the *Punch* team made merry with speculations that the 'great beast' might have been Forster.[25]

Dickens had told Chapman and Hall back on 8 September, when he wrote formally to propose to them a new work in twenty monthly numbers for which they should pay him £6,000 for the half copyright, that he would need to 'be rid of the Xmas No. here and of the Uncommercial Traveller before I can begin work to any great purpose'. Now both those commitments were dealt with and he was, as he told Forster, 'exceedingly anxious to begin my book'. It is remarkable testimony both to his passion for the theatre, and to the intensity of his friendship for Fechter, that he should about this time take the trouble to send Tom Beard on 29 October one of the longest letters he ever wrote in his life describing in great detail a highly melodramatic play in which Fechter was starring at the Lyceum. He sent it to guide Beard in writing a laudatory review of the production. With regard to his new book, he told Forster that he wanted it to start appearing in the spring but was 'determined not to begin to publish with less than five numbers done'. He had had enough health problems of recent years to make him anxious about putting himself to any greater writing pressure than was necessary. A sombre sign of the times as far as Dickens's life was concerned was that for the first time the contract with his publishers was to include provision for what should happen in the event of his death during the course of serialisation. The contract for *Our Mutual Friend*, the title having now been fixed upon, was formally signed, on the terms Dickens had proposed, on 21 November.[26]

A few days later, on 3 December, *Mrs Lirriper's Lodgings* was published and was an immediate best-seller. William Edrupt, Dickens's office-boy in Wellington Street, when he was interviewed in old age clearly remembered the stir that it had made, though he mistakenly remembered it as having been a serial. He recalled 300,000 copies of this Christmas number being sold, Wellington Street 'crowded with folks wanting to know the end of the story' and 'big posters up all over the town'. Even *The Saturday Review* capitulated, calling the number 'a great performance': 'There are only twelve pages of Mrs Lirriper, and yet she is so drawn in that short space that we can scarcely believe that there really is no such person, and that a fortnight ago no one had ever heard of her.' For Dickens himself she was as 'real' as any of his characters. 'Of course,' he wrote to the London historian Peter Cunningham on 5 December, 'Mrs Lirriper lived on the East side of the Street (how did you know it?) but not so far down as you suppose. On the Northern side of Howard street.' She was, he wrote to Wills on 20 December, presumably after receiving some very satisfactory sales figures, 'a most brilliant old lady. God bless her!' His playful prophecy about this latest Christmas story to Marguerite Power on 10 November, 'Ah! The last Roc's egg is indeed an egg! When it is fully hatched ... I intend to rest my fame upon the bird,' was more than fulfilled, and Mrs Lirriper brought him a reward that he valued even beyond sales figures: 'I doubt', he wrote to Sir Joseph Olliffe on 8 December, 'if I have ever done any thing that has been so affectionately received by such an enormous audience. I can't turn any where without encountering some enthusiasm about her.'[27]

So, with applause ringing in his ears from his last performance and with whatever private anxieties had been troubling him over the past two years or so at least assuaged, Dickens was at last ready, with the dawn of the New Year, to set out upon 'the grander journey'.

CHAPTER 23

Back to the 'big brushes'

WRITING *OUR MUTUAL FRIEND*, 1864–1865

Strange to say I felt at first quite dazed in getting back to the large canvas and the big brushes; and even now, I have a sensation as of acting at the San Carlo after Tavistock House, which I could hardly have supposed would have come upon so old a stager.

Dickens to Wilkie Collins, 25 January 1864[1]

BY 25 JANUARY 1864 Dickens had finished the first two monthly numbers of *Our Mutual Friend* (Book One, chs 1–7), a big step towards fulfilling his determination to have no fewer than five numbers safely under his belt before publication began at the end of April. As in the case of *A Tale of Two Cities*, he divided his new story into books, with the chapters being numbered to each book. In the letter to Collins cited above he called what he had written 'a combination of drollery with romance which requires a deal of pains and a perfect throwing away of points that might be amplified'. 'Drollery' certainly pervades his description of the Veneerings' dinner-party, the Wilfer ménage, Wegg and Mr Boffin, and the melancholy taxidermist Mr Venus, lovelorn among the 'lovely trophies' of his art whilst 'romance' attaches to Lizzie Hexam, a latter-day Gothic heroine glowing like a jewel in a dark setting and also the mysteriously agitated young man who later, calling himself Julius Handford re-appears at the Wilfers' home where the reader meets Bella, a second young beauty who is seemingly trapped by life. All the time Dickens, 'the story-weaver at his loom', as he was famously to call himself in this novel's 'Postscript, In Lieu of Preface' is beginning, with 'a deal of pains', to weave into these early chapters those 'finer threads' that will eventually help to reveal the whole pattern and meaning of the book without highlighting and elaborating details in such a way as to distract the reader.

Just at this moment Dickens was called upon to write an obituary of Thackeray – his 'fellow-worker' as he called him – for Thackeray's own journal *The Cornhill*. In its pages Thackeray had just embarked on a new serial story, *Denis Duval*, only four instalments of which had so far been published. Dickens asked to borrow the manuscript of the last instalment on which

Thackeray had been working and which he had not lived to finish. The empathy that clearly informs Dickens's comment on the fragment is all the more poignant when we recall that he himself was also to die in mid-story. 'That it would be sad to anyone', he wrote, '– that it is inexpressibly so to a writer – in its evidences of matured designs never to be accomplished, of intentions begun to be executed and destined never to be completed, of careful preparation for long roads of thought that he was never to traverse, and for shining goals that he was never to reach, will be readily believed.'

On the other hand, Dickens could not resist making a somewhat acerbic comment on what had been, in his view, Thackeray's unsatisfactory stance in the 'Dignity of Literature' debate: 'I thought that he too much feigned a want of earnestness, and that he made a pretence of under-valuing his art, which was not good for the art that he held in trust.' Dickens wrote to Collins on 25 January that he had tried delicately to suggest 'the two points in his character as a literary man that were bad for the literary cause' and had steered well clear of 'the fulsome and injudicious trash' written about Thackeray by other obituary-writers. He had, we are unsurprised to find, been particularly galled by those obituarists who had dwelt on Thackeray's having been ' "a gentleman", "a great gentleman", and the like – as if the rest of us were of the tinker tribe'. And it was only at proof stage that he deleted his final sentence which criticised Thackeray's partiality for titled folk: 'His funeral will always be as memorable to me in that wise [that is, for the number of colleagues present], as for its shabby representation of the order usually called "the Great": upon which he, as a man of genius, perhaps had sometimes condescended to bestow too much of his attention.'[2]

Dickens's working notes for the first number of *Our Mutual Friend* suggest that he had the main outline of the whole story already in his mind. He not only notes that there will be four books but even gives their titles. He tells himself to 'lay the ground carefully' in describing the Veneerings' dinner-party – mindful, presumably, of his plans to develop the Harmon plot and the character and behaviour of the young dandy Eugene Wrayburn. He needs also to 'lay the ground' for the Lammle marriage and its conspiratorial aftermath. Another note reads, 'Work in two witnesses by name: for end of story'. The names to be 'worked in' are Job Potterson and Jacob Kibble, the latter being taken, like so many others in this novel (Twemlow, Podsnap, Harmon, Rokesmith, Higden, and so on) from the long lists of available names in *Memoranda* which Dickens was evidently closely consulting at this stage. Already in this first number he was weaving into his narrative many of the notions he had earlier jotted down in that little volume (for example, the man who feigns to be dead 'and *is* dead to all intents and purposes external to himself', the mutually deceiving bride and groom, and the 'perfectly New people'). It is remarkable, however, that for the first time in his career, he found the need to borrow leading elements of his actual plots from elsewhere, namely from two plays by the recently-deceased playwright Sheridan Knowles. The heroine of the first, the hugely popular *The Hunchback* (1832), is educated in the value of true love by her hunchback guardian (her long-lost nobleman father in disguise) who pretends to urge her towards a mercenary marriage. Her better nature finally makes her reject this, to her father's joy. He reveals his true identity and blesses her marriage with the man she has come to love, whom she supposes to be a humble secretary but who turns out (surprise, surprise) to have been also a nobleman in disguise. The second Knowles play, *The Daughter* (1836), is set among Cornish wreckers who rob the corpses of the drowned. The heroine's father is, to her great distress, engaged in this grisly trade and is accused by a villainous colleague of having actually murdered one of those whose bodies he plunders.[3]

As for subject-matter and themes – as distinct from plot and incident – it seems clear that Dickens must have had certain of these very much in mind from the beginning of his work on this novel. Prominent among them is the dark river winding its way through the heart of London which provides the story with its arresting opening scene and which, one contemporary reviewer commented, 'We might almost mention . . . as a character', adding, 'It plays a most important part in the story, and always with great picturesqueness.' Prominent also is the all-pervading, and highly topical, theme of education, the subject of dust-heaps as a source of enormous wealth, the stifling middle-class complacency and dogmatism incarnate in the figure of Mr Podsnap (for whom Forster is traditionally supposed to have supplied some traits) and the glittering but insubstantial charade of 'Society', which acts as Chorus to the story.[4]

One of the earliest things Dickens always had to do when embarking on any of his previous monthiy-part serials was to brief Browne to produce a design for the number-covers. This time, however, it was not Browne but Dickens's young protégé Marcus Stone who needed briefing. Dickens had already got Stone commissioned to do a frontispiece for the Cheap Edition *Little Dorrit* in 1861 and to provide illustrations for *Great Expectations* and some other volumes in the Library Edition in 1862. Now, having had some sort of disagreement with Browne, he decided that Stone should illustrate *Our Mutual Friend*. He may have believed, as Browne told his partner, Robert Young, that 'a new hand would give his old puppets a fresh look'. The usual explanation for Dickens's abandonment of Browne, that he was responding to the fashion for new, more realistic, book-illustration, exemplified above all by the work of Millais, may be wide of the mark since the late nineteenth-century Dickens scholar F. G. Kitton reports Stone as affirming 'that he was much hampered by Dickens with respect to these designs, for the novelist, accustomed to the diminutive scale of the figures in Hablot Browne's etchings, was somewhat imperative in his demand for a similar treatment of the illustrations for "Our Mutual Friend" '.[5]

Neither Dickens's subsequently published letters to Stone nor the illustrations themselves seem to bear out this 'affirmation' of the artist's, however, and it may have been retrospective self-justification for work that Stone may have come to feel dissatisfied with. Generally, Dickens seems not to have been very closely engaged with the illustrations, often leaving Stone to choose his own subjects and mostly just expressing general approval of his efforts. However, his comment on Stone's second depiction of Jenny Wren shows that he would sometimes get into more detail: 'The Doll's dressmaker is immensely better than she was. . . . A weird sharpness not without beauty is the thing I want.' For the monthly-part cover, of course, Stone clearly needed some guidance beyond reading the first two numbers as Dickens suggested. The design he produced on the basis of what Dickens told him and his own reading of the numbers Dickens pronounced to be '*excellent*', in need of only one or two slight adjustments. The most dramatic change is not mentioned in this note from Dickens, however, and must have been the result of verbal communication. In the first sketch two young male figures turn their top-hatted heads to look back at each other in attitudes expressive of surprise; in the revised design they occupy a more prominent position and are bareheaded and melodramatically confronting each other, in attitudes expressive of utter astonishment. What is nowhere to be seen in either the first or the revised design is any detail suggesting that Eugene is to die, which seems odd since Stone reports Dickens as having specially asked him to work in some hint of this, having told him that 'One of the strongest features of the story . . . will be the death of Eugene after the assault by the schoolmaster.' Dickens added, 'I think it will be one of the best things I have ever done.' Presumably Dickens had second thoughts about giving so dark an ending to the Wrayburn/Lizzie story even before Stone went to work on his first design for the monthly cover.[6]

Meanwhile, as the epigraph to this chapter indicates, Dickens was having problems in adjusting to the ampler space of the old monthly number after working with the weekly instalments in which his two previous novels had had to be written. He found that he had overwritten both the first and second numbers and this forced him to hold over the description of the Lammle marriage until the third one, leaving him in need of a subject for a shorter chapter with which to conclude *Our Mutual Friend* II. He had told Stone he wanted to introduce into the story some 'peculiar avocation', one that would be 'very striking and unusual'. As it happened, Stone had been in need of someone to supply and 'set up' (that is, kill, stuff and fix into a certain pose) for him either a little dog or some pigeons (Stone's memory varied as to which unfortunate creatures were involved) and had just visited a picturesque taxidermist's shop in St Andrew's Street, Seven Dials. He described it to Dickens who must have been delighted with this piece of serendipity since the raw materials of taxidermy (bones, feathers, body parts, and so forth) fitted in so perfectly with his great dust-heap theme – as well as providing a role for Wegg's lost leg. Next day, Dickens accompanied Stone to the shop and 'with his unusually keen power of observation, was enabled during a very brief space to take mental notes of every detail that presented itself', which he was then able to reproduce as Mr Venus's shop in the last chapter of *Our Mutual Friend* II. Mr Venus himself seems to have been inspired by the taxidermist's assistant, 'a despondent melancholy youth'.[7]

As he worked on these early numbers of his new story during late January and early February Dickens was also hunting for a suitable house to rent for himself, Georgina and Mamie for the London season. He eventually settled on 57 Gloucester Place, Hyde Park Gardens, which he rented until 1 June and into which they moved on 11 February, just after Dickens had learned, on his 52nd birthday, of Walter's death six weeks earlier in Calcutta. It would have been an additional burden that Walter had died considerably and inexplicably in debt, thereby adding posthumously to all the domestic claims upon his father's purse, claims which Dickens had bewailed in a letter of 11 January, using an image that is an interesting variant on Marley's chain in the *Carol*: 'I carry through life as long and as heavy a train of dependents as ever was borne by one working man.' Burdett Coutts wrote Dickens a letter of condolence in which she evidently suggested that Walter's death might lead to some softening in Dickens's attitude towards Catherine. But, despite all his deferment to her, she could no more influence him in this respect now than she had been able to in 1858. Catherine had, as far as he was concerned, simply been written, or blotted, out of his life and that was that. 'A page in my life which once had writing on it, has become absolutely blank . . .'.[8]

In mid-March Chapman and Hall launched a truly massive advertising campaign for the new serial of which Dickens had by now managed to complete the first three numbers, among other things filling in what we should now call the back-story of Boffin's Bower. He plunged immediately into no. IV in which one of his main objectives was, according to his notes, to 'bring out Eugene'. He wrote anxiously to Forster on 29 March:

> If I were to lose a page of the 5 Nos. I have proposed to myself to be ready by the publication day, I should feel that I had fallen short. I have grown hard to satisfy, and write very slowly. And I have so much – not fiction – that *will* be thought of, when I don't want to think of it, that I am forced to take more care than I once took.

He is here presumably referring primarily to that 'long and heavy chain' he carried and to various domestic anxieties such as worries about his sons' education and careers, about his son-in-law's poor health, and, indeed, Georgina's since he believed that she suffered from the same heart trouble that killed Walter. He must have had concerns, too, about Nelly and the limbo-like existence she was now leading as a result of his take-over of her life. Having failed to make good progress with his writing as a result of all these worries, he cannot, he tells Forster, take a day off for a proposed jaunt to the seaside, tempting though it is, London being so 'beastly' in March. This very 'beastliness', however, supplies him with just the right atmosphere for this part of the story. He has had, he tells Forster, a long, unpleasant walk 'against the dust' but promptly turns this to advantage in a virtuoso description of the London streets in *Our Mutual Friend* IV (Bk I, ch.12): 'The grating wind sawed rather than blew. . . . Every street was a sawpit, and . . . every passenger was an under-sawyer, with the sawdust blinding him and choking him.'[9]

Commitments to after-dinner speaking in early April (for the Printers' Pension Society on the 6th and for University College Hospital on the 12th) perhaps threatened the completion of no.V before the publication of no.I but he seems to have achieved his goal in this respect nevertheless. He was helped by the fact that he had overwritten the fourth number and therefore had half a chapter's worth of story to carry forward into the fifth. Once he had got the business of the number done he must have enjoyed writing the final chapter describing the 'dismal swamp' of begging-letters in which Rokesmith finds himself floundering as Boffin's secretary. In the fourteen years since Dickens had excoriated begging-letter writing in *Household Words* his sufferings in this respect would not have abated and here was a fine opportunity for him once more to let off steam on the matter.

The first number of *Our Mutual Friend* appeared on the last day of April and had a nostalgically familiar look about it. Chapman and Hall, no doubt with Dickens's consent or perhaps even at his suggestion, had returned to the green monthly-part covers used from *Pickwick* to *Dombey*, abandoning the greenish-blue ones used for *Bleak House, Little Dorrit* and *A Tale of Two Cities*. There were high expectations that this new Dickens serial, coming after so long a gap and advertised so widely by the publishers, would have a very large circulation. One clear sign of this was that the 'Our Mutual Friend Advertiser' carried, as the Dickens bibliographers Hatton and Cleaver note, 'a greater volume of material than any other of the works in original parts'. The high expectations seemed at first to be fulfilled: 'Nothing can be better than *Our Friend*, now in his thirtieth thousand, and orders flowing in fast,' Dickens happily told Forster on 3 May. Forster believed that the monthly-part sales eventually surpassed this figure but it has since been shown that the print order declined during the course of serialisation until, finally, only 19,000 copies of the concluding double number were needed. In May 1864, however, Dickens certainly had grounds for optimism. He was by this time at work on no. VI which focuses on the theme of education and introduces a major new character, the National schoolmaster Bradley Headstone. Coincidentally, Dickens took the chair at a meeting on

11 May to raise money for two 'Shakespeare Foundation Schools' (one for each sex) for the children of actors. The intention was for them to impart to their students 'a sound, liberal, comprehensive education' comparable to that provided by the great public schools (the Provost of Eton was on the organising committee) and utterly different from the barren rote-learning of the National Schools as perpetrated by Headstone and his colleague, Miss Peecher. We note that in his speech Dickens was at pains to disassociate these projected Foundation Schools from the Shakespeare Tercentenary celebrations which had for some time been a source of embarrassment or irritation to him. The Tercentenary committee had been keen to involve him in fund-raising for a monument to 'the Bard' – not, presumably, like the one so vividly dreamed of in Stratford by Mrs Nickleby – but always for Dickens the best way for a writer or any other artist to be remembered was not through biographies, unless they redounded as much to the honour of the art concerned as did Forster's *Goldsmith*, nor through celebratory odes (the Veneerings' guests in Bk I, ch. 3 include 'a Poem on Shakespeare'), still less through the erection of monuments, but through the continued circulation and enjoyment of their work. Hence the concern in his speech to dispel any idea that these Shakespeare Foundation Schools were in any way 'commemorative'. They were rather to be valued as good things in themselves irrespective of any connection with Shakespeare.[10]

Dickens's life in London was inimical to steady progress with his writing. 'What with public speechifying, private eating and drinking, and perpetual simmering in hot rooms, I have made London too hot to hold me and my work together,' he told a correspondent on 15 May. Soon after his return to Gad's Hill at the beginning of June, just as No. III was published, he told Forster (10 June) that he was 'going round and round like a carrier pigeon before swooping on number seven'. As this was not due for publication until the end of October he was still comfortably ahead, even if not quite so far as when he had begun (four numbers in hand instead of five). The first part of no. VII brings in Mr Riah, described in Dickens's chapter-notes as 'The gentle Jew', his belated apology for Fagin, to be enthusiastically received by Eliza Davis in due course. Dickens may have taken this number with him to complete during what he called when writing to Wills on 26 June, on the eve of departure from London 'my present Mysterious Disappearance'. His deliberate vagueness about just where he is disappearing to, apart from its being in the direction of France, almost certainly means that he was either visiting Nelly and her mother, or else travel-ling with them. He was away for just over a week and it is piquant to note that the chapter he had either just been working on or was actually writing when with the Ternans, was the last one of No. VII (Bk II, ch. 6). Entitled 'A Riddle Without An Answer', this is the chapter in which Lightwood interrogates Wrayburn about his intentions towards Lizzie Hexam: ' "Do you design to

capture and desert this girl?" "My dear fellow, no." "Do you design to marry
her?" "My dear fellow, no." . . .'. Unable to sort out his feelings and intentions,
Wrayburn can only describe the situation as a 'riddle'. Whether Dickens is here
harking back to the beginning of his relationship with Nelly in September
1857, when he referred to her as the 'little riddle' in letters to Wills, or whether
he is writing 'to the minute', as it were, and reflecting his current emotional
state regarding Nelly we cannot know; but that a strong personal element is
pretty close to the surface in this chapter we can hardly doubt.

In his June letter to Wills Dickens shows that he had already decided to capitalise on Mrs Lirriper's enormous popularity by making her narrator-in-chief
of the next Christmas number of *All the Year Round*:

> It has occurred to me that the next Mrs Lirriper might have a mixing in it of
> Paris and London – she and the Major, and the boy, all working out the
> little story in two places. As my present Mysterious Disappearance is in that
> direction, I will turn this over on French ground with great care. I seem to
> have a sort of inspiration that may blend the undiminished attractions of
> Mrs Lirriper, with those of the Bebelle life in Paris.

Attention has been called to the difficulty of understanding what Dickens
might have meant here by the phrase 'the Bebelle life in Paris', and a solution
proposed involving that elusive child allegedly born to Dickens and Nelly,
probably in France, some time in the 1860s. Another, less thrilling, possibility
is that Dickens inadvertently omitted a comma between 'the Bebelle life' and
'in Paris'. His meaning might then be that he was thinking about 'blending'
into one narrative two attractive elements, the character of Mrs Lirriper and a
story, using Paris as the setting, like the one about Bebelle, which involved
strangers showing loving-kindness towards a neglected child. In the event, the
main action to take place on French soil in the story as published occurs in
Sens rather than in Paris, almost certainly as a result of Dickens having visited
Sens, perhaps with Nelly, during his 'Mysterious Disappearance' and being
keen, as he would have expressed it, 'to try his hand at it'.[11]

After returning to Gad's Hill Dickens had trouble with his throat and
was also beset by what Forster calls 'other anxieties'. On 29 July he reported
to Forster that he had 'fallen back' in his writing schedule, mainly because he
had been 'wanting in invention'. This may strike us as odd in that there seems
to be no lack of invention in no. VIII with its lively descriptions of Silas
Wegg's initiation of Mr Venus into 'The Friendly Move' and Bella's 'innocent
elopement' with her father to Greenwich. It also contains one of Dickens's
most elaborately-staged child death-bed scenes, which gave him, incidentally,
a novelistic opportunity to give as great a boost to the Hospital for Sick
Children as the one he had given in his superb after-dinner speech six years

earlier. Writer's anxiety does seem to have beset him nevertheless. 'Looming large before me', he continued in his letter to Forster, 'is the Christmas work, and I can hardly hope to do it without losing a number of *Our Friend*. I have very nearly lost one already and two would take away one half of my whole advance.' He is, he says, working slowly and has 'a very mountain to climb before I shall see the open country of my work'. The August heat did not help, either, and by the 26th Dickens told Emerson Tennent that he had 'dropped astern instead of going ahead'. Sales figures had also dropped but this seems not to have worried him. On 28 August he assured Frederic Chapman that the sales of the latest number to appear, no. IV, would be 'certain to pick up' (this number includes a bravura chapter on 'Podsnappery' as well as the suspenseful episodes of Rogue Riderhood's denunciation of Hexam as a murderer and the subsequent hunt for the accused man). In general Dickens had, he told his publisher, 'the strongest faith in the book's doing thoroughly well'. It was, he believed, 'GOOD, full of variety, and always rising [i.e., in interest] in its working out of the people and the story', and, he added in parenthesis, 'I know I put into it, the making of a dozen books'. He was quite happy with Chapman's proposal to publish the first ten numbers as Volume I in January and the last ten as Volume II at the end of the run. It has been pointed out that this break with the traditional method of publishing the whole novel in one fat volume at the end of the serial run was the result of some notable changes in the marketing of fiction. *Our Mutual Friend*, Dickens told Chapman, would fit well into the new procedure 'for No. Ten will end the second book'.[12]

He finished work on no. IX at the end of September, being now only three numbers ahead, and promptly turned to the impending *All the Year Round* Christmas number, *Mrs Lirriper's Legacy*: 'Mrs Lirriper is again in hand,' he told Wills on 1 October, adding that he 'hoped to make way with her apace at the office' instead of going down to Gad's Hill. He 'made way' to such effect that by the end of the week he had finished the substantial opening chapter and was 'just knocking off the couple of pages or so' that would follow the stories to be contributed by other hands and so round off the number. In the opening chapter Mrs Lirriper resumes her splendid rambling monologue. Ironically, in view of the terrible accident in which he was to be involved in the following summer, Dickens makes comic capital out of Major Jackman and Jemmy playing at railways in Mrs Lirriper's parlour. He has her admiringly describe how they made locomotives 'out of parasols broken iron pots and cotton-reels and them absolutely a getting off the line and falling over the table and injuring the passengers almost equal to the originals'. He goes on to retrieve some unfinished business from the 1863 Christmas number, namely Mrs Lirriper's ongoing feud with a neighbouring rival landlady Miss Wozenham and the fate of young Jemmy's runaway father. He gives his homely heroine two strongly pathetic scenes to play in connection with these stories and this no doubt helped to enhance her already tremendous popularity with the public when this Christmas number appeared on 1 December.[13]

The speed with which Dickens was able to polish off the 1864 Christmas number may have had something to do with the relief of turning from writing about the oppressive, dark and gloomy city of London to that very contrasting city across the Channel to which he so often escaped. Mrs Lirriper rhapsodises:

> And of Paris I can tell you no more my dear than that it's town and country both in one, and carved stone and long streets of high houses and gardens and fountains and statues and gold . . . and clean tablecloths spread everywhere for dinner and people sitting out of doors smoking and sipping all day long and little plays being acted in the open air for little people and every shop a complete and elegant room, and everybody seeming to play at everything in this world. And as to the sparkling lights my dear after dark, glittering high up and low down and on before and on behind and all round, and the crowd of theatres and the crowd of people and the crowd of all sorts, it's pure enchant-ment. (*CS*, 553f.)

In a Christmas number, too, Dickens could indulge more freely than he could in his full-length novels in that 'drollness' that came so naturally to him and gave him so much delight. In the case of *Mrs Lirriper's Legacy* he confessed to Forster that it had in it 'something – to me at all events – so extraordinarily droll, that though I have been reading it some hundred times in the course of the working, I have never been able to look at it with the least composure, but have always roared in the most unblushing manner'. Not that he wanted anyone to underestimate the sheer hard work involved in writing the number. 'It is the condensation of a great deal of subject and the very greatest pains,' he wrote when responding to Wills's enthusiastic comments. The result was that he felt confident Mrs Lirriper was 'nothing but a good 'un'. And so she indeed proved to be.[14]

The Christmas number completed, at least as far as his own contributions were concerned, Dickens turned back to the writing of No. X, the final number of Book II, 'Birds of a Feather'. At this mid-point in the writing he was concerned to bring to a point of suspenseful tension the three main intercon-nected plots that he had so carefully woven together: the Harmon/BellaWilfer/ Boffins plot, on which depend the stories of Silas Wegg and of Betty Higden; the Lizzie Hexam/Headstone/Wrayburn plot, on which depend the stories of Rogue Riderhood and of Jenny Wren; and the Lammles/Podsnaps/Twemlow plot with its social 'Chorus' of Veneerings, Lady Tippins, Boots, and Brewer on which depends the story of Fascination Fledgeby. On 13 October, accompa-nied by Georgina, Dickens retreated to Dover for a few days' peace and quiet (he always wrote well when within sight and sound of the sea). Here they were joined by Wilkie Collins, the friend with whom he could best discuss the management of plots if he felt the need to. But the number was still unfinished when he returned to Gad's Hill and shortly afterwards he was shocked and distressed by the death, on 29 October after a short illness, of John Leech, one of the best-loved of all his old friends whose special fondness for, and kindness towards Sydney Dickens, 'the Little Admiral', he now tenderly remembered. This death, he told Forster when reporting that he had still not managed to finish his number, put him out 'woefully' so that for two days he could do nothing.[15]

A day or two earlier he wrote in one of his long, *tour d'horizon* letters to Cerjat that he was 'perpetually' crossing the Channel: 'Whenever I feel that I have worked too much, or am on the eve of over-doing it, and want a change, away I go by the mail train, and turn up in Paris, or anywhere else that suits my humour, next morning.' He would always, he said, return 'as fresh as a Daisy'. Of course there is no mention of Nelly in this letter but if we accept the very plausible idea that she was living in France at this time, visiting her would certainly have been a very important feature of these recuperative excursions. Dickens evidently felt in need of such a trip by mid-November, after finally finishing No. X and dealing with sundry other matters, such as the illustrations prepared by Marcus Stone for the Library Edition of *Great Expectations*, and, of course, *All the Year Round*. He was in France from 17 to 28 November and returned, having got rid, as he claimed was always the case when he went to France, of the neuralgia that tended to plague him whenever he was writing hard. Soon after returning to Gad's Hill he sent Chapman and Hall the preliminaries for Vol. I of *Our Mutual Friend* (no preface, of course, since the story was only half-told). Presumably it was around this time, too, that he drew up an elaborate memorandum headed 'Position of affairs at the end of the Second Book (–No. X)'. In it he lists the chief characters or elements concerned in each part of the story with a concluding list of other, minor, characters who are available 'for implements and otherwise', and it contains one important piece of plot-information not yet revealed to the reader, though it is about to be ('Lizzie has disappeared, by the aid of the good Jew'). At another point he looks far ahead towards the concluding chapters of the whole book in the mention of John Harmon and Sloppy's 'check-mate' to the Friendly Move.[16]

Despite all the demands upon him, professional and domestic, Dickens was, as he had ever been, ready to give practical help and advice to friends whenever it was needed. In the case of matters theatrical it was, as we know, very much a labour he delighted in. Fechter in particular benefited greatly from his generosity in this respect. Dickens regularly helped him with regard to his managerial activities at the Lyceum – for example, he often revised and improved the scripts of plays Fechter had under production. Now, as a mark of his gratitude, Fechter presented Dickens with a small wooden Swiss châlet consisting of a lower and an upper room, the latter with six windows and a veranda. It arrived in ninety-four pieces and the delighted Dickens had it erected on the piece of land called the shrubbery that he owned on the opposite side of the Dover Road from Gad's Hill itself (he later had a tunnel dug beneath the road so that he could reach the chalet more conveniently), with the heraldic crest claimed by his father boldly affixed to the front of the veranda. 'In the summer (supposing it not to be blown away in the spring) the upper room will make a charming study,' he wrote to Forster, and the chalet did indeed become his favourite place for writing in both spring and summer. He had five mirrors fitted in the upper room and wrote a rapturous account of the place to James Fields that summer: 'they [the mirrors] reflect and refract, in all kinds of ways, the leaves that are quivering at the windows, and the great fields of waving corn, and the sail-dotted river. . . . the birds and butterflies fly in and out, and the green branches shoot in at the open windows, and the lights and shadows of the clouds come and go with the rest of the company.' It was on his plain writing-table in this chalet that on that fateful June day in 1870 he would write his last words of fiction.[17]

The sales of *Our Mutual Friend* did not pick up in the way Dickens had hoped. The print order for no. X was 28,000, 12,000 down from the order for no.I. But January 1865 saw Chapman and Hall's launch of another venture, one that was over the next two years to prove highly profitable for both themselves and Dickens. This was the People's Edition of his works, the texts being reprinted from the stereo-typed plates of the Cheap Edition. The People's Edition, aimed at the railway bookstall market, was bound in green glazed boards and sold at a shilling a volume, the longer novels being divided into two volumes. All preliminaries (prefaces, dedications, etc.) were dropped but the edition did include the original engravings. Nearly four thousand volumes of this edition were sold before it was killed off by the appearance of the Charles Dickens Edition in 1867.[18]

During the first five months of 1865 Dickens was working, as he put it in a letter of 22 April, 'like a dragon' at *Our Mutual Friend* XI–XV. Since he had now dropped back to the all-too-familiar situation of being only one number ahead of the printer, he was obliged to work under the kind of pressure he had hoped to avoid when he had started out with five numbers in hand. But the comparative brevity of the notes for each number, and the clear indications they convey of how he is developing the various plots and starting to blend them, shows that Dickens is very much in command of his materials and is quite clear about how to work them. Thus one of the notes for no. XIII reads, '*Lizzie to work an influence on Bella's character, at its wavering point*'. This is also apparent from the more detailed chapter-notes containing occasional injunctions such as (no. XI) '*Lay the ground very carefully all through*'. It was a source of great satisfaction to him to see how, as he wrote on 15 March to a correspondent who had been moved by the heroism of old Betty Higden, 'All the hits I have been patiently working up to for more than a year, are now falling into their places.'

As always, he had numerous other things clamouring for his attention, quite apart from the regular weekly grind of dealing with *All the Year Round* business with Wills. Just as he had done for Frank in late 1863 when, a promising groove having been found for him at last – the boy was preparing to go out to Calcutta to join the Bengal Mounted Police – Dickens now busied himself to find helpers and sponsors for his fourth son, Alfred, who had at last decided on a career as a sheep farmer in New South Wales. He had also to settle Alfred's tailor's bills and other debts. Another London season had to be got through in another rented West End mansion (16 Somers Place, Hyde Park, taken for three months from 6 March), with after-dinner speeches to be made to the Newsvendors' Benevolent Institution on 9 May and the Newspaper Press Fund on 20 May. It is interesting to juxtapose the generally dark and harshly satirical vision of England 'in these times of ours' (to quote the novel's opening words) that pervades *Our Mutual Friend* with the powerful passage in his Newsvendors speech in which he vividly evokes the horrors and brutality of the 'bad old days' of Georgian England which newspapers exposed and helped to abolish. Dickens saw the satire in his new novel as performing a similar function to that of the reports in certain newspapers, namely the exposure of social evils leading to their amelioration. His other speech, the one to the Newspaper Press Fund, is also noteworthy in the dashing glimpse it afforded his audience of his early life when he was a reporter for *The Morning Chronicle*, 'writing on the palm of my hand, by the light of a dark lantern, in a postchaise and four, galloping through a wild country, all through the dead of night, at the then surprising rate of fifteen miles an hour'.[19]

In addition to all this business Dickens had also, from February onwards, to contend with a major health problem, which was to plague him for the rest of his life. This was what Forster calls a 'lameness ... in his left foot' which on occasion caused him extreme pain, 'tortures' indeed, with his foot sometimes swelling so much that he was unable to force his boot on. To the end of his days Dickens was determined to regard this trouble as simply frostbite, the result of too much walking in the snow. In a letter written only three weeks or so before his death he describes suffering great pain from 'a neuralgic attack in the foot to which I am sometimes liable, and which originally came of overwalking in deep snow'. The problem was not a localised one, however, but symptomatic of Dickens's constant over-tasking of himself with damaging results for his whole nervous system. 'It is more than probable', Forster comments, 'that if the nervous danger and disturbance it [the lameness] implied had been correctly appreciated at the time, its warning might have been of priceless value to Dickens.'[20]

By May Dickens, still only one number in advance of publication, was finishing work on No. XV, the last number of Book Three (chs 15–17). Drawing on such compilations as Robert Chambers's *Book of Days: A Miscellany of Popular Antiquities* (1862–64) and F. S. Merryweather's *Lives and Anecdotes of Misers* (1850), which in late January he had asked an *All the Year Round* employee to procure for him, he had been able to provide Mr Boffin with enough fodder to assist him in his elaborate pretence of becoming a miser. This was part of the scheme, kept secret from the reader, that Boffin has concocted with his wife and Rokesmith to cure Bella of the mercenariness to which she was in danger of succumbing ('Keep Bella watching and never suspecting', runs one of the chapter-notes for Bk III, ch. 5). The scheme also deceives Wegg, emboldening him in his 'Friendly Move' against his patron. Over the course of the previous five numbers Dickens had steadily traced the busy plotting and counterplotting of different groups of characters and some individuals, notably Mrs Lammle, each of them pursuing their own agendas, and his number- and chapter-notes show how carefully he worked at 'laying the ground' for the resolution of the whole novel in Book IV. It had been strenuous, concentrated work, which he had latterly had to carry on in the febrile atmosphere of the London season, and he knew that he was in desperate need of a change of scene (that is, of another visit to France) to recruit his strength for the careful working out of the whole purpose and meaning of this long and complex story, or rather series of intertwined stories, in the final book. 'Work and worry, without exercise, would soon make an end of me,' he wrote to Forster some time in late May. 'If I were not going away now, I should break down. No one knows as I know to-day how near to it I have been.' He could not even risk waiting to see Alfred off to Australia when his departure was postponed until 5 June. From France Dickens wrote to Mamie: 'Before I went away, I had certainly worked myself into a damaged state. But the moment I got away, I began, thank God, to get well. I hope to profit by this experience, and make future dashes from my desk before I want them.'[21]

On Friday 9 June he was returning to London by the so-called 'tidal train' from Folkestone, having left Paris at 7 a.m. Nelly and an older lady, presumably her mother, were returning with him. They were alone in a compartment in the first of the seven first-class coaches which followed the engine and tender, guard's van and one second-class coach (two more second-class coaches and three luggage vans completed the train, which was carrying a total of 115 passengers). Platelayers, carrying out routine track repairs on a bridge or viaduct, ten feet high, over the little River Beult, between the Kentish villages of Headcorn and Staplehurst, had temporarily removed some of the rails. Catastrophically, their foreman had checked the wrong timetable, the one for the next day, so was not expecting any train until 5.20 p.m. whereas it was 3.11 p.m. when Dickens's train passed through Headcorn, spot on time. The flagman who was supposed always to signal any obstruction 1,000 yards in front of it had failed to do this so when the driver saw what was happening he was unable to stop the train in time. It reached the bridge at a speed of between 20 and 30 m.p.h. The engine jumped the rails and the train broke into two parts. The part that included Dickens's carriage stayed on the bridge though his carriage came to rest hanging over the side with its rear end resting on the field below. Had its rear coupling not broken it would have been dragged down into the water by the carriages behind it. 'No imagination', wrote Dickens to Thomas Mitton on 13 June, 'can conceive the ruin of the carriages, or the extraordinary weights under which the people were lying, or the complications into which they were twisted up among iron and wood, and mud and water'. He and the Ternans had been thrown down together into a corner of their tilted compartment, which like all the others would have been locked, but he quickly managed to scramble out through the window. As he told Mitton, he then hailed two of the distracted guards who were running about and called out 'tell me whether you don't know me'. One of them answered, 'We know you very well, Mr Dickens' whereupon he got the man to give him his key and then, helped by a labourer, extricated the Ternans along with all the other passengers trapped in that carriage. One of Nelly's arms had been injured but she was able to walk and Dickens's first care must have been to get her and her mother, who seems to have been unhurt, away from the scene, probably on one of the special trains that very soon began arriving from London Bridge, bringing medical assistance and providing transport back to London for all those able to travel. He would, of course, have been extremely anxious to prevent Nelly and her mother (who had been a well-known actress in her day) from being identified and he was helped in this by the situation – not only by the general confusion but also by the fact that most passengers were, according to the *Times* reporter, reluctant 'to alarm their friends by disclosing their names'.[22]

Once the Ternans had been taken care of, Dickens turned to helping other survivors, and clambered back into his wrecked carriage to fetch his brandy-flask for the purpose. Ten people had been killed and many others seriously injured. For two hours he helped to extricate those trapped in the wreckage and gave what succour he could to the injured and the dying. A sketch of him using his hat as a water-carrier and tenderly ministering to a young woman lying on the ground subsequently appeared in the *Penny Illustrated Paper* (24 June) and has been much reprinted ever since. One severely injured young man whom Dickens had helped to get out of 'a most extraordinary heap of dark ruins in which he was jammed upside down', and whom he had revived with brandy, he took back to London with him in a carriage and delivered to the Charing Cross Hospital, where he subsequently visited him several times. In the brief notes he sent to various friends from the *All the Year Round* office the following day Dickens emphasised that it was the horror of the scenes he experienced following the accident rather than the accident itself that had

49 Dickens at Staplehurst, 9 June 1865; *Penny Illustrated Paper*, June 1865

really shaken him. The phrase about working 'for hours among the dead and dying' recurs again and again in these notes. He remained in Wellington Street until the Sunday when he went down to Gad's Hill and from there wrote the long letter to Mitton quoted earlier. This is his fullest surviving account of the accident, including his description of climbing back into his wrecked compartment one more time in order to retrieve the manuscript of the No. XVI of *Our Mutual Friend* on which he had been working in France. He also gave Mitton a dramatic account of the scene that took place at the moment of the crash between himself and the 'two ladies', one old and one young, whom he does not name, who were in the compartment with him, and how the young lady 'said in a frantic way, "let us join hands and die friends" '. As has been suggested by Nelly's biographer, these words could be taken to indicate that there may have been some disagreement, or even quarrel, going on between her and Dickens just before the accident. His not naming the Ternans, even to so old and intimate a friend as Mitton, serves to remind us how very restricted was the circle that had any inkling of his relationship with Nelly.[23]

For the next three months Dickens remained quietly at Gad's Hill. At first he could not stand railway travelling because, as he told Forster, of a terrible feeling that assailed him whenever the train put on speed 'that the carriage is down on one side (and generally that is the left, and *not* the side on which the carriage in the accident really went over)' which was 'inexpressibly distressing'. Even driving his Irish jaunting-car into Rochester could leave him feeling badly shaken. Gradually, however, he steeled himself to travel again, though for some time he could not tolerate express trains, and he resumed visits to London to attend to *All the Year Round* business, and of course to visit Nelly, recuperating from her ordeal in her house in Mornington Crescent. He now began referring to her in letters as 'the Patient', something he continued to do for the rest of his life. He declined to give evidence at the inquest held on those who died at Staplehurst but did write to the head station master at Charing Cross to ask after some golden trinkets, one a seal with 'Ellen' engraved on it, that Nelly had lost in the accident. He was solicitous of his dear 'Patient' in other ways, too, and on 25 June instructed his manservant John, who was now acting as housekeeper at the office in Wellington Street: 'Take Miss Ellen tomorrow morning, a little basket of fresh fruit, a jar of clotted cream from Tuckers, and a chicken, a pair of pigeons, or some nice little bird. Also on Wednesday morning, and on Friday morning, take her some other things of the same sort – making a little variety each day'.[24]

Judging by what he said three months later, in the last paragraph of his 'Postscript' to *Our Mutual Friend*, Dickens must have virtually completed the writing of no. XVI before leaving France (referring to the accident, he describes the various characters featured in the number, including Bella on her wedding-day, which occurs in the number's last chapter, as having been 'much soiled but otherwise unhurt'). This number was due for publication at the end of June so that, unless he started work almost immediately on no. XVII, Dickens risked soon being in the highly pressured situation of not having even one number in hand (having started out with five). It still seems to have been a good three weeks before he was able to get started on no. XVII. When Forster at the beginning of July wrote assuming he had two numbers in hand Dickens answered, 'Alas! For the two numbers you write of! There is only one in existence. I have but just begun the other'. And the next day he discovered, presumably on receiving proofs of no. XVI, that he had underwritten this number by two and a half pages, 'a thing I have not done since *Pickwick*!' For the next two months he was, as he put it in a letter to Bulwer Lytton of 20 July, 'tied by the leg' to the book. He hoped, he said, that Bulwer Lytton would find 'the purpose and the plot' of the book 'very plain' when he saw it as 'a whole piece' and continued:

I am looking forward to sending you the proofs complete, about the end of next month. It is all sketched out, and I am working hard at it, giving it all the pains possible to be bestowed on a labour of love. Your critical opinion two months in advance of the public will be invaluable to me. For you know what store I set by it and how I think over a hint from you.

Bulwer Lytton did not, in fact, give Dickens his verdict on the book until after it had been published (see below, p. 542); otherwise we might perhaps have been indebted to him for another last-minute change of plan on Dickens's part – though it is hard to think that there was anything at which even Bulwer Lytton might have demurred in the resolution of either of this novel's two love-plots, since both end happily.

Dickens seems to have written no. XVII (Bk IV, chs 5–7) within a fortnight since he told Stone to expect proofs of it on 19 July. It covers a great deal of business including Headstone's murderous attack upon Wrayburn and Lizzie's dramatic rescue of her drowning lover from the river. This is only possible for her because of her old skills as an oarswoman described in the novel's first chapter ('Back to the opening of the book, strongly' reads Dickens's highlighted note for chapter 6). Work on no. XVIII would have been interrupted by Dickens's visit to Knebworth on 29 July, along with Forster and other members of the Guild of Literature and Art, to view some Gothic-style houses built by the Guild on land donated by Bulwer Lytton. It was intended that these houses should be occupied rent-free by writers or artists, either of advanced years or else in temporary need of support, and for their further comfort a public house called, by Dickens's permission, 'Our Mutual Friend' had opened up just across the road. This viewing day proved to be a very festive occasion with a 'sump-tuous luncheon' served in the picturesque old hall of Knebworth House and celebratory speeches by both Bulwer Lytton and Dickens. Percy Fitzgerald remembered Dickens as being 'in the highest spirits, gay as a bridegroom with his flower, bright costume . . . and hat set a *little* on one side'. Anxious as always to expunge the least hint of patronage from the Guild's activities, he empha-sised in his speech that those writers or artists who would be invited to occupy the houses would be invited as 'receiving a mark of respect, and assurance of high consideration, from some of their fellow workers'. He ended by praising Bulwer Lytton as 'a very great man' and a great imaginative writer. Together with Forster and other Committee members he was to spend a great deal of time and energy later in the year trying but without success to find suitable 'fellow-workers' willing to come and live in the Guild's houses.[25]

Throughout August Dickens continued working hard at the novel, charmed with his new writing-room, the Swiss chalet. He had 'never worked better anywhere', he assured Fechter on 21 July: 'It is a most delightful summer atelier.' He had certainly repaid Fechter for it, we may think, since in the same letter he gave the actor detailed advice and offered practical help, through his solicitor Frederic Ouvry, over various professional difficulties besetting the

50 The Swiss chalet at Gad's Hill

actor-manager. Despite the pressure of his own work this month, and suffering 'a little festival of Neuralgia in the face', Dickens went out of his way to help a younger fellow-writer, Eneas Sweetland Dallas, whose reviews in *The Times* he admired. Dallas was applying – unsuccessfully as it turned out – for the Chair of Rhetoric and Belles Lettres at the University of Edinburgh, and Dickens made time to read and praise his book *The Gay Science*, a bold attempt to establish literary criticism as a science, also to write to Lord John Russell and others on Dallas's behalf. Meanwhile, his 'mems' for the final double number of *Our Mutual Friend* fill a whole densely-written page with more on the verso, seeking to clarify for himself the complicated story of Old Harmon's successive wills, the actions and motives of the Boffins and of John Harmon, the fate that is to befall Riderhood and Headstone, the 'total smash' of the Veneerings and the 'End of Social chorus generally'. There is so much detail in these notes that the actual chapter-notes on the opposite page do not need to be very full. Those for chapters 13 and 14 read 'Unwind the Boffin mystery – chiefly through Mrs Boffin' and 'Unwind Venus and Wegg' with, in each case, the words 'with great care' written in a box beside the instructions. In the 'mems' Lightwood and Twemlow are the only characters, besides Riah, with queries against their names, suggesting that Dickens was not certain if he could work them into this last double number. However, the notes for the last chapter show him hitting upon an excellent role for Lightwood: the last chapter, 'The Voice of Society', is to be 'Worked through Lightwood'. Meanwhile, the underlining of Twemlow's name in the 'mems' suggests that Dickens has thought of an important use for him which we see in the last chapter as the mild little gentleman faces down the overweening Podsnap over the question of the propriety of Wrayburn's marriage to a lower-class woman like Lizzie Hexam.[26]

On 23 August Dickens began sending to the printer copy for the final double number, due for publication, alongside the second volume, on 31 October. The final section of the manuscript was sent on 2 September, together with the contents page for Volume 2 and the 'Postscript, in Lieu of Preface'. He had already given Stone the subject for the frontispiece to the volume but left it to him to choose his subjects for illustration in the final double number, subsequently supplying appropriate titles for them. The 'Postscript' follows the tradition of Dickens's prefaces in asserting the artistic unity of his work and its truth to life however outlandish some of its details may seem to be, but there is no parallel in earlier prefaces to the ferocity of his comments here on the Poor Laws. It is curious that, although in these comments he alludes to his political satire in both *Little Dorrit* and *Hard Times*, there is no mention of *Oliver Twist*; it is left to Forster to observe, 'Betty Higden finishes what Oliver Twist began.'[27]

Immediately after delivering the last section of his manuscript Dickens left for France, travelling to Paris via Boulogne, presumably accompanied by Nelly and her mother. Indeed, this, or the return journey, may have been the occasion when he came under the hostile gaze of Julia Clare Byrne, wife of the owner of the fashionable *Morning Post*, who later recorded having once seen Dickens on the Boulogne packet travelling with 'a lady not his wife, nor his sister-in-law, yet he strutted about the deck with the air of a man bristling with self-importance, every line of his face and every gesture of his limbs seemed haughtily to say – "Look at me; . . . I am the great, the *only* Charles Dickens; whatever I may choose to do is justified by that fact" '. He told Forster that he felt his bad foot to be stronger 'the moment I breathed the sea air' but was still unable to wear a boot on it after late afternoon. He was back at the office by the evening of 17 September and at Gad's Hill the next day, where he was delighted to find Sultan, a splendid Irish wolfhound, a gift from Percy Fitzgerald. Sultan was to replace Dickens's beloved mastiff Turk, killed 'by a railway-accident' and commemorated in verse by Henry Fielding Dickens in

The Gad's Hill Gazette, a record of family news and social life at Gad's Hill produced by the younger Dickens boys during school holidays.[28]

The last stages of the production of the final double number and the second volume of *Our Mutual Friend* seem to have gone smoothly and they both appeared at the end of October by which time Dickens was, as he put it, 'in the Christmas Mill' expecting 'to be flour shortly' – in other words, at work on *Doctor Marigold's Prescriptions*, his Christmas story for 1865. The new novel met with a generally favourable critical reception, apart from the usual carping by *The Saturday Review* and the famous negative review written by a disappointed young Henry James for the American journal *The Nation* (which there is no evidence Dickens ever saw). There was, however, a tendency for reviewers, whilst acknowledging the power and the great art of the new novel, to look back nostalgically to Dickens's earlier work, to *Pickwick* or *Copperfield*, as having been greater achievements. One notable exception to this was Dallas's long review in *The Times* (29 Nov. 1865). Indebted as he was to Dickens for his efforts to obtain that elusive Edinburgh professorship for him, Dallas was hardly a disinterested reviewer but nevertheless he was not wholly uncritical, deploring 'the dead weight of "The Social Chorus" '. Generally, though, he praised the work very highly indeed. 'We have read nothing of Mr Dickens's', he wrote, 'which has given us a higher idea of his power than this last tale. . . . here he is in greater force than ever, astonishing us with a fertility in which we can

51 'Our Mutual Friend', *Fun*, 17 August 1867

trace no signs of repetition. . . . It is infinitely better than *Pickwick* in all the higher qualities of a novel.' He praised the infinite pains that Dickens evidently bestowed upon his art: 'He, who of all our living novelists has the most extraordinary genius, is also of all our living novelists the most careful and painstaking in his work. In all these 600 pages there is not a careless line.' Given Dickens's lifelong insistence on the sheer hard work, the 'earnestness' (to use his favourite word) required of all true artists no matter how great might be their natural genius, this had to be his dream review. He wrote warmly to Dallas to thank him for giving him 'such heartfelt gratification and unusual pleasure' and, intending no doubt to gratify Dallas in his turn, told him about a letter received from Bulwer Lytton which praised the novel in similar terms. Dickens went even further in his gratitude to Dallas. 'As you have divined what pains I bestowed upon the book,' he wrote, 'perhaps you might set some little value on the Manuscript, as your corroboration.' In sheer monetary terms this was a very valuable gift indeed and gives us some measure of just how delighted Dickens was by this assessment of his latest, and very ambitious, work. Following the gift, motivated apparently simply by strong affection, of the *Great Expectations* manuscript to Townshend, it seems to indicate that Dickens had, for some reason, by now abandoned his practice of the last quarter-century of presenting the manuscripts of all his major works to Forster, his literary executor and appointed biographer.[29]

Back in July when the American magazine proprietor George Childs of the Philadelphia *Public Ledger* had written to Dickens asking about acquiring early proof sheets of his next novel Dickens had replied, 'As I am but now finishing Our Mutual Friend it is not likely that I shall fall to work upon another novel yet awhile.' In the event it was to be another four years, the same interval as there had been between finishing *Great Expectations* and beginning *Our Mutual Friend*, before he would begin a new book. The main reason for this was probably financial. Even though he had, because of contractual arrangements highly favourable to him, made considerably more than £12,000 from the serial publication of *Our Mutual Friend* (whereas Chapman and Hall had lost £700 on it), his potential earnings from a further series of readings, especially if the much-canvassed American tour were really to come off, was very much greater. Given that 'long and heavy train of dependents' he carried through life, and a feeling on his part that, as Forster puts it, 'for exertion of this kind the time left him was short', it is hardly surprising that he should have looked more to the platform than to the study to maximise his income during the next three years or so.[30]

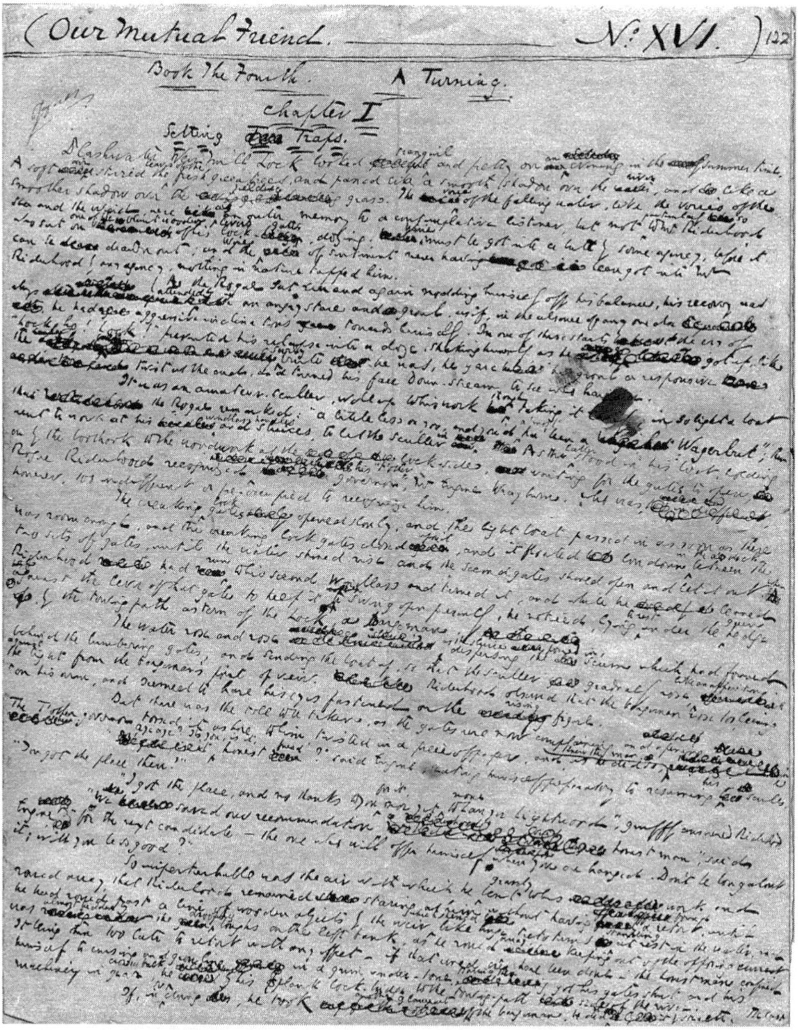
(Our Mutual Friend. No. XVI.) 122

Book The Fourth. A Turning.

Chapter I

Setting Traps.

52 Manuscript page of *Our Mutual Friend*

CHAPTER 24

Last Christmas numbers

1865–1867

Here's forty-eight original pages, ninety-six original columns, for four pounds. You want more for the money? Take it. Three whole pages of advertisements of thrilling interest thrown in for nothing. Read 'em and believe 'em. More? My best of wishes for your merry Christmas and your happy New Years, your long lives and your true prosperities. . . . You think Four Pound too much? And you still think so? Come! I'll tell you what then. Say Four Pence, and keep the secret.

Doctor Marigold's Prescriptions, 'To Be Taken Immediately'

IMMEDIATELY AFTER finishing *Our Mutual Friend* Dickens had to turn to his new Christmas number. Years before, when he had 'thought of Mr Pickwick', it was the idea for a particular character that had started him writing. Now something similar seems to have happened, but in what George Henry Lewes would have seen as a more 'hallucinatory' way. Sending Forster the completed manuscript of his part of the Christmas number, Dickens told him, 'Tired with *Our Mutual*, I sat down to cast about for an idea. Suddenly, the little character that you will see, and all belonging to it came flashing up in the most cheerful manner, and I had only to look on and leisurely describe it'. The 'little character' was Dr Marigold, a 'cheap jack' (itinerant hawker of cheap goods), a past-master of his trade, named in honour of the doctor who attended his birth in his father's van. Dickens would have seen many a cheap-jack in action in country markets and, with his keen ear for professional lingo or trade jargon would have relished his lively patter. Such a character would have been a likely one to 'flash' into his mind as he sought to find a worthy successor to those two great Christmas-number monologists Christopher and Mrs Lirriper. Moreover, cheap-jack patter offered him a perfect vehicle for parodying hustings oratory. He would have heard plenty of such speechifying during the electioneering summer of 1865, following the prorogation of Parliament in July. Marigold contrasts himself and his talking up of his wares, such as the 'pair of razors that'll shave you closer than the Board of Guardians', with the 'Dear Jacks', that is, the parliamentary candidates, their boundless promises and their often corrupt procedures:

Will you take me as I stand? You won't? Well then, I'll tell you what I'll do with you. Come now! I'll throw you in anything you ask for. There! Church-rates, abolition of church-rates, more malt tax, no malt tax, uniwersal education to the highest mark or uniwersal ignorance to the lowest, total abolition of flogging in the army, or a dozen for every private once a month all round, Wrongs of Men or Rights of Women, – only say which it shall be, take 'em or leave 'em on your own terms. . . . Take the lot on your own terms, and I'll count out two thousand seven hundred and fifty pounds on the footboard of the cart, to be dropped in the streets of your magnificent town for them to pick up that can. What do you say? Come now! You won't do better, and you may do worse. You take it? Hooray! Sold again, and got the seat![1]

Marigold is 'wonderfully like the real thing', Dickens told Forster, even though he was 'of course a little refined and humoured'. The life-story that he developed for this ebullient character deals, appropriately for a Christmas story, with the domestic affections, aiming at a greater intensity of pathos than anything Dickens had hitherto attempted in this genre and arguably surpassing even Tiny Tim. Marigold describes how his precious little daughter Sophy, who had so often suffered physical harm as a result of her mother's ungovernable temper, had died in his arms whilst he, Pagliacci-like, had been obliged to keep going with his comic sales routine. He also tells of his subsequent adoption of a little deaf and dumb waif, a second Sophy, whom he sends to be educated as a boarder to the London Deaf and Dumb Asylum, and how in her absence he collected stories to make up into a book for her that he calls *Doctor Marigold's Prescriptions*. At the end of this introductory piece Dickens the proprietor of *All the Year Round* and his Cheap Jack merge into one as Marigold cajoles the public into buying copies of the book of stories he has collected for Sophy, which is, in fact, the Christmas number, 'a general miscellaneous lot' which it has been 'no play' to get together and which is now offered to the public. From imagining himself as a cheap-jack flogging his fictional wares to the public, it could only have been a short step for Dickens to the now well-established reality of himself as a platform artist 'selling' his performances to an eager public. When, therefore, he was preparing for a new provincial readings tour the following spring *Doctor Marigold* must have seemed an obvious item to add to his repertoire.[2]

Dickens's writing for the 1865 Christmas number is not confined to his frame story about Doctor Marigold and his two Sophies. He also writes one of the inset stories called 'To be taken with a Grain of Salt', a genuinely creepy ghost-story centred on a subject that always fascinated him, a murder trial. He was 'charmed' to learn that it had given Mary Boyle 'a freeze' when she read it: 'It rather gave me a shiver up the back, in the writing', he told her on 6 January. The last section of the number, 'To Be Taken For Life', completes the frame story by describing Sophy's wooing by, and marriage to, a deaf and dumb lover, their going away and their return after some years to present Marigold with a 'grandchild', a loving little girl who can both speak and hear.

Buoyed up by his conviction that 'the Doctor' was 'nothing but a good 'un', Dickens dealt briskly with the proofs at the beginning of November and on the 8th he 'made up' the number with the printer James Birtle – 'always a tough job' as he told Wills's nephew by marriage, a young businessman called Fred Lehmann. Forster read an advance copy and pronounced it 'Neither good, gooder, nor goodest, but super-excellent'. *Doctor Marigold's Prescriptions* was published on 7 December and loyally extolled by Dallas in *The Times*. It also met with praise elsewhere and, so Forster tells us, sold the astonishing number of 250,000 copies in the first week (Dickens himself in his already-cited letter to Mary Boyle puts the figure at 200,000). Pleased as he was by the enthusiastic reception of his story, Dickens would, I feel sure, have been still more delighted by the high praise now bestowed upon *Our Mutual Friend* by Bulwer Lytton in a private letter to him, mentioned towards the end of the last chapter. Lytton's praise, however, seems to have been somewhat tempered by reservations about what he saw as Dickens's tendency to let his comic imagination run away with him (not a fault, it must be said, of which Lytton himself can ever be accused). Dickens responded that as a matter of fact he always worked 'slowly and with great care' and never gave way to his invention 'recklessly' but invariably restrained it. It was, he said, very necessary for him to do this on account of what he called his 'infirmity' that made him 'fancy or perceive relations in things which are not apparent generally'. He had, he wrote, 'such an inexpressible enjoyment of what I see in a droll light, that I dare say I pet it as if it were a spoilt child'.[3]

The autumn and winter of 1865/66 was a time of change for the Ternans. Maria had married a prosperous Oxford brewer in 1863, though she did not seem to be very settled with him and often visited her mother and sisters who by late 1865 were once more resident in Nelly's house in Houghton Place. Mrs Ternan (Frances Eleanor) had retired from the stage, Fanny was working as a singing teacher and Nelly lived, presumably, as a lady of independent means, 'using her brains to educate herself', as Katey later recalled. By 7 October, however, she had let Houghton Place and moved with her mother and sister into another, perhaps more modest, house in the same neighbourhood. She was never to live again in Houghton Place but she continued to derive rental income from it (likely to have been between £50 and £60 p.a.) until she finally sold it in 1901. Not long after the Ternans' move Dickens began helping Fechter in his preparations for a Lyceum dramatisation of Scott's *The Bride of Lammermoor* under the title of *The Master of Ravenswood*, and it may have been partly at his suggestion that Frances Ternan came out of retirement to take the part of Alice, an old blind woman. *The Master* opened at the Lyceum on 23 December and was, Dickens told Bulwer Lytton on 17 January, 'an immense success'. It ran until 20 April 1866 after which Frances played her old part of the mother of the twins in Boucicault's *The Corsican Brothers* at the Lyceum until 29 June, when she finally took her leave of the stage. It was probably at that point that she and Nelly moved again, this time to the cottage that Dickens seems to have taken for them in what was then the little market-town of Slough, where Fanny also stayed with them for some time. The Slough cottage occupied by Nelly and her mother stood in Church Street, two blocks away from the High Street in which stood Elizabeth Cottage which, it seems, had been serving Dickens as a bolt-hole since January. He paid the rates under the assumed name of John, or sometimes Charles, Tringham. This name also appears, alternating with 'Turnan', in the rate-book for the Church Street cottage during 1866–67. Dickens evidently wanted to keep his Slough retreat as private as possible and, to preserve his incognito, he seems to have borrowed the name of Tringham from the proprietress of a tobacconist's shop near the *All the Year Round Office*. It appears, however, that the true identity of 'Mr Tringham' was fairly well known locally – hardly surprising given the extent of Dickens's celebrity and the widespread dissemination of his image.[4]

We can only speculate about the reasons for Dickens renting a *pied à terre* in Slough from January 1866, and for Nelly and her mother also moving to the town later in the year, but the ease of railway travel, either from Slough or from nearby Windsor, to any one of three London termini (Paddington, Waterloo and Victoria) would undoubtedly have been an important factor in choosing this particular location. Dickens, we may assume, wanted somewhere he could easily escape to, away from the social and domestic pressures of Gad's Hill, or the London house near Hyde Park that he rented for Mamie's London season (26 Feb.–10 June) or from the social and editorial pressures of his 'London tent' in Wellington Street. As at earlier times in his life when, for example, he hired rooms at Cobley's Farm in Finchley in 1843, he was in need of a retreat where he could write in peace or (what was probably more the case now) intensively rehearse his readings – a place, too, where he could spend time with Nelly, away from London gossip. As for the Ternans themselves, a cottage in Slough would have been a more economical proposition than a house in London and, with the head of the family now definitely retired, it would have been desirable to reduce outgoings. That the Slough cottages were seen as a temporary arrangement for all concerned seems clear from certain entries in Dickens's 'pocket memorandum book', or diary, for 1867, which he lost in America at the end of that year (it ended up in the Berg Collection of the New York Public Library where it was subjected to intensive scholarly investigation and interpretation in the middle of the last century). The entry for 27 March 1867, for example, reads, 'Meet for houses at $12\frac{1}{2}$. To Peckm.' On that day Dickens, either with Nelly and her mother, or with Nelly alone, went to look for a suitable house as a permanent dwelling for the Ternans in the developing south London suburb of Peckham, linked by rail to Waterloo in 1865, and they moved there three months later.[5]

Back in the early months of 1866, the ill-health ('degeneration of some functions of the heart') from which Dickens later said he had suffered after the strain of finishing *Our Mutual Friend* does not seem to have prevented him from living life at his usual phenomenal pace. He spoke at a Mansion House banquet on 16 January, paid the usual close attention to each issue of *All the Year Round*, taking care to promote the cause of Italian unity as much as possible, and entertained a succession of friends at Gad's Hill, as at the dinner-party for twenty attended by the great *Times* journalist William Howard Russell on 25 January. As always, he read much and was hugely admiring of Bulwer Lytton's latest production, a collection of poems entitled *The Lost Tales of Miletus*. One poem in particular, 'The Secret Way', moved him deeply, almost certainly because the presentation of its heroine Argiope awakened in him thoughts of himself and Mary Hogarth. On 10 January he wrote a letter of detailed exuberant praise to Bulwer Lytton, addressing him as his 'dear friend and beloved Brother in Art' whose 'Master hand' he 'used to wonder (in the days of the Last Days of Pompeii) whether I should ever make myself famous enough to touch'. A week later he suggested that he might attend on Bulwer Lytton's behalf rehearsals of Fechter's projected revival of his ever-popular melodrama *The Lady of Lyons* (1838) at the Lyceum. He and Fechter would, he assured Bulwer Lytton, be able to 'strike a new stage picturesqueness out of it, thoroughly belonging to the play itself'. On 10 January also he had written to Wilkie Collins, busy finishing his new novel *Armadale*, to say how delighted he would be if Collins ever felt like returning to *All the Year Round* and collaborating with him in a new series of 'Idle Apprentices and such-like wanderings'. Collins did indeed return to the journal the following year at Dickens's renewed invitation but to collaborate on what was to be the last of the Christmas numbers rather than to resume the wanderings of Francis Goodchild and Thomas Idle. Mostly, however, Dickens's mind seems to have been running on a new series of readings: 'I don't like the trouble, but the money looms large,' he wrote on 18 January to his old friend and devoted admirer Charles Kent, the journalist and future author of *Charles Dickens as a Reader* (1872). After some abortive negotiations conducted through Wills with two different impresarios Dickens finally settled, on 6 March, with the music publishers and concert promoters Chappell & Co. of New Bond Street for a series of thirty readings in London and the provinces for which he was to receive the sum of £1,500 clear. It was arranged that, in addition to his valet and his gasman, Wills should go with him both as travelling-companion and to facilitate the running of *All the Year Round*. All travel arrangements, ticket-sales and other front-of-house business were to be the responsibility of

Chappell's employee George Dolby, a burly, jovial man (Mark Twain, whom he managed on his U.K. lecture-tour, called him 'a gladsome gorilla') between whom and Dickens there quickly developed an excellent rapport. Indeed, Dolby proved to be such a remarkably effective manager and so congenial to his 'Chief', as he called Dickens, that he remained Dickens's trusted and indispensable readings manager to the end. His highly readable *Charles Dickens As I Knew Him* (1885) is a major biographical source for the last four years of Dickens's life.[6]

Dickens wanted to start his tour with a new attraction and set to work to make a reading out of the first and last of *Doctor Marigold*'s 'prescriptions' – all of Marigold's autobiographical narrative contributed by himself, in other words. He also devised a reading version of *Mrs Lirriper* but, rather surprisingly, abandoned it. He had got *Marigold* up 'with immense pains', he told Forster on 11 March, having rehearsed it two hundred times. On 18 March he gave a trial performance of it before a small invited audience including Browning, Wilkie Collins, Fechter and Forster as well, of course, as Georgina and Mamie. The enthusiastic response of this group was prophetic of the enormous popularity this reading at once acquired and retained for the rest of Dickens's reading career. To quote Dolby, 'it more than realized the anticipations of even the most sanguine of Mr Dickens's friends, whilst the public, and those who in various ways were more immediately interested in the readings, were convinced that up to that time they had but a very faint conception of Mr Dickens's powers either as an adapter or an elocutionist.' *Marigold* had required very little adaptation, in fact, merely a little abridgment. It was the first item at his opening performance in St James's Hall on 10 April when it was heard, according to the *Times* critic, 'from beginning to end with the deepest attention and most manifest delight', and it was included in the programme for no fewer than fifteen of the succeeding twenty-nine readings of this tour.[7]

Shortly before this Dickens had been again troubled by a persistent irritant from his literary past. Seymour's son had revived in the columns of *The Athenaeum* his mother's claim that his father had played a significant role in the original conception of *The Pickwick Papers*, a claim that Dickens would have hoped he had finally put paid to in his 1847 preface to the Cheap Edition of *Pickwick*. Now he had to confront it yet again. He wrote to *The Athenaeum* on 28 March, quoting at length from his Cheap Edition preface, and wrote also, on 4 April, to Charley asking him to ask Catherine for a note confirming Dickens's account of his only meeting with Seymour, the one in Doughty Street just before the artist shot himself: 'It seems a superfluous precaution,', he told Charley, 'but I take it for the sake of our descendants long after'. If Catherine did write such a note it seems not to have been preserved, however. The following year Dickens inserted two paragraphs, vigorously refuting the

Seymour claims, into the Cheap Edition preface to *Pickwick* when it was being reprinted for the Charles Dickens Edition.[8]

The readings tour lasted nine weeks. After the opening night in London Dickens and his team travelled north to Liverpool, Manchester, Glasgow and Edinburgh, then back to London, then to Clifton and Birmingham, and back to London again and on 15 May an eighteen-hour journey by the Flying Scotsman to Aberdeen (in a comfortable and very well-provisioned saloon carriage). From Aberdeen they returned to Glasgow and Edinburgh, back to London, then down to Portsmouth (where Dickens joked with Dolby about his inability to identify his birthplace) and back to London again for a final three nights in St James's Hall, finishing 12 June. Everywhere, as he triumphantly reported to Georgina and others, venues were packed out and audiences as rapturous as ever, and there was always that special rapport between the reader and his public that mattered so intensely to Dickens. 'The audience', he wrote to Mamie from Edinburgh on 20 April, 'though so enormous, do somehow express a personal affection, which makes them very strange and moving to see'. It was certainly a punishing schedule, with additional stress resulting from the lingering effects of Staplehurst. Dickens told Dolby that since that horror he had never been able to travel by train 'without experiencing a nervous dread' and that whenever he was on an express train he needed always to take a draught of brandy one hour after starting 'to nerve himself against any ordeal he might have to go through during the rest of the journey'.[9]

Following the tour Dickens had to fulfil his promise to Georgina and Mamie whereby he had 'allowed himself to be disposed of for three days in each week for three months' – in other words, to be available at Gad's Hill to receive visitors. At other times he would need to be at the office or was free to escape to Slough. Fanny Ternan meanwhile was seeking to supplement her teacher's wages with income from writing and Dickens happily accepted her first novel *The Tale of Aunt Margaret's Trouble* for serialisation in *All the Year Round* (14 July–18 Aug.), praising it in a 'rapturous way' according to Percy Fitzgerald, and checking the proofs himself. (It is worth noting, by the way that, when writing about the novel's authorship to so intimate a friend as Wilkie Collins he did not reveal that it was Fanny's work.) Fanny herself had moved to Florence, where her rather footloose sister Maria had also settled for a time, to act as governess to the now motherless little daughter of Dickens's good friend the prolific writer Tom Trollope, Anthony's elder brother. As to Dickens's own family, he still had two boys on his hands at Gad's Hill, Henry and Edward ('Plorn'), but Henry at least was proving, he wrote to Emerson Tennent on 21 August, 'a very good boy ... clever and industrious', and the latest reports of Alfred's progress in Australia were also encouraging. Charley, however, was not exactly prospering in the tea trade as he steadily multiplied the number of his dependents. By now he had made Dickens a grandfather four times over ('think of the unmitigated nonsense of an inimitable grandfather!', Dickens had written to Tom Beard on 15 November 1862, after the birth of Charley's first child). And Mamie had disappointed her father by her unwillingness to contemplate matrimony with Percy Fitzgerald. Reporting this to Bulwer Lytton on 16 July (when he was writing to congratulate his friend on becoming Lord Lytton), Dickens ruefully joked, 'What a wonderful instance of the general inanity of Kings, that the Kings in Fairy Tales should have been always wishing for children! If they had but known when they were well off, having none!'[10]

Following the colossal success of his readings tour Dickens was keen to arrange for another one, the more so since he had now found in Dolby the ideal replacement for Arthur Smith. Chappell's were happy to accept his proposal for another tour in the new year during which he would give forty-two readings for £2,500. Thus, apart from the next Christmas number, still 'in the Limbo of the Unborn', as he told Wills on 11 August, any major new writing would have to be deferred until after this next tour. A new series of 'The Uncommercial Traveller' was planned for the spring of 1867 (in the event, deferred until December 1868) and he told Forster, also in mid-August, that he intended to write 'a new story' for the journal, meaning, I take it, a serialised one like *A Tale of Two Cities* and *Great Expectations*. Meanwhile, he would 'try to discover a Christmas number'. In September he was distracted from this quest into helping Fechter in his negotiations with Dion Boucicault over the Lyceum staging of Boucicault's new play *The Long Strike*, based on Elizabeth Gaskell's *Mary Barton*. Dickens was still 'unapproachable on the general subject of Xmas Nos.', he told Wills on 1 October, but by then he must certainly have begun writing the new one, probably in Slough, since only seven days later he is sending to the printer copy for the number to 'follow on' from some copy already sent and promising a further article to follow the copy now sent 'in two or three days'. The first advertisement for this number appeared in the 3 November issue of *All the Year Round*. It gives the title of the number, 'Mugby Junction', as well as the titles of the four sections Dickens wrote himself, 'Barbox Brothers', 'The Boy at Mugby', 'The Signalman', and 'Barbox Brothers and Co.'. He identifies himself as their author in the advertisement, evidently having now decided to abandon the principle of anonymity in the Christmas numbers. This was probably to counteract that 'swamping' effect of which he later complained whereby his own writing tended to be overwhelmed in the Christmas numbers by the (mostly) very inferior work of his contributors. The advertisement announced that 'other stories' would be added to Dickens's 'later', and their titles and authors were duly advertised in the 24 November issue, among the authors named being Charles Collins. From the order in which his own stories are listed in the 3 November advertisement it appears that Dickens was still at that stage planning to keep to his hallowed *Arabian*

Nights format of framing his contributors' stories within an overarching story by himself, centred on a character called Barbox. Shortly afterwards, he must have decided to abandon this plan and to give the whole of the 'frame' story first, followed by his other two pieces and then five more stories chosen from the large number sent in by would-be contributors. The contents were so ordered in an advertisement that appeared on 24 November. The fact that he had decided to write so much of the number himself meant, as he told Mrs Cowden Clarke on 3 November, that 'the always difficult work of selecting from an immense heap of contributions' was 'rendered twice as difficult as usual, by the contracted space available'.

Mugby Junction was published on 10 December. That Dickens was inspired to take a great railway junction as the setting for this particular Christmas story seems natural enough after his intensive, and at one point horrific, experience of railway travelling over the previous two years. Nine years before, after some rather more limited long-distance train travel, he had in the *Lazy Tour* given his readers a superbly atmospheric description of a great 'Junction-Station' in its two constantly alternating phases of 'Lethargy and Madness'. Now he invests his Mugby Junction nocturne with a certain nightmare quality that will be picked up again in the story of the Signalman featured later in the number, a story that clearly owes a great deal to the haunting memory of the Staplehurst horror:

> A place replete with shadowy shapes, this Mugby Junction in the black hours of the four-and-twenty. Mysterious goods trains, covered with palls and gliding on like vast weird funerals, conveying themselves guiltily away from the presence of the few lighted lamps, as if their freight had come to a secret and unlawful end. . . . Red hot embers showering out upon the ground, down this dark avenue and down the other, as if torturing fires were being raked clear; concurrently shrieks and groans and grinds invading the ear, as if the tortured were at the height of their suffering. Iron-barred cages full of cattle jangling by midway, the drooping beasts with horns entangled, eyes frozen with terror. . . . Unknown languages in the air, conspiring in red, green, and white, characters. . . .

To this confounding place comes Jackson, the story's narrator-protagonist, a depressed middle-aged man, who, feeling that he has no authentic self, has borrowed his *nom de voyage*, Barbox, from that of the pettifogging City firm for which he had drudged from youth to middle age in a 'dim den up in the corner of a court off Lombard Street'. He has at last been able to release himself from this existence but with no motivating idea as to what to do with the rest of his life. Jackson is an unfulfilled and disappointed man and his life-story as Dickens presents it contains echoes of those of two earlier Christmas protagonists, Scrooge in the *Carol* and Redlaw in *The Haunted Man* (as in Redlaw's case, Jackson's best friend and his sweetheart had betrayed him by marrying each other). Jackson's story also recalls the life-stories of Mr Lorry in *A Tale of Two Cities* and, above all, of Arthur Clennam in *Little Dorrit*. His redemption from his desiccated emotional state stems from his encounters with Phoebe, an angelically beautiful and selfless girl paralysed from the neck down, the loving daughter of the Bob-Cratchit-like railway worker 'Lamps'. Jackson's humanity is subsequently fully restored through his involvement with a seemingly lost little child called Polly whose extreme cuteness must, one imagines, have always been rather hard for all but the most sentimental of 'Dickens lovers' to endure. Polly proves, of course, to be the child of Jackson's erstwhile sweetheart and his traitor friend. The couple are now penitent and in a desperate state so there is plenty of opportunity for the converted Barbox, as there was for Scrooge and for Redlaw, to demonstrate his new-found humanity and to spread happiness all around him.[11]

The two stories Dickens himself wrote for this Christmas number in addition to the frame story are very contrasting literary productions. 'The Boy at Mugby' is not a story at all, in fact, but a comic monologue inspired, we learn from Dolby, by the extremely rude behaviour of the refreshment room staff at Rugby station towards Wills and Dickens on a particular occasion during the readings tour, when they were shrewishly informed, 'You sha'n't have any milk and sugar 'till you fellows have paid for your coffee'. The direness of railway refreshment rooms was, as we have seen, one of Dickens's abiding *bêtes noires*, already aired in his 'Uncommercial Traveller' series in 1860, and this incident at Rugby inspired him to return to the topic and to introduce some broad comic/satiric writing into this Christmas number which otherwise tended strongly towards the sombre or the sentimental. Dickens's second story, 'The Signalman', a ghost story involving a terrible railway accident, was clearly written in the shadow of Staplehurst and is a chilling tale of presentiment and foreboding, the best short story that Dickens ever wrote, in fact.[12]

Mugby Junction appeared in the shops and on the railway bookstalls on 10 December and its very warm reception showed that Dickens had mixed his ingredients in it as skilfully as he mixed them when making his celebrated punch. It surpassed even *Doctor Marigold* in popularity. By 27 December it had sold 250,000 copies and by 24 January he could tell Wills, 'We shall evidently sell our 265,000 copies' – in other words the entire print run. He was hoping, too, that it might equal or surpass *Marigold* as a reading too. In fact, he had derived three reading texts from it by mid-November, *Barbox Brothers*, *The Boy at Mugby* and *The Signalman*, and had had them printed and bound up together. He seems, for some reason, to have proceeded no further with *The Signalman* (perhaps the Staplehurst echoes were too disturbing?) but tried out the other two on audiences of family and friends. Their enthusiastic response was not shared by Dolby and 'certain of the more practical judges' as he calls them, and he and they were right. Neither *Barbox Brothers* nor *The Boy* were as successful with audiences as any of the established readings and Dickens soon dropped them from his repertoire.[13]

During the autumn and winter months of 1866 Dickens had his fair share of sad events and anxieties in his personal life. In September he was grieved to have to order the magnificent Sultan to be shot after the dog had attacked a little girl, and there are several poignant descriptions of the animal's death in letters to friends. In October he heard that his youngest brother Augustus had died in Chicago leaving his partner a widow with three children. 'Poor fellow!' Dickens wrote to Wills on 21 October, 'A sad business altogether. My mind misgives me that it will bring upon me a host of disagreeables from America.' There may also have been a problem about Nelly's finances because his bank records show six payments to 'N Trust' totalling £128 between 17 October and 14 January 1867. Then, at the beginning of November he was appalled to find that John, his trusted manservant for so many years, had been regularly pilfering money at the *All the Year Round* office, of which he had been in charge for some time. Dickens was much troubled about how to deal with this 'miserable man', whom he could not bear to have arrested. Things seem not to have been going well, either, with Katey and Mamie, who were reported as seeming distressed and behaving strangely at a London dinner-party this autumn, at which Katey appeared 'a spectacle of woe'. A month or so later she did become worryingly ill, suffering badly from a 'low nervous fever', so that it was not until after Christmas that she was able to travel to Gad's Hill with her sickly husband Charles Collins, who, Dickens told Cerjat on 1 January 1867, 'is on the whole as well as he ever is – or ever will be, I fear'.[14]

It was not all gloom and anxiety, however. Nelly was briefly away in Paris in late October attending Fanny's wedding to her employer Tom Trollope ('I little thought what an important Master of Ceremonies I was', Dickens wrote to the bridegroom on 2 November, 'when I first presented the late Fanny Ternan to you') but she would otherwise have been there for him in Slough. Mary Boyle visited Gad's Hill in mid-October and, together with Georgina, Mamie and Katey, formed a very responsive audience for a private reading of 'The Boy at Mugby' – 'I don't think I ever saw people laugh so much under the prosiest of circumstances', Dickens told Wills on 21 October. There was a large Christmas house-party at Gad's Hill, the members of which would have been much diverted by the Boxing Day sports that Dickens had organised (with, of course, the closest attention to every detail) for the local populace in the field behind his house. Dickens himself acted as judge and referee, provided and presented the cash prizes, and by means of what Austen Layard, who was of the house-party, called 'a magical kind of influence', ensured that the event was a huge success. There was no trouble or disturbance of any kind, even though between two and three thousand people turned up. Describing the event to Forster, Dickens gleefully described the man who came second in a hurdle race whilst all the time smoking his pipe, and who replied to Dickens's comment that without his pipe he would have won by answering, 'I beg your pardon, sir, . . . but if it hadn't been for my pipe, I should have been nowhere.'[15]

1 January 1867 begins a unique year in Dickens's biography in that we have a full record of his day-by-day movements in the diary he lost and which is now in New York. This enables us to see how regularly he managed to visit Slough whenever an opportunity offered itself during his strenuous readings tour, which brought him back to London for a one night's performance every ten days or so. The tour actually began in London on 15 January, with readings of the soon-to-be dropped *Barbox Brothers* and *The Boy at Mugby*, and during the next four months it took Dickens and his team to nearly all the main towns and cities in most regions of England, as well as to Glasgow, Edinburgh and Swansea. During the earlier part of the tour weather conditions were often appalling and he was 'reading in snow-storms, and down-pourings of sheets of solid ice', as he reported to Wills from Birmingham on 24 January. But he never had to cancel a reading and only very occasionally did the bad weather seem to have affected the size or dampened the enthusiasm of his audiences. From 15 to 22 March he was in Ireland despite the great fear of a major upsurge of Fenianism, which made him in prospect 'a disconsolate Voyager', as he told Wilkie Collins on 13 March. In the event, however, he achieved, as he reported to Forster, 'WONDERS!' both in Dublin and Belfast: 'Enthusiastic crowds have filled the halls to the roof each night, and hundreds have been turned away'. He and Dolby returned from Dublin to England on Saturday 23 March and his diary shows that he went directly to Slough from Euston station and remained there until the 25th when he went to his Wellington Street office. He read at St James's Hall on the 26th (*Marigold* and *Bardell and Pickwick*) and on the 27th made the expedition with Nelly to look at houses in Peckham. The next day he was on the road again, heading for Cambridge and Norwich. He continued to suffer very much from 'Railway shaking' as he called it and, Dolby records, 'kept constantly referring to the Staplehurst accident, which was ever present in his mind'. He tried to avoid travelling by express train but this proved impractical for the longer journeys.[16]

Under the circumstances of his readings tours it was, of course, impossible for Dickens to write anything apart from letters (he reckoned that his correspondence equalled that of a Secretary of State). The nearest he came to literary composition during these months was in the powerful peroration he composed for an *All the Year Round* article that he had asked Joseph Parkinson, one of his regular contributors, to write (it appeared in the issue for 2 March). The title Dickens proposed was 'What is Sensational?' and he wanted the piece to be a 'most ferocious and bitter attack' on the President of the Poor Law Board who had complained about newspapers 'sensationalising' the workhouse death of a certain pauper who had died in what Dickens called 'the most frightful circumstances'. 'Is it Sensational', runs one of his fierce rhetorical questions, 'to call the public attention to a noteworthy example of a costly Board existing under false pretences and showing mankind How not to do it?' He also committed himself to some future writing for the American market after finishing his readings. For Benjamin Wood, the flamboyant editor of the *New York Daily News*, he agreed on 27 February to write by 1 August 'a new tale of the length of "Hunted Down" ' for the same fee that he had received for that story, that is, £1,000. A month later (29 March) he told James Osgood of the Boston firm of Ticknor & Fields that he would be happy 'to write for the Child's Magazine published by your house, four little papers expressly designed for its pages, in consideration of the sum of £1,000'. Again, the length was to be the same as that of 'Hunted Down' but, if it should turn out that the series would be spoiled by compressing it into such a length, then he would write to the length required by the material. 'Your house will believe', he wrote proudly, 'that nothing would compensate me for slighting my art.' In this case his agreed final deadline was the end of October.

Dickens would have been feeling favourably disposed towards Ticknor & Fields at this time, quite apart from his personal friendship with James Fields. In early March he had received a remittance of £200 from the firm in respect of the fourteen-volume edition of his works that they had just published under the title of 'The Diamond Edition', with illustrations by Sol Eytinge, who had long worked on *Harper's Weekly* and whose work greatly pleased Dickens. On 16 April he wrote to Ticknor & Fields authorising them to state publicly that he had never profited from the reprinting of his works in America by any other publishers than themselves, except for Harper's payments to him for advance proof-sheets of the serial parts of his last three novels. Apart from these payments, he wrote, 'In America the occupation of my life for thirty years is, unless it bears your imprint, utterly worthless and profitless to me.' The publicising of this letter by Ticknor & Fields caused angry protests from other American publishers from whom Dickens had certainly received various payments. Ticknor and Fields defended themselves and Dickens as best they could and proceeded with their Diamond Edition in the anticipation that Dickens would soon commit himself to the readings tour in America that James Fields was eagerly trying to persuade him to undertake. Dickens shrank from so strenuous an undertaking but the prospective financial reward was so enormous that he found himself drawn towards America, he told Georgina on 10 May, as inexorably as Charles Darnay in *A Tale of Two Cities* had been drawn towards *his* loadstone rock, Paris. It was a grim analogy to make as the Loadstone Rock, in *The Arabian Nights*, is described as attracting all metal so strongly that ships were helplessly drawn towards it and then wrecked upon it. An American tour was not only likely to have an adverse effect upon his health but there was also the devastating prospect of several months' absence from Nelly. 'The Patient, I acknowledge to be the gigantic difficulty,' he wrote to Wills, on Nelly's own monogrammed notepaper, on 6 June, canvassing the idea of an American tour. But there might nevertheless, he believed, be ways of getting her across the Atlantic also. Overriding everything was the prospect of making no less than £10,000 'in a heap'. This was, he told Wills, 'an immense consideration' to him with 'my wife's income to pay – a very expensive position to hold – and my boys with a curse of limpness on them'. 'You don't know what it is', he continued, 'to look round the table and see reflected from every seat at it (where they sit) some horribly well remembered expression of inadaptability to anything.'[17]

Dickens may well have been thinking ahead towards a possible late-autumn visit to America when he wrote to Wilkie Collins on 1 May inviting him to collaborate with him on the next Christmas number, 'We two alone, each taking half'. Three weeks later he wrote to Forster that if he were to go at all he would need to do so before the end of 1867. The Americans, he said, were now certainly assuming that he *would* go and he and Dolby were constantly bombarded with business propositions from across the Atlantic. There would, however, be a presidential election in 1868 and 'they are a people whom a fancy does not hold long' so that he needed to decide now: 'If ever I go, the time would be when the Christmas number goes to press. Early in the next November.' This being so, he would obviously want to bring forward, simplify and streamline as far as possible the preparation of the 1867 Christmas number so that it might all be finished before he left the country. To write the entire number himself would be too burdensome but to follow the usual elaborate procedure of devising and writing substantial parts of a frame story and then dealing with the flood of offerings from would-be contributors would also be too pressuring in the time available. With Collins as his tried and tested co-writer, however, Dickens could be confident that the number could be got ready in time, especially if they began work early on it. They could jointly construct it from the beginning, since he was inviting Collins to be his co-author even 'before having approached the subject in my own mind as to contrivance, character, story, or anything else'. Collins readily agreed, and was no doubt pleased that Dickens at the same time accepted, sight unseen, his new novel, *The Moonstone*, for serialisation in *All the Year Round* later in the year. Their collaboration on the Christmas number, it was agreed, should begin 'under the trees', as Dickens puts it, at Gad's Hill, in early August.

In his 6 June letter to Wills Dickens mentioned not only the money he would make directly from touring in the States but also other profits that might accrue. 'An immense impulse', he believed, 'would be given to the C.D. Edition by my going out.' He was here referring to a new prestige edition of his works called the Charles Dickens Edition on which he had been working for some time and which Chapman and Hall launched in May with a remarkably lavish publicity campaign. Dickens wrote the prospectus published in *The Athenaeum* on 4 May.

Described as an 'Entirely New Edition of the Whole of Mr Dickens's Works', it would present each novel complete in one volume and would be reprinted from the Cheap Edition but on 'a flowing open page, free from the objection of having double columns' and the author would attach 'a descriptive head-line' to every right-hand page. A facsimile of Dickens's signature with its by now well-known flourish was stamped in gold upon the red cloth-covered boards in which each volume was bound. This might 'suggest to the Author's countrymen his present watchfulness over his own Edition, and his hopes that it may remain a favourite with them when he shall have left their service for ever'. Besides supplying the promised headlines, Dickens wrote new prefaces, admittedly often incorporating whole chunks of earlier ones, and eight of the original illustrations, 'selected as the best', were included in each volume. The whole edition was dedicated, as the Library Edition had been, and in the same terms, to Forster and was published at the rate of one volume a month until October 1868, beginning with *Pickwick* on 31 May. The price per volume was either 3s. 6d. or 3s., depending on its length, which made it cheaper than the Library Edition while still offering a handsome product at a reasonable price. Ticknor & Fields were to publish the Edition in America and in the prospectus Dickens expressed the hope that it would serve to remind 'the great American People' that the Boston firm were his appointed American publishers. This Edition sold so well on both sides of the Atlantic that by the time of his death Dickens had made a net profit of £6,250 on the sale of over half a million volumes in the United Kingdom alone.[18]

On 10 May Dickens wrote to Georgina from Wellington Street, 'Between the New Edition, correspondence, AYR, and all other cares, I have as much to do as I can manage. Last night I was so tired I could hardly undress for bed.' The chief way in which the 'New Edition' added to his work-load would seem to have been in regard to the provision of the promised 'descriptive head-lines' since he did not go in for much in the way of textual revision, with the famous exception of the regular substitution of 'Fagin' or 'the old man' for 'the Jew' in the second half of *Oliver Twist*. The new headlines, or 'running heads' as they are also called, mostly go beyond simple description and offer some sort of comment – choric, moral, humorous, ironic – on the text, not infrequently invoking Shakespeare or some other well-known literary source. The scene between Mrs Gamp and Betsey Prig in *Chuzzlewit* chapter 29, for example, has the headline 'The Weird Sisters', while the scene of Mrs Skewton making up to Mr Dombey and Carker in *Dombey and Son* chapter 36 has the headline 'Infinite Variety of Cleopatra'. The fate that has befallen Redlaw after his pact with the Phantom in *The Haunted Man* is made clear in the headline: 'All good imagination gone'. Very often headlines form a sequence commenting on the action of the chapter, as in chapter 47 of *Oliver Twist* when Fagin maddens Sikes into committing murder: 'Goading the Wild Beast' is followed by 'The Wild Beast Springs', and the phrase is picked up again three chapters later, 'The Wild Beast hemmed in' and 'The Wild Beast laid low'.

Where the scene and characters change within a chapter the headlines reflect
this, for example, chapter 23 of *Bleak House*: 'Mademoiselle Hortense', 'Richard
sinking into a Chancery Suitor', 'Put not your faith in Chancery', 'Deportment
droops', 'The real original African break-down' [Mrs Jellyby's grandiose schemes;
'break-down' was the name for a very animated tribal or other dance], and 'A
model Mother'. Perhaps most succinct of all are the two headlines for the pages
about Merdle's suicide in *Little Dorrit* Book II, ch. 25: 'The Great and Wonderful
finds his level' and 'The Chief Butler Speaks an Epitaph'.[19]

Life was not all work for Dickens, however. His diary shows that the evening
before he wrote to Georgina he had been to Fechter's Lyceum Theatre, where, as
noted above, Frances Ternan was still acting. The entry reads 'N there too'. Nelly
would have been due for a treat after having been ill, as recorded in another note,
for the latter part of April. On the 10th he went to Slough from the *All the Year
Round* office with 'N and M' ('M' who often figures in the diary as accompanying
'N' presumably stands for either 'Mother', that is, Mrs Ternan, or 'Maria'). Dickens
was back in London for one last reading (the always taxing *Little Dombey*,
followed by *Bob Sawyer's Party*) on 13 May and five days later was saddened to
hear of the death of 'dear old Stanny', Clarkson Stanfield, the best loved of all his
older friends, apart from Macready. He published a noble tribute to Stanfield in
the 1 June issue of *All the Year Round* in which he pointedly recalled how 'No
Artist can ever have stood by his art with a quieter dignity than he always did.'
And he responded both promptly and effectively to Stanfield's widow's request
for help in getting her youngest son an appointment in the Civil Service.[20]

After his four months' absorption in his readings tour Dickens was now
facing a busy summer. He had, as he told Emerson Tennent on 23 May, when
declining his friend's invitation to pay a holiday visit to Tennent's home in
Ireland, 'work to do for America which will last me through the summer' as
well as 'a vast arrear of business at All The Year Round' and the Christmas
number to be got ready to go to press in early November. He had a speech to
make, just four days before the second anniversary of Staplehurst, on behalf of
the Railway Benevolent Institution. He had also, though he could hardly have
mentioned this to Tennent, Nelly to help get settled, perhaps with her mother
also, in her new home, Windsor Lodge in Linden Grove, Peckham. In addition
to all this, he had domestic matters at Gad's Hill to attend to, not least finding
the best way to prepare fifteen-year-old Plorn to follow his brother Alfred to
seek his fortune in Australia. Over all, and obscuring his 'whole prospect' as
Dickens expressed it, loomed the great and pressing question as to whether or
not he should undertake an American readings tour in the autumn. It was
under such even more than usually pressured circumstances that he set to
work on the first piece of 'writing for America' that he had promised to deliver
this summer. It proved in the event to be one of the most haunting stories he
ever wrote and of an originality that astonished even himself.[21]

CHAPTER 25

Writing, and reading, for America

1867–1868

Well, the work is hard, the climate is hard, the life is hard: but so far the gain is enormous. . . .

Dickens to Forster, 5 January 1868

He held it as a maxim that 'No man had a right to break an engagement with the public if he were able to be out of bed.'

George Dolby, *Dickens As I Knew Him*, 227

ON 25 APRIL 1867 Dickens gave a reading in Preston and was due to give another in Blackburn the following day. The distance between the two places being only twelve miles, he and Dolby decided to walk it. Their way took them past Hoghton Tower, the sixteenth-century seat of the Hoghton family, 'standing out weird and melancholy', as Dolby later recalled, 'on the summit of the precipice on which it was erected'. The Hoghtons had ceased living there in the eighteenth-century and had let the place fall into disrepair whilst renting out a more recently built extension to a succession of local farmers. Dickens and Dolby toured the now romantically desolate old mansion, in which James I had once feasted, and the experience triggered something in Dickens's imagination that enabled him to see how to open a new story he was planning to serialise the following year in *All the Year Round*. Instead of another exhausting marathon in twenty monthly numbers like *Our Mutual Friend* he was mentally preparing for the more concentrated challenge of a novel like *Great Expectations*, written in weekly instalments over seven or eight months. Now, however, he decided to use his idea for this serial for the one-off story he had promised to write by 1 August for the New York *Daily News*. 'The main idea of the narrator's position towards the other people', he later told Wills, 'was the idea I *had* for my next novel in A.Y.R. But it is very curious that I did not in the least see how to begin his state of mind, until I walked into Hoghton Towers one bright April day with Dolby.' This suggests that the new novel he had begun thinking about was to have resembled *Great Expectations* not only in format but also in form and narrative interest. It was intended to be written in the first person with much of the interest focusing on the narrator's 'state of mind', the dramatic early experiences that had formed it, and the way in which it had subsequently determined his relations with other people and thus his destiny. Dickens transfers these things to 'George Silverman's Explanation', the first of his writings for America. Born into dire poverty in a slum cellar in Preston, George, longing for food and warmth, has a sense of guilt about his 'worldliness' instilled in him by his harshly unjust mother which later causes him to act disastrously against his own best interests at certain crucial points in his life. His attempted 'Explanation', written as an obscure country clergyman ending his days in some sequestered nook, explains nothing to him about himself and his fate. What it does do, however, is to reveal him to the reader as an incorrigibly self-tormenting egotist. In this respect his story is a free-standing successor in Dickens's oeuvre to that of Miss Wade, which had been so awkwardly inserted into the structure of *Little Dorrit*.[1]

Dickens took the name 'Silverman', which perhaps caught his eye because of its appropriateness to his elderly narrator and his twilight existence, from one of the lists of names in his *Book of Memoranda*. From the same source came the splendid name of Silverman's dishonest guardian, Brother Verity Hawkyard, and the surname of his accomplice Brother Gimblet. These two canting hypocrites and their deluded flock represent Dickens's last, and arguably most ferocious, attack on sectarian preachers and their followers. As Forster might have expressed it, Brother Hawkyard finishes what Mr Stiggins in *Pickwick* began.[2]

Dickens's rapid passing from industrial Preston with its 'notoriously high death-rate' and its thousands of slum cellars to the romantic ruin of Hoghton Tower out in the countryside surely also played its part in stimulating his novelist's imagination. What might be the effect on the awakening sensibility of a sensitive and intelligent child suddenly transported (in order to sanitise him and build up his strength) from a bare cold cellar to a place like Hoghton Tower? Dickens imagines George's imaginings. Nature, the boy thinks, seemed to pity him as the sky 'stared sorrowfully' at him through gaps and chinks in the ruined roof. Meanwhile, 'down at the bottom of dark pits of staircase into which the stairs had sunk, green leaves trembled, butterflies fluttered, and bees hummed in and out through the open doorways' while 'encircling the whole ruin were sweet scents and sights of fresh green growth and ever-renewing life that I had never dreamed of'. Humanised by his experiences, George for the first time thinks of his parents with sorrowing pity. He also falls in love with Sylvia, the beautiful young daughter of the farmer, the tenant of Hoghton Tower, with whom he has been sent to live, as young Pip had fallen in love with Estella in the setting of another picturesquely ruinous mansion. George is an even more deeply damaged child than Pip, however, and his reactions are more complex. To Sylvia's disgust, he repels her offers of friendship and hides away from her. She cannot know that he is doing this out of love, from fear that he might infect her with the taint of the Preston cellar that he fancies still clinging to him, and so interprets his behaviour as mere sullenness.[3]

Dolby tells us that 'George Silverman's Explanation' took Dickens 'but a very few days to complete', giving the impression that he dashed it off immediately after the visit to Hoghton Tower. But it was surely not until after his readings tour was over and he had cleared off some of the heavy arrears of his magazine work and other commitments (including a speech he had promised to make for the Railway Benevolent Institution on 5 June, just four days before the second anniversary of the Staplehurst disaster) that he would have been able to get down to 'Silverman'. We know from an entry in his 1867 diary that he finished the story in Windsor Lodge, Nelly's new home in Linden Grove, Peckham, on 26 June but do not know when he actually started the writing. In early June his life would have been very much dominated by the debate about whether or not he should undertake an American readings tour, with both Forster and Wills opposing the idea, the former very strongly indeed. From Dickens's letters we get the impression that his mind was in fact pretty much made up. He wrote to Fields on 3 June, 'I am trying hard so to free myself, as to be able to come over to read this next winter! Whether I may succeed in this endeavour, or no, I cannot yet say, but I am trying HARD.' Nelly was 'the gigantic difficulty', as he told Wills three days later. A four- or five-month separation from her was terrible to contemplate but, as Wills well knew, he wrote, he did not like 'to give in before a difficulty, if it can be beaten'. He evidently came to believe that this particular difficulty, 'gigantic' though it was, *might* be beaten. Nelly might come independently to America while he was there, perhaps accompanied by her sister Maria, on the pretext of a visit to her Spofford cousins in Newburyport in Massachusetts. By the 13th, following a session with Dolby in which they calculated Dickens's net profit on an American readings tour would amount to £15,500, it was decided that Dolby should cross the Atlantic in August on a reconnoitring expedition. Dolby, Dickens wrote to Fields, would confer with him and others, and would see for himself the various rooms in those cities included in the proposed itinerary in which it was intended that Dickens should read. He would telegraph his findings to Dickens who would then make a final decision on whether or not to come.[4]

It was probably immediately after this that Dickens began writing 'Silverman' and within a fortnight it was done. 'Upon myself it has made the strangest impression of reality and originality!!' he wrote to Wills on the 28th, 'And I feel as if I had read something (by somebody else) which I should never get out of my mind!!!' As this reaction suggests, the story came from a very deep layer in his psychological make-up. His remark naturally prompts us to speculate about the possible relationship of Silverman's woeful tale to some of the deepest currents in his creator's emotional life, both past and present, and particularly to that fierce sense of injured merit that flares up in Dickens's writings from time to time, notably in his response to the American press in 1842, in the autobiographical fragment a few years later, and in both his public and private comments on the break-up of his marriage in 1858. Silverman's response to the gross injustice and exploitation he has to suffer is quite the opposite. It is extremely self-abnegating, and he apparently even colludes with those who unjustly condemn and cheat him, appearing to strive after an impossible selflessness and ending up as confused about himself and his motives as when he began his 'explanation'.[5]

After finishing 'Silverman' Dickens turned to the other piece of writing for America that he had undertaken to produce this summer, the series of stories for Ticknor and Fields's children's monthly *Our Young Folks*. This was a very different, lighter-hearted, project but Dickens kept to the technique of dramatised narrators. The series is entitled *Holiday Romance* and Dickens wrote to Forster on 2 July that he hoped it was 'droll and very child-like; though the joke is a grown-up one besides'. He added, 'You must try to like the pirate story, for I am very fond of it', and Forster's enthusiastic response to the stories as a whole must have delighted him. 'They are', wrote Forster, 'the quaintest, wisest, most charming, most comical, in all ways most delightful, things I have ever read.' The format Dickens chose for *Holiday Romance* resembled the one he had used for every Christmas number since 1854. An introductory, scene-setting story told by an eight-year-old called William Tinkling, the proud editor, is followed by three more stories told by William's friends, another little boy and two girls whose ages range between six-and-a-half and nine. William's 'Introductory Romance', Dickens's first use of a child narrator since 'The Schoolboy's Story' in the 1853 Christmas number, is a less exotic variant on the harem section of 'The Ghost in Master B's Room' in *The Haunted House*. In depicting his four children as two pairs of innocent romantic lovers, this being the 'grown-up' joke that he hoped would please Forster, Dickens recalls 'Boots at the Holly-tree Inn' as well as the child David and Little Em'ly at the beginning of *Copperfield*. What is new is his giving the two little girls equal status with the boys. Both girls have their own stories and indeed it is the older one, Alice Rainbird, not William Tinkling who, like Dickens 'conducting' a Christmas number, sets up an idea for the other tales. 'Let us,' she tells the others, 'in these next Holidays now going to begin, throw our thoughts into something educational for the grown-up people, hinting to them how things ought to be. Let us veil our meaning under a mask of romance . . .'.[6]

It is in Alice's own story, a moralised fairy-tale about a magic fish-bone, that we perhaps get our last, benign, glimpse of John Dickens in his son's work for it is surely some memory of John that lies behind the figure of the harassed government clerk, 'King Watkins the First', father of a large and ever-growing family and in constant pecuniary difficulties. No comment by Dickens on Alice's story survives but, as we have seen, he did take a special pleasure in writing 'the pirate story'. Its author, 'Lieutenant-Colonel Robin Redforth' aged nine, portrays himself as 'Captain Boldheart' who, having been 'spited' by a mean-spirited Latin-Grammar-Master, 'devoted himself to the Pirate profession at a very early age'. The climax of his exotic adventures in his 'splendid schooner of one hundred guns, loaded to the muzzle' comes when he rescues his beloved from her school in Margate by threatening to bombard the town after which 'the Captain and his Bride departed for the Indian Ocean to enjoy themselves for evermore'. 'I hope', wrote Dickens to Fields from Gad's Hill on 25 July, 'the Americans will see the joke of "Holiday Romance". The writing seems to me so like Childrens', that dull folks (on *any* side of *any* water) might perhaps rate it accordingly!' He hopes especially that Fields will like the story of Captain Boldheart: 'It made me laugh to that extent that my people here thought I was out of my wits, until I gave it to them to read – when they did likewise.' Three days later he mentioned it again in a letter to Percy Fitzgerald saying he well remembered his own childhood desire to become a pirate and characteristically claiming, 'But I loved more desperately than Boldheart.' The chanting cannibals from whom Boldheart rescues the hapless Latin-Grammar-Master also come from the imaginative world of Dickens's childhood, when he would pore with delight over *Robinson Crusoe*. The last story, 'From the Pen of Miss Nettie Ashford. Aged half-past six', is about a topsy-turvy world in which adults behave like recalcitrant children and children like their sorely tried adult carers, a much softened, playfully fantastic, version of Jenny Wren and her 'bad child' in *Our Mutual Friend*. It is only here, I think, that the skilful imitation of a child's story-telling of which Dickens was so proud breaks down. He cannot resist the temptation to indulge in yet one more satirical attack on a favourite target: 'So Mrs Orange went . . . to the room where the children were having supper, to see them playing at Parliament. And she found some of the boys crying "Hear, hear, hear!" while other boys cried "No, no!" and others "Question!" "Spoke!" and all sorts of nonsense that ever you heard.'

Fields saw to it that Dickens's story was presented as attractively as possible. When Dickens wrote on 12 July that he would be sending out the manuscript of *Holiday Romance* with Dolby, together with a proof he had had specially made 'to set up again from', he remarked that the piece was 'full of subjects for illustration', suggesting it might be re-issued as a little book with plentiful illustrations 'if you can find (I can't!) a fanciful man'. Though he did not re-issue the stories in book form, Fields did commission the eminent English book and periodicals illustrator John Gilbert to produce a full-page plate to accompany each story as it appeared in *Our Young Folks* and Sol Eytinge together with another of Ticknor & Fields's house artists, G. C. White, devised four witty initial vignettes to be dropped into the text.[7]

Meanwhile, presumably, Nelly was settling into her new home in Peckham after a short sojourn in a house designated 'temporary P.' in Dickens's pocket diary. About this time Dickens's excitable amateur-actress friend Frances Elliot seems to have heard some gossip about Nelly, Dickens and their 'magic circle'. The gossip apparently included some report of suffering endured by Nelly and Elliot wrote sympathetically to Dickens, perhaps offering to try to help or comfort Nelly in some way. She had also evidently heard that Fanny Ternan, now Fanny Trollope, had also been somehow involved in the matter. Dickens's reply (4 July) assured her the 'magic circle' comprised 'but one member' and firmly rejected her kind (or inquisitive?) offer: '. . . it would be inexpressibly painful to N to think that you knew the history. . . . She would not believe that you could see her with my eyes, or know her with my mind.' If she were the kind of woman who could bear Elliot knowing her personal history, he wrote, 'she could not have the pride and self-reliance which (mingled with the gentlest nature) has borne her, alone, through so much'. We get no clue as to what the nature of this solitary ordeal of Nelly's had been but Dickens's way of mentioning it is surely very strange indeed if what he was referring to was her seduction by him and subsequent life as his mistress. Neither can we guess what was the part played by her sister Fanny in this mysterious story, the memory of which part Dickens finds 'impossible to swallow' (though it did not prevent him from continuing to pay her well for her serials in *All the Year Round*). Elliot is warned that if she should see either Fanny or her husband she should be very careful 'to make no reference to me which either can piece into any thing'. Fanny, he adds, is 'infinitely sharper than the Serpent's Tooth. Mind that'.

Nelly is here presented, in the longest piece of writing by Dickens directly about her that has so far come to light, very much in terms of a heroine of Victorian melodrama and this perhaps is how he thought of her, at least for some of the time. In his authorial life, meanwhile, he and Wilkie Collins were about to start work on an actual full-blooded melodrama, one with a remarkably self-reliant and resourceful heroine, which was initially to do duty, in narrative form, as the *All the Year Round* Christmas story for 1867. This was *No Thoroughfare* with its chapters labelled 'Overture' and then by act numbers (I–IV), the plan being that after Dickens's departure for America Collins should convert the story into a play for a Christmas production at the Adelphi with Fechter in the leading role. The part of the sinister young Swiss villain Obenreizer was clearly written with Fechter in mind. 'We put the story together in the Swiss chalet at Gad's Hill,' Collins later recalled but does not tell us who contributed what to the basic concept of the story. Two of its leading elements seem clear echoes of Dickens's *Little Dorrit*, however. The first is the crucial part played in the story by the Foundling Hospital, which recalls Tattycoram in *Dorrit*, as well as an 1853 *Household Words* article on the Hospital, 'Received, a Blank Child', written jointly by Dickens and Wills.

The second is the setting of the climactic scene high up amid the ice and snow and hospices of an Alpine pass which recalls the opening of *Dorrit* Bk II. The pass, however, is not the great St Bernard of the novel but the Simplon. The hero Vendale and Obenreizer follow the route over the Alps taken by Dickens and Collins themselves, together with Egg, in the autumn of 1853. The dramatic situation, that of a good and trusting young man alone in some icy wasteland with a powerful companion who, unbeknown to him, has a strong motive to kill him, is also an obvious reprise of the climax of Collins's *The Frozen Deep*, but Obenreizer, unlike Wardour, is no tragic hero. He remains a wholly melodramatic villain to the end, when he is 'suffocated and broken all to pieces' in an avalanche – Dickens had briefly considered suicide as an appropriate end for him but evidently decided a more spectacular, hand-of-Providence fate was what was required. Finally, the mode of Vendale's rescue recalled a more recent Dickens novel than *Little Dorrit*. He is saved by his beloved Marguerite, the Swiss peasant girl who (literally) knows the ropes, just as in *Our Mutual Friend* Lizzie Hexam's skills as an oarswoman had saved *her* lover's life after he, too, had been the victim of a murderous assault.[8]

Collins was already at work on *The Moonstone*, scheduled to begin serialisation in *All the Year Round* in January, and by 30 June Dickens had read, with strong approval, the first three numbers and had 'gone minutely through the plot of the rest' with Collins during a visit by the latter to Gad's Hill. 'It is', Dickens wrote to Wills, 'a very curious story – wild and yet domestic', and to Collins himself he predicted that it would be the most successful book he

53 Dickens kills off a character (Walter Wilding) in *No Thoroughfare*, *The Mask*, February 1868

had ever written. Collins had thus to fit his work on *No Thoroughfare* into his writing schedule for *The Moonstone*. At the beginning of August, meanwhile, Dolby departed on his reconnaissance tour to the States. Dickens saw him off at Liverpool despite being badly lamed by another attack of his foot trouble, which he consistently refused to believe was gout, attributing it to 'over-walking'. He suffered greatly after returning to Gad's Hill, telling Forster on the 6th that he had been 'on the sofa all last night in tortures', but seems to have ignored the problem when debating the pros and cons of going to America. He had promised Forster and Wills, and presumably also Georgina, Mamie and Nelly, that he would not finally decide about going until Dolby returned with a detailed report on the situation there and an estimate of the financial rewards he might expect. Nelly (referred to as 'Madame') was, Dickens wrote to Dolby on 9 August, 'very anxious' for his report and 'ready to commit herself to the Atlantic' under his care (if Dickens went, Dolby would travel out a few weeks ahead of him). To such speeches by Nelly, Dickens told Dolby, he always replied, '*If* I go, my dear; *if* I go'.

In America Dolby evidently got on very well with the Fieldses and with Fields's junior partner, James Osgood, who helped him enormously by accompanying him on a tour of the places on Dickens's proposed itinerary. As we have seen, Dolby brought with him for Fields the manuscript and first proofs of *Holiday Romance* and the manuscript of 'George Silverman' for Benjamin Wood. Wood proved so unbusinesslike, however, that Dolby, following Dickens's previously-given instructions, declined to hand over the manuscript and gave it to Fields instead. He, having paid Dickens the £1,000 agreed with Wood, subsequently published it in three parts in his journal *The Atlantic Monthly* and it was reprinted in *All the Year Round* on 1, 15 and 29 February (as was *Holiday Romance* on 25 Jan., 8 Feb, 14 March and 4 April 1868).

Various things show that, pending Dolby's return, Dickens was paving the way towards a return visit to America. For the new Charles Dickens Edition of *Martin Chuzzlewit* he revised the preface to the novel he had written for the Cheap Edition in 1850, softening down the references to America. The *American Notes* Cheap Edition preface was already emollient in tone so could be safely left to stand, but the book's appearance in the Charles Dickens Edition was nevertheless delayed until shortly after Dickens's return from America in 1868. Another sign was Dickens's prompt response to a request for an interview from the Rev. Dr G. D. Carrow, a Methodist pastor from Philadelphia, and his very friendly reception of him at the *All the Year Round* office on 9 August. Dickens's explanation to his visitor about the writing of *Chuzzlewit* and *American Notes* was, Carrow happily recorded, 'apologetic in character and I observed that the bitter criticisms of the American press had been received as partially merited and had left no resentment rankling in his heart'. He was, we may think, blessed in so believing.

Dickens, so proud of the intensity with which he had in his youth loved Maria Beadnell and now no doubt equally proud of the quality of his love for Nelly, must have been gratified indeed when Carrow, having opined that 'a man must have really loved a woman if he would fully interpret the secrets of a woman's heart', praised him for his insight into that organ. His insight in this respect was comparable only, the good pastor believed, to that possessed by 'that wonderful Galilean who knew the heart of all'. When Dickens begged him to give an example from the novels of what he was referring to Carrow cited 'the incidents of that famous scene in *Bleak House* where the "little woman" accepts her guardian's proposal of marriage'. Upon this Dickens, according to Carrow's account, seized both his visitor's hands and exclaimed, 'I see you understand me! I see you understand me! And that is more precious to the author than fame or gold.'[9]

By 23 August Dickens could tell Collins he had 'done the overture' for *No Thoroughfare* and, with an eye on the eventual Adelphi dramatisation of the story, was looking forward to the devising of a super-exciting climax to the story:

Let us arrange to culminate in a wintry flight and pursuit across the Alps. Let us be obliged to go over – say the Simplon Pass – under lonely circumstances and against warnings. Let us get into all the horrors and dangers of such an adventure under the most terrific circumstances, either escaping from, or trying to overtake (the latter, the better, I think) some one, on escaping from, or overtaking, whom, the love, prosperity and Nemesis of the story depend. There we can get Ghostly interest, picturesque interest, breathless interest of time and circumstance, and force the design up to any powerful climax we please. . . . we shall get a very Avalanche of power out of it, and thunder it down on the readers' heads.

Five days later, he had written the first two sections of 'Act I' and shortly afterwards read them to Collins in Wellington Street. Collins then wrote the next section, 'The Housekeeper Speaks', thickening the plot in his characteristic meticulously detailed fashion. Dickens took over again to introduce the new characters of Vendale the hero, Obenreizer the villain, and Marguerite the heroine and thereafter he and Collins continued to alternate as authors for the rest of the story, corresponding with each other about details of plotting, and conferring from time to time in Wellington Street or during visits by Collins to Gad's Hill. The writing did not always go fast: 'I am jogging on (at the pace of a wheelbarrow propelled by a Greenwich Pensioner) at the doomed Wilding', Dickens told Collins on 18 September, when he must have been working on the later part of the last chapter of 'Act I', which ends with the death of the unfortunate former foundling Walter Wilding. The wheelbarrow having reached its goal, Collins proceeded to write 'Act II' after which Dickens wrote 'Act III', the great climactic scene on the Simplon, and Collins then got started on 'Act IV'.

Collins later told Frederic Chapman that he and Dickens 'purposely wrote so as to make discoveries of this [of who had written which bits of Acts 1 and 4] difficult'. To this end he would insert passages into what Dickens had written and Dickens would insert passages into his sections. Yet, even if we had no external evidence to help us distinguish between what was written by Dickens and what was written by Collins, it would not be hard to deduce it from internal evidence alone. Dickens's richly descriptive prose, playful imagery and love of detail for its own sake cannot be confused with Collins's plainer, more functional, style and his concern that every detail should have a plot-significance to be revealed in the dénouement. Characteristically Dickensian, for example – indeed, a miniature sketch by Boz – is a passage in the fourth section of 'Act I', describing a little Swiss enclave in London, that 'curious colony of mountaineers' that 'has long been enclosed within that small flat London district of Soho'.[10]

Two personal elements, one relating back to the blacking factory and the other to more recent times at Gad's Hill, appear in the sections written by Dickens alone. His undying memories of Old Hungerford-stairs and Warren's warehouse, with its 'wainscotted rooms', cellars, and counting-house 'looking over the coal-barges and the river' surely haunt the vivid opening description in 'Act I' of the mouldering Thames-side area of Break-Neck-Stairs and the nearby premises of Wilding and Co., Wine Merchants, which had once been a grand merchant's mansion and therefore also has its wainscoted rooms (but which has, too, as a quintessentially Dickens touch, a cupola on its roof, like Gad's Hill). Laden coal barges would sometimes bump themselves against Break-Neck-Stairs 'and certain laborious heavers, seemingly mud-engendered, would arise, deliver the cargo in the neighbourhood, shove off, and vanish'. A scathing reference to the Lord Mayor as 'the great conserver' of the river's 'filthiness' neatly links the 'little labouring hind' of Warren's to Charles Dickens the famous writer and great campaigner for sanitary reform. The other passage in which a strongly personal element may be felt comes at the end of 'Act III' with the detailed description of the behaviour of the Alpine dogs who lead Vendale's rescuers to where he lies wounded upon an ice-shelf, deep in the abyss into which he fell when attacked by Obenreizer. The period of the writing of No Thoroughfare was, as has recently been argued, a 'likely time' for Dickens to introduce into his work the famous St Bernards of the Alpine regions. He had – remarkably for a writer so famous for his dog-portraits – omitted all mention of them in his description of the Great St Bernard hospice in Little Dorrit ten years before. Dickens's own big dogs at Gad's Hill would have been very much in his mind during 1865–67 owing to the accidental death of Turk, the severe illness of his own much-loved St Bernard Linda, the arrival of Lehmann's gift, a young black Newfoundland dog which was named Don, 'surely the finest specimen that ever was seen', and, of course, the forced execution of the magnificent but ferocious Sultan. Writing to Dolby at the end of August, just after a Gad's Hill visit by another great portrayer of dogs, his good friend Sir Edwin Landseer, Dickens mentions that he had 'six immense dogs in the yard, and tramps who open the gates look into a grove of expanded jaws and retire'. The dogs of *No Thoroughfare* did not survive into the dramatic version of the story, however.[11]

During late August and September Dickens reported himself as 'hard at it' on *No Thoroughfare* but, being Dickens, still found time and energy to entertain a stream of house-guests at Gad's Hill (he was scorer for a cricket-match that took place there on 29 August). Newspaper paragraphs stating that he was in 'a critical state of health' and had to go to America for a 'recommended change of air and scene' brought upon him such a deluge of anxious enquiries that he had to write to the papers contradicting the reports and suggesting that 'critical' was perhaps a misprint for 'cricketing'. He also found time to give Fechter regular detailed advice on a revival the actor-manager was mounting of Lytton's classic 1838 drama *The Lady of Lyons* and to keep Lytton, who was holidaying in the Pyrenees, thoroughly informed about the production. He attended the very successful first night on 16 September and felt, he reported to Lytton, that he 'should have been very proud indeed to have been the writer of the Play'. Next day, chairing a public meeting of the Printers' Readers' Association, called to demand better wages and conditions, he acknowledged 'most gratefully' the great debt that he as a writer owed to printers' readers. 'I have never', he told his audience, 'gone through the sheets of any book that I have written without having had presented to me . . . some slight misunderstanding into which I have fallen, some little lapse I have made . . ., some unquestionable indication that I have been closely followed through my work by a patient and trained mind.' A few days later he was very gratified to learn about a eulogistic *Daily Telegraph* review (14 Sept.) of the Charles Dickens Edition ('revised by the master's hand itself') praising the creations of his 'exhaustless and marvellous mind' and highlighting his great quality of 'sympathy with all the forms which human life puts on'.[12]

Dolby returned from America on 19 September and went to Gad's Hill to deliver his report, which was all in favour of going. Dickens then drew up a document which he called 'the case in nutshell' for consideration by Forster, Wills and Frederic Ouvry before he finally made up his mind. In this document he took into account the attitude of the American press. The papers were generally favourable towards his visit, despite the furore so recently caused by his letter to Ticknor & Fields (above, p. 557). This did, however, provide some ammunition for a fictitious report of an interview with him by a 'Special Correspondent' of the *New York Daily Tribune* which appeared in that paper on 6 September (indignantly denounced by Dickens in a private letter to Fields of 3 October). Also on 6 September his old enemy the *New York Herald* belittled him as a 'Homer of the slums and back alleys'. The paper's owner, James Gordon Bennett, told Dolby that if 'Dickens would *first apologise* to the American public for the "Notes" and "Martin Chuzzlewit", he would make a large amount of money'. Dickens had no intention of apologising but, as we have seen, calculated on making a substantial amount of money nevertheless. He planned a series of eighty readings in a tour that should not extend beyond Boston and New York, Philadelphia, Washington and Baltimore. Forster remained resolutely opposed to the plan. 'He was certain', Dolby recalled, 'there was no money in America, and, even if there were, Mr Dickens would not get any of it; and if he *did*, the Irish (by some means I could not quite understand), and the booksellers, between them, would break into the hotel and rob him of it.' Nevertheless, Dickens finally decided to go – probably to no-one's surprise – and telegraphed his decision to Fields. Even though he was unsure that his profits would be quite as great as he and Dolby had estimated, he could not, he wrote to Georgina on 30 September, 'set the hope of a large sum of money, aside'. His concern was understandable as he was, as noted earlier, now maintaining three households, his own (Georgina, Mamie, and the two youngest boys), Catherine's and also, presumably, Nelly's. There was also the problem of Charley, who, with a wife and four children to support, had in 1861, against Dickens's advice, become a partner with one of his brothers-in-law in a paper-making business which was now verging on bankruptcy, while the financial outlook for Charles and Katey Collins was beginning to look decidedly gloomy as a result of Collins's continuing ill health.[13]

Dickens's American 'Loadstone Rock' consisted of more than one element, however. In the end, it was probably the attraction of a huge new, and radically different, audience for him to enrapture with his readings that outweighed even financial considerations and counterbalanced even the miserable prospect of a five-month separation from Nelly. 'If I come to America this next November,' he wrote to Fields on 3 September, 'even you can hardly imagine with what interest I shall try Copperfield on an American audience, or, if they give me their heart, how freely and fully I shall give them mine.' We might juxtapose this with his alteration, just at this time, of the final paragraph of his 1850 preface to *Copperfield* to read as follows in the Charles Dickens Edition:

> Of all my books, I like this the best. It will be easily believed that I am a fond parent to every child of my fancy, and that no one can ever love that family as dearly as I love them. But, like many fond parents, I have in my heart of hearts a favourite child. And his name is DAVID COPPERFIELD.

On 12 October Dolby sailed for Boston on a Cunard steamship as an advance guard for his 'Chief'. Dickens himself was to follow on another

Cunarder, the *Cuba*, on 9 November. If there had been some idea of Nelly's travelling to America under Dolby's escort, as seems implied by the reference to her in Dickens's 9 August letter to Dolby, it had, very wisely, been dropped. Instead, Dolby was charged with what Dickens called, writing to Fields on 3 October, a 'certain delicate mission' to him. This was doubtless to get the publisher's confidential advice as to the risk of scandal involved in Nelly's following Dickens to America. Dickens was prepared, he wrote to Dolby on 16 October for an adverse answer but, as we shall see, it was not until after he himself had arrived in the States that he finally gave up the idea. Another idea that had been floated, namely that Mamie should be his travelling companion, was given up when Dickens recognised just how much of his time would have to be devoted to the readings and 'how little, indeed almost no time could be given to sightseeing'.[14]

The four weeks between Dolby's leaving for America and Dickens's departure were filled with business and arrangements. Dickens and Collins finished 'Act 4' of *No Thoroughfare* working 'side by side at two desks' in Dickens's bedroom at Gad's Hill and Dickens added the brief finale, 'The Curtain Falls'. He then planned out, in consultation with Fechter and the great scene-designer Thomas Grieve, the scenes and acts of the dramatic version to be written by Collins while the latter was also busy completing *The Moonstone*. The Christmas number was scheduled for publication on 12 December and Dickens prophesied, quite accurately, that it would be a great success. He composed a long memorandum for Wills dealing with various business matters, official and domestic, that would require attention during his absence. No reference whatever must be made to America or to Fenianism in any article published in *All the Year Round* while Dickens is in America. A section of the memo is headed 'Nelly' and tells Wills that Nelly will contact him if she needs anything; it also contains the famous instructions about the coded telegram that Dickens is to send Wills the day after arriving in America for forwarding to Nelly. Wills must be very careful to copy the exact words 'as they will have a special meaning for her'. In his diary Dickens carefully noted the key ('all well means *You come*/ safe & well means *You don't come*') but did not reveal it to Wills. Forster, Wills is told, has 'ample Power of Attorney' from Dickens, knows Nelly as Wills does, 'and will do anything for her, if you want anything done'. Another memorandum, dated 6 November and headed 'Chapman and Hall Halfyear's Accounts to Midsummer, 1867', was presumably written for Forster's guidance since he would be the one dealing on Dickens's behalf with the next half-year's accounts when Chapman and Hall would render them on 15 March 1868, when 'the balance . . . due to me is to be promptly paid, in money, and not in bills of any kind'. The memorandum goes on to note that, as Chapman and Hall have prepaid Dickens £1,500 on account of the just-published Charles Dickens Edition, that amount will need to be deducted from the total balance due to him in March.[15]

According to his diary, Dickens commuted between Wellington Street and Peckham during 21–25 October and on the 25th held a farewell dinner with Nelly and Wills at his favourite restaurant, Verrey's in Regent Street. Shortly afterwards, Nelly and her mother, who was apparently not in good health at this time, left for Florence on a visit to Fanny and Tom Trollope, whose address Dickens had given Wills in his memorandum. They were not to return to England until just before Dickens himself did in the following May. On 2 November Dickens had to brace himself for the great Farewell Banquet in his honour which had been organised by a group of his friends including Wilkie Collins, Fechter, Charles Kent (who acted as secretary to the group), Wills and Edmund Yates. Forster was, unfortunately, too ill to attend. The dinner, attended by nearly four hundred and fifty guests with a further hundred in the ladies' gallery, was held at the Freemasons' Hall with Lytton in the chair. The walls were decorated with twenty panels, each one with borders of laurel and inscribed with the name of one of Dickens's works lettered in gold, 'from our dear old acquaintance Mr Pickwick, to our dear new acquaintance, Dr Marigold', as *The Observer* described it. Tremendous enthusiasm prevailed as Dickens, leaning on Lytton's arm, processed down the hall to the sound of a march played by the band of the Grenadier Guards. It grew still greater when Lytton proposed the toast to Dickens, a speech later described by Dickens to Annie Fields as 'well written, full of good things, but delivered execrably'. Lytton, he explained, lacked 'a kind of confidence in his own powers which is necessary in a speaker'. As to Dickens's own speech, he was unable for a time to make himself heard because of the tumultuous enthusiasm of the audience with diners leaping on chairs and waving 'not only glasses but decanters and half-emptied champagne bottles over their heads . . . while the ladies fluttered fans and handkerchiefs from the gallery'.

At last he could make himself heard and delivered a fine speech in which he once more upheld 'the Dignity of Literature' claiming that 'from the earliest days of my career down to this proud night, I have always been true to my calling. [*Great cheering*]' and presenting his Copperfieldian-heroic version of his earliest steps on the path towards success as a writer: 'I began to tread it when I was very young, without influence, without money, without companion, introducer, or adviser'. In the second part of his speech he was concerned to send a placatory message to America where, he well knew, this occasion would be very extensively reported. He was returning there, he said, because of the 'immense accumulation of letters' he had received from across the Atlantic all expressing 'in the same hearty, homely, cordial, unaffected way, a kind of personal interest in me, I had almost said a kind of personal affection for me [*cheers*], which I am sure you will agree with me, it would be dull insensibility on my part not to prize'. These correspondents all pleaded with him to come and read his work in America and in addition to the motivation

FAREWELL TO DICKENS

54 'Farewell to Dickens', *Judy*, 30 October 1867

for going there that this gave him he had also 'a natural desire to see for myself the astonishing change and progress of a quarter of a century over there'. Finally, he quoted from the *Household Words* Christmas number for 1855 *The Holly Tree*, in which he had written, referring to the Americans, that 'whatever little motes my beamy eyes may have descried in theirs, they are a kind, large-hearted, generous, and great people'.[16]

Among the many letters Dickens received wishing him bon voyage came one from Catherine, to whom he sent a hurtfully terse reply written on *All the Year Round* notepaper. It was the last of the three letters he wrote to her during the twelve years following his banishment of her and read as follows: 'My dear Catherine / I am glad to receive your letter, and to accept and reciprocate your good wishes. Severely hard work lies before me; but that is not a new thing in my life, and I am content to go my way and do it./ Affectionately Yours / Charles Dickens'. The same day he sent to Lavinia Watson 'a thousand thanks' for her 'kind letter' and his 'sincere love ... always truthful to the dear old days'. He congratulated her on becoming a grandparent, joking that he never allowed the fact of his having achieved this status to be mentioned: 'Charley's children are instructed from their tenderest months only to know me as "Wenerables", which they sincerely believe to be my name, and a kind of title I have received from a grateful country'.[17]

Dickens left Liverpool on 9 November on board the *Cuba* and, following a rough passage, arrived in Boston ten days later, to be greeted by Dolby and Fields and installed in a 'quiet corner (high up)' of the luxurious Parker House Hotel. He did not really need the twelve days set aside for rest and recuperation before he began work and yearned to begin 'checking the readings off' since, for all his publicly expressed enthusiasm to see the great changes that had taken place in America during the last quarter-century, he was already looking longingly ahead to the time when he would be free to return home. Dolby meanwhile was already engaged in his long battle to outwit 'the noble army of speculators', as Dickens called them, the touts who followed Dickens from city to city buying up tickets for the readings and then re-selling them at inflated prices which resulted in much public anger being directed towards poor Dolby himself. Even one of the support team that Dickens brought out with him from England was in due course found to be colluding with these gentry.[18]

During this first free week Dickens renewed his acquaintance with Longfellow, Emerson and other Boston friends and went for his usual prodigious walks ('every day from seven to ten miles') during which he saw how enormously the city had changed, mostly for the better, since his previous visit. On 21 November he was given a festive welcome dinner at their pleasant Charles Street home by James Fields and his charming and hospitable young wife Annie (she had met Dickens once as a dinner-guest with her husband at Tavistock House in 1859, but seems not to have been so drawn to him then as she now was). She had arranged that his rooms at the Parker House should be beautifully decorated with 'choice flowers', he wrote to Mamie, chief flower-arranger at Gad's Hill, and struck him as 'a very nice woman, with a rare relish for humour and a most contagious laugh'. According to Annie's journal, Dickens himself 'bubbled over with fun' at the dinner. She despaired of being able to make an accurate record of his table-talk with 'his queer turns of expression' that so often convulsed the company with laughter but she nevertheless contrived to make some very interesting notes of various remarks he made, such as the one about a writer introducing his real self into his stories. This always happened, said Dickens, 'but you must be careful of not taking him for his next-door neighbour'.[19]

The Fieldses quickly became a very important source of emotional support and solace to Dickens during his arduous tour ('this episodical life of mine, while it lasts, is always mere bondage', he wrote to Susan Norton, wife of the Harvard classicist Charles Eliot Norton, one of his closest American friends, on 31 December). Not only did the Fieldses provide him with a congenial domestic base (he actually stayed a few days in their house in early January, breaking his otherwise cast-iron rule about never accepting private hospitality during his readings tours), they also offered him an intimate and admiring friendship, firmly based upon their love for him as a great and good man and upon their unbounded admiration for his artistic genius. Fields's reminiscences,

CHARLES [John Huffman] DICKENS'

The great Novelist appears in various characters, all, however, showing the same prolific "head" — Dickens, alias Pickwick, alias Copperfield, alias Sam Weller, &c., &c.

55 Cartoon inspired by Dickens's American reading tour 1867/68

Yesterdays with Authors, and the passages from Annie's private journal so far published richly supplement Forster and Dolby in building up a picture of Dickens's day-to-day life during the tour, the overwhelmingly enthusiastic response to his readings by capacity audiences in every city that he visited, his homesickness, and his truly astounding ability always to deliver a great performance, even after he had begun to suffer very badly from sleeplessness and appetite loss. These distresses resulted from the unshakeable catarrh that manifested itself soon after his arrival and proved impervious to all treatment, even to the 'Rocky Mountain Sneezer', an allegedly infallible cure composed of brandy, rum and snow compounded for him by the landlord of his New York hotel.[20]

Fields's record of Dickens's talk during the walks they took together show
that Dickens spoke a great deal to him about his characters and how vividly
alive they were to him in his imagination. When he was writing his earlier
stories, he told Fields, he could never get the characters out of his mind: 'while
he was writing *Oliver Twist* Fagin the Jew would never let him rest, even in his
most retired moments'. Becoming aware of the strain this was causing to his
'already overtasked brain', he trained himself when working on a story, to leave
his characters shut inside, as it were, when he left his study and just willed
himself not to think about them until he returned to his desk and 'chose to
renew their acquaintance'. On another occasion, this time at dinner, he
commented on what he saw as the miracle of character-creation:

> 'What an unfathomable mystery there is in it all!' he said one day. Taking up
> a wineglass, he continued: 'Suppose I choose to call this a *character*, fancy it a
> man, endue it with certain qualities; and soon the fine filmy webs of thought,
> coming from every direction, we know not whence, spin and weave about it,
> until it assumes form and beauty, and becomes instinct with life.'[21]

This 'second coming' of Dickens to America was quite a different affair from
the first one. Then he had primarily been on a sight-seeing tour with a secret
plan, concocted with his publishers, to write a travel-book about the country
after his return. For this he had drawn largely on the long descriptive letters
about his experiences and impressions written on the spot to Forster and
other friends back in England. This time, however, he was in America on (very
lucrative) business and had no intention whatever of writing anything about
his trip, not even in the form of sketches in *All the Year Round*. As a result, his
letters home were primarily concerned with personal news and exultant reports
of one hugely successful reading after another, with much quoting of ticket-
sales to drive home to Forster and Wills just how enormously profitable this
tour they had opposed was proving to be. His fierce schedule left him scant time
for sight-seeing in any case, though he would not have been Dickens if he had
been able to resist visiting the scene of a famous, and particularly grisly, murder
that had occurred in Boston Medical School, or accepting the Governor of
Baltimore Penitentiary's invitation to inspect a new experimental system under
which inmates worked at their own trades in prison workshops. In mid-March,
too, he took advantage of his itinerary's taking him to Buffalo to revisit Niagara
for 'two most brilliant days' and sent Forster a powerful description of the Falls
and their effect on him, but this time it is Turner rather than Mary Hogarth
who is invoked. Vividly descriptive, this letter is one of the few from this trip
that resemble those he had written twenty-five years before.

There is one group of letters written by Dickens during his 1867–68
American tour that would make headline news if they were to turn up today,

though hardly for the sake of any scenic or social description they might be found to contain. These are the ones he wrote to Nelly, almost certainly long since destroyed. Dickens told Wills in his first letter from Boston (21 Nov.) that he would be sending his letters to his 'Dear Girl' under cover to him 'since I do not quite know where she will be'. The very next day he sent Wills, for forwarding to Nelly in Florence, a telegram ending with the coded message 'Safe and well', meaning that she should *not* come to America. Presumably, Fields had repeated to Dickens in person the advice already transmitted through Dolby, namely that her coming to America at this time, even ostensibly on a visit to her Massachusetts cousins, would be highly imprudent. A mysterious second telegram to Wills, sent 4 December and ending with the words 'all well' (the agreed code for '*you come*'), perhaps indicates that Dickens had second thoughts about the matter but, if he did, Nelly must have decided against making the trip, perhaps because her mother's health was still causing concern. During the ensuing four-and-a-half months Nelly received eleven letters from Dickens through Wills, as well, apparently, as a cheque for £1,000 at one point. Enclosing one of these letters for her on 10 December, Dickens sent a covering message to Wills: 'my spirits flutter woefully towards a certain place at which you dined one day not long before I left, with the present writer and a third (most drearily missed) person'. Enclosing another when writing to Wills on Christmas Eve, he commented, 'I would give £3,000 down (and think it cheap) if you could forward *me*, for four and twenty hours only, instead of the letter'. For her part, Nelly does not seem always to have kept him very well informed about her movements (or rather, lack of movement) so that on 21 February he wrote to Wills, 'You will have seen too (I hope) my dear Patient, and will have achieved in so doing what I would joyfully give a Thousand Guineas to achieve myself at this present moment!' whereas Nelly had not, in fact, left Florence. Her continued residence there at the very heart of the sharp-eyed and gossipy English colony led by Isabella Blagden, Browning's 'dearest Isa', must surely rule out the much-canvassed idea that she bore Dickens a child during his absence in America.[22]

Dickens did indeed miss Nelly 'most drearily' but had at least the relief of being, at some point, able to talk about her and his love for her to such sympathetic friends as the Fieldses. Annie seems to have fallen very much under the spell of her dazzling visitor and wrote later in her journal, after the Fieldses had visited Dickens at Gad's Hill, that hers had been 'a most exceptional lot to have known this great man so well'. At first her knowledge of Dickens's private woes seems to have come through her husband as Dickens evidently took James Fields into his confidence on the long walks they had together. He told him, Annie recorded, that he was 'often troubled by the lack of energy his children show and has even allowed J to see how deep his unhappiness is in having so many children by a wife who was totally uncongenial' (the obvious response to this does not seem to have occurred either to her or to J.). Later, she evidently learned something about Nelly for, after Dickens had sailed for home, she fervently imagined how joyful would be his reunion with his beloved soon after his ship had docked in Liverpool:

> I cannot help rehearsing in my mind the intense joy of his beloved – it is too much to face, even in one's imagination and too sacred. Yet I know today to be *the day* and these hours, *his hours* – Surely among the most painfully and joyfully intense of his whole life. I hope and believe he is well once more. Tomorrow Gad's Hill!!

From these references to the 'sacred' nature of Nelly's joy and the pain that will mingle with Dickens's joy we may perhaps deduce that, whatever the actual relationship was between the two, the way Annie Fields came romantically to construct it, with or without encouragement from Dickens, was as a pair of high-minded, star-crossed lovers, unable to consummate their love because he was still, in the eyes of both Church and State, yoked to Catherine.[23]

Dickens spent the first six weeks of his tour reading in Boston and New York. According to Dolby, Dickens 'always regarded Boston as his American home, inasmuch as all his literary friends lived there', and he felt it only due to them that he should begin there. Weeks seven to eight were devoted to Philadelphia and Brooklyn, in which latter place Dickens was amused to find himself reading in a church and making his entry from the vestry. By this time (end of January) his health had become so bad – he had felt it necessary to consult a doctor in New York – and the profits already realised from the readings were so enormous (Dolby remitted £10,000 to Dickens's bank in London on 15 January, leaving him with over £1,000 'to go on with') that it was decided to abandon the intended tour to Chicago and St Louis, the idea of going into Canada having already been scrapped. A contributing factor to Dickens's decision to cut out Chicago was no doubt the wish to avoid an embarrassing encounter with his late brother Augustus's partner and three orphaned children. During weeks nine to eleven Dickens read in Baltimore, in Philadelphia again, and in Washington where the beleaguered Democratic President Andrew Johnson, who was under threat of impeachment, both attended a reading and received Dickens at the White House (Johnson had 'a remarkable face, indicating courage, watchfulness, and certainly strength of purpose', Dickens reported to Forster).[24]

Dolby, Fields and Osgood had by now all become very concerned over Dickens's deteriorating health and the depression that afflicted him as he thought of all the weeks that had yet to pass before he could return home. To divert him and as a tribute to his own legendary feats of pedestrianism the rather overweight Dolby and the rather short Osgood challenged each other to a 'Great International Walking Match' (England versus America) through deep New

England snow, the event to come off on 29 February. Short of organising some impromptu amateur theatricals they could hardly have hit upon anything more calculated to stimulate and amuse their suffering 'Chief'. Dickens naturally threw himself into the business with the greatest zeal and delight and was inspired to compose the only piece of non-epistolary writing that he produced during this tour, a parody of sporting journalism so good that it could almost have passed for the real thing in the pages of *Bell's Life*. He drew up in due form the Articles of Agreement between Osgood ('the Boston Bantam') and Dolby ('the Man of Ross' – Dolby's home town was Ross-on-Wye) appointing as 'umpires and starters and declarers of victory . . . JAMES T. FIELDS of Boston, known in sporting circles as Massachusetts Jemmy, and CHARLES DICKENS of Falstaff's Gad's Hill, whose surprising performances (without the least variation) on that truly national instrument, the American Catarrh, have won for him the well-merited title of The Gad's Hill Gasper'. He undertook also to write a 'sporting narrative' of the event, 'to be duly printed on a broadside', and to give a sumptuous celebratory dinner on the evening of the 29th at the Parker House attended by all participants and his other Boston friends, including 'an obscure poet named Longfellow (if discoverable)'.[25]

Dickens's 'Sporting Narrative' is a delightful *jeu d'esprit* into which he characteristically smuggled a grim little private joke of his own. The course is described as running from Boston to a place called Newton Centre six miles away and back again. Newton Centre is a little village 'with no refreshments in it but five oranges and a bottle of blacking'. One can almost believe that, even into such a seemingly ephemeral piece of writing as this broadsheet (copies of which Dickens might nevertheless have expected to be lovingly preserved by his friends and handed down by them), he deliberately introduced what we might call a 'time-lapse' reference the poignancy of which would only strike those who had read the 'autobiographical fragment', which he clearly intended should be in some form published after his death. Instead of a message in a bottle, here the bottle itself is the message.

The day before the Great Walking Match took place Congress inaugurated impeachment proceedings against President Johnson. Dickens and Dolby both judged that even the readings might prove less of a draw while such sensational political developments were beginning to unfold. Dickens therefore awarded himself a week's much-needed holiday ('simply thorough resting') in the course of which he declined attending a meeting of authors and publishers aimed at establishing an International Copyright Act as, according to Dolby, 'he felt the case to be a hopeless one'. He resumed touring on 9 March in upstate New York, visiting Syracuse, Rochester, Buffalo and Albany. He had to endure grim travelling conditions but was rewarded always with hugely enthusiastic capacity audiences. Towards the end of the month he toured in New England and on 31 March, returning by train from Portland, Maine, to Boston, he had his famous long tête-à-tête with a very articulate twelve-year-old fan, Kate Wiggin, future author of *Rebecca of Sunnybrook Farm*, who delighted him by saying that she loved *Copperfield* best of all his books, and how she and her family cried when they read about the death of Steerforth. She recalled the occasion years later in her 'A Child's Journey with Dickens': ' "Yes, I cry when I read about Steerforth," he answered quietly, and I felt no astonishment.' His *Copperfield* reading, we recall, was so arranged as to culminate in the casting ashore of the drowned Steerforth's body. For Dickens *Copperfield* was the most physically draining of all his readings before he added *Sikes and Nancy* to his repertoire. He gave it only fourteen times during the American tour.[26]

In Boston he gave six farewell readings before going finally to New York for five similar readings in that city. By now he was not only suffering terribly from his 'American catarrh' but also his old foot trouble had reappeared and was causing him great pain. He was surviving mainly on a liquid diet with a strong alcoholic content, as he reported in a letter to Mamie of 7 April in which he listed his daily intake: a tablespoonful of rum in a tumbler of fresh cream, a sherry cobbler and a biscuit, a pint of champagne, an egg beaten up in sherry (twice), and, last thing at night, 'soup and anything to drink I can fancy'. 'I don't', he told her, 'eat more than half a pound of solid food in the whole four-and-twenty hours, if so much'. He was, he told Forster at the end of March 'nearly used up' and feared that, because he was still able to rally and put on a spirited performance for two hours every evening, even Dolby did not realise how near he was to complete collapse. 'To see me at my little table at night', he wrote to Georgina on 2 April, 'you would think me the freshest of the fresh. And this is the crowning marvel of Fields's life.' Off stage James and Annie Fields cherished him as much as they could. 'They are', Dickens wrote to Mamie on 31 March, 'the most devoted friends, and never in the way, and never out of it.' They accompanied Dickens and Dolby to New York where they took him to the circus, which proved to be a very good move. He greatly enjoyed himself and astonished them by his circus knowledge: 'He knew how the horses were stencilled, how tight the wire bridles were, etc.'.[27]

Fields was, of course, present at the grand Farewell Banquet given to Dickens by the New York press at Delmonico's on 18 April with the Pickwickian-looking Horace Greeley, editor of the *New York Tribune* in the chair. Dickens was in such pain with his right foot that he could not get a shoe on it and Dolby had to scour New York to find a gout-stocking to cover the bandages. Dickens arrived late at the banqueting hall but rose magnificently to the occasion in his response to Greeley's immensely tactful toast of 'Health and happiness, honour and generous (because just) recompense, to our friend and guest, Charles Dickens'. The first part of Dickens's speech, after a graceful allusion to his own early days, as a member of the journalistic 'brotherhood', was, almost word for word, the first publication, as it were, of the 'Postscript' that, according to his promise, was subsequently appended to all editions of *Martin Chuzzlewit* and *American Notes* and appeared also, under the heading 'A Debt of Honour', in *All the Year Round* on 6 June 1868. In it Dickens expressed his 'high and grateful sense' of the 'generosity and magnanimity' of his second reception in America and his astonishment at the many 'amazing changes' he had seen in all aspects of the country, which he went on to detail. Echoing the speech he had made at his farewell banquet in Liverpool five months earlier, he said he was not so arrogant as to believe that he himself had had nothing to learn 'and no extreme impressions to correct from when I was here first', remarks which elicited great applause and a cry of 'Noble!' He had, he said, been everywhere received 'with unsurpassable politeness, delicacy, sweet temper, hospitality, consideration, and with unsurpassable respect for the privacy daily enforced upon me by the nature of my avocation here, and the state of my health'. He could hardly have gone further in seeking to counteract the effect of his earlier fierce, and still much-resented, criticisms of America and the Americans, but it would surely be unjust to Dickens to believe that this was all just a wonderfully eloquent publicity exercise since many comments in the letters he wrote during this tour testify to his greatly changed attitude towards the country. After this personal statement Dickens devoted the last part of his speech to elaborating on the idea, dear to many Victorians, that the English and the Americans were 'essentially' one people, an assertion greeted with 'great applause'. It rested with them, he ringingly declared, 'jointly to uphold the great Anglo-Saxon race' to which Horace Greeley had referred in his toast. His speech was rapturously received but as he was still in considerable pain he was obliged to retire before the end of the event.[28]

Two nights later, still suffering from what the doctor's certificate, copies of which were distributed in the hall, described as 'a neuralgic affection of the right foot', Dickens gave his last reading in America, choosing the most enduringly popular of all his programmes, the *Carol* followed by the *Trial from Pickwick*. After he had finished he made a brief farewell speech assuring his hearers that he would never recall them 'as a mere public audience, but rather as a host of personal friends' and was recalled again and again to the platform to bow his acknowledgments of the rapturous applause and cheering which broke out as soon as he had finished speaking.[29]

Having finished his battles with the speculators Dolby had one last skirmish to fight, with New York's Collector of Taxes who, disregarding the indemnity that Dolby had secured from the federal authorities, was threatening to arrest him as Dickens's manager for not having made a return of his Chief's earnings in America. He describes in his book how he contrived to get Dickens and himself and the rest of the team on board the *Russia* just in time to escape the Collector and on 22 April the ship sailed for Liverpool. Within five days Dickens's health had begun to improve greatly and he reported to Fields:

'I have got on my right boot today for the first time; the "true American" [catarrh] seems to be turning faithless at last; and I made a Gad's Hill breakfast this morning . . .'. No doubt his recovery of spirits was also greatly helped by reflecting that he had made a clear profit of some £38,000 as a result of the American tour, even after paying all expenses. This amount was reduced to just under £20,000 as a result of Dickens's insistence on exchanging dollars for gold because of his (unjustified) suspicions about American currency but this still amounted, as the Pilgrim editors point out, to 'between a quarter and a fifth of his estate at his death'. For him the United States had proved 'a golden campaigning ground' indeed.[30]

CHAPTER 26

Disappearances and deaths

1868–1870

It was a ghastly figure to look upon. The murderer staggering backward to the wall, and shutting out the sight with his hand, seized a heavy club, and struck her <u>down</u>!!

Sikes and Nancy, ch. 3

Drowsy Cloisterham ... was pretty equally divided in opinion whether John Jasper's beloved nephew had been killed by his passionate rival, treacherously, or in an open struggle: or had, for his own purposes, spirited himself away.

The Mystery of Edwin Drood, ch. 23

THE VOYAGE home of Dickens and Dolby aboard the *Russia* was, Dolby tells us, 'a very rough one' but, happily, it was also exceptionally fast. Dickens's health, as we have seen, improved rapidly; 'I sank my American Catarrh in the Atlantic on the fourth day out', he later told his Philadelphian friend George Childs, 'and disappointed all my friends by landing in the brownest and most radiant health.' Already, however, he was mentally reviving a project that would, in the event, prove highly deleterious to that health. He was committed to beginning in the autumn a six-month farewell series of one hundred readings, for which the Chappells would pay him £8,000 plus all expenses, and he wished to add a striking new item to his repertoire. Quite apart from the added strain on his physical and mental resources this would impose, the tour itself, scheduled to include Edinburgh, Glasgow, Dublin and Belfast, would inevitably involve a good deal more of that dread 'railway shaking' from which he had suffered so badly ever since Staplehurst. And, on top of all this, he was facing a greatly increased workload for *All the Year Round*. After a hunting accident, Wills, having suffered a 'concussion of the brain', was ordered complete rest for months to come resulting, Dickens wrote to one of his correspondents, in 'the complete overthrow of my usual orderly arrangements'. Given all these factors, it is hardly surprising that his 'radiant' health was destined not to last much beyond the summer.[1]

One 'rock ahead' for him (to borrow a favourite phrase of his) was the 1868 Christmas number of *All the Year Round*. The need to 'concoct' this was already haunting him in America. He wrote to Fechter on 8 March: 'after I have rested – don't laugh – it is a grim reality – I shall have to turn my mind to . . . the CHRISTMAS NUMBER!!!' He added, 'I feel as if I had murdered a Christmas number years ago (perhaps I did) and its ghost perpetually haunted me'. It seems that he may even have begun trying to devise a frame narrative for the next number during his voyage home. Writing subsequently (31 July) to Wills about two attempts he had made at producing such a frame, he mentioned that one of them had been 'aboard the American Mail Steamer'. He disliked the result, he said, 'because the stories must come limping in after the old fashion – though of course what I *have* done, will be good for A.Y.R.'. This might suggest that he later recycled and expanded this particular projected frame narrative to turn it into the evocative travel-piece 'Aboard Ship' with which, on 5 December 1868, he inaugurated a series of essays called 'New Uncommercial Samples' in the 'New Series' of *All the Year Round.*

The *Russia* docked in Liverpool on 1 May and Dickens and Dolby stayed the night there before taking the train to London the next day. The reunion with Nelly, newly returned with her mother from Florence, presumably took place as Annie Fields expected it would but Dickens did not return to Gad's Hill the next day. He did not, in fact, reach there for another week, according to reports in the local press. He had much business to attend to in Wellington Street and no Wills there to help him. No doubt he spent much time during this week with Nelly and may have stayed most nights in Windsor Lodge, Peckham, but this year we have no lost diary to enable us to track his movements and, generally, we know even less about his relationship with Nelly during these last two years of his life than we do with regard to the previous decade. His surviving correspondence contains only a few scant references to her as, for example, when he tells Dolby on 11 September that he is 'planning a small N excursion', or tells Wills that 'the patient was in attendance' at his special matinée reading of *Sikes and Nancy* for members of the theatrical profession on 21 January 1870, or when he invites Wills to a dinner to celebrate her birthday on 3 March 1870. Various payments to a 'Miss Thomas' found in his Account-book (a total of £565 between June 1868 and June 1870) seem most likely, as the Pilgrim editors note, to relate to Nelly's Peckham housekeeping expenses. The fullest and most interesting reference to her appears in Annie Fields's journal entry for 8 June 1869 when she and her husband were house-guests at Gad's Hill: 'C.D. told J. that when he was ill in his reading only Nelly observed that he staggered and his eye failed, only she dared to tell him'. This may have happened at his London reading on 13 April 1869 since it seems highly improbable that Nelly would have travelled north to attend any of the three subsequent readings that took place before Frank Beard ordered Dickens to cancel the rest of the tour on 22 April.[2]

Shortly after his return from America Dickens dashed over to Paris where Fechter was putting on a French version of Wilkie Collins's dramatisation of

No Thoroughfare, re-titled L'Abîme. Dickens had been frustrated by being unable to be involved with mounting the London production. Fechter and Collins had 'missed so many pieces of stage-effect', Dickens wrote to Annie Fields on 25 May, that he was eager to go across to Paris 'and try my stage-managerial hand at the Vaudeville Theatre' where the play was to be produced. He did, in fact, go there for a couple of days at the end of May but apparently arrived too late to be able to influence the production as much as he would have liked. This did not, however, prevent him from implying in a letter to Macready of 10 June that it was his lightning, last-minute intervention that was responsible for making the piece the great success that it was. He also at this time loaned Fechter the very substantial sum of £1,700 to enable the actor to settle a dispute with his manager.

Meanwhile, he was 'wallowing in half a year's arrears of papers' at Gad's Hill and in Wellington Street and sadly missing Wills. Fortunately, his much-valued former Household Words staffer and continuing contributor to All the Year Round, Henry Morley, was able (despite the fact that he now held a chair in English Literature at University College, London) to replace Wills, at least on a part-time basis. This arrangement lasted till November when Dickens took Charley on to the staff, having discovered, on his return from America, that the paper-making business in which his son was involved was on the verge of 'irretrievable bankruptcy, smash and ruin'. Happily, Charley was to prove himself 'a very good man of business' in Wellington Street and in May 1870 formally succeeded Wills as general manager and sub-editor. It is a relief, in this connection, to be able to record more positive than negative stories about Dickens's children during the last two years of their father's life. True, his naval lieutenant son Sydney continued to run up debts so incorrigibly that Dickens was even moved on one occasion to wish him 'honestly dead' and forbade him the house on his next shore leave. But, contrary to Dickens's gloomy blanket judgment about his sons' lassitude, which he seemed strangely moved to communicate to friends, Frank was doing well in the Bengal Mounted Police, as was Alfred, working as a land agent in Australia, while Henry was beginning to distinguish himself academically. In September 1868 he went up to Trinity Hall, Cambridge, to read mathematics and next year won the best College scholarship in that subject. Having opted for a career at the bar, he was entered by his father at the Inner Temple in January 1870. As to his daughters, Dickens seems to have ceased to worry about Mamie's not marrying but was much concerned by the continued, and sometimes severe, ill-health of Katey's husband, Charles Collins. He told Fields on 7 July 1868 that he was sure his son-in-law was actually dying.[3]

During the summer of 1868 Dickens struggled to invent a satisfactory frame story for the next Christmas number but no matter how much he 'hammered at it' he could hit upon nothing that satisfied him. 'I have begun something', he wrote to Wills in that already-cited letter dated from Peckham on 31 July, 'which is very droll, but it manifestly shapes itself towards a book, and could not in the least admit of even that shadowy approach to a congruous whole on the part of other contributors which they have ever achieved at the best.' It seems very plausible that the 'droll' piece referred to here is the so-called 'Sapsea Fragment', five pages of manuscript numbered by Dickens from six to ten and written on the same sized paper as that he used when writing material for *All the Year Round* – half the size of the paper he used for his novels. After Dickens's death Forster found these pages inserted into one of his manuscripts. It was not the *Drood* manuscript but, because the narrator-protagonist is called Sapsea (a name taken, like several others in this fragment, from the name-lists in the *Book of Memoranda*) Forster assumed that these slips must have formed part of a passage deleted from *Drood*. He supplied a title, 'How Mr Sapsea ceased to be a Member of the Eight Club. Told by Himself', and this fragment has ever since been appended to Dickens's last novel. The problematic nature of this attribution was first demonstrated by a *Drood* expert in 1986 and subsequently it was shown how well this fragment fitted the idea that it was, in fact, an aborted frame tale for the 1868 Christmas number, from which Dickens later retrieved the name Sapsea for his 'jackass' Mayor in *Drood*. Thus the 'Eight Club' business ('We were eight in number; we met at eight o'clock during eight months of the year . . .' and so on) would have allowed for the introduction of the usual number of contributors to a Christmas number.[4]

Dickens was not going to abandon the number without a struggle, he told Wills on 31 July; at Gad's Hill he had offered a £100 reward to anyone who could come up with an idea for a frame story that would satisfy him, and had found '*something* though not much' in a notion suggested by Charles Collins. But neither that nor anything else worked out well and so, presumably, he abandoned the whole idea at the end of August, as he had said he would. During this time he had had many other concerns, of course. He busied himself with fund-raising for the family of George Cattermole, that increasingly depressed and reclusive artist having died on 2 July leaving his widow and children badly off. Closer to home, he supervised, with a heavy heart, the preparations being made for Plorn's departure for Australia at the beginning of October. Henry, who accompanied his brother to Southampton, records the scene of Dickens's parting with his youngest son at Paddington: 'I never saw a man so completely overcome; giving way, as he did, to extreme sorrow, quite unconscious of his surroundings on the platform.' The sadness, tenderness and deep concern for the boy's welfare, both spiritual and temporal, shown in Dickens's going-away letter to him, are most moving, and a yearning to see Plorn again may well have been a contributing factor to the 'earnest desire' Dolby tells us that Dickens felt, amazingly enough, the following year to 'make a voyage to Australia', reviving the idea of a readings tour there. Plorn's departure was a sharper grief for him than the forlorn death in Darlington, shortly afterwards, of his ne'er-do-well, and by now pretty much derelict, brother Fred but still this had its own poignancy in the backward vista of 'a wasted life' that it opened up. 'He was my favorite when he was a child,' Dickens sadly recalled, 'and . . . I was his tutor when he was a boy.'[5]

During August and September Dickens worked hard on two items for the farewell readings tour. One of these, *The Chimes*, he had not performed since 1858 (it was, he thought, '*very* dramatic but very melancholy'). The other, the murder of Nancy in *Oliver Twist*, he had considered five years before but had rejected as 'too horrible'. His ostensible reason for all this reviving and revising was a desire to include a couple of impressive new items in his repertoire, thereby helping to guarantee the Chappells a good return on their investment in him. But he also wanted, as he told Forster in relation to the *Oliver* reading, 'to leave behind me the recollection of something very passionate and dramatic, done with simple means, if art would justify the theme'. In Forster's view art certainly did not justify performing such a Grand Guignol piece as the murder from *Oliver* but Dickens was clearly yearning for an opportunity to manifest on the reading platform that passionate histrionic power with which he had electrified audiences at performances of *The Frozen Deep. The Chimes* gave him a fine opportunity for this in Trotty Veck's agonised vision of his beloved daughter's being driven by poverty to infanticide and suicide. But this reading was utterly eclipsed in intensity by the episode from *Oliver* and in the event was performed once only during the farewell tour. The *Oliver* reading meanwhile was re-titled *Sikes and Nancy* and Dickens, drawing on chapters 45 to 49 of the novel, skilfully pruned and honed the text into three short, intensely dramatic, chapters of

56 Dickens reading *Sikes and Nancy* by Alfred Thompson, *Tinsley's Magazine*, February 1869

rising tension and horror. 'I have adapted and cut about the text with great care,' he told Forster, 'and it is very powerful.' The reading begins with Fagin (now always 'Fagin', of course, never 'the Jew') setting Noah Claypole to 'dodge' (spy on) Nancy. Chapter 2 describes her midnight rendezvous with Brownlow and Rose Maylie on London Bridge, dropping all reference to Monks and bringing in some dialogue from Nancy's earlier interview with Rose in chapter 40. Then, as in the novel, the action moves straight on to Fagin's goading of Sikes into a frenzy, followed by Nancy's brutal murder and Sikes's horror-stricken vigil by the corpse until he is put to flight by the glorious rising sun illuminating the grisly scene. Dickens planned to end the reading with the murderer rushing from the room dragging his blood-stained dog along with him.[6]

While he was working on this script and rehearsing the role of the most brutal ruffian he had ever depicted, Dickens was moved by certain newspaper police reports to write one of his white-heat articles on ruffians as a species. Titled 'The Ruffian', it appeared in *All the Year Round* on 10 October with the by-line 'By the Uncommercial Traveller,' making its authorship clear. In it Dickens rages against the idea that known ruffians should ever be allowed to remain at liberty, even when the police have insufficient evidence to arrest them: 'Why is a notorious Thief and Ruffian ever left at large? . . . he is always consignable to prison for three months. . . . I demand to have the Ruffian employed, perforce, in hewing wood and drawing water somewhere for the general service, instead of hewing at her Majesty's subjects and drawing their watches out of their pockets.' As to the ruffian who 'infamously molests women coming out of chapel on Sunday evenings', Dickens 'would have his back scarified often and deep'. Another ruffianly pastime, throwing stones in the street, is one which 'constabular contemplation' (police inaction) has allowed to become 'a dangerous and destructive offence'. This decidedly anti-social activity seems to have troubled Dickens greatly (even worse, in his view, was throwing stones at the windows of moving railway carriages – 'an act of wanton wicked-ness with the very Arch-fiend's hand in it'), as is shown later by his depiction of Deputy in *Drood*. Jasper's attempt to make this 'hideous imp' and his stone-throwing *confrères* desist from their obnoxious custom is 'received with yells and flying stones, according to a custom of later years comfortably established among the police regulations of our English communities, where Christians are stoned on all sides, as if the days of Saint Stephen were revived'.[7]

The writing of *Drood* still lay in the future at this point, however. Throughout the summer Dickens was busy entertaining Longfellow and his family and, of course, a succession of other visitors at Gad's Hill, coping with the now vastly more demanding routine work for *All the Year Round*, and preparing for the farewell readings tour. The only actual literary work on which he was (intermittently) engaged was the very unlooked-for and unwelcome job of struggling to make a coherent book out of a scattered mass of 'notes and reflections' left in his charge by his wealthy, eccentric and much loved friend, Chauncy Hare Townshend, dedicatee of *Great Expectations*. Townshend had died while Dickens was in America and left him £1,000 together with the request that he should publish 'as much of my notes and reflections as may make known my opinions on religious matters, they being such as I verily believe would be conducive to the happiness of mankind'. One can scarcely imagine a more uncongenial task for poor Dickens whom Dolby one day found 'nearly distracted by the conglomeration of ideas he had to deal with, of which he could make neither head nor tail'.[8]

The first leg of the farewell tour began in London on 6 October. During the next three months Dickens gave twenty-seven performances in Manchester and Liverpool, Brighton and London, Manchester and Liverpool again, Brighton and London again, Edinburgh and Glasgow, and finally London again for the last pre-Christmas one on 22 December. The readings were mostly concentrated in October and December on account of the General Election that took place in November. Everywhere Dickens's capacity audiences received him with as much enthusiasm and personal warmth as ever. They 'do everything but embrace me,' he told Georgina on 18 December, 'and take as much pains with the Readings as I do'. Ostensibly to help him decide whether or not to bring *Sikes and Nancy* into the repertoire but really, one suspects, to confute Forster and Wills who were strongly objecting to its inclusion, Dickens gave a trial reading of 'the Murder' (as he mostly called it) at the St James's Hall on 14 November. It was given before an invited audience of more than a hundred people, including several journalists and actors (to steady their nerves, a buffet of oysters and champagne was produced the moment Dickens had finished reading). The effect of this reading was sensational indeed as he 'flung aside his book and acted the scene of the murder, shrieked the terrified pleadings of the girl, growled the brutal savagery of the murderer, brought looks, tones, gestures simultaneously into play to illustrate his meaning', and the overwhelming majority verdict of his electrified audience was that he should by all means share such an astounding *tour de force* with his public. He was probably more gratified than worried (though, of course, he pretended to be the latter) when a 'great ladies Doctor' warned him, 'My dear Dickens you may rely upon it that if only one woman cries out when you murder the girl, there will be a contagion of hysteria all over this place.' Forster and Wills remained adamantly opposed to adding *Sikes and Nancy* to his repertoire, and both Charley and Dolby supported them, being fearful of the extraordinary physical and psychological demands it made upon Dickens. Had the verdict gone their way, Dolby comments, his 'Chief' would 'have been saved an enormity of labour and extra fatigue which he was ill prepared to endure, and which, in my opinion, and in the opinion of those who knew him the best, did more to hasten his end and to aggravate his sufferings than he himself would admit'. Dickens's decision was that *Sikes and Nancy*, carefully sandwiched between the sentimental comedy of *Boots at the Holly Tree Inn* and the uproarious fun of *Mrs Gamp*, would form the centrepiece of his programme at St Martin's Hall on 5 January and in Dublin on 13 January and, providing all went well on those two occasions, it would be brought into his regular repertoire.[9]

Initially, Dickens resisted the suggestion, made by both Wilkie Collins and Charles Kent, that the reading should be extended to cover the flight and death of Sikes. 'No audience on earth could be held for ten minutes after the girl's death,' he asserted, but then he changed his mind and before the first public performance added what has rightly been called a 'brilliantly condensed' version of the flight of Sikes into the country, his return to London, and his spectacular death followed by that of his dog (unnamed in the reading, by the way). Moreover, this additional text features 'rewriting more interesting than in any of the other Readings'. Events are seen through Sikes's eyes rather than through third-person narration as in the novel. We might note also a striking image not found in the novel when Dickens describes the dog as 'crawling as if those [blood]stains had poisoned him!!' Dickens's famous stage-direction, 'Terror to the end', written in the margin of his prompt-copy where the additional text begins, gives us, I think, some sense of how he read, or rather acted out, this final section.[10]

A less sensational preoccupation of his during November was preparations for the launch at the end of the month of a New Series of *All the Year Round*, now approaching the end of its twentieth volume. Dickens announced the New Series on the last page of the issue for 28 November. It was partly initiated for his readers' sakes, he said, since the extension of a set of large volumes beyond twenty would, he believed, be an inconvenience for them but the New Series also gave him the opportunity to make 'some desirable improvements in respect of type, paper and size of page'. He introduced an artistic heading for the first page of each number, enlarged the page-size, and caused the type to be better spaced so that there was, as Percy Fitzgerald puts it, 'altogether a brighter air' about the journal (and all this with no price increase). The biggest change was, as Fitzgerald also notes, mentioned almost casually at the end of Dickens's announcement, where he puts a good face on his failure to come up with any satisfactory notion for an 1868 Christmas number. 'The Extra Christmas Number', he wrote, 'has now been so extensively, and regularly, and often imitated, that it is in very great danger of becoming tiresome. I have therefore resolved (though I cannot add, willingly) to abolish it, at the highest tide of its success.' By way of compensation, readers could look forward to the beginning in the next issue of 'an original novel' by Edmund Yates and a series of 'occasional Papers' called 'New Uncommercial Samples' written, of course, by Dickens himself.[11]

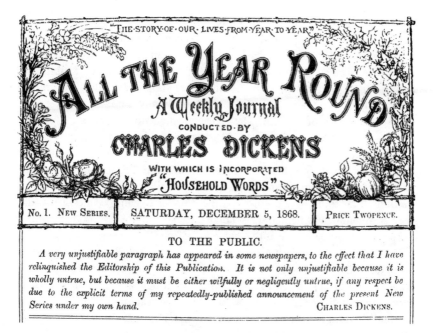

57 Mast-head for the new series of *All the Year Round*, December 1868

During the next three months Dickens found time to supply four of these new 'Samples'. 'Aboard Ship', already mentioned, appeared in the first number of the New Series (5 Dec.) and 'A Small Star in the East' in the third one (19 Dec.). The latter piece resulted from a November visit he had made, with Dr John Murray of the Middlesex Hospital, to the East London Children's Hospital. This had been established in a desperately poor area of the East End by a strongly humanitarian young couple, a doctor and his wife, using money inherited by the latter. Dickens paints a harrowing picture of famishing local families barely managing to sustain life in the most appalling conditions, and does not fail to notice the bitter irony of the disintegrating election bills he sees pasted on walls urging 'the free and independent starvers to vote for Thisman and vote for Thatman'. Being Dickens, however, he cannot help also registering certain 'droll' details in the heart-rending scenes he is observing, like the unemployed boiler-maker 'looking about him with an exceedingly perplexed air, as if for a boiler that had unaccountably vanished'. He also wrote a couple of other 'New Uncommercial Samples' this month ready for publication in the new year. The first, 'A Little Dinner in an Hour' (*AYR*, 2 Jan.), satirical reflections on the shortcomings of British hotel restaurants, was probably prompted by some of his and Dolby's recent experiences, with Dolby featured as the

Uncommercial's travelling companion Bullfinch, 'an excellent man of business'. Between Christmas and New Year Dickens was 'polishing the Murder
minutely every day', but he had also, he told Wills on 27 December, to 'hammer
out an Uncommercial – though I have not the faintest notion of a subject'. In
such a situation memories of his childhood reading never failed to stimulate
his imagination and now he quickly wrote a brilliantly comic piece inspired by
dreary memories of Thomas Day's heavily didactic children's classic *The
History of Sandford and Merton* (1783). His essay, 'Mr Barlow' (16 Jan.), takes
its title from the name of the Gradgrindian tutor in that book who seizes every
opportunity to deliver instructive and 'improving' lectures to his pupils,
and was as bent upon stifling children's imaginative life as McChoakumchild
himself: 'If he could have got hold of the Wonderful Lamp, I knew he would
have trimmed it, and lighted it, and delivered a lecture over it on the qualities
of sperm oil, with a glance at the whale fisheries.'[12]

Dickens's tour, regularly advertised in *All the Year Round*, resumed on
5 January 1869 with *Sikes and Nancy* affecting paying audiences in Belfast,
Dublin and the English South-West quite as strongly as it had the specially-
invited trial audience in November. At his Clifton reading of it on 20 January
'we had', he told Mamie a week later, 'a contagion of fainting', although the
place was not hot: 'I should think we had from a dozen to twenty ladies borne
out, stiff and rigid, at various times. It became quite ridiculous.' He delights in
a jocose epistolary identification of himself as a murderer. Back in November
he had warned Frith the painter that his enactment of the killing 'is horribly
like, I am afraid', and added, 'I have a vague sense of being "wanted" as I walk
about the streets.' And to Mary Boyle he wrote on 6 January, 'My preparations
for a certain Murder that I had to do last night, have rendered me unfit for
letter-writing these last few days' but now, 'the crime being comfortably off my
mind and the blood spilled, I am (like so many of my fellow-criminals) in a
highly edifying state to day.' Much has been made in the past of this kind of
jesting with regard to Dickens's psychological and emotional life. Its primary
interest for me, however, lies in the link that seems to suggest itself between
this epistolary jocularity about acting out the role of a murderer (a role
Dickens acted in deadly earnest on the readings platform) and what became
for Dickens the writer the main driving concern in his next novel, the exploration of 'the criminal intellect', that 'horrible wonder apart', as he calls it in
Drood chapter 20.[13]

Dickens's tour continued with readings in London, Nottingham and
Leicester, 2 to 5 February, with *Sikes and Nancy* featuring in the Leicester
programme. He then had a ten-day respite from the dreaded 'railway shaking'
before his next London reading on 16 February, to be followed immediately
by a foray into Scotland. During the ten-day pause Dickens, as he told Wills on
12 February, 'snatched out of the Readings fire' another new 'Uncommercial

Sample'. It is titled 'On An Amateur Beat' (*AYR*, 27 Feb.) and in it Dickens fancies himself walking the streets of London 'as a higher sort of Police Constable' for, however much he might playfully identify with murderers in his letters to friends, in his public, non-fictional, writing he had, of course, to stay on the right side of the law. His mind is nevertheless still running upon real-life Sikeses at the beginning of this piece ('There is many a Ruffian in the streets whom I mentally collar and clear out of them . . .') but his main purpose is to placate the owners of some East End lead mills who had protested against his apparent implication, in 'A Small Star in the East', that they had no care for their employees' safety and well-being. The most unforgettable passage in this essay, however, concerns an incident that occurs while the Uncommercial is on his 'beat'. It is a nightmarish account of how, after giving a small coin to a street-urchin he had accidentally knocked over, he found himself the epicentre of a vicious struggle for the coin among a whole mob of feral children. This was the last 'Uncommercial' piece he would write until after he had finished his last readings tour. At that point, he told the Fieldses on 9 April, 'shall the Uncommercial resuscitate (being at present nightly murdered by Mr W Sikes), and uplift his voice again'. It was not only Nancy that Sikes was killing every night but Dickens's own writing self.

Just after he had written 'On an Amateur Beat' Dickens's old foot trouble reasserted itself, causing him 'great agony', and he was compelled to cancel the London reading scheduled for the 16th. There were fears that the Scottish readings might also have to be cancelled but thanks to what Dolby called his Chief's 'extraordinary recuperative powers' he was well enough by the 21st to make the journey to Edinburgh. One of the Chappell brothers accompanied him, Dolby being already in Edinburgh, and he was able to rest upon a sofa in the saloon car that had been put at his disposal by the railway authorities. For the next two months he fulfilled a gruelling schedule (Glasgow, Edinburgh, Glasgow, Wolverhampton, Manchester, Hull, York, London, Ipswich, Cambridge, Manchester, London, Sheffield, Birmingham, Liverpool, London, Leeds, Blackburn, Bolton) with rarely more than a couple of days between readings and including many more *Sikes and Nancy* performances than Dolby thought at all wise. Dolby's one attempt to remonstrate about this made Dickens briefly furious with him but otherwise had no effect whatever. Dickens would seem to have been now driven by a strong craving for the frequent repetition of the powerful sensations he experienced when he was 'murdering'. Dolby noted that at the end of an evening during which he had performed *Sikes and Nancy* Dickens would often be seized by a 'desire to be once more on the platform' and 'a craving to do the work over again'. It seems likely that Dickens – 'being accustomed', as he was soon to write in an 'Uncommercial' piece for *All the Year Round*, 'to observe myself as curiously as if I were another man' – drew on this phenomenon in his own life when he came to depict Jasper's craving to experience again and again his opium-induced visionary journey in *Drood*.[14]

Also relevant to *Drood*, but more indirectly, was a grievous loss that Dickens sustained in his personal life at this time. Dolby, returning to their hotel in Manchester on 10 March, found his 'Chief' in 'a paroxysm of grief', having just had news of the death of his friend Sir James Emerson Tennent, the dedicatee of *Our Mutual Friend*. Tennent had worked for many years as secretary to the British colonial government of Ceylon and was a great authority on that country. In 1859 he presented Dickens with a copy of two thick volumes on the history and topography of the island that he had just published and also

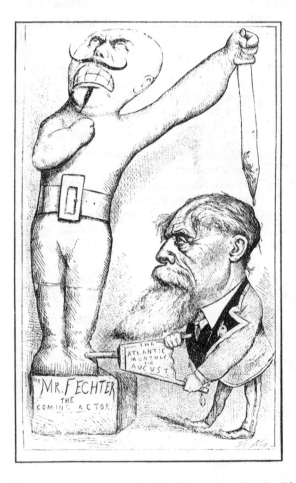

58 'Charles Dickens raising great expectations' by Thomas Nast, *Evening Telegraph* (New York), 1869; inspired by Dickens's article 'On Mr Fechter's acting' in *The Atlantic Monthly*, August 1869 (see p. 600)

contributed a number of articles on the country to *All The Year Round*. It seems likely that Dickens, when planning *Drood* a few months later and needing an exotic, but also potentially morally dangerous, setting for the early years of the Landless twins, was prompted to fix upon Ceylon either by memories of what he had heard about the place from Tennent in person, or by what he had read about it in Tennent's book and articles. Neville Landless tells Canon Crisparkle that he and his sister were subjected by their stepfather to a brutally harsh upbringing in Ceylon, 'among abject and servile dependants, of an inferior race' and adds, 'I may easily have contracted some affinity with them. Sometimes I don't know but that it may be a drop of what is tigerish in their blood' (ch.7). Dickens's 'mem' on the Landlesses in his working notes for *Drood* II reads: 'Mixture of Oriental blood – or imperceptibly acquired nature – in them. Yes'.[15]

A month later, Dickens having given three readings in Liverpool (*Sikes and Nancy* was the centrepiece in two of the programmes), the city honoured him with a grand civic banquet. This was a notable opportunity for him, in the full blaze and glory of his readings tour, to remind everyone that he was first and foremost a *writer* and one deeply committed to the 'Dignity of Literature' which he was well aware that Forster, for one, believed he was subverting through his paid platform performances, no matter how acclaimed they were. Seizing the opportunity with both hands, he proclaimed, very much in 'David Copperfield' mode, the virtues of earnestness and hard work as being the foundation of all real and lasting literary achievement. He was concerned also to allude to those lofty ideals regarding the literary profession that had inspired the foundation of the Guild of Literature and Art and did this through his references to his fellow-writers as his 'literary brethren' and 'companions-in-arms'. He and they constantly strove for 'excellence', he asserted to tumultuous applause, and in that striving lay their 'highest duty' to their 'calling', to each other, to themselves and to their public.

Nine days after this great festival, and with two more *Sikes and Nancy* performances under his belt, Dickens suddenly became very ill. He suffered bouts of giddiness and was uncertain in his sense of touch in both his left limbs. He wrote at once to Frank Beard who hurried up to Preston to meet with him and Dolby after Dickens's reading in Bolton on 20 April. Beard quickly confirmed Dickens's own belief that the readings had to be stopped at once since the combination of the 'immense exertions' they involved and 'the constant jarring of express trains' was evidently posing a very serious threat to his health. The three men returned to London and on the 23rd Dickens and Beard consulted the eminent physician Sir Thomas Watson. Watson agreed with Beard's assessment of the gravity of Dickens's state, noting that he 'had been on the brink of an attack of paralysis of his left side, and possibly of apoplexy'. The two doctors then drew up a certificate for public release stating their conviction that Dickens would not be able 'with safety to himself to resume his readings for several months to come'. Touched by the magnanimity and understanding shown by the Chappells regarding the aborted tour, Dickens was both relieved and pleased when Watson subsequently conceded that he might in the new year complete his engagement with the promoters by giving a short farewell series of readings, but all in London so as to avoid long-distance railway travelling. Whether or not he was also, as one of his earlier biographers puts it, 'sustained by the assurance that he might still slay Nancy a few more times' we cannot know.[16]

What does seem probable is that his experience of coming so close to complete physical collapse prompted Dickens to instruct Ouvry to draw up a new will for him. He signed it on 12 May, fully aware, of course, that the document, with its prominent mention of 'Miss Ellen Lawless Ternan' as a legatee, would inevitably be made public following his death. Meanwhile, the sudden curtailment of his readings tour had inevitably created something of a public sensation. He had, of course, to answer letters of enquiry from anxious friends but he would also have strongly felt the need to write some form of reassuring explanatory letter to his public. Another 'Personal Statement' in his journal might have seemed rather over-dramatic, and would also have awakened unhappy memories of the ill-advised one about the break-up of his marriage he had published eleven years before in *Household Words*. Now, however, his continuing 'Uncommercial Traveller' series gave him an ideal distancing device for such communing with his public, the Uncommercial being assumed by most readers to be pretty much identical with Dickens himself. The result was 'A Fly-Leaf in a Life' (*AYR*, 22 May 1869) which begins with a transparent allusion to the readings tour in which Dickens writes rather like a fairy-tale hero telling his own story:

> Once upon a time (no matter when), I was engaged in a pursuit (no matter what), which could be transacted by myself alone; in which I could have no help; which imposed a constant strain on the attention, memory, observation, and physical powers; and which involved an almost fabulous amount of change of place and rapid railway travelling.

This 'pursuit' leads in due course to his breakdown in health and to his being ordered that 'instant rest' that he himself knew, from his own habit of objective self-observation, was his 'only need'. Then, making fascinating use of book-writing imagery, he says his intention was 'to interpose, as it were, a fly-leaf in the book of my life, in which nothing should be written from without for a brief season'. He found, however, that people did begin to write on this leaf 'from without' – writing *him*, as it were. Some seemed to merge him into one of his own stories, echoing in their report of his collapse the rumours that fly about after Merdle's death in *Little Dorrit*, others saw it as punishment for sin, and still others, more knowing about his daily habits, saw it as the result of too much exercise. Nor were his old familiar correspondents, the begging-letter writers, at all behindhand in their contributions to this fly-leaf : 'The number of people who were prepared to live long years after me, untiring benefactors to their species, for fifty pounds a piece down, was astonishing.'

Once freed from the pressures of performing and railway travelling Dickens quickly recovered and was ready for a joyous reunion with the Fieldses on 11 May. Georgina and Mamie came up to London to stay in a hotel with him and share in showing the Fieldses round. Dickens took his friends to see the hospital he had described in 'A Small Star in the East' as well as on a two-hour tour of the main sorting-office at the G. P. O., to give them an idea of the size of London. This was followed by a trip to the Temple to see, very thrillingly for Annie, 'Pip's room and the stairs where the convict stumbled up in the dark' (Dickens was perhaps already thinking about using the Inns of Court once more as a setting for some scenes in his next novel). There was a day's outing to Richmond and Windsor, and Fields twice accompanied Dickens on one of his police-escorted tours of cheap lodging-houses, workhouse casual wards, police lock-ups and such-like 'regions of crime and woe'. Fields was greatly impressed by Dickens's unfailing kindness and compassion towards the wretched people they found in these places. In one 'miserable court' they were shown an opium den with 'a haggard old woman blowing at a pipe made of an old penny ink-bottle', on whom Dickens later modelled 'Princess Puffer' in *Drood* after going back to have another look at her in the autumn. He was, according to Dolby, at this time beginning 'to cast about for a subject for a new book' and it may be that the old woman and her clients suggested to him a way in which he might realise his notion, perhaps partly suggested by Wilkie Collins's plot in *The Moonstone*, that his story should centre on a murderer who commits his crime in a state of altered consciousness and has no knowledge of having done it when he is once more in his 'normal' state.[17]

Another experience Dickens had while showing the sights to the Fieldses was less sensational but was also to prove fruitful for the new novel he was now beginning to ponder. He took them (in some style) to Canterbury and they attended a service in the cathedral. Dickens, Fields recorded, 'noted how sleepy and inane were the faces of many of the singers, to whom this beautiful service was but a sickening monotony of repetition'. It was but one step further to conceive of there being one among the singers who was not sleepily inane but positively tormented by his monotonous duties because his thoughts and passions were so much engaged elsewhere. These apathetic choristers stayed in Dickens's mind until in due course he came to describe Jasper the Cloisterham choirmaster, obsessed with his secret passion for Rosa and astonishing her fiancé, his nephew Edwin, with his outburst beginning, 'The cramped monotony of my existence grinds me away by the grain. . . . No wretched monk who droned his life away in that gloomy place, before me, can have been more tired of it than I am.'[18]

Despite all his attention to the Fieldses and the demands of *All the Year Round* (for which, in addition to all the routine chores, he had suddenly to write a replacement article for a commissioned piece that proved unacceptable) Dickens nevertheless managed to complete two fairly substantial essays during this month. The first was a favour for a friend. Fechter was planning to make his first American tour and Dickens wrote a eulogy of him as a romantic actor, which appeared in the August number of *The Atlantic Monthly*, published by Ticknor & Fields. He especially praises the actor's Armand in Dumas's *La Dame aux Camélias* and comments with some fervour on 'the poetic and exalting influence' of Armand's love, as acted by Fechter, upon the audience's view of the heroine Marguerite, 'fallen woman' though she undoubtedly is. Can it be, one wonders, that Dickens is making a connection in his mind, at whatever level of consciousness, between Fechter's Armand and himself as Nelly's lover? Could he have been fantasising that the intensity and 'poetry' of his own passion for, and devotion to, his 'dearest girl', might, should their relationship ever become known, have in the eyes of the public a similar exalting effect upon her as Fechter's Armand does upon his Marguerite, 'so loved . . . so devotedly and romantically adored'? We can only speculate about this, of course. There does seem to be a definite connection with Nelly, a humorous one this time, in the other piece he wrote this month, 'A Plea For Total Abstinence' (*AYR*, 5 June 1869). This essay, which proved in the event to be the last of his 'Uncommercial' ones, was no doubt written because it was desirable that there should be something from his pen in the first number of Vol.II of the journal's new series. Directed against one of the oldest of Dickens's *bêtes noires*, 'A Plea' satirically describes a grand procession of Teetotalists and includes an elaborate joke about the inappropriateness of the 'lifeboat' banner carried by the contingent from landlocked Peckham. This was, presumably, introduced primarily for Nelly's amusement.[19]

The replacement article he had suddenly to write was a review of Forster's massive biography of Landor, which had just appeared. Dickens asked Eliza Lynn Linton to write an article on Landor, she having been a friend of his. She did so but ignored Forster's book. Dickens wrote to her on 19 June saying that it would pain Forster if he were to publish it: 'I am staggered and stopped short by your paper,' he tells her, 'and fear I must turn to and write another in its stead.' The result was a very personal and affectionate memoir of his old friend ('Landor's Life', *AYR*, 24 July 1869) in which Dickens is happy to refer to Forster's invocation in his biography of the Boythorn portrait in *Bleak House*. He also includes some comic-nostalgic reference to the old days of Lady Blessington's Gore House. Finally, he praises Forster highly as a biographer calling him 'so sympathetic, acute and devoted a champion'. 'It rarely befalls an author to have such a commentator,' adds Dickens, happy in the knowledge that, provided Forster should outlive him, he himself would also be so championed. Another of his comments on the work reads poignantly for us now with all our hindsight-knowledge. Forster's *Landor* (which included, of course, some mention of its subject's failed marriage) is, Dickens writes, 'essentially a sad book' and this guarantees its 'truth and worth': 'The life of almost any man possessing great gifts would be a sad book to himself.'[20]

During the next four months he was working towards his new book. In July he apparently retrieved from his *Book of Memoranda*, and communicated to Forster, an idea for a story about 'Two people, boy and girl, or very young, going apart from one another, pledged to be married after many years – at the end of the book'. The interest was 'to arise out of the tracing of their separate ways, and the impossibility of knowing what will be done with that impending fate'. On 6 August, however, he told Forster that he had put this idea aside (though he clearly returned to it to create Edwin Drood and Rosa Bud) and was now working with 'a very curious and new idea'. This was 'not a communicable idea (or the interest of the book would be gone), but a very strong one, though difficult to work'. Forster goes on to say that Dickens 'immediately afterwards' outlined to him his basic plot for the novel. An uncle was to murder his nephew only to discover almost at once that the situation motivating his crime had ceased to exist before he had committed it. As Orlick had intended to in *Great Expectations*, the murderer would use lime to destroy the corpse but a gold ring worn by the nephew would remain unconsumed and would lead to the detection and conviction of the murderer. What Forster calls the 'originality' of the story (and it is not clear whether this originality can be exactly equated to Dickens's 'very curious and new idea' since that clearly was 'communicable', Dickens having communicated it to him) 'was to consist in the review of the murderer's career by himself at the close, when its temptations were to be dwelt upon as if, not he the culprit, but some other man, were the tempted'. The last chapters were to present the murderer in the condemned cell 'to which his wickedness, all elaborately elicited from him as if told of another, had brought him'. Fagin, Sikes and Nancy being such strong presences in Dickens's mind and imagination at this time, he seems to be looking forward to writing an even more powerful condemned-cell scene than that described in the penultimate chapter of *Oliver Twist*, with an illustration that should similarly excel the *Oliver* one. Luke Fildes, the young artist commissioned to illustrate *Drood* after Charles Collins had had to withdraw from the work, recalled after Dickens's death, that the novelist had wanted to take him to 'a condemned cell in Maidstone or some other gaol' to make a drawing, aiming to 'do something better than Cruikshank'.[21]

During this gestation period of the new novel Dickens's imagination was, as always, fed from many sources, both literary and non-literary. Some of them, like the old opium woman or Tennent's writings on Ceylon, have already been noticed. Other much-canvassed sources, or literary influences on the new novel, include the grisly Parkman murder case which had so fascinated Dickens in Boston during the winter of 1867/68 (above, p. 578), Wilkie Collins's *The Moonstone*, and a story in *All The Year Round* that had greatly impressed him (Emily Jolly's 'An Experience', *AYR* 14 and 21 Aug. 1869). He was also (how consciously we can only speculate) reworking situations from earlier novels, especially his last one, as the *Dublin Review* noted after his death: 'The plot [of *Drood*] echoes that of *Our Mutual Friend* quite closely: two young people are betrothed and doubtful of the arrangement; the young man disappears and the young woman, believing him dead, is closely guarded by an eccentric friend of the vanished gentleman.' Ultimately, however, it was not his mystery plot but his exploration of the mind and behaviour of Jasper that lay at the heart of this new work for Dickens and he was, as Katey Perugini recalled, 'quite as deeply fascinated and absorbed in the study of the criminal Jasper as in the dark and sinister crime that has given the book its title'. His profound and lifelong interest in the demeanour, behaviour and psychology of murderers culminates in what proved to be his last novel.[22]

By 20 August Dickens was ready to write to Frederic Chapman inviting him to make a proposal for publishing the new work and on the same day he jotted down a list of possible titles together with some character-names. He suggested that the book should be published in twelve monthly numbers rather than in the traditional twenty and nudged his correspondent towards offering generous terms by intimating that his own personal preference would be for serialising the novel in *All the Year Round* rather than having Chapman and Hall publish it in monthly numbers. Evidently, he wished the new story to be concentrated in form, like *A Tale of Two Cities* and *Great Expectations*, rather than another 'panoramic' work such as *Our Mutual Friend*, but he and his publishers must also have been responding to the fact that the days of the twenty-monthly-part novel were now gone. By 1869 more and more people were getting their new fiction through instalments in the monthly magazines such as *The Cornhill*.[23]

One string of Dickens's list of projected titles rings the changes on the 'loss', 'flight' or 'disappearance' of a character variously named James Wakefield, Edwyn Brood, Edwyn Brude, Edwyn Drood and – finally – Edwin Drood. A different string, evidently focusing on Jasper rather than Edwin, is also considered: 'Flight and Pursuit', 'Sworn to Avenge It', 'One Object in Life' and 'A Kinsman's Devotion'. 'The Two Kinsmen' would seem to make Jasper and Edwin of equal importance, as also perhaps does 'The Mystery in the Drood Family'. A striking variant reads 'Edwin Drood in hiding'. Finally, Dickens arrives at 'The Mystery of Edwin Drood' but adds a line beneath this which reads, tantalisingly,

'Dead? Or Alive?' The editor of the Clarendon Edition of *Drood* notes some of the differing plot possibilities suggested by Dickens's variant titles but to indulge in further speculation here would soon enmesh us in that continuing, and sometimes very heated, debate about Dickens's intentions regarding his plot which has been vigorously kept up by the 'Droodians' or 'Droodists', as they are called, for the past century and a half. It is the mystery-story equivalent of Milton's Serbonian bog 'in which armies whole have sunk' and here we must tip-toe round the edges of it as best we can to avoid tumbling in. The list of character-names Dickens jotted down on the same sheet as the alternative titles provides less in the way of kindling for the debate. 'Jasper' is found among the (fairly mundane) first names he considers for his male protagonists, the names 'The Dean', 'Mrs Dean' and 'Miss Dean' show he had decided on a cathedral-town setting, and the name 'Mr Honeythunder', with its alternative 'Mr Honeyblast', shows that he already had in mind a satirical attack on professional philanthropists. His long-standing, and often expressed, scornful impatience with such people had recently been sharpened by leading philanthropists' strong support for moves to prosecute Governor Edward Eyre for his ferocious suppression of a rebellion against British rule in Jamaica in October 1865. Certain aspects of Mr Honeythunder as depicted in *Drood* might suggest that Dickens intended a recognisable caricature of the prominent Quaker M.P. John Bright, one of the leaders of the campaign to bring Eyre before a court of law.[24]

Although the formal contract for *Drood* was not drawn up until February 1870, Chapman had clearly agreed by 24 September to publish it in twelve monthly parts since on that date Dickens wrote to him to say that Charles Collins wanted to 'try his hand' at illustrating the book. Anxious, no doubt, to put his constantly ailing son-in-law in the way of earning some money, Dickens responded positively to Collins's request but wanted to see what he could do in the way of cover-design before he was formally commissioned. Chapman was asked to send him some specimen earlier monthly-part covers to serve as models. Given that these covers traditionally shadowed forth the course of the story and thus called for some briefing of the artist by the novelist, we may conclude that by this point Dickens must have worked out a much more detailed plan for his story than the one he had outlined to Forster a few weeks earlier. Whether he had begun the actual *writing* before the end of September we do not know. As always, he had many other calls upon his time, quite apart from *All The Year Round*. One was the tiresome business of preparing Townshend's *Religious Opinions* for the press, another was acting as a sort of epistolary marriage-settlement counsellor to two of his old friends, the excitable Frances Elliot and her second (or maybe third) husband the Dean of Bristol – ironically, this was just when Dickens was about to introduce an Anglican dean, presented in mildly satirical fashion, for the first time into his fictional world. He also made two public appearances. On 30 August he spoke at a banquet for the Oxford and Harvard rowing teams and continued his policy of smoothing down the Americans as much as possible ('I descried a good opportunity of saying something graceful and affectionate – and true – towards our friends in the States,' he told Charles Eliot Norton). A month later (27 Sept.) he delivered his inaugural address as President of the Birmingham and Midland Institute. This was Dickens the orator at the top of his form, reminding his hearers that he himself had had to strive as so many of them were doing against what Lord Lytton had called (and it was one of Dickens's top favourite quotations) 'Those twin gaolers of the daring heart, / Low birth and iron fortune', and also addressing with notable tact and skill the great contemporary Science *v.* Religion debate. He also made what proved in the event to be his last direct public statement about his art when he urged on his hearers the need to cultivate the quality of 'attention':

> My own invention or imagination, such as it is, I can most truthfully assure you, would never have served me as it has, but for the habit of commonplace, humble, patient, daily, toiling, drudging attention. Genius, vivacity, quickness of penetration, brilliancy in association of ideas – such mental qualities, like the qualities of the apparition of the externally armed head in *Macbeth* will not be commanded; but attention, after due submissive service, always will.[25]

Three days after his Birmingham speech Dickens told Fechter he was 'getting to work' on his new book. This involved organising his 'mems' and number-plans in the usual way as well as briefing Collins for the cover-design. To this period also belongs his sudden decision to bring to an abrupt conclusion a story by Robert Lytton, Lytton's son, called *The Disappearance of John Ackland*, which he had accepted for *All the Year Round* on 2 September and had begun serialising on the 18th. Dickens had himself suggested the title (we do not know what Lytton's original one was – presumably something like *The Murder of John Ackland*) so that the reader might be kept wondering whether Ackland 'really *was* murdered' until the end of the story. Now on 1 October he told Lytton that 'a correspondent' had pointed out to him that the story had been published before – in *Chambers's Journal*, so his informant believed – and he therefore needed to wind up the serialisation by very much truncating the story. Given that this alleged earlier published version of the story has never come to light, and also that there are some notable resemblances between the plotting of *Ackland* and that of *Drood*, various commentators have suspected Dickens's motives in this matter but the evidence does not seem to allow us either to convict or to wholly acquit him of dishonesty. However this may have been, he must surely have got started on the actual writing of *Drood* very early in October since he read it to Fields during the Fieldses' second visit to Gad's Hill on 10 October. Annie noted in her journal that Dickens sent Fields 'a queer little note inviting him to go down to his room' and when Fields presented himself Dickens

> took out the first number of his new story . . . and read it aloud acting it as he went on. To add to the interest of this was the fact that they had both seen this old woman together, with whom the scene opens, in one of their nightly peregrinations with the police. The vividness to James was mysterious and marvellous. He thinks it as powerful as anything C.D. had done.[26]

By this time Dickens had got his number-plans organised in the usual way with 'mems' on the left-hand half of the page and chapter-titles and chapter-notes on the right hand. Among his 'mems' for the first number, noting the main characters to be introduced along with some important plot-details, appears the phrase '<u>Cathedral town running throughout</u>' and indeed the beautiful, elegiac evocation of Rochester under the fictional guise of Cloisterham is a prominent feature, as well as one of the chief glories, of this number. After his death Dickens was remembered by the Cathedral verger as having often been noticed in the city during the writing of *Drood* 'studying the Cathedral and its surroundings very attentively'. Another 'mem' reads 'Miss Twinkleton and her double existence', indicating that this comic parallel to Jasper's two states of consciousness was part of Dickens's scheme from the beginning. In Miss Twinkleton herself, her confidential assistant, her school and her other existence in Tunbridge Wells, Dickens was effortlessly reprising Miss Pupford in his 1861 Christmas story, *Tom Tiddler's Ground*, but in the young 'muscular Christian' clergyman Septimus Crisparkle he is breaking new ground, as he is also with the 'droll' figure, as he would have called it, of 'Stoney Durdles' the permanently semi-intoxicated stonemason. Among the notes for chapter 2 appear the words 'Uncle and Nephew' with, immediately below them, 'Murder very far off'. This, like one of the phrases among his 'mems' for this number, '<u>You won't take warning then?</u>', suggests that Dickens wants to make the reader distinctly uneasy about Jasper's relationship with his nephew right from the beginning.[27]

Various problems connected with the new work cropped up during November. Charles Collins designed a cover that Dickens was pleased with. He also made at least eight sketches of four subjects, very likely working from verbal descriptions given him by Dickens, the text not being yet written. But then he became too ill to continue – 'collapsed for the whole term of his natural life', as Dickens later expressed it to the Fieldses, having been always noticeably exasperated by his son-in-law's ill-health, presumably because of its depressing effect on Katey's existence. Dickens meanwhile got himself into a muddle over the American rights to publish *Drood*, accepting Harper's offer of £2,000 for early proof-sheets while forgetting that he had already formally promised the American rights in all his future writings to Ticknor & Fields back in 1867, a confusion that took a deal of sorting out. Despite these problems, however, Dickens was able during the month to complete *Drood* II, in which the exotic Landless twins are introduced to Cloisterham, and sent it to the printers on the 27th.[28]

He was horrified when, on 2 December, he got back the proofs of the two first numbers from the printers and found they were a whole twelve pages too short. Never in his whole career had he so miscalculated and it suggests that he was still tending to think of this new novel in terms of weekly serialisation rather than in monthly numbers. But, incomparable professional that he was, he rose swiftly and efficiently to the situation, reporting to Forster on 22 December, nine days before he read him the revised second number (which Forster acclaimed as 'a clincher'):

> I had to transpose a chapter from number two to number one, and remodel number two altogether! This was the more unlucky, that it came upon me at the time when I was obliged to leave the book, in order to get up the readings, quite gone out of my mind since I left them off. However, I turned to it, and got it done, and both numbers are now in type. Charles Collins has designed an excellent cover.

'Excellent' as Collins's cover was, Dickens had now, as we have seen, to concern himself with finding a replacement illustrator. He was apparently impressed by Luke Fildes's engraving 'Houseless and Hungry' in the first issue of *The Graphic* (4 Dec.), which Millais, now a good friend with Dickens's 1850 attack on his work seemingly forgotten, had drawn to his attention. This night scene depicts a line of wretched men, women and children waiting in the bitter cold for admission to a workhouse casual ward. But Dickens wanted to be sure that Fildes could also draw 'pretty ladies' and asked for some specimens. These being apparently satisfactory, Dickens then requested a specimen illustration for *Copperfield*. Fildes drew Emily with Mr Peggotty and Dickens found it meritorious but 'wanting in a sense of beauty'. This concerned him because, as he explained to Chapman on 16 January 'in the new book I have two beautiful and young women [just as he had had in *Our Mutual Friend*], strikingly contrasted in appearance, who will both be very prominent in the story'. By 24 January, however, he had met and liked Fildes who, he told Chapman, promised 'admirably' and so the matter was settled. Collins's cover was retained, though probably touched up by Fildes before publication, and is now, of course, a prime piece of evidence for the 'Droodians', as is Collins's 1871 letter to the impresario Augustin Daly about it, and Fildes's various recorded reminiscences of what Dickens had found it necessary to tell him about his plans for developing the story – as, for example, that Fildes should depict Jasper wearing a long scarf 'for [he] strangles Edwin Drood with it'.[29]

Dickens passed a traditional family Christmas at Gad's Hill but was too unwell, with renewed problems with his left arm and leg, to come downstairs until the evening to join in the traditional party games. These included a memory one that involved one person saying a word or phrase to his or her neighbour that had to be repeated to his or her neighbour with another word added to it. The next player then had to repeat both words adding another, and so it went on. Henry Dickens records, 'My father, after many turns, had successfully gone through the long string of words, and finished up with his own contribution, "Warren's Blacking, 30, Strand!" ' He gave this, Henry remembered, 'with an odd twinkle in his eye and a strange inflection in his voice which at once forcibly arrested my attention and left a vivid impression on my mind for some time afterwards'. What Dickens was doing, of course, was playing with his unwitting family the private game that he had so long played with his wider family of unwitting readers, instances of which we have noted more than once. This game consisted of making private allusions in his writings, which would seem merely curious to his readers, to the blacking-factory ordeal of his younger days. The main setting of his new novel was taking him back to the scenes and memories of his happy Medway childhood (one of his chapter-notes, relating to the elaborate description of Mrs Crisparkle's dining-room cupboard and its aromatic riches in chapter 10, famously reads, 'Minor Canon Corner. The closet I remember there as a child') but the bitter memory of his time at Warren's is always with him, of course, and at this point finds a vent elsewhere than in his fiction. Not that he seems by any means to paint an idyllic picture of Rochester as Cloisterham; rather, it seems in many ways to reflect the picture of the old city as the site of stagnation and complacency drawn by the Uncommercial Traveller a decade earlier in 'Dullborough Town'.[30]

Dickens's farewell readings in London began on 11 January and ran on till 15 March, twice a week for the first fortnight and once a week thereafter. It was nothing like so demanding a schedule as his earlier touring ones had been but still Frank Beard took care to attend every reading, as also did Charley. The latter records that Beard told him, 'if you see your father falter in the least you must run up and catch him and bring him off with me, or, by Heaven, he'll die before them all!' It was, too, the first time Dickens had had to face the challenge of trying to run all three of his careers – serial novelist, editor of a weekly journal and public reader – simultaneously. It was probably, therefore, as much for his own sake and cutting down on railway travelling, as for that of giving Mamie her season ('she will probably go somewhere else, the moment we take possession!' he ruefully joked to Frances Elliot on 28 December) that he established his head-quarters in the capital for the first five months of 1870 – this would also have made it easier to visit Nelly in Peckham, of course. He rented 5 Hyde Park Place, near Marble Arch, from Thomas Milner Gibson a former governmental colleague of Lord John Russell's. Dickens did, in fact, brave the railway on

6 January despite protests from Georgina (and, for all we know, from Nelly too) to travel to Birmingham to do his presidential duty at the Birmingham Institute's prize-giving ceremony. And he took that opportunity to try (admittedly not very successfully) to clarify the statement of his political creed he had made on his previous visit. He approvingly quoted from Thomas Buckle's *History of Civilisation in England* (1857) a passage including the comment that 'lawgivers are nearly always the obstructors of society, instead of its helpers', and later (14 Jan.) wrote gleefully to the Fieldses, 'I hope you may have met with a little touch of Radicalism I gave them at Birmingham in the words of Buckle?'[31]

Dickens gave the first of two matinée readings (the *Carol*) for the benefit of members of the theatrical profession on 14 January, and a second (*Boots* and *Sikes and Nancy*), attended by Nelly, presumably accompanying her mother, on the 21st. 'These morning readings', he wrote to the Fieldses on 14 January 'particularly disturb me at my book-work' but he seems to have felt he was still making good progress on the novel: 'there is a curious interest steadily working up to No. 5, which requires a great deal of art and self-denial,' he told Fildes. A month later, *Drood* III (chs 10–12) was at the printers. A boxed chapter-note for ch.11 reads 'The two waiters' and refers to what must rank as among the most brilliantly funny of all Dickens's many, many waiter-sketches, the description of 'the immoveable waiter' and 'the flying waiter' serving up the dinner in Mr Grewgious's chambers. (Only a few months before Dickens had entertained the Fieldses with his comic impersonation of a bustling waiter as he laid out a picnic in Cooling churchyard.) The 'curious interest' that he refers to must, I think, attach to Jasper and his frequently strange behaviour in this number, including his getting Durdles to take him on an elaborate nocturnal exploration of the cathedral ('Lay the ground for the manner of the Murder, to come out at last', reads one of Dickens's notes for ch.12). Dickens anticipates the reader remembering and pondering Jasper's speeches and actions in this number two numbers later when Edwin will suddenly vanish after dining with his uncle. In the event, Edwin disappears in the fourth number and this is part of a pattern discernible in the writing of this book that shows Dickens as apparently getting through his material too fast. The note 'Done already' appears twice in his scanty 'mems' for *Drood* V, for example.

On 2 February he signed the formal contract for the novel with Chapman and Hall, with publication of the first number being set for the last day of March. The guarantee to Dickens of at least £625 per number shows that very large sales were anticipated as does the length (thirty-six pages) of the first 'Drood Advertiser'. As in the contract for *Our Mutual Friend* drawn up seven years before, there was a clause in this one providing for what should happen if Dickens were to die in the process of writing the novel.[32]

Dickens gave his last readings on 1, 8 and 15 March (*Copperfield* and *Bardell and Pickwick; Boots at the Holly-Tree Inn, Sikes and Nancy*, and *Mr Bob Sawyer's*

Party, and the *Carol* and *Bardell and Pickwick*). On the day following the second of these readings, the morning, that is, after his last public slaughter of Nancy, he was received by the Queen who wished personally to thank him for loaning her some photographs he had brought back from America with him of Civil War battlefields. During the ninety minutes the audience lasted etiquette required that Dickens should remain standing despite his painfully swollen foot (the Queen had a sofa to lean on). They discussed, among other things, such household topics – wholly appropriate, Dickens would certainly have felt, for a married woman no matter how grand her station – as the servant problem and 'the cost of butchers' meat, and bread'. He was, it seems, agreeably impressed by this exalted personage for whom he and Maclise had merrily pretended to be wildly lovesick thirty years before. Six days later came his final reading, of course a hugely emotional occasion for both himself and his audience, and one to which he rose magnificently. 'He never read better in his life than on that last evening,' Kent tells us. At the end he came forward to speak in his own person, dwelling on the 'privilege' it had been for him to read his 'cherished ideas' to audiences and to observe their response, and how it had allowed him to experience 'an amount of artistic delight and instruction which, perhaps, is given to few men to know'. In his readings, he said, as in his writings he had ever been 'a faithful servant of the public, always imbued with a sense of duty to them, and always striving to do his best'. He ended as follows:

> Ladies and gentlemen, in but two short weeks from this time I hope that you may enter, in your own homes, on a new series of readings, at which my assistance will be indispensable; but from these garish lights I vanish now for evermore, with a heartfelt, grateful, respectful, and affectionate farewell.[33]

The first number of *Drood* duly appeared on 31 March and achieved a phenomenal sale of 50,000 copies, 10,000 more than *Our Mutual Friend*. Dickens was overjoyed: '*It has very, very far outstripped every one of its predecessors,*' he told Fields on 18 April. Reviews were enthusiastic and *The Times* indeed was positively rhapsodic: 'As he delighted the fathers, so he delights the children, and this his latest effort promises to be received with interest and pleasure as widespread as that which greeted those glorious *Papers* which built at once the whole edifice of his fame'. Ten days before, he had read *Drood* IV to Forster, who was concerned by Dickens's telling him that he had been for a second time unable to read more than the right-hand half of the names over the shops he had passed in coming to Forster's – simply the effect, Dickens believed, of some medicine he had been taking. In early April, despite continuing health troubles, he fulfilled a year-old promise to preside at the annual dinner of the Newsvendors' Benevolent Institution on the 5th and the next day attended a royal levee held on behalf of the Queen by the Prince of Wales which necessitated the donning of 'fancy dress'.

59 'Charles Dickens' by André Gill (*L'Éclipse*, Paris, 14 June 1868)

But by the middle of the month he was 'most perseveringly and ding-dong-doggedly at work' on *Drood* V (chs 17–20), 'making headway but slowly' as he developed the plot. Two major new characters made their appearance, Lieutenant Tartar in London and in Cloisterham the mysterious Datchery, the latter evidently someone in disguise whose identity has always been a matter of hot debate among the 'Droodians'. The number also included the intense sun-dial scene between Jasper and the terrified Rosa – a reprise of the one between Bradley Headstone and Lizzie Hexam in *Our Mutual Friend*, less violent but more sinister. On 25 April he was greatly shaken by the sudden death of Maclise after a long period during which they had not met, Maclise having become very much a recluse. In a speech he had already agreed to give at the Royal Academy banquet on 30 April he paid a noble tribute to his greatly loved old friend and to his 'gallantly sustaining the true dignity of his vocation ... at the last as at the first'. In spite of this shock, and all the usual distractions, he somehow managed to finish Drood V in time to read it to Forster on 7 May.[34]

By now he was yearning to retreat from 'hot rooms and speechmaking' and 'the old preposterous endeavour to dine at preposterous hours and preposterous places' to the peace and quiet of Gad's Hill to get on with the writing of his novel in the chalet and to enjoy the further improvements he was making to his property. He had perhaps had anxieties about Nelly's health – in a letter of 1 May he refers to being 'in attendance on a sick friend at some distance'. As for his own health, his old foot trouble flared up again and he had besides, as he wrote to Percy Fitzgerald's wife on 9 May, 'got into that complicated state of engagements that my life is positively made wretched'. Not that all his dining out seems to have been such a misery to him. He was evidently on good form, for example, when he dined with his old friend the society hostess Lady Molesworth on 29 May and 'simply bubbled over with fun and conversation', according to a fellow-guest, Lady Dorothy Nevill. She recalled that he had confided to her that 'he had a great scheme for writing a cookery-book' and added, 'I believe the poor man really meant it'. And Dickens the theatrical manager came joyously to life again when he set about organising some private theatricals for his daughters and some friends of theirs, directing 'all the rehearsals with a boy's spirit, and a boy's interest in his favourite art' though his lameness preventing him from actually acting in the piece. The performance took place in the London home of some friends of Mamie's and Katey's on Thursday 2 June and Dickens, who had come up to town that day to sign a codicil to his will bequeathing all his share and interest in All The Year Round to Charley, was behind the scenes acting as prompter and stage-manager, 'ringing all the bells and working all the lights ... with infectious enjoyment'.[35]

Next day he returned to Gad's Hill to resume work on Drood, having now arrived at the sixth number (chs 21–23), the mid-way point of the story. He had told Fields back in January that the story was to turn in the fifth and sixth numbers 'upon an interest suspended until the end'. Since he did not live to write that end we can only speculate, along with the 'Droodians', about just what he might have been referring to. It is more to my purpose here to take note of Mrs Billickin, the wonderful London landlady with her 'overpowering personal candour', who appears in this his last piece of fictional writing. She is a worthy successor to Mrs Todgers in Chuzzlewit, as Forster noted, but is quite distinct from her. She alone, one might think, should refute Wilkie Collins's strange dismissal of Drood as 'Dickens's last laboured effort, the melancholy work of a worn-out brain'. Incidentally, the Billickin is also one of the only two characters in the book who owe anything (in her case, just one splendid speech, the one about the gas-fitter and 'your jistes' in ch. 22) to Dickens's Book of Memoranda. He seems to have had comparatively little recourse to this book in the writing of *Drood*, though, as we have seen, he did mine it for proper names when working on 'the Sapsea fragment'.[36]

On Saturday 4 June Katey went down to Gad's Hill, being anxious to consult her father about an offer she had had to go on the stage professionally which she was seriously considering in view of the parlous financial situation in which she and Collins found themselves. She was also much concerned, like the rest of the family, by the evident deterioration in Dickens's health. That his brain was 'more than usually clear and bright' during the writing of *Drood* 'no one who lived with him could possibly doubt', she later wrote, nor could anyone doubt 'the extraordinary interest he took in the development of this story'. But the very intensity of this interest made those close to him fear 'that he was trying his strength too far', though any attempt to get him to go more easily would have been 'as idle as stretching one's hand to a river and bidding it cease to flow'. It was not until late on the Sunday evening that she could talk to him about her stage offer. After strongly dissuading her from accepting it because she had 'too sensitive a nature' and was 'clever enough to do something else', Dickens promised to 'make it up' to her in some undefined way. He then went on to talk very intimately to her about himself and his life including, apparently, his relationship with Nelly, and about his hopes for the success of *Drood* 'if, please God, I live to finish it'. Apart from this one reference to finishing the book, Katey recalled, 'he spoke as though his life was over and there was nothing left'.[37]

Whatever intimations of mortality Dickens may have felt, he was back at work in the chalet a few hours later. Two summers before he had written (25 May 1868) to Annie Fields of his delight in the place, and how the mirrors 'reflect and refract in all kinds of ways the leaves that are quivering at the windows, and the great fields of waving corn, and the sail-dotted river . . . The scent of the flowers, and indeed of everything that is growing for miles and miles, is most delicious.' Now on the afternoon of 8 June when, 'much against his usual custom', he returned to the chalet after luncheon to finish the plot-thickening last chapter of *Drood* VI, it was his situation in the chalet that surely helped to inspire that beautiful, and much-quoted, description of a summer dawn in Cloisterham that was almost the last thing he ever wrote: 'Changes of glorious light from moving boughs, songs of birds, scents from gardens, woods, and fields – or rather from the one great garden of the whole cultivated island in its yielding time – penetrate into the Cathedral, subdue its earthy odour, and preach the Resurrection and the Life . . .'. The chapter ends with the words 'and then falls to with an appetite'. These were thus the last words of fiction that he ever wrote, and it would be hard indeed to imagine ones more appropriate for a writer whose multitudinous readers have been 'falling to with an appetite' ever since.[38]

******

Dickens suffered a stroke at dinner, alone with Georgina, on the evening of the
8th and died at Gad's Hill the following day, never having recovered consciousness. 9 June 1870 was the fifth anniversary, as all biographers dutifully note, of
the Staplehurst railway accident from the terrible shock of which he had never
really recovered. He had expressed a wish to be buried in the precincts of
Rochester Cathedral and the Cathedral authorities had already paid for a grave
to be prepared for him when the offer of an Abbey burial came from the Dean
of Westminster, an offer which the family felt unable to refuse, backed as it was
by strong public desire and a *Times* leader on 13 June. Dickens was therefore
buried in the Abbey, at a small and strictly private ceremony, as enjoined in his
will, early on the morning of 14 June, after which there came mourners in such
crowds that the Dean arranged for the grave to be kept open for two days so
that people might come to scatter flowers in it. They continued coming to
leave their flowers for some days even after the grave was closed.[39]

60 Scene at Dickens's graveside the day after his funeral, *Illustrated London News*, 25 June 1870

CHAPTER 27

Charles Dickens's explanations

I do not write resentfully or angrily: for I know how all these things have worked
together to make me what I am. . . .

Dickens in the 'autobiographical fragment'

D ICKENS'S LAST will and testament, dated 12 May 1869 and 'written', as *The Times* informed its readers when publishing it on 22 July, 'in his favourite blue ink on a sheet of letter paper', was a more substantial document than its most recent predecessor. This had been drawn up in 1858 and revised in 1861 when Dickens had told Ouvry, 'I wish to write it in my own hand, and I wish it to be as plain and simple as it can possibly be made'. His 1869 will is, like the earlier one, a business-like legal document but it is also, like the autobiographical fragment, the 'Personal Statement' of 1858, and the so-called 'Violated Letter', very much a *composition*, with a definite design upon the reader. Dickens knew that it would be read by vast numbers of people over the years and *The Saturday Review* correctly saw it as essentially what it called a '*pièce justicative*'. Both its style and its contents laid it open to the *Review*'s mockery of it as 'Mr Dickens's last charge to mankind', something more akin to 'a solemn rescript, *urbi et orbi*' than to a 'testamentary document'.[1]

Like Dickens's novels, his last will has an attention-grabbing opening: 'I give the sum of £1,000 free of legacy duty to Miss Ellen Lawless Ternan [misprinted by *The Times* as "Fernan"], late of Houghton Place, Ampthill Square, in the county of Middlesex'. Claire Tomalin, Nelly's biographer, rightly defines this as 'an act of defiance'. Here in this public document Dickens boldly and prominently names the woman with whom his own name has, in knowing literary and metropolitan circles, long been scandalously linked. I believe he intended this naming of Nelly to be taken as a public assertion of the innocence of his relationship with her. Such an interpretation is supported by the comparatively modest amount of the legacy itself, only £1,000 out of an estate amounting to over £90,000, as well as by surviving evidence indicating that he had almost certainly made private arrangements for further financial provision for her. The sum left to her in his will exactly equates to the amount of the

legacy left to his unmarried daughter Mamie. Thus Nelly is once again aligned
with a Dickens daughter, just as she had been eleven years earlier, in the so-
called 'Violated Letter' in which Dickens, referring to her only as 'that young
lady', had written, 'I know her to be innocent and pure, and as good as my own
dear daughters'. Anyone reading the will might well assume that this unknown
legatee (unknown to the general public, that is) must have been in some sort
of quasi-daughterly relationship to him – a cousin, perhaps, or other female
relative, or else the goddaughter that by some she was supposed to be.[2]

Immediately after the Nelly bequest in the will come the bequests of nineteen
guineas each to 'my faithful servant, Mrs Anne Cornelius' and her 'daughter and
only child', followed by the bequest of the same amount to every servant (none
of them named) in Dickens's employ at the time of his death. This singling out
of Anne Cornelius, née Brown, for her faithful service is significant. It would
have meant nothing to the general public, but those who recalled the 'Violated
Letter' might remember the mention therein of 'an attached woman servant'
who had lived with the Dickenses for many years and could 'bear testimony' to
the incompatibility and resulting unhappiness of the couple 'in London, in the
country, in France, in Italy, wherever we have been, year after year, month after
month, week after week, day after day'. And many would know that this servant
so eloquently invoked as a witness on Dickens's behalf was none other than the
Anne Cornelius of the will. As Anne Brown she had been Catherine's maid until
she left to get married in 1855. She had, Dickens told Burdett Coutts in 1858,
taken care of Catherine 'like a poor child, for sixteen years' but he doubted that
she would return to take care of her now – 'I doubt her being afraid that the
companionship would wear her to death.' Cornelius had, however, temporarily
returned to work at Tavistock House in 1857, very much as Dickens's confidential servant – it was she, we remember, whom he had commissioned discreetly to
arrange the boarding up of the door between his dressing-room and the marital
bedroom – and she evidently returned yet again as housekeeper at Tavistock
House in the autumn of 1858. Subsequently, she visited Gad's Hill more than
once, with her daughter, who as 'the demon' became, despite all Dickens's affection and gratitude towards her mother, a running joke in his correspondence
with Wilkie Collins. Now in Dickens's last will Cornelius is publicly thanked and
rewarded for her unwavering adherence to him rather than to Catherine.[3]

But the greatest heroine of Dickens's will, as of the 'Violated Letter' is
undoubtedly Georgina, to whom he leaves £8,000, most of his personal
jewellery, his private papers, all the 'little familiar objects' from his writing-
table and his room, which, he says, 'she will know what to do with' (it was
Georgina, therefore, who gave Nelly the pen he had been using to write
Drood), and finally his 'grateful blessing as the best and truest friend man ever
had'. Charley is left his library, engravings and prints while Forster gets his
gold watch and the manuscripts of most of his books. Later in the document

Dickens enjoins his children always to remember how much they owe to Georgina 'for they know well that she has been, through all the stages of their growth and progress, their ever useful self-denying and devoted friend'. It is almost as though he had turned back to his *Book of Memoranda* at this point to pick up his note there of an idea for a character that Forster tells us was 'sketched from his sister-in-law in his own home':

> She sacrificed to children, and sufficiently rewarded. From a child herself, always 'the children' (of somebody else) to engross her. And so it comes to pass that she never has a child herself – is never married – is always devoted 'to the children' (of somebody else), and they love her – and she has always youth dependent on her 'till her death – and dies quite happily.[4]

Dickens's defiance of gossip in his will can again be felt in this insistent bringing forward of Georgina as having been his 'best and truest friend' and a sort of super-nurse/governess to his children. Many of Dickens's friends had found it very strange, if not downright scandalous, that Georgina remained with him and, together with her niece Mamie, ran his household for him after its rightful mistress had been exiled. Indeed, it seemed at one point, as we have seen, that Dickens might be forced to go to law to crush the rumours regarding his relationship with his sister-in-law which, if they could have been proved, would have exposed him to the charge of incest. Even for his closest and most devoted friends Georgina seems to have been something of an embarrassment. At a Boston luncheon-party, given for Fechter by the Fieldses in February 1870, after a reference by Longfellow to Dickens's 'terrible sadness', Fechter said: 'all his fame goes for nothing since he has not the one thing. He is very unhappy in his children.' Writing up the occasion in her journal, Annie Fields expanded on this:

> Nobody can say how much too much of this the children have to bear and to how little purpose poor Miss Hogarth spends her life hoping to comfort and care for him. I never felt more keenly her anomalous and unnatural position in the household. Not one mentioned her name; they could not have, I suppose, lest they might do her wrong – Ah, how sad a name it must be to those who love him best. Dear, dear Dickens.

A few months later she was discussing Dickens's will with Fechter and recorded how shocked he had been to find the document full of 'expressions fitted to give color to the senseless and cruel accusations against Miss Hogarth'. In Fechter's view, at least, Dickens's attempt to explain Georgina's role in his own life and in that of his family had backfired. Annie herself, however, felt that Dickens and his solicitor had done 'the best they could under trying circumstances'. Neither Fechter nor Annie seems to have made any comment on the naming of Nelly in the will.[5]

Dramatically juxtaposed with Dickens's warm exhortation to his children to be always grateful to Georgina are the words, 'AND I DESIRE here simply to record the fact that my wife, since our separation by consent, has been in the receipt from me of an annual income of £600, while all the great charges of a numerous and expensive family have devolved wholly upon myself'. No wonder the American journalist and diplomat John Bigelow, who knew both Dickens and Catherine, wrote, 'There may be a great diversity of opinion as to which of Mr Dickens's works was the best, but the English speaking race, I imagine, will generally agree that his "Will" was his worst'. Dickens could not have been unaware that the clear implication of this juxtaposition of the tribute to Georgina with the cold sentence about his wife, whom he cannot even bring himself to name, is that Catherine had failed as a mother and even the separation itself (which Dickens has taught himself to believe was 'by consent') becomes, bizarrely enough, a source of grievance against her.[6]

The last section of Dickens's will deals with his funeral, and with how he wished to be remembered – his 'legacy' as we should now call it. It was, of course, hardly likely that so obsessive an organiser as Dickens would fail to leave most explicit directions about his own funeral and interment. The nature of these directions could not have come as any surprise to anyone at all aware of the scathing mockery of all funeral pomp and circumstance recurrent in his writings from *Oliver Twist* onwards. Now he 'emphatically' orders that his own funeral should be as private and simple as possible, and that the select few attending should 'wear no scarf, cloak, black bow, long hat-band, or other such revolting absurdity'. His name is to be inscribed 'in plain English letters' on his tomb 'without the addition of "Mr" or "Esquire" ' (a year before, we may recall, he had been gratified by *The Times* hailing him as the 'Great Commoner of English Fiction'). Notably, he does not here express his wish, known to his family and evidently to the Dean of Rochester also, that he should be buried in the precincts of Rochester Cathedral. Was it, we may ask, that he wanted to leave open the possibility of a Westminster Abbey burial? The answer may lie in an arresting comment on him made by one of his 'young men', the journalist John Hollingshead, 'No man in his inner mind, felt so sure of Westminster Abbey and immortality, and no man kept that inner mind more carefully concealed.' Whatever he may have privately thought, or not thought, about burial in the Abbey, Dickens certainly desired that his fame should for ever rest solely on his books, on the achievements of his writing life. It should have no need of any pompous public assertion of itself in the form of statues or other memorials. He made his desire explicit in a passage that has caused, and continues to cause, no little trouble to his descendants: 'I conjure my friends on no account to make me the subject of any monument, memorial, or testimonial whatever. I rest my claims to the remembrance of my country upon my published works . . . '. Finally, he seeks to clarify the nature of his religious faith in terms which, again, should have come as no surprise to attentive readers of his works: 'I exhort my dear children humbly to try to guide themselves by the teaching of the New Testament in its broad spirit, and to put no faith in any man's narrow construction of its letter here or there.' This passage was quoted by the 'Broad Church' Dean of Westminster, Arthur Stanley, as a fine reflection of Dickens's 'simple but sufficient faith' in his sermon at the Abbey on the Sunday following Dickens's burial.[7]

A short-lived journal called *The Period* responded to the *Saturday*'s mockery of Dickens's will by calling it 'a disgrace to English journalism' and accusing its writer of 'throwing the mud of Southampton-street', where the *Saturday*'s office was located, at both Nelly and Georgina 'in the form of a most disgraceful innu-endo'. This was a reference to the *Saturday*'s sly comments: 'To Miss Ternan and Miss Hogarth Mr Dickens very likely has duties, and he has cheerfully recognised them by word and deed. Are we told that all his duties to his wife were summed up by giving her an annuity without a single word of recognition, or, if it were needed, of forgiveness and reconciliation . . .?' Fortunately for all concerned, the matter then seems to have died away, at least in the press, though some malicious gossip continued to circulate, as shown by some comments privately recorded by Dickens's old antagonist the publisher Richard Bentley. Bentley admired the *Saturday* article and thought Dickens's will 'a lasting stigma on himself self-inflicted'. 'Had Mrs Dickens', wrote Bentley in his journal, 'been an infamous person, instead of a quiet inoffensive person (whom I personally like) he could not have treated her worse.' Just as had been the case with the publication of his 'Personal' statement in 1858, so here with his will Dickens's second public attempt to impose his own masterful interpretation on his domestic history had been, in the short run, more than a little counter-productive – at least as far as the literary world of the metropolis was concerned.[8]

Some fourteen months later, in November 1871, Forster published the first volume of his *Life of Charles Dickens* and the world was startled by another, and far more dramatic, explanation of himself by Dickens, this time the fragment of autobiography written by him over twenty years before and now presented by Forster in his second chapter. Here the public learned that young David Copperfield's grim experience of life as in Murdstone and Grinby's warehouse echoed what had happened to Dickens himself, that the Micawbers were modelled on his own parents, and their sojourn in the King's Bench Prison closely reflected what had happened in real life when John Dickens had been imprisoned for debt in the Marshalsea. To register just how sensational all this was to the vast majority of Dickens's readers, so many of whom felt themselves to be on terms of personal friendship with him, we need to remember that they knew virtually nothing of his life before he became a journalist in his late teens. This gap in his biographical record was usually filled with details about John Dickens's career in the Navy Pay Office and afterwards. 'The story of his life is soon told', said *The Times* in its obituary notice of Dickens on 10 June:

The son of Mr John Dickens, who held at one time a position in the Navy Pay Department, Charles Dickens was born at Portsmouth in the month of February, 1812. The duties of his father's office obliged him frequently to change his residence, and much of the future novelist's infancy was spent at Plymouth, Sheerness, Chatham, and other seaport towns. The European war, however, came to an end before he had completed his fourth year, and his father, finding his 'occupation gone', retired on a pension and came to London as a Parliamentary reporter for one of the daily papers. It was at first intended that young Charles should be sent to an attorney's office; but he had literary tastes, and eventually was permitted by his father to exchange the law for a post as a reporter on the staff of the *True Sun*.

All that his readers knew or surmised about Dickens's childhood, apart from the glimpse they had been given in the Cheap Edition preface to *Nickleby*, written contemporaneously with the autobiographical fragment, was what might be gleaned from some of his journalistic writings such as 'A Christmas Tree' (*HW*, 21 Dec. 1850) and 'Our School' (*HW*, 11 Oct. 1851), and especially some of the 'Uncommercial Traveller' pieces in *All the Year Round*. From these they would have derived a generalised impression of a secure middle-class background of nursemaids, children's parties, hampers and other treats, story-books, academies (as schools for middle-class children were generally called), and so on. Forster's first volume therefore came as a revelation indeed. 'Never, perhaps,' wrote the Scottish poet and critic Robert Buchanan in the February 1872 issue of *St Paul's Magazine*, 'has a fragment of biography wakened more interest and amazement than the first chapters of Mr Forster's biography'. *The Times* review, serialised in two issues (7 and 26 Dec.) extended to over five columns, Forster's friend Whitwell Elwin devoted twenty-two pages to it in the *Quarterly Review* (vol.132, Jan.–April 1872), and the volume had already been nine times reprinted before the end of 1871.[9]

Certainly the reviewers found much in Dickens's powerfully-written account of what Forster calls his 'hard experiences in boyhood' that explained why he developed into the kind of novelist that he did. In Bayham Street, wrote Elwin (no doubt taking his cue from Forster), the young boy was 'noting the humours and distresses of a new form of life, very fertile in the incidents which might make philosophers both laugh and weep'. *The Times* reviewer commented, 'Thrown among the poor and needy, and sympathising with all their sufferings, he handled their sorrows as one of themselves', and this was more than enough to counterbalance the fact that he lacked 'the manners of a gentleman'. 'As to his education,' said the reviewer in *Fraser's* (possibly Andrew Lang), 'it was perhaps the most suitable on the whole, considering the character of his mind and the career that proved to lie before him, that he could possibly have received.' Less sympathetic but making the same point was Browning, who wrote to his friend Emily Pattison, 'We are all reading the "Life of Dickens" and admiring his sensitiveness at having brushed shoes and trimmed gallipots in his early days, when, did he see with the eyes of certain of his sagest friends, it was the best education imaginable for the likes of him.' In *The Fortnightly Review*, however, J. Herbert Stack argued that Dickens's blacking-factory experience had, in fact, had a negative rather than a positive result:

> Naturally a great humorist, he resolved to be pathetic, and against the bent of his mind achieved success; but we think the effort is apparent enough. He seems driven into this line by recollections of his own past: it superinduced a sensibility almost morbid to the sufferings of unhappy children and unhappy people among the poor. . . .

Buchanan, too, saw 'the wretched soil . . . watered with tears of self-compassion' in which the great tree of Dickens's achievement was rooted as limiting that achievement. The result was a spectacular case of arrested development: 'Charles Dickens, having crushed into his childish experience a whole world of sorrow and humorous insight, so loaded his soul that he never grew any older. . . . He saw all from a child's point of view – strange, odd, queer, puzzling.'[10]

The reviewers did not spare John Dickens, despite Dickens's greater leniency towards him than towards Elizabeth in the autobiographical fragment. *The Times*, for example, observed that the young Dickens had been 'degraded by the straits and carelessness of his father to the position of a warehouse boy'. Elizabeth did find one champion, however. *Fraser's* reviewer, after quoting Dickens's bitter words about never being able to forget that it was his mother who wanted to send him back to Warren's, exclaimed: 'Poor mother! With all her trials and anxieties, five children (one a young baby) and a *Micawber* for a husband, was it wonderful if she "set herself to accommodate the quarrel" with their old friend James Lamert?' Anthony Trollope, whose readers were in time to discover, from his posthumously published *An Autobiography*, that he also had had a far rougher boyhood than they could ever have imagined, though without the class shame Dickens had suffered, did not review Forster's first volume. But in a private letter to George Eliot and George Henry Lewes he confessed that it was 'distasteful' to him: 'Forster tells of him [Dickens] things that should disgrace him, – as the picture he drew of his own father, & the hard words he intended to have published of his own mother; but Forster himself is too coarse-grained to know what is and what is not disgraceful.'[11]

We can only speculate as to whether, having incorporated a version of the auto-biographical fragment into *Copperfield*, Dickens had still wished it to be published after his death. In a footnote to his *Life* Forster, as we have seen, printed quotations from some notes of a conversation with Dickens on 20 January 1849, after he had seen the fragment in what he calls 'its connected shape'. He records

Dickens's fear that what he had written would not convey to readers the full extent of his sufferings, and also his apparent indifference as to whether or not it should ever be published, the decision being 'Left to J.F. or others. No wish.' Forster adds that, although he knew Dickens subsequently abandoned the idea of publishing an autobiography himself, that 'No wish' was never rescinded. Dickens, it would seem, never managed to resolve the struggle within himself of two powerful emotions. On the one hand, there was the strong urge to keep buried in his own heart those profound feelings of shame and humiliation over his time as 'a little laboring hind' that became rooted in him once he began to rise in the world. On the other, there was his equally strong yearning for the world's pity, love and compassion, as well as for admiration, for his neglected and exploited – but also resilient and resourceful – younger self, that mixture of Oliver Twist and the Artful Dodger that had been himself in his Warren's Blacking days.

Much as he might have been angered by certain reviewers' comments at the time, Dickens would surely, in the long term, have been content with the result of Forster's publication of the autobiographical fragment, and with Forster's biography of him in general. The revelations about his childhood sufferings naturally heightened his readers' enthusiasm for his own favourite novel *David Copperfield* now that they could understand more fully just *why* it was his favourite. When Dickens was writing it, enthused the novelist Horace Annesley Vachell, President of the Dickens Fellowship, in 1932, he had 'dipped his quill into his heart's blood'. Dickens's early sufferings gave a particular resonance and authority to his admired (and most admirable) championship of the poor and oppressed, and especially to his passionate concern for the children of the poor. Fred Barnard's poignant imagined portrayal of him, used as title-page vignette for the Household Edition of Forster's *Life* in 1892, depicting an exhausted or despairing little boy (seemingly somewhat younger than Dickens had actually been at the time) at his bench in the blacking factory, soon achieved a quasi-iconic status and was often reproduced – indeed, still is. His triumph over such early sufferings certainly made him 'the hero of his own life', and, together with Forster's loving and admiring presentation of him, to a considerable extent in Dickens's own words, ensured that for more than sixty years after his death he held a very special place – unique, in fact, – among the great writers of the century, in the hearts and minds of the English-speaking world, apart from most aristocrats and academics, as not only a very great writer indeed but also a great and good man. One of the stated aims and objects of the International Dickens Fellowship, founded in 1902, and significantly named 'Fellowship' rather than 'Society', was 'to spread the love of humanity which is the keynote of all [Dickens's] work'. As far as his private life was concerned, he was pitied as a great, wonderfully humane and extraordinarily gifted, man who had been badly treated as a child by his parents and who had later been unlucky in love and suffered much from an unhappy marriage to an inadequate wife and also from the incapacity of his many children.[12]

It was not until the mid-1930s, when revelations about his connection with Ellen Ternan began to surface, that this perception of Dickens, though not of his wife and children, began to change, and a darker, more turbulent, and altogether more complex figure began emerging into the public consciousness. But that, as the saying goes, is another story.

61 Young Dickens in the blacking factory as imagined by Fred Barnard: title-page vignette in the Household Edition of Forster's *Life of Dickens* (1892)

Abbreviations and select bibliography

1. Writings by Dickens, and works edited by him

Dates given for novels and *CHE* are dates of serialisation in monthly parts or weekly instalments; dates given for *AYR*, *BM*, *DN*, *HW* and *MHC* are the dates CD was editor (in the case of *MHC*, also sole contributor).

AMS	*A Message from the Sea* (with Wilkie Collins, 1860)
AN	*American Notes* (1842)
AYR	*All the Year Round* (1859–70)
BH	*Bleak House* (March 1852–Sept. 1853)
BL	*The Battle of Life* (1846)
BM	*Bentley's Miscellany* (1837–39)
BR	*Barnaby Rudge* (*MHC* 13 Feb.–27 Nov. 1841)
C	*The Chimes* (1844)
CB	*Christmas Books* (1852)
CC	*A Christmas Carol* (1843)
CH	*The Cricket on the Hearth* (1845)
CHE	*A Child's History of England* (*HW* 25 Jan. 1851–10 Dec. 53)
CS	*Christmas Stories* (1850–68)
DC	*David Copperfield* (May 1849–Nov. 1850)
DN	*The Daily News* (21 Jan.–9 Feb. 1846)
DS	*Dombey and Son* (Oct. 1846–April 1848)
GE	*Great Expectations* (*AYR* 1 Dec. 1859–3 Aug. 1860)
GSE	'George Silverman's Explanation' (1868)
HM	*The Haunted Man* (1848)
HR	'Holiday Romance' (1868)
HT	*Hard Times* (*HW* 1 April–12 Aug. 1854)
HW	*Household Words* (1850–59)
LD	*Little Dorrit* (Dec. 1855–June 1857)
LOL	*The Life of Our Lord*, London: Associated Newspapers Ltd (1934)
LT	'The Lazy Tour of Two Idle Apprentices' (with Wilkie Collins; *HW* 3–31 Oct. 1857)
MC	*Martin Chuzzlewit* (Jan. 1843–July 1844)

MED	*The Mystery of Edwin Drood* (April–Sept. 1870)
MHC	*Master Humphrey's Clock* (1840–41)
MJ	*Mugby Junction* (1866)
MJG	*Memoirs of Joseph Grimaldi. Edited by 'Boz'* (2 vols, 1838)
MP	'The Mudfog Papers' (*BM* 1837–38)
NN	*Nicholas Nickleby* (April 1838–Oct. 1839)
OCS	*The Old Curiosity Shop* (*MHC*, 25 April 1840–6 Feb. 1841)
OMF	*Our Mutual Friend* (May 1864–Nov. 1865)
OT	*Oliver Twist* (*BM* Feb. 1837–Jan. 1839)
PFI	*Pictures from Italy* (1846)
PP	*The Pickwick Papers* (April 1836–Nov. 1837)
RP	*Reprinted Pieces* (1858)
SB	*Sketches by Boz* ('First Series', 2 vols, 1836; 'Second Series', 1836)
SG	*The Strange Gentleman* (1836)
SUTH	*Sunday Under Three Heads* (1836)
SYC	*Sketches of Young Couples* (1840)
SYG	*Sketches of Young Gentlemen* (1838)
TTC	*A Tale of Two Cities* (*AYR* 30 April–26 Nov. 1859)
UT	*The Uncommercial Traveller* (1861, 1865)
VC	*The Village Coquettes* (1836)

2. Editions of Dickens's writings, speeches and public readings

Journalism	*The Dent Uniform Edition of Dickens' Journalism*, ed. Michael Slater and John Drew, 4 vols (London, 1994–2000)
Memoranda	*Charles Dickens' Book of Memoranda*, ed. Fred Kaplan (New York Public Library, 1981)
MP	*Miscellaneous Papers*, ed. B. W. Matz (London 1908)
P	*The British Academy Pilgrim Edition of the Letters of Charles Dickens*, 12 vols, ed. Madeline House, Graham Storey, Kathleen Tillotson et al. (Oxford, 1965–2002)
PV	*Poems and Verses of Charles Dickens*, ed. Frederic G. Kitton (London, 1903).
Readings	*Dickens: The Public Readings*, ed. Philip Collins (Oxford, 1975)
Speeches	*The Speeches of Charles Dickens*, ed. K. J. Fielding (Oxford,1960)
Stone, UW	*Charles Dickens' Uncollected Writings from Household Words 1850–1859*, ed. Harry Stone, 2 vols (London, 1968)
Stone, WN	*Dickens's Working Notes for his Novels*, ed. Harry Stone (London, 1987)

3. General

Butt and Tillotson	John Butt and Kathleen Tillotson, *Dickens at Work* (London 1957)
CD	Charles Dickens
CDM	Charles Dickens Museum, 48 Doughty Street, London
Cohen, *Illustrators*	Jane Rabb Cohen, *Charles Dickens and His Original Illustrators* (Columbus: Ohio State University Press, 1980)
Collins, *Interviews*	Philip Collins, ed., *Dickens: Interviews and Recollections*, 2 vols (London 1981)
Collins, *CH*	Philip Collins, ed., *Dickens: The Critical Heritage* (London 1972)
D	*The Dickensian* (London, 1905–)
D and W	Michael Slater, *Dickens and Women* (London, 1983)
Drew, *Journalist*	John M. L. Drew, *Dickens the Journalist* (London, 2003)
DQ	*Dickens Quarterly* (Louisville, KY, 1984–)
DS	*Dickens Studies* (Boston, MA, 1965–69)
DSA	*Dickens Studies Annual* (Carbondale, IL., 1970–)
F	John Forster, *The Life of Charles Dickens*, ed. J. W. T. Ley (London, 1928; originally published in 3 vols, London 1872–74)
JF	John Forster
Kitton, *P and P*	Frederic G. Kitton, *Charles Dickens by Pen and Pencil*, issued in 13 parts (London, 1889–90)
Kitton, *P and P, Supp.*	Frederic G. Kitton, *A Supplement to Charles Dickens by Pen and Pencil*, issued in 5 parts (London, 1890)
Langton	Robert Langton, *The Childhood and Youth of Charles Dickens* (London, 1891)
NCF	*Nineteenth Century Fiction* (Berkeley, CA: California University Press, 1949–86)
ORCD	*Oxford Reader's Companion to Dickens*, ed. Paul Schlicke, (Oxford, 1999)
Patten	Robert L. Patten, *Dickens and his Publishers* (Oxford, 1978)
RES	*The Review of English Studies* (Oxford, 1925–)
TLS	*The Times Literary Supplement* (London, 1902–)
Tomalin	Claire Tomalin, *The Invisible Woman* (London, 1990)
VPR	*Victorian Periodicals Review* (Toronto: University of Toronto, 1979–)
VS	*Victorian Studies* (Bloomington: Indiana University, 1929–)
WC	Wilkie Collins

Notes

References for quotations from Dickens's letters in the Pilgrim Edition (*P*) are not given where the date and recipient are specified in the text since such letters can easily be located by these details.

1 Early years: from Portsmouth to Chatham, 1812–1822

1. 'between eight and nine years of age': Langton 36; 'between thirteen and fourteen': *P* I, 1; Forster tells us . . . : see *F* 6; 'small tales': *F* 44.
2. 'mounted on a dining-table . . .': Langton 34.
3. 'in the signature . . .': *F* 42 (the facsimile of the letter is given only in earlier editions of *F*).
4. For details about John Dickens's career and salary in the Navy Pay Office throughout this chapter I have drawn on Michael Allen, *Charles Dickens' Childhood* (1988; hereafter cited as Allen), also Angus Easson, 'John Dickens and the Navy Pay Office', *D* 70 (1974), 35–45; date of John Dickens's birth: information from Michael Allen who established it subsequent to the publication of his book.
5. 'a most respectable locality': Allen 21; 'He has often told me . . .': *F* 2; 'water on the brain': Allen 27.
6. For the need for caution in identifying autobiographical elements in CD's journalism see my 'How Many Nurses Had Charles Dickens? *The Uncommercial Traveller* and Dickensian Biography', *Prose Studies*, 10 (1987), 250–8; 'A Christmas Tree' is collected in *CS*; for discussion of the impact of CD's earliest toys on his imagination see Angus Wilson, *The World of Charles Dickens* (London, 1970) 9–12; 'New Year's Day' is collected in *Journalism* III.
7. coming away from Portsmouth in the snow: see *F* 2.
8. 'commanding beautiful views . . .': Allen 40 (see also Allen 56–8, for CD's depiction of some of his family's Ordnance Terrace neighbours in *SB*); 'the birthplace of his fancy': *F* 8 (for more on 'Dullborough Town' see below, p. 483); 'dark corners': *Journalism* IV, 173.
9. 'the gay bright regiments . . .': *F* 8; 'full of gables . . .': 'The Seven Poor Travellers: the First' (*CS*); 'never tired of watching . . .': Langton 48.
10. *History of Rochester*: Allen 60; 'active and conspicuous member': Langton 40; 'without secretly liking him': *F* 551; 'show day': a later letter written by John Dickens to Edward Chapman recalls his coaching CD to recite a comic poem from Colman's *Broad Grins* for 'his school's show day' (MS. Martin Nason); 'such actions . . .': Langton 26; 'If you were to be very persevering . . .': 'Travelling Abroad' (*UT*), see *Journalism* IV, 86 – JF vouches for the literal truth of this memory of CD's (*F* 3); 'great precocity': *P* I, 382.
11. On John's borrowing from Milbourne see William J. Carlton, 'The "Deed" in *David Copperfield*', *D* 48 (1952), 101–6, also CD's letter to Thomas Barrow of 31 March 1836; on the borrowing from Newnham see Allen 61 (this debt was still unpaid in 1824); 'not inferior': Allen 61; 'sorrowfully remembering . . .': Langton 44.
12. 'a frank, open, and somewhat daring boy': Langton 23; 'red-cheeked baby': *F* 9 (for speculation about the lasting impact of Lucy Stroughill on CD's imagination see *D and W*, ch. 3); 'Now, Mary, clear the kitchen . . .': Langton 25; 'There were no such juvenile entertainments . . .': Langton 44.
13. Forster locates it . . .: *F* 4; 'his first desire for knowledge . . .': *F* 3f.; 'taught him regularly every day . . .': *F* 4; 'to be got up in sables . . .': *P* IX, 287; 'as thoroughly good-natured . . .': see Collins, *Interviews* 130 (for fuller discussion of Elizabeth Dickens see *D and W*, ch.1); for more information about Giles see Arthur Humphreys, *Charles Dickens and his First Schoolmaster* (Manchester, 1926).

14. 'an accomplished scholar . . .': Langton 56; 'very young indeed': *P* V, 474; 'vivid remembrance . . .': *P* I, 429; 'to the inimitable Boz': *F* 7; 'poor white hat': *F* 31; 'a much-worn little white hat': *DC*, end of ch. 10 (the connection is made by Langton 58).

15. 'rambled together through the same Kentish fields . . .': *Speeches* 51; for the story of how 'Tom-all-alone's' got its name see Langton 60; 'a very handsome boy . . .': Langton 57.

16. 'a terrible boy to read': Langton 25.

17. Forster tells us . . .: *F* 5.

18. 'attacks of violent spasm': *F* 3.

19. according to Forster: see *F* 7.

20. 'almost uninhabited': *F* 6; for fuller discussion of CD and *Misnar* see Jane W. Stedman, 'Good Spirits: Dickens's Childhood Reading', *D* 61 (1965), 150–4.

21. 'on the night before we came away': *F* 9; as Forster asserts: see *F* 9.

2 Early years: London, 1822–1827

1. 'sharp little worldly and also kindly ways': *F* 30; 'a sort of cupboard . . . over the [main] stairway': Willoughby Matchett, 'Dickens in Bayham Street', *D* 5 (1909), 147–52, 180–4 (Matchett photographed the house before its demolition in 1910).

2. *Daily Telegraph*, 7 and [?] Dec. 1871, quoted by Walter Thornbury and Edward Walford in *Old and New London* (1873–78) V, 314–15.

3. 'a *unique* of talents': *F* 836; 'famous and caressed and happy': *F* 26.

4. 'Although Charles had given promise . . .': W.J. Carlton, 'Fanny Dickens, Pianist and Vocalist', *D* 53 (1957), 133–43; 'a progidy': *F* 12; for Mr Smuggins see *SB*, 'The Streets – Night', for Little Swills see *BH*, ch.11.

5. 'a treat that served him . . .': *F* 11; 'kindhearted and generous father . . .': *F* 10 (JF quotes from what he calls a 'sketch' of John Dickens that he says CD gave him as, apparently, something separate from the autobiographical fragment but see Philip Collins's comment in his 'Dickens's Autobiographical Fragment and *David Copperfield*', *Cahiers Victoriens et Edouardiens no.20* (Montpellier, 1984, 93).

6. 'like a special correspondent for posterity': Walter Bagehot, 'Charles Dickens', *National Review*, Oct.1858 (quoted Collins, *CH*, 394); for CD's visits to Thomas Barrow see *P* I, 144; 'stole down to the market . . .': *F* 12 (the description of Covent Garden occurs in a comic poem called 'The Elder Brother' which begins: 'Centrick, in London noise and London follies, / Proud Covent Garden blooms, in smoky glory; / For chairmen, coffee-rooms, piazzas, dollies / Cabbages and comedians, famed in story'); 'attraction of repulsion': *F* 11; 'the London night-sights as he returned . . .': *F* 12; 'knew his duty and did it': *Journalism* II, 157 ('Gone Astray').

7. one distinguished Dickens scholar: see Kathleen Tillotson, 'The Middle Years from the *Carol* to *Copperfield*', *Dickens Memorial Lectures*, The Dickens Fellowship (1970), 12.

8. the father of Turner: see W.J. Carlton, 'The Barber of Dean Street', *D* 48 (1952), 8–12; 'delicate hashes . . .': *F* 12; 'to the most delicate and voluptuous palate': Alain-René Le Sage, *The Adventures of Gil Blas of Santillane*, trans. Tobias Smollett (1749), Bk. II, ch.1; 'never tired of reviewing . . .': *F* 12.

9. 'several Sums of Money': see Angus Easson, ' "I, Elizabeth Dickens": Light on John Dickens's Legacy', *D* 67 (London, 1971), 35–40; 'do something', *F* 13; 'little dens, or closets': *Journalism* I, 184.

10. 'took the liberty of using his name . . .': *F* 25; the most famous and influential discussion of CD's use of the name Fagin is Steven Marcus's Freudian take on the subject in an appendix, 'Who is Fagin?', to his *Dickens: from Pickwick to Dombey* (London, 1965).

11. For date of CD's starting work at Warren's see Michael Allen, *Charles Dickens' Childhood* (1988; hereafter cited as Allen), 81; 'the sun was set upon him for ever', 'I really believed at the time . . .': *F* 13; for the amount for which John Dickens was arrested see Angus Easson, 'The Mythic Sorrows of Charles Dickens', *Literature and History*, I (1975), 49–61; 'quarter-days are as eccentric as comets': *SB*, 'Making a Night of It'; for John Dickens's petition and pension arrangements see Angus Easson, 'John Dickens and the Navy Pay Office', *D* 70 (1974), 41.

12. For details of distances given in this para. see Allen 86.

13. 'In every respect . . . but elbow-room': *F* 30; for details about the prison see Trey Philpotts, 'The Real Marshalsea', *D* 87 (1992), 131–45, also Angus Easson, 'Marshalsea Prisoners: Mr Dorrit and Mr Hemens', *DSA* 3 (1974), 77–86.

14. 'fine, dissipated, insoluble mystery': 'Where We Stopped Growing', *HW* 1 Jan. 1853 (*Journalism* III, 105–12); 'dark arches': *F* 31; coalheavers dancing: *DC*, ch.11; the 'White Woman' of Berners Street appears in 'Where We Stopped Growing'.

15. 'a fat, good-natured, kind old gentleman . . .': *F* 30; 'quite astonishing fictions . . .': ibid.; 'smart schoolboy humour': see Gillian Thomas, 'Dickens and *The Portfolio*', *D* 68 (1972; hereafter cited as Thomas), 167–74.
16. See Angus Easson, ' "I, Elizabeth Dickens." Light on John Dickens's Legacy', *D* 67(1971), 35–42.
17. For the possible effect on CD's art of his being stared at see John Carey, *The Violent Effigy: A Study of Dickens's Imagination*, 2nd edn (London, 1991), 104; for the length of time CD worked at the blacking factory see Allen 102–03.
18. 'a poverty-stricken neighbourhood . . .': Kitton, *P and P*, 132; 'poor Spanish refugees . . .': *BH*, ch. 43.
19. For John Dickens and *The British Press* see Allen 110; for Gurney's shorthand see W. J. Carlton, *Charles Dickens. Shorthand Writer* (London, 1926); 'A circumstance of great moment . . .': *D* 9 (1913), 148, reprinted Allen 111.
20. 'with a relief so strange . . .': *F* 35; 'a very superior sort of school . . .': *F* 43; 'by far the most ignorant man . . .': *Speeches*, 240; 'like the satisfaction of a craving appetite': *DC*, ch.7.
21. 'with great energy . . .': *D* 7(1911), 229; 'more erect than lads ordinarily do . . .': *F* 41; 'very particular with his clothes . . .': *F* 835, *n.*; 'when we had finished . . .': *F* 835; for *Our Newspaper* see Langton 89; 'his wonderful knowledge . . .': *F* 43.
22. 'Our School': see *Journalism* III, 35–42; 'considering there was an illustration . . .': *F* 43f., *n.*; It has been noted . . .: see R. S. McMaster, 'Dickens and the Horrific', *Dalhousie Review* 38 (1958), 14–28; ' taste for crude sensationalism': Thomas 172.
23. For details of John Dickens's dealing with the Royal Academy of Music see W. J. Carlton, 'Fanny Dickens. Pianist and Vocalist', *D* 53 (1957), 133–43; for John Dickens and Lloyd's see Allen 110; 'a smart intelligent lad . . .': Samuel Carter Hall, *Retrospect of a Long Life; from 1815 to 1883* (1883) I, 111, quoted by Allen 110; the Polygon address is known from 'Mr George Lear's Recollections', Kitton, *P and P*, 130–3.
24. All material in this paragraph is drawn from 'Mr Edward Blackmore's Recollections' and 'Mr George Lear's Recollections' in Kitton, *P and P*, 129–33.
25. 'the Alienation Office . . .': see W. J. Carlton, 'Mr Blackmore Engages an Office Boy', *D* 48 (1952), 162–7; Dickens's 'notions of law . . .': Collins, *CH* 369; trenchant journalistic pieces: examples might be: 'A Poor Man's Tale of a Patent' (*HW*, 19 Oct. 1850; *Journalism* II, 284–90), 'Things That Cannot Be Done' (*HW*, 8 Oct. 1853; *Journalism* III, 174–9) and 'Legal and Equitable Jokes' (*HW*, 218–25; *Journalism* III, 218–25); the classic discussion of CD and the law is to be found in William S. Holdsworth, *Charles Dickens as a Legal Historian* (London, 1929).
26. 'a lawyer's office . . .': *P* I, 423.
27. See William J. Carlton, 'The Strange Story of Thomas Mitton', *D* 56 (1960), 141–52.
28. 'savage stenographic mystery': *DC*, ch. 43.

3 'The Copperfield days', 1828–1835

1. 'The Copperfield days': cf. CD's inscription in a copy of *DC* given to James Roney in 1857, quoted by William J. Carlton in *D* (see note 7 below): 'To James E. Roney, my old friend and companion in some of the Copperfield days (when Dora was beautiful) with my faithful regard'.
2. 'strong perception of character . . .': *F* 59; composed at least one original one for himself: see F. G. Kitton, *Minor Writings of Charles Dickens* (London, 1900), 221; 'really studying the bills . . .': *F* 380; for Mathews's influence on CD see Earle Davis, *The Flint and the Flame* (Columbia, MO: University of Missouri Press, 1964), Anna Zambrano, 'Dickens and Charles Mathews', *Moderna Sprache*, 66 (1972), 235–42, and Malcolm Andrews, *Dickens and His Performing Selves* (London, 2006).
3. For details about Barrow see William J. Carlton, 'Dickens's Literary Mentor' *Dickens Studies* (Boston), I (1965), 54–64, and Drew, *Journalist*, 9ff.; for CD's reading in the British Museum see *P* I, 9f. and John Bowen, 'Dickens and Digitation', *D* 100 (2004), 121–2.
4. 'wills, wives and wrecks': the Prerogative Court dealt with probate, the Court of Arches with divorce and ecclesiastical matters, and the Admiralty Court with shipwrecks among other nautical matters; 'Doctors' Commons': see *Journalism* I, 89–93; an actual case: see William J. Carlton, *Charles Dickens, Shorthand Writer* (London, 1926), ch. 4; 'lazy old nook . . .': *DC*, ch. 23.
5. 'pervaded every chink . . .': *UT*, 'Birthday Celebrations' (*Journalism* IV, 228–37); who could never even get his name right: she called him 'Mr Dickin' (*P* VII, 534); 'I have . . . too often thought': *P* I, 23; for discussion of CD's courtship letters see Duane DeVries, *Dickens's Apprentice Years* (1976, hereafter cited as Devries), 27: 'They [Dickens's surviving letters to Maria] illustrate that even this early in his writing career he had surprising control over the English language and a promising ability to express himself formally, colloquially, seriously, humorously'.

6. For fuller discussion of CD's contributions to Maria's album see *D and W*, ch. 4, and, more recently, Christine Alexander, 'The Juvenilia of Charles Dickens. Romance and Reality', *DQ* 25 (2008), 3–21 (the album itself is now in the CDM).

7. For Roney see William J. Carlton, 'A Companion of the Copperfield Days', *D* 50 (1954), 7–16; 'brooding over the choice of a career': letter from Culliford Barrow to Thomas Wright, 21 Jan. 1895 (MS. CDM).

8. 'knock up a chaunt or two': *P* I, 7; 'We take our grub . . .': *P* I, 22.

9. 'best reporter in the gallery': Charles Knight, *Passages of a Working Life*, III (1865), 37; for CD's probable authorship of the Warren's Blacking rhymes see Drew, *Journalist*, 17–19 and (ed.) *'The Pride of Mankind': Puff Verses for Warren's Blacking with Contributions attributed to Charles Dickens* (Oswestry, Shropshire: Hedge Sparrow Press, 2005).

10. See CD's letter of 9 Dec. 1832 to a would-be poll clerk (*P* I, 10).

11. 'Quadrilles 8 o'clock': *P* I, 15; 'Birthday Celebrations' (*UT*): see *Journalism* IV, 228–37; 'displays of heartless indifference . . .': *P* I, 17; 'nothing will ever afford me . . .': *P* I, 17; for CD's being summoned by Stanley see James T. Fields, *Yesterdays with Authors* (Boston, 1872), 230–31.

12. The only known copy of the printed playbill for *Clari* is in CDM; reproduced in *D* 35 (1939), 233.

13. 'in a very conciliatory note . . .' *P* I, 29; 'very coldly and reproachfully': *P* VII, 543.

14. For the surviving fragments of *O'Thello* and the music see Charles Haywood, 'Charles Dickens and Shakespeare: or, The Irish Moor of Venice, *O'Thello*, with Music', *D* 73 (1977), 67–87.

15. J. P. Collier, *An Old Man's Diary: Forty Years Ago* (London, 1872) pt. iv, 12–15.

16. For the later alteration in the 1847 preface see James Kinsley, ed., *PP* (Oxford: Clarendon Edn, 1986), 884; Bradley Deane sees the preface as part of 'a mythic narrative of the creation of Dickens the author' (*The Making of the Victorian Novelist: Anxieties of Authorship in the Mass Market*, New York: Routledge, 2003), 54.

17. re-titled as 'A Dinner at Poplar Walk': see *P* I, 32; 'rather backward . . .': *P* I, 33; Kathryn Chittick notes that Dickens's nine *Monthly* tales received 'about forty notices' whereas his newspaper sketches received none (*Dickens and the 1830s*, London, 1990), 48.

18. 'How much is conveyed . . .': *SB*, 'The Parish', ch.1 (*Journalism* I, 5); 'cut [his] proposed Novel up . . .': *P* I, 34

19. A copy of the relevant issue of the magazine being no longer traceable, the first publication of 'Sentiment' in *Bell's Weekly Magazine* is known only from Hilmer Nielsen, 'Some Observations on *Sketches by Boz*', *D* 34 (1938), 243–5; for full discussion of the influence of contemporary theatre on *SB* see Edward Costigan, 'Drama and Everyday Life in *Sketches by Boz*', *RES*, n.s. 27 (1976), 401–21; for CD's refining of his art as he wrote the *Monthly* tales see Virgil Grillo, *Charles Dickens' Sketches by Boz* (Boulder, CO: Associated University Press, 1974) and DeVries, ch. 2; 'business in the shape of masses of paper': *P* I, 34; for CD's 'French employer' see *P* I, 45 and 52.

20. 'competence in every respect . . .': Drew, *Journalist*, 22; 'rather inclined to what was once called "dandyism"': Kitton, *P and P*, 134.

21. 'A marquee was erected . . .': *Journalism* II, 4; 'having sat with exemplary patience . . .': *Journalism* II, 7.

22. 'Having been for some months past . . .': this paragraph was omitted when 'The Steam Excursion' was collected in *SB* 1836 and in all subsequent editions; for full text of 'The Story Without a Beginning' see *Journalism* II, 10–13.

23. 'A Fable (Not a *gay* one)': see *D* 28 (1932), 2–3; 'inexhaustible food for speculation': *SB*, 'Shops and Their Tenants' (*Journalism* I, 61–9); 'can chuck an old gen'l'm'n into the buss': *SB*, 'Omnibuses' (*Journalism* I, 138–41).

24. 'to instruct and provide for . . .': *P* I, 47 (for John Dickens's letter to Beard see ibid, *n.* 2); 'French employer': almost certainly an agent or businessman called André Filloneau for whom CD apparently did some part-time work (see William J. Carlton, 'Who Was Dickens's French Employer?', *D* 51 (1955), 149–54).

25. 'I have not been taken . . .': *P*, I, 45; 'to trespass at greater length . . .': *Morning Chronicle*, 15 Dec. 1834; 'left a variety of papers . . .': *Monthly Magazine*, n.s. vol.1 (Jan.–June 1835), 137.

26. 'a series of articles under some attractive title . . .': *P* I, 55; for publication details of the Sketches see table in Richard Maxwell's 'Dickens, the Two *Chronicles*, and the Publication of *Sketches by Boz*', *DSA* 9 (1981; hereafter cited as Maxwell), 21–32.

27. 'my first hearty out-and-out appreciator': *P* XII, 539; 'beautiful notice': *P* I, 129: 'able to turn round to you . . .': *P* I, 95.

28. 'if you really love me . . .': *P* I, 62.

29. 'suddenly a young sailor . . .': Mamie Dickens, *My Father as I Recall Him* (London, 1897) 30; 'stiff and formal': *P* I, 109.

30. In revising the text of *SB* for the Cheap Edition (1850) CD altered 'poverty is' to 'wretchedness and distress are' and 'until you can cure it' to 'until you improve the homes of the poor'.

31. 'a numerous concourse . . .': *Journalism* II, 16 ('cutting it fat' was contemporary slang for 'showing off').

32. That great 'magic lantern': *P* IV, 612.

33. 'Astley's', *Evening Chronicle*, 9 May 1835 ('Sketches of London, No.11; *Journalism* I, 106–11); for the fullest and most authoritative discussion of Dickens's lifelong delight in, and literary treatment of, the enjoyments of the people see Paul Schlicke, *Dickens and Popular Entertainment* (London, 1985).

34. CD eventually combined 'Bellamy's' with his earlier one of 'The "House" ' (*Evening Chronicle*, 7 March) to form 'A Parliamentary Sketch – with a Few Portraits' in *SB: Second Series*, 1836; for Mrs Newnham see William J. Carlton, ' "The Old Lady" in *Sketches by Boz*', *D* 49 (1952/53), 149–52.

35. 'in the midst of a lively fight . . .': *Speeches*, 347: 'completely worn out': *P* I, 64; attractions offered by the Colosseum: see *Journalism* II, 17–18.

36. 'How often Black and I . . .': *P* II, 275; 'We are not sufficiently acquainted . . .': 'Sketches of London: No.12 Our Parish', *Evening Chronicle*, 19 May 1835.

37. George Hogarth evidently treasured a proof . . .: see *P* I, 72.

38. For profile of *Bell's Life* see [James Grant], *The Great Metropolis* (1836) II, 132f. (see also DeVries 91, *n.* 41); for the reprinting of *Evening Chronicle* sketches in *The Morning Chronicle* see Maxwell 24; 'the first to discover . . .': see *P* I, 76, *n.* 2.

39. 'melancholy specimen . . .': *SB*, 'The Boarding House' (*Journalism* I, 275); 'most secluded portion . . .': *SB*, 'Miss Evans and the Eagle' (*Journalism* I, 225); 'the populous and improving neighbourhood . . .': *SB*, 'The Dancing Academy' (*Journalism* I, 253).

40. 'We have the most extraordinary partiality . . .': for transcript of the whole passage see Butt and Tillotson, 44.

41. Ainsworth's biographer: S. M. Ellis, author of *William Harrison Ainsworth and His Friends* (2 vols, London, 1911); Ellis states that CD and Ainsworth met in 1834 but the Pilgrim editors consider 1835 to have been more likely (*P* I, 115, *n.* 2)); 'introduced him to his own publisher . . .': Ellis, I, 274; for CD and Macrone see John Sutherland, 'John Macrone: Victorian Publisher', *DSA* 13 (1984), 243–59.

42. 'rich couches and sofas . . .': see *Journalism* II, 25; 'ignorant, drunken, and brutal electors . . .': see *Journalism* II, 28.

43. a more cumbersome joke-title: the Pilgrim editors (*P* I, 82, *n.* 1) suggest that the original title might have been 'Bubbles from the Bwain of Boz and the Graver of Cruikshank', parodying a book published in 1834 called *Bubbles from the Brunnens of Nassau* by Sir F. B. Head.

44. 'two or three new Sketches' *P* I, 83 (some of these like 'The Cook's Shop' and 'Bedlam' never got written, others appeared later); 'tortuous and intricate windings . . .': *SB*, 'A Visit to Newgate' (*Journalism* I, 201); 'rather amusing' anecdotes: *P*, I, 88.

45. 'You cannot throw the interest . . .': *P*, I, 103; 'his first proper story': Peter Ackroyd, *Dickens* (London, 1990), 170; 'an extraordinary idea': *P* I, 98; for discussion of CD's artistry in this story see DeVries 120–6.

46. 'highly gratified with . . .': *P* I, 115.

47. For detailed discussion of CD's alterations to those sketches chosen for volume publication see Butt and Tillotson, ch. 2, also Paul Schlicke, 'Revisions to *Sketches by Boz*', *D* 101 (2005), 29–38; 'here goes our glass to our lips . . .': the final para. of 'The New Year' was cancelled when it was included in *SB* Second Series, thereby causing the sketch to end on a more sombre note.

4 Break-through year, 1836

1. laying of a foundation-stone: see *P* I, 118; for CD's theatre reviews see William J. Carlton, 'Charles Dickens, Dramatic Critic', *D* 56 (1960), 11–27 (hereafter cited as Carlton).

2. 'pilot balloon': for CD's preface to the first (Feb. 1836) volume edition of *SB* see *Journalism* I, xxxix; 'it is not affectation . . .': *P* I, 123f.; 'not only *can* but *will* . . .': *P* I, 126.

3. 'in a state of exquisite torture . . .': *P* I, 119.

4. 'more irons in the fire': *P* I, 137.

5. CD had told Hullah, 'I have a little story by me which I have not yet published, which I think would dramatise well' (*P* I, 113) but the Pilgrim editors doubt that this refers to the plot eventually used for *VC* for which, as suggested above, CD seems to have turned to Goldsmith (seven years later he dismissed *VC* as follows: 'I just put down for everybody what everybody at the

St James's Theatre wanted to say and do, and that they could do best, and I have been most sincerely repentant ever since.' (*P* III, 598)).

6. For CD's favourable review of Braham and his singing of 'fine old English melodies' see Carlton, 24; 'as I should very much like you . . .': *P* I, 118; 'with the most flattering encomiums . . .': *P* I, 122.

7. *The Strange Gentleman*: of this piece CD later wrote, 'The farce I also did as a sort of practical joke, for Harley, whom I have known a long time' (*P* III, 598).

8. For a listing of all known contemporary reviews see Kathryn Chittick, *The Critical Reception of Charles Dickens 1833–1841* (London, 1989); see also Paul Schlicke, ' "Risen like a rocket": the Impact of *Sketches by Boz*', *DQ* 22 (2005), 3–18, and, for a useful anthology from which all quotations in this chapter are taken, see Walter Dexter, 'The Reception of Dickens's First Book', *D* 32 (1936), 43–50; for American publication of *SB* see Patten 95.

9. When CD came to make the final arrangement of the sketches in the 1839 volume edition 'Our Next Door Neighbours' became 'Our Next Door Neighbour' and was, rather awkwardly, tacked on to the 'Our Parish' group.

10. 'a dim recollection . . .': preface to the 'Cheap Edition' of *PP* (1847), see James Kinsley, ed., *PP* (Oxford: Clarendon Edn, 1986; hereafter cited as Kinsley), 883–5.

11. CD tells Catherine that he is 'to write and edit' the new publication 'entirely by myself' (*P* I, 128f.), which does seem to relegate Seymour to the role of contributor rather than controller.

12. 'my views being deferred to . . .': Kinsley 885; for an authoritative detailed account of the origins of *PP*, on which I have freely drawn in this chapter, see Kinsley 'Introduction'.

13. The prospectus is reprinted in full in Kinsley xx–xxi.

14. 'is a very different character . . .': *P* I, 133; Edward Costigan points out in his '*Pickwick's* Stage Manager' (re. CD's extensive use of contemporary theatre, both plays and players, in *PP*) that in Jingle CD draws on a whole sub-genre of popular farce in which the strolling player was a central figure' (*D* 99 (2003), 101–21); 'delivered with extraordinary volubility': *PP*, ch. 2; 'The Ladies' Societies': see *Journalism* I, 36–40.

15. 'the sheets are a weary length . . .': *P* I, 137 (a printer's sheet was the equivalent of 16 printed octavo pages); 'Many literary friends . . .': *P* I, 146; *The Posthumous Papers* . . . '*Boz*': like Seymour's cover-design with its sporting motif this title became less and less appropriate as CD developed his characters and story, and when the story was published in volume form the cover title became *The Posthumous Papers of the Pickwick Club* and the title on the title-page simply *The Pickwick Papers*.

16. For CD's problem with a horse on the Chelmsford–Braintree road see *P* I, 53.

17. 'altogether a very quiet piece of business': Kitton *P and P*, 10; 'the quietest possible . . .': Kitton, *P and P Supp.*, 10; 'I *must* be attended . . .': *P* I, 142.

18. For the full text of Mary Hogarth's letter see *P* I, 689.

19. 'a glass of grog': *P* I, 146; for a full discussion of Seymour's relations with CD and his death see Cohen, *Illustrators*, 39–50.

20. The print run . . . had been halved: see Patten 64f.; 'an impressive leap . . .': Kathryn Chittick, *Dickens in the 1830s* (1990; hereafter cited as Chittick), 62; 'should be very *successful*': *P* I, 147f.

21. 'graveyard' poem: belonging to the school of the so-called 'graveyard poets' of the eighteenth-century whose work tended towards gloom and melancholy, often having a graveyard setting; the young lady for whom CD wrote 'The Ivy Green' was Georgina Ross, sister of one of his fellow-journalists (see William J. Carlton, 'Dickens and the Ross Family', *D* 51 (1955), 58–66).

22. 'as soon after as I can . . .': *P* I, 150; 'preposterously small': see S. M. Ellis, *William Harrison Ainsworth and His Friends* (London, 1911), I, 306; 'most outrageous . . .': *P* I, 151.

23. '*generously angry*': George Orwell, 'Charles Dickens' (11 March 1940), see Peter Davison, ed., *Complete Works of George Orwell* (1998), XII, 56; 'directed exclusively . . .': *SUTH*, pt 2 (*Journalism* I, 486); 'sundry memorable examples . . .': *SUTH*, pt 3 (*Journalism* I, 494).

24. 'an excellent character . . .': *P* I, 207; 'merry dances round rustic pillars': 'A Little Talk about Springtime and the Sweeps', *Library of Fiction*, no. 3 (31 May 1836), reprinted as 'The First of May' in *SB*, Second Series (*Journalism* I, 168–75).

25. For Thackeray's later recalling of his rejection in a Royal Academy speech see *F* 77; for Buss and Browne as illustrators of CD see Cohen, *Illustrators* and, for Browne, see also John Harvey, *Victorian Novelists and Their Illustrators* (London, 1970) and Valerie Browne Lester, *Phiz: The Man Who Drew Dickens* (London, 2004).

26. 'specimen of London life': *P* I, 154; 'speaking highly . . .': *P* I, 151; 'high and mighty satisfaction . . .': *P* I, 159.

27. The parallel with Sterne is suggested by Kinsley (p. xliii); the 'novel character . . .': *P* I, 207, *n*.1; the Pickwick/Don Quixote comparison seems to have been first made by a reviewer of *PP* IX in *The*

Metropolitan Magazine, Jan.1837 (see Collins, *CH* 31); for the contemporary classification of CD's early novels as periodicals see Chittick, ch. 4.

28. 'make some arrangements . . .': *P* I, 157.

29. Robert L. Patten, *George Cruikshank's Life, Times and Art* II (Cambridge, 1996; hereafter cited as Patten, *Cruikshank*), 537, *n.* 37 (Patten notes that the identification was still considered sufficiently newsworthy in March 1837 for the following 'Impromptu' to be inserted into *BM*: 'Who the *dickens* "Boz" could be/Puzzled many a learned elf;/ Till time unveil'd the mystery;/ And *Boz* appear'd as DICKENS' self!').

30. 'his life-long love-affair . . .': Butt and Tillotson, 75; for CD's preface to the second edition of the First Series of *SB* see *Journalism* I, xl.

31. 'all among the nobs': *P* I, 160; 'One wonders just how happy . . .': Patten 32.

32. 'the grand object of interest . . .': see Collins, *CH* 57 (from Abraham Hayward's review of *Pickwick* I–XVII and *Sketches by Boz, Quarterly Review*, 59 (Oct. 1837), 484–518).

33. The multiplicity of CD's references and allusions to the story of Bluebeard seems relevant here; for the most bizarrely personal treatment of the subject, in the 'Bride's Chamber' story in *LT*, see p. 440.

34. For agreement with Thomas Tegg see *P* I, 163; for agreement with Bentley see *P* I, 648–9.

35. CD's book for Tegg never appeared, the volume called *Sergeant Bell and his Raree Show* which Tegg published in Dec. being attributed to George Mogridge (see *P* I, 163, *n.* 2); 'a work on which I might build . . .': *P* I, 165; 'a good round sum': [?24 Aug. 1836]; 'a very great hit': *P* I, 172.

36. For Davenport see Malcolm Morley, 'Dickens Goes to the Theatre', *D* 59 (1963), 165–71; 'clutching eye': see Lady Pollock, *Macready as I Knew Him* (1884), 59.

37. 'fast, energetic composition': see Kinsley lxxv; 'teaching him what his power was': *F* 88; synchronicity: see D. M. Bevington, 'Seasonal Relevance in *Pickwick Papers*', *NCF* 16 (1961–2), 219–30.

38. 'superintending . . . production': *P* I, 177f.; for details about the MS. of *SG* see ibid., 695; 'very well received . . .': *The Times*, 30 Sept. 1836, p. 5, col. B.

39. For detailed discussion of CD's revision of sketches for *SB Second Series* see Butt and Tillotson, 52–6, Duane Devries, *Dickens's Apprentice Years* (London, 1976), and Paul Schlicke, 'Revisions to *Sketches by Boz*', *D* 100 (2004), 29–38; 'little alterations to suit the pencil': *P* I, 183, *n.* 1; for Cruikshanks's collaboration with CD over *SB Second Series* see Patten, *Cruikshank* 28–33.

40. See Angus Easson, 'Imprisonment for Debt in *Pickwick Papers*', *D* 64 (1968), 105–12 (Easson points to a supposed 'true story' of a debtor in *Fraser's Magazine* for Aug. 1836 which CD may have plundered).

41. 'I could not get enough . . .': *P* I, 185.

42. For Hayward and his *Quarterly Review* article on CD see next chapter; 'the lingering disease . . .', *P* I, 188.

43. 'literary production': *P* I, 649; 'periodical publishers': *P* I, 189.

44. 'almost frantic': see *Wellesley Index to Victorian Periodicals* (Toronto: University of Toronto Press), IV, 5; for CD's Agreement with Bentley see *P* I, 649f.

45. 'Blast-Hope': see *P* I, 123, *n*.1; 'Great Protester': Rosemarie Bodenheimer, *Knowing Dickens* (London, 2007), 23 (Bodenheimer aptly cites CD's letters to Maria Beadnell as earlier examples of this genre of Dickensian writing).

46. 'writing on the palm of my hand . . .': *Speeches*, 347; inscribed goblet: this item is now to be seen in the CDM.

5 Editing *Bentley's Magazine*, 1836–1837

1. 'rheumatism in the face': *P* I, 199; re. date of draft prospectus for *Bentley's* see *P* I, 191; 'The management of the Wits' Miscellany . . .': *P* I, 683; 'assume a virtue': Shakespeare, *Hamlet*, III, iv, 160.

2. 'a rattling Irishman': see Miriam M. L. Thrall, *Rebellious Fraser's* (New York, 1934); much to CD's relief: see his letter to Bentley of 30 Nov. (*P* I, 202); the surmise that it was Dickens . . .: see Kathryn Chittick, *Dickens and the 1830s* (Cambridge, 1990; hereafter cited as Chittick), 102.

3. 'capital subject': *P* I, 202 (for the topicality of 'Tulrumble' with regard to national politics see Drew, *Journalist*, 41f.).

4. 'misunderstanding': *P* I, 204; 'to finish the Volume with *eclat*', 'great pains': *P* I, 208.

5. For contemporary reviews of *VC* see *D* 33 (1937), 163–72 (JF's *Examiner* review is given in full).

6. 'which blow their little trumpets . . .': *P* I, 210.

7.   'I arrived home . . .': *P* I, 217.

8.   as he told Irving: see *P* II, 268; for detailed discussion of CD's use of Washington Irving in the Christmas chapters of *PP* see Katharine Carolan, 'The Dingley Dell Christmas', *DSN* 4 (1973), 41–7.

9.   *The Man of Feeling*: in this novel, still highly popular in the early nineteenth century, the sensitive and gentle hero is depicted, like Addison's Sir Roger de Coverley, in a succession of loosely-connected scenes. For full discussion of CD the novelist's gradual move from the stance of editor to the presentation of himself as the reader's friend, a 'sympathetic and familiar narrator', seen in the wider context of authors' redefinition of themselves and their role in the new industrial age, see ch. 2 of Bradley Deane, *The Making of the Victorian Novelist* (New York: Routledge, 2003; hereafter cited as Deane).

10. *Athenaeum*, 7 Jan. 1837, 4–6; *Monthly Review*, Feb. 1837, 153–63.

11. 'really half dead . . .': *P* I, 211; 'I must beg you . . .': *P* I, 223–4; *The Extraordinary Gazette* is partly reprinted in *D* 34 (1938), 45–7 (a copy of this extremely rare document is in the BL, shelf-mark Dex. 306 [2]).

12. For the controversy aroused by Cruikshank's public claim after CD's death to have been the originator of *OT*, not only suggesting the basic idea for the story but also providing CD with outlines of the criminal characters, see Cohen, *Illustrators*, 36–8 and Robert L. Patten, *George Cruikshank's Life, Times, and Art* II (Cambridge, 1996, 50–7, hereafter cited as Patten, *Cruikshank*); 'to shame the cruel . . .': *P* IV, 201; 'his face used to *blaze* with indignation . . .': Lavinia Watson quoted in Collins, *Interviews*, 82; 'loyal to the backbone': see *P* I, 279, *n.* 2.

13. 'a day and night of watching . . .': *P* I, 221; not until baby Oliver is clothed in the 'old calico robes' . . .: as has often been noted, this comment of CD's probably owes something to the so-called 'Clothes Philosophy' developed by Carlyle in *Sartor Resartus* (*Fraser's Magazine*, 1833–34).

14. 'glance at the new poor Law Bill': *P* I, 231; Cruikshank claimed: see Patten, *Cruikshank*, 55; beadle figure . . . in popular culture: see Paul Schlicke, 'Bumble and the Poor Law Satire of *Oliver Twist*', *D* 71 (1975), 149–56 (for the accuracy of CD's New Poor Law satire generally see Humphry House, *The Dickens World* (Oxford, 1960), 92ff.); 'Theatrical Advertisement Extraordinary': see Malcolm Morley, ' "Messrs Four, Two and One" ': *D* 57 (1961), 78–81; '. . . and be very popular': Kathleen Tillotson comments, 'His hopes were fulfilled, and an extra thousand of the February number had to be printed' (*OT*, Oxford: Clarendon Edn, 1966, xix).

15. 'a very low and alarming state': *P* I, 227.

16. For Mary Hogarth's letter see *D* 63(1967), 77–9; 'little piece in one act': *P* I, 226; for a playbill for Harley's 'benefit night' (that is, a night when he would personally receive all the takings) see *D* 33 (1937), 255.

17. Cf. James Kinsley, *PP* (Oxford: Clarendon Edn, 1986; hereafter cited as Kinsley), lxii: 'He [CD] seems from early 1837 to have tried to devote the first part of the month to *Oliver Twist* and the *Miscellany* (which gave him more to do than, in his inexperienced enthusiasm, he had anticipated), and the second part to *Pickwick Papers*'.

18. 'I really have done . . .': *P* I, 227; for 'The Pantomime of Life' see *Journalism* I, 500–07; It has been persuasively argued . . .: see William Axton, *Circle of Fire: Dickens's Vision and Style and the Popular Victorian Theater* (Lexington, KY., 1966), also Edwin Eigner, *The Dickens Pantomime* (London, 1989); for a good example of CD's later use of fantasy and fairy-tale for satirical purposes see 'The Thousand and One Humbugs', *HW* 21 April 1855 (*Journalism* III, 292–8).

19. The Agreement of 17 March 1837 is printed in *P* I, 650–1.

20. 'verisimilitude': Collins, *CH* 34; 'inexhaustible fun': see Kinsley lxx; 'a series of monthly pamphlets', 'a clever series of articles': Chittick 77; for Chapman and Hall's legal action see William J. Carlton, 'A *Pickwick* Lawsuit in 1837', *D* 52 (1956), 33–8; for dramatisations of *PP* see H. Philip Bolton, *Dickens Dramatized* (Boston,1987); for the *Penny Pickwick* and other piracies and plagiarisms see Louis James, *Fiction For the Working Man* (London, 1974).

21. See John Greaves, *Dickens at Doughty Street* (1975), ch.1 (the cash-book is now held in the CDM).

22. 'as many papers for the Miscellany, . . .': *P* I, 249; for his use of the *Clergyman* book see Kinsley lxxiii; 'When I looked, with my mind's eye, . . .': *P* I, 205.

23. 'a little robber . . .': *F* 28; 'I took the liberty . . .' *F* 25; 'settled': *F* 29; I believe the first critic to put forward this explanation of CD's use of Bob Fagin's name in *OT* was John Bayley in his 'Oliver Twist: "Things As They Really Are" ' in John Gross and Gabriel Pearson, eds, *Dickens and the Twentieth-Century* (London, 1962).

24. For full discussion of the history of the text of *OT* between publication in *BM* and the first volume edition see Burton M. Wheeler, 'The Text and Plan of *Oliver Twist*', *DSA* 12 (1983), 41–61 (here-

after cited as Wheeler); Newgate interest: following the huge success of Ainsworth's *Rookwood* (1834), about the highwayman Dick Turpin, there was a great vogue for novels featuring criminals, called 'Newgate novels' after the London prison (see Keith Hollingsworth, *The Newgate Novel, 1830–1847* (Detroit: Wayne State University, 1963), hereafter cited as Hollingsworth).

25.   'resented and hated': Kitton, *P and P*, 140; for text of 'Some Particulars' see *Journalism* I, 508–12; 'Dickens sang two or three songs . . .': see *P* I, 253, *n. 2.*

26.   'overpowered by receiving . . .': *Speeches*, 1.

27.   'went up stairs to bed . . .': *P* I, 263; 'too much happiness to last': see *D and W*, 111; 'moulder away . . .': *P* I, 513; 'I cannot bear the thought . . .': *P* II, 410; 'the grace and ornament . .': *P* I, 258, 259, 263); for influence of the memory of Mary on CD's heroines see *D and W*, ch.3.

28.   'borne up through her severe trial . . .': *P* I, 263; re. topicality of Fagin's defence of hanging see Hollingsworth 114.

29.   'more than ordinarily susceptible . . .': *F* 85; 'keen animation of look': *F* 59; his biographer plausibly suggests . . .': see James Atterbury Davies, *John Forster: A Literary Life* (Leicester, 1983).

30.   'He had a capital forehead . . .': *F* 84; 'You are a part . . .': *P* III, 211; 'I have never felt so strongly . . .': see *P* I, xvii.

31.   'there was nothing written by him . . .': *F* 89; 'knocking a word's brains out . .': see *P* IV, 656; for Ainsworth's comment on JF see S. M. Ellis, *William Harrison Ainsworth and His Friends* I (London, 1911), 292.

32.   For full discussion of this wrangle over *SB* see Patten 38–44; CD later told Mitton that his total earning from the *SB* volumes published by Macrone had been about £400 while the publisher had realised ten times as much (*P* I, 550).

33.   Laing: see *P* I, 28 (CD had himself smuggled into Laing's courtroom early in June so that he would be able to describe his appearance); for Brownlow see David Paroissien, *The Companion to Oliver Twist* (London, 1992).

34.   For Buller's article see Collins, *CH* 52–5; for evidence that CD did indeed visit Waterloo on his excursion see *P* II, 236.

35.   'infernal, rich, plundering . . .': *P* I, 292; for CD's agreement with Bentley of 28 Sept. 1837 see *P* I, 654.

36.   'my long-considered intentions . . .': *OT* (Oxford: Clarendon Edn, 1966); 'Full Report of the First Meeting . . .': see *Journalism* I, 512–30; 'the best I can make it . . .': *P* I, 301.

37.   *Journalism* I, 527.

38.   Ackroyd: see Peter Ackroyd, *Dickens* (London, 1990), 238; 'fanciful photography': see *P* VIII, 668.

39.   'promote the general distress . . .': Jane Austen, *Northanger Abbey* (1818), ch.2; for details of CD's work on the monthly-part issue of *SB* see Butt and Tillotson 56–8.

40.   For Hayward's review see *Quarterly Review* 109 (1837), 484–518, reprinted in part in Collins, *CH* 56–62; 'contains a great deal that I know to be true . . .': *P* I, 316.

41.   My discussion of the *Pickwick* preface owes much to Chittick and to the analysis in Deane, 52–3; notable in it is CD's concern to defend himself against any charge of vulgarity, anticipating his own Mr Podsnap by nearly thirty years ('he trusts that, throughout this book, no incident or expression occurs which could call a blush into the most delicate cheek . . .').

42.   John Drew aptly comments on this passage: 'these opening paragraphs [of ch.17] show Dickens changing genres in midstream in a spectacular manner. In place of the spoof editor-cum-biographer . . . Dickens substitutes an authoritative narrator . . . theorising . . . the relation between art and nature, and between authors and readers, in the magisterial manner of Henry Fielding' (Drew, *Journalist*, 44).

43.   For CD's retrieving a copy of the February *BM* from the printers see *P* I, 319; 'If I can only work out . . .': *P* I, 328.

6   Periodicals into novels, 1837–1839

1.   'a glittering temple . . .': S. M. Ellis, *William Harrison Ainsworth and his Friends* I (1911; hereafter cited as Ellis), 330f.; 'under strong emotion . . .': William Toynbee, ed., *The Diaries of William Charles Macready*, I (1912; hereafter cited as Macready), 426.

2.   For the contracts see *P* I, 655–62, also Patten 71f.; for CD's long and apparently untroubled relations with Coutts's Bank see M. Veronica Stokes, 'Charles Dickens: a Customer of Coutts & Co', *D* 68 (1972), 17–30.

3.   In 1872 Collins noted in his copy of *F*: 'The character of "Nancy" is the finest thing he ever did. He never afterwards saw all sides of a woman's character – saw all round her . . .': 'Wilkie Collins about Charles Dickens', *Pall Mall Gazette*, 20 Jan. 1890.

4. For the *Grimaldi* contract see *P* I, 662–4; 'dreary twaddle': *P* I, 337; 'coughing very fiercely': *MJG* I, 73; 'chosen, as the majority . . .': *MJG* I, 66; 'telling some of the stories . . .': *P* I, 373; a 'colouring': *P* I, 373; 'diffusing himself': see *P* VII, 220 (4 Dec. 1853): 'I diffuse myself with infinite pains through Household Words'.
5. 'attention to his duties . . .': *MJG* I, 194; 'by strict attention . . .': *MJG* II, 223.
6. 'for such a little book . . .': *P* I, 630; 'a great advocate . . .': *SYG*, 'The Theatrical Young Gentleman'; for CD's review of *Pierre Bertrand* see *Journalism* II, 29–31.
7. 'suppurated abscess . . . . resolved to write about them': preface to Cheap Edition of *NN* (1848); 'guide, philosopher and friend': Pope, *Essay on Man* (1732–4), Ep.iv, l.390.
8. Pierce Egan (1774?–1849) was celebrated for his *Life in London* (1820–21), the comic adventures of two young men about town in both high and low life, told with liberal use of slang and much facetiousness.
9. 'thoughts and feelings . . .': *P* I, 629; 'merry banterings round the fire . . .': *P* I, 323; the dreams abruptly ceased: see *P* III, 483–4.
10. 'Here ends this brief attempt . . .': *P* I, 632; 'infant phaenomonon': *P* I, 338; 'looks to me like . . .': *P* I, 355.
11. 'seem disposed to think . . .': *P* I, 630; *Boz's Annual Register*: see *P* I, 378.
12. For CD on Macready's *Lear* see *Journalism* II, 170; the project to help Mrs Macrone was subject to frustrating delays and did not finally appear until 1841 when it was published as *The Pic-Nic Papers*; 'to illustrate ancient and modern London . . .': Ellis 1, 332.
13. 'containing a severe lecture . . .': *P* I, 365 (in *NN* ch. 8 the stepmother of one of Squeers's hapless pupils writes to him to say that she 'took to her bed on hearing that he wouldn't eat fat'); 'scoundrel': *P* I, 482; 'as much comicality . . .': *P* I, 482.
14. 'to keep its ground': *P* I, 370.
15. 'major change': *P* I, xxv.
16. Robert Tracy notes the difference that introducing Monks makes to *Oliver*. 'Monks's supernatural aura brings about a distinct change in the atmosphere of the novel: the sordid world of the thieves becomes one of hauntings and terror' ('Fictional Modes in *Oliver Twist*', *DSA* 17 (1988), 23; hereafter cited as Tracy).
17. For CD's deletion of sentence beginning 'Oh! Where are the hearts . . .' see *OT* (Oxford, Clarendon Edn, 1966), 186.
18. 'the grace and life of our home': *P* I, 257; 'the good in this state of existence . . .': *NN*, ch. 6.
19. Henry Fielding Dickens: see *F* 524; 'alarmingly' ill: *P* I, 392; 'never wrote without the printer at his heels': *F* 124.
20. 'as humorous and amusing . . .': *Bell's Life in London*, 1 April 1838, quoted by Kathryn Chittick in *Dickens and the 1830s* (Cambridge, 1990; hereafter cited as Chittick), 117 – Chittick also quotes another reviewer, in *Bell's Weekly Messenger* (8 April) warning CD not to get above himself in attempts to emulate Fielding and Smollett); re. notices of CD's work in *The Examiner* see Philip Collins, 'Dickens's Self-estimate: Some New Evidence' in Robert B. Partlow, ed., *Dickens the Craftsman: Strategies of Presentation* (London, 1970), 21–43 (for evidence that not all the reviews were by JF see Alec W. Brice, 'Reviewers of Dickens in *The Examiner*: Fonblanque, Forster, Hunt and Morley', *DSN* 3 (1972), 76–80).
21. For plagiarisms of CD see Louis James, *Fiction for the Working Man 1830–1850* (London, 1963), ch. 4, and H. Philip Bolton, *Dickens Dramatized* (Boston, 1987); 'involved and complicated': *P* I, 388 (after finishing *OT* CD offered to dramatise the novel for Macready at Covent Garden but Macready, having looked over the book, felt compelled, extraordinarily enough, to tell CD and JF of its 'utter impracticality . . . for any dramatic purpose' (Macready I, 475)); 'in the middle of the first scene': *F* 125.
22. 'that intrepid astronaut . . .': *P* I, 497, *n*.1; for the spoof love-letter to JF see *P* I, 422.
23. 'and if I have any fortune . . .': *P* I, 413.
24. Two surviving Cruikshank drawings showing Sikes in the condemned cell suggest that CD was considering different endings at quite a late stage – see Patten, *Cruikshank*, 76.
25. 'Full Report of the Second Meeting . . .': see G. A. Chaudhry, 'The Mudfog Papers', *D* 70 (1974), 104–12 (CD was particularly delighted by Cruikshank's illustration for this piece, an 'Automaton Police Office, and real Offenders' (*P* I, 418)); 'very moderate in tone . . .': *P* I, 428; for CD's review see *Journalism* II, 32–9 and for a full discussion of the whole topic of CD and Scott see Ian Duncan, *Modern Romance and the Transformation of the Novel* (Cambridge, 1992), chs 4 and 5.
26. 'the steam to get up afresh . . .': *P* I, 425; 'for Oliver purposes': *P* I, 428; doggerel verse: see *P* I, 432–3; for agreement with Bentley see *P* I, 666–74; for Lister's review see Collins, *CH*, 71–7 (the review was, CD told JF, 'all even *I* could wish and what more can I say!' (*P* I, 438)).

27. For CD's emendations to the *BM* text see Burton M. Wheeler, 'The Text and Plan of *Oliver Twist*', *DSA* 12 (1983), 41–61; 'such an out and outer': *P* I, 441; for CD's departure from convention with regard to heroes of mysterious origin see Tracy.

28. re. the offending *Oliver* plate Patten comments that JF's over-the-top reaction to all the later plates in the book, expressed in a letter to Bentley, may have influenced CD (Patten, *Cruikshank*, 84–7).

29. 'prodigious exertions': *P* I, 449, *n*.3; 'beautiful beyond expression': *P* I, 634; 'the birth-place . . .': *P* I, 634; payment for harpists: see *P* I, 635.

30. 'I rather suspect . . .' and 'Mr Dickens was then writing *Nicholas Nickleby* . . .': Ellis I, 340–2; another possible Nicklebeian outcome: Butt and Tillotson note that CD prepared for the possibility of introducing the cotton-mills into *Nickleby* by introducing the Cheerybles – had he located their business in Lancashire, like that of the Grants, he could have sent Nicholas to work for them there (Butt and Tillotson, 177, *n*. 1).

31. Text from Dick's Standard Plays, no. 470 (London, 1883) – CD salvaged the end of this speech for re-use in the mouth of Mr Mantalini when he is threatening to drown himself in *NN* ch. 34, written during January); 'he reads as well . . .': Macready I, 480.

32. For the Cerberus Club see *P* I, 637, and for a picture of the three goblets the friends had specially engraved with the head of Cerberus and their own initials for use at club meetings see *D* 46 (1950), 2.

33. 'enriching everybody . . .': *F* 116; 'announcing, in the pleasantest manner . . .': see R. H. Barham's letter to Bentley quoted in *P* I, 502, *n*.1 (Barham was mediating with Bentley on CD's behalf); 'Familiar Epistle . . .'; see *Journalism* I, 552–4 (John Drew notes in his 'Transport' entry for *ORCD* that the mail coaches were a matter for national pride in their day and the guards, being royal appointees, were entitled to wear the royal livery, the 'scarlet coat and golden lace' to which CD refers in his piece).

34. For the Agreement with Bentley see *P* I, 674–5 (CD bound himself to write nothing else before finishing *BR* for Bentley apart from *NN*, 'an Annual publication in one volume' for Chapman and Hall, and the book he was editing for Mrs Macrone's benefit).

35. 'looked almost verdant . . .': *The United Services Gazette*, 9 Feb. 1839, quoted by Chittick, 132; 'come out rather unique': *F* 125.

36. Lady Holland: see *P* I, *n*.2; 'presentable': see *P* I, 412 *n*.3; ' "bust" the boiler': *F* 125; 'trusty friends': *P* I, 602; 'The end of a most prosperous and happy year . . .': *P* I, 640.

37. 'Directly I build up . . .': *P* I, 454; 'The want of £15 . . .': for John Dickens's importunity see Arthur Waugh, *A Hundred Years of Publishing: Being the Story of Chapman and Hall Ltd* (London, 1930), 40–2, also Ralph Strauss, *Dickens: A Portrait in Pencil* (London, 1928), 108–10 (Strauss shows that CD's brother Alfred also solicited loans from Chapman and Hall).

38. All quotations in this paragraph come from CD's letters from Exeter to Catherine, Forster and Mitton (see *P* I, 517–25).

39. 'much athletic competition': *F* 131; 'No spoonful of soup . . .': see *Speeches*, 3.

40. 'Here we have the real identical man . . .': *Fraser's Magazine* 22 (1840), 113 (later, however, George Eliot was famously unimpressed when she saw the painting engraved for *F*: 'that keepsakey, impossible face which Maclise gave him . . . has been engraved . . . in all its odious beautification' (J. W. Cross, ed., *George Eliot's Life* (London, 1885), III,145). The portrait itself may today be seen in the National Portrait Gallery.

41. 'Maclise . . . was very handsome . . .': Kate Perugini, 'Charles Dickens, as a Lover of Art and Artists', *Magazine of Art*, n.s.,I (1902–03), 125–30; 'my inability to answer that question . . .': *P* I, 535.

42. 'literary gentleman . . . who had dramatized . . .': *NN*, ch. 48.

43. 'strain on his fancy': *F* 139.

44. 'Work': *P* I, 641–2; 'I have had pretty stiff work . . .': *F* 126.

45. 'Thank God I have lived . . .': *P* I, 642; 'Surely this is something to gratify me . . .': Macready II, 24; for CD's 29 Sept. article on Scott and his publishers see *MP* 86–89; '*too* splendid dinner': Macready II, 25; 'the bold adventure . . .': Michael Slater, ed., *The Catalogue of the Suzannet Charles Dickens Collection* (London, 1975), 183.

46. Cf. Chittick 138: 'The *Nickleby* preface and portrait were an important preparation for the initial success of *Master Humphrey's Clock*'.

47. For *Examiner* review see Collins, *CH* 47–51 (Collins attributes this review to JF but subsequent research by Alec Brice suggests that a more likely author was Leigh Hunt: see note 20 above); *The Bee*: see above, p. 13.

48. CD was anxious that his participation in the *Ballad* should not become public, no doubt because of his contract with Bentley which bound him not to write anything other than *NN* and two other specified items before delivering *BR* – see his letter to Cruikshank (*P* I, 559).

49. 'scrutinise': *P* I, 596; 'in the agonies of house-letting . . .': *P* I, 603.
50. 'going forthwith tooth and nail . . .': *P* I, 589; for the last phase of CD's stormy relations with Bentley see Patten 84–7 and for the 2 July Agreement with Bentley see *P* II, 471–5.
51. 'the old gentleman does not say . . .': *P* I, 601f.

7   The *Master Humphrey* experiment, 1840–1841

1. For detailed discussion of CD's plans in relation to his eighteenth-century models see Kathryn Chittick, *Dickens and the 1830s* (Cambridge, 1990), 139–43.
2. For CD's outline to Forster of the proposed new magazine see *F* 140.
3. For the *MHC* Agreement see *P* II, 464–71; 'at which I heartily rejoice': William Toynbee, ed., *Diaries of William Charles Macready* (London, 1912; hereafter cited as Macready), II, 56.
4. 'Saxe Humbug . . .': *P* II, 16; 'Dickens was a very clever man . . .': *P* I, 618, *n*.2.
5. re. the Halls as originals of the Chirrups see Arthur Waugh, *A Hundred Years of Publishing* (London, 1930), 6; 'rather too sumptuous a dinner . . .': see *P* II, 260, *n*. 2.
6. For Lady Blessington and Count D'Orsay see Michael Sadleir, *Blessington–D'Orsay: A Masquerade* (London, 1933); 'dandy *par excellence* . . .': Charles Mackay, *Through the Long Day* (London, 1887), I, 309; 'desperately learned': *P* II, 36.
7. 'face of dingy blackguardism . . .': Collins, *Interviews*, 18; 'I would go at all times farther . . .': *F* 839; 'did not seem to mind him overmuch . . .': C. R. Sanders et al., eds, *The Collected Letters of Thomas and Jane Welsh Carlyle*, XII (Durham, N.C.: Duke University Press, 1985), 80–1; for CD's relations with, and literary response to, Carlyle see Michael K. Goldberg, *Carlyle and Dickens* (Athens: University of Georgia Press, 1972) and William Oddie, *Dickens and Carlyle: The Question of Influence* (London, 1972).
8. 'great, London, back-slums kind of walk . . .': *P* II, 152; 'rustic walk': *P* II, 66; 'There are conveniences . . .': *P* VII, 831; 'Oh our dear friend . . .': *P* VII, 812.
9. For Macready's account of the dinner-table quarrel (at which Maclise was also present) see Macready II, 74 (under date of 16 Aug. 1840).
10. 'this old file . . .': *F* 143; for Thomas Humphrey see T. P. Cooper, 'Master Humphrey. His Shop and His Stock', *D* 27 (1931), 91–6; for the inquest on the dead baby see 'Some Recollections of Mortality' in *UT* (*Journalism* IV, 218–28); for John Overs see, for example, *P* II, 19f. where CD offers to go over one of Overs's stories with him for an hour and a half the following Sunday; 'a tendency to retreat': see Malcolm Andrews, 'Introducing Master Humphrey', *D* 67 (1971), 70–86.
11. 'England's foremost painter . . .': Cohen, *Illustrators*, 125; for Leonardo Cattermole's reminiscences see Kitton, *P and P*, 180.
12. large page size: *MHC* was printed on super royal octavo, that is, with a page size of $10 \times 6\frac{3}{4}$ inches; 'old quaint room . . .': *P* II, 8; '*most famous*': *P* II, 12; 'Believe me . . .': *P* II, 199; 'full, detailed and enthusiastic instructions . . .': John Harvey, *Victorian Novelists and their Illustrators* (London, 1970; hereafter cited as Harvey), 114; see also Joan Stevens's ' "Woodcuts dropped into the Text": the Illustrations in *The Old Curiosity Shop* and *Barnaby Rudge*', *Studies in Bibliography* 20 (1967), 13–34, and Beryl Gray, 'Man and Dog: Text and Illustration in *The Old Curiosity Shop*', *D* 103 (2007), 125–43.
13. For examples of CD's response to Bath see *PP* ch. 35 and *BH* ch. 28; 'old dark murky rooms': *Clock* 4 (*OCS*, ch.1); for discussion of CD's responsiveness to national cultural developments in his work on *OCS* see Paul Schlicke, 'Embracing the New Spirit of the Age: Dickens and the Evolution of *The Old Curiosity Shop*', *DSA* 12 (2002; hereafter cited as Schlicke), 1–35.
14. I derive my word-counts from Elizabeth Brennan, ed., *OCS* (Oxford: Clarendon Edn, 1997; hereafter cited as Brennan), xxix, *n*. 67
15. 'What will the wiseacres say . . .': *P* II, 50.
16. 'How Dickens, with his talents . . .': see review quoted in Paul and Priscilla Schlicke, *The Old Curiosity Shop: An Annotated Bibliography* (New York, 1988) no. 86 (see this volume for a thorough survey of contemporary reviews); 'Dickens is sadly flat . . .': see Gordon N. Ray, ed., *Letters and Private Papers of W. M. Thackeray*, I (London, 1945), 444 (Ray relates this letter to *Clock* 2 but Patten notes (p.110) that four or five numbers had appeared by the time Thackeray wrote it).
17. 'and to which I shall recur at intervals': this phrase does not appear in the American Lea and Blanchard edition of *MHC* that was set from first proofs but was added before UK publication (see Elizabeth Brennan, ed., *OCS* (Oxford, Clarendon Edn, 1997; hereafter cited as Brennan), 7); '[there] was taking gradual form . . .': *F* 146; 'a more removed ground': Shakespeare, *Hamlet*, I, iv, l. 43.
18. 'to give it a fair chance': *F* 147; its circulation touched . . . 100,000: see Patten 110.
19. 'room to turn . . .': *F* 147; for discussion of CD at work on *OCS* see Brennan xxvii–lxvi, also Angus Easson, '*The Old Curiosity Shop*: from Manuscript to Print', *DSA* I (1970), 93–128: Easson notes

(p.101) that 'while [CD's] superfluous writing rarely shows signs of being spun out to make up space, the passages concocted to fill underwritten episodes are often singularly vacant, occasionally mere repetition'; Sally Brass disconcertingly reveals . . .: for the significance of this change see Angus Easson, 'Dickens's Marchioness Again', *Modern Languages Review* 65 (1970), 517–18.

20. 'I *mean* to make much of him': F 146 (for the importance of CD's development of Swiveller in the evolution of *OCS* see Schlicke 24–7); '*valued suggestion*'; F 150; for the point in the serialisation of *OCS* at which CD decided Nell should die see Malcolm Andrews's review of Brennan in *D* 94 (1998), 133–5.

21. 'in common with other vagabonds': *D* 104 (2008), 142 (CD refers to the custom of 'Saint Monday' when workmen took Mondays off to allow them to recuperate from Sunday's dissipations); 'If I had read it . . .': F 147.

22. For the *MC* letters see *P* II, 86f. and 90; Thackeray: for Thackeray's powerful account of this occasion see his 'Going To See A Man Hanged', *Fraser's Magazine* 22 (1840), 150–8 in which he compares a young prostitute he saw in the crowd with CD's depiction of Nancy in *OT* and reproaches CD for sentimentalising the character; 'a ghastly night in Hades . . .': Kitton, *P and* P, 142–3.

23. For the Agreements with Bentley and Chapman and Hall see *P* II, 471–7; claret jug: see *F* 159f.

24. For details of CD's finances at this time see Patten 112–3 and *P* II, 345–6 and 348–51; 'disgusted . . .': *P* II, 350; 'the least offensive way . . .': *P* II, 350.

25. 'Such getting up of the steam . . .': K. J. Fielding and David Sorenson, eds, *Jane Carlyle: Newly Selected Letters* (Aldershot: Ashgate Publishing, 2004), 143; court dress: see *P* II, 95; 'They *seem* perfectly contented . . .': *P* II, 109.

26. 'a strong and vivid description . . .': *P* VII, 818; for the 'terrors' of Norfolk Island see Robert Hughes, *The Fatal Shore* (London, 1987), ch.13.

27. For quotations from Eleanor Christian see Collins, *Interviews*, 33–41; for Eliza Franklin's memories see David Parker and Anne and Roger Wilson, 'Letters of a Guest at Devonshire Terrace', *D* 95 (1999), 51–60.

28. In his preface to *MHC* Vol. 3 CD acknowledges a particular debt for a 'beautiful thought' in the penultimate chapter of *OCS* (describing Grandfather after Nell's death) to a passage in 'Ginevra', one of the verse tales in Rogers's *Italy* (1822–28).

29. 'would be a good thing to open a story with . . .': F 148; 'like an Allegory . . .': see Collins, *CH* 94–8; 'very pretty drawing': *P* II, 49 (for Williams, a distinguished engraver, and why he might have been asked to do this scene rather than Browne or Cattermole see Cohen, *Illustrators*, 135–8); 'books which put us in a better humour . . .': *P* II, 221, *n.* 7.

30. See Brennan, Appendix B; also Stone, *WN*, 3–15.

31. *Speeches* 5 ('The poet', said CD, was 'entitled to worship the stars; but when they contemplated him paying his adoration to stars and garters too, that was indeed a very different thing.').

32. 'none of your maudlin gentry . . .': *P* II, 139–40; re. Overs and Carlyle's *Chartism* see Sheila M. Smith, 'John Overs to Charles Dickens: a Working-Man's Letter and its Implications', *VS* 18 (1974), 195–217 (Smith suggests CD may have had Overs in mind when creating Will Fern in *C*); for Overs's making a carving of John Dickens's crest see *P* II, 139–40 and for the crest itself see *P* XII, 326.

33. 'charades and other frolics': *P* II, 169; 'Old wounds bleed afresh . . .': *F* 150; 'very melancholy to think . . .': *P* II,188; 'four mortal pages': *P* II, 190.

34. 'a panoramic vision . . .': Drew, *Journalist*, 51; in his 'Clock Work: *The Old Curiosity Shop* and *Barnaby Rudge* (*DSA*, 30 (2001), 23–43) Robert Tracy comments that this passage is 'a kind of summary for all Dickens's novels, especially those social and moral contrasts which shape them, and his readiness to show complacent middle-class readers how unjust, wicked and fragile their society is'.

35. For the Scott parallels in *BR* see Butt and Tillotson, 78.

36. Joanna Southcote: Joanna Southcote or Southcott (1750–1814) was a religious fanatic who prophesied that she would give birth to the second Messiah and underwent a prolonged false pregnancy; 'a good honest Saxon name, I think': *P* II, 207.

37. 'I didn't stir out . . .': *P* II,164; 'I want elbow room terribly': *P* II, 385; 'taking it all in all . . .': George Gissing, *Charles Dickens: A Critical Study* (1902; hereafter cited as Gissing), 224; 'like all Dickens's animals': John Ruskin *Ariadne Florentina* (E. T. Cooke and A.D.O. Wedderburn, eds, *Works of Ruskin* XXII (London, 1902–12), 467; for *BR* as a whole, however, Ruskin had no time: 'an entirely profitless and monstrous story . . .'); pet ravens: the last days of his first raven is the subject of one of CD's best comic set-piece letters (*P* II, 230–2) and he later wrote a splendid celebration of both birds in his preface to the Cheap Edition of *BR* (1849) – see also his later *HW* articles supposedly authored by a raven (*Journalism* II, 189–93); 'put in more relief': *P* II, 167.

38. 'too strong': *P*, II, 253 (in *n.*3 on this page the Pilgrim editors give some examples of JF's toning down of some of CD's more melodramatic phrasing).

39. The theme of the parent/child relationship in *BR* is explored by Steven Marcus in his *Dickens From Pickwick to Dombey* (London, 1965) in which he comments (p.170) that *BR* is 'executed with greater mastery, deliberateness and coherence than Dickens had ever revealed before'.

40. 'like a cork . . .': Collins, *Interviews*, 36.

41. For detailed discussion of the effect of these inserted paragraphs see Robert L. Patten, ' "The Story-weaver at His Loom": Dickens and the Beginning of *The Old Curiosity Shop*' in R. Partlow, ed., *Dickens the Craftsman: Strategies of Presentation* (Carbondale: University of Illinois Press, 1970); Patten misdates the writing of these paragraphs, however, believing them to have been inserted in the made-up copy of the *Shop* sent to Burdett Coutts on 20 April 1841 (*P* II, 266) whereas they were written for the first separate edition of the novel published 15 Dec. 1841– see Schlicke, 8–9; see also Ian Duncan, *Modern Romance and Transformations of the Novel: The Gothic, Scott, Dickens* (Cambridge, 1992; hereafter cited as Duncan), 216f. where Duncan notes the inserted passage 'offers one of Dickens's fullest accounts of the process of imaginative invention'.

42. See *Speeches*, 8–15.

43. 'soar to the sublime': *P* II, 323; 'such haunts as you might imagine . . .': *P* II, 324; 'perfectly horrific': *P* II, 326.

44. 'people whom politically I despise . . .': *P* II, 379; 'The Fine Old English Gentleman': for this and CD's other squibs see *PV*; 'I doubt if he ever enjoyed . . .': *F* 190; for CD and *The Edinburgh Review* see Philip Collins, 'Dickens and the *Edinburgh Review*', *RES* n.s., 14 (1963), 167–72; 'skirmisher and sharpshooter': see Drew, *Journalist*, 53.

45. Chittick, 176; 'pray give us something to love . . .': *P* II, 320; 'tumbled and bent . . .': *P* VI, 427.

46. 'Scott failed in the sale . . .': *P* II, 365; 'and put the town in a blaze . . .': *P* II, 365; for the 7 Sept. 1841 Agreement with Chapman and Hall see *P* II, 478–81; for comment on this Agreement see Patten 125–6.

47. 'some fear as to the use . . .': *F* 194; 'simple and honest hearts': *P* II, 394; 'vast solitudes': *P* II, 218; 'haunted by visions . . . *must* be managed . . .': *P* II, 380–1; 'cried dismally': *P* II, 381.

48. 'personally affectionate . . .': *P* VIII, 539; Pope: see *Essay on Man* (London, 1732–44), iv, l.390; 'manly upright thinking': *F* 171; 'old-fashioned moralising . . .': Gissing, 53f.; the full text of CD's 9 Oct. address to *MHC* readers is reprinted in Butt and Tillotson, 88–9 (see also *P* II, 389, *n.*1).

49. 'It seems like losing her . . .': *P* II, 410; 'may I not be forgiven . . .': *P* II, 411.

50. proto-cinematic: this important aspect of CD's art has been studied in depth by Grahame Smith in his *Dickens and the Dream of Cinema* (Manchester, 2003); 'In this kind of work . . .': *P* II, 418.

51. a further address to readers: see *P* II, 389, *n.*1; Protestant Associations: see Butt and Tillotson, 83; Cattermole's tailpiece illustration to *MHC*: Cohen believes (*Illustrators*, 133) this shows 'the artist's weariness'; for detailed comment on the *BR* illustrations see Cohen, also Harvey, 125–9.

52. 'for my household Gods . . .': *P* II, 440; 'piled high with . . . Travels': John D. Sherwood, quoted in Collins, *Interviews*, 44–7 (Sherwood quotes CD as saying of one of the coloured maps, 'I could light my cigar against the red-hot State of Ohio'); 'a perpetual state of weighing anchor': *P* II, 444; 'I have set my heart on . . .': *P* II, 426.

8   America brought to book, 1842

1. 'to draw wide national conclusions . . .': see Collins, *Interviews*, 45.

2. For CD's library in 1844 see *P* IV, Appendix C; in his 'Battle of the Travel Books' chapter in *Innocent Abroad: Charles Dickens's American Engagements* (Lexington: University Press of Kentucky, 1990) Jerome Meckier assumes, based on his reading of *AN* and *MC*, that CD not only knew De Tocqueville's work but was definitely engaging with it, as well as with Trollope and Martineau (on both of whom he is said to make 'an onslaught'); CD was, Meckier asserts (p.79), determined to show 'that he could evaluate a foreign country better than one Frenchman and two ladies had'.

3. 'shaking hands' with him: *P* II, 438; Pitchlynn: his full name was Peter Perkins Pitchlynn and he was only one quarter Choctaw, a fact of which CD was perhaps unaware (see *AN*, ed. Fred Schwarzbach, London: Everyman Dickens, 1997), 266; 'They are a fine people . . .': *P* II, 207; 'to go into the slave districts . . .': *P* 447, *n.* 2; transposing into his text . . . material from a pamphlet: first noted by Louise H. Johnson in 'The Source of the Chapter on Slavery in Dickens's *American Notes*', *American Literature* 14 (1943), 427–30.

4. 'cheerfulness about the whole thing': *P* III, 9, *n.*3.

5. Pier Morand: see Noel C. Peyrouton, 'Re: Memoir of an *American Notes* Original', *DS* 4 (1968), 23–31, which reproduces Morand's sketches of CD and Catherine; 'pioneer first class hotel':

Edward F. Payne, *Dickens Days in Boston* (Boston,1927; hereafter cited as Payne), 14; 'one continued shout . . .': James T. Fields, *Yesterdays with Authors* (1872), 129.

6. 'I have the correspondence of a secretary of state . . .': P III, 35; 'a reverential account': see 'Four Months with Charles Dickens', *Atlantic Monthly*, 26 (1870), 476–82, 591–9, extracts in Collins, *Interviews*, 59–61; for Putnam himself see Noel C. Peyrouton, 'Mr "Q," Dickens's American Secretary', *D* 59 (1963), 156–9.

7. 'solace of the lonely . . .': *Boston Daily Mail*, 24 Jan. 1842, quoted Payne 25 (see Payne also for other details in this paragraph); for the reaction of the Puritan press see Paul B. Davis, 'Dickens and the American Press 1842', *DS* 4 (1968; hereafter cited as Davis), 32–77; 'dwellers in log-houses . . .': *Speeches*, 20; for CD and the international copyright question see James J. Barnes, *Authors, Publishers and Politicians: The Quest for an Anglo-American Copyright Agreement 1815–1854* (London, 1974), ch. 4.

8. 'Boston is what . . .': P IV, 11; 'a glorious fellow . . .': see P III, 39, n. 2; 'The American poor . . .': P III, 50.

9. The *Aegis* notice is reprinted in full by Davis, pp. 58–61.

10. 'My blood so boiled . . .': P III, 83; all quotations from American newspapers are drawn from Davis 68–9.

11. 'with open arms': P III, 70; 'the value of your labours . . .': F 211; 'magnificent saloon . . .' 'surmounted by an eagle . . .': see W. Glyde Wilkins, *Charles Dickens in America* (London, 1911; hereafter cited as Glyde Wilkins), 109f., 112; 'into such really good society . . .': *Aurora* quotations taken from P III, 72f., n. 5.

12. 'pass through the country more quietly . . .': *Speeches*, 28; Washington Irving: for CD's indebtedness to Irving see Malcolm Andrews, 'Dickens, Washington Irving, and National Identity', *DSA* 29 (2000), 1–15; 'I have no rest . . .': P III, 87; 'out half the night . . .': P III, 161.

13. Poe's review of *OCS* is reprinted in George H. Ford and Lauriat Lane, *The Dickens Critics* (Ithaca, 1961); for other reviews of CD by Poe see Collins, *CH*, 105–11, and for detailed discussion of CD and Poe see Gerald G. Grubb, 'The Personal and Literary Relationships of Dickens and Poe', *NCF* 5 (1950), 1–22, 101–20, 209–21; 'for two mortal hours . . .': Putnam, 'Four Months with Charles Dickens: During his First Visit to America (1842)', *Atlantic Monthly* 26 (1870), 476–82, 591–9; 'perfectly game': P III, 205 (for Catherine in America see Lillian Nayder, 'The Other Dickens and America: Catherine in 1842', *DQ* 19 (2002), 141–50).

14. 'like throwing corn . . .': see Glyde Wilkins 172; 'every effort of my pen . . .': *Speeches*, 34.

15. 'feel for the humblest . . .': quoted by Glyde Wilkins 184 (for CD's response see *Speeches*, 34–6); 'like a kind of Queen and Albert': P III, 154; 'people coming in by hundreds . . .': P III, 61.

16. 'Kate sat down . . .': P III, 180;'Arabian-night city': P III, 193; Frances Trollope and the Mississippi: see her *Domestic Manners of the Americans* (London, 1832), ch. 3; 'intolerably conceited': P III, 202.

17. 'that spirit which directs my life': P III, 35; 'she has been here many times . . .': P III, 270.

18. 'a perplexingly divided . . . duty': P III, 211 (CD quotes Desdemona's famous speech in Shakespeare's *Othello*, I, iii); 'Oh! The sublimated essence . . .': P III, 211; for texts of the International Copyright documents see P III, 621–4.

19. 'The helpless hypochondriacal Cockney . . .': see Andrew Patterson, 'The Amateur Theatricals in Montreal', *D* 38 (1942), 72–4; 'I really do believe . . .': P III, 246.

20. 'FEVERED with anxiety . . .': P III, 248; for an interesting critique of CD's description of the Shaker Village and West Point in *AN* see Duncan A. Carter and Laurence W. Mazzeno, 'Dickens's Account of the Shakers and West Point: Rhetoric or Reality?', *D* 72 (1976), 131–9; 'nothing but water': P III, 231; United Vagabonds: P III, 293.

21. 'the pretty cottages . . .': *AN*, end of Book II, ch. 8; 'no man was so inclined . . .': F 835.

22. 'unrivalled quickness . . .': F 245; 'better letters I have never heard read . . .': quoted in P III, 269, n. 2.

23. See Patricia M. Ard, 'Charles Dickens' Stormy Crossing: The Rhetorical Voyage from Letters to *American Notes*', *Nineteenth-Century Prose* 23 (1996), 34–42, for the problems CD encountered in recycling private discourse for public consumption and how he dealt with them; for Hall's recommendation to CD of using letters to friends written on the spot for the compilation of travel-books see his letter of 3 Sept. 1841, quoted by David Paroissien in the 'Introduction' to his André Deutsch edition of *PFI* (1973), 30.

24. 'the *personal narrative* . . .': F 244; 'The President got up . . .': P III, 117; 'We had very queer customers . . .': P III, 178.

25. 'How long he is, growing up . . .': P III, 191; Macready and John Dickens : Macready noted in his diary on 21 Feb., 'Wrote to Mr J. Dickens. Sent him £20, desiring him not to mention it to his son.'

Forster had advised £10 – but he is Dickens's father, though –' (William Toynbee, ed., *Diaries of William Charles Macready*, II, 158).

26. 'I feel as if Providence . . .': *P* III, 76, *n.* 3; 'I have never in my life . . .': *P* III, 77; 'drop into poetry': see *P* III, 301, *n.* 4.

27. 'Her name is but a short one . . .': *P* III, 242; 'Do they commit suicide . . .': *P* III, 244 (see also his account of the life and death of John Dando, the celebrated oyster-glutton, in a later letter to Felton (*P* III, 291)).

28. no 'King or Emperor . . .': *P* III, 43; 'It is no nonsense . . .': *P* III, 34f.; the greatest Loser . . .': *P* III, 76; 'It is well known . . .': see Davis 68; 'By one side . . .': see Davis 71.

29. 'rather yellow teeth': Davis 73; 'Boz Pork and Beans': see Noel C. Peyrouton, 'Bozmania vs. Bozphobia: a Yankee Pot-Pourri', *DS* 4 (1968), 89.

30. 'People *eat* him here': see Collins, *Interviews*, 53.

31. one of the most perspicacious of modern Dickens critics: see Alexander Welsh, *From Copyright to Copperfield: The Identity of Dickens* (London, 1987), ch.3: 'The evidence suggests that he probably did go to America with the idea of doing something about international copyright, and in any event he quickly came to understand that his motives might be questioned. Either way, he felt sufficiently uncomfortable to realize subjectively the great Pecksniff' (p. 39).

32. 'pair of petticoats': *P* III, 440; harem fantasy: see also on this theme CD's Christmas story for 1859, 'The Haunted House'; for Georgina see Arthur A. Adrian, *Georgina Hogarth and the Dickens Circle* (London, 1957).

33. Quotations in this paragraph taken from CD's letter to Lady Holland of 8 July 1842 (*P* III, 262–3).

34. 'working like a dray-horse': *P* III, 268; 'seem to prepare the reader . . .': *P* III, 270.

35. For the full text of CD's letter to *The Morning Chronicle* see *P* III, 278–85.

36. For CD's rescue of the deaf and dumb child see *F* 281.

37. On problems of tone in *AN* see Drew, *Journalist*, 65: 'At times the reader is assumed to be a British armchair traveller; at times the irony is intended for *laissez aller* British government officials; at times wrath is directed at the American press . . .'; '*dash* at': *F* 279; 'very good': *P* III, 311; empathetic account of . . . a generic prisoner: 'The Solitary Prisoner' was the subject of one of the four illustrations done by Frank Stone, no doubt following CD's suggestions, for the Library Edition of *AN* in 1859.

38. 'kindly and good-humouredly': *P* III, 346; 'In reply to a question . . .': *P* 283.

39. For full text of circular see *P* III, 625–7, and 311, *n.* 4 and 312 *nn.* 1–3 for details of its circulation in the American press, and responses to it; also Davis 32–3.

40. For the full text of the forged letter see *P* III, 626; 'absolute *baseness of heart* . . .': Davis 33.

41. as one modern scholar has observed: see Drew, *Journalism*, 65.

42. The MS. of *AN* is in the Forster Collection, Victoria and Albert Museum; see Joel J. Brattin, 'Slavery in Dickens's Manuscript of *American Notes for General Circulation*', *DQ* 20 (2003), 153–65.

43. For an exhaustive account of JF's article and its reception see Sidney P. Moss, *Charles Dickens' Quarrel with America* (New York, 1984), ch. 2.

44. as has been well said: see K. J. Fielding, ' "American Notes" and Some English Reviewers', *Modern Language Review* 59 (1964; hereafter cited as Fielding), 527–37; 'are much larger than have ever been known . . .': *P* III, 344; 'Your account of the subscriptions . . .': MS. Martin Nason.

45. Macaulay had asked to review *AN* for the *Edinburgh* but withdrew after seeing the book which he thought 'at once frivolous and dull' – he did not want to offend CD by criticising it because he still hoped, as did Napier, to get CD to write for the *Edinburgh*; for details of English reviews of *AN* see Fielding, also Collins, *CH* 118–39; 'one of the most suicidal productions . . .': *Southern Literary Messenger* 9, Jan. 1843, quoted in *P* III, 348, *n.* 2, where the review is attributed to Edgar Allen Poe but there seems to be no reliable scholarly basis for this – see Richard P. Benton, 'The System of Dr Tarr and Prof. Fether: Dickens or Willis?', *Poe Newsletter* I (Washington State University, 1968), 7–9.

46. 'I have some notion . . .': *P* III, 303; 'some terribly dreary iron-bound spot . . .': *P* III, 326; 'the very dreariest . . .': *P* III, 356; Tintagel: *P* III, 358, *n.*1.

47. For CD's review of Londonderry's *Letter to Lord Ashley* see *Journalism* II, 44–51; re. possible illustrators for the new work : as late as 5 Nov. CD was willing to consider an application from John Leech to provide illustrations for the new book 'consistently with that regard which I feel bound to pay to Mr Browne' (*P* III, 359).

9 'The turning-point of his career': England, Italy, England, 1842–1845

1. 'earthy old Churches': *P* III, 414f.; CD and Cornwall: see also CD's 1855 Christmas story 'The Holly-Tree Inn' for his vivid reminiscence of the Cornish miners' Feast into which he and his companions stumbled during the tour (Ruth Glancy, ed., *CS*, London: Everyman Dickens, 1996, 99–100).

2. Forster tells us: see *F* 291.

3. 'the notion of taking Pecksniff ...': *F* 291; 'smooth self-righteousness ... conspicuous puritanism': see Peter Mandler's entry for Samuel Carter Hall in *Oxford Dictionary of National Biography*; 'the snivelling insolence ...': *P* VIII, 162.

4. See Margaret Cardwell, ed., *MC*, Clarendon Edn (Oxford, 1982; hereafter cited as Cardwell), xviii (the four MS. pages showing CD trying out variant versions are reproduced in facsimile in Stone, *WN*).

5. John Leech: see *P* III, 358, 361, also Valerie Browne Lester, *Phiz: The Man Who Drew Dickens* (London, 2004; hereafter cited as Lester), 92, and Michael Steig, *Dickens and Phiz* (London, 1978) 60–85; in *MC*, Steig comments, 'Browne's essential style is established and his ability to interpret the text by means of parallelism, antithesis, and emblematic detail emerges brilliantly.'

6. For full text of CD's Prologue see *PV*.

7. 'to the stock of cheerful ... literature': *P* III, 366; the Sanatorium: see Margaret Diane Stetz, 'Charles Dickens and "The Sanatorium": An Unpublished Letter and Manuscript', *D* 76 (1980), 23–30 (on 27 Dec. CD sent a longer version of his *Chronicle* piece to the merchant Thomas Chapman, one of the scheme's main backers, for publication in a projected pamphlet which never appeared); 'not the most pleasant in its nature': *P* III, 392; 'nothing that is so affecting': *F* 29; 'how all these things ...': *F* 35.

8. The grown-up child: see Malcolm Andrews's *Dickens and the Grown-up Child* (London, 1992) for full discussion of this important topic.

9. For full text of 'Snoring for the Million' see *Journalism* II, 51–5; 'shining facts in our early London days': Collins, *Interviews*, 177.

10. 'a sequestered Farm House': *P* III, 465; 'walking and talking ...': *F* 294; 'Old Martin's Plot ...': see Cardwell, 835; 'One of the most surprising processes ...': *P* III, 441; for cancelled opening of ch. 6 see Cardwell, Appendix B.

11. For CD's review see *Journalism* II, 55–9; for his involvement with the Society of British Authors and the Association for the Protection of Literature see *P* III, 442 *n*.5, 477, *n*.5, and 491, *n*. 7.

12. 'sleek, slobbering, bow-paunched ...': *P* III, 482.

13. For the 'Report of the Commissioners' see *Journalism* II, 59–63; the Unitarians: CD took sittings for himself and his family in the Little Portland Street Unitarian Chapel 1842–44; 'A Word in Season': *F* 294–5 reprints the whole poem.

14. For quoted sales figures see *F* 302; 'by the style of his living ...': *P* III, 493, *n*.1; 'blood-petitioners': *P* III, 601.

15. Forster tells us: *F* 302; 'a herd of rascals ...': *P* IV, 11; the *Edinburgh* review of *AN* was by James Spedding (see Collins, *CH*, 124–9), whose statement that CD went to America 'as a kind of missionary in the cause of International Copyright' was sharply contradicted by CD in a letter to *The Times* (16 Jan. 1843); 'make good': *F* 302; 'Martin has made them ...': *P* III, 541.

16. 'I mean to make a mark ...': *P* III, 520; Agreement of 7 Sept. 1841: see *P* II, 478–81; 'A wrong kind of fire ...' and 'I am bent upon ...': *P* III, 516–17; Bradbury and Evans had recently successfully ventured into publishing with the weekly satirical journal *Punch*, which they had taken over in Dec. 1842.

17. 'forfeits, picnics ...': *P* III, 551; for CD's banquet speeches see *Speeches*, 36–43.

18. 'quiet, unpretending, domestic heroism': *P* IV, 375; for the loan from Mitton: see *P* III, 525 (CD was reluctant to overdraw his account at Coutts's Bank when Angela Burdett Coutts was trying to find employment for his brother Alfred, and it was now a matter of pride with him not to exceed his monthly stipend from Chapman and Hall by even the smallest amount).

19. 'a gentleman with long hair ...': *P* III, 546; 'bang all the others': *P* III, 567.

20. 'horrible and dread': *CC*, end of Stave 3; on the same day that he wrote to Burdett Coutts CD wrote also to Macvey Napier suggesting the Ragged Schools as the topic for his still outstanding article for the *Edinburgh* but abandoned the idea once he had been inspired with the idea for *CC* and did not write directly about the Schools until his *DN* letter of 4 Feb.1846 (see Philip Collins, 'Dickens and the Ragged Schools', *D* 55 (1959), 94–109).

21. 'died within him': *Speeches*, 47 ('our great poet' is, of course, Shakespeare and CD's quotation is from *Macbeth*, II, iii).

22. 'wept and laughed . . .': *P* IV, 2; 'almost a dream reworking . . .': Peter Ackroyd, *Dickens* (London, 1990), 409; for comment on suddenness of Young Martin's conversion see Barbara Hardy, *The Moral Art of Dickens* (London, 1970), 37.

23. Kathleen Tillotson explores this autobiographical aspect of *CC* in her 'The Middle Years from the *Carol* to *Copperfield*', *Dickens Memorial Lectures* (London: Dickens Fellowship, 1970).

24. 'enlarge [his] stock of description . . .': as always, the warning figure of Scott was not far from his thoughts when anxious about his future as a writer: 'What would poor Scott have given to have gone abroad, of his own free will, a young man, instead of creeping there, a driveller, in his miserable decay!': *P* III, 591; 'putting myself before the town . . .': *P* III, 587; 'all at once . . .': *P* IV, 3; 'where, like a Napoleon . . .': see William J. Carlton, 'Dickens Studies Italian', *D* 61 (1965), 101–8.

25. Leech's illustrations: see Cohen, *Illustrators*, 142–3.

26. 'real grinding sorrows . . .': *The Britannia* (a Tory paper), 23 Dec. 1843; all the pulpits and confessionals . . .': see Collins, *CH*, 148; 'a national benefit . . .': *Fraser's Magazine* 39 (Feb. 1844), 166–9, quoted Collins, *CH*, 149; 'a most prodigious success . . .': *P* IV, 12.

27. For the definitive account of CD's battle against the pirates see E.T. Jaques, *Charles Dickens in Chancery* (1914).

28. For details of CD's *CC* earnings see Patten 149–50; 'run the expences up . . .': *P* IV, 43.

29. Thomas James Thompson, a friend of CD's since at least 1838 (see *P* I, 416), was of independent means and lived the life of a cultured man about town; for full texts of both of CD's speeches see *Speeches*, 52–65; 'It is a brave thing . . .': *P* IV, 61.

30. 'Good God what a madman . . .': *P* IV, 55; as Mrs Hogarth apparently believed: see David Paroissien, 'Dickens and the Weller Family', *DSA* 2 (1972), 7; 'disappoint him very much': see *P* IV, 55.

31. For fuller discussion of CD and Christiana Weller see *D and W*, 88–91.

32. feeling his power more than ever: *P* III, 590; 'at once the versatility . . .': see Collins, *CH* 182; 'leave the scene', 'It is impossible . . .': *P* III, 591; 'turning-point of his career': *F* 307.

33. For 'The Agricultural Interest' see *Journalism* II, 64–7; 'such scraps of descriptions . . .': *P* IV, 66; 'scattered scraps . . .': *P* IV, 37; revising key passages: see Cardwell, xliii; 'Threatening Letter . . .': see *Journalism* II, 67–73.

34. Alongside his public work for charity CD continued to respond to some among the innumerable private appeals for assistance with which he was always inundated, and was sometimes imposed upon, as in the case of the habitual begging-letter writer John Walker in the spring of 1844 (see *P* IV, 129, *n.* 7); 'odious anomaly . . .': *Speeches*, 70.

35. 'a most desirable Widow . . .': *P* IV, 134; for CD's inventory of his library see *P* IV, Appendix C; for his Agreements with Bradbury and Evans see *P* IV, Appendix A.

36. 'as interesting . . . as possible': *P* IV, 140 (for Valerie Browne Lester the *MC* frontispiece illustrates 'the moment in which his [Browne's] skill and Dickens's intent are most perfectly fused' (Lester 96)).

37. For full text of presentation to Tagart see *D* 22 (1926), 98; for full text of CD's preface to *Evening of a Working Man* see *Journalism* IV, 416–19.

38. 'good old shabby devil . . .': *P* IV, 155; 'the dear old France of my affections': 'Travelling Abroad' (*UT*), see *Journalism* IV, 87; 'Surrounded by strange and perfectly novel . . .': *P* IV, 155; 'There is no such place for material . . .': *P* IV, 177.

39. 'all the undrained, unscavengered qualities . . .': *PFI*; 'the most perfectly lonely . . .': *P* IV, 156.

40. Not being satisfied . . . very miserable': *PFI*; in his 'Dickens' *Pictures from Italy*: the Politics of the New Picturesque' (*Nineteenth-Century Prose* 29 (2002), 120–37) Joseph Phelan draws attention to this journey as exemplifying CD's evident determination 'not to allow his position as a tourist to lead to a kind of aesthetic detachment from the scenes he witnesses'.

41. For CD's report to JF on his dream see *P* IV, 196; for his later references to it see *P* VI, 277 and 'The Holly Tree Inn' (*CS*); 'We have heard THE CHIMES . . .' *P* IV, 199 (the quotation is from Shakespeare, *Henry IV Part Two*, III, ii).

42. For quotations from CD's letters to JF in this para. see *P* IV, 199–210; 'his fancies controlled him': *F* 350.

43. For detailed discussion of topicality of *C* see my 'Dickens's Tract for the Times' in Michael Slater, ed., *Dickens 1970* (London, 1970); Will Fern: Sheila Smith has suggested that CD's depiction of Fern may owe something to his memories of the recently-deceased John Overs ('John Overs to Charles Dickens: A Working-Man's Letter and its Implications', *VS* 18 (1974), 195–217).

44. 'tremendous book': *P* IV, 211; 'Keep things in their places . . .': *P* IV, 216; 'magnificent and stupendous reality': *P* IV, 217.

45. 'shrieks of laughter': see K. J. Fielding, 'Two Sketches by Maclise', *DS* 2 (1966), 7–17.

46. For CD's profits see Patten 160–1; 'Bradbury and Evans are the Men . . .': *P* IV, 296.
47. 'rolled into an impossible ball . . .': *P* XII, 443 (CD is giving a much later account of his treatment of Mme de la Rue to J. S. Le Fanu, 24 Nov. 1869).
48. 'To Be Read At Dusk' was written for *The Keepsake* in 1851, and was set in the picturesque Palazzo Doria about six miles outside Genoa and associated in CD's mind with the de la Rues because M. de la Rue had tried to get Angus Fletcher to hire it for the Dickenses; for full discussion of CD and the de la Rues see Fred Kaplan, *Dickens and Mesmerism: The Hidden Springs of Fiction* (Princeton; Princeton University Press, 1975).
49. 'a great scene . . .': *P* IV, 286 (the description duly appears in *PFI* occupying several pages); 'into the flaming bowels . . .': *P* IV, 270; 'annihilated' *PFI*; 'unmitigated humbug': *P* IV, 288; 'all well and flourishing . . .': *P* IV, 295.
50. 'such rich filling-in . . .': *F* 372; 'a story about the length . . .': *P* IV, 199.
51. re. textual revision of text of *OT*, see Kathleen Tillotson, ed., *OT* (Oxford, Clarendon Edn 1965), xxxvii–xxxviii; 'extremely nervous': *P* IV, 317, *n*. 41.
52. CD's article is called 'The Spirit of Chivalry in Westminster Hall' (*Douglas Jerrold's Shilling Magazine*, Aug. 1845; reprinted in *Journalism* II, 73–80).
53. All quotations in this para. taken from CD's letter to JF of ?early July 1845 (*P* IV, 327–8).
54. 'Railway Mania': in his *George Hudson: The Rise and Fall of the Railway King* (Stroud: Alan Sutton Publishing, 1995) Brian Bailey writes (p. 51), 'Two hundred and twenty [railway] Bills were deposited in Parliament during 1845, and ninety-four Acts received the royal assent, authorizing nearly three thousand miles of new railways.'
55. 'I have sometimes . . .': *P* IV, 423; Horne's charge appeared in his otherwise generally eulogistic profile of CD in his *A New Spirit of the Age* (London, 1844) – the relevant section is reprinted in Collins, *CH*, 99–100.
56. 'delicate and beautiful fancy . . .': *P* IV, 337.
57. For parallels with conducting *HW* see Grahame Smith, *Charles Dickens: A Literary Life* (Manchester, 1996), 6.
58. 'to blow vague Trumpets . . .': *P* IV, 444; for prospectus of *DN* see *P* IV, 444, *n*.7; for details re. terms and conditions of CD's appointment see Kathleen Tillotson, 'New Light on Dickens and the *Daily News*', *D* 79 (1982), 89–92.
59. For the illustrators of *CH* see Cohen, *Illustrators*, 141–85; for Landseer's Boxer see also Beryl Gray, 'Dickens and Dogs: "No Thoroughfare" and the Landseer Connection', *D* 100 (2004), 5–22.
60. The aristocratic *Morning Post* in its review of *CH* provides an interesting example of how CD's literary career to date might be summed up with extreme prejudice: 'Used up as a transcriber of cockney slang and Newgate dialect, and not highly appreciated as a traveller and a tenth-rate retailer of stale Americanisms, Boz bethought himself of a new line . . . and hashed up a pretty fairy tale' (22 Dec. 1845); for dramatisations see Philip Bolton, *Dickens Dramatized* (Boston,1987); 'slaughtered as gently as possible': *P* IV, 453; CD attended rehearsals of Smith's adaptations and 'took great pains' with the 'getting up' (*P* IV, 453); 'golden reasons': see Allardyce Nicoll, *A History of the English Drama*, IV: *1660–1900*, (Cambridge, 1955), 99.
61. 'Ah Charlie . . .': quoted in *P* IV, 532, *n*.1; re. Augustus's 'very small Cupid' we might note that CD showed no such reluctance to interfere in the case of his favourite brother and special protégé Fred, now aged twenty-five and eager to marry Christiana Weller's younger sister, fifteen-year-old Anna – he wrote Fred a long, affectionate letter on 7 Oct. beseeching him to think hard before committing himself to marriage at all, and especially hard before marrying someone as young and apparently flighty as Anna Weller.

10 An interlude: 'daily nooses' and the noose itself, 1846

1. For the partnership deed see Kathleen Tillotson, 'New Light on Dickens and the *Daily News*', *D* 79 (1982), 89–92
2. Justin McCarthy and Sir John R. Robinson, *The 'Daily News' Jubilee* (London, 1896), 12.
3. 'regular marking and orderly despatch . . .': see William J. Carlton, 'John Dickens, Journalist', *D* 53 (1957), 5–11; 'a more zealous, disinterested or useful gentleman . . .': *P* IV, 506; Carlton speculates that CD may also have written the obituary of his father in *DN* (1 April 1851) in which John is described as having held 'a most responsible position in connexion with its [the *News*'s] reporting staff – the acknowledged efficiency of which is mainly due to his large experience and correct judgment'.
4. 'Great attention will be paid . . .': *P* IV, 446; 'a very good fellow': *P* IV, 468 (Wills was two years younger than CD).

5. 'torn to pieces': *P* IV, 475; 'wilful and malicious murder': for CD's spoof editorial see *P* IV, 702–3.
6. 'All our efforts . . .': see Violet Markham, *Paxton and the Bachelor Duke* (London, 1935), 173; 'been at press . . .': *P* IV, 476: 'ill-printed on bad paper . . .': see Collins, *Interviews*, 75 (Russell goes on to make his much-quoted pronouncement the second part of which is definitely unjust, 'Dickens was not a good editor; he was the best reporter in London, and as a journalist he was nothing more').
7. For text of CD's *DN* editorial see Sidney J. Rust, 'Treasures at the Dickens House', *D* 34 (1938), 119–22.
8. See David Roberts, 'Charles Dickens and the *Daily News*: Editorials and Editorial Writers', *VPR* 22 (1989), 51–63; Roberts comments that none of CD's contemporaries would have considered him and his leader-writers as anything 'other than liberals and radicals who were sincere friends of the working classes' because they, like CD himself, could not accept 'a powerful, regulating government as the answer [to social problems]'.
9. For text of 'Crime and Education' see *MP*.
10. 'drawling on to . . .': *OMF*, Bk II, ch.1; 'I wish you would remember . . .': *LOL*, 24f.; *LOL*, to which CD never gave a title but always referred to as 'the children's New Testament', was not intended for publication and remained unpublished until after the death of CD's last surviving child in 1933; it was erroneously described as having been written in 1849 – see further *P* IV, 573, *n*. 2.
11. 'made some impression': *P* IV, 497; for full text of the 'Hymn' see *PV*.
12. For CD's review of Hood's *Poems* see John Drew, 'Dickens on "Poor Hood": a New Article', *D* 104 (2008), 110–22.
13. 'broke down in the mechanical business . . .': Richard Garnett, *Life of W. J. Fox, Public Teacher and Social Reformer, 1786–1864* (London, 1910), 283 – for such evidence as there is that tends to support Fox's judgment see Thomas Britton, CD's office-attendant on the paper, quoted by K. J. Fielding in his 'Dickens as J. T. Danson knew him' (*D* 68 (1972), 151–61); Danson was one of the leader-writers appointed by CD, his speciality being economic and financial affairs, and his account of CD's difficulties in dealing with him because of his own ignorance in this field rings true; 'Letters on Social Questions': all five letters are included by David Paroissien in his *Selected Letters of Charles Dickens* (Boston, 1985).
14. 'there are people . . .': *LD* I, ch.11; 'I should be glad to abolish . . .': *P* X, 345; the fullest discussion of CD's letters on capital punishment is to be found in Philip Collins, *Dickens and Crime* (1962), 225–33, see also, for the contemporary context for CD's changing attitudes towards capital punishment, V. A. G. Gatrell, *The Hanging Tree: Execution and the English People, 1770–1868* (Oxford, 1994).
15. For a detailed account of the changes made to the text of the 'Travelling Letters' for publication in *PFI* see Kate Flint, ed., *PFI* (London, Penguin Classics, 1998), xxxvi–xxxvii; for consideration of *PFI* as marking 'an influential stage in the writer's career' see Clotilde de Stasio, 'The Traveller as Liar: Dickens and the "Invisible Towns" in Northern Italy', *D* 96 (2000), 5–13.
16. CD wrote to Stanfield, 'You are the best judge of whether your Creed recognizes and includes with men of sense, such things as I have shocked you by the mention of. I am sorry to learn that it does – and think the worse of it than I did' (*P* IV, 517f.); for Palmer as illustrator of CD see Cohen, *Illustrators*, 193–6; for reception of *PFI* see Collins, *CH*, 119 and Leonée Ormond, ed., *PFI* (London, Everyman Dickens, 1997), 508–11; Patten shows (180–1) that *PFI* 'turned a nice profit' for CD.
17. 'was to do with Pride . . .': *F* 471; 'deposit men, . . .': *P* IV, 484.
18. Staggs's Gardens: see Michael Steig, '*Dombey and Son* and the Railway Panic of 1845', *D* 67 (1971), 145–8.
19. See Nina Burgis, ed., *DC* (Oxford, Clarendon Edn, 1981), xvii–xviii, for discussion of date when CD began to write the autobiographical fragment.
20. For the genesis of Burdett Coutts's asylum for homeless women see Jenny Hartley, *Charles Dickens and the House of Fallen Women* (London, 2008).
21. told Mme de la Rue: see *P* IV, 534; 'the Pit in my literary life': *P* IV, 571; overdrawn on 5 March: see *P* IV, 514; for disappointing sales of *OT* in parts see Patten, 168; 'there are many little pickings . . .': *P* IV, 534; 'to the paid magistracy . . .': *F* 388; 'radiant with happiness . . .': *P* IV, 509, *n*. 2 (a cornet was the most junior ranking cavalry officer in the British Army).
22. 'dear to him in all his visions': see last paragraph of *C*.

11 *Dombey* and other dealings, 1846–1848

1. 'a kind of beautiful bandbox': *P* IV, 561; 'something larger than a Plate Warmer': *P* IV, 570; 'good wholesome people . . .': *P* IV, 661.
2. 'one of the noblest-hearted gentlemen . . .': *P* V, 565.

3. 'always had a weird fascination ...': Charles Dickens junior, 'Reminiscences of My Father', *The Windsor Magazine* 81 (Dec. 1934, Christmas supplement), 14; quotations from Watson's diary taken from Leslie C. Staples, 'Sidelight on a Great Friendship', *D* 47 (1951), 16–21 (Staples believed erroneously that the diary belonged to Lavinia Watson); 'in these days of lecturing ...': *P* IV, 631.

4. 'if they are bad ...', *LOL* 28; 'the blessed history ...': *DS* ch. 58.

5. 'big box': *P* IV, 573; 'certain quaint ... figures': *F* 394; 'lots of little dogs ...': Charles Collins, 'Charles Dickens's Study', *The Graphic*, Christmas number for 1870; 'a Daughter after all!': this is Miss Tox's exclamation in a sentence at the end of *DS* V which accidentally dropped out of the text in the Library Edition of *DS* (1859) and was restored in the Oxford Clarendon Edition (1974).

6. 'shadowing out ...': *P* IV, 649; for detailed discussion of the *DS* monthly-part cover see Butt and Tillotson, who note that Browne includes in his design a scene of Dombey marrying, showing that CD must have told him about this major projected development; for discussion of Browne's work for *MC*, *DS* and *BH* see John Harvey, *Victorian Novelists and Their Illustrators* (London, 1970) and Michael Steig, *Dickens and Phiz* (London, 1978); 'gradually and naturally trailing away ...': *P* IV, 593; 'ultimately acquiesced': *F* 473.

7. 'brief aids in decision making ...': Stone, *WN* xvii; Stone's substantial Introduction provides the fullest discussion of this aspect of CD's working practices together with transcripts of the 'mems' and chapter-notes that amount to virtual facsimiles (see notable review by John Sutherland, *London Review of Books*, 15 Oct. 1987).

8. 'a new way of doing it ...': *P* V, 2; 'There's no writing against such power ...': see George Hodder, *Memories of My Time* (London, 1870), 277; for detailed number-by-number discussion of CD's working notes and 'mems' for *DS* see Butt and Tillotson, ch. 5.

9. 'End with the sea ...': see Alan Horsman, ed., *DS* (Oxford, Clarendon Edn, 1974; hereafter cited as Horsman), 855 and Stone, *WN* 99.

10. For fuller discussion of this more woman-centred phase of CD's novelistic career see *D and W*, ch.12.

11. 'greatly better': *P* V, 627; for the cutting in proof of *DS* I–IV see Butt and Tillotson, 97, and textual apparatus in Horsman.

12. 'a simple domestic tale': *F* 423; 'What an affecting story ...' and 'the coats and gowns ...': : *P* IV, 648; for exploration of the personal element in *BL* see Steven Marcus, *Dickens from Pickwick to Dombey* (London, 1965), 289–92, and *D and W*, 96–9.

13. 'constantly haunted ...': *P* IV, 626; 'serious danger': *P* IV, 670; 'prodigious success': *P* IV, 639; 'the good ship Boz': Collins, *CH* 212; for details of the sale of the early numbers of *DS* see Patten 185–6.

14. 'I *cannot* help it ...': *P* IV, 656; 'ogress and child-queller': *DS*, ch. 8; for discussion of CD's model or models for Mrs Pipchin see Horsman, xxv; 'I hope you will like Mrs Pipchin's establishment ...': *P* IV, 653.

15. 'Shall I leave you my life in MS. ...': *P* IV, 653.

16. 'marvellously rapid work': *F* 441; 'slaughter': *P* IV, 676; 'much better than usual': *P* IV, 681; for sales of *Mrs Perkins's Ball* see Patten 187; '*four thousand guineas ...*': see Collins, *CH*, 587 (a more authoritative figure for CD's profit on *BL* is supplied by Patten (187): £1,281.15*s.* 4*d.*).

17. 'walked about Paris ...': *P* V, 9; 'national mourning': see Patten 188 and *n.*14.

18. 'wandering into hospitals ...': *P* V, 19; for CD's earnings per no. of *DS* see *P* V, 156*n*; for CD's seeking public employment in 1846 see *P* IV, 566f: 'His accounts ...': *F*, 464.

19. For information about CD's revision of the text of *SB* for the Cheap Edition I am indebted to Paul Schlicke, editor of the forthcoming Oxford Clarendon Edition of *SB*; 'the retrospective shape of a career ...': Ian Duncan, *Modern Romance and Transformations of the Novel: The Gothic, Scott, Dickens* (Cambridge, 1992), 180.

20. 'unprecedented ... in the history of Cheap Literature': as indeed it was – see John Sutherland, *Victorian Novelists and Publishers* (London, 1976), 32 (writing to de La Rue on 24 March CD called it 'the greatest venture ... ever made in books'; Patten notes (190, *n*. 18) that CD was soon copied by Bulwer Lytton, who began issuing a Cheap Edition of his novels through Chapman and Hall in Oct. 1847; for further details and the full text of CD's 'Address' see Simon Nowell Smith, 'The "Cheap Edition" of Dickens's Works (First Series) 1847–52', *The Library* 22 (1967), 245–51; CD originally proposed dedicating the Cheap Edition to the English people 'in whose approval, if the books be true in spirit, they will live, and out of whose memory, if they be false, they will very soon die' but this idea was abandoned – 'for other reasons', says JF (*F* 448f.).

21. 'clearly moving forward ...': Horsman xxxii.

22. See K. J. Fielding, 'Two Prologues for the Amateur Players', *D* 56 (1960) 100–02.

23. For the full text of the Gamp fragment see *F* 459–63.

24. For a draft of the proposed Prospectus for the Provident Union, [Nov.] 1847, See *P* V, 700–02.

25. 'very agreeable and womanly': *P* V, 269; for reply to the author of the tragedy see *P* VII, 867–8.

26. 'forbiddingly explicit': Philip Collins, *Dickens and Crime* (London, 1962; hereafter cited as Collins), 104f.; '*tempted* to virtue': *P V*, 183; 'Home for Homeless Women': *HW* 23 April 1853, reprinted in *Journalism* III; Chesterton's report quoted by Collins, 98f.; one, at least, of the first potential recruits for Urania Cottage did have a history comparable to Nancy's, a 17-year-old 'born of drunken parents, ill used from her cradle, plundered of her clothes that they might be sold for liquor, and sent to evil courses for their gain' (*P V*, 178); see further Jenny Hartley, *Charles Dickens and the House of Fallen Women* (London, 2008).

27. CD's 'Appeal' is reprinted in *P V*, 698–9 and in *Journalism* III, 503–5.

28. 'perfectly imperturbable face': *Journalism* III, 134; 'forced open the door . . .': *P VI*, 84; 'making the same low . . . moaning . . .': *DC*, ch. 22; 'most extraordinary and mysterious study . . .': *P V*, 178.

29. 'of whom seven are now married': *Journalism* III, 129; 'A Small Star in the East' (*AYR*, 19 Dec. 1868) is reprinted in *Journalism* IV.

30. 'ghostly and wild idea': *P IV*, 614.

31. 'a most brilliant demonstration . . .': *P V*, 204; 'one cheer more . . .': see *Speeches*, 80; 'had held to [*OCS*] . . .': *P V*, 342.

32. 'a kind of inverted Maid's Tragedy': *P V*, 211; in Beaumont and Fletcher's *The Maid's Tragedy* (1619) the heroine rejects her newlywed husband because she is already the King's mistress; 'one of the few novelists . . .': *P V*, 216, *n.6*.

33. 'social miseries': *Speeches*, 86; 'a failure': *P V*, 216.

34. For Browne's extra illustrations to *DS* see *P V* 224, *n.6*; 'deep in No.18': *P V* 249; for text of CD's review of Crowe see *Journalism* II, 80–91.

35. Lord Normanby: CD presumably first became acquainted with Lord and Lady Normanby through the friendship he developed with their son, the Earl of Mulgrave, in 1842, first on board the S. S. *Britannia* and subsequently in North America; 'great faith in Dombey . . .': *P V*, 271.

12 From *Dombey* to *Copperfield*, 1848–1849

1. 'that unanimity . . .': *P V*, 335; 'His animal spirits . . .': *F* 469.

2. 'epidemic . . . special constable-ing': *P V*, 274 (150,000 Special Constables were sworn in to act in case of the expected attempt at revolution); for the texts of those articles referred to in this paragraph see *Journalism* II, 80–91.

3. 'Judicial Special Pleading': see *Journalism* II, 137–42; for discussion of CD's review of *The Poetry of Science* see K. J. Fielding and Shu-Fang Lai, 'Dickens, Science, and *The Poetry of Science*', *D* 93 (1997), 5–10, and subsequent exchange with Philip Collins, *D* 93 (1997), 136 and 205.

4. 'not being the conductor . . .': *P V*, 291; 'conducting': 'another floating fancy . . .': *F* 443*n*.

5. All quotations in this para. are from *F* 23.

6. 'perfectly recollects': *F* 27; description of the Marshalsea prisoners: *F* 33; 'literally true': *F* 5.

7. 'moved her weak head . . .': 'New Year's Day' (*HW* 12 June 1858; *Journalism* III, 494); 'vividly reawakened . . .': *F* 514; 'his tender and grateful memory': *F* 34.

8. 'a mentally matooring': *P V*, 414; CD's preface to the Cheap Edn of *OCS* is reprinted in Elizabeth Brennan, ed., *OCS* (Oxford, Clarendon Edn, 1997), 609–10.

9. 'perfectly well': *P V*, 415 (for Goldsmith's *Bee* see above, p. 13).

10. 'grinding away': the MS. of *HM* contains detailed notes for the story and, according to Ruth Glancy in 'Dickens at Work on *The Haunted Man*' (*DSA* 15 (1986), 65–85; hereafter Glancy), it is also heavily emended throughout bearing witness to the intensity of CD's work on it; for detailed discussion of the parallels and contrasts between *CC* and *HM* considered as autobiographical fictions see Harry Stone, *The Night Side of Dickens: Cannibalism, Passion, Necessity* (Columbus: Ohio State University Press, 1994), 465–70.

11. 'Of course . . . my point is . . .': *F* 508; 'pretty . . . a good Christmas tendency': *P V*, 435.

12. 'when one laughs . . .': *P V*, 448; 'crying [his] eyes out . . .': Glancy reports that the MS. of ch. 3 of *HM* is heavily blotted with tears; for CD's disapproval of Fred's marriage to Anna Weller see *P V*, 400–1; 'every word the actors say: . . .': *P V*, 460; for sales of *HM* and CD's profits see Patten 203; a satirical paper, *The Man in the Moon* (no. 25), printed a mock trial of CD for publishing a work that was 'unintelligible' with one witness saying, 'If ghosts talk such nonsense as Mr Dickens's ghost talks [he] does not wonder at people being afraid of them.'

13. CD's review is partially reprinted in *F* (492–3) and fully in *Journalism* II, 142–7; 'a secret delight': *F* 317.

14. For CD's denial that he had ever read *Jane Eyre* see Jerome Meckier, 'Some Household Words: Two New Accounts of Dickens's Conversation', *D* 71 (1975), 5–20.

15. 'a murderous look . . .': *P V*, 473; 'fit for a gigantic scoundrel's exit' and 'the strangest place in the wide world': *P V*, 473; some commentators: e.g., Peter Ackroyd, *Dickens* (London, 1990), 555; 'in

a kind of homage . . .' *F* 524; chloroform: see *P* V, 486–7 (I owe the suggestion of a possible connection between the birth of Henry Fielding Dickens and *DC* ch.1 to Beryl Gray).

16. All quotations in this para. taken from *F* ch. 2.

17. 'a picture of tragical suffering . . .': *F* 24; for interesting recent discussion of the literary craftsmanship of the autobiographical fragment see Rosemary Bodenheimer, *Knowing Dickens* (London, 2007), 68–73 and Nicola Bradbury, 'Dickens's Use of the Autobiographical Fragment' in David Paroissien, ed., *A Companion to Charles Dickens* (Oxford, 2008); for the splitting of his younger self in the fragment into versions of Oliver Twist and the Artful Dodger see Robert Newsom, *Charles Dickens Revisited* (New York, 2000), 31; 'the description may make none of the impression . . .': *F* 11*n*.

18. whether or not he was influenced by Catherine: Charley Dickens, writing in 1892, claimed that Catherine told him that CD had read the autobiographical fragment to her, and she had dissuaded him from publishing it because of its harshness towards his parents, especially his mother (see Nina Burgis, ed., *DC*, Oxford Clarendon Edn, xxi); 'itself suggested . . .': *F* 24; 'brutally conducted . . .': 'The Paradise at Tooting' is reprinted in *Journalism* II, 147–55; three further trenchant articles: published in *The Examiner* 27 Jan., 26 Feb. and 21 April (see *Journalism* II, 155–6 for summaries).

19. 'atrocious temper': *P* V, 480; 'a Stage Maniac': *P* V, 490; 'in immense black velvet hats': *P* V, 489; 'more innocent Pecksniff': *P* V, 483; *Suffolk Words and Phrases*: CD's use of Moor's book was first demonstrated by K. J. Fielding in *TLS* 30 April 1949.

20. For facsimiles and full transcripts of these experimental title-sheets see Stone, *WN* and for notable discussions of them see Donald Hawes, 'David Copperfield's names', *D* 74 (1978), 81–7, and Robert L. Patten, 'Autobiography into Autobiography: the Evolution of *David Copperfield*' in George P. Landow, ed., *Approaches to Victorian Autobiography* (Athens, OH: Ohio University Press, 1979).

13   Interweaving and connecting: writing *David Copperfield* and starting *Household Words*, 1849–1850

1. For detailed discussion of CD's working notes and 'mems' for *DC* see Butt and Tillotson, ch. 6, and Nina Burgis, ed., *DC* (Oxford, Clarendon Edn 1981; hereafter cited as Burgis).

2. 'The Verdict for Drouet' is reprinted in *MP*.

3. 'Though I know what I want to do . . .': *P* V, 526; 'If I get fierce . . .': *P* VI, 99.

4. For Carlyle delighting CD see *F* 528; 'books all round . . .': J. A. V. Chapple and A. Pollard, *Letters of Mrs Gaskell* (Manchester, 1996) 828; 'a great fight': Gordon N. Ray, ed., *The Letters and Private Papers of William Makepeace Thackeray* II (London,1945; hereafter cited as Thackeray, *Letters*), 333; 'O it is charming . . .': Thackeray, *Letters* 531.

5. 'if you are born . . .': *Speeches* 96.

6. 'It is supposed . . .': Sir Arthur Helps to Queen Victoria, 5 March 1870, quoted by John R. DeBruyn, 'Charles Dickens meets the Queen: a New Look', *D* 71 (1975), 85–90; encourage friends to look for autobiographical elements: see, for example, the letter to Mary Howitt quoted as epigraph to ch.1 above; 'People used to say to me . . .': *P* VII, 539.

7. For sales figures of *DC* see Patten 207; 'Passing influences . . .': *P* V, 611; 'read with avidity . . .': *F* 509.

8. 'see his way': *F* 496; 'dragged forth to a dungeon . . .': *P* V, 558; for CD's irritation over the way his speech was reported by *DN* see *Speeches* 98–9; 'what I know so well': see Burgis 759.

9. 'like a house afire': *P* V, 569.

10. 'It was a constant joke . . .': R. Shelton Mackenzie, *Life of Charles Dickens* (Philadelphia, 1870), 36–7, 203.

11. 'jest and merriment': *F* 498; 'the great Dickens . . .': Thackeray, *Letters*, 569.

12. 'hard Copperfieldian mornings': *P* V, 604; 'the Unparalleled Necromancer . . .': *P* V, 706–7; 'a glorious walk . . .': *P* V, 597*n*.; 'a ball of boiling fat . . .': *P* V, 605.

13. For CD and the Metropolitan Commission of Sewers see K. J. Fielding and Alec W. Brice, '*Bleak House* and the Graveyard' in Robert J. Partlow, ed., *Dickens the Craftsman* (Carbondale: Southern Illinois University Press, 1970); CD's 'Appeal to the English People on Behalf of the Italian Refugees' is reprinted in *D* 10 (1914), 320–1.

14. 'grew under his hand': Burgis xl; 'make anything out of it . . .': *F* 512; for discussion of CD's 'Shadow' idea see Audrey Jaffe, *Vanishing Points: Dickens, Narrative and the Subject of Omniscience* (Berkeley: University of California Press,1991), 15–16, and Drew, *Journalist* 106–7.

15. 'Demoralisation and Total Abstinence' is collected in *Journalism* II.

16. 'Pet Prisoners' is in *Journalism* II: for Isabella Gordon and Sesina see *P* V, 638, 641.

17. 'the girl already lost': Burgis 763; 'a piece of grotesque truth': *P* V, 654; 'His first time of getting tipsy . . .': Burgis 763.
18. For CD's *Times* letters see *P* V, 644–5, 651–4; for full discussion of CD and the Mannings' execution see Philip Collins, *Dickens and Crime* (London, 1962), 235–41.
19. one of his brilliant epistolary parodies: see *P* V, 661–3; an impressionable American tourist: Henry Colman whose *European Life and Manners, in Familiar Letters to Friends* was reviewed by CD in *The Examiner*, 21 July 1849 (see *MP* 153–61); the Cheap Edn preface to *MC* is reprinted in Margaret Cardwell, ed., *MC* (Oxford, Clarendon Edn, 1982), 846–8.
20. 'the very best actress I ever saw . . .': *P* VI, 162.
21. 'just before *Copperfield*': *P* VII, 543; 'a faithful reflection . . .': *P* VII, 539; 'No one can imagine . . .': *P* VII, 55: 'Mr Dickin': *P* VII, 537; 'Some beautiful comic love': *P* VI, 40.
22. For a full account of the Powell affair see Sydney P. and Carolyn J. Moss, *The Charles Dickens–Thomas Powell Vendetta* (New York, 1996); 'should your book be dramatised . . .': *P* V, 674, *n.* 5; 'I never represent . . .': *P* V, 675; 'serio-comic': *P* V, 676.
23. 'the slave of the lamp . . .': *P* V, 669; 'we hope to do some solid good . . .': *P* VI, 30; 'All social evils . . .': *P* VI, 41; for interesting comment on the title of *HW* see Drew, *Journalist*, 109; 'Town Tent': *P* IX, 289; for Wills see Sandra Spencer, 'The Indispensable Mr Wills', *VPR* 21 (1988), 145–51.
24. 'savage stenographic mystery': DC, ch. 43; 'Express that very delicately' and 'Carry the thread of Agnes . . .': Burgis 767; 'To carry on the thread of Uriah . . .' : Burgis, 768.
25. The Cheap Edition preface to *OT* is reprinted in Kathleen Tillotson, ed., *OT* (Oxford, Clarendon Edn, 1966) 82–4; 'one Christmas time': CD caricatured Laurie as 'Alderman Cute' in *C* (above, p. 230).
26. For circulation figures in this para. see R. D. Altick, *The English Common Reader* (1957), 394; see also Lorna Huett, 'Among the Unknown Public: *Household Words, All The Year Round* and the Mass-Market Weekly Periodical in the Mid-Nineteenth-Century', *VPR* 38 (2005), 61–8.
27. See Patten 242.
28. 'that give delight and hurt not': Shakespeare, *The Tempest*, III, ii; 'A Preliminary Word' is reprinted in *Journalism* II.
29. In 'H.W.', an article on the journal, jointly written with Henry Morley and published in *HW* 16 April 1853, CD mentions the mass of unsolicited material sent in by what he calls 'Voluntary Correspondents': 'In the last year, we read nine hundred manuscripts, of which eleven were available for this journal, after being entirely re-written'; 'an inky fishing net': see Philip Collins, ' "Inky Fishing Nets": Dickens as Editor', *D* 61 (1965), 120–5; for CD's 'autocratic' addition of 'thoroughly Dickensian touches' to contributors' work see George Augustus Sala, *Things I have Seen and People I have Known*, I (London, 1894), 78–81; for the fullest discussions of CD as editor of *HW* see Introductions to Stone, *UW* and to Anne Lohrli's *Household Words. A Weekly Journal 1850–1859 Conducted by Charles Dickens* (Toronto: University of Toronto Press, 1973).
30. 'always a wonderfully suggestive place . . .': *P* VI, 65.
31. The first two articles in the 'Doom of English Wills' series are reprinted in Stone, *UW* I; see also Katharine M. Longley, 'Charles Dickens and the "Doom" of English Wills', *Journal of the Society of Archivists*, 14 (1993), 25–38.
32. For discussion of CD's response to the Millais painting see Leonée Ormond, 'Dickens and Painting: Contemporary Art', *D* 80 (1984), 2–25.
33. For George Ruby, the crossings-sweeper rejected as a witness by a magistrate because he was ignorant of religion, see Humphry House, *The Dickens World* (Oxford, 1941), 32; for Martha Joachim see Harry Stone, *The Night Side of Dickens* (Columbus: Ohio State University Press, 1994), 336f.
34. 'looked in at the Morgue': *P* VI, 120.
35. See Burgis xlvii–viii.
36. 'hoarse music': *P* VI, 113; 'Anti-Malthusian': in his *Essay on the Principles of Population* (London, 1798) the Rev. T. R. Malthus had warned of the dangers of Population exceeding food supply and advocated measures of population control; 'Smash Uriah Heep . . .': Burgis 772; 'I hope I shall have a splendid number . . .': *P* VI, 146.
37. 'Without you we shall be quite incomplete . . .': *P* VI, 150f.
38. For revisions of *SB* for the Cheap Edition see Butt and Tillotson 59–61; 'People don't plunge into churches . . .': *P* VI, 146; 'Our Voluntary Correspondent': see 'H.W.' (*HW* 16 April 1853) reprinted in Stone, *UW* II, 467–75; 'patient and continuous energy . . .': *DC*, ch. 42.
39. 'would work up . . .': Percy Fitzgerald, *Memories of Charles Dickens* (London, 1913), 140; for discussion of CD' attitude towards the police see Philip Collins, *Dickens and Crime* (London, 1962).
40. 'into the Shadowy World': *DC*, Preface; 'half of what *Copperfield* makes me feel . . .': *P* VI, 195.

41. For discussion of Wordsworthian elements in *DC* see Robin Gilmour, 'Memory in *David Copperfield*', *D* 71 (1975), 30–42; for CD's purchase of *The Prelude* see Leon Litvak, 'What Books did Dickens Buy and Read?', *D* 94 (1998), 85–130, 94–5.
42. 'really unhappy': *P* VI, 306, *n*.1.
43. 'a dangerous break . . .': *P* V, 511; 'decidedly underrated . . .': *F* 76.
44. 'A Crisis in the Affairs of Mr John Bull' is collected in *Journalism* II.

14 The Year of the Guild, 1850–1851

1. For the Guild prospectus see *P* VI, 852–7; for the confusions and contradictions inherent in the scheme see Daniel Hack, 'Literary Paupers and Professional Authors: the Guild of Literature and Art' in his *The Material Interests of the Victorian Novel* (London, 2005).
2. One of the commissioned essays, 'Christmas in the Frozen Regions', by the naval surgeon Robert McCormick, was also partly written by CD (see Stone, *UW* I, 183–9).
3. 'There is not a drop of Tom's corrupted blood . . .': *BH*, ch. 46; 'family gout': *BH*, ch.16.
4. For Caroline Chisholm and her children see *P* VI, 53; for the ignorant crossings-sweeper see above, p. 310; notable previous evocations of London as a whole in CD's fiction are the Hogarthian one in *NN* ch. 32, the panorama in *MHC* ch.6, and, one that looks forward to the dark city of *BH*, the image of it as 'a fearful monster, roaring in the distance' in *DS* ch. 33.
5. 'elegant little theatre': *F* 535; 'wonderful clever man with his hands': see H. Snowden Ward, 'Topography of "Bleak House"', *D* I (1905), 200–03; for discussion of the role of the matronly widow Lady Clutterbuck see Susan M. Rossi-Wilcox, *Dinner for Dickens* (Blackawton, Totnes: Prospect Books, 2005; hereafter cited as Rossi-Wilcox), ch.6.
6. 'In some of the descriptions . . .': *P* VII, 135; 'with a Revolver': *P* VI, 666.
7. 'the name given by old Saxon custom . . .': *P* VI, 856.
8. *Speeches*, 117.
9. as has been pointed out: see footnote 1 above; for the Duke as patron of the arts see James Lees-Milne, *The Bachelor Duke: A Life of William Spencer Cavendish 6th Duke of Devonshire 1790–1858* (London, 1991); 'I never missed reading a number . . .': *P* VI, 306, *n*. 1; 'utmost rapture . . .': *P* VI, 222.
10. For text of 'Bill-Sticking' see *Journalism* II, 339–50 where it is noted that most of the advertisers CD refers to in the article regularly advertised in the monthly numbers of his novels.
11. 'an alarming disposition . . .': *P* VI, 311.
12. 'I am constantly striving . . .': *P* VI, 329.
13. 'a slaughter house of blood': *P* VI, 333; 'O so quietly': *P* VI, 343; 'By me as a sick child . . .': *F* 10; 'He took her in his arms . . .': E. Davey, 'The Parents of Charles Dickens', *Lippincott's Magazine* 13 (Philadelphia, 1874); to her sculptor friend Samuel Haydon Elizabeth Dickens wrote that she would not be going to live with any of her children, 'thinking it better to be independent as my beloved Charles made me immediately on the death of his Father' (MS. CDM).
14. 'a splendid paper': *P* VI, 345; '9 hours without stirring': *P* VI, 351; 'The Metropolitan Protectives': the title humorously refers to the fears that were being publicly expressed about the inability of the police to protect Londoners from the activities of the foreign criminals and political conspirators who would flood into London for the Great Exhibition (article collected in Stone *UW*).
15. See Leona Weaver Fisher, *Lemon, Dickens, and MR NIGHTINGALE'S DIARY: A Victorian Farce* (English Literary Studies Monograph, no. 41, University of Victoria, BC, 1988).
16. 'a very Fortunatus's purse . . .': *P* VI, 525; 'Last Words of the Old Year' is collected in *Journalism* II.
17. *Speeches*, 128 (Almack's was a fashionable and highly exclusive set of assembly rooms in King Street, London, administered by a committee of titled ladies).
18. 'A Cold Shower . . .': *P* VI, 520 (cf. *P* VI, 574 where he attributes his 'remarkable power of enduring fatigue' to regular cold showers); 'his cold-bath gaping for him . . .': *BH*, ch. 6; for the dummy book-backs see *P* VI, 524–5 and 851.
19. See also the passage from 'Epsom' (*HW*, 7 June 1851), a piece on Derby Day jointly written by CD and Wills, cited by Stone (*UW* 65–6) as an example of CD's remarkable anticipation of twentieth-century 'stream of consciousness' techniques.
20. 'the general features of the place . . .': *F* 40; 'One Man in a Dockyard' is collected in Stone, *UW* I, 331–42.
21. 'exceedingly': *P* VI, 448.
22. 'in the very best style of phantasmagory . . .': *The Globe*, 22 Nov. 1851, 1; for further discussion of possible connections between 'To Be Read At Dusk' and Augusta de la Rue see *D and W*, 124–5.
23. For CD's preface see *Journalism* IV, 420–21; for the book generally see Rossi-Wilcox.

24. For more detail on the items mentioned in this paragraph see Butt and Tillotson, ch. 7.
25. See Stone, *WN* 185 for a putative ordering of the various titles considered for *BH*.
26. The young American was a journalist and essayist called Grace Greenwood who dined at Tavistock House in 1852 (see Collins, *Interviews* II, 233–8).
27. 'Something with no detail in it . . .': *P* VI, 551; 'I don't believe there is . . .': *P* VI, 554.

15 Writing *Bleak House*, 1852–1853

1. For contemporary attacks on Chancery see Butt and Tillotson, ch.7 and Trevor Blount, 'The Documentary Symbolism of Chancery in *Bleak House*', *D* 62 (1966), 47–52, 106–11, 167–74; for Browne's work on *BH*, and explanation of the etching technique used to produce a 'dark plate', see John Harvey, *Victorian Novelists and Their Illustrators* (London, 1970), 152–6, also Michael Steig, *Dickens and Phiz* (London, 1978) 146–58, Cohen, *Illustrators* 107 and Valerie Browne Lester, *Phiz: The Man Who Drew Dickens* (London, 2004), 150–6; 'cher Brune': *P* VII, 111.
2. his numerous outside commitments: Robert Newsom comments (p. 98) of his *Dickens and the Romantic Side of Familiar Things* (New York, 1977; hereafter cited as Newsom) that CD 'was never busier than when planning and writing *Bleak House*'; 'very rarely more': *P* VI, 625; 'invitations to feasts and festivals': *P* VII, 34.
3. 'A Curious Dance' is reprinted in Stone, *UW* II, 381–91; for the boy in 'A Sleep to Startle Us' (collected in *Journalism* III) see Kathleen Tillotson, '*Bleak House*: another look at Jo' in Colin Gibson, ed., *Art and Society in the Victorian Novel* (Basingstoke, 1987).
4. For CD's defence of his portrait of Skimpole see *P* VII, 460 (to Leigh Hunt) and 'Leigh Hunt. A Remonstrance', *AYR*, 24 Dec. 1859 (*Journalism* IV, 14–19); 'helped to make him singularly unlike . . .': *P* VI, 623; 'the radical wrong remained': *F* 550; for Skimpole as an anti-Guild figure see K. J. Fielding, 'Leigh Hunt and Skimpole: Another Remonstrance', *D* 64 (1968), 5–9.
5. 'a most exact portrait': *P* VI, 666; re. Boythorn: George Brimley, in a mostly very critical review of *BH* in *The Spectator*, found Boythorn 'one of the most original and happiest conceptions of the book, a humorist study of the highest merit' (Collins, *CH* 285).
6. For CD's dealings with Harper & Brothers see Peter S. Bracher, 'Harper & Brothers: Publishers of Dickens', *Bulletin of the New York Public Library* 79 (1976), 315–35.
7. For the text of 'Drooping Buds' see Stone, *UW* II, 401–8; for CD's close and lasting involvement in the Great Ormond Street Hospital see Jules Kosky, *Mutual Friends: Charles Dickens and Great Ormond Street Children's Hospital* (London, 1989).
8. For Challinor see *F* 564 and see also E. T. Jaques, 'Dickens and the Court of Chancery', *D* 13 (1917), 16–17; 'would like nothing better . . .': *P* VI, 646.
9. 'rather a stunner': *P* VI, 655; 'courteous neutrality of eyebrow . . .': Gordon Haight, ed., *The George Eliot Letters* II (London, 1954), 23; 'good things': *P* VI, 670; 'for Bleak House purposes': *P* VI, 696; 'while walking about the room . . .': Mamie Dickens, *My Father As I Recall Him* (London, 1898), 62f.
10. For detailed discussion of CD at work on the MS. and proofs of *BH* see Sylvère Monod, ' "When the Battle's Lost and won . . ."': Dickens *v.* the Compositors of *Bleak House*', *D* 69 (1973), 3–12; for textual variants see George Ford and Sylvère Monod, eds, *BH* (Norton Critical Edition, New York, 1977; hereafter cited as Ford/Monod); 'Mr Dickens . . . confessed . . .': see Collins, *Interviews*, 233–8.
11. The smallpox: in her *Companion to BLEAK HOUSE* (London, 1988) Susan Shatto notes (pp. 209, 258) that there had been several smallpox epidemics in England between 1837 and 1852 and, arguing that Jo must be a carrier of the disease while not suffering from it himself, suggests he dies from pneumonia or 'the disease endemic to the slums, pulmonary tuberculosis'; the 'great turning idea': the Pilgrim editors believe (*P* VI, 805 *n.* 7) CD here refers to Lady Dedlock's revelation to Esther that she is her mother but this does not take place until No. XII and, as Newsom has pointed out (Newsom, 76), the story does not 'turn on' this in the way it does on Esther's self-denying resolve.
12. 'perfectly *lovable*': see Andrew Sanders, ed., *BH* (London, Everyman Paperback, 1994), 852; 'too often weak and twaddling', 'would either do something very "spicy" . . .': Collins, *CH*, 273, 285.
13. For details of these protests see *P* VI, 706, n. 5 and 824–8 and *nn.*
14. In her *G. H. Lewes: A Life* (London, 1991) Rosemary Ashton suggests (pp.144–5) that 'Beneath [Lewes's] attack and beneath Dickens's high-pitched response to it, lies an insecurity in both men arising from their lack of formal education.'
15. 'savage and zoological roaring': *P* VII, 19; all the articles by CD mentioned in this para. are collected in *Journalism* III while the two written jointly with Morley are in Stone, *UW*.
16. For a notable discussion of 'Where We Stopped Growing' see Malcolm Andrews, *Dickens and the Grown-up Child* (London, 1994), ch. 4.

17. 'as quaint, picturesque . . .': *P* VI, 775; 'This tremendous sickle . . .': *P* VI, 764.
18. Paxton: see p. 48 of Robert Tracey, 'Lighthousekeeping: *Bleak House* and the Crystal Palace', *DSA* 33 (2003), 25–53; 'From such evils . . .': see *Speeches*, 154–61
19. 'wooden houses like horrible old packing-cases . . .': *P* VII, 2; K. J. Fielding notes of this passage that it is the only one containing imaginative description in all CD's correspondence with Burdett Coutts, and occurs in a letter written after visiting a scene which brought back memories of his youth ('Dickens's Work with Miss Coutts: II', *D* 61 (1965), 155–60); 'the gaunt pale horse . . .': CD's first idea, as shown by the MS of *BH*, was to have Richard drive Vholes back to London in a mourning-coach that happened to be to hand but he must have decided this was overdoing the emblematic and, as Peter Ackroyd has noted (*Dickens*, London, 1990, 668), remembered the pale horse of Hickman's Folly and altered the passage in proof (see Ford/Monod 856).
20. 'purpose': *P* VII, 134 (CD does not enlarge on what this 'purpose' may be); 'noble and glorious balance': *P* VII, 48.
21. 'since I got rid of . . .': *P* VII, 60; 'Home for Homeless Women' (*HW* 23 April 1853) is collected in *Journalism* III.
22. 'North American Slavery' is collected in Stone, *UW*, II; for CD and Stowe generally see Harry Stone, 'Charles Dickens and Harriet Beecher Stowe', *NCF* 12 (1957), 188–202; 'had reason to hope that a suit . . .': *Speeches*, 164–5.
23. 'Vigorous, brown . . .': *P* VII, 101; 'at once restored to health . . .': MS. Martin Nason.
24. For the development of the friendship between CD and WC see Catherine Peters, *The King of Inventors: A Life of Wilkie Collins* (London, 1991), chs 6 and 7; 'some of the finest passages . . .': WC to his mother, 29 July 1853, quoted *P* VI, 113, *n.* 7; for CD's attack on Cruikshank and Cruikshank's response see Robert L. Patten, *George Cruikshank's Life, Times and Art*, 2 (Lutterworth, 1996), 334–47.
25. pure Skimpole: see *P* VII, 125; 'forlorn attempts at humour': *P* VII, 125; for the article on the persecution of Burdett Coutts see 'Things That Cannot Be Done', *HW*, 8 Oct. 1853, collected in *Journalism* III, 174–9.
26. re. circulation figures for *BH*: the Pilgrim editors state (VII, 134, *n.* 3) that the monthly printing run never fell below 34,000 after *BH* III, whereas the figure for *DC* never rose above 22,000, but Patten notes (p. 226) that the actual stitching order (i.e., the number of sets of parts stitched up for sale) fell from 34,000 to 31,500 during the course of the serialisation, but this nevertheless still represents 'a signal achievement'; 'would have been better away': *P* VI, 823; 'In *Bleak House* I have purposely dwelt . . .': the indispensable study of the ramifications of this comment is Newsom; 'May we meet again!': in the MS of *BH* in the Forster Collection, Victoria and Albert Museum, these words are followed by 'My labor of love is, so far, ended', deleted in proof (see Ford/Monod 815).
27. For the suggestion that CD had simply tired of *CHE* see Patten 237; 'a most amazingly gorgeous . . .': *P* VII, 158.
28. 'the immortal Bucket', *F* 561; for the reception of *BH* see Collins, *CH*, 272–99 (the *Examiner* review is reprinted in Ford/Monod 937–41; 'into the old freedoms. . . .': *F* 561.

16 Writing 'For These Times', 1853–1854

1. 'wonderfully improving': *P* VII, 163; 'an Intrepid': *P* VII, 168.
2. 'in a character that nobody else is likely to hit . . .': *P* VII, 200; 'like a sunbeam . . .': *P* VII, 201.
3. 'Art, Color, Tone and so forth': *P* VII, 197; 'the intolerable nonsense . . .: see *P* VII, 218; 'a code of morals from modern French novels': *P* VII, 204; for the opera-going Americans and the description of the Campagna see *P* VII, 201, 203 (CD makes vivid use of his memories of the Campagna in *LD* II, ch. 19).
4. Tauchnitz: since 1843 Tauchnitz had been regularly paying CD lump sums for the right to publish English-language editions of his works on the Continent and the two men had enjoyed excellent business and personal relations; 'indescribable lassitude . . .': *P* VII, 245; she did . . . write: on 9 March 1854 CD asked de la Rue if his wife had received Catherine's letter 'about the Italian dishes' – the compiler of *What Shall We Have For Dinner?* was evidently playing to her strengths.
5. For drop in *HW* profits see Patten 244; 'an insatiable relish': *F* 505; 'had intended to do nothing . . .': *P* VII, 453; 'the germ of Pip and Magwitch': *F* 733; invented ab initio: not *quite* ab initio perhaps – Philip Collins has drawn attention to the remarkable extent to which the plot and characters of *HT* reprise those of *DS* (*Dickens and Education* (London, 1963; hereafter cited as Collins, *Education*), 144–5).
6. 'Fire and Snow' is collected in *Journalism* III; 'a perfect hurricane of applause': *Speeches*, 166; 'educational of the feelings . . .': *Speeches*, 167.

7. 'fusion . . . without confusion': *Speeches*, 167.
8. fable-like tale: the best definition of the term 'fable' as applied to a work of fiction remains, I believe, F. R. Leavis's in his famous 'Analytic Note' on *HT* appended to *The Great Tradition* (London, 1948): 'in it [the fable] the intention is peculiarly insistent, so that the representative significance of everything in the fable – character, episode, and so on – is immediately apparent as we read'; 'a terrible mistake . . .': *P* VII, 367; 'the Dismal Science': Carlyle, *Latter-Day Pamphlets*, no.1 (1850); for the fullest discussion of the background to CD's educational satire in *HT* see Collins, *Education*, 148–59, Robin Gilmour, 'The Gradgrind School: Political Economy in the Classroom', *VS* 11 (1967), 207–24, and Margaret Simpson, *The Companion to HARD TIMES* (Mountfield, East Sussex: Helm Information, 1997; hereafter Simpson), which also provides much useful background information on the Preston Strike and other relevant topics; see also Geoffrey Carnall, 'Dickens, Mrs Gaskell, and the Preston Strike', *VS* 8 (1964–65), 31–48.
9. The long list of titles is reprinted in George H. Ford and Sylvère Monod, eds, *HT* (New York, Norton Critical Edn, 1966; hereafter cited as Ford/Monod) and Paul Schlicke, ed., *HT* (Oxford World's Classics, 1989), also, in facsimile, in Stone, *WN* 251; for the short-list sent to Forster see *F* 565.
10. CD's planning notes for *HT* are printed in both the Norton Critical and the Oxford World's Classics Editions. (see previous note), also in facsimile in Stone, *WN*; for detailed study of the composition of *HT* see Butt and Tillotson, ch. 8; 'CRUSHING': *P* VII, 282.
11. 'constructed it patiently . . .': *P* VII, 367; the biblical echo in the books' titles: cf. 'Whatsoever a man soweth, that shall he also reap', *St Paul's Epistle to the Galatians*, vi, 7.
12. 'I am afraid I shall not be able to get much here': *P* VII, 260.
13. For his Lancashire dialect in *HT* CD consulted *A View of the Lancashire Dialect* by 'Tim Bobbin' (John Collier) first pub.1746 (see Norman Page, *Speech in the English Novel* (2nd edn, Basingstoke: Macmillan, 1988), 67–9); in making the Coketown workers members of a Union and Slackbridge a Union official CD perhaps had in mind a strike called by the Amalgamated Society of Engineers in 1852 rather than the Preston strike (cf. his letter to F. O. Ward of 20 Jan. 1852: 'Honorable, generous and spirited, themselves, they [the workers] have fallen into an unlucky way of trusting their affairs to contentious men, who work them up into a state of conglomeration and irritation . . .'.
14. 'cracking my head': *P* VII, 274; 'any slang terms . . .': *P* VII, 279.
15. 'feelingly deplored . . .': *The Times*, 14 March 1854, p. 12, col. e; 'Who . . . knowing England at this time . . .': 'The Late Mr Justice Talfourd', *HW* 25 March 1854 (collected in *MP*).
16. as has been noted: see Joseph Butwin, 'Hard Times: the News and the Novel', *NCF* 32 (1977–78), 166–87; for *C* as forerunner of *HT* see the 1968 article by Jiro Hazama cited by Sylvia Manning in *Hard Times: An Annotated Bibliography* (New York,1984; hereafter cited as Manning).
17. Simpson supplies a table of *HW* articles relevant to topics in *HT* in her Appendix D; in 'A Note on Serialisation' in Ian Gregor, ed., *Reading the Victorian Novel: Detail into Form* (London, 1980), 243–7, Malcolm Andrews has remarked how the first instalment of *HT* is 'set in a context of writings that emphasise colour, exoticism, sentimentality, jollity and soft domesticity'; re. the passage and footnote deleted by CD in proof : this is printed in Ford/Monod and all modern editions.
18. See John D. Baird, 'Divorce and Matrimonial Causes': an Aspect of *Hard Times*', *VS* 20 (1976–77), 401–12, also Simpson 131–8 (Caroline Norton was in 1853 trying to get a legal separation from her husband whose ill-usage had caused her to desert him in 1836).
19. 'the drawbacks of his present life': *F* 638; 'so happy and yet so unhappy . . .': *P* VII, 354.
20. For CD's Garrick Club speech see *Speeches* (new ed., 1988), xxx–xxxi.; 'airy and fresh': *P* VII, 361.
21. CD did write a brief preface for one weekly serial, *TTC*, but this was because it was simultaneously published in monthly numbers, in which format a preface and other prelims were always expected with the final instalment; for contemporary reception of *HT* see Collins, *CH* 300–08, and Manning, 37–40; for CD's profits see Patten 246; we learn from Forster: see *F* 565.
22. 'and with it my hope . . .': *P* VII, 391; the seven articles, all lead articles in *HW*, are: 'It Is Not Generally Known' (2 Sept.), 'Legal and Equitable Jokes' (23 Sept.), 'To Working Men' (7 Oct.), 'Reflections of a Lord Mayor' (18 Nov.), 'Mr Bull's Somnambulist' (25 Nov.), 'That Other Public' (3 Feb.1855) and 'Prince Bull. A Fairy Tale' (17 Feb. 1855); these are all collected in *Journalism* III, except for 'Reflections of a Lord Mayor', for which see *MP*, and 'Prince Bull. A Fairy Tale', which CD was evidently pleased enough with to include in *RP*; all quotations from CD's journalism in this paragraph are from 'That Other Public'; 'My satire is against those . . .': *P* VII, 492f.
23. 'To Working Men' is collected in *Journalism* III; for CD's letter to Burdett Coutts see *P* VII, 443f.
24. This was WC's first contribution to a Christmas number of *HW* but he had been contributing to the journal since 1852.

25. CD gave Rae space in *HW* to respond and published two further articles by him; see *Journalism* III, 254–69 for fuller discussion.
26. 'An unsettled feeling . . .' *F* 635; 'Whatever it is, it is always driving me . . .', *F* 638.
27. 'a small social party . . .': *Speeches*, 169; 'to become publicly a reader . . .', *F* 572.
28. Charles Dickens junior, 'Reminiscences of my Father', *The Windsor Magazine*, 81 (Dec. 1934, Christmas supplement), 20; the *Fortunio* playbill is reproduced as frontispiece to *P* VII.
29. 'Am altogether in a dishevelled state of mind . . .': *P* VII, 523.
30. The notebook, now in the Henry W. and Albert A. Berg Collection in the New York Public Library, has been transcribed and edited by Fred Kaplan as *Charles Dickens' Book of Memoranda* (The New York Public Library, Astor, Lenox and Tilden Foundations, 1981).
31. 'walked from Gravesend to Rochester . . .': *P* VII, 528; 'literally "a dream of my childhood" ': *P* VII, 531.

17 Writing *Little Dorrit* – among other things, 1855–1857

1. For Friday as CD's lucky day see *P* VII, 254, *P* VIII, 71, *P* XII, 29; according to Georgina, she, CD and Catherine visited the Winters after their marriage (see *D and W*, 61); 'Three or four and twenty years . . .': *P* VII, 532; 'I shall never be half so good a fellow . . .': *P* VII, 539; 'Whatever of fancy . . .': *P* VII, 538; 'busy and pleasant': *P* VII, 533; 'Remember. I accept all . . .': *P* VII, 545.
2. 'toothless, fat, old, and ugly': *P* VII, 544; for Arthur Clennam's meeting with Flora see *LD*, Bk I, ch.13.
3. 'Gaslight Fairies' is collected in *Journalism* III, 276–82; for Fanny Dorrit see especially *LD* Bk I, ch. 20.
4. 'that glorious charge . . .': see Jasper Ridley, *Lord Palmerston* (London, 1971), 441.
5. 'fine little bit of satire . . .': *P* VII, 581; for the first 'Thousand and One Humbugs' article, 'The Toady Tree' and 'Cheap Patriotism' see *Journalism* III, for the second and third 'Humbugs' articles see *MP*; 'scarifier . . . my indignant soul': *P* VII, 711 (to Wilkie Collins).
6. volleys of red hot shot': *P* VII, 512; 'approved literary merit': see *Speeches*, 177; 'should be entirely in the hands . . .': *Speeches*, 178; 'utterly defective and rotten . . .': *Speeches*, 181; 'the obstructives': *P* VII, 566; for CD and the Royal Literary Fund generally see, in addition to *Speeches*, Nigel Cross, *The Common Writer: Life in Nineteenth-Century Grub Street* (Cambridge, 1985), 32–3.
7. 'the gentlemen who have been so kind . . .': *P* VII, 571; 'the story is breaking out all around me': *P* VII, 608; 'all kinds of notes': *P* VII, 613.
8. 'capital': *P* VII, 613; 'the notion . . . of a leading man . . .': *F* 623; for the fullest accounts of the genesis and composition of *LD* see Butt and Tillotson, ch. 9, and Peter Sucksmith's 'Introduction' to *LD* (Oxford, the Clarendon Edn, 1979; hereafter cited as Sucksmith).
9. 'Waiting Room . . .': see Sucksmith, 806; 'and work in what I have done . . .': *P* VII, 692.
10. 'half a dozen cannon balls to roll about the floor . . .': Charles Dickens junior, 'Personal Reminiscences of my Father', *The Windsor Magazine* 81 (Dec. 1934, Christmas supplement; hereafter Charles Dickens junior, 'Reminiscences'), 20; for the words of 'The Song of the Wreck' see John Suddaby's 'The Wrecked Dying-child Near Natal', *D* 6 (1910), 92–8, in which the link is shown between this song and CD's earlier *HW* article, 'The Long Voyage' (31 Dec. 1853); for the *Lighthouse* playbill see *P* VII, 920; for Carlyle on CD's picturesqueness' as Gurnock see *F* 575.
11. For the full text of CD's speech to the Administrative Reform Association see *Speeches*, 197–208
12. For a lengthy and very favourable review of CD's Gurnock from the *Illustrated Times* (21 July) see *D* 5 (1909), 91–4; no doubt this critic would also have marvelled at CD's comic virtuosity in *Mr Nightingale's Diary* had this been also played at Campden House but another farce was substituted for it, performed by a group of Waugh's friends and fellow-officers, under CD's stringent direction; at Lord John Russell's dinner-table: CD dined with Russell on 7 July, when Russell was still – uneasily – a member of Palmerston's cabinet (he resigned six days later) and, he told Collins in a letter the next day, 'gave them a little bit of truth about Sunday [i.e., the Hyde Park riots], that was like bringing a Sebastopol battery among the polite company' (Meyerbeer, the French composer, was present and afterwards, CD told Collins, had said to him, 'Ah mon ami illustre! Que c'est noble de vous entendre parler d'haute voix morale, à la table d'un Ministre!'); for 'Dismal London Sunday' see Stone, *W N*, 271; for 'The Great Baby' see *Journalism* III, 324–30, also Robert L. Patten, *George Cruikshank's Life, Times and Art* II (Cambridge, 1996), 346.
13. For details of Tauchnitz's publication of *LD*, in parts and vol. form, see *P* VIII, 8, *n.* 3; as scholars have noted: see Stone, *WN*, 267; 'at full explanatory length': *P* VII, 722; 'steeped': *P* VII, 704; 'heaving in the sea . . .': *P* VII, 703 (16 Sept. 1855); 'Out of Town' is collected in *Journalism* III.

14. 'sticking at it day after day': *P* VII, 711; 'the man who comfortably charges everything on Providence': in CD's 'mems' for *LD* II; 'of a book whereof the whole story . . .': *P* VIII, 33; 'weird fascination': Charles Dickens junior, 'Reminiscences', 14; 'some curious experience . . .': *P* VII, 714.

15. 'after going through unheard-of bedevilments': *P* VII, 740; 'rooms rather larger than meat-safes': *P* VII, 740; for 'A Slight Depreciation of the Currency' (*HW*, 3 Nov. 1855) see *Journalism* III, 331–8; ' "I am told", said Bishop magnate . .': *LD*, Bk 1, ch 21.

16. For discussion of the monthly part cover of *LD* see Butt and Tillotson 224–5, also Michael Steig, *Dickens and Phiz* (London, 1978), 159–61.

17. 'There is much of the personal friendliness . . .': *P* VII, 727; 'three gorgeous drawing-rooms . . .'; *P* VIII, 34; 'Just the kind of woman in appearance . . .': *P* VIII, 33; 'I cannot relieve my mind . . .': *P* VIII, 55; 'a most noble fellow': *P* VII, 758; 'sit, sit, sit': *P* VII, 758.

18. 'botheration': *P* VII 762; WC's contribution to this Christmas number was a story about the ostler haunted by fears of the return of his murderous wife (WC strengthened the ending following a suggestion by CD, and later republished the story as 'The Dream Woman'); for 'unmitigated, bawdy Rot' see *P* VII, 753.

19. 'an odd idea . . .': *P* VII, 762.

20. 'an ever-ripening genius . . .': *Athenaeum*, 1 Dec. 1855, p.1393; 'beaten even *Bleak House* out of the field': *P* VII, 759; for details of CD's earnings from *LD* ('the best figures of his career') see Patten 251; CD to Lavinia Watson: *P* VII, 771; 'Believe me, ladies and gentlemen . . .': *Speeches*, 209.

21. 'beset' by his earlier idea: *P* VIII, 33; 'A Nightly Scene in London' is collected in *Journalism* III.

22. 'mere forms and conventionalities . . .': *P* VII, 743; 'Insularities' is reprinted in *Journalism* III, 338–46.

23. 'juvenile productions': *P* VIII, 23 (for further details of CD's Hachette earnings see Patten 256–8); 'Our Wicked Mis-statements' is reprinted in Stone, *UW* (II, 550–62); 'vomit of conceit': *P* VIII, 6.

24. 'Recommend me to Dickens . . .: quoted in Collins, *CH* (p. 203); for Trollope's response see *P* VIII, 40, *n*.1.

25. 'the vulgar and common social vice . . .': *Speeches*, 212; perverting 'the project of a working literary man': *HW*, 13 (8 March 1856) 172; 'precious rascality . . . one idea and design': *P* VIII, 79.

26. Lady Franklin: see *P* VIII, 66; the leading authority on *The Frozen Deep*: Robert Louis Brannan, author of *Under the Management of Mr Charles Dickens: His Production of 'The Frozen Deep'* (Ithaca, NY: Cornell University Press, 1966; hereafter cited as Brannan) which provides a full account of the genesis of the play.

27. 'twenty mile walks in the fresh air': *P* VIII, 108.

28. 'the no-result . . .': *P* VIII, 174 (CD continues, 'Nobody at home has yet any adequate idea, I am deplorably sure, of what the Barnacles and the Circumlocution Office have done for us'); re. Lord Decimus as Palmerston see Sucksmith xxxi.

29. For CD's 'mems' for *LD* XII see Sucksmith 818.

30. 'to get all over England . . .': *P* VIII, 231; 'great service': *P* VIII, 278; for fuller discussions of CD and Collins's collaboration in *The Wreck* see Anthea Trodd, 'Collaborating in Open Boats: Dickens, Collins, Franklin, and Bligh', *VS*, 42 (1998/1999), 201–25, and Lilian Nayder, *Unequal Partners: Charles Dickens, Wilkie Collins, and Victorian Authorship* (London, 2002; hereafter cited as Nayder), in which Nayder offers an interpretation of *The Wreck* based on the contention that CD and WC were responding to problems of labour unrest in the British merchant marine, about which many articles had appeared in preceding numbers of *HW*.

31. 'Authorial sanction': *P* VIII, 203 (Brannan comments [p.34], 'if a disagreement had arisen Dickens might have deferred to Collins's "authorial sanction", but he might have been surprised if Collins had chosen to exercise it'); re. CD's alterations to Wardour's part see Nayder 94; 'to the great terror of Finchley . . .': *P* VIII, 214.

32. 'of stupefying grandeur': *P* VIII, 205; 'The mazy Berger': *P* VIII, 214; 'pegged away at the "Frozen Deep" . . .': Charles Dickens junior, 'Reminiscences', 21; 'the butcher called . . .': Charles Dickens junior, 'Reminiscences', 21; Berger recalled . . .: see Francesco Berger, *97* (London, 1931), 17.

33. the gambling mania: see 'Railway Dreaming', *HW* 10 May 1856 (*Journalism* III, 369–83); 'shewing how it came about . . .': from CD's chapter-notes for ch.14 in *LD* XIV (Sucksmith 820).

18 Drama and dénouement: performing *The Frozen Deep* and finishing *Little Dorrit*, 1857

1. 'my numerous refreshings . . .': *P* VIII, 153; 'One savage footprint . . .': CD's Prologue is reprinted in Robert Louis Brannan's *Under the Management of Mr Charles Dickens* (Ithaca, NY: Cornell University Press, 1966; hereafter cited as Brannan), 97–8; Admiral Sir William Parry: Parry commanded three expeditions in search of the north-west passage between 1819 and 1825.

2. For playbills for *The Frozen Deep* see *D* 36 (1940), 198, 199, 201; 'judges enow . . .': see my *Douglas Jerrold 1803–1857* (London, 2003; hereafter cited as *Jerrold*), 265; 'If that man . . .': see *P*VIII, 261, *n.* 4; 'remarkably, extraordinarily clever . . .': *Macready's Reminiscences*, ed. F. Pollock (London, 1875) II, 409; Oxenford's review is quoted from Brannan 81–2.
3. 'the great French people . . .': for the full text of CD's 'Address' see *D* 29 (1933), 10.
4. 'I had an idea . . .': see *P*VIII, 279; 'It quite fascinated me . . .': *P*VIII, 317.
5. For the four pages of 'Mems' 'Retrospective' and 'Prospective' see Stone, *WN*, 307–09 and Harvey Sucksmith, ed., *LD* (Oxford, Clarendon Edn, 1979; hereafter cited as Sucksmith), 825–6; for evidence that he drew on Fox Cooper's dramatisation see *P*VIII, 232, *n.* 2, 290, *n.*2 and 313, *n.*2; for discussion of CD's handling of the mystery plot in *LD* see Joel J. Brattin, 'The Failure of Plot in *Little Dorrit*', *D* 101 (2005), 111–15: Brattin notes that the plot pivots on 'the extraordinarily unlikely point that a man might plausibly leave a substantial legacy to his brother's son's lover's former friend's brother's youngest daughter' and persuasively argues from the evidence of the MS.that 'though Dickens took the mystery plot seriously, his real interests lay elsewhere'.
6. 'Stores for the First of April' is collected in *MP*.
7. 'I believe no consideration . . .': *P*VIII, 300.
8. 'to reconsider the whole of the management . . .': *Speeches*, 225; 'sic volo sic jubeo' (my will is my command): cf. Edmund Yates on CD: 'He was imperious in the sense that his life was conducted on the *sic volo sic jubeo* principle' (Collins, *Interviews*, 207); 'one of the most intelligent and attentive audiences . . .': *Speeches*, 231.
9. For CD's 'mems' for *LD* XIX/XX see Stone, *WN* 306–11, and Sucksmith 825–8.
10. For fuller discussion of the complementariness of these two illustrations see Michael Steig, *Dickens and Phiz* (London, 1978), 161.
11. For CD's letter to JF about meeting the knowledgeable small boy see *P*VIII, 321.
12. For CD's profits on *LD* see Patten 251 (Patten comments, 'These are the best figures of his career').
13. CD had an illuminated scroll made carrying a quotation from *1 Henry IV*, I, 2, 'But, my lads, to-morrow morning, by four o'clock, early at Gadshill!' which was framed and hung in the hall at Gad's Hill (now in the CDM); 'The Best Authority' is collected in *Journalism* III.
14. For details of CD's fund-raising for the Jerrold family see *Jerrold*, ch.15; for the programme of events see *P*VIII, 736–7.
15. For the *Leader* review see Collins, *Readings*, 3.
16. 'feel easy as to the social position of my daughters . . .': *P*VIII, 357; for the Queen's praise of CD's acting see *P*VIII, 366, *n.*1.
17. The detailed study of *Little Dorrit*'s contemporary reception referred to will be found in H. M. Page, *The Critical Fortunes of LITTLE DORRIT 1855–1975* (Ph. D. thesis, University of London, 1978); for extracts from the article in *Blackwood's* and from those by Hollingshead and Stephen see Collins, *CH*, 358–62, 375–77, 366–74.
18. 'Curious Misprint in the *Edinburgh Review*' is collected in *Journalism* III, 413–20.
19. 'rending the very heart out of my body': *P* VIII, 488; for CD and Andersen see Elias Bredsdorff, *Hans Andersen and Charles Dickens* (Cambridge, 1956).
20. For Walter Dickens in India see Dick Kooiman, 'The Short Career of Walter Dickens in India', *D* 98 (2002), 14–28.
21. 'too large for the ladies': *P*VIII, 370; *Manchester Guardian* review quoted *P*VIII, 393, *n.*2; 'the best who *have been* on the stage': *P*VIII, 394.

19 Writing off a marriage, 1857–1858

1. For details of the Ternans' professional careers see Tomalin, chs 3–5.
2. 'three days drill': *P* VIII, 412; 'make a family party of it': *P* VIII, 408; 'extremely unwell': *P*VIII, 409.
3. 'Dickens surpassed himself . . .': see *P*VIII, 421, *n.* 5; for CD's report of Maria Ternan's emotions see his letters to Burdett Coutts and Lavinia Watson, *P*VIII, 433, 488.
4. 'with surprising force and brilliancy': *P*VIII, 432; the 'little book' would seem to refer to his *Book of Memoranda* but, as the *P* editors note, this does not contain any entries that seem to fit, with one possible exception.
5. For JF's letter to Catherine see *P* I, vii; 'defects of temperament': *F* 635.
6. 'It was a substitution . . .': *F* 641f.
7. 'For her sake as well as mine . . .': *P*VIII, 434; 'that the world may know . . .': Gladys Storey, *Dickens and Daughter* (London, 1939), 164; 'Wardour to the life!': *P*VIII, 440.

8. 'Lord bless you . . .': *P* VIII, 449; 'Lunatics, horse-mad . . .', 'which sets women apart . . .': *LT*, ch. 5 (*HW*, 31 Oct.1857; see *Journalism* III, 467, 472); 'I am going to take the little – riddle . . .': *P* VIII, 450.
9. 'fanciful photographer': see *P* VIII, 669 ('I walked from Durham to Sunderland, and made a little fanciful photograph in my mind of Pit-country . . .'); 'tickled . . . fantastic fidelity': *P* VIII, 462.
10. For Catherine's last housekeeping cheque see p. 26 of M. Veronica Stokes, 'Charles Dickens: a customer of Coutts & Co.', *D* 68 (1972), 17–30 (Stokes notes that Georgina's quarterly allowance was increased to £12.10s (from £7.50) from Dec.1857).
11. For an exhaustive discussion of 'The Bride's Chamber' and speculation about its relationship to CD's life and psychology see the second part of Harry Stone, *The Night Side of Dickens: Cannibalism, Passion, Necessity* (Columbus: Ohio State University Press, 1994), and see also Rosemary Bodenheimer, *Knowing Dickens* (London, 2007), 159–60: the *MHC* story the dénouement of which CD recalls in 'The Bride's Chamber' is 'A Confession Found in a Prison in the Time of Charles the Second', *MHC* 3 (18 April 1840), reprinted in Peter Mudford, ed., *Master Humphrey's Clock and Other Stories* (London, Everyman Dickens, 1997).
12. For discussion of CD's collaboration with Collins over the writing of 'Perils' see Lilian Nayder, *Unequal Partners: Charles Dickens, Wilkie Collins and Victorian Authorship* (London, 2002), 115–28; 'Snorridge Bottom' is an actual place two miles outside Chatham which the young CD would have known well – see W. Laurence Gadd, 'A Kentish Landmark Located', *D* 22 (1926), 226–7; for Nelly's later public readings from 'Perils' see Katharine Longley, 'The Real Ellen Ternan', *D* 81 (1985), 27–44.
13. For Lucie Manette as a Nelly Ternan look-alike see Tomalin 125; 'maudlin proclamation': *P* VIII, 473; for discussion of 'Perils' in relation to the Indian Mutiny see William Oddie, 'Dickens and the Indian Mutiny', *D* 68 (1972) 3–15, Laura Peters, 'Dickens and the Indian Rebellion' in D. Finkelstein and D. M. Peers, eds, *Negotiating India in Nineteenth-Century Media* (Basingstoke and New York, 2000), and Grace Moore, *Dickens and Empire* (Aldershot, 2004).
14. For dramatisations of 'Perils' see H. Philip Bolton, *Dickens Dramatized* (Boston, 1987), 393–4; for reception of the 1857 Christmas number see Ruth F. Glancy, *Dickens's Christmas Books, Christmas Stories and Other Short Fiction* (New York, 1985), 388–95.
15. The two *HW* articles are 'Well-Authenticated Rappings' (20 Feb.1858; collected in *Journalism* III) and 'An Idea of Mine' (13 March 1858; collected in *MP*); for CD and Westland Marston's play see *P* VIII, 531; for a detailed account of CD's pamphlet war with the Royal Literary Fund see K. J. Fielding, 'Dickens and the Royal Literary Fund–1858', *RES*, n.s.6 (1955), 383–94 (Fielding calls CD's second pamphlet 'heavily jocose and not in his best manner').
16. For CD's speech see *Speeches*, 246–53; also, for his support of the Children's Hospital generally, Jules Kosky, *Mutual Friends: Charles Dickens and the Great Ormond Street Children's Hospital* (London, 1989); for 'Drooping Buds' see Stone, *UW* II, 401–8; '. . . as Forster ruefully recorded': *F* 647.
17. 'a gentleman who is an honour to literature . . .': *Speeches*, 262.
18. 'Nothing whatever . . .': *P* VIII, 511.
19. 'seeing the house rise at you . . .': Mary Cowden Clarke, *Recollections of Writers* (London, 1878) quoted by Collins (*Readings*, xxi); 'extraordinarily irrational': *P* VIII, 535; 'I must do something . . .': *P* VIII, 537.
20. For the misdirected jewellery story see *D and W*, 152; the chief primary sources for information about the end of the Dickens marriage are *F* 635–49 and *P* VIII, *passim*; the main secondary sources both about this, and about CD and Nelly Ternan, are Edgar Johnson, *Charles Dickens: His Tragedy and Triumph*, vol. 2 (New York, 1952), Katharine M. Longley, *A Pardoner's Tale*, unpublished typescript in the Senate House Library, University of London, MS 1003/10/1, *D and W*, and Tomalin.
21. 'Please to leave your Umbrella' is collected in *Journalism* III; 'by some constitutional misfortune . . .': see Arthur A. Adrian, *Georgina Hogarth and the Dickens Circle* (London, 1957), 57.
22. Katey's later comments: Gladys Storey quotes her as saying, 'My father was like a madman when my mother left home . . . this affair brought out all that was worst – all that was weakest in him. He did not care one damn what happened to any of us. Nothing could surpass the misery and unhappiness of our home' (Gladys Storey, *Dickens and Daughter* (London, 1939), 93–103); Helen Thomson's letter is reprinted in *P* VIII, 746–9; for the situation regarding the Divorce Laws in 1858 see *D and W*, 147–8.
23. In *Dickens, Women and Language* (Toronto, 1992) Patricia Ingham comments (p.140) on how the 'structural rhetoric' of CD's description of Catherine in his 9 May letter to Burdett Coutts 'works to negate and denature her'; as I have suggested before: see *D and W*, 146.
24. For CD's speech at St Martin's Hall and Yates's memory of it see *Speeches*, 263–4; 'a very large family party . . .': see *P* VIII, 555, *n*.2.
25. For a detailed chronology of all CD's Readings see Malcolm Andrews, *Charles Dickens and His Performing Selves: Dickens and the Public Readings* (Oxford, 2006), 269–73.

26. For the full text of the 'Violated Letter' see *P* VIII, 740–1; the 'pecuniary part' of the separation arrangement as finally worked out gave Catherine an allowance of £600 a year and a brougham, and she took up residence in a modest house in Gloucester Crescent, north of Regent's Park, where Charley lived with her (CD insisted this was at his, CD's, specific request) for a year until his departure for Hong Kong, to gain experience in the tea trade.

27. For Thackeray's letter to his mother (undated but internal evidence indicates it was written several days after 24 May) see Gordon N. Ray, ed., *The Letters and Private Papers of William Makepeace Thackeray* IV (Oxford, 1946), 85–7; given that Thackeray had often been a guest at both Devonshire Terrace and Tavistock House, it seems odd that he makes no comment on the reported assertions by CD about the 'horrible incompatibility' of his and his wife's tempers.

28. 'those amazing slanders': *P*, VIII, 568, *corr.* XII, 683; 'she has a great tenderness . . .': *P* VIII, 569; 'distress and agitation': *P* VIII, 747.

29. CD's statement is included in *Journalism* III, and reproduced in facsimile in *P* VIII, 744; 'Whoever there may be . . .': *P* VIII, 578; 'Surely he cannot mean it . . .': *P* VIII, 749.

30. Extract from *DC* ch. 37 dated 28 April 1858 sold at Bonham's 29 June 2004; extract from *DC* ch. 44 dated 2 June 1858 is in the Nason Collection; extract from *DC* ch. 44 also dated 2 June 1858, sold at Sotheby's, New York, 26 June 2000.

31. 'the extremity of his irrational behaviour': *P* VIII, xiv; for a full account of CD's break with Bradbury and Evans see K. J. Fielding, 'Bradbury *v.* Dickens', *D* 50 (1954), 73–82.

32. For full publication details regarding the Library Edition (which proved more profitable for Bradbury and Evans than it did for Chapman and Hall) see Patten 259–60; for *RP* see Stone, *UW* I, 44 (oddly, CD included one item, 'A Plated Article', which had, in fact, been jointly written by himself and Wills).

33. For CD's threatened action for slander see *P* VIII, 754–7; allegations about his fathering a child or children by Georgina have persisted to this day – see, for example, Tomalin 142, and 'Charles Dickens incest rumour acquires "ring of truth" ', *The Times* 16 Jan. 2009, p.19; for CD's letter to Richard Spofford (15 July 1858) see *P* VIII, 604.

34. 'unwholesome': *P* VIII, 687.

35. For Fred Dickens's marital troubles see *P* VIII, 699f; for the 'Garrick Club Affair' see Gordon N. Ray, *Thackeray: The Age of Wisdom* (London, 1958), 285–6.

36. 'such an odd idea': *P* VIII, 709; 'unseasonable grimness': *P* VIII.

37. 'that figure . . .': *P* IX, 230.

20 Stories into scripts: the public readings, 1858

1. Two different prompt-books of the *CH* reading are extant, one probably hastily made for the private reading in Paris – see *Readings*, 35–7; Collins's definitive ed. of CD's readings and Malcolm Andrews's *Charles Dickens and his Performing Selves: Dickens and the Public Readings* (Oxford, 2006; hereafter cited as Andrews) are the two essential sources for all information about, and discussion of, CD's readings career, and the present chapter is greatly indebted to both of them; see also the final chapter of Paul Schlicke, *Dickens and Popular Entertainment* (Boston, 1985) for discussion of the readings as the culmination of CD's lifelong devotion to entertainments for the people.

2. The *Carol* prompt-book is now in the Henry W. and Albert A. Berg Collection in the New York Public Library (hereafter cited as Berg), and the Library published a facsimile, ed. Philip Collins, in 1971; for location of this and all other surviving prompt-copies see *Readings*, xxxvi–xli.

3. 'a swim in the broader waters . . .': *P* VII, 515; last words of the reading: Alan Horsman notes at the end of his Appendix on *Little Dombey* in his Clarendon Edition of *DS* (Oxford, 1974) that the word 'too' has been pencilled in after '. . . bears us to the ocean' in the Berg prompt-copy of this reading.

4. 'playful pity': *P* VIII, 633; the prompt-copy for *Mrs Gamp* is in Berg and was published in facsimile by the New York Public Library in 1956, ed. John D. Gordan; 'the people gave themselves up . . .': *P* VIII, 621 (by 'Shillings' CD denotes the occupants of the cheapest seats).

5. 'a few hints for compassionate and merciful remembrance . . .': *Readings* 76; interestingly, he thoroughly revised the *C* reading as late as 1868 and had a new prompt-copy made, but performed the item only once, when it seems to have been a sensational success – see *Readings* 77.

6. For these published reading copies see *Readings* xlii and Patten 258f.

7. For a full account of CD's readings team and equipment see Andrews, ch. 4, also Philip Collins, 'Dickens's Public readings: the Kit and the Team', *D* 74 (1978), 8–16; 'something between a Home Secretary and a furniture-dealer . . .': *P* VIII, 617; CD's design for his readings desk and the desk itself are now in the CDM; Charles Mathews: see Andrews 119–22.

8. 'When Mr Sergeant Buzfuz . . .': *P* VIII, 682; 'such an unaffected tribute . . .': *The Nation*, 12 Dec. 1867 (quoted *Readings* 198).
9. For Burdett Coutts and Catherine see *P* VIII, 565, *n*.2.
10. 'resolve . . . one creature': *P* VIII, 584; 'there was one gentleman . . .': *P* VIII, 659.
11. For the variations CD played on Sam Weller's response see *Readings*, 209.
12. 'when he suddenly jumped from his chair . . .': Mamie Dickens, *My Father As I Recall Him* (London, 1898), 48 (quoted Andrews 103).

21 Serials, series and stories: writing for *All the Year Round*, 1859–1861

1. For details see K. J. Fielding, 'Bradbury *v.* Dickens', *D* 50 (1954), 73–82 (hereafter cited as Fielding); CD's correspondence for the next year or so contains a number of malicious remarks about Bradbury and Evans, the most distressing of which are his jocose comments on the suicide of Bradbury's son Henry (*P* IX, 302f.).
2. *Household Harmony*: see *3 Henry VI*, IV, vi, 14; 'I am afraid . . .': *P* IX, 15; 'The story of our lives . . .': adapted from 'The story of our lives, from year to year', (*Othello*, I, iii, 129–30).
3. political tensions between Britain and France: see Andrew Sanders, *The Companion to A TALE OF TWO CITIES* (London, 1988; hereafter cited as Sanders), 10–11; 'who brought his white face and his white hair . . .': 'Where We Stopped Growing' (see *Journalism* III, 105–12); for *The Dead Heart* see Carl R. Dolmetsch, 'Dickens and *The Dead Heart*', *D* 55 (1959), 178–87; Estella and Bella were first seen as based on Nelly by Hugh Kingsmill in *The Sentimental Journey: A Life of Charles Dickens* (London, 1934) and the idea was given widespread currency by Edmund Wilson in his seminal essay, 'Dickens: the Two Scrooges' in *The Wound and the Bow: Seven Studies in Literature* (London, 1941).
4. 'the children of his brain . . .': Charles Dickens junior, 'Reminiscences of My Father', *The Windsor Magazine* 81 (Dec. 1934, Christmas supplement), 25; 'little Kentish freehold': *P* VIII, 597; 'the fairy godfather': see Rosemary Bodenheimer, *Knowing Dickens* (London, 2007), 164; for the Ternans' leasing of No. 2 Houghton Place, see *D and W*, 425f.; for CD playing cards at Houghton Place see letter from Andrew de Ternant, *Notes and Queries* 165 (1933), 87; 'the charmer': see *P* IX, 318; 'a woman whom I could implicitly trust . . .': *P* IX, 415 (the Pilgrim editors here note, 'No doubt Ellen Ternan').
5. 'The drunken? – dissipated? – what? . . .': *Memoranda*, 1 (against the entry CD has noted '*Done in Carton*'); for the sending of proofs to Nelly see *P* IX, 87.
6. For the fullest account of CD's sources for *TTC* see Sanders, also his 'Monsieur heretofore the Marquis: Dickens's St Evrémonde', *D* 81 (1985), 148–56; 'two cart-loads of books': see Charles Dickens the Younger's 'Introduction' to *TTC* (London, Macmillan Edn, 1902) xx; 'no books but such as had the air of the time in them': *P* IX, 245.
7. For a critical view of Browne's work for *TTC* see Cohen, *Illustrators*, 118, and for a persuasive defence of it see Elizabeth Cayzer, 'Dickens and his Late Illustrators. A Change in Style: "Phiz" and *A Tale of Two Cities*', *D* 86 (1990), 131–41; 'rather original and bold idea': *P* IX, 35; *OCS* and *BR* had also been published in both weekly and monthly instalments but as part of a periodical, *MHC*.
8. 'very great sale . . .': *P* IX, 223; for CD's dealings with American publishers over *AYR* and *TTC* see Patten 274–6, and Drew, *Journalist*, 146–7.
9. For earlier ideas for characters used in 'Hunted Down' see *Memoranda* 8 and 13; Philip Collins suggests in *Dickens and Crime* (London, 1962) that CD may also have drawn on William Palmer the poisoner for certain of Slinkton's traits.
10. 'The Poor Man and His Beer' is collected in *Journalism* IV, 3–19; 'MISSING . . .': *AYR*, 30 April 1859, p.11(the 'Occasional Register' column ceased to appear in *AYR*, after four issues); CD's handbill advertising *AYR* is reproduced in Stone, *UW*, I, 26; for the auction of *HW* see Fielding, also Patten 269, and *P* IX, 65.
11. For all the circulation and business details included in this paragraph see Ella Ann Oppenlander, *Dickens' ALL THE YEAR ROUND: Descriptive Index and Contributor List* (Troy, N.Y., 1984), 48.
12. 'taken its place among the actual experiences . . .': *P* IX, 93; for full discussion of CD's commissioning of serials for *AYR* and his relations with fellow-writers in this connection see John Sutherland's chapter 'Dickens as Publisher' in his *Victorian Novelists and Publishers* (London, 1976); 'up to the scratch . . . sponge is thrown in': CD is here using boxing slang.
13. 'small malady': *P* IX, 84; 'my old month's advance': *P* IX, 92; 'Teaspoons': *P* IX, 113; for CD's draft agreement with Evans to undertake an American tour see *P* IX, 567.
14. 'strong hold': *P* IX, 92; *Illustrated London News* comment quoted by Linda K. Hughes and Michael Lund, *The Victorian Serial* (London, 1991) in the course of discussing the weekly serialisation and

reception of *TTC* (61–74); 'I do not positively say . . .': *P* IX, 127f. (compare with this CD's comments to Collins on his art in the early chapters of *A Woman in White*, *P* IX, 194f.).

15. For CD and Howitt see N. C. Peyrouton, 'Rapping the Rappers. More Grist for the Biographers' Mill', *D* 55 (1959), 75–89, also Harry Stone, 'The Unknown Dickens', *DSA* I (1970), 1–22; 'an idea noted in his *Book of Memoranda*': see *Memoranda*, 1, verso ('a house; abandoned by the family. . . . Inscriptions under the bells downstairs. "Mr John's Room" – "Miss Caroline's Room" . . .'); for an account of CD's work on this Christmas number, especially his extensive revision of Gaskell's contribution see Fran Baker, ed., Elizabeth Gaskell, 'The Ghost in the Garden Room', *Bulletin of the John Rylands University Library of Manchester* (2004), 86.

16. 'the simplest in the world': *P* IX, 169f; for discussion of CD's mingling of autobiography and fancy in 'The Ghost in Master B's Room' see *D and W*, 45–7.

17. For a somewhat different approach to the question of the persona of the 'Uncommercial Traveller', one related to CD's new career of public reader, see Malcolm Andrews, *Charles Dickens and His Performing Selves* (Oxford, 2006), 173–4.

18. 'that we are all Travellers . . .': *Speeches*, 292.

19. 'traits chiefly of his younger days': *F* 675.

20. For CD's bonfire of his correspondence see *P* IX, 304; my comments on 'Dullborough Town' owe much to Malcolm Andrews's fine discussion of this essay in his *Dickens and the Grown-Up Child* (London, 1994); for comment on continuities between *UT* and *GE* see Scott Foll, '*Great Expectations* and the "Uncommercial" Sketch Book', *D* 81 (1985), 109–16; in *The Novel From Sterne to James* (London, 1981) Juliet McMaster relates 'Nurse's Stories' (*UT*) to the horrific story about the cannibalistic young man with which Magwitch terrifies Pip in *GE*.

21. 'the mere sight of Dickens would almost kill her': for this comment by Catherine see *P* VIII, 749; 'an unhappy home', 'he said in a broken voice': Gladys Storey, *Dickens and Daughter* (London, 1939), 105, 106.

22. 'lying out among the marshes . . .': *F* 734f.; 'was the germ of Pip and Magwitch': *F* 733; outstandingly industrious Dickens scholar: see Harry Stone, 'The Genesis of a Novel: *Great Expectations*' in E. W. F. Tomlin, ed., *Charles Dickens 1812–1870: A Centenary Volume* (London, 1970; hereafter cited as Stone, 'Genesis').

23. 'reaches for more . . .': Robin Gilmour, 'Introduction', *GE* (London, Everyman Dickens, 1994), xxxv; for Harper's payment for the serialisation rights of *GE* see Patten 289.

24. Wisbech and Fenland Museum: the MS. of *GE* forms part of the Chauncy Hare Townshend Bequest, CD having presented it to Townshend; for description of the MS. see Margaret Cardwell, ed., *GE* (Oxford, Clarendon Edn, 1993; hereafter cited as Cardwell), lvi–lix.

25. On CD's drawing on his whole emotional and imaginative history in *GE* see Harry Stone, 'Genesis'; for discussion of the Beadnell affair as a likely biographical source for the depiction of Pip's sufferings in love see also *D and W*, 75; 'House full of Toadies . . .': *Memoranda*, 17.

26. 'The work will be written . . .': *P* IX, 734; his 'apology to Mealy Potatoes': see George Bernard Shaw, 'Foreword' to *Great Expectations* (New York Limited Editions Club, 1937).

27. For Capt. Morgan see W. J. Carlton, 'Captain Morgan – *alias* Jorgan', *D* 53 (1957), 75–82; 'a portrait . . . exactly like the man' *P* IX, 349; 'high-shouldered desperation': *P* IX, 342; for the fullest discussion of attribution problems in *AMS* see Harry Stone, 'Dickens Rediscovered: Some Lost Writings Retrieved' in Ada Nisbet and Blake Nevius, eds, *Dickens Centennial Essays* (London, 1971), 205–226.

28. For the stopping of the production of *AMS* see *P* IX, 366–7; a source of tremendous pride and pleasure: CD wrote to Bulwer Lytton on 23 Jan., 'I can honestly assure you that I never have been so pleased at heart in all my Literary life, as I am in the proud thought of standing side by side with you this great audience.'

29. For full discussion of the composition and publication of *GE*, the MS., proofs, etc., see Cardwell, and also Edgar Rosenberg, ed., *GE* (New York, Norton Critical Editions, 1999; hereafter cited as Rosenberg).

30. For Charley as original of Herbert Pocket see Rosenberg 570; for suggested connection between Nelly Ternan and the characters of Estella and Bella see note 3 above; for suggested connection between Pip's passion for Estella and CD's for Maria Beadnell see *D and W*, 75.

31. 'a certain shrinking sensitiveness . . .': *P* X, 98; 'neuralgic pains in the face': *P* IX, 424.

32. 'because its purpose would be much more apparent . . .': *P* IX, 403; 'to make himself sure . . .': *F* 736.

33. 'I work here . . .': *P* IX, 421 (Captain Barclay (1779–1854) was a celebrated long-distance walker); 'the work has been pretty close . . .': *P* IX, 424; 'I never, never, never was better loved . . .': *P* XII, 72.

34. 'accidental': see *P* IX, 259; 'extraordinarily taken . . .', 'good reasons', 'as pretty a little piece of writing . . .': *P* IX, 433; for full discussion of the two endings and their relative merits see Rosenberg 491–527.

35. For the cited contemporary reviews of *GE* see Collins, *CH*, 427ff.; for the sales of the three-volume edition of *GE* see Patten 288–93 (in the nineteenth-century less distinction was made between 'edition' and 'impression' than was the case later – the five 'editions' of *GE* published in 1861 would today be called impressions); 'tapping his forehead . . .': *P* IX, 438.

22   Christmas numbers, public readings, and 'uncommercial' travels, 1861–1863

1. 'a great deal of money': *P* X, 43; 'odious little London box': *P* X, 52; 'vanish into space': *P* X, 187; for CD and Condette see W. J. Carlton, 'Dickens's Forgotten Retreat in France', *D* 62 (1966), 69–86 and Tomalin, ch. 9; in his 'The Crisis of 1863' (*DQ*, 23 (2006), 181–91) Robert G. Garnett argues that a plausible interpretation of the surviving evidence relating to CD's frequent cross-Channel trips during the eight months between the summer of 1862 and February 1863, and of the deliberately obfuscating and confusing references to these journeys in his letters, is that Nelly discovered she was pregnant by CD in spring 1862 and moved to France, with her mother, to have the baby, which was born early in 1863.

2. 'I could perhaps see that country . . .': *P* X, 161; 'as to plan an Uncommercial Traveller Upside Down': *F* 693; 'I know perfectly well . . .': *P* X, 134.

3. 'What a great Cemetery . . .': *P* X, 66; 'in this world there is no stay . . .': *P* X, 130.

4. 'the most prosperous . . .': *Speeches*, 320; for the comment on the Queen see *P* X, 54.

5. Tomalin comments (p.140) that CD 'could not sit through *Faust* without identifying with the guilty lover', Robert G. Garnett speculates, in his article cited in note 1 that Georgina's illness may have been connected with a crisis in CD's relationship with Nelly, specifically her discovery of her pregnancy.

6. 'the poor dear fellow . . .': *P* IX, 494; 'as poor and mean a Hound as lives': *P* X, 9; 'Swearing at her …': see Elizabeth Arbuckle, ed., *Harriet Martineau's Letters to Fanny Wedgwood* (Stanford, Ca., 1983), 196.

7. 'these great experiences of the public heart': *P* IX, 553; 'blazes of triumph': *P* IX, 529; 'worthy man with a genius for mistakes': *P* X, 3; 'a continuous narrative': *P* IX, 449f.; 'far more interesting . . .': *P* X, 107.

8. For texts and discussion of all these readings see *Readings*; for further discussion of *The Bastille Prisoner* see my '*The Bastille Prisoner*: A Reading Dickens Never Gave', *Etudes Anglaises* 23 (1970), 190–6, and for further discussion of the *GE* Reading see Margaret Cardwell, ed., *GE* (Oxford, Clarendon Edn,1993), xlviii–li, and Jean Callahan, 'The (Unread) Reading Version of *Great Expectations*' in Edgar Rosenberg, ed., *GE* (New York, Norton Critical Edn, 1999), 543–6; 'Mrs Jellyby and Mr Turveydrop . . .': *Memoranda*, following p. 25.

9. 'the wholesome influences . . .': Ruth Glancy, ed., *CS* (London, Everyman Dickens, 1996; hereafter cited as Glancy), 417; 'Much more can be made of it . . .': *P* IX, 489; 'exceedingly droll': *P* IX, 548; a modern Dickens scholar: see Lilian Nayder, *Unequal Partners: Charles Dickens, Wilkie Collins and Victorian Authorship* (London, 2002), 134; 'Tom Tiddler's Ground': in this game a space is marked off as belonging to one child who represents Tom; it is supposedly covered with gold and silver and the other children venture on to it singing, 'Here I am on Tom Tiddler's Ground, picking up gold and silver' and if one of them is caught on the ground by Tom he or she has to take his place and become Tom (the relevance of the game to the recluse's situation is made clear at the beginning of the number); for sales figures for *TTG* and Lucas's response to its publication see Glancy 418.

10. 'the most pressing reasons . . .': *P* IX, 510.

11. 'In any other case . . .': *Speeches*, 302; for tentative dating of *Memoranda* entries see *Memoranda* 2–3 and 100.

12. Forster has confused the issue: see *F* 740; 'Alas! I have hit upon nothing . . .': *P* X, 75.

13. 'The difficulty of getting people to read notes . . .': *P* IX, 510 (Bulwer Lytton restored the footnotes when *A Strange Story* was published in volume form); 'Let the book explain itself': *P* IX, 543; '*wonderfully fine*': *P* X, 128; '[combining] invention and power . . .': *P* X, 128.

14. 'includes . . . everything you know about waiters . . .': *P* X, 126; 'a comic defiance . . .': *P* X, 126; 'slight leading notion . .', 'ridiculously comical . . .': *P* X, 126.

15. 'I wonder how many people . . .': *P* X, 181; 'tried to make a complete Camera Obscura . . .': *P* X, 150; It has been suggested . . .: see John Bowen, 'Bebelle and "His Boots": Dickens, Ellen Ternan and the *Christmas Stories*', *D* 96 (2000), 197–208.

16. 'Absurdly unnecessary to say . . .': *P* X, 142; see also Catherine Peters, *The King of Inventors: A Life of Wilkie Collins* (1991), 244–5.

17. 'only . . . one thing missed': *P* X, 150.

18. as her biographer speculates: see Tomalin 139.
19. 'strike in': *P* X, 237.
20. 'pervaded by boys . . .': *P* X, 281
21. 'Jew money-lender': *P* IX, 286; 'conveys that idea of him . . .': *P* X, 270; 'such an out and outer . . .': *P* I, 441; for the complete correspondence with Eliza Davis see B. W. Matz, 'Fagin and Riah', *D* 17 (1921), 144–52, and see also Harry Stone, 'Dickens and the Jews', *VS* 2 (1959), 223–53; it has to be said that in the pre-Holocaust Victorian age CD shared fairly unthinkingly in his culture's stereotyped prejudices, as when he called Bentley an 'infernal, thundering, plundering old Jew' (above, p. 104).
22. as has been suggested: see John Drew, headnote to 'Chatham Dockyard' in *Journalism* IV.
23. She has recently, however, been presented to a wider public by Miriam Margolyes in her acclaimed one-woman stage show *Dickens' Women*, also in a 2007 BBC radio adaptation by Ellen Dryden – see the review by Donald Hawes, *D* 103 (2007), 251 (an earlier BBC radio version by Mollie Greenhalgh was broadcast on 22 Dec. 1956).
24. 'really put as much into Mrs Lirriper': Percy Fitzgerald quoted by Glancy (no.1767); Glancy also quotes (no. 1768) Fitzgerald's comment that Dickens 'regretted the waste of good material in the Christmas numbers, and that in a regular story he "could have done immense things with Mrs Lirriper!" '; see also Deborah A. Thomas, 'Dickens's Mrs Lirriper and the Evolution of a Feminine Stereotype', *DSA*, 6 (1977), 154–66.
25. 'as if some great beast . . .': *P* X, 298; the joke about JF is recorded under date of 28 Oct. 1863 in Henry Silver's *Punch* diary (MS. British Library) – I am grateful to Dr Patrick Leary for help with this reference.
26. 'exceedingly anxious to begin . . .', 'determined not to begin to publish . . .': *P* X, 300; for the contract for *OMF* see *P* X, 477 and Patten 302–3.
27. For Edrupt's reminiscences see Collins, *Interviews*, 195; for extract from the *Saturday Review* notice of *Mrs Lirriper* see Collins, *CH* 413–14; Roc's egg: the roc was a fabulous bird of gigantic size featured in *The Arabian Nights*.

23   Back to the 'big brushes': writing *Our Mutual Friend*, 1864–1865

1. The San Carlo is the great theatre in Naples.
2. For CD's 'In Memoriam' notice see *Journalism* IV, 326–30.
3. For CD's *OMF* working notes and number-plans see Stone, *WN*, also Adrian Poole, ed., *OMF* (London, Penguin Classics, 1997; hereafter cited as Poole), Appendix 2; CD's debt to Knowles was first noted by Earle Davis in *The Flint and the Flame: the Artistry of Charles Dickens* (Columbia, Mo., 1963) and is discussed in detail by Poole.
4. 'We might almost mention the river itself . . .': see Collins, *CH* 458; for the topicality of education as a theme for novelists in 1864/65 see R. D. Altick, 'Education, Print and Paper in *Our Mutual Friend*' in Clyde de L. Ryals, ed., *Literary Perspectives: Essays in Honor of Lionel Stevenson* (Durham, NC, 1974); for an article CD would certainly have known on the monetary value of dust-heaps and would have recalled in planning *OMF* see R. H. Horne, 'Dust; or Ugliness Redeemed', *HW* I (13 July 1850), 379–84; for the traditional identification of JF as CD's model for Podsnap see James A. Davies, *John Forster: A Literary Life*, (Leicester, 1983), 178–83.
5. For CD and Browne in 1864 see *P* X, viii; 'that he was much hampered . . .': F. G. Kitton, *Dickens and His Illustrators* (London, 1899, hereafter cited as Kitton), 197; for assessments of Stone's work for *OMF* see Cohen, *Illustrators*, 203–9, and Elizabeth Cayzer, 'Dickens and his Late Illustrators: a Change in Style. Two Unknown Artists', *D* 87 (1991), 3–15, and note also Q. D. Leavis's acerbic judgment, 'Dickens had better have left the bereaved Stone family to starve' (F. R. and Q. D. Leavis, *Dickens the Novelist* (London, 1970), 469).
6. 'The Doll's dressmaker . . .': *P* X, 430 (Jenny first appears, with her back to the viewer, in the first plate for *OMF* VI, 'The Person of the House and the Bad Child', and again in the first plate for *OMF* VII, 'The Garden on the Roof'; the young woman in a black dress in the bottom of the right-hand corner of the monthly-part cover, mistakenly identified as Jenny by the Pilgrim editors, is clearly Bella Wilfer); 'excellent': *P* X, 361; 'One of the strongest features of the story . . .': Kitton 197; for valuable discussion of the draft and final designs for the *OMF* monthly-part cover see Michael O'Hea, 'Hidden Harmony: Marcus Stone's Wrapper Design for *Our Mutual Friend*', *D* 91 (1995), 198–208 (surprisingly, CD apparently left it to Stone to decide which of Wegg's legs should be the wooden one).
7. re. CD's overwriting the first and second numbers: see Cotsell, *The Companion to OUR MUTUAL FRIEND* (London, 1986; hereafter cited as Cotsell), 1; 'peculiar avocation': Kitton 199; 'with his

unusually keen powers of observation . . .': Kitton, *Dickens and His Illustrators*, London, 1899, 200; 'a despondent melancholy youth': Marcus Stone, *Reminiscences*, MS. at CDM.

8.   'A page in my life . . .': *P* X, 356 (see epigraph to ch.19).

9.   For details of the advertising campaign see Patten 307; for CD's concern over Georgina see *P* X, 356.

10. Hatton and Cleaver: see *Bibliography of the Periodical Works of Charles Dickens*, (London, 1933), 345; re. decline in monthly-part sales of *OMF* see Patten 308; National schoolmaster; see Cotsell 132–4; 'sound, liberal, comprehensive education': *Speeches*, 335; Tercentenary celebrations: for CD's views see *P* X, 341, 412, 426; for Mrs Nickleby's dream see *NN*, ch. 27; for CD's praise of JF's *Goldsmith* as conducing 'to the dignity and honour of literature' see *P* V, 288ff.

11. 'the Bebelle life in Paris': see John Bowen, 'Bebelle and "His Boots"': Dickens, Ellen Ternan and the *Christmas Stories*', *D* 96 (2000), 197–208.

12. See Patten 309: 'The fact is that shilling novels in monthly parts had pretty well run their course; they did not collect conveniently into three volumes for the lending libraries; they were too big for commuter customers; they were a poor bargain for the average book buyer, who could get several stories for the same price or less by purchasing a shilling magazine, or a story complete in one instalment by ordering the Christmas number of *All the Year Round*.'

13. Bowen points out (see note 11 above) that, like 'His Boots', both of the Mrs Lirriper stories, 'explore the possible fates of illegitimate children who are not cared for by their real parents, and both engineer happy endings for them'.

14. 'something – to me at all events – so extraordinarily droll . . .': *P* X, 435 (JF tells us it was 'the encounter of the major and the tax-collector'); 'It is the condensation of a quantity of subject . . .': *P* X, 441.

15. 'woefully': *P* X, 447.

16. 'Whenever I feel . . .': *P* X, 445; as he claimed always to have done: see *P* X, 469; for the 'Position of affairs' memorandum see Stone, *WN* 355, also Poole 866.

17. 'In the summer . . .': *P* XI, 3; 'they reflect and refract . . .': *P* XI, 79; the chalet may be seen today in the grounds of the Rochester Museum and the writing-table in the CDM.

18. For the People's Edition see Patten 299, also *ORCD*, 205.

19. 'writing on the palm of my hand . . .': *Speeches*, 347.

20. a 'lameness . . . in the left foot': *F* 699; 'tortures': *P* XI, 27; 'a neuralgic attack in the foot. . .': *P* XII, 528; 'it is more than probable . . .': *F* 699; see also CD's description, in a letter of 21 Feb. 1865, of how he had fallen lame on a snowy walk with his two large dogs, Turk and Linda, and was forced to limp home, 'to their remarkable terror'.

21. 'Work and worry . . .': *P* XI, 48; 'Before I went away . . .': *P* XI, 48.

22. 'tidal train': 'so called because it ran at a different time, altered every few days, depending on the state of the tide in the harbours concerned' (T. W. Hill. 'The Staplehurst Railway Accident', *D* 38 (1942), 147–52); 'to alarm their friends . . .', *The Times*, 'Dreadful Railway Accident at Staplehurst', 10 June 1865, 9e.

23. 'a most extraordinary heap of dark ruins . . .': *P* X, 61 (the young man, Edward Dickenson, was later a guest at Gad's Hill and his memories of CD and the Staplehurst accident appear in Kitton, *P and P*, 185–7); Nelly's biographer: see Tomalin 146.

24. 'that the carriage is down on one side . . .': *P* XI, 65; for CD's letter to the head station master at Charing Cross see *P* XI, 53; an unidentified cutting in the Nason Collection, evidently from some reminiscences published after CD's death, includes the following: 'The friends in the habit of meeting Mr Dickens privately recall now the energy with which he depicted the dreadful scene, and how, as the climax of his story came, and its dread interest grew, he would rise from the table, and literally act the parts of the several sufferers to whom he had lent a helping hand.'

25. For the Fitzgerald quotation and other details see *Speeches*, 349–52.

26. 'a little festival of Neuralgia . . .': *P* XI, 84; for CD's 'mems' and notes for *OMF* XIX–XX see Stone, *WN* 370–3.

27. 'Betty Higden finishes . . .': *F* 744.

28. 'a lady not his wife . . .': Julia Cara Byrne, *Gossip of the Century* I (London 1892), 225; 'the moment I breathed the sea air': *P* XI, 91; 'by a railway-accident': *F* 657; for *The Gad's Hill Gazette* see J. W. T. Ley, 'The Gad's Hill Gazette', *D* 6 (1910), 173–8, and Henry Fielding Dickens, 'The History of the Gad's Hill Gazette', *D* 25 (1929), 255–9.

29. For the critical reception of *OMF* and the reviews quoted in this paragraph see Collins, *CH* 453–73; 'as you have divined what pains . . .': *P* XI, 118; the MS. of *OMF* is now in the Pierpont Morgan Library, New York.

30. 'As I am but now finishing Our Mutual Friend . . .': *P* XI, 78; for CD's earnings from the serialisation of *OMF*, which included £1,000 from Harper's for advance proof sheets to ensure

simultaneous publication of the serial in *Harper's Monthly*, see Patten 308; 'that for exertion of this kind . . .': *F* 700.

24 Last Christmas numbers, 1865–1867

1. 'hallucinatory': G. H. Lewes's invocation of 'the phenomena of hallucination' to explain CD's extraordinary art in his review of Vol. I of JF's *Life of Dickens* in *The Fortnightly Review*, Feb. 1872 (see Collins, *CH*, 569–77) was rejected by JF in his final vol. (*F* 716–20); 'the Board of Guardians': governing board of the local workhouse; 'Will you take me as I stand . . .': Ruth Glancy, ed., *CS* (London, Everyman Dickens, 1996), 572f.
2. 'wonderfully like the real thing . . .': *P* XI, 99; Edmund Wilson was the first to suggest Marigold's keeping an audience 'entertained with his patter while his child is dying in his arms' might reflect the death of the love-child he believed CD to have had by Nelly (*The Wound and the Bow*, London, University Paperbacks edn, 1952, 65), a suggestion put forward more recently by John Bowen (see *D* 96, 2000, 207).
3. 'the "Doctor" is . . .': *P* XI, 106; 'Neither good, gooder, nor goodest . . .': *P* XI, 106; 'slowly and with great care . . .': *P* XI, 113.
4. 'using her brains to educate herself': see Gladys Storey, *Dickens and Daughter* (London, 1939), 94; for Nelly's likely income from Houghton Place see Tomalin 156; for Frances Ternan's acting at the Lyceum 1865–66 see Malcolm Morley, 'The Theatrical Ternans. Part VII', *D* 56 (1960), 41–6; for CD, the Ternans and Slough see Felix Aylmer, *Dickens Incognito* (London,1959; hereafter cited as Aylmer), J. C. Reid, 'Mr Tringham of Slough', *D* 64 (1968), 164f., letter from Katharine M. Longley, *D* 77(1981) 56, and her 'Dickens Incognito', *D* 77 (1981), 88–91.
5. intensive scholarly investigation: see Ada Nisbet, *Dickens and Ellen Ternan* (Berkeley and Los Angeles,1952); 'Meet for houses . . .': see Aylmer 40.
6. 'degeneration of some functions . . .': *P* XI, 155; dinner party for twenty: *P* XI, 142, *n*.4; for CD's response to Bulwer Lytton's 'The Secret Way' see *D and W*, 86–8; 'a gladsome gorilla': see *P* XI, 183, *n*.5.
7. For texts of, and comments on, both the *Lirriper* and the *Marigold* readings see Collins, *Readings*; 'it more than realised . . .': George Dolby, *Dickens As I Knew Him: The Story of the Readings Tours in Great Britain and America (1866–1870)* (1885; hereafter cited as Dolby); 'from beginning to end . . .': see *P* XI, 181, *n*.6.
8. 'It seems a superfluous precaution . . .': 'The Letters of Charles Dickens. Supplement V', *D* 101 (2005), 153; for CD's 1867 interpolation into the preface to *PP* see James Kinsley, ed., *PP* (Oxford, Clarendon Edn, 1986), 886.
9. For CD's joking about being unable to identify his birthplace see Dolby 38; 'without experiencing. . .': Dolby 11.
10. 'allowed himself to be disposed of . . .': *P* XI, 223; 'rapturous way': see *P* XI, 221, *n*. 8 (for discussion of *Aunt Margaret's Trouble* see also Tomalin 159–60).
11. The echoes of *HM* in *MJ* have been noted more than once; see especially Gordon Spence, 'The Haunted Man and Barbox Brothers', *D* 76 (1980), 150–7.
12. 'You sha'n't have any milk and sugar . . .': Dolby 30f.
13. 'certain of the more practical judges . . .': Dolby 53 (see also Collins, *Readings*, 421–63).
14. 'disagreeables from America': CD was in fact attacked in the American press for what was perceived as his callousness towards Augustus's bereaved partner and children – see Sidney P. and Carolyn J. Moss, *Charles Dickens and his Chicago Relatives* (Troy, NY, 1994); for payments to 'N. trust' see *P* XI, 475; 'a spectacle of woe': see letter from Frederick Lehmann quoted in John Lehmann, *Ancestors and Friends* (1962), 210.
15. 'a magical kind of influence': *F* 833; 'I beg your pardon, sir . . .': *F* 834.
16. 'WONDERS!': *P* XI, 340; 'Railway shaking': *P* XI, 314; 'kept constantly referring . . .': Dolby 67.
17. For CD's approval of Eytinge see *P* XI, 349; for the controversy stirred up by CD's letter to Ticknor & Fields see Andrew J. Kappel and Robert L. Patten, 'Dickens' Second American Tour and His "Utterly Worthless and Profitless" American "Rights" ', *DSA* 7 (1978), 1–33.
18. Prospectus for the Charles Dickens Edition: a fragment of CD's autograph MS. of this item is in the Nason Collection; for CD's profit on the Edition see Patten 312.
19. For comment on the Charles Dickens Edition and the headlines see Kathleen Tillotson, ed., *Oliver Twist* (Oxford, Clarendon Edn, 1966), xxix–xxx and xl, also George H. Ford and Sylvère Monod, eds, *Bleak House* (New York: Norton Critical Edn, 1977), 799–803; the Charles Dickens Edition headlines are given in an appendix in every volume of the Clarendon Edition of Dickens.

20. Quotations from CD's 1867 diary are taken from the partial transcript published in Aylmer; for CD's obituary notice of Stanfield see *Journalism* IV, 331–2.
21. obscuring 'his whole prospect': *P* XI, 371.

25 Writing, and reading, for America, 1867–1868

1. 'standing out weird and melancholy . . .': George Dolby, *Charles Dickens As I Knew Him* (London,1885, hereafter cited as Dolby), 78; for the history of Hoghton Tower see R. D. Butterworth, 'Hoghton Tower and the Picaresque of "George Silverman's Explanation" ', *D* 86 (1990; hereafter cited as Butterworth), 93–104; 'The main idea of the narrator's position . . .': *P* XI, 385 (CD consistently wrote 'Towers' rather than 'Tower'); 'GSE' is included in Peter Mudford, ed., *Master Humphrey's Clock and Other Stories* (London, Everyman Dickens, 1997); the story and its personal resonance for CD is very fully discussed by Harry Stone in Part 3 of his *The Night Side of Dickens: Cannibalism, Passion, Necessity* (Columbus: Ohio State University Press, 1994) and for a notable recent discussion see Rosemary Bodenheimer, *Knowing Dickens* (London, 2007; hereafter cited as Bodenheimer), 87–9, especially her analysis of Miss Wade's and Silverman's autobiographies as presenting 'quite different pathologies of deprivation'.
2. names: see *Memoranda* entries 109 and 110 ('Verity Hawkyard' is, in fact, listed among available girls' names); Brother Hawkyard finishes . . .': cf. *F* 744, 'Betty Higden finishes what Oliver Twist began'.
3. 'notoriously high death-rate': Butterworth 99.
4. 'but a very few days to complete': Dolby 78; for date of finishing 'GSE' see diary entry reproduced in Felix Aylmer, *Dickens Incognito* (London, 1959), 95; re. the possibility of Nelly's having a travelling companion to America: there is a note in CD's pocket memorandum book for 1867 about reserving a ladies' state room, '2 berths for'ard in front of machinery', for an Atlantic crossing (Berg Collection, New York Public Library); for the calculation of CD's potential profit in America see Dolby 135.
5. Bodenheimer suggests (p.89), that the story could have felt to CD 'like an exposure of his own propensity to nurture and capitalise on the resentment of feeling misunderstood'.
6. 'They are the quaintest . . .': *P* XI, 410.
7. See Philip V. Allingham, 'The Original Illustrations for Dickens's *A Holiday Romance* . . .', *D* 92 (1997), 31–47; all the illustrations are reproduced in Gillian Avery, ed., *Holiday Romance and Other Writings for Children* (London, Everyman Dickens, 1995).
8. 'We put the story together . . .': Collins to Frederic Chapman, 11 May 1873 quoted in F. G. Kitton, *The Minor Writings of Charles Dickens* (London, 1900; hereafter cited as Kitton), 173; for CD and the Foundling Hospital see Jenny Bourne Taylor, 'Received, a Blank Child: John Brownlow, Charles Dickens and the London Foundling Hospital', *NCL* 56 (2001), 293–363; Obenreizer does, in fact, commit suicide in Collins's dramatisation of the story, in which he is presented rather as a tragic figure than as a downright villain – see Lilian Nayder, *Unequal Partners: Charles Dickens, Wilkie Collins and Victorian Authorship* (London, 2002; hereafter cited as Nayder), 159.
9. For Carrow's report of his visit see Collins, *Interviews*, 323–9.
10. 'purposely wrote . . .': Collins to Frederic Chapman 11 May 1873, Kitton 173; see Nayder 141, where the sections written by Collins are identified with the help of a fragmentary MS. of *NT* in the Pierpont Morgan Library; also Nayder 157 where she notes that a certain passage, clearly very Dickensian, found in the printed text of the opening of 'Act IV', does not appear in Collins's MS.
11. 'a likely time': Beryl Gray, 'Dickens and Dogs: "No Thoroughfare" and the Landseer Connection', *D* 100 (2004), 5–22; 'surely the finest specimen . . .': *P* XI, 101; 'There are now six immense dogs . . .': *P* XI, 416.
12. 'critical state of health': *P* XI, 416, *n*.5; 'cricketing': *P* XI, 420; 'I have never gone through the sheets . . .': *Speeches*, 367 (in May 1870 CD wrote to Chapman and Hall asking for his special thanks to be passed to their printer's reader for 'his great care and attention' in correcting the sheets of the CD Edition of *CHE* for the press (*P* XII, 522)); for the *Daily Telegraph* review see *P* XI, 436, *n*.3.
13. 'the case in a nutshell' is printed in *F* (709–10) and in *P* XI, 537–8; 'Homer of the slums . . .': quoted by Andrew J. Kappel and Robert L. Patten, 'Dickens' Second American Tour and His "Utterly Worthless and Profitless" American "Rights" ' *DSA* 7 (1978), 9; 'if Dickens would *first apologise* . . ." ': Dolby 124; 'He was certain there was no money . . .': Dolby 137.
14. Mamie Dickens, *My Father As I Recall Him* (London, 1898), 97.
15. 'side by side at two desks': Collins to Frederic Chapman, 11 May 1873, Kitton 173; 'as they will have a special meaning for her': *P* XI, 475; 'all well means *You come* . . .': see Ada Nisbet, *Dickens and Ellen Ternan* (Berkeley and Los Angeles, 1952), 54; 'Chapman and Hall Halfyear's Accounts to Midsummer

1867': 'Some Unpublished Correspondence of Dickens and Chapman and Hall Annotated by Gerald G. Grubb', *Boston University Studies in English*, I (1955–56), 98–127 (see Patten 313).

16. All quotations in this and the preceding paragraph are taken from *Speeches*, 369–74, apart from CD's comments to Annie Fields about Lytton's speech for which see M. A. DeWolfe Howe, *Memories of a Hostess: A Chronicle of Eminent Friendships Drawn chiefly from the Diaries of Mrs James T. Fields* (Boston, 1922; hereafter cited as DeWolfe Howe), 177.

17. 'My dear Catherine . . .': *P* XI, 472; 'a thousand thanks . . .': *P* XI, 472.

18. 'a quiet corner (high up)': Dolby 156; 'checking the Readings off': *P* XI, 483; 'the noble army of speculators': *P* XII, 10 (see Dolby Bk II, for accounts of his battles with this 'noble army').

19. 'seven to ten miles': *P* XI, 489; 'choice flowers': *P* XI, 481; 'a very nice woman . . .': *P* XI, 488 (by 22 Dec. she had become 'one of the dearest little women in the world'); 'bubbled over with fun', 'but you must be careful . . .': DeWolfe Howe 141.

20. Annie's journal: in addition to DeWolfe Howe, see for extracts George Curry, 'Charles Dickens and Annie Fields', *Huntington Library Quarterly* 51 (1988; hereafter cited as Curry), 1–71; 'Rocky Mountain Sneezer': *P* XI, 522.

21. 'while he was writing *Oliver Twist* . . .', 'What an unfathomable mystery . . .': James T. Fields, *Yesterdays with Authors* (Boston, 1872), quoted in Collins, *Interviews*, 311–12 (cf. his comments to JF in 1843 when writing *MC* quoted above, ch. 9, pp. 212ff.; 'As to the way in which these characters have opened out . . .': *P* III, 441.

22. re. the mysterious second telegram: Katharine M. Longley in her unpublished study of the CD/Nelly relationship, *A Pardoner's Tale* (typescript in Senate House Library, University of London, Longley Papers MS 1003/10/1–2) comments: 'As Dickens continued to send letters to Wills to forward to Ellen which would have reached England after the date, 11 December, on which she would have sailed in the "City of Antwerp" had she been coming (and provided the plan was the last), it may be accepted that this telegram was not in code and does not represent a change of plan at this stage)'; for the £1,000 cheque probably destined for Nelly see *P* XII, 6.

23. 'often troubled by the lack of energy . . .', 'I cannot help rehearsing . . .': Curry 9, 27.

24. 'always regarded Boston . . .': Dolby 160; 'a remarkable face . . .': *P* XII, 39.

25. For the full text of the 'Great International Walking Match' broadsheet see *Journalism* IV, 410–15; it is also given in Dolby 261–9.

26. 'simply thorough resting': *P* XII, 65; 'he felt the case to be a hopeless one': Dolby 271; 'Yes, I cry when I read about Steerforth . . ." ': see Collins, *Interviews*, 172.

27. DeWolfe Howe 178.

28. For the full text of CD's speech see *Speeches*, 378–83.

29. 'as a mere public audience . . .': *Speeches*, 384.

30. 'between a quarter . . .': *P* XII, xi; 'a golden campaigning ground': *P* V, 396.

26   Disappearances and deaths, 1868–1870

1. 'I sank my American Catarrh . . .': *P* XII, 164; 'concussion of the brain': *P* XII, 131; 'the complete overthrow . . .': *P* XII, 115.

2. 'CD told J. . . .': George Curry, *Dickens and Annie Fields* (Los Angeles: Henry E. Huntington Library, 1988; hereafter cited as Curry), 42.

3. 'wallowing in half a year's arrears . . .': *P* XII, 105; 'irretrievable bankruptcy . . .': *P* XII, 139; 'a very good man of business': *P* XII, 378; 'honestly dead': *P* XII, 530;. for details of the careers of Alfred and Plorn in Australia see Mary Lazarus, *A Tale of Two Brothers: Charles Dickens's Sons in Australia* (Sydney, 1973) and for Henry's success story see *The Recollections of Sir Henry Dickens, K.C.* (London, 1934; hereafter cited as *Recollections*) in which a famous passage (p. 36) describes CD's moving response of pride and pleasure to Henry's informing him about the College scholarship.

4. Re. 'the Sapsea Fragment' see 'Charles Forsyte' (pen-name of Gordon Philo), 'The Sapsea Fragment – Fragment of What?', and Katharine M. Longley, 'Letter to the Editor', *D* 82 (1986), 12–16 and 84–5 and, for further correspondence on the subject, see *D* 82 (1986), 178–9, and 83 (1987), 48–9 and 110.

5. 'I never saw a man . . .': *Recollections*, 36; 'earnest desire': George Dolby, *Charles Dickens As I Knew Him* (London, 1885; hereafter cited as Dolby), 416; 'a wasted life': *P* XII, 208; 'he was my favorite . . .': *P* XII, 207.

6. '*very* dramatic . . .': *P* VIII, 712; 'to leave behind me . . .': *P* XII, 220; 'I have adapted . . . *P* XII, 203.

7. For full text of 'The Ruffian' and editorial comment on it see *Journalism* IV, 334–42.

8. For Longfellow's pleasure CD turned out a couple of post-chaises with 'postilions in the old red jacket of the old red royal Dover Road . . . like a holiday ride in England 50 years ago' (*P* XII, 149);

'nearly distracted by the conglomeration . . .': Dolby 340 (Townshend's *Religious Opinions* with a brief 'Explanatory Introduction' by CD was published in 1869 – see *Journalism* IV, 429–31).

9.   'flung aside his book . . .': Edmund Yates writing in *Tinsley's Magazine* in 1869, quoted by Collins, *Readings*, 465; 'a great ladies' Doctor': *P* XII, 247; 'would have been saved . . .': Dolby 352.

10. 'no audience on earth . . .': *P* XII, 222; 'brilliantly condensed', rewriting more interesting . . .': Collins, *Readings*, 467.

11. 'altogether a brighter air': Percy Fitzgerald, *Memories of Charles Dickens* (London, 1913), 243.

12. 'certain "droll" details': see CD's comments on these in letters to Wilkie Collins and the Fieldses, *P* XII, 235 and 248.

13. For an admirably balanced discussion of CD's penchant for performing *Sikes and Nancy* see Philip Collins, *Dickens and Crime* (London, 1962), 267–71.

14. 'the desire to be once more on the platform . . .': Dolby 386; 'being accustomed . . .': see 'A Fly-leaf in a Life' (*Journalism* IV, 388).

15. 'in a paroxysm of grief': Dolby 391; for Tennent and *MED* see Wendy S. Jacobson, *The Companion to 'The Mystery of Edwin Drood'* (1986; hereafter cited as Jacobson), 86–7.

16. 'immense exertions', 'constant jarrings . . .': *P* XII, 341; 'had been on the brink of paralysis . . .': *F* 804; 'sustained by the assurance . . .': Edgar Johnson, *Charles Dickens: His Tragedy and Triumph* (New York, 1952), II, 1110; for recent expert discussion of CD's health problems see I. C. McManus, 'Charles Dickens: a neglected diagnosis', *The Lancet*, 358 (2001), 2158–61 and David Bateman's alternative view, *The Lancet*, 359 (2002), 1253; for discussion of the circumstances surrounding the cancellation of CD's tour see R. D. Butterworth, 'Dickens's Last Provincial Readings', *D* 83 (1987), 79–87.

17. 'Pip's room and the stairs . . .': Curry 38; 'those regions of crime and woe', 'miserable court', 'a haggard old woman': James T. Fields, *Yesterdays with Authors* (Boston, 1872; hereafter cited as Fields), 205; 'to cast about for a subject . . .': Dolby 418.

18. 'noted how sleepy and inane . . .': Fields 221; 'The cramped monotony of my existence. . . .', *MED* ch. 2

19. Both 'Mr Fechter's Acting' and 'A Plea for Total Abstinence' are collected in *Journalism* IV.

20. 'I am staggered and stopped short . . .': 'The Letters of Charles Dickens: Supplement II', *D* 99 (2003), 156–63 (CD's 'Landor's Life' is collected in *Journalism* IV).

21. 'Two people, boy and girl . . . *F* 807–08: see Fred Kaplan's note on entry 72 in *Memoranda* (p. 97) for discussion of the puzzling relationship between this entry and the, perhaps spurious, mid-July letter from CD quoted by JF; 'a condemned cell . . .': William R. Hughes, *A Week's Tramp in Dickens-Land* (1893; hereafter cited as Hughes), 140.

22. For CD's sources for *MED* in general see Don Richard Cox, *Charles Dickens, The Mystery of Edwin Drood: An Annotated Bibliography* (New York, 1998; hereafter cited as Cox), Sect.12, nos 1751–98 (no. 1776 deals with Emily Jolly's story); the Parkman case: see Robert Tracy, 'Disappearances: George Parkman and Edwin Drood', *D* 96 (2000), 101–17, and response by Charles Forsyte, *D* 96 (2000), 245–6; *The Moonstone*: see Lilian Nayder, *Unequal Partners: Charles Dickens, Wilkie Collins and Victorian Authorship*, (London, 2002, ch. 6); 'the plot echoes that of *Our Mutual Friend* . . .': *Dublin Review*, April 1871 (see Cox, no. 615); 'quite as deeply fascinated . . .': Kate Perugini, ' "Edwin Drood" and the last days of Charles Dickens', *Pall Mall Magazine* 37 (1906; hereafter cited as Perugini), 643–52.

23. On the demise of the twenty-monthly-part novel see Patten 229f.

24. CD's list of possible titles and character-names is given in Stone, *WN* and in Margaret Cardwell, ed., *MED* (Oxford, Clarendon Edn, 1972; hereafter cited as Cardwell), 18; for details about the Governor Eyre case and Bright as the original of Honeythunder see Jacobson 84–6, but cf. also CD's high praise of Bright as 'one of the foremost men, and certainly one of the best speakers, if not the very best, in England' in his Birmingham speech of 27 Sept. 1869 (*Speeches*, 406).

25. 'My own invention . . .': *Speeches*, 406; it was in this speech also that CD stated his 'political creed' which had, he said, 'no reference to any party or persons': 'My faith in the people governing, is, on the whole, infinitesimal; my faith in The People governed, is, on the whole, illimitable.' This caused considerable confusion as to exactly what he meant and his later attempt at clarification (see *Speeches*, 411) did not altogether resolve the matter.

26. For a full discussion of the *John Ackland* puzzle see R. F. Stewart, 'The Mystery of *John Ackland*', *D* 98 (2002), 213–24; 'a queer little note . . .': Curry 47.

27. 'studying the Cathedral . . .': Hughes, 121; for CD's number-plans and working notes for *MED* see Cardwell 226–31, also Stone, *WN*.

28. For full discussion of Charles Collins and Luke Fildes as illustrators of *MED* see Cohen, *Illustrators*; for Collins's sketches as probably deriving from CD's verbal descriptions see Robert

Raven, 'Some Observations on Charles Collins's Sketches for *Edwin Drood*', *D* 96 (2000), 118–26; 'collapsed for the whole term . . .': *P* XII, 466; for the complications over the American rights see Cardwell xxx–xxxi, and Patten 317–19.

29. 'a clincher': *P* XII, 465; 'I had to transpose . . .': *P* XII, 454 (for details of the transpositions and adjustments made by CD see Cardwell xxii); 'pretty ladies': *P* XII, 449; for Collins's 1871 letter to Daly see *D* 51 (1955), 119; 'for [he] strangles . . .': see Cardwell xxvi.

30. 'My father, after many turns, . . .': see Collins, *Interviews*, 162.

31. 'if you see your father falter . . .': Collins, *Interviews*, 137; for Georgina's protests: see Arthur A. Adrian, *Georgina Hogarth and the Dickens Circle* (London, 1957), 129.

32. For CD's impersonation of a waiter see Fields 225; for the contract for *MED* see *P* XII, 720, also Patten 316.

33. The fullest account of CD's audience with the Queen is to be found in Dolby 455–8, though it contains one error (which, anyway, sounds pretty implausible) when Dolby describes the Queen as quoting to CD his farewell speech at his last reading which did not take place until six days later; 'he never read better in his life . . .': Charles Kent, *Charles Dickens as a Reader* (London, 1872), 268; 'an amount of artistic delight . . .': *Speeches*, 413.

34. 'As he delighted the fathers . . .': quoted in Collins, *CH*, 542; 'fancy dress': *P* XII, 505; 'most perseveringly . . .': *P* XII, 512; 'gallantly sustaining . . .': *Speeches*, 422.

35. 'hot rooms and speechmaking': *P* XII, 515; 'old preposterous endeavours . . .': *P* XII, 527; 'simply bubbled over with fun . . .': Collins, *Interviews*, 350; 'all the rehearsals with a boy's spirit . . .', 'ringing all the bells . . .': Collins, *Interviews*, 353.

36. 'Dickens's last laboured effort . . .': see Collins, *CH*, 588; for entries relating to *MED* in *Memoranda* see nos 9, 72, 81 and 114.

37. Katey's words quoted in this paragraph are here taken from Collins, *Interviews*, 354–6; see also Lucinda Hawksley, *Katey: The Life and Loves of Dickens's Artist Daughter* (London, 2006), 235–6.

38. 'much against his usual custom': *F* 851.

39. Dickens's seizure and last hours are described by JF (*F* 851–2) who based his account on information given him by Georgina. There exists an alternative oral tradition, dependent on one, of course, long-dead witness, that CD died, or became seriously ill, while visiting Nelly in Peckham and that, to avoid scandal, she arranged for his secret removal to Gad's Hill, twenty-four miles away (a three-hour journey) where, it must follow if this story be true, Georgina was able to organise things to make it seem that CD had not left Gad's Hill on the 8th and had had his fatal seizure while dining with her that evening, just as she described to JF. For detailed consideration of this version of CD's last hours see 'Postscript' to the Penguin edition (London, 1991) of Tomalin; for a reasoned and authoritative rejection of it see David Parker, 'Dickens's Death: the Peckham Conjecture' (*DQ*, 25 (2008), 190–3).

27 Charles Dickens's explanations

1. 'I wish to write it in my own hand . . .': *P* IX, 464; '*pièce justicative*': 'Mr Dickens's Will', *The Saturday Review* 30 (30 July 1870), 133–4 ('*urbi et orbi*' means 'addressed to everyone', like the Pope's Easter Message to the city [of Rome] and the whole world).

2. 'an act of defiance': Tomalin 188f.; for CD's probable private financial provision for Nelly see *P* XII, 730, *n*. i; a god-daughter: Nelly was so described in a book of reminiscences, *Keeping Off The Shelf* (London, 1928) by Mrs Thomas Whiffen (Blanche Galton), who also mentions that Nelly was with CD at Staplehurst – a statement that was strongly rejected on the authority of Sir Henry Dickens in *D* 26 (1930), 37–8.

3. 'an attached woman servant': *P* VIII, 740; 'like a poor child . . .': *P* VIII, 560; 'the demon': see *P* X, 110; CD's 'poaching' of Cornelius is noted by Jenny Hartley in her *Charles Dickens and the House of Fallen Women* (London, 2008), 86f.

4. re. the pen with which CD was writing *MED*, now in the CDM: we know that Nelly owned it as she subsequently presented it to her clergyman friend, the Dickens enthusiast Canon Edward Benham – see letter from Benham to Thomas Wright reproduced in facsimile in Wright's autobiography *Thomas Wright of Olney* (London,1936); 'sketched from his sister-in-law . . .': *F*, 753; 'She sacrificed to children . . .': *Memoranda* no. 50 (p.10).

5. 'Nobody can say how much too much . . .', 'expressions fitted to give color . . .': George Curry, 'Charles Dickens and Annie Fields', *Huntington Library Quarterly*, 51 (1988), 52, 58.

6. 'There may be a great diversity of opinion . . .': John Bigelow, *Retrospections of an Active Life, 1812–1879* (New York, 1909), IV, 383, quoted by Ada Nisbet, *Dickens and Ellen Ternan* (Berkeley and Los Angeles, 1952), 21.

7. For discussion of CD's directions for his own funeral and the suggestion that he may have been partly motivated by his wish that Nelly should be able to attend see Robert Garnett, 'The Mysterious Mourner: Dickens's Funeral and Ellen Ternan', *DQ* 25 (2008), 107–17 (Garnett comments, 'his funeral was a story that he wrote earlier, for posthumous publication . . .'); 'the "Great Commoner" of English fiction': *P* XII, 333 *n*. 3; 'No man in his inner mind . . .': see Collins, *Interviews*, 220.
8. 'a disgrace to English journalism . . .': *The Period: An Illustrated Review of what is going on*, no.14 (13 Aug. 1870; I owe this reference to Martin Nason); 'a lasting stigma . . .': Richard Bentley, *Diary*, 26 July 1870 (MS. University of Illinois at Urbana-Champagne; I am grateful to Dr Patrick Leary for supplying me with this reference).
9. Collins, *CH*, 579, 565; for the dearth of information about CD's earlier years before *F* 1 appeared see Elliot Engel, 'Dickens's Obscure Childhood in Pre-Forster Biography', *D* 72 (1976), 3–12.
10. 'As to his education . . .': *Fraser's Magazine*, n.s.5 (1872), 113 (Lang's authorship proposed by *Wellesley Index*); 'We are all reading the "Life of Dickens" . . .': see W.H.G. Armytage, 'Robert Browning and Mrs Pattison: some unpublished Browning letters', *University of Toronto Quarterly* 21 (1952), 181 (I owe this reference to Prof. Ashby Bland Crowder); 'Naturally a great humorist . . .': *The Fortnightly Review*, n. s. 9 (1872), 119; 'the wretched soil . . .': Robert Buchanan, 'The "Good Genie" of Fiction; Thoughts while reading Forster's *Life of Charles Dickens*', quoted in Collins, *CH*, 578–9.
11. 'degraded by the straits . .': *Times*, 26 Dec. 1871, p. 4, col. ?; 'Poor mother! . . .': *Fraser's*, ibid., 110; 'Forster tells of him . . .': N. J. Hall, ed., *Letters of Anthony Trollope* 2 (Stanford, CA: Stanford University Press, 1983), 557f.
12. 'dipped his quill into his heart's blood': *D* 28 (1932), 136.

Index

All Charles Dickens's separately published works are indexed under their titles